Public Finance and Public Policy

SECOND EDITION

Public Finance and Public Policy

Jonathan Gruber
Massachusetts Institute of Technology

Worth Publishers

To Andrea, Sam, Jack, and Ava

Publisher: Craig Bleyer
Acquisitions Editor: Sarah Dorger
Development Editor: Jane Tufts
Associate Managing Editor: Tracey Kuehn
Project Editor: Kerry O'Shaughnessy
Editorial Assistant: Leigh Renhard
Marketing Manager: Scott Guile
Production Manager: Barbara Seixas
Art Director: Babs Reingold
Cover Design: Kevin Kall
Interior Design: Lissi Sigillo
Photo Editor: Cecilia Varas
Composition: TSI Graphics
Printing and Binding: RR Donnelley

ISBN-13: 978-0-7167-6631-5
ISBN-10: 0-7167-6631-0
Library of Congress Control Number: 2006937926

Worth Publishers
41 Madison Avenue
New York, NY 10010
www.worthpublishers.com

About the Author

Jonathan Gruber is Professor of Economics at MIT and the Director of the National Bureau of Economic Research's Program on Children. He is a Co-Editor of the *Journal of Public Economics* and an Associate Editor of the *Journal of Health Economics*. Previously he held the position of Deputy Assistant Secretary for Economic Policy with the U.S. Treasury Department.

Brief Contents

Contents

PART I

**Introduction
and
Background**

PART III

Social Insurance and Redistribution

PART IV

Taxation in Theory and Practice

Preface

When I began writing this book four years ago, I hoped that my text would bring the excitement and enthusiasm I have for the study of public finance to the students taking this important course. I believe that a public finance text should help students understand the public finance issues that are discussed on the front page of the newspaper every day. By presenting rigorous theory, cutting-edge empirical evidence, and abundant policy-relevant applications, I hoped that students would find the main lessons of public finance accessible and appealing, perhaps even enjoyable.

With the success of the first edition of this text, I am gratified and happy to say that my approach has found wide acceptance among instructors and their students across the country. By augmenting the traditional approach of public finance texts with a true integration of theory, application, and evidence, *Public Finance and Public Policy* has enabled instructors to better engage their students. Whenever a major theoretical concept is discussed, the discussion is augmented by examples of the policy relevance of the topic and, where available, evidence on the key relationships highlighted by the theory.

For example, when discussing the impact of individual income taxation on labor supply in Chapter 21, I present the traditional theoretical analysis, discuss the available evidence on the responsiveness of labor supply to taxation, and then apply those insights to the discussion of the major tax subsidy to labor supply in the United States, the Earned Income Tax Credit. And in the discussions of externalities in Chapters 5 and 6, the theoretical analysis of private and public solutions to externalities is followed by application to the major environmental externalities facing U.S. policy makers—acid rain and global warming—and a discussion of the empirical evidence on the effects of existing U.S. regulatory interventions in those areas.

Features

Public Finance and Public Policy improves on previous texts in public finance in three ways.

Updated Selection of Topics

Any public finance textbook must devote extensive discussion to issues of externalities and public goods, taxation, and direct government spending, and this book is no exception. Yet I also devote increased discussion to the transfer and social insurance programs that dominate government activity.

The text is organized around four key areas:

▶ **Introduction and Background** The first section of the book is devoted to motivating the study of public finance beginning in Chapter 1 with a timely discussion of the government response to Hurricane Katrina and the major public policy debates of the day. The book then reviews background skills in Chapter 2 (microeconomic theory), Chapter 3 (empirical methodology), and Chapter 4 (government budgeting). I recognize that students come to their public finance courses with highly varying levels of economics skills. This course requires familiarity with introductory microeconomics, but no more: all other required skills are reviewed in these background chapters. The chapter on empirical methods provides students with all the background they need to interpret the empirical evidence boxes throughout the text. In addition, by moving the discussion of government budgeting from its traditional "orphan" spot at the end of textbooks, I allow the discussion of other topics throughout the book, such as Social Security and tax policy, to draw on the insights developed in Chapter 4 about the role of the budget in policy debates.

▶ **Externalities and Public Goods** The discussion of externalities begins in Chapter 5 with a discussion of private and public solutions to the problem of externalities, and then continues in Chapter 6 by focusing on the two major public policy issues involving externalities: environmental externalities, such as acid rain and global warming, and health externalities. The section on public goods begins in Chapter 7 with a discussion of private and public solutions to the public goods problem, and highlights two of the major issues in public provision: cost/benefit analysis (Chapter 8) and political economy (Chapter 9). I then turn to a discussion of the role of state and local governments as providers of public goods, highlighting the potential efficiencies and costs of decentralization in Chapter 10, before discussing education, one of the most important public goods in the United States, in Chapter 11.

▶ **Social Insurance and Redistribution** I have been gratified that instructors have responded positively to this book's major innovation: the expanded discussion of social insurance and redistribution, the largest and fastest growing function of government. This section begins with a novel chapter on the theory of social insurance: Chapter 12 highlights the reasons why we have social insurance, its role in crowding out private self-insurance, and the problems of moral hazard. I then include a separate chapter on the nation's largest social insurance program, Social Security (Chapter 13), and another on the three other non-health social insurance programs: unemployment insurance, disability insurance, and workers' compensation (Chapter 14). Given the enormous and growing role of governments in the provision of health care, I devote two chapters to this topic, first discussing the nature of health insurance and health economics in Chapter 15 and then focusing on the government's role in Chapter

16. Finally, Chapter 17 discusses the role of government as a redistributive agent through welfare programs.

▶ **Taxation in Theory and Practice** The feedback on the novel organization of the tax chapters has also been very positive. Nevertheless, these chapters went through a rigorous and widespread review process before the second edition, and the revised chapters reflect the excellent comments we received. The coverage of taxation begins with a chapter (Chapter 18) on the key institutional features and theoretical concepts (such as vertical equity and the Haig-Simons tax base) that are central to understanding tax policy. There are then two chapters that cover the theoretical underpinnings of tax incidence (Chapter 19) and tax efficiency analysis (Chapter 20). These chapters include applications to measuring the incidence of taxation in the United States and to designing optimal commodity and income taxes.

The next three chapters focus on the behavioral responses of individuals to income taxation, and discuss key tax policies that affect those behaviors: labor supply (and the Earned Income Tax Credit) in Chapter 21, savings (and tax-subsidized retirement savings) in Chapter 22, and the distribution of asset holdings (and capital gains, estate, and property taxes) in Chapter 23. Chapter 24 presents an overview of the corporate income tax and reviews the key equity and efficiency issues that are the focus of corporate tax debates. Finally, in a chapter that received overwhelmingly positive response from those teaching from the book, Chapter 25 concludes by discussing the motivations for, barriers to, and approaches to fundamental reform of taxation policies in the United States.

Integration of Policy Applications

The theoretical analysis that is at the core of public finance is most compelling if students can see the real-world applications that are informed by that theory. This book provides a multitude of policy applications and examples to help students appreciate the insights of public finance. Whenever a new topic is discussed, it is placed in the policy environment in the surrounding text. In addition, there are 53 separate policy applications spread throughout the book to help emphasize the importance of the material. These applications cover topics such as the difficulties policy makers face in valuing human life in cost/benefit analysis, the debate over prescription drugs in the Medicare program, appropriate and inappropriate business deductions under the income tax, and a detailed discussion of the recommendations of the recent Presidential panel on tax reform. Finally, several chapters in the text are devoted exclusively to policy applications such as global warming and education.

Integration of Empirical Evidence

Theoretical development is central to the presentation of core public finance concepts. But the presentation of theory is greatly enhanced by a careful presentation of the empirical evidence that supports, or does not support, these theoretical models. In this book, empirical evidence is presented in two ways to provide flexibility for instructors with different tastes for this material. Throughout the text, whenever a major theoretical point is made, I discuss the relevant empirical findings on this same question, as well as the certainty that we have about particular empirical findings. In addition, for those who want to teach a more empirically oriented course, Chapter 3 carefully explains how to interpret empirical results to students of public finance who may not have been exposed to sophisticated empirical methods. I have also included 26 Empirical Evidence boxes, which discuss in more detail the studies that underlie the empirical results presented in the text and illustrate for students the process of research and the methods by which empirical economists answer central policy questions. I am gratified that the inclusion of these boxes has been so widely applauded by users of the book.

Improved Presentation and Pedagogy

As inherently interesting as this material is, student interest in any text critically depends on the exposition and presentation. I have endeavored throughout the text to use a student-friendly, conversational style that emphasizes the intuition, graphics and mathematics of theory. Instructors using the book have reported that their students have found *Public Finance and Public Policy* to be an accessible, illuminating, and engaging read.

Several features make this book appealing to potential users:

▶ **Integrated Applications** As noted earlier, the 53 applications in this text allow students to step back from the main text and appreciate the policy relevance of the material. These applications are integrated directly with the text, rather than set aside, so that students understand the importance of applying the material they are learning.

▶ **Empirical Evidence Boxes** For instructors who wish to explore in more depth the nature of the empirical findings mentioned in the text, *Empirical Evidence* boxes are set aside from the main text to carefully explain the research process that generates the major empirical findings in public finance.

▶ **Integration of Relevant Statistics** Throughout the text, and in a number of graphs and tables, I present the statistics about the role of the government that emphasizes the importance of this course. It is much easier to explain to students why they should care about social insurance, for example, when they clearly see graphics that illustrate the rise in that activity as a share of the U.S. government.

▶ **Quick Hints** Throughout the text are a variety of highlighted *Quick Hints* to emphasize the intuition of key theoretical points that students often find difficult: how does one decide where to draw deadweight loss triangles (see page 52)? Why is the subsidy to employer-provided health insurance a subsidy to employees and not to employers (see page 420)? How can the income effect actually lead higher wages to cause lower levels of labor supply (see page 614)?

- **Mathematical Appendices** The text explains the material primarily through intuition and graphics, with relatively little reliance on mathematics. Nevertheless, many instructors will want to use mathematics to make key points about tax incidence, public goods provision, adverse selection in insurance markets, optimal taxation, and other topics. Five appendices develop the mathematics of these topics. Two additional appendices focus on the details of empirical analysis.

- **Marginal Definitions** Key terms are **boldfaced** throughout the text, and marginal definitions allow students to focus on the key concepts.

- **Full-Color Graphics** This is the first public finance text to use full-color graphics, allowing the students to better understand the graphical analysis that is so often confusing to them.

- **Highlights** At the end of each chapter is a summary of the key highlights from the material in that chapter.

- **Questions and Problems** At the end of each chapter are an average of 15 questions and problems. Questions on empirical analysis that draw on material in Chapter 3 are separately denoted with an **e**, and there is a careful delineation between basic and more advanced problems. The questions throughout the text have been reviewed, revised, updated, and augmented with additional problems for the second edition.

What's New in the Second Edition

New Applications

Several new applications maintain the book's focus on the interaction of theory with policy.

- **Chapter 9 Political Economy** The new application on "Contracting Out with Non-Competitive Bidding" includes examples about Hurricane Katrina cleanup and body armor providers to troops in Iraq. The application on "Direct Democracy in the United States" has also been thoroughly updated to reflect more directly the key issues raised by this section of the book.

- **Chapter 12 Social Insurance: The New Function of Government** The new application on "Flood Insurance and the 'Samaritan's Dilemma'" discusses how government-provided flood insurance has not been sufficient to solve failures in the flood insurance market because of the "Samaritan's Dilemma": individuals know that they will be bailed out by the government regardless of their insurance purchase. This application ties into discussions of Hurricane Katrina in Chapters 1 and 9.

- **Chapter 13 Social Security** The new application on "Mixed Proposals for Social Security Reform" discusses the three plans proposed by the commission President Bush appointed in 2001 to investigate solutions to Social Security's long-term fiscal problem, as well as a new bipartisan proposal to provide stable financing.

▶ **Chapter 14 Unemployment Insurance, Disability Insurance, and Workers' Compensation** The new application on "Reforming Unemployment Insurance" looks at recent proposals for reforming UI, including a system of worker self-insurance and the provision of wage insurance to displaced workers.

▶ **Chapter 16 Health Insurance II: Medicare, Medicaid, and Health Care Reform** The application on "The Medicare Prescription Drug Debate" has been thoroughly updated to discuss the initial successes and failures of this ambitious new government venture.

▶ **Chapter 21 Taxes on Labor Supply** The new application on "EITC Reform" discusses proposals to alter one of the most important redistributional features of the tax code.

▶ **Ch. 22 Taxes on Savings** The application on the "Roth IRA" has been updated to reflect recent budget shenanigans where loosening conversions to Roth IRA accounts was used to "finance" a tax extension!

▶ **Ch. 24 Corporate Taxation** A new application on "A Tax Holiday for Foreign Profits" discusses recent policy developments in how foreign profits are treated in corporate taxation.

▶ **Ch. 25 Fundamental Tax Reform** A new application on "The 2005 Panel on Tax Reform" examines the influential 2005 panel on tax reform, discussing the consensus reforms that were generally viewed as positive contributions to the debate over tax policy, as well as the controversy over some of their conclusions.

New Empirical Studies

All of the text discussions of empirical evidence on government interventions have been updated to reflect the latest developments in empirical public finance, with over 40 new empirical references incorporated into the discussion of evidence. In addition, Chapter 21 (Taxes on the Labor Supply) includes a new Empirical Evidence box on "The Effect of Child Care Costs on Maternal Labor Supply." Chapter 15 (Health Insurance I) includes an updated Empirical Evidence box on the price elasticity of demand for medical care, and Chapter 22 (Taxes on Savings) features a major update of the Empirical Evidence box on tax incentives and savings behavior, reflecting recent empirical developments.

Thoroughly Updated

Anyone using a new edition of a text expects it to have updated information. Because of the emphasis on relevant statistics, applications, and empirical evidence, however, it is essential to note that over 350 data items in text, tables, and graphs have been thoroughly researched and brought up to date.

Moreover, I received many helpful suggestions from instructors who used and reviewed the book and I implemented numerous changes in response to their comments. A sample (but much less than comprehensive) list of changes includes:

- New openings for Chapters 1 (Hurricane Katrina), 6 (pollution in China), 10 (No Child Left Behind), and 23 (Warren Buffett and the estate tax).

- Chapter 5 provides a new application of a positive production exernality by considering the case of oil drilling in an area with unproven reserves.

- Chapter 6 updates the discussion of global warming based on current events and provides updated facts on smoking in the United States and around the world.

- Chapter 9 includes a much richer discussion of the pros and cons of privatization.

- Chapter 10 includes new data on the distribution of state spending by category across the United States.

- Chapter 11 includes updated evidence on the economics of education.

- Chapter 13 includes an updated discussion of Social Security reform options, including progressive price indexing and other new proposals.

- Chapter 16 includes an updated discussion of health reform options, including a reference to the new Massachusetts health reform law that I was involved in designing.

- The basic tax example in Chapter 18 was updated to be more realistic and the background discussion of tax fairness was tightened.

- The discussion of tax distribution in Chapter 19 was augmented with interesting new results on the tax shares of the very wealthiest individuals in the United States.

- Chapter 20 was streamlined and clarified to emphasize the key concepts in tax efficiency.

- Chapter 23 includes a new overview section on the estate tax.

- Chapter 24 includes a revised discussion of the financing implications of corporate taxation which reflects new thinking in this area.

- Chapter 25 includes an updated discussion of the efficiency of consumption vs. income taxation that reflects the new "dynamic taxation" literature on this topic.

Supplements and Media Package

For many instructors, including myself, supplementary material has traditionally been irrelevant to the instruction of public finance courses. For this project, I have tried to provide supplementary material that can play a more central role in the course.

For Students and Instructors

The book's **Companion Web Site** (www.worthpublishers.com/gruber) has been created to help students learn more effectively and to provide valuable tools for professors teaching the course.

The **student side** of the Web site provides the following features:

▶ **Self-Test Quizzes** Students can test their knowledge of the material in the book by taking a multiple-choice quiz for each chapter in the text. Students receive immediate feedback, including a hint to the correct response and a page number in the text where they can study further. *All student answers are saved in an online database that can be accessed by instructors.*

▶ **Flashcards** Students may review their knowledge of key terms by studying the definitions and testing themselves with these electronic flashcards.

▶ **Research Center** This tool allows students to easily and effectively locate outside resources and readings on the Web that relate to topics covered in the textbook. Each URL is accompanied by a description of the site and its relevance to the chapter.

▶ **Student PowerPoint Slides** This version of the PowerPoint presentation created by Aaron Yelowitz of University of Kentucky is ideal for students who need extra help in understanding the concepts in each chapter. This resource enables students to review and independently prepare for classroom lectures. The PowerPoint presentation for each chapter comes complete with notes, summaries, and graphics.

The companion Web site also provides access to the following **Instructor's Resources:**

▶ **Quiz Gradebook** All student answers to the self-test quizzes are saved in an online database that can be accessed by instructors. Instructors can view and export reports of their students' practice activity.

▶ **Lecture PowerPoint Presentations** These PowerPoint slides created by Aaron Yelowitz of University of Kentucky provide comprehensive coverage of the material in each chapter. They are designed to assist with lecture preparation and presentations by incorporating key graphs from the textbook with detailed outlines of key concepts. The slides can be customized to suit instructors' individual needs and serve as a fantastic resource when building a lecture presentation. The PowerPoints are also available on the Instructor's Resource CD-ROM.

▶ **Images from the Textbook** Instructors have access to every figure and table in the new edition in high-resolution JPEG format and in the form of **Illustration PowerPoint Slides.**

Additional Resources for Instructors

Enhanced Instructor's Resources CD-ROM This **CD-ROM** includes:

- ▶ All **images from the textbook** (in JPEG and PPT formats)
- ▶ **Lecture PowerPoint presentations**
- ▶ **Solutions** to all end-of-chapter problems

With this highly accessible menu, instructors can easily customize presentations or build their own online courses. Instructors can choose from the various resources, edit, and save for use in classroom presentations.

Computerized Test Bank CD-ROM The Test Bank includes a complete set of multiple-choice and short-answer questions created to effectively test student analysis, interpretation, and comprehension of the concepts covered in the textbook. Each question is identified by level, text page reference, and key concepts. This Test Bank is powered by Brownstone for both Windows and Macintosh users. With Brownstone's Diploma application, instructors can easily create tests as well as write and edit questions. Tests can be printed in a wide range of formats. The software's unique synthesis of flexible word-processing and database features creates a program that is extremely intuitive and capable. It is accompanied by a gradebook that enables instructors to record students' grades throughout the course. It also includes the capacity to track student records, view detailed analyses of test items, and generate reports.

Acknowledgments

This book is the product of the efforts of an enormous number of people. While I'll try my best to acknowledge them all, I apologize in advance to those I have forgotten.

My initial debts are to the teachers and colleagues who taught me public finance: Peter Diamond, Marty Feldstein, Jim Poterba, and especially Larry Summers, on whose 1990 public finance course this text is very loosely based! I was very fortunate to have been able to learn at the feet of the giants of my field, and I hope that I can do them justice in passing their insights onto the next generation of public finance economists. I am also grateful to Larry Summers for making it possible for me to work at the Treasury Department in 1997–1998, which gave me an appreciation of the power of public finance analysis and the importance of educating our future generations of policy makers in the right way so that they can think about all aspects of public finance in a thorough manner.

I also owe a debt of gratitude to the generations of undergraduate students at MIT who suffered through the development of the material in this book. I am embarrassed at how much more complete my understanding is of this material because of the hard questions they asked over the years, and I only wish I could have done them the service of teaching the material as well as I am now able. Several of my students also helped in working on the book itself, and I am grateful in particular to Liz Ananat, Alan Bengtzen, David Seif, and Chris Smith for their assistance. I am also grateful to my secretary, Jessica

Colon, for her invaluable assistance in finding me materials I needed for this book, often at the last minute!

I am also extremely grateful to the hard-working team at Worth Publishers who made this book possible. Publisher Craig Bleyer shouldered the bulk of the burden of planning this revision and getting it underway. Acquisitions Editor Sarah Dorger came on later in the process to shepherd it through the final phases of production and marketing. In these efforts she was helped by the able efforts of Worth's production group: Associate Managing Editor Tracey Kuehn, Marketing Manager Scott Guile, Project Editor Kerry O'Shaughnessy, Production Manager Barbara Seixas, Art Director Babs Reingold, designer Lissi Sigillo, Photo Editor Cecilia Varas, and Editorial Assistant Leigh Renhard.

This entire project was feasible because of the assistance of several colleagues who generously devoted their time to rounding out the package of materials. David Figlio and Casey Rothschild provided the wonderful questions and problems that are found at the end of each chapter, and Kate Krause and Casey Rothschild provided the elegant solutions to the end-of-chapter problems. Aaron Yelowitz prepared the very helpful PowerPoint slides that assist teachers in bringing the text into the classroom.

A huge number of colleagues were very receptive when pestered for questions, insights, and informal reviews of the text. A less-than-comprehensive list, impressive in both its quantity and quality, includes Daron Acemoglu (MIT), Joe Aldy (Harvard University), Josh Angrist (MIT), David Autor (MIT), Steve Ansolebehere (MIT), Kate Baicker (Dartmouth College), Olivier Blanchard (MIT), Becky Blank (University of Michigan), Len Burman (Urban Institute), Ricardo Caballero (MIT), Chris Carroll (Johns Hopkins University), Amitabh Chandra (Dartmouth College), Gary Claxton (Kaiser Family Foundation), Robert Coen (Northwestern University), Jonathan Cohn (New Republic), Miles Corak (UNICEF), Julie Cullen (University of California at San Diego), David Cutler (Harvard University), Susan Dadres (Southern Methodist University), Angus Deaton (Princeton University), Peter Diamond (MIT), David Dranove (Northwestern University), Esther Duflo (MIT), Jae Edmonds (Pacific Northwest National Laboratory), Gary Engelhardt (Syracuse University), Roger Feldman (University of Minnesota), Martin Feldstein (Harvard University), David Figlio (University of Florida), Amy Finkelstein (Harvard University), Alan Garber (Stanford University), Bill Gentry (Williams College), David Green (University of British Columbia), Michael Greenstone (MIT), Jerry Hausman (MIT), Vivian Ho (Rice University), Caroline Hoxby (Harvard University), Hilary Hoynes (University of California at Berkeley), Paul Joskow (MIT), Larry Katz (Harvard University), Melissa Kearney (Wellesley College), Barrett Kirwan (Cornell University), Wojciech Kopczuk (Columbia University), Botond Koszegi (University of California at Berkeley), Jeff Leibman (Harvard University), Phil Levine (Wellesley College), Larry Levitt (Kaiser Family Foundation), Brigitte Madrian (University of Pennsylvania), Kathleen McGarry (UCLA), Bruce Meyer (University of Chicago), Kevin Milligan (University of British

Columbia), Sendhil Mullainathan (Harvard University), Robert Moffitt (Johns Hopkins University), Casey Mulligan (University of Chicago), Joe Newhouse (Harvard University), John Nyman (University of Minnesota), Ted O'Donoghue (Cornell University), Peter Orszag (Brookings Institution), Leslie Papke (Michigan State University), Franco Perrachi (Tor Vegatta University), Jim Poterba (MIT), Matt Rabin (University of California at Berkeley), Joshua Rauh (University of Chicago), Craig Ridell (University of British Columbia), Casey Rothschild (MIT), Ceci Rouse (Princeton University), Emmanuel Saez (Berkeley), Jesse Shapiro (Harvard University), Karl Scholz (University of Wisconsin), Kosali Simon (Cornell University), Jon Skinner (Dartmouth College), Joel Slemrod (University of Michigan), Kent Smetters (University of Pennsylvania), Jim Snyder (MIT), Rob Stavins (Harvard University), John Straub (Texas A & M), Chris Taber (Northwestern University), Richard Thaler (University of Chicago), Ebonya Washington (Yale University), Ivan Werning (MIT).

In addition to this gargantuan list, there was also a large number of terrific colleagues who were willing to give their time and energy to formal reviews of the textbook, particularly Julie Cullen (University of California at San Diego), Malcolm Getz (Vanderbilt University), Randall Holcombe (Florida State University), and John Straub (Texas A & M). Other invaluable reviews and comments for this edition came from Saku Aura (University of Missouri), Jon Bakija (Williams College), James E. Bathgate (Linfield College), William G. Borges (Southwest Minnesota State University), Lindsay Noble Calkins (John Carroll University), Christopher Colburn (Old Dominion University), Sewin Chan (Wagner Graduate School of Public Service, New York University), F. Trenery Dolbear Jr. (Brandeis University), Wolfgang Gick (Dartmouth College), Robert J. Gitter (Ohio Wesleyan University), Philip M. Holleran (Radford University), Gary A. Hoover (University of Alabama), Wei-chiao Huang (Western Michigan University), Wojciech Kopczuk (Columbia University), Agnieszka Bielinska-Kwapisz (Montana State University), Brigette Madrian (University of Pennsylvania), Robert Moore (Occidental College), Jessica Wolpaw Reyes (Amherst College), Robert C. Sahr (Oregon State University), Christiana Stoddard (Montana State University, Bozeman), Kurtis J. Swope (U.S. Naval Academy), and George Zodrow (Rice University)

Several individuals stand out above the others in facilitating the book as you see it now: my editor, Jane Tufts, and my research assistants, Josh Goodman, Hoai-Luu Nguyen, and Yiwei Zhang. In the first edition, Jane was responsible for taking my incoherent babble and turning into helpful exposition. Her ability to understand what I was trying to say, even when I wasn't exactly saying it, and translate it into clear text was uncanny. For the second edition, she performed more of the same. She has been a pleasure at all times to work with, and my ability to write is immeasurably improved for the experience of working with her.

Josh Goodman's contribution is no less than the roughly one-half of this book that is examples, anecdotes, statistics, and graphs. He worked tirelessly for more than a year to meet my most demanding and esoteric requests for examples and applications, in most cases turning up the ideal case study to illustrate the point I was trying to make. He turned my chicken-scratch diagrams into beautiful PowerPoint presentations. And he was a master at finding any statistic or fact, no matter how obscure. I am also extremely grateful to Hoai-Luu and Yiwei, who worked long hours to update the hundreds of facts in this edition, to expand on existing applications, and to provide new ones as well.

Finally, my greatest debt is to my family. I am grateful to my parents, Marty and Ellie, for providing me with the education and skills that allowed me to pursue this project. I hope my children, Sam, Jack, and Ava, can find some small solace for the time I spent away from them and on this book in their prominent place as examples throughout the text. And I am most of all grateful to my wonderful wife, Andrea, whose sacrifice throughout this project was the largest of all. Her unending support, from the initial decision process through the last page proof, was the backbone on which this effort was built, and I hope that someday I can make it up to her.

Why Study Public Finance?

On August 24, 2005, a tropical storm began moving from the Bahamas to the southeastern coast of the United States. As it moved toward Florida, this tropical storm became Hurricane Katrina, a Category 1 hurricane, with winds of 75 miles per hour. August 25 gave the United States its first taste of Hurricane Katrina, when nine people died in South Florida, but this was just the beginning. By August 28, Katrina had been elevated to a Category 5 hurricane, with winds of up to 175 miles per hour. It hit the southern Gulf Coast of the United States on the morning of August 29, and the devastation was enormous. Many parts of the city of New Orleans were completely destroyed as Katrina drove the sea through the levees that were supposed to keep the low-lying New Orleans safe from flooding. In the end, 1,200 people died in Hurricane Katrina and its aftermath, and there was more than $80 billion in property damage, making Katrina the costliest hurricane on record.[1]

From almost the moment Katrina hit New Orleans, there was enormous criticism of the government's role in preparing for this hurricane. Federal government officials blamed the state of Louisiana and the city of New Orleans for not adequately responding to the crisis. Shortly after the hurricane, President George W. Bush said that the magnitude of the crisis "has created tremendous problems that have strained state and local capabilities. . . . The result is that many of our citizens simply are not getting the help they need, especially in New Orleans. And that is unacceptable." But local officials claimed that the federal government bore most of the blame. "Everybody shares the blame here," said New Orleans City Council President Oliver Thomas. "But when you talk about the mightiest government in the world, that's a ludicrous and lame excuse. You're FEMA [the Federal Emergency Management Agency], and you're the big dog. And you weren't prepared either."[2]

---

[1] For a detailed timeline on Hurricane Katrina, see http://www.brookings.edu/fp/projects/homeland/katrina-timeline.pdf. Other information on Katrina is from CNN's Hurricane Katrina main page: http://www.cnn.com/SPECIALS/2005/katrina/.

[2] Details from Roig-Franzia and Hsu (2005).

The lack of coordination between levels of government was made dramatically apparent when FEMA ordered 182 million pounds of ice, much more than was needed, almost 60% of which never even reached the disaster area. The majority of the ice ended up being trucked to different storage units all over the United States with some even traveling 1,600 miles away from the Katrina damage zone to warehouses in Maine. In total, even though the majority of the ice was never used, over $100 million was spent by FEMA on ice purchases for Katrina relief (Shane and Lipton, 2005).

Equally controversial was the question of the proper government role in reconstructing New Orleans in the wake of this disaster. Politicians spoke out quickly for the need to send resources to the devastated region. In the days and weeks following Hurricane Katrina, President Bush and Congress vowed that everything would be done to rebuild the Gulf Coast, and allocated $62.3 billion to the ongoing effort. The "Bring Back New Orleans" Commission, established by New Orleans Mayor Ray Nagin, recommended an expansive reconstruction program, citing the city's importance to the petrochemical industry and the need for access to the Gulf of Mexico through its ports. This commission recommended that the government buy back heavily flooded and damaged homes at 100% of their pre-Katrina value and aggressively pursue neighborhood planning for a rebuilt city, including major new housing construction and the construction of high-speed transit in the city.

But others questioned the wisdom of pouring government resources into a city that was at risk of future devastation from natural disasters (and, indeed, New Orleans had already been catastrophically flooded in 1965 by Hurricane Betsy, the nation's costliest hurricane to that point). "It looks like a lot of that place could be bulldozed," House Speaker Dennis Hastert said in an interview with the *Daily Herald* of Arlington Heights, Ill. Asked whether it made sense to spend billions of dollars rebuilding a city that lies below sea level, he told the paper, "I don't know. That doesn't make sense to me."[3] And economist Edward Glaeser wrote that "New Orleans will remain a great city, but that great city can and should be much smaller than it has been in the past."[4] Glaeser suggested that, rather than spend $100 billion rebuilding New Orleans, the government simply give each resident a check for $200,000, which would be ten times the average annual income for city residents.[5]

Reconstruction of New Orleans has in fact proceeded at a much slower pace than initially promised. Nearly nine months after the hurricane struck, less than half of the city's residents had returned and only 1 in 10 businesses were open. Rebuilding had been stalled, in part, by the federal government's delay in releasing new building requirements and by the ruined cars and debris that still littered the streets. As Louisiana Lieutenant Governor Mitch Landrieu lamented, "The rebuild's got to start sometime, and it's not happening."[6]

---

[3] Hastert later issued a statement saying he was not "advocating that the city be abandoned or relocated."
[4] Glaeser (2006).
[5] Glaeser (2005).
[6] Facts and quotes from Rivlin (2006), Sangar and Andrews (2005), and Schwartz (2006).

The controversies about the proper role of the government in dealing with such a dramatic natural disaster raise the fundamental questions addressed by the branch of economics known as *public finance*. The goal of public finance is to *understand the proper role of the government in the economy*. On the expenditures side of public finance, we ask: What kind of services should the government provide, if any? Why should the government be in charge of rebuilding New Orleans, rather than the residents of that city? More generally, why is the government the primary provider of goods and services such as highways, education, and unemployment insurance, while provision of goods and services such as clothing, entertainment, and fire insurance is generally left to the private sector? On the revenue side of public finance, we ask: How should the government raise the money to fund expenditures such as the cost of rebuilding New Orleans? What kinds of taxes should be levied, who should pay them, and what effects do they have on the functioning of the economy?

This chapter provides an overview of the field of public finance and explains why it is an important field of study. The chapter begins with a review of the general types of questions that are addressed by public finance economists. We discuss these questions within the context of a specific example, the market for health insurance, which allows us to illustrate the importance of each question. The chapter then presents the key facts about federal, state, and local governments in the United States and places the United States' experience in an international context. Finally, the last section reviews some of the major public finance debates in the United States today.

1.1

The Four Questions of Public Finance

In the simplest terms, **public finance** is the study of the role of the government in the economy. This is a very broad definition. This study involves answering the **four questions of public finance:**

▶ *When* should the government intervene in the economy?

▶ *How* might the government intervene?

▶ *What* is the effect of those interventions on economic outcomes?

▶ *Why* do governments choose to intervene in the way that they do?

In this section, we explore these four questions within the context of a specific example: the market for *health insurance,* in which individuals pay a monthly premium to insurance companies, in return for which insurance companies pay the individuals' medical bills if they are ill. This is only one of many markets in which the government is involved, but it is a particularly useful example, since health care spending is the single largest and fastest growing part of the U.S. government's budget.

public finance The study of the role of the government in the economy.

four questions of public finance When should the government intervene in the economy? How might the government intervene? What is the effect of those interventions on economic outcomes? Why do governments choose to intervene in the way that they do?

When Should the Government Intervene in the Economy?

To understand the reason for government intervention, think of the economy as a series of trades between producers (firms) and consumers. A trade is *efficient* if it makes at least one party better off without making the other party worse off. The total efficiency of the economy is maximized when as many efficient trades as possible are made.

The fundamental lesson of basic microeconomics is that in most cases the *competitive market equilibrium is the most efficient outcome for society*—that is, it is the outcome that maximizes the gains from efficient trades. As discussed in much more detail in Chapter 2, the free adjustment of prices guarantees that, in competitive market equilibrium, supply equals demand. When supply equals demand, all trades that are valued by both producers and consumers are being made. Any good that consumers value above its cost of production will be produced and consumed; goods that consumers value at less than their cost of production will not be produced or consumed.

If the competitive market equilibrium is the most efficient outcome for society, why do governments intervene in the operation of some of these markets? There are two reasons why governments may want to intervene in market economies: market failures and redistribution.

market failure Problem that causes the market economy to deliver an outcome that does not maximize efficiency.

Market Failures The first motivation for government involvement in the economy is the existence of **market failures,** problems that cause a market economy to deliver an outcome that does not maximize efficiency. Throughout this book, and in particular in Chapters 5–17, we discuss a host of market failures that impede the operation of the market forces you learned about in basic microeconomics. Here we briefly explore a failure in the health insurance market that may cause its equilibrium outcome to be inefficient.

At first glance, the market for health insurance seems to be a standard textbook competitive market. Health insurance is supplied by a large number of insurance companies and demanded by a large number of households. In the market equilibrium where supply equals demand, social efficiency should be maximized: anyone who values health insurance above its cost of production is able to buy insurance.

In 2004, there were 45.8 million persons without health insurance in the United States, or 18% of the non-elderly population (as we'll discuss in Chapter 15, the elderly are provided universal health coverage in the United States under the Medicare program).[7] The existence of such a large number of uninsured does not, however, imply that the market doesn't work. After all, there are many more Americans who don't have a large-screen TV, or a new car, or a home of their own. That a small minority of the population is uninsured does not by itself prove that there is a problem in the market; it just implies that those without insurance don't value it enough to buy it at existing prices.

---

[7] Employee Benefit Research Institute (2005).

Is this equilibrium outcome, which leaves 45.8 million people without health insurance, the most efficient outcome for society? It may not be, as the following example shows. Suppose that I am uninsured, and as a result do not get my yearly vaccination for influenza. By not getting my flu shot, I increase my risk of getting the flu, and increase the risk of passing it on to all of the students who come into contact with me and have not had flu shots. If these students become ill, their medical costs will rise and their performance in class will worsen. Thus, the total or *social* value of health insurance is not just the improvement it causes in my health, but also the improvement it causes in my students' health, which lowers their medical costs and improves class performance. Thus, I should have insurance if the total social value, both to myself and to others with whom I have contact, exceeds the cost of that insurance.

When I make my insurance decision, however, I don't consider that total social value, only the value to myself. Suppose that I value the insurance at less than its cost because I don't mind getting the flu, but that society values the insurance at more than its cost because it is very costly for my students to go to the doctor and to perform poorly in class if they get sick. In this situation, I won't buy insurance, even though society (which includes me and my students) would be better off if I did. In this case, the competitive outcome has not maximized total social efficiency.

This is an example of a *negative externality*, whereby my decision imposes on others costs that I don't bear. As a result of this negative externality, I am underinsuring myself from society's perspective because I don't take into account the full costs that my medical decisions impose on others. We will discuss externalities in much more detail in Chapters 5 and 6, but this example illustrates the type of market failure that can cause the competitive equilibrium to deliver a socially inefficient outcome. Later chapters in the book discuss other types of market failure as well.

If the competitive equilibrium does not lead to the efficiency-maximizing outcome, there is the *potential* for efficiency improvement through government intervention. Since the government can take into account not only my costs and benefits but also the costs and benefits to others as well, the government can more accurately compare the social costs to the social benefits, and induce me to buy insurance if the total benefits exceed the total costs. As we emphasize in answering the fourth question, however, the fact that the private market outcome is not efficiency maximizing does not imply that government intervention will necessarily improve efficiency.

▶ APPLICATION

The Measles Epidemic of 1989–1991[8]

One of the illnesses for which all children are supposed to be immunized is measles. Measles is transmitted from person to person by respiratory droplets

---

[8] Wood and Brunell (1995).

and is characterized by a high fever and severe rash that lasts five to six days. In the early 1960s, there were thought to be 3 to 4 million cases annually in the United States, resulting in 500 reported deaths each year. Other costs associated with measles infection included medical expenditures and work time lost for parents in caring for sick children.

Then, in 1963, a measles vaccine was introduced. Measles vaccination greatly reduces, but does not eliminate, the chance of contracting measles, and the vaccine can wear off over time if you don't get periodic "booster" shots to reactivate the immunity. As a result of the vaccine, measles cases had become relatively rare in the United States by the 1980s, with fewer than 3,000 cases reported per year and very few deaths. Over the period from 1989 to 1991, however, there was a huge resurgence in measles in the United States, with over 50,000 cases and 123 deaths from a disease thought to be largely eradicated. What happened?

In retrospect, it is clear that this outbreak resulted from very low immunization rates among disadvantaged inner-city youths. One-third of all of the new cases were in Los Angeles, Chicago, and Houston, and one-half of those children who contracted measles had not been immunized, even though many had regular contact with a physician. These unimmunized children were imposing a negative externality on other children who had received their immunizations but for whom immunization may have worn off. There was a negative externality because the unimmunized children raised the risk that these other children would become sick, without bearing any of the costs of raising this risk.

The federal government responded to this health crisis in the early 1990s, first through publicly encouraging parents to get their children immunized, and then through an initiative that paid for the vaccines for low-income families. The result was impressive. Immunization rates, which had never been above 70% before the epidemic, rose to 90% by 1995. And, by 1995, there were only about 300 confirmed cases of measles. Government intervention clearly reduced this negative externality. ◀

redistribution The shifting of resources from some groups in society to others.

Redistribution The second reason for government intervention is **redistribution,** the shifting of resources from some groups in society to others. Think of the economy as a pie, the size of which is determined by the social efficiency of the economy. If there are no market failures, then the private market forces of demand and supply maximize the size of the pie; if there are market failures, there is the potential for the government to increase the size of the pie.

The government may care not only about the size of the pie, however, but also its distribution, or the size of each person's slice. For reasons we discuss in Chapter 2, society may decide that the resource allocations provided by the market economy are unfair; for example, society may view another dollar of consumption by a very rich person as less valuable than another dollar of consumption by a very poor person. The primary way to correct such misallocations is through government interventions that redistribute resources from those groups that society has deemed "too well off" to those groups that society has deemed "not well off enough." For example, in the United States in 2004, three-quarters of the uninsured are in families with incomes below the median income level. Thus, society may feel that it is appropriate to redistribute from those with insurance, who tend to have higher incomes, to those without, who tend to have lower incomes.

In some cases, society can undertake redistributions that change only the distribution of the pieces and not the size of the pie itself. Usually, however, redistributing resources from one group to another will entail *efficiency losses*. These losses occur because the act of redistribution causes individuals to shift their behavior away from the efficiency-maximizing point. For example, if we tax the rich to distribute money to the poor, then this tax may cause the rich to work less hard (since they don't get to take home as much money from their work) and the poor to work less hard (since they don't have to work as hard to maintain their living standards). When these groups work less hard, they don't produce goods that would be valued by consumers at more than they cost to produce, so social efficiency is reduced.

In general, then, there will be a trade-off between the size of the pie and the distribution of the pie, which we call an *equity–efficiency trade-off*. Societies typically have to choose between pies that are larger and more unequally distributed and pies that are smaller and more equally distributed.

How Might the Government Intervene?

Having decided whether to intervene, the next question is how the government should do so. There are several different general approaches that the government can take to intervention.

Tax or Subsidize Private Sale or Purchase One way that the government can try to address failures in the private market is to use the *price mechanism,* whereby government policy is used to change the price of a good in one of two ways:

1. Through *taxes,* which raise the price for private sales or purchases of goods that are overproduced, or
2. Through *subsidies,* which lower the price for private sales or purchases of goods that are underproduced.

Returning to the example of health insurance, one policy option that is currently popular in the United States is for the government to subsidize the purchase of private health insurance to reduce the number of uninsured. For example, the Bush administration has repeatedly proposed that individuals receive a credit against their taxes for expenditures on health insurance.

Restrict or Mandate Private Sale or Purchase Alternatively, the government can directly restrict private sale or purchase of goods that are overproduced, or mandate private purchase of goods that are underproduced and force individuals to buy that good. In 1994, for example, President Clinton proposed a plan that would mandate that firms provide health insurance to their employees. This plan did not succeed in the United States, but many nations, such as Germany, mandate that almost all citizens have health insurance coverage.

Public Provision Another alternative is to have the government provide the good directly, in order to potentially attain the level of consumption that maximizes social welfare. In the United States, more than one-quarter of the population has insurance that is provided to it directly by the government; Canada and many other developed nations have publicly provided health insurance for their entire populations.

Public Financing of Private Provision Finally, governments may want to influence the level of consumption but may not want to directly involve themselves in the provision of a good. In such cases, the government can finance private entities to provide the desired level of provision. For example, the 2003 legislation to add a prescription drug benefit to the United States' Medicare insurance program for the disabled and elderly involves federal government reimbursement of private insurers to provide prescription drug insurance.

As you can see, there is a wide spectrum of policy options. When considering how to intervene, policy makers should carefully evaluate alternative options before deciding which option is best. This evaluation leads naturally to the third question: How can we evaluate alternative policy options?

What Are the Effects of Alternative Interventions?

Answering this third question requires that policy makers understand the implications of each policy option under consideration. This evaluation is the focus of *empirical public finance,* which involves gathering data and developing statistical models to assess how people and firms might respond to policy interventions. We discuss empirical public finance in much more detail in Chapter 3.

In assessing the effects of government interventions, policy makers must keep in mind that any policy has *direct and indirect effects.*

direct effects The effects of government interventions that would be predicted if individuals did not change their behavior in response to the interventions.

Direct Effects The **direct effects** of government interventions are those effects that would be predicted if individuals did not change their behavior in response to the interventions. For example, suppose that the government wants to try to address the problem of the uninsured by providing free public health care, as is done in the United Kingdom. The government computes that, with 45.8 million uninsured, and an average cost of treating each uninsured person of $2,000 per year, this intervention would cost $92 billion per year. This is a huge amount, but it is much smaller than existing spending on health care by the U.S. government ($550 billion). According to this calculation, we could cover all of the uninsured for less than 4% of the federal budget.[9]

---

[9] Office of Management and Budget (2006a), Table 3.1.

Indirect Effects The **indirect effects** of government intervention are effects that arise only because individuals change their behavior in response to the interventions. For example, being uninsured is something that people can change about themselves; it is not a fixed personal characteristic such as being male or African American. By providing free health care to those who are uninsured, the government provides strong incentives for those paying for their own health insurance to drop that insurance and take part in the government's free health care program.

> **indirect effects** The effects of government interventions that arise only because individuals change their behavior in response to the interventions.

Suppose that half of the non-elderly who are privately insured behaved this way. This would add another 88 million persons to the pool using this public source of care. If each person in this group also costs $2,000 on average, the government cost of the program would almost triple, to $268 billion per year! On the other hand, if only 10% of the privately insured behaved this way, the government cost of the program would rise to only $127 billion per year.

The key question for evaluating free public health care for the uninsured is therefore: How many privately insured will drop their privately purchased coverage to join a free public option? This is an empirical question. The public finance economist needs some means of drawing on data to make the best estimate of the extent of such movement. Throughout this book, we discuss a variety of ways that empirical public finance economists make such estimates, and how economists use these to inform their understanding of the effects of alternative government interventions.

▶ **APPLICATION**

The Congressional Budget Office: Government Scorekeepers

Empirical economics is not just the plaything of academics. The methods and results derived from empirical economics are central to the development of public policy at all levels of government. A particularly good example of the power of empirical economics is provided by the Congressional Budget Office (CBO).

The CBO was created in 1975 with a mission to provide Congress with the objective, timely, nonpartisan analyses needed for economic and budget decisions.[10] The CBO increasingly plays a critical role as a "scorekeeper" for government policy debates. Legislative spending proposals that are to

"We don't use the Congressional Budget Office. We have our own figures."

---

[10] Information on the CBO comes from its Web site: http://www.cbo.gov/Policies.cfm.

become law must first have their costs estimated by the analysts at the CBO. Given budgetary pressures on the federal government, policy makers have increasingly referred their legislation to the CBO earlier and earlier in the development process. If they know what "score" their spending proposal will receive (i.e., how much the CBO says it will cost), they can tailor the proposal to fit within a given budget target.

It is not an overstatement to say that the economists who work at the CBO frequently hold the fate of a legislative proposal in their hands. Indeed, the large price tag that the CBO assigned to the Clinton administration's plan to reform health care in the United States in 1994 is often cited as a key factor in the defeat of that proposal.[11] The methods we study in Chapter 3 and many of the results that we learn about throughout this book are central to the internal deliberations of the analysts at the CBO. ◄

Why Do Governments Do What They Do?

Finally, as students of public policy, we must recognize that we cannot simply model governments as benign actors who intervene only to mitigate market failures or assure the proper distribution of social resources. In practice, the government faces the difficult problems of aggregating the preferences of millions of citizens into a coherent set of policy decisions, raising the fourth question of public finance: Why do governments do what they do? Note the important difference between this question and the second (How should governments intervene?). The second question was a *normative* question, one concerned with how things should be done. This is a *positive* question, one concerned with why things are the way they are.

political economy The theory of how the political process produces decisions that affect individuals and the economy.

To answer this question, we will turn in Chapter 9 to the tools of **political economy,** the theory of how governments make public policy decisions. Governments face enormous challenges in figuring out what the public wants and how to choose policies that match those wants. In addition, governments may be motivated by much more than simply correcting market failures or redistributing income. Just as there are a host of market failures that can interfere with the welfare-maximizing outcome from the private market, there are a host of *government failures* that can lead to inappropriate government interventions. Politicians must consider a wide variety of viewpoints and pressures, only two of which are the desire to design policies that maximize economic efficiency and redistribute resources in a socially preferred manner.

One only needs to look at the wide variety of health insurance policies in very similar countries to see that governments may have more in mind than simply efficiency or redistribution. Why does the United States rely primarily on private health insurance, while Canada, a similar country bordering the United States, relies on national public health insurance? Why does Germany mandate private health insurance coverage, while the United Kingdom pro-

---

[11] The Clinton administration had claimed that its health care reform plan would save the nation $60 billion over the 1995–2000 period, but the CBO (1994) reported that in fact it would cost the nation $70 billion over that period.

vides free national health care? Coming back to the first question (When should the government intervene?), then, we have an additional concern that must be addressed before recommending government intervention: In practice, will the government actually reduce or solve the problem? Or will government failures cause the problem to grow worse?

1.2
Why Study Public Finance? Facts on Government in the United States and Around the World

Thus far, we have clarified what public finance is. But it still may not be clear why you should spend your precious time on this topic. What makes public finance so compelling is the dominant role that governments play in our everyday lives. In this section, we detail that role by walking you through the key facts about government in the United States and other developed nations. In addition, to motivate the study of public finance, we propose some interesting questions that arise from these facts.

The Size and Growth of Government

Figure 1-1 shows the growth in federal government spending in the United States over the twentieth century. In 1930, the federal government's activity accounted for less than 3% of GDP. Since the 1970s, federal government spending has amounted to about 20% of the total size of the U.S. economy.

■ FIGURE 1-1

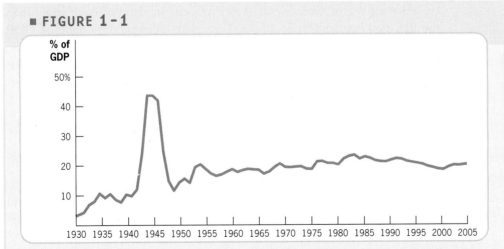

Federal Government Spending as a Percent of GDP, 1930–2005 • From 1930 to 2005, federal government spending as a share of GDP has grown from less than 3% to 20%. The huge spike in spending over the 1941–1945 period was due to the massive increase in defense expenditures during World War II.

Source: Office of Management and Budget (2006a), Table 1.2.

▪ **FIGURE 1-2**

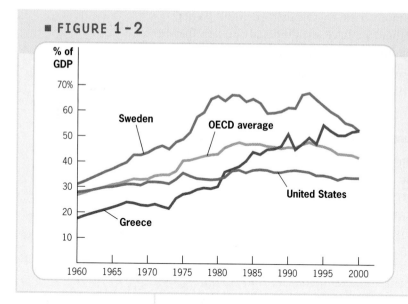

Total Government Spending Across Developed Nations, 1960–2001 • Government spending as a share of GDP has grown throughout the developed world, but the pace of growth has varied. The United States has seen a modest growth in its government share over this period, while government spending in Greece has more than tripled as a share of the economy.

Source: Organization for Economic Cooperation and Development (2001), Table 6.5 (additional data from previous editions).

This growth is mirrored in other developed nations, as seen in Figure 1-2. This figure shows the growth of government spending since 1960 in the United States, Sweden, Greece, and the average for the industrialized nations that are part of the Organization for Economic Cooperation and Development (OECD). The patterns are quite interesting. In 1960, the United States was squarely in line with the average of the OECD in terms of the government share.[12] Yet, while the government share grew on average in the OECD by 50%, it grew by only 20% in the United States. Greece started with a government share well below that of the United States in 1960, but government tripled as a share of Greece's GDP, so that today its share is much larger than the U.S. government's share. In 1960, Sweden's government's share of GDP was similar to other nations', but this share grew enormously, so that by the early 1990s government spending was about two-thirds of Sweden's GDP. Since then Sweden's government's share has fallen rapidly and now accounts for slightly more than half of GDP, similar to Greece.

▶ What explains the growth in government spending over the twentieth century?

Decentralization

A key feature of governments is the degree of *centralization* across local and national government units—that is, the extent to which spending is concentrated at higher (federal) levels or lower (state and local) levels. Figure 1-3

---

[12] Note that the size of government as a share of GDP is larger in Figure 1-2 than in Figure 1-1; this is because Figure 1-2 includes all levels of government, while Figure 1-1 is for federal government only.

shows government spending in the United States divided into the share of spending by the federal government and the share of spending by other levels of government: state, county, and local governments. The federal government provides the majority of government spending in the United States, but other government spending is quite large as well, amounting to roughly one-third of total government spending, and over 10% of GDP. The level of centralization (the share of spending done by the federal government) varies widely across nations, sometimes rising to almost 100% in countries where the federal government does almost all of the government spending.

▶ What is the appropriate extent of centralization and decentralization in government activity?

Spending, Taxes, Deficits, and Debts

When you run a household, you live on a budget. Outflows of cash for groceries, rent, clothing, entertainment, and other uses must be financed by inflows of cash from work or other sources. Any excess of income over spending is a *cash flow surplus* that can be saved to finance your own spending in future periods or, by way of an inheritance (also referred to as a *bequest*), your children's spending after you pass on. Any shortfall of income below spending is a *cash flow deficit,* and must be financed by past savings or by borrowing from others. Any borrowing results in the buildup of some household *debt,* which must ultimately be repaid from future inflows of cash.

Fundamentally, the finances of the government are no different. Its outflows are government spending and its inflows are tax revenues. If revenues exceed spending, then there is a budget surplus; if revenues fall short of spending, there is a budget deficit. Each dollar of government deficit adds to the stock of government debt. That is, the *deficit* measures the year-to-year shortfall of revenues relative to spending; the *debt* measures the accumulation of past deficits over time. This government debt must be financed by borrowing from either citizens of one's own local or national area, or by borrowing from citizens of other areas or other nations.

The three panels of Figure 1-4 show government spending and revenues, the deficit or surplus, and the level of government debt for the U.S. federal government. As shown in panels (a) and (b), with the exception of an enormous increase in spending unmatched by increased taxation during World War II (1941–1945), the federal government's budget was close to balanced until the late 1960s. From the mid-1970s through the mid-1990s, there was a relatively large deficit that rose to about 5% of GDP. This deficit shrank dramatically in the 1990s, and actually turned into a sizeable surplus by the end of the decade. But the United States was back in deficit by the early twenty-first century, at levels similar to those in the 1970s.

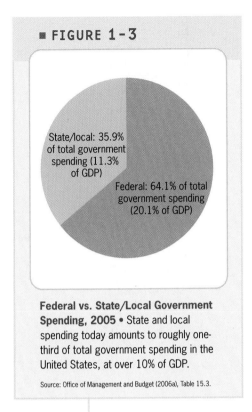

■ **FIGURE 1-3**

State/local: 35.9% of total government spending (11.3% of GDP)

Federal: 64.1% of total government spending (20.1% of GDP)

Federal vs. State/Local Government Spending, 2005 • State and local spending today amounts to roughly one-third of total government spending in the United States, at over 10% of GDP.

Source: Office of Management and Budget (2006a), Table 15.3.

■ FIGURE 1-4

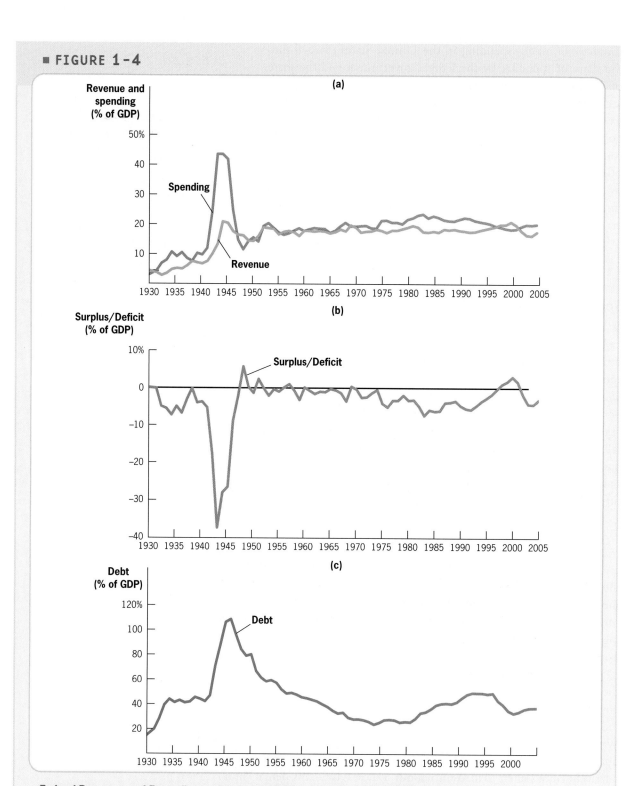

Federal Revenues and Expenditures, Surplus or Deficit, and Debt, 1930–2005 • For most of the twentieth century, except for the World War II period, federal government tax receipts have kept pace with expenditures. But expenditures have exceeded receipts by several percentage points of GDP on average since the 1970s. The resulting federal government debt is now at about 35% of GDP.

Source: Office of Management and Budget (2006a), Tables 1.2 and 7.1. (Debt figures for 1930–1939 come from the U.S. Department of the Treasury's Bureau of the Public Debt.)

■ **FIGURE 1-5**

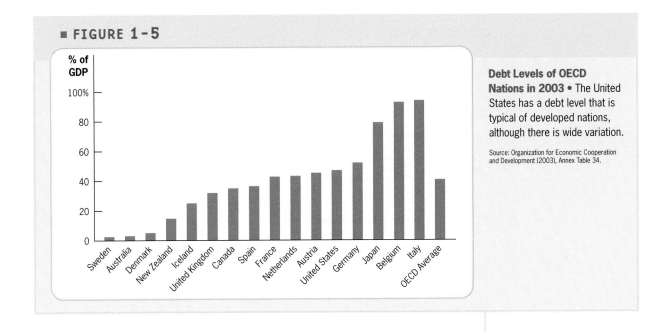

Debt Levels of OECD Nations in 2003 • The United States has a debt level that is typical of developed nations, although there is wide variation.

Source: Organization for Economic Cooperation and Development (2003), Annex Table 34.

The resulting implications for the federal debt are shown in panel (c) of Figure 1-4. The stock of debt rose sharply in World War II, then fell steadily until large deficits caused it to rise in the 1980s. The debt has risen considerably since, with a brief pause in the mid- to late 1990s, and now is roughly 35% of GDP. Figure 1-5 compares the level of U.S. debt to the level of debt of other developed nations. The United States is roughly in the middle of the pack, with debt that is much higher than that of Sweden or Australia, but much lower than that of Italy or Belgium.

▶ What are the costs of having larger deficits and a larger national debt?

Figure 1-6 (page 16) shows the spending and revenues of state and local governments over time in the United States. Interestingly, unlike the federal government, state and local governments' budgets are almost always in either surplus or balance; there is very little deficit overall across the state and local governments in any year.

▶ Why are state and local governments able to balance their budgets while the federal government is not?

Distribution of Spending

Thus far we have discussed only the sum total of government spending in the United States, and not on what these funds are spent. Figure 1-7 shows the distribution of spending across several broad categories for the federal government and state and local governments in 1960 and 2004. Several conclusions are apparent. First, the composition of federal government spending (panel (a)) has changed dramatically over time. In 1960, nearly half of federal government spending was on national defense, military expenditures either at

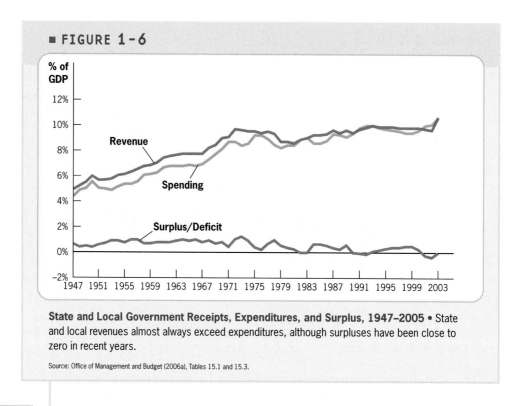

■ FIGURE 1-6

State and Local Government Receipts, Expenditures, and Surplus, 1947–2005 • State and local revenues almost always exceed expenditures, although surpluses have been close to zero in recent years.

Source: Office of Management and Budget (2006a), Tables 15.1 and 15.3.

public goods Goods for which the investment of any one individual benefits everyone in a larger group.

home or abroad. Defense is a classic example of what economists call **public goods,** goods for which the investment of any one individual benefits a larger group of individuals: if I purchased a missile to protect Boston, that would benefit not just me but all of the residents of the city. As we will discuss at length in Chapter 7, the private sector may underprovide such public goods: if I bear the full cost of buying a missile, but it benefits everyone in town, then I probably won't spend the money on that missile. This makes provision of public goods an important job for the government, as reflected in the large share of government spending in this area.

Today, however, defense spending has fallen to one-fifth of the federal budget. The offsetting spending growth can be found largely in two areas. The first is the Social Security program, which provides income support to the elderly who are retired from their jobs. This is the single largest government program in the United States today, consuming about 18% of the entire federal budget. Another large and rapidly growing category is health care programs, a variety of federal government interventions to provide health insurance for the elderly, the poor, and the disabled; this consumes almost 25% of the budget.

social insurance programs Government provision of insurance against adverse events to address failures in the private insurance market.

These types of programs are called **social insurance programs,** programs designed to address failures in private insurance markets. As we discussed earlier, private health insurance markets may not provide the appropriate amount of health insurance to the population. This market failure has motivated the government to intervene in health insurance markets; indeed, almost one-half of all health spending in the United States is done by governments. Similarly, the federal government is concerned that individuals may not plan appropri-

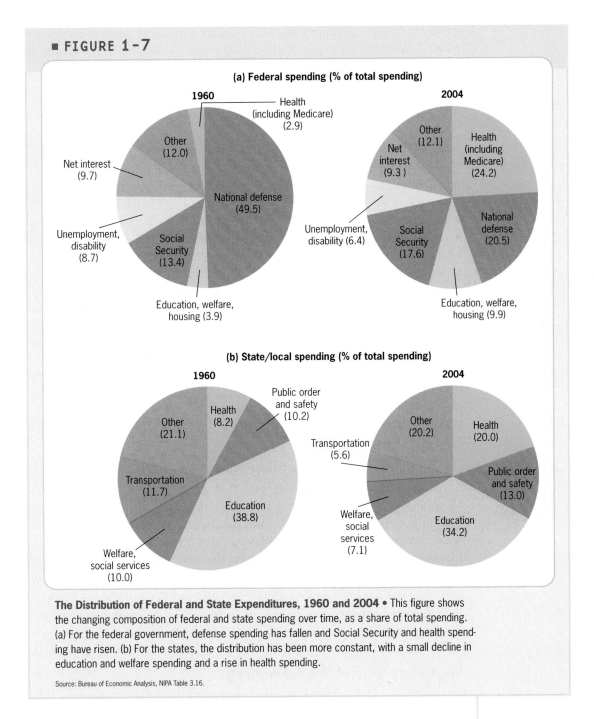

■ FIGURE 1-7

The Distribution of Federal and State Expenditures, 1960 and 2004 • This figure shows
the changing composition of federal and state spending over time, as a share of total spending.
(a) For the federal government, defense spending has fallen and Social Security and health spending have risen. (b) For the states, the distribution has been more constant, with a small decline in
education and welfare spending and a rise in health spending.

Source: Bureau of Economic Analysis, NIPA Table 3.16.

ately for the decline in income they will face when they retire, which motivates the existence of the Social Security program.

▶ Are large government interventions in insurance markets warranted,
and do they correct or exacerbate market failures?

The distribution of state and local spending (Figure 1-7, panel (b)) is much
different. At the state and local level, education, welfare, and housing account

for about 40% of spending. Only 10% of federal spending supports these programs. Likewise, there is no Social Security program or defense expenditure at the state or local level.

▶ What is the appropriate type of spending to be done at the federal versus state or local level?

Distribution of Revenue Sources

Figure 1–8 breaks down the sources of federal and state and local revenue over time. The major source of revenue for the federal government (panel (a)) is the individual *income tax,* a tax levied on the income of U.S. residents. This tax provides somewhat less than half of federal revenues and has remained roughly constant as a share of revenues over time. The major shift over time at the federal level has been the rapid shrinking of corporate tax revenues, the funds raised by taxing the incomes of businesses in the United States. While corporate tax revenues once provided almost 25% of federal government revenue, they now provide less than 14%. There has also been a sizeable reduction in *excise taxes,* taxes levied on the consumption of certain goods such as tobacco, alcohol, or gasoline.

The decrease in revenue from these taxes has been largely replaced by the growth of revenue from *payroll taxes,* the taxes on worker earnings that fund social insurance programs. Payroll taxes differ from the income tax in that the income tax includes all sources of income, such as the return on savings, while payroll taxes apply solely to earnings from work. Payroll taxes have grown from a sixth of federal revenues to well over a third.

▶ What are the implications of moving from taxing businesses and consumption to taxing workers' earnings?

At the state and local level (Figure 1–8, panel (b)), revenue sources are roughly equally divided between *sales taxes* (including state and local excise taxes on products such as cigarettes and gasoline), federal *grants-in-aid* (redistribution of funds from the federal government to lower levels of government), income taxes, and *property taxes* (taxes on the value of individual properties, mostly homes). Over the past 40 years, the substantial drop in revenue from property taxes has been made up by rising federal grants and income taxes.

▶ What are the implications of shifting from taxation of property to taxation of income?

Regulatory Role of the Government

The discussion throughout this section has focused on the government as an entity that exerts influence through its powers of taxation and spending. Another critical role the government plays in all nations is that of *regulating economic and social activities.* Consider some examples of how daily existence is affected by the government in the United States:[13]

---

[13] Information on these regulatory agencies can be found at their respective Web sites: http://www.fda.gov, http://www.osha.gov, http://www.fcc.gov, http://www.epa.gov, and http://www.uspto.gov.

■ FIGURE 1-8

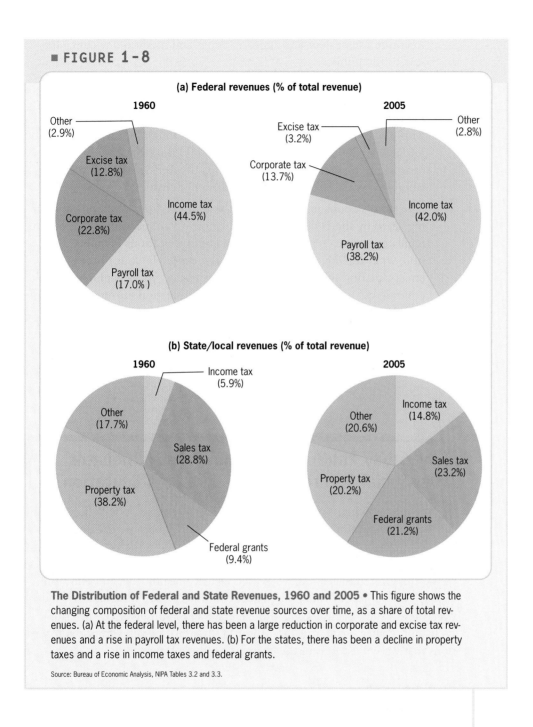

The Distribution of Federal and State Revenues, 1960 and 2005 • This figure shows the changing composition of federal and state revenue sources over time, as a share of total revenues. (a) At the federal level, there has been a large reduction in corporate and excise tax revenues and a rise in payroll tax revenues. (b) For the states, there has been a decline in property taxes and a rise in income taxes and federal grants.

Source: Bureau of Economic Analysis, NIPA Tables 3.2 and 3.3.

▶ The foods you eat and the medications you take have all been approved by the Food and Drug Administration (FDA), an agency that spends less than 0.1% of the government's budget each year, but whose regulatory powers cover $1 trillion worth of goods annually, nearly 25% of total consumer expenditures. The FDA regulates the labeling and safety of nearly all food products and bottled water, tests cosmetics to ensure their safety, and approves drugs and medical devices to be sold to the public.

▶ If you've lost a limb or developed carpal tunnel syndrome because of your work, you might want to contact the Occupational Safety and Health Administration (OSHA), which is charged with regulating the workplace safety of the 115 million Americans employed at 7.2 million job sites. In 2004, the agency sent its 1,100 inspectors on 39,000 visits to workplaces, which resulted in reports of over 87,000 workplace violations for which firms paid $85 million in penalties.

▶ The radio stations in your car and the channels you watch on cable are regulated by the Federal Communications Commission (FCC), which regulates interstate and international communications by radio, television, wire, satellite, and cable. Check any device in your home that emits radiation of communication frequencies (wireless phones, remote controls, etc.) and you'll find an FCC identification number somewhere on it.

▶ The air you breathe, the tap water you drink, and the land your home is built upon are all regulated by the Environmental Protection Agency (EPA), which is charged with minimizing dangerous pollutants in the air, water, and food supplies.

1.3

Why Study Public Finance Now? Policy Debates over Social Security, Health Care, and Education

No matter when you take a public finance course, it will be the most timely economics course you will take! This is because the questions we address in this book are the questions that are always in the news and that are the source of current policy debates. Indeed, three of the major policy issues facing the United States today—Social Security, health care, and education—are each the subject of different chapters. In this section, we review the debate over these issues, paraphrasing the "liberal" and "conservative" positions on each topic. Once again, our discussion of these issues raises important questions that we will address in the chapters on these topics.

Social Security

As just noted, Social Security is the single largest government expenditure program. As we will learn in great detail in Chapter 13, the financing structure of this program is basically that today's young workers pay the retirement benefits of today's old. As long as the number of young people remains large relative to the number of older persons, this system works. As the giant group of baby boomers (the roughly 75 million people born between 1946 and 1964) moves into old age, however, the system is running into trouble: the ratio of working-age taxpayers to elderly recipients was almost 8 to 1 in 1950, but by 2050 is projected to be less than 3 to 1.[14] Indeed, our Social Security system is projected to have insufficient funds to pay promised retiree benefits in less than 40 years.[15] What should we do about this problem? As with many questions we discuss throughout this course, conservatives and liberals provide very different answers to this question. Liberals argue that the Social Security system has worked well, and that we should simply shore it up by raising the necessary resources through higher payroll taxation or some other means. As we learn later in this book, however, higher taxes may be costly in terms of reducing the efficiency with which the economy operates. Moreover, they are not very politically popular!

Conservatives argue instead that this demographic episode points out the fundamental weakness in our system, which relies on transfers from the young to the old. They claim that we should replace this system with a system in which individuals save for their own retirement. This approach has the problem that there are currently a large number of elderly to whom Social Security benefits are owed, and the government must find some way of financing those payments.

▶ How large a role should the government play in mandating or regulating an individual's retirement savings? How can the government best reform the Social Security system to address its long-range funding shortfall?

Health Care

As noted earlier, there are currently 45.8 million Americans without any health insurance, about 18% of the non-elderly U.S. population. A large body of evidence suggests that their medical treatment and health outcomes are significantly worse as a result of their being uninsured. Moreover, after almost a decade of relatively moderate cost growth, the cost of health care is exploding again in the United States, with health insurance costs rising by 10% or more per year.[16] Projections suggest that health care will consume almost half of our GDP within the next century.

These problems have prompted liberals to suggest major changes in the way that health insurance is structured in the United States. Foremost among these suggestions are major government interventions in health insurance coverage to address the problem of the uninsured, either through mandating and/or massively subsidizing the purchase of private health insurance, or through providing more health insurance through the public sector. Liberals would rely on government regulations to control costs, for example, by limiting the prices that medical providers can charge for their services.

Conservatives, on the other hand, believe these types of interventions are much too expensive, and have recommended instead much more limited

---

[14] U.S. Bureau of the Census (2006a), Table 12. Historical data come from earlier versions of the *Statistical Abstract of the United States*. Working-age taxpayers are 18 to 64 years old.
[15] Social Security Trustees (2006).
[16] Kaiser Family Foundation (2006), Exhibit 3.3.

interventions that would bolster the existing private market through tax subsidies to purchase insurance. They argue that cost control through government price setting would cause much more damage to the system than would introducing the powers of competition. Competition could keep prices down by promoting individual choice across health plans and allowing the plans to compete through lower prices.

▶ Is this conservative approach sufficient to overcome the failures in health insurance markets and substantially increase health insurance coverage? Can either group's approach put a halt to rapidly escalating medical costs?

Education

There is an enormous dissatisfaction with our current educational system, highlighted by the dismal performance of U.S. students on international tests. A 2003 study of math and science skills in 46 countries found that U.S. students were only the 15th best at math skills and 9th best at science skills, behind nations such as Hungary, Russia, and Malaysia.[17] While this dissatisfaction is widespread, there are once again great differences across the political spectrum on how to address this problem. Liberals generally believe that the problem is that we have not put enough resources into our educational system. They argue that higher pay for teachers and more resources to schools in disadvantaged areas are required to improve the performance in the U.S. system.

Conservatives argue that our system is fundamentally broken and that more resources will not solve the problem. The problem, they argue, is that the public schools that dominate our primary and secondary educational system are local monopolies, with no incentives to improve their performance. What is needed instead, they argue, is to inject into education the same type of competitive forces that have worked so well in other sectors: give students a choice of what school to go to, public or private, and provide them with the resources to effectively make that choice by issuing vouchers for educational expenses that they can use to attend any school they like.

▶ Can more spending solve the problems of the U.S. educational system? If not, can competition work in the education market as well as it has in other markets? How do we deal with students who are "left behind" by such a system, in areas where there are bad schools and insufficient choice?

"Big deal, an A in math. That would be a D in any other country."

---

[17] International Association for the Evaluation of Educational Achievement (2004a, 2004b).

1.4

Conclusion

It is clear from the facts presented here that the government plays a central role in the lives of all Americans. It is also clear that there is ongoing disagreement about whether that role should expand, stay the same, or contract. The facts and arguments raised in this chapter provide a backdrop for thinking about the set of public finance issues that we explore in the remainder of this book.

▶ HIGHLIGHTS

- There are four key questions considered in the study of public finance. The first is: When should the government intervene in the economy? Our baseline presumption is that the competitive equilibrium leads to the outcome that maximizes social efficiency. So government intervention can only be justified on the grounds of market failure (increasing the size of the pie) or redistribution (changing the allocation of the pie).

- Having decided whether to intervene, the government needs to decide how to intervene. There are many policy options that can be pursued to achieve the same goal, such as public provision, mandates for private provision, and subsidies to private provision.

- When deciding how to intervene, the government needs some approach for evaluating the impacts of alternative interventions on the economy. The tools of empirical economics provide one such approach.

- A major question for public finance is: Why do governments choose to pursue the policies that they

do? We are particularly concerned about government failure, whereby government intervention can make problems worse, not better.

- Government, which consists of both national (federal) and local units (states, counties, cities, and towns), is large and growing in the United States and throughout the world. The nature of government spending and revenue sources is also evolving over time as governments move away from being providers of traditional public goods (such as defense) to being providers of social insurance (such as Social Security and health insurance).

- Governments also affect our lives through regulatory functions in a wide variety of arenas.

- Public finance is central to many of the policy debates that are active in the United States today, such as those over the Social Security program, health care, and education.

▶ QUESTIONS AND PROBLEMS

1. Many states have language in their constitutions that requires the state to provide for an "adequate" level of education spending. What is the economic rationale for such a requirement?

2. How has the composition of federal, state, and local government spending changed over the past 40 years? What social and economic factors might have contributed to this change in how governments spend their funds?

3. Some goods and services are provided directly by the government, while others are funded publicly

but provided privately. What is the difference between these two mechanisms of public financing? Why do you think the same government would use one approach sometimes and the other approach at other times?

4. Why does redistribution cause efficiency losses? Why might society choose to redistribute resources from one group to another when doing so reduces the overall size of the economic pie?

5. Consider the four basic questions of public finance listed in the chapter. Which of these

questions are positive—that is, questions that can be proved or disproved—and which are normative—that is, questions of opinion? Explain your answer.

6. One rationale for imposing taxes on alcohol consumption is that people who drink alcohol impose negative spillovers on the rest of society—for example, through loud and unruly behavior or intoxicated driving. If this rationale is correct, in the absence of governmental taxation, will people tend to consume too much, too little, or the right amount of alcohol?

7. What is the role of the Congressional Budget Office? Why is independence and impartiality important when conducting empirical analyses?

8. In order to make college more affordable for students from families with fewer resources, a government has proposed allowing the student of any family with less than $50,000 in savings to attend a public university for free. Discuss the direct and possible indirect effects of such a policy.

9. The country of Adventureland has two citizens, Bill and Ted. Bill has a private legal business. He earns $50 per hour. At a tax rate of 0%, Bill works 20 hours. At a 25% tax rate he works only 16 hours, and at a 40% tax rate he works only 8 hours per week. Ted works a manufacturing job. He works 20 hours per week and earns $6 per hour, regardless of the tax rate. The government is considering imposing an income tax of either 25% or 40% on Bill and using the revenues to make transfer payments to Ted. The accompanying table summarizes the three possible policies. Does either tax policy raise social welfare? Are either of the policies obviously less than optimal? Explain your answers.

Effects of Redistributive Policies in Adventureland

	0%	25%	40%
Bill's pre-tax income	$1000	$800	$400
Bill's taxes	0	$200	$160
Bill's net income	$1000	$600	$240
Ted's pre-tax income	$120	$120	$120
Ted's transfer payment	0	$200	$160
Ted's net income	$120	$320	$280

▶ ADVANCED QUESTIONS

10. In the United States, the federal government pays for a considerably larger share of social welfare spending (that is, spending on social insurance programs to help low-income, disabled, or elderly people) than it does for education spending for grades K through 12. Similarly, state and local governments provide a larger share of education spending and a smaller share of welfare spending. Is this a coincidence, or can you think of a reason for why this might be so?

11. The urban African-American community is decidedly split on the subject of school vouchers, with community leaders comprising some of the most vocal proponents and opponents of increased school competition. Why do you think this split exists?

12. Many states have constitutional requirements that their budgets be in balance (or in surplus) in any given year, but this is not true for the U.S. federal government. Why might it make sense to allow for deficits in some years and surpluses in others?

13. Proper hygiene, such as regular hand-washing, can greatly limit the spread of many diseases. How might this suggest a role for public interventions? What kinds of public interventions might be possible? Suggest three distinct types of possible interventions.

Theoretical Tools of Public Finance

2

L ife is going well. After graduating at the top of your college class, you have parlayed your knowledge of public finance into an influential job with your state's Department of Health and Human Services (HHS), which oversees, among other things, the Temporary Assistance for Needy Families (TANF) program. This program provides cash payments to single mothers whose income is below a specified level.

Your new job thrusts you into the middle of a debate between the state's governor and the head of your department, the HHS secretary. The governor believes that a major problem with the TANF program is that, by only providing income to very low income single mothers, it encourages them to stay at home rather than go to work. To provide incentives for these mothers to work, the governor wants to cut back on these cash benefits. The secretary of the department disagrees. He thinks that single mothers who are home with their children are incapable of finding jobs that pay a wage high enough to encourage them to work. In his view, if the state cuts the cash payments, it will simply penalize those single mothers who are staying home.

The secretary turns to you to inform this debate by assessing the extent to which cutting cash benefits to low-income single mothers will encourage them to work, and by evaluating the net welfare implications for the state if these benefits are cut. Such an evaluation will require that you put to work the economics tools that you have learned in your introductory and intermediate courses. These tools come in two flavors. First are the **theoretical tools,** the set of tools designed to understand the mechanics behind economic decision making. The primary theoretical tools of economists are graphical and mathematical. The graphical tools, such as supply and demand diagrams and indifference curve/budget constraint graphs, are typically all that you need to understand the key points of theory, but mathematical expositions can also help to illustrate the subtleties of an argument. In the main body of this book, we rely almost exclusively on graphical analysis, with parallel mathematical analysis presented in some chapter appendices.

theoretical tools The set of tools designed to understand the mechanics behind economic decision making.

empirical tools The set of tools designed to analyze data and answer questions raised by theoretical analysis.

Second, there are **empirical tools,** the set of tools that allows you to analyze data and answer the questions that are raised by theoretical analysis. Most students in this course will have had much less exposure to empirical tools than to theoretical tools. Yet, particularly over the past two decades, empirical tools have become as important as theoretical tools in addressing the problems of public finance, as both the quality of data and the ability to carefully analyze that data have improved dramatically.

In the next two chapters, you will be introduced to the key theoretical and empirical tools that you need for this course. In each chapter, we first provide a general background on the concepts, then apply them to our TANF example. The discussion in this chapter is intimately related to the first two of the four questions of public finance. The theoretical tools we discuss here are the central means by which economists assess when the government should intervene and how it might intervene.

The remainder of this book relies heavily on the microeconomics concepts reviewed in this chapter. This chapter does not, however, substitute for an introductory or intermediate microeconomics course. The goal here is to refresh your understanding of the important concepts that you need to undertake theoretical public finance, not to teach them to you for the first time. If the material in this chapter is very unfamiliar, you may want to supplement this text with a more detailed microeconomics text.

2.1

Constrained Utility Maximization

utility function A mathematical function representing an individual's set of preferences, which translates her well-being from different consumption bundles into units that can be compared in order to determine choice.

constrained utility maximization The process of maximizing the well-being (utility) of an individual, subject to her resources (budget constraint).

models Mathematical or graphical representations of reality.

The core of theoretical analysis in public finance is the assumption that individuals have well-defined **utility functions,** a mathematical mapping of individual choices over goods into their level of well-being. Economists assume that individuals then undertake **constrained utility maximization,** maximizing their well-being (utility) subject to their available resources. Armed with this assumption, economists then develop **models**—mathematical or graphical representations of reality—to show how constrained utility maximization leads people to make the decisions that they make every day. These models have two key components: the individual's *preferences* over all possible choices of goods and her *budget constraint,* the amount of resources with which she can finance her purchases. The strategy of economic modelers is then to ask: Given a budget constraint, what *bundle of goods* makes a consumer best off?

We can illustrate how consumers are presumed to make choices in four steps. First, we discuss how to model preferences graphically. Then, we show how to take this graphical model of preferences and represent it mathematically with a *utility function*. Third, we model the budget constraints that individuals face. Finally, we show how individuals maximize their utility (make themselves as well off as possible) given their budget constraints.

Preferences and Indifference Curves

In modeling people's preferences, we are not yet imposing any budget constraints; we are simply asking what people prefer, ignoring what they can afford. Later, we will impose budget constraints to round out the model.

Much of the power of the preferences models we use in this course derives from one simple assumption: *non-satiation,* or "more is better." Economists assume that more of a good is always better than less. This does not mean that you are equally happy with the tenth pizza as you are with the first; indeed, as we learn later, your happiness increases less with each additional unit of a good you consume. Non-satiation simply implies that having that tenth pizza is better than not having it.

Armed with this central assumption, we can move on to graphically represent a consumer's preferences across different bundles of goods. Suppose, for example, that Figure 2-1 represents Andrea's preferences between two goods, CDs (with quantity Q_C) and movies (with quantity Q_M). Consider three bundles:

Bundle *A*: 2 CDs and 1 movie
Bundle *B*: 1 CD and 2 movies
Bundle *C*: 2 CDs and 2 movies

Let's assume, for now, that Andrea is indifferent between bundles *A* and *B*, but that she prefers *C* to either; she clearly prefers *C* because of the assumption that more is better. Given this assumption, we can map her preferences across the goods. We do so using an **indifference curve,** a curve that shows all combinations of consumption that give the individual the same amount of

indifference curve A graphical representation of all bundles of goods that make an individual equally well off. Because these bundles have equal utility, an individual is indifferent as to which bundle he consumes.

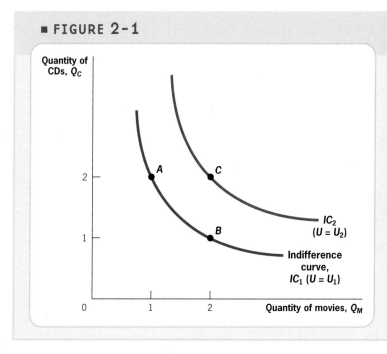

■ FIGURE 2-1

Indifference Curves for Bundles of CDs and Movies • Andrea is indifferent between consuming 2 CDs and 1 movie (point *A*) or 1 CD and 2 movies (point *B*), but she prefers 2 CDs and 2 movies (point *C*) to both. Utility is the same along a given indifference curve; indifference curves farther from the origin represent higher utility levels.

utility (and so among which the individual is indifferent). In this case, Andrea gets the same utility from bundles *A* and *B,* so they lie on the same indifference curve. Because she gets a higher level of utility from consuming bundle *C* instead of either *A* or *B,* bundle *C* is on a higher indifference curve.

Indifference curves have two essential properties, both of which follow naturally from the more-is-better assumption:

1. Consumers prefer higher indifference curves. Individuals prefer to consume bundles that are located on indifference curves that are farther out from the origin because they represent bundles that have more of, for example, both CDs *and* movies.

2. Indifference curves are always downward sloping. Indifference curves cannot slope upward because that would imply that, in this instance, Andrea is indifferent between a given bundle and another bundle that has more of both CDs and movies, which violates the more-is-better assumption.

A great example of indifference curve analysis is job choice. Suppose that Sam graduates and is considering two attributes as he searches across jobs: the starting salary and the location of the job. Sam prefers both a higher salary and a higher temperature location because he likes nice weather. We can represent Sam's preferences using Figure 2-2, which shows the trade-off between salary and weather. Sam has three job choices:

> Bundle *A*: Starting salary of $30,000 in Phoenix, AZ (hot!)
> Bundle *B*: Starting salary of $50,000 in Minneapolis, MN (cold!)
> Bundle *C*: Starting salary of $40,000 in Washington, D.C. (moderate)

■ **FIGURE 2-2**

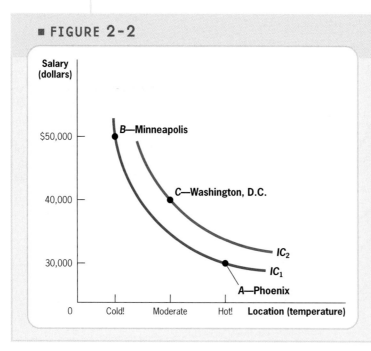

Indifference Curve Analysis of Job Choice • In choosing a job, Sam trades off the two things he cares about, salary and average temperature. On IC_1, he is indifferent between a job in Minneapolis, with a high salary and a low average temperature, and one in Phoenix, with a lower salary and a higher average temperature. However, as indicated by its position on IC_2, he prefers a job in Washington, D.C., with an average salary and an average temperature.

Given Sam's preferences, it may be that he is indifferent between bundles A and B—that is, the higher starting salary in Minneapolis is enough to compensate him for the much colder weather. But he may prefer C to either: the salary in Washington is higher than in Phoenix and the weather is much better than in Minneapolis. Compromising on salary and location leaves Sam better off than choosing an extreme of one or the other in this example.

Utility Mapping of Preferences

Underlying the derivation of indifference curves is the notion that each individual has a well-defined *utility function*. A utility function is some mathematical representation $U = f(X_1, X_2, X_3, \ldots)$, where X_1, X_2, X_3, and so on are the goods consumed by the individual and f is some mathematical function that describes how the consumption of those goods translates to utility. This mathematical representation allows us to compare the well-being associated with different levels of goods consumption.

For example, suppose that Andrea's utility function over CDs and movies is $U = \sqrt{Q_C \times Q_M}$. With this function, she would be indifferent between 4 CDs and 1 movie, 2 CDs and 2 movies, and 1 CD and 4 movies because each of these bundles would deliver a utility level of 2. But she would prefer 3 CDs and 3 movies to any of these bundles, since this would give her a utility level of 3.

Marginal Utility The key concept for understanding consumer preferences is **marginal utility,** or the additional increment to utility from consuming an additional unit of a good. This utility function described exhibits the important principle of *diminishing marginal utility:* the consumption of each additional unit

marginal utility The additional increment to utility obtained by consuming an additional unit of a good.

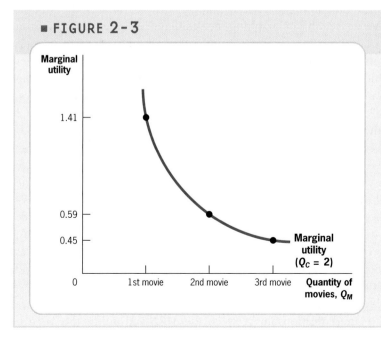

■ **FIGURE 2-3**

Diminishing Marginal Utility •
Holding the number of CDs constant at 2, with a utility function of $U = \sqrt{Q_C \times Q_M}$, each additional movie consumed raises utility by less and less.

Marginal utility

1.41

0.59

0.45

Marginal utility $(Q_C = 2)$

0   1st movie   2nd movie   3rd movie   **Quantity of movies, Q_M**

of a good makes an individual less happy than the consumption of the previous unit. To see this, Figure 2-3 graphs the marginal utility, the increment to utility from each additional movie seen, holding the number of CDs constant at 2. When Andrea moves from seeing 0 movies to seeing 1 movie, her utility rises from 0 to $\sqrt{2} = 1.41$. Thus, the marginal utility of that first movie is 1.41. When she moves from seeing one movie to seeing a second movie, her utility rises to $\sqrt{4} = 2$. The consumption of the second movie has increased utility by only 0.59, a much smaller increment than 1.41. When she sees a third movie, her utility rises to only $\sqrt{6} = 2.45$, for an even smaller increment of 0.45. With each additional movie consumed, utility increases, but by ever smaller amounts.

Why does diminishing marginal utility make sense? Consider the example of movies. There is almost always one particular movie that you want to see the most, then one which is next best, and so on. So you get the highest marginal utility from the first movie you see, less from the next, and so on. Similarly, think about slices of pizza: when you are hungry, you get the highest increment to your utility from the first slice; by the fourth or fifth slice, you get much less utility per slice.

Marginal Rate of Substitution Armed with the concept of marginal utility, we can now describe more carefully exactly what indifference curves tell us about choices. The slope of the indifference curve is the rate at which a consumer is willing to trade off the good on the vertical axis for the good on the horizontal axis. This rate of trade-off is called the **marginal rate of substitution (MRS).** In this example, the *MRS* is the rate at which Andrea is willing to trade CDs for movies. As she moves along the indifference curve from more CDs and fewer movies to fewer CDs and more movies, she is trading CDs for movies. The slope of the curve tells Andrea the rate of trade that leaves her indifferent between various bundles of the two goods.

For the utility functions we use in this book, such as Andrea's, the *MRS* is *diminishing*. We can see this by graphing the indifference curves that arise from the assumed utility function $U = \sqrt{Q_C \times Q_M}$. As Figure 2-4 shows, Andrea is indifferent between 1 movie and 4 CDs, 2 movies and 2 CDs, and 4 movies and 1 CD. Along any segment of this indifference curve, we can define an *MRS*. For example, moving from 4 CDs and 1 movie to 2 CDs and 2 movies, the *MRS* is −2; she is willing to give up 2 CDs to get 1 movie. Moving from 2 CDs and 2 movies to 1 CD and 4 movies, however, the *MRS* is −½; she is willing to give up only 1 CD to get 2 movies.

The slope of the indifference curve changes because of diminishing *MRS*. When Andrea is seeing only 1 movie, getting to see her second-choice movie is worth a lot to her so she is willing to forgo 2 CDs for that movie. But, having seen her second-choice movie, getting to see her third- and fourth-choice movies isn't worth so much, so she will only forgo 1 CD to see them. Thus, the principle of diminishing *MRS* is based on the notion that as Andrea has more and more of good *A*, she is less and less willing to give up some of good *B* to get additional units of *A*.

Since indifference curves are graphical representations of the utility function, there is a direct relationship between the *MRS* and utility: the *MRS* is the ratio of the marginal utility for movies to the marginal utility for CDs:

marginal rate of substitution (MRS) The rate at which a consumer is willing to trade one good for another. The *MRS* is equal to the slope of the indifference curve, the rate at which the consumer will trade the good on the vertical axis for the good on the horizontal axis.

■ **FIGURE 2-4**

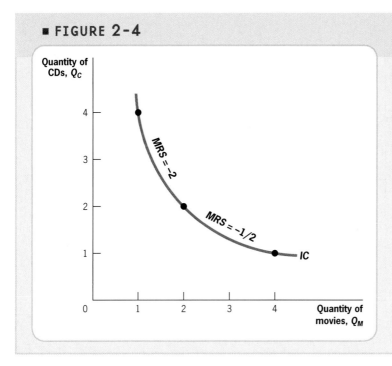

Marginal Rates of Substitution • With a utility function of $U = \sqrt{Q_C \times Q_M}$, MRS diminishes as the number of movies consumed increases. At 4 CDs and 1 movie, Andrea is willing to trade 2 CDs to get a movie (MRS = −2). At 2 CDs and 2 movies, Andrea is willing to trade 1 CD to get 2 movies (MRS = −½).

$$MRS = -\, MU_M/MU_C$$

That is, the *MRS* shows how the relative marginal utilities evolve over the indifference curve: as Andrea moves down the curve, the *MU* of CDs rises and that of movies falls. Remember that higher quantity implies lower marginal utility, by the principle of diminishing marginal utility. As Andrea moves down the indifference curve, getting more movies and fewer CDs, the marginal utility of CDs rises, and the marginal utility of movies falls, lowering the *MRS*.

Budget Constraints

If the fundamental principle of consumer choice is that more is better, what keeps folks from simply bingeing on everything? What stops them is their limited resources, or their **budget constraint,** a mathematical representation of the combination of goods they can afford to buy given their incomes. For the purposes of this discussion, we make the simplifying assumption that consumers spend all their income; there is no savings. In Chapter 22, we discuss the implications of a more realistic model where individuals can save and borrow, but for now we will assume that all income is spent in the period in which it is received. Moreover, for the purposes of this example, let's assume that Andrea spends her entire income on CDs and movies.

Given these assumptions, Andrea's budget constraint is represented mathematically by $Y = P_C Q_C + P_M Q_M$, where Y is her income, P_C and P_M are the prices of CDs and movies, and Q_C and Q_M are the quantities of CDs and movies she buys. That is, this expression says that her expenditures on CDs and on movies add up to be her total income.

budget constraint A mathematical representation of all the combinations of goods an individual can afford to buy if she spends her entire income.

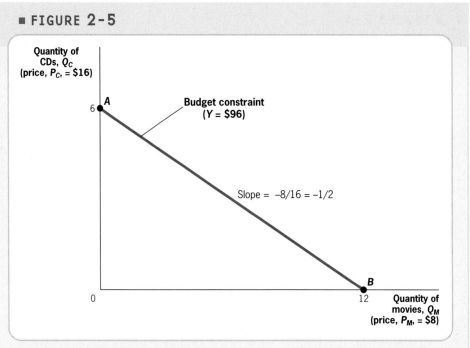

■ FIGURE 2-5

Budget Constraint • With an income, Y, of $96, a price of $16 per CD, and a price of $8 per movie, Andrea can trade off 1 CD for 2 movies, up to a total of either 6 CDs or 12 movies. The slope of the budget constraint is therefore – ½, indicating the ratio of movie-to-CD prices.

Graphically, the budget constraint is represented by the line *AB* in Figure 2-5. The horizontal intercept is the number of movies that Andrea can buy if she purchases no CDs, and the vertical intercept is the number of CDs she can buy if she goes to no movies, and the slope of the budget constraint is the rate at which the market allows her to trade off CDs for movies. This rate is the negative of the price ratio P_M/P_C: each extra movie that she buys, holding income constant, must lower the number of CDs that she can buy by P_M/P_C.

Figure 2-5 illustrates the budget constraint for the case when $Y = \$96$, $P_C = \$16$, and $P_M = \$8$. At this income and these prices, Andrea can purchase 12 movies or 6 CDs, and each CD she buys means that she can buy 2 fewer movies. The slope of the budget constraint is the rate at which she can trade CDs for movies in the marketplace, $P_M/P_C = -\,{}^{8}\!/_{16} = -\,\tfrac{1}{2}$.

Quick Hint Our discussion thus far has been couched in terms of "trading CDs for movies" and vice versa. In reality, however, we don't directly trade one good for another; instead, we trade in a market economy, in which CDs and movies are purchased using dollars. The reason we say "trading CDs for movies" is because of the central economics concept of **opportunity cost,** which says that the cost of any purchase is the next best alternative use of that money. Thus, given a fixed budget, when a person buys a CD, he forgoes the opportuni-

opportunity cost The cost of any purchase is the next best alternative use of that money, or the forgone opportunity.

ty to see two movies. In essence, he is trading the CD for two movies, even though in reality he accomplishes the trade using money rather than the goods themselves. When a person's budget is fixed, if he buys one thing he is, by definition, reducing the money he has to spend on other things. Indirectly, this purchase has the same effect as a direct good-for-good trade.

Putting It All Together: Constrained Choice

Armed with the notions of utility functions and budget constraints, we can now ask: What is the utility-maximizing bundle that consumers can afford? That is, what bundle of goods makes consumers best off, given their limited resources?

The answer to this question is shown in Figure 2-6. This figure puts together the indifference curves corresponding to the utility function $U = \sqrt{Q_C \times Q_M}$ shown in Figure 2-4 with the budget constraint shown in Figure 2-5. In this framework, we can rephrase our question: *What is the highest indifference curve that an individual can reach given a budget constraint?* The answer is the indifference curve, IC_2, that is *tangent* to the budget constraint: this is the farthest-out indifference curve that is attainable, given Andrea's income and market prices. In this example, Andrea makes herself as well off as possible by choosing to consume 6 movies and 3 CDs (point A). That combination of goods maximizes Andrea's utility, given her available resources and market prices.

■ **FIGURE 2-6**

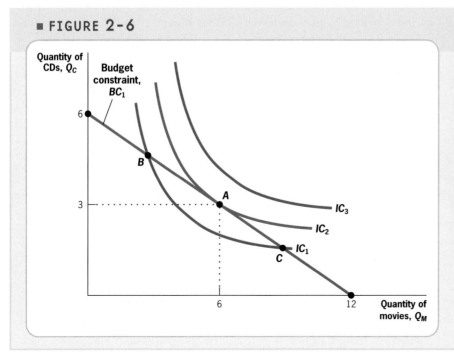

Constrained Optimization •
Given a utility function of
$U = \sqrt{Q_C \times Q_M}$, an income of
$96, and prices of CDs and
movies of $16 and $8, respectively, Andrea's optimal choice is
3 CDs and 6 movies (point A).
This represents the highest indifference curve she can reach,
given her resources and market
prices. She can also afford
points such as B and C, but they
leave her on a lower indifference
curve (IC_1 instead of IC_2).

The key to understanding this outcome is the marginal decision Andrea makes to consume the next movie. The benefit to her of consuming another movie is the *marginal rate of substitution,* the rate at which she is willing to trade CDs for movies. The cost to her of making this trade is the *price ratio,* the rate at which the market allows her to trade CDs for movies. Thus, the optimal choice is the one at which:

$$MRS = -\,MU_M/MU_C = -\,P_M/P_C$$

At the optimum, the ratio of marginal utilities equals the ratio of prices. The rate at which Andrea is willing to trade off one good for the other is equal to the rate at which the market will let her carry out that trade.

One way to demonstrate that this is the optimal choice is to show that she is worse off with any other choice. Consider point B in Figure 2-6. At that point, the slope of the indifference curve IC_1 is higher than the slope of the budget constraint; that is, the MRS is greater than the price ratio. This means that Andrea's marginal utility of movies, relative to CDs, is higher than the ratio of the price of movies to the price of CDs. Because the MRS is the rate at which Andrea is willing to trade CDs for movies and the price ratio is the rate that the market is charging for such a trade, Andrea is willing to give up more CDs for movies than the market requires. She can make herself better off by reducing her CD purchases and increasing her movie purchases, as happens when she moves from B to A.

Now consider point C in Figure 2-6. At this point, the slope of the indifference curve IC_1 is less than the slope of the budget constraint; that is, the MRS is lower than the price ratio. Relative to point B, Andrea now cares much less about movies and more about CDs, since she is now consuming more movies and fewer CDs, and marginal utility diminishes. At point C, in fact, she is willing to give up fewer CDs for movies than the market requires. So she can make herself better off by increasing her CD purchases and reducing her movie purchases, as happens when she moves from C to A. Whenever a consumer is at a point where the indifference curve and the budget constraint are not tangent, she can make herself better off by moving to a point of tangency.

Quick Hint *Marginal analysis,* the consideration of the costs and benefits of an additional unit of consumption or production, is a central concept in modeling an individual's choice of goods and a firm's production decision. All optimization exercises in economics are like climbing a hill on a very cloudy day. At any given point, you don't know yet whether you are at the top, but you do know if you are heading up or heading down. If you are heading up, then you must not yet be at the top; but if you are heading down, then you must have passed the top.

It is the same when you are maximizing your utility (or your firm's profits). Consider the mountain as your decision about how many movies to buy, and the top as the optimal number of movies given your preferences and budget constraint. Starting from any number of CDs and movies, you consider whether the next movie has a benefit (*MRS*) greater than its cost (price ratio). If the benefit exceeds the cost of that next movie, then the next step is upward, and you buy the movie and continue up the optimization mountain. If the benefit is below the cost, then the next step is downward, and you realize that you need to go backward (buy fewer movies) to get back to the top. Only when the benefit equals the cost of the next unit do you realize you are at the top of the mountain.

The Effects of Price Changes: Substitution and Income Effects

The key result from the constrained choice analysis is that $MU_M/MU_C = P_M/P_C$: Andrea consumes movies and CDs until the ratio of the marginal utility of movies to CDs equals the ratio of their prices. An implication of this result is that when the relative price of a good, such as movies in our example, rises (i.e., P_M/P_C rises), then the relative quantity of that good demanded falls. This is because, for the equality previously described to hold, when P_M/P_C rises, then MU_M/MU_C must also rise. For MU_M/MU_C to rise, the quantity of movies relative to CDs must fall (since the marginal utility of any good falls as the quantity consumed of that good rises).

This point is illustrated graphically in Figure 2-7. We have already shown that, with an income of $96, and prices of $16 for CDs and $8 for movies, Andrea chooses 6 movies and 3 CDs at point *A,* the point at which BC_1 and IC_1 are tangent. If the price of movies were to rise to $16, for example, the budget constraint would become *steeper;* it rotates inward from BC_1 to BC_2.

■ FIGURE 2-7

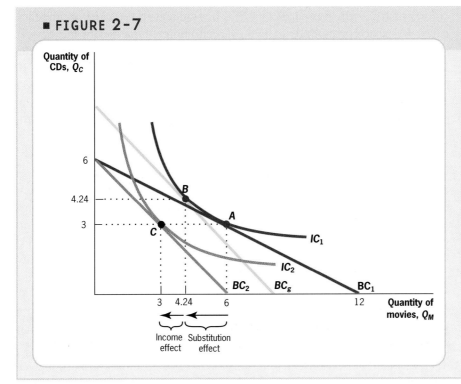

Substitution and Income Effects ● When the price of movies increases, it has two effects. First, holding utility constant, there is a substitution effect, which causes Andrea to demand fewer movies since they are relatively more expensive (moving from point *A* to point *B*). Second, holding relative prices constant, there is an income effect, which causes her to demand fewer movies because she is poorer (moving from point *B* to point *C*).

Because the price of CDs hasn't changed, Andrea can still buy 6 CDs with her $96 income (the vertical intercept of the budget constraint), but because the price of movies has risen to $16, she can only now buy 6 ($96/$16) movies (the horizontal intercept). The slope of the budget constraint rises from $-\frac{1}{2}$ to -1, as illustrated by BC_2.

With a steeper budget constraint, Andrea can no longer afford to buy the combination at point A. The optimal combination becomes point C, the point at which BC_2 is tangent to a lower indifference curve, IC_2. At this point, Andrea can buy 3 CDs, but she can now only buy 3 movies, instead of the 6 she could buy at point A. The quantity of movies she demands has fallen, because their price has gone up. She is also now worse off: her budget set, or the set of possible choices she can make given her income, has been restricted (since the budget constraint moved inward from BC_1 to BC_2). The quantity of CDs she demands has remained constant, but this is simply because of the assumed mathematical form of the utility function; in general, the number of CDs she demands would fall as well.

Income and Substitution Effects Imagine that the government could somehow insulate Andrea from the utility she loses when prices rise; that is, suppose the government was somehow able to compensate her enough that she could stay on the *same indifference curve* (IC_1 in our example), even with the new set of prices. Would this mean that the price change will have no effect on her choices? No, it wouldn't, because she would still like to choose a different bundle of CDs and movies at this new set of prices.

Figure 2-7 illustrates this point. Despite this price change, the government can hold Andrea's utility constant at these new prices by giving her a budget constraint BC_g, which is parallel to BC_2 but tangent to the same indifference curve IC_1 that corresponds to her original choice. Graphically, the budget constraint has steepened, but Andrea is on the same indifference curve (the same level of utility). Andrea chooses the bundle represented by point B: because movies are relatively more expensive, she chooses to consume fewer movies (4.24) and more CDs (4.24). This effect of a price change is called the **substitution effect:** holding utility constant, a relative rise in the price of a good will always cause a consumer to choose less of that good.

In the real world, when prices rise there is no government agency to hold utility constant. This price rise therefore leads to a second effect on demand: Andrea is now effectively poorer because she has to pay higher prices for movies. She is not poorer in an income sense (her income remains at $96), but she is poorer in a real sense because her $96 can buy fewer goods (in particular, fewer movies). This is the **income effect** of a price change: a rise in any price will make the consumer effectively poorer, causing her to choose less of all goods.[1] The quantity demanded falls because Andrea can buy fewer goods with her income.

substitution effect Holding utility constant, a relative rise in the price of a good will always cause an individual to choose less of that good.

income effect A rise in the price of a good will typically cause an individual to choose less of all goods because her income can purchase less than before.

normal goods Goods for which demand increases as income rises.

inferior goods Goods for which demand falls as income rises.

---

[1] We say "typically" here because, in theory, demand for goods can go up or down as income increases. Most goods are **normal goods,** for which demand increases as income rises, but some goods are **inferior goods,** for which demand falls as income rises. Inferior goods are those with better substitutes that might be demanded as income rises. For example, potatoes might be heavily consumed by the poor, but as income rises, fewer potatoes will be consumed as people substitute other goods, such as meat, which they can now afford.

We can measure this income effect by the change from the government-supported budget constraint BC_g to the new budget constraint BC_2. This change represents the restriction in Andrea's opportunity set at the new prices. Since she is poorer, she chooses fewer of all goods, including both movies and CDs, at point C. In this case, the income effect reinforces the substitution effect for movies: both cause the quantity of movies she demands to fall.[2] To sum up, when the price of one good increases relative to another, you choose less of that good for two reasons: because it is relatively more expensive (the substitution effect) and because you are effectively poorer (the income effect).

2.2

Putting the Tools to Work: TANF and Labor Supply Among Single Mothers

In your new position with the state government, you have now reviewed the theoretical concepts necessary to address the concerns of the secretary and the governor. Having reviewed these theoretical concepts, let's turn to the question posed at the start of the chapter: Will reducing TANF benefits increase the labor supply of single mothers? To answer this question, we can apply the tools of utility maximization to the analysis of the labor supply decision.

The TANF program was created in 1996 by a major overhaul of the *cash welfare* system in the United States. The cash welfare system distributes money from taxpayers to low-income families (as described in much more detail in Chapter 17). TANF provides a monthly support check to families with incomes below a threshold level that is set by each state. In the state of New Jersey, for example, a single mother with two children and no other source of income will receive a monthly check for $424.[3] These checks are largely targeted to single-female-headed households with children, since these families are viewed as having the worst prospects for making a living on their own.

Suppose that Joelle is a single mother who spends all of her earnings and TANF benefits on food for her and her children. By working more hours, she can earn more money for food, but there is a cost to work: she has less time at home with her children (or less time to spend on her own leisure). Suppose that she would prefer time at home to time at work; that is, suppose that leisure is a normal good. With these preferences, more work makes Joelle worse off, but it allows her to buy more food.

How does Joelle decide on the optimal amount of labor to supply? To answer this question, we return to the utility maximization framework, but with one twist relative to the decision to purchase CDs and movies. In that

---

[2] They have canceling effects on the demand for CDs, however, which is why demand for CDs doesn't change in Figure 2-7. Note also that if goods are inferior, the income effect would offset the substitution effect, rather than reinforce it.

[3] U.S. Department of Health and Human Services (2004), Table 12-2.

case, we were considering two goods. Now, the single mother is considering one good (food consumption) and one "bad" (labor, since we assume she would rather be at home than at work). The trick to modeling this decision is to model the demand for *leisure*, the good that is the counterpart of labor. That way, we can model the trade-off between two goods using our existing tools and then compute the amount of labor supplied as total work hours minus hours of leisure.

Identifying the Budget Constraint

Suppose that Joelle can work up to 2,000 hours per year at a wage of $10 per hour, that she has no other source of income, and that there is not yet a TANF program in place. By working one less hour in a year, Joelle will lower her consumption by $10 and increase her leisure time by one hour. Thus, the *"price" of one hour of leisure time is the hourly wage rate.* This fact follows from the principle of opportunity cost: when Joelle opts to take an hour of leisure, her next best alternative activity is to work. Thus, the price of the hour of leisure is $10, the forgone wage she could have earned if working.

The price of food consumption is given directly by the market; let's say that it is $1 per unit of food. This means that Joelle faces a trade-off: each hour of work brings her 10 units of food, and each hour off from work (leisure) costs her 10 units of food. If Joelle can work up to 2,000 hours per year, we can now identify her budget constraint as line *ABC* in Figure 2-8: she can consume a maximum of $20,000 of food per year, a maximum of 2,000 hours of leisure per year, or any combination in between. The slope of the

■ **FIGURE 2-8**

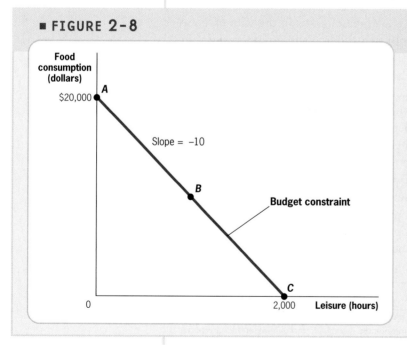

The Consumption-Leisure Trade-off • Joelle has a choice of taking more leisure and consuming less, or taking less leisure (working harder) and consuming more. If she takes no leisure, she can have consumption of $20,000 per year; but if she takes 2,000 hours of leisure, her consumption falls to 0. This is represented by the budget constraint with a slope of –10, the relative price of leisure in terms of food consumption.

budget constraint is the ratio of the price of leisure ($10) to the price of consumption ($1), −10.

The Effect of TANF on the Budget Constraint

Now, let's introduce a TANF program, and illustrate what this does to the budget constraint. Programs such as TANF typically have two key features. The first is a *benefit guarantee,* or the baseline amount of money to which recipients are entitled when they enroll in the program. The second is a *benefit reduction rate,* the rate at which the baseline amount is reduced if recipients have other income. For example, a benefit reduction rate of 100% implies that TANF recipients are entitled to the benefit guarantee if they have no other income, but that they lose a dollar of the benefit guarantee for each dollar of other income they earn. A benefit reduction rate of only 50% implies that TANF recipients once again get the full benefit guarantee if they have no other income, but that they lose $0.50 of the benefit guarantee for each $1 they earn. The benefit reduction rate is, in effect, an *implicit tax rate;* it is the rate at which TANF benefits are reduced when recipients earn other income.

We can now add the TANF program to the budget constraint in panel (a) of Figure 2-9. Let's assume the TANF program we're considering has a benefit guarantee of $5,000 and a benefit reduction rate of 50%. The original budget constraint is the line *ABC.* If Joelle chooses 1,000 or fewer hours of leisure, earning $10,000 to $20,000, the budget constraint does not change, remaining as the segment *AB.* This is because with a benefit guarantee of $5,000 and a benefit reduction rate of 50%, once she earns $10,000 ($5,000/0.5) she is no longer eligible for TANF, so it doesn't affect her budget constraint.

If Joelle chooses to take more than 1,000 hours of leisure, however, the budget constraint is now flatter. Previously, the price of leisure was $10 per hour, since that was the forgone wage. With the 50% benefit reduction rate, however, if Joelle works another hour, she earns $10 in wages, but loses $5 in TANF benefits. Under these conditions, the net return to working another hour is now only $5, so the price of leisure falls to $5 per hour. The budget constraint is therefore flatter, with a slope of only −5 rather than −10, because in the range where TANF is available, there is a lower relative price of leisure. Point *D* marks the end of the new budget constraint, and provides a new option for Joelle: she can have 2,000 hours of leisure *and* $5,000 in food consumption because of the $5,000 TANF benefit guarantee. Without TANF, if she had chosen to consume 2,000 hours of leisure, she wouldn't have been working at all and her family would have had no food (point *C*).

Effects of Changes in Benefit Guarantee Suppose that your state is considering reducing the income guarantee under TANF from $5,000 to $3,000. The effect of this change on the budget constraint is illustrated in panel (b) of Figure 2-9. If Joelle now chooses to take fewer than 1,400 hours of leisure, earning $6,000 to $20,000, the budget constraint does not change, remaining

■ **FIGURE 2-9**

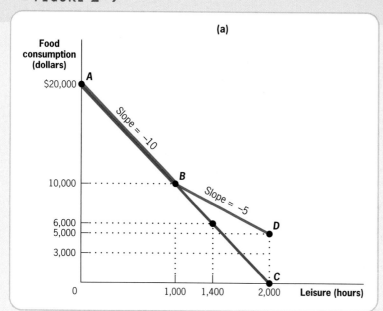

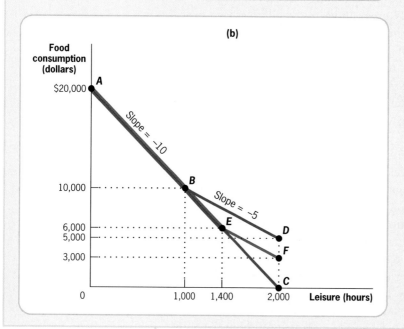

The Budget Constraint with TANF • Joelle's original budget constraint is *ABC*. With a TANF guarantee of $5,000 and a benefit reduction rate of 50% in panel (a), the budget constraint becomes *ABD*. Once she has taken more than 1,000 hours of leisure, the budget constraint flattens, and she now can enjoy $5,000 of consumption even with 2,000 hours of leisure at point *D*. When the guarantee falls to $3,000 in panel (b), the budget constraint (*AEF*) doesn't flatten until she takes more than 1,400 hours of leisure; now, with 2,000 hours of leisure, her consumption is only $3,000 at point *F*.

as the segment *AE*. This is because with the lower benefit guarantee of $3,000 and a benefit reduction rate of 50%, she is now no longer eligible for TANF once she earns $6,000. If she takes more than 1,400 hours of leisure, the budget constraint once again flattens: since she earns $10 in wages but loses $5 in TANF benefits for each hour of work in this range, the slope of the budget constraint along the segment *EF* (the net return to an hour of work) is –5.

Point F marks the end of the new budget constraint, where Joelle can have 2,000 hours of leisure *and* $3,000 in food consumption because of the $3,000 TANF benefit guarantee. How will single mothers react to this policy change?

In answering this question, it is important to return to the concepts of *income and substitution effects* introduced earlier. Suppose, for example, that Joelle earned less than $6,000 before this benefit change. In that case, there is no substitution effect associated with the policy change from a $5,000 benefit guarantee to a $3,000 benefit guarantee. There is no change in the relative price of leisure, which remains at $5 per hour, so the slope of the budget constraint doesn't change. Whether Joelle gets a $5,000 or a $3,000 check from the government has no impact on the return from working an additional hour ($5 on net), so the price of leisure is unchanged. With relative prices of food and leisure unchanged, there is no desire for substitution across the goods.

There is, however, a clear income effect for Joelle. When the TANF guarantee is reduced, she is poorer. Poorer individuals will reduce their consumption of all normal goods, including leisure. Taking less leisure means working more. In other words, since there is less money available to finance consumption, women will have to work harder. Thus, on net, there is a reduction in leisure from the income effect of reducing the TANF guarantee.

Suppose, instead, that Joelle earned between $6,000 and $10,000 before the benefit change. Once again, this benefit change would reduce her income, which will cause her to choose less leisure (and more labor). There is also, however, a change in the price of leisure. In this range of earnings, before the benefits change, an hour of work netted Joelle only $5 per hour, due to the reduction in TANF benefits from additional earnings. Now, since she is no longer eligible for TANF in this income range, an hour of work nets her $10. This relative increase in the price of leisure (taking leisure used to cost $5 but now costs $10 in forgone earnings) will lead to a substitution effect toward less leisure. Thus, in this range the income and substitution effects work together to reduce leisure.

How Large Will the Labor Supply Response Be? This example illustrates the power of economic theory. The constrained maximization model implies that a reduction in the benefit guarantee will lead to less leisure and therefore more work among single mothers. The model does not say, however, *how sizeable* this response will be. This depends on how much Joelle earned before the benefit change, and the size of the income and substitution effects on her leisure/labor decision.

To illustrate the different possible magnitudes of the response, Figures 2-10 and 2-11 show two different cases. In both cases, we consider utility functions for consumption and leisure, where the utility derived from each is proportional to its *natural logarithm (ln)*. This is a convenient form for utility functions that shares most of the properties of the square root utility function we used for CDs and movies, most notably diminishing marginal utility. As noted earlier, the square root and log forms are just two of many possible forms for utility.

■ FIGURE 2-10

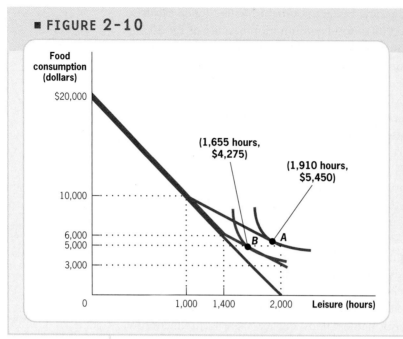

Utility Maximization for Sarah • When the TANF guarantee is $5,000, the optimal choice for Sarah is to take 1,910 hours of leisure and consume $5,450 (at point A). When the guarantee falls to $3,000, she reduces her leisure to 1,655 hours, and her consumption falls to $4,275 (at point B).

■ FIGURE 2-11

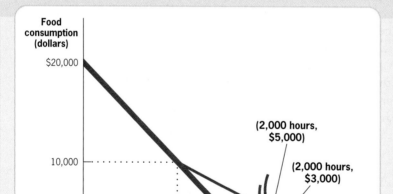

Utility Maximization for Naomi • Because Naomi values leisure more highly relative to consumption than Sarah in Figure 2-10, she chooses 2,000 hours of leisure regardless of the TANF guarantee. The reduction in guarantee therefore lowers Naomi's consumption from $5,000 (at point A) to $3,000 (at point B).

The first mother, Sarah, has a utility function of the form $U = 100 \times \ln(C) + 175 \times \ln(L)$, where C is consumption, L is leisure, and ln is the natural logarithmic function. Sarah values both consumption and leisure, but she values leisure somewhat more. Figure 2-10 shows her indifference curves and budget constraint. When the guarantee is $5,000, Sarah chooses to consume 1,910 hours of leisure and work 90 hours per year (point *A,* where her indifference curve is tangent to the budget constraint with a $5,000 guarantee). At that level of labor supply, her wage earnings are $900. Because her TANF guarantee is reduced by $0.50 for each $1 of earnings, however, her total income is the $900 in earnings plus a net TANF benefit of $5,000 − 0.5 × $900 = $4,550. So her total consumption expenditures are $900 + $4,550 = $5,450. (The mathematics of this example is shown in the appendix to this chapter.)

When the TANF guarantee is reduced to $3,000, Sarah chooses to reduce her leisure since she is now poorer (the income effect), moving to point *B* on the new budget constraint. At that point, she takes only 1,655 hours of leisure per year, works 345 hours, and earns $3,450. For this mother, the governor is right; the reduction in TANF guarantee has raised her labor supply from 90 hours to 345 hours. Note that because Sarah's TANF benefits are reduced by half her earnings, her TANF benefits are now $3,000 − 0.5 × $3,450 = $1,275. Thus, her total budget is $4,275; her consumption has fallen by $1,125 from the days of the higher TANF guarantee ($5,450 − 4,275 = $1,125). Her consumption has not fallen by the full $2,000 cut in the guarantee because she has compensated for the guarantee reduction by working harder.

Figure 2-11 illustrates the case of a different single mother, Naomi, with a utility function $U = 75 \times \ln(C) + 300 \times \ln(L)$. Naomi puts a much larger weight on leisure relative to consumption, when compared to Sarah. (Her indifference curves are steeper, indicating that a larger increase in consumption is required to compensate for any reduction in leisure.) For Naomi, the optimal choice when the TANF guarantee is $5,000 is to not work at all; she consumes 2,000 hours of leisure and $5,000 of food (point *A*). When the guarantee is reduced to $3,000, this mother *continues* not to work, and just lets her consumption fall to $3,000. That is, she cares so much about leisure than about consumption that she won't supplement her TANF guarantee with earnings even at the lower guarantee level. For this mother, the secretary is right; the reduction in TANF guarantee has had no effect on labor supply, it has simply cut her level of food consumption.

Thus, theory alone cannot tell you whether this policy change will increase labor supply, or by how much. Theoretically, labor supply could rise, but it might not. To move beyond this uncertainty, you will have to analyze available data on single mother labor supply, and the next chapter presents the empirical methods for doing so. From these various methods, you will conclude that the governor is right: there is strong evidence that cutting TANF benefits will increase labor supply.

2.3
Equilibrium and Social Welfare

The disagreement we have been discussing is over whether the labor supply of single mothers will rise or not when TANF benefits are cut. As a good public finance economist, however, you know not to stop there. What really should matter to the governor and to the secretary of your department is not a simple fact about whether the labor supply of single mothers rises or falls. What should matter is the *normative* question (the analysis of what should be): Does this policy change make society as a whole better off or not?

To address this question, we turn to the tools of normative analysis, **welfare economics.** Welfare economics is the study of the determinants of well-being, or welfare, in society. To avoid confusion, it is important to recall that the term "welfare" is also used to refer to cash payments (such as those from the TANF program) to low-income single families. Thus, when referring to cash payments in this chapter, we will use the term TANF; our use of the term "welfare" in this chapter refers to the normative concept of well-being.

We discuss the determination of welfare in two steps. First, we discuss the determinants of social efficiency, or the size of the economic pie. Social efficiency is determined by the net benefits that consumers and producers receive as a result of their trades of goods and services. We develop the demand and supply curves that measure those net benefits, show how they interact to determine equilibrium, and then discuss why this equilibrium maximizes efficiency. We then turn to a discussion of how to integrate redistribution, or the division of the economic pie, into this analysis so that we can measure the total well-being of society, or *social welfare*. In this section, we discuss these concepts with reference to our earlier example of Andrea choosing between movies and CDs; we then apply these lessons to a discussion of the welfare implications of changes in TANF benefits.

Demand Curves

Armed with our understanding of how consumers make choices, we can now turn to understanding how these choices underlie the **demand curve,** the relationship between the price of a good or service and the quantity demanded. Figure 2-12 shows how constrained choice outcomes are translated into the demand curve for movies for Andrea. In panel (a), we vary the price of movies, which changes the slope of the budget constraint (which is determined by the ratio of movie to CD prices). For each new budget constraint, Andrea's optimal choice remains the tangency of that budget constraint with the highest possible indifference curve.

For example, we have already shown that given her income of $96, at a price of $16 for CDs and $8 for movies, Andrea will choose 6 movies and 3 CDs (point A on BC_1). An increase in the price of movies to $12 will steepen the budget constraint, with the slope rising from $-\frac{1}{2}$ to $-\frac{3}{4}$, as illustrated by BC_2. This increase in price will reduce the quantity of movies demanded, so that she chooses 3 CDs and 4 movies (point B on BC_2). A decrease in the price of movies to $6 will flatten the budget constraint, with the slope falling from $-\frac{1}{2}$ to $-\frac{3}{8}$, as illustrated by BC_3. This decrease in price will increase the quantity of movies demanded, and Andrea will now choose to buy 3 CDs and 8 movies (point C on BC_3).

Using this information, we can trace out the demand curve for movies, which shows the quantity of a good or service demanded by individuals at each market price. The demand curve for movies, shown in panel (b), maps

welfare economics The study of the determinants of well-being, or welfare, in society.

demand curve A curve showing the quantity of a good demanded by individuals at each price.

■ **FIGURE 2-12**

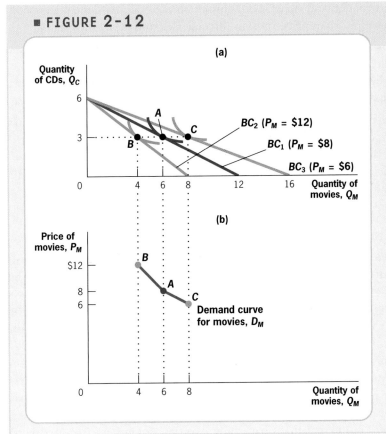

Deriving the Demand Curve • Changes in the price of movies shift the budget constraint, changing the number of movies demanded by individuals. When the price of movies rises to $12, then the number of movies demanded falls to 4, and when the price of movies demanded falls to $6, the number of movies demanded rises to 8. We can use this relationship between the price and utility-maximizing choices to trace out the demand curve for movies, D_M, as shown in panel (b).

the relationship between the price of movies and the quantity of movies demanded.

Elasticity of Demand A key feature of demand analysis is the **elasticity of demand,** the percentage change in quantity demanded for each percentage change in prices.

$$\varepsilon = \frac{\text{percentage change in quantity demanded}}{\text{percentage change in price}} = \frac{\Delta Q/Q}{\Delta P/P}$$

elasticity of demand The percentage change in the quantity demanded of a good caused by each 1% change in the price of that good.

For example, when the price of movies rises from $8 to $12, the number of movies purchased falls from 6 to 4. So a 50% rise in price leads to a 33% reduction in quantity purchased, for an elasticity of −0.666.

There are several key points to make about elasticities of demand:

▶ They are typically negative, since quantity demanded typically falls as price rises.

▶ They are typically not constant along a demand curve. So, in our previous example, the price elasticity of demand is −0.666 when the price of movies rises, but is −1.32 when the price of movies falls (a 25% reduction in price from $8 to $6 leads to a 33% increase in demand from 6 to 8 movies).

► A vertical demand curve is one for which the quantity demanded does not change when price rises; in this case, demand is *perfectly inelastic.*

► A horizontal demand curve is one where quantity demanded changes infinitely for even a very small change in price; in this case, demand is *perfectly elastic.*

► Finally, the example here is a special case in which the demand for CDs doesn't change as the price of movies changes. The effect of one good's prices on the demand for another good is the *cross-price elasticity,* and with the particular utility function we are using here, that cross-price elasticity is zero. Typically, however, a change in the price of one good will affect demand for other goods as well.

Supply Curves

supply curve A curve showing the quantity of a good that firms are willing to supply at each price.

The discussion thus far has focused on consumers and the derivation of demand curves. This tells about only one side of the market, however. The other side of the market is represented by the **supply curve,** which shows the quantity supplied of a good or service at each market price. Just as the demand curve is the outcome of utility maximization by individuals, the supply curve is the outcome of *profit maximization* by firms.

The analysis of firms' profit maximization is similar to that of consumer utility maximization. Just as individuals have a utility function that measures the impact of goods consumption on well-being, firms have a *production function* that measures the impact of firm input use on firm output levels. For ease, we typically assume that firms have only two types of inputs, *labor* (workers) and *capital* (machines, buildings). Consider a firm that produces movies. This firm's production function may take the form $q = \sqrt{K \times L}$, where q is the quantity of movies produced, K is units of capital (such as studio sets), and L is units of labor (such as hours of acting time employed).

marginal productivity The impact of a one unit change in any input, holding other inputs constant, on the firm's output.

The impact of a one-unit change in an input, holding other inputs constant, on the firm's output is the **marginal productivity** of that input. Just as the marginal utility of consumption diminishes with each additional unit of consumption of a good, the marginal productivity of an input diminishes with each additional unit of the input used in production; that is, production generally features *diminishing marginal productivity.* For this production function, for example, holding K constant, adding additional units of L raises production by less and less, just as with the utility function (of this same form), holding CDs constant, consuming additional movies raised utility by less and less.[4]

This production function dictates the cost of producing any given quantity as a function of the prices of inputs and the quantity of inputs used. The total

---

[4] A good way to see this intuition is to consider digging a hole with one shovel. One worker can make good progress. Adding a second worker probably increases the progress, since the workers can relieve each other in shifts, but it is unlikely that progress doubles. Adding a third worker raises progress even less. By the time there are four or five workers, there is very little marginal productivity to adding additional workers, given the fixed capital (one shovel).

costs of production, *TC,* are determined by $TC = rK + wL$, where *r* is the price of capital (the rental rate) and *w* is the price of labor (the wage rate). For day-to-day decisions by the firm, the amount of capital is fixed, while the amount of labor can be varied. Given this assumption, we can define the **marginal cost,** or the incremental cost to producing one more unit, as the wage rate times the amount of labor needed to produce one more unit.

For example, consider the production function just described, and suppose that the firm is producing 2 movies using 1 unit of capital and 4 units of labor. Now, holding the amount of capital fixed, it wants to produce 3 movies. To do so, it will have to increase its use of labor by 5 units (to 9 total units). If the wage rate is $1 per unit, then the marginal cost of raising production from 2 to 3 movies is $5.

The key point of this discussion is that *diminishing marginal productivity generally implies rising marginal costs.* To produce a fourth movie would require an increase in labor of 7 units, at a cost of $7; to produce a fifth movie would cost $9. Since each additional unit of production means calling forth labor that is less and less productive, at the same wage rate, the costs of that production are rising.

Recall that the goal of the firm is to maximize its **profit,** the difference between revenues and costs. Profit is maximized when the revenue from the next unit, or the *marginal revenue,* equals the cost of producing that next unit, the *marginal cost.* In a competitive industry, the revenue from any unit is the price the firm obtains in the market. Thus, the firm's profit maximization rule is to *produce until price equals marginal cost.*

We can see this through the type of "hill-climbing" exercise proposed in the Quick Hint on pages 34–35. Suppose the price of movies in the market is $8, the cost of capital is $1 per unit, the cost of labor is $1 per unit, and the firm has 1 unit of capital. Then, if the firm produces 1 movie, it will need to use 1 unit of labor, so that total costs are $2. Because revenues on that first unit are $8, it should clearly produce that first movie. To produce a second movie, the firm will need to use 4 units of labor, or an increase of 3 units of labor. Thus, the marginal cost of that second unit is $3, but the marginal revenue (price) is $8, so the second movie should be produced. For the third movie, the marginal cost is $5, as just noted, which remains below price.

But now imagine the firm is producing 4 movies and is deciding whether to produce a fifth. Producing the fifth movie will require an increase in labor input from 16 to 25 units, or an increase of 9 units. This will cost $9. But the price that the producer gets for this movie is only $8. As a result, producing that fifth unit will be a money loser, and the firm will not do it. Thus, profit maximization dictates that the firm produce until its marginal costs (which are rising by assumption of diminishing marginal productivity) reach the price.

Profit maximization is the source of the supply curve, the relationship between the price and how much producers will supply to the market. At any price, we now know that producers will supply a quantity such that the marginal cost equals that price. Thus, the *marginal cost curve is the firm's supply curve,* showing the relationship between price and quantity. As quantity rises, and

marginal cost The incremental cost to a firm of producing one more unit of a good.

profits The difference between a firm's revenues and costs, maximized when marginal revenues equal marginal costs.

marginal costs rise, the firm will require higher and higher prices to justify producing additional units.

Equilibrium

We have discussed the source of individual demand curves (utility maximization) and firm supply curves (profit maximization). To undertake welfare analysis we need to translate these concepts to their counterparts at the level of the **market,** the arena in which demanders and suppliers actually interact (such as the supermarket or a Web site). To do so, we add up the demands of each individual who is demanding goods in this market, and the supplies of each firm that is supplying goods in this market. We *horizontally sum* these curves. That is, at each price, we add up all the quantities available to be purchased at that price by demanders to obtain market-level demand, and all the quantities available to be supplied at that price by suppliers to obtain market-level supply. The result is the market-level supply and demand curves shown in Figure 2-13.

The market-level supply and demand curves interact to determine the **market equilibrium,** the price and quantity pair that will satisfy both demand and supply. This point occurs at the intersection of the supply and demand curves, such as point E in Figure 2-13. Given the equilibrium price P_E, demanders will demand the equilibrium quantity, Q_E, and suppliers will be willing to supply that equilibrium quantity. The competitive market equilibrium represents the unique point at which both consumers and suppliers are satisfied with price and quantity.

market The arena in which demanders and suppliers interact.

market equilibrium The combination of price and quantity that satisfies both demand and supply, determined by the interaction of the supply and demand curves.

■ FIGURE 2-13

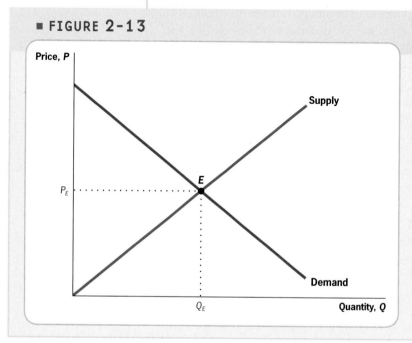

Market Outcome • The supply and demand curves for movies intersect at the equilibrium point E, where both consumers and suppliers are satisfied with price and quantity.

Social Efficiency

Armed with the analysis thus far, we are now ready to take the final step: to measure *social efficiency,* or the size of the pie. Social efficiency represents the net gains to society from all trades that are made in a particular market, and it consists of two components: consumer and producer surplus.

Consumer Surplus The gain to consumers from trades in a market for consumer goods is **consumer surplus,** the benefit that consumers derive from consuming a good above and beyond what they paid for the good. Once we know the demand curve, consumer surplus is easy to measure, because each point on a demand curve represents *the consumer's willingness to pay for that quantity.*

Panel (a) of Figure 2-14 shows a graphical representation of consumer surplus in the movie market: the shaded area below the demand curve and above the equilibrium price P_E (area WZX). This area is consumer surplus because these are units where the willingness to pay (represented by the demand curve) is higher than the amount actually paid, P_E. Consumer surplus is largest on the very first unit, since this represents the consumer who most wanted the good. (He is willing to buy the good at a very high price.) For that first unit, consumer surplus is equal to the distance WX on the vertical axis. Consumer surplus then falls as additional consumers derive less and less marginal utility

> **consumer surplus** The benefit that consumers derive from consuming a good, above and beyond the price they paid for the good.

■ FIGURE 2-14

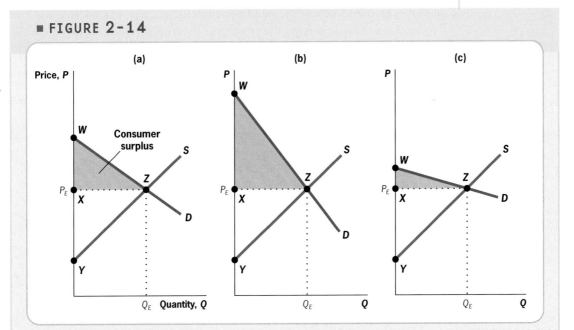

Consumer Surplus • The consumer surplus is the area below the demand curve and above the equilibrium market price, the shaded area *WZX* in all three panels of this graph. This represents the value to consumers of consuming goods above and beyond the price paid for those goods. As demand becomes more inelastic, consumer surplus rises; as demand becomes more elastic, consumer surplus falls.

from the good. Finally, for the consumer whose demand (willingness to pay) equals the price (at point Z), consumer surplus is zero.

Consumer surplus is determined by two factors: the market equilibrium price and the elasticity of demand. Panel (b) of Figure 2-14 shows the case of a good with very inelastic demand (that is, where quantity demanded is not very sensitive to prices), such as basic foods for a low-income community. In this case, the demand curve is more vertical, so the consumer surplus is a very large area. Consumer surplus is large because inelastic demand arises from a lack of good substitutes, so that consumers get enormous surplus out of consuming that particular good. Panel (c) of Figure 2-14 shows the case of a good with very elastic demand (that is, where quantity demanded is very sensitive to prices), such as going to the movies. In this case, the demand curve is nearly horizontal, so that consumer surplus is a very small area. This is because elastic demand arises from the availability of very good substitutes. Consumers don't derive very much surplus from consuming a good for which there are close substitutes.

Producer Surplus Consumers aren't the only ones who derive a surplus from market transactions. There is also a welfare gain to producers, the **producer surplus,** which is the benefit derived by producers from the sale of a unit above and beyond their cost of producing that unit. Like consumer surplus, producer surplus is easy to measure because every point on the supply curve represents the marginal cost of producing that unit of the good. Thus, producer surplus is represented graphically by the area above the supply (marginal cost) curve and below the equilibrium price P_E, the shaded area XZY in Figure 2-15. This area is producer surplus because these are units where the market price is above the willingness to supply (the supply curve). Producer surplus is, in effect, the profits made by the producer.

Panels (b) and (c) in Figure 2–15 illustrate the impact on producer surplus of varying the *price elasticity of supply,* the percentage change in supply for each percentage change in market prices. When the price elasticity of supply is very low, so that supply is very inelastic, then the supply curve is more vertical and producer surplus is very large, as in panel (b). When the price elasticity of supply is very high so that supply is very elastic, then the supply curve is nearly horizontal and producer surplus is very small, as in panel (c).

Social Surplus **Total social surplus,** also called **social efficiency,** is the total surplus received by consumers and producers in a market. Figure 2-16 shows the total social surplus for the movie market. The consumer surplus in this market is the shaded area $A + D$, and the producer surplus is the shaded area $B + C + E$. Thus, social surplus for this market is the sum of the shaded areas $A + B + C + D + E$.

Competitive Equilibrium Maximizes Social Efficiency

We can use this social surplus framework to illustrate the point known as the **First Fundamental Theorem of Welfare Economics:** the competitive equilibrium, where supply equals demand, maximizes social efficiency. This

producer surplus The benefit that producers derive from selling a good, above and beyond the cost of producing that good.

total social surplus (social efficiency) The sum of consumer surplus and producer surplus.

First Fundamental Theorem of Welfare Economics The competitive equilibrium, where supply equals demand, maximizes social efficiency.

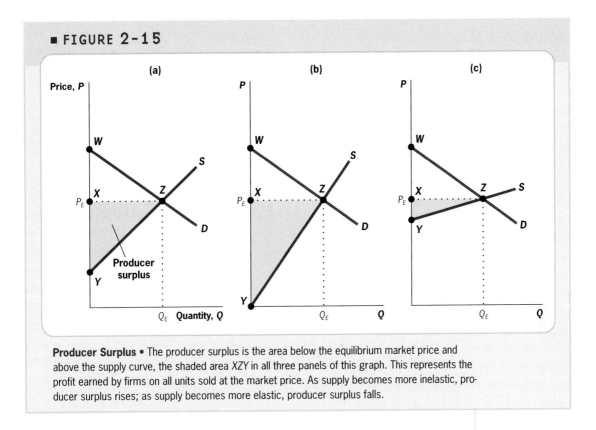

■ FIGURE 2-15

Producer Surplus • The producer surplus is the area below the equilibrium market price and above the supply curve, the shaded area *XZY* in all three panels of this graph. This represents the profit earned by firms on all units sold at the market price. As supply becomes more inelastic, producer surplus rises; as supply becomes more elastic, producer surplus falls.

theorem makes intuitive sense because social efficiency is created whenever a trade occurs that has benefits that exceed its costs. This is true for every transaction to the left of Q_E in Figure 2-16: for each of those transactions, the benefits (willingness to pay, or demand) exceed the costs (marginal cost, or supply).

Doing anything that lowers the quantity sold in the market below Q_E reduces social efficiency. For example, suppose that the government, in an effort to help consumers, restricts the price that firms can charge for movies to P_R, which is below the equilibrium price P_E. Suppliers react to this restriction by reducing their quantity produced to Q_R, the quantity at which the new price, P_R, intersects the supply curve: it is the quantity producers are willing to supply at this price. Producer surplus is now area C, the area above the supply curve and below price P_R. Thus, producer surplus falls by area $B + E$.

On the consumer side, there are two effects on surplus. On the one hand, since a smaller quantity of movies is supplied, consumers are worse off by the area D: the movies that are no longer provided between Q_R and Q_E were movies for which consumers were willing to pay more than the cost of production to see the movie, so consumer surplus falls. On the other hand, since consumers pay a lower price for the remaining Q_R movies that they do see, consumer surplus rises by area B.

On net, then, society loses surplus equal to the area $D + E$. This area is called **deadweight loss,** the reduction in social efficiency from preventing

deadweight loss The reduction in social efficiency from preventing trades for which benefits exceed costs.

■ **FIGURE 2-16**

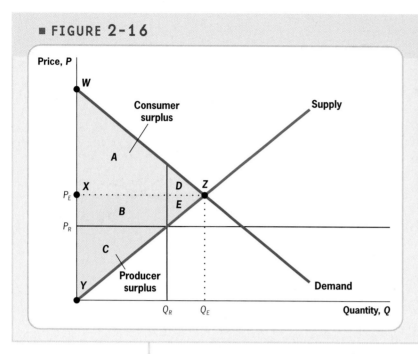

Competitive Equilibrium Maximizes Social Surplus • The sum of consumer surplus (the area below the demand curve and above the price) and producer surplus (the area above the supply curve and below the price) is maximized at the competitive equilibrium. A restriction on price to P_R lowers quantity supplied to Q_R and creates a deadweight loss of $D + E$.

trades for which benefits exceed costs. This part of the social surplus $(D + E)$ has vanished because there are *trades that could be made where benefits are greater than costs, but those trades are not being made.* Graphically, then, the social surplus triangle is maximized when quantity is at Q_E.

Quick Hint It is sometimes confusing to know how to draw deadweight loss triangles. The key to doing so is to remember that *deadweight loss triangles point to the social optimum, and grow outward from there.* The intuition is that the deadweight loss from over- or underproduction is smallest right near the optimum (producing one unit too few or one too many isn't so costly). As production moves farther from this optimum, however, the deadweight loss grows rapidly.

From Social Efficiency to Social Welfare: The Role of Equity

The discussion thus far has focused entirely on how much surplus there is (social efficiency, the size of the economic pie). Societies usually care not only how much surplus there is but also about how it is distributed among the population. The level of **social welfare,** the level of well-being in a society, is determined both by social efficiency and by the equitable distribution of society's resources.

Under certain assumptions, efficiency and equity are two separate issues. In these circumstances, society doesn't have just one socially efficient point, but a whole series of socially efficient points from which it can choose. Society can achieve those different points simply by shifting available resources among

social welfare The level of well-being in society.

individuals and letting them trade freely. Indeed, this is the **Second Funda-mental Theorem of Welfare Economics:** society can attain any efficient outcome by a suitable redistribution of resources and free trade.

In practice, however, society doesn't typically have this nice choice. Rather, as discussed in Chapter 1, society most often faces an **equity–efficiency trade-off,** the choice between having a bigger economic pie and having a more fairly distributed pie. Resolving this trade-off is harder than determining efficiency-enhancing government interventions. It raises the tricky issue of making interpersonal comparisons, or deciding who should have more and who should have less in society.

Typically, we model the government's equity–efficiency decisions in the context of a **social welfare function (SWF).** This function maps the set of individual utilities in society into an overall social utility function. In this way, the government can incorporate the equity–efficiency trade-off into its decision making. If a government policy impedes efficiency and shrinks the economic pie, then citizens as a whole are worse off. If, however, that shrinkage in the size of the pie is associated with a redistribution that is valued by society, then this redistribution might compensate for the decrease in efficiency and lead to an overall increase in social welfare.

The social welfare function can take one of a number of forms, and which form a society chooses is central to how it resolves the equity–efficiency trade-off. If the social welfare function is such that the government cares solely about efficiency, then the competitive market outcome will not only be the most efficient outcome, it will also be the welfare-maximizing outcome. In other cases where the government cares about the distribution of resources, then the most efficient outcome may not be the one that makes society best off. Two of the most common specifications of the social welfare function are the utilitarian and Rawlsian specifications.

Utilitarian SWF With a *utilitarian social welfare function,* society's goal is to maximize the sum of individual utilities:

$$SWF = U_1 + U_2 + \ldots + U_N$$

The utilities of all individuals are given equal weight, and summed to get total social welfare. This formulation implies that we should transfer from person 1 to person 2 as long as the utility gain to person 1 is greater than the utility loss to person 2. In other words, this implies that society is indifferent between one *util* (a unit of well-being) for a poor person and one for a rich person.

Is this outcome unfair? No, because the social welfare function is defined in terms of utility, not dollars. With a utilitarian *SWF,* society is *not* indifferent between giving one *dollar* to the poor person and giving one dollar to the rich person; society is indifferent between giving one *util* to the poor person and one util to the rich person. This distinction between dollars and utility is important because of the diminishing marginal utility of income; richer people gain a much smaller marginal utility from an extra dollar than poorer people. With a utilitarian *SWF,* society is not indifferent between a dollar to the rich and the poor; in general, it wants to redistribute that dollar from the rich

Second Fundamental Theorem of Welfare Economics
Society can attain any efficient outcome by suitably redistributing resources among individuals and then allowing them to freely trade.

equity–efficiency trade-off
The choice society must make between the total size of the economic pie and its distribution among individuals.

social welfare function (SWF)
A function that combines the utility functions of all individuals into an overall social utility function.

(who have a low *MU* because they already have high consumption) to the poor (who have a low *MU*). If individuals are identical, and if there is no efficiency cost of redistribution, then the utilitarian *SWF* is maximized with a perfectly equal distribution of income.

Rawlsian Social Welfare Function Another popular form of social welfare function is the *Rawlsian SWF,* named for the philosopher John Rawls. He suggested that society's goal should be to maximize the well-being of its worst-off member.[5] The Rawlsian *SWF* has the form:

$$SW = \min (U_1, U_2, \ldots, U_N)$$

Since social welfare is determined by the minimum utility in society, social welfare is maximized by maximizing the well-being of the worst-off person in society.

If individuals are identical, and redistribution does not have efficiency costs, this *SWF* would call for an equal distribution of income, as does the utilitarian *SWF*: only when income is equally distributed is society maximizing the well-being of its worst-off member. On the other hand, the utilitarian and Rawlsian *SWF* do not have the same implications once we recognize that redistribution can entail efficiency costs (and reduce the size of the pie). Suppose all individuals have identical preferences, and equal incomes of $40,000 per year, except for two individuals: Donald, who has an income of $1 million per year, and Joe, who has an income of $39,999. Now imagine a proposal to tax Donald by $960,000, take $1 of that tax revenue and give it to Joe, and throw the rest of the money into the ocean. Under a utilitarian *SWF,* this plan will lower social welfare because Donald's utility will fall more from losing $960,000 than Joe's utility will rise from gaining $1. Under a Rawlsian *SWF,* however, this plan will raise social welfare, since the utility of the worst-off person has increased, and that is all we care about! Thus, in a world of equity–efficiency trade-offs, a Rawlsian *SWF* will in general suggest more redistribution than will a utilitarian *SWF*.

Choosing an Equity Criterion

The form of the social welfare function clearly plays an important role in driving government policy. Yet the *SWF* is not handed down from some higher power, but determined in some way by the interplay of politicians and the voting public. The mechanisms through which the *SWF* might evolve through the political process are discussed at length in Chapter 9, but it is important to recognize that there are other criteria besides an *SWF* that might lead to redistributive concerns. For example, some policy makers take the **commodity egalitarianism** view, in which all that matters is that individuals have met a basic level of need for goods such as housing or medical care, and that once they have met this basic level, income distribution is irrelevant.

commodity egalitarianism
The principle that society should ensure that individuals meet a set of basic needs, but that beyond that point income distribution is irrelevant.

---

[5] See Rawls (1971), pp. 152–157, for arguments about why this should be society's goal.

Others argue that all that matters is **equality of opportunity,** whereby individuals are guaranteed an equal chance to succeed, but if some do and others do not, that is not the concern of the government. We discuss these alternative views and their implications for government policy in Chapter 17.

equality of opportunity The principle that society should ensure that all individuals have equal opportunities for success but not focus on the outcomes of choices made.

2.4

Welfare Implications of Benefit Reductions: The TANF Example Continued

The equilibrium and social welfare tools developed in Section 2.3 can be applied to evaluate the benefits and costs to society of reducing TANF benefits. The benefits are the improvement in *efficiency* from removing a barrier to labor supply by single mothers, raising single mothers' labor supply and raising the size of the social surplus. (Relying on the empirical evidence discussed in the next chapter, we assume that labor supply increases when benefits fall.) The costs are the reductions in *equity* that arise from reducing income support to one of the lowest-income groups in our society. The job of public finance economists is to measure these efficiency and equity consequences. The job of policy makers is to trade the consequences off to decide on appropriate policy choices.

Efficiency We can apply the tools of welfare analysis to model the welfare implications of cutting TANF benefits. Figure 2-17 shows the market for labor services by single mothers. The price of labor, the wage (*W*), is on the

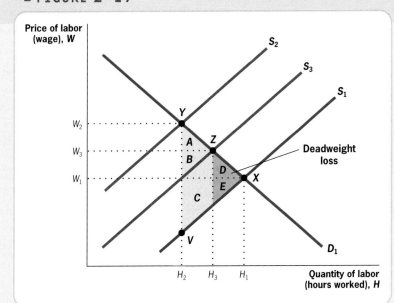

■ **FIGURE 2-17**

Welfare Implications of TANF ● Without TANF, the labor market is in competitive equilibrium at point *X*, the intersection of S_1 and D_1. When TANF is introduced, labor supply falls to S_2, and the market moves to a new equilibrium at point *Y*, creating a deadweight loss of $A + B + C + D + E$. When TANF benefits are reduced, supply increases to S_3, and social efficiency rises by $A + B + C$.

vertical axis; the amount of hours worked in aggregate in the market (H) is on the horizontal axis.

Unlike Figure 2-13, the *demand* for the good (the single mother's hours of work) comes from firms, and the *supply* comes from individuals. Nevertheless, as in Figure 2-13, the demand curve slopes downward (as wages rise, firms demand fewer hours of work) and the supply curve slopes upward (as wages rise, individuals are willing to supply more hours of work—assuming that substitution effects are larger than income effects).

Suppose that, in the absence of the TANF program, there are no other government interventions that affect the labor market. In that case, without TANF, labor supply, S_1, intersects labor demand, D_1, at point X, and the market is in competitive equilibrium, maximizing social efficiency at hours of work H_1.

When TANF is introduced, however, single mothers work fewer hours, reducing the supply of labor at every wage, so that the supply curve shifts left to S_2. The labor market will reach a new equilibrium at point Y. Relative to the original equilibrium, the number of hours worked has fallen from H_1 to H_2. This reduction in hours worked causes a deadweight loss of the area $A + B + C + D + E$. The difference between H_1 to H_2 represents hours of work that the single mother would happily provide to the firm, and the firm would happily demand from her, were it not for the TANF program. Social efficiency has thus fallen.

If TANF benefits are cut, the labor supply of single mothers increases and the supply curve shifts out to S_3. At the new equilibrium Z, the single mothers supply H_3 hours of labor, and the deadweight loss has been reduced to $D + E$. That is, social efficiency has grown by the area $A + B + C$ due to this reduction in TANF benefits.

We can now quantify the social efficiency gain to lower TANF benefits: area $A + B + C$ is gained when single mothers increase their supply of labor. If we know the slopes of these demand and supply curves, we can then measure this social efficiency gain. These slopes can be estimated using the types of empirical methods we discuss in the next chapter.

Equity Given this large efficiency gain, why not cut TANF benefits? Indeed, why have the TANF program at all? As just noted, governments have programs such as TANF because their citizens care not only about efficiency but also about *equity,* the fair distribution of resources in society. For many specifications of social welfare, the competitive equilibrium, while being the social *efficiency*-maximizing point, may not be the social *welfare*-maximizing point.

Currently, the share of single mothers living below the *poverty line,* a measure of the minimal income required to live in the United States, is 35.9%, compared to only 10.2% for all families.[6] Cutting TANF benefits would therefore worsen outcomes for a population that is already one of the worst off in society. Cutting TANF benefits could have dramatic equity costs that offset the efficiency gains.

---

[6] U.S. Bureau of the Census (2005b), Table 4.

To consider a simple example, imagine that society has a utilitarian *SWF*, and that each individual in society has a utility function of the form $U = \sqrt{C}$, where C = consumption = income. Imagine further that 10% of citizens are single mothers who have an initial income of $10,000, and the remaining 90% of citizens have an initial income of $50,000. Suppose that if we cut TANF benefits, the income of single mothers falls to $5,000, while the income of everyone else rises to $51,000. Under this policy, the average level of income in society rises from $46,000 to $46,400, so total social efficiency has risen. Yet social welfare has fallen; the average utility level has fallen from 211.2 to 210.3 (computed by averaging across all citizens the square root of income both before and after this change). This is because we are adding small amounts of income to the high-income majority, who already have a low marginal utility of income, but we are taking large amounts of income away from the low-income minority, who have a very high marginal utility of income. While this policy move raises efficiency, it harms equity even "more" in the context of this *SWF*.

Measuring empirically the cost to society from this reduced equity is quite difficult. Essentially, the analyst must make some assumption about how society values the well-being of different groups, such as single mothers versus other taxpayers.

2.5
Conclusion

This chapter has shown both the power and the limitations of the theoretical tools of economics. On the one hand, by making relatively straightforward assumptions about how individuals and firms behave, we are able to address complicated questions such as how TANF benefits affect the labor supply of single mothers, and the implications of that response for social welfare. On the other hand, while we have answered these questions in a general sense, we have been very imprecise about the potential size of the changes that occur in response to changes in TANF benefits. That is, theoretical models can help point to the likely impacts of policy changes on individual decisions and social welfare, but they cannot tell us the magnitude of those effects. To do so, we have to turn to empirical economics, which we will do in the next chapter.

▶ HIGHLIGHTS

■ Policy debates such as that over the appropriate level of Temporary Assistance for Needy Families (TANF) benefits motivate the need for theoretical modeling of individual and firm decision-making behaviors.

■ Modeling the impact of policy changes on individual behavior requires the use of utility-maximization models in which individuals maximize their well-being, subject to market prices and their available resources.

■ Individual well-being, or utility, is maximized when individuals choose the bundle of goods that equates the rate at which they want to trade off one good for another (the marginal rate of substitution) with the rate at which the market allows them to trade off one good for another (the price ratio).

■ TANF-like programs introduce complicated budget constraints with several possible segments, depending on whether a mother is on or off the program.

■ Reducing TANF benefits is likely to increase the labor supply of single mothers, but the size of the increase is unclear and depends on the mothers' preferences for leisure and consumption.

■ Social welfare is determined by considering both social efficiency (the size of the pie) and equity (the distribution of the pie).

■ Social efficiency is maximized at the competitive equilibrium, where demand (which is derived from underlying utility maximization) equals supply (which is derived from underlying profit maximization).

■ Social welfare is maximized by using a social welfare function to incorporate both efficiency and society's preferences for redistribution into policy making.

■ Since reducing TANF benefits moves the labor market closer to the competitive equilibrium, it raises total social efficiency, but at a cost of lowering the incomes of a particularly needy group. The net impact on social welfare is unclear.

▶ QUESTIONS AND PROBLEMS

1. The price of a bus trip is $1 and the price of a gallon of gas (at the time of this writing!) is $2. What is the relative price of a gallon of gas, in terms of bus trips? What happens when the price of a bus trip falls to $0.75?

2. Draw the demand curve $Q = 200 - 10P$. Calculate the price elasticity of demand at prices of $5, $10, and $15 to show how it changes as you move along this linear demand curve.

3. You have $100 to spend on food and clothing. The price of food is $5 and the price of clothing is $10.
   a. Graph your budget constraint.
   b. Suppose that the government subsidizes clothing such that each unit of clothing is half-price, up to the first five units of clothing. Graph your budget constraint in this circumstance.

4. Use utility theory to explain why people ever leave all-you-can-eat buffets.

5. Explain why a consumer's optimal choice is the point at which her budget constraint is tangent to an indifference curve.

6. Consider the utilitarian social welfare function and the Rawlsian social welfare function, the two social welfare functions described in Chapter 2.
   a. Which one is more consistent with a government that redistributes from rich to poor? Which is more consistent with a government that does not do any redistribution from rich to poor?

   b. Think about your answer to (a). Show that government redistribution from rich to poor can still be consistent with either of the two social welfare functions.

7. Since the free market (competitive) equilibrium maximizes social efficiency, why would the government ever intervene in an economy?

8. Consider an income guarantee program with an income guarantee of $6,000 and a benefit reduction rate of 50%. A person can work up to 2,000 hours per year at $8 per hour.
   a. Draw the person's budget constraint with the income guarantee.
   b. Suppose that the income guarantee rises to $9,000 but with a 75% reduction rate. Draw the new budget constraint.
   c. Which of these two income guarantee programs is more likely to discourage work? Explain.

9. A good is called *normal* if a person consumes more of it when her income rises (for example, she might see movies in theaters more often as her income rises). It is called *inferior* if a person consumes less of it when her income rises (for example, she might be less inclined to buy a used car as her income rises). Sally eats out at the local burger joint quite frequently. The burger joint suddenly lowers its prices.
   a. Suppose that, in response to the lower burger prices, Sally goes to the local pizza restaurant less often. Can you tell from this whether or not pizza is an inferior good for Sally?

b. Suppose instead that, in response to the lower burger prices, Sally goes to the burger joint less often. Explain how this could happen in terms of the income and substitution effects by using the concepts of normal and/or inferior goods.

▶ ADVANCED QUESTIONS

10. Consider an income guarantee program with an income guarantee of $3,000 and a benefit reduction rate of 50%. A person can work up to 2,000 hours per year at $6 per hour. Alice, Bob, Calvin, and Deborah work for 100, 333⅓, 400, and 600 hours, respectively, under this program.

The government is considering altering the program to improve work incentives. Its proposal has two pieces. First, it will lower the guarantee to $2,000. Second, it will not reduce benefits for the first $3,000 earned by the workers. After this, it will reduce benefits at a reduction rate of 50%.

a. Draw the budget constraint facing any worker under the original program.

b. Draw the budget constraint facing any worker under the proposed new program.

c. Which of the four workers do you expect to work more under the new program? Who do you expect work less? Are there any workers for whom you cannot tell if they will work more or less?

11. Consider a free market with demand equal to $Q = 1,200 - 10P$ and supply equal to $Q = 20P$.

a. What is the value of consumer surplus? What is the value of producer surplus?

b. Now the government imposes a $10 per unit subsidy on the production of the good. What is the consumer surplus now? The producer surplus? Why is there a deadweight loss associated with the subsidy, and what is the size of this loss?

12. Governments offer both cash assistance and in-kind benefits such as payments that must be spent on food or housing. Will recipients be indifferent between receiving cash versus in-kind benefits with the same monetary values? Use indifference curve analysis to show the circumstances in which individuals would be indifferent, and situations in which the form in which they received the benefit would make a difference to them.

13. Consider Bill and Ted, the two citizens in the country of Adventureland described in Problem 9 from Chapter 1. Suppose that Bill and Ted have the same utility function $U(Y) = Y^{1/2}$, where Y is consumption (which is equal to net income).

a. Rank the three tax policies discussed in Problem 9 from Chapter 1 for a utilitarian social welfare function. Rank the three for a Rawlsian social welfare function.

b. How would your answer change if the utility function was instead $U(Y) = Y^{1/5}$?

c. Suppose that Bill and Ted instead have different utility functions: Bill's utility is given by $U^B(Y) = Y^{1/2}$, and Ted's is given by $U^T(Y) = Y^{1/2}$. (This might happen for example, because Bill has significant disabilities and therefore needs more income to get the same level of utility.) How would a Rawlsian rank the three tax policies now?

Effects of Redistributive Policies in Adventureland

	0%	25%	50%
Bill's pre-tax income	$1000	$800	$600
Bill's taxes	0	$200	$200
Bill's pre-tax income	0	$115	$130
Bill's net income	$1000	$715	$530
Ted's pre-tax income	$120	$120	$120
Ted's taxes	0	$30	$60
Ted's transfer payment	0	$115	$130
Ted's net income	$120	$205	$190

14. You have $3,000 to spend on entertainment this year (lucky you!). The price of a day trip (T) is $40 and the price of a pizza and a movie (M) is $20. Suppose that your utility function is $U(T,M) = T^{1/3}M^{2/3}$.

a. What combination of T and M will you choose?

b. Suppose that the price of day trips rises to $50. How will this change your decision?

Appendix to Chapter 2

The Mathematics of Utility Maximization

This appendix develops the mathematics behind the utility-maximization example presented on pp. 41–43 and in Figures 2-10 and 2-11. The utility function that underlies the indifference curves in Figure 2-10 is:

$$U = 100 \times \ln(C) + 175 \times \ln(L)$$

where C is consumption, and L is leisure.

For this utility function, the marginal rate of substitution is:

$$MRS = MU_L/MU_C = (175/L) \, / \, (100/C) = 1.75 \times (C/L)$$

Sarah has a market wage of $10 per hour, and can work up to 2,000 hours per year. She is also subject to a TANF program that features a benefit guarantee of $5,000, and a benefit reduction rate of 50%. As a result, the budget constraint has two segments:

$C = 5,000 + (2,000 - L) \times 10 \times 0.5$ if leisure is more than 1,000 hours (TANF segment)

$C = (2,000 - L) \times 10$ if leisure is less than 1,000 hours (non-TANF segment)

Given this budget constraint, we can solve for the optimal amount of leisure and consumption for this single mother. We do this by first finding her optimal leisure and consumption bundle on each of the two segments of the budget constraint, and then evaluating which of those choices leads to higher total utility.

On the first (TANF) segment of the budget constraint, we solve the problem:

$$\text{Maximize } U = 100 \times \ln(C) + 175 \times \ln(L)$$
$$\text{subject to } C = 5,000 + (2,000 - L) \times 10 \times 0.5$$

Substituting from the budget constraint into the utility function, we obtain:

$$\text{Maximize } U = 100 \times \ln(5,000 + (2,000 - L) \times 10 \times 0.5) + 175 \times \ln(L)$$

We maximize this by taking the differential of utility with respect to leisure, and setting it equal to zero:

$$(100 \times - 5)/(5,000 + (2,000 - L) \times 5) + 175/L = 0$$

Solving this equation, we obtain $L = 1,910$. At that level of leisure, consumption is 5,450. This implies a utility of $100 \times \ln(5,450) + 175 \times \ln(1,910) = 2,182$.

Now, we can solve the problem again for the second (non-TANF) segment of the budget constraint:

$$\text{Maximize } U = 100 \times \ln(C) + 175 \times \ln(L)$$
$$\text{subject to } C = (2,000 - L) \times 10$$

Once again, substituting from the budget constraint into the utility function, we obtain:

$$\text{Maximize } U = 100 \times \ln((2,000 - L) \times 10) + 175 \times \ln(L)$$

Taking the differential of utility with respect to leisure, and setting this to zero, we can solve for an optimal L of 1,273, and resulting consumption of 7,270. Plugging these values back into the utility function, we get a value for utility from this choice of 2,140. This utility value is lower than 2,182, so the individual will choose point A on the first (TANF) segment of the budget constraint.

What happens when we lower the TANF guarantee to $3,000? We can solve the same problem, but now with the lower guarantee level. Doing so, we find that the single mother would still choose to be on the TANF segment of the budget constraint, with leisure of 1,655 hours (and work of 345 hours).

The utility function that underlies the indifference curves in Figure 2-11 is:

$$U = 75 \times \ln(C) + 300 \times \ln(L)$$

For this utility function, the marginal rate of substitution is:

$$MRS = MU_L/MU_C = (300/L) / (75/C) = 4 \times (C/L)$$

Naomi's Budget constraint is the same as that of Sarah's:

$C = 5,000 + (2,000 - L) \times 10 \times 0.5$	if leisure is more than 1,000 hours (TANF segment)
$C = (2,000 - L) \times 10$	if leisure is less than 1,000 hours (non-TANF segment)

On the first (TANF) segment of the budget constraint, we solve the problem:

$$\text{Maximize } U = 75 \times \ln(C) + 300 \times \ln(L)$$
$$\text{subject to } C = 5,000 + (2,000 - L) \times 10 \times 0.5$$

Doing so, we obtain an optimal value of leisure of 3,200. This value exceeds the maximum possible level of leisure, 2,000. So the mother chooses to take that maximum value, with leisure of 2,000 and consumption of 5,000, for a utility level of 2,919.

This mother will be worse off on the non-TANF segment of the budget constraint because she wants so much leisure. Likewise, solving the problem for the $3,000 guarantee, we once again find that she chooses the "corner" solution of 2,000 hours of leisure and 3,000 units of consumption.

Empirical Tools of Public Finance

3

Once again, we return to your days as an employee of your state's Department of Health and Human Services. After doing the careful theoretical analysis outlined in the previous section, you are somewhat closer to making a meaningful contribution to the debate between the governor and the secretary of Health and Human Services. You can tell the governor and the secretary that a reduction in TANF benefits is likely, but not certain, to raise labor supply among single mothers, and that the implications of this response depend on their concerns about equity versus efficiency. Yet these politicians don't just want to know that TANF reductions *might* raise labor supply, nor are they interested in the graphical calculations of the social welfare effects of lower benefits. What they want is numbers.

To provide these numbers, you now turn to the tools of **empirical public finance,** the use of data and statistical methodologies to measure the impact of government policy on individuals and markets. Many of these tools were developed more recently than the classical analyses of utility maximization and market equilibrium that we worked with in the last chapter. As a result, they are also more imperfect, and there are lively debates about the best way to approach problems like estimating the labor-supply response of single mothers to TANF benefit changes.

In this chapter, we review these empirical methods. In doing so, we encounter the fundamental issue faced by those doing empirical work in economics: disentangling causality from correlation. We say that two economic variables are **correlated** if they move together. But this relationship is **causal** only if one of the variables is *causing* the movement in the other. If, instead, there is a third factor that causes both to move together, the correlation is not causal.

This chapter begins with a review of this fundamental problem. We then turn to a discussion of the "gold standard" for measuring the causal effect of an intervention (*randomized trials*) where individuals are randomly assigned to receive or not receive that intervention. While such randomized trials are much more common in medicine than in public finance, they provide a benchmark against which other empirical methods can be evaluated. We

empirical public finance The use of data and statistical methods to measure the impact of government policy on individuals and markets.

correlated Two economic variables are correlated if they move together.

causal Two economic variables are causally related if the movement of one causes movement of the other.

then discuss the range of other empirical methods used by public finance economists to answer questions such as the causal impact of TANF benefit changes on the labor supply of single mothers. Throughout, we use this TANF example, using real-world data on benefit levels and the single-mother labor supply to assess the questions raised by the theoretical analysis of the previous chapter.

3.1

The Important Distinction Between Correlation and Causality

There was once a cholera epidemic in Russia. The government, in an effort to stem the disease, sent doctors to the worst-affected areas. The peasants of a particular province observed a very high correlation between the number of doctors in a given area and the incidence of cholera in that area. Relying on this fact, they banded together and murdered their doctors.[1]

The fundamental problem in this example is that the peasants in this town clearly confused *correlation* with *causality*. They correctly observed that there was a positive association between physician presence and the incidence of illness. But they took that as evidence that the presence of physicians *caused* illness to be more prevalent. What they missed, of course, was that the link actually ran the other way: it was a higher incidence of illness that caused there to be more physicians present. In statistics, this is called the *identification problem:* given that two series are correlated, how do you identify whether one series is causing another?

This problem has plagued not only Russian peasants. In 1988, a Harvard University dean conducted a series of interviews with Harvard freshmen and found that those who had taken SAT preparation courses (a much less widespread phenomenon in 1988 than today) scored on average 63 points lower (out of 1,600 points) than those who hadn't. The dean concluded that SAT preparation courses were unhelpful and that "the coaching industry is playing on parental anxiety."[2] This conclusion is another excellent example of confusing correlation with causation. Who was most likely to take SAT preparation courses? Those students who needed the most help with the exam! So all this study found was that students who needed the most help with the SAT

"That's the gist of what I want to say. Now get me some statistics to base it on"

---

[1] This example is reproduced from Fisher (1976).
[2] *New York Times* (1988).

did the worst on the exam. The courses did not cause students to do worse on the SATs; rather, students who would naturally do worse on the SATs were the ones who took the courses.

Another example comes from the medical evaluation of the benefits of breast-feeding infants. Child-feeding recommendations typically include breast-feeding beyond 12 months, but some medical researchers have documented increased rates of malnutrition in breast-fed toddlers. This has led them to conclude that breast-feeding for too long is nutritionally detrimental. But the misleading nature of this conclusion was illustrated by a study of toddlers in Peru that showed that it was those babies who were already underweight or malnourished who were breast-fed the longest.[3] Increased breast-feeding did not lead to poor growth; children's poor growth and health led to increased breast-feeding.

The Problem

In all of the foregoing examples, the analysis suffered from a common problem: the attempt to interpret a correlation as a causal relationship without sufficient thought to the underlying process generating the data. Noting that those who take SAT preparation courses do worse on SATs, or that those infants who breast-feed longest are the least healthy, is only the first stage in the research process, that of documenting the correlation. Once one has the data on any two measures, it is easy to see if they move together, or *covary,* or if they do not.

What is harder to assess is whether the movements in one measure are *causing* the movements in the other. For any correlation between two variables A and B, there are three possible explanations, one or more of which could result in the correlation:

- ► A is causing B
- ► B is causing A
- ► Some third factor is causing both

Consider the previous SAT preparation example. The fact is that, for this sample of Harvard students, those who took an SAT prep course performed worse on their SATs. The interpretation drawn by the Harvard administrator was one of only many possible interpretations:

- ► SAT prep courses worsen preparation for SATs.
- ► Those who are of lower test-taking ability take preparation courses to try to catch up.
- ► Those who are generally nervous people like to take prep courses, and being nervous is associated with doing worse on standardized exams.

The Harvard administrator drew the first conclusion, but the others may be equally valid. Together, these three interpretations show that one cannot inter-

---

[3] Marquis et al. (1997).

pret this correlation as a causal effect of test preparation on test scores without more information or additional assumptions.

Similarly, consider the breast-feeding interpretation. Once again, there are many possible interpretations:

▶ Longer breast-feeding is bad for health.

▶ Those infants who are in the worst health get breast-fed the longest.

▶ The lowest-income mothers breast-feed longer, since this is the cheapest form of nutrition for children, and low income is associated with poor infant health.

Once again, all of these explanations are consistent with the observed correlation. But, once again, the studies that argued for the negative effect of breast-feeding on health *assumed* the first interpretation while ignoring the others.

The general problem that empirical economists face in trying to use existing data to assess the causal influence of one factor on another is that one cannot immediately go from correlation to causation. This is a problem because for policy purposes what matters is causation. Policy makers typically want to use the results of empirical studies as a basis for predicting how government interventions will affect behaviors. Knowing that two factors are correlated provides no predictive power; prediction requires understanding the causal links between the factors. For example, the government shouldn't make policy based on the fact that breast-feeding infants are less healthy. Rather, it should assess the true causal effect of breast-feeding on infant health, and use that as a basis for making government policy. The next section begins to explore the answer to one of the most important questions in empirical research: How can one draw causal conclusions about the relationships between correlated variables?

3.2

Measuring Causation with Data We'd Like to Have: Randomized Trials

One of the most important empirical issues facing society today is understanding how new medical treatments affect the health of medical patients. An excellent example of this issue is the case of estrogen replacement therapy (ERT), a popular treatment for middle-aged and elderly women who have gone through menopause (the end of menstruation).[4] Menopause is associated with many negative side effects, such as rapid changes in body temperature ("hot flashes"), difficulty sleeping, and higher risk of urinary tract infection. ERT reduces those side effects by mimicking the estrogen produced by the woman's body before the onset of menopause.

---

[4] For an overview of ERT issues, see Kolata (2002).

There was no question that ERT helped ameliorate the negative side effects of menopause, but there was also a concern about ERT. Anecdotal evidence suggested that ERT might raise the risk of heart disease, and, in turn, the risk of heart attacks or strokes. A series of studies beginning in the early 1980s investigated this issue by comparing women who did and did not receive ERT after menopause. These studies concluded that those who received ERT were at no higher risk of heart disease than those who did not; indeed, there was some suggestion that ERT actually *lowered* heart disease.

There was reason to be concerned, however, that such a comparison did not truly reflect the causal impact of ERT on heart disease. This is because women who underwent ERT were more likely to be under a doctor's care, to lead a healthier lifestyle, and to have higher incomes, all of which are associated with a lower chance of heart disease (the third channel previously discussed, where some third factor is correlated with both ERT and heart disease). So it is possible that ERT might have raised the risk of heart disease but that this increase was masked because the women taking the drug were in better health otherwise.

Randomized Trials as a Solution

How can researchers address this problem? The best solution is through the gold standard of testing for causality: **randomized trials.** Randomized trials involve taking a group of volunteers and *randomly* assigning them to either a **treatment group,** which gets the medical treatment, or a **control group,** which does not. Effectively, volunteers are assigned to treatment or control by the flip of a coin.

To see why randomized trials solve our problem, consider what researchers would ideally do in this context: take one set of older women, replicate them, and place the originals and the clones in parallel universes. Everything would be the same in these parallel universes except for the use of ERT. Then, one could simply observe the differences in the incidence of heart disease between these two groups of women. Because the women would be precisely the same, we would know by definition that any differences would be causal. That is, there would be only one possible reason why the set of women assigned ERT would have higher rates of heart disease, since otherwise both sets of women are the same.

Unfortunately, we live in the real world and not in some science-fiction story, so we can't do this parallel universe experiment. But, amazingly, we can approximate this alternative reality through the randomized trial. This is because of the definition of *randomization:* assignment to treatment groups and control groups is not determined by anything about the subjects, but by the flip of a coin. As a result, the treatment group is identical to the control group in every facet but one: the treatment group gets the treatment (in this case, the ERT).

The Problem of Bias

We can rephrase all of the studies we have discussed so far in this chapter in the treatment/control framework. In the SAT example, the people who took

randomized trial The ideal type of experiment designed to test causality, whereby a group of individuals is randomly divided into a treatment group, which receives the treatment of interest, and a control group, which does not.

treatment group The set of individuals who are subject to an intervention being studied.

control group The set of individuals comparable to the treatment group who are not subject to the intervention being studied.

preparatory classes were the treatment group and the people who did not take the classes were the control group. In the breast-feeding example, the infants who breast-fed for more than a year were the treatment group and the infants who did not were the control group. In the ERT studies that occurred before randomized trials, those who received ERT were the treatment group and those who did not were the control group. Even in the Russian doctor example, the areas where the doctors were sent were the treatment group and the areas where the doctors were not sent was the control group. Virtually any empirical problem we discuss in this course can be thought of as a comparison between treatment and control groups.

We can therefore always start our analysis of an empirical methodology with a simple question: Do the treatment and control groups differ for any reason *other* than the treatment? All of the earlier examples involve cases in which the treatment groups differ in consistent ways from those in the control groups: those taking SAT prep courses may be of lower test-taking ability than those not taking the courses; those breast-fed longest may be in worse health than those not breast-fed as long; those taking ERT may be in better health than those not taking ERT. These non-treatment-related differences between treatment and control groups are the fundamental problem in assigning causal interpretations to correlations.

We call these differences **bias,** a term that represents any source of difference between treatment and control groups that is *correlated* with the treatment but is *not due* to the treatment. The estimates of the impact of SAT prep courses on SAT scores, for example, are *biased* by the fact that those who take the prep courses are likely to do worse on the SATs for other reasons. Similarly, the estimates of the impact of breast-feeding past one year on health are *biased* by the fact that those infants in the worst health are the ones likely to be breast-fed the longest. The estimates of the impact of ERT on heart disease are *biased* by the fact that those who take ERT are likely in better health than those who do not. Whenever treatment and control groups consistently differ in a manner that is correlated with, but not due to, the treatment, there can be bias.

By definition, such differences do not exist in a randomized trial, since the groups do not differ in any consistent fashion, but rather only by the flip of a coin. Thus, randomized treatment and control groups cannot have consistent differences that are correlated with treatment, since there are no consistent differences across the groups other than the treatment. As a result, *randomized trials have no bias,* and it is for this reason that randomized trials are the gold standard for empirically estimating causal effects.

> **bias** Any source of difference between treatment and control groups that is correlated with the treatment but is not due to the treatment.

Quick Hint The description of randomized trials here relies on those trials having fairly large numbers of treatments and controls (large *sample sizes*). Having large sample sizes allows researchers to eliminate any consistent differences between the groups by relying on the statistical principle called the *law of large numbers:* the odds of getting the wrong answer approaches zero as the sample size grows.

Suppose that a friend says that he can flip a (fair, not weighted!) coin so that it *always* comes up heads. This is not possible; every time a coin is flipped, there is a 50% chance that it will land tails up. So you give him a quarter and ask him to prove it. If he flips just once, there is a 50% chance he will get heads and claim victory. If he flips twice, there is still a 25% chance that he will get heads both times, and continue to be able to claim victory; that is, there is still the possibility of getting a biased answer *by chance* when there is a very small sample.

As he flips more and more times, however, the odds that the coin will come up heads *every* time gets smaller and smaller. After just 10 flips, there is only a 1 in 1,024 chance that he will get all heads. After 20 flips, the odds are 1 in 1,048,576. That is, the higher the number of flips, the lower the odds that we get a biased answer. Likewise, if randomly assigned groups of individuals are large enough, we can rule out the possibility of bias arising by chance.

Randomized Trials of ERT

When the National Institutes of Health appointed its first female director, Dr. Bernadine Healy, in 1991, one of her priorities was to sponsor a randomized trial of ERTs. This randomized trial tracked over 16,000 women ages 50–79 who were recruited to participate in the trial by 40 clinical centers in the United States. The study was supposed to last 8.5 years but was stopped after 5.2 years because its conclusion was already clear: ERT did in fact raise the risk of heart disease. In particular, women taking ERT were observed to annually have (per 10,000 women): 7 more coronary heart diseases (both fatal and nonfatal), 8 more strokes, and 8 more pulmonary embolisms (blood clots in the lungs). In addition, the study found that women taking ERT had 8 more invasive breast cancers as well. Thus, the randomized trial revealed that the earlier ERT studies were *biased* by differences between these groups. These new findings led some doctors to question their decisions to recommend ERTs for postmenopausal women.[5]

Randomized Trials in the TANF Context

Measuring the health impacts of new medicines is not the only place where randomized trials are useful; they can be equally useful in the context of public policy. Suppose that we want to measure the causal impact of TANF on labor supply. To begin, we gather a large (e.g., 5,000-person) group of single mothers who are now receiving a $5,000 benefit guarantee. One by one, we take each single mother into a separate room and flip a coin. If it is heads, they continue to receive a benefit guarantee of $5,000; these mothers are the *control group* whose benefits do not change. If it is tails, then the guarantee is cut to

---

[5] Results of the study are reported in Writing Group for the Women's Health Initiative Investigators (2002).

$3,000; these mothers are the *treatment group* who receive the experimental reduction in their benefits. After we have assigned a guarantee to all of these mothers, we follow them for a period of time and observe their labor-supply differences. Any labor-supply differences would have to be *caused* by the change in benefit guarantee, since nothing else differs in a consistent way across these groups.

There is a real-world randomized trial available that can help us learn about the impact of cash welfare benefits on the labor supply of single mothers. Under its Aid to Families with Dependent Children (AFDC) program (the precursor to TANF) in 1992, California had one of the most generous benefit guarantees in the United States, $663 per month ($7,956 per year) for a family of three. The state wanted to assess the implications of reducing its AFDC benefit levels, in order to reduce costs. It conducted an experiment, randomly assigning one-third of the families receiving AFDC in each of four counties to the existing AFDC program, and assigning the other two-thirds to an experimental program. The experimental program had 15% lower maximum benefits, and several other provisions that encouraged recipients to work. The experiment lasted until 1998, at which point all families became subject to the 15% lower benefit.

Hotz, Mullin, and Scholz (2002) studied the effects of these benefit changes on the employment of recipients. They found that the experiment increased the employment rate of those families assigned to the experimental treatment to 49%, relative to an employment rate for the control group of 44.5%. The difference, 4.5%, is about 10% of the employment rate of the control group. It is often convenient to represent the relationship between economic variables in *elasticity* form, which in this case means computing the percentage change in employment for each percentage change in benefits. The estimated elasticity of employment with respect to benefits here is about −0.67; that is, a 15% reduction in the benefit guarantee resulted in a 10% increase in employment in the treatment group relative to that of the control group.

Why We Need to Go Beyond Randomized Trials

It would be wonderful if we could run randomized trials to assess the causal relationships that underlie any interesting correlation. For most questions of interest, however, randomized trials are not available. Such trials can be enormously expensive and take a very long time to plan and execute, and often raise difficult ethical issues. On the last point, consider the example of a recent trial for a new treatment for Parkinson's disease, a debilitating neurological disorder. The proposed treatment involved injecting fetal pig cells directly into patients' brains. In order to have a comparable control group, the researchers drilled holes in the heads of all 18 subjects, but put the pig cells in only 10 of the subjects.[6] As you can imagine, there was substantial criticism about drilling holes in eight heads for no legitimate medical purpose.

---

[6] Pollack (2001).

Moreover, even the gold standard of randomized trials has some potential problems. First, the results are only valid for the sample of individuals who volunteer to be either treatments or controls, and this sample may be different from the population at large. For example, those in a randomized trial sample may be less averse to risk or they may be more desperately ill. Thus, the answer we obtain from a randomized trial, while correct for this sample, may not be valid for the average person in the population.

A second problem with randomized trials is that of **attrition:** individuals may leave the experiment before it is complete. This is not a problem if individuals leave randomly, since the sample will remain random. Suppose, however, that the experiment has positive effects on half the treatment group and negative effects on the other half, and that as a result the half with negative effects leaves the experiment before it is done. If we focus only on the remaining half, we would wrongly conclude that the treatment has overall positive impacts.

In the remainder of this chapter, we discuss several approaches taken by economists to try to assess causal relationships in empirical research. We will do so through the use of the TANF example. The general lesson from this discussion is that there is no way to consistently achieve the ideal of the randomized trial; bias is a pervasive problem that is not easily remedied. There are, however, methods available that can allow us to approach the gold standard of randomized trials.

attrition Reduction in the size of samples over time, which, if not random, can lead to bias estimates.

3.3

Estimating Causation with Data We Actually Get: Observational Data

In Section 3.2, we showed how a randomized trial can be used to measure the impacts of an intervention such as ERT or lower TANF benefits on outcomes such as heart attacks or labor supply. As we highlighted, however, data from such randomized trials are not always available when important empirical questions need to be answered. Typically, what the analyst has instead are **observational data,** data generated from individual behavior observed in the real world. For example, instead of information on a randomized trial of a new medicine, we may simply have data on who took the medicine and what their outcomes were (the source of the original conclusions on ERT). There are several well-developed methods that can be used by analysts to address the problem of bias with observational data, and these tools can often closely approximate the gold standard of randomized trials.

This section explores how researchers can use observational data to estimate causal effects instead of just correlations. We do so within the context of the TANF example. It is useful throughout to refer to the empirical framework established in the previous section: those with higher TANF benefits are the control group, those with lower TANF benefits are the treatment group, and our concern is to remove any sources of bias between the two groups

observational data Data generated by individual behavior observed in the real world, not in the context of deliberately designed experiments.

(that is, any differences between them that might affect their labor supply, other than TANF benefits differences). Thus, the major concern throughout this section is how to overcome any potential bias so that we can measure the causal relationship (if there is one) between TANF benefits and labor supply.

Time Series Analysis

One common approach to measuring causal effects with observational data is **time series analysis,** documenting the correlation between the variables of interest over time. In the context of TANF, for example, we can gather data over time on the benefit guarantee in each year, and compare these data to the amount of labor supply delivered by single mothers in those same years.

time series analysis Analysis of the comovement of two series over time.

Figure 3-1 shows such a time series analysis. On the horizontal axis are years, running from 1968 through 1998. The left-hand vertical axis charts the average real monthly benefit guarantee for a single mother with three children (controlled for inflation by expressing income in constant 1998 dollars) available in the United States over this period. Benefits declined dramatically from $991 in 1968 to $515 in 1998, falling by half in real terms because benefit levels have not kept up with inflation. The right-hand vertical axis charts the average hours of work per year for single mothers (including zeros for those mothers who do not work). The hours worked have risen substantially, from

■ FIGURE 3-1

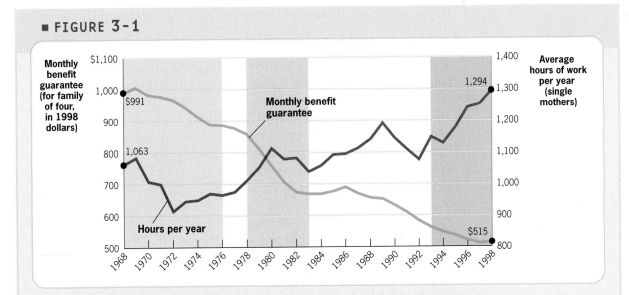

Average Benefit Guarantee and Single Mother Labor Supply, 1968–1998 • The left-hand vertical axis shows the monthly benefit guarantee under cash welfare, which falls from $991 in 1968 to $515 in 1998. The right-hand vertical axis shows average hours of work per year for single mothers, which rises from 1,063 in 1968 to 1,294 in 1998. Over this entire 30-year period, there is a strong negative correlation between the average benefit guarantee and the level of labor supply of single mothers, but there is not a very strong relationship within subperiods of this overall time span.

Source: Calculations based on data from Current Population Survey's annual March supplements.

1,063 hours per year in 1968 to 1,294 in 1998. Thus, there appears to be a strong negative relationship between benefit guarantees and labor supply: falling benefit guarantees are associated with higher levels of labor supply by single mothers.

Problems with Time Series Analysis Although this time series correlation is striking, it does not necessarily demonstrate a causal effect of TANF benefits on labor supply. When there is a slow-moving trend in one variable through time, as is true for the general decline in income guarantees over this period, it is very difficult to infer its causal effects on another variable. There could be many reasons why single mothers work more now than they did in 1968: greater acceptance of women in the workplace; better and more options for child care; even more social pressures on mothers to work. The simple fact that labor supply is higher today than it was 30 years ago does not prove that this increase has been caused by the steep decline in income guarantees.

This problem is highlighted by examining subperiods of this overall time span. From 1968 through 1976, benefits fell by about 10% (from $990 to $890 per month), yet hours of work also fell by about 10% (from 1070 hours to 960 hours), whereas a causal effect of benefits would imply a rise in hours of work. From 1978 through 1983, the period of steepest benefits decline, benefits fell by almost one-quarter in real terms (from $858 to $669 per month), yet labor supply first increased, then decreased, with a total increase over this period of only 2%. The subperiods therefore give a very different impression of the relationship between benefits and labor supply than does the overall time series.

A particularly instructive example about the limitations of time series analysis is the experience of the 1993–1998 period. In this subperiod, there is both a sharp fall in benefits (falling by about 10%, from $562 to $515 per month) and a sharp rise in labor supply of single mothers (rising by about 13%, from 1148 hours per year to 1294 hours per year). The data from this subperiod would seem to support the notion that lower benefits cause rising labor supply. Yet during this period the economy was experiencing dramatic growth, with the general unemployment rate falling from 7.3% in January 1993 to 4.4% in December, 1998. It was also a period that saw an enormous expansion in the Earned Income Tax Credit (EITC), a federal wage subsidy that has been shown to be effective in increasing the labor supply of single mothers. It could be those factors, not falling benefits, that caused increased labor supply of single mothers. So once again, other factors get in the way of a causal interpretation of this correlation over time; factors such as economic growth and a more generous EITC can cause bias in this time series analysis because they are also correlated with the outcome of interest.

When Is Time Series Analysis Useful? Is all time series analysis useless? Not necessarily. In some cases, there may be sharp breaks in the time series that are not related to third factors that can cause bias. A classic example is shown in Figure 3-2. This figure shows the price of a pack of cigarettes (in constant 1982 dollars) on the left vertical axis and the *youth smoking rate,* the percentage

■ **FIGURE 3-2**

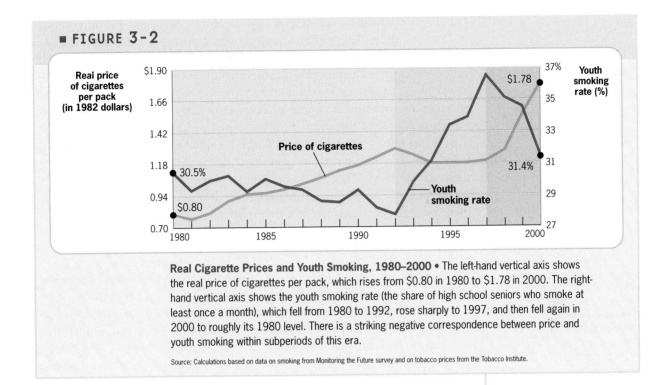

Real Cigarette Prices and Youth Smoking, 1980–2000 • The left-hand vertical axis shows the real price of cigarettes per pack, which rises from $0.80 in 1980 to $1.78 in 2000. The right-hand vertical axis shows the youth smoking rate (the share of high school seniors who smoke at least once a month), which fell from 1980 to 1992, rose sharply to 1997, and then fell again in 2000 to roughly its 1980 level. There is a striking negative correspondence between price and youth smoking within subperiods of this era.

Source: Calculations based on data on smoking from Monitoring the Future survey and on tobacco prices from the Tobacco Institute.

of high school seniors who smoke at least once a month, on the right vertical axis. These data are shown for the time period from 1980 to 2000.

From 1980 to 1992, there was a steady increase in the real price of cigarettes (from $0.80 to $1.29 per pack), and a steady decline in the youth smoking rate (from 30.5% to 27.8%). As previously noted, these changes over time need not be causally related. Smoking was falling for all groups over this time period due to an increased appreciation of the health risks of smoking, and prices may simply have been rising due to rising costs of tobacco production.

Then, in April 1993, there was a "price war" in the tobacco industry, leading to a sharp drop in real cigarette prices from $1.29 to $1.18 per pack.[7] At that exact time, youth smoking began to rise. This striking simultaneous reversal in both series is more compelling evidence of a causal relationship than is the long, slow-moving correlation over the 1980–1992 period. But it doesn't *prove* a causal relationship, because other things were changing in 1993 as well. It was, for example, the beginning of an important period of economic growth, which could have led to more youth smoking. Moreover, the rise in youth smoking seems too large to be explained solely by the price decrease.

[7] The leading hypothesis for this sharp drop in prices on "Marlboro Friday" (April 2, 1993) is that the major cigarette manufacturers were lowering prices in order to fight off sizeable market share gains by "generic" lower-priced cigarettes.

Fortunately, in this case, there is another abrupt change in this time series. In 1998 and thereafter, prices rose steeply when the tobacco industry settled a series of expensive lawsuits with many states (and some private parties) and passed the costs on to cigarette consumers. At that exact time, youth smoking began to fall again. This type of pattern seems to strongly suggest a causal effect, even given the limitations of time series data. That is, it seems unlikely that there is a factor correlated with youth smoking that moved up until 1992, then down until 1997, then back up again, as did price. That youth smoking follows the opposite pattern as cigarette prices suggests that price is causing these movements. Thus, while time series correlations are not very useful when there are long-moving trends in the data, they are more useful when there are sharp breaks in trends over a relatively narrow period of time.

Cross-Sectional Regression Analysis

cross-sectional regression analysis Statistical analysis of the relationship between two or more variables exhibited by many individuals at one point in time.

A second approach to identifying causal effects is **cross-sectional regression analysis,** a statistical method for assessing the relationship between two variables while holding other factors constant. By *cross-sectional,* we mean comparing many individuals at one point in time, rather than comparing outcomes over time as in a time series analysis.

In its simplest form, called a *bivariate regression,* cross-sectional regression analysis is a means of formalizing correlation analysis, of quantifying the extent to which two series covary. Returning to the example in Chapter 2, suppose that there are two types of single mothers, with preferences over leisure and food consumption represented by Figures 2-10 and 2-11 (p. 42). Before there is any change in TANF benefits, the mother who has a lower preference for leisure (Sarah in Figure 2-10) has both lower TANF benefits and a higher labor supply than the mother who has a greater preference for leisure (Naomi in Figure 2-11). If we take these two mothers and correlate TANF benefits to labor supply, we would find that higher TANF benefits are associated with lower labor supply.

This correlation is illustrated graphically in Figure 3-3. We graph the two data points when the benefit guarantee is $5,000. One data point, point *A,* corresponds to Naomi from Figure 2-11, and represents labor supply of 0 hours and an income guarantee of $5,000. The other data point, point *B,* corresponds to Sarah in Figure 2-10, and represents a labor supply of 90 hours per year and TANF benefits of $4,550. The downward sloping line makes clear the *negative correlation* between TANF benefits and labor supply; the mother with lower TANF benefits has a higher labor supply.

Regression analysis takes this correlation one step further by quantifying the relationship between TANF benefits and labor supply. Regression analysis does so by finding the line that best fits this relationship, and then measuring the slope of that line.[8] This is illustrated in Figure 3-3. The line that connects

---

[8] We discuss here only *linear* approaches to regression analysis; nonlinear regression analysis, where one fits not only lines but other shapes to the data, is a popular alternative.

■ **FIGURE 3-3**

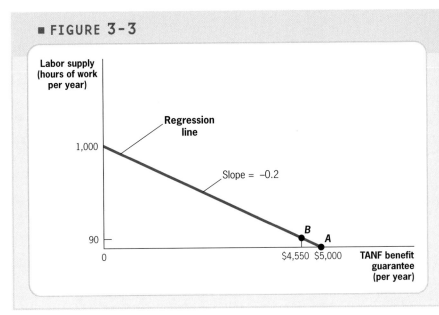

TANF Benefits and Labor Supply in Theoretical Example • If we plot the data from the theoretical example of Chapter 2, we find a modest negative relationship between TANF benefits and the labor supply of single mothers.

these two points has a slope of −0.2. That is, this bivariate regression indicates that each $1 reduction in TANF benefits per month leads to a 0.2-hour-per-year increase in labor supply. Regression analysis describes the relationship between the variable that you would like to explain (the *dependent variable,* which is labor supply in our example) and the set of variables that you think might do the explaining (the *independent variables;* in our example, the TANF benefit).

Example with Real-World Data The example in Figure 3-3 is made up, but we can replicate this exercise using real data from one of the most popular sources of cross-sectional data for those doing applied research in public finance: the Current Population Survey, or CPS.

The CPS collects information every month from individuals throughout the United States on a variety of economic and demographic issues. For example, this survey is the source of the unemployment rate statistics that you frequently hear cited in the news. Every year, in March, a special supplement to this survey asks respondents about their sources of income and hours of work in the previous year. So we can take a sample of single mothers from this survey and ask: What is the relationship between the TANF benefits and hours of labor supply in this cross-sectional sample?

Figure 3-4 graphs the hours of labor supply per year (vertical axis) against dollars of TANF benefits per year (horizontal axis), for all of the single mothers in the CPS data set. To make the graph easier to interpret, we divide the data into ranges of TANF income ($0 in TANF benefits; $1–$99 of benefits; $100–$250 of benefits; etc.). Each range represents (roughly) a doubling of the previous range (a logarithmic scale). For each range, we show the average hours of labor supply in the group. For example, as the highlighted point

■ FIGURE 3-4

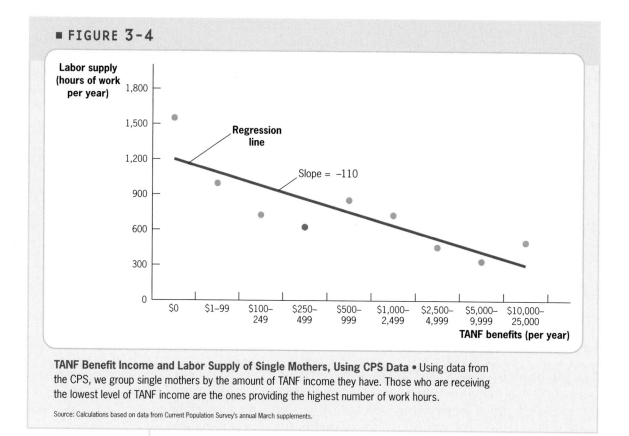

TANF Benefit Income and Labor Supply of Single Mothers, Using CPS Data • Using data from the CPS, we group single mothers by the amount of TANF income they have. Those who are receiving the lowest level of TANF income are the ones providing the highest number of work hours.

Source: Calculations based on data from Current Population Survey's annual March supplements.

shows, single mothers receiving between $250 and $499 in benefits supply just over 600 hours of labor per year.

It is immediately clear from this graph that there is a *negative relationship* between TANF benefits and hours of labor supply. The single mothers at the left of the graph, where benefits are lowest, have much higher labor supply on average than those on the right of the graph, where TANF benefits are the highest. The line in Figure 3-4 formalizes this eyeball impression. This linear **regression line** shows the *best* linear approximation to the relationship between TANF benefits and labor supply that is represented by these points. Unlike the made-up example in Figure 3-3, there is no single line that fits perfectly through this set of data points; real-world data are never that neat! What the linear regression does is find the line that comes closest to fitting through the cluster of data points.[9]

This line has a slope of −110, which indicates that each doubling of TANF benefits reduces hours of work by 110 per year (remember that each segment

regression line The line that measures the best linear approximation to the relationship between any two variables.

---

[9] Technically, this line is the one that minimizes the sum of squared distances of each point from the line. As a result, one major concern with linear regression analysis is *outliers*. An outlier, which is a point that is very far from the others, exerts a strong influence on this line, since we are minimizing the sum of *squared* distances, so a large distance has an exponentially large effect. For this reason, analysts often use other approaches that are less sensitive to such outlying observations.

on the horizontal axis represents a doubling of benefits). Once again, it is convenient to represent the relationship between economic variables in elasticity form. Based on these CPS data, the mean (average number of) hours of work in our sample is 748 hours. So we know that each 100% rise in TANF benefits reduces hours of work by 15% (110 is 15% of 748), for an elasticity of –0.15. This is a fairly *inelastic* response; there is a relatively modest reduction in hours (15%) when TANF benefits rise (by 100%).

Problems with Cross-Sectional Regression Analysis The result summarized in Figure 3-4 seems to indicate strongly that mothers who receive the largest TANF benefits work the fewest hours. Once again, however, there are several possible interpretations of this correlation. One interpretation is that higher TANF benefits are causing an increase in leisure. Another possible interpretation is that some mothers have a high taste for leisure and wouldn't work much even if TANF benefits weren't available. Because TANF benefits fall as the recipient works more, mothers who take more leisure automatically get higher levels of benefits. As a result, there may be a correlation between benefits and leisure (and therefore labor supply) because more leisure is causing higher TANF benefits, *not* because higher TANF benefits are causing more leisure. Thus, varying tastes for leisure cause a bias in our attempt to causally interpret the relationship between TANF benefits and labor supply. Differences in tastes for leisure are one reason why those with high and low TANF benefits are not exactly comparable; these differences in taste cause a consistent difference (bias) in labor supply among mothers with high and low TANF benefits.

This problem is most clearly illustrated in Figure 3-3, since we actually know the utility functions underlying the labor-supply decisions of the two mothers represented by points *A* and *B*. The mother who works less does so because she has a higher taste for leisure, and not because her TANF benefits are higher. In fact, her higher taste for leisure is what drives her TANF benefits to be higher, because TANF benefits increase as leisure increases and hours worked decrease. Thus, the negative relationship depicted in Figure 3-3 is *not causal;* it reflects, instead, differences in the taste for leisure between the two mothers we are analyzing that are correlated with their benefit levels (bias). In other words, we haven't taken two identical mothers and assigned them different benefits, which is what causal analysis demands. Rather, we took two very different mothers and compared their benefits and labor supply, which introduces bias into the analysis.

This problem is less obvious in Figure 3-4, since we don't know the utility functions of the single mothers in the CPS. But the same problematic potential exists: maybe the mothers with low TANF income are simply those who have the lowest preference for leisure. If this is true, we can't say that each doubling of TANF income *causes* a 15% reduction in labor supply. Rather, all we can say is that each doubling of TANF income *is associated with* a 15% reduction in labor supply. It could be that other consistent differences between these low- and high-benefit groups (such as different tastes for leisure) are biasing the relationship.

control variables Variables that are included in cross-sectional regression models to account for differences between treatment and control groups that can lead to bias.

Control Variables Regression analysis has one potential advantage over correlation analysis in dealing with the problem of bias: the ability to include **control variables.** Suppose that the CPS had a variable included in the data set called "taste for leisure" that accurately reflected each individual's taste for leisure. Suppose that this variable came in two categorical values: "prefers leisure" and "prefers work," and that everyone within each of these categorical values had identical tastes for leisure and work. That is, there is no bias within these groups, only across them; within each group, individuals are identical in terms of their preferences toward work and leisure.

If we had this information, we could divide our sample into two groups according to this leisure variable, and redo the analysis within each group. Within each group, different tastes for leisure cannot be the source of the relationship between TANF benefits and labor supply, because tastes for leisure are identical within each group. This "taste for leisure" control variable will allow us to get rid of the bias in our comparison, because within each group we no longer have a systematic difference in tastes for leisure that is correlated with benefits. Control variables in regression analysis play this role: they try to control for (take into account) other differences across individuals in a sample, so that any remaining correlation between the dependent variable (e.g., labor supply) and independent variable (e.g., TANF benefits) can be interpreted as a causal effect of benefits on work.

In reality, control variables are unlikely to ever solve this problem completely, as the key variables we want, such as the intrinsic taste for leisure in this example, are impossible to measure in data sets. Usually, we have to approximate the variables we really want, such as taste for leisure, with what is available, such as age or education or work experience. These are imperfect proxies, however, so they don't fully allow us to control for differences in taste for leisure across the population (e.g., even within age or education or work experience groups, there will be individuals with very different tastes for leisure). Thus, it is hard to totally get rid of bias with control variables, since control variables only represent in a limited way the underlying differences between treatment and control groups. We discuss this point in the appendix to this chapter, which includes reference to data on our Web site that you can use to conduct your own regression analysis.

Quick Hint For many empirical analyses, there will be one clear treatment group and one clear control group, as in the ERT case. For other analyses, such as our cross-sectional TANF analysis, there are many groups to be compared with one another. A cross-sectional regression essentially compares each point in Figure 3-4 with the other points in order to estimate the relationship between TANF benefits and labor supply.

Even though the treatment/control analogy is no longer exact, however, the general intuition remains. It is essential in all empirical work to ensure that there are no factors that cause consistent differences in behavior (labor supply) across two groups and are also correlated with the independent variable (TANF benefits). When there are more than two groups, the concern is the same: to ensure that there is no consistent factor that causes groups with higher benefits to supply less labor than groups with lower benefits, other than the benefit differences themselves.

Quasi-Experiments

As noted earlier, public finance researchers cannot set up randomized trials and run experiments for every important behavior that matters for public policy. We have examined alternatives to randomized trials such as time series and cross-sectional regression analysis, but have also seen that these research methods have many shortcomings which make it hard for them to eliminate the bias problem. Is there any way to accurately assess causal influences without using a randomized trial? Is there an alternative to the use of control variables for purging empirical models of bias?

Over the past two decades, empirical research in public finance has become increasingly focused on one potential middle-ground solution: the **quasi-experiment,** a situation that arises naturally when changes in the economic environment (such as a policy change) create nearly identical treatment and control groups that can be used to study the effect of that policy change. In a quasi-experiment, outside forces (such as those instituting the policy change) do the randomization for us.

quasi-experiments Changes in the economic environment that create nearly identical treatment and control groups for studying the effect of that environmental change, allowing public finance economists to take advantage of randomization created by external forces.

For example, suppose that we have a sample with a large number of single mothers in the neighboring states of Arkansas and Louisiana, for two years, 1996 and 1998. Suppose further that, in 1997, the state of Arkansas cut its benefit guarantee by 20%, while Louisiana's benefits remained unchanged. In principle, this alteration in the states' policies has essentially performed our randomization for us. The women in Arkansas who experienced the decrease in benefits are the treatment group, and the women in Louisiana whose benefits did not change are the control. By computing the change in labor supply across these groups, and then examining the difference between treatment (Arkansas) and control (Louisiana), we can obtain an estimate of the impact of benefits on labor supply that is free of bias.

In principle, of course, we could learn about the effect of this policy change by simply studying the experience of single mothers in Arkansas. If nothing differed between the set of single mothers in the state in 1996 and the set of single mothers in the state in 1998, other than the benefits reduction, then any change in labor supply would reflect only the change in benefits, and the results would be free of bias. In practice, such a comparison typically runs into the problems we associate with time series analysis. For example, the period from 1996 through 1998 was a period of major national economic growth, with many more job openings for low-skilled workers, which could lead single mothers to leave TANF and increase their earnings even in the absence of a benefits change. Thus, it is quite possible that single mothers in Arkansas may have increased their labor supply even if their benefits had not fallen.

Because other factors may have changed that affected the labor supply decisions of single mothers in Arkansas, the quasi-experimental approach includes the extra step of comparing the treatment group for whom the policy changed to a control group for whom it did not. The state of Louisiana did not change its TANF guarantee between 1996 and 1998, but single mothers in Louisiana benefited from the same national economic boom as did those in Arkansas. If the increase in labor supply among single mothers in Arkansas is driven by economic conditions, then we should see the same increase in labor supply among single mothers in Louisiana; if the increase in labor supply among single mothers in Arkansas is driven by lower TANF benefits, then we would see no change among single mothers in Louisiana. The bias introduced into our comparison of single mothers in Arkansas in 1996 to single mothers in Arkansas in 1998 by the improvement in economic conditions across the nation is *also* present when we do a similar comparison within Louisiana. In Louisiana, however, the treatment effect of a higher TANF benefit is *not* present. In this comparison, we can say that:

Hours (Arkansas, 1998) − Hours (Arkansas, 1996) = Treatment effect + Bias
from economic boom

Hours (Louisiana, 1998) − Hours (Louisiana, 1996) = Bias from economic
boom

Difference = Treatment effect

By subtracting the change in hours of work in Louisiana (the control group) from the change in hours of work in Arkansas (the treatment group), we control for the bias caused by the economic boom and obtain a causal estimate of the effect of TANF benefits on hours of work.

Table 3-1 provides an illustrative but hypothetical set of numbers that we can use to analyze the results of this quasi-experiment. Suppose that the welfare guarantee was cut from $5,000 to $4,000 in Arkansas between 1996 and 1998. Over the same period, hours of work per year among single mothers in the state rose by from 1,000 to 1,200. The time series estimate using the experience of Arkansas alone would be that the $1,000 benefit reduction (20%) increased hours of work by 200 (20%). This outcome implies an elasticity of total hours with respect to benefits of −1 (a 20% benefit cut led to a 20% labor supply rise). Notice that this estimate is considerably larger than the −0.67 elasticity found in the randomized trial in California (our gold standard).

Consider now the bottom panel of Table 3-1. This panel shows that, between 1996 and 1998, there was no change in welfare benefits in Louisiana, but hours of work increased by 50 hours per year. Thus, it appears that the economic boom did play a role in the increase in hours worked by single mothers. By looking only at time series data from Arkansas, we ignore the effect of the economic boom. If we don't take this effect into account in our study, our conclusions about the effect of TANF benefits on labor supply will be biased.

A simple solution to this problem, as we have seen, is to examine the difference between the change in Arkansas and the change in Louisiana. That is,

Arkansas had both a cut in welfare benefits and an economic boom, and hours of labor supply rose by 200; Louisiana had only the economic boom, and hours of labor supply rose by 50. These results suggest that the welfare benefit cut in Arkansas caused a 150 hour increase in labor supply, net of the economic changes. Once we've eliminated the bias caused by the improvement in overall economic conditions, the implied elasticity of hours with respect to welfare benefits is −0.75, very similar to that found in the California experiment. This technique is called a **difference-in-difference estimator:** Take the difference between the labor supply changes in the treatment group which experiences the change (in this case, single mothers in Arkansas) and the labor supply changes in the control group which does not experience the change, but is otherwise identical to the treatment group (in this case, single mothers in Louisiana). In this way, we can estimate a causal effect of TANF benefits changes on labor supply.

Difference-in-difference estimators try to combine time series and cross-sectional analyses to address the problems with each. By comparing the change in Arkansas to the change in Louisiana, the estimator controls for other time series factors that bias the time series analysis within Arkansas. Likewise, by comparing the change within each state, rather than just comparing the two states at a point in time, the estimator controls for omitted factors that bias cross-sectional analysis across the two states.

The cross-sectional estimate in this context would contrast Arkansas and Louisiana in 1998, when their benefits differed. In 1998, Arkansas had TANF benefits that were $1,000 lower than Louisiana, and single mothers in Arkansas worked 100 hours more per year. Cross-sectional analysis would therefore conclude that each $1,000 reduction in welfare benefits leads to a 100 hour increase in work, rather than the 150 hour increase that we get from difference-in-difference analysis (and that we know is true from the randomized trial).

This cross-sectional estimate is biased by the fact that single mothers tend to work more hours in Louisiana regardless of the level of TANF benefits. This is illustrated by the fact that, when TANF benefits were identical in the two states in 1996, hours of work were more in Louisiana. In principle, we might find control variables to account for the more hours of work in Louisiana, but in practice that is difficult. The difference-in-difference estimator suggests the best possible control: the hours of work in the *same state* before there was a benefits change. That is, by comparing the change within a state to the change within another state, the difference-in-difference estimator controls for cross-sectional differences across states that might bias the comparison.

■ TABLE 3-1

Using Quasi-Experimental Variation

Arkansas

	1996	1998	Difference
Benefit guarantee	$5,000	$4,000	−$1,000
Hours of work per year	1,000	1,200	200

Louisiana

	1996	1998	Difference
Benefit guarantee	$5,000	$5,000	$0
Hours of work per year	1,050	1,100	50

In Arkansas, there is a cut in the TANF guarantee between 1996 and 1998 and a corresponding rise in labor supply, so if everything is the same for single mothers in both years, this is a causal effect. If everything is not the same, we can perhaps use the experience of a neighboring state that did not decrease its benefits, Louisiana, to capture any bias to the estimates.

difference-in-difference estimator The difference between the changes in outcomes for the treatment group that experiences an intervention and the control group that does not.

Problems with Quasi-Experimental Analysis As well as the difference-in-difference quasi-experimental approach works to control for bias, it is still less than ideal. Suppose, for example, that the economic boom of this period affected Arkansas in a different way than it affected Louisiana. If this were true, then the "bias from economic boom" terms in the previous comparison would not be equal, and we would be unable to isolate the treatment effect of higher TANF benefits by simple subtraction. Instead, we get a new bias term: the difference in the impact of the economic boom in Arkansas and Louisiana. That is, when we compute our difference-in-difference estimator we obtain:

Hours (Arkansas, 1998) − Hours (Arkansas, 1996) = *AR* bias from economic boom + Treatment

Hours (Louisiana, 1998) − Hours (Louisiana, 1996) = *LA* bias from economic boom

Difference = Treatment effect + (*AR* bias − *LA* bias)

Since *AR* and *LA* biases are not equal, the estimator will not identify the true treatment effect.

With quasi-experimental studies, unlike true experiments, we can never be completely certain that we have purged all bias from the treatment–control comparison. Quasi-experimental studies use two approaches to try to make the argument that they have obtained a causal estimate. The first is intuitive: trying to argue that, given the treatment and control groups, it seems very likely that bias has been removed. The second is statistical: to continue to use alternative or additional control groups to confirm that the bias has been removed. In the appendix to Chapter 14, we discuss how alternative or additional control groups can be used to confirm the conclusions of quasi-experimental analysis.

Structural Modeling

The randomized trials and quasi-experimental approaches previously described have the distinct advantage that, if applied appropriately, they can address the difficult problem of distinguishing causality from correlation. Yet they also have two important limitations. First, they only provide an estimate of the causal impact of a *particular treatment*. That is, the California experiment found that cutting benefits by 15% raised employment rates by 4.5 percentage points. This is the best estimate of the impact of cutting benefits by 15%, but it may not tell us much about the impact of cutting benefits by 30%, or of raising benefits by 15%. That is, we can't necessarily *extrapolate* from a particular change in the environment to model all possible changes in the environment. These approaches give us a precise answer to a specific question, but don't necessarily provide a general conclusion about how different changes in benefits might affect behavior.

The second limitation is that these approaches can tell us *how* outcomes change when there is an intervention, but often they cannot tell us *why*. Consider the behavior of mothers with income between $6,000 and $10,000 in our example from Chapter 2, and how the mothers react to a cut in benefits under TANF. For these mothers, as we noted, there is both an income effect and a substitution effect leading to more work; both mothers are poorer because benefits have fallen, and they have a higher net wage since the implicit tax rate has fallen. An experimental or quasi-experimental study of the responses of these women to the benefits reduction might show us the total effect of the reduction on their labor supply, but it would tell us very little about the relative importance of these income and substitution effects.

Yet, as we will learn later in this book, we often care about the **structural estimates** of labor supply responses, the estimates that tell us about features of utility that drive individual decisions, such as substitution and income effects. Randomized or quasi-experimental estimates provide **reduced form estimates** only. Reduced form estimates show the impact of one particular change on overall labor-supply responses. This second disadvantage of randomized or quasi-experiments is thus related to the first: if we understood the underlying structure of labor-supply responses, it might be possible to say more about how labor supply would respond to different types of policy interventions.

These issues have led to the vibrant field of *structural estimation*. Using this research approach, empirical economists attempt to estimate not just reduced form responses to the environment but the actual underlying features of utility functions. They do so by more closely employing the theory outlined in the previous chapter to develop an empirical framework that not only estimates overall responses, but also decomposes these responses into, for example, substitution and income effects.

Structural models potentially provide a very useful complement to experimental or quasi-experimental analyses. Yet structural models are often more difficult to estimate than reduced form models because both use the same amount of information, yet structural models are used to try to learn much more from that information. Consider the TANF example. The earlier analysis showed you how to derive a reduced form estimate of the impact of a change in TANF benefits. Using this same information to decompose that response into income and substitution effects is not possible employing the same simple approach. Rather, that decomposition is only possible if the researcher assumes a particular form for the utility function, as we did in Chapter 2, and then employs that assumption to decompose the overall response into its two components. If the assumption for the form of the utility function is correct, then this approach provides more information. If it is incorrect, however, then the response derived from this approach might lead one to incorrectly estimate income and substitution effects.

From the perspective of this text, reduced form estimation has one other advantage (which may be obvious after reading this section!): it is much easier to think about and explain. Thus, for the remainder of the text, we will largely rely on reduced form modeling and evidence when discussing empirical results in public finance. Yet the promise of structural modeling should not be discounted, and is a topic of fruitful future study for those of you who want to go on in economics. The lessons about empirical work learned in this book

structural estimates Estimates of the features that drive individual decisions, such as income and substitution effects or utility parameters.

reduced form estimates Measures of the total impact of an independent variable on a dependent variable, without decomposing the source of that behavior response in terms of underlying utility functions.

are universal for all types of studies; they provide a basis that you can take forward to more sophisticated empirical approaches such as structural modeling.

3.4
Conclusion

The central issue for any policy question is establishing a causal relationship between the policy in question and the outcome of interest. Do lower welfare benefits *cause* higher labor supply among single mothers? Does more pollution in the air *cause* worse health outcomes? Do larger benefits for unemployment insurance *cause* individuals to stay unemployed longer? These are the types of questions that we will address in this book using the empirical methods described here.

In this chapter, we discussed several approaches to distinguish causality from correlation. The gold standard for doing so is the randomized trial, which removes bias through randomly assigning treatment and control groups. Unfortunately, however, such trials are not available for every question we wish to address in empirical public finance. As a result, we turn to alternative methods such as time series analysis, cross-sectional regression analysis, and quasi-experimental analysis. Each of these alternatives has weaknesses, but careful consideration of the problem at hand can often lead to a sensible solution to the bias problem that plagues empirical analysis.

▶ HIGHLIGHTS

■ A primary goal of empirical work is to document the causal effects of one economic factor on another, for example the causal effect of raising TANF benefits on the labor supply of single mothers.

■ The difficulty with this goal is that it requires treatment groups (those who are affected by policy) and control groups (those not affected) who are identical except for the policy intervention.

■ If these groups are not identical, there can be bias—that is, other consistent differences across treatment/control groups that are correlated with, but not due to, the treatment itself.

■ Randomized trials are the gold standard to surmount this problem. Since treatments and controls

are identical by definition, there is no bias, and any differences across the groups are a causal effect.

■ Time series analysis is unlikely to provide a convincing estimate of causal effects because so many other factors change through time.

■ Cross-sectional regression analysis also suffers from bias problems because similar people make different choices for reasons that can't be observed, leading once again to bias. Including control variables offers the potential to address this bias.

■ Quasi-experimental methods have the potential to approximate randomized trials, but control groups must be selected carefully in order to avoid biased comparisons.

▶ QUESTIONS AND PROBLEMS

1. Suppose you are running a randomized experiment and you randomly assign study participants to control and treatment groups. After making the assignments, you study the characteristics of the two groups and find that the treatment group has a lower average age than the control group. How could this arise?

2. Why is a randomized trial the "gold standard" for solving the identification problem?

3. What do we mean when we say that correlation does not imply causality? What are some of the ways in which an empirical analyst attempts to disentangle the two?

4. A researcher conducted a cross-sectional analysis of children and found that the average test performance of children with divorced parents was lower than the average test performance of children of intact families. This researcher then concluded that divorce is bad for children's test outcomes. What is wrong with this analysis?

5. A study in the *Annals of Improbable Research* once reported that counties with large numbers of mobile-home parks had higher rates of tornadoes than the rest of the population. The authors conclude that mobile-home parks cause tornado occurrences. What is an alternative explanation for this fact?

6. What are some of the concerns with conducting randomized trials? How can quasi-experiments potentially help here?

7. You are hired by the government to evaluate the impact of a policy change that affects one group of individuals but not another. Suppose that before the policy change, members of a group affected by the policy averaged $17,000 in earnings and members of a group unaffected by the policy averaged $16,400. After the policy change, members of the affected group averaged $18,200 in earnings while members of the unaffected group averaged $17,700 in earnings.

   a. How can you estimate the impact of the policy change? What is the name for this type of estimation?

   b. What are the assumptions you have to make for this to be a valid estimate of the impact of the policy change?

8. Consider the example presented in the appendix to this chapter. Which coefficient estimates would be considered "statistically significant" or distinct from zero?

9. A researcher wants to investigate the effects of education spending on housing prices, but she only has cross-sectional data. When she performs her regression analysis, she controls for average January and July temperatures. Why is she doing this? What other variables would you control for, and why?

10. It is commonly taught in introductory microeconomics courses that minimum wages cause unemployment. The Federally mandated minimum wage is $5.15, but approximately 1/3 of states have higher state-mandated minimum wages. Why can't you test the "minimum wages cause unemployment" theory by simply comparing unemployment rates across states with different minimum wages? Can you think of a better way to test it?

▶ ADVANCED QUESTIONS

11. Suppose that your friend Oscar has collected data and determined that towns with newly constructed high schools tend to have higher SAT scores than other towns. He tells you that he has proved that new high schools cause higher SAT scores. When you object that "correlation does not imply causation," he is ready with more data. He shows you convincing evidence that SAT scores tend to increase shortly after towns build new high schools, but that there is no tendency for new high schools to be built in towns which have recently seen large increases in SAT scores. Is this enough evidence to prove that new high schools cause higher SAT scores, or can you think of an alternative explanation for Oscar's data?

12. Researchers often use *panel data* (multiple observations over time of the same people) to conduct regression analysis. With these data, researchers are able to compare the same person over time in order to assess the impacts of policies on individual behavior. How could this provide an improvement over cross-sectional regression analysis of the type described in the text?

13. Suppose that your state announced that it would provide free tuition to high-achieving students graduating from high school starting in 2007. You decide to see whether this new program induces families with high-achieving children graduating in 2007 or later to purchase new cars. To test your findings, you use a "falsification exercise": you observe the new-car-purchasing behavior of families with children graduating in 2006. Why is this a useful exercise?

14. Your state introduced a tax cut in the year 1999. You are interested in seeing whether this tax cut has led to increases in personal consumption within the state.

    You observe the following information:

Year	Consumption in neighboring state
1994	260
1996	270
1998	280
2000	300

a. Your friend argues that the best estimate of the effect of the tax cut is an increase in consumption of 30 units, but you think that the true effect is smaller, because consumption was trending upward prior to the tax cut. What do you think is a better estimate?

b. Suppose that you find information on a neighboring state that did not change its tax policy during this time period. You observe the following information in that state:

Year	Consumption in your state
1994	300
1996	310
1998	320
2000	350

Given this information, what is your best estimate of the effect of the tax cut on consumption? What assumptions are required for that to be the right estimate of the effect of the tax cut? Explain.

Appendix to Chapter 3

Cross-Sectional Regression Analysis

In the text, we presented a cursory discussion of cross-sectional regression analysis, and the role of control variables. In this appendix, we provide a more detailed presentation of this approach within our TANF example.

Data For this analysis, we use data from the March 2002 Current Population Survey (CPS). From that survey, we selected all women who reported that they were unmarried and had a child younger than age 19. The total sample is 8,024 single mothers.

For this sample, we have gathered data on the following variables for each woman:

► *TANF:* Total cash TANF benefits in the previous year (in thousands of dollars)

► *Hours:* Total hours of work in the previous year, computed as reported weeks of work times usual hours per week

► *Race:* We divide reported race into white, black, and other.

► *Age:* Age in years

► *Education:* We use reported education to divide individuals into four groups: high school dropouts; high school graduates with no college; those with some college; and college graduates.

► *Urbanicity:* We use information on residential location to divide individuals into four groups: central city; other urban; rural; and unclear (the CPS doesn't identify location for some mothers for survey confidentiality reasons).

Regression Using these data, we can estimate a regression of the impact of welfare on hours of work of the form:

$$(1)\ \text{HOURS}_i = \alpha + \beta\text{TANF}_i + \epsilon_i$$

where there is one observation for each mother i. This is the counterpart of the regression analysis shown in Figure 3-4, but now we are using each individual data point, rather than grouping the data into categories for convenience.

In this regression, α, the constant term, represents the estimated number of hours worked if welfare benefits are zero. β is the slope coefficient, which

■ **APPENDIX 3 TABLE**

Cross-Sectional Regression Analysis

	Equation (1)	Equation (2)
Constant	1537	2062
	(10)	(61)
TANF benefits	−107	−93
	(3.7)	(3.6)
White		181
		(44)
Black		61
		(47)
High school dropout		−756
		(30)
High school graduate		−347
		(25)
Some college		−232
		(28)
Age		−9.3
		(0.8)
Central city		−12
		(30)
Other urban		34
		(29)
Rural		−43
		(31)
R^2	0.095	0.183

represents the change in hours worked per dollar of welfare benefits. ϵ is the error term, which represents the difference for each observation between its actual value and its predicted value based on the model.

The results of estimating this regression model are presented in the first column of the appendix table. The first row shows the constant term α, which is 1537: this measures the predicted hours of labor supply delivered at zero welfare benefits. The second row shows the coefficient β, which is −107: each \$1,000 of welfare benefits lowers hours worked by 107. This is very close to the estimate from the grouped data of −110 discussed in the text. Thus, for a mother with no welfare benefits, predicted hours of work are 1537; for a mother with \$5,000 in welfare benefits, predicted hours of work are $1537 - 5 \times 107 = 1002$.

Underneath this estimate in parentheses is the estimate's *standard error*. This figure captures the precision with which these coefficients are estimated and reminds us that we have here only a statistical representation of the relationship between welfare benefits and hours worked. Roughly speaking, we cannot statistically distinguish values of β that are two standard errors below or above the estimated coefficient. In our context, with a standard error of 3.7 hours, the results show that our best estimate is that each thousand dollars of welfare lowers hours worked by 107, but we can't rule out that the effect is only 96.6 ($107 - 2 \times 3.7$) or that it is 114.4 ($107 + 2 \times 3.7$).

In the context of empirical economics, this is a *very* precise estimate. Typically, as long as the estimate is more than twice the size of its standard error, we say that it is *statistically significant*.

The final row of the table shows the R^2 of the regression. This is a measure of how well the statistical regression model is fitting the underlying data. An R^2 of 1 would mean that the data are perfectly explained by the model so that all data points lie directly on the regression line; an R^2 of 0 means that the data are not at all explained. The value of 0.095 here says that less than 10% of the variation in the data is explained by this regression model.

As discussed in the text, however, this regression model suffers from serious bias problems, since those mothers who have a high taste for leisure will have both low hours of work and high welfare payments. One approach to addressing this problem suggested in the text was to include control variables. We don't have the ideal control variable, which is taste for leisure. We do, however, have other variables that might be correlated with tastes for leisure or other factors that determine labor supply: race, education, age, and urbanicity. So we can estimate regression models of the form:

$$(2) \ \text{HOURS}_i = \alpha + \beta\text{TANF}_i + \delta\text{CONTROL}_i + \epsilon_i$$

where CONTROL is the set of control variables for individual i.

In the second column of the appendix table, we show the impact of including these other variables. When we have a categorical variable such as race (categorized into white, black, and other), we include *indicator variables* that take on a value of 1 if the individual is of that race, and 0 otherwise. Note that when we have N categories for any variable (e.g., 3 categories for race), we only include $N - 1$ indicator variables, so that all estimates are relative to the excluded category (e.g., the coefficient on the indicator for "black" shows the impact of being black on welfare income, relative to the omitted group of Hispanics).

Adding these control variables does indeed lower the estimated impact of welfare benefits on labor supply. The coefficient falls to −93, but remains highly significant. The R^2 doubles but still indicates that we are explaining less than 20% of the variation in the data.

The control variables are themselves also of interest:

▶ *Race:* Whites are estimated to work 181 hours per year more than Hispanics (the omitted group); blacks are estimated to work 61 hours per year more than Hispanics, but this estimate is only about 1.3 times as large as its standard error, so we do not call this a statistically significant difference.

▶ *Education:* Hours of work clearly rise with education. High school dropouts work 756 fewer hours per year than do college graduates (the omitted group); high school graduates work 347 fewer hours per year; and those with some college work 232 fewer hours per year than those who graduate from college. All of these estimates are very precise (the coefficients are very large relative to the standard errors beneath them in parentheses).

▶ *Age:* Hours worked decline with age, with each year of age leading to 9 fewer hours of work; this is a very precise estimate as well.

▶ *Location:* Relative to those with unidentified urbanicity, people in cities and rural areas work less and those in the suburbs work more, but none of these estimates is statistically precise.

Do these control variables eliminate bias in the estimated relationship between TANF benefits and labor supply? There is no way to know for sure, but it seems unlikely. The fact that this large set of controls explains only 9% more of the variation in labor supply across individuals suggests that it is unlikely to capture all of the factors correlated with both labor supply and TANF benefits.

Tools of Budget Analysis

4

"We will continue along the path toward a balanced budget in a balanced economy."
PRESIDENT LYNDON JOHNSON, STATE OF THE UNION ADDRESS (JANUARY 4, 1965)

Deficit in first year in office (1964): 0.9% of GDP
Deficit in last year in office (1968): 2.9% of GDP

"We must balance our federal budget so that American families will have a better chance to balance their family budgets."
PRESIDENT RICHARD NIXON, STATE OF THE UNION ADDRESS (JANUARY 22, 1970)

Deficit in first year in office (1969): −0.3% of GDP (surplus)
Deficit in last year in office (1974): 0.4% of GDP

"We can achieve a balanced budget by 1979 if we have the courage and the wisdom to continue to reduce the growth of Federal spending."
PRESIDENT GERALD FORD, STATE OF THE UNION ADDRESS (JANUARY 15, 1975)

Deficit in first year in office (1975): 3.4% of GDP
Deficit in last year in office (1976): 4.2% of GDP

"With careful planning, efficient management, and proper restraint on spending, we can move rapidly toward a balanced budget, and we will."
PRESIDENT JIMMY CARTER, STATE OF THE UNION ADDRESS (JANUARY 29, 1978)

Deficit in first year in office (1977): 2.7% of GDP
Deficit in last year in office (1980): 2.7% of GDP

"[This budget plan] will ensure a steady decline in deficits, aiming toward a balanced budget by the end of the decade."
PRESIDENT RONALD REAGAN, STATE OF THE UNION ADDRESS (JANUARY 25, 1983)

Deficit in first year in office (1981): 2.6% of GDP
Deficit in last year in office (1988): 3.1% of GDP

"[This budget plan] brings the deficit down further and balances the budget by 1993."
PRESIDENT GEORGE H.W. BUSH, STATE OF THE UNION ADDRESS (JANUARY 31, 1990)

Deficit in first year in office (1989): 2.8% of GDP
Deficit in last year in office (1992): 4.7% of GDP

"[This budget plan] puts in place one of the biggest deficit reductions . . . in the history of this country."
PRESIDENT WILLIAM CLINTON, STATE OF THE UNION ADDRESS (FEBRUARY 17, 1993)

> Deficit in first year in office (1993): 3.9% of GDP
> Deficit in last year in office (2000): −2.4% of GDP (surplus)

"Unrestrained government spending is a dangerous road to deficits, so we must take a different path."
PRESIDENT GEORGE W. BUSH, STATE OF THE UNION ADDRESS (FEBRUARY 27, 2001)

> Deficit in first year in office (2001): −1.3% of GDP (surplus)
> Deficit in most recent year (2006): 2.6% of GDP[1]

Each of the last eight Presidents of the United States, from Lyndon Johnson on, has vowed in his State of the Union address to balance the federal budget, or at least to reduce the deficit. Yet all but one have dramatically failed to achieve these goals. Under four Presidents the deficit increased; under two, surpluses became deficits; under one, the deficit was stable, and only under President Clinton did the deficit actually shrink (and become a surplus).

Why does it seem so difficult for the federal budget to be balanced? Conservatives often blame the deficit on the growth in spending by the federal government, while liberals counter that an insufficiently progressive tax system is failing to raise revenues needed for valuable government programs. The generally persistent budget deficits could thus be due to a clash between conservatives who oppose raising taxes and liberals who oppose cutting government programs. Or it could be something deeper, a structural problem within the very nature of the U.S. budgeting process.

Dealing with budgetary issues is a problem familiar to most U.S. households that periodically consider how to match their outflows of expenditures with their inflows of income. In a similar process, budgetary considerations are foremost in many decisions that are made by government policy makers. It is therefore critical that we understand how governments budget, and the implications of budget imbalances for the economy. Budgeting for the government is far more complicated than it is for a household, however. A household has inflows from a small number of income sources, and outflows to a relatively small number of expenditure items. The federal government has hundreds of revenue-raising tools and thousands of programs on which to spend this revenue.

"Gee, Dave, a proposal to balance the budget wasn't really what I was expecting."

---

[1] Office of Management and Budget (2006a), Table 15.6.

The budgetary process at the federal level is further complicated by the dynamic nature of budgeting. Many federal programs have implications not only for this year but for many years to come. The difficulty of incorporating the long-run consequences of government policy into policy evaluation has bedeviled policy makers and budgetary analysts alike.

In this chapter, we delve into the complexity of budgetary issues that arise as governments consider their revenue and expenditure policies. We begin with a description of the federal budgeting process and of efforts to limit the federal deficit. We then discuss the set of issues involved in appropriately measuring the size of the budget and the budget deficit. After looking at how to model the long-run budgetary consequences of government interventions, we discuss why we should care about reducing the budget deficit as a goal of public policy.

4.1
Government Budgeting

In this section, we discuss the issues involved in appropriately measuring the national deficit and the national debt. As discussed in Chapter 1, government **debt** is the amount that a government owes to others who have loaned it money. Government debt is a *stock:* the debt is an amount that is owed at any point in time. The government's **deficit,** in contrast, is the amount by which its spending has exceeded its revenues in any given year. The government's deficit is a *flow:* the deficit is the amount each year by which expenditures exceed revenues. Each year's deficit flow is added to the previous year's debt stock to produce a new stock of debt owed.

debt The amount a government owes to those who have loaned it money

deficit The amount by which a government's spending exceeds its revenues in a given year

The Budget Deficit in Recent Years

Figure 4-1 graphs the level of Federal government revenue, spending, and surplus/deficit from 1965 to the present. As Figure 1-4 from Chapter 1 shows, the late 1960s marked the end of an era of post–World War II balanced budgets in the United States. The period from the late 1960s through 1992 was marked by a fairly steady upward march in government expenditures, due to the introduction and expansion of the nation's largest social insurance programs. Tax revenues did not keep pace, however, due to a series of tax reductions during this period, the most significant of which were the sharp tax cuts in the early 1980s. While government spending was rising from 17.2% of GDP in 1965 to 23.1% by 1982, taxes were roughly constant as a share of GDP at 18%. The result was a large deficit that emerged in the early 1980s and persisted throughout that decade.

The fiscal picture reversed dramatically in the 1990s. By the end of that decade, spending had fallen back to under 20% of GDP, due to reductions in military spending and a slowdown in the historically rapid growth in medical costs (a major driver of government expenditures through the nation's public health insurance programs). Tax collections rose significantly as well, due to a tax increase on the highest income groups enacted in 1993 and a very rapid

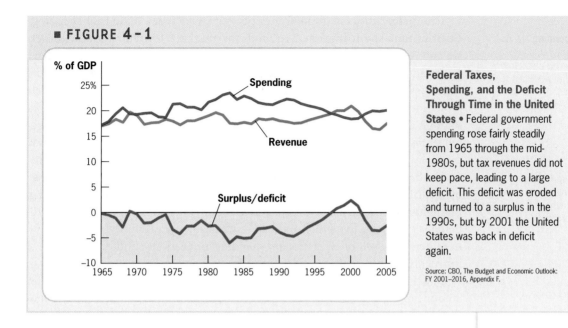

■ FIGURE 4-1

Federal Taxes, Spending, and the Deficit Through Time in the United States • Federal government spending rose fairly steadily from 1965 through the mid-1980s, but tax revenues did not keep pace, leading to a large deficit. This deficit was eroded and turned to a surplus in the 1990s, but by 2001 the United States was back in deficit again.

Source: CBO, The Budget and Economic Outlook: FY 2001–2016, Appendix F.

rise in asset values relative to GDP (which led to a large increase in *capital income taxes,* the taxes collected on asset returns).

The fiscal picture reversed itself again in the early twenty-first century, however, as a recession, growing medical costs, and a growing military budget caused government spending to rise to 20% of GDP in 2005. At the same time, falling asset values, tax cuts, and slow earnings growth led government tax receipts to fall back below 18% of GDP. For 2005, the budget deficit was 2.6% of GDP ($318 billion), a recent decrease from 2004, when the deficit reached 3.6% of GDP ($413 billion), its largest level since 1993.[2]

The Budget Process

The budget process begins with the President's submission to Congress of a budget on or before the first Monday in February. The President's budget, compiled from input by various federal agencies, is a detailed outline of the administration's policy and funding priorities, and a presentation of the coming year's economic outlook. The House and Senate then work out that year's Congressional Budget Resolution, a blueprint for the budget activities in the coming fiscal year and at least five years into the future. The resolution, which must be ready by April 15, does not require a Presidential signature but must be agreed to by the House and Senate before the legislative processing of the budget begins.[3]

---

[2] Office of Management and Budget (2006a), Tables 15.1 and 15.6.
[3] For more details on the budget process, see Martha Coven and Richard Kogan, "Introduction to the Federal Budget Process." Center on Budget and Policy Priorities (August 1, 2003), on the Web at http://www.cbpp.org/3-7-03bud.pdf.

entitlement spending Mandatory funds for programs for which funding levels are automatically set by the number of eligible recipients, not the discretion of Congress

discretionary spending Optional spending set by appropriation levels each year, at Congress's discretion

The budget process distinguishes between two types of federal spending. **Entitlement spending** refers to funds for programs for which funding levels are automatically set by the rules set by Congress and by the number of eligible recipients. The most important federal entitlement programs are *Social Security,* which provides income support to the elderly, and *Medicare,* which provides health insurance to the elderly. Each person eligible for benefits through entitlement programs receives them unless Congress changes the eligibility criteria (for example, all U.S. citizens age 65 and over who have worked for at least 10 years are eligible for coverage of their hospital expenditures under the Medicare program). **Discretionary spending** refers to spending set by annual *appropriation levels* that are determined by Congress (such as spending on highways or national defense). This spending is optional, in contrast to entitlement programs, for which funding is mandatory. Congress's budget resolution includes levels of discretionary spending, projections about the deficit, and instructions for changing entitlement programs and tax policy.

The House and Senate Appropriations Committees each take the total amount of discretionary spending available (according to the budget resolution) and divide it into 13 suballocations for each of their 13 subcommittees. The subcommittees each develop a spending bill for their areas of government, working off of the President's budget, the previous year's spending bills, and new priorities they wish to incorporate. The 13 bills must eventually be approved by the full Appropriations Committee; differences between the House and Senate versions are worked out in conference, and each of the 13 appropriations bills must be passed by both Houses of Congress no later than June 30. The bills are then sent to the President, who may sign them, veto them, or allow them to become law without his signature (after 10 days).

The budget process sets discretionary spending only, not entitlement spending. If Congress wishes to change entitlement programs, it must include in its budget resolution "reconciliation instructions" that direct committees with jurisdiction over entitlement and tax policies to achieve a specified level of savings as they see fit. In a process similar to the appropriations process, reconciliation bills must be worked out within and between the House and Senate, and are then submitted to the President by June 15. The President then has the same options as described in the appropriations process.

▶ **APPLICATION**

Efforts to Control the Deficit

The rapid rise in the deficit in the 1970s and 1980s led to a number of Congressional efforts to restrain the government's ability to spend beyond its means. In late 1985, with the government running increasing federal deficits, popular and political pressure pushed the Balanced Budget and Emergency Control Act (also known as the Gramm-Rudman-Hollings Deficit Reduction Act, or GRH) through Congress and onto President Reagan's desk, where he signed the bill on December 12, 1985. GRH set mandatory annual targets for the federal deficit starting at $180 billion in 1986 and decreasing in $36 billion increments until the budget would be balanced in 1991.

GRH also included a trigger provision that initiated automatic spending cuts once the budget deficit started missing the specified targets. In reality, the trigger was avoided by all sorts of gimmicks, for which no penalties were incurred by lawmakers. For example, when it became clear that the target for 1988 would not be met, the deficit targets were reset with a new aim to hit zero deficit by 1993 (instead of the original 1991). The divergence between projected deficits and actual ones grew larger and the projections thus became much less credible.

The continuing failure to meet GRH deficit targets led to the 1990 adoption of the Budget Enforcement Act (BEA): rather than trying to target a deficit *level,* the BEA simply aimed to restrain government *growth.* The BEA set specific caps on discretionary spending in future years that were sufficiently low that discretionary spending would have to fall over time in real terms. It also created the pay-as-you-go process (PAYGO) for revenues and entitlements, which prohibited any policy changes from increasing the *estimated* deficit in any year in the next six-year period (the current fiscal year and the five years of forecasts done by the CBO). If deficits increase, the President must issue a *sequestration requirement,* which reduces direct spending by a fixed percentage in order to offset the deficit increase.

The BEA appears to have been a successful restraint on government growth in the 1990s, contributing to the nation's move from deficit to surplus. From 1990 through 1998, discretionary government spending declined by 10% in real terms, and there were no cost-increasing changes made to mandatory spending programs (although some cost-saving changes were made to offset tax cuts in 1997). The arrival of a balanced budget in 1998, however, appears to have removed Congress's willingness to stomach the tight restraints of the BEA.

Discretionary spending grew by over 8% per year in real terms from 1998 to 2005 (when discretionary spending reached $969 billion), far in excess of the caps for those years.[4] The BEA spending caps were mostly avoided by taking advantage of a loophole in the law that allowed for uncapped "emergency spending." Some of this spending was for legitimate emergencies (Hurricane Katrina, the Iraq War, natural disasters), but much was not. A 2006 emergency spending bill ostensibly dedicated to paying for the war and hurricane recovery also included farm-program provisions totaling $4 billion; $700 million to relocate a rail line in Mississippi; and $1.1 billion for fishery projects, including a $15 million "seafood promotion strategy."[5] During the 1990s, Congress and the administration averaged only $22 billion in emergency spending per year. In recent years, however, that number has climbed to over $100 billion per year; in April 2006, the Senate Appropriations Committee approved $106.5 billion in additional "emergency" spending.[6]

---

[4] Office of Management and Budget (2006a), Table 8.1.
[5] Stolberg and Andrews (2006).
[6] Gregg (2006).

PAYGO expired on September 30, 2002. President Bush proposed its renewal only after the adoption of a 2004 budget resolution containing proposed tax cuts and spending increases, but it remains unrenewed.[7] Thus, much as GRH before it, the BEA appears to have lost most of its bite since the late 1990s.[8] ◄

Budget Policies and Deficits at the State Level

The federal government's inability to control its deficit for any long period of time contrasts greatly with state governments'. As shown in Chapter 1, state government budgets are almost always in balance, with no net deficit at the state level in most years. Why is this?

Most likely because every state in the union, except Vermont, has a **balanced budget requirement (BBR)** that forces it to balance its budget each year. Many states adopted these requirements after the deficit-induced banking crises of the 1840s. Newer states generally adopted BBRs soon after admission into the union. As a result, all existing BBRs have been in place since at least 1970.

BBRs are not the same in all states, however. Roughly two-thirds of the states have **ex post BBRs,** meaning that the budget must be balanced at the end of a given fiscal year. One-third have **ex ante BBRs,** meaning that either the governor must submit (what is supposed to be) a balanced budget, the legislature must pass a balanced budget, or both. A number of studies have found that only ex post BBRs are fully effective in restraining states from running deficits; ex ante BBRs are easier to evade, for example, through rosy predictions about the budget situation at the start of the year. These studies find that when states are subject to negative shocks to their budgets (such as a recession that causes a state's tax revenues to fall), the states with the stronger ex post BBRs are much more likely to meet those shocks by cutting spending than are states with the weaker ex ante BBRs.

balanced budget requirement (BBR) A law forcing a given government to balance its budget each year (spending = revenue)

ex post BBR A law forcing a given government to balance its budget by the end of each fiscal year

ex ante BBR A law forcing either the governor to submit a balanced budget or the legislature to pass a balanced budget at the start of each fiscal year, or both

4.2

Measuring the Budgetary Position of the Government: Alternative Approaches

The figures for the size of the budget deficit presented earlier represent the most common measure of government deficits that are used in public debate. Yet there are a number of alternative ways of representing the budgetary position of the federal government that are important for policy makers to consider.

---

[7] *New York Times* (2005a).
[8] For more information on PAYGO, see CBPP et al. (2004).

Real vs. Nominal

The first alternative way to represent the deficit is to take into account the beneficial effects of inflation for the government as a debt holder. An important distinction that we will draw throughout this text is the one between **real** and **nominal prices.** Nominal prices are those stated in today's dollars: the price of a cup of coffee today is $3. This means that consuming a cup of coffee today requires forgoing $3 consumption of other goods today. Real prices are those stated in some constant year's dollars: the cost of today's cup of coffee in 1982 dollars would be $1.48. That is, buying this same cup of coffee in 1982 required forgoing $1.48 of consumption of other goods in 1982. Using real prices allows analysts to assess how any value has changed over time, relative to the overall price level, and thus how much more consumption of other goods you must give up to purchase that good. The overall price level is measured by the **Consumer Price Index (CPI),** an index that captures the change over time in the cost of purchasing a "typical" bundle of goods.[9]

From 1982 through 2005, the CPI rose by 102%; that is, there was a 102% *inflation* in the price of the typical bundle of goods. So any good whose price rose by less than 102% would be said to have a *falling real price:* the cost of that good relative to other goods in the economy is falling. That is, the amount of other consumption you would have to forgo to buy that good is lower today than it was in 1982. Similarly, a good whose price rose by more than 102% would have a *rising real price.* For example, the cost of a typical bundle of medical care in the United States rose by 312% from 1982 through 2005. So, in real terms, the cost of medical care rose by 312% − 102%, or 210%. Thus, in 2005, individuals had to sacrifice 210% more consumption to buy medical care than they did in 1982.

Government debts and deficit are both typically stated in nominal values (in today's dollars). This practice can be misleading, however, since inflation typically lessens the burden of the national debt, as long as that debt is a nominal obligation to borrowers.

This point is easiest to illustrate with an example. Suppose that you owe the bank $100 in interest on your student loans. Suppose further that you like to buy as many bags of Skittles candy as possible with your income, and Skittles cost $1 per bag. If you pay the bank the $100 of interest, you are forgoing 100 bags of Skittles each year.

Now suppose that the price level doubles for all goods, so that a bag of Skittles now costs $2. Now, when you pay the bank $100 for interest, you only need to forgo the purchase of 50 bags of Skittles. In real terms, the cost of your interest payments has fallen by half; the consumption you have to give up in order to pay the interest is half as large as it was at the lower price level. From the bank's perspective, however, the price level increase is not a good thing.

real prices Prices stated in some constant year's dollars

nominal prices Prices stated in today's dollars

Consumer Price Index (CPI) An index that captures the change over time in the cost of purchasing a "typical" bundle of goods

---

[9] Information about the CPI comes from the U.S. Department of Labor's Bureau of Labor Statistics and can be found on the Web at http://www.bls.gov/cpi/home.htm.

They used to be able to buy 100 bags of Skittles with your interest payments; now they can only buy 50. They are worse off, and you are better off, because the price level rose.

A similar logic applies to the national debt. When price levels rise, the consumption the nation has to forgo to pay the national debt falls. The interest payments the government makes are in nominal dollars, which are worth less at the higher price level, so when prices rise, the real deficit falls. This outcome is called an *inflation tax* on the holders of federal debt (although it isn't really a tax). Due to rising prices, federal debt holders are receiving interest payments that are worth much less in real terms (like the bank in the previous paragraph).

This inflation tax can be sizeable, even in the low-inflation environment of the early twenty-first century. In 2005, the national debt was $4.59 trillion and the inflation rate was 3.4%. The "inflation tax" in that year was therefore 0.034 × 4.59, or $156 billion[10]. The conventionally measured deficit in 2005 (government expenditure minus government revenue) was $318 billion, but if we add these inflation tax revenues to the deficit, the deficit falls to $162 billion. Thus, taking account of the effects of inflation on eroding the value of the national debt reduces the measured deficit.

The Standardized Deficit

standardized (structural) budget deficit A long-term measure of the government's fiscal position, with short-term factors removed

A second alternative way to represent the deficit is to recognize the distinction between short-run factors that affect government spending and revenue and the **standardized,** or **structural, budget deficit** that reflects longer-term trends in the government's fiscal position. The standardized deficit is computed by the Congressional Budget Office (CBO) in two steps. First, it accounts for the impact of the business cycle on the deficit. When there is a recession, tax receipts fall as household and corporate incomes decline, and the many government expenditures that are linked to the well-being of households and corporations (such as the costs of benefits provided to unemployed workers) rise. Both of these factors tend to increase the deficit in the short run, but over the long run they should be balanced by the rise in receipts and the decline in spending that occurs during periods of economic growth.

cyclically adjusted budget deficit A measure of the government's fiscal position if the economy were operating at full potential GDP

To account for these factors, the CBO computes a **cyclically adjusted budget deficit.** The CBO starts with its baseline projection of revenues and outlays, which captures business cycle effects and other factors. It then estimates how much revenue loss and spending increase are due to the economy's deviation from its full potential GDP, the economy's output if all resources were employed as fully as possible.[11] For example, in 2003, the CBO calculated that the baseline budget deficit was $375 billion; $70 billion of that deficit occurred because of the slow economy, so that the cyclically adjusted deficit was only $305 billion. Similarly, in 2000, though the baseline budget surplus was $236

---

[10] That is, the value of the ongoing interest and repayment in that trust has fallen by $156 billion.
[11] This includes labor, so the economy is operating at potential GDP only when the natural rate of employment is achieved, which means the only unemployment comes from the relatively small number of people in the midst of changing jobs.

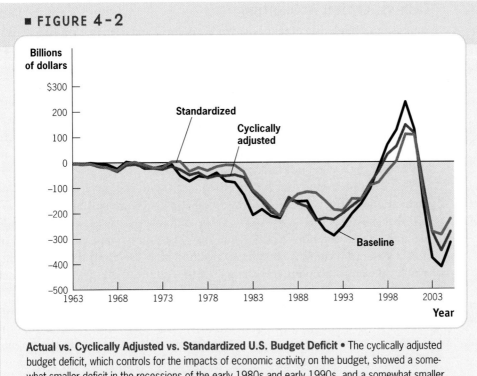

■ **FIGURE 4-2**

Actual vs. Cyclically Adjusted vs. Standardized U.S. Budget Deficit • The cyclically adjusted budget deficit, which controls for the impacts of economic activity on the budget, showed a somewhat smaller deficit in the recessions of the early 1980s and early 1990s, and a somewhat smaller surplus in the boom of the late 1990s. The standardized deficit, which also accounts for other short-term factors, showed even less movement over this period.

Source: CBO, The Budget and Economic Outlook: FY 2001–2016, Appendix F.

billion, $93 billion of that was due to the economy growing at a rapid rate. Thus, the cyclically adjusted surplus was only $143 billion that year.[12]

The second step in computing the standardized budget deficit is to take the cyclically adjusted deficit and further modify it to take into account other short-lived factors. These factors include fluctuations in tax collections due to short-run factors, changes in the inflation component of net interest payments, and temporary legislative changes in the timing of revenues and expenditures. In 1998, for instance, the cyclically adjusted surplus was $35 billion, but the CBO determined that $67 billion of revenue was coming from temporary effects, such as the increase in capital gains tax revenue (the tax revenue raised on sales of capital assets such as stocks). This increase in revenue was viewed as a temporary response of stock sales to a rapidly rising stock market. Taking account of this, the standardized budget surplus became a deficit of $32 billion, a better measure of the government's long-term fiscal health. Figure 4-2 compares the baseline budget surplus/deficit with the cyclically adjusted and standardized surplus/deficit over time.

---

[12] Information on the CBO's calculations of various budget measures comes from the Congressional Budget Office, "The Cyclically Adjusted and Standardized-Budget Measures." March 2004. http://www.cbo.gov/showdoc.cfm?index=5163.

Cash vs. Capital Accounting

Suppose that the government borrows $2 million and spends it on two activities. One is a big party to celebrate the President's birthday, which costs $1 million. The second is a new office building for government executives, which also costs $1 million. When the government produces its budget at the end of the year, both of these expenditures will be reported identically, and the deficit will be $2 million bigger if there is no corresponding rise in taxes. Yet these expenditures are clearly not the same. In one case, the expenditure financed a fleeting pleasure. In the other, it financed a lasting *capital asset,* an investment with value not just for today but for the future.

cash accounting A method of measuring the government's fiscal position as the difference between current spending and current revenues

capital accounting A method of measuring the government's fiscal position that accounts for changes in the value of the government's net asset holdings

This example points out a general concern with the government's use of **cash accounting,** a method of assessing the government's budgetary position that measures the deficit solely as the difference between current spending and current revenues. Some argue that, instead, the appropriate means of assessing the government's budgetary position is to use **capital accounting,** which takes into account the change in the value of the government's net asset holdings. Under capital accounting, the government would set up a capital account that tracks investment expenditures (funds spent on long-term assets such as buildings and highways) separately from current consumption expenditures (funds spent on short-term items such as transfers to the unemployed). Within the capital account, the government would subtract investment expenditures and add the value of the asset purchased with this investment. For example, if the building built with the second $1 million had a market value of $1 million, then this expenditure would not change the government's capital account because the government would have simply shifted its assets from $1 million in cash to $1 million in buildings.

The absence of capital accounting gives a misleading picture of the government's financial position. In 1997, for example, the Clinton administration trumpeted its victory in proposing a balanced budget for the first time in 28 years. Little recognized in this fanfare was that $36 billion of the revenues that would be raised to balance this budget came from one-time sales of a government asset, broadcast spectrum licenses (which allow the provision of wireless services such as cell phones). The government was gaining the revenues from this sale, but at the same time it was selling off a valuable asset, the spectrum licenses. So the fiscal budget was balanced, but at the expense of lowering the value of the government's asset holdings.

Problems with Capital Budgeting While adding a capital budget seems like a very good idea, there are enormous practical difficulties with implementing a capital budget because it is very hard to distinguish government consumption from investment spending. For example, is the purchase of a missile a capital investment or current period consumption? Does its classification depend on how soon the missile is used? Are investments in education capital expenditures because they build up the abilities of a future generation of workers? And if these are capital expenditures, how can we value them? For example, without selling the spectrum licenses in 1997, how could the government appropriately assess the value of this intangible asset? In Chapter 8, we discuss the difficulties of appropriately valuing these types of investments. These difficulties might make it easier for politicians to misstate the government's budgetary position with a capital budget than without one.

As a result of these difficulties, while some states use capital budgets, they have not been implemented at the federal level. The international experience with capital budgeting at the national level is mixed. Sweden, Denmark, and the Netherlands all had capital budgeting at one point but abandoned the practice because they thought it led to excessive political focus on government capital investments. Currently, New Zealand and the United Kingdom have capital budgets; while the U.K.'s capital budgeting process is very recent, New Zealand's system has been in place for more than 15 years.

Static vs. Dynamic Scoring

Another important source of current debate over budget measurement is the debate between *static* and *dynamic scoring*. When budget estimators assess the impact of policies on the government budget, they account for many behavioral effects of these policies. For example, people spend more on child care when the government subsidizes child care expenditures. Similarly, people are more likely to sell assets to realize a capital gain if the capital gains tax rate on such asset sales is reduced. While budget estimators take into account these types of effects of policies on individual and firm behavior in computing the overall effect of legislation, they do *not* take into account that a tax policy might affect the size of the economy as well. That is, budget modelers use **static scoring,** which assumes that the size of the economic pie is fixed and that government policy serves only to change the relative size of the slices of the pie.

The static assumption has been strongly criticized by those who believe that government policy affects not only the distribution of resources within the economy but the size of the economy itself. These analysts advocate a **dynamic scoring,** an approach to budget modeling that includes not only a policy's effects on resource distribution but also its effects on the size of the economy. For example, lowering taxes on economic activity (such as labor income taxes) may increase the amount of that activity (hours worked), increasing the production of society. This larger economic pie in turn produces more tax revenues for a given tax rate, offsetting to some extent the revenue losses from the tax reduction. Ignoring this reaction can lead the government to overstate the revenue loss from cutting taxes.

Budget estimators have resisted the dynamic approach largely because the impact of government policy on the economy is not well understood. Nevertheless, as proponents of dynamic scoring point out, it is not clear why policy makers and budget estimators should assume there are zero effects. The CBO took a small step toward dynamic scoring in its 2003 evaluation of the budget proposed by President Bush, which included sizable tax cuts and increased defense spending. The CBO used five different models to evaluate the long-run impacts of the administration's budget on the economy, including feedback effects on tax revenues and government spending. The message that they

static scoring A method used by budget modelers that assumes that government policy changes only the distribution of total resources, not the amount of total resources

dynamic scoring A method used by budget modelers that attempts to model the effect of government policy on both the distribution of total resources and the amount of total resources delivered was fairly consistent: unless the 2003 budget proposals were accompanied by tax increases within a decade, dynamic effects would increase their budgetary costs.[13] This is because the budgetary changes, on net, increased the deficit. As we discuss in Section 4.4, the increased government borrowing that would occur as a result would crowd out private savings, decrease investment, and ultimately decrease economic growth. Slower economic growth in the long run would cause a fall in future tax revenues, raising the deficit further.

4.3

Do Current Debts and Deficits Mean Anything? A Long-Run Perspective

Suppose that the government initiates two new policies this year. One provides a transfer of $1 million to poor individuals in the current year. The other promises a transfer of $1 million to poor individuals *next year*. From the perspective of this year's budget deficit, the former policy costs $1 million, while the latter policy is free. This view is clearly incorrect: the latter policy is almost as expensive; it is only slightly cheaper because the promise is in the future, rather than today.

Governments in the United States and around the world are always making such **implicit obligations** to the future. Whenever Congress passes a law that entitles individuals to receipts in the future, it creates an implicit obligation that is not recognized in the annual budgetary process. In this section, we discuss the implications of implicit obligations for measuring the long-run budgetary position of the government.

Background: Present Discounted Value

To understand implicit obligations, it is important to review the concept of *present discounted value*. Suppose that I ask to borrow $1,000 from you this year and promise to pay you back $1,000 next year. You should refuse this deal, because the $1,000 you will get back next year is worth less than the $1,000 you are giving up this year. If instead you take that $1,000 and put it in the bank, you will earn interest on it and have more than $1,000 next year.

To compare the value of money in different periods, one must compare the **present discounted value (PDV):** the value of each period's payment in today's terms. Receiving a dollar in the future is worth less than receiving a dollar today, because you have forgone the opportunity to earn interest on the money. Since dollars received in different periods are worth different amounts, we cannot simply add them up; we must first put them on the same basis. This is what PDV does: it takes all future payments and values them in today's terms.

implicit obligation Financial obligations the government has in the future that are not recognized in the annual budgetary process

present discounted value (PDV) The value of each period's dollar amount in today's terms

---

[13] For more information about the CBO's use of dynamic scoring, see Congressional Budget Office (2003b).

To compute the present value of any stream of payments, we *discount* payments in a future period by the interest rate that could be earned between the present and that future period. So if you can invest your money at 10%, then a dollar received seven years from now is only worth 51.3¢ today, since you can invest that 51.3¢ at 10% today and have a dollar in seven years. A dollar received one year from now is only worth 91¢ today because you can invest 91¢ at 10% today and have a dollar one year from now.[14]

Mathematically, if the interest rate is r, and the payment in each future period are F1, F2, . . . and so on, then the PDV is computed as:

$$PDV = \frac{F_1}{(1 + r)} + \frac{F_2}{(1 + r)^2} + \frac{F_3}{(1 + r)^3} + \ldots$$

A convenient mathematical shorthand to remember is that if payments are a constant amount for a very long time into the future (e.g., 50 years or more), then the *PDV = F/r*, where *F* is the constant payment and *r* is the interest rate.

Why Current Labels May Be Meaningless

Policy debates have traditionally focused on the extent to which this year's governmental spending exceeds this year's governmental revenues. The existence of implicit obligations in the future, however, suggests that these debates may be misplaced. This concept is nicely illustrated by an example in Gokhale and Smetters (2003). Suppose that the government offers you the following deal when you are 20 years old. When you retire, the government will pay you $1 less in Social Security benefits. In return, the government will reduce the payroll tax you pay today to finance the Social Security program by 8.7¢, the present value of that $1.[15] In terms of the government's net obligations throughout the future, this policy has no impact; it is lowering current tax revenues and lowering future expenditures by the same present discounted value amount. From today's perspective, however, this policy increases the deficit, because it lowers current tax revenues but does not lower current expenditures. As a result, the current deficit will rise, leading to higher national debt for the next 50 years until this payroll tax reduction is repaid through lower benefits.

This example is even more striking if we consider the following alternative: the government offers to pay you $1 less in Social Security benefits, in return for which the government will reduce your payroll tax today by only *half of* the present value of that $1. For example, if the PDV of $1 of Social

[14] Money received in the future is also worth less than money received today because of *inflation:* the goods you want to buy with that money will cost more in the future. The appropriate discount rate should account both for the interest you could have earned on that money and the rise in prices for the goods you will purchase with that money. We discuss this issue further when we cover the taxation of interest income in Chapter 22.

[15] For example, suppose that the interest rate is 5% and is projected to remain there for the foreseeable future, that you are 20 years old, and that you will claim Social Security at age 70. Then this deal would entail reducing your payroll tax by 8.7¢ today, which has the same present value as $1 in Social Security benefits in 50 years (since the present value of $1 in 50 years at a 5% discount rate is $1/(1.05)^{50} = 0.087).

Security benefits to a 20-year-old is 8.7¢, the government will reduce the pay-roll tax by 4.35¢, in return for cutting benefits by $1 when the 20-year-old retires. Such a deal would clearly be a net winner for the government: in PDV terms, the government is reducing current taxes by less than it is reducing future expenditures. Yet, from today's perspective, it is still cutting current taxes and not reducing current expenditures, so the deficit and the debt are rising. Just as in the case of capital budgeting, such a problem can lead to biased government policy making that favors policies that look good in terms of current budgets, even if they have bad long-term consequences for the fiscal position of the government.

Alternative Measures of Long-Run Government Budgets

Over the past two decades, researchers have begun to consider alternative measures of government budgets that include implicit obligations. The basic idea of these alternative measures is to correctly measure the **intertemporal budget constraint** of the government, comparing the total present discounted value of the government's obligations (explicit and implicit) to the total present discounted value of its revenues.

intertemporal budget constraint An equation relating the present discounted value of the government's obligations to the present discounted value of its revenues

Generational Accounting An influential measure of the long-run budget was the *generational accounting* measure developed by Auerbach, Gokhale, and Kotlikoff in the early 1990s.[16] This budget measure was designed to assess the implications of the government's current (or proposed) fiscal policies for different generations of taxpayers. It answers the question: How much does each generation of taxpayers (those born in different years) benefit, on net, from the government's spending and tax policies, assuming that the budget is eventually brought into long-run balance?

This is done by first estimating the government's intertemporal budget constraint:

PDV of Remaining Tax payments of Existing generations	+	PDV of Tax Payments of Future generations	=	PDV of All Future Gov't Consumption	+	Current Gov't Debt

The intertemporal budget constraint sets the present discounted value of all future inflows to the government (tax payments from both existing and future generations) equal to the current level of government debt (which must eventually be paid) plus the present discounted value of all future government consumption (which must also be paid).

These researchers then ask: What pattern of taxes is required over the future to meet this budget constraint? That is, if we raise taxes enough so that current plus future tax payments equal current debt plus future government consumption, what does that tax increase imply for the long-run burdens on

---

[16] For relatively nontechnical descriptions of this method and its implications, see Auerbach, Gokhale, and Kotlikoff (1991, 1994); for a more technical description, see Kotlikoff (2002).

each generation? To assign the burdens to different generations, they assume that taxes are raised on each generation in proportion to the growth in productivity across generations.

The results, shown in Table 4-1, are striking (although, as we discuss next, they understate the net obligations on current and future generations from very recent policy initiatives). The table shows the net tax payment that must be made by males and females of each age in 1998 in order to satisfy the intertemporal budget constraint. Males age 60 and beyond have a negative net tax: they are benefiting on net from government policy. For example, a 70-year-old male over his lifetime is projected to receive a present discounted value of $91,000 more in government benefits than he pays in taxes. On the other hand, for males below 60, the net tax payment figure is positive, indicating that the taxes required to balance the intertemporal budget constraint will exceed the value of the benefits they will receive. So, for example, a male born in 1998 (age 0) is projected to pay almost $250,000 more in taxes than he will receive in benefits.

Interestingly, at all ages, the net tax payments are smaller for women; relative to men, women pay fewer taxes and receive more benefits. For example, at age 40, while men pay a net tax of over $241,000 over their lives, women pay a net tax of only $38,000. This gap between men and women arises for two reasons. First, women tend to earn less over their lifetimes than men, at least traditionally, so they pay fewer taxes (since tax payments rise with earnings). At the same time, however, they receive higher transfers because the most sizeable transfers (through the Social Security and Medicare program) are received until a person dies, and women live longer.

The row below age 90 shows the net tax payment of future generations. For men, for example, future generations will pay on average almost $362,000 more in taxes than they collect in transfers; for women, the net tax burden will be almost $159,000. The final rows of the table show the lifetime net tax rate on future generations and on newborns, including both men and women. This lifetime net tax rate divides lifetime net tax payments by projected lifetime labor earnings. Those in future generations will have to pay 32.3% of their income in net taxes in order to satisfy the intertemporal budget constraint, while those who were infants in 1998 will have to pay 22.8%. Thus, the *generational imbalance,* or the extent to which those who are not yet born will pay more in net taxes than those who are alive today, is 42% ((32.3 − 22.8)/22.8).

■ **TABLE 4-1**

The Composition of U.S. Generational Accounts

Age in 1998	Net Tax Payment (present value in thousands of 1998 dollars)	
	Male	Female
0	$249.7	$109.6
10	272.3	104.6
20	318.7	113.7
30	313.7	95.6
40	241.4	37.9
50	129.7	−37.7
60	−5.8	−115.0
70	−91.0	−155.9
80	−56.3	−99.2
90	−25.6	−44.4
Future generations	$361.8	$158.8
Lifetime net tax rate on future generations		32.3%
Lifetime net tax rate on newborns		22.8%
Generational imbalance		**41.7%**

Currently elderly people in the United States are receiving much more in transfers over their lifetimes than they paid or will pay in taxes, but future generations will have to pay much more in taxes than they receive in transfers to bring the budget into long-run balance. Males age 70 in the current generation receive a net transfer of $91,000, while females age 0 in the current generation face a net tax of $109,600. Future generations of males will face a tax of $361,800, implying that the generational imbalance (the percentage rise in taxes on future generations relative to current generations) is 41.7%.

■ TABLE 4-2

Alternative Ways to Achieve Generational Balance in 22 Countries

Country	Cut in government transfers	Country	Cut in government transfers
Argentina	11.0%	Italy	13.3
Australia	9.1	Japan	25.3
Austria	20.5	Netherlands	22.3
Belgium	4.6	New Zealand	−0.6
Brazil	17.9	Norway	8.1
Canada	0.1	Portugal	7.5
Denmark	4.5	Spain	17.0
Finland	21.2	Sweden	18.9
France	9.8	Thailand	−114.2
Germany	14.1	United Kingdom	9.5
Ireland	−4.4	United States	21.9

Achieving balance in government spending for future generations in most countries will require that government transfers to those generations be cut (or that taxes be increased). In the United States, this would require cutting spending by more than one-fifth.

The developers of generational accounts have also considered how large a reduction in transfer program spending would be required to bring our government's finances back into "generational balance." The results of these calculations are shown for the United States and many other nations in Table 4-2. In the United States, to achieve generational balance would require cutting government transfers by 21.9%. The United States has one of the largest generational imbalances in the world (only Japan and the Netherlands have larger imbalances). On the other hand, some countries (notably Thailand) are already fiscally "overbalanced," taxing current generations more heavily than future generations (achieving generational balance would involve lowering transfers for future generations by 114%). Countries such as Canada and New Zealand have roughly achieved generational balance.

Long-run Fiscal Imbalance While generational accounting summarizes how the burden of financing the government is shared across generations, it doesn't really address the central question that might interest policy makers today: If the government continues with today's policies, how much more will the government spend than it will collect in taxes over the entire future? This question was addressed in 2003 by Jagdish Gokhale, one of the originators of generational accounts, and Kent Smetters. Rather than attempting to balance the government's intertemporal budget constraint, they measured how out of balance the government's intertemporal budget is. They computed what the government will spend, and what it will collect in taxes, in each year into the future. They then took the present discounted value of these expenditures and taxes and subtracted expenditures from taxes to get a PDV of the government's *fiscal imbalance,* how much more the government has promised in spending than it will collect in taxes.

Moreover, Gokhale and Smetters used more recent numbers than those used by the creators of generational accounts, reflecting the fact that in recent years the government has increased its future obligations by much more than it has increased its future tax collections. They highlighted in their work that the entire long-run fiscal imbalance of the federal government arises solely from the major entitlement programs for the elderly, Social Security and Medicare: there is little fiscal imbalance in the remainder of government.

More recently, this approach was adopted by the Trustees of the Medicare and Social Security Funds, who in 2006 released data on the long-run fiscal imbalance of the Social Security and Medicare programs. The results are stunning: from the perspective of 2006, the fiscal imbalance of these two programs is $84 *trillion*.[17] That is, if government policy does not change, the government has promised to pay out $84 trillion more in benefits than it will collect in taxes. Most of the fiscal imbalance ($70.5 trillion) comes from the Medicare program. The large imbalance caused by these programs reflects the fact that the government has not funded in advance the large benefits it will have to pay out as society ages. In the case of Medicare, this aging trend is compounded by the rapid rise in medical care costs.

It is worth putting this number in perspective. This figure suggests that the implicit debt of the U.S. government, that is, the extent to which future benefit obligations exceed future tax collections, is roughly 18 times as large as its existing outstanding debt. To achieve intertemporal budget balance would require a tax increase of about 32% of payroll. This would mean *nearly tripling* the existing payroll tax that finances the government's social insurance programs or more than doubling the revenue from income taxes. Eliminating all other government programs besides these large transfer programs would solve less than two-thirds of the imbalance.[18]

The U.S. government today is like a family that has 18 small children and a $15,000 balance on their credit card. The balance on the credit card is a major problem, and it is causing large interest payments. But it is a trivial problem relative to the enormous fiscal burden this family will face when its children need to go to college!

Moreover, this problem is getting worse at a rapid rate. In 2003 alone, the government added roughly $20 trillion to the fiscal imbalance. A quarter of this, $5 trillion, was the result of a series of tax reductions enacted in 2003. Most of it, over $16 trillion, was created through the addition of a new entitlement to the Medicare program, a prescription drug benefit (discussed in detail in Chapter 16). Each year, the fiscal imbalance grows by roughly 3–4%, as the nation accumulates interest obligations on the existing large implicit debt.[19]

---

[17] Medicare's fiscal imbalance is calculated from Medicare Trustees (2006), Tables III.B10, III.C15, and III.C21, by totaling unfunded future obligations and counting general revenue contributions as unfunded. Social Security's fiscal imbalance comes from Social Security Trustees (2006), Table IV.B6.

[18] Gokhale and Smetters (2003), pp. 34–35, updated to reflect more recent fiscal imbalance estimates.

[19] Gokhale and Smetters (2003), p. 25.

"These projected figures are a figment of our imagination. We hope you like them."

Problems with These Measures The facts presented in this section are sobering, yet they are typically taken with a grain of salt by policy makers. This casual attitude reflects, in part, the short-run focus of policy makers most interested in winning the next election (as discussed in more detail in Chapter 9). This casualness also reflects the fairly tenuous nature of all these computations, which depend critically on a wide variety of assumptions about future growth rates in costs and incomes, as well as assumptions about the interest rate used to discount future taxes and spending. For example, these fiscal imbalance calculations assume an interest rate of 3.6%. If the interest rate is raised to only 3.9% (an increase of less than 10% and certainly within the forecast error for this variable), the fiscal imbalance falls from $84 trillion to about $66 trillion.

There is no reason, however, to think that these estimates are biased one way or another, either always too low or always too high. If the interest rate were to fall by less than 10%, to 3.3%, for example, then the fiscal imbalance would rise to more than $111 trillion. Thus, while the assumption of an interest rate of 3.6% is a sensible central guess, there is a wide range of uncertainty around it.[20]

Moreover, not only do these calculations require potentially heroic assumptions about interest rates, costs, and incomes in the very distant future, they also assume that government policy remains unchanged. Even relatively small changes in government policy, such as a small cut in Social Security benefits, could have large implications for these estimates. This is not necessarily a problem with these measures, as long as the observer is clear that the measures are based on today's set of policies.

Another problem with these long-run imbalance measures is that they only consider the pattern over time of transfer programs, and not of other investments and government policies. Suppose that the government borrowed $1 billion today and invested it in cleaning up the environment. This would look like an increase in the fiscal imbalance of the federal government, eventually requiring higher taxes on future generations to meet the government's intertemporal budget constraint. But this conclusion would not take into account that future generations not only pay the tax bill, but also benefit from the improved environment. So a true generational or long-run fiscal accounting should include not only future taxes and transfers but also the benefits to future generations of investments made today.

What Does the U.S. Government Do?

While not adopting these types of very-long-run measures, the U.S. government has moved to consider somewhat longer-run measures of policy

---

[20] Gokhale and Smetters (2003), p. 38, updated to reflect more recent fiscal imbalance estimates.

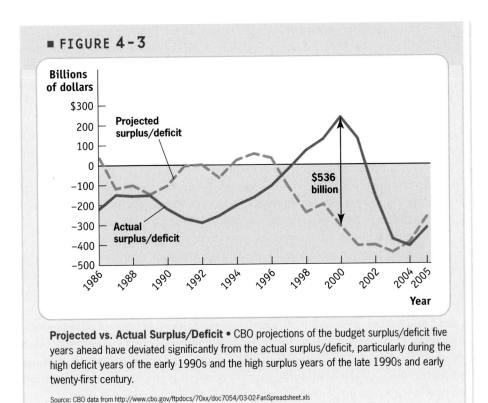

■ FIGURE 4-3

Projected vs. Actual Surplus/Deficit • CBO projections of the budget surplus/deficit five years ahead have deviated significantly from the actual surplus/deficit, particularly during the high deficit years of the early 1990s and the high surplus years of the late 1990s and early twenty-first century.

Source: CBO data from http://www.cbo.gov/ftpdocs/70xx/doc7054/03-02-FanSpreadsheet.xls

impacts. Until the mid-1990s, the budgetary impacts of most policies were considered over a one- or five-year window. This approach was viewed as having the important limitation of promoting policies that had their greatest costs outside of that window. For example, a policy that cut taxes starting in six years was viewed as having no budgetary cost, but the implicit obligation implied by this policy change could be quite large.

In 1996, the government moved to evaluating most policy options over a ten-year window to try to avoid these types of problems. In principle, this should help promote policies that are more fiscally balanced over the long run. In practice, however, moving to a ten-year window added a new problem: it worsened the forecast error inherent in projecting the implications of government programs. The further the time frame moves from the present, the more difficult it is for the CBO to forecast the government's budget position. This approach leaves policy makers dealing with very uncertain numbers when assessing the ten-year impact of a tax or spending policy.

This problem is illustrated in Figure 4-3, which shows the evolution of actual and projected budget deficits over the 1986 through 2005 period. The solid line in the figure shows the actual budget deficits or surpluses in each year. The dashed line shows what the deficits and surpluses for those years *had been project-ed to be* five years earlier.[21] In July 1981, for example, the CBO projected that in

---

[21] CBO projections and actual budget outcomes from "The Uncertainty of Budget Projections: A Discussion of Data and Methods." (CBO: April 2004). These CBO projections are corrected for the effects of subsequent legislation that were not included in the projection (e.g., laws passed after the 1981 projection that impacted the 1986 budget deficit), and for changes in the interest burden of the government due to those laws and changes in the interest rate.

1986 the federal government would have a $48 billion surplus. Instead, by 1986, there was a $211 billion deficit. The CBO's 1983 predictions for 1988 were much closer, only understating the deficit by $50 billion. The errors then got very large, reaching a peak with the 1987 projections that the government would have a balanced budget in 1992, when in reality it ended up almost $300 billion in deficit.

These errors are not one-sided, however. Beginning in 1992, the CBO began to dramatically *overstate* the deficit, so that, as shown in Figure 4-3, the CBO was projecting a larger deficit for 1997 than was actually achieved by the government. By 1995, the five-year prediction for 2000 was for a deficit of more than $300 billion. In reality the government ran a surplus of $236 billion by the year 2000—for an error of $536 billion!

The problems that such forecast errors can cause became apparent in 2001. By the time President George W. Bush was inaugurated in January 2001, the CBO was using a ten-year projection window. At that time, the CBO projected a surplus that would amount to almost *$6 trillion* over the next ten years. Indeed, at that point the concern was that the government might pay down its debt and be left with so much money it would need to start purchasing private assets with its budget surpluses. As Federal Reserve Chairman Alan Greenspan said in his January 25, 2001, testimony before the Senate Budget Committee, ". . . the continuing unified budget surpluses currently projected imply a major accumulation of private assets by the federal government. . . . It would be exceptionally difficult to insulate the government's investment decisions from political pressures. Thus, over time, having the federal government hold significant amounts of private assets would risk suboptimal performance by our capital markets, diminished economic efficiency, and lower overall standards of living than would be achieved otherwise."[22]

These projections led both candidates—Al Gore and George Bush—to propose major tax cuts during the 2000 presidential campaign, and President Bush delivered on his promise with a major tax bill in June 2001. This bill had an estimated ten-year cost of $1.35 trillion (although the likely cost is much higher, as discussed in the policy application that follows). Nevertheless, this seemed a small share of the nearly $6 trillion in future surpluses to deliver back to the American taxpayer.

The problem, as we now know, is that the $6 trillion surplus never appeared. The combination of the 2001 (and subsequent) tax cuts, a recession, and the economic shocks of the September 11, 2001, terrorist attacks had a sharply negative effect on the budget picture. By 2002, the government was already back in deficit. As noted earlier, the federal budget deficit has now increased to $318 billion, with projections of deficit through 2016.[23]

This discussion should not be taken as a condemnation of the CBO, which does an excellent job of projecting government revenues and outlays given

---

[22] Testimony of Alan Greenspan before the U.S. Senate Committee on the Budget, January 25, 2001: "Outlook for the Federal Budget and Implications for Fiscal Policy." http://www.federalreserve.gov/boarddocs/testimony/2001/20010125/default.htm.
[23] Congressional Budget Office (2006b).

the available information. Rather, the problem is that forecasting five or ten years into the future is a highly uncertain exercise. While moving to the ten-year budget window may have helped reduce trickery designed to push tax cuts outside of the budget window, it also introduced more forecast error into the process.

This reduction in forecast accuracy may have been a price worth paying if the move to a ten-year window had imposed more long-term fiscal discipline on the federal government. Unfortunately, this does not appear to be the case, as the following policy application discusses.

▶ **APPLICATION**

The Financial Shenanigans of 2001[24]

The tax reduction enacted in June 2001 was one of the largest tax cuts in our nation's history, with a revenue cost of 1.7% of GDP over the subsequent decade. The tax cut consisted of an extraordinarily convoluted set of phase-ins and phaseouts of various tax cuts in order to comply with a congressional budget plan limiting the 11-year cost (through 2011) of the cuts to $1.35 trillion. Perhaps most extreme was an infamous *sunset provision*, by which all of the tax cuts suddenly disappear on December 31, 2010, thus reducing the 2011 cost of the tax cut to zero. (The Senate originally had the sunset on December 31, 2011, but legislators realized this would push the cost beyond the $1.35 trillion limit.)

The bill itself contained numerous tax cuts operating on erratic schedules. Many of the cuts would phase in over periods longer than in any prior American legislation, backloading most of the fiscal impact toward 2010. After gradual phase-ins, many of the cuts would be fully enacted for only a short time before expiring because of the sunset provision. For example, the estate tax, which is levied on bequests over (roughly) $2 million, would be phased out entirely by 2010 and then reintroduced in 2011. This schedule led economist Paul Krugman to point out that children may want to make sure their parents die in 2010 rather than 2011, labeling this the "Throw Momma from the Train" Act! Similar tricks were played with expansions of tax credits and other tax reductions; for example, full reductions in upper-income tax rates would start only in 2006 and then expire in 2010.

Such convoluted scheduling allowed legislators to claim action had been taken on a wide range of issues, while delaying the fiscal consequences associated with these actions. Though the Joint Committee on Taxation estimated the bill's final cost at $1.349 trillion (just under the limit!), other estimates were significantly higher. The Center on Budget and Policy Priorities, for example, noted that the cost rose to $1.8 trillion once measures certain to pass in the near future were accounted for. The CBPP then calculated the cost of increased interest payments due to rising debt caused by the tax cuts, and

---

[24] See Friedman et al. (2001).

found the true cost of the bill through 2011 to be $2.3 trillion. Assuming the sunset provision was ultimately eliminated, the tax cut's cost would grow in the decade from 2012 to 2021 to $4.1 trillion, without even including the additional costs of interest payments. Indeed, over the next 75 years, these tax cuts were estimated to cost 1.7% of the GNP, which is more than twice the size of the much debated social security deficit over this same time period. ◀

4.4

Why Do We Care About the Government's Fiscal Position?

Now that we understand the complexities involved in defining the federal deficit and debt, we turn to another question: Why do we care? Continuing a theme from Chapter 1, there are two reasons why we might care: efficiency and (intergenerational) equity.

Short-Run vs. Long-Run Effects of the Government on the Macroeconomy

short-run stabilization issues The role of the government in combating the peaks and troughs of the business cycle

automatic stabilization Policies that automatically alter taxes or spending in response to economic fluctuations in order to offset changes in household consumption levels

discretionary stabilization Policy actions taken by the government in response to particular instances of an underperforming or overperforming economy

One reason to care about budget deficits has to do with **short-run stabilization issues**—that is, the role of government policies in combating the peaks and troughs of the business cycle. Short-run stabilization is accomplished on two fronts. **Automatic stabilization** occurs through policies that automatically cut taxes or increase spending when the economy is in a downturn, in order to offset recession-induced declines in household consumption levels. Such automatic stabilization is provided by, for example, the unemployment insurance program, which pays benefits to unemployed workers to offset their income losses. **Discretionary stabilization** occurs through policy actions undertaken by the government to offset a particular instance of an underperforming or overperforming economy, for example, a tax cut legislated during a recession.

There are a number of interesting questions about the stabilization role of the government. These questions have not, however, been the focus of the field of public finance for more than two decades. This lack of attention perhaps reflects the conclusion in the 1970s that the tax and spending tools of the government are not well equipped to fight recessions, given the long and variable lags between when changes are proposed and when laws become effective. Whether this conclusion is actually true is the source of considerable debate, and will continue to remain so. But this debate is largely carried out in the field of macroeconomics, and courses in that field are the place where one can learn about recessions and the role of government in combating them.[25] Public finance courses are more concerned with the longer-run impacts of government budget deficits on economic growth.

---

[25] See, for example, Mankiw (2003), Chapters 9–14.

Background: Savings and Economic Growth

The field of economic growth is a vast and rapidly growing area of academic study. There are a host of exciting issues being investigated about what drives countries to grow faster or slower, but perhaps the most long-standing issue raised by this literature is the impact of savings on economic growth. The earliest economic growth models emphasized a central role for savings as an engine of growth, and this insight remains important for growth economics today.

More Capital, More Growth The intuition behind the important role of savings in growth can be seen by returning to the production function (Chapter 2), which translates labor and capital inputs into output. Recall that for a short-run production function, the marginal productivity of labor falls as more labor is applied to a fixed level of capital. In the long run, however, capital need not be fixed. Over time, the level of capital can be increased: new plants can be built and machines can be purchased and employed for production. Employing more capital then raises the marginal productivity of labor; that is, workers are more productive if they have more and better buildings and machines with which to work.

This same type of production function analysis can be applied to the production level of an economy. As there is more capital in an economy, each worker is more productive, and total social product rises. A larger capital stock means more total output for any level of labor supply. Thus, the size of the capital stock is a primary driver of growth.

More Savings, More Capital The determination of the size of the capital stock is shown in Figure 4-4. On the horizontal axis is the size of the capital

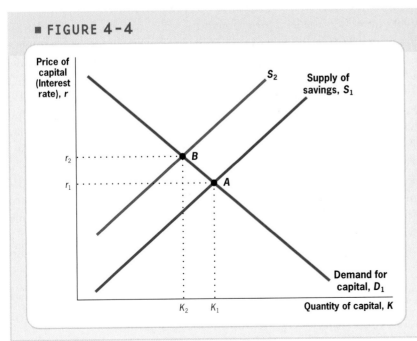

■ FIGURE 4-4

Capital Market Equilibrium • The equilibrium in the capital market is determined by the interaction of the demand for capital by firms (D_1) and the supply of savings by individual savers (S_1). When the government demands more savings to finance its deficits, this lowers the supply of savings available to private capital markets to S_2, raising interest rates to r_2 and reducing capital accumulation to K_2. This reduction ultimately reduces economic growth.

interest rate The rate of return in the second period of investments made in the first period

stock, K. On the vertical axis is the price of capital, which is the interest rate r. The **interest rate** is the rate of return in the second period on investments made in the first period. So, if the interest rate is 10%, that means that for each dollar invested in the first period, individuals receive that dollar plus ten extra cents in the second period. Firms pay the interest rate to investors to obtain the financing they need to build machines, so it is the price for their capital.

The demand for capital is driven by firms' investment demands. This demand curve is downward sloping because firms are less willing to pay high interest rates to finance their machines; the higher the interest rate, the more that firms must pay investors to obtain money to invest, so the less attractive investment becomes. The supply curve represents the savings decisions of individuals. Individuals face a decision about whether to consume their income today or save some of it for tomorrow. As the interest rate rises, each dollar of delayed consumption yields more consumption tomorrow. Because individuals are more willing to save their money and loan it out to firms at higher interest rates (rather than consuming it today), the supply curve slopes upward. That is, just as a higher wage causes individuals to take less leisure (more work) and have more consumption, a higher interest rate causes individuals to consume less and save more today in order to have more consumption in the future.[26]

In a competitive capital market, the equilibrium amount of capital is determined by the intersection of these demand and supply curves. This level of capital then enters the production function, along with the level of labor derived from the type of labor market analysis discussed in Chapter 2. The result is the equilibrium level of output for society.

The Federal Budget, Interest Rates, and Economic Growth

Now, let's introduce a federal government into this scenario. Suppose that, as in most years in recent history, there is a federal deficit, and the government must borrow to finance the difference between its revenues and its expenditures. The key concern about federal deficits is that the federal government's borrowing might compete with the borrowing of private firms. That is, if a fixed supply of savings is used to finance both the capital of private firms and the borrowing of the government, then the government's borrowing may *crowd out* the borrowing of the private sector and lead to a lower level of capital accumulation.

Figure 4-4 illustrates this crowd-out mechanism. Adding government borrowing into the capital market reduces the supply of saved funds available to the private capital market, since the government is using some of that supply of savings to finance its deficit. Thus, government borrowing to finance a deficit causes the supply of savings to the private capital market to decrease, so

---

[26] This simplified discussion presumes the substitution effects of higher interest rates (which lead to higher savings) dominate the income effects (which lead to lower savings). In fact, there is little evidence on this proposition. Chapter 22 has a more detailed discussion of these issues.

the supply shifts inward from S_1 to S_2 in Figure 4-4. This inward shift in supply leads to a higher interest rate (r_2), which in turn leads to a lower quantity of capital demanded by firms (K_2). In turn, this lower level of capital may lower economic growth, by making each unit of labor less productive. Thus, when the government competes with the private sector for limited private savings, the private sector ends up with fewer resources to finance the capital investments that drive growth.

This is a very simple model of how government financing affects interest rates and growth. In reality, there are a number of complications.

International Capital Markets In Figure 4-4, the reason that government deficits reduce capital expenditures by firms is that they drive up the interest rate. But suppose that the pool of savings is not limited by interest rates, as implied by Figure 4-4, but is essentially unlimited and unaffected by interest rates. That is, suppose that the pool of savings available to finance both private investment and public borrowing was close to perfectly elastic, so that even small rises in interest rates would call forth additional savings. In that case, federal deficits would cause only small interest rate rises, and there would be little crowding out of private capital accumulation by government borrowing.

Such would be the case if there were perfectly integrated international capital markets. While the U.S. government's deficit may be large relative to the pool of available savings in the United States, it is very small relative to the entire global pool of available savings. If the federal government can borrow not only domestically but also from abroad to finance its deficit, then there may not be negative implications for capital accumulation and growth. And, in fact, over one-third of the U.S. federal government debt is held by foreigners owning U.S. government bonds.

There is a large body of economics literature that has investigated the integration of international capital markets. It has generally concluded that while integration is present (and perhaps growing), it is far from perfect. As a result, the supply of capital to the United States may not be perfectly elastic, and government deficits could crowd out private savings.

That U.S. debt is held to some extent internationally, however, raises another issue about growing federal debt. At this time, it seems inconceivable that the United States could possibly default on (not repay) its federal debt, but if the debt gets large enough, then default could become a risk. At that point, international investors might be wary of buying U.S. government bonds. This reduction in demand from abroad would mean that more debt must be held domestically, further raising interest rates and crowding out domestic savings. No one knows how large "large enough" is, but the confidence of foreign investors that we will repay our debts is an important benchmark to consider as the federal debt grows.

Ricardian Equivalence A popular alternative model of savings determination was developed by macroeconomist Robert Barro in the 1970s. He pointed out that much of the savings in the United States is accumulated to finance *bequests*, inheritances left behind for the next generation. Suppose

Ellie has enough savings or future expected income to finance her lifetime of consumption, so that any extra income that she receives today she simply saves to leave to her children. In this case, if the government borrows more today to finance its spending, Ellie knows that the government must raise taxes or cut spending at some point in the future to pay back this borrowing. Ellie can therefore partly offset the government's actions by simply saving her extra income from the government today and leaving it to her children, who can use this savings to pay back the extra taxes (or make up for the shortfall in savings) when the government pays back its debt. The net result is that total savings does not fall: the government is saving less, but individuals like Ellie are saving more to leave to their children, offsetting the government borrowing.

While providing an innovative perspective on the role of government across generations, this model has received very little empirical support in the economics literature. Thus, it is unlikely in practice to reverse the problem of government borrowing crowding out private savings.

Expectations   A particularly important simplification that we make in Figure 4-4 is that we consider only a two-period world, in which savings done today is rewarded with interest payments that are spent tomorrow. In reality, we live in a world where businesses need to think many years ahead. As a result, there are both short-term (e.g., 30-day) and long-term (e.g., ten-year) interest rates. Short-term rates reflect the current economic environment, while long-term rates also reflect expectations about the future. If the government has a surplus today, this surplus will reduce the total demand on savings and lower short-term interest rates. If the government is expected to run a deficit starting next year, this will put upward pressure on long-term interest rates. Because businesses tend to make long-standing capital investments, they focus more on these longer-term rates. As a result, the entire future path of government surpluses and deficits matters for capital accumulation, not just the surplus or deficit today.

Evidence   Theory therefore tells us that higher deficits lead to higher interest rates and less capital investment, but it does not tell us how much higher and how much less. The existing empirical literature on this question is somewhat inconclusive, although recent evidence suggests that projected long-term deficits do appear to be reflected to some extent in long-term interest rates. Gale and Orszag (2003) conclude for every 1% of GDP increase in the U.S. government's budget deficit, long-term interest rates rise by between 0.5% and 1%; Ardagna, Caselli, and Lane (2004) use international data to show that a 1% of GDP increase in the deficit raises long-term interest rates by 1.5%.

Intergenerational Equity

intergenerational equity The treatment of future generations relative to current generations

The other reason that we might be concerned with debt and deficits is **intergenerational equity,** or the treatment of future generations relative to current generations. Just as society may care more about its worse-off than its better-off members, it may care more about its worse-off than its better-off *generations*. If the types of calculations we have discussed are accurate, then current government policy has the feature of burdening future generations for the benefit of current generations, making future generations much worse off in the process. It may therefore be deemed socially worthwhile to equalize these burdens.

Is this an accurate way to look at the question of intergenerational equity? Throughout the postindustrial era in the United States, on average, every generation of citizens has enjoyed a better standard of living over its entire adulthood than did its parents. Today most of you are living a much better life than did your grandparents. While they typed out their papers laboriously by hand, you whip them out on a computer; while they spent hours poring through encyclopedias to learn facts, you just look them up in a few minutes on the Internet; while they spent days in the hospital if they hurt their knee, you have outpatient surgery in two hours and are back on your feet in a week or so; and so on. The continual increase in productivity around the world means that every generation has more resources at its disposal than the last.

Thus, while future generations will face larger debts, they will also benefit from a better standard of living. In considering intergenerational equity, we may want to consider not just the absolute burden of debt, but that burden relative to the standard of living.[27]

4.5
Conclusion

Most of this text will focus on fiscal policy actions taken by the government, through spending or taxation. Every such action has implications for the federal budget deficit. The deficit has been a constant source of policy interest and political debate over the last decade, as the government has moved from severe deficit to large surplus and back to severe deficit again. The existing deficit is quite large, but what is more worrisome than this cash flow deficit is the long-run implicit debt that is owed to the nation's seniors through the Social Security and Medicare programs. This long-term debt is many multiples of current cash debt, and could have major negative effects on both economic efficiency (through crowding out private savings, and ultimately national growth) and intergenerational equity (by placing the enormous burden of balancing the government's obligations on future generations).

---

[27] What makes that comparison difficult, however, is that the size of the debt may determine future standards of living through the growth mechanism just discussed. Thus a large deficit, by crowding out private savings, may actually reduce the standard of living of the future generation to which the debt is being passed.

▶ HIGHLIGHTS

▪ The U.S. government's budget has generally been in deficit since the 1960s, despite many attempts to legislate balanced budgets.

▪ Defining the government's budget position appropriately raises a number of difficult issues, such as using real versus nominal budgets, current versus full employment deficits, and cash versus capital accounting.

▪ A more important issue is the short-run versus long-run debt of the U.S. government. One approach to measuring the long-run fiscal position of the government compares the long-run burdens on different generations; another adds up the total net present value of the government's promised taxes and spending.

▪ Both measures show that the U.S. government faces a major fiscal imbalance. The long-run fiscal imbalance is estimated at $84 trillion, and grows each year.

▪ The U.S. government tries to focus on longer-term issues by using a ten-year budget window, but this approach raises problems with forecasting, and does not seem to end politicians' willingness to play games with the timing of taxes and expenditures to avoid budget restrictions.

▪ The major problem with budget deficits is that they are likely to crowd out private capital accumulation, leading to lower long-term growth.

▶ QUESTIONS AND PROBLEMS

1. We say that a variable is *cyclical* if it increases with economic booms and declines with economic recessions. We say that a variable is *countercyclical* if the opposite is true. Which elements of the U.S. federal budget are cyclical and which are counter-cyclical? (To get a sense of the main elements of the budget, visit http://www.whitehouse.gov/omb/budget/fy2004/pdf/hist.pdf, Tables 2 (for revenues) and 3 (for expenditures). For fun, you can also check out Nathan Newman and Anders Schneiderman's National Budget Simulator at http://www.budgetsim.org/nbs/shortbudget04 .html,where you can experiment with what might happen to the federal budget under various taxation and spending scenarios.

2. How have the major federal laws to promote balanced budgets lost their effectiveness over time?

3. Suggest one way in which generational imbalances might be understated, and one way in which they might be overstated.

4. What is the intuition behind the notion of Ricardian equivalence? How might you look for evidence to test the suggestion that people account for future generations' tax burdens by saving more today?

5. From 1962 to 1965, federal spending on non-defense-related education and training rose from $9.6 billion to $19.5 billion, while from 2001 to 2004, it rose from $178.4 billion to $217.5 billion. Given that the Consumer Price Index (in January) was 30.0 in 1962, 31.2 in 1965, 175.1 in 2001, and 185.2 in 2004, which was the larger increase in education and training spending?

6. Why does the Congressional Budget Office construct a cyclically adjusted budget deficit for the purposes of monitoring federal income and outlays?

7. The federal government is considering selling tracts of federally owned land to private developers and using the revenues to provide aid to victims of an earthquake in a foreign country. How would this policy effect the levels of federal revenues, expenditures, and deficits under a cash accounting system? What would be different under a capital accounting system?

The e icon indicates a question that requires students to apply the empirical economics principles discussed in Chapter 3 and the Empirical Evidence boxes.

8. A government is considering paving a highway with a newly developed "wear-proof" material. Paving the highway would cost $2 billion today, but would save $300 million in maintenance costs for each of the next 10 years. Use the concept of present value to determine whether the project is worth undertaking if the government can borrow at an interest rate of 5%. Is it worth it if the interest rate is 0%? 10%? A politician says to you, "I don't care what the interest rate is. The project is clearly a good investment: it more than pays for itself in only 7 years, and all the rest is money in the bank." What's wrong with this argument, and why does the interest rate matter?

9. Table 4-1 shows the remarkable difference across generations in their likely net tax payments to the federal government. What is responsible for these large intergenerational differences?

10. Is it necessarily inequitable for future generations to face higher taxes as a result of benefits that accrue to those living today? Explain.

11. Table 6.1 from the 2004 federal budget's historical tables (http://www.whitehouse.gov/omb/budget/fy2004/pdf/hist.pdf) shows how the main categories of federal outlays have changed from 1940 to 2008 (projected). Where have the biggest changes over time occurred? Where are the biggest changes from 2004 to 2008 projected to occur?

12. Consider a one-year project that costs $300,000, provides an income of $70,000 a year for five years, and costs $30,000 to dispose of at the very end of the fifth year. Assume that the first payment comes at the start of the year after the project is undertaken. Should the project be undertaken at a 0% discount rate? How about 2%? 5%? 10%?

▶ ADVANCED QUESTIONS

13. Several public interest watchdog groups point out "pork" in the federal budget—spending that they claim would have little or no national benefit but would benefit a small number of people in a geographically concentrated area. Why are these types of spending more likely to occur in the federal budgeting process than they would be if they were each voted on individually?

14. How do you think population growth affects the degree of "generational balance" in government finance?

15. How might large federal deficits affect future economic growth? How would your answer change if foreign confidence in the ability of the United States to repay its debts erodes?

16. What is meant by dynamic scoring of the budget? Why does dynamic scoring potentially lead to more realistic estimates of the "true" effective size of a budget deficit? What are some methodological issues involved in dynamic scoring? (Note that you can read more about dynamic budget scoring in the Council of Economic Advisers' *Economic Report of the President*. In 2004, this was found in Chapter 5. The Council of Economic Advisers' Web site is http://www.whitehouse.gov/cea, and

at the time of this writing the *Economic Report of the President* could be found at http://www.gpoaccess.gov/eop/index.html.

17. Consider the same highway paving project from question 8. A second politician says to you, "At an interest rate of 6%, the project is a bad idea. Over 10 years, the project reduces maintenance costs by a total of $3 billion. But borrowing $2 billion for 10 years at a 6% interest rate means paying $1.58 billion in interest. The total cost of the project over 10 years in therefore $3.58 billion!" Use present value calculations to show that the project is, in fact, worth undertaking at a 6% interest rate. What's wrong with the second politician's argument?

18. The Budget Enforcement Act of 1990 created a PAYGO system prohibiting any policy changes which increased the estimated deficit in any year in the subsequent six-year period. Another type of possible PAYGO system would prohibit any policy changes which increase the present value of the deficit over the entire six-year period. Discuss the relative advantages and disadvantages of these "annual" and "cumulative" PAYGO systems.

Externalities: Problems and Solutions

5

In December 1997, representatives from over 170 nations met in Kyoto, Japan, to attempt one of the most ambitious international negotiations ever: an international pact to limit the emissions of carbon dioxide worldwide. The motivation for this international gathering was increasing concern over the problem of global warming. As Figure 5-1 on p. 116 shows, there has been a steady rise in global temperatures over the twentieth century. A growing scientific consensus suggests that the cause of this warming trend is human activity, in particular the use of fossil fuels. The burning of fossil fuels such as coal, oil, natural gas, and gasoline produces carbon dioxide, which in turn traps the heat from the sun in the earth's atmosphere. Many scientists predict that, over the next century, global temperatures could rise by as much as ten degrees Fahrenheit.[1]

If you are reading this in North Dakota, that may sound like good news. Indeed, for much of the United States, this increase in temperatures will improve agricultural output as well as quality of life. In most areas around the world, however, the impacts of global warming would be unwelcome, and in many cases, disastrous. The global sea level could rise by almost three feet, increasing risks of flooding and submersion of low-lying coastal areas. Some scientists project, for example, that 20–40% of the entire country of Bangladesh will be flooded due to global warming over the next century, with much of this nation being under more than five feet of water![2]

Despite this dire forecast, the nations gathered in Kyoto faced a daunting task. The cost of reducing the use of fossil fuels, particularly in the major industrialized nations, is enormous. Fossil fuels are central to heating our homes, transporting us to our jobs, and lighting our places of work. Replacing these fossil fuels with alternatives would significantly raise the costs of living

---

[1] International Panel on Climate Change (2001). Global warming is produced not just by carbon dioxide but by other gases, such as methane, as well, but carbon dioxide is the main cause and for ease we use carbon dioxide as shorthand for the full set of "greenhouse gases."

[2] Mirza et al. (2003).

■ **FIGURE 5-1**

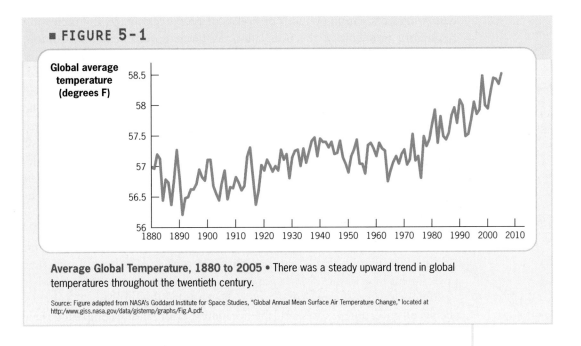

Average Global Temperature, 1880 to 2005 • There was a steady upward trend in global temperatures throughout the twentieth century.

Source: Figure adapted from NASA's Goddard Institute for Space Studies, "Global Annual Mean Surface Air Temperature Change," located at http://www.giss.nasa.gov/data/gistemp/graphs/Fig.A.pdf.

in developed countries. To end the problem of global warming, some predict that we will have to reduce our use of fossil fuels to nineteenth-century (pre-industrial) levels. Yet, even to reduce fossil fuel use to the level ultimately mandated by this Kyoto conference (7% below 1990 levels) could cost the United States $1.1 trillion, or about 10% of GDP.[3] Thus, it is perhaps not surprising that the United States has yet to ratify the treaty agreed to at Kyoto.

Global warming due to emissions of fossil fuels is a classic example of what economists call an **externality.** An externality occurs whenever the actions of one party make another party worse or better off, yet the first party neither bears the costs nor receives the benefits of doing so. Thus, when we drive cars in the United States we increase emissions of carbon dioxide, raise world temperatures, and thereby increase the likelihood that in 100 years Bangladesh will be flooded out of existence. Did you know this when you drove to class today? Not unless you are a very interested student of environmental policy. Your enjoyment of your driving experience is in no way diminished by the damage that your emissions are causing.

Externalities occur in many everyday interactions. Sometimes they are localized and small, such as the impact on your roommate if you play your stereo too loudly or the impact on your neighbors if your dog uses their garden as a bathroom. Externalities also exist on a much larger scale, such as global warming or *acid rain*. When utilities in the Midwest produce electricity using coal, a by-product of that production is the emission of sulfur dioxide and nitrogen oxides into the atmosphere, where they form sulfuric and nitric acids. These acids may fall back to earth hundreds of miles away, in the process

externality Externalities arise whenever the actions of one party make another party worse or better off, yet the first party neither bears the costs nor receives the benefits of doing so.

---
[3] Nordhaus and Boyer (2000), Table 8.6 (updated to 2000 dollars).

market failure A problem that causes the market economy to deliver an outcome that does not maximize efficiency.

destroying trees, causing billions of dollars of property damage, and increasing respiratory problems in the population. Without government intervention, the utilities in the Midwest bear none of the cost for the polluting effects of their production activities.

Externalities are a classic example of the type of **market failures** discussed in Chapter 1. Recall that the most important of our four questions of public finance is *when* is it appropriate for the government to intervene? As we will show in this chapter, externalities present a classic justification for government intervention. Indeed, 135,000 federal employees, or 5% of the federal work-force, are ostensibly charged with dealing with environmental externalities in agencies such as the Environmental Protection Agency and the Department of the Interior.[4]

This chapter begins with a discussion of the nature of externalities. We focus primarily throughout the chapter on environmental externalities, although we briefly discuss other applications as well. We then ask whether government intervention is necessary to combat externalities, and under what conditions the private market may be able to solve the problem. We discuss the set of government tools available to address externalities, comparing their costs and benefits under various assumptions about the markets in which the government is intervening. In the next chapter, we apply these theories to the study of some of the most important externality issues facing the United States and other nations today: acid rain, global warming, and smoking.

5.1

Externality Theory

In this section, we develop the basic theory of externalities. As we empha-size next, externalities can arise either from the production of goods or from their consumption and can be negative (as in the examples discussed above) or positive. We begin with the classic case of a negative production externality.

Economics of Negative Production Externalities

Somewhere in the United States there is a steel plant located next to a river. This plant produces steel products, but it also produces "sludge," a by-product useless to the plant owners. To get rid of this unwanted by-product, the own-ers build a pipe out the back of the plant and dump the sludge into the river. The sludge produced is directly proportional to the production of steel; each additional unit of steel creates one more unit of sludge as well.

The steel plant is not the only producer using the river, however. Farther downstream is a traditional fishing area where fishermen catch fish for sale to

---

[4] This estimate is from the U.S. Office of Personnel Management (2006), p. 87, as well as Web pages of agencies and departments.

local restaurants. Since the steel plant has begun dumping sludge into the river, the fishing has become much less profitable because there are many fewer fish left alive to catch.

This scenario is a classic example of what we mean by an externality. The steel plant is exerting a **negative production externality** on the fishermen, since its production adversely affects the well-being of the fishermen but the plant does not compensate the fishermen for their loss.

One way to see this externality is to graph the market for the steel produced by this plant (Figure 5-2) and to compare the private benefits and costs of production to the social benefits and costs. *Private benefits and costs* are the benefits and costs borne directly by the actors in the steel market (the producers and consumers of the steel products). *Social benefits and costs* are the private benefits and costs *plus* the benefits and costs to any actors outside this steel market who are affected by the steel plant's production process (the fishermen).

Recall from Chapter 2 that each point on the market supply curve for a good (steel, in our example) represents the market's marginal cost of producing that unit of the good—that is, the **private marginal cost (PMC)** of that unit of steel. What determines the welfare consequences of production, however, is the **social marginal cost (SMC),** which equals the private marginal cost to the producers of producing that next unit of a good *plus any costs associated with the production of that good that are imposed on others.* This distinction was not made in Chapter 2, because without market failures $SMC = PMC$, the social costs of producing steel are equal to the costs to steel producers.

negative production externality When a firm's production reduces the well-being of others who are not compensated by the firm.

private marginal cost (PMC) The direct cost to producers of producing an additional unit of a good.

social marginal cost (SMC) The private marginal cost to producers plus any costs associated with the production of the good that are imposed on others.

■ FIGURE 5-2

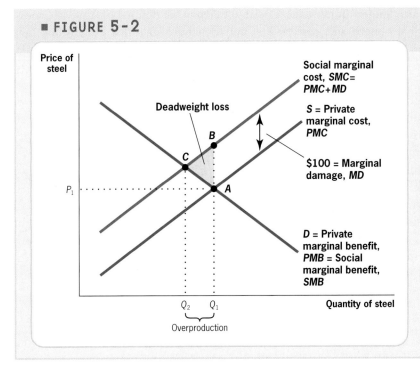

Market Failure Due to Negative Production Externalities in the Steel Market • A negative production externality of $100 per unit of steel produced (marginal damage, *MD*) leads to a social marginal cost that is above the private marginal cost, and a social optimum quantity (Q_2) that is lower than the competitive market equilibrium quantity (Q_1). There is overproduction of $Q_1 - Q_2$, with an associated deadweight loss of area *BCA*.

Thus, when we computed social welfare in Chapter 2 we did so with reference to the supply curve.

This approach is not correct in the presence of externalities, however. When there are externalities, $SMC = PMC + MD$, where MD is the marginal damage done to others, such as the fishermen, from each unit of production (marginal because it is the damage associated with that particular unit of production, not total production). Suppose, for example, that each unit of steel production creates sludge that kills $100 worth of fish. In Figure 5-2, the SMC curve is therefore the PMC (supply) curve, shifted upward by the marginal damage of $100.[5] That is, at Q_1 units of production (point A), the social marginal cost is the private marginal cost at that point (which is equal to P_1), plus $100 (point B). For every level of production, social costs are $100 higher than private costs, since each unit of production imposes $100 of costs on the fishermen for which they are not compensated.

Recall also from Chapter 2 that each point on the market demand curve for steel represents the sum of individual willingnesses to pay for that unit of steel, or the **private marginal benefit (PMB)** of that unit of steel. Once again, however, the welfare consequences of consumption are defined relative to the **social marginal benefit (SMB),** which equals the private marginal benefit to the consumers *minus any costs associated with the consumption of the good that are imposed on others*. In our example, there are no such costs imposed by the consumption of steel, so $SMB = PMB$ in Figure 5-2.

In Chapter 2, we showed that the private market competitive equilibrium is at point A in Figure 5-2, with a level of production Q_1 and a price of P_1. We also showed that this was the social-efficiency-maximizing level of consumption for the private market. In the presence of externalities, this relationship no longer holds true. Social efficiency is defined relative to social marginal benefit and cost curves, not to private marginal benefit and cost curves. Because of the negative externality of sludge dumping, the social curves (SMB and SMC) intersect at point C, with a level of consumption Q_2. Since the steel plant owner doesn't account for the fact that each unit of steel production kills fish downstream, the supply curve understates the costs of producing Q_1 to be at point A, rather than at point B. As a result, too much steel is produced ($Q_1 > Q_2$), and the private market equilibrium no longer maximizes social efficiency.

When we move away from the social-efficiency-maximizing quantity, we create a *deadweight loss* for society because units are produced and consumed for which the cost to society (summarized by curve SMC) exceeds the social benefits (summarized by curve $D = SMB$). In our example, the deadweight loss is equal to the area BCA. The width of the deadweight loss triangle is determined by the number of units for which social costs exceed social benefits ($Q_1 - Q_2$). The height of the triangle is the difference between the marginal social cost and the marginal social benefit, the marginal damage.

----

private marginal benefit (PMB) The direct benefit to consumers of consuming an additional unit of a good by the consumer.

social marginal benefit (SMB) The private marginal benefit to consumers plus any costs associated with the consumption of the good that are imposed on others.

----

[5] This example assumes that the damage from each unit of steel production is constant, but in reality the damage can rise or fall as production changes. Whether the damage changes or remains the same affects the shape of the social marginal cost curve, relative to the private marginal cost curve.

Negative Consumption Externalities

It is important to note that externalities do not arise solely from the production side of a market. Consider the case of cigarette smoke. In a restaurant that allows smoking, your consumption of cigarettes may have a negative effect on my enjoyment of a restaurant meal. Yet you do not in any way pay for this negative effect on me. This is an example of a **negative consumption externality,** whereby consumption of a good reduces the well-being of others, a loss for which they are not compensated. When there is a negative consumption externality, $SMB = PMB - MD$, where MD is the marginal damage done to others by your consumption of that unit. For example, if MD is 40¢ a pack, the marginal damage done to others by your smoking is 40¢ for every pack you smoke.

> **negative consumption externality** When an individual's consumption reduces the well-being of others who are not compensated by the individual.

Figure 5-3 shows supply and demand in the market for cigarettes. The supply and demand curves represent the PMC and PMB. The private equilibrium is at point A, where supply (PMC) equals demand (PMB), with cigarette consumption of Q_1 and price of P_1. The SMC equals the PMC because there are no externalities associated with the production of cigarettes in this example. Note, however, that the SMB is now below the PMB by 40¢ per pack; every pack consumed has a social benefit that is 40¢ below its private benefit. That is, at Q_1 units of production (point A), the social marginal benefit is the private marginal benefit at that point (which is equal to P_1), minus 40¢ (point B). For each pack of cigarettes, social benefits are 40¢ lower than private benefits, since each pack consumed imposes 40¢ of costs on others for which they are not compensated.

■ FIGURE 5-3

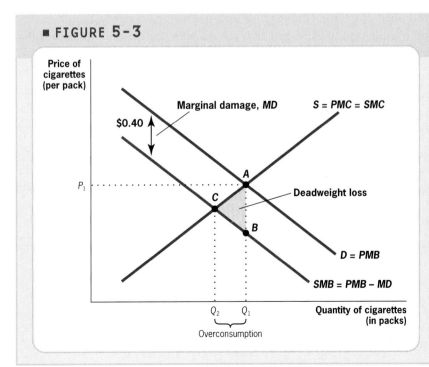

Market Failure Due to Negative Consumption Externalities in the Cigarette Market • A negative consumption externality of 40¢ per pack of cigarettes consumed leads to a social marginal benefit that is below the private marginal benefit, and a social optimum quantity (Q_2) that is lower than the competitive market equilibrium quantity (Q_1). There is overconsumption $Q_1 - Q_2$, with an associated deadweight loss of area ACB.

The social-welfare-maximizing level of consumption, Q_2, is identified by point C, the point at which $SMB = SMC$. There is overconsumption of cigarettes by $Q_1 - Q_2$: the social costs (point A on the SMC curve) exceed social benefits (on the SMB curve) for all units between Q_1 and Q_2. As a result, there is a deadweight loss (area ACB) in the market for cigarettes.

▶**APPLICATION**

The Externality of SUVs[6]

In 1985, the typical driver sat behind the wheel of a car that weighed about 3,200 pounds, and the largest cars on the road weighed 4,600 pounds. Today, the typical driver is in a car that weighs 4,089 pounds (an increase of 28%) and the largest cars on the road can weigh 8,500 pounds. The major culprits in this evolution of car size are sport utility vehicles (SUVs). The term *SUV* was originally reserved for large vehicles intended for off-road driving, but it now refers to any large passenger vehicle marketed as an SUV, even if it lacks off-road capabilities. SUVs, with an average weight of 4,500 pounds, represented only 6.4% of vehicle sales as recently as 1988, but 17 years later, in 2005, they accounted for over 25% of the new vehicles sold each year.

The consumption of large cars such as SUVs produces three types of negative externalities:

Environmental Externalities The contribution of driving to global warming is directly proportional to the amount of fossil fuel a vehicle requires to travel a mile. The typical compact or mid-size car gets roughly 25 miles to the gallon but the typical SUV gets only 18 miles to the gallon. This means that SUV drivers use more gas to go to work or run their errands, increasing fossil fuel emissions. This increased environmental cost is not paid by those who drive SUVs.

Wear and Tear on Roads Each year, federal, state, and local governments in the United States spend $33.2 billion repairing our roadways.[7] Damage to roadways comes from many sources, but a major culprit is the passenger vehicle, and the damage it does to the roads is proportional to vehicle weight. When individuals drive SUVs, they increase the cost to government of repairing the roads. SUV drivers bear some of these costs through gasoline taxes (which fund highway repair), since the SUV uses more gas, but it is unclear if these extra taxes are enough to compensate for the extra damage done to roads.

---

[6] All data in this application are from the U.S. Environmental Protection Agency (2005) and the U.S. Department of Transportation (2004).

[7] U.S. Department of Transportation (2004), p. 205.

Safety Externalities One major appeal of SUVs is that they provide a feeling of security because they are so much larger than other cars on the road. Offsetting this feeling of security is the added *insecurity* imposed on other cars on the road. For a car of average weight, the odds of having a fatal accident rise by four times if the accident is with a typical SUV and not with a car of the same size. Thus, SUV drivers impose a negative externality on other drivers because they don't compensate those other drivers for the increased risk of a dangerous accident. ◄

Positive Externalities

When economists think about externalities, they tend to focus on negative externalities, but not all externalities are bad. There may also be **positive production externalities** associated with a market, whereby production benefits parties other than the producer and yet the producer is not compensated. Imagine the following scenario: There is public land beneath which there *might* be valuable oil reserves. The government allows any oil developer to drill in those public lands, as long as the government gets some royalties on any oil reserves found. Each dollar the oil developer spends on exploration increases the chances of finding oil reserves. Once found, however, the oil reserves can be tapped by other companies; the initial driller only has the advantage of getting there first. Thus, exploration for oil by one company exerts a *positive production externality* on other companies: each dollar spent on exploration by the first company raises the chance that other companies will have a chance to make money from new oil found on this land.

> **positive production externality** When a firm's production increases the well-being of others but the firm is not compensated by those others.

Figure 5-4 shows the market for oil exploration to illustrate the positive externality to exploration: the social marginal cost of exploration is actually *lower* than the private marginal cost because exploration has a positive effect on the future profits of other companies. Assume that the marginal benefit of each dollar of exploration by one company, in terms of raising the expected profits of other companies who drill the same land, is a constant amount *MB*. As a result, the *SMC* is below the *PMC* by the amount *MB*. Thus, the private equilibrium in the exploration market (point *A,* quantity Q_1) leads to *underproduction* relative to the optimal level (point *B,* quantity Q_2) because the initial oil company is not compensated for the benefits it confers on other oil producers.

Note also that there can be **positive consumption externalities.** Imagine, for example, that my neighbor is considering improving the landscaping around his house. The improved landscaping will cost him $1,000, but it is only worth $800 to him. My bedroom faces his house, and I would like to have nicer landscaping to look at. This better view would be worth $300 to me. That is, the total social marginal benefit of the improved landscaping is $1,100, even though the private marginal benefit to my neighbor is only $800. Since this social marginal benefit ($1,100) is larger than the social marginal costs ($1,000), it would be socially efficient for my neighbor to do the landscaping. My neighbor won't do the landscaping, however, since his private

> **positive consumption externality** When an individual's consumption increases the well-being of others but the individual is not compensated by those others.

■ **FIGURE 5-4**

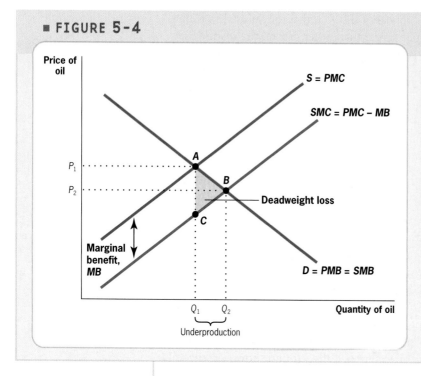

Market Failure Due to Positive Production Externality in the Oil Exploration Market • Expenditures on oil exploration by any company have a positive externality because they offer more profitable opportunities for other companies. This leads to a social marginal cost that is below the private marginal cost, and a social optimum quantity (Q_2) that is greater than the competitive market equilibrium quantity (Q_1). There is underproduction of $Q_2 - Q_1$, with an associated deadweight loss of area ABC.

costs ($1,000) exceed his private benefits. His landscaping improvements would have a positive effect on me for which he will not be compensated, thus leading to an underconsumption of landscaping.

Quick Hint One confusing aspect of the graphical analysis of externalities is knowing which curve to shift, and in which direction. To review, there are four possibilities:

▶ Negative production externality: *SMC* curve lies above *PMC* curve
▶ Positive production externality: *SMC* curve lies below *PMC* curve
▶ Negative consumption externality: *SMB* curve lies below *PMB* curve
▶ Positive consumption externality: *SMB* curve lies above *PMB* curve

Armed with these facts, the key is to assess which category a particular example fits into. This assessment is done in two steps. First, you must assess whether the externality is associated with producing a good or with consuming a good. Then, you must assess whether the externality is positive or negative.

The steel plant example is a negative production externality because the externality is associated with the production of steel, not its consumption; the sludge doesn't come from using steel, but rather from making it. Likewise, our cigarette example is a negative consumption externality because the externality is associated with the consumption of cigarettes; secondhand smoke doesn't come from making cigarettes, it comes from smoking them.

5.2

Private-Sector Solutions to Negative Externalities

In microeconomics, the market is innocent until proven guilty (and, similarly, the government is often guilty until proven innocent!). An excellent application of this principle can be found in a classic work by Ronald Coase, a professor at the Law School at the University of Chicago, who asked in 1960: Why won't the market simply compensate the affected parties for externalities?[8]

The Solution

To see how a market might compensate those affected by the externality, let's look at what would happen if the fishermen owned the river in the steel plant example. They would march up to the steel plant and demand an end to the sludge dumping that was hurting their livelihood. They would have the right to do so because they have *property rights* over the river; their ownership confers to them the ability to control the use of the river.

Suppose for the moment that when this conversation takes place there is no pollution-control technology to reduce the sludge damage; the only way to reduce sludge is to reduce production. So ending sludge dumping would mean shutting down the steel plant. In this case, the steel plant owner might propose a compromise: she would pay the fishermen $100 for each unit of steel produced, so that they were fully compensated for the damage to their fishing grounds. As long as the steel plant can make a profit with this extra $100 payment per unit, then this is a better deal for the plant than shutting down, and the fishermen are fully compensated for the damage done to them.

This type of resolution is called **internalizing the externality.** Because the fishermen now have property rights to the river, they have used the market to obtain compensation from the steel plant for its pollution. The fishermen have implicitly created a market for pollution by pricing the bad behavior of the steel plant. From the steel plant's perspective, the damage to the fish becomes just another input cost, since it has to be paid in order to produce.

This point is illustrated in Figure 5-5. Initially, the steel market is in equilibrium at point *A,* with quantity Q_1 and price P_1, where $PMB = PMC_1$. The socially optimal level of steel production is at point *B,* with quantity Q_2 and price P_2, where $SMB = SMC = PMC_1 + MD$. Because the marginal cost of producing each unit of steel has increased by $100 (the payment to the fishermen), the private marginal cost curve shifts upward from PMC_1 to PMC_2, which equals *SMC*. That is, social marginal costs are private marginal costs plus $100, so by adding $100 to the private marginal costs, we raise the *PMC* to equal the *SMC*. There is no longer overproduction because the social marginal costs and benefits of each unit of production are equalized. This example

internalizing the externality
When either private negotiations or government action lead the price to the party to fully reflect the external costs or benefits of that party's actions.

---

[8] For the original paper, see Coase (1960).

■ **FIGURE 5-5**

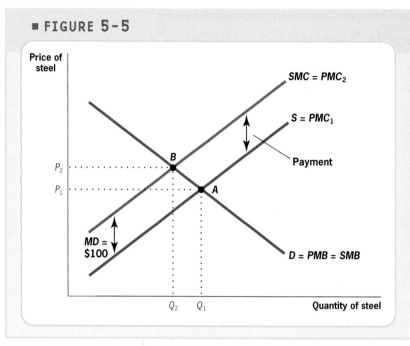

A Coasian Solution to Negative Production Externalities in the Steel Market • If the fishermen charge the steel plant $100 per unit of steel produced, this increases the plant's private marginal cost curve from PMC_1 to PMC_2, which coincides with the SMC curve. The quantity produced falls from Q_1 to Q_2, the socially optimal level of production. The charge internalizes the externality and removes the inefficiency of the negative externality.

Coase Theorem (Part I) When there are well-defined property rights and costless bargaining, then negotiations between the party creating the externality and the party affected by the externality can bring about the socially optimal market quantity.

Coase Theorem (Part II) The efficient solution to an externality does not depend on which party is assigned the property rights, as long as someone is assigned those rights.

illustrates **Part I of the Coase Theorem:** when there are well-defined property rights and costless bargaining, then negotiations between the party creating the externality and the party affected by the externality can bring about the socially optimal market quantity. This theorem states that externalities do not necessarily create market failures, because negotiations between the parties can lead the offending producers (or consumers) to *internalize the externality,* or account for the external effects in their production (or consumption).

The Coase theorem suggests a very particular and limited role for the government in dealing with externalities: establishing property rights. In Coase's view, the fundamental limitation to implementing private-sector solutions to externalities is poorly established property rights. If the government can establish and enforce those property rights, then the private market will do the rest.

The Coase theorem also has an important **Part II:** the efficient solution to an externality does not depend on which party is assigned the property rights, as long as someone is assigned those rights. We can illustrate the intuition behind Part II using the steel plant example. Suppose that the steel plant, rather than the fishermen, owned the river. In this case, the fishermen would have no right to make the plant owner pay a $100 compensation fee for each unit of steel produced. The fishermen, however, would find it in their interest to pay the steel plant to produce less. If the fishermen promised the steel plant owner a payment of $100 for each unit he did not produce, then the steel plant owner would rationally consider there to be an extra $100 cost to each unit he did produce. Remember that in economics, opportunity costs are included in a firm's calculation of costs; thus, forgoing a payment from the fishermen of $100 for each unit of steel not produced has the same effect on production decisions as being forced to pay $100 extra for each unit of steel produced. Once again, the private marginal cost curve would incorporate this extra (opportunity) cost and shift out to the social marginal cost curve, and there would no longer be overproduction of steel.

Quick Hint You may wonder why the fishermen would ever engage in either of these transactions: they receive $100 for each $100 of damage to fish, or pay $100 for each $100 reduction in damage to fish. So what is in it for them? The answer is that this is a convenient shorthand economics modelers use for saying, "The fishermen would charge at least $100 for sludge dumping" or "The fishermen would pay up to $100 to remove sludge dumping." By assuming that the payments are exactly $100, we can conveniently model private and social marginal costs as equal. It may be useful for you to think of the payment to the fishermen as $101 and the payment from the fishermen as $99, so that the fishermen make some money and private and social costs are approximately equal. In reality, the payments to or from the fishermen will depend on the negotiating power and skill of both parties in this transaction, highlighting the importance of the issues raised next.

The Problems with Coasian Solutions

This elegant theory would appear to rescue the standard competitive model from this important cause of market failures and make government intervention unnecessary (other than to ensure property rights). In practice, however, the Coase theorem is unlikely to solve many of the types of externalities that cause market failures. We can see this by considering realistically the problems involved in achieving a "Coasian solution" to the problem of river pollution.

The Assignment Problem The first problem involves assigning blame. Rivers can be very long, and there may be other pollution sources along the way that are doing some of the damage to the fish. The fish may also be dwindling for natural reasons, such as disease or a rise in natural predators. In many cases, it is impossible to assign blame for externalities to one specific entity.

Assigning damage is another side to the assignment problem. We have assumed that the damage was a fixed dollar amount, $100. Where does this figure come from in practice? Can we trust the fishermen to tell us the right amount of damage that they suffer? It would be in their interest in any Coasian negotiation to overstate the damage in order to ensure the largest possible payment. And how will the payment be distributed among the fishermen? When a number of individuals are fishing the same area, it is difficult to say whose catch is most affected by the reduction in the stock of available fish.

The significance of the assignment problem as a barrier to internalizing the externality depends on the nature of the externality. If my loud stereo playing disturbs your studying, then assignment of blame and damages is clear. In the case of global warming, however, how can we assign blame clearly when carbon emissions from any source in the world contribute to this problem? And how can we assign damages clearly when some individuals would like the world to be hotter, while others would not? Because of assignment problems, Coasian solutions are likely to be more effective for small, localized externalities than for larger, more global externalities.

The Holdout Problem Imagine that we have surmounted the assignment problem and that by careful scientific analysis we have determined that each unit of sludge from the steel plant kills $1 worth of fish for each of 100 fishermen, for a total damage of $100 per unit of steel produced.

Now, suppose that the fishermen have property rights to the river, and the steel plant can't produce unless all 100 fishermen say it can. The Coasian solution is that each of the 100 fishermen gets paid $1 per unit of steel production, and the plant continues to produce steel. Each fisherman walks up to the plant and collects his check for $1 per unit. As the last fisherman is walking up, he realizes that he suddenly has been imbued with incredible power: the steel plant cannot produce without his permission since he is a part owner of the river. So, why should he settle for only $1 per unit? Having already paid out $99 per unit, the steel plant would probably be willing to pay more than $1 per unit to remove this last obstacle to their production. Why not ask for $2 per unit? Or even more?

This is an illustration of the **holdout problem,** which can arise when the property rights in question are held by more than one party: the shared property rights give each party power over all others. If the other fishermen are thinking ahead they will realize this might be a problem, and they will all try to be the last one to go to the plant. The result could very well be a breakdown of the negotiations and an inability to negotiate a Coasian solution. As with the assignment problem, the holdout problem would be amplified with a huge externality like global warming, where billions of persons are potentially damaged.

The Free Rider Problem Can we solve the holdout problem by simply assigning the property rights to the side with only one negotiator, in this case the steel plant? Unfortunately, doing so creates a new problem.

Suppose that the steel plant has property rights to the river, and it agrees to reduce production by 1 unit for each $100 received from fishermen. Then the Coasian solution would be for the fishermen to pay $100, and for the plant to then move to the optimal level of production. Suppose that the optimal reduction in steel production (where social marginal benefits and costs are equal) is 100 units, so that each fisherman pays $100 for a total of $10,000, and the plant reduces production by 100 units.

Suppose, once again, that you are the last fisherman to pay. The plant has already received $9,900 to reduce its production, and will reduce its production as a result by 99 units. The 99 units will benefit all fishermen equally since they all share the river. Thus, as a result, if you don't pay your $100, you will still be almost as well off in terms of fishing as if you do. That is, the damage avoided by that last unit of reduction will be shared equally among all 100

holdout problem Shared ownership of property rights gives each owner power over all the others.

fishermen who use the river, yet you will pay the full $100 to buy that last unit of reduction. Thought of that way, why would you pay? This is an example of the **free rider problem:** when an investment has a personal cost but a common benefit, individuals will underinvest. Understanding this incentive, your fellow fishermen will also not pay their $100, and the externality will remain unsolved; if the other fishermen realize that someone is going to grab a free ride, they have little incentive to pay in the first place.

free rider problem When an investment has a personal cost but a common benefit, individuals will underinvest.

Transaction Costs and Negotiating Problems Finally, the Coasian approach ignores the fundamental problem that it is hard to negotiate when there are large numbers of individuals on one or both sides of the negotiation. How can the 100 fishermen effectively get together and figure out how much to charge or pay the steel plant? This problem is amplified for an externality such as global warming, where the potentially divergent interests of billions of parties on one side must be somehow aggregated for a negotiation.

Moreover, these problems can be significant even for the small-scale, localized externalities for which Coase's theory seems best designed. In theory, my neighbor and I can work out an appropriate compensation for my loud music disturbing his studying. In practice, this may be a socially awkward conversation that is more likely to result in tension than in a financial payment. Similarly, if the person next to me in the restaurant is smoking, it would be far outside the norm, and probably considered insulting, to lean over and offer him $5 to stop smoking. Alas, the world does not always operate in the rational way economists wish it would!

Bottom Line Ronald Coase's insight that externalities can sometimes be internalized was a brilliant one. It provides the competitive market model with a defense against the onslaught of market failures that we will bring to bear on it throughout this course. It is also an excellent reason to suspect that the market may be able to internalize some small-scale, localized externalities. Where it won't help, as we've seen, is with large-scale, global externalities that are the focus of, for example, environmental policy in the United States. The government may therefore have a role to play in addressing larger externalities.

5.3

Public-Sector Remedies for Externalities

In the United States, public policy makers do not think that Coasian solutions are sufficient to deal with large-scale externalities. The Environmental Protection Agency (EPA) was formed in 1970 to provide public-sector solutions to the problems of externalities in the environment. The agency regulates a wide variety of environmental issues, in areas ranging from clean air to clean water to land management.[9]

---

[9] See http://www.epa.gov/epahome/aboutepa.htm for more information. There are government resources devoted to environmental regulation in other agencies as well, and these resources don't include the millions of hours of work by the private sector in complying with environmental regulation.

▪ **FIGURE 5-6**

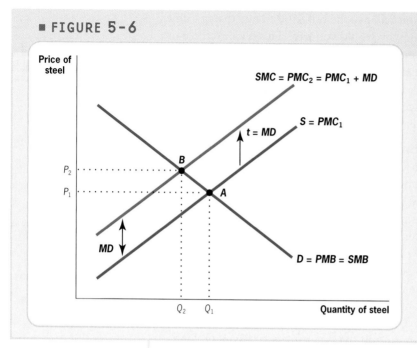

Taxation as a Solution to Negative Production Externalities in the Steel Market • A tax of $100 per unit (equal to the marginal damage of pollution) increases the firm's private marginal cost curve from PMC_1 to PMC_2, which coincides with the SMC curve. The quantity produced falls from Q_1 to Q_2, the socially optimal level of production. Just as with the Coasian payment, this tax internalizes the externality and removes the inefficiency of the negative externality.

Public policy makers employ three types of remedies to resolve the problems associated with negative externalities.

Corrective Taxation

We have seen that the Coasian goal of "internalizing the externality" may be difficult to achieve in practice in the private market. The government can achieve this same outcome in a straightforward way, however, by taxing the steel producer an amount MD for each unit of steel produced.

Figure 5-6 illustrates the impact of such a tax. The steel market is initially in equilibrium at point A, where supply ($=PMC_1$) equals demand (= PMB = SMB), and Q_1 units of steel are produced at price P_1. Given the externality with a cost of MD, the socially optimal production is at point B, where social marginal costs and benefits are equal. Suppose that the government levies a tax per unit of steel produced at an amount $t = MD$. This tax would act as another input cost for the steel producer, and would shift its private marginal cost up by MD for each unit produced. This will result in a new PMC curve, PMC_2, which is identical to the SMC curve. As a result, the tax effectively internalizes the externality and leads to the socially optimal outcome (point B, quantity Q_2). The government per-unit tax on steel production acts in the same way as if the fishermen owned the river. This type of corrective taxation is often called "Pigouvian taxation," after the economist A. C. Pigou, who first suggested this approach to solving externalities.[10]

---

[10] See, for example, Pigou (1947).

Subsidies

As noted earlier, not all externalities are negative; in cases such as oil exploration or nice landscaping by your neighbors, externalities can be positive.

The Coasian solution to cases such as the oil exploration case would be for the other oil producers to take up a collection to pay the initial driller to search for more oil reserves (thus giving them the chance to make more money from any oil that is found). But, as we discussed, this may not be feasible. The government can achieve the same outcome by making a payment, or a **subsidy,** to the initial driller to search for more oil. The amount of this subsidy would exactly equal the benefit to the other oil companies and would cause the initial driller to search for more oil, since his cost per barrel has been lowered.

subsidy Government payment to an individual or firm that lowers the cost of consumption or production, respectively.

The impact of such a subsidy is illustrated in Figure 5-7, which shows once again the market for oil exploration. The market is initially in equilibrium at point A where PMC_1 equals PMB, and Q_1 barrels of oil are produced at price P_1. Given the positive externality with a benefit of MB, the socially optimal production is at point B, where social marginal costs and benefits are equal. Suppose that the government pays a subsidy per barrel of oil produced of $S = MB$. The subsidy would lower the private marginal cost of oil production, shifting the private marginal cost curve down by MB for each unit produced. This will result in a new PMC curve, PMC_2, which is identical to the SMC curve. The subsidy has caused the initial driller to internalize the positive externality, and the market moves from a situation of underproduction to one of optimal production.

■ FIGURE **5-7**

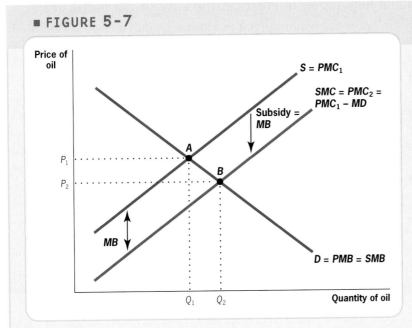

Subsidies as a Solution to Positive Production Externalities in the Market for Oil Exploration • A subsidy that is equal to the marginal benefit from oil exploration reduces the oil producer's marginal cost curve from PMC_1 to PMC_2, which coincides with the SMC curve. The quantity produced rises from Q_1 to Q_2, the socially optimal level of production.

Regulation

Throughout this discussion, you may have been asking yourself: Why this fascination with prices, taxes, and subsidies? If the government knows where the socially optimal level of production is, why doesn't it just mandate that production take place at that level, and forget about trying to give private actors incentives to produce at the optimal point? Using Figure 5-6 as an example, why not just mandate a level of steel production of Q_2 and be done with it?

In an ideal world, Pigouvian taxation and regulation would be identical. Because regulation appears much more straightforward, however, it has been the traditional choice for addressing environmental externalities in the United States and around the world. When the U.S. government wanted to reduce emissions of sulfur dioxide (SO_2) in the 1970s, for example, it did so by putting a limit or cap on the amount of sulfur dioxide that producers could emit, not by a tax on emissions. In 1987, when the nations of the world wanted to phase out the use of chlorofluorocarbons (CFCs), which were damaging the ozone layer, they banned the use of CFCs rather than impose a large tax on products that used CFCs.

Given this governmental preference for quantity regulation, why are economists so keen on taxes and subsidies? In practice, there are complications that may make taxes a more effective means of addressing externalities. In the next section, we discuss two of the most important complications. In doing so, we illustrate the reasons that policy makers might prefer regulation, or the "quantity approach" in some situations, and taxation, or the "price approach" in others.

▶ APPLICATION

Taxes and Regulation in Practice: The Case of the Baltic Sea[11]

The Baltic Sea is the world's largest brackish sea, a mixture of salt and fresh water. Considered a healthy ecosystem until the 1950s, the Baltic is now one of the most polluted bodies of water on earth. The pollution comes now largely from the former communist countries of Eastern Europe, whose inefficient industries and municipalities continue to send pollutants into the sea and the areas that surround and drain into it. Chemical plants in Poland release toxins into nearby soil, while the Russian city of St. Petersburg sends its untreated sewage directly into the Neva River, which in turn flows to the Baltic. The Western European nations are, however, not blameless. Swedish agriculture uses harmful fertilizers that leach into the Baltic's waters, and highly polluting factories in various Western European nations, though now largely closed, were responsible for some of the chemicals that remain in the sea to this day.

This pollution threatens human health, because some species of fish caught in the Baltic Sea now contain dangerously high levels of dioxin, a cancer-causing substance released when plastics and fuels are burned. Moreover, it also

---

[11] Helsinki Commission (2003).

weakens the viability of the local fishing industry on which the livelihoods of many Baltic Sea residents depend. Thus, this is a classic negative externality.

The fall of communism in 1989 opened up possibilities for international cooperation that the countries of the Baltic region were quick to exploit. In 1990, Sweden coordinated the creation of the Baltic Sea Joint Comprehensive Environmental Action Programme (JCP), an agreement to begin a massive cleanup effort among 14 nations close to the Baltic Sea. The JCP identified 132 hot spots, particularly large sources of pollution, and agreed to spend about $1 billion a year for 20 years to clean them up. Funding comes from the wealthier parties to the agreement, as well as from international institutions like the World Bank and European Union. The agreement thus allowed wealthier countries like Sweden and Finland to begin protecting their fishing industries and gave poorer countries funds to modernize industrial and municipal systems.

After the agreement was signed, a further set of questions arose. When trying to clean up a pollution hot spot, should governments use regulation (like forbidding the dumping of untreated sewage) or taxation (a charge per unit of sewage dumped)? Under the JCP, as it turns out, both regulation and taxation have been used, often simultaneously. Some examples:

▶ Poland recently succeeded in having 10 hot spots wiped off the list by quintupling (since 1990) investment in technology for environmental protection. Poland spent hundreds of millions of dollars ensuring that the vast majority of its industrial and municipal wastewater was being treated before entering the Baltic system. Surprisingly, only 6% of these funds came from external sources. The remaining 94% was raised by Poland itself, in the form of fines and fees levied on domestic polluters. A tax on pollution was thus being used to fund compliance with regulations demanding the treatment of wastewater.

▶ The Swedish city of Käppala now runs its own treatment plant through which industrial and municipal wastewater must flow before entering the Baltic system. Industries are forbidden from discharging wastewater that is corrosive or toxic (regulation) and are charged a fee by the city for the volume of wastewater and for each kilogram of pollutant present in the water sent to the treatment plant (taxation). The fees, which range from $0.50 to $10 per kilogram depending on the pollutant, reflect the cost to the city of treating the water.

▶ In 2002, the JCP was asked to develop ways of dealing with particular hot spots in Ukraine and Belarus that had arisen because of overloaded and obsolete wastewater treatment systems. The JCP noted that most European countries levy significant charges for water usage on households and industry. Belarus and Ukraine charge only $0.02 per cubic meter of water used, much less than other countries, resulting in a daily consumption of nearly 100 gallons per person, twice the European average! The JCP thus recommended that those countries raise their water fees to accurately reflect the cost of treating water being discharged into the Baltic system.

The challenges to the Baltic Sea are hardly over. To date, around 80 of the original 132 hot spots still remain heavily polluting. The main challenge, unsurprisingly, is to find the funding to deal with such spots. St. Petersburg, for example, continues as the Baltic's single largest polluter because it cannot raise the funds necessary to complete a partially built sewage treatment plant. The JCP nevertheless provides an interesting example of how to use both regulation and taxation to accomplish environmental goals. ◄

5.4

Distinctions Between Price and Quantity Approaches to Addressing Externalities

In this section, we compare price (taxation) and quantity (regulation) approaches to addressing externalities, using more complicated models in which the social efficiency implications of intervention might differ between the two approaches. The goal in comparing these approaches is to find the most efficient path to environmental targets. That is, for any reduction in pollution, the goal is to find the lowest-cost means of achieving that reduction.[12]

Basic Model

To illustrate the important differences between the price and quantity approaches, we have to add one additional complication to the basic competitive market that we have worked with thus far. In that model, the only way to reduce pollution was to cut back on production. In reality, there are many other technologies available for reducing pollution besides simply scaling back production. For example, to reduce sulfur dioxide emissions from coal-fired power plants, utilities can install smokestack scrubbers that remove SO_2 from the emissions and sequester it, often in the form of liquid or solid sludge that can be disposed of safely. Passenger cars can also be made less polluting by installing "catalytic converters," which turn dangerous nitrogen oxide into compounds that are not harmful to public health.

To understand the differences between price and quantity approaches to pollution reduction, it is useful to shift our focus from the market for a good (e.g., steel) to the "market" for pollution reduction, as illustrated in Figure 5-8. In this diagram, the horizontal axis measures the extent of pollution reduction undertaken by a plant; a value of zero indicates that the plant is not engaging in any pollution reduction. Thus, the horizontal axis also measures the amount of pollution: as you move to the right, there is more pollution reduction and less pollution. We show this by denoting *more reduction* as you move to the right on the horizontal axis; R_{full} indicates that pollution has been reduced to

---

[12] The discussion of this section focuses entirely on the efficiency consequences of tax versus regulatory approaches to addressing externalities. There may be important equity considerations as well, however, which affect the government's decision about policy instruments. We will discuss the equity properties of taxation in Chapter 19.

▪ **FIGURE 5-8**

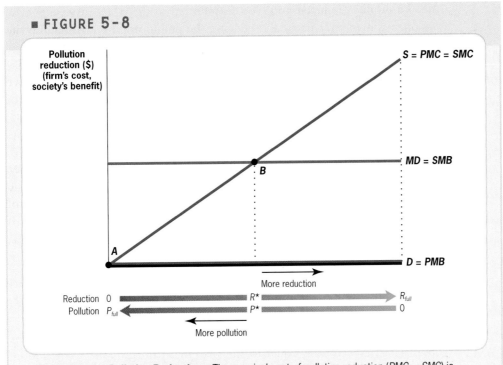

The Market for Pollution Reduction ▪ The marginal cost of pollution reduction (*PMC = SMC*) is a rising function, while the marginal benefit of pollution reduction (*SMB*) is (by assumption) a flat marginal damage curve. Moving from left to right, the amount of pollution reduction increases, while the amount of pollution falls. The optimal level of pollution reduction is *R**, the point at which these curves intersect. Since pollution is the complement of reduction, the optimal amount of pollution is *P**.

zero. *More pollution* is indicated as you move to the left on the horizontal axis; at P_{full}, the maximum amount of pollution is being produced. The vertical axis represents the cost of pollution reduction to the plant, or the benefit of pollution reduction to society (that is, the benefit to other producers and consumers who are not compensated for the negative externality).

The *MD* curve represents the marginal damage that is averted by additional pollution reduction. This measures the social marginal benefit of pollution reduction. Marginal damage is drawn flat at $100 for simplicity, but it could be downward sloping due to diminishing returns. The private marginal benefit of pollution reduction is zero, so it is represented by the horizontal axis; there is no gain to the plant's private interests from reducing dumping.

The *PMC* curve represents the plant's private marginal cost of reducing pollution. The *PMC* curve slopes upward because of diminishing marginal productivity of this input. The first units of pollution are cheap to reduce: just tighten a few screws or put a cheap filter on the sludge pipe. Additional units of reduction become more expensive, until it is incredibly expensive to have a completely pollution-free production process. Because there are no externalities from the production of pollution reduction (the externalities come from the end product, reduced pollution, as reflected in the *SMB* curve, not from the process involved in actually reducing the pollution), the *PMC* is also the *SMC* of pollution reduction.

The free market outcome in any market would be zero pollution reduction. Since the cost of pollution is not borne by the plant, it has no incentive to reduce pollution. The plant will choose zero reduction and a full amount of pollution P_{full} (point *A*, at which the *PMC* of zero equals the *PMB* of zero).

What is the optimal level of pollution reduction? The optimum is *always* found at the point at which social marginal benefits and costs are equal, here point *B*. The optimal quantity of pollution reduction is $R^\star$: at that quantity, the marginal benefits of reduction (the damage done by pollution) and the marginal costs of reduction are equal. Note that setting the optimal amount of pollution reduction is the same as setting the optimal amount of pollution. If the free market outcome is pollution reduction of zero and pollution of P_{full}, then the optimum is pollution reduction of $R^\star$ and pollution of $P^\star$.

Price Regulation (Taxes) vs. Quantity Regulation in This Model

Now, contrast the operation of taxation and regulation in this framework. The optimal tax, as before, is equal to the marginal damage done by pollution, $100. In this situation, the government would set a tax of $100 on each unit of pollution. Consider the plant's decision under this tax. For each unit of pollution the plant makes, it pays a tax of $100. If there is any pollution reduction that the plant can do that costs less than $100, it will be cost-effective to make that reduction: the plant will pay some amount less than $100 to get rid of the pollution, and avoid paying a tax of $100. With this plan in place, plants will have an incentive to reduce pollution up to the point at which the cost of that reduction is equal to the tax of $100. That is, plants will "walk up" their marginal cost curves, reducing pollution up to a reduction of $R^\star$ at point *B*. Beyond that point, the cost of reducing pollution exceeds the $100 that they pay in tax, so they will just choose to pay taxes on any additional units of pollution rather than to reduce pollution further. Thus, a Pigouvian (corrective) tax equal to $100 achieves the socially optimal level of pollution reduction, just as in the earlier analysis.

Regulation is even more straightforward to analyze in this framework. The government simply mandates that the plant reduce pollution by an amount $R^\star$, to get to the optimal pollution level $P^\star$. Regulation seems more difficult than taxation because, in this case, the government needs to know not only *MD* but also the shape of the *MC* curve as well. This difficulty is, however, just a feature of our assumption of constant *MD;* for the more general case of a falling *MD,* the government needs to know the shapes of both *MC* and *MD* curves in order to set either the optimal tax or the optimal regulation.

Multiple Plants with Different Reduction Costs

Now, let's add two wrinkles to the basic model. First, suppose there are now two steel plants doing the dumping, with each plant dumping 200 units of sludge into the river each day. The marginal damage done by each unit of sludge is $100, as before. Second, suppose that technology is now available to reduce sludge associated with production, but this technology has different costs at the two different plants. For plant A reducing sludge is cheaper at any level of reduction, since it has a newer production process. For the second plant, B, reducing sludge is much more expensive for any level of reduction.

Figure 5-9 summarizes the market for pollution reduction in this case. In this figure, there are separate marginal cost curves for plant A (MC_A) and for plant B (MC_B). At every level of reduction, the marginal cost to plant A is lower than the marginal cost to plant B, since plant A has a newer and more efficient production process available. The total marginal cost of reduction in the market, the horizontal sum of these two curves, is MC_T: for any total reduction in pollution, this curve indicates the cost of that reduction if it is distributed most efficiently across the two plants. For example, the total marginal cost of a reduction of 50 units is $0, since plant A can reduce 50 units for free; so the efficient combination is to have plant A do all the reducing. The socially efficient level of pollution reduction (and of pollution) is the intersection of this MC_T curve with the marginal damage curve, MD, at point Z, indicating a reduction of 200 units (and pollution of 200 units).

■ FIGURE 5-9

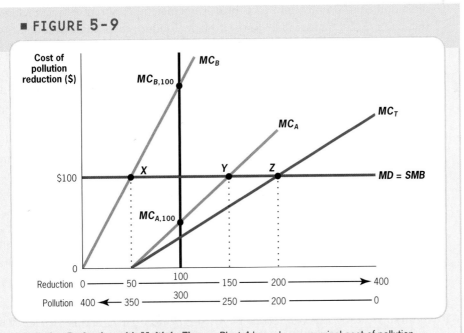

Pollution Reduction with Multiple Firms • Plant A has a lower marginal cost of pollution reduction at each level of reduction than does plant B. The optimal level of reduction for the market is the point at which the sum of marginal costs equals marginal damage (at point Z, with a reduction of 200 units). An equal reduction of 100 units for each plant is inefficient since the marginal cost to plant B (MC_B) is so much higher than the marginal cost to plant A (MC_A). The optimal division of this reduction is where each plant's marginal cost is equal to the social marginal benefit (which is equal to marginal damage). This occurs when plant A reduces by 150 units and plant B reduces by 50 units, at a marginal cost to each of $100.

Policy Option 1: Quantity Regulation Let's now examine the government's policy options within the context of this example. The first option is regulation: the government can demand a total reduction of 200 units of sludge from the market. The question then becomes: How does the government decide how much reduction to demand from each plant? The typical regulatory solution to this problem in the past was to ask the plants to split the burden: each plant reduces pollution by 100 units to get to the desired total reduction of 200 units.

This is not an efficient solution, however, because it ignores the fact that the plants have different marginal costs of pollution reduction. At an equal level of pollution reduction (and pollution), each unit of reduction costs less for plant A (MC_A) than for plant B (MC_B). If, instead, we got more reduction from plant A than from plant B, we could lower the total social costs of pollution reduction by taking advantage of reduction at the low-cost option (plant A). So society as a whole is worse off if plant A and plant B have to make equal reduction than if they share the reduction burden more efficiently.

This point is illustrated in Figure 5-9. The efficient solution is one where, for each plant, the marginal cost of reducing pollution is set equal to the social marginal benefit of that reduction; that is, where each plant's marginal cost curve intersects with the marginal benefit curve. This occurs at a reduction of 50 units for plant B (point X), and 150 units for plant A (point Y). Thus, mandating a reduction of 100 units from each plant is inefficient; total costs of achieving a reduction of 200 units will be lower if plant A reduces by a larger amount.

Policy Option 2: Price Regulation Through a Corrective Tax The second approach is to use a Pigouvian corrective tax, set equal to the marginal damage, so each plant would face a tax of $100 on each unit of sludge dumped. Faced with this tax, what will each plant do? For plant A, any unit of sludge reduction up to 150 units costs less than $100, so plant A will reduce its pollution by 150 units. For plant B, any unit of sludge reduction up to 50 units costs less than $100, so it will reduce pollution by 50 units. Note that these are exactly the efficient levels of reduction! Just as in our earlier analysis, Pigouvian taxes cause efficient production by raising the cost of the input by the size of its external damage, thereby raising private marginal costs to social marginal costs. Taxes are preferred to quantity regulation, with an equal distribution of reductions across the plants, because taxes give plants more flexibility in choosing their optimal amount of reduction, allowing them to choose the efficient level.

Policy Option 3: Quantity Regulation with Tradable Permits Does this mean that taxes *always* dominate quantity regulation with multiple plants? Not necessarily. If the government had mandated the appropriate reduction from each plant (150 units from A and 50 units from B), then quantity regulation would have achieved the same outcome as the tax. Such a solution would, however, require much more information. Instead of just knowing the marginal damage and the total marginal cost, the government would also have to know the marginal cost curves of each individual plant. Such detailed information would be hard to obtain.

Quantity regulation can be rescued, however, by adding a key flexibility: issue permits that allow a certain amount of pollution and let the plants trade. Suppose the government announces the following system: it will issue 200 permits that entitle the bearer to produce one unit of pollution. It will initially provide 100 permits to each plant. Thus, in the absence of trading, each plant would be allowed to produce only 100 units of sludge, which would in turn require each plant to reduce its pollution by half (the inefficient solution previously described).

If the government allows the plants to trade these permits to each other, however, plant B would have an interest in buying permits from plant A. For plant B, reducing sludge by 100 units costs $MC_{B,100}$, a marginal cost much greater than plant A's marginal cost of reducing pollution by 100 units, which is $MC_{A,100}$. Thus, plants A and B can be made better off if plant B buys a permit from plant A for some amount between $MC_{A,100}$ and $MC_{B,100}$, so that plant B would pollute 101 units (reducing only 99 units) and plant A would pollute 99 units (reducing 101 units). This transaction is beneficial for plant B because as long as the cost of a permit is below $MC_{B,100}$, plant B pays less than the amount it would cost plant B to reduce the pollution on its own. The trade is beneficial for plant A as long as it receives for a permit at least $MC_{A,100}$, since it can reduce the sludge for a cost of only $MC_{A,100}$, and make money on the difference.

By the same logic, a trade would be beneficial for a second permit, so that plant B could reduce sludge by only 98, and plant A would reduce by 102. In fact, any trade will be beneficial until plant B is reducing by 50 units and plant A is reducing by 150 units. At that point, the marginal costs of reduction across the two producers are equal (to $100), so that there are no more gains from trading permits.

What is going on here? We have simply returned to the intuition of the Coasian solution: we have *internalized the externality by providing property rights to pollution*. So, like Pigouvian taxes, trading allows the market to incorporate differences in the cost of pollution reduction across firms. In Chapter 6, we discuss a successful application of trading to the problem of environmental externalities.

Uncertainty About Costs of Reduction

Differences in reduction costs across firms are not the only reason that taxes or regulation might be preferred. Another reason is that the costs or benefits of regulation could be uncertain. Consider two extreme examples of externalities: global warming and nuclear leakage. Figure 5-10 extends the pollution reduction framework from Figure 5-8 to the situation in which the marginal damage (which is equal to the marginal social benefit of pollution reduction) is now no longer constant, but falling. That is, the benefit of the first unit of pollution reduction is quite high, but once the production process is relatively pollution-free, additional reductions are less important (that is, there are diminishing marginal returns to reduction).

Panel (a) of Figure 5-10 considers the case of global warming. In this case, the exact amount of pollution reduction is not so critical for the environment.

■ **FIGURE 5-10**

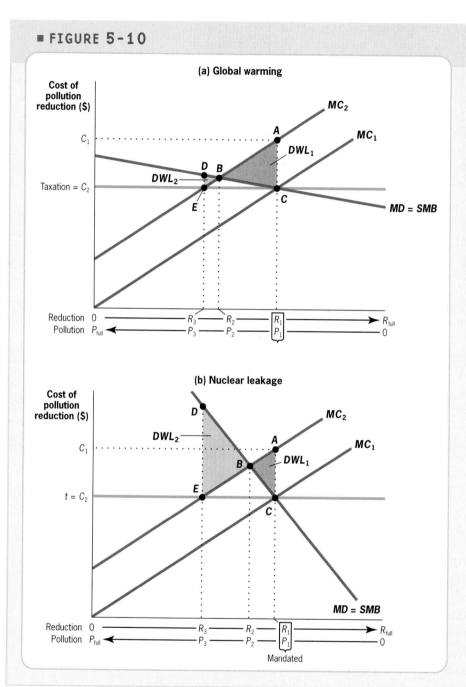

(a) Global warming

(b) Nuclear leakage

Market for Pollution Reduction with Uncertain Costs • In the case of global warming (panel (a)), the marginal damage is fairly constant over large ranges of emissions (and thus emission reductions). If costs are uncertain, then taxation at level $t = C_2$ leads to a much lower deadweight loss (*DBE*) than does regulation of R_1 (*ABC*). In the case of nuclear leakage (panel (b)), the marginal damage is very steep. If costs are uncertain, then taxation leads to a much larger deadweight loss (*DBE*) than does regulation (*ABC*).

Since what determines the extent of global warming is the total accumulated stock of carbon dioxide in the air, which accumulates over many years from sources all over the world, even fairly large shifts in carbon dioxide pollution in one country today will have little impact on global warming. In that case, we say that the social marginal benefit curve (which is equal to the marginal damage from global warming) is *very flat:* that is, there is little benefit to society from modest additional reductions in carbon dioxide emissions.

Panel (b) of Figure 5-10 considers the case of radiation leakage from a nuclear power plant. In this case, a very small difference in the amount of nuclear leakage can make a huge difference in terms of lives saved. Indeed, it is possible that the marginal damage curve (which is once again equal to the marginal social benefits of pollution reduction) for nuclear leakage is almost vertical, with each reduction in leakage being equally important in terms of saving lives. Thus, the social marginal benefit curve in this case is *very steep.*

Now, in both cases, imagine that we don't know the true costs of pollution reduction on the part of firms or individuals. The government's best guess is that the true marginal cost of pollution reduction is represented by curve MC_1 in both panels. There is a chance, however, that the marginal cost of pollution reduction could be much higher, as represented by the curve MC_2. This uncertainty could arise because the government has an imperfect understanding of the costs of pollution reduction to the firm, or it could arise because both the government and the firms are uncertain about the ultimate costs of pollution reduction.

Implications for Effect of Price and Quantity Interventions This uncertainty over costs has important implications for the type of intervention that reduces pollution most efficiently in each of these cases. Consider regulation first. Suppose that the government mandates a reduction, R_1, which is the optimum if costs turn out to be given by MC_1: this is where social marginal benefits equal social marginal costs of reduction if marginal cost equals MC_1. Suppose now that the marginal costs actually turn out to be MC_2, so that the optimal reduction should instead be R_2, where $SMB = MC_2$. That is, regulation is mandating a reduction in pollution that is too large, with the marginal benefits of the reduction being below the marginal costs. What are the efficiency implications of this mistake?

In the case of global warming (panel (a)), these efficiency costs are quite high. With a mandated reduction of R_1, firms will face a cost of reduction of C_1, the cost of reducing by amount R_1 if marginal costs are described by MC_2. The social marginal benefit of reduction of R_1 is equal to C_2, the point where R_1 intersects the SMB curve. Since the cost to firms (C_1) is so much higher than the benefit of reduction (C_2), there is a large deadweight loss (DWL_1) of area ABC (the triangle that incorporates all units where cost of reduction exceeds benefits of reduction).

In the case of nuclear leakage (panel (b)), the costs of regulation are very low. Once again, with a mandated reduction of R_1, firms will face a cost of reduction of C_1, the cost of reducing by amount R_1 if marginal costs are described by MC_2. The social marginal benefit of reduction at R_1 is once again equal to C_2. In this case, however, the associated deadweight loss triangle ABC (DWL_1) is much smaller than in panel (a), so the inefficiency from regulation is much lower.

Now, contrast the use of corrective taxation in these two markets. Suppose that the government levies a tax designed to achieve the optimal level of reduction if marginal costs are described in both cases by MC_1, which is R_1. As discussed earlier, the way to do this is to choose a tax level, t, such that the firm chooses a reduction of R_1. In both panels, the tax level that will cause firms to choose reduction R_1 is a tax equal to C_2, where MC_1 intersects MD. A tax of this amount would cause firms to do exactly R_1 worth of reduction, if marginal costs are truly determined by MC_1.

If the true marginal cost ends up being MC_2, however, the tax causes firms to choose a reduction of R_3, where their true marginal cost is equal to the tax (where $t = MC_2$ at point E), so that there is *too little* reduction. In the case of global warming in panel (a), the deadweight loss (DWL_2) from reducing by R_3 instead of R_2 is only the small area DBE, representing the units where social marginal benefits exceed social marginal costs. In the case of nuclear leakage in panel (b), however, the deadweight loss (DWL_2) from reducing by R_3 instead of R_2 is a much larger area, DBE, once again representing the units where social marginal benefits exceed social marginal costs.

Implications for Instrument Choice The central intuition here is that *the instrument choice depends on whether the government wants to get the amount of pollution reduction right or whether it wants to minimize costs.* Quantity regulation assures there is as much reduction as desired, regardless of the cost. So, if it is critical to get the amount exactly right, quantity regulation is the best way to go. This is why the efficiency cost of quantity regulation under uncertainty is so much lower with the nuclear leakage case in panel (b). In this case, it is critical to get the reduction close to optimal; if we end up costing firms extra money in the process, so be it. For global warming, getting the reduction exactly right isn't very important; so it is inefficient in this case to mandate a very costly option for firms.

Price regulation through taxes, on the other hand, assures that the cost of reductions never exceeds the level of the tax, but leaves the amount of reduction uncertain. That is, firms will never reduce pollution beyond the point at which reductions cost more than the tax they must pay (the point at which the tax intersects their true marginal cost curve, MC_2). If marginal costs turn out to be higher than anticipated, then firms will just do less pollution reduction. This is why the deadweight loss of price regulation in the case of global warming is so small in panel (a): the more efficient outcome is to get the exact reduction wrong but protect firms against very high costs of reduction. This is clearly not true in panel (b): for nuclear leakage, it is most important to get the quantity close to right (almost) regardless of the cost to firms.

In summary, quantity regulations ensure environmental protection, but at a variable cost to firms, while price regulations ensure the cost to the firms, but at a variable level of environmental protection. So, if the value of getting the environmental protection close to right is high, then quantity regulations will be preferred; but if getting the protection close to right is not so important, then price regulations are a preferred option.

5.5

Conclusion

Externalities are the classic answer to the "when" question of public finance: when one party's actions affect another party, and the first party doesn't fully compensate (or get compensated by) the other for this effect, then the market has failed and government intervention is potentially justified. In some cases, the market is likely to find a Coasian solution whereby negotiations between the affected parties lead to the "internalization" of the externality. For many cases, however, only government intervention can solve the market failure.

This point naturally leads to the "how" question of public finance. There are two classes of tools in the government's arsenal for dealing with externalities: price-based measures (taxes and subsidies) and quantity-based measures (regulation). Which of these methods will lead to the most efficient regulatory outcome depends on factors such as the heterogeneity of the firms being regulated, the flexibility embedded in quantity regulation, and the uncertainty over the costs of externality reduction. In the next chapter, we take these somewhat abstract principles and apply them to some of the most important externalities facing the United States (and the world) today.

▶ HIGHLIGHTS

■ Externalities arise whenever the actions of one party make another party worse or better off, yet the first party neither bears the costs nor receives the benefits of doing so.

■ Negative externalities cause overproduction of the good in a competitive market, while positive externalities cause underproduction of the good in a competitive market, in both cases leading to a deadweight loss.

■ Private markets may be able to "internalize" the problems of externalities through negotiation, but this Coasian process faces many barriers that make it an unlikely solution to global externalities, such as most environmental externalities.

■ The government can use either price (tax or subsidy) or quantity (regulation) approaches to addressing externalities.

■ When firms have different marginal costs of pollution reduction, price mechanisms are a more efficient means of accomplishing environmental goals unless quantity regulation is accompanied by the ability to meet regulatory targets by trading pollution permits across polluters.

■ If there is uncertainty about the marginal costs of pollution reduction, then the relative merits of price and quantity regulations will depend on the steepness of the marginal benefit curve. Quantity regulation gets the amount of pollution reduction right, regardless of cost, and so is more appropriate when marginal benefits are steep; price regulation through taxation gets the costs of pollution reduction right, regardless of quantity, so it is more appropriate when marginal benefits are flat.

▶ QUESTIONS AND PROBLEMS

1. Peterson, Hoffer, and Millner (1995) showed that air bag use has led to increases in car crashes. Despite this finding, the government mandates that new cars have air bags, rather than taxing their use. Is this policy a contradiction?

2. When the state of Virginia imposed stricter regulations on air pollution in 2003, it also authorized an auction of pollution permits, allowing some plants to emit larger amounts of ozone-depleting chemicals than would otherwise be allowed, and some to emit less. Theory predicts that this auction led to a socially efficient allocation of pollution. Describe how this outcome would occur.

3. Can an activity generate both positive and negative externalities at the same time? Explain your answer.

4. In the midwestern United States, where winds tend to blow from west to east, states tend to more easily approve new polluting industries near their eastern borders than in other parts of the state. Why do you think this is true?

5. Can government assignment and enforcement of property rights internalize an externality? Will this approach work as well as, better than, or worse than direct government intervention? Explain your answers and describe one of the difficulties associated with this solution.

6. In close congressional votes, many members of Congress choose to remain "undecided" until the last moment. Why might they do this? What lesson does this example teach about a potential shortcoming of the Coasian solution to the externality problem?

7. Suppose that a firm's marginal production costs are given by $MC = 10 + 3Q$. The firm's production process generates a toxic waste, which imposes an increasingly large cost on the residents of the town where it operates: the marginal external cost associated with the Qth unit of production is given by $6Q$. What is the marginal private cost associated with the 10th unit produced? What is the total marginal cost to society associated with producing the 10th unit (the marginal social cost of the 10th unit)?

8. In two-car automobile accidents, passengers in the larger vehicle are significantly more likely to survive than are passengers in the smaller vehicle. In fact, death probabilities are decreasing in the size of the vehicle you are driving, and death probabilities are increasing in the size of the vehicle you collide with. Some politicians and lobbyists have argued that this provides a rationale for encouraging the sale of larger vehicles and discouraging legislation that would induce automobile manufacturers to make smaller cars. Critically examine this argument using the concept of externalities.

9. Why do governments sometimes impose quantity regulations that limit the level of negative-externality-inducing consumption? Why do governments sometimes impose price regulations by taxing this consumption?

10. Answer the following two questions for each of the following examples: (i) smoking by individuals; (ii) toxic waste production by firms; (iii) research and development by a high-tech firm; and (iv) individual vaccination against communicable illness.

    a. Is there an externality? If so, describe it, including references to whether it is positive or negative, and whether it is a consumption or production externality.

    b. If there is an externality, does it seem likely that private markets will arise that allow this externality to be internalized? Why or why not?

▶ **ADVANCED QUESTIONS**

11. Warrenia has two regions. In Oliviland, the marginal benefit associated with pollution cleanup is $MB = 300 - 10Q$, while in Linneland, the marginal benefit associated with pollution cleanup is $MB = 200 - 4Q$. Suppose that the marginal cost of cleanup is constant at \$12 per unit. What is the optimal level of pollution cleanup in each of the two regions?

12. The private marginal benefit associated with a product's consumption is $PMB = 360 - 4Q$ and the private marginal cost associated with its production is $PMC = 6P$. Furthermore, the marginal external damage associated with this good's production is $MD = 2P$. To correct the externality, the government decides to impose a tax of T per unit sold. What tax T should it set to achieve the social optimum?

13. Suppose that demand for a product is $Q = 1200 - 4P$ and supply is $Q = -200 + 2P$. Furthermore, suppose that the marginal external damage of this product is \$8 per unit. How many more units of this product will the free market produce than is socially optimal? Calculate the deadweight loss associated with the externality.

14. The marginal damage averted from pollution cleanup is $MD = 200 - 5Q$. The marginal cost associated with pollution cleanup is $MC = 10 + Q$.

    a. What is the optimal level of pollution reduction?

    b. Show that this level of pollution reduction could be accomplished through taxation. What tax per unit would generate the optimal amount of pollution reduction?

15. Two firms are ordered by the federal government to reduce their pollution levels. Firm A's marginal costs associated with pollution reduction is $MC = 20 + 4Q$. Firm B's marginal costs associated with pollution reduction is $MC = 10 + 8Q$. The marginal benefit of pollution reduction is $MB = 400 - 4Q$.

    a. What is the socially optimal level of each firm's pollution reduction?

    b. Compare the social efficiency of three possible outcomes: (1) require all firms to reduce pollution by the same amount; (2) charge a common tax per unit of pollution; or (3) require all firms to reduce pollution by the same amount, but allow pollution permits to be bought and sold.

16. One hundred commuters need to use a strip of highway to get to work. They all drive alone and prefer to drive in big cars—it gives them more prestige and makes them feel safer. Bigger cars cost more per mile to operate, however, since their gas mileage is lower. Worse yet, bigger cars cause greater permanent damage to roads.

    The weight of the car is w. Suppose that the benefits from driving are $4w$, while the costs are $3/2 \times w^2$. The damage to roads is $1/3 \times w^3$. Assume that individuals have utility functions of the form $U = x$, where x are the net benefits from driving a car of a given size.

    a. What car weight will be chosen by drivers?

    b. What is the optimal car weight? If this differs from (a), why does it?

    c. Can you design a toll system that causes drivers to choose the optimal car weight? If so, then how would such a system work?

17. Firms A and B each produce 80 units of pollution. The federal government wants to reduce pollution levels. The marginal costs associated with pollution reduction are $MC^A = 50 + 3Q^A$ for firm A and $MC^B = 20 + 6Q^B$ for firm B, where Q^A and Q^B are the quantities of pollution *reduced* by each firm. Society's marginal benefit from pollution reduction is given by $MB = 590 - 3Q^{tot}$, where Q^{tot} is the total reduction in pollution.

    a. What is the socially optimal level of each firm's pollution reduction?

    b. How much total pollution is there in the social optimum?

    c. Explain why it is inefficient to give each firm an *equal* number of pollution permits (if they are not allowed to trade them).

    d. Explain how the social optimum can be achieved if firms are given equal numbers of pollution permits but *are* allowed to trade them.

    e. Can the social optimum be achieved using a tax on pollution?

6

Externalities in Action: Environmental and Health Externalities

For many years, Caldwell Pond in Alstead, New Hampshire, had been one of the state's best trout ponds, yielding brook trout that weighed upward of two pounds. By 1980, something had changed. That spring, the New Hampshire Fish and Game Department stocked the 28-acre pond with young fish, known as fingerling trout. Shortly afterward, visitors to the pond began seeing dead fish all over the pond's bottom.

What happened? Tests of the pond water uncovered the culprit: a rapid rise in the acidity of the water. Acidity is measured on a pH scale, where 7.0 is neutral and 3.0 is the acidity of vinegar. In 1948, the lake had a pH of 5.8 to 6.2; the 1980 samples of pond water had a pH of 4.2 to 4.7. The lake was over 30 times more acidic than it had been 30 years earlier.[1] The cause of this increased acidity was the phenomenon known as *acid rain*.

The primary causes of acid rain are clear. When sulfur dioxide (SO_2) and nitrogen oxides (NO_X) are released into the atmosphere, they combine with hydrogen to form sulfuric and nitric acids respectively. These acids (in liquid or solid form, also known as *particulates*) may fall back to the earth hundreds of miles away from their original source, in a process called *acid deposition,* more popularly known as **acid rain.** The majority of acid rain in North America is created by SO_2 emissions, two-thirds of which come from coal-fired power plants, which are heavily concentrated in the Ohio River Valley.[2]

Acid rain is a classic negative production externality. As a by-product of their production, power plants in the Midwest damage the quality of life along the east coast of the United States. Private-sector (Coasian) solutions are unavailable because of the problems noted in the previous chapter, such as negotiation difficulties with hundreds of polluters and millions of affected individuals. Thus, government intervention is required to address this externality. In fact, the government has intervened to reduce acid rain for over 30 years. The story of this intervention and the effects it has had on the environ-

acid rain Rain that is unusually acidic due to contamination by emissions of sulfur dioxide (SO_2) and nitrogen oxide (NO_x).

---

[1] Bryant (1980).
[2] Ellerman et al. (2000), p. 5.

ment, on health, and on the economy provides an excellent example of the possibilities and limitations of government policy toward the environment.

In this chapter, we put the theoretical tools developed in Chapter 5 to use in examining several examples of environmental and health externalities. In particular, the United States' experience with acid rain regulation highlights the enormous value of a tool introduced in the previous chapter: emissions trading. Allowing trading within the acid rain regulatory scheme lowered the costs of these regulations by half or more. This lesson has proved influential in the debate over global warming, likely the largest environmental issue that the world will face in the coming century. In this chapter, we discuss initial efforts to address global warming and the important role that trading can play in future regulatory interventions.

We then turn to another major potential source of externalities, health externalities, and in particular those caused by cigarette smoking. Health behaviors provide an excellent forum for assessing when actions cause, and do not cause, externalities on others, as well as for raising the question of whether actions an individual takes that harm only that individual should be regulated by the government.

6.1
Acid Rain

In Alstead, New Hampshire, acid rain raised the acidity of a popular fishing pond and killed the trout that lived in it. Indeed, acid rain is the primary cause of acidity in lakes and streams in the United States, and it causes a cascade of effects that harm or kill individual fish, reduce fish populations, completely eliminate fish species, and decrease biodiversity. By 1989, over 650 U.S. lakes, which once supported a variety of fish species, were now too acidic to support anything but acid-tolerant largemouth bass.[3]

The Damage of Acid Rain

Raising the acidity of lakes and other bodies of water is just one way in which acid rain affects the environment. Acid rain causes damage in a variety of other ways as well:[4]

▶ *Forest erosion:* Acid rain causes slower growth, and injury and death in a variety of trees, and it has been implicated in forest and soil degradation in many areas of the eastern United States, particularly in the high-elevation forests of the Appalachian Mountains from Maine to Georgia.[5]

---

[3] Interestingly, fishing may seem temporarily good in these acid-damaged lakes because the fish are starving (and therefore bite more!) as their food supply dies off.

[4] Acid rain information comes from the EPA's Web site at http://www.epa.gov.

[5] Acid rain does not usually kill trees directly. It is more likely to weaken trees by damaging their leaves, limiting the nutrients available to them, exposing them to toxic substances slowly released from the soil, and weakening their resistance against insects.

▶ *Damage to property:* Evaporation of acidic droplets from car surfaces causes irreparable damage to certain cars' paint jobs, forcing repainting to repair the problem, or requiring the use of acid-resistant paints. Acid rain also contributes to the corrosion of metals (such as bronze) and the deterioration of paint and stone (such as marble and limestone). In 1985, the government estimated the cost of acid rain–related damage to property at $5 billion per year.

▶ *Reduced visibility:* Sulfates and nitrates that form in the atmosphere make it hard for us to see as far or as clearly through the air. Sulfate particles account for 50 to 70% of the visibility reduction in the eastern part of the United States, a reduction that affects people's enjoyment of national parks such as the Shenandoah and the Great Smoky Mountains National Parks. Reductions in acid rain through the government programs described later in this chapter are expected to improve the visual range in the eastern United States by 30% in the long run.

▶ *Adverse health outcomes:* The harm to people from acid rain is not direct. Walking in acid rain, or even swimming in an acid lake, is no more dangerous than walking or swimming in clean water. However, the sulfur dioxide and nitrogen oxides that cause acid rain interact with the atmosphere to form fine particulates that can be inhaled deep into people's lungs. Fine particulates can also penetrate indoors. Many scientific studies have identified a relationship between elevated levels of fine particulates and increased illness and premature death from heart and lung disorders such as asthma and bronchitis. When fully implemented by the year 2010, the public health benefits of the Acid Rain Program are estimated to be valued at $50 billion annually, due to decreased mortality, hospital admissions, and emergency room visits.

History of Acid Rain Regulation

1970 Clean Air Act Landmark federal legislation that first regulated acid rain–causing emissions by setting maximum standards for atmospheric concentrations of various substances, including SO_2.

Regulation of the emissions that cause acid rain began with the **1970 Clean Air Act,** which set maximum standards for atmospheric concentrations of various substances, including SO_2. The act set New Source Performance Standards (NSPS) for any *new* coal-fired power plant, forcing any new plant to reduce emissions in one of two ways: either by switching to coal with a lower sulfur content, or by installing scrubbers, which are devices that remove a large portion of pollutants from the plant's exhaust fumes. In terms of the theory of government policy discussed in the previous chapter, the government chose a regulatory (quantity) approach over a tax (price) approach for dealing with this environmental problem.

Total emissions of SO_2 declined by the early 1980s, but some new concerns arose that motivated additional attention to the emissions issue. Most importantly, the vast majority of emissions came from older plants that were not subject to the NSPS. By mandating NSPS only for new plants, the 1970 act gave utilities great incentive to run older, dirtier plants for longer than policy makers had predicted (i.e., longer than the plants' natural "lifetimes"). Moreover, an additional requirement put in place in 1977 that all new plants have scrubbers increased the expense of building new plants and thus further encouraged the upkeep of older plants. These problems are excellent examples of the hazards of *partial policy reform*. By mandating regulations only for new plants, the government opened a major loophole in the law that encouraged firms to extend the use of outdated, more highly polluting older plants, thus undercutting the effectiveness of the law.

The 1990 Amendments and Emissions Trading In 1990, a series of amendments to the Clean Air Act were passed, most notably a regulation that mandated a reduction of more than 50% in the level of SO_2 emissions nationwide, and included all plants, even older ones. A key feature of the amendment was that it established an **SO_2 allowance system** that granted plants permits to emit SO_2 in limited quantities, based on their historical fuel utilization.[6] Plants were allowed to buy, sell, and save (for future years) these allowances. Plants that found it very costly to reduce emissions could try to purchase allowances from other plants that could more easily reduce emissions below their allowance level. The allowance market was supposed to increase the cost-effectiveness of the plan by encouraging utilities to exploit the differences in the cost of reducing emissions (something discussed theoretically in Chapter 5). Older plants, for which reductions were most expensive, could buy allowances from newer plants, for which reductions were cheaper. Heeding the advice of economists on the benefits of trading, the market for permits involved very few restrictions: trading could occur anywhere within the nation, no review or approval of trades was required, anyone (plants, brokerage firms, and so on) could trade, and the frequency and mechanism of trading were unlimited.

This amendment drew strong opposition from two different sources. On the one hand, the sizeable SO_2 restrictions were criticized on economic grounds by the utilities and coal miners, particularly those in eastern states whose coal supplies were high in sulfur content. An industry study in 1989 predicted the cost of fully implementing an acid rain program at $4.1 billion to $7.4 billion annually, with a loss of up to 4 million jobs.[7] On the other hand, the allowance and trading system was strongly criticized by environmentalists. Former Minnesota senator Eugene McCarthy likened the allowance system to the indulgences that church members could buy in the Middle Ages, which for a price forgave them their sins, calling this a "pollution absolution." McCarthy and other environmentalists opposed these amendments on the grounds that they were creating a "market for vice and virtue."[8]

> **SO_2 allowance system** The feature of the 1990 amendments to the Clean Air Act that granted plants permits to emit SO_2 in limited quantities and allowed them to trade those permits.

---

[6] For example, let's say Brian runs a power plant that in 1987 burned 10 billion Btus' (British thermal units, a measure of energy) worth of coal and emitted 15 tons of SO_2 into the atmosphere. This works out to an emissions rate of 3 pounds of SO_2 per million Btus, which means Brian runs a very dirty plant. Starting in 2000, each year the EPA would grant Brian only enough emission allowances to let him pollute as if his emissions rate in 1987 had been a much lower 1.2 pounds of SO_2 per million Btus. In this case, he would be given only six allowances, one for each ton he is now allowed to emit. Brian would thus have to reduce his emissions drastically (by 60%, from 15 to 6) or buy allowances from another power plant.

[7] Perciasepe (1999).

[8] McCarthy (1990).

ESTIMATING THE ADVERSE HEALTH EFFECTS OF PARTICULATES

The estimates of the health costs of particulates come from a large empirical literature on pollution and health outcomes. The typical approach taken in this literature is to relate adult mortality in a geographical area to the level of particulates in the air in that area. The results from this type of analysis are suspect, however, due to the key empirical problem highlighted in Chapter 3: the areas with more particulates may differ from areas with fewer particulates in many other ways, not just in the amount of particulates in the air. Imagine, for example, that researchers compared two areas, one with old plants that emit a lot of particulates, and one with newer plants that are much cleaner. If the researchers found higher mortality in the areas with the older dirty plants, they might attribute this to the effects of particulates on human health. Suppose, however, that older plants are also less safe places to work than newer plants. In this case, the higher mortality in areas with older plants might be due to workplace accidents, not pollution. It is difficult to observe valid treatment and control groups in a situation like this; you can't just compare dirty areas to cleaner ones because so many other things could differ between them, imparting bias to the estimates.

Chay and Greenstone (2003) addressed this problem in a recent study, using the regulatory changes induced by the Clean Air Act of 1970. This act applied differentially to different counties in the United States, based on whether they were above or below a mandated "attainment" of clean air levels. Counties with emissions above a mandated threshold (nonattainment counties) were subject to state regulation, while those with similar emissions, but that fell just below that threshold, were not. In the nonattainment counties, this regulation led to a very large reduction in emissions (measured as total suspended particulates, TSPs) as shown in Figure 6-1. This figure shows TSPs over time for counties above and below the mandated threshold. For areas with TSPs below the mandated threshold, there was only a slight reduction in TSPs over time, from just above 60 to just below 60 micrograms per cubic meter. For areas above the mandated threshold (those areas that were subject to this regulation), there was a very large reduction in emissions after the legislation became effective in 1971, from over 100 to 80 micrograms per cubic meter.

Applying a term we learned in Chapter 3, we have an excellent *quasi-experiment* here. The treatment group is those areas that were in nonattainment, for which TSPs fell dramatically. The control group is those areas that were in attainment, for which there was little change in TSPs. These groups were similar beforehand, and should be subject to similar changes over time *other* than the regulatory intervention. Thus, the only change in nonattainment areas relative to attainment areas is the intervention itself, so that any effect on health represents a causal impact of regulation. Chay and Greenstone make this comparison by examining a clear indicator of bad health, the *infant mortality rate* (the share of newborns who die before their first birthday). Infants can develop severe and potentially fatal respiratory problems from particulates in the air.

In fact, the costs of these regulations have been much lower than predicted due to the benefits of permit trading. Daniel Ellerman, an expert on acid rain regulations, estimates that the trading program lowered costs by more than half over the 1995–2007 period, from $35 billion to $15 billion.[9] A wider range of studies finds that the trading program has lowered estimated costs between 33% and 67%.[10]

The Clean Air Act amendments have shown that trading has worked, as economists suggested it would, to greatly improve the efficiency of regulation. Based on this success, trading regimes have gained in popularity in the environmental community in the United States and to a lesser extent around the world. Environmentalists have realized that more efficient regulation is in their

---

[9] Ellerman et al. (2000), Table 10.5.
[10] Ellerman et al. (2000), p. 296.

Chay and Greenstone's findings are striking: infant mortality declined substantially in areas with regulation-induced reductions in emissions, relative to areas where emissions were not mandated to fall. They found that each 10% decline in particulates leads to a 5% decline in the infant mortality rate. This estimate implies that 1,300 fewer infants died in 1972 as a result of the Clean Air Act of 1970, confirming in a much more convincing manner the high health costs of emissions and the benefits of regulation.

■ **FIGURE 6-1**

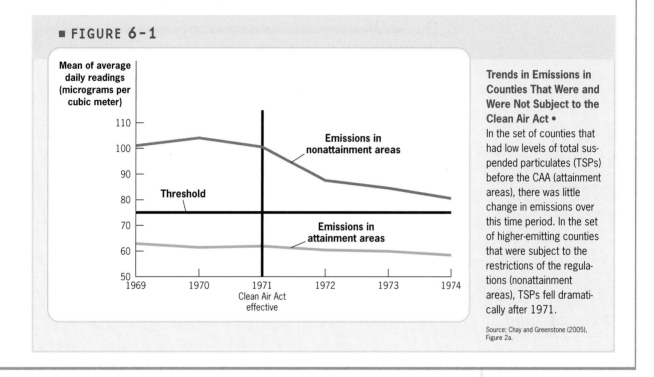

Trends in Emissions in Counties That Were and Were Not Subject to the Clean Air Act • In the set of counties that had low levels of total suspended particulates (TSPs) before the CAA (attainment areas), there was little change in emissions over this time period. In the set of higher-emitting counties that were subject to the restrictions of the regulations (nonattainment areas), TSPs fell dramatically after 1971.

Source: Chay and Greenstone (2005), Figure 2a.

interest as well, as it reduces the economic opposition to increased government regulation. According to Ellerman (2000, p. 4), "Most observers quickly judged the program to be a great success. . . . In less than a decade, emissions trading has gone from being a pariah among policy makers to being a star—everybody's favorite way to deal with pollution problems."

Has the Clean Air Act Been a Success?

Economists are best at laying out the costs and benefits of alternative interventions and leaving it to others to decide if those interventions can be called successful or not. Clearly, the Clean Air Act, particularly after the 1990 amendments, has a lot to recommend it. However, it is much harder to determine whether the net economic costs from this program are smaller than its benefits. The set of regulations imposed by this program were clearly costly: Greenstone (2002) estimates that in its first 15 years, the Clean Air Act cost almost 600,000 jobs and $75 billion in output in pollution-intensive industries. At the same time, these regulations were clearly beneficial in terms of lowering the costs of particulate emissions, particularly in terms of health improvements. The trick is to put all of these observations together into a definite conclusion. (We will discuss how economists approach this problem in Chapter 8.) In one attempt to reach such a conclusion, Burtraw et al. (1997) estimate that the health benefits alone from reducing emissions exceed by seven times the cost of reduction, once this lower-cost trading regime was in place.

6.2
Global Warming

The environmental externality that could potentially cause the most harm to humans is global warming. The earth is heated by solar radiation that passes through our atmosphere and warms the earth's surface. The earth radiates some of the heat back into space, but a large portion is trapped by certain gases in the earth's atmosphere, like carbon dioxide and methane, which reflect the heat back toward the earth again. This phenomenon is called the **greenhouse effect** because a greenhouse works by letting in sunlight and trapping the heat produced from that light. The greenhouse effect is essential to life: without it, the earth would be about 60 degrees cooler, and life as we know it would end.[11]

greenhouse effect The process by which gases in the earth's atmosphere reflect heat from the sun back to the earth.

The problem is that human activity has been increasing the atmospheric concentration of greenhouse gases such as carbon dioxide and methane, and thus the magnitude of the greenhouse effect has risen. Since the industrial revolution, for example, the amount of carbon dioxide in the atmosphere has increased by about a third, to 800 billion metric tons of carbon—its highest level in 400,000 years (amounts of carbon dioxide are measured by what the carbon alone would weigh if in solid form, sort of like a chunk of coal). Most of this carbon dioxide has come from the use of fossil fuels such as coal, oil, and natural gas. By our use of fossil fuels, humans have contributed to the warming of the earth's atmosphere as reflected in the increase of surface temperatures by more than 1 degree Fahrenheit over the past 30 years, the most rapid increase in at least 1,000 years (see Figure 5-1, p. 121). Global snow cover has declined by 10% since the 1960s, and global sea levels have risen by one-third to two-thirds of a foot over the last century.

"Gentlemen, it's time we gave some serious thought to the effects of global warming."

---

[11] Congressional Budget Office (2003a).

More worrisome are projections for the next century that temperatures will increase by as much as 6 to 10 degrees Fahrenheit, a rate without precedent in the last 10,000 years.[12] A temperature rise of 6 degrees would lower global GDP in 2100 by over 10%, with India, Africa, and Western Europe seeing reductions of more than 15%.[13] As noted in the previous chapter, the global sea level could rise by almost three feet, increasing risks of flooding and submersion of low-lying coastal areas. Perhaps the most vivid short-run illustration of the damages of global warming was the destruction of the Ward Hunt ice shelf. This ice shelf was 80 feet thick and three times the size of Boston, making it the largest ice shelf in the Arctic, but in the summer of 2003, it split into two large pieces and many small islands, an event labeled "unprecedented" by scientists. Unprecedented, but perhaps not surprising: temperatures have been rising by 1 degree Fahrenheit per decade in the Arctic, and the thickness of this ice shelf had decreased by half since 1980.[14]

Figure 6-2 shows how much carbon dioxide the most polluting nations emit annually by burning fossil fuels, the main source of greenhouse gas emissions. (In

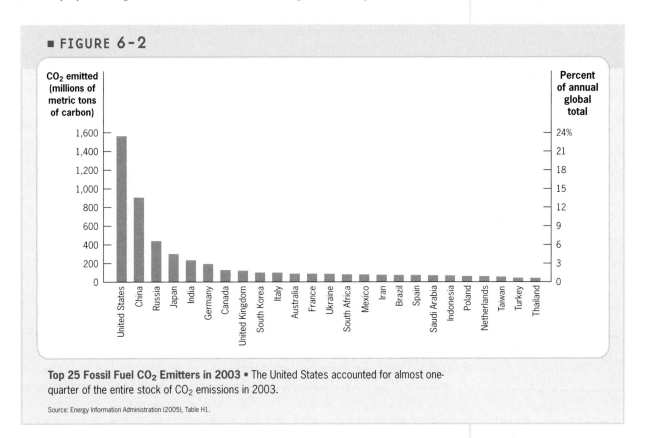

■ FIGURE 6-2

Top 25 Fossil Fuel CO$_2$ Emitters in 2003 • The United States accounted for almost one-quarter of the entire stock of CO$_2$ emissions in 2003.

Source: Energy Information Administration (2005), Table H1.

---

[12] International Panel on Climate Change (2001).
[13] Nordhaus and Boyer (2000), Figure 4.4. The damage to India and Africa will come through the impact of global warming on human health, as a number of tropical diseases will be able to spread beyond their current boundaries. India's agricultural output will also likely suffer significant harm, as increased monsoon activity reduces output. Western Europe's agriculture and quality of life will likely suffer from drastic cooling that will occur because of changing ocean currents due to global warming.
[14] Revkin (2003).

the United States today, for example, fossil fuels account for about 85% of all the energy used.) The United States is currently responsible for nearly 25% of the planet's annual carbon dioxide emissions from fossil fuels, while Japan contributes only 5% of annual emissions. Developing countries like China and India also emit large quantities of greenhouse gases, but this is a relatively recent phenomenon. If we add up such emissions over the course of the twentieth century, we find that although developed nations have only 20% of the world's population, they are responsible for 80% of the total greenhouse gas emissions from fossil fuels.

Despite this unequal role in producing emissions, global warming is truly a global problem. Carbon emissions in Boston and Bangkok have the same effect on the global environment. Moreover, it is the stock of carbon dioxide in the air, not the level of yearly emissions, that causes warming. Global warming is therefore not a problem that can be immediately solved by cutting back on carbon use. Even if all nations ended their use of all fossil fuels today, it would take centuries to undo the damage done by the industrialization of the developed world. Thus, global warming is a complicated externality that involves many nations and many generations of emitters.

The Kyoto Treaty

International conferences to address the problem of global warming began in 1988. The peak of activity was a 1997 meeting in Kyoto, Japan, which was attended by over 170 nations. At that meeting, after intense negotiation, the 38 industrialized nations agreed to begin to combat global warming by reducing their emissions of greenhouse gases to 5% below 1990 levels by the year 2010.[15] These goals were written into a treaty that has since been ratified by 35 of the 38 signatory countries, and that went into effect in early 2005. A notable omission from the ratification list is the United States, which has shown no interest in signing on to this level of emissions reduction. Given the growth in the U.S. economy since the Kyoto treaty was signed, a reduction to 7% below 1990 levels would imply reducing projected emissions in 2010 by roughly 30%.[16] Nordhaus and Boyer (2000, Table 8.6) estimate that achieving the Kyoto targets would imply a present discounted value cost to the United States of $1.1 trillion (more than twice what the government spends on its largest program, Social Security, each year). By these authors' estimates, the United States would bear over 90% of the total world cost of meeting the Kyoto targets, even though it contributes only 25% of annual greenhouse gas emissions. The United States' share of the costs is so high because its emissions are forecast to grow so rapidly, and because its emissions are very costly to reduce due to continued reliance on coal-fired power plants (as opposed to

---

[15] This is an average that reflects a compromise among that set of nations; the United States, for example, agreed to reduce to 7% below 1990 levels. Also, the deadline is not exactly 2010: emissions must be reduced to that level on average over the 2008 to 2012 period.

[16] Estimate from United Nations Environment Programme at http://www.grida.no.

the natural gas or nuclear-powered plants more frequently used in other nations such as Japan, which produce much lower levels of greenhouse gases).

Can Trading Make Kyoto More Cost-Effective?

The cost figures just presented are enormous, and one can understand the reluctance of the United States to enter such a potentially costly agreement. But these estimates ignore a key feature negotiated into the Kyoto treaty, largely at the behest of the United States: **international emissions trading.** Under the Kyoto treaty, the industrialized signatories are allowed to trade emissions rights among themselves, as long as the total emissions goals are met. That is, if the United States wanted to reduce its emissions to only 1990 levels, rather than to 7% below 1990 levels, it could do so by buying emissions permits from another nation and using them to cover the reduction shortfall.

This is an important aspect of the treaty because there are tremendous differences across developed nations in the costs of meeting these goals, for two reasons. First, there are large differences in the rate of growth since 1990: the lack of economic (and thus emissions) growth in the 1990s in Russia, for example, implies that it will not be very costly for Russia to return to 1990 emissions levels. Second, growth has been more "environmentally conscious" in some nations than in others, so economic growth has not been as much accompanied by emissions growth in nations such as Japan that use more gas and nuclear-powered production. Thus, much as with our two-firm example in Chapter 5, the total costs of emissions reductions can be reduced if we allow countries with low costs of reduction, such as Russia, to trade with countries with high costs of reduction, such as the United States. By some estimates, such trading could lower the global costs of reaching the Kyoto targets by 75%.[17]

This point is illustrated in Figure 6-3 on page 160. This figure shows the market for carbon reduction, with millions of metric tons of carbon reduction on the x axis. There is a fixed target of carbon reduction in the Kyoto treaty for the United States at 7% below 1990 levels, a reduction of 440 million metric tons. The total worldwide mandated reduction under Kyoto is 630 million metric tons, so that the rest of the world has to achieve a net reduction of 190 million metric tons.

With no trading, shown in panel (a), nations would have to meet this target from their own supply of reduction opportunities. The reduction opportunities in the United States are represented by the supply curve S^{US}. This curve slopes upward because initial reduction opportunities are low cost: for example, plants that are close to energy efficient can be fitted with relatively cheap changes to become energy efficient. Costs rise as reduction increases, however: additional reductions may require replacing energy-inefficient but perfectly functional plants with newer ones at great cost.

international emissions trading Under the Kyoto treaty, the industrialized signatories are allowed to trade emissions rights among themselves, as long as the total emissions goals are met.

---

[17] Nordhaus and Boyer (2000), Table 8.5.

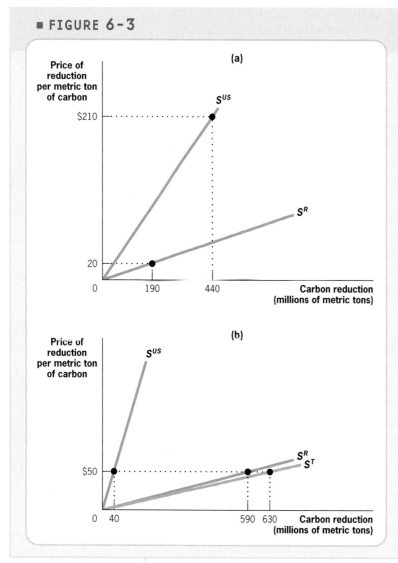

■ **FIGURE 6-3**

The Benefits of Trading • The supply curve of reductions for the United States (S^{US}) is much steeper than that for the rest of the world (S^R). If the United States has to do all of its reductions by itself (panel a), it costs $210 per ton of reduction. In that case, the United States reduces by 440 million metric tons (mmt) and the rest of the world reduces by 190 mmt. If the United States and other nations can trade (panel b), then the relevant supply curve is S^T. In that case, the price per ton falls to $50, with the rest of the world reducing by 590 mmt and the United States reducing by only 40 mmt.

In this no-trading world, the marginal cost of achieving the Kyoto target of a reduction of 440 million metric tons (as measured by the S^{US} curve) is $210 per metric ton of carbon. For ease, we combine the rest of the world into one group with reduction opportunities represented by S^R in panel (a) of Figure 6-3. The S^R curve lies far below S^{US}, indicating that these nations have much lower marginal cost reduction opportunities. For those nations to reduce by 190 million metric tons would cost them only $20 per metric ton of carbon.

Now suppose that the United States can buy permits from Russia and other nations. In panel (b) of Figure 6-3, we can measure the aggregate supply curve to the world market by horizontally summing the two supply curves S^R and S^{US} to obtain the aggregate supply curve S^T. The cost of the worldwide required level of reduction of 630 million metric tons is $50 per ton, given this supply curve. This means that, with international trading, any reductions that cost more than $50 per ton can be offset by purchasing permits instead. At that price, the United States would choose to reduce its own emissions by 40 million metric tons (since any additional reduction costs more than the $50 price per permit), and buy the remaining 400 from other nations. Other nations would reduce their emissions by 590 million metric tons, the 190 million required plus the 400 million sold to the United States. The total cost of meeting the Kyoto target worldwide would now have fallen substantially: instead of most of the reduction being done at high cost in the United States, it would now be done at low cost elsewhere.

That is, by distributing the reduction from the high-cost United States to the low-cost other nations, we have significantly lowered the price of reductions worldwide. Note that, even though the marginal cost of reduction in other nations has risen, this is because they have moved up their supply curve: these other nations are happy to supply that higher level of reduction at $50 per metric ton (they are deriving substantial producer surplus from that transaction since most of their reduction costs much less than $50 per ton). The importance that U.S. environmental negotiators placed on negotiating this trading regime shows the extent to which environmentalists in the United States have internalized the lessons from the Acid Rain Program about the benefits of allowing flexibility in meeting environmental targets.

Participation of Developing Countries The trading story does not end with the developed nations of the world, however: by the year 2030, developing nations will produce more than half of the world's emissions, with China and India leading the way.[18] As a result, an agreement that does not ultimately include developing nations is doomed to failure as a mechanism for addressing global warming.

Moreover, including developing nations in such a plan adds flexibility and lowers the costs of meeting emission reduction targets. The cost of reducing emissions in developing countries is an order of magnitude lower than in the developed world. This is because it is much cheaper to use fuel efficiently as you develop an industrial base than it is to "retrofit" an existing industrial base to use fuel efficiently. By some estimates, if we had an international trading system that included developing nations, the cost to the developed world of complying with the Kyoto treaty would fall by another factor of four.[19] That is, with both international trading *and* developing country participation, the costs of meeting the Kyoto targets would be only one-sixteenth of their costs without these "flexibilities."

The developing nations wanted no part of this argument at Kyoto, however. They pointed out, rightly, that the problem that the world faces today is the result of environmentally insensitive growth by the set of developed nations. Why, they ask, should they be forced to be environmentally conscious and clean up the mess that the United States and other nations have left behind? This conflict must be resolved for an effective solution to this global problem.

---

[18] Nordhaus and Boyer (2000), Figure 7.7.
[19] Nordhaus and Boyer (2000), Table 8.5.

Ultimately, obtaining the participation of developing nations will likely involve some significant international transfers of resources from the developed to the developing world as compensation.

What Does the Future Hold?

The Kyoto treaty of 1997 was the most significant effort made to address the global externality of greenhouse gas emissions. Developments since that time, in particular the decision of the United States to reject the Kyoto treaty, do not bode well for short-term agreement on how to combat the problem of global warming.. Does this mean that international cooperation to combat global warming is impossible? Recent evidence, reviewed in the application, suggests that the nations of the world can come together to combat a global environmental threat, but only when that threat is urgent.

An important question for future global warming debates is whether the international community should continue with Kyoto's quantity-based policy or move toward a price-based policy that would include internationally coordinated taxes on carbon usage, as advocated, for example, by Nordhaus (2006). The uncertainty model presented in Chapter 5 clearly suggests that taxation would dominate regulation (even with trading) in this context. This is because the benefits of emission reduction are related to the existing stock of greenhouse gases in the atmosphere, so that the marginal benefits of any given emission reduction are constant: given the enormous boulder that must be moved to stop global warming, each additional person pushing on the boulder has a fairly constant effect. On the other hand, the marginal costs of emissions reduction are both uncertain and not constant across nations; for some countries reduction is low cost, while for others its expensive. As we learned in Chapter 5, in such a situation (that is, one with uncertain and varying marginal costs, with flat marginal benefits) taxation dominates regulation, because regulation can lead to excessive deadweight loss when emissions reduction gets very expensive. Price and quantity approaches could even be combined in the future by pairing the quantity goals with a "safety valve" rule that allows countries to reduce their required emission reductions if the cost gets too high, so that there is a price ceiling on quantity restrictions.

▶ **APPLICATION**

The Montreal Protocol

An excellent example of international cooperation is the Montreal Protocol of 1987, which banned the use of chlorofluorocarbons (CFCs). CFCs were a popular chemical used in many facets of everyday life, including refrigerators, air conditioners, and spray cans. Their popularity partly derived from their very long life, but this longevity also led to a major environmental problem: CFCs were drifting into our stratosphere, and in the process of decaying were breaking down the ozone layer, which protects the earth from harmful UV-B radiation from the sun. As with global warming, this was a potentially enormous long-run problem: projections showed that, by 2050, ozone depletion would have reached 50–70% in the northern hemisphere, resulting in 19 million more cases of non-melanoma skin cancer, 1.5 million cases of melanoma cancer, and 130 million more cases of eye cataracts.[20]

Unlike global warming, the CFC problem was showing itself immediately and urgently: by the 1980s, a 25 million square kilometer hole had opened in the ozone layer over Antarctica! This hole spurred the international community to action, and in September 1987, the Montreal Protocol was adopted, aiming for complete phaseout of specified chemicals (mostly CFCs and halons) according to specified schedules. This agreement was ratified by 184 countries, and worldwide consumption of CFCs dropped from 1.1 million tons in 1986 to 64,112 tons in 2004.[21]

The result is that scientists predict the hole in the ozone layer will be biggest sometime in the next decade (as long-lived chemicals continue to diffuse upward into the stratosphere) but will then begin to recover and return to normal around 2050.

Thus, it may take some type of exciting and newsworthy event to spur action on global warming. The problem is that, unlike with CFCs, global warming will not be solved for centuries after emissions are greatly reduced. So if the world waits for a crisis to spur us into action, it may be too late. ◄

6.3

The Economics of Smoking

All externalities are not large-scale environmental problems. Some of the most important externalities are local and individualized. Many of these arise in the arena of personal health, and one of the most interesting is smoking.

Cigarette smoking is the single greatest self-imposed health hazard in the United States today. The number of cigarettes smoked has declined substantially over the past few decades, as shown in Figure 6-4 (page 164), yet almost one-fifth of Americans still smoke. This is despite the fact that smoking causes more than 438,000 deaths each year, *four times* as many as AIDS, motor vehicle accidents, homicide, and suicide combined. As Figure 6-5 (page 164) illustrates, smoking is the second-leading cause of death in the United States.[22] Worldwide, the problem is even worse. Of all persons alive today, 650 million will die of smoking-related disease. By 2020, 10 million persons will die annually from smoking-related disease. At that point, smoking will be the leading cause of death (not just preventable death) throughout the world.[23]

---

[20] United Nations Environment Programme (2003).
[21] United Nations Environment Programme (2006).
[22] Number of smoking-attributable deaths from Centers for Disease Control and Prevention (2005a); chart data from CDCP (2006b), Table C. In this chart, the share of deaths attributable to cancer, heart disease, and other illnesses excludes the share of illnesses that are smoking-related since those are included in the smoking category.
[23] World Health Organization. "Why Is Tobacco a Health Priority?" Accessed last on June 2, 2006, at http://www.who.int/tobacco/health_priority/en/index.html.

■ FIGURE 6-4

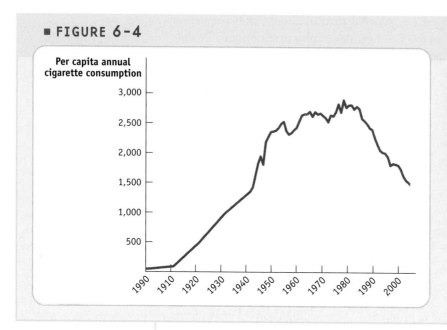

Per Capita Annual Cigarette Consumption, 1900–2004 • Cigarette consumption rose steadily throughout the first half of the twentieth century, flattened in the 1960s and 1970s, and began to decline sharply after 1980.

■ FIGURE 6-5

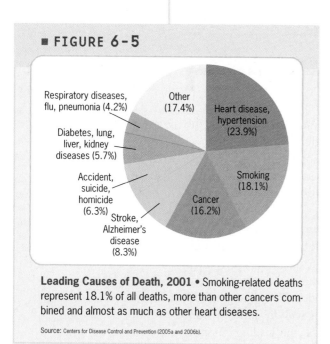

Leading Causes of Death, 2001 • Smoking-related deaths represent 18.1% of all deaths, more than other cancers combined and almost as much as other heart diseases.

Source: Centers for Disease Control and Prevention (2005a and 2006b).

Are these dire facts a cause for regulating smoking? Not in the view of traditional microeconomics. In the standard utility maximization model, any damage that individuals do to themselves from dangerous activities such as smoking results from a rational choice of trading off benefits against potential costs. The health hazards of smoking are now well known. The fact that smokers smoke given these risks, economists say, reveals their preference for the current pleasure of smoking over the distant costs of a shorter life.

Doesn't this argument ignore the fact that smoking is highly addictive? After all, leading experts on addiction rate nicotine as more addictive than either caffeine or marijuana, and in some cases, comparable to cocaine: among users of cocaine, about half say that the urge to smoke is as strong as the urge to use cocaine. Doesn't this mean that the damage that individuals do to themselves is a call to government action?

Once again, the answer from traditional economics is no. As postulated in a highly influential article by Becker and Murphy (1988), "rational addicts" understand that each cigarette they smoke today increases their addiction, leading them to smoke more tomorrow. As a result, when they buy a pack of cigarettes, they consider not only the cost of that pack but also the cost of all additional future packs that will now be purchased because their addiction has deepened. Moreover, the smoker understands that lighting up doesn't just

■ **TABLE 6-1**

The Effects of Smoking: Externalities or Not?

Effect	Not an externality if . . .	An externality if . . .
Increased health care costs	Insurance companies actuarially raise premiums for smokers.	Many individuals are insured by entities that spread the health costs of smokers among all of the insured; also, the health costs of the uninsured are passed on to others.
Less-productive workers	Employers adjust individuals' wages according to productivity.	Employers do not adjust wages according to individual productivity, so that they must lower wages for all workers to offset productivity loss.
Increased number of fires	Smokers set fire only to their own property, requiring no help from the fire department, and insurance companies adjust premiums according to smoking status.	The fires damage nonsmokers' property, raise the cost of the local fire department, or raise fire insurance premiums for all.
Earlier deaths	Smokers do not pay Social Security taxes or would not incur medical costs later in life.	Nonsmokers save money because smokers die too early to collect full Social Security benefits and because their deaths reduce the high health costs near the end of life (a positive externality).
Secondhand smoke effects	The effects are minimal or smokers account for their families' utility when deciding to smoke.	The effects are serious and smokers do not account for their families' utility when deciding to smoke.

Cigarette smoking has a number of physical and financial effects, but in many cases they may not be externalities. The first column of this table lists examples of the effects of smoking. The second column discusses the situations under which these are not externalities, and the third column discusses the situations under which they are externalities.

reduce health through the current cigarette but through all the future cigarettes that will be consumed as a result of that addiction. If the smoker consumes the cigarette anyway, then this is a rational choice, and does not call for government intervention.

The Externalities of Smoking

The key public finance implication of the traditional economics approach is that the appropriate role for government is *solely a function of the externalities that smokers impose on others*. Like all other consumption decisions, smoking is governed by rational choice. That smokers impose enormous costs on themselves is irrelevant to public finance; only the costs smokers impose on others call for government action. Measuring the externalities from smoking is complicated, however, as we discuss next (and summarize in Table 6-1).

Increased Health Costs from Smoking By one estimate, smoking-related disease increases U.S. medical care costs by $75.5 billion, about 8% of the total cost of health care in the United States.[24] This enormous number alone does not, however, justify government intervention. Suppose that all individuals in society had health insurance that they purchased on their own, and that the

---

[24] American Cancer Society (2006).

actuarial adjustments
Changes to insurance premiums that insurance companies make in order to compensate for expected expense differences.

price of that health insurance was set by insurance companies as a function of smoking status. Insurance companies would compute the extra amount they expect to spend on the medical care of smokers, and charge smokers a higher premium to compensate the insurance company for those extra costs. Such increases in insurance prices to compensate for expected expense differences are called **actuarial adjustments.** Actuarial adjustments *internalize the medical cost externality* from smoking. In this simplified model, there are no health externalities because smokers pay for the high medical costs associated with smoking through actuarial adjustments: society (in this case, the insurance companies) is fully compensated for the extra costs due to smoking through these higher premiums.

The external effects of increased health costs due to smoking arise because the real world deviates from this simplified example in three ways. First, insurance is not always actuarially adjusted for smoking behavior. At MIT, the price I pay for my group insurance is independent of my smoking behavior. If I smoke, and have high medical costs, then the insurance company will have to raise the premiums it charges to everyone at MIT by a small amount to compensate for this loss. In this case, I have exerted a negative externality on my coworkers, which I do not internalize because I do not fully pay the higher premiums associated with my smoking.

Quick Hint Externalities can be *financial* as well as *physical*. My smoking creates an externality because the social marginal benefit of my consumption of cigarettes is below my private marginal benefit by the extra amount that my coworkers have to pay for insurance.

Second, individuals who receive their insurance from the government do not pay higher premiums if they smoke. In this case, the negative externality occurs because the medical costs incurred by smokers are borne by all citizens through higher taxation. Finally, some individuals are uninsured and will not pay the cost of their medical care. Medical providers will typically make up these costs by increasing the amount they charge to other medical payers, exerting a negative financial externality on those payers.

Workplace Productivity There are many reasons why smokers may be less productive in the workplace: they may require more sick leave or more frequent breaks (for smoking) when at work. One study found that smokers impose $600–$1,100 per year in productivity and absenteeism costs on businesses, and another found that smokers miss 50% more work days each year due to illness than do nonsmokers.[25] Is this a negative externality to the firm? Once again, the answer is a qualified maybe. In this case, it depends on whether these workers' wages adjust to compensate for their lower expected productivity. That is, actuarial adjustments aren't necessarily found only in

---

[25] See Manning et al. (1991), Table 4-11 for absenteeism statistics and p. 139 for a literature review on cost estimates.

insurance markets; they may exist in labor markets as well. If wages fall to compensate the firm for a smoker's lower productivity, then the firm can internalize the productivity externalities associated with smoking. If not, these externalities will not be internalized.

Fires Smokers are much more likely to start fires than nonsmokers, mostly due to falling asleep with burning cigarettes. In 2000, for example, fires started by smokers caused 30,000 deaths and $27 billion in property damage worldwide.[26] Does this death and destruction represent an externality? If a smoker lived by himself on a mountain and burned down his house, killing himself, but with no damage to any other person, flora, or fauna, then there is no externality. But, in reality, externalities from such fires abound. There is the cost of the fire department that combats the fire; the damage that the fire may do to the property of others; and the increased fire insurance premiums that everyone must pay unless there is appropriate actuarial adjustment in the fire insurance market for smoking.

The "Death Benefit" An interesting twist on the measurement of smoking externalities is presented by the *positive* externalities for the taxpayer by the early deaths of smokers. Consider, for example, the Social Security program, which collects payroll tax payments from workers until they retire, and then pays benefits from that date until an individual dies. Smokers typically die around retirement age, so that they do not collect the retirement benefits to which their tax payments entitled them. In this situation, smokers are exerting a *positive financial externality* on nonsmokers: smokers pay taxes to finance the retirement benefits but do not live long enough to collect their benefits, leaving the government more money to pay benefits for nonsmokers. Thus, through the existence of the Social Security program, smokers benefit nonsmokers by *dying earlier.*

Moreover, the fact that smokers die earlier also offsets many of the medical cost effects of smoking. If smokers die at 65, then they won't impose large nursing home and other medical costs at very advanced ages. These avoided medical costs offset much of the additional medical costs from treatment for cancers and heart disease at younger ages.

Externality Estimates The effects of these four components, along with some other minor negative externalities, make the estimate of the external costs of smoking roughly $0.43 per pack in 2005 dollars.[27] This figure is sensitive to many factors, most importantly how one takes into account that the costs are often in the distant future while the benefits of smoking are current. Nevertheless, by most estimates the external cost of smoking is well below the average federal plus state cigarette tax in the United States, which is over $1 per pack. Of course, these estimates leave out another externality that is potentially important but very difficult to quantify: **secondhand smoke.**

secondhand smoke Tobacco smoke inhaled by individuals in the vicinity of smokers.

---

[26] Leistikow, Martin, and Milano (2000).
[27] Gruber (2001).

What About Secondhand Smoke? The damage done to nonsmokers by breathing in secondhand cigarette smoke is a classic externality because individuals do not hold property rights to the air. Without clearly defined property rights, complete Coasian solutions to this problem are not available. Yet the costs of secondhand smoke are not easily added to the list of external costs we have noted for two reasons. First, there is considerable medical uncertainty about the damage done by secondhand smoke. As a result, estimates of the externalities from secondhand smoke vary from $0.01 to $1.16 per pack![28]

Second, most of the damage from secondhand smoke is delivered to the spouses and children of smokers. If a smoking mother includes the utility of her family members in her utility function (maximizing *family* rather than just *individual* utility), she will take into account the damage she does to her husband and children by smoking. In this case, in making her choice to smoke, the smoker has decided that the benefits to her from smoking exceed the health costs both to herself *and* to her family members. When the externality is internalized in this way, the cost to other family members from being made ill must be offset by the large benefit the mother receives from smoking—or else she wouldn't smoke. On the other hand, if the smoking mother fails to fully account for the costs to her family members (fails to maximize family utility), then some of the damage she does to others will not be internalized, and should be counted in the externality calculation. Existing evidence suggests that family utility maximization is in fact incomplete, so these secondhand smoke costs are to some extent externalities.[29]

Should We Care Only About Externalities, or Do "Internalities" Matter Also?

The traditional economics approach suggests that the only motivation for government intervention in the smoking decision is the externalities that smokers impose on others, since any damage that smokers do to themselves has been accounted for in the smoking decision. But this model ignores some key features of the smoking decision that suggest that there may be other rationales for government intervention. Two such features are particularly important: the decision by youths to smoke and the inability of adults to quit. After reviewing these features, we will turn to how they challenge the traditional view of cigarette taxes based solely on externalities by suggesting that self-inflicted smoking damage matters for government policy as well.

Youth Smoking Of all adults who smoke, more than 75% begin smoking before their nineteenth birthday, but economics does not yet have a satisfactory model of the behavior of teenagers (as a matter of fact, neither do parents!).[30]

---

[28] Viscusi (1995), Table 11.

[29] See Lundberg, Pollack, and Wales (1997) for striking evidence against family utility maximization. This article shows that, in contrast to the family utility maximization model (where everyone cares equally about all the family members), shifting the control of household financial resources from husbands to wives significantly increases the expenditures made on behalf of children.

[30] In this section on internalities, all smoking facts come from Gruber (2001a) unless otherwise noted. For a broader analysis of the economics of risky behavior among youth, see Gruber (2001b).

The traditional model of smoking presumes that the decision to initiate this addictive behavior is made with a fully rational trade-off in mind between current benefits and future costs. If teens who begin to smoke do not correctly and rationally evaluate this trade-off, then government policy makers might care about the effect of the smoking decision on smokers themselves.

Indeed, there is some evidence that this monumental decision may not be made in the forward-looking fashion required by rational addiction models. A survey asked high school seniors who smoked a pack a day or more whether they would be smoking in five years and then followed the seniors up five years later. Among those who had said they would be smoking in five years, the smoking rate was 72%—but among those who said they would *not* be smoking in five years, the smoking rate was 74%! This result suggests that teens who smoke may not account for the long-run implications of addiction.

Adults Are Unable to Quit Smoking Even if They Have a Desire to Do So

Another key fact about smoking is that many adults who smoke would like to quit but are unable to do so. Consider the following facts:

▶ Eight in ten smokers in America express a desire to quit the habit, but many fewer than that actually do quit.

▶ According to one study, over 80% of smokers try to quit in a typical year, and the average smoker tries to quit every eight and a half months.

▶ 54% of serious quit attempts fail within one week.

These facts are worrisome because they hint that smokers may face a **self-control problem,** an inability to carry out optimal strategies for consumption. Economic theory assumes that individuals *can not only optimize their utility function, but that they can then carry out those optimal plans*. There is much evidence from psychology, however, that contradicts this assumption: individuals are often unable to carry out long-term plans that involve self-control when there are short-term costs to doing so. An excellent example of this is smoking, where there is a short-term cost of quitting (in terms of physical discomfort and perhaps mental distress), but a long-term health benefit. Other examples include retirement savings (short-term cost in terms of forgone consumption today, but long-term benefits in terms of a higher standard of living in retirement), or whether to diet and/or exercise (short-term costs in terms of less food or more work today, but long-term benefits in terms of a longer life). In many arenas, individuals appear unable to control their short-term desires for their own longer-term well-being.

There are two types of evidence for the existence of self-control problems. The first is from laboratory experiments in psychology. In laboratory settings, individuals consistently reveal that they are willing to be patient in the future, but are impatient today, the defining characteristics of self-control problems. A person with self-control problems has the right long-run intentions (he rationally optimizes his utility function given his budget constraint), but he just can't carry them out. For example, in one experiment, most people preferred a check for $100 they could cash today over a check for $200 they could cash two years from now. Yet the same people prefer a $200 check eight years from now to a $100 check six years from now, even though this is the

self-control problem An inability to carry out optimal strategies for consumption.

commitment devices Devices that help individuals who are aware of their self-control problems fight their bad tendencies.

same choice—it's just six years in the future.[31] This is consistent with self-control problems: individuals are willing to be patient in the future, but not today when faced with the same choice.

The second type of evidence for self-control problems is the demand for **commitment devices.** If individuals have self-control problems and are aware of those problems, they will demand some type of device that helps them fight these problems. And the search for such commitment devices is the hallmark of most recommended strategies for quitting smoking: people regularly set up systems to refrain from smoking by betting with others, telling others about the decision, and otherwise making it embarrassing to smoke. These practices help individuals combat their self-control problems by raising the short-run costs of smoking to offset the short-run benefits of smoking. The use of self-control devices is widespread in other arenas as well: individuals set up "Christmas Clubs" at their banks to make sure they have enough money to buy Christmas presents, and they buy memberships at sports clubs to commit themselves to work out when it would generally be cheaper to just pay each time they go.[32]

Implications for Government Policy Both irrationalities among youth smokers and self-control problems among older smokers seem to be sensible features of any model of the smoking decision: we all know (or were) irrational youth, and we all know (or are) individuals with problems of self-control. Yet, these sensible psychological additions to the standard economic model have dramatic implications for government policy, because in either case it is not just the external damage from smoking that matters for government intervention, but also some of the damage that smokers do to themselves. If smokers make mistakes when they are young, or would like to quit but cannot, the damage from smoking is an **internality,** which refers to the damage one does to oneself through adverse health (or other) behavior. This internality justifies government regulation of smoking in the same way that externalities do in the traditional model. The government is once again addressing a failure; in this case it is not an externality on others but rather a cost imposed on one's long-run health by one's short-run impatience or teen irrationality. If the government can make individuals better off in the long run by addressing short-run failings, then it can increase efficiency as if it were correcting a market failure.

internality The damage one does to oneself through adverse health (or other) behavior.

The stakes are large here. While the damage that smokers do to others is, on net, small, the damage that smokers do to *themselves* is enormous. Consider just one aspect of that damage: shortened lives. The average smoker is estimated to live about six fewer years than nonsmokers. A year of life is typically valued by economists at about $200,000 (using methods discussed in more detail in Chapter 8). At this estimate, the value of life lost from smoking is about $35 per pack! This is an enormous figure, on the order of 100 times larger than the typical estimate of the external damage done by smoking.

---

[31] Ainslie and Haslam (1992).
[32] DellaVigna and Malmendier (2004).

The government has several policy tools at its disposal for addressing internalities. One tool is information about the health hazards of smoking. Much of the large decline in smoking over the past 30 years has been traced to the release of information about the dangerous health implications of smoking. Information about long-run health effects will not, however, effectively combat problems of self-control or teen irrationality.[33]

An excellent commitment device available to the government is taxation, which raises the price of cigarettes to smokers. A large body of evidence shows that smokers are fairly sensitive to the price of cigarettes, with smoking falling by about 5% for each 10% rise in prices (and by even more among especially price-sensitive youth smokers). By raising taxes, the government can force smokers to face higher costs that lower their smoking, providing the desired self-control.[34] Gruber and Koszegi (2004) calculate that, for the type of self-control problems documented in laboratory experiments, the optimal tax would be on the order of $5 to $10 per pack, above and beyond any taxes imposed to combat externalities. This is a high level that is well above taxation rates today.

The notion that government policy should be determined not just by externalities but by internalities as well is a major departure from traditional microeconomic policy analysis. As such, much more research is needed to decide how large internalities really are. Nevertheless, the enormous health costs of smoking ($35 per pack) suggest that, even if such internalities are small, they might justify large government interventions.

6.4

The Economics of Other Addictive Behaviors

While cigarette smoking is a particularly interesting application, it is by no means the only health behavior where externalities (or internalities) potentially cause market failure. We briefly consider three others.

Drinking

Alcohol consumption presents an interesting alternative example to cigarette smoking. On the one hand, the externalities associated with alcohol consumption are much larger than those associated with smoking. This is largely because the major externality associated with alcohol consumption is damage due to drunk driving. Over 17,000 persons per year are killed, and half a million more are injured due to alcohol-related automobile accidents in the

---

[33] My child's school has recognized the ineffectiveness of warning youths about the very-long-run risks of smoking. His recent antismoking bookmark had ten reasons not to smoke, and only one was long-term health risks; the other nine were short-term costs such as higher likelihood of acne or worse sports performance. These are clearly less important than early death from a long-run perspective, but the bookmark serves the purpose of making youths realize short-run costs that offset the short-run benefits of smoking.

[34] Indeed, Hersch (2005) finds that smokers who plan to quit smoking are much more supportive of regulations on smoking than are other smokers.

United States.[35] Economists assess the years of life lost from these accidents at a very high value (on the order of $120 billion per year). Even though the drunk driver may lose his license and see his insurance premiums rise, he is unlikely to bear the full costs to society of his action. The central estimate for the externalities due to drinking are 80¢ per ounce of ethanol (pure alcohol), which is much higher than current alcohol taxes that amount to only 9 to 24¢ per ounce of ethanol, depending on the type of drink (since taxes per ounce of ethanol vary across beer, wine, and other alcoholic drinks).[36]

These figures do not include another potentially important externality from drinking: the increased tendency toward violence and crime. Twenty-five percent of violent crimes, and 40% of domestic abuse cases, involve victims who report that the perpetrator had been drinking before committing the crime.[37] A series of articles by Sara Markowitz and colleagues document strong effects of anti-alcohol policies (such as higher taxes on alcohol) in lowering violence, crime, risky sexual behavior, and sexually transmitted diseases.[38] Once again, if this behavior only involves family members, it may or may not be an externality; when it involves others, such as through criminal acts, the behavior is clearly an externality.

The internalities due to drinking may be much smaller than those due to smoking, however. Drinking in small quantities, while it may impair one's driving, may actually be good for long-run health. And it is only a small share of drinkers who do damage to their health and otherwise harm themselves by drinking. Thus, the major rationale for government regulation of drinking is the standard one, from externalities.

The appropriate role for government in regulating drinking is difficult because the externalities due to drinking arise from the small share of drinking that results in drunk driving and violence. In theory, the optimal policy would target drunk driving and violence with steeper fines and penalties. But it is impossible to realistically raise the cost of drunk driving or violence enough to account for the externalities of that activity. At the other extreme, raising taxes on all alcohol consumption is a very blunt instrument that will lower drinking too much among those who aren't going to drive drunk or commit violent acts, and not enough among those who are at risk for driving drunk or alcohol-related violence. Nevertheless, given the enormous damage done by drinking, higher alcohol taxes would raise social welfare overall, relative to a system that leaves taxes at a level so far below the externalities of drinking.

Illicit Drugs

Another addictive behavior that raises government concern is the use of illicit drugs, such as marijuana, cocaine, ecstasy, and heroin. In the United States, as in most countries, the government regulates these activities by prohibiting

---

[35] National Highway Traffic Safety Administration (2005).
[36] Manning et al. (1989).
[37] U.S. Department of Justice (1998).
[38] See for example Markowitz and Grossman (1999), Markowitz (2000a, b), Grossman, Kaestner, and Markowitz (2004), and Markowitz, Kaestner, and Grossman (2005).

illicit drug consumption, subject to criminal penalty. This is a particularly interesting case because most of the externalities associated with illicit drugs arise *because* of their illegality. Indeed, legal consumption of some illicit drugs is likely to have much lower externalities than consumption of alcohol. Thus, the rational addiction model would suggest that there is no more call for regulating illicit drug use than for regulating smoking. As the famous economist Milton Friedman wrote in 1972, in advocating the legalization of drugs, "The harm to us from the addiction of others arises almost wholly from the fact that drugs are illegal. A recent committee of the American Bar Association estimated that addicts commit one-third to one-half of all street crime in the U.S. Legalize drugs, and street crime would drop dramatically."[39]

Yet, despite this argument, drug legalization remains a radical idea in America and in most nations. Thus, policy makers clearly don't believe that the rational addiction model applies equally to illicit drugs and other potentially addictive activities such as drinking and smoking. For illicit drugs, but not for smoking and drinking, the government appears to have concluded that individuals are not making the right long-term decisions for themselves—otherwise it is difficult to rationalize the public policies pursued in most industrialized nations.

Obesity

A potential health externality that has recently attracted significant attention in the United States and elsewhere is obesity. There has been an enormous rise in obesity in the United States: the share of the adult population classified as obese has risen from 13% in 1960 to 31% in 2002. Indeed, the fastest-growing public health problem in the U.S. today is *diabetes*, a disease whereby the body is not able to regulate its glucose (sugar) intake. Diabetes is a progressive and often fatal disease with no known cure. It can attack every organ in the body, resulting in higher risk of heart failure, stroke, and poor circulation, which can lead to amputation. The number of diabetics has doubled in the past decade, and it is projected that one in three children born in 2000 will have diabetes. The two biggest factors driving the rise in diabetes are the rise in obesity and inactive lifestyles in the U.S.

Recent studies have suggested that both the external costs of obesity (in terms of government health costs) and the internal costs of obesity (in terms of shortened lives and lower quality years of life) may exceed those of either cigarettes or alcohol.[40] Thus, under either traditional models or models that take into account self-control problems, there may be a large role for the government in addressing this problem.

Using tax policy to reduce obesity in the United States, however, is a very complicated task, because there is a very complicated relationship between different types of food consumption and health. As Rosin (1998) writes, "Measuring fat content is not always practical. Hamburger meat has a certain

---

[39] Friedman (1972).
[40] Centers for Disease Control and Prevention (2005b), Table 73.

percentage of fat, but most of it would melt away during grilling. And what about sugary no-fat snacks such as soda and candy?" This complicated relationship suggests that the most straightforward approach to addressing the costs of obesity would be to directly tax body weight (a "fat tax"), or to perhaps subsidize weight loss (a "skinny subsidy")!

Summary

In summary, regulating other health behaviors raises many similar issues to those we raised for smoking. For drinking and obesity, however, existing taxes are already so far below the level of negative externalities that assessing the role of self-control problems and internalities is not critical: virtually any economic model would imply that if these externality calculations are correct, taxes should be higher. Yet there are difficult issues in raising taxes in both cases, ranging from the fact that a moderate amount of consumption may actually be good for people (clearly so in the case of food!) to the fact that it is difficult to appropriately design taxes to target the externality.

6.5

Conclusion

This chapter has shown that the externality theory developed in Chapter 5 has many interesting and relevant applications. Public finance provides tools to help us think through the regulation of regional externalities such as acid rain, global externalities such as global warming, and even the "internalities" of smoking. Careful analysis of public policy options requires discriminating truly external costs from costs that are absorbed through the market mechanism, understanding the benefits and costs of alternative regulatory mechanisms to address externalities, and considering whether only externalities or also "internalities" should count in regulatory decisions.

▶ HIGHLIGHTS

- Acid rain is a clear negative externality exerted primarily by power plants on wildlife, trees, structures, and (through associated particulate emissions) human health.

- The original Clean Air Act significantly (but inefficiently) reduced the amount of particulates in the air (and thus reduced acid rain). Regulation became much more efficient with the trading regime imposed by the 1990 amendments to the act.

- Global warming is a difficult problem because the effects are truly global and very long lasting.

- The Kyoto treaty would be costly (for the United States) first step in addressing global warming, but

trading and developing country participation could lower costs significantly.

- The net external costs of smoking are fairly low, suggesting a limited government role under the traditional model. Alternative models where consumers have self-control problems suggest that the government role may be larger.

- Other activities such as alcohol consumption and obesity have much larger externalities, but it is difficult to design regulatory mechanisms to target the exact source of the externality (drunk driving and fat consumption, respectively).

▶ QUESTIONS AND PROBLEMS

1. Some people were concerned that the 1990 amendments to the Clean Air Act would generate "hot spots" of pollution—localized areas with very high concentrations of pollutants. Why might the amendments lead to such "hot spots"? Are these "hot spots" necessarily a bad thing from an overall social welfare perspective? Explain.

2. The National Institute on Drug Abuse describes six-year trends in teenage smoking, drinking, and other drug use on the Web at http://www.nida.nih.gov/infofax/hsyouthtrends.html.   According to this site, for which age groups have the changes in the rates of teenage smoking and drinking been most pronounced?

3. Think about the major ways in which acid rain causes damage, such as through forest erosion, property damage, reduced visibility, and adverse health outcomes. Which of these costs are highly localized and which are borne by society more broadly? Explain.

4. Many towns and cities in the northeast and west coasts have recently passed bans on smoking in restaurants and bars. What is the economic rationale behind these bans? Would there be similar rationales for banning smoking in automobiles? Apartment buildings? Houses?

5. Think about the concerns about the original 1970 Clean Air Act described in the text. To what degree did the 1990 amendments to the act address these concerns? Explain your answer.

6. In which way could smoking exert a *positive* externality on others?

7. Some observers argue that since carbon dioxide and temperature levels have been much higher in Earth's history than they are today, the current concerns about the human contribution to global warming are overblown. How would you empirically test this argument?

8. Nordhaus and Boyer (2000) estimated that the United States would bear over 90% of the total world cost of achieving the Kyoto targets for greenhouse gas emission reductions. Explain how this can be when the U.S. produces only about a quarter of the world's greenhouse gasses.

9. Evans, Farrelly, and Montgomery (1999) found evidence that workplace smoking bans substantially reduce overall rates of smoking, particularly for those people with longer work weeks. Why should workplace smoking bans be particularly influential in affecting the behavior of people who work long hours?

10. Congressman Snitch argues that since obesity causes so many serious health problems, fatty foods should be regulated. Do you agree with him?

The e icon indicates a question that requires students to apply the empirical economics principles discussed in Chapter 3 and the Empirical Evidence boxes.

▶ ADVANCED QUESTIONS

11. Why does Chay and Greenstone's (2003) approach to measuring the effects of acid rain reduce the identification problems associated with more "traditional" approaches?

12. Imagine that it is 1970, and your parents are in college, debating the merits of the Clean Air Act of 1970. Your father supports the act, but your mother says that since it only covers new plants, it might actually make the air dirtier.

    a. What does your mother mean by her argument?

    b. How would you construct an empirical test to distinguish between your parents' hypotheses?

13. Caffeine is a highly addictive drug found in coffee, tea, and some soda. Unlike cigarettes, however, there have been very few calls to tax it, to regulate its consumption, or limit its use in public places. Why the difference? Can you think of any economic arguments for regulating (or taxing) its use?

14. When Wisconsin had lower drinking ages than its neighboring states, it experienced higher levels of alcohol-related crashes in its border counties than in other counties in its interior. What does this finding imply for the spillover effects of the policies of one state (or country) on other jurisdictions?

15. In Becker and Murphy's "rational addicts" model, smokers are perfectly aware of the potential for smoking to cause addiction, and they take this into account when deciding whether or not to smoke. Suppose a new technology—such as a nicotine patch—is invented that makes quitting smoking much easier (less costly) for an addict. If Becker and Murphy's model is correct, what effects would you expect this invention to have on people's smoking behavior? Would your answer be different for young people than for older people?

Public Goods

7

The city of Dhaka, Bangladesh, has a garbage problem. Every few days, residents of the various Dhaka neighborhoods bring their trash to large dumpsters in central areas or smaller dumpsters along their local streets. In theory, municipal employees then collect the garbage and cart it off for disposal. In practice, however, those employees often fail to show up, leaving the garbage to rot in the streets and residents to fume in frustration.

An economist might wonder why the residents of Dhaka don't simply scrap the current system of public trash collection and instead pay a private service to pick up their trash. In this way, the free market might solve Dhaka's problems. The trouble is that private trash collection, financed by a voluntary fee paid by neighborhood residents, faces the classic *free rider problem* introduced in Chapter 5: any resident could continue to throw his trash in the dumpsters, and then refuse to pay his share of the trash collection fee, with the hope that his neighbors would pick up the costs for him. If his neighbors cover the cost of collection, this free rider gets all the benefits of trash collection but pays none of the costs. Yet, if some in the neighborhood free ride, others will feel exploited by paying to have their non-paying neighbors' trash picked up; these residents might decide not to pay either. Eventually, the number of free riders might grow large enough that the town would not be able to raise sufficient funds to finance the trash collection from a private company. For this reason, only about 50 of Dhaka's 1,100 neighborhoods have been able to replace the municipal trash collection with private collection financed by voluntary trash collection fees.[1]

The problems faced by the city of Dhaka illustrate the difficulties of effectively addressing the free rider problem through a private mechanism. Goods that suffer from this free rider problem are known in economics as *public goods,* and they are the focus of this chapter. We begin by defining *public goods* and determining the optimal level of their provision. We then turn to the first

---

[1] Pargal et al. (2000).

■ **TABLE 7-1**

Defining Pure and Impure Public Goods

		Is the good rival in consumption?	
		Yes	No
Is the good excludable?	Yes	Private good (ice cream)	Impure public good (cable TV)
	No	Impure public good (crowded city sidewalk)	Pure public good (national defense)

Whether a good is private or public depends on whether it is rival and excludable. Pure private goods such as ice cream are both rival and excludable. Pure public goods such as national defense are neither rival nor excludable. Goods that are rival but not excludable, and vice versa, are impure public goods.

question of public finance and ask if the government should be involved in the provision of public goods. We show that the private sector is in fact likely to underprovide public goods due to the free rider problem. Sometimes, however, private actors successfully provide public goods, so we discuss the factors that make private provision successful.

We then discuss the public provision of public goods. In principle, the government can simply compute the optimal amount of a public good to provide, and provide that level. In practice, however, the government faces several difficulties in providing the optimal level of public goods. First, when private parties are already providing the public good, government provision may simply *crowd out* this private provision so that the total amount of the public good provided does not rise. Second, measuring the actual costs and benefits of public goods (which is required for determining optimal public goods provision) is difficult. Finally, determining the public's true preferences for public goods, and aggregating those preferences into an overall decision on whether to pursue public goods projects, raises a variety of challenges.

This chapter begins our section on public goods provision. Chapters 8 and 9 provide details on the problems of measuring the costs and benefits of public projects (*cost-benefit analysis*), and on the difficulties of effectively translating voters' preferences for public projects into public policy (*political economy*). Chapter 10 discusses the local provision of public goods and raises the important question of whether competition across localities can solve the public goods provision problems raised in Chapters 7–9. Finally, Chapter 11 focuses on one of the most important public goods provided in the United States: education.

pure public goods Goods that are perfectly non-rival in consumption and are non-excludable.

non-rival in consumption One individual's consumption of a good does not affect another's opportunity to consume the good.

non-excludable Individuals cannot deny each other the opportunity to consume a good.

impure public goods Goods that satisfy the two public good conditions (non-rival in consumption and non-excludable) to some extent, but not fully.

7.1

Optimal Provision of Public Goods

Goods that are **pure public goods** are characterized by two traits. First, they are **non-rival in consumption:** that is, my consuming or making use of the good does not in any way affect your opportunity to consume the good. Second, they are **non-excludable:** even if I want to deny you the opportunity to consume or access the public good, there is no way I can do so. These are fairly strong conditions, and very few goods meet these conditions in practice. Most of the goods we think of as public goods are really **impure public goods,** which satisfy these two conditions to some extent, but not fully.

Table 7-1 shows possible combinations of public good characteristics. Goods that are both excludable and rival are pure private goods. Private goods such as ice cream are completely rival (once you eat an ice cream cone, I cannot consume that ice cream cone at all) and they are completely excludable (you can simply refuse to sell me an ice cream cone).

There are two types of impure public goods. Some goods are *excludable, but not rival*. The best example here is cable television: the use of cable TV by others in no way diminishes your enjoyment of cable, so consumption is nonrival. It is, however, possible to exclude you from consuming cable TV: the cable company can simply refuse to hook you up to the system. Other goods, such as walking on a crowded city sidewalk, are *rival but not excludable*. When you walk on a crowded city sidewalk, you reduce the enjoyment of that walking experience for other pedestrians, who must now fight against even more foot traffic. Yet it would be very difficult for any city to exclude individuals from using the sidewalk!

Pure public goods are rare because there are few goods that are both not excludable and not rival. A classic example of a pure public good is national defense. National defense is not rival because if I build a house next to yours, my action in no way diminishes your national defense protection. National defense is not excludable because once an area is protected by national defense, everyone in the area is protected: there is no way the government can effectively deny me protection since my house is in a neighborhood with many other houses. Other classic examples of pure public goods include lighthouses and fireworks displays.

It is helpful to think about a public good as one with a large positive externality. If I set off fireworks high into the sky, it benefits many more people beyond myself, because many people will be able to see the display. I am not compensated for other people's enjoyment, however: I can't exclude others from seeing the fireworks, so I can't charge them for their enjoyment.

Optimal Provision of Private Goods

Before we model how to determine the optimal quantity of public goods to provide, let's review the conditions for optimal provision of private goods. Imagine that there are two individuals, Ben and Jerry, who are deciding between consuming cookies and ice cream, two pure private goods. For simplicity, suppose that the price of cookies is $1.

Quick Hint A convenient modeling tool in economics is the **numeraire good,** a good for which the price is set at $1. This tool is convenient because all choice models are technically written about the choice between goods, not the choice of a particular good. As a result, what matters for modeling the demand for any good (such as ice cream) is its price relative to other goods (such as cookies), not the absolute level of its price. By setting the price of cookies to $1, we make the analysis easier by making the absolute and relative price of ice cream equal.

numeraire good A good for which the price is set at $1 in order to model choice between goods, which depends on relative, not absolute, prices.

■ **FIGURE 7-1**

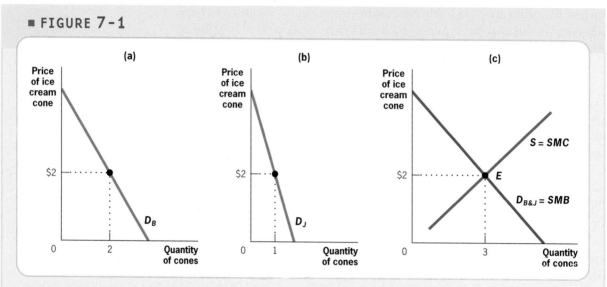

Horizontal Summation in Private Goods Markets • In private goods markets, we horizontally sum the demands of Ben and Jerry to get market demand for ice cream cones. If Ben demands 2 ice cream cones at $2, and Jerry demands 1 ice cream cone at $2, then at a market price of $2 the quantity demanded in the market is 3 ice cream cones.

Figure 7-1 shows the analysis of the market for ice cream cones. Panels (a) and (b) show Ben's and Jerry's individual demand curves for ice cream cones; that is, the number of ice cream cones that each man would demand at each price. Panel (c) shows the market demand curve, the horizontal sum of the two individual demands: for every price of ice cream cones, we compute Ben's demand and Jerry's demand, and then add them to produce a total market demand. At $2, Ben would like two ice cream cones, and Jerry would like one, for a total market demand of three cones. As we learned in Chapter 5, the demand curve in the final panel of Figure 7-1 also represents the *social marginal benefit (SMB)* of ice cream consumption, that is, the value to society from the consumption of that cone.

The market supply curve for ice cream represents the marginal cost of producing ice cream cones for a firm. As discussed in Chapter 5, in a market with no failures, this curve also represents the *social marginal cost (SMC)* of ice cream production, the cost to society from the production of that cone. In a private market, then, equilibrium occurs where *SMB = SMC,* the point at which supply and demand intersect. In Figure 7-1, equilibrium is at point *E:* at a price of $2, the market demands three ice cream cones, which are supplied by the firm.

A key feature of the private market equilibrium is that *consumers demand different quantities of the good at the same market price.* Ben and Jerry have different tastes for ice cream, relative to cookies. The market respects those different tastes by adding up the demands and meeting them with an aggregate supply. In this way, Ben and Jerry can consume according to their tastes. Since Ben likes ice cream more than Jerry, he gets two of the three cones that are produced.

It is also useful to represent this equilibrium outcome mathematically. Recall from Chapter 2 that an individual's optimal choice is found at the tangency between the indifference curve and the budget constraint. This is the point at which the *marginal rate of substitution* between ice cream cones and cookies (the rate at which consumers are willing to trade ice cream cones for cookies) equals the *ratio of the prices* of ice cream cones and cookies. That is, Ben and Jerry each consume ice cream cones and cookies until their relative marginal utilities from the consumption of these products equal the relative prices of the goods. The *optimality* condition for the consumption of private goods is written as:

(1) $$MU^B_{ic}/MU^B_c = MRS^B_{ic,c} = MRS^J_{ic,c} = P_{ic}/P_c$$

where MU is marginal utility, MRS is the marginal rate of substitution, the superscripts denote Ben (B) or Jerry (J), and the subscripts denote ice cream cones (ic) or cookies (c). Given that the price of cookies is $1, and the price of an ice cream cone is $2, then the price ratio is 2. This means that, in equilibrium, each individual must be indifferent between trading two cookies to get one ice cream cone. Ben, who likes ice cream more, is willing to make this trade when he is having two ice cream cones. But Jerry, who likes ice cream less, is only willing to make this two cookies for one ice cream cone trade at his first cone; after this, he isn't willing to give away two more cookies to get one more ice cream cone.

On the supply side, ice cream cones are produced until the marginal cost of doing so is equal to the marginal benefit of doing so, which, in this competitive market, is equal to the price. Thus, equilibrium on the supply side requires:

(2) $$MC_{ic} = P_{ic}$$

Recall that we have set $P_c = \$1$. Thus, we have from equation (1) that $MRS = P_{ic}$, and we have from equation (2) that $MC = P_{ic}$. In equilibrium, therefore, $MRS = MC$.

The private market equilibrium is also the social-efficiency-maximizing choice (the point that maximizes social surplus). This is because when there are no market failures, the MRS for any quantity of ice cream cones equals the social marginal benefit of that quantity; the marginal value to society is equal to the marginal value to any individual in the perfectly competitive market. Similarly, when there are no market failures, the MC for any quantity of ice cream cones equals the social marginal cost of that quantity; the marginal cost to society is equal to the marginal cost to producers in a perfectly competitive market. Thus, at the private market equilibrium $SMB = SMC$, which is the condition for efficiency we derived in Chapter 5 for efficiency maximization: the efficiency-maximizing point is the one where the marginal value of consuming the next unit to any consumer is equal to the marginal cost of producing that additional unit.

Optimal Provision of Public Goods

Now, imagine that Ben and Jerry are choosing not between ice cream cones and cookies but between missiles (a public good) and cookies. Once again, the

▪ FIGURE 7-2

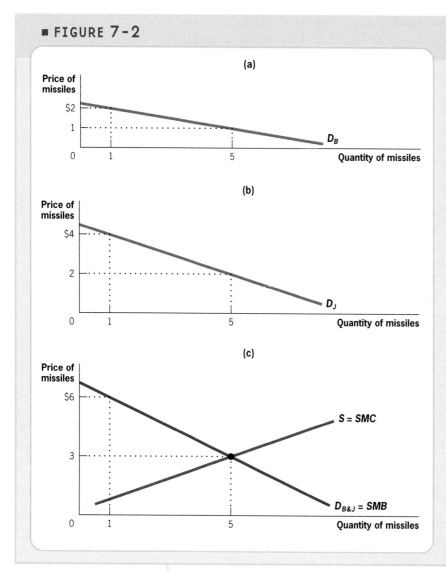

Vertical Summation in Public Goods Markets • For public goods, we vertically sum the demands of Ben and Jerry to get the social value of the public good. If Ben is willing to pay $1 for the fifth missile, and Jerry is willing to pay $2 for the fifth missile, then society values that fifth missile at $3. Given the private supply curve for missiles, the optimal number of missiles to produce is five, where social marginal benefit ($3) equals social marginal cost ($3).

price of cookies is set equal to $1. A difference between missiles and ice cream cones is that individuals cannot tailor their own specific consumption of missiles. Because missiles are a public good, whatever amount is provided must be consumed equally by all. This characteristic of the market for public goods turns the private market analysis on its head, as shown in Figure 7-2. Each person is now forced to choose a common quantity of the public good. Because Ben and Jerry have different tastes for missiles and cookies, they will be willing to pay different prices for this common quantity. Ben has a very flat demand for missiles; he is willing to pay only $2 for the first missile and $1 for the fifth missile (panel (a)). Jerry has a steeper demand, and is willing to pay $4 for the first missile and $2 for the fifth missile (panel (b)).

Whatever number of missiles is chosen applies to Ben and Jerry equally, since missiles are a public good. To arrive at the market demand for missiles, we do not sum horizontally, as with private goods (where we sum the individual quantities demanded at the given market price). Instead, we sum *vertically* by adding the prices that each individual is willing to pay for the fixed market quantity. Ben and Jerry are together willing to pay $6 for the first missile, but their willingness to pay declines as the number of missiles increases, so they are only willing to pay $3 for the fifth missile. This vertically summed demand curve is shown in panel (c) of Figure 7-2.

Panel (c) also shows a supply curve for missiles, which equals their marginal cost of production. The socially optimal level of production is the intersection of this supply with the vertically summed demand. That is, given that any missiles that are provided protect both Ben and Jerry, the producer should consider the *sum* of their valuations (their willingness to pay) in making its production decision. The resulting socially optimal level of production is five missiles.

Once again, a mathematical exposition helps clarify the mechanism underlying this result. The marginal missile is worth $MRS^B_{m,c}$ to Ben and $MRS^J_{m,c}$ to Jerry, so its total value to society is $MRS^B_{m,c} + MRS^J_{m,c}$. The social marginal benefit (*SMB*) of the next missile is the sum of Ben and Jerry's marginal rates of substitution, which represent their valuation of that missile. The social marginal cost (*SMC*) is the same as earlier: it is the marginal cost of producing a missile. Thus, the social-efficiency-maximizing condition for the public good is:

$$(3) \qquad\qquad MRS^B_{m,c} + MRS^J_{m,c} = MC$$

Social efficiency is maximized when the marginal cost is set equal to the *sum of the MRSs, rather than being set equal to each individual's MRS*. For private goods, it is optimal for firms to produce until the marginal cost equals the benefit to the marginal consumer, and that is the private competitive market outcome. For public goods, however, it is socially optimal for firms to produce until the marginal cost equals the benefit to *all* consumers combined. This is because the private good is rival: once it is consumed by any one consumer, it is gone. The public good is non-rival: since it can be consumed jointly by all consumers, society would like the producer to take into account the sum of all consumers' preferences.

7.2

Private Provision of Public Goods

We have now developed the conditions for the optimal provision of public goods: public goods should be produced until the marginal cost for producers equals the sum of the marginal rates of substitution for all consumers. With this finding in mind, the first question to ask (as always) is: Does the private sector get it right? If the private sector provides the optimal quantity of goods at the market price, then there is no market failure, and there is no potential role for the government in terms of improving efficiency.

Private-Sector Underprovision

In general, the private sector in fact *underprovides public goods* because of the **free rider problem** discussed in Chapter 5: since my enjoyment of public goods is not solely dependent on my contribution to them, I will contribute less to their provision than is socially optimal.

free rider problem When an investment has a personal cost but a common benefit, individuals will underinvest.

Let's consider this problem in the context of an example. Suppose Ben and Jerry live by themselves far away from others. It is July 4th, and they want to have a celebration. For this celebration, they care about only two consumption goods: ice cream cones and fireworks. The price of each of these goods is $1, so for every firework they buy, they forgo a serving of ice cream. Ice cream is a private good here, but fireworks are a pure public good: fireworks are non-rival since both Ben and Jerry can enjoy them without impinging on the other's enjoyment, and fireworks are non-excludable since they explode high in the sky for both Ben and Jerry to see. Neither Ben nor Jerry cares about who sends up the firework, as long as it's up in the sky for them to see. Both Ben and Jerry benefit equally from a firework sent up by either of them; what matters to them is the *total amount of fireworks*. To further simplify the example, suppose that Ben and Jerry have identical preferences over different combinations of fireworks and ice cream.

If left to their own devices, Ben and Jerry will choose to consume combinations of fireworks and ice cream cones identified by the points at which their indifference curves are tangent to their budget constraints. The slope of the budget constraints is 1, since fireworks and ice cream cones are each $1 per unit. The slope of the indifference curves is the *MRS,* or the ratio of marginal utilities. So both Ben and Jerry will set their marginal utility as $MU_F/MU_{ic} = 1$, or $MU_{ic} = MU_F$. This equivalence will determine the quantities of fireworks and ice cream cones consumed.

The optimality condition for public goods is that the marginal cost of the good should be set equal to the *sum* of marginal rates of substitution. Optimal consumption of fireworks would therefore occur at the point at which $MU^B_F/MU^B_{ic} + MU^J_F/MU^J_{ic} = 1$. Since Ben and Jerry's preferences are identical, this is equivalent to saying that $2 \times (MU_F / MU_{ic}) = 1$, or $MU_F = \frac{1}{2} \times MU_{ic}$.

Recall that marginal utilities diminish with increasing consumption of a good. In a private market equilibrium, fireworks are consumed until their marginal utility equals the marginal utility of ice cream (since the prices of both goods are $1). But the optimality calculation shows that fireworks should be consumed until their marginal utility is *half* the marginal utility of ice cream; that is, more fireworks are consumed in the optimal public goods outcome than in the private outcome.

This result is exactly what we would expect from the free rider problem. Ben and Jerry each have to forgo a serving of ice cream to provide a firework, but both Ben and Jerry benefit from each firework that is provided. There is a clear strong positive externality here: Ben's or Jerry's provision of the firework greatly benefits the other person. As we saw with positive externalities earlier, this situation leads naturally to underproduction. Thus, the free rider problem leads to a potential role for government intervention. (The appendix to this chapter works out a formal mathematical example of the free rider problem, illustrating how the private market underprovides the public good.)

▶ APPLICATION

The Free Rider Problem in Practice[2]

The free rider problem is one of the most powerful concepts in all of economics, and it applies to everything from your everyday interactions to global politics. Some everyday examples, and interesting solutions, include the following:

▶ WNYC, the public radio station in New York, has an estimated listening audience of about 1 million people, but only 75,000 (7.5%) of their listeners send in money to support the station. Contributions account for only 35% of WNYC's budget. To avoid such a free rider problem in the United Kingdom, the national television station, the BBC, charges an annual licensing fee (currently around $200) to anyone who owns and operates a TV! The law is enforced by keeping a database of addresses recorded when TV purchases are made, and periodically a fleet of BBC vans scours the country with TV detection devices that can sense the "local oscillator" that operates when a TV is being used. If you're caught without a license, the fine can run up to $1,500.

▶ A 2000 study of the file-sharing software Gnutella showed that 70% of users download files only from others, and never contribute their own files via upload. The top 1% of Gnutella users contribute 40% of the total files shared, and the top 20% of users provide 98% of all files traded. The file-sharing software Kazaa now assigns users ratings based on their ratio of uploads to downloads and then gives download priority to users according to their ratings, thus discouraging free riders.

▶ In 1994, the town of Cambridge, England, tried to provide a public good in the form of 350 free green bicycles scattered throughout the city. Users were expected to return each bicycle to one of 15 stands after its use. Unfortunately, within four days of the scheme's launch, not a single bicycle could be found, most having been likely stolen and repainted a different color. The scheme ultimately cost the city about $20,000, thus posing the ultimate in literal "free rider" problems. ◀

---

[2] Public radio data comes from Arik Hesseldahl's "Public Radio Goes Begging," a March 30, 2001, article in Forbes. The Gnutella study is described in Patti Hartigan's "Free Riders Who Don't Share in the Digital Community," an August 25, 2000, article for the *Boston Globe*. The British bicycle caper is reported in *The Times* (London) article of April 20, 1994, "Thieves Put Spoke in Freewheeling Dream."

Can Private Providers Overcome the Free Rider Problem?

The free rider problem does not lead to a complete absence of private provision of public goods. Many of us grew up in towns where there were privately financed fireworks displays, parks, even garbage collection. Indeed, one of the most famous counterarguments to the necessity of public provision of private goods was made for the case of lighthouses. Lighthouses seem to fit the definition of a pure public good: one ship's use of the light does not affect another's, and ships cannot be excluded from seeing the light when they are at sea. Indeed, for many generations, economists pointed to lighthouses as a classic example of a public good that would be underprovided by the private sector. John Stuart Mill was the first to argue that government should build lighthouses because "it is impossible that the ships at sea which are benefited by a lighthouse should be made to pay a toll on the occasion of its use." The great economist Paul Samuelson, in his classic text *Economics,* agreed that lighthouse building was "government activity justifiable because of external effects."[3]

Nonetheless, in a famous 1974 article, Ronald Coase (of Coase's theorem) conducted historical research showing that British lighthouses had been successfully provided by private interests long before the government ever took over the task. Private individuals, sensing a profitable opportunity, obtained permission from the government to build lighthouses and then levy tolls at the ports where the ships anchored. These individuals would determine how many lighthouses the ship had passed on its route and then charge them accordingly. Thus lighthouses were successfully provided by the private market until 1842, by which point the British government had purchased all private lighthouses in order to publicly provide this particular good.[4]

Thus, it appears that the private sector can in some cases combat the free rider problem to provide public goods. The previous example of file-sharing software shows one approach to doing so: charging user fees that are proportional to their valuation of the public good. The following policy application shows another example of privately financing public goods through such user fees—and the problems that such an approach can face.

► APPLICATION

Business Improvement Districts

The quality of city streets is another example of a public good. Residents all want clean, safe spaces in which to walk, but it is infeasible to charge pedestrians a fee for using the streets. For this reason, cities use tax revenues to publicly

---

[3] These quotations come from Coase (1974), described next.

[4] According to Coase (1974), the reason put forth by the government was that government ownership would actually lower prices by preventing private owners from inflating prices. Coase then argues that the government takeover did not, in fact, lower prices.

provide police departments for safety, sanitation departments for cleanliness, and public works departments to decorate the public spaces. Unfortunately, public provision of these services does not always work effectively. Take, for example, New York City's Times Square, an area of midtown Manhattan that by 1980 was infested with muggers, pickpockets, heroin dealers, prostitutes, and stores selling pornography and various kinds of weapons. The city government spent ten years attempting to clean up Times Square, but eventually gave up on the area once described as "dirty, dangerous, decrepit and increasingly derelict."[5]

Then, in 1992, a group of local businessmen decided to start a Business Improvement District (BID), a legal entity that privately provides local security and sanitation services, and funds these services with fees charged to local businesses. In theory, BIDs should fail because of the free rider problem: each business will simply hope that other area businesses will pay for the services from which they all will benefit. The New York law, however, is structured so that if the BID organizers can get over 60% of the local business community to agree to join, then the BID can levy fees on all local businesses. In the Times Square case, 84% of local businesses agreed to pay fees in order to fund the BID's services.

The Times Square BID has been a resounding success. Now with a budget over $5 million, the BID has 120 employees, half of whom do sanitation duties like sweeping, emptying trash cans, and removing graffiti, while the other half work as unarmed "public safety officers" in conjunction with the police. Crime has dropped significantly, the area is cleaner and more attractive, and as a result of these improvements business and tourism are once again booming. As the head of the BID describes it, "What BIDs are able to do is to devote an intense effort to a small place that the city itself could never afford. It's a way of localizing much of the functions of government and concentrating your community effort." The BID's power to levy fees on local businesses allows seemingly public goods (safety and cleanliness) to be provided through private channels.

Whether a BID works well depends strongly on the form of the law allowing BIDs to form in the first place. In Massachusetts, for example, BID laws allow local businesses to opt out of paying the required fees within 30 days of approval of the BID by the local government. The opt-out approach discourages businesses from pursuing plans for BIDs because of a fear that, after all the groundwork for the plans has been laid, businesses will withdraw from the program at the last minute rather than pay their fee for BID costs. As a result of the provision, only 2 BIDs have successfully formed in Massachusetts; the rest of the nation has 1,500 scattered throughout the states.[6] ◄

---

[5] For more on the Times Square BID, see McDonald (2001).
[6] Kindleberger (1999).

When Is Private Provision Likely to Overcome the Free Rider Problem?

While the free rider problem clearly exists, there are also examples where the private market is able to overcome this problem to some extent. Under what circumstances are private market forces likely to solve the free rider problem, and under what circumstances are they not? In this section, we review three factors that are likely to determine the success of private provision: differences among individuals in their demand for the public good, altruism among potential donors to the public good, and utility from one's own contribution to the public good.

Some Individuals Care More than Others Private provision is particularly likely to surmount the free rider problem when individuals are not identical, and when some individuals have an especially high demand for the public good. For example, let's assume that Ben has more income than Jerry, but total income between the two is constant, so that the social optimum for fireworks is the same as when their incomes are equal. As we show mathematically in the appendix, in this case Ben would provide more fireworks than Jerry: if the income differential is large enough, the total number of privately provided fireworks rises toward the socially optimal number of fireworks. We obtain a similar outcome if Ben and Jerry have the same income, but Ben gets more enjoyment from fireworks; even though they are a public good, Ben will still provide more of them.

The key intuition here is that the decision about how many fireworks to provide for any individual is a function of the enjoyment that the individual gets from total fireworks, net of their cost. If a person gets a lot of enjoyment, or has a lot of money to finance the fireworks, he will choose to purchase more fireworks, even though he is sharing the benefits with others: as enjoyment net of costs gets very large for any one individual, the provision of the public good starts to approximate private good provision.

Consider, for example, a driveway that is shared by a mansion and by a run-down shack. In principle, there is a free rider problem in plowing the driveway, since the costs of plowing are borne by one party but both residences benefit from a clean driveway. Despite this, the mansion owner may nevertheless plow the driveway, allowing the owner of the shack to free ride, because the mansion owner has more money and perhaps cares more about having a clear driveway.

Higher incomes or stronger tastes for the public goods can mitigate the free rider problem to some extent, but they are not likely to solve the problem. Even when one individual provides all of a public good, the individual still does not take into account the benefit to other individuals, and so the public good is usually still underproduced (as in the appendix's example). Thus, while the owner of the mansion may end up plowing the driveway, he may not bother to plow as well near the shack as the shack's owner would like.

Altruism Another reason that private agents may provide more of a public good than our model would predict is that the model assumes purely selfish utility-maximizing agents. In fact, there is much evidence that individuals are

altruistic—that is, they care about the outcomes of others as well as themselves. If individuals are altruistic, they may be willing to contribute to a public good even if the free rider problem suggests they should not. In terms of
our model, this would be equivalent to Ben caring not only about the costs of
fireworks to himself, but the cost to Jerry as well, so that he is willing to contribute more in order to lower Jerry's burden.

> **altruistic** When individuals
> value the benefits and costs to
> others in making their consump-
> tion choices.

Evidence for altruism comes from *laboratory experiments* of the kind that are
typically employed in other fields, such as psychology, but that are gaining
popularity as a means of resolving difficult economic issues. The typical public
goods experiment proceeds as follows: five college undergraduates are placed
in a room to play ten rounds of a simple game. In each round, the students are
given $1, and they have the option of keeping that $1 or placing it in a "public" fund. After all students decide whether to contribute, the amount in the
public fund is then doubled (by the economist running the experiment) and
divided up evenly among all five students, *regardless of whether or not they contributed*. Thus, if all choose to contribute $1 to the fund, they each receive $2
in return. If only 2 contribute to the fund, each of the contributors receives
$0.40 (2 × $2/5 students), while the noncontributors retain their full $1 *and*
get the $0.40 from the public fund, for a total of $1.40. In this case, the contributors lose money and the noncontributors make money. There is thus a
very clear incentive to free ride off the contributions of others, so that economists predict theoretically that no one should ever contribute to the public
fund. If we start from a point of no contributors, any particular individual
loses money by voluntarily becoming a contributor, so no one should do so.

The experimental evidence shows an outcome that is very different from
that predicted by economic theory. As reviewed in Ledyard (1995), nearly
every such public goods experiment results in 30–70% of the participants contributing to the public fund. Interestingly, in experiments with multiple rounds,
such as the one just described, contributions tend to decline as the rounds
progress, but rarely, if ever, reach zero. Thus, altruism appears to trump the
purely selfish prediction that underlies the theory of the free rider problem.

Laboratory experiments, however, suffer from some limitations as a source
of information about real-world behavior. Individuals may behave differently
in a laboratory setting, where the stakes are often small, than they do in actual
markets, where the stakes can be higher. Moreover, most of the experimental
evidence used in economics comes from laboratory work with college undergraduates, which may not provide a representative answer for the entire population of interest.

Nevertheless, some real-world evidence is also consistent with altruism in private support of public goods. For example, Brunner (1998) noted that the traditional theory of public goods suggests that as the numbers of users of a good
increases, the tendency for individuals to contribute to the financing of that
good should decrease as they feel that their contribution has less and less of an
impact (with only one user, there is no free rider possibility, but as the number of
users grows, each individual's contribution benefits that person less and less and
others more and more). Brunner therefore studied public radio stations across
the country, examining listeners' contributions in relation to the total size of a

given station's audience. Surprisingly, Brunner found that the number of listeners contributing decreases only modestly as the number of listeners increases, and that, among contributors, the amount of the contribution is unchanged. This seems to suggest that there is a subset of public goods contributors who get utility simply out of giving what they feel is their appropriate share.

What determines altruism? This is a very difficult question and has given rise to an entire field of study of **social capital,** the value of altruistic and communal behavior in society. A central finding of this field is that individuals are likely to be more altruistic when they are more "trusting" of others. For example, Anderson et al. (2003) ran a typical public goods experiment of the type described, and paired the results across individuals with both attitudinal measures of trust (do you agree with statements like "most people can be trusted"?) and behavioral measures of trust (do you loan money to friends and strangers? have you ever been a crime victim? do you purposefully leave your doors unlocked? and so on). They found that most of the attitudinal and behavioral measures of trust were positively correlated with high contributions to the public good. In the Bangladeshi trash collection example that opened this chapter, the few communities that were successful in setting up private trash collection were those neighborhoods that tended to exhibit higher levels of "reciprocity" (do you help neighbors after a householder dies? do you and your neighbors help take each other for visits to the hospital or doctor?) and "sharing" (do you send your neighbors food during festivals or other happy occasions? do you and your neighbors share fruits/vegetables grown on your own premises?).

Warm Glow A final reason that private individuals might provide more of the public good than suggested by our model is that individuals might care about their own contributions per se. Under the **warm glow model,** individuals care about both the total amount of the public good and their particular contributions as well. Perhaps they get a plaque with their name on it from making contributions, or maybe their contributions are known publicly so that their friends praise them for their generosity, or maybe they get a psychological benefit from knowing they helped a worthy cause. If individuals get utility from their particular contributions for any reason, the public good becomes like a private good, and individuals will contribute more than predicted by our original model (in which they care only about the total public good quantity). Warm glow does not fully solve the underprovision problem, however, since individuals still do not account for the positive benefits to others of their public goods provision.

social capital The value of altruistic and communal behavior in society.

warm glow model Model of public goods provision in which individuals care about both the total amount of the public good and their particular contributions as well.

7.3

Public Provision of Public Goods

The discussion in Section 7.2 highlights that the private sector will generally underprovide public goods, so that government can potentially improve efficiency by intervening. In principle, the government could solve the optimal public goods provision problem previously presented and then either provide that amount of the good or mandate private actors to provide that amount.

In practice, however, governments face some significant barriers when they attempt to solve the free rider problem in the provision of public goods. In this section, we review three of those barriers: private responses to public provision, or "crowd-out"; the difficulty of measuring the costs and benefits of public goods; and the difficulty of determining the public's preferences for public goods.

Private Responses to Public Provision: The Problem of Crowd-Out

In some instances, public goods will not be provided at all by those in the private sector unless the government tells them they must provide the good. In other cases, as we noted, the private sector is already providing the public good to some extent before the government intervenes, and this private provision will react to government intervention. In particular, public provision will to some extent **crowd out** private provision: as the government provides more of the public good, the private sector will provide less. This decrease in private provision will offset the net gain in public provision from government intervention.

crowd-out As the government provides more of a public good, the private sector will provide less.

The extent of such crowd-out depends on the preferences of the private individuals providing the public good. Let's continue to explore the fireworks example and make three assumptions:

1. Ben and Jerry care only about the total amount of fireworks provided: there is no warm glow from giving.

2. The government provision of fireworks will be financed by charging Ben and Jerry equal amounts.

3. The government provides fewer fireworks than Ben and Jerry were providing beforehand.

In this case, as we show mathematically in the appendix, *each dollar of public provision will crowd out private provision one for one.* That is, the government's intervention will have no *net effect* on the quantity of fireworks provided.

This outcome illustrates the fundamental *robustness of economic equilibria:* if a person starts from his or her individual optimum, and the market environment changes, and if the person can undo this change to get back to that optimum, he or she will do so. The private equilibrium is the preferred outcome for Ben and Jerry. If they can undo any government intervention to get back to that preferred outcome, they will do so; what was optimal before the government intervened remains optimal after government intervention given our three earlier assumptions.

For example, suppose that in the pregovernment optimum, Ben and Jerry were each providing 10 fireworks, at a cost of $10 for each person. The total private provision is therefore 20 fireworks, but let's say the social optimum is 30 fireworks. To reach the social optimum, the government decides to take $5 each from Ben and from Jerry, and use the $10 raised to buy 10 more fireworks. Ben and Jerry each have $5 less, and they observe the government providing 10 fireworks. They simply cut their spending on fireworks by $5 each, so that they spend the same ($5 on fireworks, $5 to the government), and see the same total fireworks (20). So they are exactly where they originally wanted to be, and the government intervention has done nothing. This is a case of full crowd-out.

Crowd-out is a classic example of the unintended consequences of government action that we first discussed in Chapter 1. The government intended to do the right thing by increasing fireworks to the social optimum. But, in fact, it ended up having no effect, because its actions were totally offset by changes in individual actions.

Full crowd-out is rare. Partial crowd-out is much more common and it can occur in two different cases: when noncontributors to the public good are taxed to finance provision of the good, and when individuals derive utility from their own contribution as well as from the total amount of public good.

Contributors vs. Noncontributors Suppose that some people contribute more for public goods than others, either because they are richer or because they have a stronger preference for the public good. In the extreme case, suppose that Ben contributes $20 to buy 20 fireworks, and Jerry contributes nothing, because Ben likes fireworks more than Jerry or because he is richer than Jerry. This is still below the social optimum of 30 fireworks, however.

Now, suppose that the government charges Ben and Jerry each $5 for firework contributions and then provides 10 fireworks in an attempt to bring the number of fireworks to the socially optimal level of 30. Jerry now spends $5 more on fireworks, since he was providing nothing before. Ben, on the other hand, will not reduce his firework consumption by the full $10 (to offset government provision). Ben has effectively been made better off: there are 10 more fireworks that only cost him $5 in government-mandated contributions, rather than the $10 he would have spent if he'd bought those 10 fireworks. This increase in Ben's effective wealth (the value of fireworks plus the value of other goods he can purchase) has a positive income effect on Ben's purchase of fireworks, so government intervention will not fully crowd out his spending. The total number of fireworks will rise above 20. By forcing Jerry to become a contributor, the government has increased total public goods provision.

Warm Glow Alternatively, there may not be full crowd-out if I care about my own contributions per se, as in the warm glow model. If I get utility from my particular contributions for any reason, then an increase in government contributions will not fully crowd out my giving. For example, consider the extreme case where *all* I care about is how much I give, and I don't care about gifts from others. If the government increases contributions from others, these contributions have no offsetting effects on my giving because my giving is, from my perspective, a private good. In this extreme case, there may be *no* crowd-out of my contributions by government intervention. As long as there is some warm glow from my own contributions, then crowd-out will be less than one for one, since part of my contribution is a private good.

Evidence on Crowd-Out How important a problem is crowd-out in reality? Unfortunately, the existing evidence on crowd-out is quite mixed. On the one hand, studies assessing how individual contributions respond to government spending suggest very small crowd-out. As the Empirical Evidence box reviews, however, these studies suffer from many of the bias problems discussed in Chapter 3. On the other hand, evidence from laboratory experiments suggest that crowd-out is large, but less than full. Thus, while there is no evidence for full crowd-out, there is also no consensus on the size of this important individual response to government intervention.

Measuring the Costs and Benefits of Public Goods

In the previous theoretical analysis, we assumed that the government could measure both the benefits and costs of providing public goods. In practice, this is quite difficult. Consider the example of improving a highway in order to reduce traffic slowdowns and improve safety. There is a clear free rider problem in relying on the private sector for this improvement. The benefits of highway improvement are fairly small for any one driver, although they may be quite large for the total set of drivers using the highway. Thus, no one driver will invest the necessary resources to improve the highway.

Should the government undertake these highway improvements? That depends on whether the costs of doing so exceed the sum of the benefits to all drivers who use the highway, but measuring these costs and benefits can be complicated. Consider the costs of the labor needed to repair the highway. The budgetary cost of this labor is the wage payments made by the government for this labor, but the economic costs can be different. What if, without this highway project, half of the workers on the project would be unemployed? How can the government take into account that it is not only paying wages but also providing a new job opportunity for these workers?

There are even more difficult problems facing the government as it tries to assess the benefits of the project. What is the value of the time saved for commuters due to reduced traffic jams? And what is the value to society of the reduced number of deaths if the highway is improved?

These difficult questions are addressed by the field of *cost-benefit analysis,* which provides a framework for measuring the costs and benefits of public projects. Chapter 8 provides a detailed discussion of cost-benefit analysis, within the context of this highway example.

How Can We Measure Preferences for the Public Good?

In our discussion of optimal public goods provision, the government knows each individual's preferences over private and public goods. The government can therefore compute for each individual that person's marginal valuation of public goods (his or her marginal rate of substitution of the public for the private good), sum these valuations across all individuals, and set this equal to the marginal cost of the public good (relative to the marginal cost of the private good).

EMPIRICAL EVIDENCE

MEASURING CROWD-OUT

There are a large number of studies that consider how private spending on public goods responds to public spending on the same public goods. A classic example is Kingma's (1989) study of public radio. Public radio is supported partly by contributions from its listeners and partly by government contributions. Kingma collected data on how much governments contribute to public radio stations in different cities around the country. He then gathered data on how much individuals contribute to their public radio stations in those same cities. He found that for every $1 increase in government funding, private contributions fell by 13.5¢, for only a very partial crowd-out. Other studies in this vein typically also find that crowd-out is fairly small.[7]

This is an interesting finding, but it potentially suffers from the bias problems discussed in Chapter 3: there may be reasons why areas with different government contributions to public radio might also have different tastes for private giving. For example, suppose that governments are more able to support public radio in high-income areas than in low-income areas (since the government raises more tax revenues in the high-income areas), and that individuals contribute more to charitable causes (like public radio) in high-income areas than in low-income areas. Then high-income and low-income areas are not good treatment and control groups to use for measuring the effect of government spending on individual giving. Such comparisons will be biased by the fact that high-income areas would have given more even in the absence of government intervention. In principle, regression analysis using controls for income can correct this bias, but in practice, as discussed in Chapter 3, controls are typically unable to fully correct this type of problem.

The other type of evidence that has been used in this area comes from laboratory experiments. The classic study using this approach is Andreoni (1993). He set up an experiment in which individuals contributed to a public good in a laboratory setting by contributing tokens they were given to a common fund. He set up the payoffs for this experiment so that each player, if acting as a free rider, should choose to contribute 3 tokens in order to maximize the player's likely return. This predicted contribution (3 tokens) was close to the level actually chosen by each participant (2.78 tokens).[8]

Andreoni then made the following change to the laboratory game: using the same payment schedule, he instituted a 2-token tax on every player. This tax was then contributed to the public good. This change mirrors the full earlier crowd-out example, so without warm glow effects, players should have reduced their contributions by 2 tokens to 0.78 tokens to offset the government contribution plan. In fact, however, each player cut his or her contributions by only 1.43 tokens, so that contributions fell only to 1.35 tokens. That is, crowd-out was less than full; each token of government contribution crowded out only 0.715 tokens of private contributions.

This crowd-out estimate is much higher than that obtained from empirical studies: recall that Kingma's estimate was that a dollar of government contribution would crowd out only 0.135 dollars of private contributions. At the same time, as already noted, laboratory experiments have their limitations as a source of economic evidence. Thus, the true extent of crowd-out remains an important question.

In practice, of course, there are at least three problems facing a government trying to turn individual preferences into a decision about public goods provision. The first is *preference revelation*: individuals may not be willing to tell the government their true valuation, for example, because the government might

---

[7] See Steinberg (1991) or Straub (2003) for reviews; Straub even finds that the small Kingma crowd-out is not significant when using an updated and larger sample.

[8] Andreoni's subjects did behave very much like free riders, unlike the altruistic cases discussed earlier, perhaps because they were economics students who were given time to study the structure of the game. In one public goods experiment, Marwell and Ames (1981) showed that graduate students in economics free ride much more than the general population, contributing only 20% of their tokens compared to 49% for the other subjects.

charge them more for the good if they say that they value it highly. The second is *preference knowledge:* even if individuals are willing to be honest about their valuation of a public good, they may not know what their valuation is, since they have little experience pricing public goods such as highways or national defense. The third is *preference aggregation:* how can the government effectively put together the preferences of millions of citizens in order to decide on the value of a public project?

These difficult problems are addressed by the field of *political economy,* the study of how governments go about making public policy decisions such as the appropriate level of public goods. In Chapter 9, we'll discuss the various approaches used by governments to address these problems, and their implications for the ability of governments to effectively intervene in problems such as the free rider problem.

7.4
Conclusion

A major function of governments at all levels is the provision of public goods. The potential gains from such government intervention are apparent from free rider problems, such as those impeding garbage collection in Bangladesh. In some cases, the private sector can provide public goods, but in general it will not achieve the optimal level of provision.

When there are problems with private market provision of public goods, government intervention can potentially increase efficiency. Whether that potential will be achieved is a function of both the ability of the government to appropriately measure the costs and benefits of public projects and the ability of the government to carry out the socially efficient decision. In the next two chapters, we investigate those two concerns in detail.

▶ HIGHLIGHTS

■ Pure public goods are goods that are non-rival (my consuming or making use of the good does not in any way affect your opportunity to consume the good) and non-excludable (even if I want to deny you the opportunity to consume or access the public good, there is no way I can do so).

■ For pure public goods, the optimal level of provision is the point at which the sum of marginal benefits across all recipients equals the marginal cost.

■ The private market is unlikely to provide the optimal level of public goods due to the free rider problem.

■ In some cases, the private market can overcome the free rider problem, at least partially. A solution closer to the socially optimal one is more likely if there are individuals with high incomes or high demand for the public good, individuals who are altruistic, or individuals who derive a "warm glow" from their contributions.

■ Public provision of public goods faces three important problems: crowding out of private provision; determining the costs and benefits of public projects; and effectively reflecting the public's demand for public goods.

▶ **QUESTIONS AND PROBLEMS**

1. We add the demands of *private* goods horizontally but add the demands of *public* goods vertically when determining the associated marginal benefit to society. Why do we do this and why are the procedures different for public and private goods?

2. The citizens of Balaland used to pave 120 miles of roadways per year. After the government of Balaland began paving 100 miles of roadways per year itself, the citizens cut back their paving to 30 miles per year, for a total number of roadway miles paved per year of only 130 miles. What might be happening here?

3. Bill's demand for hamburgers (a private good) is $Q = 20 - 2P$ and Ted's demand is $Q = 10 - P$.

   a. Write down an equation for the social marginal benefit of the consumption of hamburger consumption.

   b. Now suppose that hamburgers are a *public* good. Write down an equation for the social marginal benefit of hamburger consumption.

4. People in my neighborhood pay annual dues to a neighborhood association. This association refunds neighborhood dues to selected home owners who do a particularly nice job in beautifying their yards.

   a. Why might the neighborhood association provide this refund?

   b. At the most recent home owners' association meeting, home owners voted to end this practice because they felt that it was unfair that some people would not have to pay their share of the costs of maintaining the neighborhood.

What is likely to happen to the overall level of neighborhood beautification? Explain.

5. Zorroland has a large number of people who are alike in every way. Boppoland has the same number of people as Zorroland, with the same average income as Zorroland, but the distribution of incomes is wider. Why might Boppoland have a higher level of public good provision than Zorroland?

6. Think about the rival and excludable properties of public goods. To what degree is *radio broadcasting* a public good? To what degree is a *highway* a public good?

7. Think of an example of a free rider problem in your hometown. Can you think of a way for your local government to overcome this problem?

8. In order to determine the right amount of public good to provide, the government of West Essex decides to survey its residents about how much they value the good. It will then finance the public good provision by taxes on residents. Describe a tax system that would lead residents to underreport their valuations. Describe an alternative system that could lead residents to overreport their valuations.

9. Why is it difficult to empirically determine the degree to which government spending crowds out private provision of public goods?

10. Think back to Chapter 5. Why can the public good provision problem be thought of as an externality problem?

▶ **ADVANCED QUESTIONS**

11. Suppose ten people each have the demand $Q = 20 - 4P$ for streetlights, and 5 people have the demand $Q = 18 - 2P$ for streetlights. The cost of building each streetlight is 3. If it is impossible to purchase a fractional number of streetlights, how many streetlights are socially optimal?

12. Andrew, Beth, and Cathy live in Lindhville. Andrew's demand for bike paths, a public good, is given by $Q = 12 - 2P$. Beth's demand is $Q = 18 - P$, and Cathy's is $Q = 8 - P/3$. The marginal cost of building a bike path is $MC = 21$. The town government decides to use the following procedure

for deciding how many paths to build. It asks each resident how many paths they want, and it builds the largest number asked for by any resident. To pay for these paths, it then taxes Andrew, Beth, and Cathy the prices a, b, and c per path, respectively, where $a + b + c = MC$. (The residents know these tax rates before stating how many paths they want.)

    a. If the taxes are set so that each resident shares the cost evenly ($a = b = c$), how many paths will get built?

    b. Show that the government can achieve the social optimum by setting the correct tax prices a, b, and c. What prices should it set?

13. The town of Springfield has two residents: Homer and Bart. The town currently funds its fire department solely from the individual contributions of these residents. Each of the two residents has a utility function over private goods (X) and total firefighters (M), of the form $U = 4 \times \log(X) + 2 \times \log(M)$. The total provision of firefighters hired, M, is the sum of the number hired by each of the two persons: $M = M_H + M_B$. Homer and Bart both have income of $100, and the price of both the private good and a firefighter is $1. Thus, they are limited to providing between 0 and 100 firefighters.

    a. How many firefighters are hired if the government does not intervene? How many are paid for by Homer? By Bart?

    b. What is the socially optimal number of firefighters? If your answer differs from (a), why?

14. The town of Musicville has two residents: Bach and Mozart. The town currently funds its free outdoor concert series solely from the individual contributions of these residents. Each of the two residents has a utility function over private goods (X) and total concerts (C), of the form $U = 3 \times \log(X) + \log(C)$. The total number of concerts given, C, is the sum of the number paid for by each of the two persons: $C = C_B + C_M$. Bach and Mozart both have income of 70, and the price of both the private good and a concert is 1. Thus, they are limited to providing between 0 and 70 concerts.

    a. How many concerts are given if the government does not intervene?

    b. Suppose the government is not happy with the private equilibrium and decides to provide 10 concerts in addition to what Bach and Mozart may choose to provide on their own. It taxes Bach and Mozart equally to pay for the new concerts. What is the new total number of concerts? How does your answer compare to (a)? Have we achieved the social optimum? Why or why not?

    c. Suppose that instead an anonymous benefactor pays for 10 concerts. What is the new total number of concerts? Is this the same level of provision as in (b)? Why or why not?

15. Consider an economy with three types of individuals, differing only with respect to their preferences for monuments. Individuals of the first type get a fixed benefit of 100 from the mere existence of monuments, whatever their number. Individuals of the second and third type get benefits according to:

$$B_{II} = 200 + 30M - 1.5M^2$$
$$B_{III} = 150 + 90M - 4.5M^2$$

where M denotes the number of monuments in the city. Assume that there are 50 people of each type. Monuments cost $3,600 each to build. How many monuments should be built?

The e icon indicates a question that requires students to apply the empirical economics principles discussed in Chapter 3 and the Empirical Evidence boxes.

Appendix to Chapter 7

The Mathematics of Public Goods Provision

I n this appendix, we present the mathematics behind the analysis of the private provision of public goods and discuss how government intervention affects that provision. This analysis uses the tools of *game theory*, a method used by economists to solve problems in which multiple parties interact to make a decision.

Setup of the Example

Imagine that Ben and Jerry live by themselves far away from others. They choose between consuming a private good, X, with a price of $1 ($P_x = 1$), and a public good, fireworks, with a price of $1 ($P_F = 1$). They each have income of $100. Because fireworks are a public good, the total amount provided is the sum of the amount provided by each individual: $F = F_B + F_J$. Each individual (i) has a utility function of the form:

$$U = 2 \times \log(X_i) + \log(F_B + F_J)$$

which he maximizes subject to the budget constraint

$$X_i + F_i = 100$$

Private Provision Only

Initially, Ben and Jerry provide the public good on their own, with no government intervention. A question for modeling private provision is how Ben and Jerry will behave, given that each knows the other will also provide fireworks. Game theory models designed to answer questions such as these typically assume *Nash bargaining:* each actor solves for his or her optimal strategy given the other actor's behavior, and an equilibrium exists if there is a set of mutually compatible optimal strategies. The *Nash equilibrium* is the point at which each actor is pursuing his or her optimal strategy, given the other actor's behavior.

Combining the equations for the utility function and the budget constraint, Ben solves a problem of the form:

$$\text{Max } U = 2 \times \log(100 - F_B) + \log(F_B + F_J)$$

Differentiating this expression with respect to F_B, we obtain:

$$-2/(100 - F_B) + 1/(F_B + F_J) = 0$$

which we can solve to generate:

$$(100 - F_B)/(2 \times (F_B + F_J)) = 1$$

and therefore

$$F_B = (100 - 2F_J)/3$$

Note the free rider problem implied by this equation: Ben's contribution goes down as Jerry's contribution goes up.

We can solve a similar problem for Jerry:

$$F_J = (100 - 2F_B)/3$$

This yields two equations in two unknowns, which we can combine to solve for F_B and F_J. Doing so, we find that $F_B = F_J = 20$, so the total supply of fireworks is 40.

Socially Optimal Level

How does this compare to the socially optimal level of provision? The social optimum is the quantity at which the sum of the individuals' marginal rates of substitution equals the ratio of prices (which is 1 in this example). Each individual's *MRS* is the ratio of his marginal utility of fireworks to his marginal utility of private goods, which we obtain by differentiating the previous utility function with respect to fireworks and then again with respect to private goods. So the optimal amount of fireworks is determined by:

$$(100 - F_B)/[2 \times (F_B + F_J)] + (100 - F_J)/[2 \times (F_B + F_J)] = 1$$

Using the fact that total fireworks $F = F_B + F_J$, we can rewrite this equation as:

$$(200 - F)/2F = 1$$

Solving this, we obtain $F = 66.6$. This quantity is much higher than the total provision by the private market, 40, due to the free rider problem. The public good is underprovided by the private market.

Different Types of Individuals

Suppose now that Ben has an income of 125, while Jerry has an income of only 75. In that case, Ben maximizes:

$$U = 2 \times \log(125 - F_B) + \log(F_B + F_J)$$

So Ben's demand for fireworks is:

$$F_B = (125 - 2F_J)/3$$

Jerry, in this case, maximizes his utility:

$$U = 2 \times \log(75 - F_J) + \log(F_B + F_J)$$

So Jerry's demand for fireworks is:

$$F_J = (75 - 2F_B)/3$$

Solving these two equations, we find that $F_B = 45$ and $F_J = -5$. Since individuals can't provide negative fireworks, this means that Jerry provides no fireworks, and the total supply is 45. This quantity is higher than the private quantity supplied when Ben and Jerry have equal incomes. Thus, having one actor with a higher income leads the outcome to be closer to the social optimum.

Full Crowd-Out

Suppose the government recognizes that the private sector underprovides fireworks by a total of 26.6 in the original example. It therefore attempts to solve this problem by mandating that Ben and Jerry each contribute $13.30 toward more fireworks. Will this solve the underprovision problem?

In fact, it will not; such a mandate will simply crowd out existing contributions. Under the mandate, Both Ben and Jerry now maximize their utility, which has the form:

$$Max \ U = 2 \times \log(X_i) + \log(F_B + F_J + 26.6)$$

Each maximizes that utility function subject to the budget constraint:

$$X_i + F_i = 100 - 13.3$$

Solving this problem as above, we find that the optimal level of fireworks provision for both Ben and Jerry falls to 6.7 each, so that total provision (public of 26.6 plus private of 13.4) remains at 40. By reducing their provision to 6.7, Ben and Jerry can return to the private solution that they find to be optimal, which is total spending of $20 each, and a total of 40 fireworks. As discussed in the chapter, however, full crowd-out is only one of a range of possible outcomes when government provides a good that is also provided by the private sector.

Cost-Benefit Analysis

8

In November 2002, 190,000 Seattle voters went to the polls and checked boxes to select not only their politicians but also to decide whether to begin public financing and construction of a 14-mile-long monorail, an elevated train that by 2009 would connect the city's center and outer neighborhoods. Funding for the monorail's construction would come from a 1.4% excise tax on Seattle residents' and businesses' vehicles, at a median cost of about $100 per vehicle per year. Such costs angered some residents, such as Henry Aronson, founder of "Citizens Against the Monorail," who argued that "the more people [learn] about the monorail, the less confidence they have in it." Seattle Mayor Greg Nickels disagreed, describing the monorail as a "critical step" in "building a transportation system that works for the twentieth century." Ultimately, Seattle residents voted in favor of the project by a margin of fewer than 900 votes, less than half a percent of the total votes cast.

The project might never have begun if not for an important study commissioned by the city government to assess the costs and benefits of such a project for the city. The analysts first computed the project's expenditures, which consisted largely of the costs of construction and equipment purchase, as well as small costs for buying permission from certain landowners to run the monorail through their property. The analysts also addressed the nonmonetary costs of the project: for example, the monorail would have a visual impact by ruining certain views of the city; it would create noise near the train itself; and it would cause traffic delays during actual construction. The analysts concluded that these effects would be offset, however, and did not include them in project costs; for example, ruined views would be offset by the improved views that monorail passengers would have, and noise might increase near the train but would decrease as passengers switched away from even noisier buses.

Benefits from the project came in many forms. The analysts estimated that commuters would save 6.4 million hours of travel time every year, which they chose to value at about $10 per hour (half the average regional wage rate).

Many current drivers were predicted to switch to the monorail, saving themselves 4.7 million trips' worth of parking fees, which was valued based on the market value for downtown parking. The analysts also estimated that by 2020 reduced driving would save Seattle residents $11 million annually in car maintenance and operating costs. The monorail would also render travel times more reliable, increase the road capacity for those continuing to drive to work, and reduce bus and car accidents.

Ultimately, the analysts concluded that the value of the monorail's benefits were about $2.07 billion, while its costs were $1.68 billion, so the city of Seattle would benefit by the difference of $390 million if it were built. This large net benefit was an important factor in swinging public opinion toward the monorail project.[1]

The discussion in Chapter 7 relied on the theoretical concepts of the marginal social benefit and the cost of public goods. For a government making decisions about how much of a public good to provide, however, these theoretical concepts must be translated into hard numbers. To accomplish this translation, the government uses **cost-benefit analysis** to compare the costs and benefits of public goods projects to decide if they should be undertaken. In principle, cost-benefit analyses are accounting exercises, a way of adding up the benefits and costs of a project and then comparing them. In practice, however, cost-benefit analyses are rich economic exercises that bring to bear the microeconomic reasoning reviewed in Chapter 2 and a host of interesting empirical evidence.

> **cost-benefit analysis** The comparison of costs and benefits of public goods projects to decide if they should be undertaken.

This richness is clearly illustrated by the monorail example. Carrying out the cost-benefit analysis in this case required answering hard questions such as: How do we value the time savings to commuters? How do we value the costs of noise and reduced visibility? How do we value the benefits of increased safety? And how do we deal with the fact that many of these costs and benefits accrue not today but far into the future?

In this chapter, we discuss the important set of issues that must be addressed to carry out cost-benefit analysis. In doing so, we explore how policy makers use the tools of this field to apply the theory developed in Chapter 7.

8.1

Measuring the Costs of Public Projects

In this section, we introduce the example that will guide us through our discussion of cost-benefit analysis, and then turn to the difficulties associated with measuring the costs of public projects. Although the principles discussed here are general, the best way to understand cost-benefit analysis is through an example.

---

[1] DJM Consulting and ECONorthwest. "Benefit-Cost Analysis of the Proposed Monorail Green Line." Revised August 28, 2002. On the Web at http://archives.elevated.org/docs/BCA_Report_Final_revised.pdf. Mike Lindblom. "Monorail: It's a Go." *Seattle Times* (November 20, 2002), p. A1.

■ TABLE 8-1

Cost-Benefit Analysis of Highway Construction Project

		Quantity	Price / Value	Total
Costs	Asphalt	1 million bags		
	Labor	1 million hours		
	Maintenance	$10 million/year		
			First-year cost:	
			Total cost over time:	
Benefits	Driving time saved	500,000 hours/year		
	Lives saved	5 lives/year		
			First-year benefit:	
			Total benefit over time:	
			Benefit over time minus cost over time:	

The renovation of the turnpike in your state has three costs: asphalt, labor, and future maintenance. There are two associated benefits: reduced travel time and reduced fatalities. The goal of cost-benefit analysis is to quantify these costs and benefits.

The Example

Suppose that you are again working for your state government, but that instead of working on health and human services issues you are running the highway department. Your state turnpike is in poor shape, with large potholes and crumbling shoulders that slow down traffic and pose an accident risk. You have been charged by the governor with the task of considering whether the state should invest in repairing this road.[2]

As shown in Table 8-1, making the improvements will require the following inputs:

▶ 1 million bags of asphalt

▶ 1 million hours of construction labor (500 workers for 2,000 hours each)

▶ $10 million per year in the future for maintenance costs

There are two main benefits to these road improvements:

▶ Driving time for producers (trucks) and consumers will be reduced by 500,000 hours per year.

▶ The road will be safer, resulting in five fewer fatalities per year.

---

[2] Although your experience driving crowded toll roads may suggest that they are both rival and excludable, let's assume for the purposes of this example that the road in question is non-rival and non-excludable, so that the citizens of the state can't be assumed to spend the money to fix obvious problems with this road. Thus, the state government has to decide if these improvements are worthwhile.

Measuring Current Costs

The first goal of the cost-benefit analysis is to measure the cost of this public good. It seems an easy task: add up what the government pays for all the inputs just listed to obtain the cost. This method represents the **cash-flow accounting** approach to costs that is used by accountants. This does not, however, correspond to the theoretical concept of *social marginal cost* that we used in Chapter 7 to determine the optimal level of public goods. The social marginal cost of any resource (e.g., the asphalt, labor, and future maintenance costs) is its **opportunity cost:** the value of that input in its next best use. Thus, the cost to society of employing any input is determined not by its cash costs, but by the next best use to which society could put that input.

Consider first the asphalt. The next best use for a bag of asphalt, besides using it on this project, is to sell the bag to someone else. The value of this alternative use is the market price of the bag, so in this case the opportunity cost is the input's price. This is the first lesson about opportunity costs: if a good is sold in a perfectly competitive market, then the opportunity cost is equal to the price. If the price of a bag of asphalt is $100, the asphalt costs for the project will be $100 million; if in a competitive equilibrium, price equals marginal social cost.

If the labor market is perfectly competitive, then the same argument applies to the labor costs of the project. In this case, the value of an hour of labor used on this project is the market wage—that is, what that labor is worth in its next best alternative use. If the market wage for construction workers is $10 per hour, then the opportunity cost of the labor for the project is $10 million.

Imperfect Markets Suppose, however, that for some reason there is unemployment among construction workers—perhaps state law mandates a minimum wage of $20 for construction workers.[3] If $20 is above the equilibrium wage in the construction sector, there will be some workers who would happily work at the prevailing $20 per hour wage but who cannot find jobs at that wage. Instead, they sit at home and watch *The Price Is Right,* soap operas, and Oprah Winfrey. Because they value leisure, the unemployed workers do get some utility from their unemployment. Suppose that an hour of leisure is worth $10 to construction workers on average; that is, at a wage below $10, the typical construction worker would rather stay home than work.[4]

What is the opportunity cost of the time of any unemployed workers you bring onto the job? Their alternative activity is not working; it is watching

[3] As of May 2003, there are roughly 100 such "living wage" ordinances in force in U.S. localities. These laws can apply to government employees, employees of firms with government contracts, or all employees of firms above a certain size within city or county boundaries. For example, in November 2002, New York City Mayor Michael Bloomberg signed into law a living wage ordinance that covers more workers than any other such law in the country. The law will apply to about 50,000 employees of service contractors doing business with the city, principally health care workers, as well as a handful of day care, food service, and disability service workers. The current living wage is set at $9.50 plus health benefits, or $11.10 if benefits are not provided by the employer (as of June 2006). See source: http://www.livingwagecampaign.org/index.php?id=1959 for more information.
[4] Alternatively, workers may get no utility from leisure while unemployed, but may get unemployment insurance from the government at $10 per hour. This would have the same effect in our example.

---

cash-flow accounting Accounting method that calculates costs solely by adding up what the government pays for inputs to a project, and calculates benefits solely by adding up income or government revenues generated by the project.

opportunity cost The social marginal cost of any resource is the value of that resource in its next best use.

TV, an activity that is valued by the workers at $10 per hour. Thus, the opportunity cost for unemployed construction workers is only $10 per hour, not $20 per hour. If half of the million man-hours that are required for this job come from workers who are unemployed, then the opportunity cost of hiring 1 million worker hours is $20 × 500,000 + $10 × 500,000 = $15 million, even though the government is actually paying out $20 million in cash.

The cash cost to the government for labor consists of two components: the opportunity cost of the resource (labor) plus the transfer of **rents,** which are payments to the resource deliverer (the worker) beyond those required to obtain the resource. The opportunity cost of one hour of labor is only $10 per hour for the unemployed workers, since they would be willing to work for that wage. Thus, by paying them $20 per hour, we are transferring an extra $10 per hour to them. This is not a cost to society; it is simply a transfer from one party (the government) to another (unemployed construction workers). So, of the $20 million paid by the government, $5 million is a transfer of rents from government to unemployed workers ($10 × 500,000), and is not counted as a true economic cost of the project (despite being a cash accounting cost). *Economic costs are only those costs associated with diverting the resource from its next best use,* which for these unemployed workers was watching TV at a value of $10 per hour. Any other costs are transfers.

Similarly, suppose that the asphalt was sold to the government not by a perfectly competitive firm but by a monopoly, which charges a price that is above its marginal cost. In this case, the resource cost of the asphalt is the marginal cost of producing it—the cost of the asphalt in terms of what else could have been done with these resources. The difference between the price paid for the bag of asphalt and the marginal cost of its production is simply a transfer of rents from the government to the monopoly asphalt maker.

Measuring Future Costs

The last cost is maintenance, which involves both materials and labor. The analysis for those materials and labor is the same as we have pursued thus far. But there is a new wrinkle as well, because we need to combine a future stream of costs (maintenance) with the one-time costs associated with construction. To do this, we compare the **present discounted value** (*PDV*) of these costs, as reviewed in Chapter 4. A dollar tomorrow is worth less than a dollar today because I could put the dollar in a bank today, earn interest, and have more money tomorrow. So a dollar today is worth (1 + *r*) times as much as a dollar tomorrow, where *r* is the interest rate I could earn in the bank. As a result, future maintenance costs must be discounted to compare them to today's construction costs.

While applying present discounted value involves simple algebra, there are some important economic issues involved in choosing the right **social discount rate** to use for these calculations (the "*r*" in the expression for *PDV* on page 103 of Chapter 4). If a private firm were making an investment decision, the proper discount rate should represent the opportunity cost of what else the firm could accomplish with those same funds. If there is an existing

rents Payments to resource deliverers that exceed those necessary to employ the resource.

present discounted value (PDV) A dollar next year is worth 1 + *r* times less than a dollar now because the dollar could earn *r*% interest if invested.

social discount rate The appropriate value of *r* to use in computing *PDV* for social investments.

investment that yields 10% per year with certainty, and the firm pays a tax rate of 50%, then this investment would net the firm a return of 5% per year. The opportunity cost of spending money on any new project, then, is the 5% net return that the firm could earn on the existing investment. Thus, 5% is the rate that should be used to discount the payments associated with any new project.

The government should also base its discount rate on the private-sector opportunity cost. The next best use for any money by the government is its use in the hands of the private sector. Thus, if a private firm could earn a 10% return on their money, then the government counts that full 10% as its opportunity cost. Unlike the private actor, the government does not count solely the after-tax portion of the investment return as its opportunity cost, since the government is the party collecting the taxes. Thus, the social cost of removing the money from the private sector is 10%: the 5% after-tax return to the firm and the 5% in tax revenues to the government. This is the opportunity cost of devoting the funds to the government's project, so 10% should be used as a discount rate.[5]

In practice, the U.S. government uses a variety of discount rates.[6] The Office of Management and Budget (OMB) recommended in 1992 that the government use a discount rate of 7%, the historical pretax rate of return on private investments, for all public investments. Using a discount rate of 7%, and recalling the rule from Chapter 4 that the *PDV* of a long-term stream of payment is just the payment amount over the interest rate, the $10 million future stream of maintenance costs has a present discounted value of $143 million ($10 million/0.07 = $143 million). Thus, the total costs of the project in today's dollars are $100 million for asphalt, $15 million for labor, and $143 million for maintenance, for a total of $258 million. This set of costs is shown in Table 8-2.

8.2

Measuring the Benefits of Public Projects

Measuring the benefits associated with this project is more difficult than measuring the costs because it is more difficult to use market values to place a value on the benefits.

Valuing Driving Time Saved

The first benefit associated with this project is that both producers and consumers will save travel time. For producers, we can value the time savings in a

---

[5] Alternatively, one could consider the spending on public projects as being financed by increased government debt. In this case, the opportunity cost of the public funds is the interest rate paid by the government on its debt.

[6] Guidelines for the choice of discount rate were issued by the Office of Management and Budget (1992).

■ TABLE 8-2

Cost-Benefit Analysis of Highway Construction Project

		Quantity	Price / Value	Total
Costs	Asphalt	1 million bags	$100/bag	$100 million
	Labor	1 million hours	½ at $20/hour and ½ at $10/hour	$15 million
	Maintenance	$10 million/year	7% discount rate	$143 million
			First-year cost:	**$115 million**
			Total cost over time (7% discount rate):	**$258 million**
Benefits	Driving time saved	500,000 hours/year		
	Lives saved	5 lives/year		
			First-year benefit:	
			Total benefit over time:	
			Benefit over time minus cost over time:	

The cost of the asphalt for this project is dictated by the market price for asphalt, $100 per bag. The cost of labor depends not on the wage but on the full opportunity cost of the labor, which incorporates the current unemployment of any workers who will be used on the project. The cost of future maintenance is the present discounted value of these projected expenditures.

straightforward manner. The benefits to producers arise from a reduction in the cost of supplying goods, because it takes less time to transport them. The decreased costs lead to an increase in supply (a rightward shift in the supply curve), which raises the total size of social surplus. This increase in social surplus is the benefit to society from the lower cost of producing goods.

It is much trickier to measure the benefits of time saved for consumers: How do we value the benefits of being able to get from point to point more quickly? What we need is some measure of society's valuation of individuals' *time:* What is it worth to me to have to spend fewer minutes in the car? Economists have several approaches to answering this question. None are fully satisfactory, but by putting them together we can draw some general conclusions about the value of time.

Using Market-based Measures to Value Time: Wages Suppose we can show that the time that individuals save from driving faster is spent at work. Suppose, moreover, that there is a perfectly competitive labor market that allows individuals to earn their hourly wage for each additional hour spent at work. Under these assumptions, we would use drivers' wages to value their time savings. Opportunity cost is the value in the next best alternative use, and the next best alternative use in this example is being at work. The value of time at work in a perfectly competitive labor market is the wage rate that could be earned during that hour. The average wage rate for workers in the United States was $17.8 per hour in 2005.[7]

---

[7] U.S. Bureau of the Census (2006a), Table 629.

What if the time savings is spent partly at work, and partly in leisure? Once again, if we are in a perfectly competitive labor market in which individuals can freely choose how many hours they want to work, then the wage is the right measure *even if the time is spent on leisure*. This is because, in a competitive model, individuals set the value of their next hour of leisure time equal to their wage. If the marginal utility of leisure time was above the wage, individuals would work less and take more leisure (driving down the marginal utility of leisure by consuming more leisure). If the marginal utility of leisure time was below the wage, individuals would work more and take less leisure (driving up the marginal utility of leisure by consuming less leisure). Thus, in a perfectly competitive labor market with freely adjusting hours, the value of time is always the wage, even if the time is spent on leisure activities.

As you might expect, this theoretical proposition runs into some problems in practice:

▶ Individuals can't freely trade off leisure and hours of work; jobs may come with hours restrictions. Suppose I'd like to work more than 40 hours per week at my current wage, but my employer will not let me because that would involve paying me a higher overtime wage. In this case, my value of leisure could be below my wage, but I can't drive them to equality by working longer hours. So the wage *overstates* the value to me of saving time.

▶ There may be nonmonetary aspects of the job. For example, in the summertime, my office at work is air conditioned, while my home is not. This means that I value time at work at more than the wage; I also value the fact that it is more comfortable. Thus, my total compensation at work is higher than my wage. The value of leisure is set equal to total compensation from work, not just the wage, so the wage *understates* the value to me of saving time.

These problems limit the value of the wage as a value of time, leading economists to consider a variety of other approaches to time valuation.

Using Survey-Based Measures to Value Time: Contingent Valuation Before you took any economics, if I had asked you to figure out the value of time to someone, how would you have proposed to do it? Most likely you would have simply asked individuals what time is worth to them! That is, you could ask, "How much would you pay to save five minutes on your drive?" This approach is labeled by economists as **contingent valuation:** asking individuals to value an option they are not now choosing (or that is not yet available to them).

The advantage of contingent valuation is that, in some circumstances, it is the only feasible method for valuing a public good. Consider the difficulty of valuing efforts to save a rare species of owl. There is no obvious market price that you can use to value that species. But you can survey individuals and ask what it is worth to them to save the species. These preferences can then be aggregated (added up) to form a value of efforts to save the species.

The problems with contingent valuation, however, are daunting, as reviewed in the following application.

contingent valuation Asking individuals to value an option they are not now choosing or do not have the opportunity to choose.

> ▶ **APPLICATION**

The Problems of Contingent Valuation

While contingent valuation seems the most straightforward means of valuing benefits such as time savings, critics contend that the results of contingent valuation studies prove their uselessness. Two of the leading critics of contingent valuation are economists Peter Diamond and Jerry Hausman, who point out that varying the structure of contingent valuation surveys can lead to widely varying responses.[8] Examples of this problem include the following:

- ▶ *Isolation of issues matters.* When asked only one question on how much they'd be willing to pay to improve visibility at the Grand Canyon, respondents gave answers five times higher than when that question was placed third in a list with other questions.

- ▶ *Order of issues matters.* When asked how much they'd pay to save seals and whales (in that order), seals were worth $142 and whales $195. When the order was reversed, whales (first) were now worth $172 and seals only $85.

- ▶ *The "embedding effect" matters.* Asked to value preservation from logging of one, two, and three wilderness areas, respondents gave roughly the same values for all three scenarios, suggesting that the value reported was not for the task specified but for the general value of preserving wilderness. Similarly, respondents placed roughly equal value on saving 2,000, 20,000 and 200,000 birds. ◀

Using Revealed Preference to Value Time The natural way for noneconomists to value time is to ask individuals what their time is worth, but this approach runs into the previously noted problems. The natural way for economists to value time is instead to use **revealed preference:** let the actions of individuals reveal their valuation. The mantra of economics is: people may lie, but their actions, which result from utility maximization, don't!

revealed preference Letting the actions of individuals reveal their valuation.

Suppose we compare two identical houses, one of which is five minutes closer to the central city where most commuters work. If individuals are willing to pay more for the closer home, this implies that they value the time savings. We can therefore use the difference in sales prices between the two homes to assign a value to saving five minutes of commuting. This comparison provides a market-based valuation of their time that truthfully reveals the preferences of individuals.

While appealing in theory, this approach also runs into problems in practice. This example works if the two homes are identical. But what if the house that is closer to the city is also nicer? Then we would find that it sells for a lot more, and falsely assume that this implies that individuals value their

---

[8] Diamond and Hausman (1994).

VALUING TIME SAVINGS

The fundamental problem facing the revealed preference approach in practice is the type of bias we discussed in Chapter 3. When doing revealed preference analysis, the treatment is a good with a certain attribute (such as being only 10 minutes from the city), while the control is another good without that attribute (such as being 5 minutes farther from the city). The problem is that the treatments and controls may differ in ways that lead to bias. Suppose that homes built closer to the city are smaller, or that they have smaller yards. This would lead their value to be lower, so that when one compared the prices of houses farther away and closer to the city, one might not find the expected decline in prices for farther-away homes. In the Boston metropolitan area, for example, the town of Everett is on average only 4 miles from downtown Boston, while the suburban town of Lexington is 11 miles away. Yet the average home price in Everett is $225,000, while the average home price in Lexington is nearly three times higher at $614,000.[9] This is because the houses in Lexington are typically much larger and have nicer attributes than those in Everett.

Many of these attributes are observable, such as the square footage of the house or the number of bathrooms. In such cases, we can try to control for these other attribute differences using cross-sectional regression analysis with control variables. Indeed, in this context there is a name for such a strategy: *hedonic market analysis*. Hedonic market analysis proceeds by running a regression of house values on each of the bundle of attributes of housing: distance to town center, number of bedrooms, number of bathrooms, square footage, and so on. The notion is that if we control in a regression context for all of the attributes other than distance, we will essentially be comparing identical houses in different locations.

As we highlighted in Chapter 3, however, this is not likely to be a fully satisfactory approach. There are many dif-ferences between houses that are hard to observe, such as the perceived quality of the neighborhood or the care taken by the previous owner. If these things are correlated with distance to the town center, it will mean that the treatment group (close houses) and the control group (more distant houses) are not identical products, so our (biased) estimates do not give a true valuation of time differences.

In order to provide a more convincing estimate of the value of time savings, a quasi-experimental approach can be used. An example of such a study was done by Deacon and Sonstelie (1985). During the oil crisis of the 1970s, the government imposed price ceilings on the large gasoline companies, setting a maximum price that those companies could charge per gallon of gas. These low prices (relative to the true market price) led consumers to wait in long lines to get gas. These price ceilings did not apply to smaller, independently owned stations, so lines were shorter there. As a result, the amount of time individuals were willing to wait at the stations owned by large gas companies (the treatment group) relative to independent stations (the control group) can be compared to the amount of money saved by going to the treatment stations instead of the control stations to form a value of time.

The authors compared Chevron stations in California, which were mandated to lower their prices by $0.407 (in 2005) per gallon below the price being charged by the control group of independent stations. Lines formed at Chevron stations for cheaper gas, forcing customers to wait an average of 14.6 minutes more there than at competing stations. The mean purchase was 10.5 gallons, suggesting roughly that people were saving $17.60 per hour they waited. That is, individuals revealed themselves to be willing to wait an hour for $17.60—almost exactly equal to the average hourly wage in the United States.[10]

time very highly. The problem is that the price of any good values the entire set of attributes of that good, but for revealed preference analysis we are only concerned with one particular attribute (in this case, distance to the city). Because other attributes of the good differ, it is difficult to use revealed preference to distill the value of a particular attribute of the good, such as location.

---

[9] Statistics come from http://www.boston.com/realestate/community/.
[10] Consumers saved $0.407 per gallon, and purchased 10.5 gallons on average, so they saved on average $4.27 by waiting 15 minutes, which implies a valuation of 1 hour of $17.08.

The ideal way to value time would be a controlled experiment, where we varied just the attribute of the good that we are trying to value: in this example, we could take the same house and move it five minutes closer to the city. This is clearly not possible in many cases. As reviewed in the Empirical Evidence box, however, a clever attempt to resolve this problem suggests that the value of an hour of time is remarkably consistent with the estimate from market-based measures.

Valuing Saved Lives

Returning to our highway example, the other major benefit of improving the turnpike is that repairing the road will improve safety and save lives. Valuing human lives is the single most difficult issue in cost-benefit analysis. Many would say that human life is priceless, that we should pay any amount of money to save a life. By this argument, valuing life is a reprehensible activity; there is no way to put a value on such a precious commodity.

This argument does not recognize that there are many possible uses for the limited government budget, each of which could save some lives. By stating that life should not be valued, we leave ourselves helpless when facing choices of different programs, each of which could save lives. By this logic, we would have to finance *any* government program that could save lives, at the expense of, say, education or housing expenditures. Alternatively, we could claim that virtually any government expenditure has some odds of saving a life; by improving education, for example, we may reduce crime, which will save victims' lives. To escape the impotence that would be imposed by the "life is priceless" argument, one needs to be able to place some value on a human life.

▶ **APPLICATION**

Valuing Life[11]

The sticky ethical problem of valuing life arises in many instances in public policy, as shown by these examples.

1. In 1993, consumer groups demanded that General Motors recall about 5 million pickup trucks it had manufactured between 1973 and 1987. The gas tanks on these trucks were mounted on the outside of the vehicle. These groups claimed that the trucks' side-mounted gas tanks made the trucks more likely to explode on impact, causing 150 deaths over the period that the truck was manufactured. This recall would cost $1 billion and would, according to government calculations, save at most 32 more lives (since the trucks were slowly falling out of use). Using these estimates, the cost per life saved by the recall would have been $1 billion/32 = $31.25 million.

---

[11] Brown and Swoboda (1994); Jowit (2002).

GM didn't want to spend this much money and instead managed to reach a settlement with the government, agreeing to provide $50 million to support education programs about seat belts and drunk driving, to undertake research into burn and trauma treatment, and to buy 200,000 child safety seats for low-income families. Consumer advocate Ralph Nader called the settlement "the most unprecedented buyout of law enforcement officials by a culpable corporation in regulatory history." But was it? The government estimated that the child safety seats alone would save 50 lives. If this were the only benefit (and it wasn't), the cost per life saved would be $50 million/50 = $1 million, much less than the $31.25 million per life saved the recall would have cost. In other words, this alternative to the recall was saving more lives at a much lower cost. By this measure, the settlement was much better than the recall alternative, but it was only possible because the government was willing to set a value on human life.

2. In October 1999, a commuter train crash at London's Paddington Station killed 31 people and prompted calls by an outraged public for more investment in rail safety measures. The public's anger was in part focused on the fact that British Rail, once a public entity, had recently been *privatized* (sold to a private-sector entity, a policy we discuss more in Chapter 9), so that people assumed the profit-seeking companies in charge of the system had skimped on safety measures to improve their profits. Emotions ran high at the time of the crash, and one government official promised that everything possible would be done to protect rail passengers, saying, "A billion is not a lot of money when safety is at stake."

   The government responded by requiring the rail companies to install the Train Protection and Warning System (TPWS), which for $700 million would be able to quickly stop any train traveling under 75 mph if a dangerous situation were detected. But then a government investigation into rail safety recommended installing even more advanced technology, the European Train Control System (ETCS), which could stop trains traveling at any speeds. Installing the ETCS would cost between $3 billion and $9 billion (in U.S. dollars), save anywhere from one to three lives per year, and would last anywhere from 30 to 50 years. At best ($3 billion to save three lives per year for 50 years), this would mean spending $20 million per life saved; at worst ($9 billion to save one life per year for 30 years), it would mean $300 million per life saved.

   As critics noted the immensely high cost of the ETCS, government officials began to back down from promises to spend whatever it took to ensure rail safety. Furthermore, as opponents of the proposed safety measures noted, many more Britons are killed on roads than on rails, so that implementing the government's safety standards on Britain's roadways would save more lives, and at a cost of only $2 million per life saved. As a result, the government to date has not committed itself to installing the more expensive rail safety system. ◄

Using Wages to Value a Life As with valuing time, the market-based approach to valuing lives is to use wages: life's value is the present discounted value of the lifetime stream of earnings. While this seems like a logical approach, it faces a number of problems. One major problem is that using wages to value life doesn't value any time that isn't spent working. In a competitive markets model, we would want to add up not only the wages that are earned at work but also the leisure time that is valued at that market wage. Keeler (2001) calculated that a worker under 50 will spend 10–20% of her future hours working, so that, assuming she values leisure time at her wage rate, the value of her life is about 5–10 times her future lifetime earnings. Using data on employment, wages, and mortality rates, Keeler calculates that the average 20-year-old female will have future earnings of $529,000 (net present value) but will value her life at $3.4 million. Men have slightly higher values because of higher earnings, while older people have lower values because they have fewer hours of life remaining.

This approach also faces the same problem as using wages to value time, which is that the market wage may not accurately reflect the value of leisure time. Moreover, life may mean more than just wages earned or corresponding leisure. For example, an individual may internalize the enjoyment derived by others from her being alive.

Contingent Valuation The second approach to valuing a life uses contingent valuation. One way to do this is to ask individuals what their lives are worth. This is obviously a difficult question to answer. Thus, a more common approach is to ask about the valuation of things that change the probability of dying. For example, one such survey asked participants how much more they would pay for a ticket on an airline with one fatal crash out of 500,000 flights compared to the same ticket on an airline with two fatal crashes out of 500,000 flights. Another question asked how much less they would be willing to pay for a house in an area with environmental pollution that would reduce their life span by one year compared to a house in an unpolluted area.

The problems of contingent valuation just raised will clearly haunt this analysis as well, however. Perhaps for this reason, contingent valuation studies have provided a very wide range of results for life values, ranging from $876,000 to $23.7 million per life saved.[12]

Revealed Preference As with valuing time savings, the method preferred by economists for valuing life is to use revealed preferences. For example, we can value life by estimating how much individuals are willing to pay for something that reduces their odds of dying. Suppose that a passenger air bag could be added to a new car for $350, and there is a 1 in 10,000 chance that it would save the life of the car passenger. This implies that the value of lives to individuals who buy airbags is at least $3.5 million.

---

[12] Viscusi (1993), Table 2, updated to 2005 dollars.

compensating differentials
Additional (or reduced) wage payments to workers to compensate them for the negative (or positive) amenities of a job, such as increased risk of mortality (or a nicer office).

Alternatively, we can value life by estimating how much individuals must be paid to take risky jobs that raise their chance of dying. Suppose that we compare two jobs, one of which has a 1% higher risk of death each year (for example, a coal miner versus a cashier in a retail store). Suppose further that the riskier job pays $30,000 more each year. This $30,000 is called a **compensating differential.** In this example, individuals must be compensated by $30,000 to take this 1% increased risk of dying, so that their lives are valued at $3 million ($30,000/0.01).

There is a large literature in economics that uses these types of revealed preference approaches to valuing lives. The consensus from this revealed preference approach, as summarized by the renowned expert in the field, Kip Viscusi of Harvard University, is that the value of life is roughly $7.6 million.[13]

This approach, however, also has its drawbacks. First of all, it makes very strong information assumptions. In doing this type of revealed preference approach, we assume that the coal miner knows that he has a 2% higher chance of dying each year than the cashier. This type of information is often not readily available. The implied value of life from compensating differentials depends on individuals' perceptions of the risk, not the actual statistical risk, and these perceptions are often unknown to the researcher trying to estimate the value of life. Second, the literature on psychology suggests that, even armed with this information, individuals are not well prepared to evaluate these trade-offs. For example, a large experimental literature shows that individuals typically overstate very small risks (such as the odds of dying in a plane crash) and understate larger risks (such as the odds of dying on a dangerous job).

The third problem with revealed preference studies was highlighted in the discussion about housing and time savings: the need to control for other associated attributes of products or jobs. For example, suppose that a coal miner faces a 1% higher chance of dying each year than does a cashier, and also faces a 5% higher chance of being seriously injured. Then the $30,000 compensating differential incorporates both of these effects, and cannot simply be used to infer the value of life. Moreover, coal mining is a much less pleasant job along many dimensions than is being a cashier. Compensating differentials reflect both job risks and job "amenities" that determine the overall attractiveness of the job. The negative amenities of coal mining, along with other health risks, provide reasons why the compensating differential for that job overstates the value of life (since it incorporates the compensating differential for work injury and bad work conditions).

Fourth, there is the central problem of *differences in the value of life*. There is presumably not one common value of life in society, but rather a distribution across individuals of different tastes. The revealed preference approach provides an estimate of the value of life for the set of individuals who are willing to take a riskier job or buy a safer product. This may not, however, provide a representative answer for the population as a whole.

---

[13] Viscusi and Aldy (2003), p. 26, updated to 2005 dollars.

For example, suppose that there are 10,000 people in society, 1,000 of whom don't much care about on-the-job risk (risk neutral), and 9,000 of whom are very worried about on-the-job risk (risk averse). Suppose that there are two types of jobs in society, a risky job with a 1% chance of dying each year and a non-risky job with no chance of dying. The risk-neutral workers require only $1,000 more each year to work in the risky job, while the other workers require $100,000.

If there are 1,000 risky jobs in this society, who will take them, and how much more will they pay than the non-risky jobs? If the firms that offer those risky jobs pay only $1,000 in compensating differential, the jobs will be filled by the 1,000 risk-neutral workers; the risk-averse workers would not take the job at that small compensating differential. Firms would like to pay the smallest possible compensating differential, so they will pay the $1,000 to get the 1,000 risk-neutral workers.

As a result, there will be a $1,000 compensating differential in equilibrium, implying a value of life of $100,000 ($1,000/0.01). Such a difference doesn't mean that life is worth only $100,000 for the average person in society, however; it is the value only for the risk-neutral individuals who take these jobs. This estimate would provide a very misleading answer for the overall social value of life.

More generally, since risk-neutral individuals are always the first to take risky jobs, revealed preference pricing of risk will generally understate the value of life for the average person. This is because it is not an average person you are observing, but a person who (by definition) is more risk loving than average.

Government Revealed Preference Another approach to valuing lives is not to rely on how individuals value their lives but to focus instead on existing government programs and what they spend to save lives. A recent study reviewed 76 government regulatory programs that are designed to protect public safety, and computed both the associated improvements in mortality and costs of the regulation. The key conclusions from this study are summarized in Table 8-3. The costs varied from $110,000 per life saved for safety interventions such as childproof cigarette lighters, to $109 billion per life saved from regulations for solid waste disposal facilities. Forty-four of the 76

■ TABLE 8-3

Costs Per Life Saved of Various Regulations

Regulation concerning . . .	Year	Agency	Cost Per Life Saved (millions of 2005 $)
Childproof lighters	1993	CPSC	$0.1
Food labeling	1993	FDA	0.4
Reflective devices for heavy trucks	1999	NHTSA	1.0
Children's sleepwear flammability	1973	CPSC	2.4
Rear/up/shoulder seatbelts in cars	1989	NHTSA	4.8
Asbestos	1972	OSHA	6.0
VALUE OF STATISTICAL LIFE			**7.6**
Benzene	1987	OSHA	24
Asbestos ban	1989	EPA	85
Cattle feed	1979	FDA	185
Solid waste disposal facilities	1991	EPA	109,000

Morrall (2003), Table 2, updated to 2005 dollars.

Government safety regulations increase costs and save lives, and these costs and benefits can be compared to compute an implicit cost per life saved. These values range from a low of $110,000 per life saved for childproof lighters to a high of over $109 billion per life saved for solid waste disposal facility regulations.

regulations had a cost per life saved below the $7.6 million figure that comes from studies of compensating differentials, but 31 of the regulations had a cost above $10.9 million per life saved.

The fact that the government is willing to spend so much to save lives in many public policy interventions suggests that the public sector values lives quite highly. Another interpretation, however, is that the government is simply inconsistent, and does not apply the same standards in some arenas as it does in others.

Discounting Future Benefits

A particularly thorny issue for cost-benefit analysis is that many projects have costs that are mostly immediate and benefits that are mostly long-term. An excellent example of this would be efforts to combat global warming through reducing the use of carbon-intensive products (through a tax on the carbon content of goods, for example). The costs of such efforts would be felt in the near term, as consumers have to pay more for goods (such as gasoline) whose consumption worsens global warming. The benefits of such efforts would be felt in the very distant future, however, as the global temperature in 100 years would be lower with such government intervention than it would be without any such intervention.

These types of examples are problematic for two reasons. First, the choice of discount rate will matter enormously for benefits that are far in the future. For example, a dollar benefit in 100 years is worth 13.8¢ if the discount rate is 2% $(1/(1.02)^{100} = 0.138)$, 5.2¢ if the discount rate is 3%, and 2¢ if the discount rate is 4%. This sensitivity of benefit calculations to small changes in the discount rate places enormous importance on getting the discount rate exactly right.

Second, long-lived projects provide benefits not only to the generation that pays the costs but to future generations as well. Should we treat benefits to future generations differently than benefits to current generations? Some would argue that we should just weight the benefits to the current generation, who are paying the costs. But what if the current generation cares about its children? Then we should incorporate the children as well.

Cost-Effectiveness Analysis

Despite the list of clever approaches to valuing the benefits of public projects, in some cases society may be unable (or unwilling) to do so. This does not imply that the techniques of cost-benefit analysis are useless. Rather it implies that, instead of comparing costs to benefits, we need to contrast alternative means of providing the public good, and to choose the approach that provides that good most efficiently. This comparison is called **cost-effectiveness analysis,** the search for the most cost-effective approach to providing a desired public good. For example, society may decide to combat global warming even if it is impossible to put an estimate on the benefits of doing so (or if the benefit is hugely uncertain because it is so far in the future). Even so, as discussed in Chapter 6, there are many ways of combating global warming, and cost-effectiveness must be considered in choosing the best approach.

cost-effectiveness analysis For projects that have unmeasurable benefits, or are viewed as desirable regardless of the level of benefits, we can compute only their costs and choose the most cost-effective project.

■ TABLE 8-4

Cost-Benefit Analysis of Highway Construction Project

		Quantity	Price / Value	Total
Costs	Asphalt	1 million bags	$100/bag	$100 million
	Labor	1 million hours	½ at $20/hour and ½ at $10/hour	$15 million
	Maintenance	$10 million/year	7% discount rate	$143 million
			First-year cost:	**$115 million**
			Total cost over time (7% discount rate):	**$258 million**
Benefits	Driving time saved	500,000 hours/year	$17/hour	$8.5 million
	Lives saved	5 lives/year	$7 million/life	$35 million
			First-year benefit:	**$43.5 million**
			Total benefit over time (7% discount rate):	**$621.4 million**
			Benefit over time minus cost over time:	**$363.4 million**

The time savings from this project is most appropriately valued by the revealed preference valuation of time, which is $17/hour. The life savings is most appropriately valued by the revealed preference value of life, which averages $7 million. The present discounted value of costs for this renovation project is $258 million, while the *PDV* of benefits for this project is $621.4 million. Because benefits exceed costs by $363.4 million, the project should clearly be undertaken.

8.3

Putting It All Together

Table 8-4 shows the comparison of the costs and benefits of the turnpike renovation project. The present value of the costs of this project is $258 million. The benefits are 500,000 reduced hours of driving time, and five reduced fatalities per year. Let's assume that we can value both the increased time to producers and consumers at the same value, $17 per hour (which comes from the revealed preference study cited earlier). That would produce time savings benefits of $8.5 million per year. Let's also assume that we can value the lives saved at the revealed preference average of $7 million per year. That would produce a value of life savings of $35 million per year. The total benefits would therefore be $43.5 million per year.

Applying the same 7% discount rate to benefits, these benefits have a present discounted value of $621 million, more than two times the cost of this project. Even if the value of both time and lives is half as large as those assumed here, the benefits would still significantly exceed the costs of this project. Thus, society benefits from these road improvements, and the government should provide them.

Other Issues in Cost-Benefit Analysis

While the previous discussion is complicated enough, there are three other major issues that make cost-benefit analysis difficult: common counting mistakes such as double-counting benefits, concerns over the distributional impacts of public projects, and uncertainty over costs and benefits.

Common Counting Mistakes   When analyzing costs and benefits, a number of common mistakes arise, such as:

▶ *Counting secondary benefits:* If the government improves a highway, there may be an increase in commerce activity along the highway. One might be tempted to count this as a benefit of the project, but this new road may be taking away from commercial activity elsewhere. What matters in determining the benefits is only the total rise in social surplus from the new activity (the *net* increase in surplus-increasing trades that results from the improved highway).

▶ *Counting labor as a benefit:* In arguing for projects such as this highway improvement, politicians often talk about the jobs created by the project as a benefit. But wages are part of a project's costs, not its benefits. If the project lowers unemployment, this lowers the opportunity cost of the workers, but it does not convert these costs to benefits.

▶ *Double-counting benefits:* Public projects often lead to asset-value increases. For example, the fact that consumers save time driving to work when the highway is improved could lead to higher values for houses farther away from the city. When considering the value of this highway improvement, some may count both the reduction in travel times *and* the increase in the value of houses as a benefit. Because the rise in house values results from the reduction in travel time, however, both should not be counted as benefits.

Sometimes, these types of mistakes are made because of hasty or uninformed analysis. Other times, however, they are made on purpose by one side or another of a heated cost-benefit debate. The growing role of cost-benefit analysis in public policy making has raised the stakes for avoiding this type of manipulation of what should be an objective exercise.

Distributional Concerns   The costs and benefits of a public project do not necessarily accrue to the same individuals; for example, when we expand a highway, commuters benefit, but those living next to the road lose from more traffic and noise. In theory, if the benefits of this project exceed its costs, it is possible to collect money from those who benefit and redistribute it to those who lose, and make everyone better off. In practice, however, such redistribution rarely happens, partly due to economic problems (such as the informational requirements of carrying out such redistribution), and partly due to political problems of the type discussed in the next chapter.

In the absence of such redistribution, we may care specifically about the parties gaining and losing from a public project. For example, if a project benefits only the rich and hurts only the poor, we may want to discount benefits and raise costs to account for this. The problem, of course, is: How do we pick the weights? This will depend on the type of social welfare function we use, as discussed in Chapter 2.

Uncertainty As should be clear from the previous discussion, the costs and benefits of public projects are often highly uncertain. The extent of such uncertainty, however, can vary from project to project, and should be accounted for when comparing projects. For reasons we discuss in great detail in Chapter 12, for any predicted outcome, individuals prefer that outcome be more rather than less certain. As a result, for any gap between costs and benefits, governments should prefer projects that have a more certain, rather than a less certain, estimate of the gap. Much as governments might prefer projects that have their greatest benefits for the poor, they also might prefer projects that deliver their benefits with more certainty.

8.4
Conclusion

Government analysts at all levels face a major challenge in attempting to turn the abstract notions of social costs and benefits into practical implications for public project choice. What at first seems to be a simple accounting exercise becomes quite complicated when resources cannot be valued in competitive markets. One complication arises when markets are not in competitive equilibrium, so that the opportunity costs of resources must be computed. Another complication arises when benefits are not readily priced by the market, and approaches such as contingent valuation or revealed preference must be employed. Nevertheless, economists have developed a set of tools that can take analysts a long way toward a complete accounting of the costs and benefits of public projects.

▶ **HIGHLIGHTS**

- Providing optimal levels of public goods requires evaluating the costs and benefits of public projects.

- The costs of inputs to public projects are appropriately measured by their opportunity cost, or their value in the next best alternative use.

- If markets are in competitive equilibrium, the opportunity cost of an input is its market price; if markets are not in competitive equilibrium, however, the opportunity cost will differ from the market price, and some of the government spending may simply be transfers of rents.

- If costs are in the future, we must use a social discount rate to value those costs in present dollars.

- Measuring the benefits of public projects is difficult, and approaches range from using market values (such as wages to value time), to asking individuals about their valuation (contingent valuation), to using real-world behavior to reveal valuations (such as the compensating differentials for risky jobs to value life).

- Benefits are often in the future as well, which makes valuation very sensitive to the social discount rate chosen.

- Public project analysis requires considering the distributional implications of the project, the level of uncertainty over costs and benefits, and the budgetary cost of financing the project.

▶ QUESTIONS AND PROBLEMS

1. A new public works project requires 200,000 hours of labor to complete.

   a. Suppose the labor market is perfectly competitive and the market wage is $15. What is the opportunity cost of the labor employed?

   b. Suppose that there is currently unemployment among workers, and that there are some workers who would willingly work for $10 per hour. What is the opportunity cost of the labor employed? Does this vary depending on the fraction of would-be unemployed workers hired for the project?

   c. If your answers to (a) and (b) differ, explain why.

2. How does the opportunity cost of a government purchase vary depending on whether the market for the purchased good is perfectly competitive or monopolistic?

3. Two city councilors are debating whether to pursue a new project. Councilor Miles says it is only "worth it" to society if suppliers lower their costs to the city for the inputs to the project. Councilor Squeaky disagrees, and says it doesn't matter—society is no better off with these cost concessions than it would be without the concessions. Where do you stand? Explain.

4. For your senior thesis, you polled your classmates, asking them, "How much would you be willing to pay to double the amount of parking on campus?" Based on their responses, you estimated that your fellow students were collectively willing to pay $12 million to double the amount of on-campus parking. What are some problems with this type of analysis?

5. Consider the Deacon and Sonstelie (1985) approach to valuing time described in the text on page 210. Imagine that two cars are equivalent to one another in every way (such as gas mileage) except for gas tank size, and car A's tank has twice the gas capacity of car B's tank. Which driver is more likely to patronize a Chevron station mandated to lower prices below those of independent stations? Explain your answer.

6. A city government is considering building a new system of lighted bike paths. A councilor supporting their construction lists the following as potential benefits of the paths: (1) more enjoyable bike rides for current and future bikers, (2) reduction of rush-hour automobile traffic due to increases in bike commuting, (3) the creation of 15 construction-related jobs. Can all of these actually be considered to be benefits? Explain.

7. Suppose you prefer working 40 hours per week to 20 hours, and prefer working 32 hours per week to either 20 or 40 hours. However, you are forced to work either 20 hours or 40 hours per week. Is your hourly wage rate an accurate reflection of the value of your time? Explain.

8. The city of Metropolita added a new subway station in a neighborhood between two existing stations. After the station was built, the average house price increased by $10,000 and the average commute time fell by 15 minutes per day. Suppose that there is one commuter per household, that the average commuter works 5 days per week, 50 weeks per year, and that the benefits of reduced commuting time apply to current and future residents forever. Assume an interest rate of 5%. Produce an estimate of the average value of time for commuters based on this information.

9. One approach to calculating the value of life involves the use of compensating differential studies. What informational problems make these studies difficult to carry out?

The $\mathbf{e}$ icon indicates a question that requires students to apply the empirical economics principles discussed in Chapter 3 and the Empirical Evidence boxes.

▶ **ADVANCED QUESTIONS** ——————————————————————————————

10. The city of Gruberville is considering whether to build a new public swimming pool. This pool would have a capacity of 800 swimmers per day, and the proposed admission fee is $6 per swimmer per day. The estimated cost of the swimming pool, averaged over the life of the pool, is $4 per swimmer per day.

Gruberville has hired you to assess this project. Fortunately, the neighboring identical town of Figlionia already has a pool, and the town has randomly varied the price of that pool to find how price affects usage. The results from their study follow:

Swimming pool price per day	Number of swimmers per day
$8	500
$10	200
$4	1,100
$6	800
$2	1,400

a. If the swimming pool is built as planned, what would be the net benefit per day from the swimming pool? What is the consumer surplus for swimmers?

b. Given this information, is an 800-swimmer pool the optimally sized pool for Gruberville to build? Explain.

11. The U.S. Office of Management and Budget (OMB) recommends that the government use different discount rates for public investments than for the sale of government assets. For public investments, the OMB suggests a discount rate that reflects the historical pretax rate of return on private investments, while for the sale of government assets, the OMB recommends using the cost of government borrowing as a discount rate. Why might the OMB make this distinction?

12. The city of Animaltown plans to build a new bridge across the river separating the two halves of the city for use by its residents. It is considering two plans for financing this bridge. Plan A calls for

the bridge to be paid for out of tax revenues, allowing anyone to freely use the bridge. Plan B calls for imposing a toll of $6 for crossing the bridge, with the remainder of the cost to be paid out of tax revenues. City planners estimate a local demand curve for hourly use of the bridge to be $Q = 1,800 - 100P$. The bridge will be able to accommodate 2,000 cars per hour without congestion. Which of the plans is more efficient, and why? How would your answer change if congestion was predicted on the bridge?

13. You are trying to decide where to go on vacation. In country A, your risk of death is 1 in 10,000, and you'd pay $6,000 to go on that vacation. In country B, your risk of death is 1 in 20,000, and you'd pay $9,000 to go on that vacation. Supposing that you're indifferent between these two destinations, save for the differential risk of death, what does your willingness to pay for these vacations tell you about how much you value your life?

14. Jellystone National Park is located 10 minutes away from city A and 20 minutes away from city B. Cities A and B have 200,000 inhabitants each, and residents in both cities have the same income and preference for national parks. Assume that the cost for an individual to go to a national park is represented by the cost of the time it takes her to get into the park. Also assume that the cost of time for individuals in cities A and B is $0.50 per minute.

You observe that each inhabitant of city A goes to Jellystone ten times a year while each inhabitant of city B goes only five times a year. Assume the following: the only people who go to the park are the residents of cities A and B; the cost of running Jellystone is $1,500,000 a year; and the social discount rate is 10%. Also assume that the park will be there forever.

a. Compute the cost per visit to Jellystone for an inhabitant of each city.

b. Assuming that those two observations (cost per visit and number of visits per inhabitant of city A, and cost per visit and number of visits per inhabitant of city B) correspond to two points on the same linear individual demand curve for visits to Jellystone, derive that demand curve. What is the consumer surplus for inhabitants of each city? What is the total consumer surplus?

c. There is a timber developer who wants to buy Jellystone to run his business. He is offering $100 million for the park. Should the park be sold?

15. Imagine that you were the governor of Massachusetts 15 years ago and needed to decide if you should support the "Big Dig" highway and bridge construction project.

The Big Dig is estimated to take 7 years to complete. The project will require $45 million in construction materials per year and $20 million in labor costs per year. In addition, the construction will disrupt transportation within the city for the duration of the construction. The transportation disruption lengthens transport times for 100,000 workers by 30 hours per year. All workers are paid $15 per hour (assume that there are no distortions and that the wage reflects each worker's per hour valuation of leisure).

The Big Dig, when finished, will ease transportation within the city. Each of the 100,000 workers will have their transport time reduced by 35 hours per year as compared to the preconstruction transport time. In addition, part of the Big Dig project involves converting the space formerly taken up by an elevated highway into a large park. The State of Massachusetts has determined that each worker will value the park at $40 per year. We will assume that no one else will use the park.

We also assume the government has a 5% discount rate and that the workers live forever. The benefits to the Big Dig begin in year 7, assuming the project begins in year 0 (i.e., the project runs for 7 years, from $t = 0$ to $t = 6$).

a. Should you, as the governor, proceed with the project? Formally show the cost-benefit analysis.

b. It occurs to you, after completing the calculation in part (a), that it is possible that the cost estimates are uncertain. If the construction materials estimate is $45 million with 50% probability, and $100 million with 50% probability, should the project proceed? Assume that the government is risk neutral.

Political Economy

9

In 2004, President Bush threatened to use his first veto to kill a highway spending bill written by a Congress controlled by his own party. The reason? The bill contained so many projects of dubious value that he could not justify increasing the deficit further. (The bill would cost $275 billion over the next six years.) Perhaps the most egregious offenders were two bridges slated for construction in Alaska.[1]

One bridge would cost $200 million to build and would be among the tallest in America, nearly the height of the Golden Gate Bridge in San Francisco. Unlike the Golden Gate, however, it would not serve millions of travelers a year. Instead, it would connect the town of Ketchikan (population 7,845) with an island that houses 50 residents and the area's airport (offering six flights a day). The crossing from Ketchikan to the island is now made by a ferry that takes five minutes and that one resident calls "pretty darn reliable." The other bridge, which would cost taxpayers up to $2 billion, would be two miles long, connecting Anchorage to a port with one resident and almost no homes or businesses.

Such economically useless endeavors are clear examples of politicians deriving power by bringing funds, and thus jobs, to their home districts. One resident of Ketchikan observed, "Everyone knows it's just a boondoggle that we're getting because we have a powerful congressman." That congressman is Alaska's lone representative, Republican Don Young (also called "Mr. Concrete"). As chairman of the Transportation and Infrastructure Committee when the 2004 highway bill was written, he declared, "This is the time to take advantage of the position I'm in. . . . If I had not done fairly well for our state, I'd be ashamed of myself." In defending the provision of such political "pork" (federal spending for local projects that serve mostly to transfer federal dollars to a politician's constituents), Missouri senator Kit Bond once said, "Pork is a mighty fine diet for Missouri, low in fat and high in jobs."[2]

---

[1] Egan (2004).
[2] Mallaby (2004).

In July of 2005, the House and Senate approved the transportation bill, which was signed by President Bush in August. Ultimately, $286.4 billion were allocated. Over $24 billion of the total amount was set aside for spending on 6,373 pet projects.[3] In the final bill was $1 billion earmarked for over 100 pork projects in Alaska, including the Ketchikan and Anchorage bridges.[4] Although Alaska ranks 47th in the nation in terms of population, it received more pork than all but three other states. As Congressman Young said of the bill, "I stuffed it like a turkey."[5]

In Chapter 7, we learned how to determine the optimal level of public goods by setting social marginal costs and benefits equal; in Chapter 8 we learned how to use cost-benefit analysis to quantify the costs and benefits of public projects. In the real world, however, economists do not get to decide whether public policies are undertaken or not. Instead, such decisions are made in the context of a complex political system. In some countries, these decisions may be made by a single ruler or group of rulers. In others, the decisions are made by elected officials or by the direct votes of citizens. Do any or all of these mechanisms deliver the optimal interventions suggested by the theoretical analyses of this book? In some cases they will, but in other cases they will not.

This chapter discusses how government actually operates when it makes decisions about the economy, such as the provision of public goods. This chapter is the only place in the book that focuses specifically on the fourth question of public finance: *Why* do governments do what they do? We begin by discussing the best-case scenario in which a government appropriately measures and aggregates the preferences of its citizens in deciding which public projects to undertake. We then discuss the problems with this idealized scenario and turn to more realistic cases.

One more realistic case is that of *direct democracy,* whereby voters directly cast ballots in favor of or in opposition to particular public projects. We discuss how voting works to turn the interests of a broad spectrum of voters into a public goods decision. The second case is that of *representative democracy,* whereby voters elect representatives, who in turn make decisions on public projects. We discuss when it is likely or not likely that representative democracy yields the same outcomes as direct democracy.

In the final section of the chapter, we move beyond models of voting behavior to talk in broader terms about the prospects for *government failure,* the inability or unwillingness of governments to appropriately address market failures. We discuss some of the implications of government failure and discuss evidence about its importance to economic well-being.

---

[3] Rosenbaum (2005).
[4] Taxpayers for Common Sense (2005).
[5] Marsh (2005).

9.1

Unanimous Consent on Public Goods Levels

Our discussion of political economy starts with the example of a government that is able to optimally determine the level of public goods to provide through the unanimous consent of its citizens. It does so through **Lindahl pricing,** a system by which individuals report their willingness to pay for the next unit of a public good, and the government aggregates those willingnesses to form an overall measure of the social benefit from that next unit of public good. This marginal social benefit can then be compared to the marginal social cost of that next unit of public good to determine the optimal amount of the public good, and the good can be financed by charging individuals what they were willing to pay. We then discuss the problems that governments face in implementing this solution in practice, to set the stage for discussing the more realistic mechanisms that governments use to determine the level of public goods.

Lindahl pricing An approach to financing public goods in which individuals honestly reveal their willingness to pay and the government charges them that amount to finance the public good.

Lindahl Pricing

This approach, as introduced by the Swedish economist Erik Lindahl in 1919, relies on using individuals' **marginal willingness to pay,** the amount that individuals report themselves willing to pay for an incremental unit of a public good. Recall from Chapters 2 and 5 that the demand curve for any private good measures the marginal willingness to pay for that private good. Lindahl suggested that we could similarly construct a demand curve for public goods by asking individuals about their willingness to pay for different levels of public goods.

marginal willingness to pay The amount that individuals are willing to pay for the next unit of a good.

To illustrate Lindahl's procedure, suppose that we have a public good, fireworks, with a constant marginal cost of $1. This public good will be provided to two people, Ava and Jack. Remember the key feature of public goods from Chapter 7: the fireworks must be provided in equal quantities to both Ava and Jack. Lindahl's procedure operates as follows:

1. The government announces a set of *tax prices* for the public good, the share of the cost that each individual must bear. For example, the government could announce that Ava and Jack are each paying 50¢ of the cost of a firework, or that Ava pays 90¢ and Jack pays 10¢.

2. Each individual announces how much of the public good he or she wants at those tax prices.

3. The government repeats these steps to construct a *marginal willingness to pay schedule* for each individual that shows the relationship between willingness to pay and quantity of public goods desired.

4. The government adds up individual willingnesses to pay at each quantity of public good provided to get an overall demand curve for public goods (D_{A+J}).

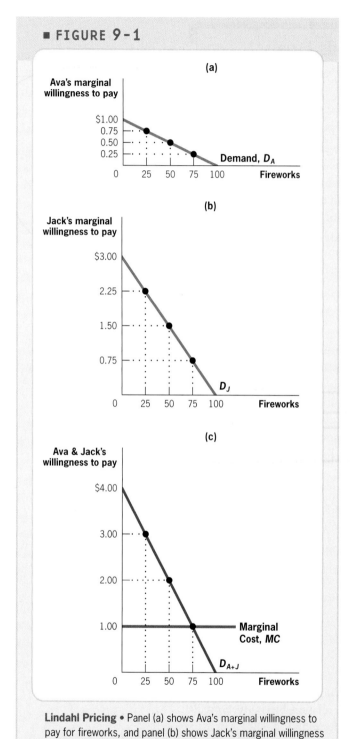

■ **FIGURE 9-1**

Lindahl Pricing • Panel (a) shows Ava's marginal willingness to pay for fireworks, and panel (b) shows Jack's marginal willingness to pay for fireworks. These marginal willingnesses to pay are summed in panel (c). The marginal cost of a firework is $1, so the optimal level of firework provision is 75 fireworks, the point at which marginal cost equals the sum of willingness to pay.

5. The government relates this overall demand curve to the marginal cost curve for the public good to solve for the optimal public good quantity.

6. The government then finances this public good by charging individuals their willingnesses to pay for that quantity of public good.

This point is illustrated graphically in Figure 9-1. Panel (a) shows Ava's marginal willingness to pay for fireworks. For the first firework, Ava has a marginal willingness to pay of $1. For the 50th firework, she has a marginal willingness to pay of 50¢. For the 75th firework, she has a marginal willingness to pay of 25¢, and by the 100th firework her marginal willingness to pay is zero. Panel (b) shows Jack's marginal willingness to pay for fireworks. For the first firework, Jack has a marginal willingness to pay of $3. For the 50th firework, he has a marginal willingness to pay of $1.50. For the 75th firework, he has a marginal willingness to pay of 75¢, and by the 100th firework his marginal willingness to pay is also zero.

Panel (c) shows the aggregate marginal willingness to pay for fireworks. Ava and Jack are together willing to pay $4 for the first firework; since this is well above the marginal cost of a firework ($1), the first firework should clearly be produced. Ava and Jack are willing to pay $2.00 for the 50th firework, which is once again well above the marginal cost of a firework. The marginal cost curve intersects their aggregate willingness to pay curve at the 75th firework, when they are together willing to pay the $1.00 marginal cost of the firework. Thus, the Lindahl equilibrium involves charging Ava 25¢ and Jack 75¢ for each of 75 fireworks.

This is an equilibrium for two reasons. First, both Ava and Jack are happy: they are both happy to pay those tax prices to get 75 fireworks. Second, the government has covered the marginal cost of producing the fireworks by charging each individual his or her marginal willingness to pay. Lindahl pricing corresponds to the concept of **benefit taxation,** which occurs when individuals are being taxed for a public good according to their valuation of the benefit they receive from the good.

benefit taxation Taxation in which individuals are taxed for a public good according to their valuation of the benefit they receive from that good.

Importantly, this equilibrium is also *the efficient level of public goods provision,* the point at which the sum of the social marginal benefits of the public good is set equal to social marginal cost. Notice the parallel between Figure 9-1 and Figure 7-2 (page 182) from Chapter 7. In both cases, we vertically sum the individual demand curves to get a social demand curve for public goods, and then set social demand equal to the social marginal cost of the public good to determine the optimal level of public goods provision. In Chapter 7, this was accomplished by maximizing utility functions to obtain each individual's demand for public goods and then adding them to get a total social demand. With Lindahl pricing, the government does not need to know the utility functions of individual voters: it gets the voters to *reveal their preferences* by stating their willingness to pay for different levels of the public good. Yet the outcome is the same: the sum of social marginal benefits (computed by the government in Chapter 7, or revealed by each voter in the Lindahl equilibrium) is set equal to social marginal cost.

Problems with Lindahl Pricing

Although Lindahl pricing leads to efficient public goods provision in theory, it is unlikely to work in practice. In particular, there are three problems that get in the way of implementing the Lindahl solution.

Preference Revelation Problem The first problem is that individuals have an incentive to lie about their willingness to pay, since the amount of money they pay to finance the public good is tied to their stated willingness to pay. Individuals may behave *strategically* and pretend that their willingness to pay is low so that others will bear a larger share of the cost of the public good. The incentive to lie with Lindahl pricing arises because of the free rider problem: if an individual reports a lower valuation of the public good, she pays a lower amount of tax but she doesn't get much less of the public good. Suppose, for example, that Jack lied and said that his preferences were identical to Ava's. Following the procedure we used earlier, we find that at the Lindahl equilibrium Jack and Ava will each pay 50¢, and 50 fireworks will be produced. Jack now pays $25 for the fifty fireworks, whereas in the previous example he paid 75¢ for each of 75 fireworks, for a total of $56.25. Thus, Jack pays less than half the total he paid before, but receives two-thirds as many fireworks; he is now free riding on Ava. Ava used to pay 25¢ for each of 75 fireworks, or $18.75. Now, she pays more ($25) to get fewer fireworks (50 instead of 75)! Especially in large groups, individuals have a strong incentive to underreport their valuation of the public good, and thus shift more of the costs to others.

Preference Knowledge Problem Even if individuals are willing to be honest about their valuation of a public good, they may have no idea of what that valuation actually is. How would you answer the question of how much you value fireworks or national defense? It is very hard for individuals to properly value goods they don't shop for on a regular basis.

Preference Aggregation Problem Even if individuals are willing to be honest and even if they know their valuation of the public good, there is a final problem: How can the government aggregate individual values into a social value? In our example, it was straightforward to keep asking Jack and Ava their willingness to pay in order to trace out their willingness to pay curves and find the correct level of public goods provision. This will clearly be considerably more difficult in reality. In the case of national defense in the United States, it is simply impossible to canvas each of 260 million U.S. citizens and ask them the value they place on the missiles, tanks, and soldiers that protect them.

Thus, the Lindahl pricing solution, while attractive in theory, is unlikely to work in practice. In the next two sections, we discuss more practical solutions to determining the optimal level of public goods. In particular, we focus on two questions. First, how can societies use voting mechanisms to effectively aggregate individual preferences? Second, how well do elected representatives carry out the preferences of individual voters?

9.2

Mechanisms for Aggregating Individual Preferences

In this section, we discuss how voting can serve to aggregate individual preferences into a social decision. We do not yet discuss the fact that voters elect representatives, who then make policy decisions. For now, we are considering only direct voting on policies, as discussed in the following application.

▶ APPLICATION

Direct Democracy in the United States[6]

On February 11, 1657, the residents of the town of Huntington, New York, held a meeting and voted to hire Jonas Houldsworth as the first schoolmaster of their town. Almost 350 years later, a similar meeting held in the town of Stoneham, Massachusetts rejected a $6 million plan to convert the local arena into a major sports complex. Through three and a half centuries, the tradition of *direct democracy,* whereby individuals directly vote on the policies that affect their lives, remains strong in America—and, indeed, has grown throughout the twentieth century.

---

[6] Information on direct democracy comes largely from the Initiative and Referendum Institute at the University of Southern California and can be accessed at http://www.iandrinstitute.org/. Matsusaka (2005) provides an excellent review of the issues surrounding direct democracy.

At the local level, the town meeting remains an important venue for decision making in many New England communities. Bryan (2003) undertook a comprehensive study of meetings in 210 Vermont towns over the 1970–1998 period, encompassing 1,435 meetings attended by 63,140 citizens. Town meetings were typically held once per year and were open to all registered voters. In some cases, votes occurred at the meeting; in others the meeting was deliberative only and voting occurred the next day. On average, over one-fifth of all Vermont residents participated in town meeting. Other towns do not have a town meeting, but have direct local voting on town budgets. For example, on April 18, 2006, voters from 549 of New Jersey's school districts voted on school board members and the budget for their local schools. Local voters approved only about half of the budgets proposed by their school boards; the remainder were sent back to the municipality, which then made changes or cuts to meet the local mandate.

Direct democracy plays an important role at the state level as well. A state **referendum** allows citizens to vote on state laws or constitutional amendments that have already been passed by the state legislature. All states allow *legislative referenda,* whereby state legislatures or other officials place such measures on the ballot for citizens to accept or reject. Twenty-four states allow *popular referenda,* whereby citizens, if they collect enough petition signatures, can place on the ballot a question of whether to accept or reject a given piece of state legislation. The important feature of a referendum is that it is designed to elicit reactions to legislation that politicians have already approved.

Much more frequent than referenda are **voter initiatives,** which allow citizens, if they can collect enough petition signatures, to place their own legislation on the ballot for voters to accept or reject. Twenty-four states allow such initiatives, the first two of which (concerning election reforms and alcohol regulation) made it to Oregon's ballot in 1904. Since that time, over 8,000 initiatives have been filed by concerned citizens. More than 2,000 of these initiatives have made it to state ballots, and 40% of these have passed. Interestingly, 60% of all initiative activity occurs in six states: Arizona, California, Colorado, North Dakota, Oregon, and Washington.

Initiatives were very popular early in the twentieth century with the rise of the Progressive political movement, and from 1911 to 1920 there were nearly 300 initiatives on various state ballots. That activity had tapered off dramatically by the 1960s, when fewer than 100 initiatives made it to state ballots. In 1978, California voters passed Proposition 13, an initiative that amended the state constitution to severely limit property tax rates that local governments could impose (discussed in more depth in Chapter 10). The measure sparked a wider "tax revolt" throughout other states, and the initiative once again became a frequently used political tool. The 1990s saw nearly 400 initiatives on state ballots (a record high of 48% were approved); in 1996 alone, almost 100 initiatives were voted on. Since 1996, however, the rate of initiatives has tapered off, with only 62 on the ballots in the 2002 elections.

referendum A measure placed on the ballot by the government allowing citizens to vote on state laws or constitutional amendments that have already been passed by the state legislature.

voter initiative The placement of legislation on the ballot by citizens.

Referenda and initiatives can be sparked by all kinds of issues. Early in the twentieth century, voters changed election rules, alcohol regulation, labor laws, and the administration of government. By the 1970s voters were interested in tax reform, environmental issues, and nuclear developments. By the 1990s, physician-assisted suicide, animal rights, gaming regulations, and politician term limits were among the many issues considered directly by the voters. ◄

Majority Voting: When It Works

The Lindahl pricing scheme had a very high standard for setting the level of public goods: only when all citizens were *unanimously* in agreement did the government achieve the Lindahl equilibrium. In practice, the government typically does not hold itself to such a high standard. A common mechanism used to aggregate individual votes into a social decision is **majority voting,** in which individual policy options are put to a vote and the option that receives the *majority* of votes is chosen. Yet even this lower standard can cause difficult problems for governments trying to set the optimal level of public goods.

In this section, we discuss the conditions under which majority voting does and does not provide a successful means of aggregating the preferences of individual voters. In this context, success means being able to *consistently* aggregate individual preferences into a social decision. To be consistent, the aggregation mechanism must satisfy three goals:

> ▶ *Dominance:* If one choice is preferred by all voters, the aggregation mechanism must be such that this choice is made by society; that is, if every individual prefers building a statue to building a park, the aggregation mechanism must yield a decision to build a statue.

> ▶ *Transitivity:* Choices must satisfy the mathematical property of transitivity: if a large statue is preferred to a medium-size statue, and a medium-size statue is preferred to a small statue, then a large statue must be preferred to a small statue.

> ▶ *Independence of irrelevant alternatives:* Choices must satisfy the condition that if one choice is preferred to another, then the introduction of a third independent choice will not change that ranking. For example, if building a statue is preferred to building a park, then the introduction of an option to build a new police station will not suddenly cause building a park to be preferred to building a statue.

These three conditions are generally viewed as necessary for an aggregation mechanism to provide a successful translation of individual preferences to aggregate decisions. In fact, however, majority voting can *produce a consistent aggregation of individual preferences only if preferences are restricted to take a certain form.*

To illustrate this point, consider the example of a town that is deciding between alternatives for school funding. Schools, an impure public good (as discussed in Chapter 11), are financed by property taxes, so a higher level of

majority voting The typical mechanism used to aggregate individual votes into a social decision, whereby individual policy options are put to a vote and the option that receives the majority of votes is chosen.

funding also means higher taxes for the town's property owners. The town is choosing between three possible levels of funding: H is the highest level of funding (and thus highest property taxes); M is a medium level of funding and property taxes; and L is a low level of funding and property taxes. There are three types of voters in this town, with equal numbers in each group:

▶ *Parents,* whose main concern is having a high-quality education for their children. This group's first choice is H, their second choice M, and their third (least-preferred) choice is L.

▶ *Elders,* who don't have children and therefore don't care about the quality of local schools, so their main priority is low property taxes. This group's first choice is L, their second choice is M, and their third choice is H.

▶ *Young couples without children,* who do not want to pay the high property taxes necessary to fund high-quality schools right now but who want the schools to be good enough for their future children to attend. This group's first choice is M, their second choice is L, and their third choice is H.

The preferences of these three groups are represented in Table 9-1.

Suppose the town uses majority voting to choose a level of funding for local schools and that to reach a decision the town compares one alternative with another through a series of pairwise votes until there is a clear winner. At each vote, individuals will vote for whichever of the presented options they prefer. Since there are three options, this will require a series of pairwise votes. For example, the town could proceed as follows:

▶ First, vote on funding level H versus funding level L. The parents will vote for funding level H, since they prefer it to funding level L. The elders and the young couples will both vote for funding level L, however, since they prefer it to the higher funding level H. Thus, L gets two votes and H gets one, so L wins the first pairwise vote.

▶ Then, vote on funding level H versus funding level M: M gets two votes (elders and young couples prefer M to H) and H gets one (parents), so M wins the second pairwise vote.

▶ Then, vote on funding level L versus funding level M: M gets two votes (parents and young couples prefer M to L) and L gets one (elders), so M wins the third pairwise vote.

Because M has beaten both H and L, M is the overall winner. Indeed, no matter what ordering is used for these pairwise votes, M will be preferred to the other options. Majority voting has aggregated individual preferences to produce a preferred social outcome: medium school spending and taxes.

■ **TABLE 9-1**

Majority Voting Delivers a Consistent Outcome

		Parents (33.3%)	Elders (33.3%)	Young Couples (33.3%)
			Types of Voters	
Preference Rankings	First	H	L	M
	Second	M	M	L
	Third	L	H	H

In this example, the option chosen by majority voting will be the medium level of funding, the choice of the median voter (the young couples).

Majority Voting: When It Doesn't Work

Suppose now that the town is the same except that the elderly are replaced by individuals who have children but are contemplating choosing private school over the local public schools to make sure that their children get the best possible education. This group's first choice is low public school spending and low property taxes: if property taxes are low, they can afford to send their children to private school. If they can't get low school spending, then their second choice is *high* school spending and high property taxes. Without the low taxes, they will not be able to afford to send their children to private schools; they will therefore choose public schools, in which case they want the highest quality public schools and are willing to pay the taxes to support them. From these new families' perspective, the worst outcome would be medium spending. They would face somewhat high property taxes, but because the schools wouldn't be top quality, they would send their children to private school anyway.

The set of preferences with this new group included is shown in Table 9-2. If the town uses the same pairwise majority voting approach to assess the spending level with these new preferences, the outcome would be:

▶ First, vote on funding level *H* versus funding level *L*: *L* gets two votes (*L* is preferred to *H* for the private school group and the young couples) and *H* gets one (*H* is preferred to *L* for the parents), so *L* wins.

▶ Then, vote on funding level *H* versus funding level *M*: *H* gets two votes (public and private school parents prefer *H* to *M*) and *M* gets one (young couples prefer *M* to *H*), so *H* wins.

▶ Then, vote on funding level *L* versus funding level *M*: *M* gets two votes (public school parents and young couples prefer *M* to *L*) and *L* gets one (private school parents prefer *L* to *M*), so *M* wins.

cycling When majority voting does not deliver a consistent aggregation of individual preferences.

This set of outcomes is problematic because there is no clear winner: *L* is preferred to *H*, and *H* is preferred to *M*, but *M* is preferred to *L*! Indeed, no matter what order the pairwise votes occur, there is never a clear winner. These results violate the principle of transitivity, resulting in **cycling:** when we aggregate the preferences of the individuals in this town, we do not get a consistently preferred outcome. So majority voting has failed to consistently aggregate the preferences of the town's voters.

Note that the failure to get a consistent winner from majority voting does not reflect any failure of the individuals in the town; as described, each individual has a sensible set of preferences across the spending levels. The problem is in aggregation: we are unable to use voting to aggregate these individual preferences into a consistent social outcome. This creates the problem that the *agenda setter*, the person who decides how voting is to be done (which mechanism and in which order), can significantly influence the outcome. For example, an

▪ **TABLE 9-2**

Majority Voting Doesn't Deliver a Consistent Outcome

		Types of Voters		
		Public School Parents (33.3%)	Private School Parents (33.3%)	Young Couples (33.3%)
Preference Rankings	First	*H*	*L*	*M*
	Second	*M*	*H*	*L*
	Third	*L*	*M*	*H*

In this example, there is no consistent outcome from majority voting.

agenda setter who wanted low spending could first set up a vote of M versus H, which H would win, and then of H versus L, which L would win, and declare that L was the winner. Or an agenda setter who wanted high spending could first set up a vote of M versus L, which M would win, and then of M versus H, which H would win, and declare that H was the winner. The inability to get a consistent winner from majority voting can, ultimately, give dictatorial power to the agenda setter.

Arrow's Impossibility Theorem

The failure to consistently aggregate individual preferences is not just a problem with majority voting. In the example with the private school parents, there is in fact *no voting system* that will produce a consistent outcome. Consider some alternative approaches:

▶ We could let everyone vote on their first choice, rather than pairwise voting, but this would just produce a three-way tie in both examples since each group is the same size and has a different first choice.

▶ We could do weighted voting by assigning, for example, 3 points for one's first choice, 2 points for one's second choice, and 1 point for one's third choice, and then pick the outcome with the most points. In the first example, M would win with 7 points while L would have 6 and H would have 5. In the second example, however, there would be a three-way tie, with each option having 6 points.

One of the most important insights of political economy theory was developed by Nobel Prize–winning economist Kenneth Arrow in 1951.[7] **Arrow's Impossibility Theorem** states that there is no social decision (voting) rule that converts individual preferences into a consistent aggregate decision without either (a) restricting the type of preferences assumed for voters or (b) imposing a dictatorship. That is, no matter what the voting rule is, one can always find examples where it cannot be used to turn individual preferences into a clear, socially preferred outcome through majority voting unless one chooses one of two shortcuts. The first is to restrict voters' preferences by imposing some additional assumptions on the general structure of preferences. The second shortcut is to impose a dictatorship: a dictator can always make a consistent social decision simply by imposing her preferences.

Restricting Preferences to Solve the Impossibility Problem

The most common restriction of preferences that is used to solve the impossibility problem is to impose what are called **single-peaked preferences**. A "peak" in preferences (also called a *local maximum*) is a point that is preferred to all its immediate neighbors. Single-peaked preferences feature only one such point, so utility falls as choices move away in any direction from the peak

Arrow's Impossibility Theorem There is no social decision (voting) rule that converts individual preferences into a consistent aggregate decision without either (a) restricting preferences or (b) imposing a dictatorship.

single-peaked preferences Preferences with only a single local maximum, or peak, so that utility falls as choices move away in any direction from that peak.

---

[7] See Arrow (1951) for more details.

choice. Multi-peaked preferences feature more than one such point, so that utility may first rise to a peak, then fall, then rise again to another peak. The key advantage of single-peaked preferences for economic theory is that *any* peak can be assured of being the *only* peak. That is, if utility falls in both directions away from any point, we can be sure that a voter prefers this option most. With multi-peaked preferences, this is not necessarily the case; utility may fall away from a peak but then rise again to a new peak.

If preferences are single-peaked, majority voting will yield consistent outcomes. We can understand this concept visually by graphing out our earlier examples. Figure 9-2 graphs the utility from each choice (the vertical axis) against the level of spending represented by that choice (the horizontal axis). For example, in both panels of Figure 9-2, parents' preferences are summarized by line *AB*: they get the largest utility value, U_{first}, at the highest level of spending. At the medium level of spending, they get a medium utility value, U_{second}. At the low level of spending, they get a low utility value, U_{third}.

In panel (a), which graphs the example shown in Table 9-1 (which is repeated at the bottom of the figure), all preferences are single-peaked. The single peak of the parents is high spending: relative to the point with high spending (point *A*), utility is always falling (as spending declines). The single peak of the elders is low spending: relative to the point with low spending (point *C*), utility is always falling (as spending rises). The single peak of the young couples is medium spending: relative to the point with medium spending (point *F*), utility is always falling (as spending either rises or falls).

■ FIGURE 9-2

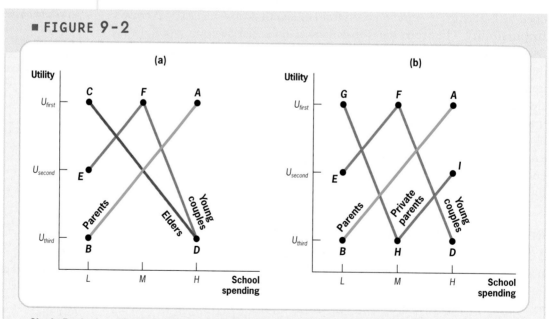

Single-Peaked vs. Non-Single-Peaked Preferencess • Panel (a) graphs the preferences from Table 9-1, which are all single-peaked; utility is always falling as each individual moves away from the preferred choice. Panel (b) graphs the preferences from Table 9-2; now the parents considering private school don't have single-peaked preferences since utility first falls then rises as spending levels increase.

Panel (b) corresponds to the second example (summarized in Table 9-2), in which the elders are replaced with parents considering private school, a group that has *double-peaked* preferences. These families have a peak at low spending (point *G*), their first choice; then, as spending rises, their utility falls to point *H* (medium spending gives them the lowest utility). Unlike the other families, however, their utility then rises again as spending moves from medium to high spending, creating a second peak (point *I*). The failure of the single-peaked preferences assumption in this second case is what leads to the inability of majority voting to consistently aggregate preferences.

Fortunately, single-peakedness is generally a reasonable assumption to make about preferences. In most cases, when choosing over public goods such as national defense, individuals will have one preferred level, with utility falling as spending either rises or falls from that level. Single-peakedness is a potentially problematic assumption, however, when there is the possibility of a private substitute for a public good. The schools example is a good illustration of this point. If private substitutes are available, individuals could be worst off with the middle option, leading to double-peaked preferences. Another example might be voting over the quality of a local park. Individuals might want either a very nice local park or no local park (in which case they'll just rely on their own backyards), but having a mediocre local park (paid for by local taxes) could be the worst option of all.

Median Voter Theory

If the preferences of voters are single-peaked, majority voting will deliver a consistent aggregation of the preferences of the individual voters. Under this assumption of single-peaked preferences, in fact, we can make an even stronger statement about the outcome of majority voting across public goods options. The **Median Voter Theorem** states that majority voting will yield the outcome preferred by the *median voter* if preferences are single-peaked. The **median voter** is the voter whose tastes are in the middle of the set of voters, so an equal number of other voters prefer more and prefer less of the public good.

In both examples, the median voters are the young couples; their first preference is for the middle option, and in each case there is one voter group that prefers low spending and another that prefers high spending. In the first case, where preferences are single-peaked, the outcome preferred by the median voter is the one chosen (medium spending). In the second case, where one voter has double-peaked preferences, the outcome is not consistent.

The Potential Inefficiency of the Median Voter Outcome

The median voter outcome from majority voting is very convenient. Taken literally, it implies that the government need find only the *one voter* whose preferences for the public good are right in the middle of the distribution of social preferences and implement the level of public goods preferred by that voter. The government need not know anything about the preferences of the many voters on either side of the median: all the government has to do is find the median voter and then implement that voter's preferences. While this

Median Voter Theorem Majority voting will yield the outcome preferred by the median voter if preferences are single-peaked.

median voter The voter whose tastes are in the middle of the set of voters.

median voter outcome is convenient, however, it might not be socially efficient. Social efficiency requires that the social marginal benefits of a public project equal its social marginal costs. This may not be true with median voter outcomes because such outcomes do not reflect *intensity of preferences*.

Recall that the social marginal benefits of a public good are the sum of the private marginal benefits that each individual derives from that good. If a small number of individuals derive enormous benefits from the public good, then they should be accounted for in computing total social marginal benefits. This will not necessarily be the case with the median voter, however, because the outcome is determined only by the *ranking* of voters and not by the intensity of their preferences.[8]

Imagine, for example, that your hometown is considering building a monument to you to recognize your wonderful successes in life. There are 1,001 voters in your town. The monument will cost $40,040, which will be financed by a $40 tax on each voter. The town takes a vote on whether this monument should be built or not. Everyone in town has single-peaked preferences so that the median voter will determine the outcome.

Five hundred of the voters in your town recognize your enormous contributions to society and are willing to pay up to $100 each to support a monument; 501 of the voters are ignorant of your contributions and are not willing to pay anything to support the monument. The social marginal benefit is therefore $500 \times 100 + 501 \times 0 = \$50,000$. The social marginal cost is $40,040. So the socially efficient outcome is for this monument to be built. Yet a proposal to build the monument, financed by a tax of $40 on each citizen, would lose by a vote of 501–500. Since the median voter doesn't want the monument at that price, it does not get built.

This socially inefficient outcome arises because the median voter outcome does not reflect intensity of preferences. That many voters were willing to pay much more than $40 to support the monument is irrelevant; all that matters is that the pivotal median voter was not willing to pay $40. Whether this inefficiency is likely depends on whether there are particularly intense preferences on one side or another of an election.

Summary

Many decisions in direct democracies are made by majority voting. In this section, we have discussed the situations under which majority voting may or may not serve to consistently aggregate the preferences of individual voters. If preferences are single-peaked, majority voting will consistently aggregate preferences, with the outcome chosen being that preferred by the median voter. This outcome, while convenient, may not be efficient.

---

[8] Technically, what matters for efficiency is the mean of valuations of a public good. If there is equal intensity of preferences on both sides of the median (if the distribution of preferences is *symmetric*), then the mean and median will be the same, and the median voter outcome will be efficient. If, however, one side is more intense than the other, then the mean will differ from the median, and the median voter outcome will be inefficient.

9.3

Representative Democracy

In reality, people in most developed nations don't vote directly on public goods. Rather, they elect representatives who are supposed to aggregate the public's preferences and take them into account when they vote on the appropriate level of spending on public goods. To understand outcomes in a representative democracy such as the United States, we therefore need a theory that explains how politicians behave. The most common theory that has been used in public finance is a version of the *median voter theory* that we discussed for direct democracy: politicians will choose the outcome that is preferred by the median voter. In this section, we review the median voter theory for representative democracies, discussing the assumptions underlying it and presenting the empirical evidence for and against it.

Vote-Maximizing Politicians Represent the Median Voter

The median voter theory in the representative democracy context rests on the single key assumption that all politicians care about is maximizing the number of votes they get. If this is true, then elected politicians will choose the outcome preferred by the median voter (as long as preferences are single-peaked). That is, with vote-maximizing politicians, the theory we used to explain direct democracy can be applied to representative democracy as well.

This point was illustrated by Downs (1957). With single-peaked preferences, we can model voters as being distributed along a line as in Figure 9-3. This line shows desired levels of defense spending as a percent of the government budget, ranging from 0% on the left to 50% on the right. Suppose voters are spaced evenly throughout this line so that the median voter would like the government to spend 25% of its budget on defense. Finally, suppose voters vote for the candidate who most closely represents their views on this issue, the candidate who is closest to the voter along this line.

Suppose now that two politicians, John and George, are running for office and vying to maximize their votes. John wants to appeal to those who don't want to spend much on defense, so he places himself initially at point J_1; George wants to appeal to those who want to spend a lot on defense, so he places himself initially at point G_1. In this case, the candidates will split the vote, because they have equal shares of voters near them on the line, as shown in panel (a) of Figure 9.3.

What if John shifts his position to J_2, where he advocates for somewhat larger defense? In that case, John would get more votes (panel (b) of Figure 9.3). He would continue to capture all those who want a small defense and would capture some of those who want a larger defense since he is closer to their preferences than is George.

What should George do in response to John's change in position? He should shift his position to G_2 (panel (c) of Figure 9.3), where he now favors a smaller defense than he did previously. After this move, George would get

■ FIGURE 9-3

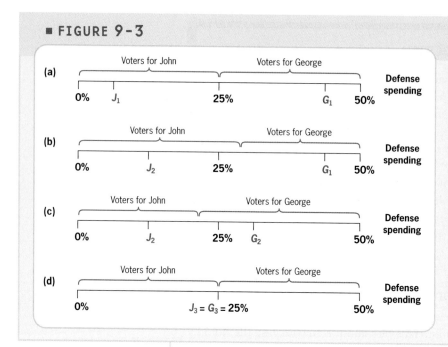

Vote Maximization Leads to the Median Voter Outcome • In panel (a), John favors small defense and George favors large defense, and they get an equal number of votes. In panel (b), John increases the level of defense spending he will support, and by doing so he obtains more than half the votes. In panel (c), George then reduces the level of defense spending he will support, and by doing so he now obtains more than half the votes. This continues until, in panel (d), both politicians support the outcome preferred by the median voter and get the same number of votes.

the majority of votes, leaving John stuck with the now minority that favors a small defense. If these politicians are purely vote-maximizing, this jockeying back and forth will continue until both candidates support the position held by the median voter (25% of budget on defense; panel (d) of Figure 9.3). If either candidate advocates more or less spending on defense than the median amount, he will reduce his number of votes, so there is no incentive for a candidate ever to deviate from the median.

In this context, as with direct democracy, the median voter model is a powerful tool. Politicians and political analysts need not know the entire distribution of preferences to predict vote outcomes in this model. All they need to understand is the preferences of the median voter.

Assumptions of the Median Voter Model

Although the median voter model is a convenient way to describe the role of representative democracy, it does so by making a number of assumptions. In this section, we review these assumptions and discuss why they may be violated, leading politicians to move away from the position of the median voter.

Single-dimensional Voting First, the median voter model assumes that voters are basing their votes on a single issue. In reality, representatives are elected not based on a single issue but on a bundle of issues. Individuals may lie at different points of the voting spectrum on different issues, so appealing to one end of the spectrum or another on some issues may be vote-maximizing. For example, if the median voter on most issues happens to advocate a lot of spending on defense, then politicians may position themselves toward high spending on defense to attract that median voter on all the other issues.

At the same time, if voter preferences on different issues are highly correlated, voting may end up close to single-dimensional. That is, if all voters who want small defense spending also want more spending on education, more spending on health care, and greater benefits for the unemployed, and all voters who want large defense spending also want less spending on education, less spending on health care, and fewer benefits for the unemployed, then voting may in effect be single-dimensional even with multiple issues.

Only Two Candidates Second, the median voter model assumes that there are only two candidates for office. If there are more than two candidates, the simple predictions of the median voter model break down. If all three candidates are at the median, then moving slightly to the left or right will increase the votes of any one candidate (since she will get all of one end of the spectrum), while the other two candidates split the other end. Indeed, there is no stable equilibrium in the model with three or more candidates because there is always an incentive to move in response to your opponents' positions. There is never a set of positions along the line where one of the politicians can't increase his or her votes by moving.

In many nations, the possibility of three or more valid candidates for office is a real one. In the United States, there are typically only two candidates, Republican and Democrat, with important exceptions, such as the 1992 presidential election when independent Ross Perot took 19% of the popular vote.

No Ideology or Influence Third, the median voter theory assumes that politicians care only about maximizing votes. In practice, politicians may actually care about their positions and not simply try to maximize their votes. Moreover, in practice, politicians with ideological convictions may be able to shift the views of voters toward their preferred position. Ideological convictions could lead politicians to position themselves away from the center of the spectrum and the median voter.

No Selective Voting Fourth, the median voter theory assumes that all people affected by public goods vote, but in fact only a fraction of citizens vote in the United States. In presidential election years, only about half the citizens vote, and in non-presidential elections, participation is even worse: only about one-third vote.[9] Even if the views of citizens on a particular topic are evenly distributed, it may be the most ideologically oriented citizens who do the voting. In that case, it could be optimal for a politician to appeal to likely voters by taking a position to the right or left of center, even if this position is not what is preferred by the majority of citizens (including both voters and nonvoters).

No Money Fifth, the median voter theory ignores the role of money as a tool of influence in elections. Votes are the outcome of a political process, but

---

[9] U.S. Bureau of the Census (2006a), Table 408.

there are many inputs into that process. One key input is resources to finance reelection campaigns, advertisements, campaign trips, and other means of maximizing votes. Running for office in the United States has become increasingly expensive.[10] From 1990 to 2004, the cost of winning a seat in the House of Representatives almost doubled, from $550,000 to over $1,000,000, while the cost of winning a seat in the Senate rose nearly 70%, from $4.3 million to $7.2 million. The cost of a campaign for President has grown even more rapidly: Governor George W. Bush spent over $345 million to get himself elected President in 2004, while his father had spent just $33 million in pursuit of the same goal in 1988, an increase of over 1000% in only 16 years. Therefore, if taking an extreme position on a given topic maximizes fundraising, even if it does not directly maximize votes on that topic, it may serve the long-run interests of overall vote maximization by allowing the candidate to advertise more.

Full Information   Finally, the median voter model assumes perfect information along three dimensions: voter knowledge of the issues; politician knowledge of the issues; and politician knowledge of voter preferences. All three of these assumptions are unrealistic. Many of the issues on which our elected representatives must vote are highly complicated and not well understood by the majority of their constituents—and often not by the representatives themselves. Democratic senator Robert Byrd was once asked if he knew what was in a 4,000-page $520 billion omnibus spending bill passed by the House of Representatives. "Do I know what's in this bill?" he replied. "Are you kidding? Only God knows what's in this conference report!"[11] Moreover, even when voters understand an issue, it is difficult for politicians to gain a complete understanding of the distribution of voter preferences on the issue.

Lobbying

These problems of information and the advantages of money make it likely that elected representatives will be *lobbied* by highly interested and informed subgroups of the population. **Lobbying** is the expending of resources by certain individuals or groups in an attempt to influence a politician.[12] Politicians find it in their interest to listen to lobbies for two reasons. First, these groups can provide relevant information about an issue to an uninformed politician: when particular subgroups have a strong interest in a complicated issue, they also typically have a thorough and deep understanding of the issue. Second, these groups will reward politicians who support their views by contributing to the politicians' campaigns and getting group members to vote for the politician, which can help the politicians' overall vote maximization.

lobbying The expending of resources by certain individuals or groups in an attempt to influence a politician.

---

[10] Statistics from the Center for Responsive Politics' Web site at http://www.opensecrets.org/bigpicture/stats.asp.
[11] McDonald (1998).
[12] This term became popular after special interest groups discovered that President Ulysses Grant spent his afternoons drinking in the lobby of the Willard Hotel in Washington, D.C., and was thus easier to extract concessions from later in the day!

In principle, lobbying can serve two useful roles: providing information and representing intensity of preferences. Indeed, given the inefficiency of the median voter outcome, some amount of lobbying is probably optimal. The problem that arises with lobbying is that when there is an issue that particularly benefits a small group and imposes only small costs on a larger (perhaps even majority) group, lobbying can lead politicians to support socially inefficient positions. Suppose, for example, there is a project where 100 U.S. citizens benefit by $1 million each, but the remaining 259.9999 million citizens lose by $100 each. Clearly, this project has negative overall social benefits (since 100 × 1,000,000 < 100 × 259,999,900). If the interested group lobbies politicians, however, promising votes and campaign contributions, and if the remainder of the citizenry is not informed about the issue and so will not vote on it, the project could be accepted by self-interested politicians.

The key point to recognize here is that large groups with a small individual interest on an issue suffer from a *free rider problem* in trying to organize politically; it is in no individual's interest to take the time to lobby policy makers over the lost $100. Small groups with large individual interest, however, may be able to overcome this problem, leading to a socially inefficient outcome. An excellent example of this result is farm subsidies, as discussed in the following application.

▶ APPLICATION

Farm Policy in the United States[13]

In 1900, 35% of workers in the United States were employed on farms. By the year 2002, this share had fallen to 2.5%, due both to increased farm efficiency and to imports of agricultural products. Yet this small sector receives $25.5 billion in direct support from the federal government each year. This support take two forms: *direct subsidy* payments to farmers of about $12.5 billion per year, and *price supports,* guaranteed minimum prices for crops, which cost about $13 billion per year. These price supports also raise the average price of food products for American consumers and cost $16 billion a year in higher prices. Together, these subsidies cost each American household about $390 per year on average, and the average recipient of the direct subsidies receives $19,600 annually, which is larger than the amount paid to most individuals that receive payments from the social insurance programs we discuss in Chapters 12–17.

Why do American families pay such large costs to support the farm sector? The typical answer provided by public policy makers of all political leanings is that this financial support is necessary to preserve the American "family farm" from larger agriculture companies and foreign competitors. Indeed, vying for

---

[13] Unless otherwise noted, statistics from Kirwan (2004) and the Organization for Economic Cooperation and Development (2002), updated to current dollars. Quotations from Allen (2002).

the Democratic presidential nomination in 2003, House Minority Leader Dick Gephardt delivered a speech at an Iowa farm lamenting the fact that "With each passing year, we lose more and more family farms to corporate agriculture." And when President Bush signed into law a 2002 farm bill estimated to cost $190 billion over the following decade, he declared that the bill "will promote farmer independence and preserve the farm way of life for generations." The only problem with this justification is that it is completely at odds with the facts. Only 8 of the roughly 400 crops grown in the United States are eligible for subsidies, and the amount of subsidy increases with the amount of crop produced, so larger farms benefit more from the subsidies than do small farms. As a result, two-thirds of all subsidies now accrue to 8% of recipients, most of whom earn over $250,000 a year. The recipients include a number of Fortune 500 firms as well as almost 9,070 farms and businesses that received over $1 million in subsidies from 1995 to 2004.[14]

If farm subsidies are so expensive and their distribution is so at odds with their stated goals, how does this program survive? The answer is that the $390 total cost per year to the typical American family of farm subsidies is dwarfed by the enormous gain of $19,600 to the typical farm from farm subsidies. These farms are able to effectively organize and lobby for the maintenance of the subsidy and price support programs, and the larger group of taxpayers hurt by these programs are not. Recognizing this imbalance, Senator Richard Lugar of Indiana, the Agriculture Committee's ranking Republican, refused to attend President Bush's signing of the 2002 farm bill, calling it "a recipe for a great deal of hurt and sadness, and at the expense of a huge transfer payment from a majority of Americans to a very few." Furthermore, candidates in presidential primaries have their first trials in Iowa, the leading recipient of farm subsidies, so opposition to farm subsidies can be quite perilous to a presidential candidate.

This example should not be taken to imply that large subsidies to farms is a uniquely American phenomenon. The European Union spends over $100 billion annually supporting its farmers. The average European cow, for example, is supported by $2 a day of government spending. Japan spends over $54 billion on its farmers, protecting them with measures like rice tariffs of nearly 500%.[15] In total, the OECD estimates that the developed world spends $225 billion annually directly supporting farmers, with $142 billion coming from tariffs and export subsidies and $83 billion from direct payments to farmers. ◀

Evidence on the Median Voter Model for Representative Democracy

While the median voter model is a potentially powerful tool of political economy, its premise rests on some strong assumptions that may not be valid in the real world. A large political economy literature has tested the median voter model by assessing the role of voter preferences on legislative voting behavior

---

[14] Data from the Farm Subsidy Database provided by the Environmental Working Group, at http://ewg.org/farm.
[15] Tariffs are taxes levied only on imported goods.

EMPIRICAL EVIDENCE

TESTING THE MEDIAN VOTER MODEL

As noted, empirical evidence on the median voter model is mixed. Some studies find strong support for the model. For example, Stratmann (2000) studied the effects of redistricting on the voting patterns of affected legislators. Every ten years when census data become available, congressional districts are reshaped to reflect population movements over the past decade. Such redistricting can change the nature of a district's median voter. Stratmann compared the preferences of the new, redistricted constituency with the old by comparing differences in the patterns of voting for presidents across redistricted districts. He asked: When districts became more conservative through redistricting (as measured by voting more often for the Republican presidential candidate in 1988 and 1992) but were represented by the same politician, did the politician start to vote more conservatively? The answer is yes, confirming that median voter preferences matter to legislators.

At the same time, there is also clear evidence that "core constituencies," as opposed to just the median voter in a district, matter for legislator behavior. Leveaux and Garand (2003) explored how voting behavior of incumbent House Republicans and Democrats changed in response to changes in the racial composition of their districts brought on by 1992 redistricting. African-American voters are typically a major component of Democratic constituencies and not of Republican ones. When the African-American population in a district increases due to redistricting, therefore, the median voter model would predict that politicians of all stripes should start voting more like Democrats: all that should matter is total number of votes, and if African Americans have more Democratic preferences, then Republicans and Democrats should both shift their positions equally to respond. These authors found, however, that the voting patterns of Democratic legislators responded strongly to changes in the African-American population in their districts, while Republican voting patterns responded only

modestly. The median voter model is clearly only part of the story.

A particularly striking test is to compare two senators from the same state but from different political parties. Since senator is a statewide office, both elected officials are appealing to the same set of voters. Thus, the median voter model would predict that they would take the same position on legislation. In fact, this is not at all true. As Levitt (1996) showed, when a state has one senator from each party, the senators vote very differently; in fact, they vote very similarly to senators from other states who are in their party. Levitt concluded that legislators care roughly equally about the median voter, voters in their own core constituencies, and the party line, but that added together these factors can explain only about 40% of voting patterns. The remainder of the voting patterns is explained by individual ideological differences.[16]

Direct evidence that ideology matters was also shown in a recent paper by Washington (2004). She compares legislators who have daughters to those with the same family size who have sons. Since a child's gender is random, two legislators with families of the same size, one of which has more daughters than the other, should form natural treatments and controls for assessing whether individual ideological factors matter for legislator behavior (they should be otherwise the same except for the sex mix of their children). She finds that as a larger share of a legislator's children are daughters, the legislator is more likely to vote in favor of women's issues such as reproductive rights (such as by opposing laws that restrict teen access to abortion) or women's safety (such as by supporting laws that increase the punishment for violence against women). Washington's findings strongly support the notion that personal ideology matters: politicians are responding to their own experience, not just to the demands of the voters.

relative to other factors such as party or personal ideology. Consider, for example, a Democratic politician who has personally liberal views but who represents a very conservative congressional district in the South. The Median Voter Theorem would predict that this politician would have a very conservative

---

[16] Levitt's work builds on a large literature in political science that provides related evidence that ideology is an important determinant of politician positioning; see in particular Kalt and Zupan (1984) and Coates and Munger (1995).

voting record to maximize his votes in the district, but other factors such as party or individual ideology could lead to a more liberal voting record.

Studies of this nature have provided mixed conclusions, as reviewed in the Empirical Evidence box. On the one hand, the preferences of the median voter clearly matter: where the median voter is more conservative, politicians vote more conservatively. The median voter model is therefore a sensible starting point for modeling politician behavior. On the other hand, the preferences of the median voter do not completely explain legislator voting behavior. There is strong evidence that legislators consider their own ideology when they vote on policies and seem not only to cater to the median voter in their district or state but also to pay particular attention to the position of their own "core constituency" (the minority of voters who particularly agree with the beliefs of the politician, such as the minority of liberal Democrats who strongly support a Democratic senator in a Republican state).

9.4

Public Choice Theory: The Foundations of Government Failure

public choice theory School of thought emphasizing that the government may not act to maximize the well-being of its citizens.

The policy analysis in most of this book assumes a benign government intent on maximizing social welfare. Similarly, in this chapter we have discussed the assumption that in both direct democracy and representative democracy, politicians will ultimately strive to represent the will of the people. Starting in the 1950s, however, a school of thought known as **public choice theory** began to question this assumption. Begun by James Buchanan and Gordon Tullock (the former of whom won the 1986 Nobel Prize), public choice theorists noted that governments often do not behave in an ideal manner, so that the traditional assumption of benevolent social-welfare-maximizing government may not be appropriate.[17] In this section, we review some of the important sources of **government failure,** the inability or unwillingness of the government to act primarily in the interest of its citizens.

government failure The inability or unwillingness of the government to act primarily in the interest of its citizens.

Size-Maximizing Bureaucracy

bureaucracies Organizations of civil servants, such as the U.S. Department of Education or a town's Department of Public Works, that are in charge of carrying out the services of government.

Some of the earliest critiques of idealist conceptions of government began with the idea that **bureaucracies,** organizations of civil servants in charge of carrying out the services of government (such as the U.S. Department of Education or a town's Department of Public Works), might be more interested in their own preservation and growth than in carrying out their assigned missions efficiently. In 1971, William Niskanen developed the model of the *budget-maximizing bureaucrat.* In this model, the bureaucrat runs an agency that has a monopoly on the government provision of some good or service. For example, a town's Department of Public Works might be charged with collecting trash, maintaining the sewers, and so on. This bureaucracy is part of

---

[17] For an early text on public choice theory, see Buchanan and Tullock (1962).

the larger town government, and the politicians running the larger government will decide on the bureaucrat's power and pay.

Niskanen notes that while the private sector rewards its employees for efficient production, a bureaucrat's salary is typically unrelated to efficiency. In Niskanen's model, a bureaucrat's compensation (wages, benefits, status, quality of support staff, and so on) is based on the total measurable output of his bureaucracy. For example, the compensation of the director of the Department of Public Works rises as that department fixes more problems in the town. The goal of the bureaucrat is therefore to maximize the size of the agency he controls, and thus maximize its budget, not to choose the level of service that maximizes efficiency. Even if the larger town government knows that the bureaucrat is pursuing a self-interested, inefficient goal, it is hard to enforce efficient production in the agency because the bureaucrat knows much more than the town government knows about the true cost of the service he is providing.[18]

Private vs. Public Provision The key question raised by this discussion is whether goods and services are provided more efficiently by the public or the private sector. For the production of purely private goods and services, such as steel, telecommunications, or banking, it seems abundantly clear that private production is more efficient. Mueller (2003) lists 71 studies that compared the performance of state-owned public companies to private companies: in only 5 of these studies did state-owned companies outperform their private counterparts in terms of efficiency; 56 studies found that the private companies were more efficient, and in 10 studies the performance was similar. Majumdar (1998), for example, studied Indian industrial companies and rated their efficiency. Majumdar used 1.0 to indicate a perfectly efficient company, and he found that state-owned companies scored about 0.65, mixed ownership (partly private/partly public ownership) companies scored 0.91, and privately owned companies averaged 0.975.

Correspondingly, a large literature finds that when state-owned companies are *privatized*—that is, sold to private (presumably) profit-maximizing owners—efficiency improves dramatically, and a smaller company is required to produce the same level of output.[19] Several studies have investigated the sources of the efficiency gain from privatization, and they conclude that the productivity increase from installing new, profit-oriented management in place of government-appointed bureaucrats is the source of most of the gains in efficiency. Indeed, in privatized firms that retain their government managers, productivity gains are not nearly as large as when new managers are brought in.

Problems with Privatization

The strong presumption of the benefits of privatization implied by the Niskanen model, however, is subject to two limitations. First, some markets may be **natural monopolies,** markets in which, because of the nature of the good,

natural monopoly A market in which, because of the uniformly decreasing marginal cost of production, there is a cost advantage to have only one firm provide the good to all consumers in a market.

---

[18] A number of subsequent studies have criticized Niskanen's model as unrealistically assuming an uninformed and perhaps even unintelligent legislature. Miller and Moe (1983), for example, argued that large bureaucracies would arise only through failings of legislative oversight.

[19] A review of these studies is provided in Megginson and Netter (2001).

there is a cost advantage to have only one firm provide the good to all consumers in a market. Examples of such markets are those for utilities such as water, gas, or electricity. The provision of natural monopoly goods requires sufficient *scale* or size of the producer: it is not efficient for, say, five or six water companies to lay the pipes for water delivery all over town. The high level of the fixed costs associated with the provision of natural monopoly goods leads to *economies of scale,* whereby the average cost of production falls as the quantity of the output increases. Thus, in natural monopoly markets, only one firm will exist in the private market equilibrium.

As a result, in natural monopoly markets, private provision will not be associated with competitive pressure; privatization in such markets can therefore lead to higher costs to consumers than does government provision. Evidence on this point comes from Kemper and Quigley (1976), who used data from municipalities in Connecticut to compare public and private refuse collection. They showed that private collection was much more expensive than direct public collection because the private vendors exploited their natural monopoly power to charge very high prices.

In natural monopoly markets, therefore, pure privatization may end up costing consumers more than a middle ground option of **contracting out,** an approach through which the government retains responsibility for providing the good or service, but hires private sector firms to actually provide the good or service. Governments can harness the forces of competition in this context through *competitive bidding,* asking a number of private firms to submit bids for the right to perform the service or provide the good. In principle, the government then grants the right to provide the good or service to the private entity that can provide the good most efficiently. When the government contracts out, it exploits its own monopoly power for good, not evil, by finding the most efficient provider and delivering the savings to the taxpayer. Indeed, Kemper and Quigley found that contracting out refuse collection was the most efficient option of all.

In practice, however, the bidding in contracting out is often far from competitive. In many situations, government bureaucrats may exploit their power and award contracts not to the most efficient lowest-cost bidder, but to the one that assists them in maximizing their own bureaucratic power (or, in the case of kickbacks and bribes, personal wealth). The application shows some examples of the problems with contracting out. If these problems are severe, then pure government or pure monopoly private provision may be more efficient than contracting out. Thus, whether contracting out is best depends on the nature of the contract.

In addition, while privatization of goods markets may increase efficiency, it is not clear that private provision of *social services,* such as health insurance, cash welfare, or public safety, is more efficient than public provision. As we highlight in Chapters 12–17, markets for social services often involve market failures that impede efficient private provision, such as the externalities of health insurance noted in the opening chapter.[20] One example of the prob-

---

contracting out An approach through which the government retains responsibility for providing a good or service, but hires private sector firms to actually provide the good or service.

---

[20] Blank (2000) also reviews the arguments for and against private provision of social services.

lems of privatizing social services was provided by Hart, Shleifer, and Vishny (1997), who compared private to public prisons. They found that private prisons are roughly 10% cheaper per prisoner, but that those savings are achieved by paying lower wages to prison guards. The low pay led to staffing with lower-quality guards, resulting in higher instances of violence (and in one case a major riot). Thus lowered costs were achieved at the demonstrable expense of quality.

▶ APPLICATION

Contracting Out with Non-Competitive Bidding

In principle, contracting out may be the best way for the government to arrange for the provision of public services. Contracting out is much more likely to deliver efficiency gains, however, if potential contractors compete to deliver cost savings or quality gains to the government. In practice, however, such competitive bidding can be the exception rather the rule, as shown by the following examples.

In the late 1990s, Science Applications International Corporation (SAIC), one of the government's largest contractors, was hired to conduct a series of environmental testing and cleanup jobs at Kelly Air Force Base in Texas. The contracts had been awarded without competitive bidding, and the government paid the negotiated price of $24 million. However, in 2002 the government brought a fraud suit against SAIC. Charges were first brought forth by a whistleblower, a former project manager for the company, and they accuse SAIC of having encouraged its managers to list higher-paid employee categories on job descriptions but use lower-paid employees to do the actual work; describing to the Air Force a pattern of expenses that would result in a profit of 10% even while internal documents indicated that the "actual profitability" would be 23%; and failing to disclose to the Air Force knowledge that the effective profit had continued to rise several months into the one-year contract.[21]

Since the early 2000s, Wackenhut Corporation has been the primary security contractor at weapons plants across the United States. In January 2004, the inspector general of the Energy Department revealed that in running drills to test security at weapons plants, Wackenhut attackers had told Wackenhut defenders which buildings and targets were to be attacked, in addition to whether any diversionary tactic would be used. Consequently the defense teams were found to have performed remarkably well in these drills but, as the inspector general reported, the results were "tainted and unreliable." Nonetheless, in August 2004, the Nuclear Energy Institute announced that it would be hiring Wackenhut, who at the time was already responsible for security at over half of the country's civilian reactors, to train and manage "adversary teams" to attack these reactors in drills. Representative Edward J. Markey of Massachusetts protested that allowing Wackenhut to test security at plants where it

---

[21] Eckholm (2005).

was the security contractor was akin to allowing athletes to conduct their own drug tests.[22]

In 2003 and 2004, DHB Industries was awarded contracts worth hundreds of millions of dollars to supply body armor to troops in Iraq. DHB, however, already had a shaky history with regard to product quality: in 2002, the New York Police Department returned 6,400 vests to DHB for replacement after state government tests showed that some of the vests were defective, and in 2003, a confrontation with the union representing DHB's employees in Florida led to workers accusing the company of sloppy quality control. DHB was still awarded the contract, but in 2005 the *Marine Corps Times* reported that the Marines had acquired the vests despite warnings from the Army that the vests had "critical, life-threatening flaws." In the end, 23,000 DHB vests were recalled from the field.[23]

In the weeks following Hurricane Katrina, concerns were raised over the fact that more than 80% of the $1.5 billion in contracts signed by FEMA were awarded without bidding or with limited competition. Richard L. Skinner, the inspector general for the Department of Homeland Security, complained that bills were coming in for deals that were apparently clinched with a handshake without any documentation to back them up.

One company that has come under scrutiny is Ashbritt, a company based in Pompano Beach, FL, which was awarded a $568 million contract for debris removal. Ashbritt is a client of the former lobbying firm of Governor Haley Barbour of Mississippi. According to its contract, Ashbritt was to be paid $15 per cubic yard to collect and process debris and was also to be reimbursed for costs if it had to dispose of materials in landfills. However, three communities in Mississippi that refused Ashbritt's offer and found their own contractors had negotiated contracts of as low as $10.64 per cubic yard, which included disposal, in addition to collection and processing.[24] ◄

Leviathan Theory

Niskanen's theory assumes that individual bureaucrats try to maximize the size of their own agencies and that a larger government tries to rein them in. In contrast, Brennan and Buchanan (1980) see these two entities as one monopolist (which they call "Leviathan") that simply tries to maximize the size of the public sector by taking advantage of the electorate's ignorance. Under this theory, voters cannot trust the government to spend their tax dollars efficiently and must design ways to combat government greed.

This view of government can explain the many rules in place in the United States and elsewhere that explicitly tie the government's hands in terms of taxes and spending. In Chapter 4, we discussed rules for limiting the size of the government budget. Likewise, a number of U.S. states have passed laws limiting the ability of local communities to raise property taxes (taxes

---

[22] Wald (2004a,b).
[23] O'Brien (2006).
[24] Lipton and Nixon (2005).

imposed on the value of homes and businesses and the land they are built on), as discussed in more detail in the next chapter. There is no reason to have these types of "roadblocks" if a benevolent government is maximizing social welfare, but with a Leviathan government they may be a means of putting a brake on inefficient government growth.

Another way to combat the Leviathan tendencies of government is to ensure that politicians face electoral pressure to deliver public services efficiently, as suggested by a recent study by Besley, Persson, and Sturm (2005). These authors studied the impact of the increased "political competition" in the southern United States during the twentieth century due to the enfranchisement of blacks and other groups. They measure political competition as the extent to which voters choose a fairly balanced slate of candidates in local elections, as opposed to always voting for one party or another. They find that areas with more political competition had much faster economic growth (25% higher growth in the long run), partly because of lower taxes and higher quality jobs.

Corruption

The theory of size-maximizing bureaucrats and Leviathan governments describes how governments will take action to maximize their size and power in carrying out their legitimate functions. Even more problematic is **corruption,** the abuse of power by government officials seeking to maximize their own personal wealth or that of their associates. As the following policy application illustrates, corruption is an international phenomenon.

corruption The abuse of power by government officials in order to maximize their own personal wealth or that of their associates.

▶ APPLICATION

Government Corruption

Corruption can take many forms, but the common theme is government officials using their power to enrich themselves or their associates. Two recent examples from different areas of the world:

1. In December 2003, former governor of Illinois George Ryan was indicted by a federal grand jury for selling state contracts to his friends in exchange for cash, gifts, loans, and trips for his family. The scandal unfolded only because of an unfortunate accident in which six children were killed when the minivan their parents were driving burst into flames after running over a piece of metal that had fallen off a truck in front of them. The deaths sparked Operation Safe Road, an investigation that revealed that the truck driver (as well as many other truck drivers) had bribed officials at the office of then Secretary of State Ryan to obtain a driver's license. In total, at least 20 people had died in accidents involving drivers who had bribed officials for their licenses. The investigation resulted in 70 indictments with over 60 convictions, many of whom were close friends and allies of Ryan who had kicked some of the bribe money into his campaign funds.

"But how do you know for sure you've got power unless you abuse it?"

Ryan was indicted for, among other things, accepting at least $167,000 from friend and businessman Larry Warner, who benefited in the millions from state contracts signed under Ryan's oversight. The federal prosecutors also charged Ryan with signing leases with Warner and another real estate developer for office space, in exchange for staying in their California and Jamaica homes for free (though Ryan arranged scam payments to make it appear that he had paid for the privilege). In exchange for other help from Ryan, political allies allegedly invested $6,000 in his son's cigar store, lent $145,000 to a company founded by his brother, and paid in part for a trip to Disney World for the family of one of his children. Ryan was eventually found guilty on all charges in his 2005 trial. In August, 2006, he was sentenced to 6½ years in prison.[25]

2. Carlos Menem was elected President of Argentina in 1989 and immediately rewarded members of his political party with cushy government jobs requiring only the occasional appearance to pick up a paycheck. Menem himself traveled on a private jet with his own hairdresser, both paid for by the state, and privatized a number of industries while ensuring that bidding was rigged and that he and his colleagues received lucrative kickbacks. To be sure that his corrupt schemes would run smoothly, Menem not only involved other legislators in his corruption but stacked the courts with appointees who would always decide the law in his favor. In 1994 he had the constitution amended to allow him a second five-year term in office, and he tried but failed to amend it again for a third term. Argentines suffered directly from the corruption. The average Argentine was, for example, unable to get a mortgage, both because the government was borrowing all available surplus funds to feed its habits and because, in such a lawless environment, banks could not trust their customers to repay the loans.

In 2001, Swiss authorities froze $10 million in Menem's various bank accounts, and Argentines were surprised only that he had stolen so little money from them. By 2001, Argentines had so little faith in their elected officials that when four presidents resigned within a two-week period, the popular joke was: "Five more presidents, five more millionaires." Even so, Menem ran again in 2003, but he withdrew from a vote he was certain to lose to his opponent, Nestor Kirchner. President Kirchner has since enjoyed approval ratings around 70% in part for firing a number of corrupt and useless officials within weeks of taking office.[26] ◄

---

[25] More information about the George Ryan trial can be found at http://cbs2chicago.com/politics.
[26] Leight (2006).

Why does corruption exist? Some public choice theorists might agree with Lord Acton's famous observation: "Power tends to corrupt and absolute power corrupts absolutely." In this view, a government's monopoly power over some spheres of its citizens' lives is sufficient to explain corruption. Why shouldn't the clerk at your local Department of Motor Vehicles ask for $10 to speed up your application for a driver's license? Doesn't he have complete power over who gets and who does not get a license? Ultimately, of course, he is unlikely to ask for a bribe, in part because rampant corruption in the DMV might motivate voters to elect a politician who vows to clean up that particular department.

This view suggests that the only thing keeping corruption in check is *electoral accountability,* the ability of voters to throw out corrupt regimes. The notion that electoral accountability is a primary deterrent of corruption is supported by the evidence in Persson and Tabellini (2000). They measured the extent of government corruption using surveys of business leaders, the most direct victims of such corruption. They compared systems of government in which voters choose individual candidates, such as the United States, to systems of proportional voting where voters choose a party slate of candidates, such as the United Kingdom. They reasoned that in the latter type of system, individual politicians are less accountable to the electorate since the voter votes only for the party and not for the individual. Indeed, they found that corruption is much more prevalent in systems with proportional voting.

Corruption also appears more rampant in political systems that feature more *red tape,* bureaucratic barriers that make it costly to do business in a country. Djankov et al. (2002) examined data from 85 countries that pertain to the procedure a citizen must go through to start a business. The procedures varied widely, taking as few as 2 days in Canada and Australia to as many as 152 days in Madagascar before the business may begin. The costs of these bureaucratic procedures ranged from less than 0.5% of per capita GDP in the United States to over 460% of per capita GDP in the Dominican Republic. This study found that countries where entrepreneurs must go through large numbers of bureaucratic procedures to start a business tend to have higher levels of corruption.

Another key determinant of corruption appears to be the wages of government bureaucrats. Paying bureaucrats higher wages makes them less willing to risk losing their jobs by being caught in a corrupt act and thus lowers rates of corruption. Goel and Nelson (1998) used convictions for public abuse of office to measure the corruption of state-level government employees in the United States, and they found that higher wages led to a lower level of government corruption.

The Implications of Government Failure

There is clear evidence that governments fail in some instances to benevolently serve the interests of their citizens. Do these failures have important implications? Or can citizens use policies such as property tax limitations to limit harms imposed by government structure? Some evidence suggests that

GOVERNMENT FAILURES AND ECONOMIC GROWTH

There are several recent studies that suggest that poor government structure can have long-lasting negative impacts on economic growth. One such study is Mauro (1995), which used data collected by a private firm whose agents in various countries rated the quality of government along various dimensions such as the amount of red tape involved in government procedures and the amount of corruption. Mauro found that nations with higher levels of corruption and red tape have slower growth rates and that these effects are large: if the most bureaucratically inefficient nation in his sample (Zaire) improved its efficiency to the level of the least inefficient nations (Switzerland, New Zealand, the Netherlands, or Singapore), his model predicts that Zaire's growth rate would be 4.9% per year higher!

The difficulty with studies such as Mauro's, however, is that the nations with high-quality governments (the treatment group) may differ from those with low-quality governments (the control group) for other reasons as well, biasing the estimates of the effect of government quality. Suppose, for example, that the efficiency of a bureaucracy rises as the wages of government workers rise. Then slow-growing low-income nations who cannot pay their government workers well will have poorly functioning governments. In this case, slow economic growth may cause government failure, not vice versa.

A recent attempt to surmount this problem using a historical perspective was taken by Acemoglu, Johnson, and Robinson (2001). They denoted two sets of nations that were quite similar when they were colonized by the same set of European powers and therefore could be considered comparable treatments and controls, but for which colonization took very different forms. The treatment nations in the Caribbean, Central America, and Africa were governed from afar: their European colonizers focused solely on extracting from these countries as many natural resources (such as diamond, silver, and copper) as possible. The colonizers were not interested in setting up institutions in these nations to foster economic success (such as effective property rights or bureaucratic institutions). The control nations in North and South America, and Australia and New Zealand, were governed from within: the European colonizers moved to these nations in large numbers and set up institutions to foster economic success.

The reason for the lack of hands-on governing in the treatment nations was simple: the odds of colonists dying from infectious diseases such as malaria was much higher in these nations than in the control nations. In the nations of the Caribbean, Central America, and Africa, while native people were immune to local disease, settlers were not. So these nations were governed from afar with little long-term interest in settlement. In nations in North and South America, and in Australia and New Zealand, settlers were less likely to suffer from local infectious diseases, so they settled there in large numbers. In doing so, they set up institutions that would foster their success. The reason for this difference should not be otherwise associated with economic success, since native people were immune to disease; these two sets of nations were comparable other than through the type of colonization.

Despite their precolonization similarity, these sets of nations have performed very differently in the postcolonial era. The treatment nations in the Caribbean, Central America, and Africa have grown much more slowly post colonization than have the control nations in North and South America and Australia and New Zealand. These treatment nations appear to suffer from the long-run detrimental effects of inefficient government institutions. For example, the authors compute that if the quality of Nigeria's government institutions could be improved to the level of Chile's, Nigeria would see a sevenfold increase in per capita income.

Acemoglu (2003) made a similar "historical accident" argument with relation to North and South Korea, two halves of a region that had been a single region (Korea) under Japanese control until the end of World War II. There were no inherent differences between the northern and southern regions of Korea until World War II: they were culturally and economically very similar. After World War II, however, the Soviet Union occupied the northern half of Korea, which became a communist nation, and the United States occupied the southern half, which adopted a capitalist system. The results of this division of the nation into two different systems have been dramatic. Maddison (2001) showed that the two countries had similar income levels in 1950 of $770 per capita, and North Korea was actually more heavily industrialized than the south. Fifty years later, North Korea had per capita income of only $1,200, compared to South Korea's $12,200.

government failures can have long-lasting negative impacts on economic growth, as reviewed in the empirical evidence discussion.

9.5
Conclusion

In most of this book and in most of public finance, the government is assumed to be a benign actor that serves only to implement the optimal policies to address externalities, to provide public goods and social insurance, and to develop equitable and efficient taxation. In reality, however, the government is a collection of individuals who have the difficult task of aggregating the preferences of a large set of citizens. Will governments operate to pursue policies in the ways suggested by the economic analyses presented in other chapters of this book?

The core model of representative democracy suggests that governments are likely to pursue the policies preferred by the median voter, which in most cases should fairly represent the demands of society on average. Yet, while that model has strong evidence to support it, there is offsetting evidence that politicians have other things on their mind. In particular, there are clear examples of government's failure to maximize the well-being of its citizens, with potentially disastrous implications for economic outcomes. The extent to which government serves or fails to serve the interests of its citizens is a crucial one for future research in political economy.

▶ HIGHLIGHTS

- In theory, a government can efficiently finance public goods by simply asking individuals to pay their valuation of the good (Lindahl pricing).

- In practice, such a solution faces the problems of preference revelation (individuals not honestly reporting their preferences), preference knowledge (individuals not knowing their preferences), and preference aggregation (the government being unable to collect data on each individual's preferences).

- One way to aggregate preferences is through direct democracy, where votes are directly cast on particular issues. This voting mechanism will consistently aggregate preferences only if preferences are restricted to a particular form (single-peaked preferences).

- If preferences are single-peaked, the option chosen will be the one preferred by the median voter. This

will not be the efficient outcome, however, if voters on one side or another of an issue have particularly intense preferences.

- Representative democracies will also support the policy preferred by the median voter if politicians are vote-maximizing and if other fairly restrictive assumptions hold. In practice, it appears that factors such as ideology, not just vote maximization, are important in determining legislator behavior.

- Public choice theory directly models the preferences of legislators and the government failures that can arise when legislators pursue their own interests rather than the common good. Government failures such as corruption can have serious negative ramifications for the economic well-being of societies.

▶ QUESTIONS AND PROBLEMS

1. In a recent study, Americans stated that they were willing to pay $70 billion to protect all endangered species and also stated that they were willing to pay $15 billion to protect a single species. Which problem with Lindahl pricing is demonstrated? Explain.

2. The preference revelation problem associated with Lindahl pricing becomes more severe as the number of people in society increases. Why do you think this is true?

3. Matsusaka (1995) showed that states that provide for voter initiatives tend to have smaller government growth than do states without such a provision. Why might this be so?

4. Major League Baseball uses what is known as a 5-3-1 system to vote for the Most Valuable Player (MVP) in each league. Each voter gets to vote for three different players they consider worthy of the award. Their first place candidate gets 5 points, their second place candidate gets 3 points, and their third place candidate gets 1 point. Points are then added up across all voters, and the player with the most total points wins the award. Suppose there are three voters—Neyer, Law, and Phillips—and five potential candidates for the award—Alex, David, Raffy, Manny, and Mario. The table below shows how each voter ranks the candidates. Raffy is embroiled in a substance abuse scandal. The "guilty" or "innocent" verdict will come out the day before voting, and a guilty verdict will ban him from MVP voting.

Rank	Neyer	Law	Phillips
Best	David	David	Raffy
Second Best	Alex	Alex	Alex
Third Best	Raffy	Raffy	Manny
Fourth Best	Manny	Manny	Mario
Fifth Best	Mario	Mario	David

a. Who will win the MVP if Raffy is found innocent?

b. Who will win the MVP if Raffy is found guilty?

c. What problem with consistent aggregation does this illustrate?

5. Fletcher (2003) shows that when congressional districts are redrawn to include more elderly people, members of Congress become more likely to take pro-elderly positions in congressional votes. Why does the median voter model predict that this would be so?

6. Stratmann (1995) documented a condition of "logrolling" in Congress, in which members of Congress trade votes on one bill for votes on another. Is logrolling efficient, or should it be banned? Explain.

7. A problem with the median voter outcome is that it does not take into account intensity of preferences. Suppose that the government decided to give multiple votes to people with strong preferences, pro or con. Would this solve the problem? Why or why not?

8. When local telephone companies wish to raise the rates they charge to phone customers, they must first argue their case at a public hearing before a regulatory body. How does the free rider problem explain why telephone companies are usually successful in getting permission to raise their rates?

9. Figlio (2000) found that legislators are more likely to mirror their constituents' preferences during election years than in earlier years of their terms. This is particularly true for relatively inexperienced legislators. Why might this be the case?

10. Every year, the World Bank rates countries on the basis of their quality of governance, along a number of different dimensions (such as political stability, government effectiveness, and the rule of law). These indices are on the Web at http://www.worldbank.org/wbi/governance/pubs/gov/matters4.html. Identify some countries where the quality of governance has improved from 1996 to the present. What does this improvement portend for future economic growth in these countries?

▶ **ADVANCED QUESTIONS**

11. Alfie, Bill, and Coco each value police protection differently. Alfie's demand for the public good is $Q = 55 - 5P$, Bill's demand is $Q = 80 - 4P$, and Coco's demand is $Q = 100 - 10P$. If the marginal cost of providing police protection is $13.5, what is the socially optimal level of police provision? Under Lindahl pricing, what share of the tax burden would each of the three people pay?

12. Carrboro has three equal-size groups of people: (1) Type A people consistently prefer more police protection to less; (2) Type B people prefer high levels of police protection to low levels and they prefer low levels to medium levels; (3) Type C people most prefer medium levels to low levels, which they in turn prefer by a modest amount to high levels.

    a. Which types of people have single peaked preferences? Which have multi-peaked preferences?

    b. Will majority voting generate consistent outcomes in this case? Why or why not?

13. In business, there is a tension between the principals (stockholders) and agents (managers). The managers may choose policies that increase short-term profitability (and their bonuses) at the expense of long-term profitability. Describe why the same types of problems may exist in government, where elected officials are the agents and voters are the principals.

14. Voters rarely get to choose the exact level of spending on a public good. Instead, they are provided with two options—a proposed spending level posed by the government and a default (or "reversion") level that would be enacted if the proposal were rejected by voters. The Leviathan theory suggests that governments will intentionally select large proposed spending levels and default levels that are well below the desired level of spending. Why is this behavior consistent with a size-maximizing government?

15. Refer back to Table 4-1, which reports the composition of the U.S. Generational Accounts. Why might the political system in the U.S. have led to this pattern of intergenerational transfers?

State and Local Government Expenditures

10

In 2002, President Bush signed into law what would become one of his most significant contributions to domestic policy: the No Child Left Behind Act (NCLB). NCLB sought to address the problem of substandard educational opportunities for poor and minority children by requiring standardized testing starting in Grade 3 and continuing in high school. In addition, NCLB mandated that schools publish their scores categorized by race and ethnic group. Harsh penalties, including the possibility of the elimination of principals and teachers and the installation of new management, were to be imposed on schools that failed to show progress. NCLB represented the greatest expansion of federal power over schools in half a century.

The first years of NCLB have been marked by intense controversy nationwide and a fierce battle between the states and the federal government. While some concerns have arisen due to technical shortcomings with the law and lower-than-expected federal funding, the central issue of contention has been the intervention on the part of the federal government into public education, a domain that has historically been reserved for the local and state governments. On the one hand, supporters of the law have applauded the federal government for intervening when it is clear that many states have either failed or not even tried to close the achievement gap between white and minority students. An April 2005 editorial in the *New York Times* supporting NCLB stated that, historically, "the federal government has looked the other way when the states have damaged the national interest by failing to educate large swaths of the population. That approach has left us with one of the weakest educational systems in the developed world . . . the Bush administration must stand firm against the districts that simply don't want to make the effort."[1]

On the other side, critics of NCLB have countered that the federal government's imposition of a standardized criterion across the nation has interfered

---

[1] *New York Times* (2005b).

with ongoing local attempts to improve educational systems in a manner most suitable for each state. By March 2005, at least 15 state legislatures were considering challenges to the law and in Utah the state Senate had approved a bill requiring state officials to give higher priority to local educational goals than to those of the federal law.[2] As State Representative Kory M. Holdaway argued, "No Child Left Behind is one of the most important issues of federal intrusion in state affairs that we've faced. This is a message bill. We want to send a message to the federal government that Utah has a great education system and we know best how to manage it."[3] In February 2006, under the pressure of continued calls for greater flexibility in the law, the federal Department of Education finally agreed to review requests from 20 states to significantly alter the manner in which student progress is measured.[4]

At heart, the central issue in these debates over NCLB is the question of who should control educational policy. A 2005 report compiled by a bipartisan panel of lawmakers directly addressed this issue by calling into question whether NCLB is even constitutional because the Constitution does not delegate the powers to educate the nation's citizens to the federal government.[5] As Utah State Senator Thomas Hatch explained, "This issue is a lot bigger than the details of teacher qualifications and student testing. This is about who controls education—the states or Washington."[6]

This debate raises the important issue of **optimal fiscal federalism,** the question of which activities should take place at which level of government. Representative Holdaway was correct in asserting that an advantage of local provision of government services is that it allows communities to choose the package of services that best matches the tastes of their residents, potentially improving the efficiency of public goods delivery. The Bush Administration was also correct in asserting that in some cases, matching local interests may not be in the national interest.

In this chapter, we discuss the set of issues surrounding state and local, or "subnational," government spending, and the division of responsibilities across different levels of government. We begin with a discussion of the current division of responsibilities in the United States and other developed nations. We then turn to a discussion of whether local government provision of public goods solves the problems with government provision of public goods highlighted in the previous chapter. In particular, by allowing individuals to choose the jurisdiction that most matches their tastes, local government provision of public goods may allow local governments to provide the optimal amount of public goods, surmounting the problems of preference revelation and preference aggregation that hamper decisions about national public goods provision.

> **optimal fiscal federalism** The question of which activities should take place at which level of government.

---

[2] Dillon (March 6, 2005c).
[3] Dillon (February 16, 2005a).
[4] Schemo (2006).
[5] Dillon (February 24, 2005b).
[6] Dillon (March 6, 2005c).

The remainder of the chapter asks whether and how the government should redistribute resources across communities. There are enormous differences across U.S. communities in the ability to finance local public goods, largely due to differences in the value of property on which local taxes are levied. Should the state and federal governments care about these differences? If so, what tools can these higher levels of government use to redistribute resources across communities?

10.1

Fiscal Federalism in the United States and Abroad

The last amendment (Amendment X) in the Bill of Rights of the United States Constitution states: "The powers not delegated to the United States by the Constitution, nor prohibited by it to the states, are reserved to the states respectively, or to the people." Early in the history of the United States, therefore, the federal government played a relatively limited role in many aspects of the nation's life, including the economy. As Figure 10-1 shows, in 1902 the federal government accounted for only 34% of total government spending, with local governments accounting for 58% and state governments accounting for the remaining 8%. The federal government limited itself to spending on national defense, foreign relations, judicial functions, and the postal service. State and local governments were responsible for education, police, roads, sanitation, welfare, health, hospitals, and so on. The various levels of government operated in their own spheres, rarely overlapping or interfering with each other. Furthermore, the state and local governments funded their spending largely from their own sources. Less than 1% of state and local revenues at the time came from federal government grants. **Intergovernmental grants** are payments from one level of government to another.

intergovernmental grants
Payments from one level of government to another.

■ FIGURE 10-1

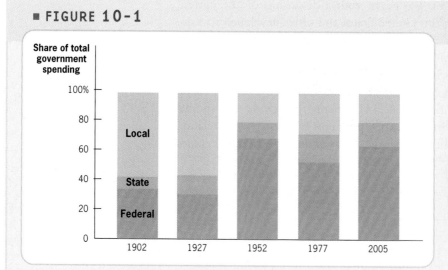

Changing Fiscal Federalism • In the last hundred years, the federal government has grown significantly relative to state and local governments.

Source: 1902–1977 data from Wallis and Oates (1998), Table 5.1; 2005 data on direct expenditures (grant spending attributed to recipient level of government) from Office of Management and Budget (2006a), Table 15.2, with state and local expenditures divided according to the proportion of direct spending in U.S. Bureau of the Census (2006a), Table 443.

Over the next 50 years, the situation changed dramatically. By 1952, the federal government accounted for 69% of total government spending, while local and state governments accounted for 20% and 11% respectively. In addition, 10% of state and local revenue now came from federal grants. This change was largely due to three factors. The first was the Sixteenth Amendment to the Constitution (enacted in 1913), which allowed the federal government to levy income taxes on individual citizens (before this amendment, the Constitution had basically forbidden such taxation), thus providing a centralized source of revenue. The second factor in the growth of the federal government was the New Deal programs of the 1930s, which were the federal government's response to the Great Depression. These programs initiated a number of federal government projects that fundamentally changed the relationship between the federal government and state and local governments. Federal grants to lower governments ballooned, and many of the new programs, like the Works Progress (later Work Projects) Administration (WPA) and highway programs, were funded by the federal government but administered locally. The third factor in the growth of federal government was the introduction of large social insurance and welfare programs by the federal government, most notably the Social Security old-age income support program and the system of matching grants to encourage states to provide assistance to the elderly, blind, and disabled.

The share of spending done at the local, state, and federal levels has remained fairly constant over the past 50 years. There has been a growth in the share of state financing coming from the federal government, largely due to the introduction in the 1960s of jointly federal- and state-financed welfare programs such as cash welfare and public Medicaid insurance for the poor. Federal grants now account for 30% of state and local revenues.[7]

Spending and Revenue of State and Local Governments

As noted in Chapter 1, the sources of revenue and the types of spending done by state and local governments differ dramatically from those of the U.S. federal government. On the spending side, the largest element of state and local spending is education, followed by health care and public safety; the largest elements of federal spending are health care, Social Security, and national defense. The federal government plays a very small role in financing education. On the revenue side, states receive only 15% of their revenues from income taxes, while the federal government obtains nearly half its revenues from income taxation.

A major source of revenue raising at the local level is the **property tax,** the tax on land and any buildings on it, such as commercial businesses or residential homes. Property taxes raised $286 billion in revenue in 2003 and accounted for almost half of the (nongrant) revenues of local governments.[8]

property tax The tax on land and any buildings on it, such as commercial businesses or residential homes.

---

[7] Office of Management and Budget (2006a), Tables 12.1 and 15.1.
[8] U.S. Bureau of the Census (2006b), Table 1.

▪ TABLE 10-1

Comparison of State Spending and Revenue Across the United States

		State	Dollars per capita
Spending	**Education**	Alaska	$2,370 (high)
		New Mexico	1,368 (median)
		Kentucky	958 (low)
	Health Care	New York	2,320 (high)
		North Dakota	1,212 (median)
		Utah	650 (low)
Taxes	**Income Taxes**	New York	1,583 (high)
		Nebraska	671 (median)
		AK/SD/FL/NV/WY/WA/TX	0 (low)
	Sales Taxes	Washington	1,540 (high)
		Nebraska	749 (median)
		DE/OR/MT/NH	0 (low)

Source: Statistics from the U.S. Department of Education (2006a), the U.S. Bureau of the Census (2003), the National Association of State Budget Officers at www.nasbo.org/publications.php, and the Rockefeller Fiscal Studies at http://rfs.rockinst.org/data/comprev.

We will discuss property taxation at length in Chapter 23 as part of the broader discussion of wealth taxation.

There is tremendous variety in spending and revenue raising behavior across U.S. states. Table 10-1 illustrates this variation by showing for a number of fiscal measures the state with the highest value, the median value, and the lowest value. For example, the state of Alaska has the highest education spending per capita in the nation, at $2,370, while the median state, New Mexico, spends $1,368 per capita, and the lowest state, Kentucky, spends under $1,000 per capita. Health care spending per capita is twice as much in New York as in the median state, North Dakota, and four times as much as the lowest state, Utah. Income taxes per capita are highest in New York, at almost $1,600, and are zero in the seven states without an income tax, while sales taxes are highest in Washington, D.C., at $1,540, and are zero in the four states without a sales tax.

Fiscal Federalism Abroad

Compared to most other developed nations, U.S. subnational (state and local) governments collect a much larger share of total (national plus subnational) government revenues and spend a somewhat larger share of total government spending. A recent survey of OECD nations, summarized in Table 10-2, showed that the average nation's subnational governments collect only 22% of total government revenue, while in the United States subnational governments collect 40% of total revenue. The cross-national differences on the spending side are slightly less dramatic: the average OECD nation's subnational government accounts for 32% of spending, compared to about 40% in the United States.

The higher level of centralization in other nations exists because in many countries, such as Mexico, Austria, and Norway, subnational governments have almost no legal power to tax citizens: this power is reserved for the central government. Moreover, in most countries, central governments redistribute a larger share of their revenues to subnational governments. Many countries practice **fiscal equalization,** whereby the national government distributes grants to subnational governments in an effort to equalize differences in wealth. This can be accomplished by providing larger national grants on a per capita basis to poorer subnational areas. In Austria, for example, the federal government offsets more than half of the difference across subnational areas in the revenues they are able to raise through taxation. The federal government in the United States is notable because it does not use grants for equalization; the only such program, initiated by President Richard Nixon in the early 1970s, was eliminated by 1986.[9]

Other nations also have a very different distribution of spending across national and subnational governments. In the United States, for instance, 30–40% of state and local spending is devoted to education, while the average in OECD nations is about 20%, highlighting the larger role the central government plays in education in other countries.[10]

Recent years have seen a move toward fiscal decentralization around the globe. In the United States, there have been increased efforts to shift control and financing of public programs to the states, as demonstrated by the welfare reform example. In countries as diverse as Hungary, Italy, Korea, Mexico, and Spain there have been efforts to shift responsibility for health care, education, and welfare from national to subnational governments. Thus, in most countries spending by subnational governments has increased over the past couple of decades, often financed through grants from the national government. This increased funding and control has typically been accompanied by increasing imposition of national norms and quality standards on locally provided goods (such as increasingly rigid national curricula in education).

■ **TABLE 10-2**

Subnational Government Spending/Revenue as Share of Total Government Spending/Revenue in 2001

	Spending %	Revenue %
Greece	5.0	3.7
Portugal	12.8	8.3
France	18.6	13.1
Norway	38.8	20.3
United States	40.0	40.4
Denmark	57.8	34.6
OECD Average	32.2	21.9

Source: Joumard and Kongsrud (2003), Table 1.

Compared to the subnational governments of other nations, state and local governments in the United States account for a relatively large portion of total government activity.

fiscal equalization Policies by which the national government distributes grants to subnational governments in an effort to equalize differences in wealth.

---

[9] Some implicit equalization still exists through the joint federal and state financing of social insurance and welfare programs since the federal share of those costs rises as state income falls.
[10] Joumard and Kongsrud (2003), Table 4.

10.2

Optimal Fiscal Federalism

The different approaches to fiscal federalism seen in various nations raise a natural question: What is the optimal division of responsibilities across different levels of government? Why should anything be done by local governments? Alternatively, why is there any role for a central government? And which particular types of programs are most appropriately administered at which level of government? A theory of how the efficiency of public goods provision may differ at different levels of government will help answer these questions.

The Tiebout Model

Two major problems with government provision of public goods, as discussed in the previous chapter, are the problems of *preference revelation* and *preference aggregation:* it is difficult to design democratic institutions that cause individuals to honestly reveal their preferences for public goods, and it is also difficult to aggregate individual preferences into a social decision. As a result, governments are often unable to deliver the optimal level of public goods in practice.

In 1956, economist Charles Tiebout (pronounced TEE-bow) asked: What is it about the private market that guarantees optimal provision of private goods that is missing in the case of public goods?[11] His insight was that the factors missing from the market for public goods were *shopping* and *competition.* Shopping is the fundamental force that induces efficiency in private goods markets. If a firm is selling an inferior good relative to its competitors, consumers will purchase from the competitors, not from the firm. This competition leads firms to produce efficiently in the perfectly competitive private goods market.

With many public goods, however, there is no shopping. Individuals don't debate whether to live in the United States or in Canada based on whether the marginal missile is produced by the federal government. Voters can shop across political parties based on their promises to provide public goods, but this is only one of a large number of factors that determine votes for federal office, and the process of changing federal decision making is slow. Since there is little real competition facing the federal government when it makes its decisions to provide public goods, the decisions can result in inefficient public goods provision (as we saw in Chapter 9).

Tiebout pointed out, however, that the situation is different when public goods are provided at the local level by cities and towns (and to a lesser extent, states). In this case, he argued, competition will naturally arise because individuals can *vote with their feet:* if they don't like the level of public goods provision in one town, they can move to the next town over, without nearly as much disruption to their lives as moving to another country.

---

[11] For the original paper, see Tiebout (1956).

Suppose, for example, that you read that the U.S. Department of Defense was spending $110 on an electronic diode worth $0.04, or $435 on a single claw hammer, or $437 on a measuring tape (as was revealed to be true in the United States in the 1980s).[12] What could you do about this? You are unlikely to move to another nation. You could vote out the party in power, but your vote for congressman or president is based on a large number of factors, of which this is only one. So there is really little you can do to end such inefficiency.

Now suppose instead that you found out when your local high school was being renovated that the school was paying $75 each for the little metal covers that are placed on electric sockets (which cost $0.80 apiece), as happened in Chicago in 1992.[13] This waste clearly raises the property taxes you pay to finance the town government. In this case, you have a realistic option: you can move to the town next door, which may be similar along most dimensions but better in terms of fiscal discipline. With local public goods, we have a new *preference revelation device:* mobility.

Tiebout argued that this threat of exit can induce efficiency in local public goods production. Indeed, he went one step further and argued that under certain conditions public goods provision will be *fully efficient* at the local level. By the same logic that the competitive equilibrium delivers the efficient level of private goods, competition across localities in public goods provision will deliver the efficient level of public goods. Towns that don't provide efficient levels of public goods will lose citizens to towns that do achieve efficiency— and will eventually go out of business.

The Formal Model In this section, we discuss the formal model that underlies Tiebout's intuition. This model makes a number of assumptions that are unrealistic, as we discuss in the next section. Yet the main message of the model, that competition across local jurisdictions places competitive pressures on the provision of local public goods, is an important one that is consistent with the evidence that we review later in this chapter.

The Tiebout model assumes that there are many people who divide themselves up across towns that provide different levels of public goods. Each town i has N_i residents, and finances its public goods spending, G_i, with a uniform tax on all residents of G_i/N_i. Tiebout showed that in this model individuals will divide themselves up so that each resident in any town has the same taste for public goods, and so demands the same level of public goods spending, G_i.

This model solves the problems of preference revelation and aggregation that cause difficulties with public provision of public goods. There is no problem of revelation because there is no incentive for people to lie with a uniform tax that finances the public goods. To illustrate this, let's return to the example of Jack and Ava from Chapter 9 (Figure 9.1), but now let's assume that fireworks cost 75¢ each. Suppose that Jack joins a town of 100 individuals identical to himself. Such a town would vote to have 75 fireworks, with each person paying 56¢ to finance the fireworks. Now suppose that once again Jack

[12] Barron (1983).
[13] Oclander and Rossi (1995).

lies by saying that he has the same preferences as Ava. In Tiebout's model, to carry out that lie he would have to actually move to a town of individuals like Ava (since those in his town want 75 fireworks, so that is the level provided). In Ava's town, they choose to only purchase 25 fireworks, with each individual paying 19¢ for each firework. By moving to Ava's town, Jack pays only one-third as much for fireworks—but he only gets one-third as many fireworks as a result. Jack has no incentive to lie because he must act on his lie by moving to a different town that matches his stated preferences. That is, Jack can't free ride when individuals in each town are identical and equally share the financing of the public good. The problem of preference aggregation is also solved because everyone in town wants the same level of public goods G_i, and the town government can simply divide that amount by the population to get the appropriate financing.

With the preference revelation and aggregation problems solved, Lindahl pricing works in the Tiebout model. Each individual reports his or her true valuation of the public good, the valuations are added, and then each individual is billed for the total cost of the public good divided by population size. This is an equilibrium because every person is happy to pay his or her share of the tax to get the public good, and the condition for optimal public goods provision is met because the level of public goods provided is determined by the sum of the individual benefits.

Problems with the Tiebout Model

Although the Tiebout model is interesting, it is obviously extreme. A number of problems stand in the way of the prediction of the Tiebout model that local public goods provision will be efficient.

Problems with Tiebout Competition The Tiebout model requires a number of assumptions that may not hold in reality. The first assumption is perfect mobility: individuals must not only want to vote with their feet, they must be able to actually carry out that vote. This is difficult in practice. For example, I am now quite settled in the town of Lexington, Massachusetts (of Revolutionary War fame), with many friends and other comforts. It would take a lot more than the purchase of expensive electric socket plates for the high school to get me to move now.

Perhaps even more implausible is the assumption that individuals have perfect information on the benefits they receive from the town and the taxes they pay. Even if Lexington High School were buying expensive socket plates for its renovation, I would never find out unless it was somehow exposed by the local media (and I was paying attention).

Moreover, for the Tiebout model to hold, I must be able to freely choose among a range of towns that might match my taste for public goods. This range exists in the suburbs of Boston, where there are many towns that are fairly close to my job at MIT. But it might not be true in other areas, where towns are more spread out and voting with my feet would mean moving considerably farther from my job. Such restrictions on suitable substitutes for one's town could limit the usefulness of the Tiebout mechanism for smaller or declining metropolitan areas.

Finally, the provision of some public goods requires sufficient *scale* or size. It is not efficient to run a school with only a few students or to build a park that will be used by only a few residents because of the large fixed costs of constructing the school or the park. These fixed costs lead to *efficiencies of scale*, whereby the efficiency of a public good is much higher if it is used by many rather than few. A school that is used by 1,000 students can be financed by a much lower property tax per household than a school that is used by 10 students, since the large fixed costs of schooling (e.g., the building, the principal) can be spread among the larger set of households.

At the same time, the Tiebout model requires that there be enough towns so that individuals can sort themselves into groups with similar preferences for public goods. This raises a clear tension: Can we divide the population into groups of people who all have similar preferences for public goods, yet also ensure that these groups are large enough to support the economies of scale required by public goods?

Problems with Tiebout Financing A second major problem with the operation of the Tiebout model is that it requires equal financing of the public good among all residents. This kind of financing is called a **lump-sum tax,** a fixed sum that a person pays in taxation independent of that person's income, consumption of goods and services, or wealth. As we will discuss in the tax chapters, this form of taxation is viewed as highly inequitable by the public, since both rich and poor pay the same amount of tax (most forms of taxation place higher tax burdens on the rich than on the poor). As a result, lump-sum taxation is very rarely used to finance government expenditures. Indeed, the most high-profile attempt to impose lump-sum taxes, by the British government of Margaret Thatcher in 1990, resulted in major riots that led to the resignation of the once incredibly popular Prime Minister.

> **lump-sum tax** A fixed taxation amount independent of a person's income, consumption of goods and services, or wealth.

Towns typically finance their public goods instead through a property tax that is levied in proportion to the value of homes. The problem that this property taxation causes is that the *poor chase the rich*. Richer people pay a larger share of the public goods bill than do poorer people, so people who value those goods would like to live in a community with people richer than they are. That way, the poorer people can benefit from the higher taxes paid by their richer neighbors. In other words, everyone wants to live in towns with people who are richer than they are so that they can free ride on their neighbors' higher tax payments.

One way that towns have endeavored to solve this problem is through the use of **zoning.** Zoning regulations are restrictions that towns place on how real estate property can be used, ostensibly with the goal of preserving the character of the local community. For example, one common zoning regulation requires that houses be built a certain distance back from the street to preserve some yard space and thus the aesthetic character of the neighborhood. Other examples of zoning regulations include prohibitions against

> **zoning** Restrictions that towns place on the use of real estate.

using one's home to run a business in a residential neighborhood, restrictions on the maximum number of occupants a lot or building may house, requirements for minimum lot sizes, constraints on the maximum size of buildings, and bans on multifamily housing.

Zoning regulations protect the tax base of wealthy towns by pricing lower-income people out of the housing market. For example, a town that prohibits multifamily dwellings (such as two-family houses and apartment buildings) lowers the available amount of housing and thus inflates the value of existing housing so that poor people can't afford to move in and free ride on the tax payments of higher-income neighbors. Indeed, Glaeser and Gyourko (2002) compared areas with different zoning laws and found that the prices of land in zoned areas are higher by a factor of 10 than prices in unzoned markets.

No Externalities/Spillovers A third problem with the Tiebout model is that it assumes that public goods have effects only in a given town and that the effects do not spill over to neighboring towns. If such spillovers exist, there is a case for provision of public goods at a higher level of government, or grants that subsidize local purchases.

Imagine that my town is considering building a large new public park. This park will be enjoyed primarily by individuals in my town, but many people from neighboring towns will visit its beautiful grounds as well. Under the Tiebout mechanism, when my town decides whether to build the park, it will consider only the preferences of residents in my town, not the preferences of residents of other towns who might enjoy the park. Thus, we face the standard problem with public goods provision: since people in other towns are free riding on my town's park, my town will underprovide park services. If the social benefits (to my town and all surrounding towns) exceed the cost of building the park, it should be built, but if the private benefits to my town are smaller than the costs of building the park, then it will not be built, which is socially inefficient.

Many local public goods have similar externality or spillover features: police (if my town's police department is not large enough, criminal activity in my town might spill over to other towns); public works (if my town's streets are covered in potholes, the drivers from neighboring towns might suffer as they drive through my town); education (the entire nation benefits from a more educated citizenry), and so on. Thus, there is a fundamental trade-off with the Tiebout approach. There are advantages to locally provided public goods for small towns of similar individuals, but it may be optimal to provide public goods that have external effects or spillovers to other towns at a higher level of government that can internalize the externalities.

Evidence on the Tiebout Model

The Tiebout model clearly imposes a very restrictive set of assumptions if taken literally, yet the basic intuition that individuals vote with their feet is still a strong one. Indeed, two types of tests reveal that the provision of local public goods is generally consistent with the Tiebout description.

Resident Similarity Across Areas A clear prediction of the Tiebout model is that people living in a given local community (such as a town) should have similar preferences for local public goods. The more local communities there are from which to choose, by the logic of this model, the more residents can sort themselves into similar groupings. If a city has only one suburb within commuting distance, it will be hard for residents working in the city to vote with their feet if they don't like the level of public goods provision in that one suburb. Thus, a testable implication of the Tiebout model is that when people have more choice of local community, the tastes for public goods will be more similar among town residents than when people do not have many choices (and so can't sort themselves into like-minded Tiebout communities).

Supportive evidence on this point comes from Gramlich and Rubinfeld (1982), who surveyed Michigan households on their demand for public goods. They found that in larger metropolitan areas (that is, in suburbs near cities), where people have greater choice of which community they can live in, preferences for public goods were more similar within towns than in smaller areas with fewer independent towns to choose from. Moreover, in urban/suburban areas, residents were much more satisfied with the level of public goods spending than in nonurban areas where there are fewer ways to vote with one's feet because there are fewer towns to move to. Bergstrom et al. (1988) used the data from Michigan suburbs to estimate individual demands for public goods and showed that the provision of local public goods appeared to satisfy the efficiency condition that the marginal cost equals the sum of marginal rates of substitution of residents.

Capitalization of Fiscal Differences into House Prices For many individuals, the decision about where to live is not primarily determined by the level of local public goods. Indeed, many residents don't even demonstrate the basic knowledge of local taxes and spending that is required for the Tiebout mechanism to operate.[14] At the same time, the Tiebout mechanism requires not that *all* residents are willing to vote with their feet but that *enough* residents are willing to vote with their feet to enforce the optimal provision of public goods. A town does not have to completely empty out before local officials get the message that the residents are unhappy with public goods provision; all that is required is that there be sufficient mobility among an informed minority in response to public goods decisions.

In fact, very little actual mobility is required for the Tiebout mechanism to operate because people not only vote with their feet, they also vote with their pocketbook, in the form of *house prices*. The Tiebout model predicts that any differences in the fiscal attractiveness of a town will be **capitalized into house prices.** The price of any house reflects the cost (including local property taxes) and benefits (including local public goods) of living in that house. Thus, towns that have a relatively high level of public goods, given taxes paid, will have more expensive housing; conversely, towns that have relatively high property taxes, given the public goods provided, will have less expensive housing. House pricing

house price capitalization Incorporation into the price of a house the costs (including local property taxes) and benefits (including local public goods) of living in the house.

---

[14] See Dowding et al. (1994) for a review of the evidence on Tiebout and Teske et al. (1993), and Dowding et al. (1995) for evidence on knowledge of public services and taxes among movers.

EVIDENCE FOR CAPITALIZATION FROM CALIFORNIA'S PROPOSITION 13

There is a large literature in state and local public finance that tests for capitalization effects. Typically, this literature proceeds by regressing house prices on school quality or on local property tax rates and assessing whether higher-quality schools lead to higher house prices and higher taxes lead to lower house prices. These simple comparisons are potentially biased, however. For example, towns with better public schools may attract higher-income families, so finding that house prices are higher where schools are better does not prove that higher-quality schools are causing higher house prices. This correlation could just reflect that higher-income groups pay more for houses.

More convincing evidence for capitalization effects comes from Rosen's (1982) study of the effects of California's Proposition 13, a voter initiative that became law in 1978 and has proved to be one of the defining events of state and local public finance of the past half century. Proposition 13 was the first of a series of state laws that limit the ability of localities in a state to levy property taxes. Since its passage, nearly 40 statewide tax-limiting measures have been passed by voters in 18 states through the initiative process.

Proposition 13 mandated that the maximum amount of any tax on property could not exceed 1% of the "full cash value" of the property. The full cash value was defined as the value as of 1976, with annual increases of 2% at most, unless the property was sold, in which case its full cash value would just be its sale value.[15] Proposition 13 therefore restricted local property tax collections in two ways. First, it limited the rate that could be charged: the rate could not exceed 1% of a home's assessed value. Second, despite the high inflation of the late 1970s, it limited the rate at which the tax base (the house's value) could be increased to 2% per year. This was a strict limitation: the typical Los Angeles home saw its property tax increase 80% between 1973 and 1977.[16]

Rosen (1982) studied over 60 municipalities in the San Francisco metropolitan area, examining tax rates and housing prices six months before and six months after the vote on Proposition 13. He compared towns with high property tax rates before 1978 (the treatment group), which were mandated by Proposition 13 to have large reductions in their property tax rates, to towns with lower property tax rates before 1978 (the control group), which did not see much change in their property tax rates. As long as there was nothing else changing differently between treatment and control towns at this time, the passage of Proposition 13 provides a quasi-experiment for assessing the impact of property taxes on house values.

therefore represents voting with your pocketbook: people will pay more for a house in a town that more efficiently delivers local public goods.

There is strong evidence for voting with the pocketbook, as reviewed in the Empirical Evidence box. Thus, even if some residents do not choose their location based on Tiebout factors, enough residents do make choices that way that it drives the pricing of housing across local communities.

Optimal Fiscal Federalism

Although the Tiebout model is an imperfect description of reality, changes in local taxation and spending do affect mobility and house prices. Given these *positive* findings (that is, they support the predictions of the model about behavior), what are the *normative* implications of the Tiebout model for the optimal design of fiscal federalism? That is, what does the Tiebout model

---

[15] Property taxes are levied on the assessed value of a house, which can differ substantially from the house's market value, as discussed in more detail in Chapter 23.

[16] Sears and Citrin (1982), pp. 21–22.

[17] *Washington Post* (1983).

Rosen found a strong association between reductions in property taxes and increases in house values: each $1 of property tax reduction increased house values by about $7. Given that buying a house means committing to a stream of future property tax payments, full capitalization of lower property taxes into house prices would imply that house prices should rise by the present discounted value of reduced future tax payments (the price should rise today to reflect the entire future benefit from lower property taxes). Mathematically, full capitalization would require that house prices rise by $1/r$ for each dollar reduction in property taxes, where r is the interest rate (recall from Chapter 4 that the present discounted value of a long future stream of payments is $1/r$ times the payment). Interest rates at the time of Proposition 13 were about 12%, so a $7 rise in house prices for each $1 reduction in property taxes suggests close to full capitalization (with full capitalization, house prices would have risen by $1/0.12 = 8.33 for each dollar reduction in property taxes).

This result implies very large capitalization of this policy change because, in principle, the fall in property taxes would result in a future reduction in public goods and services, which would lower home values. If, for example, each $1 of taxes was going to finance public goods and services worth $1 to residents, then house prices should not have

changed, since the gain of lower property taxes would be offset by falling local goods and services. The fact that house prices rose by almost the present discounted value of the taxes suggests that Californians did not think that they would lose many valuable public goods and services when taxes fell.

Rosen conjectures that Californians were not worried about falling public goods and services because the state used supplementary funds to offset the losses to local communities. Residents apparently perceived that these state offsets would continue or, alternatively, that the cut in taxes was simply reducing "wasteful" local spending. That optimism appears to have been unfounded, however. San Jose, a fairly prosperous area with good public services, found itself having to cut services dramatically in the wake of Proposition 13. The school district laid off art and music teachers in the elementary schools, cut bus transportation, fired school nurses and guidance counselors, and shortened the school day from six to five periods—all to no avail. In 1983, the district became the first American public school system in 40 years to declare bankruptcy. The rest of the town suffered too, as library hours shortened, parks became overgrown, and mental health nurses were fired. A poll of San Jose residents showed that a majority believed that Proposition 13 had worked out "unfavorably" for most people.[17]

imply *should be* the principles that guide the provision of public goods at different levels of government?

The Tiebout model implies that the extent to which public goods should be provided at the local level is determined by three factors. The first is **tax-benefit linkages,** the extent to which residents view their tax payments as directly tied to goods and services that they receive. Goods with strong tax-benefit linkages, such as local roads, should be provided locally. There is a direct tax-benefit linkage to spending on local roads: higher property taxes fund better-quality roads that benefit most residents of a town. Goods with weaker tax-benefit linkages, such as welfare payments to the lowest income residents of a town, should be provided at the state or federal level. There is a very limited tax-benefit linkage to spending on welfare: the majority of residents in a town do not benefit from redistribution to low-income groups (unless they have altruistic preferences toward the local poor).

If residents can see directly the benefits they are buying with their property tax dollars, they will be willing to pay local taxes. If they cannot see a benefit from their property tax payments, they will vote with their feet by moving

tax-benefit linkages The relationship between the taxes people pay and the government goods and services they get in return.

to a town that has lower property taxes. If a town instituted a cash welfare program, higher-income residents would have an incentive to leave and move to a town that did not have such a program and had lower local property taxes as a result. The ability of individuals to vote with their feet is a fundamental limitation on a town's ability to pursue programs that benefit only a minority of residents.

The second factor that determines the optimal level of decentralization is the extent of positive externalities, or spillovers, in public goods provision. If local public goods have large spillover effects on other communities, the goods will be underprovided by any locality. In this case, higher levels of government have a role in promoting the provision of these public goods, for example, through grants.

The third factor that determines the optimal level of decentralization is the economy of scale in the nature of public goods. Public goods that have large economies of scale, such as national defense, are not efficiently provided by many competing local jurisdictions; public goods without large economies of scale, such as police protection, may be provided more effectively in Tiebout competition.

As a result of these factors, the Tiebout model predicts that local spending should focus on broad-based programs with few externalities and relatively low economies of scale, such as road repair, garbage collection, and street cleaning. Similarly, local communities should play a more limited role in providing public goods that are redistributive (such as cash welfare), have large spillovers (such as education), and have very large economies of scale (such as national defense). The nature of fiscal federalism in the United States is largely consistent with this prediction. Public works are financed primarily at the local level, redistributive programs are financed at the state and federal levels, and defense is a national program. Education is roughly one-half financed by localities and one-half financed by higher levels of government (mostly state government), which is consistent with the spillovers associated with education. The only question here is whether the externalities from education are sufficiently large on a nationwide basis that the federal government, which currently provides less than 10% of educational spending, should play a larger role in financing education, as is true in most other industrialized nations. The remainder of this chapter discusses the financing of education in more detail.

10.3
Redistribution Across Communities

The Tiebout model provides a framework for considering one of the most important problems in fiscal federalism: Should there be redistribution of public funds across communities? There is currently enormous inequality in both the ability of local communities to finance public goods (the value of the property tax base) and the extent to which they do so. For example, in the state of Massachusetts, the city of Fall River raises only $1,699 in local tax revenue per public school student, while the town of Weston raises $12,603, over seven times more.[18] Some of this difference comes from decisions about the level of local taxation: the tax per $1,000 of property value is $8.21 in Fall River and $9.67 in Weston. Most of this difference, however, comes from underlying differences in the values of taxed property: the median single-family home is worth $180,539 in Fall River and $1,162,135 in Weston.[19] In the state of Illinois, one study found that the property values per public school student varied by a factor of more than 10, with the poorest 5% of communities having property values per student of less than $45,000 and the richest 5% of communities having property values per student of more than $467,000.[20]

Should We Care?

Should this inequality in revenue bases (as reflected in property values) or revenues raised (the product of property values and property tax rates) across communities concern public policy makers? Should higher levels of government mandate redistribution across lower levels of government to offset these differences? As noted earlier, such redistribution is an important feature of fiscal federalism in some nations, where the national government distributes grants to poorer communities that largely offset differences in revenues across communities.

The broad answer to the "Should we care?" question is that it *depends on the extent to which the Tiebout model describes reality*. In a perfect Tiebout world, we would *not* redistribute across communities: communities would have formed for the efficient provision of public goods, and any redistribution across them would impede efficiency. If a town has low revenues or low spending, it is because the residents of the town have chosen to provide a low level of public goods, and this is the efficient outcome given their tastes. Government redistribution in this case should focus on individuals, not on communities.

To the extent that Tiebout does not perfectly describe reality, however, there are two arguments for redistributing from high-revenue, high-spending communities to low-revenue, low-spending communities. The first is *failures of the Tiebout mechanism*. For example, suppose that there are reasons why people cannot effectively vote with their feet, such as restrictive zoning rules that cause houses to be very large and expensive in communities with high public goods (e.g., each house must be on at least a one-acre lot). In this situation, there may be people who desire high levels of public goods but who cannot afford the high quality of house mandated by the zoning rules. These people could remain stuck in a town with low public goods provision, the only place they can afford a house. In this case, it could be efficient to redistribute to the low public goods towns to help the individuals stuck in a situation where they are forced to underconsume public goods.

The second reason for redistribution is *externalities*. If a large share of local tax revenue is spent on local public goods with spillovers or externalities for

---

[18] Data from the "Public School District Finance Peer Search" provided by the Department of Education's Education Finance Statistics Center, at http://nces.ed.gov/edfin/links/findata.asp.
[19] Data from http://www.boston.com/realestate/community/.
[20] Steiner and Schiller (2003), p. 34.

other communities, there is a standard externality argument for higher levels of government to subsidize spending in the communities providing the externalities. For example, suppose that high-quality elementary education in a town leads to lower crime rates in both that town and neighboring towns. In this case, it may be optimal for the state government to tax high-revenue towns and redistribute to low-revenue towns to ensure that low-revenue towns can provide a high-quality elementary education.

Tools of Redistribution: Grants

If higher levels of government decide for one of the two reasons stated to redistribute across lower levels of government, they do so through *intergovernmental grants,* which are cash transfers from one level of government to another. Grants are a large and growing share of federal spending. From 1960 to 2005, grants to lower levels of government grew from 7.6% to 17.2% of federal spending.[21] State governments, however, have always sent a large portion of the budget to local governments. From 1960 to 2002, state grants to local governments actually dropped slightly, from 34.1% to 28.1% of state spending, the bulk of which funded local education.[22] Higher levels of government use several different types of grants. In defining these types, we will use the example of a state redistributing to local communities (although the same description applies to other forms of higher-to-lower level of government redistribution, such as national to state).

Suppose that the town of Lexington provides only one public good to its residents—education. It finances education through property taxes, and any money families have after taxation is spent on private goods (such as cars or clothing). Figure 10-2 shows the situation in Lexington before any grant is provided. Residents of Lexington have a total budget of $1 million to spend on education and other private goods, and we model how they choose to divide this budget. At point *A,* Lexington residents choose to spend nothing on education and spend their entire $1 million budget on private goods. At point *B,* Lexington spends its entire budget of $1 million on education and nothing on private goods.

The voters of Lexington have some preferences for education and private goods that can be represented as an indifference curve IC_1 between these two sets of goods. That is, we can analyze Lexington's choice between education and private goods in the same way that we might analyze an individual's choice between these same items; IC_1 represents the aggregation of the indifference curves of the voters through a voting mechanism. Before there are any state grants in place, Lexington chooses to spend $500,000 per year on education and $500,000 per year on private goods. This spending combination is represented by point *X,* where the town's indifference curve is tangent to its budget constraint.

[21] Office of Management and Budget (2006a), Table 12.1.
[22] U.S. Bureau of the Census (1962), Table 547; U.S. Bureau of the Census (2006a), Table 427.

■ FIGURE **10-2**

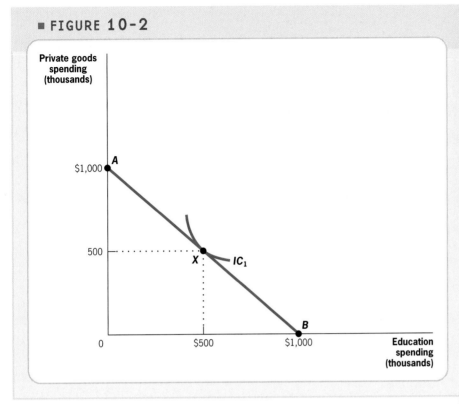

A Town's Choice Between Education and Private Goods • With $1 million to spend on some combination of education and private goods, Lexington chooses point X on its budget constraint AB, spending $500,000 on each, at the point where its indifference curve, IC_1, is tangent to its budget constraint.

Matching Grants One type of grant the state government might use is a **matching grant,** which ties the amount of funds transferred to the local community to the amount of spending it currently allocates to public goods. For example, a one-for-one matching grant for education would provide $1 of funding from the state for each $1 of education spending by the local community. While we use a one-for-one match as the example here, match rates can vary from 0.01 to more than 1.

This one-for-one matching grant reduces the price of education by half; each dollar of education spending now costs Lexington only $0.50 because the state of Massachusetts provides the other $0.50. This change pivots the budget constraint outward from AB to AC in Figure 10-3. This grant unambiguously increases spending on education through both the income and substitution effects. In our example, total education spending increases from $500,000 to $750,000 at point Y. Lexington contributes $375,000 toward education and receives the other $375,000 in matching grants. Of its original $1 million budget, Lexington now has $625,000 to spend on private goods (the original $500,000 it was spending plus the $125,000 it no longer spends on education). As a result of the matching grant, then, total spending on both education and private goods has increased.

matching grant A grant, the amount of which is tied to the amount of spending by the local community.

■ FIGURE 10-3

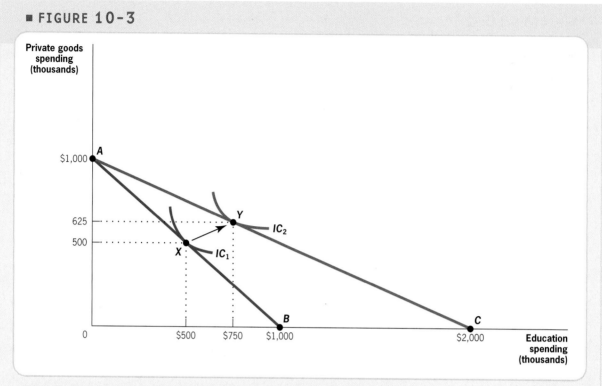

The Impact of a Matching Grant on the Town's Budget Constraint • When Lexington is offered a matching grant for educational spending, with $1 of grant for each $1 of local spending, the budget constraint pivots outward from *AB* to *AC*. Lexington chooses point *Y* on *AC*, as it spends $250,000 more on education (with education spending rising from $500,000 to $750,000) and $125,000 more on private goods.

block grant A grant of some fixed amount with no mandate on how it is to be spent.

Block Grant Another grant option is a **block grant,** whereby the state simply gives the local community some grant amount *G* with no mandate on how it is to be spent. To keep the cost to the state government constant, suppose that the state government gives Lexington a $375,000 block grant. Because the block grant makes Lexington wealthy enough to afford to spend up to $1.375 million on either education or private goods, it shifts the budget constraint out from *AB* to *DE*, as Figure 10-4 illustrates.

While Massachusetts is giving Lexington the same amount of money with the block grant, it has a very different effect on the town's behavior. Some of this newfound wealth will be used to increase education spending, while some will be used to increase consumption of private goods. In this example, the town moves to point *Z*, raising education spending by only $75,000 and private goods spending by $300,000 (from $500,000 to $800,000).

The increase in education spending is lower with the block grant ($75,000) than it was with the matching grant ($250,000) because there is now only an income effect on education spending for Lexington, whereas the matching grant had both a substitution and an income effect. The income effect raises

■ FIGURE 10-4

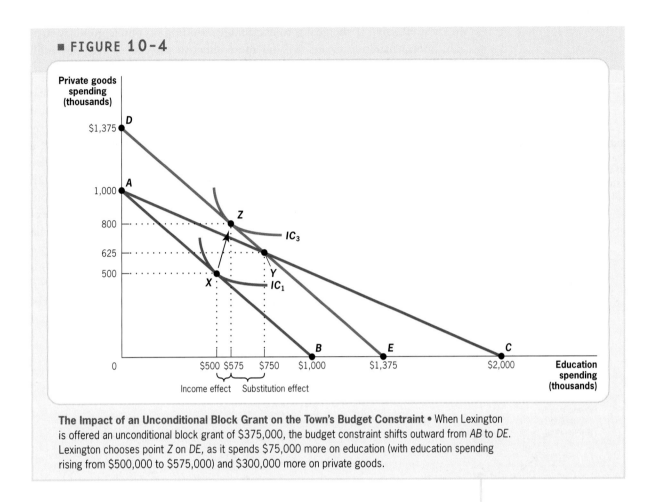

The Impact of an Unconditional Block Grant on the Town's Budget Constraint ● When Lexington is offered an unconditional block grant of $375,000, the budget constraint shifts outward from *AB* to *DE*. Lexington chooses point *Z* on *DE*, as it spends $75,000 more on education (with education spending rising from $500,000 to $575,000) and $300,000 more on private goods.

spending on education from $500,000 to $575,000, moving the town from point *X* to point *Z*. The substitution effect that is added with the matching grant then raises education spending by an additional $175,000 to $750,000, as reflected by the move from point *Z* to point *Y*.

On the other hand, Lexington has been made better off with the block grant than with the matching grant. This can be seen graphically by the fact that, with the new budget constraint under the block grant (*DE*), the town *could have* afforded its choice at point *Y*, with education spending rising to $750,000 and private goods spending rising to $625,000, but it chose a different combination. Since the town chose point *Z* instead, it must be on a higher indifference curve. That is, given the freedom to spend its grant money as it likes, without the restriction of a matching condition, the town would rather spend most of the money on private goods and relatively little on education. The matching grant leads to more spending on education than the town would otherwise choose given that amount of money, so it leaves the town on a lower indifference curve.

Thus, the optimal choice of grant mechanisms for higher levels of government (such as states) depends on the goal of the grant program. If the goal is to maximize the welfare of the lower level of government, block grants will be most effective. If the goal is to encourage spending on public goods such as education, matching grants will be most effective since they will put both income and substitution effects to work to increase town spending.

Conditional Block Grant Suppose that Massachusetts likes the fact that it has made Lexington better off with a block grant than with a matching grant, but it doesn't like the fact that education spending hasn't gone up as much. One way the state could try to remedy this is through a **conditional block grant,** a fixed amount of money distributed to the town with a mandate that the money be spent only on education. In this case, the state could provide Lexington with a $375,000 block grant and mandate that it spend the entire grant on education.

The effect of this conditional block grant is illustrated in Figure 10-5. Lexington can now spend up to $375,000 (the grant amount) on education while continuing to spend its original $1 million budget on private goods. Thus, the first segment on the budget constraint is now *AF.* Once Lexington spends beyond $375,000 on education, however, it faces the same trade-off between spending on education and spending on private goods that it did when it got the unconditional grant: the condition imposed on this grant doesn't matter if

conditional block grant A grant of some fixed amount with a mandate that the money be spent in a particular way.

■ **FIGURE 10-5**

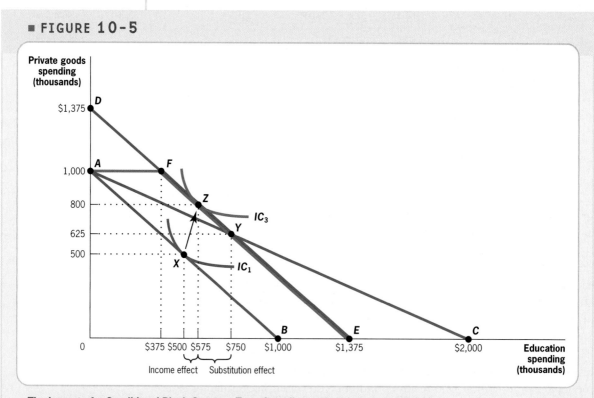

The Impact of a Conditional Block Grant on Town Spending • When the town is offered a conditional block grant for education spending, it can spend up to $375,000 on education while still spending $1 million on private goods. Beyond point *F*, the conditional block grant operates like the unconditional block grant, so the budget constraint is *AFE*. For towns that already have high educational spending, like Lexington, the conditional grant has the same effect as the unconditional grant, causing education spending to rise by $75,000.

the town is already spending more than $375,000 on education. The new budget constraint is therefore *AFE*. Beyond the $375,000 point on the horizontal axis, this new budget constraint is the same as the budget constraint from the unconditional block grant.

As is clear from Figure 10-5, adding this condition has *no effect* on Lexington's behavior: the town still chooses to spend the same $575,000 on education that it spent with the unconditional block grant (at point *Z*). Because Lexington was already spending more than $375,000 on education, this grant is effectively *not conditional* for the town—it has the same effect as if the state had simply given it $375,000 to spend on anything. The town has therefore undone the mandate to spend the money on education by reallocating existing spending to meet the mandate. This is an example of the type of *crowd-out* that we discussed in Chapter 7. The state government gave the town $375,000 to spend on education, but the town spent only $75,000 net of that money on education; it spent the remaining $300,000 on private goods. Thus, 80% ($300,000/$375,000) of the state spending was crowded out by the town's reaction. Despite a large state grant, local education spending rose by only a small amount.

The effect of a conditional block grant will differ from that of an unconditional block grant *only* if the town receiving the grant would have spent less than the grant amount without the condition being imposed. That is, adding the condition to the block grant would affect Lexington's behavior only if it would have chosen to spend less than $375,000 on education with the unconditional block grant. In that case, making the block grant conditional would increase Lexington's educational spending by more than just $75,000. If towns such as Lexington would spend more than $375,000 on education regardless of this restriction, then there is no effect of imposing the restriction.

Redistribution in Action: School Finance Equalization

Perhaps the most dramatic examples of attempts of higher levels of government to use grants to influence lower levels of government are **school finance equalization** laws that mandate redistribution across communities in a state to ensure more equal financing of schools. Local school districts in the United States receive about 45% of their funding from local sources, primarily from local property taxes. This dependence on property taxes can lead to vast disparities in the revenue base from which towns fund education because of the wide variation in property values across towns. As a result of the disparity in property values, levels of education funding can differ substantially across localities within a state. In Texas, for example, the Leonard district spends $7,067 per student, while the Bruceville-Eddy district spends $19,276, or 2.7 times as much.[23]

States can try to offset these inequities by using the types of grants just discussed. By collecting tax revenues from all communities, then redistributing the revenues in block or matching grants to particular communities with low property values or low education spending, the state can attempt to equalize

school finance equalization Laws that mandate redistribution of funds across communities in a state to ensure more equal financing of schools.

---

[23] Data from the "Public School District Finance Peer Search" provided by the Department of Education's Education Finance Statistics Center, at http://nces.ed.gov/edfin/links/findata.asp.

THE FLYPAPER EFFECT

Block grants are simply income increases to communities if the grants are unconditional, or if the grants are conditional but are below the town's desired level of spending on that public good. As a result, a community should react to a block grant in the same way Lexington did in the example, by substantially reducing its own contribution to the public good (a type of *crowding out*, as discussed in Chapter 7) so that spending on the public good goes up by only a fraction of the total grant amount.

This theory has been put to the test in the context of federal grants to states. Researchers have compared the spending of states that receive larger and smaller grants from the federal government to assess whether these federal grants largely crowd out the states' spending. In fact, this does not appear to be the case. Hines and Thaler (1995) reviewed the evidence on this issue and found that the crowd-out of state spending by federal spending is low and often close to zero (so that total spending rises by $1 for each $1 in federal grants). Referring to Figure 10-5, towns such as Lexington appear unlikely to end up at point *Z,* as the theory implies, and instead seem to spend roughly the same amount on private goods ($500,000 in that example) and to devote the entire block grant to education. Economist Arthur Okun described this as the *flypaper effect* because "the money sticks where it hits" instead of replacing state spending.

These studies suffer from potential bias, however. As Knight (2002) noted, states that value public goods the most may be the most successful at lobbying for federal grants. If this is true, then there would be a positive correlation between grants and spending—not because of a flypaper effect, but simply because states that get grants are the ones that like spending the most. Thus, states that don't get grants might not be a good control group for states that do since they might differ in their taste for public spending.

Knight proposed a quasi-experimental approach to solving this problem by noting that highway grants from the federal government to states are determined by the strength of the state's political representatives. Congresspeople and senators have more power to determine the nature of highway spending if they (a) are on the transportation committees of the House and Senate, (b) are in the majority party, and (c) have long tenures in Congress. In the type of vote-maximizing model discussed in Chapter 9, congresspeople will use this power to bring grants to their states.

Knight compared the level of spending in treatment states that see increases in the power of their congressional delegations (e.g., because a senator from that state gets appointed to the Senate transportation committee or because the control of Congress changes to the party of the state's senator) with the level of spending in control states that see decreases in the power of their congressional delegations (e.g., because a congressperson with long tenure is not reelected). Knight found, as expected, that federal grants rise for states that see increases in the power of their congressional delegations. He also found, as the standard model (but not the flypaper effect) would predict, that this grant money largely crowds out the state's own spending: each additional $1 of federal grant money increase due to rising congressional power leads to a $0.90 reduction in the state's own spending (so that total combined state and federal spending rose by only $0.10 per dollar of federal grant).

Knight's study therefore throws some doubt on the previous literature on the flypaper effect. Additional studies by Duggan (2000), Gordon (2004), and Lutz (2004) also find evidence inconsistent with the flypaper effect, suggesting that the traditional conclusion of substantial crowd-out from block grants is supported by the evidence.

education spending across districts. Since 1970, every state has made at least one attempt at school finance equalization, some prompted by state courts, others by the voting public.

The Structure of Equalization Schemes School finance equalization schemes can take very different forms. Some states have systems that attempt to completely or nearly completely equalize spending across school districts. California, for example, provides a base level of education financing for its school districts and prohibits differences between school districts of more than $300 in per-pupil spending. Once a district is spending $300 more than the lowest-spending district, all additional property taxes raised by the town are given to the state for distribution to other districts. Thus, under this scheme a town receives no benefit from raising its own local property taxes because the extra revenue is divided among districts across the state.[24]

Less extreme are states that have instituted a statewide property tax that is redistributed in a way that guarantees a certain "foundation level" of per-pupil funding for each town. For example, in the state of New Jersey, towns with property values above the 85th percentile of the property values in the state simply receive a small foundational grant from the state and have to raise other educational revenues locally. Towns with property values below the 85th percentile of the property values in the state receive a matching grant that is a multiple of their own educational spending, which thus gives towns an incentive to raise their spending.[25]

The Effects of Equalization A number of economics studies have evaluated the effects of school finance equalization. These studies generally agree that equalization laws have had the intended effect of equalizing school spending across communities, and spending equalization appears to have led to an equalization in student outcomes as well. Murray, Evans, and Schwab (1998), for example, concluded that court-ordered equalizations reduced in-state spending inequality by 19 to 34%. Card and Payne (2002) found that equalizations narrowed the gap in average SAT scores between children with highly educated and children with poorly educated parents by 8 points, or roughly 5% of the gap.

There is less agreement about whether this equalization has come about by raising spending among low-spending districts, lowering spending among high-spending districts, or both. A careful study of this question is provided by Hoxby (2001), who computed the **tax price** of school equalization schemes, the amount of revenue a local district would have to raise in order to gain $1 more of spending. California districts face an infinite tax price: no matter how much revenue they raise through local taxation, they can't raise their local education spending to more than $300 per pupil above the lowest district. New Jersey's districts mostly have tax prices of less than 1: a district might raise $0.60 of its own revenue in order to receive $0.40 in state aid for a total of $1 in increased spending. This district would thus have a tax price of 0.6.

Hoxby found that extreme equalization schemes with very high tax prices, such as California's, lead to an overall reduction in per-pupil spending. Since any taxes that towns raise beyond the minimum level (plus $300) are simply taken by the state and redistributed to other districts, there is an incentive to cut taxes and reduce spending. California's equalization caused a drop in per-pupil spending of 15%; New Mexico's spending dropped by 13%; and Oklahoma's, Utah's, and Arizona's spending dropped by 10%. States like California equalized per-pupil spending but only by "leveling down"—that is, lowering the overall education

tax price For school equalization schemes, the amount of revenue a local district would have to raise in order to gain $1 more of spending.

---

[24] Data from "A Guide to California's School Finance System," provided by EdSource Online at http://www.edsource.org.
[25] Data available from Education Law Center at http://www.edlawcenter.org/index.htm.

spending across all districts. The result has been a general deterioration in the quality of public schools and a flight to private schools by students who can afford it. Equalization schemes with low tax prices, such as those in New Jersey, New York, and Pennsylvania, actually raised per-pupil spending by 7–8%; these states thus managed to "level up." Thus, school finance equalization can achieve its intended effects of improving the educational spending of low-wealth districts only if the system is designed in a way that gives those districts incentive to raise their spending without excessively penalizing higher-wealth districts.

▶ **APPLICATION**

School Finance Equalization and Property Tax Limitations in California

William Fischel (1989) asked a very interesting question about the property tax limitations under Proposition 13 in California: If residents perceived that property taxes were "too high" in California, why did they wait until 1978 to lower them? Indeed, earlier referenda in 1968 and 1972 proposing property tax limitations had failed. What had changed by 1978?

Fischel's answer is that Proposition 13 was actually a response to the court case (*Serrano v. Priest*) that led to school finance equalization in California in 1976. The key feature of this decision was that it broke the link between local property taxes and spending on schools by imposing the infinite tax price discussed earlier. As a result, Fischel notes, this ruling also *broke the Tiebout mechanism*. Under the Tiebout model, property taxes are essentially prices paid for local services. In this model, individuals shop across communities (much as they shop across goods) to find the package of prices and spending that best matches their tastes. They know that if they choose a community with high taxes, they will be getting a high level of spending as well. Thus, there is a full tax-benefit linkage: their higher taxes buy them better public services (primarily schooling).

The California equalization decision severed the link between taxes paid and benefits received. Taxes were no longer a price: they were just taxes. As a result, it was natural for communities to vote to lower taxes, since they did not perceive any benefit from them anymore. Fischel claimed that wealthy voters would have opposed Proposition 13 in the absence of the school finance equalization because their high taxes were paying for schooling they desired for their town without subsidizing anyone else's schooling. School finance equalization changed this so that wealthy property-tax payers now saw that their taxes were paying for benefits accruing to other, poorer citizens in other towns. Thus, these wealthy taxpayers were happy to approve Proposition 13. ◀

10.4

Conclusion

In every country, the central government collects only part of the total national tax revenues and does only part of the national public spending.

The remainder of taxation and spending is done by subnational governments, such as state and local governments in the United States. Relative to other developed countries, the United States places a large share of governmental responsibilities on its subnational governments. This chapter presented a theory to explain why spending might be divided between national and subnational governments. When spending is on goods for which local preferences are relatively similar, and where most residents can benefit from those goods, the Tiebout model suggests that the spending should be done locally. When spending is for goods that benefit only a minority of the population, such as income redistribution, the Tiebout model suggests that it might be difficult to do this spending locally because the majority of people who do not benefit will "vote with their feet" and move elsewhere. These outcomes are consistent with the division of responsibility for spending on education and public safety (local) and redistribution (national). In addition, if spending has external effects on other communities, local provision may be inefficient as well, which is consistent with the financing of education in the United States shared between local and state governments, although it raises the question of whether the federal government should play a larger role.

Higher levels of government may not believe the conclusions of the idealized Tiebout model, in which case they will want to redistribute across lower levels of government. If the higher-level government decides that it wants to redistribute across lower levels, it can do so through several different types of grants. The appropriate choice depends on the goal (redistributing to offset Tiebout failures or redistributing to offset externalities).

▶ HIGHLIGHTS

- A large share of public spending and revenue raising is done at the subnational level in the United States, relative to other industrialized countries.

- The Tiebout model suggests that the provision of local public goods can be efficient if individuals "vote with their feet" by moving to towns with others who share their tastes for public goods.

- While the strict version of the Tiebout model is unlikely to hold, there is strong evidence that local spending and taxation respond to local preferences as reflected in mobility (voting with one's feet) and that the value of local public goods and local tax differences are capitalized into house prices.

- The Tiebout model suggests that spending with strong tax-benefit linkages (such as public safety) should occur at the local level and that spending with weaker tax-benefit linkages (such as redistribu-

tion under cash welfare) should occur at higher levels of government.

- When higher levels of government want to redistribute to lower levels of government, they use grants. Matching grants (under which the grant amount matches the amount to be spent by the lower level of government) are the best way to encourage a certain behavior by subnational governments, but unconditional block grants (under which the grant is a fixed dollar amount) maximize the welfare gains to communities from redistribution.

- A classic example of redistribution across governments is school finance equalization efforts, which have reduced inequality in local school spending but at the cost in some cases of a reduction in overall educational spending.

▶ QUESTIONS AND PROBLEMS

1. The (identical) citizens of Boomtown have $2 million to spend on either park maintenance or private goods. Each unit of park maintenance costs $10,000.

    a. Graph Boomtown's budget constraint.

    b. Suppose that Boomtown chooses to purchase 100 units of park maintenance. Draw the town's indifference curve for this choice.

    c. Now suppose that the state government decides to subsidize Boomtown's purchase of park maintenance by providing the town with one unit of maintenance for every two units the town purchases. Draw the new budget constraint. Will Boomtown purchase more or fewer units of park maintenance? Will Boomtown purchase more or fewer units of the private good? Illustrate your answer, and explain.

2. Why does the Tiebout model solve the problems with preference revelation that are present with Lindahl pricing?

3. Some have argued that diversity in communities and schools leads to positive externalities. What implications does this view have for the efficiency of a Tiebout equilibrium? What implications does it have for government policy?

4. Brunner, Sonstelie, and Thayer (2001) studied how home ownership and community income influenced votes on a proposed initiative in California to allow children to obtain their locally funded education at any public or private school rather than being districted to their local school. Think about how public services such as education are capitalized into house prices. Why would renters in high-income communities be more likely than owners to support this school choice plan? Why would the reverse be true in low-income communities?

5. Think about two public goods—public schools and food assistance for needy families. Consider the implications of the Tiebout model. Which of the goods is more efficiently provided locally? Which is more efficiently provided centrally? Explain.

6. Describe the externalities argument for distributing money from one community to another. Provide an example of this kind of redistribution based on externalities.

7. The state of Minnegan is considering two alternative methods of funding local road construction, matching grants and block grants. In the case of the matching grant, Minnegan will spend $1 for every $1 spent by localities.

    a. What is the price of an additional dollar of local spending in each case?

    b. Which of the two methods do you think would lead to higher levels of local spending on roads? Explain your answer.

8. The state of Massachusetts recently ran an advertising campaign for the state lottery which claimed "Even when you lose, you win." The gist of the advertisement was that lottery revenue was used for particularly good ends like education. Suppose that lottery revenues are indeed earmarked for education. How would traditional economic theory evaluate the claim behind their ad campaign? How would an economist who believed in the flypaper effect evaluate it?

9. Why does California's school finance equalization policy have a high associated marginal tax price? Explain.

▶ ADVANCED QUESTIONS

10. Rhode and Strumpf (2003) evaluated a century of historical evidence to investigate the impact of changes in moving costs within the Tiebout model.

  a. What does the Tiebout model predict should happen to the similarity of residents within a community as the costs of moving fall?

  b. Rhode and Strumpf found that while mobility costs have steadily fallen, the differences in public good provision across communities have fallen as well. Does Tiebout sorting explain this homogenization of public good provision, or must other factors have played a larger role? Explain.

11. The state of Delaland has two types of town. Type A towns are well-to-do, and type B towns are much poorer. Being wealthier, type A towns have more resources to spend on education; their demand curve for education is $Q = 100 - 2P$, where P is the price of a unit of education. Type B towns have demand curves for education which are given by $Q = 100 - 5P$.

  a. If the cost of a unit of education is $15 per unit, how many units of education will the two types of town demand?

  b. In light of the large discrepancies in educational quality across their two types of town, Delaland decides to redistribute from type A towns to type B towns. In particular, they tax type A towns by $5 for each unit of education they provide, and they give type B towns $5 for each unit of education they provide. What are the new tax prices of education in the two towns? How many units of education do the towns now purchase?

  c. Delaland wants to completely equalize the units of education across towns by taxing type A towns for each unit of education they provide and subsidizing type B towns for each unit of education they provide. It wants to do this in such a way that the taxes on type A towns are just enough to finance the subsidies on type B towns. If there are 4 type A towns for every 5 type B towns, how big a tax should Delaland levy on type A towns? How big a subsidy should they provide to type B towns?

12. The Individuals with Disabilities Education Act mandates that states and localities provide appropriate education for all students identified as having special needs. States have responded by funding special education using several different mechanisms. Two of these mechanisms are "census" approaches (in which states estimate how many children should have special needs based on student characteristics and allocate money to localities based on these predictions) and "marginal subsidy" approaches (in which states pay localities a percentage of the amount of money that the localities say they spend on special education).

  a. It has been found that the marginal subsidy approach leads to more students being classified by their localities as needing special education than does the census approach. Why might this be the case?

  b. Suppose that you analyze cross-sectional data on the level of subsidy and the number of students enrolled in special education. You find that, in cross section, states that reimburse localities the most for their special education students tend to have the highest rates of students enrolled in special education. Think of one possible problem with this analysis.

13. As described in the text, Fischel (1989) argued that California's *Serrano v. Priest* school finance equalization induced voters to limit property taxes in California. Following this argument, would an alternative school finance equalization that produced increased spending for low-wealth communities using *state* funds be more, less, or equally likely to induce a property tax limitation in California? Explain.

14. There are two types of residents in Brookline and Boston, professors and students. Professors have an income of $Y = 200$; students have an income of $Y = 100$. Both Brookline and Boston provide road repair services for their citizens. Professors value road repair more than students because they have nicer cars. In fact, the value of road repair to an individual takes the form $((Y \times R)/10) - (R^2/2)$. The *per-resident* cost of road repair is $5R$.

The ⓔ icon indicates a question that requires students to apply the empirical economics principles discussed in Chapter 3 and the Empirical Evidence boxes.

a. What is the marginal value of road repair for each type of individual? What is the marginal cost to each type of individual?

b. How much do professors want to spend on road repair? How much do students want to spend?

c. Assume that residents are distributed as follows:

	Brookline	Boston
Professors	50	25
Students	25	50

If each town uses majority voting to determine how much road repair to provide, how much will each town provide? Are any residents unsatisfied with the amount of road repair?

d. Now assume that professors and students are able to migrate between Brookline and Boston. Which residents will choose to move? What will the equilibrium distribution of residents be? Are any residents unsatisfied with the amount of road repair now? Is the provision of road repair efficient? Why or why not?

e. Consider again the premigration equilibrium. The state of Massachusetts decides to pass a law about road repair. It requires that professors in the state must contribute 75 units toward road repair in the town where they live; students must contribute 25 units toward road repair in the town where they live. How much road repair will there be in each town under the new regime? Will any residents want to move and, if so, where and why?

Education

I n the United States, the single largest expenditure item for state and local governments is education: state and local governments spend 30% of their budgets to provide their citizens with this government service. In fact, the United States spends more money per pupil on education than nearly every other nation on earth. Yet U.S. students perform only around the international average on tests of reading, math, and science ability. Even worse, U.S. eighth-graders are less proficient in math than students in much less wealthy countries, like Bulgaria, Latvia, Malaysia, and Slovenia, which have a combined GDP that is 3% of that of the United States. Figure 11-1 compares the United States with other nations in terms of money spent per pupil and the resulting educational outcomes in mathematics for eighth-graders.

While there is widespread agreement on the problematic state of education in the United States today, there is much less agreement about the causes of or solutions to the nation's educational shortcomings. In his 2000 campaign for the presidency, George W. Bush claimed that overly bureaucratic systems were to blame for educational troubles, and he worried that government involvement in education often gives power not to "the parents, or even the teachers, but some distant central office."[1] In his view, schools are not subject to enough fiscal discipline. The centerpiece of his education proposal was to hold schools accountable for learning outcomes through standardized testing and to link the outcomes to federal aid, thus giving schools financial incentive to perform.

Al Gore, in the same campaign, responded, "We need to invest more and demand more. . . . Accountability without investment is doomed to fail." Emphasizing that the central problem in American education was a lack of funding, Gore proposed spending $115 billion over the next decade to hire more teachers, provide universal preschool, and build new schools.[2]

---

[1] Bruni (2000).
[2] Gore (2000).

■ FIGURE 11-1

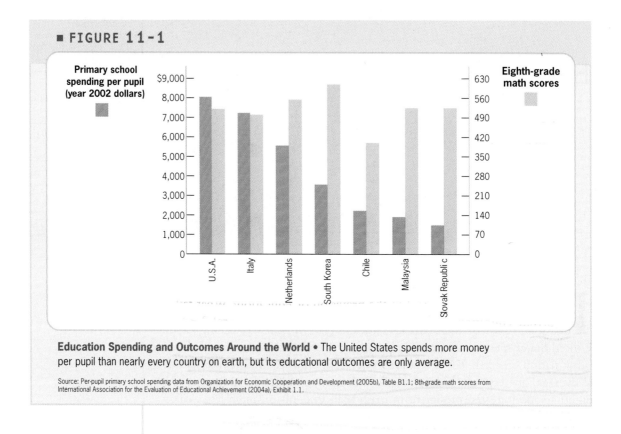

Education Spending and Outcomes Around the World • The United States spends more money per pupil than nearly every country on earth, but its educational outcomes are only average.

Source: Per-pupil primary school spending data from Organization for Economic Cooperation and Development (2005b), Table B1.1; 8th-grade math scores from International Association for the Evaluation of Educational Achievement (2004a), Exhibit 1.1.

One of President George W. Bush's first legislative accomplishments was the No Child Left Behind Act discussed in Chapter 10, which required states to test students in grades 3 through 8 and to use the exam results to judge school performance. Schools that do not make adequate progress are at risk of losing their students to other area schools or being shut down altogether by the state. Was this the right approach? Should we go further, as some propose, in moving to a more competitive and accountable education system? Or would educational improvement be larger if we simply invested more in our existing educational system?

In this chapter, we review the public finance issues involved in providing education. We begin with the first question of public finance: Why should the government be involved in education at all? We discuss a number of rationales for public involvement and their implications for the second question of public finance: How should the government be involved? We address this question in two steps. First, we consider the structure of government involvement, showing that public provision of a fixed level of education can crowd out private education. This result implies that efficiency may be increased with vouchers that can be used at either public or private schools. We extensively review the debate over school choice and school vouchers, discuss the theoretical arguments for and against vouchers, and look at the limited empirical evidence available on this debate.

The second step of our analysis is to ask, for a given structure, how much the government should spend on education. A central determinant of how much the government should spend on education is the return provided by this investment. We review the existing evidence on the returns to education and what they imply for government involvement. Finally, we turn to a discussion of higher education, a market that appears to work much better in the United States than elsewhere in the world but that still raises many difficult policy issues.

11.1

Why Should the Government Be Involved in Education?

In the United States, 90% of elementary and secondary students are in public educational institutions instead of privately financed institutions. Should the public sector be so dominant in the provision of education? What failure in the private education market justifies government's dominant role? Education is not a pure public good because it does not meet the conditions of non-rivalry (that my consumption of the good does not reduce your enjoyment of the good) and non-excludability (I cannot deny you the opportunity to consume or access the good). Education is clearly a rival good: having more children in a classroom may lower the quality of classroom instruction. Education is clearly also to some extent excludable: private schools can decide which students to accept.

At the same time, there are a number of public benefits (positive externalities) to education that might justify a government role in its provision.

Productivity

The first potential externality from education is productivity. If a higher level of education makes a person a more productive worker, then society can benefit from education in terms of the higher standard of living that comes with increased productivity. As discussed in Chapter 6, however, this higher standard of living is not an externality if the worker is the only one who reaps the benefits from her higher productivity. For example, if more education raises Stacey's marginal product of labor, but the increase is fully reflected in her receiving a higher wage from her employer, then there is no positive externality to society from Stacey's education.

Social benefits from higher productivity occur through one of two channels. The first is "spillovers" to other workers: Stacey's increased productivity could raise the productivity of her coworkers, thus raising their wages and well-being. Since Stacey herself is unlikely to be fully compensated for the rise in her coworkers' wages, this is a positive externality to her coworkers from her education. The second is through taxes: if Stacey's higher productivity is reflected in higher pay, then the government collects more tax revenues as a result.

Citizenship

Public education may improve the quality of life in the United States in indirect ways as well. Education may make citizens more informed and active voters, which will have positive benefits for other citizens through improving the quality of the democratic process. Education may also reduce the likelihood that people turn to a life of crime, an outcome that has positive benefits for other citizens by improving their safety and reducing the public costs of policing. More generally, education may play a role in enabling immigrants, who are some of the most productive members of U.S. society, to establish themselves in the United States. These arguments are fairly compelling for public intervention in basic education such as elementary school, but they provide less rationale for public financing of secondary and especially higher education.

Credit Market Failures

Another market failure that may justify government intervention is the inability of families to borrow to finance education. In a world without government involvement, families would have to provide the money to buy their children's education from private schools. Suppose, in this private-education-only world, there is a poor family with a talented child, and this child could earn a comfortable living as an adult if properly educated. It would be socially optimal for this child to be educated, yet the family cannot afford the costs of education.

In principle, the family could borrow against the child's future labor earnings to finance the education. Yet, in practice, banks and other lenders are unlikely to make such loans since there is no source of *collateral* (assets owned by a person that the bank can claim if the person doesn't pay back the loan). If the family takes a loan to finance a home purchase (a *mortgage*), the collateral is their house; if they don't repay the loan, the bank can claim their house to offset its losses. Because the bank cannot claim the family's child if they don't repay the loan, banks may be unwilling to lend for education; after all, despite the family's claims, the bank can't really tell if their child is a good investment or not. This situation is an **educational credit market failure:** the credit market has failed to make a loan that would raise total social surplus by financing productive education.

The government can address this credit market failure by making loans available to families to finance education. Yet the government in the United States and the governments of most industrialized nations do not play this role except in financing higher education (discussed at the end of this chapter). Instead of providing loans to finance elementary and secondary education, the government directly provides a fixed level of publicly funded education.

educational credit market failure The failure of the credit market to make loans that would raise total social surplus by financing productive education.

Failure to Maximize Family Utility

The reason governments may feel that loans are not a satisfactory solution to credit market failures is that they are concerned that parents would still not choose appropriate levels of education for their children. In a world with well-functioning credit markets (or with government loans available), private education would probably still involve some sacrifice on the part of parents, such as paying the cost of schooling not covered by loans or making interest payments on the loans. Even if total family utility would rise with a more highly educated child, some parents may not be willing to reduce their consumption in order to finance their children's education because they care more about their own consumption than their children's future income. (As noted in Chapter 6, evidence suggests that parents are not maximizing the utility of their entire family.) Children can be harmed by the unwillingness of their parents to finance their education, and making loans available to parents cannot solve that problem. In this case, public provision of education is a better alternative. Otherwise, smart children would be penalized for having selfish parents.

Redistribution

A final justification for government involvement is redistribution. In a privately financed education model, as long as education is a normal good (demand for which rises with income), higher-income families would provide more education for their children than would lower-income families. Since more education translates to higher incomes later in life (as we will show later in this chapter), this situation would limit income mobility because children of high-income parents would have the best opportunities. *Income mobility,* whereby low-income people have a chance to raise their incomes, has long been a stated goal for most democratic societies, and public education provides a level playing field that promotes income mobility.

In summary, then, there are various reasons for government involvement in education: potential productivity spillovers; more informed and less criminally inclined citizens; failures in credit markets; failures of family utility maximization; redistribution. We next turn to the question of how governments are involved in education and what effects their involvement has on educational attainment.

11.2

How Is the Government Involved in Education?

In Chapter 5, we discussed two alternative means for governments to deal with positive externalities: the price mechanism and the quantity mechanism. In the context of education, the price mechanism approach would be to offer discounts on private educational costs to students, and the quantity mechanism approach would be to mandate that individuals obtain a certain level of education. In practice, the governments of most developed nations pursue neither of these approaches, instead providing a fixed level of education for no cost. In this section, we discuss the effects of providing free public education on the level of *educational attainment* (the amount and quality of education received by individuals) in society.

Free Public Education and Crowding Out

We can model public education using the same approach we used to model the provision of a public good (fireworks) in Chapter 7: education is a public good that is provided to some extent by the private sector. As such, an important problem with the system of public education provision is that it may *crowd out* private education provision. Indeed, as economist Sam Peltzman argued in 1973, it is possible that providing a fixed amount of public education can actually *lower* educational attainment in society through inducing choice of lower-quality public schools over higher-quality private schools.[3]

In Peltzman's model, individuals are choosing how much to spend on their children's education. He assumes that the more individuals spend, the higher quality education they can buy for their children (later in the chapter we review the evidence for the strength of this spending–quality link). The public sector provides some fixed level of expenditure and thus of quality. If parents want higher quality education than that provided by the public sector, then they must send their children to private school.[4] By sending their children to private school, however, parents forgo their entitlement to free public education for their children. As a result, some parents who might desire higher quality education for their children decide not to use private schools; they reduce their desired education in order to take advantage of free public education. For this group, free public schools have therefore lowered the quality of education they "purchase" for their children.

Figure 11-2 illustrates the choice families face between spending on education and spending on all other goods. Before there is any provision of public education, families face the budget constraint *AB*, with a slope that is dictated by the relative prices of private education and other goods. Any money that is spent on a child's education reduces the family's budget for purchasing other goods.

The government then provides free public education of a quality that costs E_F. For now, we ignore the financing of this educational expenditure (since all the policy alternatives we discuss involve financing as well, we discuss financing separately later in the chapter). The provision of free public education means that individuals can spend their full budget on other goods and still get educational spending of E_F (at point *C*). To spend more than E_F on education, however, the family would have to entirely forgo the free public education; although the public education is free, it can be used only up to amount E_F. Thus, the new budget constraint runs from *A* to *C* (since education is free to a spending–quality level of E_F), then drops down to point *D*, after which it is the same segment *DB* as the original budget constraint. What does the provision of free public education do to educational spending (and thus quality) choices?

---

[3] See Peltzman (1973). This discussion is couched in terms of school quality, but the same argument could be made about quantity of education received.

[4] The model assumes that individuals cannot simply "top off" public education by supplementing it with private spending, for example on tutoring.

■ FIGURE 11-2

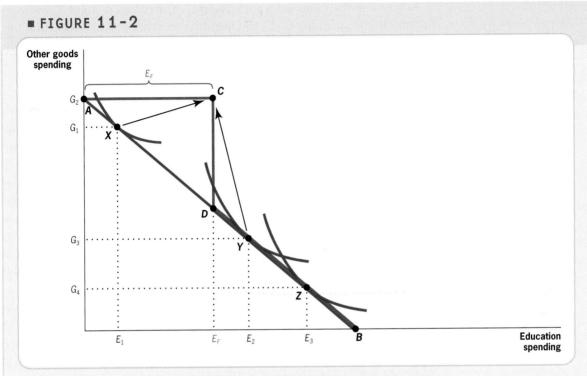

Public Education Spending Crowds Out Private Spending • When the government introduces free public education in the amount of E_F, the budget constraint changes from AB to $ACDB$. This leads families such as X to increase the amount of education they obtain from E_1 to E_F and families such as Z to maintain their educational spending of E_3. Families such as Y, however, reduce their educational spending from E_2 to E_F.

In Figure 11-2, we compare three families, X, Y, and Z, all of whom have children. Before public schooling is introduced, these families choose different-quality (and thus different-cost) private schools. Family X initially chooses bundle X, the point at which their indifference curve is tangent to the private-market budget constraint AB. This bundle consists of relatively little education spending for their children (a low-quality private school) at E_1 and relatively high spending on other goods of G_1. After the free public system is introduced, family X moves from point X to point C, a bundle that consists of higher levels of education spending (E_F) and higher levels of spending on other goods (G_2 at point A). The family is on a higher indifference curve (indicating greater utility) at this kink in the budget constraint because its consumption of both education and other goods has increased.

Family Z initially chooses bundle Z, very high educational spending (a very high-quality private school at E_3) and relatively low spending on other goods (G_4). When the public system is introduced, there is no change in family Z's spending on either education or other goods; this family wants such a high-quality education for its children that the public school option is irrelevant.

Family Y initially chooses a medium level of spending at point Y, with initial educational spending of E_2 and spending on other goods of G_3. After free public education is introduced, however, the family moves to point C, a bundle in which their education spending has fallen a bit from E_2 to E_F, but their consumption of other goods has increased greatly from G_3 to G_2. Their utility has increased because point C is on a higher indifference curve than point Y is. Thus, the introduction of free public education has *reduced* family Y's spending on education. By spending somewhat less on education, the family can dramatically increase how much they can spend on other goods, and this is a trade-off they are willing to make. It is true that children in family Y would have gotten more education by staying in their original private school (level E_2), but this would have required the family to forgo a lot of consumption of other goods; the family is better off by sacrificing a small amount of education to obtain a lot more consumption of other goods. For group Y, public educational spending has *crowded out* private spending on education as the family reduced their overall education spending levels in response to this free public option.

Thus, free public education increases educational quality for children in families such as X, lowers it for children in families such as Y, and has no effect on families such as Z. In principle, if group Y is big enough relative to group X, total educational spending (and thus educational quality) could actually *fall* when free public education is introduced.

Solving the Crowd-Out Problem: Vouchers

One solution to the crowd-out problem would be the use of **educational vouchers,** whereby parents are given a credit of a certain value (for example, the average spending on a child of a given age in the public education system) that can be used toward the cost of tuition at any type of school, public or private. Figure 11-3 illustrates how a voucher system could work: families would be given a voucher for an amount E_F, which they could either give to their local public schools in return for free education for their children or apply toward private school tuition. The availability of this voucher would lead to a new budget constraint ACE: families get an amount E_F to spend on education without lowering other consumption. The voucher has the same effect as a conditional lump-sum grant to local governments: it raises incomes but forces the families to spend a minimum amount on education.

With this system, educational spending (and therefore quality) would increase for all three types of families. Family X would still move to point C, at which both education and other consumption have increased. Once again, family X's utility has increased and they will be on a higher indifference curve at this point.

Family Y would no longer move to point C and purchase less education (E_F instead of E_2) as they did in Figure 11-2 because now they *no longer have to forgo the public subsidy to get higher-quality private education.* Now, they can move to a point such as Y_2 in Figure 11-3, using some of their higher income (from the voucher) to purchase more education (E_4 instead of E_2) and some

educational vouchers A fixed amount of money given by the government to families with school-age children, who can spend it at any type of school, public or private.

■ FIGURE 11-3

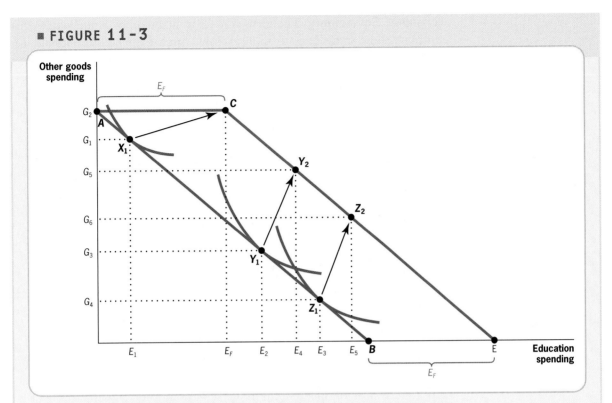

Vouchers Offset Public School Crowd-Out • When the government provides vouchers in the amount of E_F, the budget constraint changes from *AB to ACE*, leading all families to increase educational spending. Low-spending families like *X* will spend the full amount (E_F) on public schools, families such as *Y* will switch from public education in an amount E_F to private education in an amount E_4, and higher-spending families like *Z* will also increase their educational spending somewhat (from E_3 to E_5) because the voucher increases their effective incomes.

to purchase more of other goods (G_5 instead of G_3). This is a preferred outcome to point *C*, since they get both more education and more consumption of other goods.

Instead of continuing to purchase the same amount of education as they did in Figure 11-2, family *Z* would now choose a point such as Z_2 and use some of their higher income to purchase more education (E_5 instead of E_3) and some to purchase more of other goods (G_6 instead of G_4). Under the voucher program, total education has clearly increased.

This type of analysis motivates support for educational vouchers as a policy option in the United States. A number of analysts have proposed voucher systems whereby individuals are given the choice of either attending free public schools or applying their local public school spending to their private school education. Supporters of vouchers make two arguments in their favor, which mirror the two arguments in favor of free choice in most economic markets.

Consumer Sovereignty The first argument in favor of vouchers is that vouchers allow individuals to more closely match their educational choices with their tastes. By forcing individuals either to choose free public education or to forgo this large public subsidy and choose private education, today's system does not allow people to maximize their utility by freely choosing the option that makes them best off. This restriction has the unintended consequence of crowd-out that could be solved with vouchers.

Competition The second argument in favor of vouchers is that they will allow the education market to benefit from the competitive pressures that make private markets function efficiently. Critics contend that the public education sector is rife with inefficiency. They point to the fact that per-pupil spending has doubled in real terms since 1970, yet the math and reading scores of 17-year-olds have risen by only about 5% in that same time period. Furthermore, the number of administrative staff in public schools has grown by 65% since 1970, while the number of enrolled students has grown by only 2%.[5]

This inefficient bureaucracy has been allowed to grow, critics contend, because there is no competitive pressure to keep it in check. Vouchers would bring that pressure to bear on public schools by making private schools a more affordable option. If students choose schools based on which delivers the best product, not based on the financial advantage of local public schools, then schools that are inefficient will not be chosen since they deliver less education per dollar of spending. If these schools are not chosen, they will be forced out of the education market, just as competition forces inefficient firms out of the market. Thus, competitive pressures will cause schools to serve the needs of students and parents rather than bureaucrats. Vouchers "level the competitive playing field" between private and public schools by removing the financial advantage currently held by public schools.

One response to this claim is to note that there is already competitive pressure on local schools through the Tiebout mechanism (voting with your feet to choose the right mix of property taxes and public goods provision for you). If local schools are inefficient, families will move to other towns where their property-tax dollars are spent more efficiently to produce better education for their children. Indeed, one study found that areas with more school districts from which parents can choose (e.g., many small suburbs) feature both better educational outcomes and lower school spending than do areas with fewer school districts (just several large suburbs).[6] This finding is consistent with Tiebout pressures on schools to improve their educational productivity.

It is unlikely, however, that the Tiebout mechanism works perfectly in this case. Individuals choosing towns are choosing a bundle of attributes, not just educational quality. Vouchers allow for Tiebout unbundling: individuals can live in a town they like for noneducation reasons while sending their children to any public or private school they like.

---

[5] U.S. Department of Education (2006a), Tables 32, 78, 108, and 162.
[6] Hoxby (2000). This important study has been the subject of some controversy; see Rothstein (2005) and Hoxby (2005).

Problems with Educational Vouchers

The consumer sovereignty and competition arguments provide strong support for the use of educational vouchers. There are, however, a number of compelling arguments that can be made against using education vouchers as a means to improve the quality of education in the United States.

Vouchers Will Lead to Excessive School Specialization Many of the arguments in favor of public financing of education relate to the externalities that come from having a common educational program, particularly at the elementary school level. The first argument made here for vouchers, that schools will tailor themselves to meet individual tastes, threatens to undercut the benefits of a common program. In principle, a free educational market could produce "football schools," with little educational provision but excellent football programs, or "art schools," with little education other than in the arts. By trying to attract particular market segments, schools could give less attention to what are viewed as the central elements of education (such as basic reading, writing, and mathematical skills).

In principle, this problem could be dealt with through regulations that require all schools to provide a certain set of common skills. These regulations could also be supported by testing regimes that ensure that students at each school are maintaining an acceptable level of achievement in basic skills.

In practice, however, such regulation could become so onerous and costly to enforce that it would defeat the purpose of school choice. Moreover, as we discuss later, such efforts to hold schools accountable for student performance often have unintended side effects. Ultimately, what determines the optimal level of uniformity across schools is the value to society of educational conformity at each level of schooling. If this value is low, which may be true at the high school level, there will be large gains from free choice. If this value is high, which may be more true at the elementary school level, public provision may be more efficient than private competition with regulation.

Vouchers Will Lead to Segregation A major achievement over the past 60 years in the United States, in the eyes of many citizens, is the reduction in segregation in education. A public education system that once provided African Americans and other minorities with separate and unequal educational quality has become more integrated, so in principle, all citizens have the right to high-quality public education. Critics of voucher systems argue that vouchers have the potential to reintroduce segregation along many dimensions, such as race, income, or child ability. These critics envision a world where children of motivated parents move to higher-quality private schools, while children of disinterested or uninformed parents end up in low-quality public schools. If the children of interested and motivated parents differ

"I'm taking my voucher and going to circus school."

along the lines of race, income, or child ability from those of uninterested and unmotivated parents, segregation could worsen.

Supporters of vouchers note that, in fact, vouchers may serve to reduce the natural segregation that already exists in our educational system. Currently, students are trapped by the monopoly that their local school system has over education production. Vouchers allow motivated students and their parents to choose a better education and end the segregation imposed on them by location. In a famous example, Nobel Prize–winning economist Milton Friedman pointed out that it is unfair that an inner-city child who wants to use his money to buy a new car can do so, but if he wants to use that same money to buy better education, he cannot do so without giving up his public educational subsidy.

Both sides of this argument make valid points. It is true that segregation remains a significant problem in the U.S. educational system. Although white students are only 60% of the student population, the typical white student attends a school that is 80% white. Forty percent of black students and 30% of Latino students attend intensely segregated schools, where 90–100% of students are from minorities. And in almost 90% of these intensely segregated minority schools, the majority of students are poor. California and New York are among the states with the most segregated schools, with the typical black student attending a school that is 80% minority.[7] As a result, supporters of vouchers are undoubtedly correct in pointing out that some individuals would benefit from using vouchers to escape to higher-quality education.

At the same time, vouchers might increase segregation by student skill level or motivation. As the motivated and high-skilled students flee poor-quality public schools for higher-quality private schools, the students left behind will be in groups that are of lower motivation and skill. That is, school choice is likely to reduce segregation along some dimensions (e.g., by allowing minority students with greater ability and motivation to mix more with students at higher-quality schools) but increase it along others (e.g., by separating the education system into higher and lower ability/motivation schools).

Vouchers Are an Inefficient and Inequitable Use of Public Resources

One issue that was set aside in the theoretical discussion about the effects of vouchers was the financing of education and of vouchers. Education is financed mostly by local property taxes and state taxes (as discussed in the previous chapter). If the current financing were replaced by vouchers, total public-sector costs would rise, since the government would pay a portion of the private school costs that students and their families are currently paying themselves.

For children from families such as X in Figures 11-2 and 11-3, costs would not increase: the children would stay in public school, so costs to the public sector for educating the children in family X would remain at E_F. Children from families such as Y would move to private schools, thus spending more on education, but the cost to the public sector would still only be E_F since this is the

---

[7] Frankenberg and Lee (2002).

amount of the voucher that is provided; the families are paying the extra costs of the private school. For children such as those from family Z, however, public-sector costs would increase. Previously, family Z was paying the entire cost of their children's private education, but now because family Z receives a voucher, the local government is picking up a portion, E_F, of this cost. This increased government spending is associated with only a very small rise in their educational attainment, the rise from E_3 to E_5, which occurs because the families are richer by the amount of government transfer (E_F).

Thus, one cost of substantially increasing the level of education chosen by families such as Y is the cost incurred by providing large new subsidies to families such as Z who don't much change their educational attainment. That is, crowd-out of private educational spending has been reduced for Y, but it has been introduced for Z. If vouchers are most used by families (like family Z) who were already paying for private school for their children on their own, then this is a fairly inefficient use of public resources. On the other hand, if the vouchers are most used by families (like family Y) who are switching from public education to much higher private levels of education (from E_F to E_4 in Figure 11-3), this may be an efficient use of public resources. The goal of government policy here is to direct resources to the currently undereducated (such as the children in family Y); if most of the gain from the use of vouchers goes to families such as Z, the goal is not being met.

Equity considerations further strengthen this point. Income and use of private schools are strongly positively correlated; families like Z are much more likely to be high income than families such as Y. Granting much of the voucher expenditure to higher-income families who are already sending their children to private schools is an inefficient and inequitable use of public funds.

Ideally, the government could solve this problem by identifying whether families are in group Y or Z and directing more resources to those in group Y (whose use of more education we want to encourage). Unfortunately, the government cannot perfectly identify which group families are in, so it cannot carry out this type of targeting exactly. One way to approximate this targeting would be to target the voucher's value to the family's income. Having vouchers for which the value falls as the family's income rises would accomplish three goals. First, such a program would target resources to groups who are most likely to use them to increase educational attainment. Second, it would reduce the inequity of a system that mostly benefits higher-income private school attendees. Finally, to the extent that lower-income children are "left behind" in public schools by their higher-ability and more motivated peers, it would provide resources for the remaining public schools to succeed (since income-targeted vouchers would provide higher levels of funding to low-income schools through their larger voucher amounts).

The Education Market May Not Be Competitive The arguments of voucher supporters are based on a perfectly competitive model of the education market. Yet the education market is described more closely by a model of *natural monopoly*, in which there are efficiency gains to having only one monopoly provider of the good. Economies of scale in the provision of education mean that it may not be efficient to have many small schools competing with one another for students; it may be much more (naturally) efficient to have one monopoly provider instead.

The fact that education markets may be natural monopolies can lead to failures in the educational market. If a large inner-city school closes due to lack of demand, for example, what happens to its core of unmotivated students who have not taken advantage of choice to enroll elsewhere? There may not be a small school in the city that can meet their needs, and the closing of their school would potentially leave them without educational options. Similarly, how could a rural area without much population density support enough schooling options to effectively introduce competition?

Given these problems, it is unlikely that the government would actually allow certain schools to go out of business and leave local students without educational options. Yet if schools know that they are "too important to fail," the competitive pressure on the schools would be mitigated: Why should a school work hard to improve its efficiency if it knows it will retain its funding regardless of performance? Thus, there is a tension between government efforts to ensure educational opportunities for all and the ability of the educational market to put pressure on underperforming schools.

The Costs of Special Education In the type of voucher system described here, each child would be worth a voucher amount that represents the average cost of educating a child in that town in that grade, but all children do not cost the same to educate. Children with diagnosed disabilities, for example, have much higher costs associated with their need for **special education,** programs for educating disabled children that require extra resources (such as trained teachers, smaller classes, or special equipment). In the United States, 5.8 million students aged 6–21 are provided with special education services, and the average student with a disability costs about $12,700 a year to educate, more than twice the cost of educating a regular education student. The United States now spends about $50 billion a year on special education, or 14% of total elementary and secondary education spending.[8]

The higher cost of special education students raises problems in the context of a voucher system because schools will have an incentive to avoid special education students. These students bring vouchers of the same amount, yet they cost much more to educate. Schools will want to take only the students who can be educated effectively for the voucher amount and will shun the highest-cost special education students. This student selection by schools will reduce the options available to special education students. In principle, the government could use antidiscrimination regulations to deal with this problem, but in practice schools may have many subtle ways of deterring applications from such students. They might, for example, institute a very low quality special education program that would deter special education students from applying.

---

special education Programs to educate disabled children.

[8] U.S. Department of Education (2003).

The government could address this problem by making the voucher amount for any child match the cost of educating that child. Children with special education needs who cost more to educate could receive larger voucher amounts to offset the extra costs associated with educating them. Because it is very hard to adjust voucher amounts for the specific educational needs of each child, however, this potential problem with vouchers will remain.

11.3

Evidence on Competition in Education Markets

In the previous section, we discussed the theory of how vouchers may or may not improve the efficiency with which education markets function in the United States. There is substantial uncertainty about the ultimate effects of vouchers. In this section, we review the evidence on the effects of competition in education markets in an effort to understand what impact widespread use of vouchers might have in the United States and other nations.

Direct Experience with Vouchers

There have been several small-scale voucher programs put in place in the United States in recent years. Probably the most studied program has been the one used in Milwaukee. Starting in 1990, the state of Wisconsin allowed families with income no more than 175% of the poverty line to apply for a voucher worth about $3,200 that could be used for tuition at any nonsectarian (not religiously affiliated) private school. Studies of this program, reviewed in the Empirical Evidence box, provide some support for the notion that vouchers can allow students to improve the quality of their education. The effects might be much larger with widespread adoption of vouchers, which would put competitive pressure on all schools to improve their performance.

Experience with Public School Choice

Some school districts have not offered vouchers for private schools but have instead allowed students to choose freely among public schools. In some cases, students are allowed to choose any local school, not just the one nearest them. Other possible choices include **magnet schools,** special public schools set up to attract talented students or students interested in a particular subject or teaching style, and **charter schools,** small independent public schools that are not subject to many of the regulations imposed on traditional public schools, including restrictions on teacher qualifications.

Cullen, Jacob, and Levitt (2003) provided an evaluation of one of the most ambitious such school choice plans, in the city of Chicago, where students can apply for any school in the public school system. Schools that had too many applicants used a lottery to determine who would be admitted. The authors found that lottery winners, who won the chance to attend a more selective

magnet schools Special public schools set up to attract talented students or students interested in a particular subject or teaching style.

charter schools Schools financed with public funds that are not usually under the direct supervision of local school boards or subject to all state regulations for schools.

ESTIMATING THE EFFECTS OF VOUCHER PROGRAMS

A number of recent studies, both in the United States and abroad, attempt to estimate the impact of voucher programs on student achievement. In the United States, Rouse (1998) studied the effect of the Milwaukee voucher program on the achievement of students who used their vouchers to finance a move to private schools.[9] She noted that one cannot directly compare students who do and do not use vouchers, since they may differ along many dimensions; for example, students who take advantage of a voucher program may be more motivated than those who do not. This selective use of vouchers would bias any comparison between the groups. An important feature of the Milwaukee program, however, is that participating private schools had to accept all students who applied unless the school was oversubscribed (too many applicants for the available slots). Oversubscribed schools had to select randomly from all applicants, using a lottery.

This administrative solution has the benefit of approximating the type of randomized trial that is the gold standard in empirical research. The randomized lottery allowed Rouse to form a control group (students who applied to oversubscribed schools but were randomly rejected) and a treatment group (students who applied to the same schools and were randomly accepted). These groups should be comparable, except that the treatments go to the private schools rather than remaining in the public schools like the controls. Rouse found that the treatment group saw an increase in academic performance: there was a rise in math test scores of 1–2% per year relative to the control group,

although there was no difference in reading scores across the two groups.[10]

In the United States, about 10% of students are enrolled in private schools, a proportion that doubles or triples in the low-income developing world, where public schools may be of particularly low quality. Introducing a voucher program may therefore have a great effect in developing countries, where private schools are a closer substitute for public schools, than in developed countries. Angrist et al. (2002) studied a Colombian voucher program called PACES that gave over 125,000 pupils vouchers that covered somewhat more than half the costs of private secondary school. Many of the vouchers were distributed by lottery, thus allowing Angrist to compare the randomly selected lottery winners (the treatment group that received vouchers) and losers (the control group that did not receive vouchers).

The study found that students who won vouchers were 10% more likely than lottery losers to finish eighth grade, primarily because they didn't repeat as many grades before the age of school leaving. The study also found that lottery winners scored significantly higher on standardized achievement tests than did losers. Winners were also less likely to be married or cohabiting and worked 1.2 fewer hours per week, suggesting an increased focus on schooling among lottery winners. The study concluded that the vouchers cost the government $24 per winner, yet the improved schooling attainment and quality increased the wages earned by this group by between $36 and $300 per year, making this an enormously successful program.

public school, saw no improvement in their academic outcomes relative to lottery losers, who were not able to attend a more selective school. There was no improvement in test scores and no increase in the odds of dropping out of high school. Bifulco and Ladd (2004) and Hanushek, Kain, and Rivkin (2002) also found that charter schools do not have a positive impact on student performance relative to the traditional public school alternative. These findings cast doubt on the ability of "better" public schools to dramatically improve

---

[9] Her work builds on earlier conflicting analyses by Greene et al. (1996) and Witte (1997).

[10] The other major experience with vouchers in the United States has been several privately financed "experiments" in which low-income public school children were given scholarships to attend private schools. Recent studies of such a program in New York have provided only mixed evidence on its success, however, in contrast to the positive evidence in Milwaukee.

education. At the same time, this does not mean that more competition from *private* schools could not improve the educational process.[11]

Experience with Public School Incentives

Although the United States has limited experience with vouchers and school choice, it has much larger experience with another aspect of educational reform: school accountability. Any move to an increase in school choice in the United States would bring with it an increased use of testing to ensure that schools are meeting educational standards, and the country has a large body of experience with accountability measures. As of 2002, 25 states explicitly linked student promotion or graduation to performance on state or local assessment tests, 18 states rewarded teachers and administrators on the basis of successful student performance on exams, and 20 states penalized teachers and administrators on the basis of subpar student exam performance.[12] This approach to school accountability was codified in federal law through the No Child Left Behind Act of 2001.

Making schools accountable for student performance can provide incentives for schools to increase the quality of the education they offer. By some measures, accountability requirements have had this intended effect. Hanushek and Raymond (2004) found that states that implemented strong accountability programs—programs with sanctions for poor performance on standardized tests (such as no graduation without passing the test) and rewards for good performance on standardized tests—saw sizeable improvements in their test scores over time.

At the same time, accountability programs can have two unintended effects. First, they can lead schools and teachers to "teach to the test"—that is, to narrowly focus their teaching on enabling students to perform well on the test that determines school accountability, not on a broadly improved education. Indeed, recent studies find that improved performance of students on tests that determine school accountability is not reflected on more general tests of student ability.[13] Second, schools can manipulate the pool of test takers and the conditions under which they take tests to maximize success. For example, Jacob (2002) and Figlio and Getzler (2002) found that the introduction of accountability in Chicago and Florida led schools to reclassify low-skilled students as special education or disabled students (and thus exempt from testing) in order to raise average school scores. Figlio and Winicki (2002) found that schools even manipulated their cafeteria menus around

---

[11] There are several recent studies of the impact of competition from private schools on overall school performance, but they have reached differing conclusions. Hoxby (2002) found that the public schools that faced the most competition from private schools under the Milwaukee voucher program were the ones that most improved their performance on standardized tests after 1998. A recent study by Figlio and Rouse (2004), however, found that a new voucher program introduced in Florida did not cause improvements in the performance of local public school students. And Hsieh and Urquiola (2003) found that there was no aggregate improvement in student performance with a large-scale voucher-type program in Chile.

[12] Hanushek and Raymond (2004).

[13] See, for example, Jacob (2002).

testing time, increasing calories to improve student energy levels and test scores! Teachers may even cheat to improve test scores; Jacob and Levitt (2003) found that a teacher is more likely to provide the answers to standardized tests to students if the teacher has more at stake (through accountability regimes).

Bottom Line on Vouchers and School Choice

Given the mixed evidence reviewed in the previous section, several conclusions seem apparent. First, school accountability measures have been successful in improving test outcomes, but there are offsetting school responses that undercut their intended effect. There is also little evidence to support the notion that public school choice has major beneficial effects on outcomes. There is some evidence that vouchers improve the academic performance of students who move to private schools, particularly in nations where such systems are widespread. Yet voucher systems raise serious concerns about equitable treatment of the "worst" students, who might get left behind as their higher-ability, higher-motivation friends move on to better schools. These systems may also hinder access to high-quality education for special needs students.

The United States is currently in a phase of experimentation with both choice and accountability that will provide further evidence on the most effective way to improve elementary and secondary education. From all existing evidence, it appears that there may be benefits to a voucher plan with some sort of targeted vouchers that vary with income and special needs. Some sort of guarantee of educational access must be provided to ensure that every student has the option of at least one educational alternative, however, even if this reduces the pressure of competition on schools that will not be allowed to fail.

11.4

Measuring the Returns to Education

Regardless of the use of public education or private education, the government must still make some decision about the share of its budget to devote to education. For the government to decide how much to invest in education, it must undertake the type of cost-benefit analysis discussed in Chapter 8. Measuring the costs associated with education is fairly straightforward, using the techniques of opportunity cost introduced in Chapter 8. Measuring the benefits, however, is much trickier. There is an enormous economics literature devoted to measuring the **returns to education,** the benefits that accrue to society when individuals get more schooling or when they get schooling from a higher-quality environment (such as one with better-qualified teachers or smaller class sizes).

returns to education The benefits that accrue to society when students get more schooling or when they get schooling from a higher-quality environment.

Effects of Education Levels on Productivity

The topic that has received the most attention from economists studying education is the effect of education on worker productivity. In a competitive labor market, workers' wages equal their marginal product, so wages are typically used as a proxy for productivity. The idea of these studies is to let the market reveal whether education has raised productivity: if individuals are more productive as a result of being more highly educated, then firms should be willing to pay more to employ them.

There is a large literature that shows that more education leads to higher wages in the labor market. A typical estimate, which comes from comparing the earnings of those with more and less education, is that each year of education raises earnings by about 7%. There is little controversy over the question of whether those with more education earn more. There is substantial controversy, however, over the implications of this correlation. Two very different interpretations have been offered for this result.

"It is my wish that this be the most educated country in the world, and toward that end I hereby ordain that each and every one of my people be given a diploma."

Education as Human Capital Accumulation

The typical view of education is that it raises productivity by improving worker skills. Just as firms invest in physical capital, education is the individual's means of investing in **human capital.** More education raises a worker's stock of skills and allows her to earn more in the labor market.

Education as a Screening Device An alternative view is also consistent with the correlation between higher levels of education and higher levels of earnings. In the **screening** model, education acts only to provide a means of separating high- from low-ability people and does not actually improve skills. In this model, more highly educated workers would be more productive and have higher wages, but it would not be because education has improved their human capital. Rather, it would be because only those who turn out to be the most productive workers have the *ability* to pursue higher levels of education, so the very fact of having more education has signaled their high ability (and productivity). The school system in this model is not adding any value in terms of raising productivity; its only value is in screening for the most able and productive workers, who can obtain the most education.

Thus, in the screening model, employers pay more to more highly educated workers *not* because education has raised their productivity but because education is serving as a signal of underlying motivation by screening out unmotivated workers. In the human capital model, more educated workers earn more because education has raised their marginal product; in the screening model, more educated workers earn more because their education has signaled high ability.

human capital A person's stock of skills, which may be increased by further education.

screening A model that suggests that education provides only a means of separating high- from low-ability individuals and does not actually improve skills.

Policy Implications The human capital and screening models may have the same prediction for the correlation between wages and education, but they result in very different recommendations for government policy. Under the human capital model, government would want to support education or at least provide loans to individuals so that they can get more education and raise their productivity. Under the screening model, however, the government would *not* want to support more education for any given individual. In this model, the returns to education are purely private, not social: higher education serves as a signal that a person is more productive, but it does not improve social productivity at all. In fact, by getting more education, a given worker exerts a negative externality on all other educated workers by lowering the value of their education in the labor market. In the cartoon on page 303, the King's declaration would lower the signaling ability of a degree because all of the productive workers who worked hard to actually earn a degree would suffer when unproductive workers are able to raise their education level.

EMPIRICAL EVIDENCE

ESTIMATING THE RETURN TO EDUCATION AND EVIDENCE FOR SCREENING

A simple approach to estimating the return to a year of education in terms of higher wages is to compare people with more education (the treatment group) to people with less education (the control group), but this approach suffers from the type of bias problems discussed in Chapter 3: people who obtain more education may be of higher ability than people who obtain less. Thus, the estimated difference in wages between these groups can arise either from human capital accumulation or from the underlying ability differences in the groups.

Two methods try to control for this bias in estimating the true human capital effects of education. The first tries to control directly for underlying ability in a wage regression so that any remaining effect of education represents true productivity effects. Researchers include, for example, standardized test scores of students as youths to try to control for their ability. The problem with this approach is that this crude measure of the differences between individuals does not take into account unobserved factors such as motivation (e.g., Dick can be less intelligent than Jane, but because he studies harder he is still of higher ability).

The other approach to control for bias in estimating the human capital returns to education has been quasi-experimental studies that try to find treatment and control

groups that are identical except for the amount of schooling they receive. One quasi-experimental approach was taken by Duflo (2004), who studied the impact of a large-scale public school construction project in Indonesia. Between 1973 and 1978, more than 61,000 new primary schools were opened in Indonesia, with more schools in some areas than in others. Duflo studied students who were of primary schooling age when schools were built. The treatment group of students lived in areas with more school construction; the control group of students lived in areas with less school construction. Since school location was decided by essentially random political factors, these two groups should have been of comparable ability. Indeed, Duflo found that these treatment and control areas were very similar before the construction program. Despite this ex ante similarity, Duflo found that the treatment group saw a larger rise in educational attainment relative to the control group after the school construction project. Years later, this group saw much higher wages as adults, proving that there was a true productivity gain from increased education.

Another example is the use of the quasi-experiment provided by the passage of mandatory schooling and child labor laws in the United States in the late 1800s and early 1900s. Before this time, there was no requirement that

At the same time, education does play a valuable social role as a screening device in the screening model, allowing the labor market to recognize and reward the most able workers. Thus, the appropriate government policy in this model would be to support the establishment of educational institutions, if they are the best screening device, but not to subsidize an individual to get the education since this has no social return and simply lowers the value of education to others.

Differentiating the Theories While these theories have radically different policy prescriptions, in practice it is hard to tell the theories apart. An enormous literature in labor economics has proposed a wide variety of approaches to differentiating the theories, and the conclusion is very clear: most of the returns to education reflect accumulation of human capital, although there may be some screening value to obtaining a high school or higher education degree. The details of these studies are reviewed in the Empirical Evidence box.

children attend school and no limit on child labor. These laws set up the minimum age at which children had to start school, the minimum age at which they could drop out, and the minimum number of years of education required before children could engage in full-time work. Studies have shown that mandatory schooling and child labor laws significantly increased the level of education attained by students in the United States. These studies compare individuals born in states where schooling/child labor laws changed to require more education (the treatment group) to those born in states where laws did not change (the control group). Once again, these groups were of similar ability other than the laws that affected their mandatory level of schooling. Later in life, however, the people who received more (mandatory) education had higher wages than the control group, showing once again that more education raised productivity relative to another group with the same level of ability.

Although all of these approaches have some limitations, the result of the analysis is surprisingly consistent: each year of education raises wages by 7–10%. This is strong evidence for the human capital model of educational attainment.

At the same time, some clever studies have found evidence for an important type of screening, often called the "sheepskin effect": getting a degree from high school, college, or graduate school has a particularly high rate of return relative to obtaining the same amount of education but no degree. For example, Tyler, Murnane, and Willet (2000) compared students who took a test to earn a General Educational Development (GED) degree for high school credentials. The standard for passing this exam varied across states, so a student in one state could pass while a student in another state with an identical score (and presumably identical human capital) would not pass. They found that students who passed the GED exam earned wages 10–19% higher than students with comparable scores who didn't pass the exam. Since these students have similar human capital, the higher wages must reflect the screening value of the exam. Similarly, Jaeger and Page (1996) show that there is a particularly large benefit to obtaining higher education degrees, regardless of the number of years of schooling. If two individuals both have four years of college but one doesn't graduate, the one with a bachelor's degree will earn 25% more, despite (presumably) similar human capital across the two students, suggesting that the degree clearly signals higher ability levels for graduates relative to nongraduates.

Effect of Education Levels on Other Outcomes

As discussed earlier in this chapter, a major motivation for government intervention in education is the externality generated by more education. In recent years, a number of studies have assessed the impact of increased education on external benefits. Key findings include the following:

▶ Higher levels of education are associated with an increased likelihood of participation in the political process and more awareness of current policy debates (Milligan, Moretti, and Oreopoulos, 2004; Dee, 2004).

▶ Higher levels of education are associated with a lower likelihood of criminal activity (Lochner and Moretti, 2004).

▶ Higher levels of education are associated with improved health of the people who received more education and of their children (Currie and Moretti, 2003).

▶ Higher levels of education of parents are associated with higher levels of education of their children (Oreopoulos, Page, and Stevens, 2003).

▶ Higher levels of education among workers are associated with higher rates of productivity of their coworkers (Moretti, 2004).

These findings, along with the findings that more education results in higher wages, suggest that there are large private *and* public returns to increasing human capital through increasing years of education.

The Impact of School Quality

A smaller but growing literature has investigated a different question: What is the impact of higher-quality schools on the returns to education? This literature must initially grapple with the question of how to define school quality. The most common measures used are average class size (the ratio of students to teachers within a school) and school spending per student.

As reviewed in the Empirical Evidence box, a number of approaches have been taken to estimate the impact of school quality on student test scores. Experimental evidence from Tennessee suggests that smaller class sizes lead to much higher student test scores. Yet a recent attempt to dramatically reduce class sizes in California did not have the expected positive effects, perhaps because the associated rapid rise in the number of classes required led the state to hire underqualified teachers. These findings suggest that the outcomes of efforts to improve school quality can be very dependent on the approach taken to improvements.

11.5

The Role of the Government in Higher Education

The focus of our discussion thus far has primarily been on elementary and secondary education, yet there is an enormous higher education sector in the United States, which comprises 151 universities, 2,382 four-year colleges, and 1,683 two-year degree-granting institutions. Institutions of higher education spend about \$315 billion per year, about 40% of total educational spending.[14] Interestingly, in contrast to other levels of education, the higher education system in the United States is viewed as an enormous success. U.S. research universities are consistently rated as the best in the world. The clear market evidence for the success of higher education in the United States is the vast inflow of foreign students to U.S. institutions of higher education: 565,000 foreign students each year spend over \$13 billion to enroll in American colleges and universities. The number of foreign students studying here has nearly doubled in the last 20 years and now represents 4.0% of all higher education enrollment in the United States. This compares to only 12,000 American students who are studying abroad for more than one semester in any given year.[15]

EMPIRICAL EVIDENCE

ESTIMATING THE EFFECTS OF SCHOOL QUALITY

A major focus of research in labor economics is estimating the impact of school quality on student outcomes. Recent studies in this area have recognized that we cannot simply compare school districts with better and worse schools and look at the resulting implications for students. Districts with better schools (the treatments) differ in many ways from districts with worse schools (the controls). For example, residents in the treatment districts are likely to be the ones who provide a better home environment for their children. Therefore, it is necessary to find an approach that allows researchers to identify the effects of school quality alone on educational outcomes.

Two approaches have been used to address this issue. The first is using experimental data. The state of Tennessee implemented Project STAR in 1985–1986, randomly assigning 11,000 students (grades K–3) to small classes (13–17 students), regular classes (22–25 students), or regular classes with teacher's aides. Krueger (1999) analyzed the data from this experiment and found that there was a large improvement on standardized test scores for the first year and a slight improvement for each year thereafter in a small class. These effects were largest for poor and minority students. Krueger and Whitmore (2001) found that small class size effects persisted later in life; that is, being in a small class for those four years increased test scores in middle

school and increased the likelihood of taking a college entrance exam. Overall, their estimates imply that the real rate of return to smaller class sizes (doing a standard cost-benefit analysis of the experiment) is roughly 5.5% per year.

The other approach is a quasi-experimental analysis of changes in school resources. An interesting example is California, which by the mid-1990s had the largest class sizes in the nation (29 students per class on average). The California state government in 1996 provided strong financial incentives for schools to reduce their class size to 20 students per class in grades K–3, at a cost of over \$1 billion per year. Bohrnstedt and Stecher (2002) reviewed the evidence on the impacts of this major reform, using variation across schools in the rate at which they implemented smaller class sizes: schools that implemented smaller class sizes quickly were the treatment group, while schools that went more slowly were the controls. They found that there was little beneficial impact of smaller classes on student outcomes, perhaps because the state hired underqualified teachers to fill the extra classes or perhaps because the state was forced into educationally unproductive approaches such as combining different grades in one class. Thus, there remains some controversy about the returns to increased public-sector investments in school inputs.

[14] U.S. Department of Education (2006a), Tables 25, 243, and 244.
[15] Institute of International Education (2005).

The major difference between higher education and primary/secondary education in the United States is the degree of private provision and competition. Only 12% of students are enrolled in private elementary/secondary schools, and public schools typically have a local monopoly. In higher education, 24% of students attend private institutions, and students have free choice over the entire nation of where to go to college.[16] The relative success of higher education, where the United States is the world leader, and primary/secondary education, where the United States performs relatively poorly, provides some evidence for the power of competition to improve educational performance. As noted in our discussion of privatization, even with a minority of students enrolled in private schools, the competition from the private schools can lead to efficiency in the public sector.

Current Government Role

As seen in Figure 11-4, the U.S. government currently intervenes in the higher education sector through four channels.

State Provision The primary form of government financing of higher education is direct provision of higher education through locally and state-supported colleges and universities. These institutions offer subsidized low tuition for in-state students and somewhat less subsidized costs for out-of-state students. Currently, state and local governments spend about $156 billion per year on their institutions of higher education.[17]

Pell Grants The Pell Grant program is a subsidy to higher education administered by the federal government that provides grants to low-income families to pay for their educational expenditures. For a student from a family with

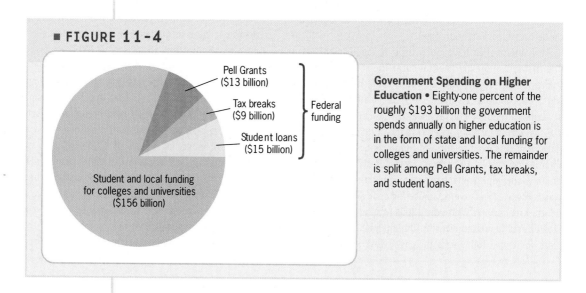

▪ **FIGURE 11-4**

Pell Grants ($13 billion)

Tax breaks ($9 billion)

Student loans ($15 billion)

Federal funding

Student and local funding for colleges and universities ($156 billion)

Government Spending on Higher Education • Eighty-one percent of the roughly $193 billion the government spends annually on higher education is in the form of state and local funding for colleges and universities. The remainder is split among Pell Grants, tax breaks, and student loans.

[16] U.S. Department of Education (2006a).
[17] U.S. Department of Education (2006a), Table 28.

annual income below $15,000, the Pell Grant program provides a grant of $4,050. For a somewhat higher-income student, the grant amount is reduced according to parental income and assets and student income and assets. The Pell Grant program currently provides $13 billion per year in grants to about 5 million students.[18]

Loans The federal government also makes loans available to students for higher education expenditures. These loans come in two types. **Direct student loans** are loans taken directly from the federal Department of Education, while **guaranteed student loans** are loans taken from private banks for which the government guarantees repayment. For students who qualify on income and asset grounds, the government subsidizes the loan cost to students by (a) guaranteeing a low interest rate (the 2005–2006 rate for the 10-year loan was 5.30%, compared to 15-year home mortgage rates, the cost to the private sector of borrowing, of about 6% over that period), and (b) allowing students to defer repayment of the loan until they have graduated. Students who do not qualify can still receive loans at the same low interest rate but must start repaying them immediately rather than deferring them until their education is complete. A dependent undergraduate can borrow up to $23,000 per degree program, an independent undergraduate can borrow up to $46,000, and a graduate or professional student up to $138,500.[19] The total amount of loans made each year under this program is $85 billion, with 23% of the loans made through the direct student loan program. The net cost to the government of student loans is $15 billion per year.[20]

> **direct student loans** Loans taken directly from the Department of Education.
>
> **guaranteed student loans** Loans taken from private banks for which the banks are guaranteed repayment by the government.

Tax Relief The final way in which the government finances higher education is through a series of tax breaks for college-goers and their families. The largest of these are the Lifetime Learning Tax Credit and the HOPE tax credit, which were put into place in 1998. These provisions provide tax credits to lower- and middle-income families of up to $2,000 per year per person for the costs of higher education. Alternatively, individuals can deduct from their taxable income up to $4,000 per year in higher education expenses. Interest paid on student loans is also tax deductible. These four tax breaks add up to about $9 billion per year in forgone government revenue.[21]

What Is the Market Failure and How Should It Be Addressed?

The arguments discussed earlier to motivate public intervention in education markets, such as provision of a common set of values, apply much less strongly in the context of higher education, where a larger share of the returns are private. Some of the recent studies cited show public returns to college education (in terms of improved health or productivity spillovers), but these benefits have not yet been shown to be large relative to government expenditures on higher education.

---

[18] U.S. Department of Education (2006b), Table 1.
[19] U.S. Department of Education (2006c).
[20] Congressional Budget Office (2006b), Table 3-3.
[21] Office of Management and Budget (2006b), Table 19-1.

The major motivation for government intervention in higher education is not to produce positive externalities but rather to correct the failure in the credit market for student loans. As noted at the start of this chapter, it is much harder to get a loan to finance education than it is to obtain a loan to finance the purchase of a car or a home since there is no collateral for banks to repossess if the loan is not repaid. As a result, in the absence of government intervention, banks may be unwilling to loan money to finance higher education. Government intervention is motivated by the need to ensure credit to students for higher education so that they can obtain higher education if it is productive for them to do so.

The major source of government expenditure on higher education is not through loans (see Figure 11-4), however, and the rationale for other types of government intervention is less clear. One rationale for Pell Grants, for example, could be the concern that low-income individuals will avoid loans because of shortsighted fears about loan repayments, thereby forgoing valuable education. The importance of this concern is illustrated by a recent study of a program at New York University law school where admitted students were randomly assigned either loans or grants of the same financial value (Field, 2006). Students who were randomly assigned grants were twice as likely to enroll at that university as those assigned loans, and students assigned grants were also about 40% more likely to take low-paying public interest jobs after graduation rather than higher-paid private sector legal work. This suggests that moving from grants to loans can have real effects on behavior.

At the same time, there is no real rationale for providing subsidies only to the higher-income individuals who benefit from tax deductions. There is an even less clear rationale for state education provision, which, as Figure 11-4 shows, is by far the largest source of public spending on higher education. Presumably states provide public education to improve the skill level of their workforce. This goal is undercut, however, by the mobility of college graduates to other states. A recent study by Bound et al. (2004) found that for every ten students educated by state schools, only three of the state school graduates remain in the state in the long run. Given that the major market failure for higher education is in credit markets, shifting state resources away from direct provision and toward loans would likely improve efficiency.

11.6

Conclusion

The provision of education, an impure public good, is one of the most important governmental functions in the United States and around the world. Because of external returns, market failures, or redistribution, governments have traditionally decided to be the majority providers of educational services. In this chapter, we learned that one cost of the government role can be a reduction in the level of educational attainment of children. Voucher systems can address this problem, but they raise a host of additional issues about segregation and the feasibility of private educational markets. The optimal amount of government intervention in education markets depends on the extent of market failures in private provision of education and on the public returns to education. A large literature suggests sizable private returns to education, with some evidence of public returns as well.

▶ HIGHLIGHTS

■ Education is primarily provided by state and local governments in the United States, and only a small share of students go to private schools.

■ The rationales for public intervention in education include positive externalities, failures in credit markets, failures of family utility maximization, and redistribution.

■ Publicly provided free education may crowd out the educational attainment of those who would like to choose higher levels of education but don't want to forgo the free public good.

■ Vouchers might solve this crowd-out problem by allowing people to choose the optimal level of education for themselves, as well as interjecting competition into the education market.

■ At the same time, vouchers may lead to increased educational stratification, and the education market may face difficulties in implementing competition.

■ Existing evidence suggests that private school choice through vouchers can move students to better schools, but a much richer evaluation of the total social effects of vouchers is needed before policy conclusions can be drawn.

■ There is a sizable private return to additional schooling that appears to reflect increased human capital accumulation rather than screening. There is also some evidence of public returns in terms of outcomes such as increased voting and better health.

■ The government supports higher education through direct spending, grants, loans, and tax breaks. The rationale for non-loan interventions, and particularly for public universities, is unclear.

▶ QUESTIONS AND PROBLEMS

1. State and federal governments actively support education at the primary, secondary, and collegiate levels. But they *mandate* education at the primary and secondary levels, while merely providing subsidies and loan guarantees at the collegiate level. Of the key rationales for public provision of education described in section 11.1 of the text, which do you think underpins this differential treatment?

2. Consider two metropolitan areas, one that has many small school districts and one that has only a few large school districts. How are the efficiency and equity effects of introducing a voucher system likely to differ across these two areas?

3. Suppose that a family with one child has $20,000 per year to spend on private goods and education, and further suppose that all education is privately provided. Draw this family's budget constraint. Suppose now that an option of free public education with spending of $4,000 per pupil is introduced to this family. Draw three different indifference curves corresponding to the following three situations: (a) a free public education would increase the amount of money that is spent on the child's education; (b) a free public education would decrease the amount of money that is spent on the child's education; (c) a free public education would not affect the amount of money spent on the child's education.

4. Empirical evidence suggests that better-educated adults donate more to charity than do less-educated adults with similar income levels. Why might this evidence justify public subsidization of education? What potential biases may make it difficult to interpret this empirical relationship?

5. Some have argued that introducing a voucher system would be particularly good for two groups of students: those who are the *worst* off under the current system, and many of the students who are the *best* off under the current system. Why might this be the case?

6. Several researchers have found evidence of sheepskin effects in which the labor market return to twelfth grade is higher than the return to eleventh grade and the return to the fourth year of college is higher than the return to the third year of college. Why does this evidence of sheepskin effects bolster the screening explanation for the relationship between education and earnings?

7. What are the advantages of comparing twins to investigate the relationship between education and earnings? What are the drawbacks of doing so?

8. Suppose you want to evaluate the effectiveness of vouchers in improving educational attainment by offering a vouchers to any student in a particular town who asks for one. What is wrong with simply comparing the educational performance of the students receiving vouchers with those who do not receive vouchers? What would be a better way to study the effectiveness of vouchers?

9. Seven in ten students attending publicly funded universities leave the state after graduation, indicating that a very large fraction of states' investments in human capital bears fruit elsewhere. Why, then, might states still play such a large role in higher education financing?

10. The U.S. Department of Education regularly conducts the National Assessment of Educational Progress (also known as the "Nation's Report Card") to monitor student achievement in subjects such as reading, writing, and mathematics. Visit their data Web site at http://www.nces.ed.gov/nationsreportcard/naepdata/search.asp (or start at the main Web site at http://www.nces.ed.gov/nationsreportcard/). Compare the progress from 1998 to 2003 of students in your state with the progress of students in one other state. In which subject areas or grade levels has your state compared most favorably with the other state?

The e icon indicates a question that requires students to apply the empirical economics principles discussed in Chapter 3 and the Empirical Evidence boxes.

▶ ADVANCED QUESTIONS

11. Many state constitutions explicitly require that the state provide an "adequate" level of school funding. How might raising this level of "adequacy" actually lead to reduced overall levels of educational spending?

12. Epple and Romano (2002) describe theoretical evidence that school vouchers will lead to "cream-skimming," where private schools will pick off the better students and leave public schools with lower-ability average students. They propose targeted vouchers, in which different-sized vouchers go to different groups of students, to combat this potential concern. How would you design a targeted voucher system that would lead to a reduced level of cream-skimming?

13. The town of Greenville has three families, each with one child, and each of which earns $20,000 per year (pre-tax). Each family is taxed $4,000 per year to finance the public school system in the town, which any family can then freely attend. Education spending is $6,000 per student in the public schools. The three families differ in their preferences for education. Though families A and B both send their children to the public school, family B places a greater value on education than family A. Family C places the greatest relative value on education and sends its child to private school.

   a. Graph the budget constraints facing each of the three families and draw a possible indifference curve that could correspond to the choice each family makes.

The town is considering replacing its current system with a voucher system. Under the new system, each family would receive a $6,000 voucher for education, and families would be still be able to send their children to the same public school. Since this would be more costly than the current system, they would also raise taxes to $6,000 per household to pay for it.

b. Draw the budget constraint the families would face under this system.

Suppose that, when the new system is introduced, family A continues to send their child to public school, but family B now sends their child to private school (along with family C's child).

c. Explain how you know that family C is made better off and family A is made worse off by the voucher policy.

d. Show, using diagrams, that family B could be made better or worse off by the voucher policy.

14. Lazear (2001) noted that when one simply compares the performance of students in small and large class sizes, there is little difference, despite the presumption (and experimental evidence) that smaller class sizes improve performance. He argued that one reason for the lack of an observed relationship between class size and student outcomes is that schools may put more disruptive children in smaller classes. How would this practice bias the estimated effect of class size on student outcomes?

15. One way to structure a student loan repayment plan is to make it income-contingent—that is, to relate the amount that a student would have to repay in any given month to how much income he or she earns. How might the existence of such a plan alter a student's choice of college major?

Social Insurance: The New Function of Government

12

In the preamble to the United States Constitution, the framers wrote that they were uniting the states in order to "establish justice, insure domestic tranquility, provide for the common defense, promote the general welfare, and secure the blessings of liberty to ourselves and our posterity." For most of the country's history, one of those goals, "common defense," was the federal government's clear spending priority. In 1953, for example, 69¢ of each dollar of federal government spending went to fund national defense (Figure 12-1). Another 4¢ went to pay for Social Security, a 17-year-old program that provided only 18% of the income of the typical elderly household.[1] Only 0.4¢ out of each dollar of federal government spending was devoted to providing health care to U.S. citizens.

Since then, the government's spending priorities shifted dramatically, away from "common defense" and toward promoting "the general welfare." By 2005, only 20¢ of each dollar of federal government spending went to fund national defense (second panel of Figure 12-1 on page 315). Twenty-one cents were paid for Social Security, which now represents 67% of the income of the typical elderly household.[2] Another 22¢ were devoted to health care spending, primarily on two programs that did not exist in 1953: the Medicare program, which provides universal health insurance coverage to the elderly, and the Medicaid program, which provides free health insurance to many poor and disabled people. The dramatic shift in spending led economist Paul Krugman to observe that "loosely speaking, the post-cold-war federal government is a big pension fund that also happens to have an army."[3]

This radical change in the nature and scope of government spending is one of the most fundamental changes in public policy in the United States over the past 50 years. The programs that have grown are labeled collectively as

---

[1] Income statistics on the elderly from Social Security Administration (2006a).
[2] Social Security Administration (2006a, 2006b).
[3] Krugman (2001).

■ FIGURE 12-1

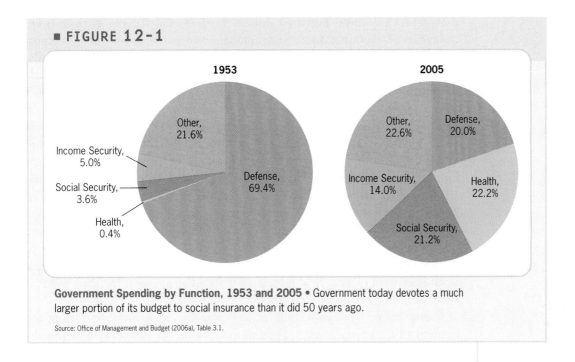

Government Spending by Function, 1953 and 2005 • Government today devotes a much larger portion of its budget to social insurance than it did 50 years ago.

Source: Office of Management and Budget (2006a), Table 3.1.

social insurance programs, government interventions to provide insurance against adverse events. In this chapter, we discuss social insurance programs in the United States in general terms. The following chapters focus on specific social insurance programs, such as:

▸ *Social security,* which provides insurance against earnings loss due to death or retirement

▸ *Unemployment insurance,* which provides insurance against job loss

▸ *Disability insurance,* which provides insurance against career-ending disability

▸ *Workers' compensation,* which provides insurance against on-the-job accidents

▸ *Medicare,* which provides insurance against medical expenditures in old age

Social insurance programs have several common features. Workers participate by "buying" insurance through payroll taxes or through mandatory contributions that they or their employers make. These contributions make them eligible to receive benefits if some measurable event occurs, such as disability or on-the-job injury. Program eligibility is conditioned only on making contributions and on the occurrence of the adverse event. Eligibility is typically not **means-tested;** that is, eligibility does not depend on one's current *means,* the level of one's current income or assets.

Throughout the next several chapters, we will discuss particular social insurance programs, but before we get into the details of these programs, we need to understand the general economics of insurance markets. This chapter begins by explaining the nature of insurance and why it is a product that is

social insurance programs
Government interventions in the provision of insurance against adverse events.

means-tested Programs in which eligibility depends on the level of one's current income or assets.

valued by consumers. We then discuss the potential failures in the private insurance market that might warrant government intervention. Foremost among these is the problem of *adverse selection:* the fact that the insured individual knows more about her risk level than does the insurer might cause insurance markets to fail. As we have discussed throughout this book, market failures potentially warrant government intervention.

The value of government intervention is mitigated, however, by the availability to individuals of *self-insurance:* to the extent that individuals can insure themselves against risks (for example, by savings or borrowing), government intervention may not have large benefits and may serve only to *crowd out* that self-insurance. Moreover, social (or any type of) insurance carries with it the important problem of *moral hazard:* when you insure individuals against adverse events, you can encourage adverse behavior. If individuals are insured against on-the-job accidents, they might be somewhat less careful on the job; if individuals are insured against long unemployment spells, they might not work very hard to find new jobs; if individuals are insured for their medical costs, they might overuse their doctors.

Moral hazard problems will occur naturally whenever individuals are insured against adverse events. Thus, in this chapter we lay out the *central trade-off with social insurance programs:* governments can improve efficiency by intervening when insurance markets fail (due, for example, to adverse selection) and individuals are not self-insured against such risks, but those interventions themselves have offsetting efficiency costs (moral hazards) that undercut their goals.

12.1

What Is Insurance and Why Do Individuals Value It?

Any discussion of government insurance provision must start with an understanding of what insurance is and why it is so valuable to consumers.

What Is Insurance?

Insurance is provided for a wide variety of different circumstances, but it has a common structure. Individuals, or those acting on their behalf (their employers or their parents, for example) pay money to an insurer, which can be a private firm or the government. These payments are called **insurance premiums.** The insurer, in return, promises to make some payment to the insured party, or to others providing services to the insured party (such as physicians or auto repair shops). These payments are conditioned on a particular event or series of events (for example, an accident or a doctor's visit).

This broad definition covers the wide variety of private insurance products that exist in the United States. A sampling includes:[4]

insurance premiums Money that is paid to an insurer so that an individual will be insured against adverse events.

---

[4] American Council of Life Insurers (2005), Insurance Information Institute (2006).

▶ *Health insurance:* Individuals and employers pay $550 billion of premiums each year to insure against health problems and the medical bills associated with them.

▶ *Auto insurance:* Drivers pay $160 billion in premiums each year to insure against the cost and physical damage of auto accidents and theft.

▶ *Life insurance:* Individuals and employers pay $140 billion in premiums each year to provide income to the heirs of those who die.

▶ *Casualty and property insurance:* Individuals and businesses pay $440 billion in premiums each year to insure their homes and other properties and possessions against fire, natural disasters, and theft.

Why Do Individuals Value Insurance?

Insurance is valuable to individuals because of the principle of *diminishing marginal utility* discussed in Chapter 2. Recall that we typically assume that the marginal utility derived from consumption falls as the level of consumption rises: the first pizza means a lot more to you than the fifth. This intuitive assumption means that, if given the choice between (a) two years of average consumption and (b) one year of excessive consumption and one year of starvation, individuals would prefer the former. Individuals prefer two years of average consumption because the excessive consumption doesn't raise their utility as much as the starvation lowers it.

For example, given the utility functions we typically use in economics, having consumption of $30,000 in both year one and year two delivers a higher utility level than having consumption of $50,000 in year one and $10,000 in year two. The gain in utility from raising consumption from $30,000 to $50,000 in year one is much smaller than the loss in utility from lowering consumption from $30,000 to $10,000 in year two. Thus, individuals desire **consumption smoothing:** they want to translate consumption from periods when it is high (so that it has a low marginal utility) to periods when it is low (so that it has a high marginal utility).

When outcomes are uncertain, people want to smooth their consumption over possible outcomes, or **states of the world,** just as they want to smooth their consumption over time. And, just as utility is maximized by having the same consumption in year one and year two in the previous example, utility is maximized by having the same consumption regardless of the outcome of some uncertain event.

Imagine that, over the next year, there is some chance that you will get hit by a car, and as a result you will have high medical expenses. There are two possibilities, or states of the world, for the next year: you get hit by a car or you don't get hit by a car. Your goal is to make a choice today that determines your consumption tomorrow in each of these states of the world, so that your utility across the two states of the world (accident, no accident) is maximized.

Individuals choose across consumption in states of the world by using some of their income today to *buy insurance against an adverse outcome tomorrow.* By buying insurance, individuals commit to make a payment regardless of the

consumption smoothing The translation of consumption from periods when consumption is high, and thus has low marginal utility, to periods when consumption is low, and thus has high marginal utility.

states of the world The set of outcomes that are possible in an uncertain future.

state of the world, in return for getting a benefit if the uncertain outcome is negative (an accident). The larger the payment to the insurer (the insurance premium), the larger the benefit in the negative outcome case (the insurance payout). Thus, by varying the amount of insurance they buy, individuals can shift their consumption from one state of the world to another. For example, by buying a lot of insurance, an individual shifts consumption from the positive outcome state of the world (when he only pays premiums) to the negative outcome state of the world (when he also gets benefits).

The fundamental result of basic insurance theory is that individuals will demand *full insurance in order to fully smooth their consumption across states of the world*. That is, in a perfectly functioning insurance market, individuals will want to buy insurance so that they have the same level of consumption regardless of whether the adverse event (such as getting hit by a car) happens or not. Given diminishing marginal utility, this course of action gives individuals a higher level of utility than does allowing the accident to lower their consumption. The intuition is the same as the example over time at the start of this section: it is better to have constant consumption in all states of the world than to have consumption that is high in one state and low in another.

Formalizing This Intuition: Expected Utility Model

expected utility model The weighted sum of utilities across states of the world, where the weights are the probabilities of each state occurring.

To better understand this difficult intuitive point, it is useful to turn to the standard mechanism that economists use for modeling choices under uncertainty: the **expected utility model.** This model is similar to the consumer choice model we introduced in Chapter 2, but it allows individuals to maximize utility across states of the world rather than across bundles of goods. In particular, suppose that there is an uncertain outcome, with some probability p of an adverse event. Then expected utility is written as:

$$EU = (1 - p) \times U \text{ (consumption with no adverse event) } + p \times U \text{ (consumption with adverse event)}$$

We can use this model to examine an individual's decision over how much insurance coverage to buy. For example, suppose there is a 1% chance ($p = 0.01$) that Sam will get hit by a car next year and that his injuries will result in $30,000 in medical expenses. Sam has a choice of insuring some, none, or all of these potential medical expenses, but this will cost him $m¢$ in insurance premiums per dollar of expenditures covered. Thus, if Sam buys an insurance policy that pays b if he is hit, his premium is mb (for example, if he fully insures the risk, then he pays $m \times 30,000$). If Sam buys insurance, in the state of the world where he doesn't get hit by the car he will be mb poorer than if he doesn't buy the insurance. In the rare state of the world where he does get hit by the car, he will be $b - mb richer than if he hadn't bought the insurance (since he paid the mb premium, and the insurance covered b of expenses). Thus, purchasing insurance is the way Sam can effectively translate consumption from periods when consumption is high, and therefore has low marginal utility (doesn't get hit), to periods when consumption is low, and therefore has high marginal utility (does get hit).

■ **TABLE 12-1**

The Expected Utility Model

If Sam . . .	And Sam is . . .	Consumption (C)	Utility $\sqrt{C}$	Expected Utility
Doesn't buy insurance	Not hit by a car (p = 99%)	$30,000	173.2	$0.99 \times 173.2 + 0.01 \times 0 = 171.5$
	Hit by a car (p = 1%)	0	0	
Buys full insurance (for $300)	Not hit by a car (p = 99%)	$29,700	172.34	$0.99 \times 172.34 + 0.01 \times 172.34 = 172.34$
	Hit by a car (p = 1%)	$29,700	172.34	
Buys partial insurance (for $150)	Not hit by a car (p = 99%)	$29,850	172.77	$0.99 \times 172.77 + 0.01 \times 121.86 = 172.26$
	Hit by a car (p = 1%)	$14,850	121.86	

Sam has a choice over how much insurance to buy against the risk of getting hit by a car. This table shows the consumption, and associated utility, for the states of the world where Sam is and is not hit by a car. Expected utility, the weighted average of utility in the two states of the world (weighted by the odds of each state of the world), is higher with the purchase of insurance.

Sam's interest in translating consumption from the no-accident state to the accident state will depend on the price that is charged for insurance. A starting point is to assume that insurance companies charge an **actuarially fair premium;** that is, they charge a price equal to the insurer's expected payout. This assumption implies that insurers have no administrative costs and make no profits; they simply recycle their premium payments into insurance claims. If, for example, there is a 1% chance that the insurer must pay out $30,000, then its expected payout is 0.01 × 30,000 = $300. So the premium that the insurer charges will be $300. At that premium, given the 1% chance of an accident, the insurer breaks even, collecting $300 from each person and paying out $30,000 to 1 in 100 people ($300 each on average). More generally, for any amount of coverage $b and an odds of payout of p, the insurance companies will charge premiums equal to $p × b.

actuarially fair premium
Insurance premium that is set equal to the insurer's expected payout.

Full Insurance Is Optimal The central result of expected utility theory is that *with actuarially fair pricing, individuals will want to fully insure themselves to equalize consumption in all states of the world.* This point is illustrated in Table 12-1. Suppose that Sam's income, which he fully consumes, is $30,000 per year. That first row shows the case where Sam doesn't buy any insurance to pay his medical bills if he is in a car accident. There is a 99% chance that Sam will have consumption of $30,000 next period, and a 1% chance that he will have consumption of zero, since he will have to pay $30,000 in medical bills if he has an accident. Suppose also that his utility function is of the form $U = \sqrt{C}$, where C denotes his consumption, which is equal to his income. (There are no savings.) With no insurance, Sam's expected utility is therefore:

$$(0.99 \times \sqrt{30,000}) + (0.01 \times \sqrt{0}) = (0.99 \times 173.2) + (0.01 \times 0) = 171.5$$

Suppose instead that Sam buys insurance that pays all of his medical bills if he is hit by a car. This insurance costs Sam $300, which he pays regardless of whether he gets hit. If he is hit, however, he doesn't have to spend his $30,000 of income on medical bills. With insurance, Sam's expected utility becomes:

$$(0.99 \times \sqrt{30,000 - 300}) + (0.01 \times \sqrt{30,000 - 300}) = (0.99 \times 172.34) + (0.01 \times 172.34) = 172.34$$

Sam's utility is higher if he buys the insurance, even though he will almost certainly end up paying the premium for nothing. This is because Sam wants to use insurance to smooth his consumption across both states of the world, due to the principle of diminishing marginal utility. Moreover, Sam will prefer this full insurance for $30,000 to any other level of benefits b. For example, suppose Sam were to choose only $15,000 of coverage, half of the costs if there is an accident. In that case, Sam would pay premiums only half as large, $150 per year. But his utility would fall to 172.26, below the level of utility he gets from purchasing full insurance.

Thus, even if insurance is expensive, so long as its price (premium) is actuarially fair, individuals will want to fully insure themselves against adverse events. This intuition is formalized mathematically in the appendix to this chapter. The key lesson here is that *with actuarially fair premiums, the efficient market outcome in the insurance market is full insurance and thus full consumption smoothing.*[5]

The Role of Risk Aversion One important difference across individuals is the extent to which they are willing to bear risk, or their level of **risk aversion.** Individuals who are very risk averse are those with a very rapidly diminishing marginal utility of consumption; they are very afraid of consumption falling, and are happy to sacrifice some consumption in the good state to insure themselves from large reductions in consumption in the bad state.[6] Individuals who are less risk averse are those with slowly diminishing marginal utility of consumption; they aren't willing to sacrifice very much in the good state to insure themselves against the bad state. Individuals with any degree of risk aversion will want to buy insurance when it is priced actuarially fairly; so long as marginal utility is diminishing, consumption smoothing is valued. When insurance premiums are not actuarially fair, as in some cases we describe next, those who are very risk averse may be willing to buy insurance even if those who are not very risk averse are unwilling to buy, since the former group is willing to sacrifice more in the good state to insure the bad state.

risk aversion The extent to which individuals are willing to bear risk.

---

[5] It is possible, of course, that when there is an adverse event your taste for consumption might change. For example, if you are disabled, you may need to spend less on consumption (other than medical expenditures, which are covered by health insurance), since you do not pay work expenses, don't partake in as much entertainment, and so on. In this circumstance, you wouldn't desire full consumption smoothing; maximizing utility would mean allowing your consumption to fall when disabled. This is called a *state-dependent utility function.* We ignore that case here and assume individuals have the same taste for consumption in all states (regardless of whether the adverse event occurs). As a result of this assumption, all an adverse event does is change the budget constraint, not the utility function.

[6] More generally, the degree of risk aversion bears a more complicated relationship to the shape of the utility function, but the intuition that more rapidly diminishing marginal utility equates to more risk aversion is a fairly general (and helpful) one.

12.2

Why Have Social Insurance? Asymmetric Information and Adverse Selection

If the world functioned as described in Section 12.1, there would be no need for government intervention in insurance markets: individuals would fully insure themselves in the private market at actuarially fair prices. Yet such government intervention is enormous and growing. In this section, we review the most common motivation suggested by economists for government intervention in insurance markets: asymmetric information between insured and insurer, which leads to the problem of *adverse selection*.

Asymmetric Information

Insurance markets may be marked by **information asymmetry,** which is the difference in information that is available to sellers and to purchasers in a market. Information asymmetry can arise in insurance markets when individuals know more about their underlying level of risk than do insurers. This asymmetry can cause the failure of competitive markets.

The intuition of the market failure caused by information asymmetry is best illustrated using the market for used cars, the example used by Nobel Prize–winning economist George Akerlof in 1970.[7] Sellers of used cars know their vehicles' problems, while potential buyers may not. Individuals selling a car may be doing so because they have a "lemon," a car that has major, serious defects. Buyers of cars don't know whether they are getting a lemon, and they can't necessarily trust the information provided by sellers, since sellers will want to dump their lemons on unsuspecting buyers. Therefore, buyers might avoid the used car market altogether. As a result, overall demand in the used car market is low, and sellers of used cars on average receive less for their cars than they are worth. Even if you have a car in excellent condition, and even if you are willing to attest to that fact, buyers will not pay enough for it because they can't be sure that you are being honest. You may be unwilling to sell your high-quality used car for a low price, so the used car sale may not be completed.

This outcome is a market failure because some trades that are valued by both parties may not be made due to the asymmetry of information. Buyers might be perfectly happy to pay a high price for a high-quality used car, and sellers might be perfectly happy to sell at that high price. The fact that buyers are wary of getting a lemon, however, stops that trade from happening.

In the used car market, the imperfection arises from the fact that sellers know more than buyers, making buyers wary of the market. In insurance markets, the information asymmetry is reversed: the purchasers of insurance may know more about their insurable risks than the seller (insurer) does. In

information asymmetry The difference in information that is available to sellers and to purchasers in a market.

---

[7] For the original paper, see Akerlof (1970).

this case, the insurer will be reluctant to sell insurance, since he will be worried that only those with the insured-against problems will demand insurance; the insurer will worry that only the sick demand health insurance, for example, or only those about to lose their job will demand unemployment insurance. As a result, insurers will charge higher than actuarially fair premiums, or they may not sell insurance at all if they are particularly suspicious about someone's risk status. The next sections use a health insurance market example to formalize this intuition.

Example with Full Information

Imagine that there are two groups, each with 100 persons. One group is careless and absentminded and doesn't pay attention when crossing the street. As a result, members of this group have a 5% chance of being hit by a car each year. The other group is careful and always looks both ways before crossing the street. Members of this group have only a 0.5% chance of being hit by a car each year. What effect would the existence of these two different types of pedestrians have on the insurance market? The effect depends on what we assume about the relative information available to the individuals and to the insurance company.

For example, suppose that the insurance company and the street crossers have full information about who is careful and who is not. In this case, the insurance company would charge different actuarially fair prices to the careless and careful groups. The people in the careless group would each pay 5¢ per dollar of insurance coverage, while those in the careful group would each pay only 0.5¢ per dollar of insurance coverage. At these actuarially fair prices, individuals in both groups would choose to be fully insured (as proved in Section 12.1), with the careless paying $30,000 \times 0.05 = 1500 per year in premiums and the careful paying $30,000 \times 0.005 = 150 per year in premiums. The insurance company would earn zero profit, and society would achieve the optimal outcome (each group is fully insured).

The first row of Table 12-2 illustrates the full information example, with separate prices for the two groups of consumers. At these premiums, the 100 careful people pay a total of $15,000 in premiums, and the 100 careless people pay a total of $150,000. Total premiums paid are $165,000. The insurer expects to have 0.5 accidents among the 100 careful consumers, for a payout of $15,000 (0.5 × $30,000 cost per accident), and 5 accidents among the careless consumers, for a payout of $150,000 (5 × $30,000). So the total expected insurance payout is $165,000, and the insurance company will break even.

Example with Asymmetric Information

Now suppose that the insurance company knows that there are 100 careless consumers and 100 careful consumers, but it doesn't know which category any given individual belongs in. In this case, the insurance company could do one of two things.

■ TABLE 12-2

Insurance Pricing with Separate Groups of Consumers

Information	Pricing Approach	Premium per Careless (100 people)	Premium per Careful (100 people)	Total Premiums Paid	Total Benefits Paid Out	Net Profits to Insurers
Full	Separate	$1,500	$150	$165,000 (100 × $1,500 + 100 × $150)	$165,000	0
Asymmetric	Separate	$1,500	$150	$30,000 (0 × $1,500 + 200 × $150)	$165,000	–$135,000
Asymmetric	Average	$825	$825	$82,500 (100 × $825 + 0 × $825)	$150,000	–$67,500

If the insurer has full information about whether insurance purchasers are careful or careless (first row), then he will charge $1,500 to the careless and $150 to the careful, making a net profit of zero. If the insured know whether they are careless or careful, and the insurer does not, then the insurer may try setting separate premiums for the groups (second row) or one common premium for all individuals (third row). In either case, the insurer loses money due to adverse selection, so the insurer will not offer insurance, leading to market failure.

First, the insurance company could ask individuals if they are careful or careless, and then offer insurance at separate premiums, as in the second row of Table 12-2: the premium would be only $150 if you say you are careful when you cross the street, and $1,500 if you say you are careless. In this case, however, *all consumers* will say that they are careful so that they can buy insurance for $150 per year: why voluntarily pay ten times as much for insurance? From the consumers' perspective this is a fine outcome, because everyone is fully insured and paying a low premium. But what about the insurer? The company is collecting $30,000 in total premium payments (200 persons × $150 per person). It is, however, expecting to pay out 5 claims to the careless and 0.5 claims to the careful, for a total cost of 5.5 × 30,000, or $165,000. So the insurance company, in this example, loses $135,000 per year. Companies will clearly not offer *any* insurance under these conditions. Thus, the *market will fail:* consumers will not be able to obtain the optimal amount of insurance because the insurance will not be offered for sale. This outcome is summarized in the second row of Table 12-2.

Alternatively, the insurance company could admit that it has no idea who is careful and who is not, and then offer insurance at a *pooled,* or average, cost. That is, on average, the insurer knows that there are 100 careless and 100 careful consumers, so that on average in any year the insurer will pay out $165,000 in claims. If it charges each of those 200 persons $825 per year, then, in theory, the insurance company will break even.

Or will it? Consider the careful consumers, who are faced with the decision to buy insurance at a cost of $825 or to not buy insurance at all. Careful consumers would view this as a bad deal, given that they have only a 0.5% chance of being hit. So they would not buy insurance. Meanwhile, however, all of the careless consumers view this as a great deal, and they would all buy insurance. The insurance company ends up collecting $82,500 in premium payments (from the 100 careless customers), but paying out $30,000 × 5 = $150,000 in benefits to those careless customers. So the insurance company again loses money. Moreover, half the consumers (the careful ones), who would ideally choose to fully insure themselves against getting hit by a car, end up with no insurance. Once again, the *market has failed* to provide the optimal amount of insurance to both types of consumers. This outcome is shown in the third row of Table 12-2.

The Problem of Adverse Selection

The careful/careless pedestrian example in the previous section is an example of an asymmetric information problem that plagues insurance markets, the problem of **adverse selection:** the fact that insured individuals know more about their risk level than does the insurer might cause those most likely to have the adverse outcome to select insurance, leading insurers to lose money if they offer insurance. The general operation of the adverse selection problem is illustrated by our example. Only those for whom the insurance is a fair deal will buy that insurance. With one price that averages the high- and low-expense groups, only those in the high-expense group will find the insurance to be a fair deal. (For them it's actually better than a fair deal.) If only the high-expense (highest risk of adverse outcome) group buys (selects) the insurance, the insurance company loses money because it charges the average price but has to pay out the high expected expenses of careless individuals. If the insurance company knows that it will lose money when it offers insurance, it won't offer that insurance. As a result, in this case no insurance will be available to consumers of any type.

Adverse selection can therefore lead to failure in the insurance market, and perhaps the eventual collapse of the market. This might occur because it may not be in the interest of any individual company to offer insurance at a single, pooled price, so that no companies offer the insurance. For example, in the 1980s, the California health insurer HealthAmerica Corporation was rejecting all applicants to its individual health insurance enrollment program who lived in San Francisco, on the belief that AIDS was too prevalent there. According to the San Francisco district attorney, HealthAmerica would pretend to review San Franciscans' applications, but would actually place these in a drawer for several weeks before sending them rejection letters.[8]

adverse selection The fact that insured individuals know more about their risk level than does the insurer might cause those most likely to have the adverse outcome to select insurance, leading insurers to lose money if they offer insurance.

---

[8] *Journal of Commerce* (1988).

This is a market failure because, with full information, individuals from San Francisco were likely to buy insurance at the actuarially fair premium, even if that premium was higher due to the risk of AIDS.

Does Asymmetric Information Necessarily Lead to Market Failure?

Are insurance companies destined to fail whenever there is asymmetric information? Not necessarily. First of all, most individuals are fairly risk averse. Risk-averse individuals so value being insured against bad outcomes that they are willing to pay *more* than the actuarially fair premium to buy insurance: they are willing to pay a **risk premium** above and beyond the actuarially fair premium. In our example, it is possible that the careful individuals are so risk averse, and therefore so afraid of being uninsured, that they are willing to buy insurance even at the average price. That is, even if the actuarially fair price for the careful is $150, and the market is charging $825, so that their risk premium is $675 ($825 − $150), they will still buy insurance. This situation is technically called a **pooling equilibrium,** a market equilibrium in which all types buy full insurance even though it is not fairly priced to all individuals. The pooling equilibrium is an efficient outcome: both types are fully insured and the insurer is willing to provide insurance.

Even if there is no pooling equilibrium, the insurance company can address adverse selection by offering *separate products at separate prices*. Think about the source of the adverse selection problem in our example: careless individuals are pretending to be careful in order to get cheap insurance. The insurance company would like to get individuals to reveal their true types (careless or careful), but the company faces the type of preference revelation problem we saw with public goods. Even if individuals aren't willing to voluntarily reveal their types, however, they might make choices that involuntarily reveal their types.

Suppose that the insurance company offered two polices: full coverage for the $30,000 of medical costs associated with accidents, at $1,500 (the actuarially fair price for the careless), and coverage of up to $10,000 of medical expenses, at a price of $50 (the actuarially fair price for that level of coverage for the careful). If these two products were offered, it is possible the careless would purchase the more expensive coverage and the careful would purchase the less expensive coverage. This outcome occurs because the careless don't want to bear the risk of having only $10,000 of coverage, given their relatively high odds of having an accident; they would rather pay a high price to make sure they have full coverage. The careful can take that risk, however, because of their very low odds of having an accident. By offering different products at different prices, the insurance company has caused consumers to reveal their true types. This market equilibrium is called a **separating equilibrium.**

Sound far-fetched? Consider what happened in health insurance markets 25 years ago. At that time, insurance companies were offering very generous insurance to all consumers at one high price. As health insurance costs began

risk premium The amount that risk-averse individuals will pay for insurance above and beyond the actuarially fair price.

pooling equilibrium A market equilibrium in which all types of people buy full insurance even though it is not fairly priced to all individuals.

separating equilibrium A market equilibrium in which different types of people buy different kinds of insurance products designed to reveal their true types.

to escalate, however, companies could no longer make profits with this strategy. In response to the higher costs they faced, insurance companies began to offer two products: a traditional insurance plan, and a new product called the health maintenance organization (HMO). HMOs offered care that was much more tightly monitored, typically featuring much less access to medical specialists, for example. But HMOs also had a much lower premium. The result, as we will discuss at length in Chapter 15, was a major shift by largely healthy consumers to this new, relatively low-cost/low-benefit option: a classic separating equilibrium.

Unlike the pooling equilibrium, however, the separating equilibrium _still represents a market failure._ The careless are getting what they would get in a model of full information: full coverage at a high price, which they are willing to pay. The careful are not getting their first choice, however, which would be full coverage at a lower, actuarially fair price. To address this market failure, insurers have forced the careful to choose between full coverage at a very high price and partial coverage at a lower price. Since many of the careful will choose the partial coverage, this is not the optimal solution: the optimum is full coverage for both groups, at different prices that reflect each group's relative risks of injury. Thus, even with separate products, adverse selection can still impede markets from achieving the efficient outcome.

▶ APPLICATION

Adverse Selection and Health Insurance "Death Spirals"

A particularly compelling example of the damage done by adverse selection in health insurance markets comes from a study of Harvard University by Cutler and Reber (1998). Harvard offered its employees a wide variety of health insurance plans, some much more generous than others (e.g., covering more expensive procedures). The prices charged to the university by the insurance companies for these plans were a function of how much each plan's enrollees made use of the medical care paid for by the plan. If a plan had many sick enrollees, for example, then its costs were higher, and the insurance companies would charge the university higher premiums. Such a pricing system is called **experience rating:** charging a price for insurance that is a function of realized outcomes. This is the "ex post" equivalent of actuarial adjustments: while actuarial adjustment charges a price based on _expected_ experience, experience rating charges a price based on _actual_ or _realized_ experience.

Health insurance plan costs were shared by Harvard University and its employees. Traditionally, the university shielded its employees from the fact that some plans were more expensive than others by paying a larger share of the more generous, more expensive health insurance plans and leaving employees with similar costs whichever plan they chose. Thus, from the employees' perspective, there was relatively little penalty for choosing a more expensive, more generous insurance plan. In 1995, however, Harvard moved

experience rating Charging a price for insurance that is a function of realized outcomes.

to a system in which the university paid the same amount for each plan, regardless of the plan's cost, so that employees had to pay more for the more generous and expensive health plans.

Cutler and Reber found that this new system greatly increased the extent of adverse selection across Harvard health insurance plans. Before 1995, many healthy individuals would choose the generous and expensive plan because prices were so similar—there was a *pooling equilibrium,* with both sick and healthy choosing generous (full) insurance. When employees had to pay much more for the generous plan, however, some healthy enrollees chose cheaper plans, and the less healthy employees continued to choose the more generous plans; that is, the insurance group moved to a *separating equilibrium,* with the healthy getting less-generous insurance at cheaper prices, and the less-healthy getting more generous insurance at high prices.

Because these less-healthy employees used much more medical care, however, the experience-rated premiums (which reflect the average medical utilization of enrollees) of the more generous plans increased substantially. Given Harvard's new system (the university picked up a flat amount of costs, regardless of the total cost of the plan), the rising costs of these generous plans were borne completely by plan enrollees, which caused even more healthy employees to leave the generous plans for ones that were more affordable. This led to a spiral of higher premiums, causing the healthy to give up the generous plan, leading to even higher costs for that plan (since the remaining enrollees were sicker on average), which led to even more of the healthy leaving the plan. This spiral continued until, by 1998, the most generous plan had gotten so expensive that it was no longer offered. Adverse selection had led to a "death spiral" for this plan.

This was clearly an inefficient outcome, because individuals who wanted very generous insurance could no longer buy it at *any* price. The insurance market had failed for Harvard employees; a product that was demanded at (or above) its cost of production was no longer available. This case study illustrates how adverse selection can produce market failure. ◄

How Does the Government Address Adverse Selection?

There are many potential government interventions that can address this problem of adverse selection. Suppose that, in the careful/careless pedestrian example, the government mandated that everyone buy full insurance at the average price of $825 per year. This plan would lead to the efficient outcome, with both types of pedestrians having full insurance. This would not be a very attractive plan to careful consumers, however, who could view themselves as essentially being taxed in order to support this market, by paying higher premiums than they should based on their risk. That is, at a premium of $825, many careful consumers would prefer to be uninsured rather than being mandated to buy full insurance, so the government is making them worse off.

Another option is public provision: the government could just provide full insurance to both types of consumers, so that all consumers have the optimal full insurance level. Alternatively, the government could offer everyone subsidies toward the private purchase of full insurance to try to induce (optimal) full coverage. These government interventions would have to be financed, however. If the interventions were financed by charging all consumers equally, then the situation would be the same as that with the mandate: careful consumers would be paying more than they would voluntarily choose to pay for the full insurance (now in the form of tax bills rather than insurance premiums). Thus, the government can address adverse selection, and improve market efficiency, in a number of ways, but they involve redistribution from the healthy to the sick, which may be quite unpopular.

12.3

Other Reasons for Government Intervention in Insurance Markets

Adverse selection is the most common but far from the only reason offered for government intervention in insurance markets. Other rationales include the following.

Externalities

A classic case for government intervention in insurance markets is the negative externalities imposed on others through underinsurance. As discussed in Chapter 1, your lack of insurance can be a cause of illness for me, thereby exerting a negative physical externality. Alternatively, if you don't have auto insurance, and you injure me in an auto crash, then my insurer and I bear the cost of my injury, a negative financial externality. Just as the government intervened to solve externalities in Chapters 5 and 6, it can do so in insurance markets as well by subsidizing, providing, or mandating insurance coverage.

Administrative Costs

The administrative costs for Medicare, the government-run national insurance program for the elderly, are less than 2% of claims paid. Administrative costs for private insurance, on the other hand, average about 12% of claims paid.[9] Why does this matter? Return to the case of perfect information, where the insurance company can appropriately price insurance for the careless and careful consumers. As we noted, the insurance company in this case would charge $150 to the careful consumer and $1,500 to the careless consumer, and at those prices all consumers would fully insure themselves against injury. If the insurance company has administrative expenses of 15% of premiums, however, it would have to charge $172.50 to the careful consumer ($150 × 1.15 = $172.50), and $1,725 to the careless consumer ($1,500 × 1.15 =

---

[9] Woolhandler et al. (2003).

$1,725) in order to break even. At those higher (actuarially unfair) prices, some not-very-risk-averse consumers may decide against buying insurance. In this way, administrative inefficiencies can lead to market failure because not all people will be fully insured, as is optimal.

Redistribution

With full information, the optimal outcome is for the careless consumer to pay ten times as much for his insurance as the careful consumer. This outcome may not be very satisfactory to many societies from a distributional point of view. Governments may want to intervene in insurance markets, perhaps by taxing the low-risk individuals and using the revenues to subsidize the premiums paid by high-risk individuals, thereby achieving a more even distribution of insurance costs.

Interestingly, technologies that make private insurance markets work better are also the ones that worsen the redistribution problem. Genetic testing, for example, may ultimately allow insurers to remove many problems of asymmetric information via the testing of individuals to accurately predict their health costs. Such testing has the implication, however, that those who are genetically ill-fated will pay much higher prices for insurance than those who are genetically healthy. Will modern societies tolerate an insurance market that charges many times more for insurance to individuals who happen to have been born with the wrong genes?

Paternalism

Paternalism is another major motivation for all social insurance programs. Governments may simply feel that individuals will not appropriately insure themselves against risks if the government does not force them to do so. This motivation for intervention has nothing to do with market failures. Instead, it has to do with the failure of individuals to maximize their own utility. Thus, governments may insist on providing social insurance for individuals' own good, even if the individuals would choose not to do so themselves in a well-functioning private insurance market.

▶APPLICATION

Flood Insurance and the Samaritan's Dilemma

Another social insurance rationale goes by the name of the *Samaritan's Dilemma*. Compassionate governments find it difficult to ignore individuals who have suffered adverse events, especially when the events are not the fault of the individual. When a disaster hits, the government will transfer resources to help those affected to get back on their feet. Since individuals know that the government will bail them out if things go badly, they will not take precautions against things going badly (leading to the moral hazard problem we will learn about shortly). As a result, the Good Samaritan government foots the bill for risky behavior.

Insurance against flood damage to homes is an example of the Samaritan's Dilemma. There should be, in principle, a well-functioning market for flood insurance: because insurers know as much if not more than homeowners about the flood risks that each household faces, adverse selection would not be a major concern in this market. Yet, until the late 1960s, few homeowners had flood insurance for their homes, even in the most dangerous, flood-prone areas. Because individuals and businesses knew they would receive federal disaster assistance if they were flooded, there was no reason for them to insure themselves against that eventuality. This government safety net therefore led people to continue to develop residential communities in areas at high risk for flooding and other natural disasters. As noted in Chapter 1, for example, New Orleans had already suffered major hurricane damage in 1965, but was rebuilt with large infusions of government funds shortly thereafter.

To reduce taxpayer-funded federal expenditures on flood control and disaster assistance and to shift some of the burden onto the beneficiaries themselves, the federal government established the National Flood Insurance Program (NFIP) in 1968.[10] Under the NFIP, the Federal Emergency Management Agency (FEMA) maps areas along floodplains across the United States that are known as special flood hazard areas (SFHAs)—areas with a 1% chance of flooding in any given year. Communities located in SFHAs are given the option of buying flood insurance through the program, but only if they adopt and enforce federal floodplain management regulations. If a community agrees to enroll in the NFIP, the responsibility then falls upon individual homeowners and business owners in the community to assess their own risk and to determine whether or not to buy a flood insurance policy. Through an arrangement with the NFIP, the majority of policies are written by major property insurance companies which collect the premiums and return them, minus the fee paid for their involvement in the program, to the National Flood Insurance Fund. The financial responsibilities of NFIP are met using these premium revenues; in emergency situations, however, the NFIP is also allowed to borrow from the Treasury.[11]

Since 1969, FEMA asserts that the NFIP has paid out $11.9 billion in losses that would otherwise have been paid through taxpayer-funded disaster assistance or borne directly by the victims themselves. In addition, they claim that NFIP floodplain management regulations have significantly reduced the frequency and severity of flood-related damages: structures built according to NFIP criteria generally experience 80% less damage and these building restrictions are estimated to save $1 billion per year.[12]

However, the myriad failures of the NFIP following Hurricane Katrina have made it clear that the program has failed to deliver on many of its original goals. In the weeks after the hurricane, it was revealed that nearly half of the victims did not have flood insurance. Moreover, the $25 billion of claims from those who did have flood insurance bankrupted the program, which

---

[10] Drew and Treaster (2006).
[11] FEMA.
[12] FEMA.

brings in a mere $2.2 billion in premiums each year. In the end, the government was forced to commit to $15 billion in additional taxpayer money for rebuilding in Louisiana and Mississippi.[13]

The failures of the NFIP have many sources. First among these is that even within communities who are members of the NFIP, many individuals opt out of paying for insurance.[14] According to Linda Mackey, flood program manager at the Independent Insurance Agents and Brokers Association, "After every catastrophic event, we see more requests to quote flood insurance. Typically, they finally see that they could be at risk and buy coverage only to let it lapse again until the next disaster and they rush to buy it again."[15] This is a classic example of the Samaritan's Dilemma in practice: If the government is going to continue to help individuals in disasters, and people are not required by law to buy flood insurance, then why buy it? Indeed, the federal government continues to repair coastal infrastructure along hurricane-prone areas; 12 counties along the Eastern Seaboard and Gulf Coast that are especially vulnerable to flooding damage from natural disasters are among the top 100 most rapidly developing counties in the nation.[16]

A solution to this problem would be to mandate purchase of flood insurance at actuarially fair prices in areas at risk of flooding. But such an approach runs squarely into strong opposition from developers who want to develop scenic, water-view areas at high risk of flooding (but without the extra costs of flood insurance), and from politicians who represent those areas and who feel that their constituents should not face a higher cost of living. Another problem with mandated purchase of flood insurance is the antiquated and imperfect assignment of risks around the country by the NFIP, which has not updated its flood risk information in more than ten years because it does not have the funding to do so. Premiums are the same in any area with a more than 1% chance of flooding each year, despite widely varying risks. Thus, while residents in Michigan and Louisiana are charged the same premiums, the actual incidence of flooding in Louisiana has been much higher. Residents in Michigan have paid four times more in premiums than they have received in claims over the past ten years. Homeowners in just three states—Florida, Louisiana, and Texas—have received more than half of all claims paid out by the program since 1978. Such inequities between paying and receiving areas have all led to very strong opposition against any expansion of the flood insurance program and in some states, such as Michigan, representatives have even considered urging their states to withdraw from the program entirely. As Representative Candice S. Miller of Michigan said, "You've got people living in dry areas paying for people who want to keep living in wet ones. They're sticking it to us, and I don't like to be stuck."[17]

---

[13] Drew and Treaster (2006).
[14] FEMA.
[15] Pasha (2005).
[16] Singer (2006).
[17] Drew and Treaster (2006).

12.4

Social Insurance vs. Self-Insurance: How Much Consumption Smoothing?

The arguments just presented suggest a number of reasons why private insurance markets may not make it possible for a risk-averse individual to satisfy his or her desire for consumption smoothing. Yet they do not suggest that consumption smoothing is completely unavailable, because individuals may have other private means to smooth consumption: their own savings, the labor supply of family members, borrowing from friends, and so on. The justification for social insurance depends on the extent to which social insurance is necessary, given consumers' use of private forms of consumption smoothing. For ease of exposition, we will call these other forms of consumption smoothing **self-insurance,** although most of these forms are not actually insurance. If people have extensive self-insurance against adverse risk, the benefits of social insurance will be reduced.

self-insurance The private means of smoothing consumption over adverse events, such as through one's own savings, labor supply of family members, or borrowing from friends.

Example: Unemployment Insurance

To better understand how self-insurance might work, let's consider the case of unemployment insurance (UI), which provides income to workers who have lost their jobs. Individuals do not generally have a private form of unemployment insurance upon which they can draw, but they do have other potential means to smooth their consumption (self-insurance) across unemployment spells:

▶ They can draw on their own savings.

▶ They can borrow, either in *collateralized* forms (such as borrowing against the equity they have in their homes) or in *uncollateralized* forms (on their credit card, for example).

▶ Other family members can increase their labor earnings.

▶ They can receive transfers from their extended family, friends, or local organizations, such as churches.

The importance of social insurance programs as a source of consumption smoothing depends on the availability of self-insurance. If there is no self-insurance, then social insurance will provide an important source of consumption smoothing. Once we allow for private forms of consumption smoothing through self-insurance, we have a problem similar to that raised in Chapter 7 in the context of public goods: public intervention (social insurance) can *crowd out* private provision (self-insurance). If social insurance simply crowds out self-insurance, there may be no net consumption-smoothing gain to social insurance. Given that there is an efficiency cost to raising government revenues (see Chapter 20), government insurance market interventions that do not provide consumption-smoothing gains (that simply crowd out private sources of support) are harder to justify.

Illustration We can illustrate this point using the unemployment example. Unemployment insurance benefits replace some share of the worker's lost wage income; that share is called the **UI replacement rate.** The benefits of UI to a worker are determined by the extent to which raising the replacement rate improves the worker's ability to smooth her consumption over a period of unemployment. The effect of the replacement rate on consumption smoothing is determined, in turn, by the availability of other forms of private consumption smoothing (self-insurance) during unemployment spells.

Figure 12-2 on page 334 shows some examples of the possible relationship between the UI replacement rate (the horizontal axis) and the percentage drop in consumption when Ava becomes unemployed (the vertical axis). A larger fall in consumption means less consumption smoothing. Ideally, Ava does not want her consumption to fall at all when she becomes unemployed—she wants her consumption to be the same in states of employment and unemployment. Ava's optimum, then, is a 0% reduction in consumption at unemployment; this outcome represents full consumption smoothing.

Panels (a) to (c) show how the drop in consumption at unemployment depends on the UI replacement rate. Each of these three top panels represents different levels of self-insurance. That is, *within* each panel we consider the relationship between UI and consumption smoothing, and *across* panels we consider how that relationship changes with the level of self-insurance.

Panel (a) shows the scenario in which Ava has no self-insurance—for example, no savings, credit cards, or friends who can loan money to her. With no UI (a zero replacement rate), consumption falls by 100% (point *A*) when Ava becomes unemployed because her earnings are gone and she has no self-insurance or UI to replace them. Thus, her consumption drops to zero. In this example of no self-insurance, each percent of wages replaced by UI benefits reduces the fall in consumption by 1%, as shown by the upward-sloping relationship between the replacement rate and the consumption drop (which has a slope of 1). When UI replaces the full previous income (a UI replacement rate of 100%), consumption doesn't fall at all. (There is a 0% change in consumption at point *B*.) In this case, *UI plays a full consumption-smoothing role: there is no crowd-out of self-insurance* (because there is no self-insurance)*; each dollar of UI goes directly to reducing the decline in consumption from unemployment.*

Skipping to panel (c), we see the other extreme, full self-insurance, as would be the case if a private unemployment insurance product existed and were sold at an actuarially fair price, or if Ava had rich parents who would happily lend her as much money as she needed. We know from the insurance theory explained earlier in the chapter that individuals, in the absence of government intervention, will choose full insurance if it is available. This implies that Ava will choose to fully smooth her consumption when she becomes unemployed, either from private sources if there is no public insurance, or from public insurance if it is available.

In this case, even with a zero replacement rate (no UI), Ava's consumption does not fall at all when she becomes unemployed (point *D*); self-insurance allows her to fully maintain her desired consumption. As the replacement rate

UI replacement rate The ratio of unemployment insurance benefits to pre-unemployment earnings.

■ FIGURE 12-2

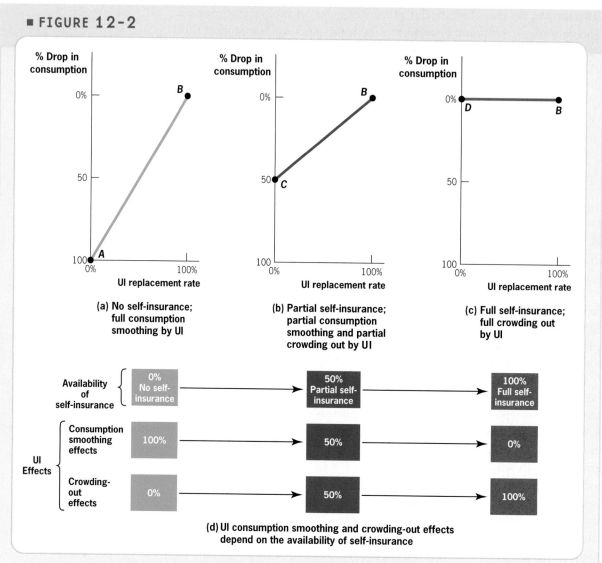

Consumption-Smoothing Benefits of UI • Panels (a) to (c) show the relationship between the UI replacement rate (horizontal axis) and the drop in consumption upon unemployment (vertical axis) for three situations: no self-insurance (panel (a)), partial self-insurance (panel (b)), and full self-insurance (panel (c)). If there is no self-insurance (panel (a)), then each dollar of UI benefits leads to $1 more of consumption smoothing; with partial self-insurance (panel (b)), each dollar of UI benefits leads to 50¢ more of consumption smoothing; with full self-insurance (panel (c)), each dollar of UI benefits simply crowds out a dollar of self-insurance and has no effect on consumption smoothing. Panel (d) shows the extent to which UI smoothes consumption and crowds out self-insurance as a function of the amount of self-insurance available.

increases, there is no change in consumption smoothing, since it is already at its desired level. (At any replacement rate, the change in consumption is always zero.) Rather, the only effect of increases in UI benefits is a reduction in the extent to which Ava purchases private insurance or borrows from her parents.

In this situation, *UI plays no consumption-smoothing role, and plays only a crowd-out role: each dollar of UI simply means that there is one less dollar of self-insurance.*

This example, while hypothetical, is not implausible. My wife's aunt worked for a large Midwestern manufacturing company that closed its operations every summer, but essentially promised to hire its workers back the following fall. During the year she saved for this event out of her earnings, and was pleased to spend her summers as a state champion softball pitcher! As UI generosity increased over time in her state, she simply saved less, maintaining her desired level of consumption smoothing. UI did nothing to help her smooth her consumption; it only reduced (crowded out) the amount of saving she needed to do during the year to ensure constant consumption throughout the year.

Finally, panel (b) presents the middle-ground case where partial, but not complete, self-insurance is available. Suppose, for example, that in the absence of UI (replacement rate of 0%), Ava has sufficient self-insurance so that her consumption falls by only 50% (point *C*). As the UI replacement rate becomes more generous, Ava has less need for her self-insurance, so she reduces that self-insurance by 50¢ for each dollar provided by UI: that is, if UI replaced all lost earnings (UI replacement rate of 100%), Ava would not use self-insurance at all (at point *B*). Relative to the outcome shown in panel (a), UI plays a *partial consumption-smoothing role: it is both smoothing consumption and crowding out the use of self-insurance.* Each dollar of UI leads to 50¢ more consumption smoothing and 50¢ crowd-out of individual savings.

Summary The bottom panel (d) of Figure 12-2 summarizes the lessons from the first three panels. The first line of this panel shows the availability of self-insurance, running from 0% (no self-insurance) on the left to 100% (full self-insurance) on the right. The next two lines show how the effect of UI on both consumption smoothing and crowd-out depends on the extent of self-insurance. If there is no self-insurance, UI plays a 100% consumption-smoothing role: each dollar of UI is translated directly into a dollar of consumption. Likewise, with no self-insurance, UI does no crowding out, since there is nothing to be crowded out by the government program. As self-insurance grows, the amount of consumption smoothing provided by UI falls, because individuals have self-insurance they can rely on instead. Likewise, as self-insurance grows, the amount of crowding out done by UI increases, since the government program is increasingly simply replacing private sources of consumption smoothing. When there is full self-insurance, UI plays a 100% crowding-out role: each dollar of UI crowds out a dollar of self-insurance. In this case, UI has no consumption-smoothing effect.

Thus, *the availability of self-insurance determines the value of social insurance to individuals suffering adverse events.* If self-insurance is very incomplete, then social insurance is as valuable, providing extensive consumption smoothing. If self-insurance is nearly complete, then social insurance is not very valuable, as it simply serves to crowd out that self-insurance.

Social insurance may still be of value, however, even if there is crowd-out, for the reason noted earlier: social insurance may be more efficient than self-insurance. This discussion assumes that self-insurance is efficient, such as buying private insurance at actuarily fair rates, or borrowing from very rich parents. In practice, self-insurance may be inefficient relative to social insurance. My wife's going to work may be a very inefficient means for me to insure against the consumption loss from unemployment, since we have to arrange child care, buy new clothes for her job, etc. Likewise, my saving to smooth consumption over adverse events is inefficient because I will likely save too much (if the adverse event doesn't occur) or too little (if it does). Insurance, by pooling risk across many individuals, allows me to smooth consumption efficiently. Thus, even if social insurance is largely crowding out self-insurance, it may be still of some value, since it is a more efficient means of insuring against adverse events. The main point of this section is that social insurance will be less efficient if there is self-insurance than if there is not.[18]

Lessons for Consumption-Smoothing Role of Social Insurance

While the example we used was specific to unemployment insurance, the lessons are general for all of the social insurance programs we look at in the next few chapters. For example, as we discuss in Chapter 13, an important source of self-insurance for retirement is one's own savings. To what extent does the Social Security program, which provides retirement income, simply crowd out savings that individuals would do on their own for retirement, and to what extent does it provide consumption smoothing across the years between working and retirement? We deal with these specific issues in the next chapter.

In general, the importance of social insurance for consumption smoothing will depend on two factors:

▶ *Predictability of the event:* social insurance plays a smaller consumption-smoothing role for predictable events because individuals can prepare themselves for predictable events through other channels (such as savings). Thus, the benefits of social insurance are highest when events are not predictable.

▶ *Cost of the event:* savings or borrowing are possible channels of consumption smoothing for a few weeks of unemployment, but may be much less feasible for years out of work due to a long-term or permanent disability. Thus, the benefits of social insurance are highest when events are most costly.

Understanding the extent of consumption smoothing provided by any social insurance program is important for evaluating the central trade-off mentioned in the introduction to this chapter. The benefits of social insurance are measured by the amount of consumption smoothing provided by the program. Next, we turn to measuring the costs.

---

[18] See Chetty and Looney (2005) for an excellent discussion of this point in the context of developing countries.

12.5

The Problem with Insurance: Moral Hazard

When we discussed externalities in Chapter 5, the analysis was straightforward: there was a failure in the market and, in principle, the government could achieve efficiency by forcing the relevant actors to internalize the external costs (or benefits) they were imposing. When governments intervene in insurance markets, however, the analysis is one step more complicated because of another asymmetric information problem called **moral hazard,** which is the adverse behavior that is encouraged by insuring against an adverse event. Moral hazard is a central feature of insurance markets: if families buy fire insurance for their homes, they may be less likely to keep fire extinguishers handy; if individuals have health insurance, they may be less likely to take precautions against getting ill; if workers have unemployment insurance, they may be less likely to search hard for a new job. The existence of moral hazard means that it may not be optimal for the government to provide the full insurance that is demanded by risk-averse consumers.

> **moral hazard** Adverse actions taken by individuals or producers in response to insurance against adverse outcomes.

Consider the example of workers' compensation insurance, a $55 billion program that insures workers against injury on the job (discussed in detail in Chapter 14).[19] Clearly, getting injured on the job is a bad thing, and individuals would like to insure against it. There is a big problem with workers' compensation insurance, however: it is difficult to determine whether individuals are really injured, and whether that injury occurred on the job. Many injuries are impossible to precisely diagnose, particularly chronic problems like back pain or mental impairment, and it is hard to tell whether injuries, particularly chronic injuries, have occurred on the job or during a weekend softball game.

The difficulty of assessing injuries is a problem because it can be quite attractive to qualify for the workers' compensation program. Workers' compensation benefits include payment of the medical costs of treating an injury, and cash compensation for lost wages, which can amount to two-thirds or more of a worker's pre-injury wages. Recall that in standard economic models we assume that leisure is a normal good and that, all else equal, individuals would rather be home than at work. If you can claim that you have an on-the-job injury, even if you really don't, you can stay home from work and continue to take home two-thirds of what you earned when working. Thus, the existence of this program may actually encourage individuals to fake injury.

By trying to insure against an adverse event (true injury), the insurer may encourage individuals to pretend that the adverse event has happened to them when it actually hasn't. This scenario is a primary example of moral hazard. Imagine how bad this problem would be if, as in the Social Security systems of some European countries we study in the next chapter, you actually receive as much (or more) money from staying home than you do from working!

---

[19] Social Security Administration (2006b), Table 9.B2.

▶APPLICATION

The Problems with Assessing Workers' Compensation Injuries

Excellent examples of the difficulties in assessing whether a worker is truly injured come from stories of workers who are collecting workers' compensation when they are clearly not injured:[20]

▶ Thirty-five-year old Ricci DeGaetano had been a guard in a Massachusetts prison until he slipped and fell on the job in 1997. He returned to work the next year, but soon after claimed he was injured while fighting with an inmate. He collected $82,500 in workers' compensation claims for the next three years. The problem? DeGaetano, a certified black belt, was operating a karate school the entire time, teaching there almost daily. Pictures of him with his students from this period were even available on the Internet. He was fired by the Department of Correction and charged with two counts of fraud and larceny.

▶ New Orleans police officer David Dotson started getting workers' compensation after an April 2001 claim that he received a shoulder injury while on patrol. His story began to unravel, however, when his supervisors saw him give an emotional television interview upon his return from the 9/11 World Trade Center attacks. They wondered how Dotson's shoulder injury allowed him to work with a bucket brigade at Ground Zero. Further investigation found that Dotson spent his nights moonlighting as a supermarket security guard. He was eventually convicted of collecting $16,532 in fraudulent claims and sentenced to 21 months in prison.

▶ Los Angeles police detective Rocky Sherwood managed a Little League baseball team for 7-to-8-year-olds so successfully that they won the California World Series in June 2001. Two on-the-job traffic accidents in 1998 had given Sherwood what he described as constant pain in his spine and right knee, rendering him unable to work and thus eligible for workers' compensation. Unfortunately for him, the LAPD suspected deception and made a videotape of him coaching his Little League team. According to the investigating officer, the tape showed Sherwood engaged in "strenuous activity," including hitting, pitching, fielding, and demonstrating for the kids how to slide into a base. He was charged with felony workers' compensation fraud. ◀

Moral hazard is an inevitable cost of insurance, private or social. Because of optimizing behavior by individuals and firms, we increase the incidence of adverse events simply by insuring against them. The existence of moral hazard problems therefore creates the *central trade-off of social insurance:* by fixing fail-

---

[20] Rothstein (2002), Perlstein (2004), and http://www.lapdonline.org/ (Article #1236).

ures in private insurance markets, the government can worsen the underlying problem that is being insured against.

What Determines Moral Hazard?

The extent of moral hazard varies with two factors. The first factor is how easy it is to observe whether the adverse event has happened. If an employer truly knows whether a worker has been injured on the job, the moral hazard problem with workers' compensation is greatly diminished. The second factor is how easy it is to change behavior in order to establish the adverse event. When it is neither easy nor attractive to change behavior in order to qualify for insurance, such as in the case for insurance against death, moral hazard is unlikely to be a problem. When the insurance is for an adverse event that is easily and costlessly attained (or faked), however, moral hazard may be a larger problem.

Moral Hazard Is Multidimensional

Moral hazard can arise along many dimensions. In examining the effects of social insurance, four types of moral hazard play a particularly important role:

▶ *Reduced precaution against entering the adverse state.* Examples: because you have medical insurance that covers illness, you reduce preventive activities to protect your health, or because you have workers' compensation insurance, you aren't as careful at work.

▶ *Increased odds of entering the adverse state.* Examples: because you have workers' compensation, you are more likely to claim that you were injured on the job, or because you have unemployment insurance, you are more likely to become unemployed.

▶ *Increased expenditures when in the adverse state.* Examples: because you have medical insurance, you use more medical care than you otherwise would, or because you have workers' compensation, you don't work hard to rehabilitate your injury.

▶ *Supplier responses to insurance against the adverse state.* Examples: because you have medical insurance, physicians provide too much care to you, or because you have workers' compensation, firms aren't as careful about protecting you against workplace accidents.

In the next few chapters, we often will not draw a strong distinction between these different types of moral hazard, but it is important to recognize the alternative dimensions along which it can exist.

The Consequences of Moral Hazard

Why is moral hazard a problem? Even if social insurance encourages individuals to, for example, spend more time at home pretending to be injured than being at work, why is that an important cost of social insurance?

Moral hazard is costly for two reasons. First, the adverse behavior encouraged by insurance lowers social efficiency, for example, because it reduces the provisions of socially efficient labor supply. In a perfectly competitive labor market, a worker's wage equals his marginal product, the value of the goods he is producing for society. With no workers' compensation, workers will supply labor until their wage (their marginal product) equals their marginal valuation of the next hour of leisure time (such as their value of watching TV). If the wage is above the value of leisure time, it is socially efficient for individuals to work, since the benefit of work (the marginal product of that labor) exceeds the cost (the value of the foregone TV).

When workers' compensation is introduced, the value of leisure rises: each hour of leisure not only provides one hour of TV, but also a workers' compensation payment. Thus, individuals will supply labor only until the wage equals their marginal value of leisure *plus* the workers' compensation income they can receive by pretending to be injured. This will lead individuals to work less than is socially efficient: even if the wage (and therefore the marginal product) is above the value of watching TV, individuals may still choose not to work because of the promise of workers' compensation benefits.

This moral hazard cost arises in any insurance context, such as health insurance. In the case of health insurance, individuals should use medical care only until the point where the marginal benefit to them (in terms of improved health) equals the marginal cost of the service. If individuals are completely insured, however, and don't pay any costs for their medical care, they will use that medical care until the marginal benefit to them is zero (their marginal cost, which is zero with full insurance). This will lead to an inefficiently high level of medical care if the true marginal cost is greater than zero.

The second cost for social insurance due to moral hazard is revenue raising. Whenever the government increases its expenditures, it must raise taxes to compensate (at least in the long run). As we discuss at length in the tax chapters, there are efficiency costs associated with government taxation through the negative impacts it has on work effort, savings, and other behaviors. Thus, when social insurance encourages adverse events, which raise the cost of the social insurance program, it increases taxes and lowers social efficiency further.

12.6

Putting It All Together: Optimal Social Insurance

There are four basic lessons from the discussion in this chapter. First, individuals value insurance because they would ideally like to smooth their consumption across states of the world. That is, they would like to have the same consumption whether or not an adverse event such as unemployment or injury befalls them. Second, there are a number of reasons why the market may fail to provide such insurance, most notably adverse selection. Third, even if the market fails to provide such insurance, the justification for social insurance depends on whether other private consumption-smoothing mechanisms are available. The key question is the extent to which the social insurance provides new consumption smoothing versus just crowding out existing self-insurance. Fourth, expanding insurance coverage has a moral hazard cost in terms of encouraging adverse behavior.

These lessons have a clear policy implication: *optimal social insurance systems should partially, but not completely, insure individuals against adverse events.* As with all government policies in this book, the appropriate role for the government in providing social insurance reflects the trade-off between the benefits and costs of such intervention. The *benefit of social insurance is the amount of consumption smoothing provided by social insurance programs.* If individuals become injured on the job and the government smoothes their consumption by insuring that injury, social efficiency rises because a market failure has been fixed. If, on the other hand, people are fully self-insured and the government provides no consumption smoothing with social insurance, there is less benefit to the intervention (although perhaps some benefit if self-insurance was itself inefficient).

The *cost of social insurance is the moral hazard caused by insuring against adverse events.* If individuals join a workers' compensation program even when they are not in fact injured, social efficiency falls for two reasons. First, these individuals are not employed, so social product is smaller than is efficient. Second, the government must raise more tax revenues to pay for their workers' compensation benefits, and higher taxes also lower social efficiency.

Thus, higher social insurance improves social efficiency by fixing a market failure but reduces social efficiency by reducing production and raising taxes. As with most trade-offs in economics, the resolution of this full insurance–adverse behavior trade-off will generally be somewhere in the middle, optimally providing some insurance against adverse events, but not full insurance.

12.7
Conclusion

Asymmetric information in insurance markets has two important implications. First, it can cause *adverse selection,* which makes it difficult for insurance markets to provide actuarially fair insurance to those who would demand it if it were available to them. Second, it can cause *moral hazard,* whereby the provision of insurance encourages adverse behavior in those purchasing the insurance. The ironic feature of asymmetric information is therefore that it simultaneously motivates *and* undercuts the rationale for government intervention through social insurance.

In the remainder of this section of the book, we will investigate the role of the government in insuring several major life events: unemployment, on-the-job injury, career-ending disability, retirement, and illness. In each case, we see that there is a trade-off between the benefits of completing imperfect insurance markets and the costs of encouraging adverse behavior. The extent of this trade-off will vary with the nature of the adverse events being insured. The purpose of these chapters will be to assess how the extensive literature on these social programs can inform policy makers of appropriate reforms to the programs.

▶ **HIGHLIGHTS**

■ The largest and fastest-growing function of the government is the provision of social insurance against adverse events such as retirement, unemployment, injury, or illness. Social insurance programs are mandatory, contribution-based systems that tie the payout of benefits to the occurrence of a measurable event.

■ Insurance is demanded because it allows individuals to smooth their consumption across various states of the world; with actuarially fair premiums, the optimal outcome is for individuals to fully insure themselves against adverse events.

■ The major motivation for government-provided social insurance is the failure in private insurance markets caused by adverse selection. Adverse selection causes insurance markets to fail because imperfect information leads insurers to be unable to offer full insurance to different types of consumers.

■ Other motivations for social insurance include externalities, administrative inefficiencies in the private insurance market, the desire for redistribution, and paternalism.

■ The consumption-smoothing benefits of social insurance are determined by the ability of individuals to use other forms of self-insurance to smooth their consumption.

■ Moral hazard is an offsetting cost to the benefits of social insurance. By insuring individuals against adverse events, we may increase the incidence of these events among the insured.

■ Full insurance is unlikely to be optimal: the optimal social insurance benefit level trades off moral hazard costs against consumption-smoothing benefits.

▶ **QUESTIONS AND PROBLEMS**

1. A number of Web sites, such as www .quickquote.com, offer instant quotes for term life insurance. Use one such Web site to compare the prices of $1 million 5-year term life policies for 50 year old men and women. Explain the difference in quotes for the man and the woman. Suppose the U.S. government were to pass a law requiring insurers to offer the same prices for men and women. What effect would you expect this to have on prices and insurance coverage?

2. What is consumption smoothing? How does insurance help people smooth consumption?

3. Suppose that you have a job paying $50,000 per year. With a 5% probability, next year your wage will be reduced to $20,000 for the year.

   a. What is your expected income next year?
   b. Suppose that you could insure yourself against the risk of reduced consumption next year. What would the actuarially fair insurance premium be?

4. Small companies typically find it more expensive, on a per employee basis, to buy health insurance for their workers, as compared with larger companies. Similarly, it is usually less expensive to obtain

health insurance through an employer-provided plan than purchasing it directly from an insurance company—even if your employer requires you to pay the entire premium. Use the ideas from this chapter to explain these observations.

5. The problem of adverse selection in insurance markets means that it is generally a bad deal for companies to offer insurance at the same price for all potential customers. Why then do we observe some insurance companies (such as those selling "trip insurance" that refunds money to people who purchase trips that they are unable to take) do exactly this?

6. Why might government provision of insurance lead to a larger number of insurance claims than private provision of insurance would?

7. Why does the government mandate individuals to purchase their own insurance in some cases—such as automobile liability insurance—but directly provide insurance to people in other situations—such as health insurance?

8. Your professor is paid only nine months out of the year (really!!). Suppose that she were fired each spring and rehired each fall, and thereby be

eligible for unemployment insurance benefits. (After all, all those students going away for the summer creates economic hardship for your university!) Do you think that would affect her consumption smoothing over the year, relative to what she does right now, when she is not fired annually? Explain your answer.

9. Currently, in order to receive workers' compensation, a claimant's injury claims must be verified by a physician of the claimant's choosing. Suppose that the workers' compensation policy changed so that only government-assigned physicians could verify injury claims. What is likely to happen to the rate of reported on-the-job injury? Explain.

10. Describe the dimensions along which moral hazard can exist. Can you think of ways in which the government can reduce the prevalence of moral hazard along each dimension?

▶ ADVANCED QUESTIONS

11. Suppose you think that poorly educated families are less able to smooth consumption in the absence of unemployment insurance than are well-educated families. How would you empirically test this supposition? What types of data would you want to use?

12. There are two types of drivers on the road today. Speed Racers have a 5% chance of causing an accident per year, while Low Riders have a 1% chance of causing an accident per year. There are the same number of Speed Racers as there are Low Riders. The cost of an accident is $12,000.

    a. Suppose an insurance company knows with certainty each driver's type. What premium would the insurance company charge each type of driver?

    b. Now suppose that there is asymmetric information so that the insurance company does not know with certainty each driver's type. Would insurance be sold if:
       i. Drivers self-reported their types to the insurance company?
       ii. No information at all is known about individual driver's types?

    If you are uncertain whether insurance would be sold, explain why.

13. Your utility function is $U = \log(2C)$ where C is the amount of consumption you have in any given period. Your income is $40,000 per year and there is a 2% chance that you will be involved in a catastrophic accident that will cost you $30,000 next year.

    a. What is your expected utility?
    b. Calculate an actuarially fair insurance premium. What would your expected utility be were you to purchase the actuarially fair insurance premium?
    c. What is the most that you would be willing to pay for insurance, given your utility function?

14. Billy Joe has utility of $U = \log(C)$, while Bobby Sue has utility of $U = \sqrt{C}$. Which person is more risk averse? Which person would pay the higher insurance premium to smooth consumption?

15. Chimnesia has two equal-sized groups of people: smokers and nonsmokers. Both types of people have utility $U = \ln(C)$, where C is the amount of consumption that people have in any period. So long as they are healthy, individuals will consume their entire income of $15,000. If they need medical attention (and have no insurance), they will have to spend $10,000 to get healthy again, leaving them with only $5,000 to consume. Smokers have a 12% chance of requiring major medical attention, while nonsmokers have a 2% chance.

    Insurance companies in Chimnesia can sell two types of policies. The "low deductible" (L-) policy covers all medical costs above $3,000, while the "high deductible" (H-) policy only covers medical costs above $8,000.

    a. What is the actuarially fair premium for each type of policy and for each group?
    b. If insurance companies can tell who is a smoker and who is a nonsmoker and charge the actuarially fair premiums for each policy and

group, show that both groups will purchase the L-policy.

Suppose that smoking status represents *asymmetric information*: each individual knows whether or not they are a smoker, but the insurance company does not.

c. Explain why it is impossible, at any price, for both groups to purchase L-policies in this setting. Which groups, if any, do you expect to buy L-policies, and at what price?

d. Show that it *is* possible for both group to purchase insurance, with one group buying L-policies and one group buying H-policies.

16. The country of Adventureland's two citizens, Bill and Ted, both earn $1,000 per week working the same job at the same company. Bill and Ted each face some risk of being laid off due to bad market conditions next year, in which case they will have an income of only $250 from an alternative part-time job they would fall back on. There is a 10% probability that Bill we be laid off, and a 30% probability that Ted will be laid off. Bill and Ted have the same utility function $U = \ln(C)$.

The government is considering providing some social unemployment insurance. In particular, they are considering two plans: The first would pay any worker who loses his job $100, and the second would pay any worker who loses his job $600. Both would be financed by collecting a tax from any worker who *keeps* his job.

a. Under each plan, how high would the government have to set the tax so that it would not expect to lose money on the plan?

b. Assuming it sets the tax rate you found in part a, compute the well-being of Bill and Ted under each of the plans. How do Bill and Ted rank the three possibilities (the two policies and the *status quo*)? Explain the pattern you see in terms of *redistribution* and *risk aversion*.

c. Which plan is best if the society has a utilitarian social welfare function? A Rawlsian social welfare function? (See Chapter 3 if you need a reminder about social welfare functions!)

The ℮ icon indicates a question that requires students to apply the empirical economics principles discussed in Chapter 3 and the Empirical Evidence boxes.

Appendix to Chapter 12

Mathematical Models of Expected Utility

This appendix presents the mathematical model of expected utility that underlies the discussion in Chapter 12. This model illustrates the consequences of adverse selection in insurance markets.

Expected Utility Model

The model is described by the following parameters:

- ▶ You are hit by the car with some probability p.
- ▶ Your income is W, regardless of whether you get hit or not.
- ▶ But, if you get hit, you incur medical costs δ.
- ▶ You can buy insurance, with premium m per dollar of insurance.
- ▶ That insurance will pay you $\$b$ if you are hit by the car.

In this case, we can write your expected utility (EU) as:

$$EU = (1 - p) \times U(W - mb) + p \times U(W - \delta - mb + b)$$

The problem with this expression is that we have one equation, with two unknowns (m and b). To solve this equation, we need to add one more condition: that insurance is priced in an actuarially fair manner, so that insurance companies make zero expected profits (we assume, for now, zero administrative costs). In that case, the zero expected profit ($E\pi$) condition for the insurer is:

$$E\pi = m \times b - p \times b = 0$$

The expected profit of the insurer, which equals premiums received minus expected benefits paid out, equals zero. This, in turn, implies that the premium equals:

$$m = p$$

That is, if the risk is 10%, then $m = 10¢$ per dollar of insurance. We can now go back and maximize expected utility, by plugging in b from this equation. As in the example in the text, we assume that utility is of the form $U = \sqrt{C}$. So:

$$\text{Maximize} \quad EU = (1 - p) \times \sqrt{(W - b \times p)} + p \times \sqrt{(W - \delta - bp + b)}$$

Maximizing this equation with respect to b, we obtain:

$$-(1 - p) \times p / \sqrt{(W - bp)} + p \times (1 - p) / \sqrt{(W - \delta - bp + b)}$$

Setting this equal to zero and solving for the optimal level of insurance benefits ($b\star$), we get: $b\star = \delta$. That is, individuals should buy enough insurance so that if they have the adverse outcome, their benefits exactly offset their costs: individuals should buy *full insurance* to smooth their consumption across states. Another way to see this is to plug the optimal benefit level ($b\star = \delta$) back into the utility function:

$$EU = \sqrt{(W - p\delta)} + \sqrt{(W - \delta - p\delta + \delta)}$$
$$= \sqrt{(W - p\delta)} + \sqrt{(W - p\delta)}$$

That is, we obtain the result that *consumption is equalized* (at $W - p\delta$) *in both states of the world*. This result motivates the key conclusion of Chapter 12: facing actuarially fair insurance markets, individuals will want to fully insure themselves against risk.

Adverse Selection

To understand more formally the implications of adverse selection, we now consider two groups, the careful and the careless, where the probability of accident for the careful is p_c, and the probability of accident for the careless is $p_a > p_c$.

As discussed in this chapter, if there is full information, then the insurance company charges prices such that $m_a = b \times p_a$ for the careless, and $m_c = b \times p_c$ for the careful. The former premium is higher, since $p_a > p_c$; those who are more likely to have an accident have to pay more for insurance.

But if there isn't full information, so that insurance companies know only the proportions of types in the population, then there are two possible pricing strategies. One is to assume that individuals are honest and charge them according to their reported types. As discussed in the chapter, however, this strategy will lead all individuals to claim that they are careful. In this world, the profits earned on the careful are: $E\pi = m_c - b \times p_c = b \times p_c - b \times p_c = 0$; that is, the insurance company breaks even on the share of the population that is careful. However, the profits earned on the careless are $E\pi = m_c - b \times p_a = b \times p_c - b \times p_a < 0$, since $p_a > p_c$ profits are negative overall and insurance is not offered.

The other strategy considered in this chapter was to offer insurance at an average price, m_v, that is based on the average of the accident probabilities $p_a > p_v > p_c$. At this price, insurance is a good deal for the careless but a bad deal for the careful, and may only be bought by the careless. In that case, the expected profits of the insurer are again negative:

$$E\pi = m_v - b \times p_a = b \times p_v - b \times p_a < 0, \text{ since } p_a > p_v.$$

It is possible, however, that the careful would still buy full insurance (the pooling equilibrium). They would, for example, buy insurance if expected utility with insurance (at the unfair price) is still higher than expected utility without insurance, that is, if:

$$EU \text{ (with insurance)} = (1 - p_c) \times U(W - p_v\delta) + p_c \times U(W - p_v\delta) >$$

$$EU \text{ (no insurance)} = (1 - p_c) \times U(W) + p_c \times U(W - \delta)$$

Whether this inequality holds or not will depend on two things: the extent of risk aversion of the careful individuals and the relationship between p_c and p_a. If the careful individuals are more risk averse, they will be more willing to buy insurance (even at an unfair premium) to guard against the odds of being left with low consumption. And the closer the average risk is to the risk faced by the careful, the closer the premium is to being actuarially fair, and the more likely it is that the careful individuals will buy the insurance.

Social Security

13

Social Security A federal program that taxes workers to provide income support to the elderly.

In October 2000, near the end of a televised debate, presidential candidates Al Gore and George W. Bush started to argue over how to save the federal government's **Social Security** program, which taxes workers to provide income support to the elderly. Over the next several decades, the aging of the huge "baby boom" cohort that was born in the United States in the wake of World War II will lead to a large rise in the number of elderly relative to the number of workers. Because there will be more elderly to be supported by fewer workers, the Social Security program faces a stark financing problem: over the next 75 years, the program has promised *$4.6 trillion* more in benefit payments than it plans to collect in taxes from workers.[1]

Candidate Bush proposed to address this problem by changing the existing transfer system to one in which workers save for their own retirement. Bush proposed to viewers that his administration would "take a trillion dollars of your own money and let you invest it under safe guidelines to get a better rate of return on the money than the paltry 2% that the federal government gets for you today. . . . Workers should have their own assets. It's who you trust, the government or people."

Gore objected, saying that "[Bush] has promised a trillion dollars out of the Social Security trust fund for young working adults to invest and save on their own, but he's also promised seniors that their Social Security benefits will not be cut." Gore argued that there were not enough government revenues to accomplish both goals, and that the funds Bush would be giving back to workers are "also used to give your mothers and fathers the Social Security checks that they live on."[2]

Since that debate more than six years ago, little progress has been made on Social Security reform. A presidential commission, formed to examine the system, issued a report with a number of recommendations, but no politician

---

[1] Social Security Trustees (2006).
[2] *New York Times* (2000).

348

has been willing to pursue any of the options seriously. Reforming Social Security is difficult because the program is the largest single source of income for the elderly population in the United States: 60% of beneficiaries derive more than half their income from Social Security, and for almost 30%, it provides more than 90% of income.[3] Any reform that is perceived as reducing the generosity of this program is therefore subject to withering political attack.

Politicians are wary of making changes to Social Security, not only because it is the single largest government expenditure today, but also because it is the nation's largest social insurance program. By making payroll tax payments to the Social Security program, workers purchase insurance against earnings loss when they die or retire. Thus, the tools we used in the last chapter to analyze the benefits and costs of social insurance programs help us evaluate the role that Social Security should play in the United States.

This chapter begins with a review of the institutional features of Social Security, then turns to a discussion of why the government would want to intervene to provide income security to the elderly. Following on our

"Forget about me—save Social Security."

discussion in the last chapter, we then discuss the ability of individuals to self-insure through savings against income loss in retirement, and the extent to which Social Security crowds out that self-insurance. We then examine the cost of providing such income security, and the possibility that it might encourage adverse behavior in terms of early retirement, and review the theory of and evidence for this moral hazard. Finally, we look at possible reforms for Social Security, including options that propose changes to the existing program and options that change the nature of the program itself.

13.1

What Is Social Security and How Does It Work?

In this section, we discuss the basic structure of Social Security.[4] This program began in 1935, at the height of the Great Depression, during which asset values had plunged, wiping out the lifetime savings of many elderly. One

---

[3] American Institute of Certified Public Accountants (2005).

[4] As with all of the social insurance and welfare programs that we will discuss in Chapters 12–17, this chapter presents the minimal institutional details necessary to understand the economics of the program. For much more detail on all of these programs, there are two excellent sources. The "Green Book," compiled by the Committee on Ways and Means of the U.S. House of Representatives, is available at http://waysandmeans.house.gov/Documents.asp?section=813 and has incredible detail on program structure. Robert Moffitt's (2003) edited volume *Means-Tested Transfer Programs in the United States* has details on some of these programs, along with a rich review of the economics literature. For up-to-date information on the Social Security program, see http://www.ssa.gov.

major motivation for the establishment of Social Security was to provide a means of income support for this unfortunate generation of the elderly.

The basic operation of the program is straightforward. Workers pay a tax on their earnings, and the money from this tax is deposited into a trust fund that is invested in government bonds. Checks written on this trust fund are paid to those who enroll in the Social Security program, which is open to most people over age 62. Checks are paid until the recipient dies, and, if there is a surviving spouse, he or she receives a payment until his or her own death.

Program Details

There are a variety of details on how the Social Security program operates in practice. Descriptions of some of the most important details follow. Note that all numbers and eligibility requirements described in this section reflect the Social Security program in place in 2006.

How Is Social Security Financed? Almost all workers in the United States pay the Federal Insurance Contributions Act (FICA) tax on their earnings. This tax is currently 6.2%. In addition, their employers (or the workers themselves, if they are self-employed) pay a 6.2% tax on these same earnings, for a total tax burden of 12.4%. This tax is levied only on the first $94,200 of earnings.[5]

Who Is Eligible to Receive Social Security? To be eligible to collect Social Security benefits, a person must have worked and paid this payroll tax for 40 quarters over their lifetime (the equivalent of 10 years), and must be age 62 or older.

How Are Social Security Benefits Calculated? When eligible, the Social Security claimant receives an **annuity payment,** a payment that lasts until the recipient's death. The amount of this annuity payment is a function of the recipient's average lifetime earnings, where each month's earnings are expressed in today's dollars by inflating their value for increases in the wage level since the earnings occurred. In particular, the government averages a person's earnings over the person's 35 highest earning years. If a person has worked for fewer than 35 years, say for 30 years, the formula just treats those missing years as years of zero earnings, so the benefit would be based on averaging 30 years of earnings and five years of zeros. If a person has worked for more than 35 years, the lowest earnings years are thrown out when computing the average. This 35-year average of real monthly earnings is called the *Average Indexed Monthly Earnings*, or *AIME*.

> **annuity payment** A payment that lasts until the recipient's death.

▶**APPLICATION**

Why Choose 35 Years?

The choice of a 35-year averaging period by Social Security reflects the trade-off of two considerations. First, individuals should not be penalized for years of part-time work or particularly low earnings. If you graduate and earn

---

[5] Social Security Administration (2006).

a large salary for 35 years, you should not have your benefits reduced because you worked at McDonald's when you were in high school.

Second, if the averaging period is too short, it can have perverse incentives for behavior by older workers. A classic example of such behavior is the case of a 61-year-old subway driver for the Boston MBTA who fell asleep at the wheel, causing a crash in which 18 people were injured.[6] An investigation revealed that this driver had been working 25 hours straight in an effort to maximize his overtime pay. This was partly because the pension that the driver would be able to claim was a function of his earnings during his last 5 years of work. As the chairman of the MBTA stated in the wake of this accident: "Unfortunately, a system has developed which provides a double incentive; overtime income now, more pension income in the future. . . . Neither the seniority system nor the pension system was originally designed to tempt a man to work himself to exhaustion for retirement income which shortens his life expectancy and jeopardizes public safety." In the wake of this accident, the MBTA changed its pension plan to no longer reward such excessive work at the end of one's career.

A similar problem has arisen in Brazil, whose pension scheme for civil servants is among the most generous in the world and is exerting enormous financial pressure on the country. This is due in part to the fact that pension benefits are determined as 100% of a worker's last month's salary. The World Bank has found that therefore "it was not uncommon for public-sector workers to receive ample promotions in the months just before they retire." ◄

Benefits are then calculated as a *redistributive function of past earnings,* whereby low earnings are more strongly translated to higher benefits than are high earnings. This point is illustrated in Figure 13-1 (page 352), which shows the formula for translating the AIME into the monthly benefit, also known as the *Primary Insurance Amount (PIA).* Workers who have an AIME of less than $612 per month receive $0.90 in benefits for every dollar of AIME. For $656 to $3,955 of AIME, workers receive only $0.32 in benefits for every dollar of AIME. Between an AIME of $3,955 and $6,316, they receive only an additional $0.15 in benefits for each dollar in AIME. Beyond an AIME of $6,316, there are no additional benefits, because this corresponds to the earnings level beyond which the worker no longer pays the payroll tax. The result of these two criteria is that (a) workers who earn more get higher benefits, but (b) benefits do not rise nearly as fast as earnings. This is what is meant by a *redistributive function of past earnings:* past earnings are translated to increased benefits at a slower rate as earnings rise.

A key measure of social insurance program generosity is the **replacement rate,** which is the ratio of benefits received to earnings prior to the entitling event. For Social Security, the replacement rate represents the ratio of benefits to preretirement earnings, because retirement is the event that entitles one to receive benefits. For the average person on Social Security, benefits are roughly

replacement rate The ratio of benefits received to earnings prior to the entitling event.

---

[6] Radin (1980).

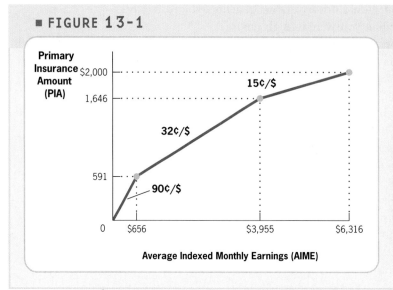

■ FIGURE 13-1

Translating Earnings into Social Security Benefits • Social Security's Primary Insurance Amount (PIA) is a redistributive function of Average Indexed Monthly Earnings (AIME). Figures in bold show the benefits increment per dollar of AIME in that range of AIME. For example, if your AIME is between $3,955 and $6,316, you receive $0.15 in additional benefits for each additional dollar of AIME.

40% of preretirement earnings.[7] For the typical low-income worker, this replacement rate is closer to 60%, while for high-income earners, the replacement rate is only 20% on average, because a smaller share of high earnings is translated to benefits (Figure 13-1). Once individuals retire and receive a benefit, that benefit is adjusted upward for inflation each year by the Consumer Price Index (CPI) to protect the elderly against rising prices.

How Are Social Security Benefits Paid Out? Individuals can receive their PIA starting at age 65, which is the **Full Benefits Age (FBA).** As a result of 1983 legislation (discussed in more detail later in this chapter), the FBA is currently slated to rise to age 67 for those born in 1960 or later.[8]

It is possible to receive benefits as early as age 62, the **Early Entitlement Age (EEA).** For each year of benefits claimed before age 65, however, there is an *actuarial reduction* in benefits of 6.67% per year so that individuals who claim their benefits at age 62 receive 20% less in benefits than those who claim their benefits at age 65. This is called an "actuarial" reduction because it is designed to compensate for the fact that individuals who take benefits early receive them for more years. That is, if you and I are the same age, and I claim benefits at age 62 and you claim them at age 65, and we both live to age 75, then I get three more years of benefits than you do. The reduction in benefits that I receive each year is designed to compensate for the fact that I get three additional years of benefits. With the actuarial adjustment, we can both expect to get the same total amount of benefits in our retirement years. Similarly, if you decide to wait past age 65 to claim benefits, you receive a delayed retire-

Full Benefits Age (FBA) The age at which a Social Security recipient receives full retirement benefits (Primary Insurance Amount).

Early Entitlement Age (EEA) The earliest age at which a Social Security recipient can receive reduced benefits.

---

[7] Social Security Administration (2004).

[8] Traditionally, this age was called the Normal Retirement Age, but this is a misnomer since 80% of workers today have retired by this age. What is critical about age 65 (eventually 67) is that this is the age at which a worker becomes entitled to their full PIA.

ment credit (DRC), which raises your benefits for each year of delay by 6% (rising to 8% by 2008).

Can You Work and Receive Social Security? Another key feature of Social Security is the *earnings test,* which reduces the benefits of 62 to 64-year olds by $0.50 for each dollar of earnings they have above $12,480.[9] This reduction is popularly viewed as a tax on benefits for the elderly with earnings. In fact, this is not true: these benefits are not lost to the worker, but are returned later (with interest, in the form of an actuarial adjustment) when the worker's earnings fall below this threshold. Thus, the earnings test is actually not a tax but a "forced savings" mechanism that takes benefits from workers when they have high earnings and returns these benefits when the workers are truly retired. Because this program is so misunderstood by the public, many people believe that the program causes the elderly to reduce their earnings, or even retire altogether, rather than subject themselves to this "tax."[10]

Are There Benefits for Family Members? Social Security claimants aren't the only ones who derive benefits from this program. Spouses of claimants also receive benefits equal to the higher of their own benefit (based on their earnings) and half of the benefit of their spouse (the spousal benefit). So spouses who have low earnings (or who didn't work the 40 quarters required to qualify for Social Security) can benefit by receiving half of their spouse's benefit level. Children of deceased workers are also entitled to a share of benefits as well, but the total family benefit level cannot exceed 185% of the worker's benefit amount.

In addition, surviving spouses are entitled to Social Security benefits. Spouses who survive a Social Security recipient receive whichever is higher: their own benefit or the deceased's benefit.

> **Quick Hint** That was a lot of acronyms! To review:
> ▶ AIME is Average Indexed Monthly Earnings, a measure of lifetime average earnings
> ▶ PIA is the Primary Insurance Amount, which determines benefit levels
> ▶ FBA is the Full Benefits Age (currently age 65, rising to 67) at which one can claim benefits and get one's PIA
> ▶ EEA is the Early Entitlement Age (currently age 62), the earliest age at which one can claim benefits
> ▶ DRC is the Delayed Retirement Credit amount (currently 6%, rising to 8%) by which the PIA is increased if one delays retirement beyond the FBA (if one starts receiving benefits at the EEA, there is a corresponding downward actuarial adjustment in the PIA)

---

[9] Social Security Trustees (2006), Table V.C1.

[10] In fact, there is no evidence that there is a large effect of the earnings test on the labor supply of the elderly; see Gruber and Orszag (2003) for updated estimates and a literature review. Until 2000, there was also an earnings test that applied to those over age 65, but that has since been removed, so that now workers over 65 can both claim benefits and earn as much as they like.

funded Refers to retirement plans in which today's savings are invested in various assets in order to pay future benefits.

unfunded Refers to retirement plans in which payments collected from today's workers go directly to today's retirees, instead of being invested in order to pay future benefits.

How Does Social Security Work Over Time?

The best way to think about the operation of Social Security is to contrast it to a private pension plan. Private pension plans are **funded** plans: savings today are invested in assets such as government bonds, corporate bonds, or stocks, and the accumulated assets pay for (fund) the future benefits promised by the pension. Social Security, on the other hand, has traditionally been an **unfunded** plan: taxes collected from a worker today go directly to today's retirees, rather than being saved to pay for benefits when the taxed worker retires (this is often referred to as a "Pay-As-You-Go" system).

There is no guarantee, however, that the system will actually work this way. What if the Social Security program goes bankrupt, or if workers in 40 years refuse to pay their taxes to fund retirees' benefits? If this were to occur, retirees would be out of luck: they would have paid into the program but would be getting nothing back from it. In contrast, with a funded plan that is based on accumulated assets, retirees would be assured that there are assets that can be sold to finance their retirement income.

In other words, the promises of a funded private pension plan are backed by the actual assets held by that plan. The promises of Social Security are backed by the policies of the government. It seems highly unlikely that the government would break those promises. Yet, as we noted in Chapter 4, the United States (and other nations) face a very large long-term fiscal imbalance that will have to be met somehow, and lower Social Security benefits are one way to meet that imbalance. It is perhaps for this reason that, when polled, nearly three-quarters of young people (18–34) believe that Social Security will not provide them with significant income by the time they retire.[11]

As some of you may know, Social Security today is not an unfunded system, but rather a partially funded system. The taxes collected from today's workers finance not only the benefits to today's retirees but also a Social Security trust fund that is invested in U.S. government bonds. As we discuss later in the chapter, that trust fund is a temporary solution to the financing problems that face the Social Security system over the next half century. Yet, by 2042, this trust fund is projected to run out of money, so Social Security will return to a purely unfunded system.

How Social Security Redistributes Income The unfunded nature of Social Security has important implications for the redistribution of income across generations, as the following example illustrates. Consider the simplified world illustrated in Table 13-1, in which people live for two periods. In the first period, when they are young, they work and pay a tax to support the Social Security program. In the second period, when they are old, they retire and live on their Social Security benefits. In each period, the number of young people grows by 5% (population growth), and their wages go up by 5% (due to productivity increases).

---

[11] See the 1999 poll "Young Americans and Social Security," commissioned by The 2030 Center from Peter Hart Research Associates, located at http://www.2030.org/pdf/report1.pdf.

■ TABLE 13-1

Social Security in a Two-Period World

Period	Number of Young Workers	Earnings Per Young Worker	Taxes Paid Per Young Worker	Total Taxes Paid	Number of Old Retirees	Benefits to Old Retirees	Taxes Paid by Old Retirees	Rate of Return
1	100	$20,000	0	0	0	0	—	—
2	105	$21,000	$2,100	$220,500	100	$2,205	0	Infinite
3	110	$22,050	$2,205	$242,550	105	$2,310	$2,100	10%
4	115	$23,153	$2,315	$266,225	110	$2,420	$2,205	10%
5	121	$24,310	0	0	115	0	$2,315	Negatively infinite

In period 1, 100 young people work, and there is no Social Security program. Each young person earns $20,000 per period.

In period 2, the 100 initial young people are now retirees, and an unfunded Social Security program has been established that is financed by a 10% payroll tax; the taxes are collected from workers today and are paid immediately to today's retirees.

There are 105 young workers in period 2, each of whom earns $21,000 and pays a 10% payroll tax of $2,100. The tax collection of $220,500 (105 × 2100) is then spent on the 100 older people in that period, for a benefit of $2,205 per retiree. Because these older people paid no taxes when they were young, their rate of return is infinite: they get a benefit without having paid anything in. Thus, the *initial generation is the big winner from an unfunded Social Security system:* they receive retirement benefits even though they contributed relatively little during their working lives. As previously noted, this was the explicit goal of the U.S. Social Security system when it was established in 1935.

In this two-period model, workers in period 1 pay no taxes when young, but do receive benefits when old in period 2. In period 2, young workers pay $2,100 in taxes each, so each retiree receives $2,205 in benefits—an infinite rate of return. In periods 3 and 4, the retirees pay taxes when young, so they receive a 10% rate of return, which is determined by population and wage growth. In period 5, the last generation pays in when young, but get nothing when old, so there is a negatively infinite rate of return.

▶ APPLICATION

Ida May Fuller[12]

The very first beneficiary of Social Security was Ida May Fuller. Ida May was born on September 6, 1874, on a farm in Vermont, and attended school with future president Calvin Coolidge. Ida May worked for only three years after the establishment of the Social Security system, and paid a total of $24.75 in Social Security taxes. On November 4, 1939, she dropped by the Social Security office in Rutland, Vermont; as she later said, "It wasn't that I expected anything, mind you, but I knew I'd been paying for something called Social Security and I wanted to ask the people in Rutland about it." Ida May's case was the first one

---

[12] Information on Ida May Fuller comes from Social Security's Web site, at http://www.ssa.gov/history/imf.html and http://www.ssa.gov/history/idapayroll.html.

processed by the new Social Security Administration, and so the first Social Security check in U.S. history was issued to her on January 31, 1940, for $22.54.

Ida May went on to live for 35 more years, dying at age 100 in 1975. Over those 35 years, she collected a total of $22,888.92 in Social Security benefits. Quite a return on her $24.75 investment! Ida May is a striking example of the first generation of Social Security beneficiaries who were the big winners under this new social program. ◄

In period 3, the elderly are the first generation that paid taxes when they were young in period 2. These retirees paid $2,100 per person in taxes when they were working but receive $2,315 in benefits when they are old, roughly 10% more than they paid in. Where does this extra money come from? First, there is the *wage growth effect:* each current worker is earning more than these retirees did when they were young, due to higher productivity. Because taxes are paid on the higher earnings of the period 3 young, there are more funds to be paid as benefits to the retirees. Second, there is a *population growth effect:* because more workers are paying taxes, there are more funds to be paid as benefits to retirees.

In our example, we have assumed that population and wages each grow by 5% in each period. In the real world, however, these growth rates vary and the impact of an actual Social Security system on the "middle generations" of recipients is ambiguous. The impact depends on the size of this population and on wage growth effects. If both are large, beneficiaries can receive a high rate of return on the taxes they've paid in. If either or both are small or negative, the beneficiaries can receive a very poor rate of return on their tax payments.

In periods 3 and 4, retirees earn a 10% rate of return on the amount of money they put into the system when they were young. Imagine, however, that in period 5 the young workers decide that they no longer want to participate in the Social Security program. They haven't yet paid taxes, so there is no cost to them if they leave the system. Who bears the cost of this decision? The period 5 retirees: they paid $2,315 per person in taxes when they were working in period 4 but receive no benefits in return now that they are retired. Thus, the *final generation is hurt by unfunded Social Security*.

Lessons Learned To summarize, this example illustrates two points. First, the rate of return provided by an unfunded Social Security to "middle generations" depends on the rates of population and wage growth. Second, unfunded Social Security carries with it what Diamond and Orszag (2004) call a **legacy debt.** The unfunded transfers to the Ida Fullers and others in the first generation of retirees receiving Social Security put the system immediately into a large debt. If society decided to end the Social Security program, the existing generation of older workers and retirees, who paid the taxes to support the program, would receive no benefits, and so their past tax payments would end up paying off the debt.

It seems unlikely that the political process would allow a single generation of workers to be held accountable for this large debt. Thus, reforms of the Social Security system must all grapple with the fact that this debt must be somehow paid before we can bring our unfunded Social Security system into balance.

legacy debt The debt incurred by the government because early generations of beneficiaries received much more in benefits than they paid in taxes.

How Does Social Security Redistribute in Practice?

The example in Table 13-1 shows how an imaginary Social Security system can lead to redistribution across generations: the first generation was a big winner, middle generations got a rate of return determined by wage and population growth, and the final generation, if there ever is one, is the big loser. Reality is more complicated than this simple example. In this section, we look at the evidence on the actual redistribution due to the Social Security system in the United States. Which generations have won from the existence of this system, which have lost, and by how much?

We measure redistribution by computing the **Social Security Wealth (SSW)** accruing to different generations in the United States. SSW is the expected present discounted value of future Social Security benefits over a person's lifetime, minus the expected present discounted value of payroll taxes that the person will pay. SSW is computed as follows:

▶ Calculate the entire future stream of benefits that a person expects to receive before he or she dies, accounting for the fact that the date of death is not certain (which is why this is the *expected* present discounted value), by multiplying each period's benefits by the odds that the individual will live to receive them (e.g., benefits at age 68 are valued much more highly than those at age 80, since the odds of living to receive the benefits at age 80 are lower).

▶ Use a discount rate to calculate the present discounted value (PDV) of that stream of benefits (as discussed in Chapter 4 on pages 102–103).

▶ Calculate the entire future stream of taxes that a person expects to pay before he or she dies.

▶ Compute the PDV of that stream of taxes.

▶ Take the difference between these two to get the SSW.

Table 13-2 shows the SSW for unmarried males turning age 65 in 1960, 1995, and 2030 (that is, born in 1895, 1930, and 1965). For each age group, the table also shows the SSW separately for low-, medium-, and high-earning workers. The figures in each cell in the table are the SSW for the group indicated on the top and to the left of the table. An average wage earner turning 65 in 1960, for example, would have received $36,500 more in benefits than he or she paid in taxes. An average wage earner turning 65 in 1995 would

Social Security Wealth The expected present discounted values of a person's future Social Security payments minus the expected present discounted value of a person's payroll tax payments.

■ **TABLE 13-2**

Redistribution Under Social Security for a Single Male

Earnings Level	Retirees Turn 65 in 1960	Retirees Turn 65 in 1995	Retirees Turn 65 in 2030
Low earner	$26,100	$12,500	–$4,100
Average earner	$36,500	–$5,100	–$56,200
High earner	$36,800	–$37,100	–$248,500

The Social Security Wealth of single males varies both across generations, with older generations getting more than recent generations, and within generations, with the rich first getting more, and more recently less, than the poor.

Steuerle and Bakija (1994), Table A.6.

have received $5,100 less in benefits than he or she paid in taxes. An average wage earner turning 65 in 2030 can expect to receive $56,200 less in benefits than he or she pays in taxes.

Why do we see this redistribution from those born later to those born earlier? First, the oldest retirees in the table (those who are 65 in 1960) benefit somewhat from the same feature we saw in period 2 of Table 13-1. These retirees were born in 1895. If they began working in 1913 (when they were 18), they would have worked for 24 years without paying any Social Security tax because Social Security tax payments didn't start until 1937. Thus, these retirees paid into the system for only part of their lives but received benefits throughout their retirement.

Second, over much of the life of the Social Security program, not only were there population and wage growth effects (as in our earlier example), there was also a *tax rate growth effect:* that is, the size of the payroll tax has risen throughout the years (in our earlier example, the payroll tax remained fixed at 10%). In 1937, the payroll tax rate used to finance the Social Security system was 2%; today, it is 12.4%. When the tax rate grows along with population and wages, the benefits of this system to early generations also increase.

For those turning 65 in 1995, Social Security has generally become a losing proposition, for three reasons. First, unlike those turning 65 in 1960, these workers did have to pay taxes their entire working lives to finance their benefits. Second, slowing tax rate growth meant that they received a much smaller tax rate growth effect. Finally, there has been a very significant reduction in the wage and population growth effects, beginning in the early 1970s. Before 1973, for example, the population growth effect averaged 1.5% per year, and the wage growth effect averaged 2.5% per year; since 1973, the population growth effect has averaged only 1% per year, and the wage growth effect has averaged only 0.9% per year.[13] Those turning 65 in 2030 have the worst outcome, since payroll taxes are no longer rising at all, and wage and population growth are slow.

In addition to showing how the Social Security system has treated different generations, this table also shows how the system has treated workers with different levels of earnings. In particular, the Social Security system has shifted from one that favored the rich, with a higher SSW for the rich than for the poor, to one that favors the poor, with a higher SSW for the poor than for the rich. The reason for this change is that higher-income earners pay more money into the system through payroll taxes. So when the returns to Social Security are high (through high wage growth, population growth, and tax rate growth), they benefit more than lower-income earners. But when the returns to Social Security are low, higher-income earners have more of their income in an underperforming asset, and they are worse off than low-income earners.

The treatment of different earnings levels is only one example of the redistribution that Social Security causes across different groups within any gener-

---

[13] Population and wage growth rates derived from U.S. Bureau of the Census (2003) and previous editions of that publication.

ation. Some examples of how SSW varies within groups that are the same ages include the following:

▶ Females have more SSW than males: they pay the same taxes but receive a larger stream of benefits because they live longer.

▶ Married couples have more SSW than single people: spouses of workers are automatically entitled to 50% of the workers' benefits, and surviving spouses receive 100% of the workers' benefits. So a married worker who pays Social Security tax is purchasing not only his benefits but those for his wife as well, which provides a higher return.

▶ Single-earner couples have more SSW than two-earner couples: a couple in which only one person has worked gets 150% of the earner's benefit even though the nonworking spouse has paid no taxes. Both earners of a two-earner couple have to pay taxes on their full earnings, even though they may not get much more in benefits than the single-earner couple.[14]

▶ The gains to the poor relative to the rich from Social Security are overstated because the length of life rises with income, so that the rich generally receive their benefits for more years than the poor. While sizeable, this effect is not large enough to overturn the basic conclusion that the poor win and the rich lose from the current Social Security system.

13.2

Consumption-Smoothing Benefits of Social Security

The fundamental motivation for Social Security is the notion that the elderly will not have sufficient income to support themselves in retirement or to support their dependents when they die. As a result, the government needs to force workers to provide for their retirement years by paying taxes when working that entitle them to benefits when retired.

Rationales for Social Security

Given that retirement is an anticipated event that is largely the decision of the individual, why does the government need to be involved in providing retirement income? What is the argument for social insurance when the event is highly predictable?

There are basically two rationales offered for Social Security, along the lines of our discussion in Chapter 12. The first rationale is that there are market

---

[14] For example, suppose that I am entitled to a Social Security benefit of $10,000 per year. If my wife never worked, we will receive $15,000 per year (150% of my benefit). If my wife has earnings identical to mine and has paid identical payroll taxes, we will, as a couple, receive $20,000 in benefits per year. Even though we've paid 100% more in payroll taxes, our benefits are only 33% larger.

failures in the *annuities market*. A pure annuity is a contract whereby a person pays some amount of money up front to an insurance company, and in return the insurance company pays the person a fixed payment until he or she dies. Annuities should be valued by consumers facing an uncertain date of death because they facilitate the type of consumption smoothing we described in Chapter 12. That is, they allow people facing an uncertain date of death to smooth their consumption over their remaining years, solving the problem of saving too little (and therefore going hungry in old age) or too much (and therefore not fully enjoying their wealth).[15]

Yet adverse selection can lead the annuities market to fail. Recall that adverse selection can cause insurance market failure when the insured party has an informational advantage over the insurer. This is clearly the case with annuities, because individuals know more about their potential life expectancy than do insurers: they know more about their family's health history (did all their ancestors live to be over 100?) and about outside behaviors they engage in that are likely to result in a particularly short or long life (do they like health food and never drive over the speed limit?). The longer a person lives, the less money the insurer makes from an annuity contract. Insurance companies will therefore be reluctant to sell annuities for fear that they will be purchased only by the longest-lived individuals (adverse selection). This reluctance could lead to such a high price for annuities that most potential buyers would not want to buy them.[16] By providing public annuities, Social Security can solve this market failure.

While annuities market failure is the classic economic rationale for Social Security, the true reason that most policy makers favor the program is *paternalism;* that is, they are concerned that people won't save enough for their own retirement. And, in fact, most workers have very little savings other than Social Security (and private pensions) when they retire. In 1991, the median American aged 51–61 had $107,000 in Social Security Wealth, $16,000 in private pension wealth, and $3,000 in other personal retirement assets.[17] This balance is slowly changing because more young workers are participating in personal retirement accounts like 401(k) plans (discussed in more detail in Chapter 22), but Social Security will nonetheless remain a crucial component of many retirees' incomes.

Does Social Security Smooth Consumption?

Regardless of the reason, market failure in the annuities market or paternalism, Social Security's existence is motivated by the notion that individuals are not appropriately protected for their retirement consumption. Whether this leads to a

---

[15] A useful way to understand annuities is to compare them to life insurance contracts, whereby a person pays an insurance company up front, and the insurance company pays the person's descendants once the person dies. Life insurance is insurance against living too few years (so that one's family is left without resources once one is dead); annuities are insurance against living too long (so that one is left without resources while one is still alive).

[16] Finkelstein and Poterba (2004) provide striking evidence for adverse selection in annuities markets. Those who lead long lives are much more likely to buy annuities than the short lived. Moreover, those who lead long lives are much more likely to buy "true" annuity products, while short-lived people are much more likely to buy products that are partial annuities that pay their heirs something if they die soon.

[17] Poterba, Venti, and Wise (1998a), Table 2.11.

failure of consumption smoothing, and thus a need for government intervention, is an open question. On the one hand, once workers retire, they have many years of consumption to finance. On the other hand, retirement is generally a very predictable event for which most workers can readily prepare. So it is not clear how important Social Security is for smoothing consumption across the working life and retirement years. In particular, all that Social Security may be doing is crowding out the savings that individuals would otherwise set aside for their retirement (a situation illustrated in panel (c) in Figure 12-2.) The important question of the extent to which Social Security provides real insurance, as opposed to just crowding out savings, has been the subject of many studies, in two different areas.

Social Security and Private Savings

The major form of self-insurance for retirement is private savings. In a world without Social Security, people would have to rely on their own savings (either as individuals or through firm pension plans) to finance their retirement. Social Security might crowd out that private savings by allowing people to count on a government transfer to support their income in old age. The larger this crowd-out is, the less consumption smoothing Social Security provides for retired individuals. Existing research suggests that each dollar of Social Security Wealth crowds out $0.30 to $0.40 of private savings, so that crowd-out exists, but it is partial.

Living Standards of the Elderly

The other piece of evidence on Social Security and consumption smoothing comes from examining the living standards of the elderly. Figure 13-2 (page 362) shows the poverty rate of the elderly from 1959 through 2001. The *poverty rate* is the percent of a population whose income is below the *poverty level,* which is the amount of income required to buy a "minimum acceptable" bundle of food, housing, and other goods (this concept is defined more precisely and discussed in more detail in Chapter 17). For a family of four, the poverty level in 2004 is $18,850. The elderly poverty rate is graphed against the size of the Social Security system, as a share of GDP. In 1960, 35% of the elderly lived in poverty (compared to only 21% of the non-elderly); by 2001, only 10% of the elderly were living in poverty (compared to 12% of the non-elderly).

This change corresponds closely to the evolution of the Social Security system; the steepest reductions in poverty were during the 1960s and 1970s, when the program grew the fastest. Indeed, Engelhardt and Gruber (2004) analyzed how poverty fell for birth cohorts that particularly benefited from expansion of Social Security relative to those that did not, and concluded that the expansion of Social Security can explain the entire reduction in poverty among the elderly over this period. That Social Security's growth had such a dramatic effect on elderly poverty suggests that individuals were not in fact protecting themselves appropriately for their retirement, so that there were large consumption-smoothing benefits to the program. Taken together, both pieces of evidence point to only very partial crowd-out of private savings by the Social Security program.

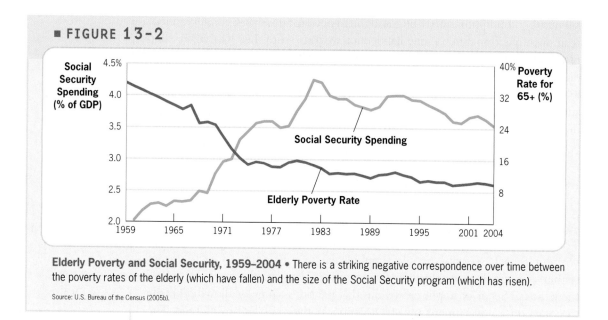

■ FIGURE 13-2

Elderly Poverty and Social Security, 1959–2004 • There is a striking negative correspondence over time between the poverty rates of the elderly (which have fallen) and the size of the Social Security program (which has risen).

Source: U.S. Bureau of the Census (2005b).

13.3

Social Security and Retirement

The fundamental motivation for Social Security is to insure against the adverse events of dying or being too old to work by providing income support to those who are retired or to the survivors of deceased workers. This goal leads to a natural moral hazard problem: workers may retire early to start collecting their benefits. As we noted earlier, there is no need to retire at an early age to start collecting benefits in the United States: you can keep working, have your benefits reduced by the earnings test, and receive those benefits back (with actuarial adjustment) when you do fully retire. Yet almost all people (wrongly) perceive the earnings test as a tax on their earnings, and feel that benefits collection must be associated with full retirement. Thus, as with the moral hazard examples discussed in Chapter 12, insuring against the adverse event of retirement may encourage that adverse event, which lowers social efficiency and raises program costs (and associated taxes).

Theory

In theory, there are two effects of Social Security on retirement decisions. The first is the *implicit taxation* that Social Security may levy on work at older ages by reducing the value of Social Security benefits if retirement is delayed. Gruber and Wise (1999) define the implicit tax rate from Social Security as the reduction in Social Security Wealth (the expected present discounted value of Social Security benefits received minus the expected present discounted benefits of taxes paid) if one continues working another year relative

MEASURING THE CROWD-OUT EFFECT OF SOCIAL SECURITY ON SAVINGS

The effect of Social Security on private savings has been the subject of a large number of studies over the past 30 years. Feldstein (1974) used a time series analysis of Social Security Wealth and private savings to suggest that Social Security was lowering the private savings rate in the United States by 50%, but subsequent analyses found flaws in this approach and have produced mixed results. Moreover, this application is a classic example of the difficulties of time series analysis. Movements in national savings over time are driven by a number of factors, of which Social Security is only one. With few distinct changes in Social Security at a particular point in time, it is difficult to tease out any effects on savings from time series alone.

Another approach to modeling the impact of Social Security on savings is cross-sectional regression analysis of the type discussed in Chapter 3. A number of articles have looked at whether people who are entitled to higher Social Security benefits in the future save less today. Such articles typically find some reduction in savings from higher Social Security benefits, although the reduction is much less than one for one.

But recall the key issue raised in Chapter 3: results of empirical analyses can be biased by the inability to find comparable treatment and control groups. To get a valid measure of the impact of Social Security on savings from econometric analysis, there must be a way to compare people with different levels of Social Security benefits who are otherwise identical. What determine Social Security benefits are largely individual characteristics: average lifetime earnings, marital status, age, and retirement age. Thus, any two people with different benefits are also likely to differ along some or all of these dimensions. Because factors such as earnings and age are likely to be correlated with individual tastes for savings, it is difficult to assume that any

association between Social Security benefits and savings is due to the program itself.

To answer this question requires some type of quasi-experiment that allows us to compare people with similar characteristics but very different levels of Social Security benefits. Such a quasi-experiment has proven hard to find in the United States because Social Security is a national program that applies to almost all workers; very similar people usually have very similar benefits. However, two recent studies have provided quasi-experimental evidence on the impact of Social Security–like programs on private savings in Italy and the United Kingdom.[18] Both studies focused on reforms to the social security systems that changed the social security wealth of some types of workers, but not others.

In Italy, for example, reforms in 1992 substantially reduced the benefits, and thus future SSW, for younger workers in the public sector, while reducing much less the benefits of older workers and those in the private sector. This change set up a natural quasi-experimental analysis, in which the researchers could assess whether the savings of younger workers in the public sector rose to offset the fall in future SSW. The authors compared the change in savings of young public-sector workers (the treatment group) before and after the reforms to the change in savings of older public-sector and private-sector workers (the control groups) at the same time. This allowed the authors to remove any bias arising from other time series changes in savings (the "difference-in-difference" estimate of Chapter 3). According to the authors' estimate, 30–40% of the reduction in SSW was offset by higher private savings. The results from the UK study were similar. That is, social security does crowd out private savings to some extent, but not fully.

to the wage that could be earned by working that year. The numerator for this variable is calculated by computing the SSW at a possible age of retirement, and then measuring how it changes if the person works another year. Consider, for example, a 62-year-old worker. If she works until 63, instead of

[18] Attanasio and Brugiavini (2003) and Attanasio and Rohwedder (2004).

retiring at 62 and claiming her Social Security benefits, four things happen through the Social Security system:

▶ She pays an extra year of payroll taxes on her earnings.

▶ She receives one year less of Social Security benefits.

▶ She gets a higher Social Security benefit level through the actuarial adjustment.

▶ Since earnings generally rise with age, she gets to replace a low-earnings year with a high-earnings year in the 35-year benefits average.

The first two factors reduce the return to working that extra year and the second two increase the return. If the first two factors dominate (as we will show below to be the case in most countries), there will be an implicit tax on work, and thus more retirement: the system designed to protect individuals from income loss in retirement will actually be inducing them to retire.

The second effect of Social Security on retirement is through the redistribution discussed earlier. This system results in some groups becoming richer over their life, and others becoming poorer. These changes in wealth will have income effects on retirement, as the groups that are richer use some of their wealth to buy themselves more retirement, and the groups that are poorer work longer.

Evidence

There are three types of evidence that suggest that Social Security is a powerful determinant of retirement decisions. This evidence is largely focused on males, since the rapid increase in labor force participation by females since World War II makes it difficult to discern an effect of Social Security on retirement for women.

The first piece of evidence is time series evidence, as illustrated in Figure 13-3. The Social Security program grew rapidly through the 1960s and 1970s, with a corresponding reduction in elderly *labor force participation* (LFP) rates, the percentage of the elderly population that is either working or looking for work. Then, when program growth flattened out in the mid-1980s, labor force participation flattened out as well (although with a several-year lag). On its own, however, this evidence is not fully convincing because many other factors were changing over this period, and these other factors could explain the changes in elderly LFP.

The second piece of evidence that Social Security matters for retirement behavior comes from examining the age pattern of retirement in the United States. Figure 13-4 shows the **retirement hazard rate,** the rate at which workers of a certain age retire. The retirement hazard rate rises slowly until age 62, at which point it jumps up and then rapidly falls back down. At age 61, 10% of workers retire, and at age 63 only about 8% retire; but at age 62, the retirement rate is 25%. Recall that age 62 is the Early Entitlement Age (EEA), the age at which benefits can first be claimed. There is then another spike at age 65, the Full Benefits Age (FBA) for the program.

retirement hazard rate The percentage of workers retiring at a certain age.

■ FIGURE 13-3

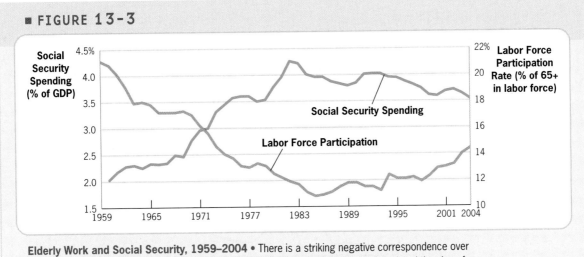

Elderly Work and Social Security, 1959–2004 • There is a striking negative correspondence over time between the labor force participation (LFP) rates of the elderly (which have fallen) and the size of the Social Security program (which has risen).

Source: U.S. Department of Labor (2005b) and the Bureau of Labor Statistics, accessed at http://www.bls.gov/emp/home.htm.

That workers happen to retire in large numbers at these particular ages is not evidence that Social Security *caused* this behavior; people may have other reasons for choosing these ages to retire. As Figure 13-5 (page 366) shows, however, there was no such spike at age 62 in 1960, before the EEA was introduced. The spike emerged slowly, with a small spike in 1970, and a larger one by 1980. This pattern suggests that it was the introduction of the EEA in 1963 that led to the evolution of this spike.

The third, and most compelling, type of evidence that Social Security matters for retirement decisions comes from international comparisons. There are enormous spikes in other countries at their early and normal retirement ages

■ FIGURE 13-4

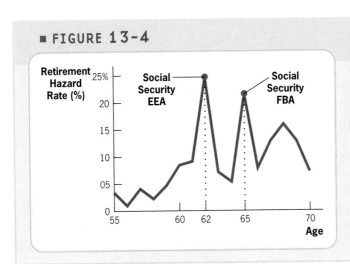

Hazard Rate of Retirement for Males in the United States • The male hazard rate, or exit rate at each age given that a man has worked to that age, has a distinct spike at age 62 (the Early Entitlement Age, EEA) and 65 (the Full Benefit Age, FBA), key ages for the Social Security system.

Source: Diamond and Gruber (1999), Figure 11.12.

■ FIGURE 13-5

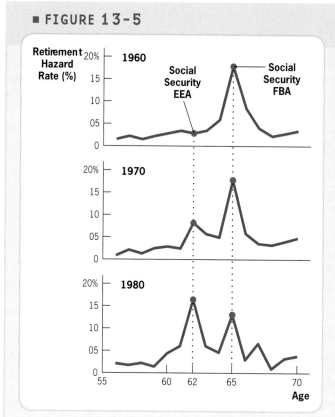

The Evolution of the U.S. Male Retirement Hazard • In 1960, before the EEA of 62 was introduced for men, the hazard rate for men was highest at age 65 (the FBA), with no spike at age 62. By 1970, the spike at 62 had begun to emerge, and by 1980 it was larger than the spike at age 65.

Source: Gruber and Wise (1999), Figure 12.

that mirror closely what we see in the United States. Perhaps the most compelling example comes from France, where age 60 is both the age at which you can first claim benefits and is the full benefits age. As Figure 13-6 shows, there is an enormous spike in the hazard rate of retirement at age 60 in France: 60%

■ FIGURE 13-6

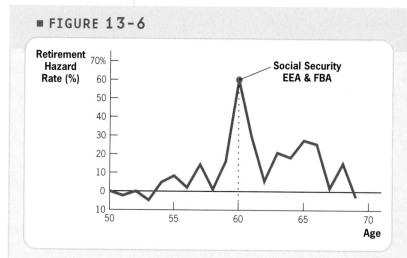

Hazard Rate of Retirement in France • In France, there is an enormous exit rate from the labor force at age 60, which is both the EEA and FBA.

Source: Gruber and Wise (1999), Figure 11.

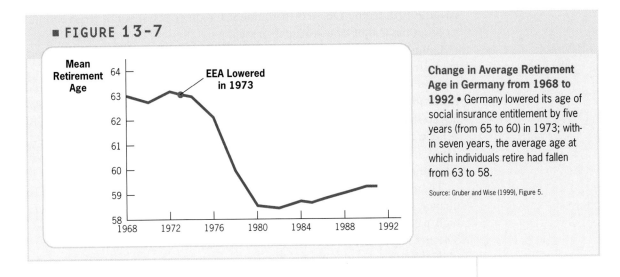

■ FIGURE 13-7

Change in Average Retirement Age in Germany from 1968 to 1992 • Germany lowered its age of social insurance entitlement by five years (from 65 to 60) in 1973; within seven years, the average age at which individuals retire had fallen from 63 to 58.

Source: Gruber and Wise (1999), Figure 5.

of those working when they turn 60 retire during the next year. Once again, what is striking about this example is that 30 years ago, when retirement at age 60 was not an option, only about 10% of those working at age 60 retired at that age; retirement was concentrated at the EEA/FBA at that time, age 65.

Germany provides another compelling example of the effects of social insurance on retirement age. In 1973, Germany lowered the early entitlement age for benefits from 65 to 60. Figure 13-7 shows that, within seven years, the average retirement age in that nation had fallen by five years, from 63 to 58. This is a striking change in a short period of time, and further confirms the important role that social insurance plays in retirement decisions.

► APPLICATION

Implicit Social Security Taxes and Retirement Behavior

Gruber and Wise (1999) presented data from a series of countries on the implicit taxes from Social Security, computed as previously described. For the United States, they found, there is a zero implicit tax on working another year at age 62: the fact that (1) the worker has to pay one extra year of payroll taxes, and (2) the worker receives one less year of benefits is exactly cancelled by the fact that (3) benefits are higher when the worker does retire and (4) the worker's benefit is based on a higher earnings average.[19] The implicit tax is effectively zero through the FBA of age 65. At that point, the implicit tax becomes positive, since the reward for getting one less year of benefits (which,

---

[19] This raises the interesting question of why, then, we see this large spike in retirement at age 62 in the United States. This is indeed one of the great mysteries of retirement behavior. One view is that people are "liquidity constrained": they would like to actually retire before age 62, but they have no savings, so they can't afford to retire until benefits become available at age 62. The other view is that people don't fully understand the system, and think that they are penalized if they work past 62 (or, equivalently, that they are too impatient and retire at 62 without thinking out the consequences).

past the FBA, is the Delayed Retirement Credit (DRC)) is not large enough to offset the loss of one year of benefits.

Contrast what happens in the United States to what occurs in the Netherlands. In the Netherlands, at the early retirement age of 60, there is a 91% replacement rate—that is, benefits amount to 91% of what individuals would earn if they work that year. Moreover, there is *no actuarial reduction for early claiming,* so that working past age 60 simply means that you receive one less year of benefits, without a compensating rise in benefit levels (as in the United States). Think of it this way: if you work at age 60, you get a wage; if you retire at age 60, you get 91% of that wage without working and with no other penalty.

There is even one more benefit to early retirement in the Netherlands. To finance their generous retirement system, the Netherlands must impose a very high payroll tax on workers. By retiring, you can also avoid paying this tax. The net result of these factors is that people in the Netherlands *lose money by working past age 60*: the net wage, after taxes, that they take home from working is less than their benefit if they retire. What would you do in this situation? Probably what most persons in the Netherlands do: quit work by age 60!

Indeed, across the nations in the Gruber and Wise study, there is a strong relation between these "implicit taxes" and decisions to work. Figure 13-8

■ FIGURE 13-8

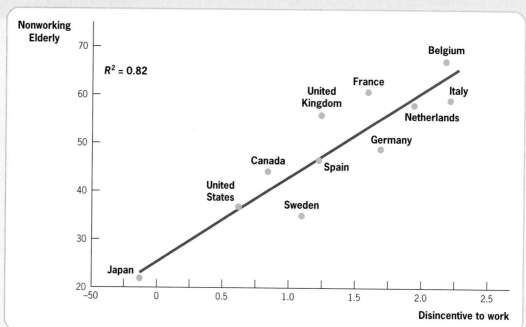

Implicit Taxes on Work and Nonwork • There is large variation across nations in the social security disincentives to work at older ages. The disincentive to work is measured here as the natural logarithm of the sum of implicit taxes on work at older ages. Those nations with greater disincentives to work tend to have much higher nonwork among older workers.

Source: Gruber and Wise (1999), Figure 17.

shows on the horizontal axis the disincentive to work in each nation due to implicit taxation.[20] The vertical axis measures the extent of nonwork at older ages: the percentage of the population that is not working, on average, from ages 55 to 65. There is a striking positive correspondence between the two. In nations such as the United States, Sweden, and especially Japan, there is little implicit tax (i.e., the system doesn't penalize work past the early retirement age), and there is relatively little nonwork. In nations such as the Netherlands, Belgium, France, and Italy, there is a large implicit tax, and the vast majority of people do not work at older ages. The variation in this one measure of implicit taxes can explain 82% of the variation in the rates of nonwork across this sample of nations. ◄

Implications

This evidence suggests that it is potentially very costly to design Social Security systems that penalize additional work beyond the retirement age. Systems such as those in Europe that do not increase benefits for additional years of work appear to have led to a mass exodus from the labor force by older workers. Adjusting systems to more fairly reward work at old ages can mitigate much of the moral hazard effect of Social Security.

13.4
Social Security Reform

Social Security is currently facing a major fiscal imbalance. In the United States in 1950, there were 12 people over the age of 65 for every 100 people of working age. By 2050, as Figure 13-9 (page 370) shows, there will be more than 35 people over the age of 65 for every 100 working-age people. This rise is due to the aging of the enormous baby-boom generation that was born in the wake of World War II. This may seem abstract, but think of it this way: by the year 2025, the share of elderly people in the United States will be larger than it is in Florida today! As noted earlier, over the next 75 years, the present discounted value of the program's obligations exceeds the present discounted value of the taxes it will collect by $4.6 trillion.[21]

Three factors are coming together to cause this fiscal imbalance. The first factor is the dramatic improvement in life expectancy that was ongoing throughout the twentieth century, which means that the elderly receive a larger number of years of benefits. The second factor is a reduction in birth rates, so that there are fewer workers to support the increased number of elderly. Finally, the growth in wages has slowed dramatically. Thus, returning to our

---

[20] This measure is the natural logarithm of the "tax force" to retire across these nations: the sum of the implicit taxes on work at all ages from the early retirement age to age 69.
[21] Calculation based on projected GDP growth rates from Social Security Trustees (2006), Table IV.B6.

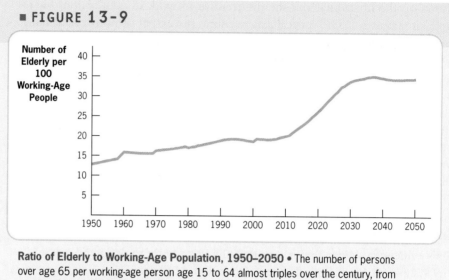

■ **FIGURE 13-9**

Ratio of Elderly to Working-Age Population, 1950–2050 • The number of persons over age 65 per working-age person age 15 to 64 almost triples over the century, from 13 per 100 in 1950 to 35 per 100 in 2050.

Source: Historical statistics from U.S. Bureau of the Census (2005) and previous editions; projections from http://www.census.gov/ipc/www/usinterimproj/usproj2000-2050.xls.

discussion of Table 13-1, we have promised benefits to retirees based on a high rate of wage and population growth, so the slower actual rates of growth leave us unable to meet that promise. In addition, the Social Security system continues to carry the "legacy debt" that was built up by our unfunded payments to the first generation of Social Security recipients, which adds a major component to the long-run fiscal imbalance of the system. The problem of Social Security underfunding is not just a problem of the baby-boomer cohorts retiring, but a much longer-run problem due to those factors previously listed. Over the entire future (not just the next 75 years), the Social Security Administration projects the unfunded obligation of this program to be $13.4 trillion![22]

Reform Round I: The Greenspan Commission

The United States first faced up to this Social Security financing problem in 1983, when it was projected that the Social Security trust fund would run out of money to pay its claims in July of that same year. The government established the Greenspan Commission, headed by former Council of Economic Advisors chair (and future Federal Reserve Chairman) Alan

"I had another bad dream about Social Security."

[22] Social Security Trustees (2006), Table IV.B6.

Greenspan.[23] The commission's primary recommendation was that the Social Security system should move away from an unfunded system to some extent, and that the government should accumulate savings in the Social Security trust fund so that when the baby boomers retire and there are fewer workers to support them, there would be enough money to pay their benefits. To increase the trust fund, the Greenspan Commission made a number of changes, including speeding up increases in payroll taxes that were scheduled for the future, and cutting benefits.

The Social Security Trust Fund and National Savings

In theory, one benefit of the partial funding of Social Security through the build-up of the trust fund is an increase in national savings, with the associated benefits for the capital stock and productivity growth highlighted in Chapter 4. In practice, however, the trust fund may not actually add to national savings. This trust fund is, by law, "off budget," meaning that the government is supposed to consider its other revenue and spending obligations distinct from the trust fund. But this has not traditionally been the case. When the government reports its budget deficit or surplus for each year, it typically reports the "unified budget," which incorporates off-budget categories. For example, for 2005, the federal government reported a deficit of $318 billion. In fact, however, this is composed of an on-budget deficit of $494 billion, and a Social Security *surplus* of $173 billion (along with a postal service surplus of $2 billion), meaning that the true deficit ($494 billion) is over 50% more than that popularly reported.[24]

Suppose, as seems to be the case, that the government ignores the distinction between on-budget and off-budget and just pays attention to the unified deficit. Suppose further that the government, and the public to which it is accountable, has some budget target, such as a balanced budget. By allowing policy makers to hide deficits in other areas, the Social Security trust fund is displacing other government savings. That is, in the absence of the trust fund, to get the budget to balance policy makers would have to save more, which would require either tax increases or spending cuts, neither of which are very popular.

By hiding the deficit, the trust fund allows policy makers to avoid these tough decisions—until the bill comes due. When the baby boomers start to retire, the trust fund will get drawn down, and suddenly the unified budget, which looked to be in balance, will plunge sharply into deficit. Thus, if policy makers only pay attention to the unified budget, then the trust fund is not new savings—it just displaces other government savings. The trust fund isn't

---

[23] The commission's final report can be found at http://www.ssa.gov/history/reports/gspan.html.
[24] Congressional Budget Office (2006b), Table 1-1.

necessarily increasing national savings by $173 billion in 2005; it may simply be enabling the government to avoid tough decisions that would raise national savings by this amount.[25] ◄

Incremental Reforms

While the 1983 commission staved off Social Security's financing problems to some extent, these financial problems will come back with a vengeance as the baby boomers age. What can we do to move beyond the 1983 reforms and deal with the long-term funding problem? There are several approaches. In this section, we review approaches that build on the existing structure of the system, before turning to more fundamental changes in the nature of the program.

Raise Taxes Further While the problems of financing Social Security are large, they are not insurmountable. Increasing the payroll tax by 2.0 percentage points, from 12.4% to 14.4%, is projected to solve the financing problem for the next 75 years, and raising it by 3.7 percentage points is projected to solve the financing problem forever.[26]

Extend the Base of Taxable Wages Another tactic would be to try to delay the pain by extending the base of wages that can be taxed by Social Security to finance retirement benefits. Since the problem is that the number of elderly are growing rapidly relative to the number of young, we could try to increase the number of young who pay into the system. For example, many state and local government workers are now excluded from Social Security (since they were given the option to enroll instead in their state or local pension plans); we could mandate that they come into the system. Or we could ease immigration restrictions for young workers. These expansions improve the finances of the system in two ways. First, they raise the base on which payroll taxes can be collected in the short run. Second, the system now is charging workers, on average, more in payroll taxes than they will ultimately expect to collect in benefits. So new workers who can be pulled into the system represent a net gain in the financial position of the program (and a net loss for the workers).

Another means of extending the base of taxable wages would be to increase the maximum income on which the payroll tax that finances Social Security is paid. In 2006, workers pay the payroll tax on income up to $94,200 per year. Since the system is progressive, such a change would once again improve the finances of the system both in the short and long run. We will discuss how to evaluate such tax changes in Chapters 20 and 21.

---

[25] Existing results are mixed on whether the trust fund, in fact, just crowds out other government spending. Nataraj and Shoven (2004) suggested such crowd-out is full, and Bosworth and Burtless (2004) found that OECD nations that attempted to accumulate social security surpluses ended up running larger deficits in the rest of government than nations that did not. On the other hand, Bosworth and Burtless found no evidence that state governments offset the saving in their government employee pension trust funds with larger deficits in the rest of government.

[26] Social Security Trustees (2006), p. 55.

Raise the Retirement Age Relative to life expectancy, the Social Security Full Benefits Age has been *falling*. In 1950, males who were age 65 could expect to live 12.7 more years on average; today, that figure is 16.3 years. For females, life expectancy at age 65 has risen from 15 years in 1950 to 19.2 years today.[27] It seems sensible that, as people live longer, they should work longer as well, so that they don't have an increasingly long retirement to finance. Yet the FBA has remained fixed for many years at 65, and has only slowly started to move to age 67. Expenditures on the Social Security program could be significantly reduced by either speeding up or increasing the rise in the FBA.

It is important to recognize that the FBA is simply the point at which individuals are entitled to their full Primary Insurance Amount (PIA). This so-called "normal retirement" age is no longer normal; in fact, many more people retire at the EEA of 62 than at the FBA of 65. So raising the FBA simply means *cutting benefits* at any age. Since the actuarial reduction penalizes people for each year that they claim benefits before the FBA, as the FBA moves out, a claimant at a given age faces a larger penalty. For example, those retiring at age 62 today receive 80% of their PIA; due to the increase in the Full Benefits Age, those retiring at age 62 in 2025 or later are scheduled to receive only 70% of their PIA. So increases in the FBA are most accurately viewed as a benefits cut, as opposed to a radical restructuring of the program.

A much more radical option would be to raise the EEA past age 62. Evidence from the United States and other countries suggests that this could significantly reduce retirement rates, since there are such high retirement rates right at the EEA. This change could thereby save the government money by reducing the years of benefits received by older people. But the trade-off here is that there may be people who have a very difficult time working past age 62, and they would be excessively burdened by raising this age.

Lower Benefits Another option is to just lower the benefit amounts paid by Social Security. There are different ways this can be accomplished. Benefits can just be cut, for example by lowering the rates at which the Average Indexed Monthly Earnings is translated to PIA. Alternatively, the government could reduce the indexation rate of Social Security benefits. Currently, benefit levels for recipients rise each year by the increase in the cost of living, as measured by the Consumer Price Index (CPI). If we reduced that adjustment, say, to 1% below the CPI increase, this would significantly reduce expenditures—in a way that is less obvious to the voting public (and thus more attractive to politicians).

While this is politically advantageous, however, it would be much better policy to cut benefits across the board than to reduce indexing. When indexing is reduced, it has its biggest impact on those who live the longest, since benefits fall every year relative to what they were before the reform.[28] But if there remains a

---

[27] See Table 11 of the Centers for Disease Control and Prevention's *National Vital Statistic Reports* 51, no. 3 (December 19, 2002).

[28] To see this, consider a reduction in the inflation adjustment of 1% each year. In the first year of the inflation adjustment, all elderly people receive 1% lower benefits than the baseline without reduction. In the second year, those elderly people who die are unaffected, but those who live now receive 2% lower benefits. Over time, it is those elderly who live to the oldest ages who see the greatest cuts in their benefits relative to the alternative of no reform (or a simple across-the-board benefits cut).

group of elderly that still face poverty problems, it is exactly the "oldest old," particularly widows. Of the elderly over age 80, 11.3% live in poverty, compared to only 9.2% between ages 65 and 69.[29] A straight benefits cut would affect all groups equally, but a reduction in inflation adjustment would have a much more pernicious effect on the neediest group of the elderly.

Reduce Benefits for Higher Income Groups Another alternative to an across-the-board cut in benefits is a reduction in benefits only for higher income groups. After all, over one-third of benefits are paid to those in families with incomes of over $50,000 per year, so that some reduction in their benefits would be unlikely to impose great hardship.[30]

A simple means of accomplishing this would be to increase the taxation of Social Security benefits. Under current law, Social Security income is taxed only if other income plus one-half of Social Security income exceeds $25,000. As a result, only 20% of recipients are taxed on their benefits, and only 6% of Social Security benefit dollars are returned to the federal government in the form of taxes.[31] It is unclear why an elderly person with $25,000 of income should pay less in taxes than a younger family with the same income, particularly since many of the major expenditures that must be financed out of income (home mortgage, child's education) are largely behind the elderly family.

Another alternative that has gathered significant attention is the "progressive price indexing" proposal of Pozen (2005). As noted above, Social Security benefits are based on historical earnings inflated to today by using increases in the wage level. Pozen suggested that, for higher income workers, earnings be inflated by using the rate at which the price level increases instead, which is typically below the rate at which wages increase. Over time, this change would reduce benefits for higher-earning workers relative to lower-earning workers, and in the process could save enough in benefit payments to meet 75% of the 75-year shortfall in Social Security.

Opponents of reducing benefits only for the wealthy fear that doing so would endanger the widespread support for the Social Security program. Should the program become viewed as a "welfare program" for the poor, rather than a universal entitlement for all retirees, it would likely not be defended by such a uniform block of elderly voters. It seems unlikely, however, that the types of changes proposed above are enough to cause this change in attitude about Social Security.

Fundamental Reforms

In addition to the type of incremental reforms previously discussed, there are two more fundamental reforms that have been posed as a solution to Social Security's fiscal imbalance.

---

[29] Social Security Administration (2006a), Table 8.2.
[30] Calculation based on Current Population Survey's March 2003 Supplement.
[31] Social Security Trustees (2006), Table II.B.1. In 2005, the OASDI Trust Fund paid out $435.4 billion in benefits and received about $14 billion from taxation of benefits, which represents roughly half of the total taxes levied on benefits. Thus the total taxation of benefits, $28 billion, is roughly 6% of $435.4 billion.

Invest the Trust Fund in Stocks One problem with the Greenspan Commission's solution in 1983 was that the trust fund is very inefficiently invested. Consider an individual planning for his own retirement. He has a choice of two investment options that are very different: *stocks* and *bonds*. Stocks are an investment that is much riskier over the short run, but which over long time periods (e.g., 30 years) consistently yield a higher rate of return. Thus, when saving for retirement, most experts recommend that individuals, particularly when young, have the majority of their assets in stocks. Since they won't need to access the assets for many years, and since stocks have traditionally done much better in the long run, this compensates for the higher short-term risk of investment in stocks.

By this logic, because the Social Security trust fund is, in essence, savings for future generations of retirees, it should be at least partially invested in stocks. But it is not: 100% of the assets in this trust fund are held in government bonds. Thus, one problem with the trust fund is that it is inefficiently invested. Any private pension manager that had invested his private pension 100% in government bonds would be immediately fired! A slow investment of the trust fund in the stock market, with a limit of 40% of the trust fund in the market, could cover half or more of the 75-year projected deficit in the system.[32] So why not just invest the trust fund in the stock market, earn higher long-run returns, and reduce the long-run fiscal imbalance in the program?

There are two serious concerns with such an approach. First, if we can't keep the politicians out of the cookie jar, why put more cookies in the jar? If the trust fund is going to be used to finance other government projects, Social Security's long-term problems will not be solved by investing in the market.

Second, do we want the government investing such huge sums in the private stock market? If the government invested half the trust fund in the stock market, it would own almost 6% of the entire stock market today; that share could grow substantially over time as the trust fund grows. Thus, there is a legitimate concern that the government might abuse its position to manipulate capital markets for its own good. For example, politicians who didn't like nonunion labor could vote to have the government sell all stock in nonunion firms, or politicians who didn't like smoking could vote to sell all stock in tobacco-producing firms. As Federal Reserve Chairman Alan Greenspan testified in 1999, "Investing a portion of the Social Security trust fund assets in equities, as the Administration and others have proposed, would arguably put at risk the efficiency of our capital markets and thus, our economy. Even with Herculean efforts, I doubt if it would be feasible to insulate, over the long run, the trust funds from political pressures—direct and indirect—to allocate capital to less than its most productive use."[33]

In theory, both of these concerns could be addressed by appropriate design of the investment strategy. The government could place the earnings from

---

[32] Social Security Advisory Board (2001), p. 23.
[33] See Alan Greenspan's January 28, 1999, testimony at http://www.federalreserve.gov/boarddocs/testimony/current/19990128.htm.

stock investments off budget in a more "iron-clad" manner than it does with the current trust fund. And it could establish an independent, Federal Reserve–like institution to manage those stock holdings, to immunize the holdings from political pressure. In practice, it is not clear how successful these safeguards would be.

privatization A proposal to reform Social Security by allowing individuals to invest their payroll taxes in various assets through individually controlled accounts.

Privatization Finally, the most radical alternative for reform is **privatization,** whereby we move toward a fully funded system with individually controlled accounts. That is, Social Security would become like a private pension, where individuals invest their payroll taxes and receive those taxes back with interest when they retire.

Such an approach has two major advantages. First, the system would be funded by individual savings, thereby increasing the capital stock and long-run well-being of the United States.[34] Moreover, since the capital would be in an individual's hands, and not in the government's hands, it would be truly "off budget," so that the government would not be tempted to spend against this account. Second, such an approach would respect consumer sovereignty with respect to their investment decisions. Some consumers are very risk averse, and would like to invest their retirement savings conservatively. Others would like to take risks and invest their retirement savings aggressively. By forcing people to invest in the same way, the Social Security program potentially reduces welfare by restricting their choices.

In spite of its positive attributes, this approach also has major problems. The most pressing, of course, is: How can we have individuals save money for their own retirement, while at the same time continuing to support the existing generation of retirees? If we privatize the system, we still have to pay off the legacy debt from the first generation of recipients, which requires either enormous double taxation of existing generations or huge deficits. If the latter course is chosen, then it completely offsets the savings benefits promised by privatization! That is, if we pay off the existing retirees by building up a large debt, we are simultaneously increasing national borrowing and saving, with no net effect on the capital stock.

This point relates to a claim commonly made by proponents of privatization: that privatization will allow individuals to earn a higher rate of return on their Social Security payroll taxes. As many have noted, the Social Security system pays a much lower rate of return (the sum of the wage and population growth effects) than the rate of return provided by private savings. The return on Social Security is currently only about 2%, while the historical real return on stock investment is about 7%. Thus, a strong argument for privatization has been the ability to allow individuals to take their money out of poorly performing Social Security investments and put it into more efficient private investment opportunities.

Geanakoplos, Mitchell, and Zeldes (1999) argued, however, that once we account for the need to pay back the legacy debt, a privatized Social Security

---

[34] This argument presumes that individuals wouldn't just offset this change by reducing other private savings they had for retirement. We will discuss the importance of such offsets in Chapter 22.

system *would not* provide a higher rate of return than our current system. They considered a move to a privatized system where all future generations pay an additional tax to pay off the legacy debt. They demonstrated that this tax is sufficiently large to *exactly offset* the higher returns from private investment. So we would move from a system where people are forced to save inefficiently to one where they can save efficiently but have to pay taxes owed on the legacy debt that offset any efficiency gains. There is no net gain in investment efficiency for participants in the Social Security program.

Another problem with privatization is that such a system could have much higher administrative costs. The Social Security program has very low administrative costs in terms of both investing (since the trust fund simply buys government bonds) and in terms of annuitization (due to the large pool of recipients over which the fixed costs of annuitization can be spread). The total administrative costs of the Social Security program are only 0.2% of the program's asset balances.[35]

On the other hand, nations that have privatized all or part of their social insurance systems have much higher administrative costs. In the United Kingdom, for example, the cost of administering the investment accounts alone is 1.24% per year. These higher costs result from the administrative inefficiencies of smaller investment pools, the profits earned by private administrators, and the advertising expenditures associated with competition for individual retirement accounts. This may not seem like a very big difference, but earning 1.24% less each year adds up to a large effect when one is investing for the long term. For example, an administrative cost of 1.24% per year on a 40-year investment results in an account that is only two-thirds as large as one with administrative costs of 0.19% per year. Moreover, these are only the costs for administering the accounts, and not for the annuitization that will be provided when individuals retire. In the United Kingdom, those administrative costs amount to another 15% of account balances, so that costs and fees in total reduce the average account's value by 43%.[36]

The United Kingdom is not an unusual example; in Chile, for example, the administrative costs of its privatized system were initially over 5% per year, and even after 15 years of program operation, the costs had fallen only to 1.36% per year.[37] In the U.S. context, with our sophisticated mutual fund and life insurance industries, it is possible that administrative costs could be much lower, but international evidence is not very heartening on this front.

A third problem with privatization is that policy makers may not *want* to respect consumer sovereignty with respect to retirement savings. After all, the main motivation in most policy makers' eyes for having the Social Security program is that individuals are too short-sighted or uninformed to save for their own retirement. Yet privatization would suggest that individuals *can be trusted* with the much more complicated decision of how to optimally invest

---

[35] Social Security Trustees (2006), Table II.B.1.
[36] Orszag (1999).
[37] James, Smalhout, and Vittas (2001).

their (forced) retirement savings. This seems a clear contradiction. Just as the government may have a paternalistic role in forcing consumers to save, it may also have a role in telling them how to save.

▶ **APPLICATION**

Company Stock in 401(k) Plans

An important feature of retirement savings in the United States has been the growth of 401(k) plans. These plans, discussed in more detail in Chapter 22, allow individuals to save for their own retirement, in self-directed investment choices. A number of recent studies have documented problems, however, with how these choices are made, illustrating the hazards of allowing individuals to direct their Social Security investments.

One option in many company 401(k) plans is to invest money in company stock. But it is an option that almost never makes sense, particularly for large parts of one's retirement portfolio. There are two major sources of financial uncertainty in a worker's life: their job security, and the performance of their savings. Investing in company stock *binds these sources of uncertainty together*. If the company does well, the worker will do very well. But if the company does badly, the worker is both out of a job *and* out of savings. Once again, given our desire for smooth consumption, we should much prefer an outcome where these two aspects of uncertainty are unrelated: a middle path is always preferred to a feast-or-famine outcome.

Despite this logic, investing in company stock is a popular option for 401(k) account holders. Half of people with 401(k)s have the option of investing in company stock, and in total, company stock makes up one-sixth of aggregate 401(k) assets. Of those workers who have the option to invest in company stock, one-seventh have over 80% of their assets invested in company stock.[38]

The hazards of this approach are illustrated by the experience of workers at Enron, once one of the largest energy companies in the world. When large accounting irregularities were exposed at Enron in 2001, the company went bankrupt, over 4,000 workers lost their jobs in a single day, and more had their retirement savings wiped out. Sixty-two percent of Enron's 401(k) assets had been invested in its own stock, which lost over 99% of its value over the course of the year surrounding its bankruptcy.[39] Fortunately, these workers still had Social Security to support them in their retirement, but if privatized Social Security had been invested as poorly as their 401(k) funds, those Social Security benefits would have disappeared as well! ◀

The Trade-offs Between Fundamental Reforms To summarize, there is a clear and important trade-off between equity investment of the trust fund and individual accounts. Government equity investment is likely more effi-

---

[38] Holden and VanDerhei (2003).
[39] Davis (2002).

cient than individual private accounts, since it reduces administrative costs and solves the failures of optimization that appear to mark individual retirement savings decisions. But it is risky to give the government such a large stake in private equity markets, and it doesn't solve the problem of the government spending the trust fund surplus.

One potential middle ground is *government regulated accounts*. Under such a plan, each person would get an account, but the government would limit investment choices and force annuitization. In the application, we review the nature of such "mixed" proposals. As with most middle grounds, however, this approach may leave no one happy: it is too risky for the traditionalists, and not private enough for the privatizers. Thus, Social Security reform remains one of the most daunting problems facing our nation today and in the future.

► APPLICATION

Mixed Proposals for Social Security Reform[40]

In 2001, President Bush appointed a commission to propose solutions to Social Security's long-term fiscal problem. This commission proposed three plans, each of which included government-regulated individual accounts. None of the plans proposed fully replacing the existing pay-as-you-go Social Security system with a system of private accounts; rather, each proposal reflected a hybrid between the current structure and a privatized structure. Under one of the options, for example, workers would have the choice of investing up to 2% of their wages in a personal account. If they chose this option, they would then see their future Social Security benefits reduced by the amount of wages they invested in personal accounts, assuming an interest rate of 3.5%. Thus, if people could earn a rate of return in excess of 3.5%, they might choose to opt out of part of the traditional Social Security plan.

Each of the three plans tried to address some of the concerns about privatization, for example by suggesting government-regulated investments in personal accounts. But the major issue facing all of the plans is their cost. Because all of the plans divert some payroll tax revenues away from the Social Security program and into private accounts, offsetting revenue increases need to be found so that the Social Security benefits we are currently obligated to pay can be paid. Under one plan, these revenues would come purely from other sources; other plans propose that the financing would come partly from decreases in Social Security benefits.

A more recent mixed proposal comes from Leibman et al. (2005). This proposal represents a consensus plan drawn up by three people who have advised politicians at very different points in the political spectrum. This plan has four key elements. First, cut Social Security benefits by (a) reducing the values of

---

[40] Information about the President's Commission to Strengthen Social Security (CSSS) can be found at http://www.csss.gov/.

the rate at which the PIA is converted to the AIME (as shown in Figure 13.1) to 67.6, 15, and 7.5, and (b) raising the Full Benefits Age to 68 and the Early Entitlement Age to 65. Second, raise new revenue through (a) a 1.5%-of-payroll mandatory contribution into personal retirement accounts, and (b) an increase in the maximum earnings that can be taxed, so that 90% of all earnings is taxed (in current terms, that would imply an increase to $171,600, or roughly a doubling of the current maximum). Third, establish individual retirement accounts with the following rules: a 3%-of-earnings contribution rate, investment options restricted to five broad options provided by no more than 15 companies (to restrict administrative costs and the possibility of poor investment choices), and mandatory annuitization. Leibman et al. estimated that this plan would break even, although it would deliver larger benefits to higher earners. ◀

13.5
Conclusion

Social Security is the largest social insurance program in the United States, and the largest single expenditure item of the federal government. Not surprisingly, this program has major implications for the standard of living of the elderly, as well as for the non-elderly who pay the taxes to support this program. Social Security faces a long-run financing problem to which there are no easy solutions. The question of how to resolve this problem will be one of the most contentious sources of political debate for at least the first part of the twenty-first century.

▶ HIGHLIGHTS

- Social Security is the largest social insurance program in the United States.

- Social Security is financed by a tax on earnings, and pays benefits to retired workers. These benefits are a redistributive function of the workers' average lifetime earnings.

- Social Security is an unfunded system that has paid excessive returns to early generations. As a result, Social Security has a "legacy debt" that must be paid back.

- The government provides Social Security to remedy failures in private annuity markets and to paternalistically ensure that workers are saving appropriate amounts for their retirement.

- The Social Security program crowds out savings to some extent, but the consumption-smoothing value of this program to the elderly is shown by the dramatic reduction in elderly poverty rates over the past 40 years.

- At the same time, Social Security has been shown to significantly increase retirement rates in the United States and other nations.

- The system faces a major shortfall over the next 75 years because people are living longer, birth rates are falling, wages are growing more slowly, and payroll taxes are not scheduled to rise.

- There are a variety of options for reforming the Social Security program to move it to more sound financial footing, ranging from the basic (raising payroll taxes further) to the radical (privatizing the system).

▶ QUESTIONS AND PROBLEMS

1. The government of Westlovakia has just reformed its social security system. This reform changed two aspects of the system: (1) it abolished the actuarial reduction for early retirement, and (2) it reduced the payroll tax by half for workers who continued to work beyond the early retirement age. Would the average retirement age for Westlovakian workers increase or decrease in response to these two changes, or can you tell? Explain your answer.

2. When you called her last night, your grandmother confided that she is afraid to sell her home because doing so will affect her Social Security benefits. You told her that you'd call her back as soon as you read Chapter 13. Now that you've read it, what will you say to her about how her benefits will change when she sells her house?

3. Congressman Snicker has proposed a bill that would increase the number of years of earnings counted when computing the Social Security Average Indexed Monthly Earnings amount from 35 to 40. What would be the effects of this policy change on the retirement behavior of workers? Would the Social Security trust fund balance increase or decrease? Why?

4. Suppose the Social Security payroll tax were increased today to 16.4% in order to solve the 75-year fiscal imbalance in the program. Explain the effect of this change on the value of the Social Security program for people of different ages, earning levels, and sexes.

5. Senator Deal proposes to offer a choice to future retirees: if you retire before age 70 the benefits are calculated on the last 35 years of your income; if you retire at age 73, however, you receive benefits calculated on only the last 15 years of income. Which option are high-income workers likely to choose? Low-income workers? Why?

6. Consider two households, the Smiths and the Joneses. The Smiths are a two-earner household: both Dick and Jane Smith work and earn the same amount each year. The Joneses are a one-earner household: Sally Jones works while Harry Jones is a homemaker and stay-at-home dad. Use the way spousal benefits are treated in the Social Security system to address the following:
    a. How do the relative rates of return on Social Security payroll taxes compare for the two families?

    b. After the kids go off to college, Harry considers taking a small part-time job. How might the Social Security system of taxes and benefits affect his decision?

    c. Suppose that both families have retired and have started to receive Social Security benefits. By what fraction will these benefit fall for each of these families if one member of the household dies? What implications does this have for relative consumption smoothing in these two households?

7. Senator Dare suggests lowering Social Security benefits by reducing the rate at which Average Indexed Monthly Earnings are converted to the Primary Insurance Amount for future retirees. Senator Snow instead proposes reducing the rate at which benefits are indexed to inflation so that when the Consumer Price Index rises by one percentage point, Social Security benefits rise by less than one percent. Which proposal will be worse for current retirees? For future retirees?

8. What are the political and economic ramifications of investing a large part of the Social Security trust fund in the stock market, as has been recently proposed?

9. Prior to 1982, college-age children of deceased workers received college tuition subsidies as benefits of the Social Security program. Drawing on the lessons of Chapter 11, what do you think the rationale for such a program was?

10. Dominitz, Manski, and Heinz (2003) present survey evidence suggesting that young Americans are extremely uncertain about the likelihood that they will receive any Social Security benefits at all. How might demographic trends in the United States contribute to this concern?

11. The Social Security Administration Web site has a link to a publication entitled *Social Security Programs Throughout the World.* The European version is online at http://www.ssa.gov/policy/docs/progdesc/ssptw/2002-2003/europe/index.html. Pick any two countries in Europe and compare the key attributes of their social security programs. Which of these two countries do you think will have the greater rate of early retirement? Why?

▶ ADVANCED QUESTIONS

12. Lalaland is an extremely stable country with 200,000 residents, half of whom are young workers and half of whom are retirees. At the end of each "year," the 100,000 retirees die, the 100,000 young workers retire, and 100,000 new young workers are born. Workers earn a total of $5,000 for the year. Lalaland operates a "pay as you go" social security system, where each current worker is taxed $2,500 and the revenue collected is used to pay a $2,500 pension to each retiree. The neighboring country, Gogovia, is larger and more dynamic. Gogovia has an active stock market that Lalalandians could invest in and earn a 10% rate of return. It also has an active banking sector, which will gladly lend the Lalalandian government money, charging them 10% interest per year.

    Lalaland is considering moving to a system of personal accounts, where each Lalalander would take her $2,500 and invest it in Gogovian markets (and earn a much higher rate of return!). The government would borrow $250 million ($2,500 × 100,000) from Gogovian bankers to pay for current retirees. It would then tax retirees each year by just enough to pay the interest on this debt. Would this new system be better or worse for Lalaland?

13. Does Social Security provide much benefit in terms of consumption smoothing over the retirement decision? Contrast Social Security with a different social insurance program, unemployment insurance, which provides income support for half a year to people who have lost their job. Do you think that unemployment insurance is likely to provide more or less consumption smoothing than Social Security?

14. Edwards and Edwards (2002) describe evidence that, following a social security reform in Chile that reduced the implicit tax on working in the formal sector, informal sector wages rose. What do you think is the mechanism at work here?

15. Suppose that you had information about the amount of private savings during the years before and after the introduction of the Social Security program. How might you carry out a difference-in-difference analysis of the introduction of the Social Security program on private savings?

16. Suppose you find evidence that high-school-dropout workers are more likely to retire at age 62 than are college-educated workers. You conclude that the high-school-dropout workers do so because they are more liquidity-constrained than are other workers. Can you think of alternative explanations for this finding?

17. Consider an economy that is composed of identical individuals who live for two periods. These individuals have preferences over consumption in periods 1 and 2 given by $U = \ln(C_1) + \ln(C_2)$. They receive an income of 100 in period 1 and an income of 50 in period 2. They can save as much of their income as they like in bank accounts, earning an interest rate of 10% per period. They do not care about their children, so they spend all their money before the end of period 2.

    Each individual's lifetime budget constraint is given by $C_1 + C_2/(1 + r) = Y_1 + Y_2/(1 + r)$. Individuals choose consumption in each period by maximizing lifetime utility subject to this lifetime budget constraint.

    a. What is the individual's optimal consumption in each period? How much saving does he or she do in the first period?

    b. Now the government decides to set up a social security system. This system will take $10 from each individual in the first period, put it in the bank, and transfer it to him or her with interest in the second period. Write out the new lifetime budget constraint. How does the system affect the amount of private savings? How does the system affect national savings (total savings in society)? What is the name for this type of social security system?

    c. Suppose instead that the government uses the $10 contribution from each individual to start paying out benefits to current retirees (who did not pay in to a social security system when they were working). It still promises to pay current workers their $10 (plus interest) back when they retire using contributions from future workers. Similarly, it will pay back future workers interest on their contributions using the contributions of the next generation of workers. An influential politician says, "This is a free lunch: we help out current retirees, and current and future workers will still make the same contributions and receive the same benefits, so it doesn't harm them, either." Do you buy this argument? If not, what is wrong with it?

18. For each of the reforms listed below, briefly discuss the pros and cons of the reform, paying attention in particular to efficiency implications (through potential behavioral responses to the change) and equity implications (who wins and who loses). (Note that all reforms are intended to save the system money, so you do not need to list this as a benefit.)

    a. Increase the number of years used to calculate benefits from 35 to 40.

    b. Reduce benefits for beneficiaries with high asset levels (wealth).

    c. Add new state and local government workers to the pool of covered workers (i.e., they pay payroll taxes now and receive benefits when they are old).

    d. Gradually increase the normal retirement age (NRA) from 65 to 70 (under current laws, the NRA will gradually rise to 67 by 2022; the proposal is to speed up this process so the NRA will be 70 by 2022).

The ℮ icon indicates a question that requires students to apply the empirical economics principles discussed in Chapter 3 and the Empirical Evidence Boxes.

Unemployment Insurance, Disability Insurance, and Workers' Compensation

14

In December of 2002, 8.5 million Americans were out of work, and the unemployment rate had reached 6%, a level not seen since mid-1994. Many of the unemployed were receiving unemployment benefits under their state unemployment insurance programs, but such benefits typically ended after 26 weeks. Having recognized in March 2002 that 26 weeks might not be enough time to find a job in a sluggish economy, the Congress passed the Temporary Extended Unemployment Compensation Act (TEUC), granting an additional 13 weeks of benefits to those whose state unemployment benefits had run out. When TEUC expired on December 31, 2002, however, the additional 13 weeks of benefits would no longer be available.

There was tremendous controversy over how to address the fact that these extra benefits were ending. Some policy makers advocated an additional extension of a modest 5 weeks of benefits (at a cost of $1 billion). Others advocated a larger 12-week extension (at a cost of over $2 billion). The result of this disagreement was a stalemate, and on December 31, 2002, 800,000 unemployed persons stopped receiving the extra weeks of unemployment insurance benefits.

The public was in an uproar. Clearly sensing a groundswell in public opinion, Congress revisited this issue and within a week passed legislation even more generous than the large extension advocated earlier in the year. It retroactively restored benefits to those 800,000 and granted a 13-week extension to those becoming unemployed between January and May of 2003, a number estimated at about 1.6 million people.[1]

This debate illustrates that public provision of insurance for unemployment is considered an important role for government in the United States. Chapter 12 taught us, however, that public finance economists must step back and ask *why* there is a role for the government in providing this insurance. We must also consider whether the benefits of extending unemployment insurance

---

[1] Hulse (2003).

(the additional consumption smoothing for displaced workers) exceeds the costs (the moral hazard effects on unemployment).

In this chapter, we discuss in detail the issues that arise in providing unemployment insurance and two other major forms of social insurance: workers' compensation insurance against on-the-job injury, and disability insurance against career-ending disabilities. These are three of the largest social insurance programs in the United States, and they share many common features. Benefits are conditioned on the occurrence of some adverse event (unemployment, disability, injury), and are based on past earnings on the job. Most important, benefits are based at least partly on unobservable or difficult-to-verify conditions, such as job search effort and the true inability to work due to disability or injury. The unobservability of some aspects of the adverse event raises moral hazard problems that must be considered in program design.

We begin the chapter with a description of the structure of these three programs, comparing their similarities and differences. The next section presents the empirical evidence on the costs and benefits of these programs, and uses the framework from Chapter 12 to discuss the implications for optimal program benefit levels. We then look at the impact of these programs on employer decision making over issues such as worker layoffs and workplace safety. We conclude with a discussion of the implications of these findings for program reform.

14.1

Institutional Features of Unemployment Insurance, Disability Insurance, and Workers' Compensation

As with Social Security, it is difficult to discuss the economic implications of these social insurance programs without first understanding how they work. In this section, we provide a brief overview of the institutional features of these three programs.

Institutional Features of Unemployment Insurance

Unemployment insurance (UI) is a federally mandated program that is administered by each of the 50 U.S. states and the District of Columbia, which are free to set their benefit levels and other aspects of the program.[2] That UI is administered by the states is an excellent feature of this program for the purposes of empirical economics, because economists can learn about the consumption-smoothing and moral hazard effects of UI by studying how these effects vary as the generosity of state benefits vary. Indeed, the large empirical literature discussed in this chapter derives its success from the wide variation in UI programs across the states.

> **unemployment insurance** A federally mandated, state-run program in which payroll taxes are used to pay benefits to workers laid off by companies.

---

[2] For more information on UI, see Section 4 of the Green Book (U.S. House of Representatives Committee on Ways and Means, 2004).

partially experience-rated
The tax that finances the UI program rises as firms have more layoffs, but not on a one-for-one basis.

Unemployment insurance is financed by a payroll tax that is levied on employers and averages 2.1% across the states. As with the Social Security payroll tax, this tax is only paid on earnings up to a certain level, a fairly low level in most states. The UI payroll tax is **partially experience-rated;** that is, it rises as firms have more layoffs, but not on a one-for-one basis. Thus, firms with twice as many layoffs do not typically pay twice as much in payroll taxes.

An important feature of UI is that not all those out of work qualify for benefits. To be eligible, workers must meet three criteria. First, workers must have earned a minimum amount over the previous year; in most cases, states require minimum earnings in several previous calendar quarters before individuals are eligible for benefits. Second, workers cannot quit or be fired for cause; UI is available only to those who are laid off from their jobs for economic reasons. Third, workers have to be actively looking for work and willing to accept a job comparable to the one they lost. Even if eligible, individuals don't automatically receive benefits. They must go to the UI office and enroll in the program, and must show evidence that they are looking for a new job.

Between eligibility requirements and the effort required to claim UI, only 40% of unemployed workers actually receive UI benefits.[3] Even among those eligible, take-up of benefits is only about two-thirds (Blank and Card, 1991). The reasons for this lack of participation among those eligible for benefits are unclear, but they are usually divided into two issues. The first is information: some individuals may not understand that they are entitled to UI when they lose their jobs. The second is the stigma attached to being unemployed: individuals may be reluctant to sign up for what they see as a government handout, particularly since they would actually have to go to a public office and state that they can't find a job.

Once an individual qualifies for UI, he receives a benefit that is a function of his pre-unemployment earnings, which is typically measured by the average weekly wage in the quarter of the past year when earnings were highest. The benefits schedule for a typical state, Michigan, is shown in Figure 14-1. There is a minimum benefit level of $81 per week for all workers who earned over $152 per week on average in their highest-earning quarter of the past year. If earnings were less than $152 per week on average during the quarter, no benefits are paid. Benefits are increased by $0.53 for each dollar of pre-unemployment earnings (4.1% of wages earned in their highest-earning quarter), until reaching a maximum benefit level of $362 per week.

As with Social Security, a key measure of the generosity of the UI program is the *replacement rate,* the extent to which benefits replace pre-layoff earnings. The replacement rate under the United States' UI system is high for the lowest-paid workers but can be low for higher-earning workers, because their benefits are capped at the maximum benefit level (such as $362 per week in Michigan). Replacement rates also vary substantially across states. Replace-

---

[3] For the most recent figures on UI benefits recipient rates, see the U.S. Department of Labor's Web site on UI data at http://workforcesecurity.doleta.gov/unemploy/content/data.asp.

■ FIGURE **14-1**

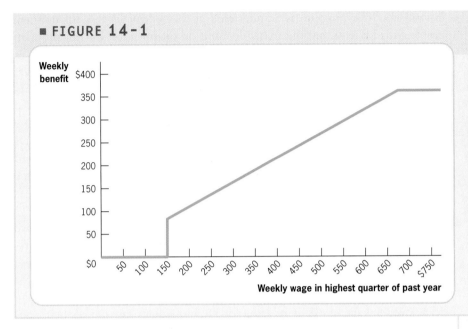

Unemployment Benefit Schedule for Michigan ● In the state of Michigan, no unemployment benefits are paid to those earning less than $152 per week in the highest quarter of the past year. Once the $152 level has been reached, unemployment benefits rise with the weekly wage in the highest quarter of the past year, with a maximum benefit of $362.

Source: U.S. Department of Labor (2006b).

ment rates average 47% nationally, but unemployed Alaskans have an average replacement rate of only 31%, while unemployed Rhode Islanders average about 56%.[4] Unlike most other social insurance programs, the benefits received from UI are taxed as if they were wage income.

The other key aspect of benefit payments under UI is their duration. Benefits generally last for 26 weeks, with some exceptions. First, workers who have sporadic work histories can qualify for benefits, but only for a shorter period of time. Second, there is an automatic extended UI program that goes into effect whenever a state's unemployment rate exceeds some (fairly high) threshold; when this program is in effect, individuals are entitled to 13 more weeks of benefits. Finally, in recessionary periods, the federal government has typically intervened to mandate further extensions in UI availability, as seen in the example at the start of this chapter. In the early 1980s, during the deepest recession since World War II, the combination of state-extended benefits programs and federal extensions led to a maximum entitlement of 65 weeks, or 2.5 times the typical benefits availability period.

Institutional Features of Disability Insurance

The **disability insurance (DI)** program was introduced in 1957 to provide insurance against career-ending disabilities. Along with Social Security, DI is part of the Old Age Security and Disability Income (OASDI) program. The DI program currently has benefits expenditures of $85.4 billion, over 15% of the total OASDI budget.[5] It is financed by a portion of the Social Security

disability insurance A federal program in which a portion of the Social Security payroll tax is used to pay benefits to workers who have suffered a medical impairment that leaves them unable to work.

---

[4] U.S. Department of Labor (2004), Chart A.17.
[5] Social Security Trustees (2006), Table II.B1.

payroll tax. The program is administered at the federal level, with uniform nationwide benefits, but the initial decision on qualification for this program is made at the state level.

To apply for DI, individuals must have a medical impairment that leaves them unable to work. In order to prove disability, the DI program mandates that individuals cannot receive benefits until they have been disabled for five months; that is, individuals who want to receive DI must first go five months without working to demonstrate that they are truly disabled. DI applications go to state medical determination boards for a decision, and these boards are fairly stringent in awarding benefits; the DI acceptance rate—the share of those applying who are accepted into the program—is only about one-third.

If awarded benefits, workers receive the same amount they would have received if they retired at the Full Benefit Age of 65 under the Social Security program (their Primary Insurance Amount). As with Social Security, these benefits are largely untaxed. Two years after disability, workers also qualify for health insurance coverage under the Medicare program available to all Americans over the age of 65. If rejected for DI, individuals can appeal their cases through the court system. Ultimately, because of successful appeals, about half of those applying for DI receive benefits. Once receiving DI, individuals are very unlikely to leave the program, and eventually move into the old-age portion of OASDI at age 65.

While the disability evaluations are made by trained professionals, it is nevertheless difficult to perfectly assess disability. An illustration of these problems is provided by Parsons (1991), who reported on a study in which a set of disability claims was initially reviewed by a state panel and then, one year later, resubmitted to the same panel, but as anonymous new claims. For the majority of claims (78%), the panel made the same decision that it had the previous year. For the other 22%, however, the panel switched its decision: 22% of those who had initially qualified for DI were rejected one year later, and 22% of those initially rejected for DI were found to be qualified one year later. That the same set of experts cannot provide a consistent judgment of disability for such a large share of cases highlights the difficulties in assessing true disability.

Institutional Features of Workers' Compensation

workers' compensation
State-mandated insurance, which firms generally buy from private insurers, that pays for medical costs and lost wages associated with an on-the-job injury.

Workers' compensation (WC) differs from UI and DI in that it is not publicly provided insurance. Instead, state governments *mandate* that all employers buy insurance against on-the-job accidents. WC insurance is typically provided by private companies, but in some states the state government may sell WC insurance as well. The nature of this program, including benefits determination, varies greatly across the states (similar to UI). The premiums that firms pay for this insurance are experience-rated more tightly than with UI, however: for most large firms, WC premiums are based purely on their past history of WC claims. (For small firms, there is less experience rating at the firm level.)

■ TABLE 14-1

Maximum Indemnity Benefits Paid to Selected Types of Work Injuries in 2005

State	Type of permanent impairment					Temporary injury (10 weeks)
	Arm	Hand	Eye	Leg	Foot	
Georgia	$ 95,625	$ 68,000	$ 63,750	$ 95,625	$ 57,375	$ 4,000
Hawaii	194,064	151,768	99,520	179,136	127,510	5,800
Illinois	137,618	104,589	82,571	123,859	85,323	10,044
Indiana	86,500	62,500	50,500	74,500	50,500	5,880
Michigan	185,341	148,135	111,618	148,135	111,618	6,530
Mississippi	70,228	52,671	35,114	61,450	43,893	3,311
Missouri	82,140	61,958	49,567	72,388	54,878	6,493
New Jersey	161,370	98,000	62,200	154,035	81,650	6,380
New York	124,800	97,600	64,000	115,200	82,000	4,000
Washington, DC	239,148	187,026	122,640	220,752	157,388	10,220

The benefits for different types of injuries differ greatly across this sample of states. The last column shows the benefits (from 2003) over 10 weeks for a temporary total injury that leaves the worker unable to work.

WC insurance has two components. The first is medical coverage for the costs associated with the injury. The second is cash payments to compensate the worker for lost wages during recuperation from the injury. In most states, WC systems are designed to replace two-thirds of workers' wages, but, unlike UI, WC benefits are not taxed by the federal income tax system.[6] As a result, the after-tax replacement rate can be considerably higher: a worker with a tax rate of 25% (roughly the median) can work and receive $0.75 of each dollar earned (net compensation after tax), or the worker can receive WC and get $0.67 tax-free, so that the after-tax replacement rate is actually 89% (67/75).

Workers' compensation benefits vary significantly across the country, as shown in Table 14-1, which shows the compensation under WC systems in ten states for permanent impairment to different body parts. Losing a leg in Washington, DC, entitles a worker to nearly four times as much compensation as in the state of Mississippi, for example ($220,752 versus $61,450).[7] Most benefits payments are made for what are called "temporary total injuries," which keep the worker from working, but only for a short period of time. Classic examples of temporary total injuries include lacerations or back sprains. The problems in consistently diagnosing these types of injuries are even harder than those faced by the DI program. Temporary injuries are typically harder to diagnose than permanent disabilities, and it is often even more difficult to assess whether an injury is truly work-related.

---

[6] For more information on WC, see Section 15-WC of the Green Book (U.S. House of Representatives Committee on Ways and Means, 2004).
[7] U.S. Department of Labor (2005a), Table 9a.

▪ **TABLE 14-2**

Comparing Unemployment Insurance, Disability Insurance, and Workers' Compensation

Characteristic	UI	DI	WC
Qualifying event	Unemployment and job search	Disability	On-the-job injury
Duration	26–65 weeks	Indefinite	Indefinite (with medical verification)
Difficulty of verification	Unemployment: Easy Job search: Nearly impossible	Somewhat difficult	Very difficult
Average after-tax replacement rate	47%	60%	89%
Variation across states	Benefits and other rules	Only disability determination	Benefits and other rules

Source: U.S. Department of Labor (2004), Chart A.17; National Academy of Social Insurance (2005); Hunt (2004).

UI, DI, and WC differ along many dimensions, such as the qualifying event, the duration of benefits, the difficulty of verifying eligibility for the program, the average after-tax replacement rate, and the extent to which the program varies across states.

no-fault insurance When there is a qualifying injury, the workers' compensation benefits are paid out by the insurer regardless of whether the injury was the worker's or the firm's fault.

A key feature of WC is that it provides **no-fault insurance** against accidents. Prior to the creation of WC systems at the beginning of the twentieth century, if workers were injured on the job they had to sue their employers for compensation. This system was viewed as unfair because injured low-income workers may not have had the resources to bring suit against employers. Moreover, there was substantial deadweight loss involved in using the courts as a means to settle injury claims. Since all that was at stake was a transfer of money from employers to employees, all the costs associated with these cases (such as lawyers' fees and other court costs) were a waste to society.[8] WC, in contrast, does not assign blame for injuries: regardless of whose fault it is, workers are entitled to insurance benefits if they are injured on the job. As a result of this approach, the transaction costs of the transfer are greatly reduced by the existence of no-fault WC.

Comparison of the Features of UI, DI, and WC

Table 14-2 compares the major features of these three programs. UI provides benefits that are the least generous and have the shortest duration. The event of unemployment is easy to verify, but confirming whether an individual is actually searching for a job is close to impossible. The benefits under DI are somewhat more generous, and are of indefinite length. Disability for DI is

---

[8] Recall from the cost-benefit analysis of Chapter 8 that transfers from one party to another do not affect social costs, so any costs in enabling these transfers are wasteful from a social perspective.

somewhat difficult to verify. WC has the most generous benefits of all, and the duration of benefits is as long as a physician is willing to say that the worker is not recovered. Injury for this program is often much harder to verify than for DI.

► APPLICATION

The Duration of Social Insurance Benefits Around the World

The three U.S. programs we study in this chapter have very distinct time patterns: UI is paid out for a limited period of time (usually 26 weeks); DI is paid out indefinitely, with relatively little effort to reassess the readiness of the disabled individual to work again; and WC is paid out for as long as the injury can be medically verified. These are not the only time patterns possible. For example, for UI, we could simply pay out a lump-sum amount when individuals lose their jobs. Or, we could follow Europe's example, which is illustrated for several representative nations in Figure 14-2. The typical European approach is to pay out benefits for a fairly long period (a year or more) at a fairly high replacement rate. Then, when that time limit is reached, rather than simply cutting off the benefits, workers are moved to a welfare system that usually features lower benefits for an indefinite period of time. (In Sweden, benefits actually rise after 15 months of unemployment.)

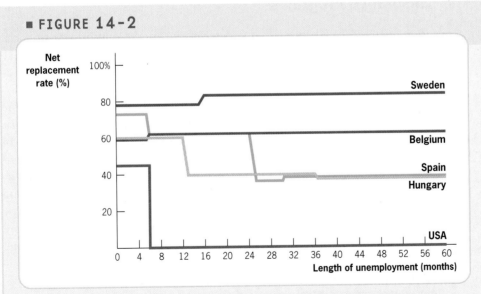

■ FIGURE 14-2

Duration of UI Benefits • In most European countries, UI benefits are available for much longer than the six months (26 weeks) available in the United States. The United States is the only nation in this sample that leaves workers with no benefits entitlement within five years of unemployment.

Source: Organization for Economic Co-operation and Development (2002b).

The appropriate time pattern for benefits under social insurance programs must balance the trade-off among three considerations. The first consideration is moral hazard: the longer benefits last, the longer individuals will choose leisure over work. This is the motivation for the relatively short (compared to Europe) duration of UI benefits in the United States, which are paid for only 6 months (26 weeks).

The second consideration has to do with consumption smoothing. As noted in Chapter 12, individuals will be more able to self-insure their consumption over shorter adverse events than longer ones. As the duration of unemployment grows, the ability of individuals to self-insure their consumption falls, for example, as their savings run out.[9] This consideration would suggest that benefits rise, rather than fall, with duration.

The final consideration has to do with targeting the benefits to those who need them the most. Workers away from work (due to either unemployment or injury) for the longest period may be most in need of assistance from the government in finding a new job; if they could readily find one, they would have done so already. Under this logic, cutting benefits off after some fixed time is exactly the wrong thing to do. Given these three considerations, the optimal duration of social insurance benefits is quite difficult to compute, which may explain the differences in structures across similar industrialized nations. ◄

14.2

Consumption-Smoothing Benefits of Social Insurance Programs

As discussed in Chapter 12, one determinant of the optimal size of social insurance programs is the extent to which they crowd out self-insurance rather than providing consumption smoothing. Unfortunately, there is relatively little evidence on the consumption-smoothing implications of these programs. The most direct study is that of Gruber (1997), who measured the consumption-smoothing benefits of unemployment insurance. He found that individuals are not fully insured by other sources against the income loss of unemployment, that their consumption falls significantly when they lose their jobs, and that higher levels of UI do lessen the negative effects of this fall. Gruber's study also found, however, that the role of UI in consumption smoothing is limited: each dollar of UI benefits only reduces the fall in consumption by about 30¢. Referring to Figure 12-2, we see that the case of UI appears more readily described by the imperfect self-insurance case shown in the middle panel than by the no-self-insurance case shown in the first panel. UI smoothes consumption in a limited way because other forms of self-insurance enable unemployed workers to maintain part of their pre-unemployment consumption.

---

[9] Gruber (2001c) shows that the wealth holdings of the unemployed are sufficient to weather average unemployment spells for most workers, but that those who have the longest unemployment spells typically do not have enough wealth to cover their consumption for that extended period.

Another way to phrase this conclusion is that UI *crowds out* other forms of income support when people are unemployed. Other research shows directly that crowd-out occurs: when individuals face more generous unemployment insurance benefits, they save less, and their spouses are less likely to work when they lose their jobs. These studies estimate that crowd-out of UI is about $0.70 on the dollar, consistent with the consumption findings just noted. That is, these findings imply that, of each dollar of UI, $0.30 is going to increase consumption, and $0.70 is crowding out other forms of insurance that individuals were using for their unemployment spells.[10]

There is no parallel evidence on the consumption-smoothing properties of DI and WC. It seems clear that DI should play a stronger consumption-smoothing role than UI: disability is usually unexpected and permanent, so individuals are unlikely to be able to use their own savings (for example) to fully finance their consumption. The case for WC is less clear. On the one hand, true on-the-job injuries are probably even more unexpected than is unemployment, and can often last longer. On the other hand, many claimed on-the-job injuries are really planned, according to the moral hazard evidence presented next, so individuals may be well prepared to smooth their consumption.

14.3

Moral Hazard Effects of Social Insurance Programs

In contrast to the small amount of research that has been done on consumption-smoothing effects of these social insurance programs, there is a large literature on their moral hazard effects. In this section, we review that evidence.

Moral Hazard Effects of Unemployment Insurance

The major moral hazard effect of UI is seen in the duration of unemployment spells. The question of how UI affects the odds of becoming unemployed is a separate one that we take up when discussing the behavior of firms later in this chapter.

There is a voluminous economics literature on the effect of UI benefit levels on unemployment durations. The literature is motivated by facts such as those illustrated by Figure 14-3 (page 394). This figure shows the hazard diagram for exiting unemployment (akin to our hazard diagrams for retirement from the previous chapter); that is, the percent of unemployed workers exiting unemployment each week. There is a fairly steady exit pattern through the first 25 weeks of unemployment spells, with 5–7% of unemployed workers exiting each week. However, in the 26th week (when UI benefits run out), the exit rate jumps to 16.5%. This pattern suggests that UI benefits are a key factor in a person's decision about when to return to work.

---

[10] Engen and Gruber (2001), Cullen and Gruber (2000).

■ FIGURE 14-3

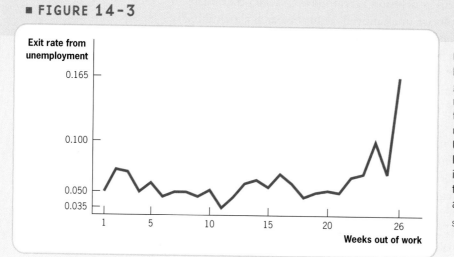

Unemployment Hazard Rate • Each point on this graph represents the hazard rate of unemployed workers, the rate at which they exit unemployment. Workers in the United States are much more likely to leave unemployment in the 26th week, the week that UI benefits end, than in any earlier week.

Source: Adapted from Meyer (1990), Table 4.

The most convincing studies in this literature use the quasi-experimental approach discussed in Chapter 3. In particular, because UI programs differ so much across states, researchers can use differences in benefits across state UI systems to measure the response of unemployment durations to benefit levels. Such analyses have suggested that higher benefits lead to a large increase in unemployment durations; the best estimate, reviewed in the Empirical Evidence box, suggests that each 10% rise in the amount of unemployment insurance benefits leads to unemployment durations that are 8% longer.

Normative Implications of Longer Durations

The clear conclusion from empirical research is that higher UI benefits have a significant causal effect on unemployment durations. The normative implications of this positive finding are, however, unclear, and depend on what the worker is doing during a longer unemployment duration. Suppose that unemployed workers can find jobs relatively easily, but that when benefits are high enough they delay taking those jobs while they take extra weeks of leisure in front of the TV. This outcome would imply that the increase in duration is inefficient, both because workers are not being productive when sitting at home and because higher taxes must be levied on productive workers to finance these benefits.

If instead workers spend this time looking for better jobs, however, longer durations might be an efficient outcome of UI. The productivity of

"I do intend to seek employment, but it will be at a time and place of my own choosing."

any worker in any job will depend on how well the worker is suited to that particular job. Workers who are highly productive in some jobs may be unproductive in others. Moreover, when workers with specialized skills lose their jobs, it may take them some time to find new ones. Taking the first job they are offered could be inefficient; society's productivity will clearly not be maximized if brain surgeons end up working in the fast-food sector! If UI is increasing duration by subsidizing effective (but time-intensive) job searches, then society may gain from the improved **job match quality.**[11]

How can we distinguish whether UI subsidizes unproductive leisure or productive job searches? The best way to do so is to study the quality of the post-UI job matches. If higher UI benefits are leading to longer durations because of more productive job searches, then we should see higher benefits leading to better job matches. But if higher UI benefits are simply subsidizing leisure, then there will be no better job matches when benefits increase, since individuals will just take jobs they would have taken without the benefits increase (with the benefits increase simply raising leisure before that job is taken).

While it is difficult to measure the quality of job matches, jobs' wage rates should be some indication of their quality. A finding that higher UI leads to higher post-unemployment wages would indicate that job matches are better. In fact, however, this is not the case: Meyer (1989) found that the post-unemployment wages of UI recipients are no higher when benefits rise, despite the longer unemployment durations. Thus, it appears that higher UI benefits are not leading to better job matches, and that UI has a significant moral hazard cost in terms of subsidizing unproductive leisure.

Evidence for Moral Hazard in DI

Concerns about moral hazard in the DI program arise because of the difficulty of determining if individuals are truly disabled. There have been a number of studies of the degree of moral hazard in the DI program. Essentially, all of these studies attempt to assess whether higher levels of DI benefits lead to more use of the program and/or less labor force participation. If there is no moral hazard, and individuals using these programs are truly disabled, then use of the programs (and labor supply) should be unaffected by benefit levels; individuals are either too disabled to work, or they are not. If benefit levels have a significant effect on the incidence of disability and the level of work effort, then these programs may have moral hazard effects.

The literature on moral hazard in disability insurance grows out of the facts shown in Figure 14-5 (page 398), from Parsons (1984). From 1957—when the DI program was introduced—until 1980, there was a tremendous concurrent expansion in the number of males age 45–54 receiving DI benefits and

> **job match quality** The marginal product associated with the match of a particular worker with a particular job.

---

[11] With a perfectly functioning capital market, this argument doesn't make much sense: workers who need to wait to find the right job matches could just take loans. In fact, however, the market for loans to unemployed workers is likely to be highly imperfect, so that providing income to the unemployed could improve their search.

MORAL HAZARD EFFECTS OF UNEMPLOYMENT INSURANCE

Perhaps the best illustration of the quasi-experimental approach is Bruce Meyer's (1989) classic study (Figure 14-4). Suppose the UI program in New Jersey pays a maximum benefit of $350 per week; any worker with earnings above $700 per week is eligible for the maximum benefit. New Jersey then changes its UI program so the maximum benefit is $400 per week. After the change, any worker with earnings above $800 per week (workers in group *H*) is eligible for the new maximum benefit. Workers with earnings above $800 per week have therefore seen an increase in their benefits of $50 per week.

This policy change sets up a natural quasi-experiment. Workers in group *H* in New Jersey (the treatment group) can be compared to workers with the same earnings ($800 or more per week) in another state that did not increase benefits, such as Pennsylvania (the control group). By doing this comparison, we can control for any changes over time that might affect unemployment durations, for example, a recession that affects both New Jersey and Pennsylvania. The change in unemployment duration in the control state (Pennsylvania) is a measure of how much the change in duration is due to the recession. The difference between the treatment state and the control state accounts for the recession effect and provides a causal estimate of the impact of the benefit change on the duration of unemployment spells.

To accomplish this analysis, Meyer computed the difference-in-difference estimate shown below:

By comparing the change in duration in the treatment state to that in the control state, Meyer rid the estimates of the impact of changes over time such as a recession. In doing so, he found that a 10% rise in benefits leads to an 8% increase in the length of durations.

As Meyer noted, however, this difference-in-difference approach may not provide a truly causal estimate. Suppose that the recession has a different effect in different states; in particular, New Jersey is hit hardest, which may even be the reason it raised its benefits. In this case, using Pennsylvania as a control would not be sufficient to eliminate any bias, because unemployment durations in New Jersey would have risen more due to the steeper recession in New Jersey, not due to higher benefits. If the treatment and control states are affected differently by the recession, bias would continue to be a problem in this cross-state comparison.

To try to eliminate the remaining bias in this comparison, Meyer suggested an additional control: group *L* in Figure 14-4, low earners in New Jersey, for whom benefits did not change. Since this group is in the same state as group *H*, they are subject to the same (New Jersey-specific) recession, and thus to the same source of potential bias from that recession. Thus, we can compute a similar difference-in-difference estimate to Meyer's original, but using workers in group *L* in New Jersey as the control, rather than using group *H* in Pennsylvania as the control. Meyer undertook both these checks on his results (comparing group *H* to both group *L* within the same state and to group *H* in

$$\frac{\begin{aligned} \text{Duration(treatment, after)} - \text{Duration(treatment, before)} &= \text{Treatment effect} + \text{Recession effect} \\ \text{Duration(control, after)} - \text{Duration(control, before)} &= \text{Recession effect} \end{aligned}}{\text{Difference} = \text{Treatment effect}}$$

the number of men in that age group dropping out of the labor force. This striking correspondence suggests that DI plays a large role in reducing labor force participation, which is consistent with moral hazard. It is hard to draw strong conclusions from this evidence, however, because many other things were changing in the 1960s and 1970s that may have led older men to work less. For example, many of the disabled could have been World War II veterans who, because of their war injuries, may have been less physically able to work at older ages, and so would have dropped out of the labor force even if other states), and his conclusions were unchanged. (Note that it is possible to use both checks simultaneously in an effort to rid the estimates of bias; this approach is described in detail in the appendix to this chapter.)

There is also some randomized trial evidence to draw on in evaluating the impact of UI benefits on unemployment durations. In the 1980s, a number of states pursued "reemployment bonus experiments," in which a treatment group of individuals on UI was offered a bonus if they found a job more quickly, and in which a control group of UI recipients was not offered this bonus. For example, in the Illinois experiment, treatment UI recipients were offered cash bonuses of $500 (equivalent to 4 weeks of UI benefits for the typical worker at that time) if they found a job within 11 weeks of filing for UI. These experiments generally showed a significant decline in unemployment durations of treatments, relative to controls, when the bonuses were offered; on average, across experiments, the offer of such bonuses caused unemployment durations to decline by about half a week, or 3% of average duration.[12] Thus, we can confirm from a randomized trial that unemployment durations are indeed responsive to benefit levels.

■ FIGURE 14-4

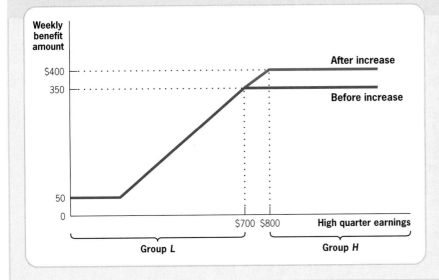

Quasi-Experiments for Studying the Effect of UI Benefits on Unemployment Durations ● The treatment state of New Jersey originally provides a maximum benefit of $350 for workers earning more than $700 per week. It then raises its maximum benefit to $400, which applies to all workers earning more than $800 per week (group *H*). Workers earning less than $700 per week (group *L*) are not affected by this policy change.

Source: Adapted from Meyer (1989), Table 1.

there were no DI program. In addition, the growth of private pension programs over this period may have made retirement more attractive.

A second source of evidence for a moral hazard effect of DI comes from the role of the business cycle. A number of studies have documented that disability applications rise sharply during recessions.[13] It seems highly unlikely

---

[12] Woodbury and Spiegelman (1987).
[13] See, for example, Lewin Group (1995).

■ FIGURE 14-5

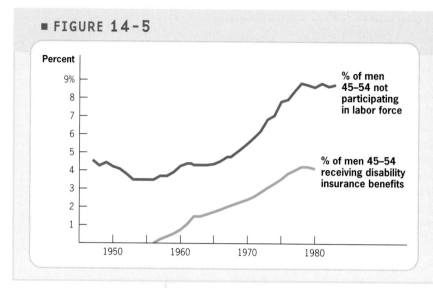

Labor Force Nonparticipation of Older Men and Growth in DI ● There is a striking correspondence between the growth in the DI program from the mid-1950s to the mid-1970s, and the rise in nonparticipation rates of men age 45–54 during this same period. This correspondence may indicate that the availability of DI induced older men to leave the labor force, but other factors may also explain the correspondence.

Source: Parsons (1984), Figure 1.

that more individuals become disabled in recessions than in other times, so this finding is consistent with a moral hazard effect: workers are out of work anyway due to the recession, so the five-month waiting period for DI is less of a barrier, and they are willing to take a chance at applying even if they are not "truly" disabled.

Another test of moral hazard is to assess how changes in the generosity of the DI benefits affect work effort. One recent study, reviewed in the Empirical Evidence box, finds that labor supply does respond to benefits generosity, but fairly modestly, with an elasticity of labor supply with respect to benefits of 0.3: that is, for every 10% increase in DI benefits, the numbers of older workers in the labor force fall by 3%.[14] This is much lower, for example, than Meyer's estimate of an elasticity of 0.8 for unemployment durations with respect to UI benefits, indicating that moral hazard is less of an issue in the DI program than it is in the UI program.

Evidence for Moral Hazard in WC

There is much evidence that points to a major moral hazard effect of the WC program. The first is Krueger's (1990) study of the incidence of injuries, where he asked: Does the rate of reported injury on the job depend on the generosity of the WC system? Krueger answered this question by using the fact that benefits for WC vary across the states and looking at how reported rates of on-the-job injury change when states increase their WC benefits. In the absence of moral hazard, there would be no reason for the injury rate to rise just because a state increased its benefits. In fact, however, that is exactly

---

[14] Gruber (2000).

MORAL HAZARD EFFECTS OF DI

The problem researchers face in assessing the effect of DI benefits generosity on work and disability in the United States is the same as that faced by those studying Social Security. Because DI is a national program, there are few good quasi-experiments for assessing the impact of the program changes on outcomes within the United States. Cross-sectional regression analysis of how DI benefits affect work effort are not convincing because the differences in DI benefits across individuals is mostly determined by characteristics of the individuals themselves, such as their past earnings. These characteristics might be correlated with the taste for leisure. For example, the treatment group with high DI replacement rates (because of low labor market earnings) and the control group with low DI replacement rates (because of high labor market earnings) may also have very different tastes for leisure. Since it is difficult to control for factors such as taste for leisure, cross-sectional models can be subject to bias.

There is some suggestive international evidence, however. Gruber (2000) studied Canada's DI system, which is similar to that in the United States with one major exception: the province of Quebec has a DI program that is different from the one in the rest of Canada. Beginning in 1973, the benefits in Quebec rose more rapidly than did the benefits in the rest of Canada. Then, in January 1987, the rest of Canada increased its benefits to equal those in Quebec, raising the replacement rate for the typical disabled worker from 25% to 33%. This event provides a quasi-experiment for studying the impact of DI on labor supply: the treatment group is workers in the rest of Canada, for whom there was a major rise in benefits, and the control group is workers in Quebec, where there was little change.

This research found that around 1987 there was a decline in the labor force participation rates of older men in the rest of Canada (the treatment group) that corresponded to the timing of the benefits increase. This decline amounted to 1.7 percentage points of the total older male population. Because participation rates for older males in Quebec actually rose by 1 percentage point, the net relative decline in the rest of Canada was actually 2.7 percentage points (the difference-in-difference estimate). While this response (a 12% increase in nonparticipation among older men) was large, it remained modest relative to the enormous 36% increase in benefits, so that the implied elasticity of labor supply with respect to benefits was only about 0.3.

what Krueger found: every 10% increase in benefits generosity led to a 7% rise in the rate of reported injury (a large elasticity of 0.7).

The second piece of evidence comes from Krueger's (1991) study of the impact of WC benefits on injury durations, which is similar to earlier studies of the impact of UI on unemployment durations. In this study, reviewed in the Empirical Evidence box, Krueger found enormous impacts of benefits on injury durations, with each 10% rise in benefits leading to durations that were 17% longer! This is a much larger response than for UI, where 10% higher benefits led to 8% longer unemployment durations.

Another piece of evidence for moral hazard in WC comes from the *types of injuries* reported. Recall that the problem of moral hazard is a problem of unobservability of true injury status. Unobservability implies that moral hazard would be worse for injuries that are hard to observe or verify, such as sprains or strains, and less of a problem for verifiable injuries, such as lacerations or broken or missing limbs. In fact, Krueger (1991) found that the response of injury durations to benefits increases is much stronger for hard-to-verify injuries than

KRUEGER'S STUDY OF WORKERS' COMPENSATION

Figure 14-6 illustrates the excellent quasi-experiment for the state of Minnesota used by Krueger (1991). Minnesota had a WC program with three flat rates, along with two sloped segments connecting these flat rates. On October 1, 1986, the state increased the benefits along each of the flat-rate portions but left the slopes unchanged. This policy change sets up three treatment groups, the workers on each of the flat-rate portions (groups A, C, and E), and two control groups, the workers on the sloped portions (groups B and D). It seems unlikely that there are other factors changing that affect only the three treatment groups and not the two control groups, except for the benefits change that affects the treatments but not the controls. Thus, the treatment and control groups should be comparable; this condition made it possible for Krueger to estimate a causal effect of the benefits change.

The numbers along each segment of this schedule show the percentage change in injury durations from before to after October 1, 1986. For groups A, C, and E (for whom benefits increased), there were large rises in injury durations: 23.5% for group A, 10.7% for group C, and 13.2% for group E. For groups B and D (for whom benefits did not increase), however, the rise in injury durations was negligible (1.4% for group B and 4.5% for group D).[15] Thus, increases in benefits appear to be associated with increases in injury duration. The estimated response of injury duration to increased benefits is enormous, with an implied elasticity of 1.7; that is, each 10% rise in benefits led to an injury duration that was 17% longer.

for easier-to-verify injuries. That is, a rise in benefits causes a very large increase in reported back sprains, for example, but a smaller increase (or none at all) for lacerations.

A final interesting piece of evidence for the moral hazard effects of WC comes from the infamous "Monday effect." By examining the types of claims made for WC by day of the week, one sees that on Mondays there is a large rise in sprains and strains relative to lacerations.[16] This suggests that many of the reported injuries on Mondays may actually arise from injuries incurred over the weekend, and then claimed on Monday in order to qualify for WC. If you strain yourself playing softball on Sunday, it may be quite easy to pretend that it happened at work on Monday; but if you cut yourself with a power saw on Sunday, it will be much harder to pretend that this is a work accident on Monday!

14.4

The Costs and Benefits of Social Insurance to Firms

Thus far, our analysis has focused on the impact of the social insurance programs on workers. Yet because employers play an important role in both layoffs and work injuries, both UI and WC programs can have important

---

[15] Referring to our discussion of regression analysis in the appendix to Chapter 3, the estimates for the three treatment groups were all statistically significant, while neither of the estimates for the two control groups was statistically significant.

[16] Smith (1989).

■ FIGURE 14-6

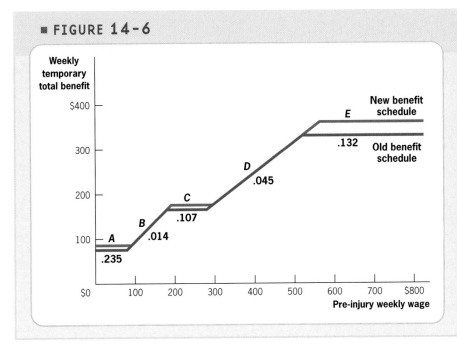

WC Benefits Changes and Injury Duration • On October 1, 1986, the state of Minnesota raised benefits for workers on segments A, C, and E of this schedule, while leaving benefits unchanged for segments B and D. Krueger found a sizeable rise in the duration of workplace injuries for workers at segments A, C, and E, but not for workers at segments B and D. Numbers below segments of the curve are differences (in log [weeks of benefits received]) between workers injured before and after the benefits change.

Source: Adapted from Krueger (1991), Figure 2.

impacts on firms' decision making as well. We first discuss the impact of UI on firms and then turn to the impact of WC.

The Effects of Partial Experience Rating in UI on Layoffs

The key feature of UI from the firm's perspective is that it is *partially experience-rated*. A fully experience-rated system would be one in which a firm pays additional tax each time it lays off a worker. The amount collected through the tax would equal the expected UI benefits paid to that worker. In the current UI system, payroll taxes do rise with past layoffs, but much less than one for one.

The degree of partial experience rating is illustrated in Figure 14-7, which shows the relationship between the UI payroll tax rate and past layoffs in Vermont, which has a typical state experience-rating system. There is a minimum payroll tax rate of 0.4% paid by all firms in the state. Beyond that point, the payroll tax rate rises with what is called the *benefit ratio,* the ratio of the payments made by the UI system to the firm's laid-off workers, relative to the size of the firm's payroll, averaged over the past four years. Thus, a benefit ratio of 10 means that UI paid benefits equal to 10% of the firm's payroll on average over the past four years. Once this measure of past layoffs reaches a particular level, the payroll tax rate climbs, continuing to ratchet upward in this fashion until it reaches a maximum rate of 5.4% for firms with a benefits ratio of 11 or higher.

Partial Experience Rating Subsidizes Layoffs A fully experience-rated system would follow the path of a 45-degree line from the origin, which would

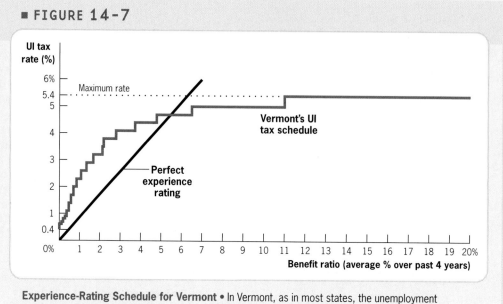

■ FIGURE 14-7

Experience-Rating Schedule for Vermont • In Vermont, as in most states, the unemployment insurance tax rate paid by employers rises as past layoffs rise, as measured by the benefit ratio, which is the ratio of unemployment insurance benefits paid to the firm's workers relative to the firm's payroll. This rise is not on the one-for-one basis, however, that would follow the perfect experience rating line. As a result, high-layoff (high-benefit ratio) employers are relatively subsidized by the system.

Source: State of Vermont (2005).

indicate a one-for-one increase in tax payments for each increase in benefits payouts. Relative to full experience rating, the Vermont system causes firms with a low level of layoffs to pay too much (since the actual schedule is above the 45-degree line), and firms with many layoffs to pay too little (since the actual schedule is below the 45-degree line). Thus, relative to a full system of experience rating, partial experience rating *subsidizes firms with high layoff rates.* This conclusion is best illustrated by the maximum condition: once firms reach the maximum UI tax rate, there is no additional tax cost to them for additional layoffs. This is a general phenomenon in states across the nation: high-layoff firms are subsidized for additional layoffs, relative to a fully experience-rated system.

How is this a subsidy? Think about the firm and the worker as making a joint decision about whether to place the worker on *temporary layoff,* where the worker spends some time laid off but with a promise (explicit or implicit) to be hired back after the layoff is over (like my wife's aunt in the example in Chapter 12). From the worker's perspective, a temporary layoff is some time off at a partial wage—a partially paid vacation. From the firm's perspective, the attractiveness of a temporary layoff depends on the extent of experience rating. If there is no experience rating, the firm pays nothing when a worker is temporarily laid off. So this is a vacation for workers, paid for by the government—a good deal for both firms and workers.

Contrast this with full experience rating. In that case, the benefits paid to the worker would be exactly canceled by the taxes paid by the firm, so that, on net, there would be no money flowing from the government to this worker–firm pair. Thus, if the worker wants a paid vacation, the firm has to pay for it; there is no subsidy to layoffs from the government because the firm pays the full costs of any layoffs.

Evidence on Effect of Partial Experience Rating on Layoffs It is clear from the previous discussion that firms should have more layoffs when a state's experience-rating system is more partial (that is, the more that the government, and not the firm, pays for benefits when the worker is laid off). In fact, there are several careful investigations of the impact of the experience-rating structure on layoff decisions. These studies investigated state systems with different degrees of experience rating and found that partial experience rating increases the rate of temporary layoffs, as predicted by the theory. The studies suggest that partial experience rating alone can account for 21–33% of all temporary layoffs in the United States.[17]

The "Benefits" of Partial Experience Rating

If partial experience-rating systems increase the number of layoffs in the U.S. labor market, why are they so common in state UI programs? Once again, the benefit that offsets this moral hazard cost is consumption smoothing. Having a fully experience-rated system would "hit firms while they are down": just when firms have laid off the most workers (presumably because the firm is not doing well), their taxes would increase the most.

At the same time, by having partial experience rating, UI programs systematically subsidize high-layoff firms. These firms may be particularly inefficient firms that, in a capitalist economy, should go out of business, leaving the field to their more efficient rivals. In particular, the system of partial experience rating subsidizes seasonal firms, which can afford to hire workers for just part of the year because the workers can receive UI for the remainder of the year, at no marginal cost to the firm. Anderson and Meyer (2000) computed that, in Washington state, the one-eighth of firms that are subsidized by the UI system for four continuous years account for one-third of all UI benefits payments.

▶ APPLICATION

The "Cash Cow" of Partial Experience Rating

The United States is actually relatively unique among industrialized nations in having *any* experience rating of its UI system, however partial. Most nations finance their UI systems through a flat payroll tax that is unrelated to the firm's actual layoff experience. Such a system can turn the UI system into a "cash cow" that subsidizes the existence of highly inefficient firms.

---

[17] Topel (1983), Anderson and Meyer (1993).

Consider the case of Canada's UI system, where workers traditionally had to work only 10 weeks to qualify for 42 weeks of UI with a replacement rate of 60%, at no extra cost to their firms. One can assess the implications of such a generous system by posing a hypothetical example. You and four friends want to figure out a way to work only 10 weeks a year, and take vacation the rest of the year. The five of you are considering buying a fishing boat, with each of you working 10 weeks out of the year, for a total of 50 weeks. You know that with this fishing boat you can catch $40,000 worth of fish during the entire year. That is only $8,000 of fish for each 10-week period, a sum that is not large enough to support each one of you for an entire year. In the absence of UI, then, you would not purchase this fishing boat, which is the socially efficient outcome: it would be inefficient for your combined group of workers to only produce $40,000 worth of goods per year.

Given the structure of the Canadian UI system, however, this purchase will be more attractive. In this system, you and your friends each work 10 weeks, for a total of 50 workweeks. Each of you would report earning $800 per week for the 10 weeks worked and then report being laid off. Because you report being laid off, you would each receive $20,160 of UI during the rest of the year (60% of the $800 per week reported earnings, for 42 weeks). So the total UI benefits income across all five recipients is $20,160 × 5 = $100,800. Adding the $40,000 of fish produced, that is a total income to the five of you of $140,800, or $28,160 per worker per year for only 10 weeks of work each! This makes the purchase of the fishing boat much more attractive.

This example illustrates the fundamental problem with partial experience rating: it subsidizes the existence of inefficient firms. Your firm is not an economically viable employer of five employees; it could pay each employee $8,000 per year only if there were no UI system. But by exploiting partial experience rating, the firm can remain viable, with each employee earning $28,160 for the year. Thus, UI is not simply a system of insurance against true unemployment risk in Canada, but also a large government transfer to inefficient firms and their laid-off workers. ◄

Workers' Compensation and Firms

A similar set of issues arises in the context of workers' compensation. With UI, partial experience rating means that firms and workers have an incentive to increase layoffs to exploit this government payment for leisure. With WC, firms and workers can get together to increase "injuries" if the insurance is less than fully experience-rated. There is an additional problem as well: firms have less incentive to invest in safety when there is no-fault insurance for injuries. In the past, when injuries could lead to lawsuits against a firm, firms had to trade off the cost of making workplaces safer against the costs of getting sued if someone was injured. Now, for the partially experience-rated firm, there are relatively little savings to making the workplace safer because the firm pays relatively little of the cost of the WC benefit if the worker is injured. Thus, an additional moral hazard for firms is that no-fault WC can lead to less-safe workplaces.

The potentially important role played by experience rating in WC is illustrated in Krueger's (1991) study. He compared the injury durations of employees of firms that *self-insure* their WC costs to the durations of employees of firms that buy their WC in a partially experience-rated insurance market. Self-insured firms pay their own injury claims, so by definition they are fully experience-rated (more injuries lead to higher costs for the firm). Krueger found that workers in self-insured firms came back to work more quickly from a given type of injury than did workers in comparable non-self-insured (partially experience-rated) firms. Moreover, in self-insured firms, worker injury durations were much less responsive to benefits increases than durations in non-self-insured firms. These findings suggest that firms that are more fully experience-rated are much more aggressive in monitoring worker injury durations.

14.5

Implications for Program Reform

This chapter has presented a large body of evidence on the costs and benefits of three of the most important social insurance programs in the United States. We can use this evidence, along with the theory presented in Chapter 12, to draw lessons for program reform.

Benefits Generosity

The optimal level of benefits generosity reflects the trade-off between moral hazard and consumption-smoothing benefits. It is clear that for all three programs studied here, the replacement rate should be less than 100%, because there is significant moral hazard associated with each type of insurance. The literature also indicates that the negative behavioral responses to these programs (such as longer unemployment or injury durations) are very large for WC, fairly large for UI, and smaller for DI. At the same time, the consumption-smoothing benefits are likely largest for DI, and have been shown to be only partial for UI (and likely for WC as well). Taken together, these facts suggest that benefits should be highest for DI and lowest for WC, with UI in the middle.

As Table 14-2 showed, however, this is not the case; in fact, WC has the most generous benefits of all of these programs. This is clearly inconsistent with the evidence presented here.

Targeting

Another issue that is raised by the discussions of Chapter 12 and the evidence in this chapter is the need to better target program benefits toward those who benefit the most from consumption smoothing and/or for whom the moral hazard problems of social insurance are smallest. Consider those who regularly have temporary unemployment spells and receive implicit promises from their employers that they can return to their old jobs. For this group, there is little consumption-smoothing benefit of UI because the predictability and regularity of such layoffs should allow them to use self-insurance to smooth consumption. Moreover, empirical analyses have shown that this is the group that is the most responsive to UI benefit levels in terms of extending unemployment durations. For this group, the costs of high UI benefits appear to outweigh their benefits. Thus, efficiency could be improved if UI benefits could be targeted away from this group and toward those who have been permanently laid off.

Targeting is also possible within the DI and WC programs, based on the type of injury or disability. Some injuries or disabilities are easier to diagnose, minimizing problems of moral hazard. Becoming blind or paralyzed, or having a laceration or losing a limb, is unlikely to represent a negative behavioral response to social insurance program generosity. In principle, it would be possible to arrange these programs so that higher benefits were paid to people with less ambiguous (easier to verify) disabilities or injuries, people for whom the consumption-smoothing benefits are more likely to outweigh the moral hazard costs. In practice, however, this approach raises difficult issues of how to classify injuries into these different categories.

Experience Rating

Partial experience rating at the firm level has been shown to increase both the number of layoffs and the duration of workers' compensation claims. It also allows inefficient firms to continue to exist at the expense of more productive firms that pay payroll taxes despite few layoffs; this is especially true in nations with no experience rating for their UI systems. Thus, we once again confront the trade-off between insurance and incentives: we want to insure firms against downturns, but by doing so we subsidize inefficient firms to stay in business.

In this case, however, the argument for insurance seems somewhat weak. Businesses that are fundamentally sound but going through a rough spell should be able to access capital markets (say, by taking out a bank loan) in a much easier fashion than can unemployed workers. That is, there are more formal structures for self-insurance by firms than there are for individuals. So it is somewhat harder in this context to appeal to consumption smoothing to justify insurance for firms. It seems likely that fuller experience rating would do more to put inefficient firms out of business than to hurt firms that are fundamentally sound but having a downturn.

Worker Self-Insurance?

A more radical reform of the three social insurance systems would be to move toward *worker self-insurance* against these adverse events. For example, the government could replace payroll taxes and mandated WC insurance with individual "social insurance savings accounts," to which workers would contribute some fixed amount. If they qualified for social insurance because they experienced one of these adverse events, they could then draw on this savings account, with provisions for borrowing (and repaying) if they exceed the account. If there are positive balances in these accounts at retirement, they could be used to finance retirement consumption. The pros and cons of such an approach are discussed in the following policy application.

▶ **APPLICATION**

Reforming UI

A system of worker self-insurance for UI would be similar to a privatized Social Security system, and it has many of the same advantages and disadvantages. One major advantage in this context is that there is much clearer evidence for moral hazard effects of programs such as UI and WC than for Social Security, and likely much less consumption smoothing provided by government insurance. By making unemployed or injured workers pay for their income support out of their own savings accounts, the program would minimize moral hazard. Feldstein and Altman (1998) conclude that a UI payroll tax of 4% invested in such accounts could cover the costs of unemployment spells for virtually all workers. But a disadvantage of such a self-insured system is that we would lose the redistribution of income from those who are have not lost their jobs to those who have.

Kling (2006) suggested an alternative approach that combines partial UI self-insurance with a new mechanism: *reemployment earnings insurance*. On average, full-time workers displaced from a job due to economic reasons (such as a plant closing) who then find another full-time job see their earnings decline by 17% relative to comparable workers who do not lose their job (Farber, 2005). This is a much bigger reduction in lifetime resources than a 26-week temporary loss of earnings, yet there is no social insurance to protect against this loss in earnings. Moreover, many of the workers who suffer lower earnings after job loss are the same workers who would suffer the loss of redistribution from moving to a self-insured UI system.

Kling therefore suggested that UI be replaced by a two-part program. The first part would be self-insurance for unemployment: workers who lose their jobs could either draw funds from a voluntary savings account to which they had contributed while working, or take loans from the government which are to be paid back out of future labor earnings. Low-wage workers or those who are unable to find a new job would receive forgiveness on the part of their loan that financed the unemployment spell (essentially converting the loan back to UI benefits). The second part of Kling's program would be wage insurance: workers would receive a transfer from the government equal to 25% of the difference between their old hourly wage and their new hourly wage. The duration of payments (up to a maximum of six years) would be determined by the number of hours worked in the two years prior to the job loss. Partial replacement, only 25% of the wage difference, ensures that workers will still try to find a high-wage new job. Indeed, a social experiment of a similar type of program in Canada found that it provided significant insurance for wage losses without adverse effects on job search or work behavior. The net result of this two-part unemployment and wage insurance program would be a system that has lower moral hazard, yet redistributes to both low-wage workers and to workers suffering a large wage loss. ◄

14.6
Conclusion

The three social insurance programs studied in this chapter (unemployment insurance, disability insurance, and workers' compensation) provide excellent applications of the general principles of social insurance learned in Chapter 12. In each case, individuals clearly value the consumption smoothing provided by the program. And, in each case there are significant moral hazard costs associated with the provision of the insurance. These moral hazard costs dictate that insurance be less than full. The many empirical analyses of all three programs can be used to inform policy makers' decisions as program reforms move forward.

► HIGHLIGHTS

- Unemployment insurance (UI) provides 26 weeks of benefits to workers who are laid off and searching for work.

- Disability insurance (DI) provides income replacement at Social Security levels for workers who are disabled and can no longer work.

- Workers' compensation (WC) provides generous cash benefits and medical insurance to workers injured on the job.

- The consumption smoothing provided by UI is only partial because the program seems to a large extent to be crowding out other forms of self-insurance. The effects of DI and WC on consumption smoothing have not been studied enough to reach any conclusion about their consumption-smoothing effects.

- Existing evidence suggests that the moral hazard costs of UI are large, with an elasticity of unemployment durations with respect to benefits of 0.8. (Each 10% rise in benefits raises unemployment durations by 8%.)

- There are also significant moral hazard effects associated with DI, although they are smaller, with each 10% rise in benefits leading to only a 3% rise in the odds of leaving the labor force.

- The largest moral hazard effects appear to be associated with WC, with each 10% rise in benefits leading to a 7% rise in the odds of claiming a workplace injury, and leading to a 17% rise in injury durations.

- Partial experience rating of both the UI and WC programs appears to raise the rate of layoffs and the duration of injury-related job leave.

- The evidence in this chapter implies that the WC program is likely too generous, and the DI program perhaps not generous enough; that benefits should be targeted toward groups such as the long-term unemployed and seriously disabled; and that firms should be more fully experience-rated for social insurance payments to their workers.

▶ QUESTIONS AND PROBLEMS

1. The unemployment insurance payroll tax is said to be partially experience-rated, because the tax rate on earnings is higher for firms with a history of laying off workers. What is the rationale for making the payroll tax rate a function of a firm's layoff history?

2. Describe the effects of raising the maximum benefit level for unemployment insurance on the savings rate of high income workers. How big are the consumption-smoothing benefits of this policy change likely to be? Are there other potential benefits of raising this maximum benefit level?

3. Workers' compensation benefits vary across states and types of injuries. How can you employ this information to estimate the elasticity of injury with respect to workers' compensation benefits generosity?

4. The Organization for Economic and Cooperation and Development (OECD) compares net replacement rates for unemployed families of different types across countries. These data are available online through the "Statistics" link at http://www.oecd.org/els/social/workincentives. In which countries has the replacement rate provided by unemployment benefits increased the most over the 40 years? Has the replacement rate declined in any countries?

5. What does the empirical evidence on the consumption-smoothing benefits of unemployment insurance indicate about the degree to which individuals are, on average, insured against the income losses associated with unemployment?

6. Consider Meyer's (1989) study of the effects of unemployment benefits on unemployment spell durations. How does this study deal with the likelihood that unemployment spells and unemployment benefits may both increase during economic recessions?

7. Gruber (2000) found evidence that the elasticity of labor supply with respect to disability insurance benefits is considerably smaller than the estimates of the elasticity of unemployment durations with respect to unemployment insurance benefits. Why might moral hazard be less of an issue in the disability insurance program than in the unemployment insurance program?

8. Governments typically provide disability insurance and unemployment insurance to workers. In contrast, governments typically *mandate* that firms provide workers' compensation insurance to their workers but do not provide the coverage. Why the difference? Why don't governments provide workers' compensation instead of mandating it?

9. In May 2004, the state of Vermont significantly reformed its workers' compensation system. One key provision of this reform was to reduce the window of time during which a claimant could file an initial workers' compensation claim. Will this help to reduce the degree of fraudulent use of the workers' compensation system? Explain.

10. Senator Doppelganger has proposed rules that will make it easier for workers to apply for and receive disability benefits. What is this likely to do to rates of application for disability benefits? To the reported unemployment rate?

▶ ADVANCED QUESTIONS

11. Are individuals more likely to maintain their pre-injury consumption levels after an easily preventable on-the-job injury than after a difficult-to-prevent on-the-job injury? Explain.

12. The empirical evidence on unemployment spell durations suggests that workers who leave unemployment earlier (that is, find or take a job sooner) have no higher post-unemployment wages than do workers who leave unemployment later. This result could be interpreted as evidence that the quality of the job match does not improve as the unemployment spell grows longer.

    a. What does this interpretation of the evidence imply about the moral hazard costs of unemployment insurance?

    b. An alternative explanation for this evidence is that workers with longer unemployment spells are less qualified than are workers with shorter unemployment spells. How could you empirically distinguish between this explanation and the explanation put forth in (a)?

13. The U.S. Department of Labor's Web site, http://workforcesecurity.doleta.gov/unemploy/sigprojul2006.asp, includes a table of the major differences in unemployment insurance programs across states. At the time of this writing, the state of Kentucky had a much wider range in the payroll tax rates paid by different experience-rated firms than did Oregon. Which state's system subsidizes firms with high layoff rates to a greater degree? Explain.

14. You are hired by the presidential administration to review the unemployment insurance (UI) program, which currently replaces approximately 45% of a worker's wages for 26 weeks after she loses her job.

    Consider two alternative reforms of the current UI system. The first is to experience-rate firms fully, so that the taxes firms pay are set exactly equal to the benefits their workers receive (benefits remain at 45% of wages). The second is a system of *individual* full experience rating—the government would loan individuals 45% of their wages while unemployed, but they would have to pay this back when they get new jobs.

    a. Contrast the effects of these alternative policies on unemployment durations and the likelihood of worker layoffs.

    b. What are the consumption-smoothing properties of each alternative policy?

The ℮ indicates a question that requires students to apply the empirical economics principles discussed in Chapter 3 and the Empirical Evidence boxes.

Appendix to Chapter 14

Advanced Quasi-Experimental Analysis

As discussed in the chapter, Meyer's study of the effect of UI benefits on unemployment durations considers two possible control groups: high-earning workers in other states and lower-earning workers in the same state. The chapter describes how these two different control groups can be used to compute two difference-in-difference estimators. This appendix describes how these estimates can be combined to form an even more convincing quasi-experimental estimate (known as a "difference-in-difference-in-difference" estimate) of the impact of UI benefits on unemployment durations.

Carrying Out the two Difference-in-Difference Estimates To define these estimates, we must use eight measures of unemployment durations, which we will call $DUR(e, s, p)$, where:

e stands for earnings level for each group: H is the high-earning treatment group with the benefits change (those earning more than \$800 per week), L is the low-earning control group with no benefits change;

s indicates the state of residence of each group: T is the treatment state with the benefits change (New Jersey), C is the control state with no benefits change (Pennsylvania);

p identifies the time period: B is before the benefits change and A is after the benefits change.

Thus, $DUR(H, T, B)$ is the unemployment durations of high-earning workers in the treatment state (New Jersey) before the benefits change.

As described in the chapter, we can compute two different difference-in-difference estimators. The first estimator contrasts the change in unemployment durations (from before to after the policy change) of high-earning workers in the treatment and control states:

$$DD1 = [DUR(H, T, A) - DUR(H, T, B)] - [DUR(H, C, A) - DUR(H, C, B)]$$

This is a causal estimate of the effect of higher UI benefits on unemployment durations, under the assumption that other changes over time, such as a recession, affect both states in the same fashion. In that case, the first term picks up the effect of benefits increases plus the recession, the second term picks up the effect of the recession, and the difference between the two is the effect of the benefits increase.

The second difference-in-difference estimate contrasts the change in unemployment durations (from before to after the policy change) of high- versus low-earning workers in the treatment state:

$$DD2 = [DUR(H, T, A) - DUR(H, T, B)] - [DUR(L, T, A) - DUR(L, T, B)]$$

This is a causal estimate of the impact of higher UI benefits on unemployment durations under the assumption that the recession in the treatment state has the same effect on workers in groups H and L. In this case, the first term picks up the effect of the benefits increase plus the recession, the second term picks up the effect of the recession, and the difference is the effect of the benefits increase.

It is possible that neither of these assumptions is true. If the recession has a stronger effect in the treatment state than in the control state, then DD1 will not measure just the impact of higher UI benefits on unemployment durations, but also will measure a partial impact of the recession as well. Suppose, moreover, that recessions have a stronger effect on low-earning than on high-earning workers. In this case, DD2 would suffer from the same problem: it would measure the effect of higher benefits *and* a partial effect of the recession.

Difference-in-Difference-in-Difference Estimates Even if both of these difference-in-difference estimators have limitations individually, they can be *combined* to form a more convincing estimator. That is, one can take the difference of these difference-in-difference estimators to account for *both* the fact that the recession may be stronger in New Jersey than in Pennsylvania, *and* the fact that recessions may affect higher-earning workers differently than lower-earning workers. This is accomplished by using a difference-in-difference-in-difference estimator: compare the unemployment durations of high-earning workers to the duration of low-earning workers in treatment states, then do the same comparison in the control states, and then take the difference of these two DD estimates. That is, one can compute:

$$DDD =$$

$$\{[DUR(H, T, A) - DUR(H, T, B)] - [DUR(L, T, A) - DUR(L, T, B)]\}$$

$$- \{[DUR(H, C, A) - DUR(H, C, B)] - [DUR(L, C, A) - DUR(L, C, B)]\}$$

This is a causal estimate of the impact of higher UI benefits on unemployment durations under the following assumption: the impact of recessions on high-earning workers relative to low-income workers is the same in both the treatment and control states. Under this assumption, even if the impact of the recession is different in the two states, and even if the impact is different on the two groups of workers, we can rid the estimate of bias with this difference-in-difference-in-difference estimator.

Even the assumption laid out in the previous paragraph may not be met. As highlighted in Chapter 3, quasi-experimental approaches are imperfect mechanisms for replicating the "gold standard" of the randomized trial. Yet this appendix shows how the use of data from different groups in different states can help to address some of the concerns about bias that arise with quasi-experimental estimates.

Health Insurance I: Health Economics and Private Health Insurance

15

O n March 30, 1981, only two months after entering office, President Ronald Reagan was shot by John Hinckley, a deranged fan of Jodie Foster who thought the actress would pay more attention to him if he killed the President. Reagan was rushed to George Washington Hospital, where he underwent three hours of surgery to remove a bullet that had entered his lung. Though the injury was potentially fatal, Reagan made a full recovery and went on to serve a full eight years in office.

One hundred years earlier, President James Garfield was not so lucky. He too was shot two months after entering office, on July 2, 1881, by Charles Guiteau, who thought God had ordered him to kill the President. Garfield was brought back to the White House, where for 80 days a dozen doctors attempted to find one bullet that, unbeknownst to them, had lodged itself near Garfield's spine. The doctors probed the President's wound with their unsterilized fingers and metal rods, succeeding only in widening the wound, infecting it, and puncturing his liver. Alexander Graham Bell ran a metal detector over Garfield's body and soon announced that he'd found the bullet. Surgeons went to work but still failed to locate it, not realizing that Bell had mistakenly detected one of the bedsprings underneath the President. The infection resulting from his poor medical care soon caused Garfield to have a heart attack, and when he eventually died, his coroner declared that Garfield would have survived if only his doctors had left him alone.[1]

Between President Garfield's death and President Reagan's election, the field of health care had clearly made great strides, so that doctors were now helping rather than harming people. This improvement in the quality of health care in the United States has been accompanied by an enormous increase in the share of the U.S. economy devoted to health care. In 1950, only 4% of U.S. GDP was accounted for by the health care sector. At that time, Americans spent less on health care than on cars, fuel, or clothing. By 2004, health care accounted for 16% of GDP, surpassing spending on housing

---

[1] The story about President Garfield comes from www.anecdotage.com.

and food.[2] This growth is not expected to stop: health care is forecast to consume 38% of U.S. GDP by 2075, which would represent a greater share than the United States currently spends on cars, fuel, furniture, food, clothing, housing, utilities, and recreational activities combined.[3]

Is such high and rapidly growing health care spending a problem? After all, what is more important than our health? And, by some measures, we are buying wonderful things with our health care dollars. Consider the treatment of knee injuries in the 1950s and today. Fifty years ago, if you tore the meniscus (the cartilage under the kneecap), the only option was to have open surgery, during which the surgeon cut open your knee and removed the entire meniscus. You would spend days in the hospital, months recovering, and 15 years down the road you'd have an increased chance of developing arthritis in that knee. If you tear your meniscus today, you can often have only a small piece of it removed by arthroscopic surgery, which allows the surgeon to make tiny incisions in your knee and repair the damage in an average of 30 minutes. You go home that same day, can do light work within a few days, and be up and running (or whatever other sport you enjoy) within three to six weeks.

Similarly, in 1950, 6 out of every 1,000 Americans died from a heart attack. Since then, that number has fallen by half.[4] In 1950, 29 out of every 1,000 infants born died in their first year of life; today, that figure is less than 7 out of 1,000.[5]

Despite the huge benefits reaped from the U.S. health care system, all is not completely well. First, there are enormous disparities in medical outcomes. For example, in 2003 the white infant *mortality rate* in the United States, the share of infants who die in their first year, was 0.7%, which was in line with other developed nations like the United Kingdom and Australia. The 2003 black infant mortality rate, however, was 1.4%, which was somewhat higher than the infant mortality rate in Barbados (1.1%) and twice as high as the rate in Malaysia (0.7%).[6]

Second, the United States is the only major industrialized nation that does not endeavor to provide universal access to health care for its citizens. Almost 46 million persons, one-sixth of the U.S. non-elderly population, are without health insurance, and this number has grown fairly steadily for the past 20 years despite a strong economy for much of that period.

Despite the perceived "private" nature of the U.S. health care system, governments account for almost half of all health spending in the United States. Health care spending is now more than a fifth of the federal government budget and state and local government budgets.[7]

---

[2] Historical health spending statistic comes from Cutler (2004, p. 4); 2004 spending from Centers for Medicare and Medicaid Services (2006c); comparisons to spending on other goods come from the Bureau of Economic Analysis's National Income and Product Accounts, Table 1.1.5 and Table 2.3.3.

[3] Chernew et al. (2003).

[4] See the technical appendix to Chapters 3 and 4 of Cutler (2004), located at http://post.economics.harvard.edu/faculty/dcutler/book/technical_appendix.pdf.

[5] Data from the Centers for Disease Control at http://www.cdc.gov/nchs/fastats/pdf/mortality/nvsr52_03t31.pdf.

[6] U.S. statistics come from Centers for Disease Control and Prevention (2006a). International statistics come from United Nations Development Programme (2005).

[7] See Figure 1-7.

Furthermore, growth in health spending is projected to account for most of the long-run fiscal problems faced by the U.S. government because of the aging of the U.S. population and the rapid rise in medical care costs. Thus, there are clear public finance issues raised by this large and growing health economy.

In the next two chapters, we discuss many issues relative to health care and its importance to the economy and to government policy. In this chapter, we discuss the nature of health care and the set of general health insurance issues relevant to government involvement in the delivery of health insurance. This chapter provides the basis for understanding the health economy and allows us to contemplate reforms in the government role in the delivery of health care. In the next chapter, we examine the two largest public-sector interventions in health insurance markets, the Medicaid and Medicare programs, and the implications of past evidence for future directions in health care reform.

15.1

An Overview of Health Care in the United States

In 2004, the United States spent $1.9 trillion on health care, or 16% of GDP.[8] As noted previously, this represents a dramatic increase from 50 years earlier. This is also much higher than the amount spent in comparable industrialized nations. As Figure 15-1 (page 416) shows, in 2003 the United States spent nearly twice as much on health care as did Japan or the United Kingdom. This health spending amounts to $6,470 on average for each man, woman, and child in the United States.[9]

Individuals typically fund these expenditures by purchasing insurance. As discussed in Chapter 12, risk-averse individuals generally prefer insurance as a means of financing uncertain expenditures, at least if that insurance is available on an actuarially fair basis. There are several major sources of health insurance in the United States; the distribution of the population across these sources in 2004 is illustrated in Table 15-1 on page 417.

How Health Insurance Works: The Basics

Health insurance parallels the general structure of insurance discussed in Chapter 12. Individuals, or firms on their behalf, pay monthly premiums to insurance companies. In return, the insurance companies pay the providers of medical goods and services for most of the cost of goods and services used by the individual (the individual's medical claims). Under most health insurance plans, however, the patient also pays the provider for part of the costs of medical goods and services and the insurance company pays the remainder. There are three types of patient payments:

---

[8] Centers for Medicare and Medicaid Services (2006c).
[9] Information on medical spending comes from the Centers for Medicare and Medicaid Services (2006c), while information on the U.S. population comes from U.S. Bureau of the Census (2006c).

▪ **FIGURE 15-1**

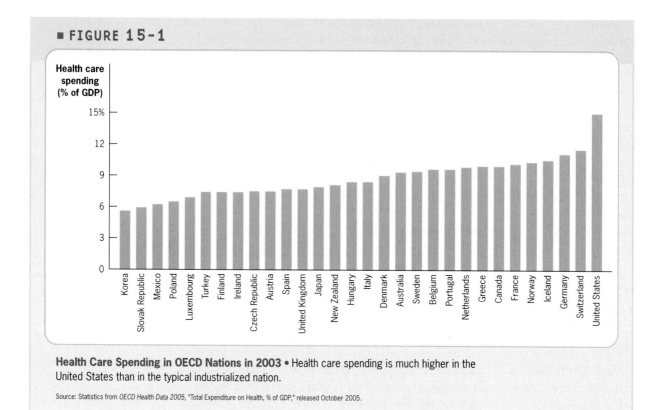

Health Care Spending in OECD Nations in 2003 • Health care spending is much higher in the United States than in the typical industrialized nation.

Source: Statistics from *OECD Health Data 2005*, "Total Expenditure on Health, % of GDP," released October 2005.

▶ *Deductibles:* Individuals face the full cost of their care, but only up to some limit; for example, a $100 deductible would mean that you pay the first $100 of your medical costs for the year, and the insurance company pays some or all of the costs thereafter.

▶ *Copayment:* Individuals make some fixed payment when they get a medical good or service; for example, a $10 copayment for a doctor's office visit or a new prescription.

▶ *Coinsurance:* The patient pays a percentage of each medical bill (the coinsurance rate, e.g., 20%), rather than a flat dollar amount (as with a copayment).

Private Insurance

The most important source of health insurance in the United States is private insurance; in 2004, 68.1% of the population (80.8% of those with some kind of health insurance), or 198.2 million persons, had private health insurance. Within that group, the predominant source of private insurance is employer-provided health insurance. Only 14% of those with private insurance purchase insurance on their own, through the **nongroup insurance market**.[10]

nongroup insurance market
The market through which individuals or families buy insurance directly rather than through a group, such as the workplace.

[10] See Table 15-1.

Employers offer insurance to qualified employees in the firm, typically those who work full-time and have completed some minimal service requirement (such as six months of employment at the firm); employers also typically charge employees some share of the employers' premium payments for insurance. As a result of these employee premiums, some employees choose not to take up the insurance even if it is offered.

There are two reasons why employers are the predominant source of insurance.

Why Employers Provide Private Insurance, Part I: Risk Pooling

The first reason that employers provide most private insurance is the nature of insurance risk pools. An insurance **risk pool** is the group of individuals who enroll in an insurance plan. When insurers sell an insurance plan to a group, they don't care about the medical experiences of any one member of the group. What matters to the insurer is the total premium collected from, and medical claims paid out on behalf of, that insurance pool as a whole. Recall our example from Chapter 12: actuarially fair pricing simply requires that the insurance company collect enough in premiums from the entire group to cover its costs for that group.

As a result, the goal of all insurers is to create *large insurance pools with a predictable distribution of medical risk*. So long as the insurer can accurately predict the claims that it will pay out for that insurance pool, it can charge a premium to cover its claims costs (along with administrative costs and profits). If it can't make that prediction accurately, there is a risk that the premiums will not cover the pool's medical costs.

Two features increase the predictability of medical risk distributions for insurance risk pools. The first is the absence of adverse selection. Insurers predict medical risk based on the observable characteristics (such as age and sex) of the individuals in the risk pool, and such predictions will only be valid if those individuals have the average medical risk of their age and sex group. If individuals are forming a pool based on their (unobserved to the insurer) health status as well,

■ TABLE 15-1

Americans' Source of Health Insurance Coverage, 2004

	People (millions)	Percentage of population
Total population	291.1	100.0%
Private	198.2	68.1
Employment-based	174.1	59.8
Individually purchased	27.1	9.3
Public	79.2	27.2
Medicare	39.9	13.7
Medicaid	37.6	12.9
TRICARE/CHAMPVA	10.8	3.7
Uninsured	45.8	15.7

Source: U.S. Bureau of the Census (2005a). Estimates by type of coverage are not mutually exclusive; people can be covered by more than one type of health insurance during the year.

More than two-thirds of insured Americans have private health insurance, largely through employers, while the remaining have public health insurance. Roughly one-sixth of Americans are uninsured.

risk pool The group of individuals who enroll in an insurance plan.

"Kids, your mother and I have spent so much money on health insurance this year that instead of vacation we're all going to go in for elective surgery."

then the insurer can't predict the expected costs of that pool very well. The second factor that increases predictability is group size. The statistical *law of large numbers* (introduced in Chapter 3) states that as the size of the pool grows, the odds that the insurer will be unable to predict the average health outcome of the pool falls.

Employees of firms, particularly large firms, constitute a risk pool that has a good chance of meeting these two conditions. Workers generally do not take their health status into account when choosing which firm to work for, so there is no reason to believe that there will be adverse selection in this risk pool. That is, there is no reason to suspect that particularly sick or healthy individuals band together to work in a firm (particularly a large firm), so that on average within a firm, workers of a given age and sex will have the expected medical expenditures for that age and sex. In addition, most employees work in firms that are sufficiently large that the law of large numbers can be employed in predicting medical risks.

For these reasons, firms provide an attractive risk-pooling mechanism for insurers. Individuals, on the other hand, do not. Large groups of individuals could be formed to deal with the second concern, group size, but the first concern, adverse selection, always remains: the individuals who band together to come to the insurer looking for coverage might be doing so simply because they are sick. Because of adverse selection, insurers would much rather sell insurance to large employer groups than to small groups or individuals.

The preference for large groups by insurers is reinforced by another aspect of insurance provision, administrative costs. Many of the costs of administering insurance are *fixed* at a certain level no matter the size of the pool (e.g., the costs of selling the insurance product). As a result, the larger the pool, the lower per capita administrative costs can be spread. For individuals or small groups, these fixed administrative costs can amount to a large share of the premium, but the costs are a very small share of the premium for large firms.

These issues are reflected in the pattern of private insurance coverage in the United States. Large employers in the United States almost universally offer health insurance to their employees; 98% of firms with more than 200 employees offer health insurance. Among smaller firms, however, health insurance offering rates are much lower; only 47% of firms with fewer than 10 employees provide insurance, and only 72% of firms with 10–24 employees provide insurance.[11] This difference is partly because the insurer cannot appeal to the law of large numbers for these smaller pools: one cancer or AIDS patient in a small firm could cause medical claims costs to exceed the insurance company's projection and thus exceed premiums collected. As a result, insurers are more reluctant to insure small firms, since they can't predict with certainty the insurance costs that their premiums must cover. The difference is also due to the higher (fixed) administrative costs per worker at small firms. As discussed in Chapter 12, the demand for insurance will fall if administrative costs cause insurance premiums to rise above their actuarially fair level.

---

[11] Kaiser Family Foundation (2006), Exhibit 2.4.

Why Employers Provide Private Insurance, Part II: The Tax Subsidy The second reason why employers are the predominant providers of health insurance is the **tax subsidy to employer-provided health insurance.** Under current U.S. tax law, employee compensation in the form of wages is subject to taxation, but employee compensation in the form of health insurance expenditures is not. If your employer pays you $1 in wages, you keep only $1 $\times (1 - \tau)$ of those wages, where τ is your tax rate; if you have a 33% tax rate, you only keep $0.67 of each $1 you earn. If your employer pays you in health insurance, on the other hand, you keep the full $1 of health insurance. This tax subsidy is *only available* for employer-provided health insurance. Thus, there is a large subsidy to purchasing health insurance through your employer rather than on your own.

For example, suppose that Jim and Peter are both working for the same employer (see Table 15-2). The labor market is perfectly competitive, so their wage is equal to their marginal product, which is $30,000 per year for each employee. Assume that both employees face a flat tax rate of 33%, so that, without insurance, their after-tax income is $30,000 $\times (1 - 0.33)$ = $20,000. The employer now offers both employees the opportunity to have health insurance at a cost of $5,000, but the employer will reduce their wages by $5,000 if they take this insurance, so that their total compensation is still equal to their marginal product.

Jim can purchase insurance on his own for $4,000, so he turns down the employer. He has an after-tax income of $20,000, out of which he pays $4,000 for insurance, so that he ends up with $16,000 in after-tax, after-insurance income. Peter takes the health insurance. His earnings fall to $25,000, which is $25,000 $\times (1 - 0.33)$ = $16,666 after tax. But Peter now has a higher after-tax, after-insurance income than does Jim, even though his insurance is much more expensive ($5,000 rather than $4,000). This is because Peter has benefited from the tax advantage to employer-provided health insurance, lowering the taxes he has to pay by $1666 (33% of $5,000), which more than offsets the $1000 higher cost of the employer-provided insurance.

tax subsidy to employer-provided health insurance Workers are taxed on their wage compensation but not on compensation in the form of health insurance, leading to a subsidy to health insurance provided through employers.

■ **TABLE 15-2**

Illustrating the Tax Subsidy to Employer-Provided Insurance

	Marginal Product, Wage	Employer Health Insurance Spending	Pre-Tax Wage	After-Tax Wage	Personal Health Insurance Spending	After-Tax, After-Health Insurance Income
Jim	$30,000	0	$30,000	$20,000	$4,000	$16,000
Peter	$30,000	$5,000	$25,000	$16,666	0	$16,666

Jim and Peter both have the same marginal product of labor, but Peter chooses to take insurance through his employer, accepting a $5,000 reduction in wages as a result, while Jim purchases it on his own for $4,000. Even though Jim's insurance is cheaper, Peter ends up with $666 more income after taxes than Jim due to the subsidy to employer-provided insurance.

Quick Hint The subsidy to employer-provided health insurance is generally not well understood. This is not a subsidy to *employers* but rather a subsidy to *employees* for insurance purchased in the employment setting. From the employer's perspective, whether she pays you in wages or health insurance is irrelevant; either way, a dollar of employer spending has the same effect on the firm's bottom line (since any type of employee compensation is deductible from corporate taxation). From the worker's perspective, however, there is a large difference: by being paid in health insurance rather than wages, the worker reduces her tax payments. If the government wanted to end the tax subsidy, it would not do so by increasing the corporate tax paid by the firm; it would instead include employer spending on health insurance as part of an employee's taxable income.

The Other Alternative: Nongroup Insurance Of the approximately 70 million individuals who are not covered by employer insurance (or public insurance sources described later in this chapter), only around 37% (27.1 million) turn to the nongroup health insurance market. This relatively small percentage is explained partly by the problems we highlighted with the small group market (potential for adverse selection and high administrative costs per enrollee), which are even greater when the insured is a single individual or family. As a result, the nongroup insurance market is not a well-functioning market. Furthermore, nongroup insurance is not always available; those in the worst health are often unable to obtain coverage (or obtain it only at an incredibly high price). Often, nongroup policies will have "preexisting conditions exclusions," which state that the health insurance will refuse to pay for the expenditures associated with any illness that the purchaser has when he or she buys the insurance (e.g., recurrences of cancer would not be covered for those with past episodes of cancer).

Medicare

Medicare A federal program that provides health insurance to all people over age 65 and disabled persons under age 65.

The second major source of health insurance is the **Medicare** program, which provides health insurance for all people over age 65 and disabled persons under age 65. Medicare is financed by a payroll tax of 1.45% each on employees and employers.

Every citizen who has worked for ten years in Medicare-covered employment (and their spouse) is eligible for Medicare at age 65. (Unlike Social Security, individuals cannot access Medicare coverage before the age of 65.) In 2004, about 35.3 million elderly persons were eligible for Medicare. After a two-year waiting period, Medicare insurance is also available to those receiving disability insurance. Disabled persons under age 65 add another 6.3 million people to the Medicare program.[12]

---

[12] Social Security Administration (2006b), Tables 8.B4 and 8.B5.

Medicaid

The other major public health insurance program in the United States is the **Medicaid** program, which provides health care for the poor. The federal and state governments share the financing of this program, which is paid for out of general tax revenues.

> **Medicaid** A federal and state program that provides health care for the poor.

Medicaid benefits are targeted at several groups:

▶ Those who qualify for cash welfare programs, mostly single mothers and their children

▶ Most low-income children in the United States (typically below 200% of the Federal poverty level)

▶ Most low-income pregnant women (typically below 200% of the poverty level, for the expenses associated with their pregnancies only)

▶ The low-income elderly and disabled (for non-Medicare health costs and long-term care costs for facilities such as nursing homes)

Medicaid is best known for its coverage of the young poor population, particularly mothers and children, who make up nearly 70% of program recipients. However, over two-thirds of the costs of the program are accounted for by disabled and elderly program recipients. Expenses for this group include those for long-term care, either from providers visiting their homes or from institutions such as nursing homes, which account for 20% of total Medicaid spending.[13]

TRICARE/CHAMPVA

Another large source of insurance in the United States is health insurance for those currently or formerly in the military and their dependents. TRICARE is a program administered by the Department of Defense for military retirees and the families of active-duty, retired, or deceased service members. CHAMPVA, the Civilian Health and Medical Program for the Department of Veterans Affairs, is a health care benefits program for disabled dependents of veterans and certain survivors of veterans. Together, these two programs provide health coverage for nearly 11 million Americans.

The Uninsured

Finally, there are the 45.8 million in the United States without any insurance coverage at all. Who are they?[14]

▶ The uninsured have lower-than-average incomes; nearly two-thirds of the uninsured are in families with incomes below twice the poverty line. Not all of the uninsured are poor, however: 21.1% of the uninsured are in families with incomes above $40,000 per year.

---

[13] Social Security Administration (2006b), Table 8.E1 and 8.E2.
[14] U.S. Bureau of the Census (2005a).

▶ In 2004, almost 70% of the uninsured came from families where one or more members were full-term workers, but were either not offered health insurance by their employer, or were offered insurance by their employer but did not enroll in that insurance to cover themselves or their family members.

▶ Over one-fifth of the uninsured are children.[15]

Why Care About the Uninsured? What does it matter if there are people without health insurance? There are several possible answers to this question. First, there are physical externalities associated with communicable diseases; uninsured people are less likely to receive vaccinations and care for communicable diseases. (Recall the measles example in Chapter 1.) Second, there is a significant financial externality imposed by the uninsured on the insured through **uncompensated care.** When the uninsured get served by medical providers and don't pay their bills, those costs are passed on to other users of the medical system through high medical prices, a practice called *cost-shifting.* The latest estimates suggest that the amount of uncompensated care delivered in the United States is $41 billion each year.[16] This is a classic negative financial externality because the uninsured are raising medical costs for others without bearing the full costs themselves.

The third reason we might care whether individuals are uninsured is that care is not delivered appropriately to the uninsured, thus jeopardizing their health and further raising the costs of uncompensated care that are paid by those who are insured. A classic example is the uninsured's use of the emergency room (which is designed for acute medical emergencies) for primary care, such as treatment of the common cold. There is enormous anecdotal evidence of such inefficient use of medical services; for example, a recent survey of individuals in a Los Angeles emergency room revealed that 38% of those surveyed would trade their current emergency room visit for a doctor's office visit within three days![17] This misuse of services is a problem because the emergency room is a very expensive place to treat a minor illness; the efficiency of the medical system would be improved by sending these individuals to physicians' offices instead.

Fourth, there are paternalism and equity motivations for caring about the uninsured. In particular, individuals may irrationally underinsure themselves because they do not appreciate the risks they face, and governments may view such irrational underinsurance as justifying intervention in insurance markets. In addition, many feel that health care is a basic right, like food or shelter, and since the uninsured are generally poorer than average, they may be a group to whom we want to redistribute health care resources.

The final reason for caring about the uninsured is that *becoming uninsured* is a concern for millions of individuals who currently have insurance. Many individuals are afraid to search for or move to jobs where they may be more productive because they are afraid of losing their health insurance coverage.

---

uncompensated care The costs of delivering health care for which providers are not reimbursed.

---

[15] Kaiser Commission on Medicaid and the Uninsured (2006).
[16] Kaiser Commission on Medicaid and the Uninsured (2006).
[17] Grumbach et al. (1993).

HEALTH INSURANCE AND MOBILITY

Is job lock an important problem in reality? A large literature has investigated this question and concluded that it is. Initially, this literature compared the mobility rate of those who have and do not have health insurance, and showed that those who have health insurance are less likely to leave their jobs than those who do not, suggesting job lock. However, these groups do not form sensible treatments and controls, since they are likely to be dissimilar in at least two ways. First, those who choose to enter jobs that offer health insurance may be quite different from those who do not; for example, they may be in worse health. If worse health is associated with less job mobility, then this may be the reason for the observed correlation of health insurance and mobility. (Those with insurance are less likely to leave jobs because they are most ill, not because of insurance coverage.) Second, jobs that provide health insurance are typically "better jobs" along many dimensions, such as higher wages and other benefits (such as pension plans or vacation). Individuals may be reluctant to leave these jobs not because they fear losing health insurance coverage but because these jobs are too good to leave! As a result of this lack of comparability between treatment groups (those with health insurance) and control groups (those without), these estimates are biased.

A more sophisticated literature in the 1990s surmounted this problem in two different ways.[18] First, studies used a difference-in-difference strategy that compared a treatment group of those who valued health insurance particularly highly with a control group of those who did not. These studies asked, for example: Does having health insurance lower the mobility rate among those who don't have any other source of insurance coverage (treatments), relative to those who do have coverage from their spouses or some other source (controls)? If job lock is an important problem, it should be found most prominently among those who don't

have coverage from a spouse; other reasons for the correlation of insurance with mobility (bias that does not represent true health insurance effects) are captured by the control group of those who don't have spousal coverage.

Second, studies examined the impact of state laws that allowed workers to continue to purchase their employer-provided health insurance for some period of time after leaving their jobs. These laws mitigated the problem of job lock to some extent because workers could be sure to have coverage for a period of time even if they left a job with health insurance for one without health insurance. These laws were passed in some U.S. states in the 1970s and 1980s, so that a quasi-experimental analysis was possible: individuals in states passing laws were the treatment group (since job lock should be loosened) and those in states without laws were the control group, and any difference in mobility was due to a loosening of job lock through these laws. Federal legislation in 1986 (part of the Consolidated Omnibus Reconciliation Act, or COBRA) then made continuation coverage available nationally (which is why it is often known as COBRA coverage). The passage of COBRA provided another opportunity for quasi-experimental analysis in which those workers in states that did not already have laws were the treatment group, and those in states that already had laws (and were thus unaffected by the federal law) were the control group.

The results from these studies support the notion that job lock is quantitatively important. Madrian's (1994) estimates, for example, suggest that it reduces mobility across jobs among those with health insurance by as much as 25%. Subsequent studies in this same vein have found that a lack of health insurance coverage for retirees reduces the odds that someone will retire before age 65 from his or her job, since older persons do not want to risk being uninsured before they become entitled to Medicare at age 65.

This reluctance to change can lead to a mismatch between workers and jobs that can lower overall U.S. productivity. This is often referred to as **job lock,** the unwillingness to change to a better job for fear of losing health insurance.

To illustrate this problem, suppose that Brigitte has utility over only two goods, health insurance and consumption, so that her utility function is of the form $U = U(C, HI)$, where C is consumption, and HI is a variable equal to 1 if she is covered by health insurance and to 0 otherwise. Suppose that she works

job lock The unwillingness to move to a better job for fear of losing health insurance.

---

[18] For a review of this literature, see Gruber and Madrian (2004).

in a well-functioning labor market so that the wage that she is paid is equal to her marginal product, net of the cost of providing health insurance, and that she consumes her net income.

Suppose that Brigitte is currently on job 1 (an accountant), but has an offer to move to job 2 (a start-up software firm), where she has a higher marginal product ($MP_1 < MP_2$). This move would be an efficiency improvement from society's perspective. Suppose, however, that job 1 is at a large firm where health insurance is relatively cheap and is therefore provided at a cost P, while job 2 is at a small firm where health insurance is very expensive and is therefore not provided. Brigitte enrolls in health insurance in job 1, so that she earns a wage $MP_1 - P$. Consumption is equal to net compensation, so Brigitte has utility $U(MP_1 - P, 1)$ if she stays on job 1, and utility $U(MP_2, 0)$ if she moves to job 2. On job 1 she has a lower marginal product, from which is subtracted the cost of health insurance, but she gets health insurance; on job 2, she has a higher marginal product and doesn't have to pay the costs of health insurance, but she doesn't get insurance.

In this case, if Brigitte values health insurance at above its cost (if there is a lot of weight on the second term in her utility function relative to the first), she might stay at her old job, even though $MP_2 > MP_1$, because of her disutility of losing insurance. *Health insurance availability may inhibit productivity-increasing job switches.*[19] In fact, as we review in the Empirical Evidence box, it appears that job lock is an important phenomenon in the United States: workers with health insurance are about 25% less likely to change jobs because of that insurance.

15.2

How Generous Should Insurance Be to Patients?

In considering government intervention in health insurance markets, the first question is: How generous should health insurance be? As with other insurance discussed in Chapters 12–14, the optimal generosity of health insurance will be determined by trading off the consumption-smoothing benefits and moral hazard costs of insurance. Yet generosity is measured in a very different way with health insurance than with the other programs we have studied. For Social Security or unemployment insurance, generosity reflects the share of pre-event wages replaced, or perhaps the duration of benefits. In the context of health insurance, generosity reflects the share of medical spending that will be reimbursed by the health insurer.

The generosity of health insurance is therefore measured along two dimensions. The first is generosity to *patients:* what share of the bill for med-

---

[19] This conclusion assumes that (a) firms can't offer health insurance only to some workers, or (b) firms can't set worker-specific wages to address their valuation of health insurance. If firms could do these two things, then firm 2 could lure Brigitte away from firm 1 by offering health insurance just to her, and reducing wages accordingly. But assumption (a) is legally justified; firms cannot restrict eligibility for health insurance based on characteristics other than hours of work or tenure with the firm. Assumption (b) is trickier; we'll discuss this point in Chapter 18.

ical services should be paid by the insurer, and what share by the patient, through deductibles, copayments, and coinsurance? The most generous health insurance plan is one that provides **first–dollar coverage**, reimbursing providers fully with no cost to the patients themselves. Plans can be less generous to consumers either by refusing to reimburse some services, so that patients pay the full cost, or by raising the amount that patients need to pay when they get the service. So the question we discuss in this section is: What share of a patient's medical spending should be reimbursed by the insurer, and what share should be paid by the patients themselves?

The second dimension of insurance generosity is generosity to *providers:* How should insurers reimburse providers for the services they deliver? Should insurers just pay the amount billed by the provider for medical services, or should the insurer limit in some way how much the provider will be reimbursed? In the next section, we discuss this alternative dimension of generosity.

> **first-dollar coverage** Insurance plans that cover all medical spending, with little or no patient payment.

Consumption-Smoothing Benefits of Health Insurance for Patients

Applying what we learned in Chapter 12, the benefits of health insurance to individuals are clear. Risk-averse individuals will value health insurance as a means of smoothing their consumption with respect to the cost of medical events. Not all types of medical events are created equal, however. Some are minor and predictable, such as a quick physician visit for a checkup. Others are more extensive and unpredictable, such as hospitalization for a heart attack. The key insight of expected utility theory is that insurance is much more valuable for the latter types of medical events, and that there is relatively little consumption-smoothing benefit from covering the former type of (minor) events. Thus, first-dollar coverage does not provide much more consumption smoothing than does health insurance that makes patients pay the minor costs of medical care and has insurance pay only the higher costs of major medical events (what is often called "catastrophic care").

The consumption-smoothing benefit from first-dollar coverage of minor and predictable medical events is small for two reasons. First, risk-averse individuals gain little utility from insuring a small risk: the disutility to the individuals from paying insurance premiums for small risks is roughly the same as the utility they gain from insuring those risks. We can illustrate this point by returning to the initial example from Table 12-1 (page 319 of Chapter 12). In that example, Sam faced an actuarially fair premium for insurance against a catastrophic risk: the 1% risk of being in a car accident and having medical expenses that wiped out his income ($30,000). We showed that Sam could greatly increase his utility by buying full insurance against that small but catastrophic risk.

Consider the same example now, but imagine that the medical care costs of the accident were only $100 rather than $30,000. In that case, Sam's utility with no insurance is:

$$(0.99 \times \sqrt{30,000}) + (0.01 \times \sqrt{29,900}) =$$
$$(0.99 \times 173.2) + (0.01 \times 172.9) = 173.2$$

Suppose instead that Sam buys insurance that pays the $100 if he is hit. Since the odds of an accident are 1%, the actuarially fair premium for such insurance is $1, which Sam pays regardless of whether he gets hit. With insurance, Sam's expected utility becomes:

$$(0.99 \times \sqrt{[30,000 - 1]}) + (0.01 \times \sqrt{[30,000 - 1]}) =$$
$$(0.99 \times 173.1) + (0.01 \times 173.2) = 173.2$$

Thus, *Sam's utility does not measurably increase if he buys insurance.* This outcome stands in contrast to the earlier example, when there was a large increase in utility from buying insurance, and illustrates that insurance has little value to individuals for very small risks. Technically, the consumption-smoothing gains from insuring small risks is small because there is extremely little diminishing marginal utility for small changes in consumption: the losses from reducing consumption by a dollar are roughly equal to the gains from increasing consumption by a dollar. For risks that involve very small income loss, then, individuals are no longer particularly averse to risk (they are approximately *risk neutral*).

The second reason that the consumption-smoothing benefits of first-dollar coverage are small when medical spending is small and predictable is that individuals are much more able to self-insure such spending than to self-insure large and unpredictable medical events. Individuals can save in advance for their expected physician visit, but it would be very inefficient for them to save an extra $200,000 against the small chance that they might have a heart attack.

Moral Hazard Costs of Health Insurance for Patients

Offsetting the consumption-smoothing benefits of health insurance to individuals is the risk of moral hazard. The classic analysis of patient-side moral hazard in health insurance is provided in Feldstein (1973), and illustrated in Figure 15-2, in the example of a doctor's office visit (although the theory applies generally to most medical goods and services). On the horizontal axis is the number of office visits by Marty; on the vertical axis is the price that Marty must pay for each office visit. Assume that the marginal cost of producing an office visit (physician's time, supplies, and so on) is constant at $100, so that the supply curve for medical care is the horizontal line *S*. Assume also that Marty has a downward-sloping demand curve for health care such as office visits: he is willing to pay less for more health care (due to diminishing marginal utility). Finally, assume that Marty is in a large group, so that his medical spending is irrelevant for the insurance premium that he pays. (There is no individual-level experience rating in insurance prices.) The only costs to him for using medical care, then, are the copayments that he makes for that care.

If Marty faced the full price for medical care (that is, if he had a 100% coinsurance rate), he would consume Q_1 visits per year (point *A*). At point *A*, his marginal benefit of receiving care (summarized by the demand curve) equals his full price of that care, $100. Q_1 is also the socially optimal level of medical care: at this point, social marginal benefits (demand) equal social marginal costs (supply).

■ **FIGURE 15-2**

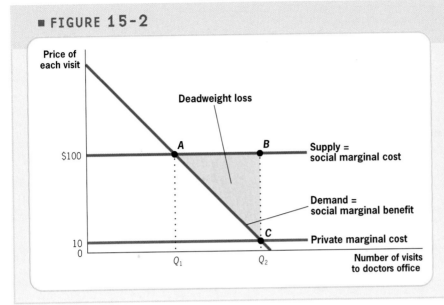

Patient-side Moral Hazard • With no insurance, at a cost of $100 per visit, individuals would consume Q_1 doctor's office visits, where marginal costs and benefits are equal. With only a $10 copayment, however, individuals consume Q_2 worth of visits, where private marginal costs equal social marginal benefit; this overconsumption of health care leads to a deadweight loss of *ABC*.

Now suppose that Marty must pay a $10 copayment when he goes to the doctor, as is typical in many health plans today. In this case, he will face a private marginal cost of only $10, and will choose Q_2 visits (point *C*). Q_2 is an inefficiently large amount of medical care, because at this quantity private marginal costs ($10) are far below social marginal costs ($100). Thus, there is an inefficiency of the area *ABC*, which represents all of the units of medical care that are delivered with a marginal benefit (demand) below their social marginal cost. The moral hazard associated with not charging Marty for the full cost of care leads to a deadweight loss of the area *ABC*.

The benefit of this small copayment is consumption smoothing: individuals such as Marty value the fact that they are insured against paying the full cost when they go to the doctor. A 100% coinsurance rate may induce efficient medical care use, but it provides no insurance against large medical costs, something that is valued by risk-averse consumers. Here we see the fundamental trade-off of health insurance: the gains in terms of consumption smoothing (paying $10 instead of $100 when you go to the doctor) versus the costs in terms of overuse of medical care (consuming Q_2 instead of the socially optimal Q_1).

The "Flat of the Curve" This inefficient overuse of medical care has led some to claim that we practice "flat of the curve" medicine. This notion is illustrated in Figure 15-3 (page 428), which graphs the relationship between medical spending and the associated improvement in health, or the "health effectiveness curve." The horizontal axis in this figure measures the *level* of medical spending. The vertical axis measures the *marginal health benefit* from the next dollar of medical spending. Health benefits in this stylized figure are represented in dollar terms, or the monetary value of improving one's health;

■ FIGURE 15-3

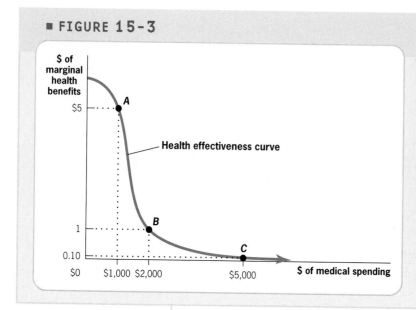

The "Flat of the Curve" • Spending on health care is assumed to initially be very productive in terms of improved health care outcomes, but that productivity dwindles as spending rises. The curve shows the value of improved health for each dollar in medical spending. At point *A*, when individuals are spending $1,000 on health care, each dollar of medical spending buys $5 worth of improved health, and at point *B*, when individuals are spending $2,000 on health care, each dollar of medical spending buys $1 worth of improved health. Beyond point *B*, however, there is much less than $1 in improved health for each $1 in medical spending.

an improvement of $1 means that this improved health is worth $1 to the individual. Each point on this curve is the marginal improvement in health for spending the next dollar on health care.

Initially, health spending is very productive in terms of improving health status, because there are a series of very cost-effective medical interventions (such as vaccination against influenza for the elderly). Point *A*, for example, measures the marginal health benefits to spending another dollar of health care once one has spent $1,000 on health care. This next dollar of spending improves the individual's health at that point by $5 (vertical axis), or five times the increase in health spending. As health spending rises, however, we move from clearly cost-effective interventions to less clearly cost-effective interventions. At point *B*, moving from $2,000 to $2,001 of health care spending improves the value of health by $1, equal to the spending increase. At point *C*, moving from $5,000 to $5,001 in health care spending improves health by only $0.10, or one-tenth the spending increase. Eventually, additional spending does no good in terms of improving health and the effectiveness curve flattens out; some claim that overuse may actually reduce one's health, with the curve sloping downward at very high levels of spending.

Optimally, people should stop getting medical care when the additional health benefit is smaller than the additional medical cost. When we look at Figure 15-3, we see that people should not get medical care beyond point *B*, the point at which each dollar of spending buys a dollar of improved health. If individuals paid the full cost of their health care, point *B* would be the socially optimum level of health care that would be chosen in a competitive market. If individuals do not pay much for their additional health care, however, they will demand health care as long as the effectiveness curve is not perfectly flat. This demand pushes our society to the right of point *B*, into the region where each dollar of medical care buys much less than $1 in improved health.

As a result, some studies have judged that as many as one-third of all medical procedures delivered in the United States are "of questionable benefit."[20] In an influential series of articles, researchers at Dartmouth University have shown that high-cost areas in the United States spend about 30% more on health care without any measureable benefit in terms of improved health outcomes (Fisher et al., 2003a,b).

How Elastic Is the Demand for Medical Care? The RAND Health Insurance Experiment

"You're responding beautifully. Let's go ahead and see what happens if we increase your deductible."

The extent to which moral hazard causes the actual quantity of health care consumed to exceed the socially optimal quantity depends on both the copayment amount and the elasticity of demand for medical care. Many years ago, policy makers assumed that this elasticity was close to zero; individuals went to the doctor when they were sick and didn't if they weren't sick. Several decades of empirical economics research has shown this not to be the case.

The best evidence on the elasticity of demand for medical care comes from one of the most ambitious social experiments in U.S. history: the RAND Health Insurance Experiment (HIE), which was conducted in the mid-1970s at several sites in the United States. In the HIE, individuals were randomly assigned to plans with different coinsurance rates; for example, some individuals were placed in plans with no coinsurance, while others were in plans with a coinsurance rate of 95% (they paid 95% of all their health costs), with a range of coinsurance rates in between. One limitation of this approach was that individuals who were assigned less-generous plans had to pay more, which is unethical (and might have made it hard to recruit participants). As a result, each plan had an "out-of-pocket maximum" of $1,000; once families had spent $1,000 on their medical care, they did not have to pay any additional costs of care, regardless of their plan. The findings of the HIE were striking.[21] First, medical care demand is price sensitive: individuals who were in the free care plan used about one-third more care than those paying 95% of their medical costs. The implied elasticity across the entire study was 0.2, meaning that each 10% rise in the price of medical care to individuals led them to use 2% less care. This is a low elasticity, but even with this relatively modest elasticity the implied deadweight loss from insurance coverage in the

---

[20] RAND has conducted "appropriateness of care" studies for a number of medical situations. See Winslow et al. (1988) for an example of a procedure that is inappropriately conducted roughly a third of the time.

[21] For an excellent comprehensive summary of the study's findings, see Newhouse and the Insurance Experiment Group (1993). For a shorter summary, see Gruber (2006).

ESTIMATING THE ELASTICITY OF DEMAND FOR MEDICAL CARE

Initial research on the elasticity of demand for medical care proceeded by comparing individuals in different types of health plans. Some health plans provided first-dollar coverage, where individuals had no coinsurance; others had large coinsurance, with coinsurance rates of 20% (the patient pays one-fifth of the cost of the visit) or more. These studies showed that individuals in plans with higher coinsurance used less care, which suggested that medical care demand was somewhat elastic.

It is likely, however, that these earlier studies were seriously biased, because insurance plans are not randomly assigned to individuals. Individuals who spend a lot on health care are likely to buy plans with low coinsurance, so the correlation between low coinsurance and high use of medical care is not a causal effect of coinsurance on utilization. Instead, the correlation reflects that high-utilization individuals have chosen low-coinsurance plans. This is a classic example of the bias problem that arises when trying to assign causal interpretations to correlations.

The RAND HIE was designed to address this shortcoming. Because of random assignment, we can use the data from the HIE to assess the causal impact of coinsurance on utilization by comparing individuals in different plans. By definition, individuals with different coinsurance rates were identical other than for their coinsurance rates, so it is possible to compare the utilization of those with high- and low-coinsurance rates to identify the elasticity of demand for medical services.[22]

Recent studies have used quasi-experimental approaches to estimate the price elasticity of medical demand. As reviewed in Gruber (2006), these studies compare utilization before and after a copayment change in a plan, relative to other plans that do not change copayments. These studies have the weakness that the copayment changes are not experimental; for example, firms may raise copayments for prescription drugs in the face of rising demand, leading to the appearance that higher copayments lead to more drug utilization! In fact, however, a large number of studies in many different settings have now been completed of this type, and the results are fairly uniform. These studies confirm the RAND HIE conclusion that higher copayments reduce care, particularly for prescription drugs, although, as noted below, they find that the reduction in care has deleterious effects on health for the chronically ill, highlighting the value of targeted copayment polices. Thus, when the ideal experiment is not available, there is an advantage to using multiple imperfect tests to assemble a consensus conclusion.

United States is huge. One study estimates this loss in the range of $125 billion to $400 billion per year in today's economy.[23]

Second, those who used more health care due to the lower price did not, on average, see a significant improvement in their health. This finding suggests that the typical person is indeed on the flat of the health effectiveness curve when responding to changes in coinsurance. The finding *does not imply*, however, that insurance isn't valuable at all, because everyone in this experiment was insured; once a family's health spending reached $1,000, it had full insurance. The RAND results imply that once individuals are insured for large expenditures, varying the coinsurance for small expenditures does not seem to affect their health on average.

---

[22] As noted in the text, the RAND HIE involved making a $1,000 payment to all participants to ensure that no one was made worse off. This payment did not cause any bias, however, because it was made equally to treatments and controls. So any income effect from the money was the same across both groups, and they could still be compared to assess the impact of coinsurance variation.

[23] Feldman and Dowd's (1991) deadweight loss calculation has been updated by multiplying by GDP growth since that time.

Third, for those who are chronically ill and don't have sufficient income to easily cover copayments, there was some deterioration in health. In particular, low income individuals who were hypertensive (had high blood pressure) saw dangerous increases in their blood pressure arising from lack of care. More recent studies have confirmed that finding, concluding that those who have treatable but chronic illnesses may be made worse off by copayments. Indeed, some studies find that for the chronically ill raising copayments actually raises total medical costs because the reduced use of prescription drugs and physician visits results in more expensive hospitalizations due to health deterioration.[24]

Optimal Health Insurance

The finding of significant deadweight loss from moral hazard in the health insurance market suggests that the *optimal health insurance policy is one in which individuals bear a large share of medical costs within some affordable range, and are only fully insured when costs become unaffordable.* This structure is optimal because first-dollar coverage has little consumption-smoothing benefit but a large moral-hazard cost.

As we showed, the consumption-smoothing benefit of first-dollar coverage is small. But first-dollar coverage also has substantial moral-hazard cost because it encourages individuals to overuse the medical system, demanding care for which the social costs exceed the social benefits. In other words, coverage for small amounts of medical spending has little benefit (since individuals don't much value consumption smoothing for small risks) and significant cost (since individuals are using care where marginal benefit is less than marginal cost), so the optimal insurance plan should not provide such coverage. Rather, it should insure only large medical expenses for which the consumption-smoothing gains are large (and for which the moral hazard might be smaller, such as for heart attacks).

An example of an optimal insurance plan would be Feldstein's (1973) "Major Risk Insurance" plan, in which individuals would make a 50% copayment on all services until they spent 10% of their income on medical care, beyond which there would be no more copayments. But the findings of particular damage to those with chronic illness from copayments suggest some targeting of copayments, such as waiving copayments for treatment of chronic illness. These findings suggest the value of using insurance structure to encourage appropriate care and discourage inappropriate care, as well as to protect against bankruptcy.

---

[24] See Gruber (2006) for a review of these studies. One example is Chandra, Gruber, and McKnight (2006), who studied the effects of copayment increases for physicians and prescription drugs on retired public employees in California. They found that all retirees had many fewer physician visits and prescriptions, and that total spending for the group was lower. But for those retirees who were chronically ill, there was an offsetting rise in hospital spending, presumably because lack of outpatient care led to more inpatient care. This rise in hospital care was large enough to offset the savings from lower physician/prescription use by the chronically ill.

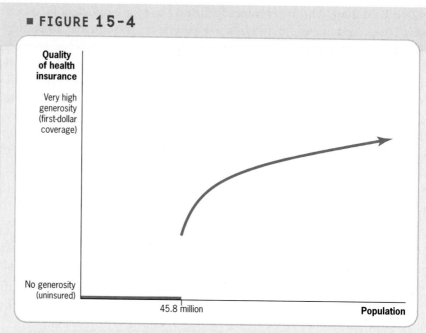

■ FIGURE 15-4

The Generosity of Health Insurance in the United States • The vertical axis in this diagram shows the generosity of health insurance, running from no insurance (uninsured) at the bottom to very generous insurance (first-dollar coverage) at the top. There are 45.8 million uninsured persons in the United States, who are at the bottom of this axis. The remaining persons in the United States almost all have insurance of high to very high generosity, leading to a jump upward in the curve. The mystery is: Why is there so little insurance of low to medium generosity in the United States, such as catastrophic coverage?

Why Is Insurance So Generous in the United States?

Feldstein's proposal is much less generous than the typical private insurance plan in the United States, which features relatively low copayments for enrollees. As a result, the insurance coverage distribution in the United States is best described by a line such as that in Figure 15-4. On the horizontal axis is the population of the United States, arrayed from least generous insurance (uninsured) to most generous, and on the vertical axis is the generosity of health insurance products. The 45.8 million Americans with no health insurance lie at zero on the vertical axis (no insurance = zero generosity).[25] The line then jumps up to reasonably high generosity insurance, and there is an increasing generosity of insurance for the remainder of the population. The mystery is: Why the jump? Why aren't more individuals requesting lower generosity insurance that would cover only their catastrophic risks? Why are people either uninsured or "overinsured"? There are three possible reasons.

---

[25] See Table 15-1.

The Tax Subsidy As previously noted, health insurance expenditures by employers are tax subsidized: payments to employees in the form of wages are taxed, while payments in the form of health insurance are not. This is a major reason health insurance is offered through firms. It also has the effect of increasing consumption of health insurance relative to other goods, by lowering the relative price of health insurance. For the typical worker, the marginal dollar spent on better health insurance buys a dollar's worth of insurance, while the marginal dollar paid in wages buys only $0.70 of other consumption because $0.30 of that dollar goes to pay taxes. This situation will lead employees to devote a larger share of their compensation to health insurance than they would in the absence of the subsidy; even if individuals would not demand generous insurance at unsubsidized prices, they may choose it when there is a tax subsidy to its purchase. Estimates suggest that eliminating the tax subsidy to health insurance purchases by employers could lower employer-provided insurance spending by almost half.[26]

This estimate does not imply that removing the tax subsidy today would necessarily be good health policy. Many individuals (more than 20 million by one estimate) would lose their employer-provided health coverage if the subsidy were eliminated and would then face the difficulties of obtaining insurance in the nongroup market, with its high prices and incomplete coverage.

One compromise policy that has been suggested is to *cap* the tax subsidy. Ending the tax subsidy would be accomplished by taxing workers on all employer contributions to health insurance as if these were earnings to the workers. Capping the tax subsidy would mean continuing to exclude from income taxation employer health insurance spending up to some level (perhaps the median cost of a health insurance plan in the area), but taxing as worker earnings any employer spending above that level. For example, your employer would add to your reported wage income any amount he spends on insurance above the ceiling level, and you would be taxed on this in the same way you are taxed on wages. This approach would retain the tax subsidy to employers for some basic insurance spending, thus encouraging them to provide some insurance coverage. The subsidization to excessively generous coverage, however, would end: there would no longer be a reason for employees to choose a very generous insurance plan over cash compensation, once employers are spending the cap amount.

▶ **APPLICATION**

Health Savings Accounts

Removing or capping the tax subsidy to employer-provided health insurance is a straightforward means of addressing overinsurance, but undertaking such an action would be politically difficult because it would be attacked as a large tax increase on workers. An alternative to this "stick" approach that may be

---

[26] Gruber and Lettau (2004).

health savings account (HSA) A type of insurance arrangement whereby patients face large deductibles, and they put money aside on a tax-free basis to prepay these deductibles.

more politically feasible is a "carrot" approach: extend additional tax subsidies to those individuals who choose more efficiently designed health care plans. A recent attempt to do so is the introduction of **health savings accounts (HSA)** as part of the Medicare prescription drug legislation of 2003 (discussed in detail in the next chapter). HSAs are plans with high deductibles (at least $1,000 for individuals and $2,000 for families per year) under which individuals prepay the deductible amount into a savings account, and then draw down that account as they spend the deductible. Importantly, the amount put into the HSA is not taxed, so that spending on insurance and spending on deductibles are treated the same for tax purposes (as opposed to other insurance plans, where insurance spending is tax subsidized but employee coinsurance is not).[27] Individuals who do not spend down their accounts in any year can roll the money over to the next year, and any money left at retirement can be withdrawn either for the retiree's health care needs, in which case it's tax-free, or for any other purpose, in which case the gains are taxed. Thus, HSAs provide a large tax subsidy to those whose plans have a high deductible, hopefully encouraging increased use of such (closer to optimal) insurance arrangements.

Unfortunately, HSAs have a number of disadvantages as well. First, this new tax break will be expensive in terms of forgone tax revenue, and the tax benefits of HSAs are targeted mostly to higher income individuals who can afford large deductibles (and who have the high tax rates that allow them to benefit most from HSAs). Second, a flat deductible alone is not the right structure for encouraging the proper use of medical care. For individuals who are very poor, this may represent too much out-of-pocket risk relative to the optimal design of a copayment with an income-related out-of-pocket limit. For individuals who are well off, and who know that they will certainly use at least that much health care during the year (e.g., at least $2,000 for the family), the deductible is too low—since individuals know that they will surpass the deductible for sure during the year, they ignore it. Finally, if the right way to address overinsurance is to limit the employer exclusion, then HSAs represent the wrong direction for tax policy because they try to offset the distortions of the existing tax subsidy with a new tax subsidy. ◄

The Access Motive A second reason why insurance may be so generous is that the traditional analysis overstates the costs of moral hazard. In traditional models of insurance, the additional medical care used is all due to moral hazard. Nyman (1999) highlights a problem with this view: some of the additional medical care used because of insurance is not due to moral hazard, but rather to the fact that individuals can now afford better treatments. Suppose, for example, you have an illness that costs $1 million to treat. Suppose further that you care enough about your health that if someone handed you $1 mil-

---

[27] In many workplaces, however, employers have set up *flexible spending accounts* whereby employees can set money aside at the start of the year to pay their coinsurance costs on a tax-free basis.

lion today, you would immediately use the money to treat your illness. Likewise, if you had insurance that covered the treatment of illness, you would also get it treated. In this case, there is no moral hazard: all insurance has done is allow you to afford a treatment you value.

Moral hazard is technically the difference between what health care you buy with $1 million of insurance or with $1 million of cash. If you would get treated when you have insurance, but if handed the actual cash you would use it for other expenditures, then insurance is causing moral hazard. If, on the other hand, you would buy the expensive treatment with either the insurance or the cash, then there is no moral hazard; all insurance has done is allow you to transfer sufficient resources from the situation (state) in which you are healthy to the situation that occurs when you are ill. Moral hazard is measured only by the *substitution effect* of social insurance programs, the extent to which you change behavior because relative prices are changing. The *income effect* of social insurance programs, the extent to which you change behavior because you are richer, is not moral hazard.

This analysis suggests that some of the deadweight loss associated with increased expenditures due to insurance is not pure moral hazard, but an income effect. As a result, we are overstating the deadweight loss associated with health insurance, which is why insurance may be more generous than our analysis would suggest is optimal.

Unfortunately, it is difficult to decompose the increase in the use of medical care into access and moral-hazard effects. The access motive is a more important consideration for very expensive treatments, and not for everyday treatments, such as physician's visits. Thus, the access motive may explain the strong demand for catastrophic limits on spending out of pocket, but it is unlikely to explain why individuals don't face higher co-payments for more minor medical procedures, such as those performed in physician office visits.

Psychological Motivations Finally, the third reason why insurance may be so generous is that there may be motivations for holding insurance that go beyond the simple expected utility model developed in Chapter 12. For example, individuals with self-control problems may use insurance as a commitment device. I may know that without insurance I will spend all of my money today and save nothing for possible future medical expenditures. By buying insurance I am effectively forcing my impatient self to save for illness. I may be buying overly generous insurance because otherwise my impatience would leave me with no money at all to pay large medical bills that may arise. Once again, however, this is unlikely to explain the aversion of patients to modest coinsurance for minor medical events.

Alternatively, it may be that individuals simply don't like associating financial transactions with medical care. They would rather pay higher insurance up front to avoid dealing with the difficult decisions about whether they want to pay at the time of care. Clearly, more analysis is needed to understand the causes of overinsurance among Americans today.

15.3

How Generous Should Insurance Be to Medical Providers?

The other type of moral hazard that is relevant for health care is on the provider side. Even if insurers could perfectly assess your true level of illness, they cannot always perfectly assess how much it costs to treat that illness. For many illnesses there is no clearly delineated course of treatment, and major illnesses can progress very differently in different individuals. As a result, insurers have traditionally reimbursed medical providers according to their reported costs of treatment; if two physicians billed different amounts to treat a heart attack, they were typically paid those different amounts, even if characteristics of the heart attack patients were similar. Such a reimbursement system is called **retrospective reimbursement,** since insurers simply reimburse physicians for the costs they have already incurred.

Retrospective reimbursement removes any incentive for providers to treat their patients cost-effectively. Suppose that all a doctor cares about is making her patients as healthy as possible. In that case, if there is a medical procedure or test that has any possible medical benefit that exceeds the private costs to the patient (the coinsurance plus any discomfort or time lost due to the procedure), then she will provide that care. After all, why skimp when you are risking someone's health? The problem is that the *social* cost of these procedures may greatly exceed the private costs (and the private benefits) to the patient, particularly if health care is being delivered on the "flat of the curve." Thus, there is overuse of medical care, and a deadweight loss from provider-side moral hazard.

Moreover, the overuse problem can be exacerbated if providers care about their incomes as well. Suppose that your doctor cares not only about maximizing your health but also about maximizing her income. In that case, if there is a procedure that does you no good (but no harm, or at least not much harm), and on which she makes a net profit, then she will undertake that procedure.

Managed Care and Prospective Reimbursement

The twin problems of patient- and provider-side moral hazard were assumed to be major drivers of the rapid rise in health care costs during the postwar period. Initially, the insurance market responded to these moral-hazard concerns through increased patient cost-sharing, but this approach did not slow the rise in health care costs: throughout the 1960s, 1970s, and 1980s, health care costs were rising sharply in real terms.

In the late 1980s and 1990s, the private market (as well as public insurance programs) turned to an alternative approach to cost control: **managed care,** which implemented supply-side controls on the delivery of medical care. Managed care comes in two forms.

Preferred Provider Organizations One fundamental failure in medical markets is that it is very difficult to shop for a medical provider. How can a consumer of medical care effectively compare hospitals or physicians? And how

retrospective reimbursement Reimbursing physicians for the costs they have already incurred.

managed care An approach to controlling medical costs using supply-side restrictions such as limited choice of medical provider.

can consumers possibly shop for cost-efficient providers even if they wanted to, since prices for specific procedures are not posted by hospitals or physicians? This dilemma is particularly true for emergency care; no one will tell the ambulance driver to "take me around to a few hospitals to see which is cheapest"! This lack of price shopping means there are few competitive pressures on providers' pricing decisions and thus providers have no incentives to lower medical care costs.

In the 1980s, a new type of health organization called the **preferred provider organization (PPO)** gained popularity as a means of solving this problem. Essentially, PPOs are middlemen: they shop across providers on behalf of the insured, striking deals that can lower the cost of care. For example, a PPO might first go to an area employer and offer it 20% savings off its medical care costs *if* it is willing to restrict the set of hospitals its employees can use to the PPO's hospital "network." The PPO would then tell area hospitals that *if* they wanted the business from this firm (or other firms using that PPO), they would have to cut prices by 20%. Those hospitals that agreed would lower their prices for the PPO client in return for being part of the restricted PPO network. The employer would tell his employees that they can use only those hospitals that are in this PPO network. In principle, this shopping strategy could lead not only to lower prices but also to more efficient delivery of medical care, in the same way that shopping in other markets increases efficiency.

> **preferred provider organization (PPO)** A health care organization that lowers care costs by shopping for health care providers on behalf of the insured.

Health Maintenance Organizations

The other type of managed care organization is a **health maintenance organization (HMO)**. As with PPOs, HMOs restrict enrollee choice of medical providers, but HMOs go one step further by integrating the insurance and the delivery of medical care. In the classic *staff model,* HMOs hire their own physicians and may have their own hospitals. They put the providers on a salary that is independent of the amount of care they deliver. This approach removes any income incentive for the delivery of excess care.

> **health maintenance organization (HMO)** A health care organization that integrates insurance and delivery of care by, for example, paying its own doctors and hospitals a salary independent of the amount of care they deliver.

The more typical HMO model is the Independent Practice Association (IPA), in which the HMO contracts with independent providers (within a restricted network) to deliver care to its enrollees. In this case, HMOs counteract moral hazard through the use of **prospective reimbursement,** the practice of paying providers based on what treating patients should cost, not what the provider spends. The HMO might, for example, pay a primary-care physician (e.g., a family doctor) $100 per month for each person in her practice, regardless of how much medical care that person uses.[28]

> **prospective reimbursement** The practice of paying providers based on what treating patients should cost, not on what the provider spends.

Prospective reimbursement completely reverses the financial incentives of physicians. Under retrospective reimbursement, where the physician is just reimbursed for her billed costs, the more care the physician delivers, the more money she makes. Now, the *less* care she delivers, the more money she makes;

---

[28] These are also often referred to as "capitated" payment schemes because providers are paid a given amount per capita (per patient enrolled), rather than for treatments.

the physician gets the $100 no matter what she does, so by delivering less care she can pocket a larger share of that payment. Thus, just as retrospective reimbursement offers financial incentives for excessive care, prospective reimbursement offers financial incentives for insufficient care.

Prospective reimbursement can come in many different forms, and there is indeed an enormous variety of prospective payment schemes used by HMOs. Some HMOs augment the flat payment to primary care providers with disincentives to use specialty care or hospital visits. For example, the HMO might reduce compensation every time the primary care physician recommends a specialist or a hospital visit, or raise compensation if such recommendations aren't made. In this way, HMOs try to give incentives to any given provider to not only limit the care he delivers, but also limit the care delivered by the system as a whole.

Over the late 1980s and 1990s, the vast majority of insured persons in the United States moved into some form of managed care along the spectrum from PPOs to staff-model HMOs. Currently, 97% of the privately insured are in managed care plans.[29]

The Impacts of Managed Care

The key question from our perspective is whether managed care has improved the functioning of the insurance market. In particular, has managed care lowered the deadweight loss of excessive medical care utilization? If so, has prospective reimbursement perhaps even gone too far, and begun to restrict medical care that is valued by individuals at its cost?

Spending There is now a very large literature in health economics that addresses these questions. The consistent finding of this literature is that HMOs spend much less per enrollee than do traditional retrospective reimbursement plans. Interpreting this finding is not as straightforward as it seems, however. It is difficult to compare spending per person in these two types of plans because different types of people enroll in the plans. Many studies have found that managed care plans attract the healthiest enrollees, as measured, for example, by how much the individuals were spending before they switched to the HMO. This type of *selection* of the lowest-cost individuals into HMOs means that there is not a simple comparison between the HMOs and traditional insurance plans: even if HMOs didn't change the delivery of medical care, their costs would be lower because they have the healthiest enrollees.

In assessing the impact of HMOs on costs, there have been a number of attempts to control for this selection problem. Perhaps the most convincing is evidence from the RAND HIE previously discussed, which had a second component that randomly assigned individuals into one of the nation's earliest HMOs, in Puget Sound, Washington. Since individuals were randomly assigned, they were otherwise comparable to individuals in traditional insur-

---

[29] Kaiser Family Foundation (2006), Exhibit 2.3.

ance plans, and thus any differences in costs reflect the effects of the HMO on medical utilization. This study found that the cost of medical care for the HMO enrollees was only 72% of the cost for enrollees in traditional insurance plans, in large part because the HMO admitted patients to hospitals at a much lower rate (7.1% of patients were admitted to hospitals by HMOs, compared to 11.2% in the traditional plans).[30] Thus, the cost savings to HMOs do not purely reflect selection (the fact that healthier people enroll in HMOs).

Quality As we saw earlier, retrospective reimbursement of providers may lead to excessive provision of care. We also saw that prospective reimbursement under HMOs might lead to *underprovision* of care. Do HMOs underprovide, or do they simply serve to correct some of the natural excesses of retrospective reimbursement? There is now an enormous literature on the impact of HMOs on patient treatment, and the answer is a definite maybe. Roughly equal numbers of studies find that HMOs deliver care that is better, worse, or the same as traditional health insurance. At this point, there is no real consensus on the impact of HMOs on care quality: it is clear that they are paying lower prices for medical services, but it is not clear that they are actually providing significantly fewer of those services or having any measurable adverse effects on health outcomes.

How Should Providers Be Reimbursed?

The managed care "revolution" does not appear to have had the negative effect on patient health that some feared. The advent of managed care has clearly lowered reimbursement to providers, but it has not measurably lowered the quality of care those providers deliver. Thus, the move from retrospective to prospective reimbursement appears to have improved efficiency in the health care sector. The key question for the future is whether additional "tightening" of the prospective reimbursement system is needed. We discuss this issue at length when we discuss the Medicare program in the next chapter.

15.4

Conclusion

This chapter provided an overview of the health care economy in the United States. We began with a discussion of the nature of health insurance in the United States and learned that most individuals have private health insurance, and that for those employed by large firms this is a well-functioning insurance market. For small firms and individuals there are more failures in the insurance market, one possible reason that almost 46 million Americans are uninsured.

The benefits of health insurance are clear from the theory presented in Chapter 12: risk-averse individuals greatly value the consumption-smoothing

[30] Manning et al. (1984).

benefits of having their medical bills paid. There are clear moral hazard costs as well, both on the patient and provider side. Some cost sharing has been used to address moral hazard on the patient side, and managed care has arisen as a means of addressing moral hazard on the provider side. The success or failure of these approaches is not yet fully apparent. In the next chapter, we discuss how the government has approached the trade-off between providing insurance for those who need it and inducing excess medical care through moral hazard.

▶ HIGHLIGHTS

■ Health care has improved dramatically in the United States over the past 50 years, but substantial inequalities remain.

■ Most individuals have private insurance, which is largely provided through firms because of risk pooling and the tax subsidy to employees for employer-provided health insurance.

■ The 45.8 million uninsured persons concern policy makers for these reasons: externalities, labor market inefficiencies (job lock), and paternalism.

■ There is a clear potential for moral hazard on the patient side of the medical care system because medical demand has been shown to be somewhat elastic, with few health improvements attributable to more generous health insurance plans.

■ Despite this, individuals still demand very generous health insurance coverage in the United States, which could be due to the tax subsidy to insurance, access to the most expensive treatments that insurance provides, or psychological motivations.

■ The potential for moral hazard on the provider side of the medical care system has given rise to managed care, which uses shopping and prospective reimbursement to control medical costs.

■ Existing research suggests that managed care has controlled costs, with no clear evidence that the quality of medical care has suffered as a result.

▶ QUESTIONS AND PROBLEMS

1. Matt is an employee at a large university, where he pays $120 per month in insurance premiums and his employer pays $300 per month. He finds that if he quits his job, the same quality of insurance would cost him $600 per month. Why is there a difference in the premium?

2. The U.S. Bureau of the Census reports trends over time in health insurance coverage, by race and sex, at http://www.census.gov/hhes/hlthins/historic/hihistt1.html. Which racial or ethnic group has seen the largest increase in its rate of health insurance coverage from 1987 to 2002? Is this increase largely coming from increases in the rates of government-provided insurance, employer-provided insurance, or privately purchased insurance?

3. Suppose the U.S. government gets rid of the tax-exemption for employer-provided health insurance. Instead, the government provides a 20% subsidy on employer-provided health insurance, so that the employer only has to pay 80% of the cost of such policies. How might this policy change affect the type of workers to whom firms will offer health insurance? Which types of firms is this policy most likely to affect?

4. Many privately purchased health insurance plans have stringent "preexisting conditions" exclusions, which deny coverage to insured persons for any health conditions that were known at the time of enrollment. Why does this exclusion reflect a market failure in the insurance market?

5. What negative externalities arise when an individual does not have health insurance?

6. An individual's demand for physician office visits per year is $Q = 10 - (1/20)P$, where P is the price of an office visit. The marginal cost of producing an office visit is $120.

   a. If individuals pay full price for obtaining medical services, how many office visits will they make per year?

   b. If individuals must pay only a $20 copayment for each office visit, how many office visits will they make per year?

   c. What is the deadweight loss to society associated with not charging individuals for the full cost of their health care?

7. Jack has three types of medical expenditures: contact lenses, prescription drugs for a condition he has, and accidents and acute illnesses (such as broken bones and pneumonia). He has been paying for all of his medical expenditures out of pocket and he is now considering purchasing health insurance. Different plans he is considering offer coverage for different types of expenditures. Describe the consumption-smoothing benefits and moral hazard costs of coverage for contact lenses, prescription drugs, and accidents and acute illnesses.

8. As Figure 15-1 illustrates, the United States leads all OECD countries in health care expenditures, spending almost double the average OECD country's share of gross domestic product on health care. But American health care outcomes are not dramatically better than those of other OECD countries. What could explain this disconnect between differential spending and differential outcomes?

9. Senator Snead, making the case for universal, free health care, argues that people are not price sensitive to health care costs; when they need to go to the doctor, they go, regardless of the cost. Evaluate this argument in light of the empirical evidence on the price sensitivity of health care demand.

10. Catastrophic injuries and illnesses account for two-thirds of total health care costs in the country of Gnut. The Gnuti government is deciding between two different universal health insurance programs: program X would pay for two-thirds of any health care expense that a Gnuti citizen incurred, while program Y would pay only for catastrophic illnesses and injuries, but would cover 100% of those costs. Which program is likely to better allow Gnuti citizens to smooth consumption? Which program is likely to cost the Gnuti government less? Explain your answers.

11. You observe that states with higher income tax rates also tend to have higher rates of employer-provided health insurance. Is this a good test of the effects of tax policy on the demand for employer-provided health insurance? Explain.

12. Given that subsidized health care leads to increased health care usage, is this necessarily due to moral hazard? Explain.

13. Your employer-provided health insurance coverage allows you to choose either a health maintenance organization—in which your doctor is paid the same amount by the insurance company when you select her as your physician, regardless of how many visits you make—or a preferred provider organization—in which your doctor is reimbursed by the insurance company based on the quantity of care provided—for your health benefits. In which organization would you expect to have an easier time getting an appointment to see your doctor? Explain.

The e indicates a question that requires students to apply the empirical economics principles discussed in Chapter 3 and the Empirical Evidence boxes.

▶ ADVANCED QUESTIONS

14. Suppose the government of Orwellia decides to genetically test all individuals for the risk of major illness, and reports the results of these tests to potential insurers when people apply for individual health insurance coverage. Will healthy people find working for large firms more, less, or equally attractive than before this testing program began? How about unhealthy people? Explain.

15. The following question considers the possibility that employer-provided health insurance reduces job mobility—a phenomenon that has been termed *job lock*. Job lock prevents workers from transitioning to jobs in which their marginal productivity would be higher than at their current jobs.

Consider three workers with the following preferences:

$$U_{ij} = W_{ij} + (50 \times H_{ij})$$
$$U_{kj} = W_{kj} + (110 \times H_{kj})$$
$$U_{lj} = W_{lj} + (150 \times H_{lj})$$

where W_{ij} is the wage at job j for worker i, H_{ij} is an indicator variable (i.e., it takes on a value of one or zero) for whether or not employer-provided health insurance (EPHI) is offered to worker i at job j. Assume that there are no employee copayments for the insurance and that the labor market is perfectly competitive. Workers i, k, and l all have a marginal product of $200. There is an arbitrarily large number of firms in the economy, and they cannot offer worker-specific compensation packages. If they provide EPHI to one worker, they must provide it for all of their workers. EPHI costs firms $100 per worker. Assume that there is full employment—all three workers will be employed.

a. What wage does each of these workers earn? Do they have EPHI? What is the compensating wage differential for EPHI (the labor-market-wide decrease in wages at a job that provides EPHI)?

b. Now assume that there are two types of firms: type 1 and 2. Type 1's cost of providing EPHI is $200 per worker and type 2's cost of providing EPHI is $100. At which type of firm is each of the three workers employed? Why? Which workers have EPHI?

c. Now assume that firms of type 1 develop a new technology that increases the marginal productivity of their workers to $230. At what firms do the workers work now? Are any of them suffering job lock?

16. The Consolidated Omnibus Budget Reconciliation Act of 1985 (COBRA) mandated that employers with over 20 employees allow workers who are separated from their job to purchase insurance through their health-insurance plan (if they offer one). How might you use this law to test for health-insurance-related job lock?

17. The country of Cheapland currently has a national health insurance system that reimburses citizens for 90% of all heath care costs incurred. Cheapland's government is considering a policy change that would provide medical care providers with a fixed reimbursement level for each diagnosed illness so that citizens would no longer bear any out-of-pocket expenses for medical care. In what ways will this policy change reduce moral hazard? In what ways will it increase it?

Health Insurance II: Medicare, Medicaid, and Health Care Reform

16

From 1998 through 2003, one of the most heated topics of public policy debate in the United States was the addition of a prescription drug benefit to the Medicare program. Medicare, which provides universal health insurance coverage to those over age 65 and to those on the disability insurance program, was established in 1965. The original program covered most medical needs for the elderly and disabled, including hospital and doctor costs, but it excluded coverage for prescription drugs.

This omission was not perceived as a major one in the early years of the Medicare program, but in the 1990s the advancement of prescription drug treatments for common illnesses among the elderly drew attention to this gap in Medicare coverage. In the 1960s, there were few outpatient drugs for hypertension (high blood pressure), depression, peptic ulcers, diabetes, and many other common afflictions of Medicare recipients, but all were treatable with prescription drugs by the late 1990s. Medicare recipients, for example, spent an average of $2,500 each on prescription drugs in 2003, more than twice what the average American spent on all health care in 1965![1] As a result, there was strong demand for adding a prescription drug benefit to the Medicare program. This was a major issue in the 1998 congressional campaigns, the 2000 presidential elections, and the 2002 congressional campaigns.

The debate in Congress over adding this benefit was a contentious one. Advocates of adding a prescription drug benefit to Medicare saw this as an unnecessary and unfair "hole" in the supposed universal coverage provided to our nation's elderly and disabled. Opponents saw it as an unwarranted expansion of the government's role in the provision of health insurance. Representative Mike Pence, a Republican from Indiana, upset that his own party was considering this augmentation to Medicare, lamented that "a Republican

---

[1] Data for prescription drug spending comes from the Congressional Budget Office (2002). Data for average Americans' health spending comes from the "National Health Expenditures" section of the Centers for Medicare and Medicaid Services' *National Health Accounts*. All other health-spending statistics in this chapter come from the *National Health Accounts* unless otherwise noted.

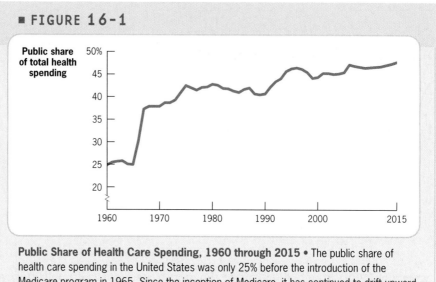

■ FIGURE 16-1

Public share of total health spending

Public Share of Health Care Spending, 1960 through 2015 • The public share of health care spending in the United States was only 25% before the introduction of the Medicare program in 1965. Since the inception of Medicare, it has continued to drift upward.

Source: Centers for Medicare and Medicaid Services (2006c).

president and a Republican Congress are poised to create the largest entitlement since 1965."[2] Finally, in 2003, the Bush administration and Congress reached agreement on a far-reaching prescription drug benefit package at a projected cost to the federal government of $40 billion per year for its first ten years.

Despite the large amount of energy expended on this debate, adding prescription drug coverage to Medicare increases the government's spending on health care by less than 8%. The government already plays an enormous role in the provision of health care in the United States: almost half of all health care spending today is done by the government.[3] This is a dramatic rise over the past 40 years, as illustrated in Figure 16-1.

Public health spending is targeted to three specific groups: the **Medicare** program targets the elderly and the disabled, and the **Medicaid** program targets low-income families, including low-income elderly and disabled who do not qualify for Medicare. Medicaid and Medicare represent the most rapidly growing expenditure item for federal and state governments, rising from less than 0.1% of total government expenditures in 1962 to nearly 20% today.[4] Because of their large and growing role, these programs are a constant source of policy debate.

To help you become familiar with the functions of these programs, this chapter provides a description of how and for whom they operate. We also review the major policy issues concerning these two programs. We begin by

Medicare Federal program, funded by a payroll tax, that provides health insurance to all elderly over age 65 and disabled persons under age 65.

Medicaid Federal and state program, funded by general tax revenues, that provides health care for poor families, elderly, and disabled.

---

[2] Stone (2003).
[3] Centers for Medicare and Medicaid Services (2006c).
[4] Office of Management and Budget (2006a).

assessing the impact of the Medicaid program for low-income families on the health insurance coverage and health of those families: Has expanding public insurance to low-income groups proved a cost-effective means of improving their health? We then turn to the major source of policy debate in Medicare, how to control the rapidly rising costs of this program. We discuss the two major government efforts to control costs: moving to prospective reimbursement of providers and enabling consumer choice of managed care plans. Next, we discuss the set of issues surrounding long-term care of the elderly, which involves both public programs.

Finally, the last section of the chapter pulls together the lessons from both Chapters 15 and 16 to discuss the broad question of health care reform in the United States. The discussion focuses on the twin crises of health care (rising costs and the large numbers of uninsured) and the key issues involved in moving forward to address these crises.

16.1

The Medicaid Program for Low-income Mothers and Children

The major public health intervention for low-income populations in the United States is the Medicaid program. The Medicaid program serves two types of groups: low-income women and children and low-income disabled and elderly. Because the majority of program enrollees are in the first group, our discussion focuses on low-income families; there will be a brief discussion of the disabled and the elderly later in the chapter.

How Medicaid Works

Medicaid, like unemployment insurance (UI), is a program that is federally mandated but administered by the states.[5] It is financed on a shared basis between the states and the federal government out of general revenues rather than a payroll tax. The rate at which the federal government shares in Medicaid spending is an inverse function of state income, with the federal government paying half the costs of the program in high-income states, such as Massachusetts, and more than three-quarters in low-income states, such as Mississippi. The federal government mandates some minimal levels of eligibility and service coverage, and states are free to increase generosity beyond these mandates.

Individuals qualify for Medicaid on the basis of their income and family structure, as described next. If eligible, individuals may then enroll in the Medicaid program. Medicaid insurance coverage is similar to private insurance, reimbursing providers for the services they provide to enrollees, although there is little or no patient coinsurance.

---

[5] For details on the programs discussed in this chapter, see the 2004 Green Book (U.S. House of Representatives Committee on Ways and Means, 2004).

Who Is Eligible for Medicaid?

Medicaid was introduced in the late 1960s as a health insurance component for state cash welfare programs that targeted low-income single-parent families. Beginning in the mid-1980s, the Medicaid program was slowly separated from cash welfare programs, first by extending benefits to low-income children in two-parent families and then by raising the income eligibility thresholds for two groups—children and pregnant women (who were covered only for the costs associated with pregnancy, not for other health costs).

In 1997, the Medicaid program for children was augmented by the **Children's Health Insurance Program (CHIP).** The goal of CHIP was to expand the eligibility of children for public health insurance beyond the existing limits of the Medicaid program. This program provides $4 billion per year (on average) through 2007 for states to expand their health insurance coverage beyond Medicaid levels, using either expansions of the Medicaid program or a new program that more closely mimics private health insurance. To provide incentives for states to expand their low-income health care coverage using CHIP funds, the federal government pays a higher share of each state's CHIP costs than it pays of the state's Medicaid costs. In the remainder of this chapter, we will typically refer to both Medicaid and CHIP coverage as Medicaid.

Currently, all individuals age 18 or younger are eligible for Medicaid or CHIP up to 100% of the poverty line ($20,000 for a family of four), and children under age 6 and pregnant women are covered up to 133% of the poverty line ($26,600). In most states, eligibility extends further for both children and pregnant women: a typical state covers both groups up to 200% of the poverty line ($40,000). Eligibility extends much further in some states: children in New Jersey, for example, are eligible up to 350% of the poverty line ($70,000).[6]

Children's Health Insurance Program (CHIP) Program introduced in 1997 to expand eligibility of children for public health insurance beyond the existing limits of the Medicaid program, generally up to 200% of the poverty line.

What Health Services Does Medicaid Cover?

Besides eligibility, states have leeway along two other dimensions. The first is service coverage. While federal Medicaid rules require states to cover major services, such as physician and hospital care, they do not require states to pay for optional services, such as prescription drugs or dental care. Even so, all states have chosen to cover the most expensive optional benefits; all states cover prescription drugs and optometrist services, for example, and all but one cover dental services. For the traditional Medicaid population, these services are provided with little or no copayment required. (In states that have CHIP, copayments are allowed to be somewhat higher for those above 150% of the poverty line.) This package of services is much more generous than that of virtually any private insurance plan. Thus, Medicaid is really the best insurance money can't buy!

---

[6] Poverty line information from Office of the Federal Register (2006), pp. 3848–3849; Medicaid eligibility information from Centers for Medicare and Medicaid Services (2006d); and New Jersey eligibility information from U.S. Department of Health and Human Services, Health Resources and Services Administration (2006).

How Do Providers Get Paid?

States can also regulate the rate at which health service providers are reimbursed. Unlike the situation for services covered (in which all states cover basically the same health care services), there is more variability across the states in provider reimbursements. In most states, Medicaid reimburses physicians at a much lower level than does the private sector, which often leads physicians to be unwilling to serve Medicaid patients. For childbirth, for example, the reimbursement rate to physicians under Medicaid averages about half of the private-sector reimbursement rate for the same services. In one survey, one-third of all physicians reported that they serve no Medicaid patients, and another third reported that they limit access of Medicaid patients to their practice.[7] Thus, while the coverage provided by Medicaid is very generous in all states, in a number of states individuals may have trouble availing themselves of that coverage because physicians do not want to accept them as patients.

16.2
What Are the Effects of the Medicaid Program?

The Medicaid program is not only enormous, with spending of $292 billion in 2004, but is growing rapidly—an average of 17% per year since its inception (11% per year since 1990).[8] The goal of this large and rapidly growing program is to provide health insurance coverage to low-income populations who cannot afford private coverage and thereby improve their health. Whether Medicaid has had this intended effect is an empirical question, and in this section we review the evidence on this question.

How Does Medicaid Affect Health? A Framework

Can expanding eligibility for public insurance programs improve health? Figure 16-2 provides an organizing framework for answering this question, in several steps.

Step 1: Translate the eligibility change into a change in actual coverage by the Medicaid program. There are two channels through which eligibility increases can increase coverage. The first is the "take-up" channel: eligibility changes make people who were previously uninsured eligible for coverage, and only some of these newly eligible people will enroll in the program. The second is the "crowd-out" channel: eligibility causes some people with private insurance to discontinue their private insurance and enroll in public insurance. This outcome is another form of the substitution of social insurance for self-insurance (crowd-out) we discussed in Chapters 12–14.

---

[7] Gruber (2004).
[8] Centers for Medicare and Medicaid Services (2006c).

■ FIGURE 16-2

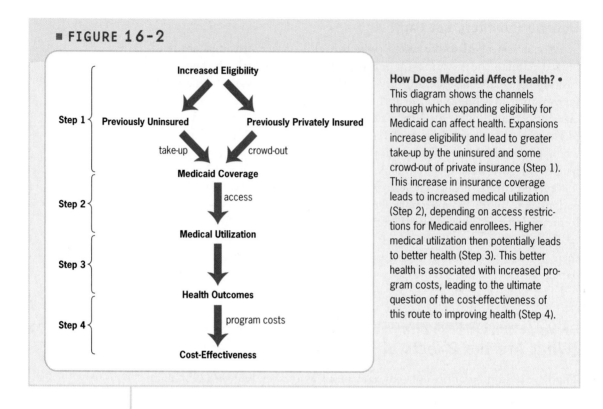

How Does Medicaid Affect Health? • This diagram shows the channels through which expanding eligibility for Medicaid can affect health. Expansions increase eligibility and lead to greater take-up by the uninsured and some crowd-out of private insurance (Step 1). This increase in insurance coverage leads to increased medical utilization (Step 2), depending on access restrictions for Medicaid enrollees. Higher medical utilization then potentially leads to better health (Step 3). This better health is associated with increased program costs, leading to the ultimate question of the cost-effectiveness of this route to improving health (Step 4).

Step 2: Translate the increases in Medicaid coverage into actual increases in utilization of care. As noted earlier, many providers will not see Medicaid patients because of low reimbursement rates. As a result, it is not clear that covering more people with Medicaid will greatly increase utilization; if the supply of providers willing to see Medicaid enrollees is fixed, increasing demand for care will not increase the total amount of care provided.

Step 3: Translate the increase in utilization of care into improved health. It is not clear how important increased medical care will be for health improvements. The RAND Health Insurance Experiment results reviewed in the previous chapter, for example, suggest that varying the generosity of health insurance does not improve health outcomes very much.

Step 4: Determine the cost-effectiveness of the Medicaid expansion. The value of any Medicaid-induced improvements in health must be weighed against their costs. Even if Medicaid improves health, if we could improve health more cost-effectively through other policies, then we may want to pursue those other policies instead.

How Does Medicaid Affect Health? Evidence

What is the evidence concerning the various steps shown in Figure 16-2? In this section, we provide a quick overview of the relevant economics literature.

Take-Up The Medicaid expansions of the 1980s and 1990s led to an explosion in eligibility for the program. In 1982, 12% of individuals nationwide aged 18 or under were eligible for public insurance under Medicaid. By 2000, 46% of individuals in that age group were eligible, an increase of almost 400%. There was a parallel rise for pregnant women, with some small increase for parents of eligible children in selected states that chose to expand to that population.[9]

Relatively few of the newly eligible people enrolled, however. By most estimates, only about one-quarter of those made eligible for Medicaid in the late 1980s and early 1990s enrolled in the program, and only about 10% of those made eligible through the CHIP expansions of the late 1990s enrolled. Just as we saw with UI in Chapter 14, some of this low enrollment may be caused by a lack of information about eligibility for the program, and some may be caused by stigma about taking a public handout. Another reason that is particular to the Medicaid expansions, however, is that most of those made eligible *already had private health insurance coverage*. For those individuals, switching from private to public coverage might not be very attractive; for example, individuals may be wary of leaving their private insurance for a public program they could be disqualified for if their incomes rise.

Crowd-Out Unlike people who prefer to hold on to their private health insurance, some individuals might find it attractive to leave private insurance for public insurance because the Medicaid insurance package is much more generous than that provided by the typical private insurance plan and it doesn't cost anything. In terms of benefits, many employer-provided insurance plans don't include the "optional" benefits covered by virtually all state Medicaid programs, such as dental or vision care. In terms of costs, the typical employer that offers health insurance charges families over $226 per month, or almost $2,720 per year, to enroll in an insurance plan, while Medicaid is free.[10] Moreover, while copayments are low in employer-provided insurance relative to the optimal level recommended by economic theory, they are much higher than those in Medicaid, which has close to zero copayments mandated by law. As a result of all these cost and coverage differences between private and public insurance, some privately insured individuals may find it advantageous to switch to public insurance when they are made eligible. This is another example of the ways government intervention can crowd out private provision, as we saw with fireworks, education, and social insurance.

There are a number of empirical studies that estimate the extent of crowd-out. These studies find that there is some crowd-out, but it is far from complete, with private insurance declines amounting to 20–50% of the public insurance increases.[11]

Health Care Utilization and Health Even at the largest estimates of crowd-out, expanding Medicaid still substantially reduces the number of uninsured,

---

[9] Calculations from the author's research with Kosali Simon at Cornell University.
[10] Kaiser Family Foundation (2005), Exhibit B.
[11] See Gruber and Simon (2006) for a review of this literature.

so expansions may affect the utilization of health care services (such as doctor's office visits) and ultimately the health of those newly covered. In fact, the existing evidence suggests that both utilization of health care services and health care outcomes improved when Medicaid expanded (Steps 2–3 in Figure 16-2). Preventive care, particularly early prenatal care and preventive medical visits by children, rose by more than 50% when individuals were made eligible for Medicaid. At the same time, there were large corresponding reductions in both infant and child mortality: infant mortality, for example, declined by 8.5% as a result of the expansion of Medicaid coverage to pregnant women.[12]

The finding that providing health insurance to the uninsured can improve their health is echoed in other studies as well. Hanratty (1996) studied the introduction of national health insurance in Canada and found that it was associated with a 4% decline in the infant mortality rate and an 8.9% decrease in the incidence of low birth weight among infants of single mothers. Lurie et al. (1984) studied a large group of individuals in California who lost their eligibility to receive public insurance (due to a fiscal crisis in the early 1980s that forced the state to cut back its insurance coverage) and found that health deteriorated significantly among this group afterward. For example, blood pressure rose among hypertensive patients, leading to a 40% increased risk of dying: overall, 5 of the 186 patients who had lost insurance subsequently died, compared to 0 of the 109 patients in a comparable group of individuals that did not lose insurance coverage.

Do these findings contradict the conclusions of the RAND Health Insurance Experiment, which found that varying the extent of insurance (through the coinsurance rate) had no impact on health? They don't, because the HIE made no one uninsured; all individuals were fully insured for expenditures above $1,000. So putting these two pieces of evidence together, we can trace the type of medical effectiveness curve we showed in Figure 15-3. Moving individuals from being uninsured to having some insurance, as is done by the Medicaid expansions, has an important positive effect on health. But once someone is insured, varying the amount of insurance coverage, as is done in the RAND HIE, doesn't seem to cause significant changes in health.

Cost-Effectiveness Finally, we come to cost-effectiveness, the last arrow in Figure 16-2; evidence indicates that expanding public insurance does improve health, but at what cost? Currie and Gruber (1996) estimated that it cost Medicaid roughly $1 million per infant life saved through its expansions. This is much lower than the typical estimate of the value of a life from compensating differential studies discussed in Chapter 8 ($3 million to $7 million). One million dollars is also much lower than the cost of many alternative government interventions designed to save lives, such as food regulation or seat-belt safety. This finding suggests that investing in low-income health care may be a cost-effective means of improving health in the United States.

---

[12] Currie and Gruber (1996a,b).

USING STATE MEDICAID EXPANSIONS TO ESTIMATE PROGRAM EFFECTS

A natural way to measure the effect of Medicaid on health status would be to compare those who choose to enroll in the program with those who are not enrolled. Such an approach suffers from two types of bias, however. First, eligibility for Medicaid is determined by factors, such as income, that might also determine outcomes such as health status (for example, the poor individuals eligible for Medicaid may also be the least healthy individuals in a state). Second, only some individuals who are eligible for Medicaid will take up the program, and these individuals may be different from those who do not take up the program (for example, those enrolled may be in worse health). As a result, the treatment group (those on Medicaid) will be different along many dimensions from the control group (those not on Medicaid), biasing estimates of the effect of the program on outcomes.

Fortunately, the expansions in Medicaid eligibility over the 1980s and 1990s provide a natural means of overcoming this limitation. An important feature of the Medicaid expansions is that they occurred at a very different pace across the states and at a different pace for different age groups of children within states, as illustrated in Table 16-1. In Missouri, for example, which had fairly restrictive

eligibility for Medicaid before these expansions, Medicaid eligibility for children rose from 12% of children in 1982 to 76% of children in 2000. In Michigan, in contrast, 20% of children were already eligible in 1982, and that figure had risen to only 34% by 2000.

This differential pace of expansion across the states provides an excellent setting for quasi-experimental analysis of the effects of these programs. Studies can compare outcomes (such as degree of illness) in the treatment states, those that expand eligibility more, to outcomes in the controls, those that expand it less. As long as nothing else is changing in these states that is correlated with both the eligibility expansions and the outcome variables, such as health, then this approach controls for the bias inherent in comparing individuals on and off Medicaid.

It is possible, however, that other things were changing along with state insurance expansions; for example, states may have been more willing to expand Medicaid when there was a state recession, which would independently affect health (if parents have less money, they are less able to afford food and health services for their children). As in the case of UI, however, there are "within-state" control groups that can further limit bias, because eligibility expands for some age groups of children and not for others. Researchers could, for example, compare what happened to outcomes of 13-year-olds in Washington, D.C., the treatment group, for whom eligibility rose by over 40% of the population from 1982 to 2000 (from 18% to 59%), with what happened to newborns there, the control group, for whom eligibility rose by less than 10% of the population (from 48% to 56% because a large percentage of newborns were already eligible in 1982). Both groups are subject to the same outside factors, such as a recession, but they face very different Medicaid policies. As shown in the appendix to Chapter 14, we can combine the across-state comparisons with the within-state comparisons to develop a more convincing quasi-experimental estimate.

■ **TABLE 16-1**

Medicaid Eligibility Changes Across and Within States

	Eligibility for All Children, by State	
Year	Missouri eligibility	Michigan eligibility
1982	12%	20%
2000	76%	34%
	Eligibility for Children by Age, in Washington, D.C.	
Year	Age 13 eligibility	Age 0 eligibility
1982	18%	48%
2000	59%	56%

Over the 1982–2000 period, Medicaid eligibility rose much more in Missouri than in Michigan (top panel). There were also dramatic differences in eligibility growth within states: eligibility rose much more for 13-year-olds in Washington, D.C., than for 0-year-olds (bottom panel).

Source: Calculations from the author's research with Kosali Simon at Cornell University.

―16.3

The Medicare Program

The largest public health insurance program in the United States is Medicare, which, as previously discussed, was started in 1965 as a universal health insurance system for the elderly and nonelderly disabled (those receiving disability insurance from the federal government). To help you organize your thoughts about Medicaid and Medicare, Table 16-2 compares the key features of the two programs.

How Medicare Works

The Medicare program is administered at the federal level. All U.S. citizens who have worked and paid payroll taxes for ten years, and their spouses, are eligible for coverage; other citizens who do not have the requisite work experience can purchase Medicare coverage at its full cost. Medicare operates similarly to a private insurance plan, with the government reimbursing providers for their costs and with patients responsible for coinsurance. There are two key features of Medicare to keep in mind as we learn about this program and think about reforms to it.

▪ TABLE 16-2

Medicaid and Medicare

	Medicaid	Medicare
Eligibles	Families on welfare	Retirees and spouses 65 and older
	Low-income children, pregnant women	Certain disabled individuals under 65
	Low-income elderly, disabled	People with kidney failure (requiring dialysis or transplant)
Premiums	None	Hospital coverage: none
		Physician coverage: $66.60 per month
		Prescription drug coverage: Variable
Deductibles/copayments	None (or very small)	Hospital coverage: $876 deductible for first 60 days
		Physician coverage: $100 deductible, 20% coinsurance
		Prescription drug coverage: Variable
Services excluded	None (or very minor)	Prescription drugs (until 2006)
		Routine checkups, dental care, nursing home care, eyeglasses, hearing aids, immunization shots
Provider reimbursement	Very low	Moderate (but falling)

Medicaid provides health insurance for low-income individuals, covering a wide range of health services at little cost to those individuals. Medicare provides health insurance for those age 65 and over, covering many, though not all, health services at some cost to those individuals.

Medicare Is Really Three Different Programs Medicare really consists of three different programs. **Medicare Part A** covers inpatient hospital costs and some costs of *long-term care* (care for the elderly, either in institutions such as nursing homes or in their own homes). This part of the program is financed from the Medicare Hospital Insurance trust fund, which is funded by a 1.45% payroll tax on both employers and employees. **Medicare Part B** covers physician expenditures, outpatient hospital expenditures, and other services. About 25% of the cost of this part of the program is financed by enrollee premiums ($88.50 per month in 2006), which are deducted directly from Social Security payments; the remaining 75% of the cost is paid from general government revenues.[13] **Medicare Part D** provides coverage for prescription drug expenditures. As described below, individuals can choose from a large variety of private insurance plans for their prescription drug coverage. Part D coverage is financed by a mix of enrollee premiums (which vary widely across available plans) and general revenues.

Medicare Part A Part of the Medicare program that covers inpatient hospital costs and some costs of long-term care; financed from a payroll tax.

Medicare Part B Part of the Medicare program that covers physician expenditures, outpatient hospital expenditures, and other services; financed from enrollee premiums and general revenues.

Medicare Part D Part of the Medicare program that covers prescription drug expenditures.

Medicare Has High Patient Costs Relative to private health insurance, and certainly relative to Medicaid, the Medicare program has fairly high copayments and deductibles and a relatively lean benefits package. Part A of the program has an $952 deductible for the first 60 days of a hospital stay (with costs to the patient rising to $238 per day for days 61–90, $476 per day for days 91–150, and full payment required after that), and Part B has a $124 deductible and a 20% coinsurance rate.[14] It is important to note that the Part B coinsurance is not capped at some level of out-of-pocket expenditures; if an individual has $10,000 in physician bills in a year, he or she must pay $2,000 in coinsurance. This greatly lowers the consumption-smoothing value of Medicare, since there is still some risk of very high medical expenditures if you are ill. Part D coverage also features high patient costs (see the application that follows) although there is wide variation across Part D insurance plans, with some plans charging higher premiums and in return covering a much larger share of prescription expenditures. Moreover, Medicare does not cover many benefits provided by private-sector insurance plans, including dental and vision care.

▶ APPLICATION

The Medicare Prescription Drug Debate

As noted in the introduction to this chapter, one of the liveliest health policy debates of the early twenty-first century was over the addition of a prescription drug benefit to the Medicare program. Because outpatient

---

[13] Centers for Medicare and Medicaid Services (2006a).
[14] Centers for Medicare and Medicaid Services (2006a).

drugs were only a very small share of medical spending when Medicare was established in 1965, their absence from the benefits package was not viewed as a terrible omission. As prescription drugs grew in importance, particularly for the elderly, the fact that Medicare differed from private health plans, 99% of which cover prescription drugs, became a glaring deficiency.

Democrats and Republicans proposed two different approaches to deal with this problem. Democrats suggested adding a drug benefit to the Medicare program, with the government negotiating directly with drug companies to ensure the lowest drug prices. Republicans suggested that the government subsidize private insurers to offer prescription drug coverage to the elderly, either through HMOs or as a stand-alone prescription drug–only plan.

There are advantages and disadvantages to both these approaches. On the one hand, the federal government would represent an enormous buying pool for prescription drugs, which would allow it to both minimize administrative costs and strongly negotiate for low prices. On the other hand, the federal government could become too heavy-handed and lower prices so much that new drug development becomes unprofitable and pharmaceutical innovation is reduced.[15]

Private insurance approaches would not suffer from this problem as they would negotiate prices with manufacturers, but the private model would introduce the new problem of adverse selection, whereby plans might suffer from getting only those enrollees who need the most prescription drugs.

In December 2003, President Bush signed into law a bill that followed the Republican approach, but provided government *reinsurance* to deal with potential problems of adverse selection. Under this reinsurance arrangement, the federal government reimburses insurers for a share of very large drug bills to ensure that insurers do not suffer unduly from enrolling sick individuals.

Enrollment in the new Part D program was initially fraught with problems. Starting shortly before the official opening of the enrollment period on November 15, 2005, Medicare and state officials were bombarded by hundreds of calls per day from frustrated Medicare recipients who felt hopelessly lost among the 44 different plans they were expected to choose from, some of which continued to be adjusted by fiercely competing private insurers even as consumers were trying to make a decision.

This confusion was exacerbated by the technical difficulties that plagued the actual transition on January 1, 2006. The biggest problems arose for low-

---

[15] Finkelstein (2003) shows that innovation in pharmaceuticals responds to the incentives provided by government insurance coverage.

income Medicare beneficiaries who were supposed to have their drug coverage heavily subsidized by Medicare. Across the country, low-income Medicare beneficiaries went to a pharmacist to pick up their medications only to be turned away when pharmacists were unable to verify beneficiaries' eligibility for drug benefits or the low-income subsidies. Due to the widespread pattern of problems, governors in at least four states were forced to intervene and provide the drugs that low-income beneficiaries had been unable to acquire or afford on their own. In a period of less than a week, the state of Maine incurred over $2 million in expenses providing medication to those in need. In New Hampshire, where the state had also agreed to pay for drugs that should have been covered by Medicare, Governor John Lynch reported that the start of the Medicare drug program "has been a nightmare for many of our citizens."[16]

Despite this rocky start, in the following months the federal government was able to iron out many of the problems that had arisen during the initial transition and, by May 2006, the new program was filling more than three million prescriptions per day.[17] Moreover, surveys showed that while only roughly 37% of seniors felt they understood the new Medicare program in November 2005, that number had risen to almost 50% by April 2006.[18]

The ultimate verdict on the success of this private market-based approach is not in. What is clear, however, is that the basic structure of this drug benefit is illogical. For basic Part D plans, individuals receive coverage for:

▶ none of the first $250 in drug costs each year

▶ 75% of costs for the next $2,250 of drug spending (up to $2,500 total)

▶ 0% of costs for the next $3,600 of drug spending (up to $5,100 total)

▶ 95% of costs above $5,100 of drug spending

This is a very odd structure, featuring generous coverage for low spending amounts (between $250 and $2,500 of drug spending), followed by a "donut hole" where there is no coverage (up to $5,100), and then almost full coverage above a catastrophic level (above $5,100). There is no coherent economic rationale for such a structure. The optimal insurance arrangement discussed in the previous chapter would feature little coverage of initial spending, to avoid moral hazard, with insurance coverage rising as spending rises to ensure consumption smoothing. The first and last brackets of this plan, with an initial deductible and catastrophic coverage above

---

[16] Pear (2006a).
[17] Pear (2006b).
[18] Kaiser Family Foundation (2006a).

$5,100, follow that arrangement. Yet there is no economic rationale for the two middle brackets, which provide fairly generous coverage of drug spending, between $250 and $2,500, and then *no coverage* for the next $3,600 of spending. This is an upside-down benefit structure that is exactly the reverse of an optimal insurance design.

The rationale for this structure is clearly political. The majority of seniors have modest drug costs; 54% of Medicare recipients, for example, have drug costs of less than $2,000 per year.[19] The goal of the bill was, for a given federal budgetary cost, to deliver benefits to the largest number of elderly, regardless of their ultimate need for insurance coverage. This was accomplished by this upside-down drug benefit. Efforts to maximize votes by politicians therefore led to the use of low coinsurance for low expenditures and higher coinsurance for higher expenditures. The effect of this donut hole on the use of prescription drugs for the elderly is likely to be an important source of debate in the coming years. ◀

16.4

What Are the Effects of the Medicare Program?

Unlike Medicaid, the focus of public policy debate on Medicare has not been about who should be eligible; there appears to be broad support for a program that universally covers the elderly and disabled. Despite this broad support, however there is surprisingly little evidence that the Medicare program actually improves the health of the elderly.[20] This does not mean that Medicare is not valuable. Recall that the role of insurance discussed in Chapter 12 was not to improve outcomes; rather, it was to ensure consumption smoothing over adverse events. And Medicare is clearly successful in this goal. As Finkelstein and McKnight (2005) document, the introduction of Medicare was associated with a large reduction in out-of-pocket spending on medical care, particularly for those who had the highest medical spending. Using the type of insurance model described in Chapter 12, these authors compute that the consumption-smoothing gains from Medicare have been at least half as large as the expenditures on the program, so that even without positive effects on health, there have been sizeable benefits to universal coverage of the elderly.

Given the broad consensus for universal coverage of the elderly, the focus of debate has been on controlling the rapidly rising costs of this program. In

---

[19] Congressional Budget Office (2002).

[20] Card et. al. (2004) finds that there are little health gains at age 65, either for those insured or uninsured before reaching that age.

its first 15 years of existence, the Medicare program grew exponentially, from $64 million in federal expenditures in 1966 to $32.1 billion in 1980. This rapid rise led policy makers to focus on controlling costs, through two different channels.

The Prospective Payment System

Like those in the private sector, the administrators of Medicare realized that its retrospective reimbursement of medical providers on the basis of their billed costs was a recipe for rapidly rising costs. This program was therefore a pioneer in moving toward prospective reimbursement, in which reimbursement is based on expected costs, not actual services delivered, in an effort to control overuse of medical care. In 1983, Medicare moved to a **Prospective Payment System (PPS)** for reimbursing hospitals. This system had several key features:

1. All diagnoses for hospital admissions were grouped into 467 "Diagnosis Related Groups," or DRGs.

2. The government reimbursed hospitals a fixed amount based on the DRG of patient admission, regardless of the actual treatment costs of those patients. The reimbursement amounts were higher for more "severe" (higher-cost) DRGs.

3. The fixed amount of reimbursement was determined by a national standard for the cost of treating that DRG and a hospital-specific adjustment that more highly reimbursed teaching hospitals and those hospitals that treat many poor patients.

> **Prospective Payment System (PPS)** Medicare's system for reimbursing hospitals based on nationally standardized payments for specific diagnoses.

Empirical Evidence on the Move to the PPS

In theory, PPS represented a classic prospective payment system, with incentives to treat patients as cost-efficiently as possible, since hospitals are paid a fixed amount regardless of treatment intensity. Indeed, the effects of the PPS were striking. There was an enormous reduction in the treatment intensity of the elderly within hospitals, a result consistent with the move from retrospective to prospective reimbursement incentives. The average length of a hospital stay for elderly patients fell from 9.7 days to 8.4 days in just one year, which was four times the rate of decrease over the previous two decades. In one Indiana hospital, the length of stay for hip fractures fell from almost 22 days to only 13 days. There was a 15% drop in admissions to intensive care units and a 16% drop in admissions to coronary (heart) care units.[21]

Moreover, despite this enormous reduction in treatment intensity, there was no evidence of an adverse impact on patient outcomes. Mortality rates within one year of treatment were the same before and after this major policy

---

[21] Fitzgerald et al. (1987); Leibson et al. (1991).

change. This result is further evidence for the "flat of the curve" model shown in Figure 15-3: as long as individuals are insured, treating them less intensively leads to little decline in their health.

The move to a PPS led to a sharp reduction in the rate of growth of hospital costs: after growing at 9.6% per year from 1967 to 1982, hospital costs under Medicare grew at only 3.0% per year from 1983 to 1988. Unfortunately, the PPS appears to lose its effect over time: from 1988 to 1997, hospital costs rose at a rate of 5.4% per year.

Problems with PPS

Why didn't the PPS solve the long-run cost growth problems of the Medicare program? Perhaps because it was not prospective enough. Almost immediately, the system ran into the problem of "DRG creep." Medicare was paying a fixed price per diagnosis, but the choice of a diagnosis is something the hospital has some control over when patients are admitted (particularly for elderly patients, who often have many problematic conditions on admission). Thus, by labeling an admitted patient as having a more severe diagnosis, hospitals could change their DRG categorization to one for which the hospital would be reimbursed more highly. Indeed, there was a large increase in reported severity of admission diagnoses for the elderly around the time of PPS!

Some examples were so egregious that they led to criminal persecution of the largest hospital chain in the United States, the Columbia/HCA corporation. For example, in 1995 the Columbia's Cedars Medical Center in Miami coded 93% of their Medicare cases with respiratory illness in the DRG for complex respiratory infection (with a reimbursement rate of $5,700), and only 7% in the DRG for pneumonia with complications (with a rate of only $1,700). Meanwhile, at Jackson Memorial, a non–Columbia-operated hospital located just across the street, only 28% of billings were in the complex respiratory infection category. Moreover, a pronounced shift in Cedars' billing pattern was shown to coincide exactly with its acquisition by the Columbia Corporation. In 1992, the hospital's last year of independent operation, only 31% of respiratory cases were billed at the highest rate; only one year later, afer Columbia Corporation had bought the hospital, that number had risen to 76%. Ultimately, in 2000, HCA (as the company later renamed itself) pleaded guilty to 14 felonies, and agreed to pay $1.7 billion in civil and criminal penalties, the largest amount ever secured by federal prosecutors in a health care fraud case.[22]

This short-run problem has a longer-run manifestation, which is a problem with the design of the DRGs themselves. Almost half of the DRG designations are based not purely on diagnosis but also on the actual treatment used for the patient. For example, someone entering the hospital with severe heart trouble might be given a diagnosis of "cardiac arrest, unexplained" (DRG

---

[22] Eichenwald (2002); Gottlieb et al. (1997).

129), for which the hospital might be reimbursed $5,000. Or he or she might receive one of many surgeries, including coronary bypass (DRG 106, with a reimbursement of $33,000), pacemaker implantation (DRG 551, reimbursement of $15,000), or in the most extreme case, a heart transplant (DRG 103, with a reimbursement of $88,000).[23] With this categorization, there is effectively retrospective reimbursement: by performing a certain procedure, a provider can move the patient's case to a higher DRG and raise the reimbursement level.

Finally, another problem with the PPS has been that it applies only to one part of the medical system for treating the elderly, but there is enormous substitutability across different pieces of the medical system. One excellent example of this is provided by Newhouse and Byrne (1988), who studied rehabilitation hospitals, which are designed for longer-term hospital stays that require little acute medical care (little constant monitoring and more long-term rehabilitation, such as for recovery from hip replacement surgery). Rehabilitation hospitals were originally exempt from the restrictions of the PPS. As a result, around the time of the PPS, there was an enormous shift of patients from acute-care hospitals to these exempt rehabilitation institutions, undoing a large part of the savings from the PPS change.

Lesson: The Difficulty of Partial Reform

These findings highlight a key problem with *partial reform* of provider reimbursement. If policy makers don't address systemwide incentives for overtreatment due to retrospective reimbursement, then partial solutions are like squeezing one corner of a pillow: the costs just move to the other corners. Pay hospitals based on diagnosis and patients suddenly appear sicker; reimburse one type of hospital more strictly and patients are moved elsewhere. In 1997, recognition of this fact motivated the federal government to mandate that the prospective reimbursement system eventually be applied to other sectors that were currently receiving retrospective reimbursement. The implementation of these changes has been slow, however, so we do not currently have evidence on their effects on costs or health.

Just as with designing optimal insurance systems for workers, designing optimal reimbursement systems for providers reflects a trade-off. On the one hand, retrospective reimbursement systems do not provide sufficient incentives to control medical costs. On the other hand, a purely prospective system, which we have not yet achieved, might lead providers to cut care too much in order to make money. Thus, the optimal system would probably include some combination of both approaches. The existing evidence for the Medicare program suggests that it may err too much toward retaining key features of retrospective reimbursement.

---

[23] Office of the Federal Register (2005).

Medicare Managed Care

The other avenue pursued by policy makers to control the costs of Medicare is to increase use of managed care in the Medicare program. Since managed care plans cost less per enrollee without obviously reducing the quality of care, the government could in theory save money by shifting enrollees to managed care.

Traditionally, all enrollees in Medicare received the same type of retrospectively reimbursed health insurance. Then, starting in 1985, the federal government allowed Medicare enrollees a choice of Medicare HMOs as well. These plans typically covered many of the out-of-pocket costs of Medicare, so that enrollees were less exposed to the program's copayments and deductibles. The plans also often provided other benefits not available through Medicare, most notably prescription drug coverage. A disadvantage for patients was that HMOs restricted their choice of provider and potentially engaged in other rationing devices to keep down costs that were not present in the traditional system. Despite this disadvantage, as Figure 16-3 shows, enrollment in Medicare HMOs rose steadily to a peak of 16% of all enrollees in 1999.

The Medicare program endeavored to lower its costs by reimbursing HMOs only 95% of the average annual medical costs of enrollees who stayed in traditional Medicare (the "adjusted average per capita costs," or AAPCC). In this way, everyone won: the patients who chose Medicare HMOs got a package they preferred, and the government saved money.

But was the government actually saving money? Recall from the previous chapter that there is strong evidence for positive selection into HMOs—only the healthiest patients choose this option. Such selection also operated strongly for the elderly in Medicare. As a result, many Medicare HMOs had annual medical costs *for their enrollees* that were well below 95% of the AAPCC, since

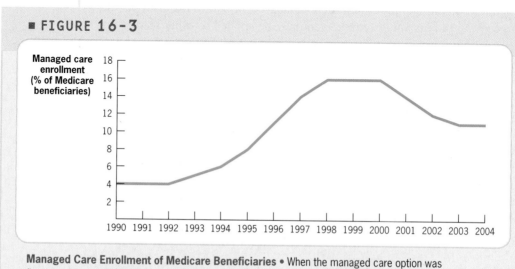

■ **FIGURE 16-3**

Managed Care Enrollment of Medicare Beneficiaries • When the managed care option was first introduced to Medicare, enrollment rose steadily, to a peak of 16% of Medicare beneficiaries by 1999. In recent years, enrollment has declined because of the government's decision in 1997 to lower reimbursement rates to managed care providers.

Source: Kaiser Family Foundation (2006), Exhibit 2.17.

■ FIGURE 16-4

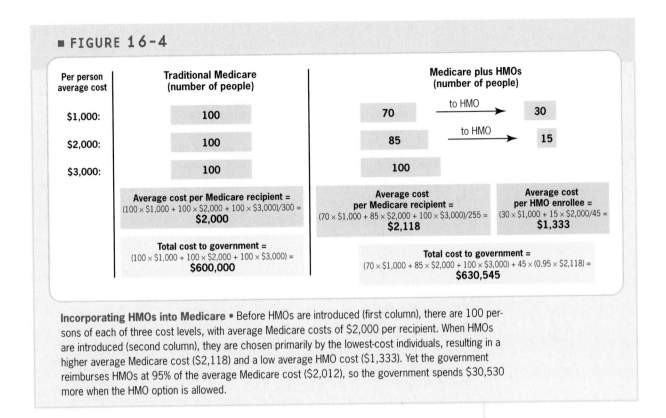

Incorporating HMOs into Medicare • Before HMOs are introduced (first column), there are 100 persons of each of three cost levels, with average Medicare costs of $2,000 per recipient. When HMOs are introduced (second column), they are chosen primarily by the lowest-cost individuals, resulting in a higher average Medicare cost ($2,118) and a low average HMO cost ($1,333). Yet the government reimburses HMOs at 95% of the average Medicare cost ($2,012), so the government spends $30,530 more when the HMO option is allowed.

they were enrolling only the healthiest people. Thus, most estimates suggest that the government was actually *losing money* on the HMO option.

How could the government lose money when it was paying only 95% of the average? Because the government was paying 95% of the average cost of the sickest enrollees remaining on Medicare, while the HMO's true cost for its healthy enrollees was much lower. Figure 16-4 illustrates the process of selection with a mythical Medicare program. Before HMOs are available, there are 300 individuals in this program. One-third of enrollees have average costs of $1,000 per year, one-third have average costs of $2,000 per year, and one-third have average costs of $3,000 per year. So the average cost to the Medicare program is $2,000 per enrollee, and the government spends a total of $600,000.

When HMOs are introduced, they are chosen by 30 of the individuals who cost $1,000 per year, by 15 of the individuals who cost $2,000 per year, and by none of the individuals who cost $3,000 per year (since HMOs are preferred by the healthy). So the set of individuals in the HMOs cost on average $1,333, while the set of individuals remaining in Medicare cost on average $2,118. The government reimburses the HMOs 95% of the average cost of those on Medicare, or $2,012 ($2,118 × 0.95 = $2,012) per year. So the government is losing $679 annually (the $2,012 reimbursement minus the $1,333 those individuals actually cost) on the average HMO enrollee. In other words, the government now has to pay for its remaining enrollees (70 × $1,000) + (85 × $2,000) + (100 × $3,000) = $540,000, plus it pays the HMO

$2,012 for each of its 45 enrollees, or $90,540, for a total of $630,530. So the government has lost over $30,000 by introducing this HMO option!

Recognizing this problem, in 1997 the government lowered further payments to HMOs. This led many HMOs, presumably the ones unable to attract the most healthy enrollees, to drop their Medicare lines of business. As a result, Medicare HMO enrollment, which peaked at 16% of enrollees in 1999, fell to 12.6% by 2003. Disturbed by this trend, Congress reversed itself as part of the Medicare Modernization Act of 2003 (better known for its introduction of prescription drug benefits for Medicare) and raised HMO reimbursement to at least 100% of the level of reimbursement for traditional Medicare (in 2004 they received 107%). This change has had the effect of increasing managed care enrollment in Medicare, which rose to 14% by the end of 2005. It is unclear, however, why managed care enrollment per se should be a government goal; what is clear is that the government is once again losing money on reimbursing HMOs, relative to traditional Medicare![24]

Should Medicare Move to a Full Choice Plan? Premium Support

The problem with the current approach to choice in Medicare is that the government must make some estimate of how much to reimburse managed care plans, and that estimate may be too high (costing the government money) or too low (leading the HMOs to exit the program). Another alternative is to move to a system of full choice among health plans, leaving the elderly with the type of decision faced by employees at firms that offer multiple health insurance plans. In this type of system, commonly known as **premium support,** the elderly would receive a voucher for a certain amount. They could then choose from a range of options, including the traditional Medicare program. If they choose an option that costs less than their voucher amount, they keep the difference; if they choose an option that costs more, they pay the difference. As we discuss in the application, such a system would introduce competition into Medicare and allow the government to more easily set a reimbursement level, but at the cost of redistributing from the sickest enrollees to the most healthy.

premium support A system of full choice among health care plans for Medicare enrollees, whereby they receive a voucher for a certain amount that they can apply to a range of health insurance options (either paying or receiving the difference between plan premiums and the voucher amount).

▶ **APPLICATION**

A Premium Support System for Medicare

A typical premium support plan is illustrated in the top panel of Table 16-3. An elderly person would have a choice in his or her area of, for example, three plans, A, B, and C. The cost of those plans per year are $1,800, $2,000, and

---

[24] It is true that Medicare HMOs provide a richer benefits package than does traditional Medicare, but it is unclear why the government should be subsidizing that richer package just for those who happen to choose HMOs. Indeed, Pizer et al. (2003) find that those choosing HMOs do not value these extra benefits at or above their costs, suggesting little reason to be subsidizing their provision.

$2,500. The government could set its voucher at any level, but suppose the government chooses to reimburse the cost of the median-cost plan in the area ($2,000 in this case). Then individuals who choose plan A would get a rebate of $200; individuals who choose plan B would get nothing; and individuals who choose plan C would have to pay $500.

The advantages of a premium support system mirror the advantages of voucher systems for education (discussed in Chapter 11). First, such a system respects consumer sovereignty by allowing individuals to choose the health plan that best matches their taste rather than forcing them into one government-provided option. Second, such a system promotes efficiency in medical care delivery by allowing individuals to shop across plans. Both HMOs and Medicare will have to produce care as efficiently as possible so that they can offer the lowest possible premiums to attract enrollees. There is less incentive to do so under today's Medicare program, since enrollees pay the same premium amount regardless of which option they choose.

Finally, such a system solves the problem of "appropriate" reimbursement levels for managed care plans by simply letting the market work. The government would simply announce that it would reimburse, for example, the amount of the median-cost plan in the area. Plans would then compete to have low costs in order to attract enrollees, and after this competition the government could simply find the median price and set that as its reimbursement level. There would be no more guessing at the right reimbursement level that fits all HMOs.

There are many positive attributes of health care choice under Medicare, but choice has one key disadvantage that is much worse for health care than it is for education: adverse selection. If the government simply reimburses a flat amount and makes individuals pay on the margin for more expensive plans (or allows them to pocket savings on less expensive plans), then we run into the same problem we first discussed in the context of Harvard University in Chapter 12 (pp. 326–327): healthy individuals choose the less expensive plans, raising costs even further for sicker individuals, who prefer the more generous plans.

■ TABLE 16-3

Premium Support Systems With and Without Adverse Selection

Full-choice Medicare (before adverse selection)			
Plan	Plan cost (per person)	Voucher (median plan cost)	Individual payment
A	$1,800	$2,000	–$200
B	$2,000	$2,000	0
C	$2,500	$2,000	$500
Full-choice Medicare (after adverse selection)			
Plan	Plan cost (per person)	Voucher (median plan cost)	Individual payment
A	$1,600	$2,100	–$500
B	$2,100	$2,100	0
C	$3,000	$2,100	$900

Under a typical premium support system, individuals pay the difference between the cost of their plan and the median-cost plan, as shown in the top panel. Adverse selection, however, will cause sicker patients to choose the most expensive plans, making these plans even more expensive, while the least costly plans fall in price as they are chosen by healthier individuals. In the long term, a voucher scheme thus ends up rewarding the healthy and costing the sick more (bottom panel).

The bottom panel of Table 16-3 illustrates what the premium support system might look like after adverse selection has taken its toll. The healthiest individuals have moved into plan A, lowering its costs further to $1,600 per year. Some of these individuals came from plan B, so plan B now has sicker enrollees on average, and its costs have risen to $2,100. A few individuals from plan C might have moved to plan A, and more from plan C have moved to plan B, so plan C now has just the sickest enrollees, and its costs have risen to $3,000. Now, with the voucher amount tied to the median-cost plan, those in plan A get a rebate of $500 per year, while those in plan C must pay $900 per year.

In a system that reimburses the cost of the median health plan offered, the adverse selection problem could lead to very large rebates for the healthy (who generally choose plan A) and very large costs for the sick (who generally choose plan C). At its heart, therefore, this adverse selection problem is primarily an income distribution issue: Are we willing to permit the healthier elderly to save money and the sicker elderly to pay more in order to introduce competition into the Medicare system? The appropriate level of plan choice in Medicare reflects the trade-off between the benefits of competition and the costs of redistribution from the sick to the healthy. ◀

Gaps in Medicare Coverage

While most of the policy debate around Medicare has focused on cost control, another important source of debate has been whether and how to enrich the Medicare benefits package. Medicare insurance is significantly less generous than most private insurance because of its high copayments and deductibles and because it leaves some medical goods and services uncovered. Individuals fill these coverage gaps in Medicare in one of three ways:

1. Low income elderly individuals are entitled to more generous coverage under the Medicaid program or through subsidies to private prescription drug plans.

2. About one-third of all retirees over 65 are covered by retiree health insurance from their former employers, which fills in many of these gaps.

3. Many retirees not covered by Medicaid or their own retiree health insurance buy individual "Medi-gap" policies from insurance companies that fill these gaps.

An important problem with these three means of filling the gaps in Medicare coverage is that they exert a *negative financial externality* on the Medicare program. As discussed earlier, patient coinsurance for medical care costs reduces the total amount of medical care used by Medicare enrollees. Thus, when other forms of insurance cover Medicare's deductibles and coinsurance, the amount of medical care used increases. Because the costs of most of this medical care (what is spent beyond copayments) is covered by Medicare, there is a negative externality imposed on Medicare by these other forms of insurance: those holding this supplementary insurance raise Medicare costs without bearing the costs of doing so. If I have to pay $20 for my $100 doctor's visit under the traditional Medicare plan, I may not go to the doctor, so Medicare incurs no costs; but if my Medi-gap policy covers that $20, then I will go, and the Medicare program will see its costs increase by $80 through no action of its own. The availability of Medi-gap has caused me to spend $80 more of Medicare's money, but my Medi-gap insurer and I bear none of this $80 in increased public sector costs.

16.5

Long-term Care

The discussion of health care thus far in this chapter has focused on acute medical care, such as for flu or a heart attack. A growing share of medical spending, however, is devoted to chronic long-term care needs, such as nursing home stays for the elderly and disabled. In 1960, only 3.4% of health care dollars was spent on **long-term care.** In 2004, 8.4% of health care spending, or $158 billion per year, was on long-term care.[25]

This care is delivered primarily in two forms:

1. *Institutional care* provided in nursing homes. Reimbursement of the cost of such institutions (where infirm individuals live full-time) accounts for 73% of long-term care costs. Medicaid is the primary insurer of nursing home costs, covering 44% of such costs nationally; Medicare pays only for the small share of costs associated with the first 100 days in a nursing home.[26]

2. *Home health care,* where nurses and other aides provide care in the patient's home, accounts for the remaining 27% of long-term care costs. Medicare is the primary insurance payer for home health care, covering 38% of such costs nationally through its Part A home health care benefit.[27] Since 1980, there has been an enormous shift from institutional to home health care.

long-term care Health care delivered to the disabled and elderly for their long-term rather than acute needs either in an institutional setting (a nursing home) or in their homes.

Financing Long-term Care

The major debate over long-term care is about financing. Currently, nursing home costs are financed mostly by private payers (individual self-insurance and to a small but growing extent by private long-term care insurance) and by Medicaid. Individuals who enter nursing homes begin by paying costs out of their own savings; usually those savings are rapidly drawn down by nursing home stays, which cost on average over $61,000 per year.[28] When savings are drawn below a threshold level, individuals qualify for state programs that pick up the cost of nursing homes under Medicaid. Individuals are therefore insured against nursing home costs, but only if they use up all their personal

---

[25] Centers for Medicare and Medicaid Services (2006c), Table 2.
[26] Centers for Medicare and Medicaid Services (2006c), Table 2 and Table 8.
[27] Centers for Medicare and Medicaid Services (2006c), Table 2 and Table 11.
[28] MetLife Mature Market Institute (2004).

savings first. In this sense, Medicaid imposes an implicit tax on assets: Medicaid will provide financing only once assets are low, so having a lot of assets implies forgoing the right to a government-financed nursing home stay.

This financing system has several problems. First, those who wish to leave money behind when they die have no protection against losing their entire estate to nursing home costs. Second, individuals have an incentive to cheat by hiding their wealth in forms that cannot be found or accessed by Medicaid authorities, thereby more quickly qualifying for public insurance while preserving their wealth. Finally, this system *crowds out* savings for old age, since people can qualify for Medicaid only once they have spent their wealth. This situation parallels our discussion of education in Chapter 11: it leads those who would like to save for a somewhat higher-quality nursing home when they are old to instead not save at all in order to take advantage of the free Medicaid entitlement.

There is a private long-term care insurance market that could, in principle, solve these difficulties. Despite rapid growth in the past decade, however, this market remains small, paying for nursing home costs for only about 8% of patients.[29] There are many potential causes of failure in this market, most notably adverse selection based on private information about the likely risk of nursing home stays. Thus, there may be an argument for replacing the government's current patchwork of long-term care financing with a social insurance system; indeed, there are many proposals for a "Medicare Part C" that would finance nursing home stays out of a higher payroll tax. As always, the cost of such a move would be increased by moral hazard, in the form of increased and longer-term use of nursing homes by the elderly if the costs of such care are insured.

16.6

Lessons for Health Care Reform in the United States

The current debate over health care reform in the United States is concerned with two crises: rapidly rising health care costs and the large and growing number of uninsured persons. In this section, we first discuss the causes of these problems and the fundamental issues that must be addressed in solving them. We then discuss several potential approaches to health care reform in the United States in light of these issues.

Rising Health Care Costs

Since 1950, the Consumer Price Index for medical care has risen by 1.8 percentage points more per year than the Consumer Price Index for all items in the U.S. economy.[30] This dramatic rise in health care costs must be caused by

---

[29] Centers for Medicare and Medicaid Services (2006c), Table 8.
[30] Bureau of Labor Statistics (2006).

something so powerful that it could not be surmounted by the strong incentives embodied in managed care health insurance plans, which now dominate the private insurance industry. While managed care did lead to lower costs in the 1990s, medical cost growth since 2000 has continued to greatly outstrip the growth of the U.S. economy. What drives ever-increasing health care costs? A large health economics literature has studied this question, and the general conclusion is a simple one: the rapid rise in health care costs has been driven by quality-improving technological change in the delivery of health care.

An excellent example of this technology effect is shown in the study of the treatment of heart attacks over time by Cutler et al. (1998). The authors note that there is a wide variety of treatments for heart attacks, ranging from the least-intensive (and lowest-cost) treatments, such as drugs and monitoring of heart activity, to the most-intensive (and highest-cost) treatment, bypass surgery. They report that from 1984 to 1991 the average cost of treating heart attacks rose by 4% per year in real terms. But over this same period, the prices paid for each type of heart attack treatment by Medicare (the primary payer, since heart attacks are concentrated in the elderly) actually fell. Thus, if the types of treatments individuals were receiving for heart attacks had not changed, the cost of treating heart attacks should have fallen, not risen.

The fact that costs did rise shows that there was a shift from cheaper, less-intensive treatments to more expensive, intensive treatments, which raised costs per heart attack treated. For example, the share of patients receiving only low-cost medical management (costing an average of $9,829 per case) fell from 89 to 59%, and the share receiving high-cost bypass surgery (costing $28,135 per case) rose from 5 to 13%. At the same time, this shift was associated with a dramatic improvement in the health outcomes of heart attack patients; over this period, the life expectancy of heart attack patients rose by 8 months, or 13% of the baseline life expectancy. Thus, there was a lot of health improvement purchased with these extra dollars spent on heart attack victims.

In principle, the prospective reimbursement strategies used by managed care organizations and the Medicare program *could* control this type of expensive technological progress. But it is not clear that they *should,* given the enormous quality improvements that may be associated with medical progress. The bottom line is that it is not clear whether society actually *wants* health care costs to be controlled. Cutler (2004) makes a compelling argument that the increase in health spending has led to improvements in health that are of even higher value to our citizens, and he asks: Would you rather buy 1950s health care with 1950s prices or today's health care at today's prices? For almost everyone, the answer is the latter.

Isn't this argument inconsistent with the fact that we seem to be on the "flat of the curve," where the reduced health care use (because of higher copayments or prospective reimbursement) doesn't seem to cause worse health? Not necessarily. The key is to distinguish the *average* value of medical technological advance from the *marginal* value of a given additional procedure. On average, technological advance in medicine has been enormously beneficial, justifying the higher costs patients pay. But, on the margin, there are many cases of inappropriate and ineffective use of medical care. If the government could figure out some way to target those cases, then perhaps it could reduce the size of the health sector without sacrificing health.

Such targeting is, however, easier said than done. It is easy to look back and highlight wasteful medical care; it is much harder to look ahead and know which care will be wasteful. For example, a common fact cited by analysts to declare our health care system "wasteful" is that 30% of medical spending is on people in the last six months of their lives so that we are "wasting" money on a population that will die anyway. The problem with this argument is that doctors don't know in advance who are in the last six months of their lives and who might live for many more years. Only a small share of this spending during the last six months of life is for those we *know* are at the end of life. The rest of the spending may not be wasteful, in that it may have some chance of significantly extending life. If you had an illness that would be likely to end your life in six months but that could possibly be cured (or at least your length of life significantly extended) by expensive modern medical procedures, wouldn't you want your doctor to try those procedures?

In summary, controlling medical care costs is a tremendously difficult proposition for two reasons. First, it is not clear that costs *should* be controlled: evidence suggests that the cost growth of the past half century has resulted in greatly improved health. Second, even if costs should be controlled, it is not clear how this can be done.

The Uninsured

The other major problem to be addressed by health care reform is the high and rising number of Americans without health insurance. This is a much easier problem, at least in economic (if not political) terms, than controlling health care costs. There are a number of policies that could end or greatly reduce the problem of uninsurance. Debates over these policies focus on three central issues.

Pooling As discussed in Chapter 15, efficient provision of insurance requires large pools of participants that are created independently of health status. A major problem faced by the currently uninsured is that they do not have access to any such pooling mechanism (for example, most uninsured do not work for an employer that offers insurance). Solving the problem of the uninsured requires developing some new pooling mechanism, either through government insurance or through private insurance pools. The success of attempts to create a new pool will depend on its scale; existing attempts to create state-level pools for small businesses have generally failed because they did not attract a sufficient number of enrollees to deal with concerns about adverse selection and to spread administrative costs.

Affordability Health insurance is expensive. For example, the average cost of employer-provided insurance (counting both the employer and employee portions) in 2006 is $4,024 per year for individuals and $10,880 for families.[31] For a family of four with income of $40,000 (200% of the poverty line), for example, this $10,880 would represent 27.2% of family income, a huge share of income to devote solely to health care. What is an "affordable" level of health insurance spending? There is no right answer, but these high costs highlight the fact that it is impossible for the government to substantially reduce the number of uninsured individuals without providing large subsidies to low-income groups to cover those costs.

Mandates Even large subsidies for health insurance coverage will not be sufficient to end the problem of uninsurance. To come close to full insurance in the United States would require a **mandate** that employers offer insurance or that individuals obtain some type of insurance coverage. This mandate would be similar to auto insurance in most states, where individuals are required to have insurance if they want to drive a car. Mandates are politically unpopular, as witnessed by the major defeat of the Clinton administration's attempts to mandate employers to provide health insurance in 1994.

> **mandate** A legal requirement for employers to offer insurance or for individuals to obtain some type of insurance coverage.

Incremental Reforms

With these issues in mind, there are a number of incremental (minor) reforms that could be considered to deal with the problems of rising costs and the uninsured.

Incremental Cost Controls The most popular option for controlling health care costs is to reduce fraud and waste in the system. Estimates of the size of such fraud and waste vary, but some claim it is well over 10% of health care spending. While reducing fraud and waste is an admirable goal, it does not hold much promise as a long-term cost-control strategy. First, we don't know much about how to reduce fraud and waste without also reducing the quality of care delivered. Second, this approach does nothing to address the root cause of cost increases, which is technology improvement. Even if we could suddenly lower health care costs by 10% today by rooting out fraud and waste, with 10% per year cost growth, in one year we would be right back at the same place! If policy makers want to effectively control costs in the long run, they must deal with the rapid rate of cost increase, not just with cost levels.

One approach that has been used extensively in recent years by the Medicare program is to restrict provider reimbursement, either by lowering prices or moving to more prospective reimbursement. This approach has the advantage of directly lowering spending without (for Medicare at least, so far) significantly lowering the quality of care provided. There are limits to this approach, however. Once physician fees become too low, patients can run into access problems of the type experienced by Medicaid enrollees today. Moreover, as the Prospective Payment System (PPS) experience shows, such

---

[31] Kaiser Family Foundation (2006), Exhibit 3.1.

reforms tend to be undone by a complicated medical system that can always seem to find ways to get around reimbursement restrictions. Perhaps for this reason restricting provider reimbursement has yet to limit the underlying rate of cost growth for very long, once again making it an untenable long-run solution to rising costs.

Incremental Reforms to Cover the Uninsured There have been a wide variety of incremental reforms implemented, and others proposed, to partially reduce the number of uninsured. One option is to try to make the small employer and nongroup markets more hospitable to the uninsured, in the hopes of inducing the uninsured to buy insurance. Many states, and the federal government, have passed regulations in the past decade to guarantee access of small firms and individuals to insurance markets and to regulate the prices that can be charged for that insurance (by mandating, for example, that sick applicants can be charged no more than healthy applicants).

The existing evidence on these reforms suggests, however, that they have not been successful in reducing the number of uninsured. Faced with the inability to deny applicants coverage, insurers will charge astronomical prices that have the same effect. And, faced with the inability to price-discriminate between healthy and sick enrollees, insurers will charge very high prices to all customers. This pricing change makes insurance more attractive to unhealthy enrollees but less attractive to healthy enrollees. Evidence suggests that, on net, such regulations may actually lower insurance coverage among the healthy by more than they raise coverage among the sick, thus actually decreasing net coverage.

Another possibility for increasing insurance coverage for the uninsured is to continue to expand the public insurance safety net. A politically popular option is to continue to expand eligibility to middle-income children. The problem with this approach is that the vast majority of uninsured children in the United States are already eligible for either Medicaid or CHIP, so that further expansions of entitlement will go largely to populations that are already insured. Among those children between 200% and 250% of the poverty line, only 13% are uninsured, and almost 75% already have private health insurance. This raises the prospect of significant crowd-out with additional expansions, with most of those moving onto public insurance coming from the ranks of the insured and with little new coverage of the uninsured as a result. In contrast, among parents below the poverty line, for example, 42% are uninsured, while 47% of adults below the poverty line but without children are uninsured.[32] Expanding insurance to cover this poor adult population would lead to much less crowd-out and more coverage of the uninsured.

A third possibility (which is currently very popular) is to offer individuals new tax subsidies with which to purchase health insurance. A typical proposal of this type is a tax credit equal to $1,000 for individuals or $2,500 for families toward the purchase of insurance. This alternative has the advantage of

---

[32] Kaiser Commission on Medicaid and the Uninsured (2006), Figure 14.

directly addressing affordability concerns within the context of the existing private health insurance system. But this approach typically does not provide any pooling mechanism and sends individuals into the harsh nongroup market with their relatively small (compared to the cost of nongroup insurance) tax credits. This method is unlikely to be broadly successful unless credits are large enough to cover a very sizeable share of the costs of insurance and unless individuals have a more hospitable (pooled) environment in which to use their credits.

Fundamental Reform: Public National Health Insurance

In terms of more fundamental reforms to the health care system, one approach would be to follow the lead of many other nations, such as Canada, and move to a public **national health insurance** system (often called a "single payer" system). Under such a system, the government would insure all citizens, putting them into a publicly run health insurance plan. Costs would be controlled through an explicit nationwide health care budget that imposed true prospective reimbursement on the health care system as a whole. For example, the government would establish a network of providers (physicians, hospitals, and so on) in each region and would pay that network a fixed amount to cover all the medical costs for every person in that region. This amount could then be increased slowly to limit medical care spending growth.

> **national health insurance** A system whereby the government provides insurance to all its citizens, as in Canada, without the involvement of a private insurance industry.

Such a plan has major advantages. First, it would fully solve the problem of the uninsured. Second, it would reduce the administrative costs inherent in the U.S. medical care system: the administrative costs of Canada's national health insurance system are only 1.3%, compared to the 12% costs on average for private health insurance in the United States.[33] Third, it has the potential to be successful in controlling costs because cost controls are comprehensive, not piecemeal. Finally, it would solve the many inequities and inefficiencies arising from the patchwork of health insurance coverage available in the United States; for example, it would resolve the problem of job lock incurred by individuals afraid to leave their employer-based insurance.

Public national health insurance also has major disadvantages, however. First, it would require massive new government expenditures, because the government would now be paying the insurance costs of every citizen. A large part of this cost would be offset by reduced spending on existing public insurance for the non-elderly, but most would require new public-sector revenues.

> **Quick Hint** One confusing aspect of discussions of public health insurance is that while public expenditures would rise dramatically, there would be an almost equally large reduction in private insurance expenditures. Thus, the rise in total *social* costs of health care would be small compared to the actual costs

---

[33] Woolhandler et al. (2003).

to the government. In theory, it is these social costs that matter, not the budgetary expenditures of the government. In practice, however, the expenditures by the government matter for two reasons. First, as discussed at more length in the tax chapters, there may be a deadweight loss arising from the need to increase government revenues to pay for these expenditures that does not arise from private spending (whether that deadweight loss is larger than the administrative gains from public insurance is unclear). Second, and more important in practice, moving from private financing of health insurance through employer expenditures to public financing is like moving from a hidden tax to an explicit tax. While economists can talk until they are blue in the face about how this is just shifting from one payer to another, the typical voter sees it as a massive tax increase and will be reluctant to support it.

Second, nationwide budgeting as a means of controlling health care costs is a very blunt instrument that may not allow doctors to use a technology that is worth its high cost. For example, suppose that the U.S. government had imposed a global budget on health care spending of 5% of GDP in 1950. While the health care sector would likely be much more efficient today, it is also likely that many beneficial medical advances would not be available. Once again, it seems unlikely that many of us would return to the world of 1950 medical care, even at 1950s prices, if we had the choice. It is quite possible that the same statement could be true in 2054 with respect to 2004 prices and medical care.

Finally, national health insurance has the disadvantage that politicians rather than individuals are in charge of choosing their health benefit package. If chosen wisely to conform to principles of optimal insurance, national health insurance could increase efficiency, but there is no guarantee that these principles would be followed. Moreover, some individuals may wish to purchase insurance that economists might not consider optimal, and it is not clear that the government can or should restrict such choice.

Fundamental Reform: Private-Sector Solutions

An alternative approach to fundamental reform would be to build on the existing hybrid of private and public insurance in the United States by offering a new set of private health insurance options to the uninsured. For example, state governments could each set up new pools of insurance plans, akin to the pools offered by employers, from which individuals could choose insurance. These pools would feature a variety of plan choices, ranging from limited (e.g., no prescription drug coverage, high copayments) to more generous insurance. The government could then offer large subsidies to low-income individuals to address the affordability problem, subsidizing the cost of insurance for those below 300% of the poverty line, for example. The government could mandate that all individuals obtain coverage through an employer, a public program, or this new pooling option. An option along these lines that was recently passed in Massachusetts featured a new central insurance purchasing authority that would offer insurance plans, subsidies for those below 300% of poverty to buy those plans, and a mandate that all individuals have health insurance.

Such an approach has three major advantages relative to public national health insurance. First, it would involve much less new public financing, since it would build on, rather than displace, existing insurance arrangements. The cost would still be large, however, because there would be substantial crowd-out, with low-income individuals dropping coverage that they pay for and instead taking up coverage that is subsidized by the government. Estimates of the costs of these types of programs typically are in the range of $150–$200 billion per year. While large, this total government cost is far below the budgetary cost of national health insurance (although not necessarily the total social cost)

Second, this approach would use consumer choice to search out cost-effective health care options rather than blunt government cost controls. This approach would work similarly to the premium support system discussed for Medicare, with government subsidies to the poor tied to the median-cost plan in each area. With such a plan in place, individuals would face the consequences of their decisions to choose more expensive plans that provide more generous coverage. If all individuals were willing to pay for some expensive but effective new technology, then all plans would include that technology; costs would go up, but only because the perceived health benefits exceed the costs. If only some individuals were willing to pay for some new technology that is of more questionable effectiveness, then only some plans would include that technology, and individuals, not society, would pay the higher price of choosing those plans.

Finally, this approach is much more politically feasible. As discussed in Chapter 9, it is difficult to achieve political reforms that harm a very concentrated interest. The health insurance industry in the United States has over $550 billion per year in revenues, and this makes for a concentrated interest that would work very hard against any reform that essentially removed its role in the U.S. economy.

At the same time, this approach has disadvantages relative to public national health insurance. The existing problems with private health insurance, such as high administrative costs, would remain. The inequities and inefficiencies of a patchwork health insurance system would remain as well. There is also a difficult tension between the desire to induce cost-conscious decision making across plans and the problem of adverse selection that led to the Harvard "death spiral" discussed in Chapter 12. Allowing choice across plan types has the advantage of reflecting consumer sovereignty, but it could lead the sick to end up in much more expensive plans than the healthy. Finally, such a system would explicitly lead to two-tier medical care in the United States, in which higher-income groups are more able to afford the more expensive plans that cover more technologies. This may be undesirable from an equity perspective.

16.5

Conclusion

The Medicare and Medicaid programs play a central and growing role in the delivery of health care in the United States. As a result, any policies to address the twin crises of rising medical costs and the high number of uninsured must learn from, and potentially improve upon, these programs. A large economics literature on these programs offers some useful lessons for moving forward with health care reform.

In particular, two lessons are apparent that can help guide health care reform efforts. First, expanding health insurance to those without coverage can increase medical utilization and improve health in a cost-effective manner. Moreover, reductions in the generosity of health insurance coverage (such as increases in coinsurance rates) or provider reimbursement (such as retrospective versus prospective reimbursement) appear to reduce use without worsening health. This suggests that a system that provided less generous coverage to a broader population would cause better overall health than the current U.S. system of very generous coverage that excludes a sizeable minority of our citizens. Large expansions of health insurance coverage are likely to be expensive, however, because it is hard to distinguish the uninsured from the insured, leading to a problem of crowd-out as we try to cover the uninsured.

Second, there are no easy answers when it comes to controlling health care costs. Efforts made in the past, such as reducing provider reimbursement, have been unable to constrain the rate of health care cost growth. If costs are to be controlled, more wide-ranging efforts are necessary.

▶ **HIGHLIGHTS**

■ The Medicaid program serves low-income families, the low-income disabled, and the low-income elderly.

■ Low-income families are eligible for Medicaid if they are on cash welfare; in most states, low-income children and pregnant women are eligible if they have incomes below 200% of the poverty line.

■ The Medicaid program has been shown to reduce the number of uninsured people (although there is also significant crowd-out of private health insurance coverage), increase health care utilization, and improve health in a cost-effective manner.

■ The Medicare program serves the elderly and disabled, providing universal coverage with significant enrollee copayments.

■ The Medicare program has tried to limit its cost growth through restrictions on provider reimbursement, most notably with a move to prospective reimbursement of hospitals (PPS), which has lowered costs without significantly reducing quality of care.

■ The Medicare program has also tried to introduce choice across insurance options with limited success. A premium support plan, which would more aggressively induce choice in Medicare, could control costs but would have adverse effects on the living standards of the least healthy beneficiaries.

■ A large and rising share of medical spending is on long-term care, and there is a major debate over appropriate division of the financing of these costs between individuals and the government.

■ The problem of controlling health care costs in the United States is a hard one, since on average these cost increases have delivered significant improvements in health. The problem of increasing insurance coverage is more straightforward to solve, but it can be expensive due to the crowd-out of the existing insured.

■ Incremental solutions such as reducing "fraud and waste" and expanding public insurance programs can

partially solve the problems of cost and insurance coverage, but they cannot move the United States most of the way toward solving these problems.

■ More fundamental solutions, such as public national health insurance or new private insurance options with subsidies for low-income groups, can address these problems, but each has large economic and political costs.

▶ QUESTIONS AND PROBLEMS

1. When your governor took office, 100,000 children in your state were eligible for Medicaid and 200,000 children were not. Now, thanks to a large expansion in Medicaid, 150,000 children are eligible for Medicaid and 150,000 children are not. Your governor boasts that, under her watch, "the number of children without access to health care fell by one-quarter." Is this a valid statement to make? Why or why not?

2. Explain why takeup rates—the fraction of eligible individuals who enroll in the program—are so much higher for Medicare than for Medicaid.

3. Describe the empirical evidence of the relationship between Medicaid expansions and improved children's health. How cost-effective have these Medicaid expansions been? Explain your answer.

4. Beginning in the mid 1980s, there was a large expansion in the Medicaid eligibility of children. How do you think this affected the job-mobility of low to middle income parents? How could you test this?

5. What are the similarities between Medicare vouchers and education vouchers (described in Chapter 11)? What are the differences?

6. Is the rapidly expanding share of total GDP of the health sector in the United States necessarily evidence of wasteful health care spending? Why or why not?

7. Suppose the government decided to subsidize health insurance for the currently uninsured,

requiring participants to pay half of their health insurance costs up to 10% of total family income.
   a. How might this policy affect the use of medical care by the uninsured and their health?
   b. How might this policy affect the employer provision of health insurance?
   c. How might this policy affect hours of labor supplied by workers in the state?

8. Artie, Bella, and Carmen are Medicare Part D recipients. Artie currently has $1000 in prescription drug costs each year. Bella and Carmen have $3000 and $6000, respectively. Each has a mild case of insomnia, and a new drug has just been introduced to treat their condition. It will cost $1000 per year. Which of the three are most likely to take the new drug?

9. One disadvantage of a national health insurance system such as Canada's is "queuing"—people often need to wait long periods of time to receive desired treatments. What elements of a national health insurance system could lead to this situation?

10. The fact that such a large fraction of U.S. health care costs are spent on people in their last six months of life has led many people to call the American health care system "wasteful." Why might this be an overgeneralization?

The ℮ indicates a question that requires students to apply the empirical economics principles discussed in Chapter 3 and the Empirical Evidence boxes.

▶ ADVANCED QUESTIONS

11. In response to the State Children's Health Insurance Program in 1997, 37 states (including the District of Columbia) expanded Medicaid coverage to children in families below 200% of the poverty line, with even higher thresholds in some states.

    a. In some of these states, the eligibility expansions have covered all children. How would you design a quasi-experimental analysis to evaluate the impact of these expansions?

    b. In other states, the eligibility expansions covered only certain age groups of children. How could you design a quasi-experimental analysis to evaluate the impact of these expansions? How could you make this more convincing than the evaluation in (a)? Explain.

12. After the Medicare program adopted the Prospective Payment System (PPS), researchers observed that people tended to receive less care for any given diagnosed condition.

    a. One explanation for this finding is that the PPS provides incentives to provide lower levels of treatment for any given diagnosis. Why would PPS provide this incentive?

    b. Another explanation for this finding is that PPS offers incentives for physicians to diagnose marginal health conditions as more serious than they are. Why would PPS provide these incentives?

    c. Since this reduction in quantity of care was not accompanied by a reduction in observable health outcomes, what, if anything, can you infer about the efficiency of the Medicare program *before* the policy change? Explain your answer.

13. One feature of Medicare coverage is that individuals are responsible for 20% of their Part B (primary physician) costs, without limit. Individuals have traditionally purchased Medi-gap policies that cover this gap by paying for the out-of-pocket costs not covered by Medicare. But some Medi-gap policies did not cover this 20% copayment.

    Finkelstein (2002) studied the effects of a federal mandate that Medi-gap plans cover this 20% copayment. She found that this mandate would lead fewer individuals to buy Medi-gap coverage.

    a. Why would the mandate lower the demand for Medi-gap coverage?

    b. What do you think would be the net effect of this policy on the costs of the Medicare program itself?

14. In 1981, the federal government passed a law that gave states permission to change the structure of their Medicaid program. States could now, if they wished, require Medicaid beneficiaries to enroll in a Medicaid "managed care organization" (MCO), as long as Medicaid recipients were offered a choice of several plans. Medicaid recipients would be required to receive their medical care only through their MCOs. These MCOs would receive fixed, regular payments from the state and, in return, would cover the medical expenses of their Medicaid enrollees.

    a. Using what you know about Medicaid and managed care, explain several reasons why policy makers might support the requirement that Medicaid beneficiaries enroll in MCOs.

    b. Again, applying what you know about Medicaid and managed care, how do you think this requirement would affect the decision of people who are eligible to enroll in Medicaid? Be specific about which individuals eligible for Medicaid are likely to change or not change their decision to enroll.

    c. How might this requirement affect overall access to care for Medicaid eligibles?

15. Their current government-provided system in the country of Puceland provides free health insurance for all children but to no adults. There are two types of adults in Puceland: high earners and low earners. All of the 100,000 high earners receive insurance coverage through their employer, but only half of the 100,000 low earners do. The remaining adults are uninsured.

    You are hired to analyze the effectiveness of a proposed plan to offer coverage to all low earners. You have read the economics literature in Puceland and your best estimates are as follows: (1) only 80% of uninsured workers who are offered government health insurance will choose to enroll; (2) 60% of currently insured low earners work at firms who will drop insurance coverage for them after the policy change, and the other 40% will remain in their current employer-provided plan; (3) 10% of high earners will choose to become low earners (at firms who do not offer health insurance) and take up the government insurance once they can get it.

a. Estimate the increase in the number of insured adults.

b. Estimate the dollar cost per additionally insured adult. Why is it so much higher than $5000?

c. Suppose that, without access to any insurance, each adult has a 5% chance of dying in a given year. Access to government-provided health insurance reduces this to 3%, while access to employer-provided health insurance reduces it to 2%. If it costs the government $5,000 to provide health insurance per year to an adult, estimate the dollar cost of the program per life saved.

Income Distribution and Welfare Programs

17

On August 22, 1996, President Bill Clinton signed into law the Personal Responsibility and Work Opportunity Reconciliation Act of 1996 (PRWORA), more commonly known as the welfare reform law. (Note that the use of the term *welfare* in this context does *not* refer to a measure of economic well-being but rather to government programs that make cash payments to low-income populations). This law fulfilled the promise that President Clinton (and many other policy makers) had made to "end welfare as we know it." Before this law, cash welfare in the United States was a system in which states received *matching grants* to provide time-unlimited benefits to low-income single mothers: the federal government paid states a certain percentage of the state's spending on welfare, without limit. After the law, states received a *lump-sum block grant*, a flat amount, independent of state spending on welfare, earmarked to provide time-limited benefits to a broader range of low-income families. The association between the timing of this law and the reduction in welfare caseloads (the number of persons receiving cash welfare), documented in Figure 17-1, is striking. After reaching a peak in 1994, welfare caseloads had declined by more than two-thirds by 2005.[1]

At its peak, cash welfare spending by the federal government amounted to only 1.7% of the federal budget.[2] Yet virtually no other public policy intervention has generated as much controversy as cash welfare programs. To some conservatives, the negative effects of cash payments to low-income single mothers are responsible for many of the social ills in the United States. Newt Gingrich, then the newly elected Speaker of the House, said in a televised address on the steps of the Capitol on April 7, 1995, "The welfare system's greatest cost is the human cost to the poor. In the name of 'compassion' we have funded a system that is cruel and destroys families. Its failure is reflected by the violence, brutality, child abuse and drug addiction in every local TV

---

[1] Administration for Children and Families (2006).
[2] Welfare spending data come from the U.S. Department of Health and Human Services (2003a), while data on total government spending come from the U.S. Office of Management and Budget (2006a).

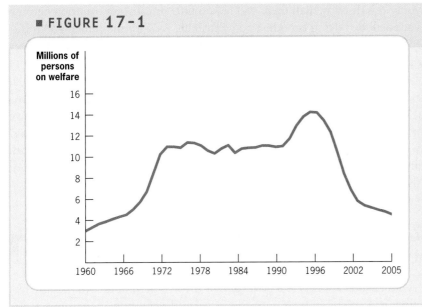

■ FIGURE 17-1

Welfare Caseloads in the United States, 1960–2005 • The number of persons on welfare rose rapidly in the 1960s, then was fairly constant until rising again in the recession of the early 1990s. Welfare enrollments fell dramatically after 1994; some of this reduction was due to the 1996 welfare reform law and related earlier state policy initiatives.

Source: Data come from the Administration for Children and Families (2006).

news broadcast."[3] To some liberals, it is wrong to force low-income families off welfare and into the labor market. In a debate on work requirements for welfare recipients, Massachusetts senator Edward Kennedy said, "We cannot throw workers into low-wage, dead-end jobs and expect them to support their families. We cannot force workers into jobs for which they have no skills and expect them to succeed."[4] Who is right? Has cash welfare played a constructive or destructive role in the lives of lower-income groups?

Most important from the perspective of this text, we must start with the first question of public finance: Why is the government involved in the business of redistributing income? In Chapter 2, we discussed why the socially efficient outcome of a nation's economy was not necessarily the outcome that maximizes social welfare (here meaning well-being). If society cares equally about the utility of all its members, then social welfare may be maximized by redistributing from high-income individuals (for whom the marginal utility cost of losing a dollar is low) to low-income individuals (for whom the marginal utility gain of getting a dollar is high). Arguments for redistribution are even stronger if society cares in particular about low-income persons, a philosophy embodied in the Rawlsian social welfare function discussed in Chapter 2.

The private sector, however, is unlikely to provide such income redistribution, since redistribution faces the same free-rider problems encountered in private provision of other public goods. The consumption of the poor is a public good: I would like the poor to consume more, but I would prefer if others provide them the means of doing so, since I would then get the benefits of seeing the poor consume more but not bear the costs of their increased consumption. If

---

[3] Gingrich (1995).
[4] Leonard (2002).

everyone feels this way, then there will be too little private redistribution because everyone will be relying on others to contribute. As with the public goods discussed in Chapter 7, there may be a role for a government in solving this free-rider problem by taxing its citizens to provide public redistribution.

This chapter begins with facts on the distribution of income in the United States and around the world to motivate our concern with income redistribution. We then discuss the effects, both in theory and reality, of alternative means of income redistribution. We focus initially on cash welfare programs, but we also discuss alternatives, such as food stamps, free child care, and work training. Finally, we review the evidence on the effects of the radical reform of our nation's welfare system in 1996.

17.1

Facts on Income Distribution in the United States

To understand appropriate government involvement in income redistribution, it is useful to start with the facts on distribution of income in the United States.

Relative Income Inequality

relative income inequality
The amount of income the poor have relative to the rich.

There are two ways of thinking about the distribution of income: relative income inequality and absolute deprivation. **Relative income inequality** measures the share of a nation's total income that accrues to the poor relative to the rich. The facts on relative income inequality for the United States over time are given in Table 17-1, which shows the share of aggregate income accruing to each income quintile (each fifth of the income distribution) in the United States. For instance, in 1967, the bottom fifth of the U.S. income distribution accrued only 4% of aggregate income in that year. The top 20%, by contrast, accrued almost 44% of aggregate income. In a society with no

■ TABLE 17-1

Share of Aggregate Income Received by Quintile, 1967–2004

Income	1967	1970	1975	1980	1985	1990	1995	2000	2004
Lowest 20%	4.0	4.1	4.4	4.3	4.0	3.9	3.7	3.6	3.4
Second 20%	10.8	10.8	10.5	10.3	9.7	9.6	9.1	8.9	8.7
Third 20%	17.3	17.4	17.1	16.9	16.3	15.9	15.2	14.8	14.7
Fourth 20%	24.2	24.5	24.8	24.9	24.6	24.0	23.3	23.0	23.2
Highest 20%	43.8	43.3	43.2	43.7	45.3	46.6	48.7	49.8	50.1

In 1967, the poorest 20% of households received 4% of the national income, and the richest 20% received almost 44%. Today, the poorest 20% receives 3.4% of the national income, and the richest 20% receives over 50%.

U.S. Bureau of the Census (2005c), Table H-2.

relative income inequality, each quintile would accrue an equal share of income (20%). Relative income inequality is measured by the difference between the share of incomes accruing to the higher-income groups and the share accruing to lower-income groups.

There has been an interesting evolution of relative income inequality over time in the United States. From the late 1960s through the late 1970s, income inequality was falling as the share of income accruing to the bottom income quintile grew and the share accruing to the top income quintile fell. From 1980 to the present, however, income inequality has been sharply rising: the share of income accruing to the bottom income quintile has fallen by more than 20%, while the share of income accruing to the top income quintile has risen by about 15%. Today, more than half of all income in the United States accrues to the richest 20% of the nation. Much of this inequality has been driven by enormous increases in income at the very top of the income distribution. As documented in Piketty and Saez (2006), the share of income accruing to the top 1% of the income distribution grew from 8% in the 1960s and 1970s to 15% by the end of the 1990s.

Relative income inequality in the United States is much higher than it is in other developed nations, as Table 17-2 shows. Looking at the unweighted average row in Table 17-2, we see that the poorest fifth of households in the United States receives less than half the share of income of the poorest fifth of households in the typical industrialized nation (3.4% versus 7.7%).[5] In fact, the lowest three quintiles of households in the United States all receive a smaller share of the nation's income than they do in the OECD nations. The difference is shifted to the top fifth of households in the United States, who accrue nearly 10% more of the nation's income than their OECD counterparts (50.1% versus 40.5%).

Absolute Deprivation and Poverty Rates

The second way to think about income distribution is to think about **absolute deprivation:** how much the poor have relative to some measure of a reasonable "minimally acceptable" income level. In the United States the standard for measuring absolute deprivation is the **poverty line.** This measure was developed in 1964 by Molly Orshansky, an employee of the Social Security Administration, who wanted to compute a minimal living standard for the United States. She started with nutritional standards for a minimally acceptable diet, and applied average national food costs to price out the cost of buying this bundle of goods for families of different sizes. She then determined that the average (not just poor) family of three or more persons spent one-third of their after-tax income on food, so she multiplied the food bundle cost by three. This became the poverty line. These same amounts have simply been updated for inflation ever since, resulting in the poverty lines we

absolute deprivation The amount of income the poor have relative to some measure of "minimally acceptable" income.

poverty line The federal government's standard for measuring absolute deprivation.

---

[5] This table uses the typical measure of industrialized nations for economic comparisons, the set of nations in the Organisation for Economic Co-operation and Development (OECD).

■ TABLE 17-2

Share of Aggregate Income Received by Quintile of Households for OECD Nations

Country (year)	Income Quintile				
	Lowest	Second	Third	Fourth	Highest
Austria (2000)	8.6	13.3	17.4	22.9	37.8
Belgium (2000)	8.5	13.0	16.3	20.8	41.1
Canada (2000)	7.2	12.7	17.2	23.0	39.9
Czech Republic (1996)	10.3	14.5	17.7	21.7	35.9
Denmark (1997)	8.3	14.7	18.2	22.9	35.8
Finland (2000)	9.6	14.1	17.5	22.1	36.7
France (1995)	7.2	12.6	17.2	22.8	40.2
Germany (2000)	8.5	13.7	17.8	23.1	36.9
Greece (2000)	6.7	11.9	16.8	23.0	41.5
Hungary (2002)	9.5	13.9	17.6	22.4	36.5
Italy (2000)	6.5	12.0	16.8	22.8	42.0
Korea (1998)	7.9	13.6	18.0	23.1	37.5
Luxembourg (2000)	8.4	12.9	17.1	22.7	38.9
Mexico (2002)	4.3	8.3	12.6	19.7	55.1
New Zealand (1997)	6.4	11.4	15.8	22.6	43.8
Norway (2000)	9.6	14.0	17.2	22.0	37.2
Poland (2002)	7.5	11.9	16.1	22.2	42.2
Portugal (1997)	5.8	11.0	15.5	21.9	45.9
Slovak Republic (1996)	8.8	14.9	18.7	22.8	34.8
Sweden (2000)	9.1	14.0	17.6	22.7	36.6
Turkey (2003)	5.3	9.7	14.2	21.0	49.7
United Kingdom (1999)	6.1	11.4	16.0	22.5	44.0
Unweighted average	7.7	12.7	16.8	22.3	40.5
United States (2004)	3.4	8.7	14.7	23.2	50.1

The share of income received by the lowest quintile in the United States is smaller than in any other nation, and is less than half of the worldwide average. The share of income received by the highest quintile in the United States is higher than in any nation except Mexico, and is nearly 25% higher than the worldwide average.

World Bank (2006).

see in Table 17-3. In the United States in 2006, a family of four with income below $20,000 was considered to be living in poverty.

Figure 17-2 shows the evolution of the poverty rate in the United States for all persons, as well as for two particular age groups: those under 18 and those 65 and older. The poverty rates fell both for all persons and for both age groups in the 1960s and early 1970s. From 1973 to 1995, however, all individuals and especially children under 18 lived in increasingly poor circumstances. For children, the poverty rate rose from 14.4% in 1973 to over 20.8% in 1995. For the elderly, on the other hand, poverty rates continued to decline throughout this period. The late 1990s saw improvements again for all groups, although the overall poverty rate and the rate for children remain above their level in 1973.

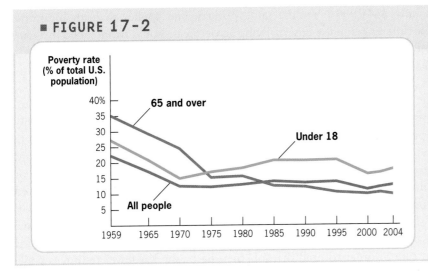

■ **FIGURE 17-2**

Poverty Rates over Time in the United States • The poverty rate for all persons fell substantially in the 1960s but has risen somewhat since. The poverty rate for children fell in the 1960s as well, and has risen even more since, while the poverty rate of the elderly has declined throughout this period.

Source: U.S. Bureau of the Census (2005b), Tables 2, 3.

▶ APPLICATION

Problems in Poverty Line Measurement

Despite its humble origins, the poverty line has remained a mainstay of U.S. public policy, with its exact placement influencing billions of dollars of government spending each year. There have, however, been a wide variety of criticisms of the poverty line, which suggests that it would be valuable to revisit its calculation.[6] These criticisms are of three types:

Bundle Has Changed: The share of food in family consumption has fallen over time relative to clothing, shelter, medical care, and other goods: by 1998, the typical family spent only 16% of its budget on food, down from 33% in 1964, when the poverty line was calculated.[7] As a result, using the cost of food times three is no longer an appropriate way to compute a minimum standard of living. A better solution might be to use the cost of a "typical" bundle of consumption for families in each year, and then to take a certain percentage of that to be the poverty line.

Differences in Cost of Living Across Areas Are Ignored: In 2005, the median single-family home in the Boston–Cambridge–Quincy area of Massachusetts cost $413,000. In that same year, the median single-family home in St. Louis, Missouri,

■ **TABLE 17-3**

Poverty Lines by Family Size (2006)

Size of family unit	Poverty line
1	$9,800
2	$13,200
3	$16,600
4	$20,000
5	$23,400
6	$26,800
7	$30,200
8	$33,600
For each additional person, add	$3,400

A family of four with an income of less than $20,000 per year is considered to be living below a minimum acceptable standard in the United States.

Office of the Federal Register (2006), pp. 3848–3849.

---

[6] This section echoes the conclusions of a National Academy of Sciences panel convened to study this issue.

[7] Johnson, Rogers, and Tan (2001), Table 1.

cost only $141,000.[8] Yet the same poverty line applies to both locations. These differences in the cost of living across areas should be included in a true measure of the cost of achieving a minimal standard of living.

Income Definition Is Incomplete: The computation of the poverty rate compares an individual's cash income to the poverty standard. Cash income is not a true representation of the individual's available resources, however, for several reasons. First, such a representation must also include other noncash transfers provided to the individual, such as through the Medicaid program. If two individuals have the same cash income but only one of them has Medicaid coverage, then the individual with Medicaid is effectively richer because he or she doesn't have to pay for medical costs, and this transfer should be reflected in computing poverty. Second, the income that is compared to the poverty line should also include the cost of earning a living. If two individuals have the same job and earn the same wage but one of them has to pay more for child care in order to hold that job, then he or she has fewer resources available to spend, so the measure of his or her income should be adjusted to reflect that fact. Third, what determines a family's ability to consume is their after-tax income, not their before-tax cash income. Since poverty rates are designed to measure the ability of a family to achieve a given standard of consumption, they should be computed based on after-tax income.

In the early 1990s, these types of problems with the poverty line motivated a blue-ribbon panel appointed by the National Academy of Sciences to recommend radical changes to the way the U.S. poverty line is calculated, in accord with the suggestions just given. These recommendations have run into two major problems, however. First, these changes are difficult to carry out in practice. How, for example, can we include the true value of Medicaid in someone's income? It is clear from our analysis of the economic theory of social insurance in Chapter 12 that the true value of Medicaid is not just the cost of medical bills reimbursed, but rather the utility benefit of having consumption smoothed across healthy and ill states, the value of which is very difficult to compute.

The second major problem is the political ramifications of making these changes. For example, accounting for area variation in the cost of living would mean that the poverty rate would go up sharply on the East and West coasts and fall in most of the South and Midwest. Such a shift would lead to an enormous relative redistribution in government income transfers across regions of the country, with more transfers to the newly poor East and West coasts, and fewer transfers to the newly rich South and Midwest. Such changes would be politically unpopular with those in the South and Midwest. Thus, such radical changes in the distribution of government resources may not be politically feasible, even if they make for good economic science. ◄

What Matters—Relative or Absolute Deprivation?

An important question for government redistribution policy is whether relative or absolute deprivation is the more appropriate measure for driving redis-

---

[8] National Association of Realtors (2006).

tribution: Should the government care about how much the poor have relative to the rich or relative to some absolute standard? It seems intuitive that it is the latter that matters for government policy. After all, once the poor can reach an acceptable level of consumption, why does it matter how much money the rich have? If the income of the rich doesn't matter, given an acceptable level of consumption by the poor, then it is not relative income inequality that a nation cares about but rather some measure of absolute deprivation.

On the other hand, there are two reasons why relative income inequality measures may matter. First, the "minimal" standard of living for a society may be best defined relative to the standard of living of others. In 1950, a poor family could be living a minimally acceptable life without a television or a car, but that is clearly not true today. This concern could be addressed, as noted in the previous application, by defining the poverty line as a fraction of the "typical" consumption bundle in the United States, which would move us toward a relative income measure.

Second, there is some interesting recent evidence that the level of inequality in society is itself negatively related to measures of well-being. There are a number of studies, for example, that find that mortality rates across nations or states are highly correlated with the degree of income inequality.[9] A recent study by Luttmer (2004) also finds that individuals' self-reported well-being rises as their own income rises, but falls as their neighbors' incomes rise, suggesting that it is relative income, and not absolute income, that determines well-being. This evidence is just suggestive at this point, however, and the channels of causation from inequality to well-being are not yet established.

17.2
Welfare Policy in the United States

In this section, we briefly discuss the nature of programs that redistribute income to low-income groups in the United States; the other side of the equation, taxing higher-income groups to finance these programs, is discussed in the next set of chapters on taxation.

In discussing welfare policy, it is important to understand two characteristics of each policy:

1. *Categorical and Means-Tested Programs:* **Categorical welfare** programs are programs that are restricted by some demographic characteristic, such as single motherhood, disability, and so on. **Means-tested welfare** programs are programs that are tied to income and asset levels. A means-tested program might specify, for example, that benefits are available only to those with incomes below the poverty line. Most redistributive programs in the United States, such as cash welfare for low-income single mothers, are both categorical (single mothers) and means tested (low-income).

categorical welfare Welfare programs restricted by some demographic characteristic, such as single motherhood or disability.

means-tested welfare Welfare programs restricted only by income and asset levels.

---

[9] See Deaton (2003) for an excellent review of this literature.

cash welfare Welfare programs that provide cash benefits to recipients.

in-kind welfare Welfare programs that deliver goods, such as medical care or housing, to recipients.

2. *Cash and In-Kind Programs:* **Cash welfare** programs provide cash benefits to recipients. **In-kind welfare** programs deliver goods, such as medical care or public housing, rather than money.

Cash Welfare Programs

There are two major cash welfare programs in the United States: Temporary Assistance for Needy Families (TANF) and Supplemental Security Income (SSI). A third redistributive program, the Earned Income Tax Credit (EITC), which subsidizes labor supply for low-income families, is discussed as part of tax policy in Chapter 21.

Temporary Assistance for Needy Families (TANF) The TANF program, which is jointly funded by the federal government and the states, provides support to low-income families with children in which one biological parent is absent.[10] As part of the major overhaul of welfare discussed at the start of this chapter, TANF replaced the Aid to Families with Dependent Children (AFDC) program, which was begun in 1935 to support widows and orphans. In the decades that followed, however, the AFDC program had become focused primarily on women who were either divorced or never married. As part of the 1996 welfare reform, states are allowed to use their TANF funds for either single mothers or two-parent families, although the vast majority of recipients remain single-parent families (only 3.5% of recipient families have two parents present). TANF is a relatively small program compared to the other government programs we have been discussing in this section of the book, with expenditures of $25.8 billion in 2004 compared to $529.9 billion for Social Security and $330 billion for Medicare in 2005).[11]

benefit guarantee The cash welfare benefit for individuals with no other income, which may be reduced as income increases.

benefit reduction rate The rate at which welfare benefits are reduced per dollar of other income earned.

Families become eligible for TANF by having sufficiently low income, in which case they qualify for a cash payment from the state, called a **benefit guarantee.** For a family with one parent and two children, for example, the benefit guarantee in 2003 varied from $170 per month in Mississippi to $923 per month in Alaska; in no state were the payments from this program high enough to lift a family over the poverty line. This payment is means tested: it is reduced as the family's income from other sources grows. The **benefit reduction rate** (the rate at which benefits are reduced as other income grows) varies widely across the states, with states typically exempting some level of income from reduction, then reducing benefits by 50–100% as income grows.

The major role of the federal government is financial: it supports TANF through the provision of large block grants to finance the state programs. In addition, the federal government imposes *time limits* and *work requirements* on TANF recipients. The federal government mandates that individuals cannot receive TANF benefits more than 60 months (five years) over the course of their

---

[10] For detailed information on AFDC/TANF, see Section 7 of the 2004 Green Book, published by the U.S. House of Representatives Committee on Ways and Means.
[11] TANF: Administration for Children & Families (2005), Table F. Social Security: Social Security Trustees (2006), Table II.B.1. Medicare: Centers for Medicare and Medicaid Services (2006b), p. 2.

lives. The federal government also requires welfare recipients to work after receiving at most 24 months of TANF benefits, although states can choose shorter deadlines, and more than 12 states require some immediate work activity. Overall, the federal government requires that half of a state's TANF recipients be working at a point in time. There are some loopholes in these requirements, however: states may exempt up to 20% of their welfare recipients from these time limits for "hardship" reasons; and the definition of "work" is somewhat flexible, as up to 30% of recipients can count education or job-skills training as work.

Supplemental Security Income (SSI) SSI is a program that provides cash welfare to the aged, blind, and disabled. Essentially, the job of SSI is to fill holes that are left by the incomplete nature of two of our major social insurance programs, Social Security and disability insurance (DI). Some individuals who have not worked enough in the past may not qualify for benefits under either of these social insurance programs, so they qualify for SSI: for example, a young person who has never worked and is disabled in a car accident would not qualify for DI but can receive SSI. Indeed, a large share of the SSI caseload is youth, as the result of a 1990 court decision that qualified youth with learning disabilities as disabled for SSI purposes. This decision led to a rise in the number of youths on the program from under 300,000 in 1990 to over 800,000 in just four years.[12] This rapid rise in enrollment highlights the problems in truly defining disability, particularly in a population such as children. SSI is not very widely known, nor is it debated with the ferocity of TANF, but it is in fact a bigger program, with expenditures of over $36 billion in 2004.[13]

In-Kind Programs

Along with these two cash programs, there are four major types of in-kind benefits provided to the poor in the United States.

Food Stamps The food stamps program traditionally provided vouchers to individuals that they could use to pay for food at participating retailers. These vouchers have been replaced by debit-card-like systems whereby individuals are issued a card for a certain value of food, which is drawn down as they make purchases.

Food stamps is a national program, with spending of $27 billion in 2004.[14] Households composed entirely of TANF, SSI, or other state cash welfare recipients are automatically eligible for food stamps; otherwise, monthly cash income is the primary eligibility determinant. Households without elderly or disabled members must have income below 130% of the poverty line to receive food stamps, and the amount of the food stamps benefit falls as income rises. In addition, able-bodied adults are required to register for work and be willing to take any job offered; if they violate these conditions, the welfare agency may discontinue benefits for one to six months. Finally, many

---

[12] See Garrett and Glied (2000) for a discussion of this change.
[13] Social Security Administration (2005), p. ii.
[14] National Governors Association (2005), p. 1.

noncitizens are ineligible: permanent residents must have been in the United States for at least five years to receive food stamps.

Medicaid We discussed the Medicaid program extensively in the previous chapter, but it is worth remembering that this is by far the largest categorical welfare program in the United States, with expenditures of $292 billion in 2004.[15]

Public Housing The public housing system in the United States consists of two separate programs. The first is the provision of housing in public housing projects, typically large apartment buildings. The second is the provision of "section 8 vouchers," which individuals can use to subsidize private rentals from participating landlords. Both benefits are restricted to low income families, typically those with incomes below 50% of the median income in a metropolitan area (in FY 2006, median income ranged from a low of $17,500 in Buffalo County, South Dakota, to a high of $116,300 in Stamford–Norwalk, Connecticut), and the level of benefits is reduced as incomes rise.[16] In FY 2007, $33.6 billion was allocated for spending on public housing, , with about two-thirds spent on private-sector vouchers and one-third spent on public housing projects.[17]

Other Nutritional Programs The other major type of in-kind welfare in the United States is additional nutritional programs. One such program is the Special Supplemental Nutrition Program for Women, Infants, and Children (WIC), which provides funds for nutritious food purchases specifically intended to improve fetal development and infant health. Women who are pregnant or recent mothers, as well as children under five years old, are eligible if they are on cash welfare, are on Medicaid, or have incomes below 185% of the poverty line. In 2005, the program served about 8 million people at a cost of $5 billion.[18]

Other programs in this category are the School Lunch and Breakfast Programs, which offer free or reduced-price meals to schoolchildren to help them meet federal nutrition standards. Children in families below 130% of the federal poverty line receive free meals in school, and those between 130% and 185% receive meals for no more than 40¢. In FY 2003, 28.4 million free or reduced-price lunches and 8.4 million free or reduced-price breakfasts were served, at a cost of $8.7 billion.[19]

17.3

The Moral Hazard Costs of Welfare Policy

As with social insurance programs, the benefits of redistributing to the poor (in terms of raising social welfare) come with potentially large

[15] Centers for Medicare and Medicaid Services (2006c).

[16] Median income statistics come from "FY 2006 Income Limits," located on the Web site of Department of Housing and Urban Development (HUD) at http://www.huduser.org/intercept.asp?loc=/Datasets/IL/IL06/Section8_IncomeLimits_2006.pdf.

[17] U.S. Department of Housing and Urban Development (2006).

[18] USDA, Food and Nutrition Service (2006).

[19] USDA, Food and Nutrition Service (2005a,b).

moral hazard costs. It's one thing to say that we are going to take $1 from a rich person and give that $1 to a poor person; it is another thing to actually accomplish this. The prominent economist Arthur Okun once compared the process of income redistribution to a "leaky bucket": we are carrying money from the rich to the poor, but some money leaks out along the way. Okun's question was: At what level of leakage are we no longer willing to undertake this income transfer?[20] The answer depends on the nature of the country's social welfare function (SWF), which quantifies this *efficiency-equity trade-off* between less redistribution with more social efficiency, and more redistribution with less social efficiency. By providing an overall measure of social well-being, the SWF allows public finance economists to ask whether the nation is better off with a larger social pie, distributed unequally, or a smaller social pie, distributed more equally.

There are three sources of leakage from Okun's bucket as society transfers money from high to low income groups. The first is the administrative costs of enabling this transfer, which are fairly modest (roughly 10% of total TANF spending). The second leakage occurs because higher income individuals are taxed to pay for income transfers. This taxation lowers returns to work and savings and might cause higher income people to work less hard or save less (this leakage is the deadweight loss from taxation that we discuss in detail in the coming taxation chapters).

The third source of leakage is the major focus of this section, the moral hazard effects on the poor individuals who are potential recipients of these transfers. As the government insures individuals against being poor, it raises the incentive for individuals to be poor in order to qualify for these transfers, raising the cost of these means-tested transfers. This effect also matters for social efficiency because of the deadweight loss caused by reduced incomes. When individuals reduce their labor supply in order to become poor and qualify for cash welfare, social surplus falls because fewer goods are produced (see Figure 2-17). A key component of the efficiency-equity trade-off is the social surplus (efficiency) lost due to reduced labor supply by welfare recipients.

Moral Hazard Effects of a Means-Tested Transfer System

We can illustrate this moral hazard problem using a pure means-tested transfer system, as discussed in Chapter 2. This system is a simplified version of TANF or other redistributive programs, but it allows us to clearly show the effects of moral hazard that come with redistribution. Under this system, the government would guarantee every individual an income transfer (the benefit guarantee), but this transfer would be reduced as labor earnings increase, at the benefit reduction rate (the implicit tax rate). The benefit to any individual would be equal to

$$B = G - \tau \times w \times h$$

where G is a benefit guarantee level, τ is the benefit reduction (implicit tax)

---

[20] For Okun's original discussion, see Okun (1975).

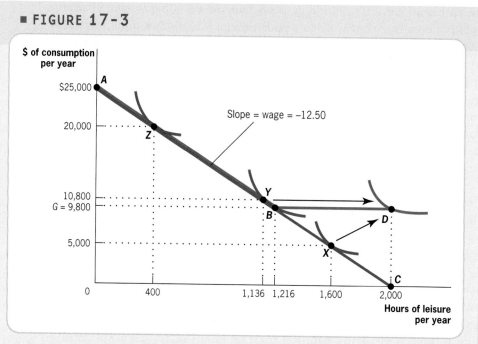

■ FIGURE 17-3

Labor Supply Decisions with a 100% Benefit Reduction Rate (BRR) • If workers are subject to a welfare system with a 100% BRR, then their budget constraint changes from *ABC* to *ABD*. Persons such as Mr. X (earning below $9,800 without welfare) will no longer work (he takes 2,000 hours of leisure). Some persons earning just above $9,800 without welfare, such as Ms. Y, may also be induced to drop out of the labor force and join welfare. Here, Ms. Y moves from point Y to point *D*. Persons such as Mr. Z will be unaffected.

rate, w is the wage rate, and h is hours of work. For example, with a guarantee level of $10,000 and a benefit reduction rate of 1, individuals would get a benefit equal to $10,000 minus their labor income (until their labor income reaches $10,000, at which point they get nothing).

In fact, it would be possible to actually end poverty in the United States today using such a system. Suppose that the government established a system with a guaranteed benefit level (G) equal to the poverty line, and a benefit reduction rate (τ) of 1 (a 100% implicit tax, so that the benefit falls by $1 for each $1 in earnings). Under this system, the government would pay any family below the poverty line the difference between the poverty line and their income. Taking the families below the poverty line and giving each the difference between the poverty line and their income would cost $104 billion dollars.[21] By this calculation, everyone in the United States could be brought up to the poverty line for only 20% of what the government spends on the Social Security program each year.

---

[21] These and subsequent calculations are based on the March 2003 Supplement to the U.S. Bureau of the Census's Current Population Survey.

But this $104 billion estimate is misleading because it doesn't consider individual reactions to such a system. Figure 17-3 considers the individual's choice of leisure and consumption in a world with a welfare program that has a benefit guarantee of the poverty line ($9,800 for a single-person family) and a 100% benefit reduction rate. Assume that each family just has one member, and that member works. This worker has a maximum of 2,000 hours per year of leisure (so hours of labor = 2,000 − hours of leisure), and a market wage of $12.50 per hour. Before this means-tested welfare program is in place, the budget constraint is the line *ABC*, with a slope equal to the negative of the wage (−$12.50).

Suppose a program is introduced that provides each (single person in our example) family a guaranteed benefit level (*G*) of $9,800 with a benefit reduction rate (*τ*) of 1, so that for every $1 that the family earns above $9,800, it loses $1 in its guaranteed benefit. This changes the individual's budget constraint to *ABD*. For those working more than 784 hours (taking less than 1,216 hours of leisure), the budget constraint segment *AB* is unchanged: with a benefit guarantee of $9,800 and a benefit reduction rate of 1, an individual who earns more than $9,800 is no longer eligible for this program. Individuals working less than 784 hours (1,216 hours or more of leisure), however, now qualify for this program. Their benefit is $9,800 regardless how hard they work, since any earnings are offset one for one against the benefit guarantee, so the budget constraint is flat from point *B* to point *D*.

What effects does this have on the individual's labor supply decision? Consider three individuals, characterized by their choice of leisure in the absence of this welfare program. In the pre-welfare world, Mr. X chooses to be at point *X* on the graph: he enjoys 1,600 hours of leisure and $5,000 of consumption. After the welfare program is introduced, Mr. X's optimal decision is to move to point *D* and enjoy 2,000 hours of leisure, with $9,800 of consumption from the government benefit guarantee. The introduction of the welfare program has raised both Mr. X's leisure and his consumption, so he is unambiguously better off.

The effects of the welfare program on the behavior of individuals located above point *B* on the budget constraint depend on their preferences, as indicated by the shape and location of their indifference curves. Consider Ms. Y, who currently takes 1,136 hours of leisure, working 864 hours and earning $10,800 per year. If she decides to join the welfare program, she would move to point *D*: given the 100% tax rate, once people are in this program there is no reason to work, since they get more leisure and the same amount of consumption by not working. If Ms. Y moves to point *D*, her consumption would fall by $1,000 per year (to $9,800), but her leisure would rise by 864 hours per year. So Ms. Y may well choose to take that trade-off and move to point *D*. She will do so if she can achieve a higher indifference curve at point *D* than at point *Y*; this is the case in Figure 17-3 (since her old indifference curve passes under the new budget constraint), so she moves into the new welfare program.

Now consider Mr. Z, whose pre-welfare consumption/leisure combination is shown at point *Z* in Figure 17-3. He currently works 1,600 hours, taking

400 hours of leisure and earning $20,000 per year. He is better off if he stays off the welfare program; point D would place him on a lower indifference curve than point Z.

What do these behavioral reactions imply for the costs of the poverty eradication program just described? First, they imply that all families with income below the poverty line (like Mr. X) would immediately stop earning income so that they could get both more leisure and more consumption for their family. This means that now the transfer amount to every family below the poverty line becomes the poverty line itself (in our example, $9,800 for a family of one), since the family has no earnings against which this transfer is reduced. The cost of the program becomes the poverty line for each family size times the number of families of each size below the poverty line, or $244 billion. Our $104 billion estimate was off because we made the *static* (no behavior change) assumption that individuals maintain their pretransfer income; if all pretransfer income falls to zero (as it does for Mr. X), the cost of the program increases substantially.

Second, many individuals above the poverty line (like Ms. Y) will stop earning money so that they can gain a huge amount of leisure with little reduction in consumption. If all individuals with incomes up to 25% above the poverty line behave this way, $80 billion will be added to the costs of the program. Thus, the poverty eradication program would cost a total of $324 billion, not the $104 billion first estimated.

More generally, Figure 17-3 illustrates the type of efficiency loss caused by the moral hazard effects of cash welfare systems such as TANF. By providing income transfers to low-income groups, the program makes being low-income more attractive, encouraging individuals to work less hard. This moral hazard effect reduces the labor supply of low-income groups, and the resulting inward shift in their labor supply curve lowers social surplus (as in Figure 2-17 on p. 55). In other words, the moral hazard response to this program adds a leak to the redistributive bucket.

Solving Moral Hazard by Lowering the Benefit Reduction Rate

One answer to this moral hazard problem would be to lower the benefit reduction rate. With a 100% tax rate on work, it is no surprise that individuals quit working; with a lower tax rate there might be a less dramatic reduction in work effort. Consider instead a system with a benefit reduction rate $\tau = 0.5$. Such a system is illustrated in Figure 17-4, with a new budget constraint AB_2D. (The budget constraint from Figure 17-3 is also represented here, as AB_1D). Compared to the pre-welfare budget constraint, the segment AB_2 is unchanged; with a benefit guarantee of $9,800 and a benefit reduction rate of 50%, once income reaches $19,600, individuals are no longer eligible for benefits. The second segment of the budget constraint, B_2D, has a slope of −$6.25: for every hour worked by a welfare recipient, each one gains $12.50 in wages but loses $6.25 in benefit reduction.

Does this type of system reduce the disincentives to work relative to a system with a 100% benefit reduction rate? In fact, it is not clear. Consider the

■ FIGURE 17-4

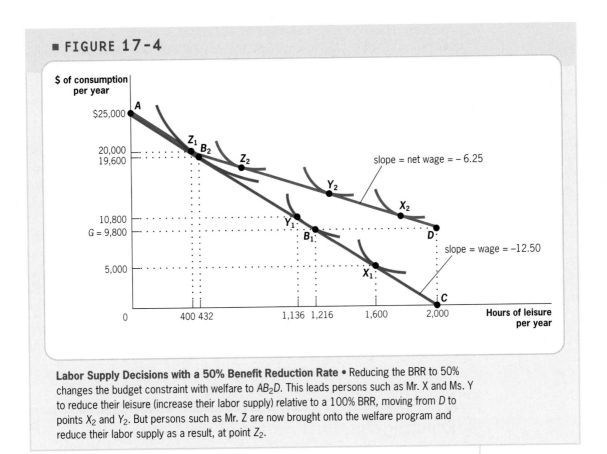

Labor Supply Decisions with a 50% Benefit Reduction Rate • Reducing the BRR to 50% changes the budget constraint with welfare to AB_2D. This leads persons such as Mr. X and Ms. Y to reduce their leisure (increase their labor supply) relative to a 100% BRR, moving from D to points X_2 and Y_2. But persons such as Mr. Z are now brought onto the welfare program and reduce their labor supply as a result, at point Z_2.

same three persons we've been discussing. For Mr. X, the disincentive is definitely reduced, since the tax rate on work is lower. Under the old system, there was no incentive for Mr. X to work, since each $1 of earnings simply reduced benefits one for one, so he chose point D. Now, because Mr. X gets to keep 50¢ of each $1 he earns, he will move to a new point such as X_2, which features less leisure (more labor supply) but more consumption than at point D.

For Ms. Y, the disincentive is also reduced. She also faced a 100% tax rate on earnings before, so when she joined the welfare program she automatically chose not to work at all (point D). Now, with a lower tax on earnings, she chooses a point such as Y_2, with much less leisure than at point D but more consumption as well.

For Mr. Z, however, there is a new disincentive to supply labor that was not present before. Under the old program, the welfare segment of the budget constraint left him on a much lower indifference curve, so he ignored the welfare option. Now, welfare becomes a relevant choice: his indifference curve falls below the new welfare segment B_2D of the budget constraint, so he chooses to receive welfare and operate at point Z_2, with much higher leisure (less work) and only slightly lower consumption. While labor supply has increased (leisure has fallen) for Mr. X and Ms. Y, labor supply has fallen (leisure has increased) for Mr. Z. Thus, the net impact of the new welfare program on labor supply is ambiguous, and depends on the relative sizes and preferences of these different groups. For example, if there were 100 persons each like Mr. X and Ms. Y, but 1,000 persons like Mr. Z, then total labor supply could fall from this cut in the benefit reduction rate.

The "Iron Triangle" of Redistributive Programs

This example illustrates the **iron triangle** of cash welfare programs: there is no way to reform a simple cash welfare program (like that used here) to simultaneously achieve three goals: (a) encourage work, (b) redistribute income, and (c) lower costs. In such a system, the government has two tools at its disposal: the level of the benefit guarantee (G) and the benefit reduction rate (τ). There is no change in these two parameters that can achieve all three of these goals. As we showed, if the government lowers the benefit reduction rate for a given guarantee level, it doesn't necessarily encourage work or lower costs. If the government reduces the guarantee for a given benefit reduction rate, it will definitely encourage work and lower costs, but it will lower the amount of income redistribution (since the poor will receive less in a system with a lower guarantee). If the government raises the guarantee, it will definitely increase income redistribution, but it will discourage work and increase costs.

17.4

Reducing the Moral Hazard of Welfare

The main lesson from section 17.3 is that the disincentive effects of welfare systems cannot necessarily be overcome by lowering the benefit reduction rate. Is it possible to design a welfare program that gets around this iron triangle? There are three approaches that might work.

Moving to Categorical Welfare Payments

The moral hazard effects of cash welfare arise because the government cannot observe an individual's earning capacity. If the government knew for sure what each individual was capable of earning, it could set up a cash welfare system with no moral hazard. For example, suppose that we were all born with our earning capacity stamped on our heads, that we could not change this, and that the government could observe it perfectly. The government would then set up a system that gave larger cash welfare checks to those who had the least earning capacity. This system would have no moral hazard effects since there would be no way that we could change our behavior to affect our welfare payment.[22]

---

[22] Under this system, the transfers would affect work behavior, since leisure is a normal good. Those who are of low earning capacity, who received the transfers, would work less hard as a result. As with the access effect and health insurance, however, this is not a moral hazard effect, since individuals are working less simply because they are richer, not due to welfare per se. Moral hazard only arises when individuals change their behavior in response to the incentives put in place by a government program (only through substitution responses to government programs, not through income effects).

The problem is that the government does not know what each person is capable of earning; the government only observes what each person actually does earn. This figure is related to earning capacity, but it is also determined by an individual's labor supply decisions. So a poor person might either be low-ability and working his or her hardest, or high-ability and lazy. By targeting welfare payments to observed earnings, the government introduces incentives for individuals to work less hard in order to qualify for larger welfare payments.

This problem could be eliminated if the welfare program could target those who are truly less capable of earning, to ensure that benefits go to those who really need them, not just to those who are working less hard in order to qualify for benefits. In the absence of our being born with an earning capacity tattoo, the government can attempt to target benefits by classifying individuals according to other characteristics that they cannot easily change.

For example, consider a program that redistributed money to the blind. Blindness is an excellent measure of earning capacity, since being blind makes it difficult to earn a high wage; and using blindness as a target for cash welfare removes moral hazard as well, since individuals are unlikely to change their behavior (blind themselves) to qualify for the welfare benefit. By directing resources toward the blind, the government can redistribute income to those with low potential earnings without distorting an individual's incentive to supply labor to the market. This type of targeting can overcome the iron triangle: the less able (for example, the blind) can be made better off without discouraging work.

What Makes a Good Targeting Mechanism? The best targeting mechanisms have two features. First, they are unchangeable. Moral hazard in welfare programs and the resulting leaks from the bucket come from substitution: individuals change their behavior in order to receive welfare benefits. If an unchangeable characteristic is used to determine benefits, individuals have no way to change behavior in order to qualify.

Second, the best mechanisms target those with low earning capacity. For example, the government could announce a program today that gave a one-time bonus to the 500 persons who *last year* were the CEOs of the Fortune 500 companies. This program would meet the first test for a good targeting mechanism; there is nothing that an individual could do today to qualify for the program, so there would be no substitution effect on behavior. This program would not meet the second criteria, however, since this is clearly not a group with low earning capacity!

Targeting by Single Motherhood The means of targeting that the United States traditionally used for cash welfare was single motherhood. Does this targeting device meet the two criteria? It seems clear that this group meets the second criterion, low earning capacity: the poverty rate for single-female-headed families with children is over 35%.[23] It is less clear that this group

---

[23] U.S. Bureau of the Census (2005b), Table 4.

■ FIGURE 17-5

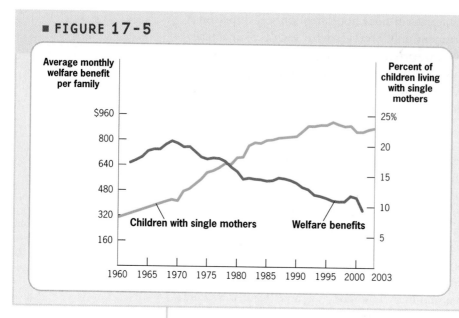

Welfare Benefits and Single Motherhood, 1960–2003 • The average monthly welfare benefit per family rose along with single motherhood in the 1960s, but single motherhood has continued to rise even as welfare benefits have fallen over the past three decades.

Source: Welfare benefit data come from the U.S. Department of Health and Human Services (2005), Table TANF 6. Data on children with single mothers come from the U.S. Bureau of the Census (2004), Table CH-1.

meets the first criterion, that of being unchangeable. Women can choose to become single mothers, either by having a child out of wedlock or by divorcing, in order to qualify for welfare. Just as there are efficiency costs from reduced work effort with means-tested welfare programs, there are efficiency costs associated with women becoming single mothers in order to qualify for welfare benefits (such as the negative implications for their children from growing up with only one parent).

Indeed, perhaps the most controversial aspect of welfare has been its incentives for the dissolution of the nuclear family. After the 1992 Los Angeles riots, then Vice President Dan Quayle declared that "the lawless social anarchy which we saw is directly related to the breakdown of family structure, personal responsibility and social order in too many areas of our society. For the poor the situation is compounded by a welfare ethos. . . . A welfare check is not a husband."[24]

Theoretically, it is possible that women might become single mothers in order to qualify for welfare. But two types of evidence suggest that this theoretical possibility is not very common in practice. First, time series evidence (Figure 17-5) shows that in the 1960s single motherhood and welfare benefits rose in lockstep, which is consistent with the notion that higher welfare benefits were causing more single motherhood. In subsequent years, however, single motherhood continued to rise despite dramatic declines in welfare benefits in real terms. As always, however, these slow-moving time series trends may be driven by other factors that make it difficult to draw a causal interpretation from this graph. Second, a large number of studies have assessed whether rates of single motherhood grow in states that raise their benefits rel-

[24] Quayle (1992).

ative to other states where benefits are constant or falling. The consensus from this research is that this effect is either nonexistent or very small.[25]

Thus, single motherhood does appear to meet the first criteria of targeting mechanisms: it is unlikely that a woman will become a single mother just to receive welfare benefits. Single motherhood, then, appears to be a reasonable targeting mechanism: it targets a low-income group using a characteristic that is not very responsive to program incentives (small moral hazard effects). As a result, targeting to single motherhood allows us to overcome the iron triangle.

Despite the general consensus on this point in the empirical literature on cash welfare programs, the supposed negative effects of cash welfare on the formation of stable families remain a major source of opposition to cash welfare among policy makers. This opposition led to the removal (at least in theory) of the distinction between single-female-headed families and other types of families when TANF was introduced in 1996 (although most recipients remain single mothers). What policy makers must recognize, however, is that the benefits of reducing such distinctions (removing disincentives to marriage) are offset by two costs. First, by removing targeting, we subject ourselves once again to the iron triangle: a program designed to make married families better off will reduce their labor supply (because married families are like Mr. Z in Figures 17-3 and 17-4: welfare used to be irrelevant but could now induce them to work less hard). Second, we are now paying out benefits to a much larger group, at higher costs. Thus, if the target is not responsive to welfare benefits, as appears to be true with single motherhood, then the benefits of removing the target are likely outweighed by the budgetary distortionary and budgetary costs of doing so.

Using "Ordeal Mechanisms"

The first approach just discussed was to use observable characteristics of individuals to target programs at the least able. That approach faces the problem that it might be difficult to assess ability based on a limited set of observable characteristics. An alternative approach is to try to get individuals to *reveal themselves as less able* by setting up a welfare program that is unattractive to the more able persons in society but continues to redistribute to those who are truly less able. The government can accomplish this through the use of **ordeal mechanisms,** features of welfare programs that make them unattractive: if welfare programs are sufficiently unattractive, only the least able will want to sign up for them.[26]

Suppose that there are two types of individuals who want to be on welfare: hard-working but low-ability individuals, and lazy but high-ability individuals. The government would like to set up a welfare system to redistribute income to the low-ability individuals, but not to high-ability individuals who have low income just because they are lazy. One way to do this is to find characteristics, such as education, that are correlated with ability, but this correlation is far from perfect. Another way is to set up a welfare system that the

ordeal mechanisms Features of welfare programs that make them unattractive, leading to the self-selection of only the most needy recipients.

---

[25] See Moffitt (1992) or Hoynes (1997).
[26] An excellent discussion of this set of issues is provided by Nichols and Zeckhauser (1982).

high-ability lazy individuals would not find attractive so that the high-ability individuals *self-select* out of welfare.

An excellent example of such an ordeal mechanism is the *work* or *training requirements* that are a feature of the TANF program. Such requirements impose a cost on lazy individuals who are just using welfare as a means of increasing their leisure. For those who are using welfare because they simply can't make ends meet despite working hard, however, these requirements are not costly. Indeed, such low-ability individuals might welcome the training that is provided.

Another example of an ordeal mechanism is the provision of in-kind rather than cash benefits through welfare programs. Targeting is hard to do with cash, because everyone values cash! If the government gives away cash, then individuals who aren't needy will pretend to be needy in order to qualify for the cash. If the government gives away apartments in a somewhat run-down public housing project, however, those with high ability may not be interested in taking up the benefit; they would rather work than live in a bad apartment. Once again, however, those who are truly needy will likely prefer the bad apartment to living on the street.

The use of an ordeal mechanism may not be the only reason for providing transfers in-kind instead of in the form of cash, however. It may also be that voters are more willing to support redistribution through in-kind mechanisms, perhaps because of paternalistic concerns that low-income groups will not spend their money appropriately. Evidence that this might be the case comes from an innovative study by Jacobsson et al. (2005). These authors ran a number of laboratory experiments in which participants were given the choice of providing assistance to others in the form of cash or in-kind; for example, they were offered the choice between helping smokers with diabetes by providing them with cash or with a quit-smoking product with an equivalent value. In 90% of cases, when given this choice participants chose the in-kind transfer.

The Paradox of Ordeal Mechanisms The fundamental efficiency problem in transfer programs is that the non-needy might *masquerade* as needy in order to qualify for benefits, and as a result the government cannot target benefits only to the needy. If the government provides a benefit that is not attractive to the non-needy but helps out the truly needy, then the non-needy won't pursue this masquerade and targeting will be more efficient.

The paradox of ordeal mechanisms is therefore that *apparently making the less able worse off can actually make them better off.* This is because the government has a fixed amount of money it will spend on welfare. If the less able have to share that budget with the (masquerading) more able, then that is less money they can receive. If an ordeal mechanism can get the more able off the welfare rolls, then the less able can receive more money, even if it involves putting them through an ordeal along the way. If the government can assess who is truly less able through an ordeal mechanism, then it can surmount the iron triangle by having a generous program targeted to that less-able population.

This ordeal mechanism intuition suggests a rationale for making the process of receiving welfare less pleasant, such as by making individuals use food stamps at the supermarket, where others can see them, or making them wait in line at a public welfare office. By more effectively targeting benefits, such approaches make recipients better off: they remove the drain on the system by weeding out higher-income individuals who pretend to be poor in order to claim benefits.

▶**APPLICATION**

An Example of Ordeal Mechanisms

An example illustrates the power of ordeal mechanisms as a targeting device. The government wants to set up a soup kitchen for low-ability individuals who are poor, but the government cannot tell whether individuals are truly low-ability, or high-ability and just lazy. The government can either hire a large number of workers for this soup kitchen, so that no one has to wait very long for a bowl of soup, or they can hire a small number, so that there is always a line outside. It seems inefficient to make needy and hungry individuals wait in line for their soup, but doing so might reveal who truly needs the free food: the long line might prevent the more able from using resources that they don't need and are not really intended for them.

More specifically, suppose that the utility that low-ability individuals gain from the soup kitchen's soup is $U_l = 240S - W$, where S = soup and W = wait in minutes. The utility of high-ability individuals for soup is $U_h = 120S - 2W$; the high-ability person gets less utility from each serving of soup (because the high-ability are not as hungry), and more disutility from waiting (because the high-ability have more productive things they can do with their time). Suppose further that the government endeavors to maximize a utilitarian social welfare function that weights equally the utility of each member of society, $SWF = U_l + U_h$. Finally, suppose that there are two bowls of soup to give away, and that the government is trying to figure out how long to make individuals wait for those bowls.

The government first attempts a system with no waiting ($W = 0$). Under such a system, both the high-ability and low-ability will take the free soup, so let's assume that they each get one bowl. Thus, the low-ability individual gets $U_l = 240$, and the high-ability individual gets $U_h = 120$, so that social welfare = 360.

The government then moves to a system that requires individuals to wait 61 minutes to get free soup. Under such a system, the high-ability person will no longer demand the soup, since the utility would be negative ($U_h = 120 - (2 \times 61) < 0$), so that person won't wait in line. The low-ability person would therefore get both bowls of soup, for a utility that would be $U_l = 480 - 61 = 419$. Social welfare has therefore risen from 360 to 419. Thus, making the low-ability person wait in line raises both that person's individual utility and that of society as a whole!

This outcome is possible because the gains from efficient targeting (not having to share benefits with the high-ability) outweigh the costs of having the low-ability person wait in line. Through the use of ordeal mechanisms, such as waiting in line, welfare programs can use the fact that the low-ability want the good more, and have a lower disutility from this ordeal, to more effectively target the redistribution of scarce resources. ◄

Increasing Outside Options

The third approach to reducing the moral hazard effects of welfare is to increase the outside options available to individuals so that it is no longer attractive to be on welfare. Figure 17-6 replicates the choice set depicted in Figure 17-3, focusing just on one worker from that earlier case (Ms. Y). As in that earlier graph, individuals such as Ms. Y initially face an hourly wage of $12.50 (represented by the budget constraint ABC), and choose 1,136 hours of leisure and $10,800 of consumption at point Y_1. If welfare is introduced as

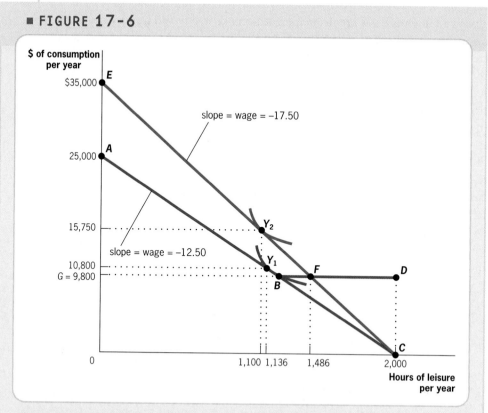

■ FIGURE 17-6

Increasing the Cash Welfare Opportunity Set • One way to reduce use of welfare without changing the benefit reduction rate (and thus running into the iron triangle problem) is to increase the outside opportunities of single mothers so that they can literally "work their way off welfare." By raising the single mother's wage to $17.50, we move her budget constraint with welfare from ABD to EFD. With this new budget constraint, she will no longer choose to be on welfare.

earlier, with a guarantee of $9,800 and a benefit reduction rate of 100%, the budget constraint becomes *ABD*, and she chooses to work not at all at point *D*. At this point, she loses only $1,000 of consumption, but she gains 864 hours of leisure.

Suppose now that Ms. Y's wage rises to $17.50 per hour, so her budget constraint now becomes *EFC* without welfare, or *EFD* with welfare. At this higher hourly wage Ms. Y earns $15,750 and chooses 1,100 hours of leisure (point Y_2) regardless of the existence of welfare; even when welfare is introduced, she is on a higher indifference curve at point Y_2 than at point *D*. Thus, raising the wage rate to $17.50 per hour reduces the inefficiencies of welfare by making it a less attractive option relative to work, without penalizing those on welfare by actually lowering benefits. This theory underlies the "carrot" approach to welfare reform: reduce the welfare rolls by providing women with the means to work their way off welfare rather than by making welfare less generous.

There are five different approaches the government can take to increase outside opportunities for welfare recipients.

Training The traditional approach to increasing outside opportunities is through *training* of welfare recipients. Most women on welfare have very low skills; they are typically high school dropouts without many of the skills necessary to earn a reasonable living in America's high-tech economy. If these women can learn the skills valued in the current economy, their potential wage will increase as shown in Figure 17-6, and they will find welfare less attractive relative to outside labor market opportunities.

State welfare programs have actually run a series of randomized trials to evaluate how well this training approach (including classroom training, workplace training, and job search assistance) works. The evidence from these randomized trials is that training does work; training programs lead to modest declines in welfare receipt and increase the earnings for welfare recipients.[27] Most experts agree, however, that while the effects of training programs are positive, they are minor, and that such programs cannot induce sizeable reductions in the welfare rolls.

Labor Market Subsidies Another approach to increasing outside options for welfare recipients is to directly subsidize their market wages in order to make market work more attractive to them so that they leave welfare. These types of subsidies can come in two forms. The first form is a general subsidy to the labor supply of the lowest-income workers. An example of this approach is the Earned Income Tax Credit (EITC), which provides a subsidy for each dollar of earnings for those with income less than a certain level. In 2006, to be eligible for the EITC a family with two or more children had to earn less than $36,348; a family with one child had to earn less than $32,001; and a family with no children had to earn less than $11,750.[28] As will be discussed

---

[27] For a review of the literature, see Gueron (1990).
[28] Furman (2006).

THE CANADIAN SELF-SUFFICIENCY PROJECT

A particularly interesting example of a wage subsidy program is the Self-Sufficiency Project (SSP) in Canada.[29] This program randomly offered wage subsidies to a treatment group of Canadian welfare recipients who had been on welfare for more than one year: if these individuals found a full-time job within one year of leaving welfare, the program would on average double their earnings over the first three years they held the job. By choosing only those who had been on welfare for a long period of time, the program minimized the concern about individuals claiming welfare in order to receive the benefit, but at the cost of excluding many individuals who could benefit from this program. This treatment group was compared to a control group of long-term welfare recipients randomly selected to not receive this wage subsidy.

The results of this randomized trial are striking: the employment rates of those offered the subsidy (the treatment group) rose by 12 percentage points (43%) relative to those who were not offered the subsidy (the control group), and the rate of welfare enrollment fell by roughly the same amount. This short-term subsidy did not have long-lasting effects, however. After five years the treatment and control groups appeared similar in terms of work and welfare utilization. An open question is whether a longer-term version of this subsidy would have had longer-lasting impacts.

Over the entire five-year period studied by researchers, each $1 of government spending translated into $2 in increased income for former welfare recipients who took this subsidy. Thus, this program is the opposite of a leaky bucket: government transfers raised total income by more than the amount of the transfer. This finding suggests that well-targeted, large wage supplements can be an effective means of reducing the welfare rolls.

in detail in Chapter 21, this approach has been shown to be very successful in terms of increasing the labor supply of low-income earners. At the same time, it is fairly expensive, with current EITC expenses of over $35 billion per year.[30]

An alternative is to target wage subsidies to those already on welfare in order to reduce the costs of the subsidy program. Blank, Card, and Robins (2000) review evidence from a series of programs designed to increase returns to work among families on welfare. They found that subsidizing work increases employment and reduces the number of people on welfare and that this impact rises with the size of the subsidy. Moreover, such targeted programs are much less expensive than general wage subsidies such as the EITC.

Such a targeted approach has two disadvantages, however. First, there are many individuals who could benefit from wage subsidies but who do not qualify for them. For example, a single mother who loses her job, but who does not want to enroll in welfare, is penalized by her reluctance to accept the government's help if the benefits are restricted to welfare recipients. This leads to the second disadvantage: Blank, Card, and Robins also found that subsidizing those on welfare when they go to work increases the number of people enrolling to receive welfare benefits. Since individuals have to be on welfare to get these wage subsidies (in contrast to general subsidies like the EITC), individuals will join welfare programs in order to qualify. The mother in our

[29] For details on the implementation and results of SSP, see Ford et al. (2003).
[30] Office of Management and Budget (2006a), Table 8.5.

example is now more likely to join welfare in order to qualify, offsetting some of the costs savings from the more targeted subsidy program.

Thus, there is a clear trade-off between more general and more targeted (to existing welfare recipients) wage subsidy programs. More targeted subsidy programs will save costs relative to general programs, but at the risk of leaving out some of the truly needy and increasing welfare enrollment among those trying to qualify for the program.

Child Care In reality, for families with children the budget constraint shown in Figures 17-2 and 17-6 should represent the wage that the mother can earn in the labor market, *net* of the costs of the child care she must buy for her children while she is at work. The more a mother must pay others to care for her children while she is working, the less she takes home at the end of the week. As a result, another means of increasing outside opportunities for women is to subsidize their child care costs, or even to provide free child care. This is equivalent to raising the wage and thus the slope of the non-welfare budget constraint.

Subsidizing child care has been shown to raise female labor supply: recent estimates suggest that for each 10% rise in child care subsidies, female labor supply increases by about 2%. But increases in child care use also imply more nonparental care for children, and there is an open debate over whether this is beneficial or not. The available evidence suggests that children attending high-quality preschool programs have better outcomes than comparable children not in the programs. This outcome justifies the existence and possible expansion of the Head Start program, which provides such high-quality preschool services for disadvantaged youth. But evidence on the benefit of more generally defined child care is much more mixed: increased use of child care appears to clearly worsen child outcomes in the short run (e.g., more aggressiveness, lower motor and social skills), but has more mixed effects in the longer run (with some studies finding an improvement in school performance).[31]

Child Support A fourth means of increasing outside opportunities is to more fully enforce the **child support** obligations of the fathers of children whose mothers are welfare recipients. When individuals divorce, or children are born out of wedlock, the court system will often order the absent parent (typically the father) to provide some means of financial support to the parent who retains custody of the children (typically the mother). The problem is that only half of these court-ordered child support payments are actually made in the United States today. As a result, women are unable to leave welfare because they cannot finance consumption for themselves and their children on their wage earnings alone without these child support payments. If more child support were paid, there would be an outward shift in the non-welfare budget constraint in Figure 17-6, and welfare would become less attractive.

This is a very appealing approach to reducing welfare dependence; after all, there isn't a large constituency to defend the "deadbeat dads" who aren't paying

child support Court-ordered payments from an absent parent to support the upbringing of offspring.

---

[31] See Baker et al. (2005) for a review of the economics literature on child care.

their child support. The appeal of this approach probably explains why, in nearly every year from 1981 to 1999, there was major federal legislation to continue to tighten child support enforcement in order to find deadbeat dads and make them pay their court-ordered obligations. A state (the entity that enforces child support laws) now has the power to order possible fathers to undergo genetic testing to establish paternity, investigate fathers' financial records in order to facilitate court-ordered determinations of child support payments, and enforce child support orders by withholding deadbeat dads' wages or seizing and selling their property.[32]

The problem with this approach to solving welfare dependence, however, is that many of these deadbeat dads are poor as well, so there is not much money that can effectively be collected from them. Moreover, under the current structure of the TANF system in most states, virtually all the money collected from deadbeat dads in child support for women on welfare goes directly to the state to offset the women's welfare costs, with the women keeping only a small nominal amount. So the current system is effectively taxing low-income deadbeat dads to finance welfare programs.

This system provides little incentive for women on welfare to help in tracking down deadbeat fathers, since the state gets the money, not the mothers. That is why some states are experimenting with "passing-through" to mothers on welfare the entirety of the child support payments collected from absent fathers.

On the other hand, the major advantage of stronger enforcement of child support is that it potentially reduces the incidence of single motherhood by making it financially costly for fathers to abandon their families. There is little convincing evidence, however, to demonstrate that stronger child support enforcement is associated with lower divorce rates or with lower rates of out-of-wedlock childbearing.

Remove "Welfare Lock" Finally, a fifth approach to improving outside incentives is to unlink cash welfare from other in-kind benefits. For example, until the mid-1980s, receipt of public health insurance under Medicaid for low-income, nondisabled mothers was restricted to those on welfare. If they left welfare, most of these women could not find jobs that offered health insurance. This linkage between cash welfare and insurance had the potential effect of causing women to stay on welfare solely to receive the health insurance benefit.

This point is illustrated in Figure 17-7. The starting point is Figure 17-4, showing a pre-welfare budget constraint with a slope of $12.50 (the hourly wage), *ABC*. A welfare program is introduced that provides a benefit guarantee of $9,800 with a 50% benefit reduction rate (recipients lose 50¢ in benefits for each $1 earned), shifting the budget constraint to *ABD*, as in Figure 17-4. Now suppose that the poverty reduction program offered by the government includes free health insurance only for those on welfare, and that this health insurance is worth $3,000. This causes an additional upward shift in the

---

[32] U.S. House of Representatives Committee on Ways and Means (2004), Section 8.

■ FIGURE 17-7

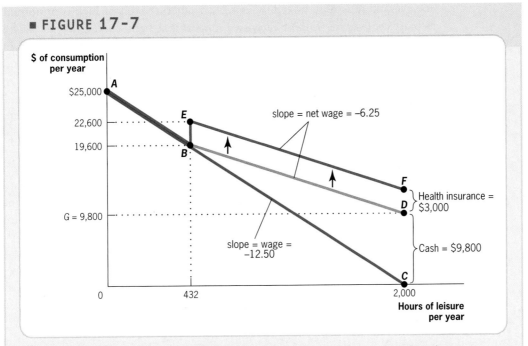

Tying Health Insurance to Cash Welfare • The linking of health insurance coverage through Medicaid to cash welfare creates an additional large disincentive to leave welfare. The budget constraint with the welfare program moves from *ABD* to *ABEF* when insurance is tied to welfare, with an extra portion (*BEF*) that reflects the value of Medicaid, but that ends when the individual leaves welfare. Thus, when Medicaid is linked to welfare, it is never sensible to leave welfare for a job that pays only slightly more, unless that job offers health insurance.

budget constraint when an individual is on welfare by $3,000; as long as the individual is on the welfare program, he or she receives health insurance worth $3,000. Once they leave welfare, however, individuals lose their health insurance as well as cash payments. The budget constraint on welfare (and public health insurance) thus becomes *ABEF*.

The implication is that for the woman who is considering working her way off welfare, that last $1 of earnings that moves her off the welfare program doesn't just cost her 50¢ of welfare benefits; it also costs her the entire value of the health insurance package! Thus, there is a huge disincentive to working one's way off welfare; women will not leave welfare until their earnings exceed what they could get on welfare by a large amount, enough to cover the cost of the lost health insurance. In terms of Chapter 15's discussion of job lock, there is "welfare lock": even if they can increase their income in the labor market, women may be unwilling to leave welfare because they will lose their public health insurance.

Thus, one way to increase the outside opportunities of women is to uncouple their eligibility for health insurance from their receiving cash welfare payments. This was one major motivation for the Medicaid expansions of the 1980s and 1990s, which were not tied to cash welfare. Unfortunately, however, there is only mixed evidence on whether welfare lock is important in practice; even the largest estimates suggest that such uncoupling of health insurance from welfare results in only very modest decreases in the number of people on the welfare rolls.

17.5

Welfare Reform

As noted in the introduction to this chapter, welfare reform in the United States has been one of the most contentious sources of political debate over the past two decades. This debate culminated in the most important reform of the welfare system since its inception, the Personal Responsibility and Work Opportunity Reconciliation Act of 1996 (PRWORA).

Changes Due to Welfare Reform

PRWORA was an incredibly detailed piece of legislation that made many changes to the welfare system that existed as of 1996. Some of the most important changes follow.

1. Cash welfare was changed from an *entitlement,* for which the federal government paid at least half of a state's benefits costs, to a *block grant,* where the federal government simply sent each state a check for a fixed amount to finance welfare programs. This change is equivalent to moving from retrospective to prospective federal reimbursement of states for welfare costs.

2. States were allowed, and encouraged, to experiment with alternative structures of cash welfare payments, such as reducing the benefit reduction rate or allowing women to keep more of the child support payments made by their children's fathers.

3. Time limits were imposed on welfare recipients, as described earlier in this chapter; these time limits did not exist before PRWORA.

4. Work requirements were imposed on welfare recipients. Work requirements were much weaker before PRWORA.

5. New efforts to limit unwed motherhood were introduced: teenagers who want to qualify for benefits must live with their parents and attend school; there is a 25% reduction in benefits for mothers who do not identify the paternity of their children; and states are allowed to impose a "family cap" whereby benefits don't increase as women have more children.

Effects of the 1996 Welfare Reform

What have been the effects of this welfare reform? First, as illustrated in Figure 17-1, there has been an enormous reduction in welfare caseloads, of more than 50% nationally and of more than 80% in some states. The best available evidence, using methods reviewed in the Empirical Evidence box, suggests that about one-third of this decline can be explained by welfare reform.

ESTIMATING THE IMPACT OF WELFARE REFORM

As you might expect, the time series evidence for the effects of welfare reform in Figure 17-1 is not entirely convincing, for two reasons. First, the caseload decline began in 1994, well before welfare reform began taking effect. Second, this period also saw one of the largest economic booms in the history of the United States, and better labor markets have always been associated with reductions in welfare rolls. Similar problems plague attempts to assess the impact of welfare reform on other outcomes such as labor supply and childbearing.

It is very hard to move beyond time series analyses of welfare reform, however, because the reform was instituted on a national, not state-by-state, basis. The law did have different manifestations in different states, due to decisions each state made with its new flexibility, but so many different aspects of the welfare laws changed that it is hard to assign a causal impact to any one of the changes.

Analysts of the 1996 welfare reform have proposed two solutions to this problem, neither entirely satisfactory, but which together can begin to paint a picture of the effects of reform. The first approach is to compare the outcomes of single mothers (the treatment group) to other control groups, such as married mothers, who were subject to similar economic shocks but were not much affected by welfare reform. The second approach is to use the fact that some states received waivers from the federal government to experiment with particular aspects of welfare reform before the national law was in place, such as changing the benefits reduction rate and other incentives for work or sanctions for non-work. The fact that these policies were tried in some states and not others in the mid-1990s provides a quasi-experimental setup for evaluating their effects.[33]

One unambiguous impact of welfare reform is that it has led to a large financial windfall for the states. This is because the block grant amounts that states receive to finance this program are tied to their level of welfare expenditures in 1994, a level that dramatically exceeds current levels in every state. States have used some of the extra funds from this windfall to finance programs such as subsidized child care for single mothers in order to further encourage the move from welfare to work.

There has also been extensive investigation of the effects of this welfare reform on the income and well-being of single mothers. Most studies find that despite the enormous reduction in use of welfare, single mothers as a group have *not* seen a drop in their income or their consumption due to welfare reform. This surprising finding is accounted for by the large increase in the labor supply of single mothers over this period, so that rising earnings fully offset falling welfare benefits. The rise in single mother labor supply, in turn, is due partly to the strong economy of this era, partly to expansions of wage subsidies through the EITC, and partly to welfare reform itself. At the same time, some subgroups of single mothers, those with particularly low skills who were unable to increase their earnings, have suffered from the reduction in their entitlement to cash welfare.

Finally, one of the major motivations for welfare reform was to reduce out-of-wedlock childbearing. Yet, consistent with the evidence described earlier in

---

[33] For reviews of the effects of welfare reform, see Blank (2002). For evidence on welfare reform and consumption, see Meyer and Sullivan (2004).

this chapter's section on targeting to single mothers, there has been no noticeable effect of welfare reform on fertility rates. For example, a recent study of the state-level family caps by Kearney (2004) found that capping benefit levels did not at all reduce the rate at which single mothers had children.

Was Welfare Reform a Success? From the evidence thus far on the effects of welfare reform, the 1996 reforms have much to recommend them. These reforms, and earlier state reforms that preceded them, appear to have lowered welfare rolls without lowering the incomes of single mothers in the United States.

Whether these reforms were ultimately "successful," however, depends on four additional factors. First, while incomes did not fall on average, they did fall for some women; if society cares in particular about those at the very bottom of the income distribution, these costs for a small share of women may exceed the gains from reduced government welfare spending.[34] Second, although incomes for single mothers were not down on average, they did not rise much either, and leisure clearly fell, so in a standard utility-maximizing framework these single mothers are worse off. The benefits of reduced government spending on welfare must be weighed against the reduction in the utility of these single mothers from reduced leisure. Third, this reform was passed in the midst of one of the largest economic expansions in U.S. history, and it remains to be seen how this system will weather a major recession, which would force states to spend their full block grant allocations and, possibly, run out of money to pay welfare benefits.

Finally, the most important long-run effects of welfare reform are likely to be on the children in welfare-eligible families. Such children did not see much change in their income on average from welfare reform, but they are now increasingly cared for by others rather than by their own mother (who is working instead of staying at home on welfare). Whether this is on net a positive or negative outcome for their own well-being remains to be seen.

17.6

Conclusion

One of the major roles of governments in the United States and in the rest of the world is to redistribute resources to low-income groups. In the United States, this redistribution occurs through cash and in-kind benefits, which are targeted to low-income groups in general, and often to low-income single mothers in particular. These welfare programs have been a source of contentious debate for many years, and the past decade has witnessed the most radical reform of cash welfare since the program's inception. Despite the apparent success of the 1996 welfare reform, welfare debates will no doubt continue in the future.

---

[34] Bitler, Gelbach, and Hoynes (2003) emphasize the differential effects of welfare incentives throughout the earnings distribution.

▶ HIGHLIGHTS

■ Redistribution may be concerned with either relative income inequality or absolute deprivation, where the latter is measured by the poverty line. Income inequality is high in the United States both relative to other nations and to historical standards.

■ There are two major cash welfare programs in the United States (TANF and SSI) and four major in-kind welfare programs (food stamps, Medicaid, public housing, and other nutritional programs).

■ Welfare policy may distort the incentives for low-income populations to work (to supply labor). This disincentive problem cannot be solved simply by lowering the benefit reduction rate because the increased labor supply incentives for some groups are offset by new labor supply disincentives for other groups (the iron triangle problem).

■ One potential solution to the iron triangle problem is to use categorical welfare programs, which are effective if (a) individuals cannot (or will not) easily change to appear to be one of the targeted group and (b) the targeted group has low earnings capacity. Single motherhood appears to be a good targeting device using these criteria.

■ Another potential solution to the iron triangle problem is to make use of ordeal mechanisms (such as in-kind benefits or welfare stigma) that reduce the value of welfare to higher-ability groups and so can be used to effectively target public spending to lower-ability groups.

■ Another solution to the iron triangle problem is to increase the outside opportunities for welfare recipients, through training, wage subsidies, child care, or child support, or by uncoupling in-kind from cash benefits.

■ Welfare reform in 1996 appears to have been successful in reducing welfare rolls without significantly reducing the incomes of welfare recipients.

▶ QUESTIONS AND PROBLEMS

1. As Table 17-2 shows, members of the poorest fifth of U.S. households have a much smaller share of total U.S. income than is typical in other developed countries. Does this mean that the poorest fifth of U.S. households are worse off in the United States than are the poorest fifth of households elsewhere? Why or why not?

2. The U.S. federal government definition of poverty is the same in all communities around the country. Is this appropriate? Why or why not?

3. Suppose there are two types of people in the country of Dipolia: unskilled people who value only food and skilled, lazy people who value only alcoholic drinks. The government of Dipolia is considering moving from a cash-welfare system to a food stamps system. The new system will provide the same benefit levels, but recipients will get stamps allowing them to buy food instead of cash. Explain how this change will affect the work efforts and utility levels of the two types of people in Dipolia. How would your answer differ if unskilled people value both food and alcoholic drinks?

4. Suppose that currently the government provides everyone with a guaranteed income of $12,000 per year, but this benefit level is reduced by $1 for each $1 of work income. The government is considering changing this policy such that the benefit level is reduced by $1 for every $2 of work income. What effect would this policy have on work effort? Explain your answer.

5. Senator Ostrich suggests that "in order to end poverty, all we need to do is pay everyone making less than the poverty line the difference between what they are earning and the poverty line." Ostrich argues that, based on the set of people currently below the poverty line, this would cost $98 billion per year. Why is Ostrich understating the costs of this program?

6. An individual can earn $12 per hour if he or she works. Draw the budget constraints that show the monthly consumption-leisure trade-off under the following three welfare programs:

   a. The government guarantees $600 per month in income and reduces that benefit by $1 for each $1 of labor income.

b. The government guarantees $300 per month in income and reduces that benefit by $1 for every $3 of labor income.

c. The government guarantees $900 per month in income and reduces that benefit by $1 for every $2 in labor income, until the benefit reaches $300 per month. After that point, the government does not reduce the benefit at all.

7. Suppose that you wanted to test the hypothesis that welfare benefit generosity induces people to become single mothers.

a. Which population would you choose to study in answering this question?

b. How would you use variation in welfare benefits to estimate the impact of welfare on single motherhood?

c. How would you know whether welfare benefit generosity influences single motherhood?

8. Several recent studies have documented a "race to the bottom" in welfare benefit levels, whereby states respond to their neighbors' benefit reductions with reductions in their own welfare generosity. Why might a state respond to its neighbors' change in generosity?

9. The Earned Income Tax Credit (EITC) provides a cash subsidy for every $1 earned by those with incomes below $33,700 per year. How might the EITC raise an individual's over-all work effort? How might the EITC lower an individual's work effort?

10. An issue that arises when designing a welfare system is whether to make the benefits available to all low-income families with children or only to families headed by a single mother. Explain the trade-offs involved in this decision.

11. Consider the major changes in the welfare system that occurred in the 1996 welfare reform, described in section 17.5. Which of these changes are likely to reduce the number of people on welfare? Which of these changes are likely to increase the number of people on welfare?

12. Congressman Snowball, having read Chapter 11 of this text, informs his colleagues that people who have higher levels of education have higher earnings capacities. He argues, based on Chapter 17, that one way to reduce the moral hazard of welfare is to pay larger benefits to those with limited earning capacities. Therefore, according to Congressman Snowball, a way to accomplish this would be to provide large welfare payments to poorly educated Americans. Does this eliminate moral hazard?

The **e** indicates a question that requires students to apply the empirical economics principles discussed in Chapter 3 and the Empirical Evidence boxes.

▶ ADVANCED QUESTIONS

13. The Women, Infants, and Children food assistance program provides needy families with easily identifiable coupons good for very specific types of food, while in most states the food stamps program provides recipients with an Electronic Benefit Transfer card that looks and works very much like a standard debit card. Which program is more likely to surmount the problem of the iron triangle? Explain your answer.

14. The Personal Responsibility and Work Opportunity Reconciliation Act of 1996 imposed limits on the amount of time that a family could receive cash welfare payments during its members' childhoods. Grogger and Michalopoulos (2003) found that these time limits led to immediate reductions in the number of people receiving welfare benefits, even though nobody in the family had reached his or her time limit. Which group of families should be particularly sensitive to the introduction of these time limits: those with younger children or those with older children? Explain your answer.

15. Jackie spends her money on food and all other goods. Right now, she has an income of $600 per month. Compare two alternative welfare programs in which she could participate: program A would provide her with a monthly check of $300 and program B would provide her with $400 a month in credits that can be spent only on food.

a. Draw Jackie's budget constraints in each of these two cases.

b. Draw representative indifference curves that would reflect each of these three scenarios:

(i) Jackie prefers program A to program B;

(ii) Jackie prefers program B to program A;

(iii) Jackie is indifferent between the two programs.

16. Polly, Molly, and Dolly are all single mothers. They each can earn $10 per hour working for up to 2,000 hours per year. Their government runs a welfare system that gives income benefits of $5,000 per year for single mothers with no income. The welfare benefits are reduced by $1 for every $2 in earned income. Currently, the government also provides free health care for children of single mothers with less than $25,000 in income. Each mother values this benefit at $2,000 per year. Under this system, Polly works 200 hours per year, Molly works 1,025 hours per year, and Dolly works 1,500 hours, so only Polly receives welfare.

a. Draw the set of hours worked and consumption combinations that these mothers face (carefully labeling the slopes of the budget constraint). Draw a representative indifference curve for each mother.

b. In an effort to save money, the government decides to cut back on insurance provision. It dictates that to receive free health care for their children, single mothers will henceforth have to be on welfare. On a new set of axes, draw the new budget constraint for the three mothers. Describe what will happen to the number of hours each mother works.

17. Consider the following welfare program, designed to ensure that needy people get adequate income to buy food. The government offers cash assistance to any worker earning more than $100 and less than $980, according to the following schedule.

Income	Food Stamps Received
$100	$264
$200	$234
$300	$204
$400	$174
$500	$144
$600	$114
$700	$84
$800	$54
$900	$24
$980	$0

There are two types of consumption goods, food (F) and other goods (X), and people have utility functions

$$U = 1/3\ln(F) + 2/3\ln(X)$$

over these goods. The prices of food and other goods are both normalized to 1; therefore, the budget constraint is

$$F + X = Y$$

a. Determine the optimal level of food and other-good consumption for an individual with earned income of $300.

b. Now consider replacing the cash welfare program with a food stamps program. Instead of receiving the cash amount indicated in the table above, workers would receive an equal amount of stamps that they could spend only on food. Determine the optimum level of food and other-good consumption for the individual with $300 in earned income. Does this make the individual better or worse off than the cash welfare system?

c. Repeat (a) and (b) for an earned income of $900 and explain any differences in outcomes.

Taxation in the United States and Around the World

18

In August 1988, Republican presidential candidate George H. W. Bush was in trouble. Despite being the sitting Vice President at the end of the very popular presidency of Ronald Reagan, Bush was trailing badly in the polls behind Democratic candidate Michael Dukakis. Part of Bush's difficulty was that people were concerned over his resolve to act on core Republican issues, such as cutting taxes and restraining spending to shrink the size of government. At the Republican convention that month, Bush's speechwriter found inspiration in a popular Clint Eastwood character, the resolute and righteous cop Dirty Harry Callahan. On August 18 Bush made a startling promise to project his strength and resolve: "Read my lips," he declared, "No new taxes." The pithy phrase worked miracles. Within days of the national broadcast of the convention, polls showed that the gap between Bush and Dukakis had all but disappeared. Bush won the election convincingly, carrying all but ten states, with 53% of the popular vote to Dukakis's 46%. But his promise would come back to haunt him.

By 1990, the federal deficit was projected to reach $225 billion. Though hardly a record deficit, the Gramm-Rudman-Hollings budget act (discussed in Chapter 4 on pages 94–96) required that the deficit that year be no more than $64 billion or automatic, across-the-board cuts in federal spending would ensue. Forced to achieve a more balanced budget, President Bush publicly abandoned his "no new taxes" pledge in June, saying that "tax revenue increases" would be a necessary part of any deficit-reducing legislation. Many Republicans were furious, but by November the President had signed into law a bill raising taxes by $140 billion over the next five years, including an increase in the tax rate paid by the highest-income taxpayers from 28% to 31%.

Subsequent polls showed that five out of ten Americans disapproved of Bush's backtracking on his promise, while four out of ten actually approved of his willingness to raise taxes. To his most conservative allies, Bush's U-turn made him look weak when it came to restraining the size of government. This opened the door in 1992 for third-party candidate H. Ross Perot, whose campaign focused largely on bringing fiscal responsibility back to Washington. Perot ultimately drew votes away from Bush in a number of key states, allowing Bill Clinton to win the majority of electoral votes while garnering only 43% of the popular vote.[1]

The "no new taxes" episode highlights the important role that taxes play in both the political arena and government policy making in the United States. In this section of the book, we move beyond our study of government expenditures to the study of government revenue raising through taxation. This chapter begins the study of taxation by setting the institutional and theoretical stage for understanding tax policy and its effects. Once we understand these basic concepts, our study of taxation proceeds in three steps. Chapters 19 and 20 cover the basic theory of taxation. Chapters 21–24 apply this basic theory to the study of how tax systems affect economic behavior by individuals and by corporations. Finally, Chapter 25 discusses the implications of our analysis for fundamental tax reform in the United States.

"How about 'No new taxes after these new taxes'?"

We begin our study by providing a brief overview of the types of taxation that exist in the United States, at the federal, state, and local levels, and around the world. We then discuss in more detail the main tool of revenue raising in the United States, the federal income tax. We provide an overview of the structure of the income tax and discuss alternative means of measuring the "fairness" of the income tax system. We then turn to the question of how to measure the base on which income taxes should be levied. Should all forms of income be taxed, or only some forms? Should the government use the tax code to encourage private provision of public goods by exempting contributions toward such goods from taxation? Should the government tax individuals on the basis of their own income or on the basis of the income of all those in their family? This part of the chapter discusses how governments should, and do, form the bases for taxing income.

18.1

Types of Taxation

The governments of the United States and other nations raise revenues through a wide variety of mechanisms. Our study of taxation will focus on the five most common types of taxes, which we review in this section. (Other, more specific types of taxes will also be discussed, when appropriate, in the remaining chapters of the book.)

Taxes on Earnings

The first type of taxation is the **payroll tax,** a tax levied on the earnings of workers. Payroll taxes are the primary means of financing social insurance programs, such as those discussed in the preceding chapters (Social Security, unemployment insurance, Medicare, and so on).

payroll tax A tax levied on income earned on one's job.

---

[1] Balz and Yang (1990), Oreskes (1990), Woodward (1992).

Taxes on Individual Income

individual income tax A tax paid on individual income accrued during the year.

The second type of taxation is the **individual income tax,** a tax paid by individuals on income accrued during the year. Income for income tax purposes includes labor earnings, but the tax is distinguished from the payroll tax by (a) applying to a broader set of income sources (such as interest earnings from household savings as well), and (b) applying in many cases to the entire income of a family, not just to the income of one individual worker. A form of income taxation that is of particular interest is the taxation of **capital gains,** the earnings from selling capital assets, such as stocks, paintings, and houses.

capital gains Earnings from selling capital assets, such as stocks, paintings, and houses.

Taxes on Corporate Income

corporate income tax Tax levied on the earnings of corporations.

In addition to taxing individual income, many countries also separately tax the earnings of corporations through the **corporate income tax.** The purpose of the separate taxation of corporations, above and beyond taxes on individuals, is to tax earnings of owners of capital that might otherwise escape taxation by the individual-based income tax system.

Taxes on Wealth

wealth taxes Taxes paid on the value of the assets, such as real estate or stocks, held by a person or family.

property taxes A form of wealth tax based on the value of real estate, including the value of the land and any structures built on the land.

estate taxes A form of wealth tax based on the value of the estate left behind when one dies.

Wealth taxes are taxes paid not on income as it is accrued but on the value of the assets held by a person or family, such as land, jewelry, artwork, real estate, and stocks. Included in this category are state and local **property taxes,** which are based on the value of land and any structures built on the land, and **estate taxes,** which are based on bequests (money, property, and so on) left behind when one dies.

Taxes on Consumption

consumption tax A tax paid on individual or household consumption of goods (and sometimes services).

sales taxes Taxes paid by consumers to vendors at the point of sale.

excise tax A tax paid on the sales of particular goods, for example cigarettes or gasoline.

The form of taxation that is most common around the world is the **consumption tax,** which is paid on individual or household consumption of goods (and sometimes on services as well). Consumption taxes are often levied in the form of **sales taxes,** taxes that are paid by consumers to vendors at the point of sale. These taxes can be applied either to a broad variety of consumption goods or to a particular good alone. When applied to only certain goods, for example cigarettes or gasoline, the sales tax is called an **excise tax.**

Payroll, income, and wealth taxes are called *direct taxes* because they are assessed directly on individuals. Consumption taxes are called *indirect taxes* because they tax individuals indirectly by taxing their transactions.

Taxation Around the World

Figures 18-1 and 18-2 show the distribution of tax revenues across these different types of taxes in the United States and in other nations.[2] The U.S.

---

[2] Note that the figures for the U.S. differ somewhat from those in Figure 1-8, since these figures are percentages of tax revenue only, while in Chapter 1 we were examining shares of total revenues, including non-tax sources (such as lottery revenues at the state level).

■ FIGURE 18-1

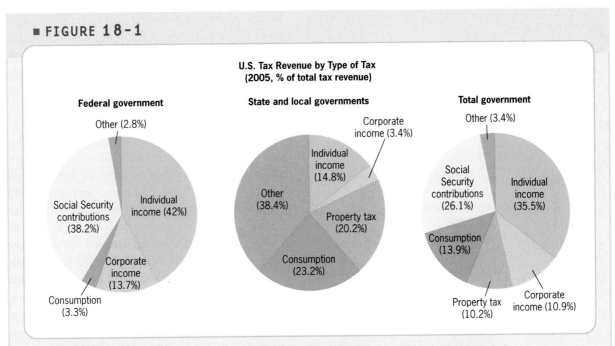

Tax Revenues by Type of Tax • Almost 85% of the federal government's tax revenue comes from individual income taxation (income and payroll taxes). For state and local governments, revenue is more evenly split among taxes on wealth (property), consumption, and individual income. In total, U.S. governments receive about two-thirds of their revenue from individual income taxes and payroll taxes.

■ FIGURE 18-2

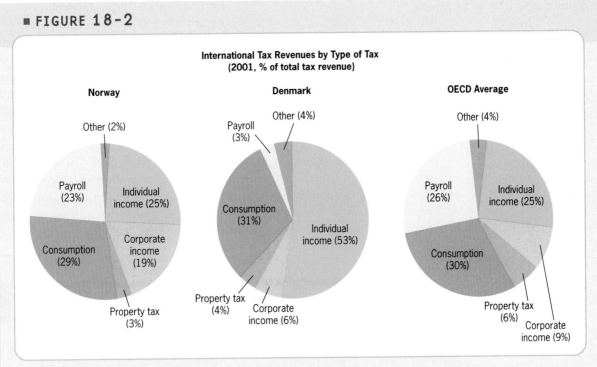

International Tax Revenues by Type of Tax • Consumption taxes provide a greater portion of national government revenue in all OECD countries than in the United States.

■ **TABLE 18-1**

Computing Jack's Income Tax

Gross income	$60,000
– Deductions	– $2,000
= Adjusted gross income (AGI)	= $58,000
– Exemptions	– $16,500
– Standard (or itemized) deduction	– $10,300 (or $9,000)
= Taxable income	= $31,200
Use income tax schedule (Figure 18–3)	
= Taxes owed	= $3,925
– Credits	– $3,000
= Total tax payment	= $925
– Withholding	– $2,000
= Final payment (refund) due	= ($1,075)

Jack has gross income of $60,000, from which he subtracts some deductions to get adjusted gross income (AGI). From AGI, he subtracts his family exemptions and either the standard deduction or itemized deductions (Jack chooses the former), yielding taxable income. A tax schedule is applied to determine taxes owed, and tax credits are then subtracted to arrive at the final tax payment.

federal government receives most of its tax revenue (43%) from the individual income tax, and another large share (39%) from payroll taxes. A more moderate share comes from the corporate income tax (14%), with very small shares from consumption and other taxes (such as wealth taxes).

The distribution of tax revenue sources at the state and local levels is quite different. For states and localities, individual income tax revenues are only 24% of total revenues, and corporate income tax revenues are even smaller than the federal level at 5% of the total. The two major sources of revenues for subnational governments in the United States are consumption taxes (both sales and excise taxes) and local property taxes on homes and commercial property. While some states collect payroll taxes, payroll tax data are not available at the state level. For the United States as a whole, combining all levels of government, the most revenues are raised by income taxation, followed by payroll taxes, and consumption taxes, while property taxes and corporate income taxes are about the same.

The distributions are quite different in other nations. Figure 18-2 shows the distribution of taxes in two sample countries with very different tax systems, Norway and Denmark, and then for the set of developed OECD nations as a whole. In Norway, revenue is raised almost equally from income taxes, payroll taxes, consumption taxes, and corporate income taxes, with a very small share of revenues from property taxation. In Denmark, in contrast, more than half (53.1%) of revenues are raised from individual income taxes, with a large portion of the remainder from consumption taxes; there are small shares from corporate income taxes, property taxes, and payroll taxes. On average, the other developed OECD nations have a share of tax revenues from consumption taxes that is about twice as large as that of the United States, a share from payroll taxes that is similar to that in the U.S., and smaller shares of tax revenues from individual income taxes, corporate income taxes, and property taxes.

18.2

Structure of the Individual Income Tax in the United States

As shown in the previous section, the most important source of revenue in the United States is the federal individual income tax. In this section, we review the structure of this tax, which is shown graphically in Table 18-1, both in general terms and with some sample calculations for an individual we'll call Jack.

Computing the Tax Base

The income tax calculation begins by adding up one's various sources of income to compute **gross income,** which is $60,000 for Jack. This includes wages and salaries; capital income, such as interest, dividends, or rental income; and other business income. Once the taxpayer determines his or her gross income, the taxpayer is allowed to adjust it downward by subtracting the amounts spent on several items; the amount that remains after these deductions is called **adjusted gross income (AGI).** These adjustments have varied over time, but as of 2004 they include:

▶ Contributions to retirement savings through Individual Retirement Accounts (IRAs) or self-employed pension plans

▶ Alimony paid to a former spouse

▶ Health insurance premiums paid by the self-employed

▶ One-half of the payroll taxes paid by the self-employed

In our example, Jack makes a $2,000 contribution to his IRA, so he deducts $2,000 from his gross income, leaving him with an AGI of $58,000.

The taxpayer then subtracts exemptions from AGI. An **exemption** is a fixed amount of money that can be deducted for the taxpayer, the taxpayer's spouse, and any other dependents who live in the house (such as children or elders who depend on the taxpayer and spouse for financial support). In 2006, the exemption amount was $3,300 per person.[3] Jack has a wife and three children, so he deducts a total of $16,500 in exemptions from his AGI.

After taking these exemptions, the taxpayer then gets to make further deductions from his or her taxable income. There are two forms of deductions from which to choose:

1. The **standard deduction** is a fixed amount that taxpayers can deduct from taxable income. In 2006, the standard deduction was $5,150 for single taxpayers and $10,300 for married couples.

2. Alternatively, taxpayers can forgo the standard deduction and choose **itemized deductions.** Under this route, the taxpayer deducts from his or her income the sum of amounts from several categories:

▶ Medical and dental expenses exceeding 7.5% of AGI

▶ Other taxes paid, such as state or local income tax (or sales tax if the state has no income tax), real estate tax, and personal property tax

▶ Interest the taxpayer pays on funds borrowed to make investments and on home mortgages

gross income The total of an individual's various sources of income.

adjusted gross income (AGI) An individual's gross income minus certain deductions, for example contributions to individual retirement accounts.

exemption A fixed amount a taxpayer can subtract from AGI for each dependent member of the household, as well as for the taxpayer and the taxpayer's spouse.

standard deduction Fixed amount that a taxpayer can deduct from taxable income.

itemized deductions Alternative to the standard deduction, whereby a taxpayer deducts the total amount of money spent on various expenses, such as gifts to charity and interest on home mortgages.

---

[3] Exemptions and some deduction amounts (discussed next) are *phased out* (begin to decline) for very high incomes (ranging from AGI above $109,475 for married persons filing separately to $218,950 for married persons filing jointly). Internal Revenue Service (2005a).

  ▶ Gifts to charity

  ▶ Casualty and theft losses

  ▶ Unreimbursed employee expenses, such as union dues or expenses incurred on job travel

Taxpayers are free to choose the method (standard or itemized deductions) that maximizes their deductions and minimizes their tax bill. Most home owners have sufficiently high mortgage interest and property tax payments that it makes sense to itemize. Jack has paid $6,000 in interest on his mortgage, paid $2,500 in state and local taxes, and has given $500 to charity, so his item- ized deductions total $9,000. Because this amount is less than the standard deduction for married couples ($10,300), he chooses the standard deduction. Nationwide, 65% of taxpayers chose the standard deduction in 2003, with the remaining 35% using itemized deductions.[4]

The remainder after subtracting exemptions and deductions from AGI is called **taxable income.** Jack's taxable income is $31,200.

taxable income The amount of income left after subtracting exemptions and deductions from adjusted gross income.

Tax Rates and Taxes Paid

The next step for Jack is to figure out the amount of tax he owes to the gov- ernment on his taxable income of $31,200. To find out how much he owes, Jack can look at a tax schedule, such as that shown in Figure 18-3. The typical tax system in the United States and around the world is one in which the tax rate on one's next dollar of income rises as income rises. For example, the 2006 U.S. tax rate schedule (for a married couple, filing taxes jointly) is:

  ▶ For any dollar of taxable income below $15,100, there is a tax of 10¢ on each dollar of taxable income.

  ▶ For the next $46,200 of taxable income, there is a tax of 15¢ on each dollar of taxable income.

  ▶ For the next $62,400, there is a tax of 25¢ on each dollar of taxable income.

  ▶ For the next $64,750, there is a tax of 28¢ on each dollar of taxable income.

  ▶ For the next $148,100, there is a tax of 33¢ on each dollar of taxable income.

  ▶ For all income above $336,550, there is a tax of 35¢ on each dollar of taxable income.

Applying this tax schedule, Jack owes $3,925 in taxes: he owes 10% of his first $15,100 of taxable income ($1,510) plus 15% of the remaining $16,100 of taxable income ($2,415).

Taxpayers can then reduce their tax payments through certain **tax cred- its,** flat amounts that are subtracted from taxes owed. These include credits

tax credits Amounts by which taxpayers are allowed to reduce the taxes they owe to the gov- ernment through spending, for example on child care.

---

[4] IRS statistics located at http://www.irs.gov/taxstats/article/0,,id=102886,00.html.

■ **FIGURE 18-3**

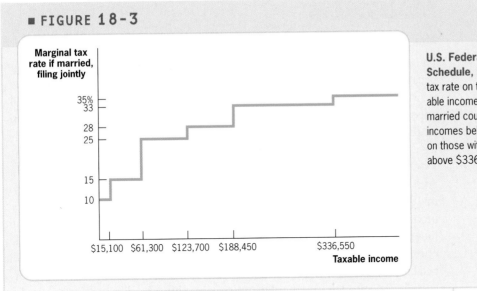

Marginal tax rate if married, filing jointly

35%
33
28
25

15

10

$15,100 $61,300 $123,700 $188,450 $336,550

Taxable income

U.S. Federal Income Tax Rate Schedule, 2006 • In 2006, the tax rate on the next dollar of taxable income varied from 10% on married couples with taxable incomes below $15,100 to 35% on those with taxable incomes above $336,550.

for having children (the Child Tax Credit), for paying for care of children and elderly dependents (the Credit for Child and Dependent Care Expenses), for being poor and either elderly or disabled (the Credit for the Elderly or Disabled), for paying for educational expenses of family members (the Hope and Lifetime Learning Credits), for hiring as employees welfare recipients, ex-felons, veterans, or other members of groups with high unemployment rates (the Work Opportunity Credit), and for earning income if family income is very low (the Earned Income Credit). Jack qualifies for a child credit of $3,000 for his three children, so that he now owes $925 ($3,925 − $3,000) in taxes.

The taxes for each year must be paid by April 15 of the following year. For most taxpayers, taxes are subtracted from their wage and salary income as it is earned, a process called **withholding**.[5] The amount withheld is an estimate of the taxes the worker will owe based on his or her earnings, but this estimate is rarely perfectly accurate. In Jack's case, for example, the government has withheld $2,000 from his earnings during the year. Thus, Jack is due a tax **refund** of $1,075, the difference between what was withheld from his earnings and the amount he owes in taxes. In other cases, withholding may fall short of taxes due, in which case the taxpayer must pay additional taxes when he files his tax return.

withholding The subtraction of estimated taxes owed directly from a worker's earnings.

refund The difference between the amount withheld from a worker's earnings and the taxes owed if the former is higher.

---

[5] There is also optional withholding for other forms of income, such as pension and transfer payments. Some taxpayers have large earnings in non-withheld forms, such as interest on savings or self-employment income; these taxpayers make *estimated tax payments* four times per year based on their best guess of their taxable income for that year.

▶APPLICATION

The Coming AMT Timebomb[6]

Figure 18-3 presents a somewhat simplified schedule of marginal tax rates because it does not account for features such as the Earned Income Tax Credit (a tax subsidy paid to low income earners to redistribute income while encouraging work, to be discussed in Chapter 21), or the **Alternative Minimum Tax (AMT),** an additional tax schedule that applies to taxpayers who have a very high ratio of deductions and exemptions to total income. In a 1969 televised hearing, Treasury Secretary Joseph W. Barr produced for Congress's Joint Economic Committee a list of 155 high-income households that in 1966 had earned over $200,000 ($1.1 million in 2004 dollars) but paid no income taxes whatsoever. None of these households, including the 21 with incomes over $1 million ($5.8 million in today's dollars), had committed a crime; they had simply taken advantage of existing tax laws to minimize their taxable income (through the types of exemptions and deductions just discussed). An outraged public demanded something be done about this and in 1969 President Nixon signed into law a minimum tax intended to ensure that all wealthy households paid some amount of income tax. By 1986, 659 wealthy American households still managed to avoid all income taxes, so Congress strengthened the law, now called the Alternative Minimum Tax.

All taxpayers who have high exemptions/deductions are required to compute their tax under both the regular schedule and the AMT. Under the AMT, you compute your income without the personal and dependent exemptions, the standard deduction, state and local tax write-offs, and other tax benefits. You then deduct the AMT exemption, which is $40,250 for individuals and $58,000 for joint filers. The remaining amount up to $175,000 is subject to a 26% tax, while income above $175,000 is taxed at 28%.

Congress did not index any of these AMT figures with inflation, so as nominal incomes have risen over time, more and more taxpayers have become subject to the AMT, which was originally intended to affect only the few taxpayers who would otherwise have avoided paying taxes altogether. By 2010, nearly one-third of all taxpayers (or a total of 31 million taxpayers) will be subject to the AMT, making it as common as the mortgage interest deduction is now. Ninety-four percent of households with income between $200,000 and $500,000 will pay the AMT, and 37% of AMT payers will have household incomes under $100,000 (in 2005 dollars).

Because the AMT calculations add so much complexity and increasingly apply to the middle class rather than the wealthy households originally targeted, there is broad political agreement for a reform that will once again make the AMT a last-resort tax that applies only to the very wealthy. The reform will, however, be expensive primarily because the 2001–2004 tax cuts introduced cuts into the regular income tax system without making any significant, lasting

Alternative Minimum Tax A tax schedule applied to taxpayers with a high ratio of deductions and exemptions to total income.

---

[6] Burman, Gale, and Rohaly (2003).

changes to the AMT. Before the 2001–2004 legislation, only 14% of taxpayers were slated to pay the AMT in 2010; after the legislation was passed, that number had risen to 31%. Furthermore, the recent tax cuts will more than double the share of AGI subject to the AMT in 2010 from 22% to 50%. By 2009, the AMT is projected to produce more revenue than the ordinary federal income tax and repealing it would cost $670 billion between 2006 and 2015. As of this writing, neither political party has been willing to shoulder the responsibility for addressing this problem.[7] ◄

18.3
Measuring the Fairness of Tax Systems

In March 1990, rioters in London set fire to parked Jaguars and Porsches, smashed store windows, destroyed a Renault showroom, and ultimately caused the injury of over 400 people and the arrest of nearly 350 people. The cause of the riot was a tax reform proposal by British Prime Minister Margaret Thatcher's government. Thatcher had proposed to replace the system of property taxes (based on real estate value) with a poll tax, a flat charge levied equally on all individuals, regardless whether they were rich, poor, or somewhere in between. The proposal provoked enormous outrage because the tax burden was being shifted away from wealthy citizens owning valuable property and onto poorer citizens, who didn't previously pay property taxes but would now have to pay the poll tax. Because of the poll tax's unpopularity, Thatcher was eventually ousted as leader of the Conservative Party and the proposal was quickly abandoned. Thatcher may have gotten off easily: the last attempt to impose such a tax in England, in 1381, led to the beheading of several prominent citizens.[8]

As this example illustrates, tax *fairness* is an important concern to citizens worldwide. Yet fairness is an elusive goal: what is a fair tax system to me may seem unfair to you. To carry out the evaluation of a tax system's fairness requires a particular concept of fairness, or *equity,* and a means of measuring how a tax system redistributes income to make the distribution more equitable. This section defines the common concepts that are used to measure fairness and the statistics that are used to assess whether tax systems meet those fairness goals. But we must first define some important terms that are used to measure the distributional nature of tax systems.

Average and Marginal Tax Rates

Two key concepts describe the set of tax rates on income. The first is the **marginal tax rate,** the percentage of the next dollar of taxable income that is paid in taxes. With a system such as that in the United States, the marginal tax rate rises with income; for those with taxable income below $15,100, the

marginal tax rate The percentage that is paid in taxes of the next dollar earned.

---

[7] Burman, Gale, and Rohaly (2005 update).
[8] Slemrod and Bakija (2000), p. 49.

marginal tax rate is 10%, but for those with taxable income above $336,550, the marginal tax rate is 35%.

The second concept is the **average tax rate,** the percentage of total income that is paid in taxes, which is computed as the ratio of total tax payments to total income. The average tax rate for any individual is a weighted average of the marginal rates the individual pays as he or she moves along the tax schedule. For example, suppose that Josh has gross income of $150,000, and has taxable income (after adjustments, deductions, and exemptions) of $130,000 (and no tax credits). His total tax bill is

$$(\$14{,}600 \times 0.1) + (\$44{,}800 \times 0.15) + (\$60{,}550 \times 0.25) + (\$10{,}050 \times 0.28) = \$26{,}131.50.$$

We compute Josh's total tax bill by walking him up the marginal rate schedule until we get to his income level. Josh's marginal rate is 28% because this is the rate he pays on his next dollar of income. His average tax rate is 17.4%, which is his tax bill ($26,131.50) divided by his gross income ($150,000); this is a weighted average of all the marginal rates Josh is paying, where the weights are the share of his income in each tax bracket (including the $20,000 of his income that is not taxed, and therefore faces a zero marginal rate)

Vertical and Horizontal Equity

Two distributional goals are frequently considered in measuring tax fairness. The first is **vertical equity,** the principle that groups with more resources (higher income, higher wealth, higher profits) should pay higher taxes than do lower-resource groups. This idea is related to the concept of equity discussed in Chapters 2 and 17, which referred to the distribution of resources between higher- and lower-income (or –ability) groups. Concerns over vertical equity in taxation could be motivated, for example, by a utilitarian social welfare function that calls for redistribution from lower to higher marginal utility of consumption groups in society.

Another concept of equity that is often raised in tax policy discussions is **horizontal equity,** the principle that individuals who are similar but who make different economic or lifestyle choices should be treated in the same way by the tax system. Consider two state sales tax systems. One state sets a sales tax of 5% on all goods. Another state implements a system whereby whenever you make a purchase the cashier flips a coin, and you pay no sales tax if it is heads and a 10% sales tax if it is tails. This latter system will raise the same amount of money as the former system on average, but it is much less horizontally equitable because two identical individuals could end up paying very different taxes.

This extreme example clearly illustrates a horizontal inequity, but in reality horizontal inequities are hard to define. Imagine that my friend and I are identical in terms of intelligence, education, and motivation. I choose to spend more of my time at home with my children, while my friend chooses to spend more time on his job. Even though we are the same in many respects, my friend has higher income than I do, and will pay higher income taxes as a result.

average tax rate The percentage of total income that is paid in taxes.

vertical equity The principle that groups with more resources should pay higher taxes than groups with fewer resources.

horizontal equity The principle that similar individuals who make different economic choices should be treated similarly by the tax system.

Does this outcome violate horizontal equity? On the one hand, we have different amounts of income, so we pay different taxes, which seems horizontally equitable. On the other hand, we are two identical people in terms of abilities and underlying resources, yet because of the different choices we have made we pay different amounts of taxes, which seems horizontally inequitable.

Whenever the amount of taxes paid depends on choices made by individuals, such a dilemma will exist: individuals of identical underlying resources who make different choices will pay different amounts of tax. The only time that horizontal inequities are unambiguous is when taxes differ for reasons independent of choice, such as in the previous random taxation example. Thus, violations of horizontal equity are ultimately in the eye of the beholder, an unfortunate fact because horizontal equity concerns are constantly raised in tax debates and are often distorted to fit the views of the proponents or opponents of a particular tax proposal.[9]

Measuring Vertical Equity

While horizontal equity is often difficult to define and measure, there are more standard measures of vertical equity that are central to debates over tax policy. Most analysts conclude that to be vertically equitable tax systems must be **progressive:** effective average tax rates must rise with income, so that the rich pay a higher share of their income in taxes than do the poor. (For example, a progressive tax system would be one in which individuals pay 10% of their income in tax at an income of $10,000, but they pay 30% of their income in tax at an income of $100,000.) Tax systems in which the effective average tax rate does not change with income are **proportional** tax systems, since everyone pays the same proportion of his or her income in taxes. (For example, individuals pay 15% of income in taxes regardless of whether they earn $10,000 or $100,000.) Tax systems in which effective average tax rates fall with income are **regressive** tax systems. (For example, individuals pay 15% of their income in tax at an income of $10,000, but pay only 10% of their income in tax at an income of $100,000.)

> **progressive** Tax systems in which effective average tax rates rise with income.
>
> **proportional** Tax systems in which effective average tax rates do not change with income, so that all taxpayers pay the same proportion of their income in taxes.
>
> **regressive** Tax systems in which effective average tax rates fall with income.

▶ **APPLICATION**

The Political Process of Measuring Tax Fairness[10]

As the previous discussion suggests, measuring tax fairness can be challenging. There are several different ways to measure fairness, and politicians are likely to choose the one that best fits their agendas in advocating or opposing a tax change. An excellent example of this process is the debate over the income tax cuts proposed by President Bush and signed into law by Congress in 2003.

---

[9] Vertical and horizontal equity are illustrations of the "ability to pay" approach to tax fairness. There is an entirely different approach called the "benefits" approach, which states that tax fairness should be measured by comparing the tax burdens born by individuals to the benefits they receive from the public sector. This principle is rarely used in tax policy debates, but we do discuss the importance of tax-benefit linkages in Chapter 20.

[10] Lee and Friedman (2003).

These tax cuts accelerated already scheduled reductions in income tax rates, expanded tax breaks for married couples, increased the credit paid to families with children, and increased tax breaks for corporations.

Democratic critics opposed these tax cuts on grounds of "fairness." They pointed out, for example, that 44% of the tax reductions from this bill would go to the top 1% of taxpayers. The Bush administration acknowledged that fact but responded by pointing out that these top taxpayers already pay 38% of all income taxes. So this reduction in their tax bill was roughly in proportion to their existing income tax payments. Thus, in the view of the bill's proponents, this was a fair reduction in taxes for those paying the most in taxation today.

Democrats responded by highlighting that while the top 1% of taxpayers pay 38% of income taxes, they pay only 30% of *all taxes,* since our payroll tax system is less progressive than our income tax system (because the payroll tax rate is flat rather than rising, and because the base of taxation for OASDI taxes is capped for high earners). So the top 1% was getting a tax break (44% of the tax cut) that was far out of proportion to its share of total payments (30% of total taxes paid). This, they contended, was unfair.

The administration fired back by noting that 34 million families with children would receive an average tax cut of $1,549 each. But critics noted that this was a misleading use of the word "average." These average figures were inflated by the fact that the lion's share of the tax cut accrues to households with the highest incomes. As economist and *New York Times* columnist Paul Krugman put it, "When Bill Gates enters a bar, the average net worth of the patrons soars, but that doesn't make everyone in the bar a billionaire."[11] While it is true that 34 million families with children would get a $1,549 tax cut on average, this average consisted of both 10 million families that would receive a tax cut of less than $100 and 200,000 families (with incomes over $1 million per year) receiving a $93,500 tax cut. Families in the middle of the income distribution received an average tax cut of only $217.

As is often said in Washington, D.C., where you stand on an issue depends on where you sit. For most Republicans, this tax cut fairly rewarded those who were most burdened by the current income tax. For most Democrats, this tax cut unfairly rewarded the rich out of proportion to their current overall tax burden. Neither party to the debate really emphasized the economist's generally preferred measure of the distributional effects of tax policies, which is how they affect the after-tax distribution of income. Progressive tax reforms will narrow the after-tax distribution of income; regressive tax reforms will widen it. According to the non-partisan Tax Policy Center's evaluations of both the 2001 and 2003 tax cuts, the lowest quintile of the income distribution saw their after-tax incomes rise by 0.5% as a result of these tax cuts, while the top quintile saw their after-tax incomes rise by 3.4%, and the top 0.1% of taxpayers saw their after-tax incomes rise by 7.5%. Clearly, by this measure, the tax changes were highly regressive, resulting in a widening in the after-tax distribution of incomes.[12]

---

[11] Krugman (2003).
[12] Data from TPC Web site.

18.4

Defining the Income Tax Base

As was clear from Table 18-1, income taxes are not determined by simply taking all income accrued during the year and applying a tax rate schedule. In the U.S. tax system, as in most other income tax systems, there are a variety of tax exemptions, deductions, and credits that cause the tax base to be smaller than total income. What are the rationales for these "holes" in the tax base? What are their implications for the equity of the tax system? In this section, we discuss the theoretically appropriate income tax base and carefully review the sources of deviation of income taxes from that theoretical ideal and their implications.

The Haig-Simons Comprehensive Income Definition

The benchmark that public finance economists use for defining income is the **Haig-Simons comprehensive income definition,** which defines taxable resources as an individual's *ability to pay taxes.* This ability to pay is equal to an individual's *potential annual consumption,* the individual's total consumption during the year, plus any increases in his or her stock of wealth.

The U.S. tax system deviates from the Haig-Simons standard in many ways. For example, the amount employers spend on employer-provided health insurance is not currently included in taxable employee income, but it would be included under a Haig-Simons definition because it contributes to an individual's ability to consume: because you don't have to pay for health insurance yourself, you have that much more of your income to spend on other things or to save.

Does the Haig-Simons definition make sense as a goal of tax-base design? Recall that there are two aspects to measuring the equity of a tax system. Vertical equity is achieved when high-income taxpayers pay a larger share of their income in taxes and horizontal equity is achieved when identical taxpayers pay the same amount in taxation regardless of their choices.

Using the Haig-Simons income definition to determine the base on which taxes are paid improves vertical equity because those who have more resources pay more tax, even though they get those resources through a nontaxed channel (such as with employer-provided health insurance). Thus, if you and I have the same cash wages, but I have more valuable health insurance, I should pay more tax.

The Haig-Simons approach also improves horizontal equity by ensuring that people who are the same in terms of their underlying resources pay the same amount of tax regardless of the form in which they choose to receive or spend their resources. Under the current U.S. system, if I choose to take my compensation in wages and you choose instead to take part of your compensation in the form of employer-provided health insurance, you pay less tax than I do. Moving to a Haig-Simons approach, which treats all forms of compensation as income, would improve horizontal equity.

> **Haig-Simons comprehensive income definition** Defines taxable resources as the change in an individual's power to consume during the year.

Thus, adhering to a Haig-Simons definition could greatly improve the equity of a tax system along both vertical and horizontal equity dimensions. However, implementing a Haig-Simons definition in practice is challenging. In the remainder of this section, we discuss two of the major difficulties with implementing a Haig-Simons definition in the U.S. tax system: (a) the difficulty of how to define a person's power to consume/ability to pay, and (b) how to deal with expenditures that are associated with earning a living and not personal consumption.

Deviations Due to Ability-to-Pay Considerations

The first difficulty with implementing Haig-Simons is the question of how to define an individual's ability to pay taxes. Suppose two individuals have the same income in any year but that one suffers a large fire in his home and has to spend 20% of his income to repair the damage. In that year, this person will have lower consumption and increases in wealth, or a lower ability to pay taxes, and this should be reflected by adjusting his tax base. The desire to take into account expenditures that are not associated with desired consumption is the rationale for one of the major deductions from taxable income allowed by the tax code, the deduction for *property and casualty losses*.

Another major deduction that may be justified on ability-to-pay considerations is the deduction for *medical expenditures*. Itemizers can deduct from their taxable income any medical expenditures that exceed 7.5% of their AGI. The motivation for this deduction is that large medical expenditures are not a choice but are beyond the taxpayer's control, like the fire.

As we discussed in Chapter 15, however, this assumption may not be valid in the context of medical spending. When individuals have some control over their level of medical spending, a part of that spending may be consumption, and thus should be included in Haig-Simons income. By providing the medical expenditure deduction, the government may be subsidizing that optional part of medical consumption. The ideal tax system would provide a deduction only for nondiscretionary medical expenditures. The key question is whether 7.5% of income is "high enough" so that it covers only large expenditures over which individuals have little control.

Another deduction that is often justified on ability-to-pay grounds is the deduction for *state and local tax payments*. If Jim and Rob have the same income, but Jim lives in a state or town with high taxes and Rob lives in a state or town with low taxes, then some argue that Jim has a lower ability to pay federal income taxes, so state and local taxes should be subtracted from his Haig-Simons income. The problem with this argument, however, is that Jim's higher taxes are also buying him a higher level of state and local public goods. Indeed, if Jim lived in a perfect Tiebout equilibrium, then his local taxes would simply be the user fee he was happily paying for his local public goods. Since at least some of the state and local taxes collected from individuals are providing them with valuable benefits, full deductibility of state and local tax payments is hard to justify on Haig-Simons grounds.

Deviations Due to Costs of Earning Income

Another rationale for deviations from Haig–Simons is that some expenditures are not for consumption but rather reflect the cost of earning a living. Because the comprehensive income definition refers only to the *net* increment to resources over the period, any legitimate costs of doing business should be deducted from a person's income.

Difficulties arise in defining "legitimate" business costs, however. Consider business meals. Suppose that you have a new business and you have two types of promotion expenditures: magazine ads and lunches with prospective clients. Advertising expenditures are fully deductible from your reported business income as a cost of doing business, but lunches are not. Why are lunches different? Because you are deriving some consumption value yourself from those lunches, and this consumption value should be included in your Haig–Simons income. In theory, you should only be able to deduct from your income the total cost of the lunch minus your own consumption value from that lunch.

This point seems to have been gradually realized by U.S. policy makers. Up until 1962, businesses were allowed to deduct expenses related to business entertainment, which included meals. After President Kennedy's 1961 call for a crackdown on this business tax advantage, the Revenue Act of 1962 required that deduction claimants supply proof to demonstrate the "business purpose" of each entertainment claim. In the case of business meals and drinks, however, Congress said that no business discussion need occur before, during, or after the meal. The only requirement was that the meal be under circumstances "of a type generally considered to be conducive to a business discussion." Thus meals remained 100% deductible.

In the 1976 presidential election, Jimmy Carter campaigned vigorously against the "$50 three-martini lunch," but, though he won the election, he was never able to reduce the 100% deduction to the 50% he desired. The first reduction occurred under President Reagan, who reduced the deduction rate to 80% in 1987 (under the 1986 Tax Reform Act). In 1994, under President Clinton, business meals became only 50% deductible.

▶ APPLICATION

What Are Appropriate Business Deductions?

In the movie *Ghostbusters*, lovable loser Louis is an accountant throwing a big party one evening. He brags to his guests that the smoked salmon cost $24.95 a pound, but only $14.12 after tax. How? Because of an accounting trick, he explains: "I'm giving this whole thing as a promotional expense. That's why I invited clients instead of friends."

As Louis's explanation points out, the U.S. tax code distinguishes between expenditures for business and expenditures for pleasure: the former are wholly or partially deductible from one's taxable income, while the latter are not. Yet Louis's party shows how vague this distinction is. The difficulties in defining an appropriate, or inappropriate, business deduction are well illustrated by some classic examples from U.S. tax law[13]:

▶ A high school geography teacher claimed a $5,047, six-month, 18-country world tour as a business expense. Visiting Victoria Falls, South Africa, Rio (during Carnival week), Tahiti, and Australia helped him, the teacher claimed, to collect experiences and slides of exotic places to aid his teaching. The tax court disallowed the deduction, concluding that "any actual educational benefit gained from these experiences was de minimis."

▶ A rabbi claimed as a business expense the $4,031 he spent on 700 guests who attended his son's bar mitzvah. The rabbi claimed that his position obliged him to invite all 725 families from his congregation to the celebration. The tax court disagreed, finding that the rabbi "was not required to invite the entire membership of the congregation to David's bar mitzvah service and reception as a condition of his employment."

▶ A man claimed $30,000 worth of business expenses for the costs of goods he was selling in 1981. The goods? Amphetamines, cocaine, and marijuana. The IRS disallowed the deductions because the man hadn't documented his business thoroughly, but a tax court overturned the decision based on his candid testimony about his business practices. Allowed to claim the deductions, he was then sentenced by a criminal court to four years in prison for possessing cocaine with intent to distribute it.

▶ The entertainer Dinah Shore claimed several dresses as business expenses, prompting an investigation by the IRS. She argued that the gowns had been worn only onstage during her performances. In what is now called the "Dinah Shore ruling," the IRS decreed that a dress may be deducted as a business expense only if it is too tight to sit down in!

▶ Traditionally, U.S. companies were at a disadvantage in international business efforts because other countries (but not the United States) allowed their companies to write off as a business expense the cost of bribing foreign officials! The United States, in 1996, convinced 26 OECD nations to revise their tax codes so that such bribes were no longer considered a deductible expense. ◀

18.5

Externality/Public Goods Rationales for Deviating from Haig-Simons

One classic rationale for deviations from a comprehensive income definition is the possibility that reducing taxes on certain activities will yield external benefits to society. In this section, we discuss two major deviations from the Haig-Simons

[13] Reid (1981a,b), Swardson (1986).

definition that are typically justified by the fact that the private market is likely to underprovide some good or activity: charitable giving and housing expenditures.

Charitable Giving

An excellent example of the application of the external benefits rationale is that donations to charitable organizations can be deducted from taxable income. Because of the free rider problem discussed in Chapter 7 (when costs are private but benefits are public, individuals will underprovide public goods), the private market is likely to underprovide charitable support for many public goods.

Suppose, for example, that the government is concerned that the private sector is not providing sufficient funds to build shelters for the homeless, which is a classic case of a public good. One way to address this problem would be to subsidize charitable giving to the homeless in order to increase private sector support, and one means of subsidizing charitable giving is to allow individuals to deduct from their taxable income the amount they give to charity. By doing so, the government makes charitable giving cheap relative to other types of consumption, which must be financed by after-tax dollars. The tax system in the United States allows those who itemize their deductions to subtract contributions to charitable organizations from taxable income.

Suppose that Ellie is deciding whether to buy a $1 cup of coffee or to donate $1 to a homeless shelter. If she spends the $1 on coffee, she will have to pay income tax on that dollar at a tax rate τ. So to get $1 worth of coffee, Ellie will have to earn $\$1/(1 - \tau)$ first. For example, if her tax rate is 50%, then she will have to earn $2 to buy a $1 cup of coffee. If Ellie spends the dollar on the donation, however, she doesn't pay any tax on the dollar. So she can use $1 of her earnings to give $1 to the shelter. Thus, the *relative price* of charitable giving, relative to other consumption, is $\$1/[(\$1/(1 - \tau)]$, or $\$(1 - \tau)$. At a tax rate of 50%, the relative price of charitable giving is only 50¢ because Ellie has to earn $1 to get a 50¢ cup of coffee, but she only has to earn 50¢ to give 50¢ to charity. This tax treatment yields a benefit (it makes giving to charity much more attractive) at the cost of deviating from the Haig-Simons standard, since the part of taxable income given to charity is not taxed, so taxes are applied to a less-than-comprehensive measure of ability to pay.

There is another approach the government could take to support the provision of the public good, however; it could provide the good itself. Rather than indirectly inducing private individuals to raise their charitable contributions by giving them a tax break, the government could simply spend its own money to improve homeless shelters. So why does the government choose to deviate from the Haig-Simons standard rather than increase government spending? There are at least two possible reasons.

Spending Crowd-Out Versus Tax Subsidy Crowd-In

First, as we discussed in Chapter 7, government provision may crowd out private contributions to the public good. If the government subsidizes homeless shelters, the amount of private charitable giving to those shelters would most likely fall.

When the government tax subsidizes charitable giving, however, it may "crowd in," or increase, private contributions. This occurs because the government tax subsidy lowers the relative price of charitable giving. A lower relative price for charitable giving increases private giving, through both substitution effects (the "price" of charitable giving has fallen) and income effects (because Ellie is paying fewer taxes, she is richer and can give more to charity).

Marginal Versus Inframarginal Effects of Tax Subsidies At the same time, when the government tax subsidizes charitable giving, it is also giving a tax break to those who *would have already supported the homeless even without this tax break.* This may be viewed as horizontally equitable, since the tax break applies to everyone who is giving to charity. But it adds significantly to the cost of this "hole" in the Haig-Simons base: the government subsidizes not only new giving to charity but also old giving to charity that would have existed even without this tax break.

For example, suppose that there would be $1 million of private giving to the homeless without any tax break. The government then allows individuals to deduct charitable giving from their taxable income, at a 50% tax rate, and this raises giving to the homeless to $1.5 million. The government has therefore encouraged $500,000 in new giving through this tax break, achieving its goal of expanding private giving. Yet for those who would have given the $1 million anyway, there is also now a $500,000 tax break that rewards what they were already doing.

When economists discuss the impact of tax breaks such as that for charitable contributions, they often distinguish the *marginal* and *inframarginal* impacts of these tax breaks. The **marginal impacts** are the changes in behavior the government hopes to encourage by offering this tax incentive. In the case of charitable giving, the government wants to encourage people to give more to charity; in our example, the marginal impact is the $500,000 increase in giving to the homeless that was encouraged by the tax subsidy to giving. The **inframarginal impacts** are the tax breaks the government gives to those whose behavior is not changed by this policy. In the case of charitable giving, the inframarginal impact is the revenue lost in rewarding (with a tax break) those who were going to give to charity anyway; in our example, the inframarginal impact is $500,000 in new tax deductions offered to those individuals who were going to give to the homeless even without this tax incentive.

What determines the efficiency of a tax break designed to encourage behavior (such as increasing charitable giving) is the share of the tax break that goes to those who are changing their behavior versus the share going to those whose behavior is unaffected. The most cost-efficient tax breaks have large marginal impacts that come from those who change their behavior. In that case, a relatively small government expenditure can deliver large marginal impacts. The least cost-efficient tax breaks have small marginal impacts and large revenue costs because of those who were already engaging in the subsidized behavior. In that case, there can be very large government expenditures without much of a marginal impact.

marginal impacts Changes in behavior the government hopes to encourage through a given tax incentive.

inframarginal impacts Tax breaks the government gives to those whose behavior is not changed by new tax policy.

Effects of Tax Subsidies Versus Direct Spending Thus, there is a trade-off to be considered when deciding which of these two approaches to use, direct spending or tax subsidies. If the government spends the money directly, it raises the public resources available to the homeless but, through crowd-out, potentially lowers the private resources available. If the government provides a tax break, it induces new giving but also spends money to subsidize existing giving. This trade-off can be summarized with the following question: If the government has a dollar of revenue that it wants to spend on charitable causes such as homeless shelters, what is the best way to spend that dollar? Mathematically, the government should use a tax break instead of direct spending if:

the increase in charity per dollar of tax break >
            1 − the reduction in charity per dollar of government spending.

If this inequality holds, the government can increase the total amount of charitable giving by tax subsidizing private charity rather than directly spending its revenues on charitable goods or services.

Evidence on Crowd-Out Versus Crowd-In There are a large number of studies that have endeavored to estimate the effect of tax subsidies on charitable giving. The general conclusion of these studies is that the elasticity of charitable giving with respect to its subsidy is about −1: for each 1% reduction in the relative price of charitable giving, the amount of giving rises by 1%. This means that the increase in charity (the *marginal* effect of the tax subsidy) equals the tax revenues lost from tax breaks to existing giving (the *inframarginal* effect of the tax subsidy). This corresponds to the previous example. The elasticity is −1 since a fall in the tax price of 50% raises charitable contributions by 50%; the $500,000 increase in contributions is exactly equal to the $500,000 in lost revenues from existing givers.

The extent of government crowd-out referenced in the right-hand side of the inequality is unclear and depends on a variety of factors, as discussed in Chapter 7. The available evidence suggests some, but less than complete, crowd out (between 10 and 70%). Thus, $1 of government spending raises overall spending by 30 to 90¢. This gives us the right-hand side of the equation above (1 − the reduction in charity per dollar of government spending = 0.3 to 0.9).

Thus, it appears that, using this criterion, subsidizing private giving is a more efficient way of providing resources to the homeless than direct spending. Subsidies to private giving deliver $1 in new spending for each $1 in reduced government revenues, while direct spending delivers only 30¢–90¢ in new spending for each $1 in increased government spending (due to private crowd-out).

Consumer Sovereignty Versus Imperfect Information

In addition to being a more efficient means of increasing charitable giving, tax subsidization may also be preferred to direct government spending on consumer sovereignty grounds. When the government provides spending directly, then it imposes its preferences on how the funds are spent. The types of government failures discussed in Chapter 9 suggest that the preferences of legislators may not be the same as those of citizens. By offering tax subsidies to private individuals to donate as they wish, the government directly respects the preferences of its citizens.

The disadvantage of this decentralized provision of charity is that the private sector may not have the appropriate mechanisms in place to ensure efficient distribution of charitable spending. This issue is highlighted by a number of recent stories, such as this 2003 story from the *New York Times*:

> The American Relief Organization, a nonprofit, tax-exempt group based in Phoenix, raises money throughout the United States, mainly through telephone solicitation. Its mission is "to provide food, clothes, medical and school supplies for needy and abused children, homeless people and Native Americans on reservations," but its tax return indicates that it raised $665,844 in 2001 and donated $6,424. Its grants, which included items like a "disposable camera and developing of pictures" for $11, made up about 1 percent of the total it collected. The rest went to expenses, including salaries totaling more than $450,000.[14]

Of course, there are also inefficiencies in direct government provision of public goods. The important question, to which there is no clear answer at this point, is whether the private or public sector is more effective at translating each dollar of charitable spending into beneficial outcomes.

Housing

A second example of a deviation from Haig-Simons that is potentially justified on externality grounds is the *tax subsidy to home ownership*. Suppose that you are looking for a place to live and you find a home you like with a market rental value of $1,000 per month. The owner offers to either rent it to you for $1,000 per month or sell it to you for $100,000. To finance that $100,000 purchase, you would have to take a home loan, a **mortgage,** with interest payments of $1,000 per month (in this example). Your tax rate is 50%, and you earn $4,000 per month.

A true Haig-Simons approach to defining your income in either case would be to add to your income the net consumption value to you from living in that home, and to subtract the cost to you of doing so. Whether you rent or own, you are consuming $1,000 worth of housing services each month, which we call the *imputed rental value* of your home. And, in either case, you are paying $1,000 for the right to live in that home.[15] So your Haig-Simons tax burden would be unaffected by your decision to rent or buy.

The current U.S. tax system does not include the rental value of one's home in taxable income. Nevertheless, the income tax does allow individuals

mortgage Agreement to use a certain property, usually a home, as security for a loan.

---

[14] Stamler (2003).

[15] If you buy the home, you may also be paying some money each month toward the principal on your mortgage. This doesn't affect the Haig-Simons tax burden, since you are simply converting one form of asset (cash) into another (housing).

to deduct mortgage interest from their taxable income—but does not allow them to deduct rental payments. Under the U.S. tax system, if you decide to buy, your taxable income is reduced from $4,000 to $3,000, and you pay only $1,500 in taxes. If you decide to rent, however, you pay taxes on the full $4,000, for a tax burden of $2,000. Because of this mortgage interest deduction there is a financial advantage to buying rather than renting. This subsidy is a major budgetary cost to the government: the federal tax revenues forgone by allowing mortgage interest deductions are $80 billion per year (that is, if the mortgage interest deduction were ended, federal tax revenues would rise by $80 billion per year).

Why Subsidize Home Ownership? The most common justification provided for this subsidy to home ownership in the United States is that home ownership has *positive externalities* that renting does not. As Glaeser and Shapiro (2002) write: "To its supporters, the home mortgage interest deduction is the cornerstone of American society. Home ownership gives people a stake in society and induces them to care about their neighborhoods and towns. By subsidizing property ownership, the deduction induces people to invest and then to have a stake in our democracy. Ownership makes people vote for long-run investments instead of short-run transfers."

Glaeser and Shapiro reviewed a large body of empirical evidence that supports the existence of these positive externalities: relative to renting, home ownership is positively correlated with political activism and social connection, and home owners take better care of their properties, leading to a higher value for surrounding houses (a positive financial externality for their neighbors). Unfortunately, however, the empirical research in this area has yet to convincingly deal with the types of problems we discussed in Chapter 3. Those who own homes may be more inclined to social connection and better maintenance regardless of their ownership status. That is, the set of persons who buy homes might be the types of persons who would have presented these characteristics even if they were renting. This is the classic bias problem we encountered in Chapter 3, and it has been difficult to find a means of surmounting it in the context of home ownership. Thus, there is yet to be compelling, unbiased evidence for positive externalities associated with home ownership.

Effect of Tax Subsidies for Housing There is a large body of evidence that suggests that this tax subsidy to home ownership increases expenditures on housing, with an elasticity of spending with respect to tax subsidies of roughly 1; that is, each dollar of tax subsidies leads to $1 more spending on housing.[16] At the same time, there is no evidence that this subsidy causes more people to buy homes. Indeed, despite wide variation in this tax subsidy, the home ownership rate has remained essentially constant since the 1950s, at about 65%. Given that the tax subsidy doesn't appear to increase

---

[16] Rosen (1985).

home ownership but does increase housing expenditures, it appears that the tax subsidy is inducing individuals to spend more on houses they would have bought anyway, even without the tax subsidy.

Most arguments for positive externalities, however, focus on the benefits from home ownership, not the benefits from having larger, more expensive houses. Thus, even if there are externalities from ownership, the existing subsidy does little to address this issue. This finding suggests that the case for tax subsidizing of home ownership is weak on positive externality grounds.

From the evidence that the home mortgage interest deduction does not have external benefits, there is no clear rationale for this deviation from the Haig-Simons comprehensive income definition. Yet the home mortgage deduction remains one of the most popular provisions in the tax code, and politicians rarely criticize or try to limit this provision. The likely reason is that discussed in Chapter 9: the beneficiaries of this subsidy are organized and aware of its benefits, while the losers (taxpayers in general, who have to pay $80 billion more each year in taxes) are neither organized nor aware of the cost.[17] Nevertheless, if policy makers want to subsidize home ownership, there are much more efficient and equitable ways to do so, such as the first-time home buyer's credit discussed in Gale et al. (2006), which would directly subsidize first-time home purchase through a tax credit rather than allowing a deduction for mortgage interest paid.

Tax Deductions Versus Tax Credits

tax deductions Amounts by which taxpayers are allowed to reduce their taxable income through spending on items such as charitable donations or home mortgage interest.

Another important question that arises when a tax system deviates from the Haig-Simons comprehensive income definition is whether to apply those deviations in the form of tax deductions or tax credits. **Tax deductions** allow taxpayers to reduce their *taxable income* by a certain amount (e.g., the amount of charitable giving or home mortgage interest deduction); deductions therefore lower the price of the behavior in question to $\$(1 - \tau)$, where τ is the marginal tax rate. *Tax credits* allow taxpayers to reduce the *amount of tax they owe* to the government by a certain amount (e.g., the amount they spend on child care). If an individual's expenditure is less than the amount of the credit, the tax credit lowers the price of the behavior in question to zero.

Efficiency Considerations Which approach is preferable? The answer is unclear on efficiency grounds. For example, consider replacing the current deductibility of charitable giving with a 100% tax credit for charitable giving up to $1,000. For those who are giving less than $1,000 now, the credit provides a much stronger incentive to increase giving up to the $1,000 level, since it is free (tax payments fall by $1 for each dollar of giving). Once a person gives more than $1,000, there is no more benefit from the tax credit. The deduction, however, continues to provide some incentive to give even beyond the $1,000 limit (after the credit's incentive has run out). The trade-off the

---

[17] U.S. Joint Committee on Taxation (2006).

government faces is between a system that subsidizes all giving partially (the deduction), versus one that subsidizes some giving fully and some not at all (the credit).

Which policy, deduction or credit, is more efficient is dictated by two considerations. The first is the nature of the demand for the subsidized good. Our discussions in this book have generally assumed constant elasticities of demand for goods, but in reality elasticities of demand may differ depending on the magnitude of the price change. For some goods, individual demand may be very elastic in response to large reductions in the price, but not very elastic in response to small reductions in price; in such cases, credits may cause a larger increase in charitable giving (for example) than deductions, since credits lead to larger reductions in price.

Second, policy makers must decide how important it is to achieve some minimal level of the behavior. With charitable giving, for example, there is no obvious reason why $1,000 should be the target, so it may be better to simply subsidize individuals to give as much as they like. With some behaviors, however, the government may want to subsidize some minimal level of provision but not subsidize a particularly generous provision. As we discussed in Chapter 15, health insurance probably fits this case, where the government may want to subsidize individuals so they can have some basic level of coverage but does not want to subsidize expensive health insurance on the margin. Similarly, with the subsidy to housing, we may want to subsidize some basic level of housing consumption but not particularly large houses that don't have obvious external benefits.

Equity Considerations On vertical equity grounds, tax credits are more equitable than deductions. The value of a deduction rises with one's tax rate, and therefore one's income, making deductions *regressive* (deduction amounts are higher, as a share of income, for higher-income taxpayers). Credits, on the other hand, are available equally to all incomes, so that they are *progressive* (credit amounts are lower, as a share of income, for higher-income taxpayers). This difference is further heightened by the nature of the itemized deductions in our tax system. The rate of itemization among high-income groups is very high: 94% of households with income over $200,000 itemize deductions. Yet only 10% of those with incomes less than $30,000 do so.[18] Since deductions are typically only available to those who itemize, they will be used more by the higher-income groups that do itemize, a fact that further reduces their equity.

▶ APPLICATION

The Refundability Debate[19]

While tax credits are more progressive than tax deductions, the extent of their progressivity depends on whether they are **refundable,** or available to

refundable Describes tax credits that are available to individuals even if they pay few or no taxes.

---

[18] Internal Revenue Service (2004), Tables 1.1 and 2.1.
[19] This discussion draws heavily on Firestone (2003).

individuals who owe few or no taxes. Refundable credits result in a net payment to such individuals; that is, refundable credits increase the tax refund that such taxpayers receive. Refundability is important because many of the lowest-income families in the United States that can benefit from tax credits do not currently owe taxes. As a result, if credits are not fully refundable, they are not as powerful in terms of vertical equity.

Nevertheless, many conservatives object to the notion that those who owe little or no income taxes get a refund. "It's not a credit, it's someone else's money," said Representative Spencer Bachus (R-Alabama). "If we want to turn our income tax code into a welfare system, let's be honest with the American people that's what we are doing." Supporters of refundability respond to this point by noting that while low-income families pay little income tax, they do pay a large portion of their income in the form of other taxes, such as the payroll and sales tax, and that the credit could thus be seen as a refund for those payments. Moreover, most individuals who receive a refund in any year actually pay positive taxes over a ten year period.[20]

An excellent example of this conundrum is the debate over the child credit, a tax credit for low- and middle-income families introduced in 1997, but on a nonrefundable basis for most families. In 2001, this credit was expanded from $500 to $600 per child and made partially refundable. If the credit were fully refundable, then families would receive $600 per child, regardless of their tax payment status. Instead, for families that pay less income tax than the child credit to which they are entitled, the 2001 law allowed them to receive a refund of 10% of earnings over $10,500 (in 2003), up to a maximum of $600 per child.

Consider, for example, a married couple with two children and an annual income of $20,000, who because of the standard deduction and personal exemptions owe no federal income tax. Under the 2001 tax cut, that family receives a $950 credit [$0.10 \times (20,000 - 10,500)$], or $475 per child. If the credit were not refundable, the family would receive no credit because they pay no taxes; if it were fully refundable, the family would receive $1,200, or $600 per child. This $950 was a compromise between forces in favor of and opposed to refundability.

This issue became much more difficult during the next round of tax cuts, in 2003, when the child tax credit was increased by $400 to $1,000, accelerating a raise already scheduled in the 2001 bill. The President made frequent public mention of the $400 checks that would be mailed to families eligible for the credit, but criticism began to mount over last-minute changes that had been inserted into the bill before he signed it into law. These changes prevented low-income families from receiving the benefits of this $400 increase by retaining the 10% cap from the 2001 bill. The married couple just mentioned, for instance, would continue to be limited to the $475 credit per child and would thus not benefit from the newly increased child tax credit. Because of

---

[20] Batchelder et al. (2006), the source for this fact, presents an elegant defense of refundabilty as a tax principle.

this, some proposed raising the 10% cap to 15%. This 15% cap would mean the married couple in our example would receive $712.50 per child [0.15 × (20,000 − 10,500)/2] and would thus see some benefit from the increased credit.

This provision was left out of the final law, however; by one estimate, of the 12 million children that would have been helped by this accelerated refundable tax credit, 8 million would now see no benefit because of the 15% provision's removal. This effect was viewed by many as particularly appalling given that adding the 15% provision would have cost $3.5 billion, about 1% of the bill's $350 billion total cost. Indeed, in 2004 the Congress passed legislation to raise the cap to 15% to remedy this perceived shortcoming. In October 2005, however, the tax credit once again came under close scrutiny when a study released by the Tax Policy Center found that more than a quarter of American children (19.5 million in total) and half of the nation's black children belonged to families who were too poor to qualify for the full $1,000 benefit. In response, various changes to the structure of the child tax credit have been proposed, including the possibility of lowering the earnings threshold from $10,500 to $10,000 and barring it from rising with inflation, as it does under current law.[21] ◄

Bottom Line: Tax Expenditures

The end result of the existing set of deviations from the Haig-Simons comprehensive income definition is a set of **tax expenditures,** defined by the government as "revenue losses attributable to provisions of the Federal tax laws which allow a special exclusion, exemption, or deduction from gross income or which provide a special credit, a preferential rate of tax, or a deferral of liability." Since 1976, the federal government has included a separate section of the budget that shows the amount of these tax expenditures. For example, the government measures how much revenue is lost by excluding health insurance from taxable compensation, or how much revenue is lost by allowing individuals to deduct charitable contributions from their taxable income.

tax expenditures Government revenue losses attributable to tax law provisions that allow special exclusions, exemptions, or deductions from gross income, or that provide a special credit, preferential tax rate, or deferral of liability.

The major tax expenditures are shown in Table 18-2. In 2007, the government is projected to lose $872 billion through all tax expenditures (including many smaller expenditures not shown here), which amounts to over 30% of direct government spending. The largest single tax expenditure is the exclusion of employer-provided health insurance premiums from taxable income, which will cost the federal government $147 billion in forgone income tax revenues in 2007. Other large expenditures include the exclusion of employer contributions to pensions ($52.5 billion) and 401(k)s ($39.8 billion) and the deduction of mortgage interest ($79.9 billion). The total amount of tax expenditures is half as large as total tax revenues projected for 2007, and more than three times as large as the projected federal deficit for 2007. Thus, the debate over the tax base is not an academic one; the holes in the Haig-Simons tax base for the United States allow large sums of money to escape the U.S. Treasury every year.

---

[21] DeParle (2005).

▪ **TABLE 18-2**

Top 10 U.S. Federal Government Tax Expenditures (projected for 2007)

Major categories of tax expenditures	
Exclusion of employer contributions for medical insurance	$146.8
Deductibility of home mortgage interest	79.9
Exclusion of pension contributions and earnings: employer plans	52.5
Child credit	42.1
Exclusion of pension contributions and earnings: 401(k) plans	39.8
Deductibility of charitable contributions	34.5
Preferential treatment of capital gains income	32.5
Deductibility of state and local taxes	29.6
Exclusion of interest on state and local bonds	29.6
Exclusion of interest on life insurance savings	20.8
Total of all tax expenditures	**$871.8**

Tax Expenditure Comparisons	Value (in billions of $)	Ratio
Tax expenditures/tax receipts	$872/$1,516	0.56
Tax expenditures/federal deficit	$872/$270	3.2

In 2007, the government will lose $871.8 billion in revenue because of various exclusions and credits in the tax code. The largest such tax expenditures are shown here; the most important tax exclusions are those that favor employer contributions to health insurance and pension plans.

Source: Congressional Budget Office (2006b), Tables 1-1 and 3-1; Congressional Budget Office (2006c), Tables 14-1 and 19-1.

18.6

The Appropriate Unit of Taxation

Another important aspect of the tax base has been absent from our discussion of the Haig-Simons principle: How should the government choose the appropriate *unit of taxation*? That is, how should the government share the tax burden among individuals who are in the same family? Should taxes be levied on total family income or just on the incomes of individuals?

The Problem of the "Marriage Tax"

Suppose you were hired by the federal government to design a tax system that had three goals:

▶ *Progressivity:* marginal tax rates rise as family incomes rise

▶ *Across-Family Horizontal Equity:* Families with equal incomes would pay equal taxes

▶ *Across-Marriage Horizontal Equity:* Tax burdens would be *marriage neutral,* independent of whether two individuals decide to wed

■ TABLE 18-3

The Impact of Marriage on Tax Liabilities

	Individual income	Individual tax	Family tax with individual filing	Total family income	Family tax with total family income
Hillary	$140,000	$32,000 ⎤	$33,000	$150,000	$35,000
Bill	$10,000	$1,000 ⎦			
George	$75,000	$13,000 ⎤	$26,000	$150,000	$35,000
Laura	$75,000	$13,000 ⎦			

Table from U.S. Office of Management and Budget. "Analytical Perspectives: Budget of the United States Government, Fiscal Year 2004." Washington, DC: U.S. Government Printing Office, 2003.

A progressive tax system that is based on the individual incomes of each person in a married couple leads Hillary and Bill to pay a much higher tax ($33,000) than George and Laura ($26,000), despite having the same family income ($150,000). On the other hand, a progressive tax system based on total family income imposes a "marriage tax" on both couples, as they both pay more in tax as married couples ($35,000) than they would as singles.

These all seem like worthwhile goals. There is one problem, however: it is literally impossible to achieve all three goals at once.

This impossibility is easiest to see through a simple example. Consider a tax system with a 10% tax rate on income up to $20,000, a 20% marginal rate up to $80,000, and a 30% marginal rate on any income above $80,000. Now consider two successful couples. The first couple, Hillary and Bill, get the bulk of their income from Hillary, who makes $140,000 a year, while Bill makes only $10,000. George and Laura, on the other hand, each contribute equally to their partnership, earning $75,000 a year. Both couples have the same total income of $150,000.

We have two choices for how to tax these couples. If the government taxes the couples on an *individual basis,* it would compute the tax burden on each individual, then add burdens to find the family's tax bill. As Table 18-3 shows, such an approach leads to a tax bill of $33,000 for Hillary and Bill, but only $26,000 for George and Laura. Thus, this approach violates our second condition: families with equal incomes are not paying equal taxes.

The alternative is to tax the couples on a *family basis.* Under this system, the government would first add the incomes of the individuals to get the family income, and then compute a family tax based on that family income. As Table 18-3 shows, such an approach leads to tax bills of $35,000 on both families, so that the second condition is met. Such a system violates our third condition, however, since both couples now pay more tax as families ($35,000) than they would as individuals living together ($33,000 or $26,000). That is, there is now a **marriage tax,** a rise in the total tax burdens of two individuals simply from marrying.

These problems crop up because of the first condition, progressivity. If we tax on an individual basis, rising marginal rates mean that individuals with higher income pay a higher share of their income in taxes. Thus, families with a more equal distribution of income will pay lower taxes, violating our second

marriage tax A rise in the joint tax burden on two individuals from becoming married.

condition. Rising marginal rates also mean that when individuals combine their income into families, a larger share of the total family income is subject to the higher marginal tax rate. Thus, families will pay more taxes when married than when single, violating our third condition.

Referring to our example, when we tax on an individual basis, Hillary pays 23% of her income in taxes, Bill pays 10%, and George and Laura each pay 17%. Adding up the individual taxes owed by each family, Hillary and Bill pay a larger share of their total income (22%) than do George and Laura (17%), violating the second condition. If we then move to family taxation, Bill's $10,000 of earnings, which used to be taxed at a low rate of 10%, are now taxed at a much higher rate of 30%. Under the individual tax, both Bill and Hillary benefited from having the first $10,000 of income taxed at only 10%, but with a family tax, Hillary "uses up" that $10,000 bracket with her first $10,000 of earnings. Thus, Bill's earnings are added on top of Hillary's income so it is in the higher marginal tax rate bracket. A similar phenomenon occurs with George and Laura: while they used to both benefit from low taxation on the first $10,000 of earnings, now only one of them does. This causes the marriage tax, violating the third condition. The only way to satisfy both the second and third conditions would be to have a proportional tax, which would violate the first condition (progressivity).

Marriage Taxes in Practice

Note that the third condition was couched in terms of having marriage *neutrality,* not in terms of having *no marriage taxes*. In fact, we could have a system with no marriage taxes by providing very large deductions for married couples relative to single tax filers. Suppose that we augmented our tax system with a deduction for married couples of $20,000 per year, with no deduction for singles. In this case, each couple would now have a taxable income of $130,000 and thus pay $29,000 in taxes. Under this system, Bill and Hillary would have a marriage *subsidy* (a reduction in their tax bill from marrying), while George and Laura would have a marriage tax. We could even increase the deduction to $40,000, and then both families would have a marriage subsidy.

The point is not that the government can't get rid of marriage taxes; it can. The point is that there is no set of deductions we could establish that would make the system of family-based taxation marriage *neutral,* rather than providing subsidies to some marriages and taxing others. Given the differences between these couples, and the other goals of tax policy, there is no way to design a system that yields zero marriage tax/subsidy on both couples. This is the essence of the problem facing family-based tax systems.

Marriage Taxes in the United States There has been much debate over the marriage tax in the United States. In 2001, Republican House Majority Leader Dick Armey said the IRS was sending the message that "if you fall in love and get married, we will punish you."[22] In fact, despite this rhetoric, the tax system in the United States looks very much like the previous example

---

[22] O'Rourke (2001).

with a $20,000 deduction: some families face marriage subsidies and some face marriage taxes. Indeed, according to one report on taxpaying couples in 1999, 48% of couples receive a marriage penalty, 41% receive a marriage subsidy, and 11% receive neither a penalty nor a subsidy.[23] The mean penalty paid by such couples is $1,140, for a total penalty of $28.3 billion. The mean subsidy received is $1,270, for a total subsidy of $26.7 billion.

So when individuals say that there are marriage taxes in the United States, what they really mean is that *some* families pay marriage taxes. The only way to get rid of marriage taxes completely would be to give a joint filer deduction that is so large that no one would have a marriage tax. Under such a program, most families would receive large marriage subsidies.

Despite the rhetoric around this topic, however, there has been little attention paid to the more fundamental question: Should we care about marriage taxes? One reason to care is the horizontal equity point previously made. The other reason to care is that society might actually want to encourage marriage, not discourage it through marriage taxes. Once again, if the government were to use a tax incentive to encourage marriage, it would have to consider the marginal and inframarginal effects of this incentive: Do taxes actually matter for marriage decisions, or does such a policy simply give a large tax break to those who would have married anyway? The answer appears to largely be the latter; most research on this topic suggests that taxes exert little effect on the decision to get married. Thus, encouraging marriage is not a strong argument for the large revenue costs of ending marriage taxes imposed on some families (and increasing marriage subsidies for others).

Finally, the reason we might care is not marriage at all but the high marginal tax rate on secondary earners. In our example, moving from an individual tax to a family tax has raised the marginal tax rate on Bill's earnings from 10% to 30%. Such a high tax rate could reduce the labor supply of secondary earners, causing Bill not to work at all, for example. One proposal to address this problem (which is a lot less expensive than raising the deduction for joint filers) is to reintroduce a secondary earner deduction that was in place in the early 1980s, which would allow families to deduct some amount of earnings by a secondary earner. Under such a policy, for example, couples could deduct from taxation the first $10,000 of earnings by a secondary earner, which would remove the higher tax rates on Bill's labor under family taxation than under individual taxation. This deduction would greatly reduce both the marriage tax and the distortion to secondary earner labor supply. At the same time, however, it would reduce vertical equity, since families with two earners tend to have more money than families with one earner.

Marriage Taxes Around the World The United States is almost alone in having a tax system based on family income. Of the industrialized nations in the OECD, 19 tax husbands and wives individually, and 5 (France, Germany, Luxembourg, Portugal, and Switzerland) offer marriage subsidies to virtually all couples through family taxation with *income splitting*.[24] This means that the

---

[23] Bull et al. (1999).
[24] Congressional Budget Office (1997), Appendix A.

family income is totaled and then divided equally, either between husband and wife (in Germany, as in the United States between 1948 and 1969), or among all family members including children (in the other 4 nations). As we saw in Table 18-3, under family taxation with rising marginal tax rates, families with more equally divided income (George and Laura) pay lower taxes than those with more unequal incomes (Bill and Hillary). Thus, allowing families to divide their income equally, along with other provisions generous to families, leads to marriage bonuses in most cases in these nations. Only 2 other nations have a "pure" family taxation system similar to that used in the United States: Ireland and Norway.

18.7
Conclusion

The debate over taxation in the United States neither began nor ended with George H. W. Bush's 1988 pledge for no new taxes. Nevertheless, the public focus on this pledge, and the implications of Bush's breaking it, highlight the key role that taxes play in debates over public policy in the United Sates. In this chapter, we set the stage for our study of taxation by discussing the different types of taxation used by the United States and the rest of the world, how to measure tax "fairness," and the key issues policy makers face in designing the base of income taxation. In the remaining chapters of the book, we discuss the economic considerations that drive the determination of both the tax base and the tax rate.

▶ HIGHLIGHTS

▪ There are many different types of taxes, which can be sorted into four broad categories: taxes on individual income, taxes on corporate income, taxes on wealth, and taxes on consumption. The federal government depends heavily on individual income taxes, while state and local governments get most of their revenue from taxes on wealth and consumption. Other national governments receive a much greater share of their revenue from consumption taxes than the United States does.

▪ The major source of revenue raising in the United States is the individual income tax, which starts with total income accrued during the year, subtracts a variety of exemptions and deductions, and then applies a schedule of tax rates to determine tax liability.

▪ Measuring the "fairness" or equity of the income tax is difficult and involves considerations such as how to measure tax rates and how to define equity.

▪ The "gold standard" for defining the income tax base is the Haig-Simons definition, which defines the ability to pay taxes as consumption plus change in net worth. The tax base in the United States deviates in significant ways from this gold standard.

▪ Some deviations are based on ability to pay or the cost of earning income, both of which should be deductible under Haig-Simons in theory but raise some difficult issues in practice.

▪ Some deviations are based on externality arguments, which can justify tax subsidies if these subsidies have large marginal impacts (such as encouraging more charitable giving) without very large inframarginal impacts (the revenue lost on subsidizing those already giving to charity). The existing evidence suggests that tax breaks for charitable giving may be justified on these grounds, but that tax breaks for home ownership are not.

■ Deviations from Haig-Simons can come in the form of tax credits or deductions from taxable income. The relative efficiency implications of these alternative approaches are unclear, but credits are clearly more vertically equitable, so long as they are refundable to taxpayers who pay little or no taxes.

■ The ideal tax system would not distort the decision to become married, but that is not possible if the tax system wants to also meet the goals of progressivity and equal treatment of families with equal income. The U.S. tax code currently provides roughly as many marriage subsidies as it does marriage taxes.

▶ QUESTIONS AND PROBLEMS

1. The nation of Fishkasar has a tax rate of 10% on the first 20,000 walops (the national currency) of taxable income, then 25% on the next 30,000 walops, then 50% on all taxable income above 50,000 walops. Fishkasar provides a 4,000-walop exemption per family member.

   a. Jamil's family has three members and earns 50,000 walops per year. Calculate the family's marginal and average tax rates.

   b. Boba's family has five members and earns 85,000 walops per year. Calculate the family's marginal and average tax rates.

   c. Suppose that Fishkasar changed its tax code to a flat tax of 30% with an 8,000-walop per family member exemption. Would this change in the tax system make the system more progressive, more regressive, or neither?

2. What is the rationale behind having an Alternative Minimum Tax?

3. Suppose that the U.S. personal income tax system became a flat tax system, in which all taxpayers paid a certain percentage of their incomes in tax, and in which there are no exemptions or deductions. In which way(s) could this flat tax be more *regressive* than the present U.S. system? In which ways could it be more *progressive* than the present system?

4. Why should casualty losses or large medical expenditures be fully tax-deductible only in certain circumstances?

5. Many employers sponsor "cafeteria" plans. These plans allow employees to have some of their earnings put into an account that can be used for medical expenditures incurred in that tax year. The income put in this account is not considered part of the individual's tax base. It what ways is it desirable to exclude this income from the tax base? In what ways is it undesirable?

6. Professor Slither attended the Antarctic Economic Association meetings. She is able to fully deduct from her taxes the hotel expenses that she incurred, but can deduct only half of the meals expenses that she incurred. Why does the U.S. tax code make this distinction? Does this tax policy make sense, from a Haig-Simons perspective?

7. Ed and Wendy are a married couple with no children. Each earns $75,000 per year, and their combined household adjusted gross income is $150,000. John and Kristen also have $150,000 in combined household adjusted gross income and no children. However, Kristen earns all of the income; John does not work.

   a. Use the 2006 tax rates for married couples filing jointly described in this chapter to compute how much income tax each couple owes. Assume that both take the standard deduction.

   b. Does either couple pay a "marriage tax"? Does either couple receive a "marriage benefit"? [Note: To answer this question, you will need to look up the 2006 tax rates for single individuals. These can be found at the IRS Web site at http://www.irs.gov/formspubs.]

8. Chapter 7 argued that private provision of public goods is inefficiently low, and that subsidization can help attain the optimal level of public goods. Why might offering tax breaks for public goods provision be an inefficient method of bringing about this goal?

9. Your roommate and you had identical high school grade point averages and SAT scores. In many respects, one would expect that you would be equally successful. But because you chose economics as a major and your roommate chose geology, you will be paying a larger amount of tax in the future than your roommate will because your income will be higher. Is this attribute of the tax code vertically equitable? Is it horizontally equitable?

10. The government of Utopia plans to offer a transportation tax credit in which families receive a share of their expenditures on transportation to and from work or school as a reduction in their tax bill. Utopia is considering two forms of this tax credit, one that is fully refundable and one in which the tax credit is limited to the amount of taxes the family pays. Which form of the tax credit is more progressive? Explain.

11. Suppose that the government adopts a Haig-Simons comprehensive income definition. Will this make employers more likely or less likely to offer employer-provided pension plans or health insurance coverage? Why?

▶ **ADVANCED QUESTIONS**

12. Your employer allows you to purchase a parking permit with "pretax dollars"—that is, you don't have to pay taxes on the money that you used to purchase this permit. Does allowing some people to purchase certain goods or services using pretax dollars increase or decrease equity in the U.S. tax system? Explain.

13. Oregon has an income tax but no state sales tax, while Washington has no state income tax but does have a state sales tax. Oregon residents can deduct the state taxes they pay (the income tax payments) from their federal income taxes, while Washington residents cannot deduct the state taxes they pay (the sales tax payments). What are the equity implications of this difference?

14. Suppose a researcher compared charitable contribution levels across counties and found that, all else equal, counties with higher home-ownership levels have higher levels of charitable contributions. Give an explanation of this finding that draws on the U.S. personal income tax code. Can you think of a reason this estimated relationship might not, in fact, be an effect of the tax code?

15. You are interested in estimating the effects of tax breaks on the level of charitable contributions. How could observing changes over time in tax rates and associated charitable contribution levels help you to distinguish between marginal and inframarginal effects of the tax break?

16. The largest tax break for most Americans is the mortgage interest tax deduction, which allows home owners to deduct from their taxable income the amount of money they pay in interest to finance their homes. This tax break is intended to encourage home ownership. Compare this tax deduction to a uniform *tax credit* for home ownership on equity and efficiency grounds.

The *e* indicates a question that requires students to apply the empirical economics principles discussed in Chapter 3 and the Empirical Evidence boxes.

The Equity Implications of Taxation: Tax Incidence

19

In early 2002, with New Jersey facing a $5.3 billion budget gap, Governor James McGreevey called for changes in the state's corporate tax system. The outdated system based corporate tax payments on the corporation's profits earned in the state of New Jersey, thus encouraging businesses to use accounting tricks to shift reported profits to their subsidiaries in other states. As a result, 30 of the state's 50 companies with the biggest payrolls each paid just $200 annually in corporate taxes. McGreevey wanted to institute a 1% tax on corporate gross sales in New Jersey to ensure that all corporations would pay tax. Arthur Maurice, vice president of the NJ Business and Industry Association, objected: "Where are companies going to get the money to pay these taxes? They're going to cut jobs. It will be the people who work at these companies who will ultimately pay the price for this counterproductive tax."

A version of the tax reform was eventually enacted, leading one company, Federated Department Stores, to publicly announce layoffs that they attributed to the tax increase. Governor McGreevey responded angrily, claiming that these statements were just a cover for those wealthy corporate owners who would really bear the brunt of this new tax: "All that we're asking is that they pay their fair share: not a dollar more, not a dollar less. But when you have a CEO making $1.5 million and upwards of $14 million in stock options threatening people who are making $25,000, that's what's wrong."[1]

The fundamental disagreement between the governor and the business community concerned who would ultimately pay this new tax. The business community claimed workers would bear the burden, while the governor claimed the burden would be shouldered by wealthy companies and their executives.

This debate focuses on the central question of **tax incidence:** Who bears the burden of a tax? A simple answer to this question would be that whoever sends the check to the government bears the tax. Yet such an answer ignores

tax incidence Assessing which party (consumers or producers) bears the true burden of a tax.

[1] Kocieniewski (2002a, 2002b).

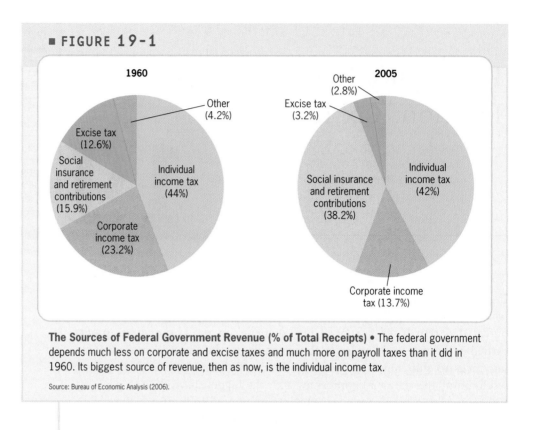

■ FIGURE 19-1

The Sources of Federal Government Revenue (% of Total Receipts) • The federal government depends much less on corporate and excise taxes and much more on payroll taxes than it did in 1960. Its biggest source of revenue, then as now, is the individual income tax.

Source: Bureau of Economic Analysis (2006).

the fact that markets respond to taxes and that these responses must be taken into account to assess the ultimate burden, or *incidence,* of taxation.

To see the importance of this question, let's return to the facts on the distribution of federal taxation over time from Chapter 1. Figure 19-1 shows these facts again. In 1960, 23% of federal taxes was collected from corporations, and 62% was collected from individuals through income and payroll taxes. Today, 14% of taxes is collected from corporations, and 80% is collected from individuals. Is this an equitable shift in the burden of taxation? Your first reaction might be "No, it's not at all equitable! Corporations are rich, and individuals aren't, so this imbalance is not fair." Your indignant reaction, however noble, is misplaced because corporations don't pay taxes; corporate taxes are paid by the individuals who own, work for, and buy from the corporations. When we study tax incidence, then, we are always comparing taxes collected from one set of people to taxes collected from another set. This comparison makes the issue of figuring out who bears the burden of a tax less clear than if we view it simply as a matter of pitting rich corporations against poor individuals.

This chapter examines the equity implications of taxation. We begin with the *three rules of tax incidence* that guide our modeling of the distributional implications of taxation. We then turn to the study of *general equilibrium tax incidence,* the effect of taxes on one sector in a multisector world. Finally, we present empirical evidence on the burden of taxation in the United States over time.

19.1

The Three Rules of Tax Incidence

The goal of determining a tax's incidence is to assess who ultimately bears the burden of paying a tax. Economic tax incidence can be described by *three basic rules*. We describe these rules with reference to the incidence of a tax of a fixed amount on a specific commodity, or a *specific excise tax*. An alternative form of taxation of commodities is *ad valorem* taxes, a fixed percentage of the sales price (such as with state sales taxes). All of the lessons drawn here apply equally to both types of taxes; the major difference with ad valorem incidence analysis is that taxes shift the demand or supply curve proportionally (e.g., quantity rises by 10%) rather than by fixed amounts (e.g., quantity rises by 5 units).

The Statutory Burden of a Tax Does Not Describe Who Really Bears the Tax

The first and most important rule of tax incidence is that tax laws do not accurately identify who actually bears the burden of the tax. The **statutory incidence** of a tax is determined by who pays the tax to the government. For example, the statutory incidence of a tax paid by producers of gasoline is on those very producers. Statutory incidence, however, ignores the fact that markets react to taxation. This market reaction determines the **economic incidence** of a tax, the change in the resources available to any economic agent as a result of taxation. The economic incidence of any tax is the difference between the individual's available resources before and after the tax has been imposed.

> **statutory incidence** The burden of a tax borne by the party that sends the check to the government.
>
> **economic incidence** The burden of taxation measured by the change in the resources available to any economic agent as a result of taxation.

When a tax is imposed on producers in a competitive market, producers will raise prices to some extent to offset this tax burden, and the producers' income will not fall by the full amount of the tax. When a tax is imposed on consumers in a competitive market, the consumers will not be willing to pay as much for the taxed good, so prices will fall, offsetting to some extent the statutory tax burden on consumers. Technically, we can define the tax burden for consumers as

consumer tax burden

= (post-tax price − pre-tax price) + per-unit tax payments by consumers.

For producers the tax burden is

producer tax burden

= (pre-tax price − post-tax price) + per-unit tax payments by producers.

For example, suppose that tomorrow the federal government levied a 50¢ per gallon tax on gasoline, to be paid by the producers. Will gas producers receive 50¢ less on each gallon they produce as a result of this tax?

To answer this question, we need to consider the impact of the gas tax on the market for gas, as shown in panel (a) of Figure 19-2. The vertical axis in this graph shows the price per gallon of gas, and the horizontal axis shows billions

▪ **FIGURE 19-2**

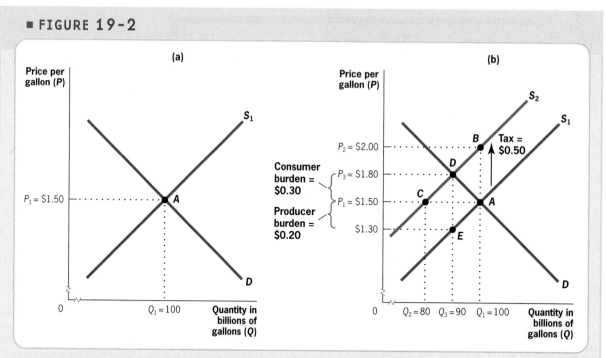

Statutory Burdens Are Not Real Burdens • Panel (a) shows the equilibrium in the gas market before taxation (point A). A 50¢ tax levied on gas producers (the statutory burden) in panel (b) leads to a decrease in supply from S_1 to S_2 and to a 30¢ rise in the price of gas from P_1 to P_3 (point D). The real burden of the tax is borne primarily by consumers, who pay 30¢ of the tax through higher prices, leaving producers to bear only 20¢ of the tax.

of gallons of gas. Recall from Chapter 2 that the supply curve shows the quantity that suppliers are willing to sell at any given price. In a competitive market, the supply curve is determined by the firm's marginal cost: the producer will sell any units for which the market price is at or above its marginal cost of producing that unit. In Figure 19-2, the market is initially in equilibrium at point A: at the market price of $1.50 ($P_1$), producers will supply 100 billion gallons (Q_1) of gasoline. Producers are willing to supply 100 billion gallons at $1.50 per gallon because $1.50 is the producers' marginal cost of producing that quantity of gas.

Panel (b) of Figure 19-2 shows the effects of imposing a tax of 50¢ per gallon of gas sold on the producers of gas. For these producers, this is equivalent to a 50¢ per gallon increase in marginal cost. Because firms must pay both their original marginal cost and the 50¢ tax, they now require a price that is 50¢ higher to produce each quantity. To supply the initial equilibrium quantity of 100 billion gallons after the tax is imposed, for example, firms would now require a price of $P_2 = $2.00 (50¢ higher than the initial $1.50 equilibrium price, at point B). Because the tax acts like an increase in marginal cost, the entire supply curve shifts upward by 50¢ from S_1 to S_2 and the supply of gas falls.

At the initial equilibrium price of $1.50, there is now excess demand for gasoline. Consumers want the old amount of gasoline (100 billion gallons) at $1.50, but with the new tax in place producers are willing to supply only 80 billion gallons (point C). At $1.50, there is a shortage of Q_1 (point A) minus Q_2 (point C), or 20 billion gallons. Consumers therefore bid up the price as they compete for the smaller quantities of gas that are now available from producers. Prices continue to rise until the market arrives at a new equilibrium (point D) with a market price of $1.80 ($P_3$) and a quantity of 90 billion gallons (Q_3). The market price is now 30¢ higher than it was before the tax was imposed.

Burden of the Tax on Consumers and Producers The tax has two effects on the participants in the gas market. First, it has changed the market price that consumers pay and producers receive for a gallon of gas; this price has risen by 30¢ from $1.50 to $1.80. Second, producers must now send a check to the government for 50¢ for each gallon sold.

From the producers' perspective, the pain of the 50¢ tax is offset by the fact that the price the producers receive is 30¢ more than the initial equilibrium price. Thus, the producers have to pay only 20¢ of the tax, the portion that is not offset by the price increase.

From the consumers' perspective, they feel some of the pain of the tax since they pay 30¢ more per gallon. Even though consumers send no check to the government and producers send a 50¢ check to the government, consumers actually bear more of the tax (30¢ to the producers' 20¢). The price increase has transferred most of the tax burden from producers to consumers.

These burdens are illustrated in Figure 19-2 by the segments labeled "Consumer burden" and "Producer burden." Using the formulas on p. 547, we can compute the burdens on consumers and producers. The consumers' burden is

$$\text{consumer tax burden}$$
$$= (\text{post-tax price} - \text{pre-tax price}) + \text{per-unit tax payments by consumers}$$
$$= P_3 - P_1 + 0 = \$1.80 - \$1.50 = \$0.30.$$

The producers' burden is

$$\text{producer tax burden}$$
$$= (\text{pre-tax price} - \text{post-tax price}) + \text{per-unit tax payments by producers}$$
$$= P_1 - P_3 + \$0.50 = \$1.50 - \$1.80 + \$0.50 = \$0.20.$$

The key insight is that the burden on producers is not the 50¢ tax payment they make on each gallon but some lower number, because some of the tax burden is borne by consumers in the form of a higher price. The sum of these burdens is $0.50, the total **tax wedge** created by this tax, which is the difference between what consumers pay ($1.80) and what producers receive net of tax ($1.30, at point E) from a transaction.

tax wedge The difference between what consumers pay and what producers receive (net of tax) from a transaction.

The Side of the Market on Which the Tax Is Imposed Is Irrelevant to the Distribution of the Tax Burdens

The second rule of tax incidence is that the side of the market on which the tax is imposed is irrelevant to the distribution of the tax burdens: tax incidence

▪ FIGURE 19-3

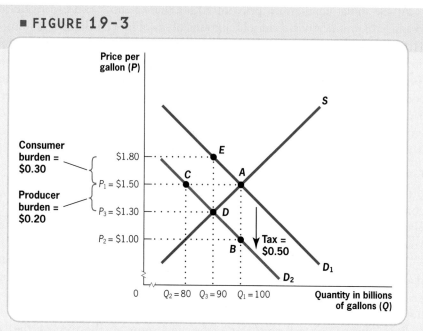

The Side of the Market Is Irrelevant ▪ A 50¢ tax levied on gas consumers (the statutory burden) leads to a decrease in demand from D_1 to D_2 and to a 20¢ fall in the price of gas from P_1 to P_3 (with the market moving from the pre-tax equilibrium at point A to the post-tax equilibrium at point D). The real burden of the tax is borne primarily by consumers, who pay the 50¢ tax to the government but receive an offsetting price reduction of only 20¢; producers bear that 20¢ of the tax.

is identical whether the tax is levied on producers or consumers.[2] In terms of the previous rule and Figure 19-2, this rule means that whether the 50¢ tax is imposed on producers or consumers, consumers will always end up bearing 30¢ of the tax and the producers will end up bearing 20¢.

Figure 19-3 considers the impact of a 50¢ per gallon tax on consumers of gas. In this case, the tax is collected from consumers at the pump when they pay for their gas rather than from producers, as in Figure 19-2. Recall from Chapter 2 that the demand curve represents consumers' willingness to pay for any quantity of a good. Each point on the demand curve shows the quantity demanded for any market price encountered by consumers. With consumers having to pay a 50¢ tax in addition to the market price at every quantity, they are now willing to pay 50¢ less for each quantity. Thus, because the tax causes a reduction in consumers' willingness to pay (before adding in their tax payments), the entire demand curve shifts downward by 50¢, from D_1 to D_2. Before the tax, consumers were willing to pay a price of $P_1 = \$1.50$ for the

---

[2] Technically, this rule is just an application of the first rule of tax incidence, but it is useful to think of it as a distinct rule when applying tax incidence principles.

100 billionth gallon of gas at point A. Now they are willing to pay only a price of $P_2 = \$1.00$ for the 100 billionth gallon (point B), since they also have to pay the 50¢ tax on each gallon purchased.

At the old market price of $1.50, there is now an excess supply of gasoline: producers are willing to sell the old amount of gasoline (100 billion gallons, at point A), but consumers are willing to buy only 80 billion gallons at that price, at point C. There is an excess supply of gasoline of $Q_1 - Q_2 = 20$ billion gallons at the initial equilibrium price of $1.50 after the demand curve shifts. Producers therefore lower their price to sell their excess supply until the price falls to $1.30 ($P_3$) at point D, with an equilibrium quantity of 90 billion gallons (Q_3). The market price is now 20¢ lower than it was before the tax was imposed.

As in the previous example, this tax has two effects on the participants in the gas market. First, it has changed the market price that consumers pay and producers receive for a gallon of gas; this price has fallen by 20¢ from $1.50 to $1.30. Second, the consumer must now pay the government 50¢ for each gallon purchased. At the equilibrium price of $1.30, adding the 50¢ tax yields a cost to consumers (price plus tax) of $1.80 at point E.

From the consumers' perspective, the pain of the 50¢ check is offset by the 20¢ per gallon decline in the market price. From the producers' perspective, they are feeling some of the pain of this tax since they are receiving 20¢ less per gallon. Even though producers send no check to the government, and consumers send a 50¢ check to the government, both parties bear some of the ultimate burden of the tax, since the price decrease has transferred some of the tax burden from consumers to producers.

These burdens are illustrated in Figure 19-3 by the segments labeled "Consumer burden" and "Producer burden." Using our formulas, we can compute the burdens on consumers and producers:

consumer: $P_3 - P_1 + \$0.50 = \$1.30 - \$1.50 + \$0.50 = \$0.30$

producer: $P_1 - P_3 + 0 = \$1.50 - \$1.30 = \$0.20$.

Once again, the sum of the burdens on consumers and producers, the difference between what consumers pay ($1.80) and what producers receive ($1.30), is the tax wedge of 50¢.

Note that *these tax burdens are identical to the burdens in the previous example.* Consumers now have to pay the 50¢ at the pump, but they are facing a lower price ($1.30) to which they have to add that tax. Adding the two together, the consumer pays exactly the same amount ($1.80, price plus tax) as in the previous case. Producers now don't have to pay a tax, but they receive a lower price for their gas ($1.30 instead of $1.50), so they end up receiving the same amount ($1.30) as well.

Gross Versus After-Tax Prices While there is only one market price when a tax is imposed, there are two different prices that economists often track in these types of tax incidence models. The first is the **gross price,** the price paid by or received by the party *not* paying the tax to the government; it is the

gross price The price in the market.

after-tax price The gross price minus the amount of the tax (if producers pay the tax) or plus the amount of the tax (if consumers pay the tax).

same as the price in the market. The second is the **after-tax price**, the price paid by or received by the party that *is* paying the tax to the government; it is either lower by the amount of the tax (if producers pay the tax) or higher by the amount of the tax (if consumers pay the tax).

When the gas tax is levied on producers, as shown in Figure 19-2, the gross price paid by consumers is $1.80, and the after-tax price received by producers is $1.80 − $0.50 = $1.30. When the gas tax is levied on consumers, as in Figure 19-3, the gross price received by producers is $1.30, and the after-tax price paid by consumers is $1.30 + $0.50 = $1.80. The after-tax price is equal to the gross price *plus* the tax wedge if the tax is on consumers, but is equal to the gross price *minus* the tax wedge if the tax is on producers.

Parties with Inelastic Supply or Demand Bear Taxes; Parties with Elastic Supply or Demand Avoid Them

In the previous example, we described a particular case in which consumers bear more of the burden of a tax than do producers. This is, however, only one of many possible outcomes. The incidence of taxation on producers and consumers is ultimately determined by the *elasticities of supply and demand* on how responsive the quantity supplied or demanded is to price changes.

Perfectly Inelastic Demand Consider again the case in which the 50¢ per gallon tax is levied on gasoline producers, but let's assume this time that consumers have a perfectly inelastic demand for gas, as shown in Figure 19-4. At initial equilibrium, the price for 100 billion gallons is P_1 ($1.50). When the tax is levied on producers, they once again treat this as equivalent to a 50¢ rise

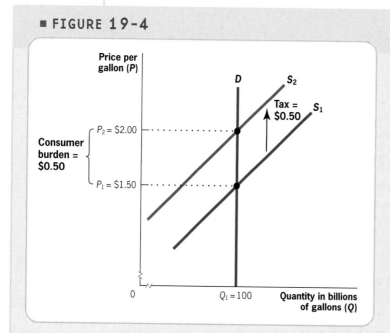

■ FIGURE 19-4

Inelastic Factors Bear Taxes • A tax on producers of an inelastically demanded good is fully reflected in increased prices, so consumers bear the full tax.

in marginal cost, raising the price that they require to supply any quantity; supply falls and the supply curve shifts from S_1 to S_2. The new equilibrium market price is $2.00 ($P_2$), a full 50¢ higher than the original price P_1. When demand is perfectly inelastic, the tax burdens are

$$\text{consumer burden}$$
$$= (\text{post-tax price} - \text{pre-tax price}) + \text{tax payments by consumers}$$
$$= P_2 - P_1 = \$2.00 - \$1.50 = \$0.50$$

$$\text{producer burden}$$
$$= (\text{pre-tax price} - \text{post-tax price}) + \text{tax payments by producers}$$
$$= P_1 - P_2 + \$0.50 = \$1.50 - \$2.00 + \$0.50 = \$0.$$

When demand is perfectly inelastic, producers bear *none* of the tax and consumers bear *all* of the tax. This is called the **full shifting** of the tax onto consumers.

> **full shifting** When one party in a transaction bears all of the tax burden.

Perfectly Elastic Demand Contrast that outcome with the case in which consumers' demand for gas is perfectly elastic, as shown in Figure 19-5. Initially, the market is in equilibrium at $P_1 = \$1.50$ and $Q_1 = 100$ billion gallons. In this case, when a 50¢ tax causes the supply curve to shift from S_1 to S_2, the equilibrium price remains at P_1, $1.50, but the quantity falls to Q_2, 80 billion gallons.

When demand is perfectly elastic, the tax burdens are therefore

consumer: $P_1 - P_1$ $= \$1.50 - \$1.50 = 0$
producer: $P_1 - P_1 + 0.50 = \$1.50 - \$1.50 + \$0.50 = \$0.50.$

In this case, producers bear *all* of the tax and consumers bear *none* of the tax.

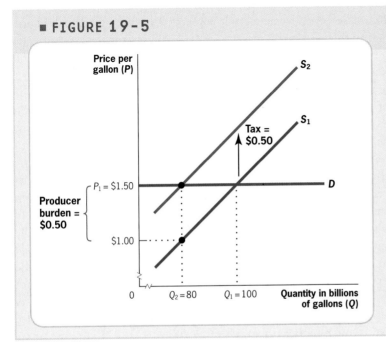

■ FIGURE 19-5

Elastic Factors Avoid Taxes ● A tax on producers of a perfectly elastically demanded good cannot be passed along to consumers through an increase in prices, so producers bear the full burden of the tax.

General Case These extreme cases illustrate a general point about tax incidence: *parties with inelastic demand (or supply, as we show below) bear taxes; parties with elastic demand (or supply) avoid them.* Demand for goods is more elastic (the price elasticity of demand is higher in absolute value) for goods with many substitutes. For example, the demand for fast food is fairly elastic because higher-quality restaurant meals or home cooking can be substituted for fast food fairly easily. Thus, if the government levied a tax on fast food, fast-food restaurants would find it difficult to raise prices in order to pass all of the tax onto fast-food consumers; if they did, individuals would substitute one of these alternatives for their fast food. Thus, because the demand for fast food is elastic, the producers (the restaurants) bear most of the burden of the tax.

For products with an inelastic demand, the burden of the tax is borne almost entirely by the consumer. For example, the demand for insulin is highly inelastic because it is essential to the health of diabetics. If the government taxes the producers of insulin, they can easily raise their price and completely shift most of the tax burden onto consumers because there are no substitutes available that allow consumers to leave this market because of a higher price.

Supply Elasticities Supply elasticity also affects how the tax burden is distributed. Supply curves are more elastic when suppliers have more alternative uses to which their resources can be put. In the short run, a steel manufacturer has fairly inelastic supply; having invested in the steel plant and expensive machinery to produce steel, there are few alternative choices for production. The plant cannot easily convert from making steel to making plastic pipes or wood furniture. So the supply curve for steel will be fairly inelastic (vertical). The supply of sales from sidewalk vendors (of items such as watches, purses, scarves, and so on) in New York City, in contrast, is very elastic. Since the individuals selling these goods have a very low investment in that particular business, if it is taxed they can easily move to other activities, such as working in a store selling the same items. So the supply curve for sidewalk vendor sales will be very elastic (horizontal).

Compare the incidence of a tax on steel (levied on steel producers) to the incidence of a tax on sidewalk vendors (levied on the vendors) for any given demand curve (assuming that the demand curve is neither perfectly elastic nor inelastic). Panel (a) of Figure 19-6 shows the impact of a tax on steel producers. The steel market is initially in equilibrium at point A. The steel company can reduce the amount of steel it produces only slightly because it is committed to a level of production by its fixed capital investment. As a result, even when the steel company is paying 50¢ to the government for each unit of steel produced, it still wants to produce almost the same amount. Overall, the steel company's supply curve shifts upward from S_1 to S_2. Price rises only slightly from P_1 to P_2, and quantity of steel sold falls only from Q_1 to Q_2; the new equilibrium is at point B. Since the price rise is very small, it does not much offset the tax that the steel company must pay. The steel company therefore bears most of the tax, and consumers of steel bear very little (since they don't pay a much higher price).

■ **FIGURE 19-6**

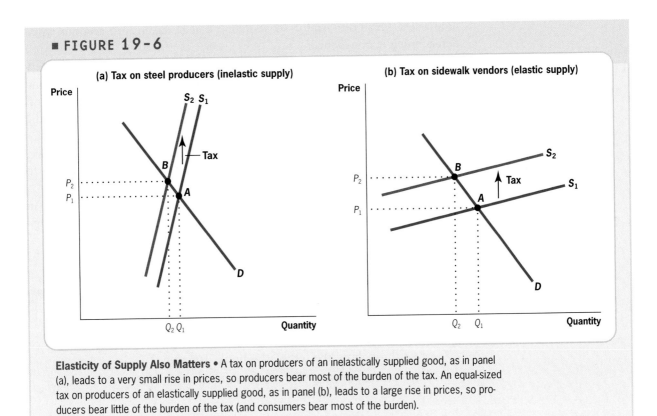

Elasticity of Supply Also Matters • A tax on producers of an inelastically supplied good, as in panel (a), leads to a very small rise in prices, so producers bear most of the burden of the tax. An equal-sized tax on producers of an elastically supplied good, as in panel (b), leads to a large rise in prices, so producers bear little of the burden of the tax (and consumers bear most of the burden).

Panel (b) of Figure 19-6 shows the impact of an equal-sized tax on sidewalk vendors. These vendors are very sensitive to the costs of production in their production decisions, leading to the very elastic supply curve. They are initially willing to provide a quantity Q_1 of goods at a price of P_1. If the government makes them pay 50¢ per good they sell, then many vendors will move out of the sidewalk vending business into some more lucrative line of work. The supply curve therefore shifts from S_1 to S_2, with prices rising from P_1 to P_2, and the quantity of goods sold falling from Q_1 to Q_2 (at point B). The large increase in price in the sidewalk vendors' market greatly offsets the taxes the vendors have to pay, so they bear little of the burden of the tax. Consumers of goods sold by sidewalk vendors will see much higher prices for these goods, however, so they will bear most of the tax.

Thus, the same principles hold for supply as for demand elasticities; elastic factors avoid taxes, while inelastic factors bear them.

In the appendix to this chapter, we develop the mathematical tax incidence formulas that formalize this intuition.

Reminder: Tax Incidence Is About Prices, Not Quantities

When the demand for gas is perfectly elastic, as in Figure 19-5, we claimed that consumers bore none of the burden of taxation, and yet the quantity of gas consumed fell dramatically. Doesn't this decrease in consumption make consumers worse off? And if so, shouldn't that be taken into account when determining tax incidence?

The answer to both questions is "no" because, at both the old and new equilibria, consumers in this case are indifferent between buying the gas and spending their money elsewhere. Each point on a demand curve represents consumers' willingness to pay for a good. That willingness to pay reflects the value of the next best alternative use of their budget. If the demand curve for gas is perfectly elastic, consumers are truly indifferent, at the market price, between consuming gas and consuming some other good. So if they have to shift to buying more of another good and less gas, they are no worse off.

More generally, when we analyze tax incidence we ignore changes in quantities and only focus on the changes in prices paid by consumers and suppliers. This assumption makes tax incidence analysis simpler.[3]

19.2

Tax Incidence Extensions

Section 19.1 presented the fundamental rules that will guide tax incidence analysis throughout the rest of this book. To recap:

- ▶ The statutory burden of a tax does not describe who really bears the tax.

- ▶ The side of the market on which the tax is imposed is irrelevant to the distribution of tax burdens.

- ▶ Parties with inelastic supply or demand bear taxes; parties with elastic supply or demand avoid them.

In this section, we apply these rules to cases different from those previously considered, including taxes on factors of production, taxes in markets with imperfect competition, and accounting for (tax-financed) expenditures in tax incidence analysis. As we will see throughout the remainder of this book, the three basic rules of tax incidence are largely all we need to know to understand more complicated cases and issues in taxation.

Tax Incidence in Factor Markets

Our discussion thus far has focused on taxes that are levied in the goods markets, such as the markets for gas or fast food. Many taxes, however, are levied in

---

[3] Technically, the tax incidence analysis discussed here applies strictly only to very small changes in taxes. For those very small changes, the sole consumers who no longer consume the good are those for whom the value of the good is the same as the value of the next best alternative purchase (consumer surplus is zero). Similarly, the only suppliers who no longer sell the good are those for whom the cost of producing that good is the same as the revenues gained from selling it (producer surplus is zero). So, as in the perfectly elastic demand case, there is no implication of changing quantity for the well-being of either consumers or suppliers; only the change in price matters. In practice, we use the same formulas for larger changes in taxes, continuing to ignore any effects of changes in quantities. A full welfare analysis of the equity effects of a larger tax change should incorporate the entire change in consumer and producer surplus, which would involve both quantity and price effects. But the key intuitions for tax incidence analysis are best demonstrated in this simpler framework.

factor markets, such as the market for labor. The analysis of tax incidence in factor markets is identical to that in goods markets; the only difference is that consumers of the factors are the firms (they demand factors such as labor) and producers of factors are individuals (who provide factors such as labor).

Consider, for example, the market for labor shown in panel (a) of Figure 19-7. Hours of labor supplied in the market are shown on the x-axis; the market wage is on the y-axis. There is a downward-sloping demand for labor from firms (D_1) and an upward-sloping supply of labor from individuals (S_1). The market is initially in equilibrium, before taxes, with a wage W_1 of $5.15 per hour at point A.

Suppose that the government levies a payroll tax of $1 per hour on all workers. This tax lowers the return to work by $1 at every amount of labor. As a result, individuals require a $1 rise in wages to supply any amount of labor and the supply shifts up from S_1 to S_2 in panel (a) of Figure 19-7. With demand remaining at its original level, this shift results in a higher market equilibrium wage of $5.65 ($W_2$) at point B. The incidence of the tax is shared by workers (suppliers) and firms (demanders) according to the elasticities of demand and supply. If these elasticities are equal, the burden is shared equally:

■ **FIGURE 19-7**

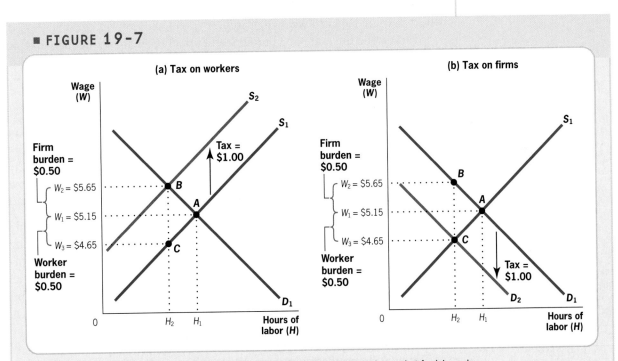

Incidence Analysis Is the Same in Factor Markets • These figures show the market for labor where firms are the consumers and workers are the producers of hours worked at a wage rate *W*. A $1.00 tax per hour worked that is levied on workers, shown in panel (a), leads the supply curve to rise from S_1 to S_2 and the wage to rise from its initial equilibrium value of $5.15 (point *A*) to a higher value of $5.65 (point *B*). A tax of $1.00 per hour worked that is levied on firms, shown in panel (b), leads the demand curve to fall from D_1 to D_2 and the wage to fall from $5.15 to $4.65 at point *C*. Thus, regardless who pays the tax, workers and firms each have a burden of 50¢ per hour.

the wage will rise to $5.65 per hour, and workers will take home $4.65 per hour after paying their $1 per hour tax. The firms and the workers each bear 50¢ of the $1.00 tax, split as indicated on the vertical axis. The firms pay a 50¢ higher wage ($5.65) and the workers receive a 50¢ higher wage ($5.65), but because they must pay $1 an hour in tax, they receive 50¢ less in after-tax wage ($4.65). The gross wage in the market has risen to $5.65, but the after-tax wage of workers has fallen to $4.65.

According to the second rule of tax incidence, what matters for the burdens on workers and employers from this tax is the total tax wedge and the elasticities of supply and demand, not who sends the check to the government. Panel (b) of Figure 19-7 shows the effect on the labor market if the payroll tax in our example were instead paid only by firms and not by workers. In that case, the supply curve would remain at S_1, and, because the tax on consumers (the firms) acts like an increase in the price of labor, the demand for labor would fall and the demand curve would shift inward to D_2. Market wages would fall by $1.00 from $5.65 to $4.65, the new equilibrium (point C), and the burdens of taxation would be unchanged. Firms bear the same 50¢ burden as before; rather than paying a 50¢ higher wage, however, they now pay a wage ($4.65) that is 50¢ lower than the initial equilibrium wage of $5.15. In addition, firms now must send a $1 check to the government, so in effect they are paying a wage of $5.65.

Workers see the same 50¢ burden; rather than receiving a 50¢ higher wage and sending a $1 check to the government, however, they now receive a 50¢ lower wage ($4.65). The gross wage in the market has fallen to $4.65, but the after-tax wage paid by firms is $5.65.

The tax incidence analysis of a payroll tax shows that it makes no difference that the Social Security payroll tax is levied half on workers and half on firms, rather than being levied 100% on workers or on firms. The second rule of tax incidence tells us that what matters for determining the burden of the Social Security tax is the total size of the tax (the total tax wedge), not how the tax is distributed across demanders and producers.[4]

Impediments to Wage Adjustment These conclusions from comparing panels (a) and (b) in Figure 19-7 will not be correct, however, if anything impedes the free adjustment of wages in the labor market. One such impediment is a **minimum wage,** a mandated minimum amount that virtually all workers must be paid for each hour of work. The current U.S. minimum wage is $5.15 per hour. Panels (a) and (b) of Figure 19-8 show how the analysis of Figure 19-7 changes when a minimum wage, W_M, is introduced at the initial equilibrium wage of $5.15.

Panel (a) shows the case where the payroll tax is levied on workers. In that case, the minimum wage has no effect on incidence analysis: when the tax is

minimum wage Legally mandated minimum amount that workers must be paid for each hour of work.

---

[4] You will recall from Chapter 13 that the FICA tax that finances Social Security is an ad valorem tax (a fixed percentage of wages) rather than the specific $1/hour tax modeled here. The conclusions of this section would not change in any way if we instead modeled the ad valorem tax, but the shift in demand or supply resulting from the tax would be a rotation (a percent shift) rather than a linear outward shift.

■ FIGURE 19-8

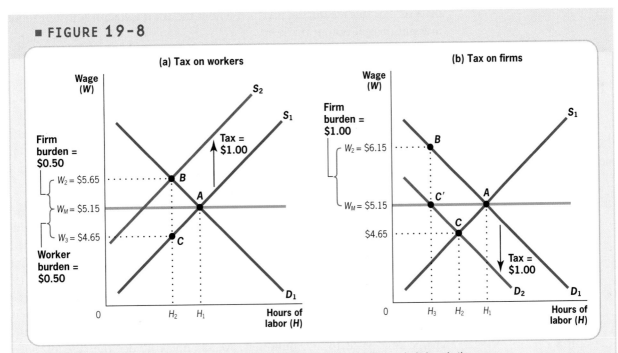

Incidence Analysis in Factor Markets Differs with a Minimum Wage • The analysis here is the same as in Figure 19-7, with the addition of the constraint that the wage cannot fall below $5.15 per hour. If the payroll tax is levied on workers, as shown in panel (a), this constraint has no effect: the wage rises to $5.65, as in Figure 19-7, and workers and firms equally share the burden of the tax. If the payroll tax is levied on firms, as shown in (panel b), however, the firms cannot lower the wage to the desired $4.65 per hour, so the firms bear the full amount of the tax.

implemented, wages rise to $5.65 at point B (firms pay 50¢ in higher wages), workers send $1 to the government in taxes, and they earn an after-tax wage of $4.65.

Panel (b) shows the case where the payroll tax is levied on firms. In that case, the supply curve remains at S_1 and the demand curve shifts to D_2. However, the firms cannot lower the wage to the desired level of $4.65 (point C), because this is an illegally low wage. The wage must stay at $5.15, and the *firm must bear all of the burden*. The workers' wage doesn't fall from $5.15, and the firm sends the check to the government, so the firm bears the full incidence of the payroll tax and pays an after-tax wage of $6.15. The quantity of labor in the market falls to H_3, where the new demand curve D_2 intersects the minimum wage line (point C').

When there are barriers to reaching the competitive market equilibrium (as in this minimum wage example), the side of the market on which the tax is levied can matter. There are a number of potential barriers, ranging from the minimum wage to workplace norms, that do not allow employers to explicitly cut workers' wages. Such rigidities are often not present in output markets. For this reason, the party on whom the tax is levied may matter more in input than in output markets.

Tax Incidence in Imperfectly Competitive Markets

Our analysis thus far has focused on perfectly competitive markets in which there are a large number of demanders and suppliers consuming very similar goods. Very few markets are perfectly competitive in practice. Unfortunately, modeling *imperfectly competitive* markets is an imperfect science. In this section, we discuss the one case that we can model clearly, a **monopoly market,** a market in which there is only one supplier of a good.

monopoly markets Markets in which there is only one supplier of a good.

Background: Equilibrium in Monopoly Markets
Monopolists maximize profits just as competitive firms do: they produce a good or service until the marginal cost of the next unit produced equals the marginal revenues earned on that unit. For competitive firms, the marginal revenue earned on the next unit is the market price, so they set marginal cost equal to price. Because monopolists are *price makers,* not *price takers,* however, marginal revenue is *not* a price determined in the market but a price chosen by the monopolist. (In our analysis of tax incidence in monopoly markets, we assume that monopolists charge one price to all consumers; we do not consider the case of *price-discriminating monopolists.*)

Panel (a) of Figure 19-9 shows the determination of equilibrium in monopoly markets. The monopoly seller has an upward-sloping marginal cost curve and faces a downward-sloping demand curve. For a monopolist, there are two aspects to the decision about whether to produce and sell the next unit. The first is the price that the monopolist will earn on the next unit. The second is that in order to sell the next unit, the (non–price discriminating) monopolist must lower the price because he or she faces a downward-sloping demand curve. Consumers will buy another unit only if the market price is less than it was at the previous quantity. However, because the monopolist charges only one price to all customers, he or she must lower the price on all previous units for sale as well. Thus monopolists face a trade-off as price makers: additional sales at a given price will increase revenue, but they will also force the monopolist to lower prices on all existing units to achieve equilibrium at the new higher quantity produced, lowering revenue.

The result of this pricing decision is that the monopolist's *marginal revenue curve* is the line MR_1 in panel (a) of Figure 19-9, which lies everywhere below the demand curve D_1. The marginal revenue that the monopolist gets from additional sales is below the consumers' willingness to pay for the given unit (the demand curve) because it incorporates the negative effect of lowering prices on all other units. In our example, the monopolist chooses to produce the quantity Q_1, the quantity at which marginal revenue equals marginal cost at point A. As measured on the demand curve D_1, consumers are willing to pay price P_1 for quantity Q_1. Thus, the monopolist produces Q_1 and charges price P_1. Note that even though the monopolist sets the price, the demand curve still must be respected. The monopolist cannot, for

■ FIGURE 19-9

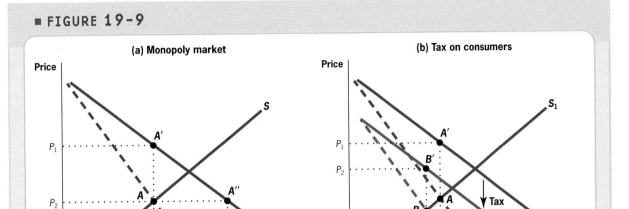

Tax Incidence in Monopoly Markets • Panel (a) shows the equilibrium in a monopoly market. The monopolist sets quantity produced where the marginal revenue curve intersects the supply curve (at Q_1) and then sets the price using the demand curve for that quantity (at P_1). When a tax is imposed on consumers in this market, as in panel (b), the demand curve shifts downward from D_1 to D_2, leading the marginal revenue curve to also shift downward from MR_1 to MR_2. The new equilibrium quantity is Q_2, with a new price of P_2.

example, produce quantity Q_1 and charge price P_2 because at that price consumers would demand Q_2 far more than Q_1 (where the monopolist's marginal revenue equals marginal costs). The mathematics of the monopolist's profit maximization, and its implications for tax incidence, are developed in the appendix.

Taxation in Monopoly Markets Suppose that the government imposes a tax on consumers in a monopoly market, as shown in panel (b) of Figure 19-9. You will recall from Chapter 13 that the FICA tax that finances Social Security is an ad valorem tax (a fixed percentage of wages) rather than the specific $1/hour tax modeled here. The conclusions of this section would not change in any way if we instead modeled the ad valorem tax, but the shift in demand or supply resulting from the tax would be a rotation (a percent shift) rather than a linear outward shift.

This tax causes consumers to be less willing to pay a given market price for the monopolist's good, shifting the demand curve to D_2. This reduction in willingness to pay leads to an associated shift in the marginal revenue curve to MR_2. The new equilibrium (at the intersection of MR_2 and the marginal cost curve) is at a lower quantity Q_2, and the new lower price is P_2.

The monopolist bears some of the tax, just as the competitive firm does: even though consumers are paying the tax to the government, the monopolist receives a lower price (P_2) in the market, so he or she shares the tax burden. The three rules of tax incidence therefore apply in monopoly markets as well. In this case, as we show in the appendix to this chapter, the side of the market on which the tax is imposed remains irrelevant: even though the monopolist has market power, a tax on either side of the market results in the same sharing of the tax burden. So monopolists cannot "exploit their market power" to avoid the rules of tax incidence.

Tax Incidence in Oligopolies Very few markets are perfectly competitive or monopolistic. Most markets operate somewhere in between, with some degree of imperfect competition. **Oligopoly markets** are markets in which firms have some market power in setting prices but not as much as a monopolist. While there are widely accepted models of how competitive and monopolistic markets work, there is much less consensus on models for oligopolistic markets. As a result, economists tend to assume that the same rules of tax incidence apply in these markets as well, but there is more work to do to understand the burden of taxes in oligopoly markets.

Balanced Budget Tax Incidence

The model we have used thus far to examine the burden of taxation in perfectly competitive markets and monopolies has focused on the incidence of the tax alone. Taxes also raise revenues, however, and these revenues will ultimately be spent. Thus, a complete picture of tax incidence would consider not only who bears the tax but also who receives the *benefit* of the spending that is financed out of the tax revenues.

Consider, for example, the federal gas excise tax, a tax levied by the federal government on the sale of gasoline. Suppose that demand for gasoline is very inelastic (or supply is very elastic), so that the price of gas to consumers rises by the full amount of this tax . At the same, however, 80% of the revenues collected by this 18.4¢ gas tax are spent on highway improvements and repairs through the highway trust fund.[5]

In this case, it would be wrong to say that drivers fully bear the tax: they do pay the tax, but they also reap some of the rewards in terms of better roads on which to drive. Tax incidence that takes into account the incidence of both the tax and the benefit is called **balanced budget incidence.**

It is often difficult, however, to trace the spending associated with a given tax increase. Thus, we typically ignore the spending side when we do tax incidence analysis. It is important to remember, however, that in reality the full burden of a tax policy will depend on the distribution of the both the tax payments and the spending of the associated revenues.

oligopoly markets Markets in which firms have some market power in setting prices but not as much as a monopolist.

balanced budget incidence Tax incidence analysis that accounts for both the tax and the benefits it brings.

---

[5] U.S. Dept of Transportation, Federal Highway Administration (2006).

19.3

General Equilibrium Tax Incidence

The model of tax incidence that we have used thus far is what economists call a **partial equilibrium** model, which considers the impact of a tax on a market in isolation. In reality, however, a given market does not exist in isolation; it is integrated with a number of other markets. To study the effects on related markets of a tax imposed on one market, economists use the model of **general equilibrium tax incidence.**

partial equilibrium tax incidence Analysis that considers the impact of a tax on a market in isolation.

general equilibrium tax incidence Analysis that considers the effects on related markets of a tax imposed on one market.

Effects of a Restaurant Tax: A General Equilibrium Example

I live in the town of Lexington, Massachusetts, which is nestled among a number of neighboring similar towns. Suppose that Lexington were to announce tomorrow that it was levying a tax of $1 on all restaurant meals in that town. The demand for restaurant meals in Lexington is fairly elastic because there are many substitutes, such as cooking at home or going to a restaurant in a nearby town. For ease, let's suppose that the demand for Lexington restaurant meals is perfectly elastic.

The effect of the restaurant meal tax under this assumption is illustrated in Figure 19-10. The restaurant meal market in Lexington is initially in equilibrium at point A: at a price of $20 per restaurant meal ($P_1$), 1,000 restaurant meals are sold per day in the town (Q_1). The meal tax acts like an increase in the restaurants' marginal costs and shifts the supply curve inward from S_1 to

■ FIGURE 19-10

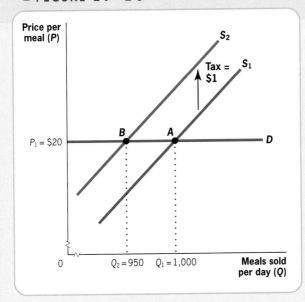

The Incidence of a Tax on Lexington Restaurants • The demand for restaurants in Lexington is perfectly elastic, so prices cannot increase when they are taxed; as a result of a $1.00 tax on restaurant meals, the supply of meals falls from S_1 to S_2, and the quantity of meals demanded and supplied falls to Q_2 (950). The price of a restaurant meal remains at $20, so the restaurant, which is paying the tax, bears its full burden.

S_2, with quantity falling to 950 meals sold per day (Q_2). Note that this tax has no effect on the price charged by restaurants: because demand is perfectly elastic, any increase in price to consumers would drive all business away. Thus, the restaurant bears the entire burden of the tax, and consumers bear none of it.

The story can't end there, however, for the simple reason that *restaurants cannot bear taxes*. As Nobel Prize–winning economist Milton Friedman once said in discussing energy taxes, "How do you 'burden' industry or 'tax' a factory? Do you squeeze it until it screams? Send it to jail? Only people can bear a 'burden' or pay a tax. An industry, a factory, or a utility can do neither."[6]

In the standard microeconomics model, firms are not self-functioning entities but are a technology for combining capital and labor to produce an output. In the context of our restaurant example, capital is best thought of as *financial* capital, the money that buys physical capital inputs, such as the building, the ovens, tables, and so on. By labor, we mean the hours of labor workers supply to the restaurant. When we say that the $1 Lexington meals tax is borne by restaurants, we mean that it is borne by the factors (labor and capital) that restaurants have organized to produce meals. To accurately identify who bears the burden of the meals tax, we need to move the analysis back one step and ask: In what proportions do these factors of production bear the restaurant tax?

General Equilibrium Tax Incidence Consider first the market for labor employed by restaurants in Lexington, shown in panel (a) of Figure 19-11. In this market, supply is likely to be very elastic, because workers can always choose another job in Lexington or go to work in a restaurant in a nearby town. Once again, for ease, let's assume that the labor supply available to restaurants in Lexington is perfectly elastic. At the initial market equilibrium (point A), the wage is $8/hour ($W_1$) and the quantity of labor is 1,000 hours per year (H_1). When the new tax goes into effect, and restaurants bear its full burden (since the demand for restaurant meals is perfectly elastic), they will reduce their demand for workers. Each worker is worth less because the restaurant's willingness to pay for an hour of labor falls when it is taxed on the fruits of that labor (the meals).[7] The demand curve in the Lexington restaurant labor market shifts downward from D_1 to D_2, but because labor supply is perfectly elastic, wages do not fall and workers bear none of this tax. If restaurant owners try to pay their workers a wage lower than W_1, the workers will simply go work someplace else.

Now consider the market for capital in Lexington restaurants, shown in panel (b) of Figure 19-11. In the short run, having invested in a Lexington restaurant, the capital owner is stuck, unable to pull out money that has already been spent on stoves, tables, and a building. In principle, the capital owner could resell goods, such as chairs, tables, and buildings, but in reality the owner would receive only a fraction of the purchase price. Thus, while the supply of capital isn't perfectly inelastic in reality, we assume for convenience in panel (b) of Figure 19-11 that capital supply is perfectly inelastic.

---

[6] Friedman (1977).

[7] The demand for labor is determined by its after-tax marginal value: the marginal product of the worker times the value of the goods produced net of taxes paid on those goods.

■ FIGURE 19-11

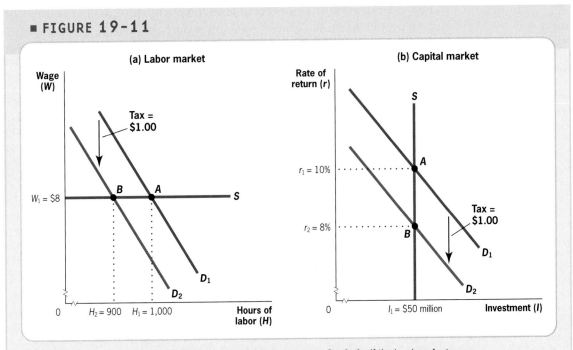

The Incidence of a Lexington Restaurant Tax on Labor versus Capital • If the burden of a tax on restaurants is borne by the restaurants, it must be borne by the factors of production used by the restaurants. In panel (a), the supply of labor to restaurants in Lexington is perfectly elastic, so when demand for labor falls to D_2, it cannot be reflected in lower wages; the wage is unchanged and workers do not bear any of this tax. In panel (b), the supply of capital to restaurants in Lexington is perfectly inelastic, so when demand for capital falls to D_2, the rate of return to capital falls by the full amount of this tax to r_2.

The initial equilibrium in this capital market is at point A: the rate of return to capital is 10% (r_1) and the investment in restaurants is $50 million. Since the tax is borne fully by the restaurants, it reduces their demand for capital just as it reduced their demand for labor. Capital is also worth less when the restaurant is taxed on the fruits of that capital (meals), so the restaurant will demand capital only from those who are willing to charge a lower rate of return. The lower demand is reflected in the fall in the demand curve from D_1 to D_2; the new equilibrium is at point B, with a lower rate of return of 8% (r_2). Because the supply of capital is inelastic in the short run, capital owners will bear the meals tax in the form of a lower return on their investment in the restaurant. Thus, when Lexington levies a tax on restaurant meals, its incidence ultimately rests on the investors in Lexington restaurants. This spillover of incidence to other markets is an example of general equilibrium tax incidence.

Issues to Consider in General Equilibrium Incidence Analysis

General equilibrium analysis is a game of "follow the tax burden": the analysis does not stop with the effects on the market in which a tax is levied, but expands to all related markets until it identifies the persons who ultimately bear the tax burden. This process raises three interesting issues that must be considered when using general equilibrium analysis.

Effect of Time Period on Tax Incidence: Short Run Versus Long Run Under the assumptions we made, we have just shown the correct general equilibrium analysis of the tax burden of a restaurant meals tax in Lexington. These assumptions are likely to be valid for a short-run (say, one-year) analysis of a restaurant tax. In the long run (for example, over ten years), however, these assumptions may no longer be valid. Over time, capital invested in Lexington restaurants is no longer inelastic; investors can close or sell the restaurants, take their money, and invest it elsewhere. Indeed, in the long run, capital supply is likely to be perfectly elastic because there are many substitutes for investing in restaurants in Lexington. In the long run, then, capital owners will not bear any of the tax.

Quick Hint What does it mean for capital supply to be elastic? Think of capital investments already made as irretrievable; that is why capital supply is inelastic in the short run. In the long run, however, restaurants need new infusions of capital to stay afloat: equipment and furnishings need to be replaced, buildings need to be renovated, and so on. The elasticity of capital supply in the long run arises from the ability of investors to choose whether to reinvest in a firm. If there is a tax on the good produced by the firm, and this tax is passed on to capital investors in the form of a lower return, then they are less likely to reinvest in the restaurant.

The rule that the market participants with the most elastic supply or demand avoid taxes is *always* the guide to the game of "follow the tax burden." We've just seen that in the long run the supply of capital is perfectly elastic. The supply of labor was already elastic in the short run, and it should be even more elastic in the long run as workers with restaurant-specific skills can move out of Lexington to other towns where the restaurants are not taxed and can pay higher wages as a result. This finding leaves us with a puzzle: If neither capital nor labor bears the tax in the long run, who does?

There is one more inelastic factor in the restaurant production process: the *land* that the restaurants are built on. This land is in fixed supply and is therefore inelastic by definition. When labor and capital avoid the tax, its burden falls squarely on the owners of the land in Lexington. With workers unwilling to accept a lower wage to work at Lexington restaurants and owners of capital unwilling to accept a lower return, the only way restaurants can stay open is if they pay lower rent on their land. Thus, factors that are always inelastically demanded or supplied in both the short and long run bear taxes in the long run.

Effect of Tax Scope on Tax Incidence The incidence of a tax is also affected by the share of the product market to which it applies. Compare the incidence of the tax on restaurant meals in Lexington with a tax imposed on all restaurant meals in the state of Massachusetts. While demand for meals in Lexington may be very elastic, demand for all restaurant meals in the state of Massachusetts is less elastic because it is more costly to find substitutes. Individuals can still eat at home instead, but there aren't easily available substitutes for dining away from home unless you live very near a neighboring state. Since demand is less elastic, restaurant consumers will bear some of the tax burden.

In the short run, the remainder of the tax burden not borne by consumers is shared once again between labor and capital. The incidence on labor has changed, however: workers are less mobile because they cannot move into other restaurant jobs as easily as they could when the restaurant tax was imposed only in Lexington. (In that case, they could avoid the Lexington tax burden by working at a restaurant in a neighboring town.) With the labor supply to the entire state restaurant industry less elastic than it was to just Lexington restaurants, labor will bear some of the meals tax: restaurants will be able to pay their workers somewhat less in response to this tax because the workers have fewer employment alternatives. As before, capital is inelastic in the short run, so it will continue to bear much of the tax burden.

As a result, the short-run burden of a tax on all restaurants in Massachusetts will be shared among consumers, workers, and capital, rather than being fully borne by capital. The exact proportions in which the burden will be shared depend on the exact elasticities of demand and supply in each of these markets. Once again, the goal of general equilibrium tax analysis is to follow the burden until it is distributed across all payers. When demands or supplies are not perfectly elastic or perfectly inelastic, the tax burden may be spread across many parties. The scope of the tax matters to incidence analysis because it determines which elasticities are relevant to the analysis: taxes that are broader based are harder to avoid than taxes that are narrower, so the response of producers and consumers to the tax will be smaller and more inelastic.

Spillovers Between Product Markets While the discussion thus far has focused solely on the consumers and producers in the restaurant market, the incidence of a tax may extend beyond this market to other goods markets as well. When consumers of a good bear any of the tax on that good, this burden will affect their consumption of other goods by shifting their budget constraint. This spillover to other goods markets means that a tax in one market can have a burden or benefit on the consumers and producers in other markets too.

Consider the tax on restaurant meals in the state of Massachusetts. This tax reduces demand for restaurant meals by raising the after-tax price to consumers. This higher after-tax price has three effects on other goods as well:

1. Consumers have lower incomes and may therefore purchase fewer units of all goods (the income effect).

2. Consumers may increase their consumption of goods and services (such as movies) that are substitutes for restaurant meals because they are now relatively cheaper than the taxed meals (the substitution effect).

3. Consumers may reduce their consumption of goods or services (such as valet parking services) that are complements to restaurant meals because they are consuming fewer restaurant meals (the complementary effect).

So, for example, a tax on restaurant meals could lower the demand for babysitters, since incomes will be lower and individuals will go out to eat less frequently. On the other hand, the meals tax could raise the demand for concerts, since individuals might attend a concert instead of eating out.

A complete general equilibrium tax analysis must account for effects in all other markets. Playing "follow the tax burden" means not only following it up and down within a market, but also following it horizontally across markets and then vertically within those other markets. For example, if the tax on restaurants raises demand for movies (shifting out the demand curve), it leads to higher prices for moviegoers (so that movie consumers bear some of the tax on restaurants), higher wages for movie workers, and a higher return on capital in the movie sector. Indeed, a full general equilibrium analysis must also incorporate supply spillovers as well. As highlighted in the important article by Bradford (1978), a tax that shifts capital or labor out of any one jurisdiction will raise the supply of capital or labor to other jurisdictions, lowering the return to capital or labor elsewhere.

19.4

The Incidence of Taxation in the United States

The central role of tax fairness in debates over tax policy has motivated extensive analysis of tax incidence in the United States. The best-known study of tax incidence in the United States is the periodic analyses of the Congressional Budget Office (CBO). In this section, we review the lessons from its analyses.

CBO Incidence Assumptions

The CBO analysis considers the incidence of the full set of taxes levied by the federal government. To do so, CBO must use the type of analysis we employed to guide their assumptions about the incidence of each type of taxation in the United States. Their key assumptions follow:

1. *Income taxes* are borne fully by the households that pay them.
2. *Payroll taxes* are borne fully by workers, regardless of whether these taxes are paid by the workers or by the firm.
3. *Excise taxes* are fully shifted to prices and so are borne by individuals in proportion to their consumption of the taxed item.
4. *Corporate taxes* are fully shifted to the owners of capital and so are borne in proportion to each individual's capital income.

These assumptions are generally consistent with both theory and empirical evidence. For example, as we show in Chapter 21, the low response of the labor supply of primary earners in the United States to taxation (inelastic supply) means that taxes on labor will be borne by workers. There is also substantial evidence that excise taxes on goods such as tobacco and alcohol are shifted forward to the prices charged to consumers, as discussed in the Empirical Evidence box on p. 569.

THE INCIDENCE OF EXCISE TAXATION

In the United States, excise taxes on goods such as gasoline, alcoholic beverages, and cigarettes vary widely across the states, and there are frequent changes within states over time in these taxes as well. This variation in taxation allows for quasi-experimental estimation of the impact of excise taxes on prices of the taxed goods. Analysts can compare the change in goods prices in the states raising their excise tax (the treatment group) relative to states not changing their excise tax (the control group), to measure the effect of each 1¢ rise in excise taxes on goods prices.

An excellent example is excise taxes on cigarettes. The excise tax on cigarettes varies widely across the U.S. states, from a low of 2.5¢ per pack in Virginia to a high of $1.51 per pack in Connecticut and Massachusetts. Moreover, there have been large changes in cigarette taxation within states over time. Since 1990, for example, New Jersey has increased its tax rate nearly sixfold (from 27¢ per pack to $1.50), while Arizona has increased its tax nearly eightfold (from 15¢ to $1.18).[8] A number of studies have examined the change in cigarette prices when there are excise tax increases on cigarettes, comparing states increasing their tax (treatments) to other states that do not raise taxes (controls). These studies uniformly conclude that the price of cigarettes rises by the full amount of the excise tax.[9]

Another example is the reaction of consumer goods prices to increases in general sales taxes. Poterba (1996) uses data from 1947 to 1977 for a sample of eight cities that had sales tax changes at some point during that period. He relates the change in prices for clothing and other personal care items to the change in sales taxes in each city, and he finds that these goods prices rose fully by the amount of the sales tax increase (full shifting to prices).

The most difficult assumption to assess is the incidence of the corporate tax. As we discuss at length in Chapter 24, it seems likely that at least some of the corporate tax is borne by consumers and workers, rather than its full incidence being solely on capital owners, although there is no convincing empirical evidence on this question. This means that the corporate tax is not as progressive as the CBO analysis indicates, because some of that tax is borne by lower income workers (whereas the CBO assumes that the corporate tax is fully borne by higher income owners of capital).

Results of CBO Incidence Analysis

The results of this CBO analysis (published in 2005 for analysis through the year 2003) are shown in Tables 19-1 and 19-2. Table 19-1 shows the computed average tax rates (taxes paid relative to total income) by income group for the years 1979, 1985, 1990, 1995, 2000, and 2003.. We show the results for all households and for the lowest and highest quintile. The top panel in Table 19-1 shows the average tax rates for all taxes combined; the remaining panels show the average tax rates by type of tax.

Several interesting conclusions emerge from Table 19-1:

1. The total average tax rate, combining all taxes across all households, declined from 22.2% in 1979 to 20.9% in 1985, then climbed to 23% in 2000 before dropping back down to 19.8% in 2003.

---

[8] Orzechowski and Walker (2003), Table 7.
[9] Chaloupka and Warner (2000).

■ TABLE 19-1

Effective Tax Rates

	1979	1985	1990	1995	2000	2003
	Total effective tax rate					
All households	22.2%	20.9%	21.5%	22.6%	23.0%	19.8%
Bottom quintile	8.0%	9.8%	8.9%	6.3%	6.4%	4.8%
Top quintile	27.5%	24.0%	25.1%	27.8%	28.0%	25.0%
	Effective income tax rate					
All households	11.0%	10.2%	10.1%	10.2%	11.8%	8.5%
Bottom quintile	0.0%	0.5%	−1.0%	−4.4%	−4.6%	−5.9%
Top quintile	15.7%	14.0%	14.4%	15.5%	17.5%	13.9%
	Effective payroll tax rate					
All households	6.9%	7.9%	8.4%	8.5%	7.9%	8.4%
Bottom quintile	5.3%	6.6%	7.3%	7.6%	8.2%	8.1%
Top quintile	5.4%	6.5%	6.9%	7.2%	6.3%	7.2%
	Effective corporate tax rate					
All households	3.4%	1.8%	2.2%	2.8%	2.4%	2.0%
Bottom quintile	1.1%	0.6%	0.6%	0.7%	0.5%	0.3%
Top quintile	5.7%	2.8%	3.3%	4.4%	3.7%	3.4%
	Effective excise tax rate					
All households	1.0%	0.9%	0.9%	1.0%	0.9%	0.8%
Bottom quintile	1.6%	2.2%	2.0%	2.4%	2.3%	2.3%
Top quintile	0.7%	0.7%	0.6%	0.7%	0.5%	0.5%

Congressional Budget Office (2005), Table 1A.

The top panel of this table shows the total effective federal tax rate on all households and on the top and bottom quintiles of the income distribution. The other panels show the effective tax rates of various other types of federal taxes.

2. The total average tax rate on the bottom quintile rose sharply from 8% to 9.8% from 1979 to 1985, then fell throughout the rest of the period, reaching 4.8% by 2003.

3. The average tax rate on the top quintile fell from 27.5% in 1979 to 24% in 1985, rose to 28% by 2000, and then fell back to 25% by 2003.

4. The bottom quintile pays much more in payroll taxes than in income taxes, and this disparity has been growing over time. In 1979, the bottom quintile had an average income tax rate of zero but an average payroll tax rate of 5.3%; by 2003, the average income tax was −5.9% (on net, the income tax system paid out more to lower income individuals through tax credits, primarily the Earned Income Tax Credit, than it collected through tax payments) but the average payroll tax rate had risen to 8.1%. Indeed, over 70% of all households paid more in payroll taxes than in income taxes in 2003.

■ TABLE 19-2

Top and Bottom Quintile's Share of Income and Tax Liabilities

	1979	1985	1990	1995	2000	2003
Top quintile						
Share of income	45.5%	48.6%	49.5%	50.2%	54.8%	52.2%
Share of tax liabilities	56.4%	55.8%	57.9%	61.9%	66.6%	65.7%
Bottom quintile						
Share of income	5.8%	4.8%	4.6%	4.6%	4.0%	4.2%
Share of tax liabilities	2.1%	2.3%	1.9%	1.3%	1.1%	1.0%
Top 1%						
Share of income	9.3%	11.5%	12.1%	12.5%	17.8%	14.3%
Share of tax liabilities	15.4%	14.8%	16.2%	20.1%	25.5%	22.6%

Congressional Budget Office (2005), Tables 1B and 1C.

This table shows the share of income and tax liabilities accruing to the top and bottom income quintiles over time.

5. Average corporate tax rates are small relative to income and payroll tax rates and have fallen at both the top and bottom of the income distribution.

6. Average excise tax rates are also small and have risen for the bottom of the income distribution while falling at the top. (This is due to a much larger decline in consumption of taxed goods, such as cigarettes, by higher income groups than by lower income groups.)

The general conclusion from Table 19-1 is that the United States has a fairly progressive tax system overall, although some elements (the income tax) are progressive while others are not (the payroll tax). Table 19-2 presents the share of tax liabilities paid by the top and bottom quintiles over time, and it compares this to their share of the income earned in the United States.[10] The bottom quintile of taxpayers has always paid a very small share of taxes, and that share has fallen (from 2.1% of taxes paid to 1.1% of taxes paid) along with its share of national income (which has fallen from 5.8% of national income to 4.2% of national income). The top quintile of taxpayers has always paid the majority of taxes, and that share has risen (from 56.4% of taxes paid to 65.3% of taxes paid) along with its share of national income (from 45.5% of national income to 52.4% of national income). Today, the top quintile earns more than half of all the income earned in the United States, and pays almost two-thirds of the taxes paid, under the CBO's incidence assumptions.

Of particular interest is the tax burden on the very richest members of society, which is also shown in Table 19-2. The top 1% of the income distribution now controls 14.3% of pretax income, or about one in every seven

---

[10] These income shares differ from what was presented in Table 17-1 because that table was based only on cash incomes, and CBO's income definition includes imputed income from the corporate sector, employer contributions for health and retirement plans, and the value of in-kind benefits, such as food stamps and public health insurance.

dollars of income, an increase of 50% from 1979. But the tax burden on this group rose as well until 2000, although it has fallen since that time.

Current Versus Lifetime Income Incidence

current tax incidence The incidence of a tax in relation to an individual's current resources.

lifetime tax incidence The incidence of a tax in relation to an individual's lifetime resources.

A final important distinction that must be drawn in incidence analysis is between **current** and **lifetime tax incidence.** The CBO analysis just presented measures individual incomes on an annual basis. This approach can be misleading given the extensive mobility across income classes observed in the United States. Recent estimates show that between 25 and 40% of Americans change income quintiles within a one-year period, and 60% change within a decade.[11]

Closer to home, suppose that we were to assess the incidence of a tax on college textbooks. College students are typically living independently and would be measured as having fairly low incomes. Thus, such a tax would be viewed as highly regressive on an annual or current basis. Yet most of the students reading this book certainly hope that their incomes will be much higher later on in life as a result of their valuable college education. Indeed, the lifetime incomes of college graduates are, on average, more than twice as high as the lifetime incomes of those who do not attend college. Thus, on a lifetime basis, taxes on college textbooks are *progressive*, since they tax those who earn high incomes on a lifetime basis.

The importance of this point is illustrated by Poterba (1989a), who examined the incidence of alcohol, gasoline, and tobacco taxes. Poterba first divided people in 1984 by quintiles of income and observed that the share of income spent on gasoline and alcohol of the lowest quintile was five times the share of the highest quintile. The share of tobacco of the bottom quintile was nine times the share of the top quintile. Thus it seems that taxes on such goods would be highly regressive.

Poterba then divides people by quintiles of *consumption,* which may be a better measure of lifetime resources. For example, low income college students who know they will someday be rich will reflect that in their spending by borrowing from parents; similarly, rich elderly people who currently have low income but high savings will also have high consumption. Relating taxes paid to consumption rather than to current income, Poterba found that the tax burden is still regressive but much less so. In fact, the lowest four quintiles spend roughly the same share of their total expenditures on gasoline and alcohol, which is less than twice the highest quintile's share. For tobacco, the lowest quintile's share of total expenditures is only three times the share of the highest quintile.

19.5

Conclusion

Debates over tax incidence have been central to tax policy for decades. The "fairness" of any tax reform is one of the primary considerations in policy

---

[11] McMurrer and Sawhill (1996).

makers' positions on tax policy. Therefore, it is crucial for public finance economists to have a deep understanding of who really bears the burden of taxation so that we can best inform these distributional debates over the fairness of a proposed or existing tax. The techniques developed in this chapter can provide that deep understanding and allow you to think more carefully through the distributional implications of any tax change.

▶ HIGHLIGHTS

■ Tax incidence is the study of the distribution of tax burdens across economic agents, and it takes into account not only who pays the tax to the government but also the effects of the tax on market prices.

■ Tax incidence does not depend on who pays the taxes to the government or on whether taxes are levied on suppliers or demanders. In all cases, elastic parties avoid taxes and inelastic parties bear them.

■ The incidence of taxes on factor markets is analyzed in the same way as taxes in goods markets, although impediments to price adjustment such as minimum wages can complicate the analysis. Like-

wise, the analysis of tax incidence in imperfectly competitive markets is similar to the analysis in competitive markets.

■ General equilibrium tax incidence is a game of "follow the tax burden" from goods markets to their associated input markets and from one output market to another.

■ Taxes are fairly progressive overall in the United States, although the overall progressivity of taxation is subject to key assumptions about tax incidence.

■ Tax incidence can be based on current or lifetime income, and the results can differ greatly for some types of taxes.

▶ QUESTIONS AND PROBLEMS

1. Why do most analysts assume that payroll taxes in the United States are borne by workers rather than by employers?

2. The demand for rutabagas is $Q = 2,000 - 100P$ and the supply of rutabagas is $Q = -100 + 200P$. Who bears the *statutory* incidence of a $2 per unit tax on the sale of rutabagas? Who bears the *economic* incidence of this tax?

3. The demand for rutabagas is still $Q = 2,000 - 100P$ and the supply is still $Q = -100 + 200P$, as in Question 2. Governor Sloop decides that instead of imposing the $2 sales tax described in Question 2, the government will instead force stores to pay the tax directly. What will happen to the "sticker price" on rutabagas? How will the size of the consumer tax burden change?

4. The demand for football tickets is $Q = 360 - 10P$ and the supply of football tickets is $Q = 20P$. Calculate the gross price paid by consumers after a per-ticket tax of $4. Calculate the after-tax price received by ticket sellers.

5. The government is considering imposing taxes on the sellers of certain classes of products. The first tax they are considering is a tax on 2% milk. The second is a tax on all dairy products. The third is a tax on all food products. Which of these three taxes would you expect to have the largest impact on the sticker prices of the taxed products?

6. To finance a new health insurance program, the government of Millonia imposes a new $2 per hour payroll tax to be paid by employers.

   a. What do you expect to happen to wages and the size of the workforce?

   b. How will this answer change in markets where labor is inelastically demanded?

7. You have determined that producers, rather than consumers, will bear the lion's share of the burden associated with a new tax. How does the elasticity of labor supply influence whether this tax burden will, in turn, be borne more by workers or more by property owners?

8. Why can some taxes that appear to be regressive in terms of current income be thought of as progressive from a lifetime tax incidence perspective?

9. Consider a labor market in which workers are paid the minimum wage. When will it matter for tax incidence whether a payroll tax is imposed on workers or on employers?

10. Consider the changes over time in the U.S. effective tax rates presented in Table 19-1. How did the total effective tax burden change for the lowest and highest deciles of the population between 1979 and 2003? How did the composition of this burden across different types of taxes change over this period?

▶ ADVANCED QUESTIONS

11. The elasticity of demand for maracas is −2.0 and the elasticity of supply is 3.0. How much will the price of maracas change with a per-unit tax of $2? Who bears the larger burden of the tax, consumers or producers?

12. The government of Byngia has introduced a new tax on airline travel. Byngia has two types of travelers, business travelers and leisure travelers. Business travelers in Byngia have an elasticity of demand of −1.2, while Byngian leisure travelers have an elasticity of −3.0. Airlines can price-discriminate between these groups; that is, they can charge different prices to the different types of fliers in the market. Which type of travel will bear the larger burden of the tax? Explain.

13. Massive Products, Inc., is a monopolist whose cost of production is given by $10Q + Q^2$ (so its marginal cost curve—equivalently, its inverse supply curve—is given by $10 + 2Q$). Demand for Massive Products' massive products is $Q = 200 − 2P$.

   a. What price will the monopolist charge, and what profits will the monopolist earn? What will the consumer surplus be?

   b. How will the monopolist's price and profits change if a tax of $15 per unit is imposed on the buyers of the product?

   c. What is the deadweight burden of the tax?

14. In which case will workers bear a larger share of the tax burden, when taxes are imposed in a single locality or when taxes are imposed throughout an entire state? Why will your answer differ between the short run and the long run?

15. The city of Malaise is considering a 10% tax on the revenues of all hotels/motels inside the city limits. Although not completely different from hotels and motels in the nearby suburbs, the ones in Malaise have a distinct advantage in their proximity to interesting sights and convention centers. So individuals will pay some premium to stay in Malaise rather than to stay nearby.

   Furthermore, all land is used equally well by hotels/motels and other forms of business; any Malaise land not taken by a hotel/motel is readily absorbed by other forms of business.

   Mayor Maladroit calls you in to advise him on the incidence of such a tax. He is particularly concerned with who will bear this tax in the short run (one month) and the long run (five years).

   a. What is the incidence of the tax in the short run? Answer intuitively, and use a diagram if possible.

   b. What is the long-run incidence? Once again, use a diagram if possible.

   c. How would your analysis in (b) change if hotels/motels in the suburbs were perfect substitutes for those in Malaise? What would happen to tax revenues?

Appendix to Chapter 19

The Mathematics of Tax Incidence

In this appendix, we develop the mathematical formulas that lie behind the incidence discussion in Chapter 19. We then use them to examine various aspects of tax incidence in a monopoly market.

Tax Incidence Formulas

To analyze tax incidence, we need to measure how imposing a tax changes the price in a market. Consider first the case of a tax that is *paid by consumers* so that the total price change to consumers is

$$\text{total price change} = \Delta P + \tau$$

where ΔP is the change in market price (presumably negative) and t is the tax payment. The price change to producers is just ΔP, the reduction in price.

We can determine the effect of tax on price in three steps:

Step 1: Start with the definitions of elasticity of demand and supply:

$$\text{elasticity of demand} = \eta_d = \Delta Q/(\Delta P + \tau) \times (P/Q)$$
$$\text{elasticity of supply} = \eta_s = \Delta Q/\Delta P \times (P/Q)$$

Step 2: Rearrange terms so that the two expressions can be set equal to each other:

$$\Delta Q/Q = \eta_d \times (\Delta P + \tau)/P$$
$$= \eta_s \times \Delta P/P$$

Step 3: Set these expressions equal to each other, and solve for the change in price as a function of the tax (which is what we need to know in order to do incidence analysis):

$$\Delta P = [\eta_d/(\eta_s - \eta_d)] \times \tau.$$

This equation formalizes our intuition on inelastic and elastic factors. For example, if demand is inelastic ($\eta_d = 0$), then $\Delta P = 0$. The price does not change, so since the consumer is sending the check to the government, he bears the full tax. Alternatively, if demand is perfectly elastic ($\eta_d = \infty$), then $\Delta P = -\tau$. The price falls by the full amount of the tax, offsetting the consumer tax payment so that the consumer has no remaining tax burden.

Similarly, if we redo the exercise for a tax paid by producers, we obtain

$$\Delta P = [\eta_s/(\eta_s - \eta_d)] \times \tau.$$

Tax Incidence in a Monopoly

We can put these mathematical insights to work to explore the implications of tax incidence in a monopoly. Suppose that a monopoly firm has a cost function of

$$C = 12 + q^2.$$

Its marginal cost, the increment to cost from one additional unit of production, is therefore $2q$ (the derivative of the cost function with respect to quantity).

Suppose further that the monopolist faces a demand function of

$$p = 24 - q.$$

Given the cost and demand functions, we can determine the monopolist's revenue and marginal revenue:

$$\text{revenues} = p \times q = (24 - q) \times q = 24q - q^2$$
$$\text{marginal revenues} = \text{derivative of revenues with respect to } q = 24 - 2q.$$

Marginal revenues are set equal to marginal costs to maximize profits:

$$24 - 2q = 2q.$$

Solving for q, we find that $q = 6$; marginal revenues equal marginal costs (and profits are maximized) by selling 6 units. Once the monopolist has determined the quantity at which profits are maximized, the price per unit is determined by the demand curve $p = 24 - 6 = 18$. Initially, then, the monopolist produces 6 units and sells them for $18 each.

Now suppose that the government levies a tax on the monopolist of $4 per unit sold. The cost function becomes $12 + q^2 + 4q$, and marginal costs are $2q + 4$. Re-solving for the profit-maximizing quantity, we obtain $q = 5$. As before, once the monopolist sets the quantity, the price is determined by the demand curve, $p = 24 - q = 19$. After the tax is imposed, the monopolist therefore produces 5 units at a price of $19. The monopolist bears three-quarters of this tax; the price goes up by only $1, but the monopolist pays $4 in tax.

How would this outcome change if the government levies the tax on consumers of this monopoly product? After tax, the demand function becomes $p = 24 - q - 4 = 20 - q$. Revenues are therefore $(20 - q) \times q = 20q - q^2$. Differentiating with respect to q, we obtain a marginal revenue function of $20 - 2q$. Re-solving for the profit-maximizing quantity, we once again find that $q = 5$. On the new demand curve, this implies a price of $15 to consumers and an after-tax cost to consumers of $19 (because they pay the $4 tax). So, once again, consumers bear only $1 of the tax (since price has decreased from $18 to $15 to offset the $4 tax payment), and the monopolist bears $3 (as the price has decreased). This analysis confirms our earlier finding that the side of the market on which the tax is imposed is irrelevant to the determination of which side bears the burden of the tax.

Tax Inefficiencies and Their Implications for Optimal Taxation

20

Arnold Harberger, one of the pioneers of the general equilibrium tax incidence model we discussed in Chapter 19, once wrote of his experience in Indonesia, where cars are taxed more heavily than motorcycles. This tax difference provided a great incentive to make motorcycles more carlike. As Harberger reports, "Three-wheel cycles were converted, by artful additions, into virtual buses, or at least taxis. Sometimes a single bench was added, with the passenger looking backward. Other times the cycle was stretched at the back, with two benches going down each side, and maybe even with an extra little running board cutting laterally across the rear (where the rear bumper of the car would be). I must say I was truly astounded when I saw my first eight-passenger motorcycle."[1]

This example highlights a simple fact: markets do not take taxes lying down. If there is some action that market participants can undertake to minimize the burden of taxation, they will do so. As long as there are substitutes for the consumption of any taxed good, some consumers will shift to those substitutes to avoid the tax, and as long as there are alternatives to the production of taxed goods, some producers will shift into producing those alternatives.

In this chapter we learn how attempts to minimize tax burdens have *efficiency costs* for society. In the absence of market failures, social efficiency is maximized at the competitive equilibrium without government intervention. When the government taxes market participants, they change their behavior to avoid the tax and move the market away from the competitive equilibrium, thereby reducing social efficiency. Put simply, it is costly for society to transport people in dangerous eight-passenger motorcycles instead of cars.

The remainder of the chapter uses these general lessons to explore the determination of the optimal taxation of commodities (goods such as cereal and cars) and income. We show how the tools of economic theory can be used to describe the ideal tax system across goods or people and discuss how

---

[1] Harberger (1995), p. 307.

economists use empirical evidence to advise policy makers on constructing more efficient tax systems in the real world.

20.1
Taxation and Economic Efficiency

$\mathbf{A}$s we move from discussing the effects of taxation on equity (how the economic pie is distributed among market participants, the topic of Chapter 19) to discussing the effects of taxation on efficiency (how taxes affect the size of the economic pie), we shift our focus from the effect of taxes on market *prices* to their effect on market *quantities*. The discussion of tax incidence was about who bore the burden of taxation through tax payments and price changes. This discussion of tax efficiency is about the amount of social efficiency sacrificed by society when trades are impeded by the presence of taxation; the social efficiency effects of taxation are determined by the effect of taxes on quantities.

Graphical Approach

For modeling the efficiency consequences of taxation, it is useful to start with a graphical approach. Figure 20-1 shows the impact of a 50¢ per gallon tax levied on producers of gasoline. Before the tax is imposed, the demand curve for gasoline is D_1, the supply curve is S_1, and the market is initially in equilib-

■ **FIGURE 20-1**

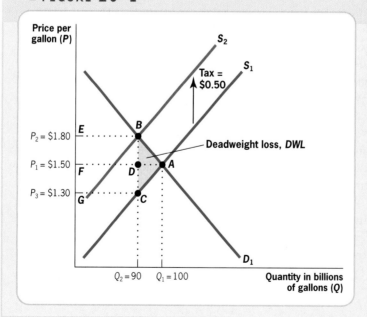

Deadweight Loss of a Tax ● When a tax is imposed, the supply curve shifts from S_1 to S_2 and the equilibrium quantity in the market falls from Q_1 to Q_2, creating a deadweight loss triangle *BAC*. The *DWL* arises because there are trades ($Q_1 - Q_2$) for which social marginal benefits (demand curve) exceed social marginal costs (supply curve) that are not made.

rium where they intersect at point A, with quantity Q_1 (100 billion gallons) and price P_1 ($1.50 per gallon).

Recall from Chapter 2 that in a perfectly competitive market the demand curve measures the social marginal benefit of gasoline consumption, and the supply curve measures the social marginal cost of gasoline production. At the competitive market equilibrium (point A), all gallons of gasoline that have a social marginal benefit greater than their social marginal cost are produced and consumed. The 100 billionth gallon (Q_1) has both a social marginal benefit and social marginal cost of $1.50, so this is the competitive market equilibrium. All previous units sold have a social marginal cost below $1.50 (since they are farther down on the supply curve) and a social marginal benefit above $1.50 (since they are higher up on the demand curve). At equilibrium, the sum of consumer surplus and producer surplus is at its maximum.

The 50¢ tax acts like an increase in producers' costs, causing them to decrease the quantity supplied at each price, which shifts the supply curve in from S_1 to S_2. The new equilibrium is at point B; the quantity of gasoline sold has fallen from Q_1 (100 billion gallons) to Q_2 (90 billion gallons) and the price has risen from P_1 ($1.50) to P_2 ($1.80). The reduction in sales to a level below the competitive equilibrium quantity Q_1 means that, because of the tax, trades that would be beneficial to both producers and consumers of gasoline (trades on which there is positive consumer and producer surplus) are not being made. The units between 90 billion and 100 billion (between Q_2 and Q_1) are units for which the social marginal benefit of consumption exceeds the social marginal cost of production: they are valued at more than $1.50 by consumers and cost less than $1.50 to produce (the pre-tax demand curve is above the pre-tax supply curve). Yet these units are not being produced and consumed once the tax is in place.

This reduction in quantity creates a *deadweight loss* (*DWL*) of the area *BAC*. Since the competitive equilibrium quantity maximizes social efficiency, the reduction in quantity below Q_1 causes social efficiency to fall. Because consumers value the units between Q_2 and Q_1 above their price of $1.50, they would have purchased them. After the tax is levied, they forgo these purchases and consumer surplus falls by the trapezoid *EBAF*. Because producers could make profits on the forgone sales of the units between Q_2 and Q_1, producer surplus falls by the trapezoid *FACG*. Much of this reduced social surplus is transferred to the government in the form of higher tax revenues (the rectangle *EBCG*), but some of it (triangle *BAC*) disappears because many surplus-producing trades are not made. Deadweight loss therefore measures the inefficiency of taxation, the amount of consumer and producer surplus society loses by imposing a tax, that is, surplus that is lost and not recaptured in the form of tax revenues. Deadweight loss is determined by changes in quantities when a tax is imposed, since this change captures the number of socially efficient trades that are not being made.

From the second rule of tax incidence, it should be clear that the outcome of this efficiency analysis would be the same if the tax were imposed on consumers instead of producers. In that case, market prices would fall (to $1.30 per gallon) instead of rising (to $1.80 per gallon), but the change in quantity would be the same. Since the efficiency effects of a tax are determined by the change in quantity, this would not affect the computation of deadweight loss.

Elasticities Determine Tax Inefficiency

Just as the price elasticities of supply and demand determine the distribution of the tax burden among market participants, they also determine the inefficiency of taxation: as demand and supply elasticities rise, the deadweight loss of taxation grows. This lesson is illustrated in Figure 20-2 for a tax on producers in two different markets. In panel (a), demand is relatively inelastic. A tax on producers shifts the supply curve upward from S_1 to S_2. This leads to a large rise in market prices from P_1 to P_2 and a relatively small reduction in market quantity from Q_1 to Q_2. Since deadweight loss is determined by the reduction in socially efficient trades, the deadweight loss in this case (area BAC) is small. If the government were to tax insulin, for example, there would be very little effect on the quantity of insulin demanded, and therefore little deadweight loss.

In panel (b), demand is more elastic. Thus, when the tax on suppliers shifts the supply curve from S_1 to S_2, there is a small rise in market prices from P_1 to P_2, but a relatively large reduction in market quantity from Q_1 to Q_2. As a result, the deadweight loss triangle (BAC) is much larger because many social-

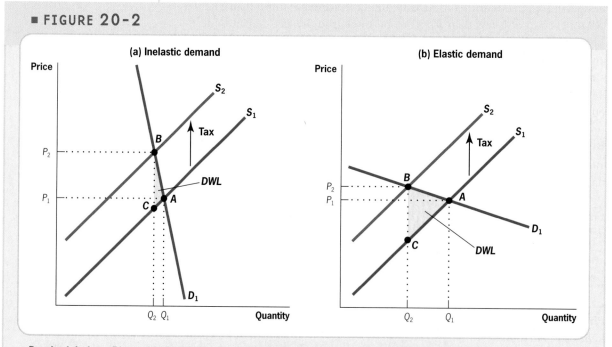

■ FIGURE 20-2

Deadweight Loss Rises with Elasticities • The deadweight loss of a given tax is smaller when the demand curve is less elastic, as in panel (a), than when it is more elastic, as in panel (b).

ly efficient trades (where the pre-tax demand is above the pre-tax supply) are not being made. Suppose, for example, that the government levied a tax on a particular fast-food restaurant, McGruber's. This tax would cause a large reduction in demand for McGruber's meals because individuals would shift their consumption to close substitutes (like Gruber King). This change is inefficient, however, because the fact that individuals were eating at McGruber's before the tax indicates that McGruber's meals are their preferred choice. The large deadweight loss occurs because many individuals move away from their preferred choice in response to the tax.

As these two examples show, the *inefficiency of any tax is determined by the extent to which consumers and producers change their behavior to avoid the tax; deadweight loss is caused by individuals and firms making inefficient consumption and production choices in order to avoid taxation.* The competitive equilibrium quantity maximizes social surplus. Any change in quantity from the equilibrium point leads to inefficiency because trades that have a benefit larger than their cost are not made. Inefficiency is therefore proportional to the change in quantity induced by the tax. For insulin, there is little change in quantity induced by the tax, so there is little inefficiency. The tax on McGruber's fast-food restaurant induces a large change in quantity, so there is substantial inefficiency. The more elastic the demand or supply of a good is, the larger the change in quantity induced by the tax, and the larger the inefficiency of the tax.

▶ APPLICATION

Tax Avoidance in Practice

The legendary economist John Maynard Keynes once remarked, "The avoidance of taxes is the only pursuit that still carries any reward." His comment appears to have been taken to heart by many individuals whose elastic behavior allows them to avoid taxes. Some examples:

1. The British boat designer Uffa Fox lived in a home he constructed from a floating bridge. When the Inland Revenue (Britain's tax collectors) attempted to collect property tax on the home, Fox began sailing it up and down the river. By the time he was done, Fox had collected so many different addresses that the Inland Revenue gave up their attempts.[2]

2. An Englishman visiting Cyprus in the early 1980s asked a tour guide why so many of the houses seemed to have steel reinforcement bars jutting out from their top floors. The guide informed him that Cyprus had a building tax that applied only to finished structures. Owners of those houses could thus claim that they were still in the process of finishing the roof. The process, of course, never ended.[3]

3. The Thai government levies a tax on signs in front of businesses. The tax is levied only on external signs and the rate depends on whether the sign

---

[2] Angus and Robertson (1978).
[3] See Doug Porter's letter at http://www.wirksworth.org.uk/MAIL-1.htm.

is completely in Thai (low), in Thai and English (medium), or completely in English (very high). A walk around Bangkok thus reveals many businesses hanging English signs with a small amount of Thai writing in the upper-right-hand corner. Some businesses manage to avoid the tax entirely by printing the message on curtains that are hung in the front window, rendering the sign "internal" and thus tax-exempt.[4] ◀

Determinants of Deadweight Loss

The appendix to this chapter mathematically derives the formula for deadweight loss as a function of the elasticities of supply and demand and the size of the tax. We show that the formula for *DWL* is

$$DWL = -\frac{1}{2}\frac{\eta_s \eta_d}{\eta_s - \eta_d} \times \tau^2 \times \frac{Q}{P}$$

where η_d is the elasticity of demand, η_s is the elasticity of supply, and τ is the tax rate. From this equation, we learn two important lessons. First, deadweight loss rises with the elasticities of demand and supply: the more opportunities market participants have to consume or produce substitutes (the more elastic is demand or supply), the greater the inefficiency they will create by substituting.

As we discuss in the appendix, the appropriate elasticities to use for this calculation are ones that reflect substitution effects only, not income effects (called the *compensated* elasticity). This is because any government revenue raising has income effects, since income is transferred from individuals to the government, so what determines the inefficiency of a particular tax is how much the tax distorts behavior due to substitution effects. In practice, however, it is typically difficult to distinguish the substitution and income effects of a price change, so we generally rely on the total (or *uncompensated*) elasticity when computing deadweight loss; we use the overall response of quantity to price, not the theoretically appropriate response that reflects substitution effects only.

Second, the deadweight loss rises with the square of the tax rate (τ^2), so that the distortion from any given amount of tax is greater as the existing tax rate increases. Thus, the distortion from a nickel tax on gas is much greater if it is the last nickel of a 25¢ tax increase than if it is the first nickel of a 5¢ tax increase. The **marginal deadweight loss,** the increase in deadweight loss per unit increase in the tax, rises with the tax rate.[5]

This point is illustrated graphically in Figure 20-3. The gas market is initially in equilibrium at point *A*, with quantity Q_1 and price P_1. The government then imposes a 10¢ per unit tax on producers, causing the supply curve to shift in from S_1 to S_2 as producers face a higher cost per unit produced (and so produce less at each price). Quantity falls to Q_2 at the new equilibrium point *B*. This tax creates a deadweight loss triangle with area *BAC*.

---

marginal deadweight loss
The increase in deadweight loss per unit increase in the tax.

---

[4] http://angkor.com/cityrain/got0201.shtml.
[5] *DWL* rises with the square of the tax rate only when elasticities are constant, as they are here. The more general point is the last one: the marginal deadweight loss of any tax rises with the tax rate.

■ FIGURE 20-3

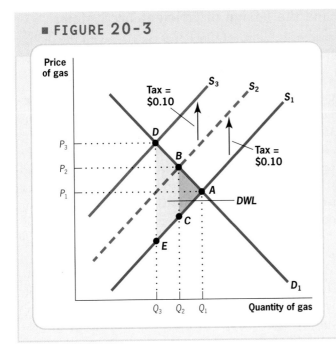

Marginal Deadweight Loss Rises with Tax Rate • An initial $0.10 tax on suppliers causes a deadweight loss triangle *BAC*. An additional $0.10 tax causes a much larger deadweight loss, *DAE*. The trapezoid *DBCE* is the marginal deadweight that is added to the initial deadweight loss of triangle *BAC*.

The government then levies a second tax of 10¢ per unit on producers, which causes the supply curve to shift in even farther to S_3. Quantity now falls to Q_3 at the new equilibrium point D. The additional deadweight loss from this second tax is the trapezoid *DBCE,* which is much larger than the triangle *BAC.* The marginal deadweight loss from the second 10¢ tax (which brings the total tax to 20¢) is much larger than the marginal deadweight loss from the first 10¢ tax. After both taxes have been levied, the total *DWL* from the 20¢ tax is the triangle *DAE.*

The intuition behind this outcome relates to the Quick Hint about deadweight loss on page 52 of Chapter 2. Small deviations from the competitive market equilibrium are not very costly in terms of lost social surplus, because the transactions made close to the equilibrium are not the ones that generate a lot of social surplus. Indeed, a tax that reduced the quantity sold by only one unit would have approximately zero deadweight loss because the last trade was one for which consumers valued the good at roughly its price (no consumer surplus) and producer costs were roughly equal to price (no producer surplus). The 100 billionth gallon of gas has neither producer nor consumer surplus, so ending the sale of that particular gallon has little consequence for society.

As the market moves farther and farther from the competitive equilibrium, however, the trades that are impeded by taxation (trades for quantities between Q_2 and Q_1 for the first 10¢ tax, and trades for quantities between Q_3 and Q_2 for the second 10¢ tax) are trades that have more and more social surplus, as indicated by the widening gap between demand and supply. The loss of these higher-surplus trades means that deadweight loss is larger as the market moves farther from the competitive equilibrium.

Deadweight Loss and the Design of Efficient Tax Systems

The insight that the marginal deadweight loss of a tax rises with the the tax rate has a number of important implications for the design of efficient tax policy. In this section we provide two examples.

A Tax System's Efficiency Is Affected by a Market's Preexisting Distortions

preexisting distortions Market failures, such as externalities or imperfect competition, that are in place before any government intervention.

The fact that the marginal deadweight loss rises with the tax rate means that **preexisting distortions** in a market, such as externalities, imperfect competition, or existing taxes, are key determinants of the efficiency of a new tax. Consider the two goods markets depicted in Figure 20–4. In the first market, shown in panel (a), there are no externalities, and the initial equilibrium is at point A, where quantity is Q_1. In the second market, shown in panel (b), there are positive production externalities (like the donut shop and the policemen in Chapter 5). The positive externalities cause the social marginal cost of production (the SMC curve) to be below the private marginal cost (the S_1 curve), since the firm does not incorporate the positive benefits for others into its supply decision. The firm chooses to produce at point E, where supply equals demand, but social surplus is maximized at point D, where SMC equals demand. So the firm underproduces at quantity Q_2, where the social efficiency maximum is at quantity Q_1. Any reduction in production below Q_1 is inefficient because units for which social marginal benefit (measured by the

■ FIGURE 20-4

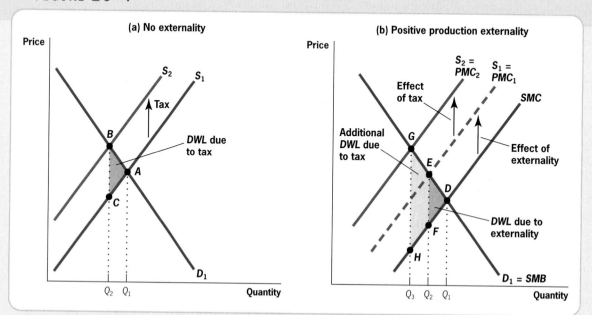

Preexisting Distortions Matter • In panel (a), a tax in a market with no preexisting distortions (such as externalities) creates a deadweight loss equal to triangle *BAC*. In panel (b), a positive externality in the market has created a deadweight loss triangle *EDF*; imposing a tax on this market results in a deadweight loss that is larger by the area of trapezoid *GEFH*. The total *DWL* in the market with a positive externality and a tax is the area of triangle *GDH*.

demand curve) exceeds social marginal cost (the SMC curve) are not being produced. Thus, there is underproduction of the good, and a deadweight loss of area EDF, because trades with a positive social surplus (those between Q_1 and Q_2) are not being made.

Now suppose the government imposes an equal-sized tax of $1 per unit sold on suppliers in both markets. This tax shifts the supply curves up from S_1 to S_2 in both panels, and causes the producer to cut back production to Q_2 in panel (a) and Q_3 in panel (b). For the market in panel (a), which has no externalities, the tax causes a small deadweight loss of BAC. For the market in panel (b), the market that already has a pre-tax deadweight loss because of its positive production externalities, the tax adds a a large deadweight loss (the area of trapezoid $GEFH$). This trapezoid is much bigger than the triangle BAC in panel (a), because the tax in the second market moves the market outcome to Q_3, even farther away from the social efficiency maximizing level of production Q_1 than is Q_2. Once a market is already underproducing, the drop in quantity from a tax is especially costly because the trades that are not occurring are ones for which marginal social benefits significantly exceed marginal social costs.

This point also has important implications for taxation in markets that are imperfectly competitive, such as monopolies. Because imperfectly competitive firms already underproduce their goods relative to competitive equilibrium, the efficiency cost of imposing a tax on them is greater than the cost of imposing the same size tax on a market that is initially in competitive equilibrium. Of course, if there are negative externalities in a market, then the conclusion of the analysis is the opposite: a tax might have *no* deadweight loss, rather than a small deadweight loss, because it is correcting an externality (as in Chapter 5).

Governments Should "Smooth" Tax Rates Over Time The fact that the marginal deadweight loss rises with the tax rate implies that governments should not raise and lower taxes as they need money but should instead set a long-run tax rate that will meet their budget needs on average, using deficits and surpluses to smooth out its short-run budget fluctuations. For example, suppose that a nation has a tax rate of 20% that finances its revenue needs. Now also suppose that the nation decides to enter a one-year war, which it estimates will double its revenue needs for one year, after which these will return to normal. The government should *not* finance its needs by raising the tax rate to 40% next year, and then lowering the rate back to 20% in the year after. Rather, the government should raise its tax rate by a small amount in all future years, for example by 1% for 20 years, to finance this war.

This course of action is suggested by the fact that the marginal deadweight loss rises with the tax rate. A tax of 40% in one period and 20% in the next causes more deadweight loss than a tax of 21% for 20 years, because the marginal deadweight loss associated with the increase in rates from 20% to 40% in one year is larger than the savings in deadweight loss going from a rate of 21% to a rate of 20% for 20 years. Just as individual utility is maximized by full consumption smoothing, government efficiency in taxation over time is maximized by *tax smoothing,* by having a relatively constant tax rate over time rather than high taxes in some periods and low taxes in others.

▶**APPLICATION**

The Deadweight Loss of Taxing Wireless Communications

Hausman (2000) estimated the deadweight loss from a particularly dynamic sector of our economy: wireless communications services, those communications carried out with cell phones, PCs, and other wireless devices. In 1999, the state and federal tax burden on wireless communication in the typical state was 14.5%, although the rate was 25% in high-tax states such as California, New York, and Florida. Hausman estimated that the deadweight loss from this taxation averaged 53¢ per dollar of revenue: for every dollar the government raised in taxes, social welfare was reduced by 53¢.

This figure is high for three reasons. First, demand for wireless communications is fairly price sensitive; Hausman estimated a price elasticity of demand of –0.51. Second, there is already a large preexisting distortion in this market because wireless prices are well above marginal cost; the marginal cost of wireless services is only 5¢ per minute, while the typical wireless plan charges many multiples of that. Thus, there is already underproduction of wireless services relative to the competitive equilibrium, which is exacerbated by taxation. Finally, the taxes are fairly high, and the marginal deadweight loss rises with the tax rate; in California, New York, and Florida, the deadweight loss is 70¢ per dollar raised.

This is only the average deadweight loss. Hausman also computed the marginal deadweight loss from additional increments to wireless taxation. This deadweight loss is higher than the average, since deadweight loss grows as we move farther from the undistorted equilibrium. Hausman estimated that the marginal deadweight loss caused by an additional tax on wireless services ranged from 72¢ to 90¢ per dollar raised. Thus, in high-tax states, for every additional dollar in revenue raised, society would lose almost another dollar in efficiency losses. ◀

20.2

Optimal Commodity Taxation

Section 20.1 has provided us with the necessary tools to turn from the *positive* question of how to measure deadweight loss to the *normative* question of how the existence of *DWL* should be taken into account in the design of the tax system. We address this normative question with reference to two different types of taxes. This section looks at *commodity taxation,* the taxation of goods. The next section discusses the taxation of income.

Ramsey Taxation: The Theory of Optimal Commodity Taxation

The theory of **optimal commodity taxation** began with the early-twentieth-century economist Frank Ramsey, who considered the problem of a government with a given budgetary requirement and the ability to set dif-

optimal commodity taxation
Choosing the tax rates across goods to minimize deadweight loss for a given government revenue requirement.

ferent tax rates for different commodities (food, clothing, tobacco, and so on). Ramsey formulated the problem of optimal taxation by asking the question: How can we raise a given amount of revenue with the least amount of distortion? In other words, how should a government set its tax rates across a set of commodities to minimize the deadweight loss of the tax system while meeting its budgetary requirement?

The appendix to this chapter presents the mathematics of Ramsey's elegant solution. Here, we discuss the key lesson of his model: *The government should set taxes across commodities so that the ratio of marginal deadweight loss to marginal revenue raised is equal across commodities:*

Ramsey Rule: set commodity taxes such that $\dfrac{MDWL_i}{MR_i} = \lambda$

where *MDWL* is the marginal deadweight loss from increasing the tax on good *i*, *MR* is the marginal revenue raised from that tax increase, and λ is the **value of additional government revenues.** This constant measures the value of having another dollar in the government's hands relative to its next best use in the private sector. If λ is large, it implies that additional government revenues are quite valuable relative to keeping the money in private hands; if λ is small, then additional government revenues have little value relative to the value private individuals place on having that money.

This rule states that the deadweight loss per dollar of tax revenue associated with an additional dollar of taxes on commodity *i* should be equal for all commodities. If the tax on good *A* has an *MDWL/MR* that is higher than the *MDWL/MR* from taxing good *B*, taxing good *A* causes more inefficiency per dollar of revenue raised than does taxing good *B*. Recall that *MDWL* is a positive function of the tax rate; as discussed earlier, higher taxes lead to a higher marginal deadweight loss because they move the market farther from the competitive equilibrium (the deadweight loss is determined by the square of the tax rate). Therefore, to minimize inefficiency in the market, the government should reduce taxation of good *A,* thus reducing its *MDWL*, and raise the tax on good *B,* increasing its *MDWL*. These adjustments should continue until the *MDWL/MR* ratios for both goods are equal to λ, so that both goods have the same efficiency cost per dollar of revenue raised.

If λ is large, then additional resources to the government have a high value, so the *MDWL/MR* should be large for all commodity taxes (tax rates should be high); if λ is small, then additional resources to the government have a low value, so the *MDWL/MR* should be small for all commodity taxes (tax rates should be low). In other words, the government should be willing to have potentially inefficient (high *MDWL*) taxes when it has large budgetary needs. This tells the government to set the *marginal cost* of taxation (*MDWL/MR*) equal to its *marginal benefit* (λ).

In principle, the Ramsey Rule can tell us the optimal *level* of taxation across commodities. In practice, policy analysts typically do not have a measured value for λ, the value of additional revenues to the government, so the Ramsey Rule is typically used when talking about *tax reform* and the costs and benefits of shifting from an existing pattern of commodity taxes to another

Ramsey Rule To minimize the deadweight loss of a tax system while raising a fixed amount of revenue, taxes should be set across commodities so that the ratio of the marginal deadweight loss to marginal revenue raised is equal across commodities.

value of additional government revenues The value of having another dollar in the government's hands relative to its next best use in the private sector.

pattern that raises the same amount of revenue. The application on page 589 discusses the use of the Ramsey Rule to inform tax reform.

Inverse Elasticity Rule

It is convenient to express the Ramsey result in a simplified form that allows us to relate it to elasticities of demand. As we show in the appendix, if we assume that the supply side of commodity markets is perfectly competitive (elasticity of supply is infinite), then the Ramsey result implies that

$$\tau_i^\star = -1/\eta_i \times \lambda$$

where $\tau_i^\star$ is the optimal tax rate for commodity i, and η_i is the elasticity of demand for commodity i. This equation indicates that the government should set taxes so that the tax rate on each commodity is proportional to 1 over the elasticity of demand; elastically demanded goods (a higher value of η_i) should be taxed less and inelastically demanded goods taxed more.

This formulation of Ramsey's rule shows that two factors must be balanced when setting optimal commodity taxes:

▸ *The elasticity rule:* When elasticity of demand for a good is high, it should be taxed at a low rate; when elasticity is low, the tax rate should be high. The deadweight loss from any tax rises with the elasticity of demand, so efficiency is enhanced by taxing inelastically demanded goods more than elastically demanded goods.

▸ *The broad base rule:* It is better to tax a wide variety of goods at a moderate rate than to tax very few goods at a high rate. Because the marginal deadweight loss from a tax rises with the tax rate, the government should spread taxes across a large number of commodities and not tax any one commodity at a very high rate. This is a corollary of the "tax smoothing" result described earlier: better to tax many goods at 1% than just a few goods at 2%, since the rise from 1 to 2% in the tax rate has a larger marginal *DWL* than moving from 0 to 1%.

To balance these two recommendations, the government should tax inelastically demanded goods at a higher rate, but should not look to collect *all* its taxes from these goods unless the price elasticity of demand is perfectly inelastic. If a government cared only about the elasticity rule, it would find the most inelastic good and raise all revenues from taxing that good. The broad base rule, however, tempers that tendency. Thus, while the government should tax inelastic goods more highly, it should tax other goods as well.

Equity Implications of the Ramsey Model

This inverse elasticity formulation of the Ramsey model highlights the fairly nasty equity implications of the Ramsey approach. Imagine that the government had only two goods it could tax, cereal and caviar. The elasticity of demand for caviar is much higher than that for cereal, so the inverse elasticity rule would suggest that the government tax cereal much more highly than caviar. This would mean imposing a tax on a good consumed exclusively by higher-income groups that was much lower than the tax imposed on a good consumed by all. This outcome, while efficient, might violate a government's sense of tax fairness across income groups (vertical equity).

An optimal commodity tax framework can address equity concerns by taking into account not only the elasticity of each commodity but also the income distribution of its consumers. Goods that are disproportionately consumed by higher-income consumers could have a tax rate above that implied by the inverse elasticity rule, and goods that are disproportionately consumed by lower-income consumers could have a tax rate below that implied by the inverse elasticity rule. How much of this "reweighting" of optimal taxes across commodities should be done is a function of the extent to which governments want to trade efficiency for equity. As the government moves away from the Ramsey efficiency rule by bringing in equity issues, the tax system becomes less efficient but more equitable.

Perhaps because of these distributional concerns, there is relatively little reliance on commodity taxation in the United States. Most of our tax revenues come from taxing individual incomes, which we discuss after the following application.

▶ APPLICATION

Price Reform in Pakistan

Although commodity taxes are not widely used in the United States, they are a primary source of revenue in developing nations, where income is very difficult to measure and consumption is a more reliable basis for taxation. Moreover, in developing nations, another important tool of public policy is to *subsidize* many staple consumption goods, such as rice. Such subsidies usually work in the following manner: the government purchases the good from producers at market prices and then sells it to consumers at below market prices (with the government making up the difference in price from its revenues). These subsidies are motivated by equity concerns (the government is subsidizing the cost of living of low-income groups), but they also have efficiency costs. The logic of tax inefficiencies works with subsidies as well: any government intervention that moves consumption away from its optimal level is inefficient. With taxation, there is underconsumption of a good relative to the efficiency-maximizing point; with subsidies, there is overconsumption. Since the good is made artificially cheap for consumers, they consume in a range where their social marginal benefit of consumption is actually below the social marginal cost of production.

Angus Deaton (1997) studied the demands for commodities in several developing nations. He used variation in prices encountered by consumers of rice, wheat, and other commodities to estimate their elasticities of demand. He also estimated the preexisting distortions to demand from the existing subsidies or taxes on these goods. He then put this information together to develop estimates of the optimal changes in commodity taxes and subsidies in each nation.

His analysis of the data from Pakistan is particularly revealing. In 1984–85, the Pakistani government was paying subsidies of 40% to wheat and to rice, so that consumers paid 40% less than the market price for these goods, and the government was collecting a 5% tax on oils and fats. Demand for wheat was price inelastic, with a price elasticity of demand of −0.64, while demand for rice and for oils and fats was very price elastic, with a price elasticity of demand of −2.08 for rice and −2.33 for oils and fats: for the latter two categories of goods, demand fell by more than 2% for every 1% rise in price (or rose by more than 2% for every 1% subsidy to price). There were also other taxes and subsidies in place, but we focus our discussion on these three goods to illustrate the lessons of Deaton's analysis.

These conditions are summarized in Table 20-1, and the markets for these commodities are illustrated in Figure 20-5. Panel (a) of the figure shows the market for wheat. This market is initially in equilibrium at point A, where D intersects S_1 at a price of P_1 and a quantity of Q_1. The subsidy to wheat increases the supply of wheat, shifting the supply curve out to S_2, and raising the consumption of wheat to Q_2. The consumption of wheat between Q_1 and Q_2 is inefficient, because the social marginal benefit (the demand curve) is below the social marginal cost (S_1), so there is a deadweight loss of BAC. Panel (b) of the figure shows the market for rice. The analysis here is similar to that in panel (a), but the deadweight loss from the subsidy is much larger, since the demand for rice is more elastic than the demand for wheat. As with taxes, a higher elasticity of demand leads to a larger deadweight loss from subsidies, so there is more socially inefficient consumption (between Q_1 and Q_2). Panel (c) shows the market for oils and fats. Here, the market is initially in equilibrium at

---

▪ **TABLE 20-1**

Demand for Various Commodities in Pakistan

Good	Subsidy	Price elasticity	Policy change	Welfare gain	Include distributional concerns
Wheat	40%	−0.64	Reduce subsidy	Small	Don't reduce subsidy
Rice	40%	−2.08	Reduce subsidy	Large	Reduce subsidy
Oil/fat	−5%	−2.33	Reduce tax	Large	Reduce tax further

Deaton (1997).

Different goods in Pakistan have different levels of subsidies and taxes, as well as different price elasticities. This table shows the welfare gain from government reforms to the subsidies/taxes on three of these goods. Optimal tax simulations suggest that there are small welfare gains from reducing the subsidy on wheat (since it is inelastically demanded), and that income distribution concerns further argue against subsidy reduction. On the other hand, there are large welfare gains from reducing the subsidy on rice (since it is elastically demanded), and large welfare gains from reducing the tax on oils and fats, and income distribution considerations only strengthen those conclusions.

■ FIGURE 20-5

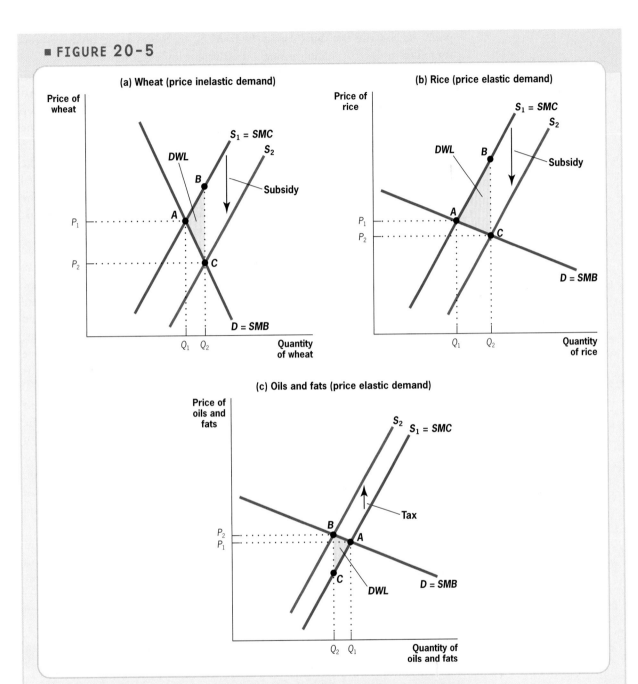

Efficiency Consequences of Subsidies and Taxes in Pakistan • In panel (a), the market for wheat, demand is fairly inelastic and supply is subsidized, leading quantity to increase from Q_1 to Q_2 with a deadweight loss of BAC. In panel (b), the market for rice, demand is very elastic, so when supply is subsidized the quantity rises by much more (from Q_1 to Q_2), and the deadweight loss is larger (BAC). In panel (c), the market for oils and fats, demand is also very elastic, so even the small tax leads to a large reduction in quantity from Q_1 to Q_2, with a deadweight loss of BAC.

point *A,* and the tax shifts supply in from S_1 to S_2, lowering quantity consumed from Q_1 to Q_2 and causing a deadweight loss of *BAC.*

Using a framework similar to Ramsey's, Deaton computed the social cost of raising the tax or reducing the subsidy on particular goods. He found that there was a modest social benefit to reducing the subsidy on wheat, as shown in the fifth column of Table 20-1, and a large social benefit to reducing the subsidy on rice. This is apparent from Figure 20-5: reducing the subsidy on wheat would remove a small deadweight loss triangle, while removing the subsidy on rice would remove a larger deadweight loss triangle. The social benefits of reducing the subsidy for rice are larger than those for reducing the subsidy for wheat because rice demand is much more price elastic than wheat demand, so the distortions from subsidizing rice are even larger.

Deaton also found that there were social costs to the taxation of oils and fats, and that society would be better off reducing that commodity tax (removing the deadweight loss of *BAC* in panel (c) of Figure 20-5). Because oils and fats are very elastically demanded, they should be taxed at a lower rate than other goods for which the demand is less elastic. Thus, Deaton suggested a tax reform that would increase efficiency: reduce the tax on oils and fats, while making up for the lost tax revenues by reducing the subsidies to rice (especially) and to wheat. Without changing net government revenues, efficiency would be improved.

Deaton also considered whether distributional considerations offset these tax reform conclusions. He found that wheat is consumed quite heavily by the poor. Thus, if redistributional concerns are important, subsidies for wheat should not be scaled back. In contrast, rice is consumed fairly evenly by people at all income levels, so rice subsidies should end even if society places high weight on helping the poor. The tax on oils and fats should be reduced even further if helping the poor is a concern because fats and oils are consumed relatively heavily by the poor.

Thus, the rather abstract notions of optimal commodity taxation can find very useful application in practice. Armed with these concepts and the tools of empirical analysis, economists can provide important advice to policy makers on appropriate reforms to commodity tax and subsidy systems.[6] ◀

_20.3_

Optimal Income Taxes

In the United States and most other developed countries, income taxation is a much more important source of revenue raising than commodity taxation. In designing optimal income taxes, the government's goal is still to meet its revenue requirements while minimizing the distortions due to taxation, but with income taxes the government also explicitly cares about another goal: the vertical equity of the resulting tax system. The goal of the government is

---

[6] For a more recent application of this method to price reforms in Mexico, see Nicita (2004).

to raise revenues in a manner that maximizes the nation's *social welfare function,* the function that aggregates individual utilities into an overall level of social well-being. In this section, we develop the theory of **optimal income taxation** and then illustrate how this theory can be applied to construct examples of optimal income tax systems. Just as the optimal commodity tax system consists of a set of tax rates (and subsidies) across commodities, the optimal income tax system consists of a set of tax rates (and income transfers) across income groups. Rather than setting optimal tax rates across goods, the optimal income tax is setting optimal tax rates across individuals.

optimal income taxation
Choosing the tax rates across income groups to maximize social welfare subject to a government revenue requirement.

A Simple Example

It is helpful to begin with a simple example that makes the following assumptions:

1. Everyone in society has the same utility functions ($U_1 = U_2 = \ldots$).

2. These utility functions exhibit diminishing MU of income.

3. The total amount of income in society is fixed (so incomes are not determined by individual choices that might respond to tax rates).

4. Society has a utilitarian social welfare function ($V = U_1 + U_2 + \ldots$) under which each individual's utility is weighted equally in determining social welfare.

Under these assumptions, the optimal income tax system is one that leaves everyone with the *same level of post-tax income,* which is the total post-tax income in society divided by the number of persons in society. Any individuals with incomes below this level would receive a transfer from the government that would increase their incomes to the average amount. Any individuals with incomes above this level would have their incomes taxed away until their post-tax income equaled the average amount.

With this system, the marginal tax rate is 100%: each additional dollar of earnings either reduces one's transfer by $1 (if below the average income level) or raises one's tax by $1 (if above the average income level). The average tax rate is negative below the average income level, since those individuals receive a transfer (pay negative taxes), positive above the average income level, and everywhere rising with income.

This may sound like an extreme system, but it is not as far from historical reality as one might think. At its peak (in 1945), the top marginal tax rate in the United States was 94%! But this example imposes very unrealistic assumptions. Perhaps the most unrealistic is the assumption that incomes are fixed, which implies that individuals won't work less if they face a 100% marginal tax rate. This is at odds with common sense and empirical evidence.

General Model with Behavioral Effects

As discussed in Chapters 2 and 17, in redistributing resources across individuals, the government typically faces an *equity-efficiency trade-off.* When society redistributes resources, it likely shrinks the total size of the economic pie by reducing income generation while at the same time it equalizes the distribution of the slices of the pie. In the previous example, there was no trade-off: since total incomes in society were fixed, there was no efficiency cost of raising taxes. Thus, the optimal system focused solely on equity, ensuring that all individuals had equal incomes.

In reality, taxation affects the size of the pie too: the rate at which incomes are taxed will generally determine the size of the incomes that are subject to taxation. Thus, in designing optimal income taxes the government needs to consider the effect of raising tax *rates* on the size of the tax *base*.

Consider the example of a tax on labor income. The revenues raised by this tax are equal to the tax rate times the tax base of labor earnings. Assume that workers reduce the amount of labor they supply to the market as their after-tax wage falls (we discuss this assumption in more detail in Chapter 21). An increase in the tax rate on labor income will therefore have two effects on tax revenues. First, tax revenues will rise for a given level of labor income. Second, however, at some point workers will reduce the amount of labor income they earn and the tax base will shrink. For low tax rates, the first effect will dominate: if we start from a tax rate of zero, there is no tax base to shrink by raising the tax rate, so only the first effect can operate. But as tax rates rise, the second effect will become increasingly important: at a tax rate of 100%, no one would work, the base would be zero and taxes would raise no revenue.

These two effects are the genesis of the famous *Laffer curve,* which was an intellectual underpinning of the large tax cuts of the early 1980s in the United States. Figure 20-6 shows that curve, with tax revenues on the vertical axis and the tax rate on the horizontal axis. When the tax rate is either zero or 100%, the tax raises no revenues. As the tax rate moves upward from zero, revenue increases, but after reaching its maximum at the tax rate $\tau^\star$, revenues

■ **FIGURE 20-6**

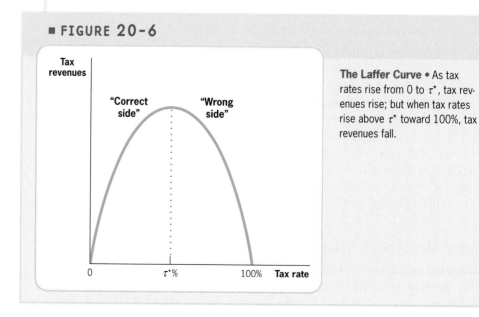

The Laffer Curve • As tax rates rise from 0 to τ^*, tax revenues rise; but when tax rates rise above τ^* toward 100%, tax revenues fall.

eventually decrease and fall back to zero again at a 100% tax rate. Thus, when we are on the "wrong" (right-hand) side of the Laffer curve, we can actually *raise revenues by cutting the tax rate*. In the early 1980s, the belief that we were on the wrong side of the Laffer curve led Congress to pass tax cuts on higher-income individuals. In fact, evaluations of the type that we discuss later in this chapter and in Chapter 25 suggest that we were still on the "correct" (left-hand) side of the Laffer curve at this point, and that cutting taxes on the wealthy reduced revenues.

The goal of optimal income tax analysis is to identify a schedule of tax rates across income groups that maximizes social welfare, while recognizing that raising tax rates has conflicting (and, if taxes are high enough, negative) effects on revenues. The appendix to this chapter shows the mathematical formulation of this analysis, and concludes that the optimal income tax system meets the following condition:

set income tax rates across groups such that $MU_i / MR_i = \lambda$

where MU is the marginal utility of individual i, MR is the marginal revenue raised from taxing that individual, and λ is the value of additional government revenues (as discussed in the context of optimal commodity taxation). The optimal income tax system is one in which the marginal utility per dollar of revenue raised is equalized across individuals.

Individual marginal utility is a declining function of individual consumption, due to the principle of diminishing marginal utility discussed in Chapter 2. By lowering after-tax income, higher taxes lead to lower individual consumption and higher marginal utility of consumption for individual i. If the income tax system is such that it leaves individual i with a higher marginal utility per dollar of revenue than individual j, then this formulation suggests that taxes should be lowered on individual i and raised on individual j. Such a shift will raise the after-tax income of individual i, increasing her consumption and lowering her marginal utility, and it will lower the after-tax income of individual j, decreasing his consumption and raising his marginal utility. These adjustments should continue until the MU/MR ratios for all individuals are equal to λ.

Much like optimal commodity taxation, this outcome represents a compromise between two considerations. In the case of commodity taxation, optimal taxes trade off the elasticity rule (tax inelastic commodities more highly) and the broad base rule (spread taxes broadly to minimize tax rates). In the case of income taxation, the optimal tax system reflects a different balancing:

▶ *Vertical Equity:* Social welfare is maximized when those who have a high level of consumption, and thus a low marginal utility, are taxed more heavily, and those who have a low level of consumption, and thus a high marginal utility, are taxed less heavily; those with high consumption will "miss the money less" when it is taxed away.

▶ *Behavioral Responses:* As taxes rise on any one group, individuals in that group may respond by earning less income. This means that an additional increase in taxes will raise less revenue, because the base of taxation is smaller.

In considering whether to move to a more progressive tax system, therefore, the government needs to balance the fact that this will bring the marginal utilities of the rich and poor into equality (by lowering the consumption of the rich) against the fact that by taxing the rich more highly, they will work less hard, thus lowering the marginal revenue raised by taxation. This latter point is strengthened by that previously noted: the marginal inefficiency of a tax rises with the tax rate, and the rich are the most productive elements of society, so the reduction in output will be the greatest. So raising taxes on the rich while lowering them on the poor leads to an overall efficiency reduction.

An Example

Imagine a world with no taxation, where the government wants to introduce a small income tax of 1%. In such a world, MU/MR is much lower for a rich person than a poor one. MU is much lower for the rich person since he or she already has such a high level of consumption, and MR is also higher for that rich person since a 1% tax raises more money off a higher base of income. So the ratio MU/MR is much lower for the rich than the poor.

As we tax the rich more, however, their ratio of MU/MR rises. The numerator rises because their consumption is falling, so MU is higher. The denominator falls through behavioral responses of labor supply: the higher tax causes them to work less hard, the tax base gets smaller, and thus the tax raises less revenue. At some point, when the tax on the rich is high enough, their MU/MR will actually fall below that of the poor. Tax rates should be higher for the rich than for the poor, but the government shouldn't totally "soak" the rich; it should drive their MU up, but not so much that their MR from the tax becomes very small (or even negative, as on the wrong side of the Laffer curve).

Figure 20-7 illustrates this point. On the x-axis in this diagram is the tax rate, and on the y-axis is the ratio of MU/MR. The curves on the graph show how

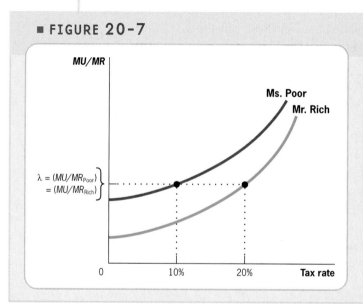

■ **FIGURE 20-7**

Optimal Income Taxation • The ratio of marginal utility to marginal revenue rises as tax rates rise for any taxpayer, but this ratio for Mr. Rich is everywhere below the ratio for Ms. Poor. Optimal income tax rates are those that equate this ratio across taxpayers. Here, the optimal rates are 10% for Ms. Poor and 20% for Mr. Rich.

MU/MR changes as tax rates rise. These curves slope upward: as tax rates rise, *MU* rises (as a result of diminishing marginal utility) and *MR* falls (as a result of the reductions in labor supply when tax rates rise). Indeed, the simultaneous rise in the numerator and reduction in the denominator lead to curves that not only slope upward but slope upward at an increasing rate (the curves are becoming steeper as tax rates rise). In the limit, with a 100% tax rate, *MU/MR* is infinity for everyone (the curve is perfectly vertical) since the tax raises no money.

Consider two individuals, Mr. Rich, who has a high income, and Ms. Poor, who has a low income. Mr. Rich's curve starts below Ms. Poor's, because Mr. Rich has a lower *MU* for each additional dollar of income. If we tax both individuals at 10%, then *MU/MR* for Mr. Rich is well below *MU/MR* for Ms. Poor.

As we raise the tax on Mr. Rich, his *MU* rises and his *MR* falls. By the time the tax rate on Mr. Rich is 20%, his *MU/MR* equals Ms. Poor's at the 10% rate. This is the optimal pair of income tax rates, since $MU/MR = \lambda$ for both taxpayers.

The Structure of Optimal Income Tax Rates: A Simulation Exercise

There is a long history of attempts by economists to estimate the structure of the optimal income tax. Economists do so through **simulation exercises,** which use economic theory to formulate optimal tax rates as a function of key economic parameters, such as the elasticity of the supply of labor. The analyst can then present results for optimal taxes as a function of different values of these parameters.

Gruber and Saez (2000) provided a simulation exercise along these lines. They considered a tax rate that has a guaranteed income level, as with welfare. There is, therefore, a two-sided income tax: if a person's income is low enough, the government sends him a check, but if the person's income is high enough, he sends the government a check. For example, a system with a guaranteed income level of $10,000 and a constant tax rate of 50% would be one in which the tax bill is 50% of your income, minus $10,000. If your income is $15,000, the government sends you a check for $2,500 ([0.5 × 15,000] − 10,000 = −2,500). If your income is $100,000, you send the government a check for $40,000 ([0.5 × 100,000] − 10,000 = 40,000).

Gruber and Saez's simulations maximize a utilitarian social welfare function, while raising the same amount of revenue as the existing tax code. To make their analysis feasible, they divided individuals into four taxable income categories: $0 to $10,000; $10,000 to $32,000; $32,000 to $75,000; and above $75,000.[7] They then used the type of optimal tax theory we've discussed to compute the optimal guaranteed income level and the optimal marginal tax rate for each of these four income classes.

> **simulation exercises** The numerical simulation of economic agents' behavior based on measured economic parameters in an attempt to determine optimal tax rates or other outcomes of interest.

---

[7] Gruber and Saez consider a variety of social welfare functions, but that presented here is one where utilities are assumed to be such that the social welfare function weights additional dollars to the bottom income group at twice the value of additional dollars to the second income group; weights additional dollars to the second income group at twice the value of additional dollars to the third income group; and does not value at all additional dollars to the top income group.

To do so, they compared the equity gains from a redistributive tax system to the efficiency costs of having high marginal tax rates. These efficiency costs depend on how responsive, or elastic, taxable income is to tax rates: if taxable income is more responsive for any group, it will lower optimal tax rates, since *MR* will fall rapidly with taxes. Gruber and Saez used tax data to estimate the elasticities of taxable income by income group. They found that there is little elasticity of taxable income for most taxpayers: for the first three income groups, changes in taxes did not cause a sizeable change in their taxable income. For the highest income group, however, there was a sizeable response of taxable income to taxes, with each 10% rise in tax rates causing taxable income to fall by almost 6%.

Before reviewing the results of Gruber's and Saez's simulations, it is important to recall the difference between *marginal* and *average* tax rates. Marginal tax rates determine the efficiency properties of an income tax system. The models we've used to discuss tax efficiency consider individuals who are deciding whether to earn the marginal dollar of income, for example, and that decision will be determined by the tax rate they will pay on that dollar of income. Average tax rates determine the equity properties of an income tax system. What matters for equity is the tax burden on each individual relative to his or her income, which is the average tax rate. Marginal and average tax rates will differ under a nonproportional (progressive or regressive) tax system, such as a system that exempts low-income individuals from paying taxes, or a system that features higher marginal tax rates on higher-income groups.

Figure 20-8 and the associated table show the results from this study's simulations. The figure graphs family tax payments against family income, while the table summarizes the key results by income group. The income guarantee is set at $11,000 for a family of four. The resulting tax schedule is as follows:

- ▶ Families with an income of zero receive a transfer of $11,000.

- ▶ In the income range from $0 to $10,000, the marginal tax rate is 68%, so that each dollar of earnings reduces the transfer by 68¢. Thus, a family with an income of $10,000 receives a transfer of $11,000 − (0.68 × 10,000) = $4,200.

- ▶ In the income range from $10,000 to $32,000, the marginal tax rate is 66%. Thus, by the time families have an income of $16,364, their transfer has become zero, and they begin to pay taxes. At an income of $32,000, families are paying $10,320 in taxes.

- ▶ In the income range from $32,000 to $75,000, the marginal tax rate is 56%. Thus, a family with an income of $75,000 pays $34,400 in taxes.

- ▶ In the income range above $75,000, the marginal tax rate is 49%. Thus, a family with an income of $100,000 pays $46,650 in taxes.

The most important point about this proposed tax schedule is that marginal tax rates are actually *highest* on the poor and *lowest* on the rich, while average tax rates rise with income. This finding highlights the important difference between average and marginal tax rates. The optimal income tax structure features a large grant to low-income taxpayers that is taxed away

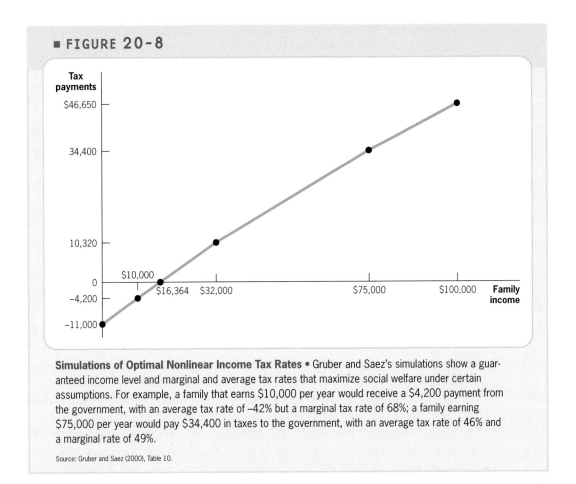

■ FIGURE 20-8

Simulations of Optimal Nonlinear Income Tax Rates • Gruber and Saez's simulations show a guaranteed income level and marginal and average tax rates that maximize social welfare under certain assumptions. For example, a family that earns $10,000 per year would receive a $4,200 payment from the government, with an average tax rate of –42% but a marginal tax rate of 68%; a family earning $75,000 per year would pay $34,400 in taxes to the government, with an average tax rate of 46% and a marginal rate of 49%.

Source: Gruber and Saez (2000), Table 10.

| Optimal Tax Results | | | | | |
Income groups	$0–$10K	$10K–$32K	$32K–$75K	$75K and above	Guaranteed income level
Marginal tax rates	68%	66%	56%	49%	$11,000
Average tax rates	–161%	12%	40%	47%	

rather quickly as income rises (as with high-benefit reduction rates under cash welfare systems). Thus, although those with no income get $11,000 from the government, by the time income has risen to $16,434, which is still a fairly low income level, that transfer has been reduced to zero. This reflects the large equity gains to targeting the very lowest income group: due to this group's low income, they have very high marginal utility of consumption, so the optimal tax system subsidizes their consumption.

Once incomes rise, however, marginal tax rates should be lower, since higher-income groups have a higher elasticity of taxable income. The inefficiency of taxation rises with income because higher-income groups are more responsive to taxation, and so there are greater efficiency costs for high marginal tax rates on those groups. But *average* tax rates continue to rise with income. So this is a very progressive tax schedule; the rich pay a much higher share of their income in tax (47% of income on average in the top income group) than do the poor (the bottom group receives on average a transfer of 161% of their income). It is also, however, a system that minimizes work disincentives for the highest-income taxpayers, who are the most responsive to tax.

While these types of simulation exercises are useful, the particular results are very sensitive to the authors' assumptions about inputs such as the structure of the social welfare function. Nevertheless, the main lesson from such work is that, even with redistributive social tastes, the optimal tax system should not punish the rich with very high marginal tax rates, but should use a combination of an income grant and relatively flat marginal rates to achieve progressivity.

20.4

Tax-benefit Linkages and the Financing of Social Insurance Programs

tax-benefit linkages Direct ties between taxes paid and benefits received.

In the previous two chapters, we have focused on the equity and efficiency implications of taxation while ignoring the disposition of tax revenues. By doing so, however, we have ignored the possible effects of **tax-benefit linkages,** direct ties between taxes paid and benefits received. These linkages can significantly affect the equity and efficiency of a tax. This point was made forcefully by Summers (1989) in the context of government social insurance programs. He showed that the link between payroll taxes and the social insurance benefits they finance can cause the incidence of payroll taxation to fall more fully on workers than might be presumed from the analysis of Chapter 19. The link can also lead the efficiency cost of financing social insurance programs to be lower than might be presumed from the analysis of this chapter. Because payroll taxes to finance social insurance programs constitute such a large share of the tax burden in the United States and elsewhere, it is important to understand and assess this argument.

The Model

To illustrate the effect of payroll taxes that finance social insurance programs, we consider a *workers' compensation* program (which provides reimbursement to injured workers) financed by a payroll tax. Consider a labor market that starts with no workers' compensation program, as shown in panel (a) of Figure 20-9. This market is initially in equilibrium at point A where quantity of labor L_1 is supplied at a wage of W_1. The government then introduces a workers' compensation program, financed by a payroll tax on employers. This tax imposes a significant new cost of production on employers, causing them to decrease the quantity of labor they demand at all wage levels and shifting the demand curve in from D_1 to D_2. The equilibrium moves to point B, the intersection of D_2 and the original supply curve S_1. The equilibrium wage

■ **FIGURE 20-9**

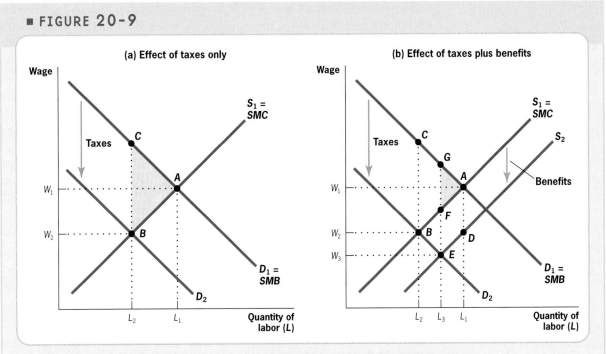

Tax-Benefit Linkages • (a) A pure tax on labor would shift the demand curve from D_1 to D_2, reducing labor from L_1 to L_2 and creating the deadweight loss triangle (CAB). (b) If those taxes are tied to benefits provided to workers, then supply shifts out to S_2 because the benefits act as an effective rise in wages and make supplying labor more attractive. Labor supply falls only to L_3, and the deadweight loss triangle shrinks to (GAF).

falls to W_2 and the equilibrium quantity of labor falls to L_2. At this reduced quantity of labor, there are many workers ($L_1 - L_2$) who would like to work and would accept a wage that would be profitable for the firm if there were no tax. The hiring of these workers is not profitable for the firm once the tax is in place, however, so these efficient labor market matches are not made, causing a deadweight loss of the area CAB.

This analysis is accurate as far as it goes, but it does not go far enough because it ignores the reason the tax is in place. The payroll tax is financing a benefit for workers: insurance if they are injured. Before workers' compensation existed, if a worker on a risky job was injured and had to miss work, then the worker lost his or her wages for the time away from work *and* the medical costs of recovering from the injury. Workers in risky jobs would therefore demand compensating differentials of the type discussed in Chapter 8: they would demand wages higher than those paid for comparable jobs without risk to compensate for these potential post-injury costs. With workers' compensation, however, workers don't require such a large compensating differential from their employer because the government will reimburse them for lost income and medical expenditures. Workers are therefore willing to supply their labor to the market for a lower wage.

Figure 20-9 panel (b) shows what happens to the deadweight loss from the tax when benefits are taken into account. At wage W_1, workers were initially willing to supply quantity of labor L_1 (point A), but after workers' compensation is introduced, they are willing to supply the same quantity for the lower wage of W_2 (point D). Because this change occurs at every quantity, the supply curve shifts outward to S_2. The new equilibrium occurs at point E, the intersection of D_2 and S_2: the wage falls to W_3 and labor supply increases to L_3. The increase in the quantity of labor in the market relative to panel (a) reduces the efficiency cost of the tax, since there are now fewer efficient employer-worker matches that are not occurring because of the tax (only those between L_3 and L_1, instead of the larger set of those between L_2 and L_1). The deadweight loss triangle therefore shrinks to GAF.

Why is the deadweight loss triangle GAF when the new equilibrium is at point E? This is an excellent illustration of the hazards of correctly identifying deadweight loss triangles. Remember that deadweight loss is defined as the reduction in social surplus due to units that are not sold and that have a social marginal benefit exceeding their social marginal cost. The social marginal benefit of labor is measured by the preintervention demand curve (D_1), and the social marginal cost of labor is measured by the preintervention supply curve (S_1), so deadweight loss must be drawn with reference to those curves. At the new quantity of labor L_3, the social-efficiency-increasing trades that are not made are those between L_3 and the original equilibrium L_1. Thus, deadweight loss consists of the difference between the social marginal benefit (curve D_1) and the social marginal cost (curve S_1) for those units between L_3 and L_1.

Indeed, if workers fully valued the benefit of the workers' compensation insurance at its cost to the employer, then there would be *no deadweight loss* from this program. This possibility is illustrated in Figure 20-10, which shows an outward shift in the supply curve to S_2 that fully offsets the downward shift in the demand curve to D_2. The quantity of labor remains at L_1 in the initial equilibrium (point A) and the new equilibrium (point B). Equilibrium wages fall by the full cost of the program to W_2, which is below W_1 by the exact program cost. Thus, *the cost of the workers' compensation tax is fully shifted to the workers* in the form of lower wages. When the government puts in a workers' compensation program, and workers value that benefit at its cost to employers, the government is essentially replacing workers' wages with this insurance benefit, with no change in labor cost to employers, and therefore no deadweight loss.

Issues Raised by Tax-benefit Linkage Analysis

This analysis of the efficiency of tax-benefit linkages raises a series of interesting questions.

If There Is No Inefficiency to Providing a Benefit, Why Doesn't the Employer Just Do So Without Government Involvement? In Figure 20-10, there is no inefficiency associated with providing workers' compensation; workers value the benefits from the program at its employer cost and are will-

■ FIGURE 20-10

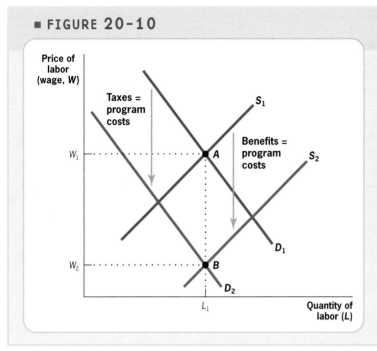

Taxation with No Deadweight Loss Due to Linkages • When workers value the tax-financed benefit so highly that they are willing to accept its full cost in lower wages, there is no change in employment when the tax is imposed. Since the increase in labor supply exactly offsets the reduction in labor demand, wages fall to W_2, while the quantity of labor remains at L_1.

ing to reduce their wages by the full cost to finance the program. In this case, why didn't the employer simply provide the program in the first place? Why does the government need to get involved?

The answer is that there may be market failures that lead employers to not reflect workers' valuation of this program without a government mandate. For example, there could be adverse selection in the market. Suppose you owned a firm and your employees came to you offering to reduce their wages by the full amount of a new workers' compensation insurance policy if you will buy one. No other firms in town have such a plan. You might be worried that if you were the first to offer such a plan, all the clumsy workers in town (or those who like to pretend to be injured) will come to work for you, driving up your workers' compensation costs. This standard adverse selection problem may keep employers from offering benefits that are fully valued by employees.[8]

When Are There Tax-benefit Linkages? The tax-benefit linkage is strongest when taxes paid are linked directly to a benefit for workers. When those taxes are used to provide benefits for nonworkers as well, the tax-benefit link is broken. Consider a new payroll tax that will be used to finance national health insurance for all citizens. As in our workers' compensation example, this tax

---

[8] Indeed, if there is such a market failure, it is feasible that a program such as workers' compensation could *raise* the quantity of labor in the market. If workers value workers' compensation at more than its cost to employers (as might be the case if workers are risk averse), the labor supply curve would shift out by more than the demand curve shifted in; workers would be willing to accept a wage cut of *more* than the cost of workers' compensation in order to have this benefit. This would actually raise employment.

A GROUP-SPECIFIC EMPLOYER MANDATE

Gruber (1994) examined the impact on wages and labor supply of a *group-specific mandated benefit,* a benefit mandated for a specific group within the workplace. This paper studied the effect of state laws (and a follow-up federal law) that mandated in the mid-1970s that the costs of pregnancy and childbirth be covered comprehensively. Before this time, health insurance plans provided very little coverage for the costs associated with normal pregnancy and childbirth, while providing generous coverage for other medical conditions. This distinction was viewed as discriminatory by some state governments, leading to the state laws mandating that pregnancy costs be covered as completely as other medical costs.

These laws significantly increased the insurance costs for women of childbearing age in those states, thereby raising the costs of employing a specific group of workers (or their husbands, who may provide them with insurance). These workers became the treatment group for the analysis. There were two possible control groups: similar workers in other states that did not pass these laws, or other groups of workers within the states that did pass these laws. Gruber's study compared the changes in wages and labor supply of the treatment group around the time of the passage of these laws to the changes in both of these control groups, using the type of difference-in-difference estimation techniques described in the appendix to Chapter 14. The results show that the cost of this new mandate was fully passed on to the wages of the affected groups, with little effect on their labor supply.

In the wake of these state laws, the federal government passed the Pregnancy Discrimination Act of 1978, which mandated equal coverage of pregnancy and other medical conditions in all states. This law allowed for a "reverse" quasi-experimental analysis: now the states that had originally passed their own laws were the control group (since there was no change), and the states that had not yet passed laws were the treatment group (since they were now newly subject to this mandate). Gruber studied this "reverse" quasi-experiment as well and found similar results, confirming the conclusion that the costs of the mandate were fully passed through to wages.[9]

These findings have important implications for debates over group-specific mandates, such as mandated maternity leave (unpaid or paid time off for mothers or fathers when new children are born). These laws are typically criticized as lowering the demand for women of childbearing age and reducing their employment prospects. The evidence from these studies suggests that the total employment of such groups will not fall; only their wages will fall. This outcome is good for efficiency; there is no deadweight loss created by the regulations. The outcome may be viewed as bad from an equity perspective, however, because women are fully absorbing the cost of this new benefit in the form of lower wages.

---

will reduce labor demand. In this case, however, there will be no associated rise in labor supply, because one doesn't have to work to get the benefits financed by this tax. There is no link between paying taxes and receiving benefits; everyone receives the national health insurance, regardless whether they pay the tax. So standard tax analysis involving deadweight losses applies here.

What Is the Empirical Evidence on Tax-benefit Linkages? There are numerous studies that have investigated the impact of social insurance contributions on wages and employment. Many of these studies compare wages and employment across states or groups of workers where social insurance contribution rates change. For example, Gruber and Krueger (1991) estimated the impact on wages and employment of changes in the costs of workers' compensation across states over time, and Anderson and Meyer (2000) studied the

---

[9] Further corroborating evidence on this point is provided by Sheiner (1999), who found that when health care costs rise in a city, the wages of workers who have the highest costs (older and married workers) fall the most. See Gruber (2001) for a review of this literature.

impact of changes in unemployment insurance payroll taxes across firms over time. Both studies concluded that, on average, the costs of financing these programs are largely paid through (shifted to) lower wages, with relatively little effect on employment.

Thus, the existing literature suggests that the cost of social insurance financing is borne by workers in the form of lower wages and not lower employment. The taxes that fund the social insurance programs do not appear to cause significant deadweight loss, as Summers's original analysis suggested.

20.5
Conclusion

The fundamental issue in designing tax policy is the equity-efficiency trade-off. In Chapter 19 we discussed the distribution of the tax burden, or how taxes affect equity (the distribution of the economic pie). In this chapter we discussed how taxes affect efficiency (the size of the economic pie), and the implications of those effects for the optimal design of commodity and income tax systems. While this analysis can be complicated, understanding tax efficiency really comes down to remembering two key principles. First, the more elastically supplied or demanded the good, the larger the deadweight loss from the tax. Second, the higher the tax rate, the larger the incremental deadweight loss of taxation. Trading off these two considerations is the key to understanding the efficiency aspects of the tax policies that we analyze throughout the remainder of this book.

▶ HIGHLIGHTS

■ The efficiency cost of taxation is measured by the deadweight loss arising from reduced consumption of a good.

■ This efficiency cost rises with the elasticities of supply and demand, and with the square of the tax rate.

■ The latter point implies that taxes have larger efficiency costs in the presence of preexisting distortions, such as externalities, subsidies, and existing taxes, and that progressive taxes have a larger efficiency cost than proportional taxes.

■ Optimal commodity taxation involves trading off the desire to tax inelastically demanded goods at a higher rate against the desire to tax the broadest set of commodities and minimize overall tax rates, leading under some assumptions to the "inverse

elasticity" rule of taxing goods in inverse proportion to their elasticity of demand.

■ Optimal income taxation involves trading off the desire for equity against the distortion costs associated with taxing higher-income groups at a higher rate. Simulations suggest that, as a result, the optimal income tax system has flat or falling marginal tax rates but rapidly rising average tax rates.

■ Accounting for tax-benefit linkages can reduce the measured deadweight loss of payroll taxation and increase the expected burden of payroll taxes on workers. Since such linkages are prominent in social insurance programs, both theory and evidence suggest that the burdens of those taxes are fully borne in the form of lower worker wages.

▶ **QUESTIONS AND PROBLEMS** ────────────────────

1. The market demand for super-sticky glue is $Q = 240 - 6P$ and the market supply is $Q = -60 + 4P$.

   a. Calculate the deadweight loss of a tax of $4 per unit levied on producers of super-sticky glue.

   b. How does deadweight loss change if the tax is levied on consumers of super-sticky glue?

2. The government of Washlovia wants to impose a tax on clothes dryers. In East Washlovia the demand elasticity for clothes dryers is −2.4 while in West Washlovia the demand elasticity is −1.7. Where will the tax inefficiency be greater? Explain.

3. On a recent visit to Amsterdam, you noticed that houses facing the canals are tall, deep, and extremely narrow. Your host tells you that this is a consequence of builders' desires to avoid taxes. Describe a tax system that would induce this kind of behavior.

4. Suppose that the government of Michconsin imposes a tax on cheese curd production. When will the efficiency costs of the tax be greater, in the short run or in the long run, and why?

5. Bob's Bees is a small boutique honey manufacturer in Massachusetts. Bob's neighbor is Jon's Jams. The more honey Bob produces, the more jam Jon is able to produce; that is, there is a positive production externality.

   a. Suppose that the government of Massachusetts imposes a new tax on jam and honey production. Will the deadweight loss of this tax be greater, smaller, or the same as if there were no production externality? Explain.

   b. How would your answer change if the production externality were negative (perhaps because Bob's bees sting Jon's jam-makers)?

6. The city of Johnstown decides to build a new stadium to attract a basketball team from the city of Rosendale. One economic advisor suggests that the stadium should be financed by a 2-year sales tax of 10%, while another advisor suggests that the stadium should be financed with a 20-year sales tax of 1%. Assume that the interest rate is zero. Which approach will yield a more efficient outcome? Why?

7. You are a consultant to the government of Buttony. The government has decided to cut taxes on either apples, bananas, or cantaloupe, and it wants your input on which fruit would be the best choice for a tax cut. It provides you with the following information. What is your recommendation, and why?

Good	Unit Price	Sales (thousands)	Unit tax	Marginal tax revenue (thousands of dollars per $1 additional tax)	Marginal deadweight loss (thousands of dollars per $1 additional tax)
Apples	$1	100	$0.10	20	5
Bananas	$2	100	$0.25	30	20
Cantaloupe	$4	50	$0.15	10	20

8. Luxury goods often have much higher elasticities of demand than do goods purchased by a broad base of people. Why, then, are governments more likely to tax luxuries than these "staple" goods?

9. Consider a social insurance program that is financed by a payroll tax. How does the incidence of this tax differ if the benefits of the insurance program are restricted to workers, rather than if the benefits are available to all citizens? Under what circumstances will these differences be particularly large?

▶ **ADVANCED QUESTIONS** ────────────────────

10. The market demand for stuffed rabbits is $Q = 2,600 - 20P$, and the government intends to place a $4 per bunny tax on stuffed rabbit purchases. Calculate the deadweight loss of this tax when:

   a. Supply of stuffed rabbits is $Q = 400$.

   b. Supply of stuffed rabbits is $Q = 12P$.

   c. Explain why the deadweight loss calculations differ between (a) and (b).

11. How is it possible for marginal tax rates to decline as income increases while average tax rates rise with income? How does the optimal tax system simulated by Gruber and Saez (2000) represent an optimal trade-off between equity and efficiency concerns?

12. Gruber and Krueger (1991)[1] found that mandated increases in the costs of workers' compensation benefits in the 1970s and 1980s led to substantial wage offsets for workers. Some of the wage reductions they found were even larger than the total cost to firms of providing the additional benefits. What does this suggest about the deadweight loss from the implicit "benefit tax" involved in imposing these mandatory benefits?

13. Schmeezle and Schmoozle are two advisors for the government of Feldspar. Schmeezle says that since the elasticity of demand for granite countertops is −3 and the elasticity of demand for sinks is −1.5, taxes should be raised entirely from granite countertops. Schmoozle argues that it is better to levy taxes on both goods anyway. Which advisor should the Feldspar government listen to? Why?

14. What is the theoretical justification for the Laffer curve? Basing your view on the empirical evidence described in the text, should the United States raise or lower its tax rates in order to increase tax revenues? Explain.

15. The demand for snorkels in Berhama is given by $Q_S = 500 − 8P_S$, and the supply of snorkels in Berhama is given by $Q_S = 200 + 4P_S$. The demand for kayaks is given by $Q_k = 650 − 6P_k$ and the supply of kayaks is given by $Q_k = 50 + 1.5P_k$. Both goods are currently untaxed, but the government of Berhama needs to raise $5,000 (to finance a new lighthouse) by taxing snorkels and kayaks. What tax should it levy on each of the two goods?

16. Suppose that a state mandates that both women and men be provided family leave by their employers following the birth of a child.

    a. How would you empirically test how this policy change affected the relative wages of men and women in the state?

    b. Based on the empirical evidence on group-specific employer mandates described in the text, what do you expect to happen to the relative wages of men and women in the state?

17. The government of Granita is thinking about imposing a very small tax on one or more of the following goods: anvils, books, and cardigans. Anvils and books are both produced in competitive markets with constant marginal costs, while cardigans are produced by a monopoly with constant marginal costs. The elasticities of demand for the three goods are −3, −1.5, and −1. What good or goods should the government put the very small tax on if it wants to minimize the deadweight burden?

---

[1] Jonathan Gruber and Alan Krueger, "The Incidence of Mandated Employer-Provided Insurance: Lessons from Workers' Compensation Insurance," in *Tax Policy and the Economy*, D. Bradford, ed. (Cambridge, MA: MIT Press and NBER, 1991).

The **e** icon indicates a question that requires students to apply the empirical economics principles discussed in Chapter 3 and the Empirical Evidence boxes.

Appendix to Chapter 20

The Mathematics of Optimal Taxation

In this appendix, we develop mathematically a number of points made intuitively and graphically in the text.

Deriving the Formula for Deadweight Loss

The most straightforward means of computing the deadweight loss of a tax is to use the formula for the area of a triangle: area = $1/2 \times$ base $\times$ height. The base of the deadweight loss triangle is the change in quantity induced by the tax (ΔQ) and the height is the size of the tax, so

$$DWL = -1/2 \times \Delta Q \times \tau.$$

The DWL is positive because quantity is falling ($\Delta Q < 0$).

Recall from the appendix to Chapter 19 that

$$\Delta Q/Q = \eta_s \times \Delta P/P \text{ and}$$

$$\Delta P = \frac{\eta_d}{\eta_s - \eta_d} \times \tau.$$

Combining and rearranging these equations yields an equation for ΔQ, the tax-induced change in quantity:

$$\Delta Q = \frac{\eta_s \eta_d}{\eta_s - \eta_d} \times \tau \times \frac{Q}{P}$$

Substituting this equation into the formula for DWL above, we obtain

$$DWL = -\frac{1}{2} \frac{\eta_s \eta_d}{\eta_s - \eta_d} \times \tau^2 \times \frac{Q}{P}$$

Behavioral Responses to Taxation and Deadweight Loss: A Technical Point

Taxes have two effects: they redistribute income and they cause market participants to substitute untaxed activities for taxed activities. The deadweight loss of taxation arises only from the second of these effects, the actions that economic agents take to avoid taxation.

The best way to see the contrast between the distribution and substitution effects of taxation is to compare the types of taxes we have discussed thus far with a *lump-sum tax,* a fixed sum that a person pays in taxation independent of that person's income, consumption of goods and services, or wealth. A lump-sum tax would tax individuals a fixed amount regardless of their income, and there would be no way to change the amount of tax owed by changing one's behavior. In contrast, the taxes we have discussed thus far are *distortionary taxes*, whereby economic agents can change their tax payments by changing their behavior. A lump-sum tax is the most efficient way possible to raise revenues, since individuals will not change their behavior in response to the tax.

It is unfair to compare the efficiency effects of a tax to a world without taxation, since the government has some revenue requirement that is being met by taxation. As a result, to analyze tax efficiency in raising a given amount of revenue, we should compare the efficiency of any existing or proposed tax to the most efficient tax, the lump-sum tax. Lump-sum taxes have no substitution effects on behavior, only income effects. Thus, the efficiency cost of distortionary (non-lump-sum) taxes results only from the substitution effect of taxation, not the income effect.

Since we want to avoid counting changes in demand or supply due to income effects as distortionary, we cannot carry out efficiency analysis with standard demand and supply curves. For example, a standard demand curve would show demand falling from a lump-sum tax: consumers would be poorer because of higher prices (due to income effects). So the decrease in equilibrium quantity would appear to cause a deadweight loss, but this is not the case; a deadweight loss occurs only when individuals substitute across goods due to the tax.

To be technically accurate when looking at the efficiency costs of a tax, we should use a *compensated demand curve,* or a demand curve along which utility is constant, so that it reflects only the substitution effects of price changes. Similarly, when we compute the deadweight loss of taxation, we should not use the overall elasticity of demand but the *compensated elasticity of demand,* or the percentage change in quantity demanded in response to a percentage change in price, holding utility constant. A parallel point arises with supply curves; we should analyze supply responses to taxation using a *compensated supply curve* and the *compensated elasticity of supply.*

The distinction between the measured elasticity of demand or supply and the compensated elasticities is a clean one in theory but is often hard to carry out in practice. As a result, many of the studies that we will discuss in this set of tax chapters simply focus on measured (or *uncompensated*) elasticities rather than on the appropriate compensated elasticity.

Deriving Optimal Commodity Tax Rates

The Ramsey optimal commodity tax problem is to minimize the deadweight loss associated with a set of commodity taxes, subject to a revenue-raising constraint:

$$\min (DWL_1 + DWL_2 + DWL_3 + \ldots + DWL_n)$$
$$\text{subject to the revenue target: } R_1 + R_2 + R_3 + \ldots + R_n = \underline{R}$$

where R_i stands for the revenues raised by tax $i,$ $\underline{R}$ is the government's total revenue target, and the indicators $1, 2, \ldots n$ are the various commodities that can be taxed by the government. The government chooses a set of tax rates $\tau_1, \tau_2, \ldots \tau_n$ to solve this maximization problem.

To solve this problem, we set up the *Lagrangian,* which is a mathematical formulation for constrained optimization. The Lagrangian is equal to the maximand (such as utility) minus the budget constraint times a multiplier, λ. Differentiating these expressions with respect to the tax rate on each commodity and setting them equal to zero gives us a set of equations that can be solved to yield the solution to the problem. This procedure is equivalent to the mathematics we used in the appendices to Chapters 2 and 7, where we plugged the budget constraint into the utility function. In cases such as the Ramsey problem, however, we can't easily avail ourselves of this shortcut, so we must use the formal Lagrangian analysis.

In this Ramsey problem, the Lagrangian is

$$(DWL_1 + DWL_2 + DWL_3 + \ldots) - \lambda \times (R_1 + R_2 + R_3 + \ldots - \underline{R}).$$

Differentiating these expressions with respect to the tax rate on each commodity and setting them equal to zero, we obtain expressions of the form (labeled *first order conditions*)

$$MDWL_1 = \lambda MR_1$$
$$MDWL_2 = \lambda MR_2$$
$$\text{etc.} \ldots$$

where
$$MDWL = \delta(DWL)/\delta\tau$$
$$MR = \delta R/\delta\tau.$$

This implies the general Ramsey Rule: set $MDWL_i / MR_i = \lambda$, for all i.

From the previous, we know that the general deadweight loss formula is

$$DWL = -\frac{1}{2}\frac{\eta_s\eta_d}{\eta_s - \eta_d} \times \tau^2 \times \frac{Q}{P}$$

We can simplify by assuming that $P = 1$, and that there is a perfectly competitive supply side (η_s = infinity). Then the expression for DWL is

$$DWL = -1/2\eta_d Q\tau^2.$$

From this, we can derive that

$$- MDWL = \delta DWL/\delta\tau = -\eta_d Q\tau.$$

We also know that revenues $= \tau \times Q$, so that marginal revenues are simply Q. Thus, implementing the Ramsey Rule we obtain

$$MDWL/MR = \lambda \longrightarrow \tau = -1/\eta_d \times \lambda.$$

Deriving Optimal Income Tax Rates

The goal of optimal income tax analysis is to choose the pattern of tax rates across individuals that maximizes social welfare, subject to a revenue target. Thus, for a Utilitarian SWF, the problem can be expressed as

$$\max V = U_1 + U_2 + \ldots$$
$$\text{subject to } R_1 + R_2 + \ldots = \underline{R}.$$

As above, we can set up a Lagrangian expression and solve this, yielding expressions of the form

$$MU_i/MR_i = \lambda.$$

Taxes on Labor Supply

21

Between 1987 and 1988, Iceland overhauled its tax system. Before the overhaul, workers had paid taxes on the previous year's income (much as we do in the United States), and the average tax burden was 14.5% of income, with marginal rates as high as 56.3%. The new system was "pay-as-you-go," with workers paying a flat 32.5% income tax as they earned each paycheck. During the transition to this new system, workers paid taxes on their 1986 income in 1987, and paid taxes on their 1988 income in 1988. Their 1987 income was thus never taxed! For one year both average and marginal tax rates on labor income were zero.

Did this radical change in the tax burden actually affect workers' decisions about how many hours to work? Bianchi, Gudmundsson, and Zoega (2001) investigated this issue by examining the response of Icelandic workers to this one-year "tax holiday," and they found large effects on labor supply and economic growth. On average, each 1% rise in after-tax wages led workers to work 0.4% more weeks than they had previously, so that by one measure overall employment spiked in 1987 from 78% to 81%, as shown in Figure 21-1.

■ **FIGURE 21-1**

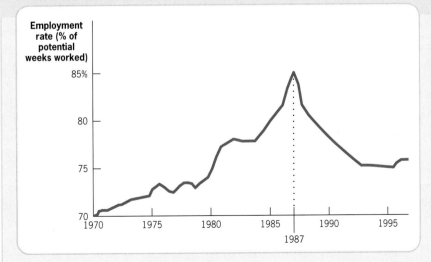

Iceland's Supply-Side Experiment • For a single year in 1987, Icelandic citizens paid no tax on their income. The result was a noticeable one-year spike in employment rate.

Source: Bianchi, Gudmundsson, and Zoega (2001).

"I suppose one could say it favors the rich, but, on the other hand, it's a great incentive for everyone to make two hundred grand a year."

Real GDP also leapt from an annual growth rate of 4.3% to 8.5%. The effects were, however, transitory. By 1988, these figures had dropped back to levels comparable to the pre-tax-reform levels.

This striking response to a change in tax policy shows that taxes can have effects on important decisions, such as how much to work. The existence of such responses highlights the tension between equity and efficiency in the design of government tax policy. As we saw in Chapter 20, a society's desire for a more equitable distribution of income may lead to a higher desired level of taxes, but the higher level of taxes may have a detrimental effect on the economy: higher taxes may discourage people from earning income and shrink the size of the economic pie on which those taxes can be levied. Whether this reduction in the tax base actually occurs depends on how responsive the size of the pie is to the taxes that are levied on various economic activities.

In an effort to understand how tax rates affect the economy, in the next three chapters we address the question of how responsive individual economic decisions are to taxation. We discuss three types of taxation: taxes on labor, taxes on savings, and taxes on wealth and risk taking. In each case, we begin by discussing the theory of how taxation might affect individual decisions, such as how hard to work, how much to save, and how much risk to take with one's investments. We then turn to the empirical evidence on the impact of taxation on these behaviors. Finally, in each case we discuss key tax policies in the United States that affect these behaviors.

This chapter begins with a discussion of the taxation of the earnings from work in the market, which economists generally refer to as *labor supply*. In this case, we draw on a rich body of evidence from both public finance and labor economics developed over the past three decades, which allows us to draw some fairly general and uncontroversial conclusions. We then turn to one of the most important current government tax polices to promote labor supply, the Earned Income Tax Credit (EITC), a wage subsidy program for low-income families. Studying the EITC presents an opportunity to apply the theoretical analysis of taxation and labor supply and to understand, based on solid empirical evidence, how government tax policy can affect labor supply in practice. Finally, we consider the appropriate tax treatment of child care expenditures, which may be a primary determinant of the work behavior of parents.

21.1

Taxation and Labor Supply—Theory

The optimal income tax analysis of Chapter 20 illustrated the importance of understanding how labor supply responds to changes in taxation. If individuals greatly reduce their work effort as income taxes rise, income taxes could impose large deadweight losses on society.

Basic Theory

The theoretical framework for assessing how income taxes affect labor supply is the same as that used to model the effect of cash welfare on labor supply in Chapters 2 and 17. Figure 21-2 illustrates Ava's possible choices between hours of leisure and dollars of consumption. Recall that we solve for optimal leisure, then compute labor as total possible hours per year minus hours of leisure. Recall also that the slope of the budget constraint, the wage rate, 12.50, is the price of leisure because it is the opportunity cost of taking leisure rather than working. Before taxes are imposed, Ava enjoys an initial level of leisure of 900 and a level of consumption of $C_1 = 13,750$ (point A). Now let's suppose that a tax τ of 30% is imposed on each dollar of wages earned. The slope of Ava's budget constraint is now the *after-tax* wage, $12.50 \times (1 - 0.3) = 8.75$, since this is what she (and all workers with the same gross wage) see as the monetary return for their work. A flat tax on earnings at rate $\tau = 0.3$ causes the budget constraint to pivot inward from BC_1 to BC_2. At the

■ FIGURE 21-2

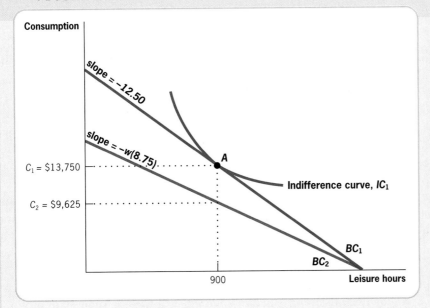

Taxation and the Consumption-Leisure Trade-off ● Before taxes are introduced, Ava loses $12.50 worth of consumption for each hour of leisure she takes. After tax $\tau = 0.3$ is imposed, Ava's after-tax wage is $12.50 \times (1 - 0.3) = 8.75$. Because some of Ava's wages go to pay taxes, Ava now gets less consumption ($C_2 = 9,625$) for the same amount of work/leisure.

same amount of labor, 900 hours, and thus the same amount of leisure, Ava can now consume fewer goods, $C_2 = 9{,}625$, since some of her income goes to tax payments.

Substitution and Income Effects on Labor Supply We cannot tell for certain what will happen to labor supply as a result of this tax because it has two offsetting effects. The after-tax wage is the effective price of leisure. Since the after-tax wage is lower than the pretax wage, the price of leisure has fallen. The decrease in the price of leisure will induce a *substitution* effect toward more leisure and less work. However, the decrease in the returns to work also means that Ava is poorer at any given level of labor supply. This reduction in income will have an *income effect* that causes her to buy fewer of all normal goods, including leisure; and fewer hours of leisure means more hours of work. Because the substitution and income effects on labor supply pull in opposite directions, we cannot predict clearly whether labor supply rises or falls in response to tax τ.

> **Quick Hint** For understanding the intuition of the income effect on labor supply it is sometimes helpful to think about an individual's *income target,* his or her goal of earning a fixed amount of income. Imagine that the only reason Ava works is to buy one CD each week. If she earns $5 per hour, and a CD costs $20, she will work four hours each week. If the government imposes a 20% tax on labor earnings, her after-tax wage will fall to $4. To buy that same CD, Ava will now have to work five hours per week. Thus, she works harder even though her after-tax wage has fallen, because she has a target income she wants to earn. In this case, the income effect dominates the substitution effect and the quantity of labor supplied increases.

The two panels of Figure 21-3 illustrate two possible effects of taxing labor income. In panel (a), the substitution effect of taxation (which reduces the price of leisure, leading Ava to desire more leisure) is larger than the income effect of lower after-tax income (which leads to less leisure). In this case, Ava's leisure rises from 900 hours to 1,200 hours, implying lower labor supply. In panel (b), the income effect of the lower after-tax income is larger than the substitution effect of taxation, and Ava works harder to earn more income so that she can afford more consumption. In this case, Ava's leisure falls from 900 to 600, implying higher labor supply.

These two possibilities imply different shapes for the supply curve in the labor market. If substitution effects dominate, as in the first case, then the labor supply curve is the typical upward-sloping shape we have discussed thus far. If income effects dominate, as in the second case, then the labor supply curve will slope downward, with higher wages leading individuals to supply a lower quantity of labor. It seems very unlikely that labor supply curves can be everywhere downward sloping, since income effects on labor supply are proportional to hours worked before the wage change. If individuals have not been

▪ FIGURE 21-3

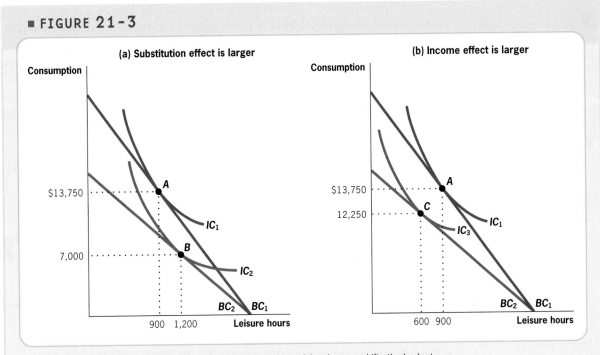

Substitution Versus Income Effect ▪ In both panels, a tax on labor income shifts the budget constraint inward from BC_1 to BC_2. (a) If the substitution effect of the change in the after-tax wage is larger, work is less attractive and Ava chooses to have more leisure, moving to 1,200 hours of leisure at point B. (b) If the income effect is larger, Ava feels poorer and thus reduces her leisure (increases her work hours) in order to regain some of that lost income, moving to 600 hours of leisure at point C.

working at all, and wages are taxed, then there is a substitution effect on their labor supply decision, but no income effect: they can't be poorer since they weren't earning anything before taxation. Thus, at low levels of labor supply, it seems unlikely that income effects could be larger than substitution effects. At higher levels of labor supply, where there is a larger income loss from taxation of wages, income effects could become larger than substitution effects, and taxation could lead to more, not less, labor supply.

Limitations of the Theory: Constraints on Hours Worked and Overtime Pay Rules

The basic theory of taxation's effect on labor supply assumes an idealized view of the labor market, where individuals can freely adjust their hours incrementally as government tax policy changes. In most labor markets, however, individuals cannot freely adjust their hours of work to find the exact tangency of their indifference curve and budget constraint. Firms may, for example, require workers to be on the job for a certain number of hours. This restriction could be due to *production complementarities,* features of the production process that make it important to have many workers on the job at the same time. A worker who is part of a production line in a manufacturing plant can't work only 32 hours per week, even if that is his or her optimum, when all the other workers on the line are working 40 hours per week.

Another constraint on increasing worker hours is the existence of **overtime pay rules,** which mandate that workers paid by the hour be paid one and a half times their regular hourly pay if they work more than 40 hours per week.[1] These laws make it very expensive for firms to have workers work more than 40 hours per week, which means that they will be reluctant to allow workers to do so even if that is the optimum for the worker. Overall, such hour constraints will force workers toward uniform work schedules, thus lowering the responsiveness of hours worked to after-tax wages.

overtime pay rules Workers in most jobs must legally be paid one and a half times their regular hourly pay if they work more than 40 hours per week.

21.2

Taxation and Labor Supply—Evidence

There is an extensive econometric literature that estimates the effects of taxes on labor supply. This literature typically makes a distinction between primary and secondary earners. **Primary earners** are the family members who are the main source of labor income for a household, while **secondary earners** are other workers in the family. Since primary earners are the family members most attached to the labor force, secondary earners are likely to be the family members in charge of other household activities, like child care. Traditionally, primary earners were husbands and secondary earners were wives who assumed charge of child care.

primary earners Family members who are the main source of labor income for a household.

secondary earners Workers in the family other than the primary earners.

The general conclusion from the literature is twofold. First, the work decisions of primary earners are not very responsive to changes in their wages (such as those induced by taxes). For every 10% reduction in after-tax wages, primary earners work about 1% fewer hours, for an elasticity of labor supply with respect to after-tax wages of 0.1. These studies also find that secondary earners are much more responsive to wages (and thus taxes), with elasticities of labor supply with respect to after-tax wages typically estimated to range from 0.5 to 1; for secondary earners, each 1% rise in after-tax wages increases labor supply by 0.5% to 1%. Most of the response of secondary earners comes from the decision to work at all (labor force participation), with a smaller part of the response coming from the decision over how many hours to work.

These findings are sensible in the historical context. The elasticity of labor supply with respect to after-tax wages is determined by the availability of substitute options for labor supply: when there are better substitutes for work, labor supply will be more elastic. Traditionally, primary-earning males had few outside alternatives to work, given the expectation that primary earners in the United States would work full-time. Secondary-earning females, however, had a natural

---

[1] There are exemptions from overtime regulations for certain classes of employees, such as executive, administrative, and professional employees. Professors, for example, qualify as professional employees because their fields require "advanced knowledge." More details on the law can be found at http://www.dol.gov/dol/topic/wages/overtimepay.htm.

ESTIMATING THE ELASTICITY OF LABOR SUPPLY

Three approaches have been used to estimate the elasticity of labor supply with respect to the after-tax wage:

Cross-Sectional Linear Regression Evidence: The first type of evidence comes from cross-sectional studies using linear regression analysis of the type discussed in Chapter 3 (p. 74). These studies estimate regressions of labor supply as a function of the after-tax wage and other control variables. Models such as these typically estimate a large effect of after-tax wages on the labor supply of secondary earners, but a very small (or even negative) effect on primary earners.

These cross-sectional regression analyses suffer, however, from potentially important bias in estimating the effects of wages on labor supply. Recall from Chapter 3 that bias can arise whenever there are factors that differentiate the treatment group (high-wage individuals) from the control group (low-wage individuals) that are correlated with the decision to supply labor. In fact, such bias seems likely. Those individuals who earn high wages may be driven personalities who would work long hours no matter the wage. Since the included *X* variables can't effectively control for underlying "drive" in this regression analysis, there is a bias to these estimates of the impact of wages on labor supply.

Experimental Evidence: Another approach suggested in Chapter 3 for assessing the causal impact of taxation on labor supply is a randomized experiment. In fact, one of the most significant social experiments in the United States was a randomized evaluation of a negative income tax (NIT) system. The NIT experiment was run between 1968 and 1976, initiated by the Office of Economic Opportunity, a federal agency established by President Johnson. In this study, randomly selected individuals were placed into treatment and control groups. For the treatment group, the government replaced their existing tax schedule with a fixed income guarantee, with a benefit reduction/tax rate. For example, a family of four might be offered a $4,000 guarantee (at the time, half of the poverty level, which was about $8,000 for a family that size) and a benefit reduction/tax rate of 50%. If a family had no income it would receive $4,000; once it had income of $8,000 it would receive nothing, and half of any income above $8,000 would be paid in tax. The amount of the guarantee and the reduction rate were randomly varied across treatment groups in various parts of the country, and the results for each treatment group were compared to the other treatment groups and to the control groups. Because assignment to treatment and control groups was random, this study provided a means by which economists could understand how income and variation in the after-tax wage affect labor supply.[2]

The evidence from the NIT experiment is primarily focused on males. The findings are surprisingly consistent with the cross-sectional regression estimates. The overall responsiveness of male labor supply to after-tax wages is small, with the elasticity of labor supply with respect to after-tax wages estimated at around 0.1.

Quasi-Experimental Evidence: A third approach to estimating the elasticity of labor supply is to use quasi-experimental studies of the type discussed in Chapter 3. Perhaps the best known of these studies is Nada Eissa's studies of the impact of the Tax Reform Act of 1986 (TRA 86) on labor supply. Eissa noted that this major tax reform lowered the tax rates on the very-highest-income taxpayers much more than it lowered rates on those who were moderately high-income. Her treatment group was therefore wives of very high-earning men (above the 99th percentile of the earnings distribution), whose tax rates were greatly reduced by this tax law change. The problem she faced was that other factors were changing over time that would naturally cause the labor supply of high-earning women to increase (e.g., increasing opportunities for women in the labor force during the late 1980s). To deal with this problem, she compared this treatment group to a control group of wives of moderately high-earning men (at the 75th percentile of the earnings distribution), who did not see much change in their tax rates.

Eissa pursued a "difference-in-difference" approach to analyzing this quasi-experiment, as discussed in Chapter 3: she compared the change in labor supply from before to after TRA 86 for wives of very high-earning men, who saw a large reduction in tax rates, to the change in labor supply over this same period for wives of moderately high-earning men, who saw little change in their tax rates. She found that labor supply went up significantly for the wives of men who experienced a reduction in tax rates, relative to the less-rich group, which did not experience a reduction in tax rates: each 10% rise in after-tax wages led to 8% more labor supply by wives. Using the same approach, Eissa found that these tax changes had little effect on the labor supply of these very-high-income men, relative to a control group of somewhat less high-income men.

---

[2] For more information on the negative income tax, see http://www.econlib.org/library/Enc/NegativeIncomeTax.html.

outside option: providing child care. Thus, they were more elastic in their decisions to supply labor. The findings are also sensible given the hour constraints discussed in the previous section: men traditionally had the types of production-sector jobs for which hour constraints were important, so that there was little leverage for adjusting their hours to a desired level. Women traditionally worked in service-sector jobs for which work hours were more flexible.

Limitations of Existing Studies

One important issue raised by this literature is the blurring of lines between primary and secondary earners. Although only 50% of married women worked in 1970, by 2004 nearly 60% were working. The majority of married couples in the United States now have both partners working, and in 46% of those couples the men and women work roughly the same number of hours each year. Indeed, in about 30% of married couples, the woman works more hours than the man, and in 25% of married couples where both spouses have earnings, the woman earns more over the year than does the man.[3] This makes it hard to decide who should be called the primary earner and who should be called the secondary earner when analyzing labor markets. Blau and Kahn (2005) find that the married female labor supply elasticity fell by half from 1980 to 2000, from an elasticity of 0.8 in 1980 to an elasticity of 0.4 by 2000. Thus, as secondary earners become more established in the labor force, their wage elasticities are falling toward those of primary earners, so that they are also becoming less responsive to taxation in their work decisions.

Another important limitation of this literature has been its focus on only a subset of the possible measures of labor supply, labor force participation and hours of work. In fact, other measures of labor supply might respond to taxation. For example, suppose that you can earn a higher wage by providing more effort per hour of work at your job, but this effort is costly, so you will provide more effort only if the rewards in terms of higher wages are great enough. When tax rates are low, you may put in this effort, since the after-tax wage is high enough to reward you for the effort; once tax rates rise, however, the after-tax wage may not be enough of a reward to offset the costs of increased effort, and you may not put in the effort. Similarly, suppose you are considering two jobs: in one you are more productive but more stressed out, and in the other you are less productive but more relaxed (which, we'll assume, you prefer!). You will take the higher stress job only if the after-tax wage earned is high enough to compensate you for the higher level of stress. In this example, as tax rates rise you will be less likely to take the more stressful, higher-paying job. Another measure of labor supply that might respond to changes in taxes is the decision over how much *human capital* to obtain; the effects of taxes in this realm, which are more complicated, are discussed in Chapter 23.

What matters for the social efficiency consequences of taxation is how taxes affect the *total product* of society. If individuals don't change their work

---

[3] Information on percentage of married women who are employed and relative earnings of married couples comes from U.S. Bureau of Labor (2005). Information on relative working hours in married couples comes from Cancian and Reed (2004).

hours as a result of taxation, but take less productive jobs or work less hard per hour, then taxation distorts individual labor supply decisions and reduces total social efficiency. In Chapter 25 we will come back to the question of how total incomes (not just hours of work) are affected by taxation.

21.3

Tax Policy to Promote Labor Supply: The Earned Income Tax Credit

In the previous sections, we discussed in general how income tax rates can affect the labor supply decisions of primary and secondary earners. In this section we apply those lessons to study the effects of the **Earned Income Tax Credit (EITC),** an income tax policy aimed specifically at low-income wage earners. The EITC subsidizes the wages of low-income earners to accomplish two goals: redistribution of resources to lower-income groups and increases in the amount of labor supplied by these groups.

In Chapter 17, we discussed the standard trade-off in programs that redistribute income: they increase vertical equity by redistributing but may lower social efficiency by reducing the incentives for lower-income groups to earn income. The EITC holds out the promise of breaking this "iron triangle." By redistributing income through wage subsidies, the program aims to increase vertical equity and promote work among low-income populations.

> **Earned Income Tax Credit (EITC)** A federal income tax policy that subsidizes the wages of low income earners.

Background on the EITC

The EITC was introduced in 1976 and has grown tremendously over time, as shown in Figure 21-4. The federal government now spends $34.6 billion annually on the EITC, making it the nation's single largest cash antipoverty

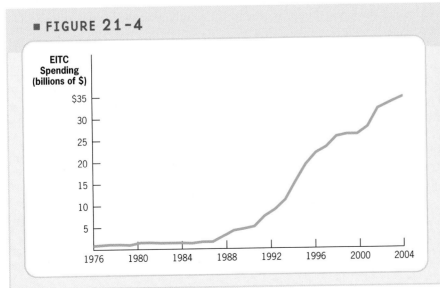

■ **FIGURE 21-4**

The Growth of the Earned Income Tax Credit • The EITC program has grown from less than $1 billion in 1976 to over $34 billion today. Numbers are measured in current dollars.

Source: Office of Management and Budget (2006a), Table 8.5.

■ **FIGURE 21-5**

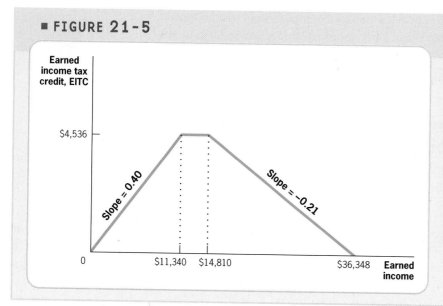

The Earned Income Tax Credit • For the first $11,340 of earned income, Stacey receives an EITC payment of 40¢ per dollar of earnings, to a maximum of $4,536. Between $11,348 and $14,810 of earnings, the EITC payment is flat at $4,536. From $14,810 to $36,348 of earnings, the EITC payment falls by 21¢ per dollar earned, until it reaches zero.

Source: Furman (2006).

program.[4] The EITC has clearly been successful in vertical equity terms: more than 90% of its benefits go to those with incomes below $30,000. In this section, we review evidence on the other goal of the program, to promote the labor supply of low-income groups.

To be eligible for the EITC, a family must have annual earnings greater than zero and below about $34,000, if supporting one child, or $36,000 if supporting more than one child. A family that supports no children must have earnings greater than zero and below about $12,000. For childless families, the EITC is significantly smaller (about 15% of the maximum amount a family with one child can receive). Importantly, for all types of families the EITC is *refundable:* even if the family owes no other taxes, it can still qualify for this credit, and the government will send the family a check for the amount as a tax rebate.[5]

The current structure of the EITC is illustrated in Figure 21-5 for Stacey, a single earner with two children. For the first $11,340 of Stacey's earnings, the government pays her 40¢ per dollar of wages earned (40%), up to a maximum credit of $4,536 (40% of $11,340). So the slope of the first segment in Figure 21-5 is 0.4. For the next $3,470 of earnings (up to a total of $14,810) the credit is held constant at $4,536, so the graph is flat between $11,340 and $14,810. Once Stacey's earnings exceed $14,810 however, the government begins to reduce this credit, at a rate of about 21¢ per dollar earned (21%), so that for those earning $36,348 and above, there is no EITC.

---

[4] Office of Management and Budget (2006a), Table 8.5
[5] For current details on the EITC, see IRS Publication #596.

■ FIGURE 21-6

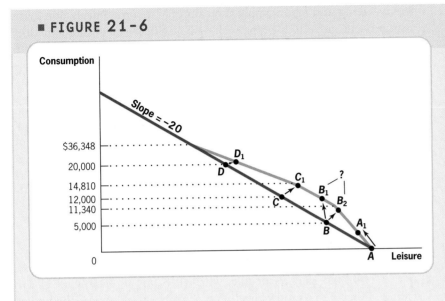

EITC's Effect on Labor Supply •
The EITC unambiguously raises the labor supply of those not working (such as person A, who moves to point A_1); has an ambiguous effect on the labor supply of those with low earnings, who receive the wage subsidy (such as person B, who may move to either point B_1 or point B_2); reduces the labor supply of those on the flat maximum subsidy (such as person C, who moves to point C_1); and reduces the labor supply of those on the phase-out portion (such as person D, who moves to point D_1). Note that the figure is not to scale.

Impact of EITC on Labor Supply: Theory

Like most income tax policies, the EITC has both income and substitution effects on labor supply decisions. This can be seen by adding the EITC to our standard consumption-leisure trade-off diagram, as in Figure 21-6 (the figure is not drawn to scale in order to provide space to illustrate the labor supply effects clearly). The blue line is the original budget constraint before the EITC is introduced, assuming a wage rate of $20/hour; the green line represents the new budget constraint after the EITC is added (until $36,348, at which point it reverts to the old blue budget constraint). This figure illustrates the impact of the EITC on four distinct groups:

1. For people not in the labor force at all, such as person *A,* the EITC will likely raise their labor supply, since the only way they can get the credit is to enter the labor force. The EITC has no income effect on this group, since they start with no labor income. The EITC does have a substitution effect, however: by raising the returns for being in the labor force at any earnings level below $33,750, it encourages nonworkers to enter the labor force, moving to point A_1.

2. People already in the labor force who earn less than $11,340, such as person *B* earning $5,000, are on the upward-sloping "phase-in" portion of the EITC schedule, receiving more EITC for each hour of work. The effects on this group's labor supply are ambiguous. The subsidy has substitution effects leading to more work, since each hour of work brings a higher wage, but the subsidy also has income effects that lead to less work, since workers are wealthier as a result of this subsidy. If substitution effects dominate, workers will move to a point such as B_1, with

leisure falling and labor supply increasing; if income effects dominate, workers will move to a point such as B_2, with leisure rising and labor supply falling.

3. People already in the labor force and earning between $11,340 and $14,810, such as person C earning $12,000, are on the "flat portion" of the EITC schedule, receiving the same amount of EITC no matter how little or how much they work within this range. This benefit configuration amounts to a parallel shift outward in the budget constraint, which will lower labor supply. Since the EITC does not raise their hourly wage for additional hours of work, there is no substitution effect. Because they are richer from the subsidy earned on past hours of work, however, the income effect may lower the number of hours they work, moving them to a point such as C_1.

4. People already in the labor force earning between $14,810 and $36,348, such as person D earning $20,000, are on the downward-sloping "phase-out" part of the EITC schedule, where the amount of their EITC is falling as they work more. This outcome causes the slope of the budget constraint to fall relative to the previous segments. The substitution effect now works to reduce labor supply, since the government transfer falls with each additional hour of work, and the income effect continues to work to reduce labor supply, since there is still some transfer of income to the worker. So labor supply definitely falls for this group, moving to a point such as D_1.

If we put all these groups together, theory's prediction about the net impact of the EITC on the total labor supply of low-income populations is ambiguous. This ambiguity has motivated many studies of the EITC's labor supply impacts.

Impact of EITC on Labor Supply: Evidence

The empirical literature on the impact of the EITC has focused on studying how changes in the structure of the EITC over time have affected labor supply. An example of this is shown in Figure 21-7, which illustrates the change in the EITC due to the Tax Reform Act of 1986 (TRA 86). Before this law change, the EITC was much more modest than it is today, with a subsidy rate of only 11%, a maximum credit of only $550, and a phase-out rate of 12.2%. The 1986 law raised the subsidy rate to 14% and the maximum credit to $851, and lowered the phase-out rate to 10%. The combination of the higher maximum credit and the slower phase-out led to a large expansion in eligibility for the credit: workers with earnings between $11,000 and $15,432 became eligible for the first time. Note, however, that both of these programs were much less generous than the current EITC (Figure 21-5), because there have been even larger expansions since 1986, particularly in 1993. Also, unlike today, both before and after TRA 86 the EITC was only available to families with children.

■ **FIGURE 21-7**

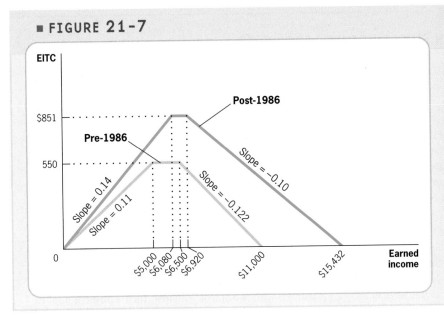

Changes in the EITC Structure • The Tax Reform Act of 1986 changed the structure of the EITC, raising the subsidy rate, increasing the maximum rate, and reducing the phase-out rate, so that a wider range of earnings was eligible for the subsidy. These changes in turn allowed economists to test the effects of the EITC by comparing those who were affected by these changes to those who were not.

Source: Eissa and Leibman (1996).

The post–1986 expansion in EITC generosity had ambiguous effects on labor supply. For those not working, there was a clear increase in the return to work, so labor supply should have increased. For those already working, the substitution effect toward *more* work was strengthened, both by increasing the subsidy rate along the phase-in portion, and by reducing the rate at which the subsidy was phased out. At the same time, the income effect toward *less* work was strengthened by increasing the maximum level of the EITC from $550 to $851. Moreover, recalling the discussion of the iron triangle in Chapter 17, a new set of individuals for whom the EITC had been previously irrelevant (those earning between $11,000 and $15,432) were now eligible, and for those individuals there were income and substitution effects, both of which led to a lower labor supply.

The literature assessing the effect of the EITC has reached several clear conclusions:

Effects on Labor Force Participation Most studies in this area have examined the impact of the EITC on the labor force participation of single mothers (that is, on their decision to work). There is a strong consensus across these studies that the EITC has played an important role in increasing the share of single mothers who work. For example, as described in the Empirical Evidence box, Eissa and Leibman (1996) estimated that single mothers were 1.4 to 3.7 percentage points more likely to work as a result of an expansion of the EITC in 1986.

Effects on Hours of Work Following the theory we just discussed, the 1986 expansion in the EITC would have been expected to increase labor force participation, but it might also have reduced hours worked by those already in

THE EFFECT OF THE EITC ON SINGLE MOTHER LABOR SUPPLY

As noted, studies of the effect of the EITC on single mother labor supply typically exploit quasi-experimental changes in the nature of the EITC over time. One example of this analysis is the paper by Eissa and Leibman (1996), who studied the major expansion of the EITC in 1986 just discussed. Eissa and Leibman studied the impact of the EITC policy change by comparing the labor supply of single women with children (the treatment group, which was affected by this policy change) to the labor supply of single women without children (the control group, for whom the EITC was not available in this era, although they became eligible in the 1990s). The researchers found a large effect of the EITC expansions on the labor supply of single mothers: they estimate such women were 1.4 to 3.7 percentage points more likely to work as a result of this program.

Although this is an interesting set of findings, one may still be concerned that single women without children do not form a valid control group for single women with children, causing bias in the estimates of the EITC. This could arise if any other factors besides the EITC were changing over this period in a way that affected these groups differently. For example, over this period there was an increasing acceptance of mothers of small children working for pay, which could have led single mothers to enter the labor force at a higher rate even without the EITC expansion.

Eissa and Leibman's paper, as well as work by Meyer and Rosenbaum (2000), proposed a series of additional tests to confirm that these labor supply changes are true EITC effects. These tests seek to provide additional treatment-control comparisons that can confirm the causal effect of the EITC, much as with the study of unemployment insurance in Chapter 14. For example, there were additional expansions of the EITC in 1993, which were modest for families with only one child, but much larger for families with two or more children. Thus, an alternative difference-in-difference strategy is to compare the labor supply of single mothers with two or more children (the treatment group) to the labor supply of those with only one child (the control group) around the 1993 change in the EITC. Since both groups of women have children, this comparison would be free of any bias caused by changing norms about working mothers. These additional tests confirmed the large role of the EITC in increasing single mother labor supply.

the labor force, particularly people with incomes in the phase-out range. In most of that range, the marginal tax rate on additional earnings was 51.3% (a 15% federal marginal tax rate, a 15.3% payroll tax, and a 21% phase-out rate for the EITC). This high tax rate might have discouraged labor supply.

Eissa and Leibman also examined the impact of the EITC expansion on hours of work among those in the labor force, and, surprisingly, they found no effect. That is, the wage subsidy of the EITC has had a large effect on getting people into the labor force; however, once people are in the labor force and working, taxes on marginal earnings through the EITC don't have a huge effect on how many hours they work. This outcome could occur because the decision to participate in the labor force with respect to wage subsidies is elastic, but the decision on how many hours to supply with respect to the taxation of wages is not elastic. Alternatively, this outcome could occur because individuals in the phase-out income range don't really understand the complicated disincentives of the phaseout, so they don't respond to it by cutting back their hours of work despite the financial incentives to do so.

Impact on Married Couples Although the EITC appears to have positive effects for the labor supply of single mothers, it might have negative impacts on a married couple's labor supply decisions. Consider a married couple making a sequential labor supply decision: the husband first decides how many hours he will work, then the wife decides how many hours she will work. For the husband, the theoretical impacts of the EITC are the same as for a single mother (those who are not in the labor force will start to work, but the labor supply effects on those already working are ambiguous). For the wife, however, the effects of the EITC will be more negative because the EITC is computed on the basis of *total family earnings*. For most low-wage families with children, this means that the family will already be at the maximum credit level based on the husband's earnings, so that the wife will face only the downward-sloping phase-out range in her decision on how much to work. Indeed, among couples with low education and children, 9% are on the phase-in, 6% are on the plateau (maximum benefit), and 43% on the phaseout.[6] As noted, on the phaseout there are strong disincentives to work, because each additional dollar of earnings lowers EITC payments by 21¢. Thus, secondary earners have a strong disincentive to work through the EITC.

Eissa and Hoynes (1998) studied the impact of the EITC on married couples. They found that there was no effect on men's work. This outcome is consistent with the single mother findings (that the EITC increased the labor force participation of single mothers but did not affect their hours once they were working) because almost all men participate in the labor force to begin with. At the same time, the researchers found a modest reduction in the labor supply of married women, an effect that offsets to some extent the labor supply increases for single women.

Summary of the Evidence

Overall, the United States' experience with the EITC seems fairly successful. It is a powerful redistributive device that now delivers more cash to low-income families than any other welfare program in the United States. And it has done so without reducing overall labor supply, the problem with standard cash welfare; rather, this redistribution has been associated with increased labor supply among single mothers (increased labor force participation with no offsetting reduction in hours worked), no effect on fathers, and a modest reduction in labor supply among married mothers.[7]

▶ **APPLICATION**

EITC Reform

While the EITC has been a major success story, there are significant flaws in its design, as discussed at length in Furman (2006). For example, there is only a very small EITC for childless workers, with a maximum of only $412 per year. As a result, the federal tax rate for families with children at the Federal

---

[6] Eissa and Hoynes (1998), Table 2.

[7] These findings *do not* imply that cash welfare should be abolished and replaced by a larger EITC. Some household heads simply cannot earn a living (perhaps because they are too unskilled), so there is still a need for a purely income-related transfer that does not require work. Simulation work by Saez (2000) suggests that if an EITC is available, the optimal redistributive scheme should continue to feature a guaranteed income such as that discussed in the optimal income tax section of Chapter 20, with EITC-like incentives to work for the lowest income earners.

poverty level has fallen from 15% in 1986 to 10% today, while for those without children it has remained at roughly 15%. Given the powerful effects that the EITC can have on labor supply, while redistributing income to the needy, the EITC could be increased for childless adults to encourage work among this population.

Another flaw is that families receive no additional EITC transfer as family size grows beyond two children; the EITC maximum is $2,747 for families with one child, and rises to its highest value of $4,536 for families with two children. Perhaps as a result of this feature of the EITC, while the poverty rate for those with one or two children is about 12%, it rises to over 20% for those with three children, and almost 35% for those with four children. Poverty among families with children could therefore be decreased by raising the EITC for larger families. Even a budget-neutral shift to a lower maximum for those with two children and a higher maximum for those with three or more would likely lower overall poverty rates for this population.

Another major objection to the current form of the EITC is that it penalizes many single parents who subsequently marry because the credit is based on the income of the tax filing unit, regardless of whether that includes one or two people. For example, if a single mother with two children and annual income of $12,000 marries a man whose income is also $12,000, together their $24,000 income qualifies them for an EITC of $2,601, even though the mother on her own would have received the maximum credit of $4,536.[8] Getting married thus costs the woman nearly $2,000, a *marriage penalty* of the type discussed in Chapter 18. Because of this penalty, one editorial lamented that "the federal government, through the EITC, says, 'If you get married, it'll cost you. And it'll cost you big time.'"[9]

Not all marriages are, however, penalized by the EITC. Take the case of a single mother with two children and no income. If she marries a man whose annual income is $12,000, then together they qualify for the maximum credit of $4,536, even though on her own she would not receive any credit. The EITC thus tends to penalize single mothers with low earnings who marry men with their own earnings, while it subsidizes single mothers with no earnings who marry men with low earnings.

Ellwood (2000) investigated the balance between marriage penalties and bonuses and found that newly married couples with children prior to their marriage are three times as likely to receive a lower rather than a higher credit because of their marriage. Ellwood also found that the average marriage penalty is around $1,600, a figure that agrees roughly with one estimate placing the total cost of the EITC marriage penalty at around $5 billion for low-income families.[10] One way to address the marriage penalty would be to raise the EITC level for married couples, relative to single parents with children. Alternatively, Ellwood and Sawhill (2000) suggested allowing low-income

---

[8] EITC credit amounts calculated using Figure 21-5.
[9] Sawhill and Horn (1999).
[10] Ellwood (2000), Table 9; Holtzblatt and Rebelein (2000).

couples to calculate their EITC using an income splitting method. Under this system, couples divide their total income in half and calculate their EITC based on that number. For the couple each earning $12,000, this would return their EITC to the woman's level before she married, thus removing the penalty she receives for marrying.

Finally, the EITC is very complex. The IRS documentation explaining the EITC is 56 pages long. Perhaps as a result, about one-seventh of those eligible for the EITC do not participate, and the majority of EITC recipients spend some of their low incomes to hire professionals to prepare their taxes. Simplifying the EITC could expand its power as a poverty-fighting tool. ◄

21.4

The Tax Treatment of Child Care and Its Impact on Labor Supply

A primary lesson from the empirical literature on labor supply is that the labor supply decisions of secondary earners are very sensitive to after-tax wages. Yet wages are clearly not the only factor that determines such work decisions. Another important factor is likely to be the cost of **child care** for the children of working parents. Currently, only one-fourth of preschool-age children are cared for solely by their parents. Some of the remaining three-fourths are cared for by relatives, but the majority (56%) are placed in child care centers. As parents work and earn more, the figures become even more dramatic. In households with income over $75,000, only 13% of preschool-age children are cared for solely by their parents, with three-fourths of the remaining children placed in child care centers. Between parents' expenditures and government subsidies, total child care expenditures in the United States are well over $70 billion annually.[11]

> **child care** Care provided for children by someone other than the parents of those children.

Theoretically, child care expenditures for working parents operate in exactly the same way as wage taxation. The higher the child care expenditures, the lower the net returns from working. Thus, child care expenditures have substitution effects leading to less work and income effects leading to more work; for secondary earners, the empirical literature suggests that the substitution effects dominate, causing secondary earners to work less (Anderson and Levine, 2000).

The Tax Treatment of Child Care

The tax treatment of child care also raises interesting additional questions that relate to the discussion of the Haig-Simons comprehensive income standard introduced in Chapter 18. Under the U.S. income tax system, labor delivered

---

[11] Johnson (2005); National Child Care Information Center (2006). Expenditures were determined by summing total expenditures on monthly child care payments made by families with total government child care funding across the nation.

THE EFFECT OF CHILD CARE COSTS ON MATERNAL LABOR SUPPLY

The potential barrier to secondary earner participation in the labor market posed by child care costs has led to a number of studies of the responsiveness of labor supply to child care costs. Most past literature, nicely reviewed by Anderson and Levine (2000), has investigated this question by modeling female labor force participation as a function of the costs of child care in a given area, asking in essence whether mothers are less likely to work when child care is more expensive. The problem with this approach, however, is that the main determinant of the cost of child care is the wages of child care workers, which in turn reflect the general demand for labor in the area. Thus, in areas where labor demand is high, child care worker wages will be high, and child care will be expensive. But expensive child care will not necessarily be associated with less female labor supply because the high demand for labor may bring women into the labor force. In other words, we have a classic bias problem: there is a third factor (the level of labor demand) that affects both the dependent variable (whether a mother works) and the explanatory factor of interest (child care costs).

Several studies have suggested clever approaches to surmounting this problem. Berger and Black (1992) looked at women on welfare who applied for a limited pool of child care subsidies. These subsidies were allocated randomly in the county Berger and Black analyzed, so that women who received subsidies and those who did not were otherwise identical: the only difference between them was their luck in the lottery. As a result, the only difference between these women in their labor supply was the receipt of child care subsidies by the lottery winners. Berger and Black found that labor supply is higher among lottery winners, but that the effect is relatively modest, with an elasticity of labor supply with respect to child care costs of only –0.1 to –0.35.

Gelbach (2002) pursued an alternative innovative strategy: he took advantage of kindergarten birthday cutoffs. Consider two children born one day apart, on August 31

(Emily) and September 1, 2002 (Caroline). Suppose that they live in a school district that has a kindergarten birthday cutoff of August 31: that is, children can attend kindergarten as long as they were born before September 1 five years earlier. In this situation, Emily can attend kindergarten in the fall of 2007 when she has just turned five. But Caroline, who differs only in being born one day later, cannot; she must wait a full year to attend, until she is almost six. Gelbach used this fact to compare the labor supply of mothers whose youngest child was born before (treatment group) and after (control group) school cutoff dates; the women whose children could go to kindergarten essentially got free child care from the public schools one year before those whose children had to wait a year. As expected from theory, he found that mothers whose youngest children were born before the cutoff date are more likely to work than mothers with children born after the cutoff date, although once again the elasticity with respect to child care costs is fairly modest, at –0.16 to –0.35.[12]

Baker et al. (2005) considered a third approach. In the late 1990s, the Canadian province of Quebec passed a law providing universal access to child care for all families in the province for only \$5/day, reflecting a subsidy of about 85% off the market price for child care at the time. There were no notable changes in the price of child care for married women in other provinces (there were many other changes for single women throughout Canada due to that nation's version of welfare reform). Thus, Baker et al. pursued a quasi-experimental difference-in-difference analysis of the labor supply of married women before and after this policy change in Quebec, relative to the rest of Canada. Similar to these other studies, they found a relatively modest elasticity of labor supply with respect to child care costs of only –0.24. Similarly to the types of checks pursued in EITC studies, they confirmed their finding by showing that there was no effect on the labor supply of married women with older children at this same time.

---

[12] To compute an elasticity, Gelbach used area child care costs to impute a value on the free child care provided by the public schools.

■ TABLE 21-1

Child Care Choices

	Pretax, pre-child-care earnings	Child care costs	Child care deduction	Imputed earnings	Taxes owed if work tax rate = 50%	Taxes owed if home	After-tax value of work	After-tax value of home
Base	$1,000	$600	0	0	$500	0	$500	$600
Impute	$1,000	$600	0	$600	$500	$300	$500	$300
Deduct	$1,000	$600	$600	0	$200	0	$800	$600

In the first row of this table, when individuals work they earn an after-tax wage of only $500 but they have to pay a pre-tax cost of $600 for child care, so they won't work. In the second row, the value of child care delivered at home is imputed as income, so after-tax income is higher if individuals work ($500 versus $300). In the third row, child care costs are deductible from taxable income, so after-tax income is also higher if individuals work ($800 rather than $600).

through the market is taxed, while labor delivered through nonmarket activities, such as home child care, is not taxed. This approach is inequitable because families that choose to provide child care themselves, rather than earn income and then buy child care services, pay lower taxes. It is also inefficient because it subsidizes home over market child care.

Consider my family, where I am the primary earner. We have the choice of my wife's looking after our three children or sending them to child care and going into the market to work. Suppose that my wife can earn $25 per hour and that child care for each of our children costs $5 per hour, for a total of $15 per hour. Suppose further that the tax rate on my wife's market earnings is 50%, including federal income taxes, payroll taxes, and state income taxes. Finally, suppose that my wife is equally happy working or caring for our children, so we decide to make this decision purely on financial grounds. This example is illustrated in Table 21-1.

If my wife works 40 hours per week, she would make $1,000 each week, but we would have to put our children in child care for those 40 hours, costing us $600. We would owe $500 in taxes on her market earnings, so that after taxes she would be earning $500 for the week, which is less than the $600 we pay in child care. So, even though my wife's pre-tax wage of $1,000 is higher than the cost of child care, her after-tax wage is lower. In other words, in after-tax terms, the child care my wife delivers at home is worth $600 per week (the last column), while the after-tax wage she brings home from market work is only $500 (the next-to-last column). The taxation of market work but not home work (her value in caring for our children) has created a *tax wedge* that puts market work at a disadvantage. Tax wedges are created whenever two comparable activities are taxed at different rates.

Quick Hint We have used the term "tax wedge" in two different ways in Chapter 19 and in this discussion. In Chapter 19 we discussed tax wedges within a single market; in that context, tax wedges are the difference that taxes

broadest definition of tax wedges Any difference between pre- and post-tax returns to an activity caused by taxes.

cause between producer and consumer prices in this one market. Here, we refer to tax wedges across input markets, where tax wedges are the difference between the returns to the input (labor supply) in the different markets. Both of these are valid definitions, and are a subset of the **broadest definition of tax wedges:** any difference between pre- and post-tax returns to an activity caused by taxes.

Options for Resolving Tax Wedges

This example raises a general point about tax wedges between taxed and untaxed activities: *such tax wedges distort behavior by encouraging people to undertake the untaxed activities and cause deadweight loss.* By taxing market labor but not home labor, we reduced total productivity by $400, since my wife gave up the chance to earn $1,000 in order to stay home and deliver $600 worth of child care. This reduction in productivity increases deadweight loss: the social efficiency pie is now smaller by $400 because my wife is engaging in the activity for which she has a lower marginal product. Public finance economists often say that such tax wedges create an *uneven playing field* across economic activities, where individuals are treated differently because of the choices they make.

Imputing Home Earnings In this case, there are two ways that policy makers could level the playing field in favor of market work, as illustrated in the next two rows of Table 21-1. One would be to tax at-home work just as we tax work in the market. The government would do so by **imputing home earnings,** or assigning a home earnings value to my wife based on the amount of child care she delivers. Thus, the government could impute that she delivers $600 worth of home child care, since that is what it would cost us if we had our children in market care. My family would then be taxed on that home child care, so that if she didn't work in the market we would pay $300 in taxes (50% of the $600 in imputed home earnings) and have an after-tax value of home work of $300. With this tax system in place, we increase our income by $200 if she works ($500 rather than $300), so she will go to work.

   As you might suspect, this is an impractical solution. There are a number of daunting issues facing policy makers as they attempt to tax a good with no clearly assigned market value, such as child care delivered at home.

Deductible Child Care Costs The other alternative is to *make market child care costs deductible.* Suppose now that work at home is not taxed but that the government allows each family to deduct the cost of child care from its taxable income. Under this rule, my wife's taxable income would fall from $1,000 to $400 (since we would deduct the $600 paid for child care), and our tax bill on her earnings would fall to $200. Her after-tax earnings from work would be $800, exceeding the $600 in child care costs; on net, we would gain $200 per week from her market work, the same amount as if home work were taxed. Thus, there are two ways to even a playing field: by taxing all activities equally or by subsidizing all activities equally.

imputing home earnings Assigning a dollar value to the earnings from work at home.

Comparing the Options

While both these solutions level the playing field, their effects on the tax base are not identical: allowing a deduction for child care costs has *lowered the tax base*. When the government taxes home work, and my wife decides to go to work, the government collects $500 in taxes. But when the government subsidizes child care, and my wife decides to go to work, the government collects only $200 in taxes. Thus, the cost of leveling the playing field for this child care decision is the $300 reduction of the entire size of the tax base. As the size of the tax base falls, rates must increase to raise a given level of revenue, and deadweight loss will rise as the tax rates rise.

Thus, we are faced with three choices, all of which have drawbacks. We can continue to have an uneven playing field, which lowers social efficiency by deterring mothers from market work. We can even the playing field by taxing home work, which makes the most economic sense but is an administrative nightmare. We can level the playing field by offering subsidies to market work, which reduces the overall efficiency of the tax system.

Ruling out the second option (taxing home work) on administrative grounds, how do we decide which of the remaining two option causes less distortion overall to the economy and is thus more efficient? A system that has no deduction for child care costs has the cost of distorting mothers away from market work toward home work, but a system that has a deduction for child care costs lowers the tax base and thus the overall efficiency of the tax system. Which is worse?

As highlighted in the previous chapter, these efficiency costs will depend on the elasticities of the taxed activities. The efficiency cost of lowering the overall tax base will be determined by the overall elasticity of economic activity to taxation: as we discuss in Chapter 25, most estimates suggest that this elasticity is modest. The efficiency cost of distorting mothers away from market work will be determined by the elasticity of mothers' market labor supply with respect to the wage: as discussed earlier in this chapter, most estimates suggest that this is very large. Thus, it seems that subsidizing child care to reduce the tax wedge is the better of the two options.

In the United States, we have chosen a position between these two alternatives by partially subsidizing market child care. In particular, families receive a tax credit for child care costs up to $3,000 for one child or $6,000 for two or more. The credit is calculated as an income-dependent percentage of those costs, so that households with income under $10,000 may claim 30% of child care costs (up to $900 or $1,800) while households with income over $28,000 may claim 20% of child care costs (up to $600 or $1,200).

21.5
Conclusion

The discussion of optimal income taxation in Chapter 20 illustrated the key role played by behavioral responses to tax rates. If higher taxes lead people to change their behavior to supply less labor, these changes can offset the gains from tax increases and there might be a natural limit to the revenue that can be raised by income taxation.

In this chapter, we reviewed the evidence on how labor supply responds to taxation. Most studies show that tax rates have little impact on the labor supply of primary earners but a more substantial impact on secondary earners. We have also reviewed one of the major tax policies to promote labor supply, the Earned Income Tax Credit (EITC), and discussed evidence showing that the EITC has raised the labor supply for low-income earners. Finally, we discussed the appropriate tax treatment of child care, one of the major impediments to labor supply by secondary earners.

▶ HIGHLIGHTS

■ Taxes on labor income have theoretically ambiguous impacts on behavior: the substitution effect leads to more labor supply, but the income effect operates in the opposite direction if leisure is a normal good.

■ A wide variety and number of studies indicate that the labor supply of primary earners is inelastic with respect to taxes, while the labor supply of secondary earners is fairly elastic.

■ The largest federal subsidy to labor supply is the Earned Income Tax Credit, which provides a wage subsidy to the lowest-income families. The EITC is reduced when income rises above a certain level.

■ The EITC has ambiguous theoretical implications for labor supply, but available evidence suggests that it clearly raises the labor supply of single mothers overall.

■ A potential impediment to labor supply by secondary earners is the cost of child care. This impediment is worsened by income taxation in the United States because market work is taxed while home work (such as child care) is not.

■ The tax wedge between market and home work can be resolved either by taxing home work, which is administratively impractical, or making the costs of child care deductible, which the United States does to some extent.

▶ QUESTIONS AND PROBLEMS

1. Suppose that for every hour you work you can earn $10 before taxes. Furthermore, suppose that you can work up to 16 hours per day, 365 days per year. Draw your annual budget constraint reflecting the consumption-leisure trade-off under the following income tax schemes:

   a. a flat income tax of 20% on all income earned

   b. an income tax where you pay no tax on the first $10,000 earned and a tax of 25% on all income over $10,000

   c. an income tax where you pay 10% on the first $5,000 earned, 20% on the next $10,000 earned, and 30% thereafter

2. For which group of workers is the substitution effect associated with a tax increase more likely to outweigh the income effect: primary earners or secondary earners? Explain.

3. Over time, more women have become the primary (or sole) wage earners in their households. How does this fact complicate the empirical analysis of the effects of taxation on women's labor supply?

4. What is likely to happen to overall labor supply if

   a. the Earned Income Tax Credit (EITC) compensation rate increases from 30% to 50% for each dollar earned?

   b. the rate of reduction in the EITC phase-out period increases?

5. The country of Akerlovia currently has a tax system that gives each citizen $5,000 in cash up front, exempts the first $10,000 in earned income from tax, and taxes all earned income over $10,000 at a 25% rate. It is considering replacing this system with an Earned Income Tax Credit

system. The proposed new system would drop the $5,000 cash give-away and would instead subsidize the first $10,000 in earned income at a 50% rate. All income earned over $10,000 would still be taxed at the same 25% rate, and the EITC benefits would never be phased out. Describe the effects of this policy change on the labor supply of workers with various incomes.

6. How does making child care costs tax-deductible reduce the "tax wedge" associated with the fact that market work is taxed but home work is not? Does making child care costs deductible increase or decrease social efficiency?

7. Suppose that you can earn $16 per hour before taxes and can work up to 80 hours per week. Consider two income tax rates, 10% and 20%.

   a. On the same diagram, draw the two weekly consumption-leisure budget constraints reflecting the two different tax rates.

   b. Draw a set of representative indifference curves such that the income effect of the tax increase outweighs the substitution effect.

   c. Draw a set of representative indifference curves such that the substitution effect of the tax increase outweighs the income effect.

8. Suppose that the government introduces an Earned Income Tax Credit such that for the first $8,000 in earnings, the government pays 50¢ per dollar on wages earned. For the next $3,000 of earnings, the credit is held constant at $4,000, and after that point the credit is reduced at a rate of 20¢ per dollar earned. When the credit reaches zero, there is no additional EITC.

   a. Draw the budget constraint that reflects this earned income tax credit for a worker who can work up to 4,000 hours per year at an hourly wage of $10 per hour.

   b. Illustrate on your graph the portions of the budget constraint where the labor supply effects of the policy are positive, negative, or ambiguous, relative to the "no policy" status quo.

9. Congressman Pinkie proposes reducing the tax exemption for children in married families where only one parent works outside the home. Why would this proposal improve equity, from a Haig-Simons perspective?

▶ ADVANCED QUESTIONS

10. Suppose that you estimate the following female labor supply relationship:

    Labor supply$_i$ = −320 + 85(after-tax wage)$_i$ + 320(college graduate)$_i$ − 120(married)$_i$, where labor supply is measured in annual hours worked and wages are expressed in hourly wages.

    a. Interpret the coefficient on after-tax wages. What does this coefficient imply about the effect of increasing wages from $6 to $10 per hour on labor supply?

    b. What can we learn from this estimate about the income and substitution effects of wages on labor supply?

    c. How might this coefficient estimate be biased? Explain.

11. Why does the Earned Income Tax Credit exacerbate the marriage penalty for low-income workers? Suggest an alternative method of calculating the EITC that reduces this penalty.

12. The National Bureau of Economic Research's TAXSIM model (http://www.nber.org/~taxsim/taxsim-calc5/) allows you to calculate tax liabilities for a given individual in different years. Go to this Web site and fill in the blanks to "construct" two individuals—a lower-income individual with $20,000 in income and a higher-income individual with $100,000 in income. Assume that both individuals are 45-year-old single parents of two children who do not own homes and have no child care expenses. Use the model to calculate these individuals' federal marginal tax rates and federal income tax liability in 1985, 1995, and 2005. Explain the pattern you find.

13. You graduate from college and take a job at a consulting firm with a wage of $25 per hour. Your job is extremely flexible: you can choose to work any number of hours from 0 to 2,000 per year.

a. Suppose there is an income tax of the following form:

Income up to $10,000: no tax

Income from $10,000 to $30,000: 20% tax rate

Income from $30,000 up: 30% tax rate

Draw a graph in hours worked/consumption space, showing your opportunity set with and without the tax system. With the tax system in place, are there any points that you are particularly unlikely to choose? Why or why not?

b. Say you choose to work 1,500 hours per year. What is your marginal tax rate? What is your average tax rate? Do these rates differ? Why or why not?

c. Suppose that the two tax rates are increased to 25% and 50%. What is the likely effect on the labor supply of men? What is the likely effect on the labor supply of married women? Explain how the responses might differ between these groups, both in terms of underlying economic effects and in terms of the empirical evidence on labor supply responses.

14. Fligrenia's tax system has several tax brackets, ranging from a 0% marginal rate to a 50% marginal rate. The marginal tax rate paid by married couples under the current system is based on the last dollar earned by either spouse. Fligrenia is changing its tax system, however. Under the new system, the higher earner in a household will continue to be taxed as before (i.e., based on the marginal rate associated with total household income). The marginal rate for the lower earner will now be based on that worker's income only, however.

a. Which families do you expect to be most affected by this tax change, and why?

b. Describe a difference-in-difference analysis that could be used to estimate the effects of taxation on married female labor supply.

The **e** icon indicates a question that requires students to apply the empirical economics principles discussed in Chapter 3 and the Empirical Evidence boxes.

Taxes on Savings

22

On January 31, 2003, the Bush administration proposed the creation of Lifetime Savings Accounts and Retirement Savings Accounts, allowing families to place up to $30,000 each year into special savings accounts on which the interest earned would not be subject to income taxation. These new accounts featured fewer restrictions than existing tax-subsidized savings vehicles: individuals could withdraw from their Lifetime Savings Account for any reason at any age, and from their Retirement Savings Account for any reason after age 58. When withdrawn, any interest earned on these accounts, or increases in the value of the assets in the accounts, would be exempt from taxation. The administration's stated goal was to simplify the current set of savings incentives and to increase Americans' retirement savings by reducing the taxation of the returns from that savings. Assistant Treasury Secretary for Tax Policy Pamela Olson declared that "These bold new accounts will give more hardworking Americans the chance to save."[1]

Opponents of the new plans, like the *Washington Post* editorial board, claimed that "the new accounts would drain tax revenue—potentially huge amounts—from the government down the road, when the money was withdrawn and no taxes were paid."[2] Furthermore, many opponents, such as Democratic representative Charles Rangel, argued that "the new tax break will be used by people of means to shelter what they already will save," so that savings would not actually increase.[3]

Politically, most Democrats and many Republicans agreed with Rangel's view that the revenue costs of such a plan would outweigh the benefits gained from any possible increase in savings. Within a week of the announcement, the Bush administration realized the new accounts had very little political support and began focusing on other tax-cutting measures. Nonetheless, the

---

[1] U.S. Department of the Treasury (2003a).
[2] *Washington Post*, "Stealth Tax Reform," February 4, 2003, p. A24.
[3] Howe (2003).

capital income taxation The taxes levied on the returns from savings.

proposal provoked a number of questions, which we will address in this chapter. Does the existing structure of income taxation in the United States reduce the amount that individuals save in this country? Should the government use the tax code to encourage Americans to save more? If so, how should the tax incentives be structured?

This chapter, the second in our series of three chapters on taxation and individual behavior, focuses on savings decisions. As discussed in Chapter 4, the amount a society saves, which makes more capital available to businesses, can be a key determinant of economic growth. Thus, a major source of policy debates in the United States and around the world is the appropriate role of **capital income taxation,** the taxation of the return from savings.

Recall that we began Chapter 21 by discussing the traditional theory of how income taxation affects labor supply. Similarly, this chapter begins with a discussion of the traditional theory of how income taxation affects savings decisions. Unlike our findings about labor supply, however, there is relatively little evidence on the key question raised by this model, how responsive savings are to the after-tax interest rate. We then turn to two alternative models of saving, the precautionary model (where savings are primarily serving as self-insurance against risk) and the self-control model (where savings are determined through a competition between short-run impatience and long-run patience). These alternatives have important implications for the major policy initiative proposed to raise savings in the United States: tax-subsidized retirement savings accounts. We review the structure of these accounts, their likely effects on savings, and the limited evidence on their effectiveness.

22.1
Taxation and Savings—Theory and Evidence

The decision about how much of one's income to save and how much to spend, like the decision about how much labor to supply, is another major individual behavior that is affected by taxation. In this section, we discuss how taxes might affect savings decisions.

Traditional Theory

In the traditional theory of savings, the role of savings is to smooth consumption across periods of time. Individuals have more income in some periods (such as their working lives) and less in others (such as retirement). With no savings, individuals would be forced to consume much less in periods when income is lower. Yet, due to diminishing marginal utility, such a consumption pattern is unlikely to be utility maximizing: individuals would prefer to smooth their consumption over time, consuming a constant amount rather than feasting in some periods and starving in others. By reducing spending in periods when it is high, and raising spending in periods when income is low, savings play that consumption-smoothing role.

intertemporal choice The choice individuals make about how to allocate their consumption over time.

Under this model, called an **intertemporal choice model,** the choice about how much to save is really the choice about how to allocate one's consumption over time. As with modeling labor supply, we do not model savings directly, but rather model consumption over time. Since labor is a "bad," we analyze the complementary "good," leisure, and then compute labor supply as the difference between time available and leisure time taken. Similarly, saving is a "bad"—it is something that we do today to finance future consumption, but we don't get any direct utility out of the savings.[4] The corresponding "good" is today's consumption. **Savings** is the difference between a person's income and his or her current consumption.

savings The excess of current income over current consumption.

A Simplified Model Suppose that Jack lives for two periods. Period one is his working life, during which he earns income Y; period two is his retirement, during which he earns nothing. His consumption during his working life, C^W (for working), is his income in period one minus any saving (S) that he does. Those savings are put in the bank and earn a rate of interest r. In period two, retirement, Jack's consumption, C^R (for retirement), is his savings from period one plus the interest earned on those savings, $S \times (1 + r)$. Given this information, Jack chooses his optimal level of consumption in both periods.

In Figure 22-1 (page 638), we derive savings by analyzing Jack's choice between consumption in periods one (C^W) and two (C^R), using the intertemporal choice model. This choice is made using the same type of utility maximization discussed throughout the book, where the choice is now between consumption in two different periods instead of between two different goods. The indifference curve IC_1 represents the set of combinations of consumption in periods one and two, between which Jack is indifferent. Jack's taste for current versus future consumption (essentially his impatience), along with his desire for consumption smoothing over time (how quickly his marginal utility diminishes), determine the shape and position of his indifference curves.

Before there is any taxation of savings, Jack maximizes his utility subject to an **intertemporal budget constraint** (BC_1), which relates his first- and second-period consumption to his earnings and savings decisions. If Jack saves nothing, he can consume Y in the first period. If he saves his total income, he can consume $Y \times (1 + r)$ in the second period. The relative price of first-period consumption is therefore $1 + r$, the slope of the budget constraint. This is because the *opportunity cost of first-period consumption is the interest income not earned on savings for second-period consumption.* Just as the price of leisure in the labor supply model is the wage rate (the opportunity cost of leisure), the price of first-period consumption in this two-period model is the opportunity cost of first-period consumption, $1 + r$.

intertemporal budget constraint The measure of the rate at which individuals can trade off consumption in one period for consumption in another period.

Figure 22-1 illustrates a typical intertemporal consumption choice of C^W_1 and C^R_1 (point A). At this level of consumption, savings in the first period is $S = Y - C^W_1$, and consumption in the second period is then $S \times (1 + r) = (Y - C^W_1) \times (1 + r)$. We can next consider what happens when the government taxes interest payments on savings. Before doing so, however, it is important to

---

[4] At least not in standard models; some have proposed alternative models of savings which suggest that individuals actually derive utility from having savings.

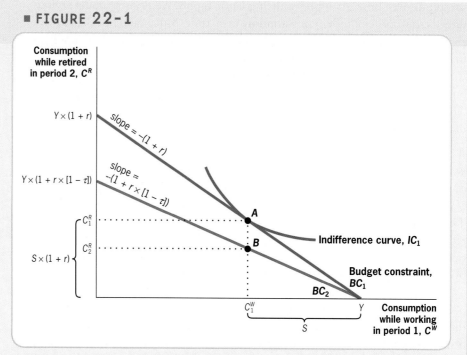

■ **FIGURE 22-1**

Taxation and the Intertemporal Consumption Decision • Before taxes are introduced, individuals lose $-(1 + r)$ worth of consumption in period two (C^R) for every dollar of consumption in period one (C^W). Based on this budget constraint (BC_1), individuals will choose to do some amount of savings, S, in the first period, and consume $S \times (1 + r)$ in the second period. When taxes rise, the budget constraint pivots inward to BC_2. Individuals lose only $-(1 + r \times [1 - \tau])$ worth of consumption in period two for every dollar of consumption in period one. This may raise or lower savings depending on which is more powerful, the income or substitution effect.

remember that we are *not directly modeling savings:* just as in Chapter 21 we modeled leisure, and solved for labor as a residual, here we model consumption while working, C^W, and solve for savings as a residual.

Suppose now that the government taxes interest income. Such a tax would cause the after-tax return to savings to fall from r to $r \times (1 - \tau)$, since the government takes a portion $r \times \tau$ in taxes. This would flatten the budget constraint from BC_1 to BC_2, as shown in Figure 22-1, lowering the slope of the budget constraint from $1 + r$ to $1 + (r \times [1 - \tau])$. That the budget constraint is flatter reflects that the price of first-period consumption, C^W, has fallen: the opportunity cost of consuming in the first period has fallen because each dollar of savings yields less consumption in the second period. At a given level of first-period consumption, Jack can now afford less second-period consumption, since his savings earn a lower rate of return.

Substitution and Income Effects of Taxes on Savings As always, the price change that results from the tax on savings interest will have two effects. The lower after-tax interest rate (lower price of C^W) will cause consumption in period one to rise through the substitution effect. This will in turn lead savings to fall. There is also, however, an income effect of lower after-tax income. Jack is now poorer at all levels of savings because the amount of interest he keeps from each dollar of savings has fallen, and a given level of savings buys him less C^R. For example, in Figure 21-1, at the same level of first-period consumption (and thus the same level of savings) of C^W_1, Jack can only afford second-period consumption of C^R_2. This drop in income will cause C^W_1 to fall, and S to rise.

> **Quick Hint** When thinking about the income effect of changes in the after-tax interest rate on savings, it is helpful to reflect on the extreme case of a target level of consumption for retirement in period two (as we did in Chapter 21 with target earnings in the labor supply case). If Jack has a certain amount of consumption he wants in period two (such as a certain standard of living in his retirement), then when the after-tax interest rate falls, he must save more and reduce C^W in period one to achieve that target.

Because the substitution and income effects work in opposite directions, the net effect of interest taxation on savings is uncertain. The two panels of Figure 22-2 on page 640 illustrate this point. In panel (a), the substitution effect of the lower after-tax interest rate (the lower price of period-one consumption C^W causes Jack to prefer more period-one consumption) is larger than the income effect of the lower after-tax income (lower income causes Jack to consume less of everything, including period-one consumption). Jack initially consumes at point A (C^W_1, C^R_1). After a tax on interest is imposed (seen in the move from BC_1 to BC_2), Jack moves to point B, with higher first-period consumption, C^W_2, lower savings (fall from S_1 to S_2), and much lower second-period consumption, C^R_2.

In panel (b), the income effect of the lower after-tax income is larger than the substitution effect of the lower after-tax interest rate, and Jack moves to point C. First-period consumption falls from C^W_1 to C^W_3, implying a rise in savings from S_1 to S_3. Second-period consumption still falls in this case (to C^R_2), but not by as much as in panel (a). This is because the income effect isn't large enough to lead Jack to fully undo the reduction in income by saving more; if C^R didn't change at all, this would be the target income case described earlier, with savings rising by exactly enough to offset the reduction in the return to savings.[5]

---

[5] This is a simplified example where Jack only has earnings in the first period. In a more general model where Jack has earnings in both the first and second period, and where he can borrow against second-period earnings to consume in the first period, there is another effect that further strengthens the negative effect of taxes on savings: the human wealth effect highlighted by Summers (1981). Jack's consumption in both periods in this model is determined by the present discounted value of his entire lifetime stream of income. Jack discounts his second-period labor earnings by the after-tax interest rate—from today's perspective, having earnings in the future is worth less at a higher interest rate. Rising taxes lower the discount rate and raise the net present value of second-period labor earnings. With a higher present value of lifetime labor earnings, Jack will consume more and save less in response to the higher taxation.

■ FIGURE 22-2

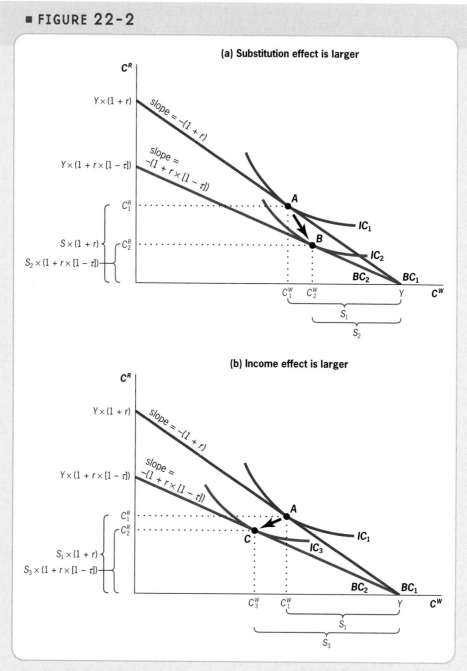

Intertemporal Substitution Versus Income Effect • If the substitution effect is larger than the income effect (panel (a)), individuals will move from point A to point B, consuming more in the first period (C_2^W) and thus saving less (S_2). As a result, their consumption in period two (C_2^R) falls by a lot. If the income effect is larger (panel (b)), individuals will move from point A to point C, consuming less in the first period (C_3^W) and thus saving more (S_3). Their consumption in period two (C_2^R) still falls, but not by as much.

Evidence: How Does the After-Tax Interest Rate Affect Savings?

In contrast to the case of labor supply, there is little consensus on the impact of taxes or the interest rate on savings decisions. Indeed, economists aren't even in agreement on whether there is a negative, zero, or even positive impact of interest income taxes on savings. Hall (1988) uses time series evidence to argue that there is no impact of the after-tax interest rate on consumption and savings. More recent studies suggest that consumption decisions do respond strongly to the after-tax interest rate (Attanasio and Weber, 1995; Gruber, 2006).

To be fair, studying the connections between after-tax interest rates and savings is a difficult problem. Determining the appropriate interest rate to use is one of the most difficult aspects of this problem: although we can measure a given worker's wage, it is hard to measure the appropriate interest rate for any given saver. Which interest rate is "appropriate" depends on the set of savings opportunities available to an individual, ranging from bank accounts to tax-subsidized pensions. Moreover, the interest that can be earned on any type of savings typically changes over time in the same way for all individuals, making it hard to find appropriate treatment and control groups for studying how savings respond to interest rate changes. Nevertheless, the elasticity of savings with respect to the after-tax interest rate remains a crucial parameter for policy analysis, and future work is clearly needed to assess its magnitude.

Inflation and the Taxation of Savings

For a number of years in the 1970s and 1980s, the United States struggled with very high inflation rates, peaking at 13.5% in 1980. Before 1981, the tax brackets on which taxation is based (as shown in Figure 18-3 on page 519) were denominated in constant dollars that did not change with inflation. This practice led to a phenomenon known as *bracket creep,* whereby individuals would see an increase in their tax rate despite no increase in their real (constant dollar) income. From 1979 to 1980, for example, prices rose by 11.3%. If incomes had risen by that same amount, consumers would have had constant earnings in real terms, so that their purchasing power would have been unchanged. The tax bracket amounts, however, remained the same in 1979 and 1980, which meant that individuals whose incomes rose just to offset inflation would pay more taxes, since more of their income would appear in higher tax brackets.

Suppose, for example, that Steve had an income of $16,500 in 1979. That year, he would have faced a 21% marginal tax rate and would have paid taxes of $2,370, leaving him an after-tax income of $14,130. In 1980, Steve's income rose to $18,365, exactly offsetting the 11.3% inflation of that year, so that Steve's *real income* (the amount of goods he could purchase with his income) did not change. Since the tax brackets were not indexed in 1980, however, Steve would then have faced a higher marginal rate of 24%, because the 21% bracket ended at $16,600 in income. He would have paid $2,815 in taxes and would have had an after-tax income of $15,550. Note that Steve's after-tax income grew by only 10.0%, while prices rose by 11.3%. Because of the fixed nominal tax brackets, his salary increase was too small to keep up with inflation. The solution to this problem was fairly straightforward: in 1981, Congress indexed the tax brackets for the regular income tax (although not for the Alternative Minimum Tax), so that the marginal tax rate was based on real income, not nominal income.

Inflation and Capital Taxation Indexing the income tax brackets did not remove inflation's impact on income taxation altogether because the rules about capital income taxation had remained the same. The interest rate earned on a bank account is determined by the **nominal interest rate,** while the actual improvement in purchasing power from savings is the **real interest rate.** Instead of being concerned about how much money you get next year, you should be concerned about how many goods you will be able to consume with that money next year.

Table 22-1 illustrates the impact of capital taxation in an inflationary environment. Suppose that Robin is going to save $100 at a nominal 10% interest rate, and that she spends all of her money on Skittles, at $1 per bag. Initially, there is no tax on interest earnings. She earns $10 in interest, so her after-tax resources are $110. At a Skittles price of $1, with no inflation (first row of the table), she can buy 110 bags as a result of this savings. In the second row, a tax on capital income is introduced at 50%, which means that Robin gets to keep only half of her interest earnings, $5. So she can only buy 105 bags of Skittles after taxation.

Suppose now that there is inflation, at a 10% rate, so that a bag of Skittles costs $1.10. In this case, with no taxation (third row) Robin can only buy 100 bags with her $110 in resources, the same as today. Her purchasing power has

nominal interest rate The interest rate earned by a given investment.

real interest rate The nominal interest rate minus the inflation rate; this measures an individual's actual improvement in purchasing power due to savings.

▪ TABLE 22-1

Capital Taxation in an Inflationary Environment

Case	Inflation	Tax rate on interest	Savings	Nominal interest rate	Interest earnings	After-tax resources	Price of skittles	Bags of skittles
No inflation	0%	0%	100	10%	$10	$110	$1.00	110
	0%	50%	100	10%	$10	$105	$1.00	105
Inflation	10%	0%	100	10%	$10	$110	$1.10	100
	10%	50%	100	10%	$10	$105	$1.10	95.5
Constant real rate	10%	0%	100	21%	$21	$121	$1.10	110
	10%	50%	100	21%	$21	$110.5	$1.10	100.5

In the first two rows, there is no inflation. Robin earns $10 in interest on her $100 in savings. With no taxation in the first row, she can buy 110 bags of Skittles; with interest taxation at 50% in the second row, she can buy only 105 bags of Skittles. The next two rows introduce 10% inflation but keep the nominal interest rate fixed at 10%; now Robin can afford only 100 bags of Skittles without taxation, and 95.5 bags with a 50% tax rate. The final two rows raise the nominal interest rate to 21%, so that the real interest rate remains at 10% despite the 10% inflation. With no taxation, Robin is as well off as before inflation. With capital income taxation, however, she is worse off; she can now afford only 100.5 bags of Skittles, compared to the 105 bags she could buy in the second row when there was taxation but no inflation.

not increased because her 10% interest earnings have been offset by 10% inflation. With taxation of capital income at 50%, she now only has $105 after taxes, and can only buy 95.5 bags of Skittles.

When there is inflation, however, it will affect the interest rate that Robin can earn on her savings. We can define the relationship between the real and nominal interest rates as:

$$\text{Real interest rate } (r) =$$
$$[1 + \text{Nominal interest rate } (i)] \,/\, [(1 + \text{Inflation rate } (\pi)] - 1$$

When individuals make their savings decisions, they care about the real interest rate, or how much of an improvement in buying power they can obtain from their savings (in this example, how many bags of Skittles they can buy next year). As a result, when inflation rises, banks and corporations will have to pay a higher nominal interest rate to attract individual savings.

In principle, banks and corporations will offset inflation by raising nominal interest rates to keep the level of real rates the same. If inflation were 10%, a bank would pay a nominal interest rate of 21% to provide the same 10% real return that was received before inflation (since $121/$1.10 = 110 bags of Skittles). As the third row of the table shows, with a 21% interest rate, and no taxation, Robin can once again purchase 110 bags of Skittles at a price of $1.10 (as in the first row). So, if banks raise nominal interest rates to fully offset inflation, in the absence of taxation, inflation will not erode the purchasing power of savings.

The problem is that *taxes are levied on nominal, not real, interest earnings.* The final row of Table 22-1 reintroduces taxes on interest earnings. Now, when Robin earns $21 in interest, she pays $10.50 in taxes on those interest earnings, leaving her with $110.50 in after-tax resources. With that $110.50, she can purchase only 100.5 bags of Skittles—which is below what she could purchase after-tax before inflation (105 bags in the second row).

Because taxes are levied on nominal interest rates, the increase in nominal interest rates by banks in inflationary periods will not fully compensate for the fall in real interest rates. Thus, even though bracket creep ended in 1981, the impacts of inflation on the tax code remain important. In particular, higher inflation lowers the after-tax real return to savings.

22.2
Alternative Models of Savings

In the standard intertemporal choice model, saving is undertaken solely to smooth consumption over time. Recent economic research has focused on two augmentations to this model that suggest other factors that might be important in determining savings, and that the after-tax interest rate may be less important than proposed by the traditional theory.

Precautionary Savings Models
Another factor that will determine savings is the amount of uncertainty individuals face in their financial prospects and their desire to use savings to ensure

precautionary savings model
A model of savings that accounts for the fact that individual savings serve at least partly to smooth consumption over future uncertainties.

liquidity constraints Barriers to credit availability that limit the ability of individuals to borrow.

against negative financial shocks. Just as savings can smooth consumption over time, they can smooth consumption over states of the world as well, as highlighted by our discussion of self-insurance in Chapter 12. Indeed, when people were asked about their reasons for saving, the top answer, along with saving for retirement, was saving for "emergencies," such as unemployment or health problems.[6] This finding has led to the development of the **precautionary savings model** of savings in which saving is motivated not only by the desire to smooth consumption across time but also to self-insure against risk.

In this model, people face the risk of adverse events happening in the future: adverse health shocks (such as having a heart attack), unemployment, divorce, and so on. This model assumes that individuals are unable to borrow if they experience an adverse shock because they face **liquidity constraints,** barriers to borrowing. Such liquidity constraints may arise because, for example, banks are unwilling to loan to an individual with a major illness or who has just lost his job. As a result, individuals must build up a *buffer stock* of savings that is available should one of these adverse shocks occur, so they can smooth consumption between periods of good luck and periods of adverse shocks. The desire to have a buffer stock is another reason, besides intertemporal smoothing, that individuals have savings.

Evidence for the Precautionary Model In support of the precautionary savings model, a number of studies have shown that more uncertainty leads to more savings, and that reducing uncertainty reduces savings. Other studies have shown that expansions in social insurance programs that lower income uncertainty also lower savings, an outcome that is consistent with the notion that saving is motivated by precaution against risk.

Self-Control Models

An alternative formulation of the savings decision draws on the self-control type of models discussed in Chapter 6 in the context of smoking. In this model, individuals faced the conflict between impatient short-run preferences (I need a cigarette today) and patient long-run preferences (I would like to quit tomorrow). Such a self-control problem is also likely to be important in the context of savings.[7] Individuals have a long-run preference to ensure enough savings for smooth consumption throughout their lives, but their impatient short-run preferences may cause them to consume all of their income and not save enough for future periods. In this model, a key determinant of savings behavior is the ability of individuals to find ways to commit themselves to save, so that they can keep their income out of the hands of their impatient "short-run self."

Evidence for the Self-Control Model There is growing evidence that is consistent with self-control models of savings. Recall from our discussion of self-control models in Chapter 6 that individuals with self-control problems

---

[6] Aizcorbe et al. (2003), Table 2.
[7] Laibson et al. (1998).

EMPIRICAL EVIDENCE

SOCIAL INSURANCE AND PERSONAL SAVINGS

A central prediction of the precautionary savings model is that when the government provides insurance against income uncertainty, individuals will reduce the buffer stock of precautionary savings they have built up to deal with that uncertainty. This is a natural implication of the crowd-out discussion of Chapter 12: as the government expands social insurance, self-insurance, of which savings is a primary form, falls.[8] A number of papers have shown that this prediction holds true.

Perhaps the most striking is the study by Chou et al. (2003) of the introduction of National Health Insurance (NHI) in Taiwan in 1995. Before NHI was introduced, health insurance in Taiwan was incomplete. The introduction of NHI led to comprehensive health insurance coverage for all citizens, greatly reducing their need to save for their own medical expenses. In principle, one could then assess whether savings fell around 1995 in Taiwan to find out whether individuals were saving for medical expenses but no longer felt the need to do so. In practice, this is difficult because other things were changing in Taiwan around 1995 that might also have affected savings rates; in particular, strong economic growth in this era could have led to rising savings that masked any true reduction in savings from NHI.

Chou et al. recognized this difficulty and posed a sensible solution. They note that before 1995, private-sector workers typically had health insurance for themselves through their jobs, but not for family members. Government workers, however, were provided with health insurance for their families as well as themselves. Thus, the introduction of NHI would likely have a relatively modest effect on government workers, who were completely insured before and after 1995, and a much larger effect on other workers, who were now gaining coverage for family members. In their difference-in-difference framework, Chou et al. compared the change in savings for the treatment group (nongovernment workers, who saw a large reduction in their uncovered family medical expenses) to that of the control group (government workers, who saw little change in their uncovered family medical expenses).

The results of this analysis were striking. Among government workers, from before NHI to after, savings rose by $30,000 Taiwanese dollars (U.S.$1,165) on average, consistent with the strong economic growth of this era. Among nongovernment workers, from before NHI to after, savings *fell* by $20,585 Taiwanese dollars (U.S.$800), despite economic growth. Thus, the expansion of health insurance to nongovernment workers was associated with a reduction in their savings, consistent with the notion that individuals had been saving against medical uncertainty (and no longer had to do so).

Similar evidence is available for the United States as well. For example, Gruber and Yelowitz (1999) found that the Medicaid expansions discussed in Chapter 16, which greatly reduced the risk of uncovered medical costs and thereby lowered the need for precautionary savings, significantly reduced the savings of low-income groups.

will demand *commitment devices* to help curb their self-control problems. Such commitment devices are widespread in the context of savings. A classic example is the "Christmas club," a bank account into which individuals put money throughout the year, at low or no interest, to make sure they have money available at Christmastime to buy gifts. Another example is retirement savings accounts of the type described in the next section.

A second piece of evidence that is consistent with self-control explanations is the pattern of asset accumulation in the United States, which has a very strange feature: individuals have substantial savings in forms that are hard to access (housing or retirement accounts), but very little in more easily accessible forms, such as checking accounts. Even more puzzling, many individuals

---

[8] This crowd-out is modeled formally by Hubbard, Skinner, and Zeldes (1995), among others.

save money in forms that are hard to access, such as retirement accounts, at fairly modest interest rates (5% or less), while simultaneously borrowing money on their credit cards at high interest rates (10% or more). In the standard model, these individuals could make themselves better off by saving somewhat less at 5% and not borrowing at 10%. The fact that they don't is very consistent with the self-control model: individuals are worried that if they have the money in their hands, they will spend it recklessly, but if they can commit to keeping it away from themselves, it will be saved. Thus, individuals can successfully save in forms such as housing or retirement accounts, but they can't successfully save once they get their hands on the money!

Finally, very convincing evidence for self-control models is found in an experiment run by economists Richard Thaler and Shlomo Benartzi (2004), who offered a unique retirement savings plan to employees at a midsize manufacturing firm. With their "save more tomorrow" plan, employees committed a portion of their *future* pay increases to their retirement savings. Employees were given the option to make this savings commitment long before the actual pay increase appeared, so that the decision seemed less difficult. Once employees joined, their contribution to the savings plan went up with every raise the employees received.

Such a plan should have had no attraction for the type of rational, forward-looking savers in the standard intertemporal consumption model. They could save as much as they like from their income, so there was no need to precommit to a fixed savings plan. In other words, in the standard model, there is rarely a reason to restrict one's behavior in this way; if a worker wants to save a share of future raises, she can simply do so when the raise is provided. Yet this plan would have great attractiveness to those with self-control problems, who would like to keep some of their future raises out of the hands of their impatient short-term selves. Individuals with self-control problems might fear that if they don't commit now to saving their raises, then when the raises actually happen they will spend them in a fit of short-run impatience.

In fact, when this plan was introduced, 78% of employees offered the plan decided to join it, and 80% of those employees stayed on the plan through four pay raises. Most strikingly, the savings rates for plan participants jumped from 3.5% to 13.6% over the course of 40 months. The fact that a form of commitment that is useless in the standard model has such a large effect on savings behavior is once again consistent with the notion that employees have self-control problems over their savings. Ashraf et al. (2006) documented a similar result for a commitment device for savings in the Philippines, proving that self-control problems are a worldwide phenomenon!

22.3

Tax Incentives for Retirement Savings

As discussed in Chapter 4, some economists and policy makers argue that we save too little in the United States and that our economic growth suffers as a result. Moreover, despite the existence of the Social Security program, some remain concerned that worker shortsightedness may cause workers to undersave for retirement. As a result of these concerns, the U.S. government has introduced a series of tax subsidies to encourage retirement savings. In this section, we review the structure and effects of these subsidies.

Available Tax Subsidies for Retirement Savings

In the United States there are a variety of tax-subsidized mechanisms available for retirement savings. In this section, we briefly review the four major tax incentives for retirement savings.

Tax Subsidy to Employer-Provided Pensions One of the largest fringe benefits provided by employers to their employees is the **pension plan,** whereby employers save to provide retirement income to their workers. Traditionally, employer-provided pension plans were **defined benefit pension plans,** in which workers accrued pension rights during their tenure at the firm, and when they retired the firm paid them a benefit that was a function of that workers' tenure at the firm and of their earnings. Over time, employer-provided pension plans have shifted to **defined contribution pension plans,** in which employers set aside a certain proportion of a worker's earnings (such as 5%) in an investment account, and the worker receives these savings and any accumulated investment earnings when she retires.

Similar to employer-provided health insurance, the contributions that employers make to pension plans are not taxed as income to employees. Likewise, any interest that accumulates on this pension savings is not taxed as it is accrued. Instead, employees are taxed on their pension savings as regular income when it is withdrawn in retirement.

401(k) Accounts The most rapidly growing form of retirement savings is the **401(k) account,** an individually controlled savings program offered through the workplace. These 401(k) accounts allow individuals to save for their retirement on a tax-favored basis through a paycheck withdrawal, with employers often matching employee contributions. A typical 401(k) option at a firm allows the worker to contribute up to 10% of her income to a retirement account, and any dollars contributed are not counted as taxable income. In addition, the employer matches, say, the first 5% of employee contributions, by contributing to the account an amount equal to the worker's contribution. There is a limit on 401(k) contributions of $13,000 per year (as of 2004, rising to $15,000 by 2006). 401(k) account balances are taxed as ordinary income when withdrawn in retirement.

Individual Retirement Accounts The problem with employer-provided pensions or 401(k) plans as retirement savings vehicles is that many individuals are not offered such plans by their employers; only 49% of workers in the private sector participate in an employer-provided pension plan.[9] In 1974, Congress introduced the **Individual Retirement Account (IRA),** a tax-favored

pension plan An employer-sponsored plan through which employers and employees save on a (generally) tax-free basis for the employees' retirement.

defined benefit pension plans Pension plans in which workers accrue pension rights during their tenure at the firm, and when they retire the firm pays them a benefit that is a function of that workers' tenure at the firm and of their earnings.

defined contribution pension plans Pension plans in which employers set aside a certain proportion of a worker's earnings (such as 5%) in an investment account, and the worker receives this savings and any accumulated investment earnings when she retires.

401(k) accounts Tax-preferred retirement savings vehicles offered by employers, to which employers will often match employees' contributions.

Individual Retirement Account (IRA) A tax-favored retirement savings vehicle primarily for low- and middle-income taxpayers, who make pre-tax contributions and are then taxed on future withdrawals.

---

[9] Data from Bureau of Labor Statistics' 2003 *Employee Benefits Survey*, "Incidence of Employees in All Retirement Plans."

retirement savings vehicle for individuals not covered by employer-provided pensions. For low- and middle-income households (income below $60,000 for a single head of household, or $85,000 for a married couple), IRAs function as follows:[10]

▶ They are not a special type of savings. Almost any form of asset can be put in an IRA (from stocks to bonds to holdings of gold).

▶ Individuals can contribute up to $4,000 tax-free each year (deducted from their taxable income).

▶ Unlike the interest on a regular savings account, the interest earned on IRA contributions accumulates tax-free.

▶ IRA balances can't be withdrawn until age 59½, and withdrawals have to start at age 70 (or there is a 10% tax penalty).

▶ IRA balances are taxed as regular income on withdrawal.

For higher income households, however, IRAs were restricted by the Tax Reform Act of 1986. Higher-income households now only have access to *nondeductible* IRAs, IRAs for which the annual contributions are part of taxable income but for which the interest earned accumulates tax-free.

The tax subsidization of saving through an IRA was expanded in 2001 through the introduction of the "saver's tax credit." This program matches the contributions to IRA accounts by low-income families. For example, for married couples jointly filing taxes with incomes below $30,000, the saver's credit equals 50% of their IRA contribution up to $2,000, so that the after-tax cost of contributing $2,000 to an IRA is only $1,000. The match rate then falls, and for joint filers with incomes between $32,501 and $50,000, the credit rate is only 10%. The saver's credit also can apply to 401(k) contributions as well, under a somewhat more complicated formula.

Keogh Accounts   The final large form of tax-subsidized retirement savings is **Keogh accounts,** which are retirement savings options specifically for the self-employed. Individuals with Keogh accounts can save up to $44,000 per year from their self-employment earnings tax-free, for withdrawal (and taxation) upon retirement. Thus, Keogh accounts function in the same way as do 401(k) accounts (without matching), except that they are not run through employers.

Why Do Tax Subsidies Raise the Return to Savings?

All of the tax subsidies just described have a similar structure: individuals are shielded from taxation on their savings, as well as on any interest earnings on those savings. In addition, individuals are taxed on their retirement savings as regular income when they withdraw the funds from their retirement savings accounts.

Keogh accounts Retirement savings accounts specifically for the self-employed, under which up to $44,000 per year can be saved on a tax-free basis.

---

[10] For more information on IRAs, see IRS publication #590.

If retirement savings are taxed anyway when individuals are retired, how is this a tax subsidy? This is a subsidy because instead of paying the taxes on the savings up front, you defer the payment of taxes (on both the initial contribution and on any interest earned) until you withdraw those retirement savings. Recall from our discussion of present discounted value (PDV) in Chapter 4 that money received today is worth more than money that will be received in the future because you can earn interest on the money if you have it today. By the same token, taxes paid in the future are less costly than taxes paid today, because you can earn interest on the tax payments that you avoid today.

In other words, with savings that are not tax-preferred, you pay taxes as you earn the money. In turn, the government can take these tax payments, deposit them, and earn interest on them. With tax-preferred retirement savings, you get to hold on to any taxes you would have paid on both your initial contribution and any interest earnings, and *you get to earn the interest on the money that would have otherwise been paid in taxes*. The difference between paying the taxes up front (and letting the government earn the interest on them), and paying the taxes at withdrawal (so that you earn the interest on them) can be quite large.

Suppose that Ted is a 70-year-old who has earned $100 at his job that he wants to save for one year in a bank account and then withdraw. His tax rate is 25% and the interest rate he can earn on the bank account is 10%. He is trying to decide whether to label his bank account an IRA; the implications of his decision are shown in Table 22-2. If he doesn't label the account as an IRA, he has to pay taxes on his earnings. In that case, he keeps $75 of earnings after tax, puts it in the bank, earns $7.50 in interest, but then pays $1.88 in taxes on that interest. When he withdraws his money after one year, he has $80.62. If he labels his account as an IRA, however, he gets to invest the entire $100 of earnings (since IRA contributions are tax-deductible). He earns $10 of interest on this investment. Then, when he withdraws the money after one year, the government collects 25% of his $110, or $27.50. He ends up with $82.50, $1.88 more than the amount withdrawn from the non-IRA account.

Moreover, the IRA's advantage of deferring tax payments increases the longer one holds the asset. For example, if you hold an asset for 30 years at an

■ **TABLE 22-2**

The Tax Advantage of IRA Savings

Account type	Earnings	Tax on earnings (tax rate = 25%)	Initial deposit	Interest earned (interest rate = 10%)	Taxes paid upon withdrawal	Total amount withdrawn
Regular	$100	$25	$75	$7.50	$0.25 × ($7.50) = $1.88	$75 + 7.50 − $1.88 = $80.62
IRA	$100	0	$100	$10	$0.25 × ($110) = $27.50	$100 + 10 − $27.50 = $82.50

If Ted deposits his $100 earnings in a regular bank account, those earnings are taxed before deposit at a rate of 25%, and the interest earned on the remaining $75 is also taxed at 25%. He ends up with more money if he deposits his earnings in an IRA because those earnings are untaxed before the deposit, so that he can gain interest on all $100 of his earnings (rather than just 75% of them).

interest rate of 10% and a tax rate of 25%, an IRA would leave you with *twice* as much money as a non-IRA account.[11] Another advantage is that many taxpayers will find themselves in a lower tax bracket when they retire because their income is lower than when they were working. As a result, deferring taxes to retirement lowers the amount of taxes paid.

This same logic applies to all forms of tax-subsidized retirement savings. Thus, these types of tax incentives can dramatically increase the after-tax rate of return to retirement savings.

Theoretical Effects of Tax-Subsidized Retirement Savings

Theoretically, tax subsidies to retirement savings act in the opposite way that the tax on interest income worked in Figure 22-1. The effects are illustrated in Figure 22-3, which once again shows the intertemporal consumption trade-off. We start with the after-tax budget constraint, BC_2, from that figure, with a slope $-(1 + r \times [1 - \tau])$; remember that the slope is after-tax interest rate, the price of first-period (working-life) consumption, C^W.

When retirement savings is in a tax-subsidized form, however, savings are taxed much more lightly, since taxes are not paid until retirement (lowering the PDV of tax payments). If this delay in tax payments reduces the tax burden on savings from τ to $\tau \times \rho$, where ρ is the share of the tax burden that remains after accounting for the delay in tax payments. Suppose, for example, that $\tau = 0.3$ and ρ equals 0.33; this would imply that individuals saving through tax-subsidized retirement plans have an effective tax rate on savings of $0.3 \times 0.33 = 0.1$ when subsidies are accounted for. In this case, the availability of tax-subsidized savings raises the slope of the budget constraint to $-(1 + r \times [1 - \tau \times \rho])$, so that the budget constraint moves from BC_2 to BC_3, raising the price of first-period consumption. (With a higher interest rate, there is a higher opportunity cost to consuming rather than saving.) This leads to a substitution effect toward more savings and an income effect toward less savings. Individuals will save more because the price of current consumption (the after-tax interest rate) has risen (the substitution effect); but they will save less because they can now more easily reach their retirement savings goals (the income effect).

As discussed earlier, the effect of this change in the after-tax interest rate is ambiguous. Figure 22-3 shows two possible outcomes of savings subsidies. If the substitution effect is larger than the income effect, then such subsidies will raise savings (from S_2 to S_3), with first-period consumption falling from C^W_2 to C^W_3 (moving from point A to point B). If the income effect is larger than the substitution effect, then such subsidies will lower savings (from S_2 to S_4), with first-period consumption rising from C^W_2 to C^W_4 (moving from point A to point C).

---

[11] In fact, even the nondeductible IRAs available to higher income taxpayers after 1986 are valuable opportunities for long-term investors because they allow investors to defer the taxation on interest earnings until the investment is withdrawn. Indeed, over the long run, most of the benefits of an IRA come not from the initial deductibility of the IRA contributions but from the tax-free accumulation of interest earned by the account.

■ FIGURE 22-3

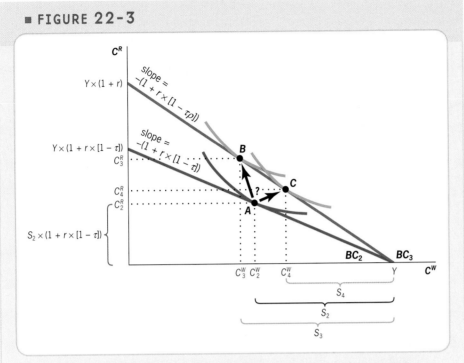

Tax Subsidies and the Intertemporal Consumption Trade-off • Individuals initially face a budget constraint BC_2 with a slope $-(1 + r \times [1 - \tau])$. When retirement savings is tax-subsidized, the budget constraint moves to BC_3, with a higher slope $-(1 + r \times [1 - \tau \times \rho])$. This leads to a substitution effect toward more savings, and an income effect toward less savings. If the substitution effect is larger, then first-period consumption will fall from C_2^W to C_3^W, and savings will rise from S_2 to S_3. If the income effect is larger, then first-period consumption will rise from C_2^W to C_4^W, and savings will fall from S_2 to S_4.

Limitations on Tax-Subsidized Retirement Savings Most of the vehicles for tax-subsidized retirement savings we reviewed earlier feature a limit on annual contributions, such as the $3,000 limit for IRAs. These limits complicate the theoretical analysis. Suppose that Andrea is making savings decisions in a world with and without an IRA available. Figure 22-4 shows the impact of the IRA on her budget constraint. Her original after-tax budget constraint, BC_2, between consumption in period one and period two is the line AB, with a slope of $-(1 + r \times [1 - \tau])$, where r is the interest rate earned on her savings and τ is the tax rate paid on interest earnings. Before the IRA is available, the price of first-period consumption, in terms of forgone second-period consumption, is $1 + r \times (1 - \tau)$, since that is how much second-period consumption she could have if she consumed one dollar less today.

If Andrea decides to put money in an IRA, the after-tax rate of return to savings changes. The slope of the new budget constraint, BC_3, for the first

▪ **FIGURE 22-4**

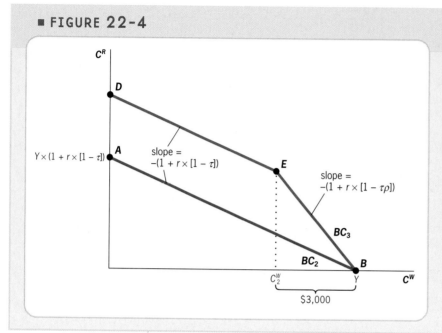

IRAs and the Intertemporal Consumption Decision • The availability of IRAs raises the return to saving less than $3,000 from $-(1 + r \times [1 - \tau])$ to $-(1 + r \times [1 - \tau \times \rho])$, where ρ is the net tax preference from using an IRA. Once savings is above $3,000 (period-one consumption less than C_2^W), the IRA simply increases period-two income, and the return to each dollar of savings returns to $-(1 + r \times [1 - \tau])$.

$3,000 of savings (which corresponds to period-one consumption of C_2^W) rises to $-(1 + r \times [1 - \tau \times \rho])$, where $\tau \times \rho$ is once again the effective tax rate on tax-subsidized savings. This change is reflected in a new, steeper budget constraint between points E and B. Above $3,000 of savings (with period-one consumption of less than C_2^W), there is no change in the rate of return to savings, due to the cap on IRA contributions. Above $3,000 of savings then, the slope of the budget constraint returns to its original value $-(1 + r \times [1 - \tau])$, but the budget constraint is higher, as seen in segment DE.

What effect does the IRA have on savings? Consider two types of individuals, shown in Figure 22-5. In panel (a), Mr. Grasshopper saves little before the IRA is introduced (point A), consuming C_1^W and saving only $S_1 = \$1,000$. For Mr. Grasshopper, the effect of the IRA on savings is ambiguous due to offsetting substitution effects (which tend to increase savings as the after-tax interest rate rises) and income effects (which tend to reduce savings as after-tax income falls). If substitution effects dominate, Mr. Grasshopper will move from point A to point B, reduce period-one consumption to C_2^W, and raise savings to $S_2 = \$1,500$. If income effects dominate, Mr. Grasshopper will move from point A to point C, increase period-one consumption to C_3^W, and lower savings to $S_3 = \$500$. Thus, for consumers such as Mr. Grasshopper, the effect of IRAs is ambiguous.

Panel (b) shows the analysis for Ms. Ant, who was a high saver before the IRA was introduced, consuming C_1^W and saving $5,000 (point A). For Ms. Ant, the introduction of the IRA does not change the price of first-period consumption, which remains at $1 + r \times (1 - \tau)$, so that the budget constraints without (BC_1) and with (BC_2) IRAs have the same slope for her. The introduc-

■ FIGURE 22-5

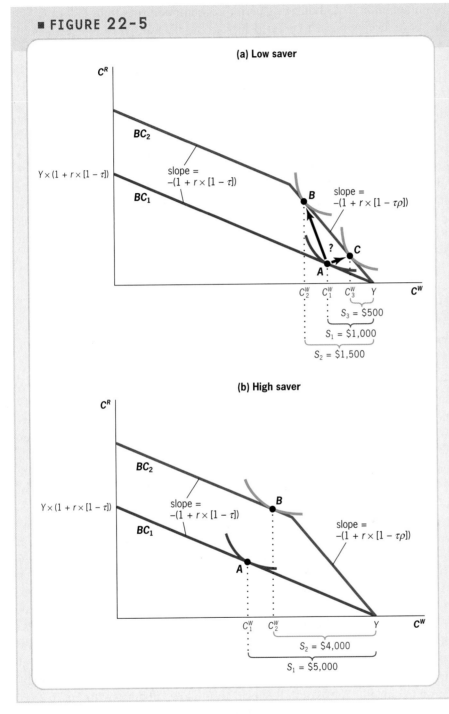

(a) Low saver

(b) High saver

Low Savers Versus High Savers • In panel (a), Mr. Grasshopper saves little before the IRA is introduced (point A), consuming C_1^W and saving only $1,000. For Mr. Grasshopper, the effect of the IRA on savings is ambiguous: if substitution effects dominate, he will move from point A to point B (with savings rising); if income effects dominate, he will move from point A to point C (with savings falling). In panel (b), Ms. Ant was a high saver before the IRA was introduced, consuming C_1^W and saving $5,000 (point A). For Ms. Ant, the introduction of the IRA does not change the price of first-period consumption, but it does have an income effect, causing her period-one consumption to rise to C_2^W and her savings to fall to S_2, $4,000.

tion of IRAs does have an income effect, however, since she is now richer from having a tax subsidy to her first $3,000 of savings: with the higher return, she doesn't need to save as much ($5,000) to achieve the same level of period-two consumption. She will therefore use her increased income to purchase more consumption in period one: first-period consumption rises from C_1^W to C_2^W as she moves from point A to point B. Her savings fall from S_1 to $S_2 = \$4,000$.

The income effect for high savers such as Ms. Ant arises as they "reshuffle" their existing assets into an IRA; they take $3,000 of the savings they were already putting aside and relabel it as tax-preferred IRA savings. For high savers, therefore, the IRA is a subsidy to existing savings: the government gives them a higher rate of return on savings they had already planned on making. If such reshuffling is likely, then it is possible that IRAs could actually *lower* overall private savings through this income effect.

This analysis used IRAs as an example, but it applies to other forms of retirement savings as well. The difference with these other forms is that the limits are much higher, so there are likely to be more individuals like Mr. Grasshopper than like Ms. Ant; for example, relatively few self-employed individuals would have saved above the $44,000 Keogh account limit for their retirement without a Keogh account.

▶ **APPLICATION**

The Roth IRA

Roth IRA A variation on normal IRAs to which taxpayers make after-tax contributions but may then make tax-free withdrawals later in life.

In 1997, Congress enacted legislation that established a major new tax-preferred retirement savings vehicle, the **Roth IRA.** This account has many similarities to a regular IRA, but has two key differences. First, unlike traditional IRAs, where contributions are made pre-tax and taxed upon withdrawal, individuals contribute *after-tax* dollars to a Roth IRA, and when withdrawals are eventually made, the withdrawals are not taxed. Third, individuals are never required to make withdrawals from their Roth IRAs (whereas withdrawals must start from a traditional IRA by age 70), so that earnings on assets can build up tax-free indefinitely.

Why did policy makers introduce this new option? If policy makers wanted to expand IRAs, why didn't they just do so (e.g., by raising contribution limits or income eligibility), rather than introduce this "reversed" structure? One clear reason was budget politics.

Over the near term on which budgetary forecasts are based, expanding traditional IRAs is very costly: under the regular IRA plan, the government loses the taxes on contributions today and doesn't collect tax revenue on withdrawals until far in the future. Over this same near term, however, Roth IRAs look much better: the government collects tax revenues today and loses them in the future (since we don't tax interest earnings on the account or withdrawals from it). The Roth IRA plan thus allows politicians to enact a tax break while delaying the budgetary pain of paying for it.

The Joint Tax Committee (the congressional counterpart of the Congressional Budget Office for estimating the revenue implications of tax changes) estimated that instituting the Roth IRAs, along with a simultaneously proposed expanded availability of traditional IRAs, would cost the government only $1.8 billion over the 1997–2002 window (with the Roth IRA actually saving money, while the traditional IRA expansion cost money). This low price tag was one reason that Congress was able to include Roth IRAs in the 1997 legislation. Yet over the 2003–2007 window, when these tax-free payments begin to be made to holders of Roth IRAs, the payments were estimated to cost the government $18.4 billion, ten times more—and costs will rise even further into the future.[12] This is a good example of the problems of short-term thinking about the budget.

Recently, the budget politics of the Roth IRA have been exploited even further to pass a tax reconciliation bill that would extend the capital gains and dividend tax cuts currently slated to expire in 2008 (and discussed in more detail in Chapters 23 and 24). In its original form, this extension would cost $51 billion in lost revenues over ten years, with $31 billion in losses occurring in 2011–2015. According to current Senate rules, any reconciliation bill that increases deficits in years after the reconciliation period (after 2010, in this case) is barred (unless 60 votes can be gathered to support passage, which is not possible given the current partisan split of the Senate). To meet this test, it seems the Senate would have to raise taxes elsewhere in the system, an unpopular option. Ironically, however, the Senate proposed to help meet this test by *cutting taxes further,* in the form of an expansion of the Roth IRA.

Currently, individuals who have incomes below $100,000 are allowed to "roll over" savings from their traditional IRAs into Roth IRAs. That is, these individuals could close their IRAs, pay taxes on the proceeds, and then put those proceeds into a Roth IRA. To pay for the tax cuts in the most recent tax reconciliation bill, the Senate proposed to eliminate this $100,000 income limit, so that anyone could convert their regular IRA into a Roth IRA.[13]

Higher income households would find the removal of this limit attractive for a number of reasons, as summarized in Burman (2006). For example, unlike traditional IRAs, Roth IRAs have no withdrawal requirements, so that high-income individuals can now leave their money in a tax-preferred savings account for more years, raising their total tax savings. Moreover, these conversions would essentially amount to a timing shift in when an individual pays taxes: funds converted from a traditional IRA are taxed immediately but then are allowed to accumulate tax-free under the Roth IRA plan even when withdrawn in retirement. Thus, households who expect that their tax rate will be higher in retirement (such as those with large payouts from pension plans), or who are just worried that the fiscal imbalance of the government will lead to higher future tax rates, can lower their lifetime taxes by paying them now rather than later. In both cases, these gains to higher-income individuals in terms of lower future tax payments imply a corresponding future federal revenue loss.

Finally, and most significantly, allowing this conversion essentially amounts to removing the income limit on Roth IRAs. This is because, while higher income individuals are barred from contributing to regular IRAs, they are currently allowed to contribute to a *non-deductible IRA,* for which they cannot

---

[12] Joint Committee on Taxation (1997).
[13] Friedman and Greenstein (2006).

deduct their initial contributions but can benefit from the non-taxation of interest earnings. Under the new law, this non-deductible IRA can then be turned around and converted into a Roth IRA. Thus, higher income individuals can contribute to a Roth IRA in two simple steps: start a non-deductible traditional IRA, then convert it to a Roth IRA.[14]

For these reasons, many higher-income individuals are expected to convert their traditional IRAs into Roth IRAs. This action implies that removing the conversion limit will lead to a short-term increase in tax revenues (as households pay taxes on the funds transferred into their Roth IRA) and a long-term net reduction in tax revenues (since tax-sheltered savings opportunities are extended to higher-income groups). Indeed, the Joint Committee on Taxation concluded that while lifting the Roth IRA income limits would raise nearly $5 billion in the first four years it was in effect, the proposal would then lose more than $9 billion over the following six years with the losses exceeding $2 billion a year by the end of the ten-year period.[15]

This outcome is fine for the Senate's purposes, because they conveniently set 2010 as the date at which IRAs could be converted (for one year only). Thus, the money raised by the conversion would apply to the 2011–2015 period for which financing was needed, while the long-run higher costs would not be included in the revenue costs of the bill. Thus, the trick of financing a tax cut with a tax cut, Roth IRA style![16] In May 2006, the bill was signed into law by President Bush.[17] ◄

Implications of Alternative Models

As noted, there is strong evidence to suggest that savings decisions are determined by both precautionary and self-control considerations. Both of these alternatives suggest that retirement tax incentives may have stronger positive effects on savings than implied by the traditional theory.

Precautionary Savings This asset reshuffling just discussed will be likely if two conditions are met: if a large share of IRA contributors would have saved $4,000 anyway in the absence of the IRA, and if IRA savings and non-IRA savings are viewed as highly substitutable. Consider someone who was going to save $4,000 for retirement even without an IRA. Such an individual would not feel constrained by the fact that she couldn't withdraw the money before retirement, so that IRA and non-IRA savings would be substitutes for each other, and reshuffling would be likely (so that there is no net new savings).

On the other hand, consider people who had more than $4,000 in savings but were using their savings for precaution against job loss. Since it cannot be accessed if they lose their job before age 59½, the savings in an IRA would not be viewed as very substitutable for them, so they would not just reshuffle

---

[14] Burman (2006).
[15] Friedman and Greenstein (2006).
[16] Friedman and Greenstein (2006).
[17] Lieber (2006).

$4,000 of their (precautionary) savings in the IRA. The analysis in Figures 22-3 to 22-5 refers to retirement savings only: those with precautionary savings over $4,000 do not reshuffle, but those with *retirement* savings over $4,000 do reshuffle. The fact that many contributors to tax-subsidized retirement savings accounts have high savings doesn't necessarily imply that they will be reshuffling those savings into the tax-subsidized account, if the savings are for precautionary reasons instead of for retirement. Thus, there may be more new savings due to retirement incentives than are suggested by the traditional model discussed earlier.

Self-Control Models The hallmark of self-control models of savings is the search for commitment devices to provide self-control. Retirement accounts such as pension and 401(k) accounts provide excellent commitment devices because the contributions are *taken directly out of the paycheck* and individuals can't access their money until retirement. Thus, the money in these accounts can't be accessed to satisfy short-term impatience, allowing the individual to commit to long-term patience. Retirement savings accounts may therefore increase savings by more than is suggested by the previous analysis. In addition to the demand for these accounts because of tax incentives, there will also be a demand that arises because individuals can effectively commit to save.

Private vs. National Savings

The discussion of savings incentive effects thus far has focused on the impacts on private savings. What matters ultimately for the determination of investment (and potentially growth) is *national* savings, the sum of private and government savings. Recall from Chapter 4 that increasing the government deficit can lower investment by reducing the pool of available capital. While retirement tax incentives may increase private savings, they have an offsetting negative effect on national savings because they are financed by a tax break. The reduced tax revenue lowers national savings and offsets any increase in private savings.

Suppose that we found that 401(k)s raised private savings by 30¢ per dollar of contribution: of each dollar saved in 401(k)s, 70¢ is retirement saving that would have been saved even absent the 401(k) (but which is now saved through the 401(k) for tax reasons), and 30¢ is new saving that is induced by the 401(k). Suppose also that the typical tax rate of contributors was 43%. Under these assumptions, the cost of each dollar of IRA contribution in terms of forgone tax revenue on existing savings reshuffled into 401(k)s would be 30¢ (0.43 × 70¢ of existing savings). Thus, there would be no national savings impact of 401(k)s: the increase in *private* savings due to the 401(k) would be completely offset by the reduction in *national* savings due to the tax break on savings that would have occurred even without the 401(k) (and would have been taxed in that case).

The comparison of private to national savings comes back to the notion of *marginal impacts* of tax incentives (new behavior encouraged) versus *inframarginal impacts* of tax incentives (old behavior rewarded) that we introduced in

Chapter 18. In the example here, there is some marginal response: each dollar of contribution raises private savings by 30¢. But there is also a large inframarginal response: 70¢ on each dollar of 401(k) savings was going to happen even if 401(k)s never existed. This large inframarginal response significantly lowers tax revenues, offsetting any national savings gain from 401(k) incentives. Thus, unless there is a large marginal increase in savings from the availability of retirement savings plans, these plans will lower overall national savings.

The size of the marginal and inframarginal response to tax incentives for savings will depend on two factors. The first is the size of the income and substitution effects for retirement savers below the savings limit (e.g., for those with less than $4,000 of retirement savings). The second is the share of retirement savers who are above the savings limit, for whom there is only an

---

EMPIRICAL EVIDENCE

ESTIMATING THE IMPACT OF TAX INCENTIVES FOR SAVINGS ON SAVINGS BEHAVIOR

The difficulties in assessing the impact of savings incentives on savings are illustrated by studies on the effect of IRAs on savings. Researchers began explicitly testing the reshuffling hypothesis by asking whether individuals who contribute to IRA accounts withdrew funds from other assets to finance that contribution. In fact, this does not seem to be true: when IRA contributions increased, other savings actually rose, rather than falling, as the reshuffling hypothesis would predict.

These studies are unconvincing, however, because they have not surmounted the problem of bias in comparing contributors (the treatment group) to noncontributors (the control group). Those who contribute to IRAs may be "savers," who save more in *every form* than the "non-savers" who don't contribute to IRAs. Thus, even in the absence of the IRA, these individuals would have saved $4,000 more anyway, in some other form. In contrast, the noncontributors may be non-savers, who would not have saved at all. In that case, noncontributors are not a good control group: there is a bias in comparing them to the savers because that treatment group would have saved more even in the absence of IRAs. More sophisticated tests designed to surmount this bias have reached mixed conclusions, but no one has yet designed a very convincing test of the impact of IRAs on savings behavior.

The literature on 401(k)s has taken a different approach, with researchers comparing the amount of savings put aside by workers in firms with 401(k)s (the treatments)

with the savings put aside by workers in firms that do not offer 401(k)s (the controls). The problem with this approach is that the treatments and controls may not be comparable, because workers in firms that offer 401(k)s may have different tastes for savings than those in firms that do not offer 401(k)s. If people who work in firms that offer 401(k)s save more in general than people in other firms, there is a clear bias in comparing these two groups: the fact that having access to a 401(k) is associated with higher levels of savings doesn't prove a causal effect of 401(k)s on savings.

This concern is heightened by the observable sharp differences across employees in firms that do and do not offer 401(k)s. For example, in 1991, those eligible for a 401(k) had average incomes of $39,000, while those not eligible for a 401(k) had average incomes of $27,000; 69% of eligibles were married, while only 58% of noneligibles were married.[18] If these groups are so different among factors that determine savings, such as income and marital status, it is hard to imagine that they are identical in their underlying tastes for savings. And if they are different in their tastes for savings, then they are not comparable treatments and controls.

Two studies have, however, developed convincing means of assessing the impact of these savings incentives on savings. One such study is Engelhardt's (1996) analysis of the Canadian Registered Home Ownership Savings Plan (RHOSP). Introduced in 1974, this plan gave individuals a

---

[18] Poterba, Venti, and Wise (1998b).

tax deduction of up to $1,000 per year if this money were deposited into an RHOSP account for the future purchase of a first home. In addition, withdrawals from these accounts were tax-free if used for the purchase of a first home. Unlike IRA or 401(k) plans, the RHOSP was not simply a tax-deferred savings incentive but a truly tax-free savings opportunity.

Moreover, substantial quasi-experimental variation arose as a result of the structure of the RHOSP savings subsidy program.

■ The program was available only to renters, not owners, so researchers could compare the savings of renters versus owners.

■ The program ended in 1985, so researchers could compare the savings of renters before and after 1985.

■ The tax benefit of the program was larger when the marginal tax rate was higher (since it was a tax deduction), and marginal tax rates varied widely across the Canadian provinces.

Engelhardt (1996) used this quasi-experimental variation to estimate the impact of the RHOSP program on savings. He used the difference-in-difference approach described in Chapter 3 to compare the change in savings by renters from before to after 1985 to the change in savings by home owners over this same period. He found strong evidence that total renter savings fell when the RHOSP program ended, relative to home owners, suggesting that this program was encouraging renters to save.

Engelhardt augmented his analysis by comparing savings changes for high-tax-rate renters, for whom the RHOSP provided a bigger tax incentive to savings (since the value of a deduction from taxes rises with the tax rate), to savings changes for low-tax-rate renters, for whom the RHOSP provided a smaller tax incentive to savings (if one's tax rate is zero, there is no value from a tax deduction). He found that it was indeed the high-tax-rate renters whose savings fell most sharply in 1985, which is consistent with a causal effect of RHOSP. Overall, Engelhardt's estimates suggest that each dollar contributed to the RHOSP represented 56¢ to 93¢ of new private savings, and 20¢ to 57¢ of new national savings. This substantial effect suggests that savings incentives, if generous enough, can encourage people to save more than they had planned to.

This quasi-experimental study succeeds where studies of U.S. savings incentives fail because Engelhardt was able to construct comparable treatment and control groups by using a change that affected one group (renters) and not another (home owners). The 401(k) studies, in contrast, do not have a change to study, so they are simply comparing two groups that might be quite different for other reasons.

In terms of Chapter 3, this comparison highlights the benefits of having a difference-in-difference approach over a simple "difference" approach.

More recent evidence on the impact of retirement savings incentives on savings behavior comes from a randomized trial run by Duflo et al. (2005). These authors contracted with a tax processor in St. Louis to randomly provide different match rates to low-income individuals contributing to IRA accounts. By randomizing the match rates, the study was able to avoid bias in assessing the impact of matches on savings decisions, since the treatments (match rate) and controls (no match rate) are otherwise identical. The study found that those who randomly received a 20% match contributed four times as much to their IRA accounts, and that those who randomly received a 50% match contributed seven times as much relative to the control group that received no match. Thus, providing further incentives for people to contribute to their retirement savings can raise the level of savings.

At the same time, several studies suggest that it is not tax savings, but other factors in program design, that have the most impact on the effect of retirement incentives. For example, Madrian and Shea (2001) followed 401(k) participation in a firm that changed from (a) a system in which workers had to actively sign up for a 401(k) plan if they wanted to participate, to (b) a system in which workers were placed by default in the 401(k), and had to opt out if they *didn't* want to participate. Under standard economic theory, these two systems should have identical effects, since individuals have a choice about whether to participate or not in each case. In practice, however, changing the default from one in which individuals are not automatically enrolled (and have to actively enroll) to one in which individuals are enrolled (and have to actively disenroll) had enormous effects, raising participation rates in company 401(k) plans among new hires from about 50% to almost 90%. These effects were particularly large for disadvantaged groups: for those with incomes under $20,000 per year, participation in 401(k) plans rose from 13% to 80% from this simple change!

The enormous effects of such a simple change in "framing" the participation decision suggests that tax subsidies may play a secondary role in driving retirement savings to other behavioral factors. This conclusion is confirmed by the findings in Duflo et al. (2005) that their randomized match plan was much more successful than the existing (more complicated) saver's tax credit for low income families. Reframing the match as a simple choice for individuals, rather than as a complicated part of an overall tax calculation, had large effects on participation in subsidized savings plans for their low-income population.

inframarginal response: there is no new savings encouraged for this population since there is no substitution effect.

Evidence on Tax Incentives and Savings

There are a number of studies of the impacts of employer-provided pensions, IRAs, and 401(k)s on savings behavior.

As discussed in the Empirical Evidence box, identifying a causal estimate of the impact of these incentives on savings has proved to be surprisingly difficult. But evidence from recent studies suggests that individuals do respond to these savings incentives by saving more—and might even respond enough to raise not only private but national savings.

22.4

Conclusion

One of the most important decisions made by taxpayers in the United States is how much to save, and it seems likely that taxes factor into that decision. Unfortunately, neither theory nor existing empirical evidence offers a clear lesson for the magnitude (or even the direction) of the effect of taxes on savings. Despite this lack of evidence, tax incentives for savings continue to grow in importance. In 1975, the tax expenditure on incentives for savings was less than $20 billion; in 2006, it had grown to $105 billion.[19] Clearly, policy makers believe that tax incentives can make a difference in the savings decisions of individuals. Future research is needed to assess the validity of that belief.

---

[19] Office of Management and Budget (1976), Table F-1, and Office of Management and Budget (2006b), Table 19-1. These figures include net exclusions for pension contributions and earnings, but no other forms of saving.

▶ HIGHLIGHTS

- Taxes lower the rate of return to savings, which causes a substitution effect away from savings but an income effect toward savings, with ambiguous overall effects.

- There is little evidence on the impact of taxes on the decision to save, but there is strong evidence that deciding to save is at least partially determined by the desire to take precautions against income uncertainty and by the desire for self-control.

- By deferring tax payments, tax subsidies for retirement savings (such as IRA and 401(k) plans) significantly increase the return to retirement savings.

- Retirement tax subsidies have ambiguous effects on savings. A key factor in determining their effects is the substitutability between the subsidized retirement savings and other savings.

- Despite the availability of a variety of mechanisms for tax-subsidized retirement savings, there is little consensus on their effects on savings decisions. The best available evidence, from Canada, suggests that these effects can be large if savings subsidies are very generous.

▶ **QUESTIONS AND PROBLEMS** ─────────────────────

1. Suppose that a person lives for two periods, earning $30,000 in income in period 1, during which she consumes or saves for period 2. What is saved earns interest of 10% per year.

 a. Draw that person's intertemporal budget constraint.

 b. Draw that person's intertemporal budget constraint if the government taxes interest at the rate of 30%.

2. Suppose that the government increases its tax rate on interest earned. Afterward, savings increase. Which effect dominates, the income effect or the substitution effect? Explain.

3. Mallovia has two tax brackets. The first $20,000 in income is taxed at a 10% marginal rate, and income above $20,000 is taxed at a 30% marginal rate. All income—earned income and nominal interest, dividend, and capital-gains income—is treated the same. The threshold for the 30% rate is currently indexed for inflation, and the real interest rate is 5%.

 a. How does inflation affect the returns to saving in Mallovia? Compare the likely savings rate when expected inflation is 10% with the likely savings rate when expected inflation is zero.

 b. How would your answer change if the threshold for the 30% rate were not indexed for inflation?

4. The government of Maupintania introduces a new insurance program that pays for 100% of unexpected catastrophic medical costs. Before this time, only low-income households had this benefit.

 a. Describe an empirical test of the effects of this policy change on the savings of high-income households in Maupintania.

 b. What do you expect to happen to the overall rate of savings in Maupintania?

5. Shiz University has introduced a new plan that allows employees to automatically deduct after-tax money from their paychecks to be deposited in a pension plan. Why might people participate in this plan when there are no financial incentives to do so?

6. The government introduces a tax incentive program in which the first $5,000 of savings can be tax-deferred. Draw the resulting budget constraint that illustrates the trade-off between current and future consumption.

7. Gale and Scholz (1994) estimate that increasing the contribution limits for Individual Retirement Accounts would have little effect on the overall rates of savings. Why do you think this might be the case?

8. Discuss whether IRAs have increased savings in the United States in the past 15 years, paying attention to the fact that people vary along many dimensions and that there are numerous definitions of savings. What can we learn by comparing the non-IRA assets of people who do and don't have IRAs? Can you suggest alternative means of estimating the impact of IRAs on savings?

9. Two countries with comparable levels of income per capita each propose raising the amount of savings that can be tax-deferred by $2,000. In Wenti, the current maximum amount of savings that can be tax-deferred is $2,000, while in Schale, the current limit is $5,000. In which country are savings likely to rise by more? In which country is the inframarginal response likely to be greatest? Which savings incentive will likely cost its government the most? Explain.

10. Jack is a 48-year-old consultant who earns $480,000 per year. Hector is a 19-year-old college student who has just finished a summer job that paid him $5,000. Both are planning on putting some of their earnings into IRA accounts. Who should be more likely to use a Roth IRA instead of a traditional IRA?

▶ **ADVANCED QUESTIONS** ━━━━━━━━━━━━━━━━━━━━━

11. Generational accounting techniques (recall Chapter 4) suggest that future income tax rates will be higher than current tax rates. How should this information affect the savings rate? How should it affect the relative appeal of Roth versus traditional tax-deferred IRAs?

12. In some cultures, when a member of the community who is ineligible for government-provided social insurance faces some adverse condition, the rest of the community lends that member money until his condition improves. In these cultures, would you expect more or less buffer-stock savings than occurs in the United States? Explain.

13. Consider a model in which individuals live for two periods and have utility functions of the form $U = \ln(C_1) + \ln(C_2)$. They earn income of $100 in the first period and save S to finance consumption in the second period. The interest rate, r, is 10%.

    a. Set up the individual's lifetime utility maximization problem. Solve for the optimal C_1, C_2, and S. (Hint: Rewrite C_2 in terms of income, C_1, and r.) Draw a graph showing the opportunity set.

    b. The government imposes a 20% tax on labor income. Solve for the new optimal levels of C_1, C_2, and S. Explain any differences between the new level of savings and the level in part (a), paying attention to any income and substitution effects.

    c. Instead of the labor income tax, the government imposes a 20% tax on interest income. Solve for the new optimal levels of C_1, C_2, and S. (Hint: What is the new after-tax interest rate?) Explain any differences between the new

level of savings and the level in part (a), paying attention to any income and substitution effects.

14. Consider a model in which an individual lives for two periods. There are two individuals, John and Jules, and both have utility functions of the form $U = \ln(C_1) + \ln(C_2)$. John earns $100 in the first period and saves S to finance consumption in the second period. Jules will receive $110 in the second period, and she borrows B to finance consumption in the first period. The interest rate r is 10%.

    a. Set up each individual's lifetime utility maximization problem. Solve for the optimal C_1, C_2, and S (or B) for Jules and John. (Hint: Rewrite C_2 in terms of C_1, income, and r.)

    b. The government now imposes a 20% tax on interest income. Solve for John's new optimum level of S. (Hint: What is the new after-tax interest rate?) Explain how your answer relates to the saving you found for John in part (a), paying attention to any income and substitution effects.

    c. Suppose that the government also provides a 20% tax credit on interest, so if Jules borrows $10—and consequently owes $1 in interest—the government will give her $0.20 back. Solve for Jules's now optimum level of B. Explain how your answer related to the borrowing you found in part (a), paying attention to any income and substitution effects.

─────────────────────────────

The **e** icon indicates a question that requires students to apply the empirical economics principles discussed in Chapter 3 and the Empirical Evidence boxes.

Taxes on Risk Taking and Wealth

23

I n June 2006, Warren Buffett, the world's second-richest man, made the shocking announcement that he is giving 85% of his fortune to the Bill and Melinda Gates Foundation, a philanthropic organization headed by Microsoft Corporation Chairman Bill Gates and his wife Melinda. The Gates Foundation is dedicated to addressing social issues such as child mortality, disease control, and education. The gift, valued at $30.7 billion, will turn the Gates Foundation into a $60 billion philanthropic giant with the power to effect significant changes worldwide; in comparison, the United Nations and its related agencies spend only about $12 billion per year.[1]

The decision to donate the vast majority of his wealth to charity rather than bequeathing it to his own children was seen by many as a culmination of Buffett's long-standing advocacy against the transfer of large estates from generation to generation. In keeping with this position, Buffett, along with other wealthy Americans such as William Gates, Sr., and George Soros, has long been an outspoken critic of moves to repeal the *estate tax,* a tax levied on large estates upon the death of their owners.

Buffett has argued that allowing children to inherit all of their parents' riches causes them to be spoiled and sapped of all motivation, and keeping the tax in force helps to preserve America's meritocracy. Allowing savings to pass untaxed from one generation to the next is, Buffett claims, akin to "choosing the 2020 Olympic team by picking the eldest sons of the gold-medal winners in the 2000 Olympics."[2] He has also said that he "would hate to see the estate tax gutted. . . . It's a very equitable tax. It's in keeping with the idea of equality of opportunity in this country, not giving incredible head starts to certain people. . . ."[3]

---

[1] Richardson (2006).
[2] Jenkins (2001).
[3] Reuters (2006).

Many others have also defended the estate tax for its progressivity: they note that because of the high exemption levels, the tax affects only a very small portion of the wealthiest citizens upon death. Tom Daschle, then the Democratic Senate Minority Leader, opposed repeal of the estate tax in 2003 because "helping billionaires ought not to be our business."[4] Larry Summers, who was the deputy secretary of the treasury in 1997 (he later became the secretary), declared that, "When it comes to [cutting] the estate tax, there is no case other than selfishness. In terms of substance, this estate tax argument is about as bad as it gets."[5]

Opponents of the estate tax, however, have well-reasoned and strong views on the topic as well. They point out that much of the income taxed by the estate tax was already taxed when estate holders were alive, so it amounts to a double taxation of their income. This double taxation may lead the wealthy to earn and save less. Opponents of the estate tax also view it as a "death tax" that imposes a government penalty for the act of dying itself, an insult added to the ultimate injury. As Grover Norquist, president of Americans for Tax Reform, says, "The rich have paid every damn tax that was ever devised. Why should they get taxed just because they pass away?"[6] The arguments made by opponents appear to be carrying the day in recent years: the 2001 tax bill (discussed in the Application box on page 111 of Chapter 4) has substantially increased the thresholds at which estates are subject to tax, and the estate tax itself is scheduled to disappear in 2010 (although, as noted in Chapter 4, it is also scheduled to reappear again in 2011).

In Chapter 22, we discussed government policies that affect individual decisions on how much to save by directly altering the rate of return to savings. In this chapter, we focus on two other aspects of taxation that might affect the savings decisions of taxpayers. The first is the taxation of *risk taking*. Individuals not only decide how much to save but also what form their savings will take. Should you save in the form of government bonds, for example, which are very safe but yield a low return on average, or in the form of corporate stock, which is much riskier but yields a higher return on average? Just as taxes might influence how much individuals save, they can also influence the form that savings take. A particular tax policy that might affect risk taking is the taxation of *capital gains,* the earnings realized on the sale of capital assets.

Individuals can also be taxed not only on the return from their savings in each period but on the amount of *wealth* they have accumulated through past savings. In the United States, such taxation occurs in two forms. The first form of wealth tax consists of *transfer taxes,* a set of taxes on gifts from one party to another, including the contentious estate tax we discussed. The second type of wealth tax is the *property tax,* which (you may recall from Chapter 10) is the largest source of revenue for localities in the United States. Because the major source of savings for most Americans is their homes, property taxation can significantly affect the level of savings as well.

---

[4] Thompson (2003).
[5] Chandler (1997).
[6] Thompson (2003).

23.1

Taxation and Risk Taking

As discussed in Chapter 12, we face risk and uncertainty in many dimensions of life. Some are risks of purely adverse outcomes (car accidents, major illness, or injury), and we attempt to insure against these. Other risks are more balanced, with some chance of a positive outcome and some chance of a negative outcome. One example of a more balanced risk is the risk that comes with financial investments: Will a business succeed or fail? Will a stock portfolio go up or down? The decision about whether to make risky investments can be affected by taxation. In this section, we discuss the impact of taxation on risk taking.

Basic Financial Investment Model

The basic model of taxation and risk taking was developed by Domar and Musgrave in 1944 in the context of financial investment risk. In their model, individuals have a choice between investing in a safe asset that yields no real return and investing in a risky asset that yields some positive rate of return. The government taxes any positive return on the risky asset but allows a deduction against taxable income for the full amount of any negative return. In this situation, Domar and Musgrave pointed out that *taxing the returns from the risky asset would increase risk taking* because any tax on the returns could be completely undone by taking more risk.

This point is best illustrated through an example, shown in Table 23-1. Suppose that Sam has invested $100 in a small business venture that has a 50% chance of rising in value to $120 (so that he makes $20) and a 50% chance of falling in value to $80 (so that he loses $20). This investment has an **expected return** of $0: the return to a successful investment times the probability of success plus the return to an unsuccessful investment times the probability of failure is $0 ([$20 × 0.5] + [–$20 × 0.5] = $0). There is no tax initially, so these pre-tax returns are also his after-tax returns, as shown in the first row of Table 23-1.

The government then announces that it is introducing a tax of 50% on investment income, with a deduction against taxable income for any losses. Any positive return from this investment is taxed, so Sam keeps half of his payoffs and pays the other half in taxes. Since any loss from the investment is deducted against taxable income, Sam only bears half of the loss; losses are subtracted from taxable income so that reduced taxes offset by half the loss amount. (Because the government gets 50% of each dollar of taxable income, allowing a deduction against taxable income means that the government also gets 50% of each dollar of loss.) Under this policy, as shown in the second row, Sam will net only $10 if the investment goes well, since he has to pay $10 in additional tax; he will lose only $10 if the investment goes poorly, since he can deduct the $20 loss from taxable income so that his taxes are reduced by $10. This new outcome has the same expected return, $0, but it leaves Sam with less risk than he would like—as revealed by his initial investment

expected return The return to a successful investment times the odds of success, plus the return to an unsuccessful investment times the odds of failure.

▪ TABLE 23-1

Taxation and Risk-Taking by Sam

Policy	Investment	Payoff If Win	Payoff If Lose	Tax Rate If Win	Tax Deduction If Lose	After-Tax Winnings	After-Tax Loss
(1) No tax	$100	$20	–$20	0	0	$20	–$20
(2) Tax	$100	$20	–$20	50%	50%	$10	–$10
(3) Loss offset	$200	$40	–$40	50%	50%	$20	–$20
(4) No loss offset	$200	$40	–$40	50%	0	$20	–$40
(5) Progressive tax	$200	$40	–$40	75%	50%	$15	–$20

In row 1, Sam makes a $100 investment that yields $20 if the investment is successful and –$20 if the investment fails. In row 2, the government imposes a 50% tax on his investment, so that Sam now earns only $10 if successful and loses $10 if the investment fails. Sam can undo the government's actions, as in row 3, by doubling his investment to $200, leaving him with the same returns as in row 1, so that taxation has increased risk taking. If, however, there is no loss offset, as in row 4, or progressive taxation, as in row 5, Sam will be unable to undo the government's action, so his risk taking won't necessarily increase under taxation.

decision, he wanted a risk of winning $20 or losing $20, not a risk of winning $10 or losing $10 (which he could have had initially by investing only $50 but which he chose not to do).

Sam can, however, completely undo the effects of this tax policy on his portfolio by investing more money in the risky investment. Suppose that he doubles his risky investment to $200, as in the third row of Table 23-1. After tax, there is once again a 50% chance of earning $20 if things go well (since Sam earns $40 before tax, then pays half of it in taxes) and a 50% chance of losing $20 if things go poorly (since Sam loses $40 before tax and deducts half of the loss from his taxes). By investing more in this risky asset, Sam has completely undone the government tax scheme and arrived back at the after-tax winnings and losses from row 1, where there were no taxes to be paid or losses to be deducted. This outcome is an example of the lesson we learned in Chapter 7: if an economic agent can undo government interventions to return to his original equilibrium, he will do so.

This result has an important implication for tax policy: by raising taxes on capital income, the government can raise revenues without reducing the individual's well-being. The only change is that $100 has been shifted from Sam's riskless asset to the risky asset, but since that riskless asset earns no return, this shift has no effect on expected utility. The government is essentially a "silent partner" in this investment: because the government bears some of the risk of success or failure, an individual will want to increase his or her risky investment. Taxation of risky investments, in this case, actually increases risk taking.

Real-World Complications

Under the simplified Domar-Musgrave model just presented, investment-income taxation will actually increase risk taking. In reality, this may not be true, due to two important complications that the model does not take into account.

Less-Than-Full Tax Offset In the model, individuals can deduct the full losses from their taxable income when computing taxes. When Sam loses his gamble, he can deduct the full losses from his taxable income, just as when he wins the gamble, his full gains are added to his taxable income. In reality, most tax systems allow individuals to deduct only a portion of their losses from taxable income when computing taxes. The amount of a loss that can be deducted is called a **tax loss offset.**

In the United States, individuals are allowed to deduct only $3,000 of investment losses in any tax year from their other taxable income.[7] These rules are in place to keep people from generating tax losses by undertaking clearly losing investments in order to wipe out some of their taxable income (a problem discussed at more length in Chapter 25). The rules have the additional implication, however, that a taxpayer cannot simply undo government taxation by making increasingly risky investments, because the losses from these investments will not be fully deductible from taxation.

Continuing the example from Table 23-1, suppose that the government did not allow individuals to deduct *any* investment losses under its 50% tax system. In that case, Sam could not simply undo government tax policy by investing more, as he did in the third row. In the fourth row of Table 23-1, if Sam raises his investment to $200 in the small business, there is a 50% chance that he will earn $40, which is $20 after tax, and a 50% chance he will lose $40, which cannot be deducted against taxable income, and so remains a loss of $40 after taxes. Thus, with no deductibility of losses, Sam cannot simply offset the tax policy by raising his investment, since that will put him in a losing position of a 50% chance of earning $20 after taxes and a 50% chance of losing $40 after taxes, an expected after-tax return of ($20 × 0.5) + (−$40 × 0.5) = −$10.

Since Sam cannot simply undo government policy by taking more risk, he will not necessarily increase his risk taking in response to taxation. It is impossible to predict for sure what effect limits on loss offsets will have on risk taking, but less-than-full tax offsets definitely limit the applicability of the simple Domar-Musgrave model.

Redistributive Taxation The idealized model of risk taking also assumes a constant rate of tax on investment income. In reality, tax systems are typically progressive, with higher marginal tax rates as income rises. Under such a system, if investors win a large gamble, they can move themselves into a higher tax bracket (higher marginal tax rate); if they lose a large gamble, they can move themselves into a lower tax bracket. Thus, winning gambles may be taxed at a higher rate than the rate at which losing gambles are deducted. As with the limited loss offset, this can lead investors to reduce their risk taking.

tax loss offset The extent to which taxpayers can deduct net losses on investments from their taxable income.

---

[7] More specifically, individuals are allowed to offset any investment losses in a year against investment gains in that same year; any remaining net losses can be deducted against other taxable income, up to $3,000.

Suppose that, instead of a flat 50% tax rate, the government imposes a tax rate of 50% on income up to $20 and 75% on income above $20. Assume that there is a full loss offset so that any losses can be deducted from taxable income at the 50% rate. In this case, Sam once again cannot undo the effects of the tax on his "winnings," as shown by the final row of Table 23-1. If he raises his investment to $200 and the investment outcome is a good one, he takes home only $15 after tax: 50% of the first $20 in earnings and 25% of the next $20. If the investment outcome is a bad one, however, he loses $20 after tax, just as shown. Once again, Sam will not simply offset the tax policy by raising his investment, since that will put him in a losing position with a 50% chance of earning $15 after tax and a 50% chance of losing $20 after tax (an expected return of [$15 × 0.5] + [−$20 × 0.5] = −$2.50).

Evidence on Taxation and Risk Taking

Due to these complications, as well as others, there is no clear prediction about how taxation will affect risk taking in the real world. Ultimately, what the effect of taxes is on risk taking is an empirical question. Unfortunately, however, there is very little evidence about the effect of capital income taxation on risk taking, making this another of the important mysteries in the economics of taxation.

Labor Investment Applications

Financial investments are not the only risky investments individuals make—they can also invest in *human capital* through education or other job training (as discussed in more detail in Chapter 11). Investing in human capital is risky because individuals are making an up-front sacrifice in return for some expectation of higher earnings in the future. The extent to which this investment in human capital will lead to higher earnings is, however, uncertain.

Consider the decision to attend a year of college. Attendance has two costs: the cost of the year of college (tuition, books, and so on), and the forgone earnings that the individual passes up by going to college for a year instead of working. The benefit is the prospect of higher earnings from being more educated. On average, there is about a 7% rise in earnings for each year of education. This is only an average estimate, however, and for any given individual the return on more education could be lower or higher.

How do income taxes affect the decision to accumulate human capital? The analysis is similar to that for financial investments. The net return to the investment in human capital is the rise in wages minus the direct costs of education and the indirect opportunity cost of forgone earnings. Suppose initially that there is a flat single-rate income tax and that the financial costs of obtaining human capital (such as tuition) are fully deductible against taxable income. Because income taxes are only levied on income earned, the opportunity cost of education is also fully deductible since obtaining education means *not* earning wages, thereby lowering taxes. In this case, as with financial investment, higher taxation would simply increase investment in human capital so that individuals could preserve the desired amount of net (of taxes) expected investment return.

Once again, however, real-world features of taxation complicate the picture. In reality, the costs of primary and secondary education are not deductible from taxation, and the cost of higher education is only partially deductible from taxation, through the tax subsidies to higher education discussed in Chapter 11. Moreover, the progressive tax system in place in most nations implies that the gains from successfully increasing human capital will be taxed at a higher rate than would the wages earned if work were chosen instead of education. If you don't go to college and instead work in the fast-food sector, you lose the chance to earn a high wage, but at least you pay low taxes; if you sacrifice the fast-food earnings to go to college, the returns to that education are taxed at a high rate. This makes investments in human capital less attractive. Thus, as with financial investments, the net impact of income taxation on human capital investments is ambiguous.

23.2

Capital Gains Taxation

The discussions in the last two chapters have focused on the taxation of *earned income,* income generated either by labor earnings or interest earnings. Many assets, however, yield a return to investors that is not in terms of annual interest earnings, but rather in the form of a **capital gain,** the difference between an asset's purchase price and its sale price. This is the form of return for investments in art and housing, as well as the primary source of return for many investments in businesses or stocks. The question of how to tax these returns has been one of the most contentious tax policy issues of the past several decades.

capital gain The difference between an asset's purchase price and its sale price.

Current Tax Treatment of Capital Gains

Assets (such as bank accounts or government bonds) that earn interest are **taxed on accrual;** taxes are paid each period on the interest earned in that period. Capital gains, in contrast, are **taxed on realization:** taxes are only paid when the asset is sold, and the tax payment is based on the difference between the sale price of the asset and its purchase price. Taxation upon realization, rather than upon accrual, generally leads to a reduction in tax obligations for the asset holder. The intuition for this claim is the same as what we used in our discussion of tax-subsidized retirement savings accounts. By paying taxes upon sale of the asset rather than as value is accrued, you can earn the interest on what would have been your tax obligation.

Suppose, for example, that you buy a painting for $100, and it increases in value by 10% per year, so that after seven years you sell the painting for $195. At that point, you pay tax on the $95 difference between the sale and the purchase price. If the capital gains tax rate is 20%, you will pay $19 in capital

taxation on accrual Taxes paid each period on the return earned by an asset in that period.

taxation on realization Taxes paid on an asset's return only when that asset is sold.

gains tax and pocket a net gain of $76. If, instead, you had invested that $100 in a bank account earning 10% per year, with a 20% tax rate on interest earnings, at the end of seven years you would have only $71 in interest earnings. You earn less when you pay taxes on accrual since the government collects its revenues earlier and therefore earns the interest on those revenues instead of you doing so. This is a tax preference for savings in the form of capital gains-producing assets.

The tax preference for capital gains is hard to eliminate for many capital goods for two reasons. First, it may not be possible to measure accrual for many assets. For stocks, it is feasible that the government could tax on yearly accrual, by using the year-to-year change in the value of the stock. This might work for stocks, but how do we estimate the year-to-year accrual in the value of a house or a painting? In principle, we could get an expert valuation of each capital asset at the end of each year, but the virtue of the realization system is that it relies on market valuations, not expert opinion, which is both imperfect and subject to manipulation.

The second problem is that even if the government could appropriately measure accrual, individuals may not have the ability to finance the required tax payment. Suppose that a very volatile stock has just doubled in value. The resulting gain to a person's wealth may be so large that there is no way he could pay the annual tax bill without actually selling a large share of his stock. It could be inefficient to force individuals to divest themselves of productive assets simply to make tax payments.

In addition to the preference for capital gains through taxation on realization, there are two additional preferences for capital gains in the U.S. tax code.

"Step-up" of Basis at Death

basis The purchase price of an asset, for purposes of determining capital gains.

For assets that an individual purchases and then sells before she dies, the capital gains tax burden is based on the sale price minus the purchase price. That purchase price is called the **basis** for capital gains taxation. For assets that are passed on to heirs, this basis is "stepped up" to the value at the time of death. The capital gains tax burden on an asset sold after the purchaser dies is based on the sales price minus the price of the asset at the time of death, not the purchase price. Thus, a family will owe no capital gains taxes on an asset that has greatly increased in price if it is sold the day after the purchaser dies.

Suppose that Betty buys a painting for $100 when she is 20, and by the time of her death at 75 it is worth $10,000. If she sells this painting the day before her death, she would pay capital gains taxes on the $9,900 capital gain on the painting. Instead, if she leaves this painting to her children and they sell it the day after her death, they would pay no capital gains tax because the painting is worth $10,000 and its new basis is also $10,000.

Exclusion for Capital Gains on Housing

The tax code in the United States has also traditionally featured an exclusion for capital gains on houses. For many years the exclusion allowed individuals not to pay capital gains on home sales if they put those gains into a new house purchase. There was also a one-time exemption from gains up to $125,000 for those over age 55. In 1997, this exclusion was changed to a flat $500,000 exemption from capital gains for sales of a principal residence.

Capital Gains Tax Rates Through the Years Even with this long list of tax preferences for capital gains, this form of income has traditionally borne lower tax rates than other forms of income:

1. From 1978 through 1986, individuals were taxed on only 40% of their capital gains on assets held for more than six months.

2. The Tax Reform Act of 1986 ended this difference and treated capital gains like other forms of income for tax purposes, with a top tax rate of 28%.

3. The Tax Reform Act of 1993 raised top tax rates on other forms of income to 39% but kept the tax rate on capital gains at 28%.

4. The Taxpayer Relief Act of 1997 reduced the top rate on long-term capital gains to 20% (though certain items, like collectibles such as art and coins, are still taxed at 28%).

5. The 2003 Jobs and Growth Act reduced the top rate further, to 15%, for gains realized after May 5, 2003 (collectibles are still taxed at 28%).

Applying different tax rates to different types of capital income is not unique to the United States. Table 23-2 shows the tax treatment of various forms of capital income in eight large industrialized nations. In only two cases (Canada and the U.K.) are capital gains taxed at the same rate as other capital income. In Germany, despite a tax rate over 50% on other forms of capital income, there are no taxes paid on capital gains.

What Are the Arguments for Tax Preferences for Capital Gains?

Although it may not seem fair to tax capital gains at a rate that is much lower than rates on other forms of income, three major arguments are commonly made for these lower tax rates: to protect asset owners against the effects of

■ **TABLE 23-2**

Capital Income Taxation in Selected OECD Countries (2000)

	United States	Canada	France	Germany	Italy	Japan	Spain	United Kingdom
Highest tax rates on capital income								
Interest from bank deposits	46.8%	48.6%	25.0%	53.8%	27.0%	20.0%	48.0%	40.0%
Dividends	46.8	48.6	61.2	53.8	12.5	50.0	48.0	40.0
Capital gains	20.0	48.6	26.0	0	12.5	26.0	20.0	40.0

Source: Herd and Bronchi (2001), Table 1.

In most industrial nations, the taxes on capital gains are lower relative to other forms of capital income taxation.

inflation; to improve the efficiency of capital markets; and to promote entrepreneurship. We evaluate each of these arguments in turn.

Protection Against Inflation Because of inflation, current tax policy overstates the value of capital gains. Consider the example of the painting that rises in value by 95% over seven years, but now imagine that the price level has also risen by 95% over those seven years. In this case, the painting is no more valuable in real terms, and so the owner is not wealthier in real terms. Her tax bill, however, is based on nominal, and not real, gains. So even though she has seen no real capital gain and is no richer, she will have to pay $19 in capital gains taxes, making her worse off. This argues for lower capital gains tax rates to offset the inflation disadvantage of capital gains realizations.

Although this is a valid point, the capital gains inflation problem is no worse than it is for other kinds of savings. As we pointed out in Chapter 22, inflation leads to the excessive taxation of interest earnings as well. Thus, inflation protection is not a reason to have tax policies that favor capital gains over other types of capital income. Moreover, for both capital gains and other forms of capital, the appropriate reaction to the inflation problem is not to lower the capital gains tax rate but to index the tax system (as the government has done for noncapital income).[8]

Improved Efficiency of Capital Transactions A second major argument in favor of lower capital gains tax rates is that individuals will delay selling their capital assets to lower the present discounted value of their tax burdens. The value from having a capital asset that is taxed on realization, compared to another investment (like a bank account) that is taxed on accrual, is that tax payments can be delayed until sale. The longer this delay is, the lower the present discounted value of tax payments is (since money paid in the future is worth less than money paid today). Indeed, a person could reduce his family's capital gains taxes to zero by holding on to an asset until he dies and passing it to his children. This plan can lead to a **lock-in effect,** whereby individuals delay selling their capital assets in order to minimize the present discounted value of capital gains tax payments.

Lock-in effects are costly because much of the success of capital markets rests on their fluidity, which allows investors to deploy their assets to the assets' most productive use. Suppose you have a great idea for a new product but you must sell your art collection to finance the new product's development, triggering capital gains taxes on your art sales. If you don't sell the art collection to finance this new product, the art collection will pass on to your children, avoiding capital gains taxation altogether. You therefore might not sell your paintings in order to minimize capital gains taxes, and as a result you may

lock-in effect In order to minimize the present discounted value of capital gains tax payments, individuals delay selling their capital assets, locking in their assets.

---

[8] Other nations have managed to index their capital gains taxes: India uses a cost inflation index when computing capital gains to be taxed. (Source: Department of Revenue of India, Income Tax Department, available at http://incometaxindia.gov.in/general/computation.asp#c3.) The United Kingdom also indexes their capital gains taxes to inflation by providing for "indexation allowances." (Source: HM Revenue & Customs, *Notes on Capital Gains*, available at http://www.hmrc.gov.uk/pdfs/2002_03/capital_gains/sa108_notes.pdf.)

never start that new company. This may be an efficiency cost to society if social efficiency would be higher because you started the company instead of hanging on to your paintings. This is an argument for lowering capital gains taxes to reduce the lock-in effect.

Encouraging Entrepreneurial Activity When you graduate from college and start your own company, the major return that you expect is not the income you will earn each year but rather the increase in the value of the underlying company. *Entrepreneurs,* individuals who start their own businesses, obtain most of their wealth not from accrued income early on in the life of the business but from increases in the value of the underlying business asset over time. The relevant tax rate for entrepreneurs is therefore not the income tax rate, since the returns entrepreneurs receive aren't taxed as accrued income, but rather the capital gains tax rate, since their main return will be in selling their assets when they become valuable. Thus, a higher capital gains tax rate may deter entrepreneurship. The capital gains tax is fundamentally a tax on risk taking, but risk taking is an engine of growth for the economy. Therefore, encouraging entrepreneurship is one reason to have a lower capital gains rate.

There are three countervailing arguments to this point, however. First, as discussed earlier, it is not clear if taxing risk taking will encourage or discourage risk taking. There is no good evidence to date on whether capital gains taxes raise or lower risk taking. Second, only a very small fraction of capital gains go to entrepreneurs. Poterba (1989b), for example, estimated that less than 1% of capital gains in the mid-1980s were realized by venture capitalists who financed entrepreneurial ventures; the most recent estimate, for 2001, is 5.5%.[9]

Finally, while capital gains rate reductions today may increase entrepreneurial activity now and in the future, they also yield enormous benefits to those who have made capital investments in the past. The lower capital gains tax is not only an incentive for investors to take entrepreneurial risks; it is a reward for having taken risks in the past. As a result, much of the revenue lost through lower capital gains taxes is not encouraging risk taking but rather just rewarding past risks.

This point adds a nuance to the discussions in Chapters 18 and 22 of the *marginal* and *inframarginal* effects of tax incentives. In the previous cases we considered, IRAs and charitable giving, the marginal effect was the new behavior encouraged (new savings or charitable gifts) and the inframarginal effect was the behavior that would have taken place anyway but was now tax-preferred (previously planned savings or charitable gifts). Both of these effects are present with capital gains taxes: the government is subsidizing investments that would have happened anyway, as well as encouraging new investment today. With capital gains, however, there is another inframarginal effect: the

---

[9] Of course, much entrepreneurship is not financed by venture capitalists, so this is only a lower bound on the share of capital gains accruing to entrepreneurship.

prospective capital gains tax reduction Capital gains tax cuts that apply only to investments made from this day forward.

government not only subsidizes investments that would be made anyway today, it also subsidizes the returns on investments that were *made in the past.* This is an additional revenue cost that must be traded off against the marginal gains in terms of encouraging entrepreneurial risk taking.

In other words, cutting the capital gains tax rate is a very blunt instrument for encouraging entrepreneurship. It may raise the returns to entrepreneurship in the future, but at the large revenue cost of also rewarding investments in the past. To see this, contrast a capital gains tax reduction to a **prospective capital gains tax reduction,** where the capital gains tax rate is reduced only on sales of investments made from this day forward, not on any sales of investments made in the past. Both an overall capital gains tax cut and a prospective capital gains tax cut would have identical impacts on entrepreneurial activity in the future, since any investments made starting today reap the benefits of a lower capital gains tax rate. Yet the prospective reduction would be much less expensive because it does not also deliver a tax break to investments made in the past.

Evidence on Taxation and Capital Gains To summarize this discussion, there are two main arguments for lowering the capital gains tax rate below that on other forms of capital income: unlocking past gains and encouraging entrepreneurship. Cutting the rate on all capital gains, including those on past investments, is a very costly way to encourage entrepreneurship, relative to simply cutting the rate only on investments made from today forward. The main argument for an overall capital gains tax reduction that includes previously earned capital gains, then, is that a lower capital gains tax rate will lead to more capital gains realizations (asset sales). This has two advantages: it unlocks assets for their most productive use, and it increases tax collections on those gains.

If there is a large "unlocking" effect, that is, if a lower capital gains tax encourages people to sell assets now instead of waiting or not selling them at all, it is possible that a reduction in the capital gains rate could actually raise revenues: we would be applying a smaller tax rate to a much larger base of capital gains. That is, the government may be on the wrong side of the Laffer curve (page 594) with respect to capital gains taxes. If, however, reductions in capital gains do not affect asset sales, or if they only affect the timing of sales in one year versus the next, then reductions in the capital gains tax rate will simply lower tax revenues and provide a transfer to those holders of capital gains who were going to realize them anyway.

Figure 23-1, which shows capital gains realizations over time, suggests that taxes play a powerful role in determining capital gains realizations. There was an enormous spike in realizations in 1986: realizations were $172 billion in 1985, $328 billion in 1986, and $148 billion in 1987. This spike was driven by the large relative increase in capital gains taxation that was scheduled to go into effect in 1987 but was announced in 1986; as noted earlier, in 1987 capital gains realizations moved from being taxed much less than other forms of income to being taxed in the same way as other income. Individuals anticipated this relative increase in the tax and sold their assets before the tax increase took place.

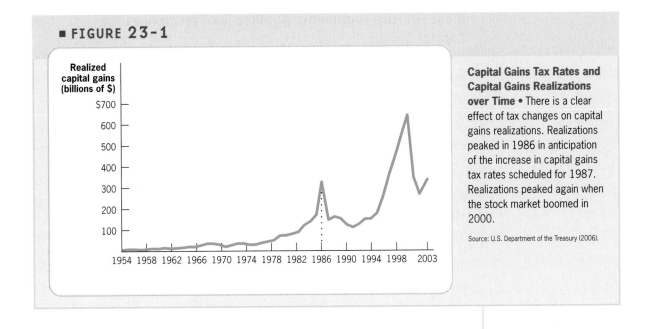

■ FIGURE 23-1

Capital Gains Tax Rates and Capital Gains Realizations over Time • There is a clear effect of tax changes on capital gains realizations. Realizations peaked in 1986 in anticipation of the increase in capital gains tax rates scheduled for 1987. Realizations peaked again when the stock market boomed in 2000.

Source: U.S. Department of the Treasury (2006).

The fact that capital gains realizations returned to their original level in 1987, however, suggests that the response to the capital gains tax increase was only a temporary one. Indeed, Burman and Randolph (1994) estimated that virtually *all* the response of capital gains realizations to taxation is transitory, or short-term, and that there is little long-term increase in the rate of capital gains realizations when tax rates are lower. When capital gains taxes are cut, individuals simply speed up the sales of assets they were going to sell anyway. Revenues may rise in the short run as these assets are sold, but they fall in the long run because the remaining base of gains is smaller, and a lower tax rate is applied to that base. Burman and Randolph estimate that the long-run elasticity of capital gains with respect to the tax rate is only –0.18; at this elasticity, lowering the capital gains tax rate by 1% would reduce revenues by roughly 0.82% (since there would be such a small offsetting increase in realizations). Thus, we are clearly on the correct side of the Laffer curve with capital gains taxes. Furthermore, there does not appear to be much long-run misallocation of assets that is resolved by lowering the capital gains tax rate; rather, changes in the capital gains rate appear to largely effect only the short-run retiming of asset sales.

Moreover, some of the revenue raised by lower capital gains tax rates comes at the expense of other sources of tax revenue. For example, many highly compensated workers have the choice, to some extent, over whether to be compensated in the form of cash wages or stock that yields capital gains-taxable stock returns. When capital gains taxes are lowered relative to wage taxes, individuals will choose the latter route, receiving less in (high-tax) wages and more in (low-tax) stock. This shift will lead to a rise in capital gains taxes when those stocks are sold, but the increase in tax revenue comes at the expense of lower tax revenue on the smaller base of wages.

What Are the Arguments Against Tax Preferences for Capital Gains?

There are two arguments against the existing favoritism shown to capital gains income in most nations. First, capital gains taxes are very progressive. Capital gains income accrues primarily to the richest taxpayers in the United States. In 2000, 90% of capital gains went to the richest 15% of income tax filers, with the richest 0.2% (those with incomes over $1,000,000) receiving 55% of all capital gains.[10] Thus, any reductions in those taxes primarily benefit the highest income taxpayers.

Second, lower tax rates on capital gains violate the Haig-Simons principle for tax systems. The goal of taxation should be to provide a level playing field across economic choices, not to favor one choice over another, unless there is some equity or efficiency argument for doing so (such as a positive externality that justifies a tax preference). Having a capital gains tax rate that is lower than that on other income introduces a *tax wedge* that provides incentives for individuals to engage in inefficient choices in order to access the lower tax rate. As noted earlier, for example, when capital gains taxes are lowered relative to wage taxes, individuals will choose to receive less in wages and more in stock. As we discuss in the next chapter, such a shift in compensation may not be efficient, in that it encourages excessive risk taking and perhaps even cheating by executives. Yet this shift is encouraged by a tax wedge between capital gains taxation and taxation of other forms of income, such as wages.

Similarly, taxing capital gains at a lower rate than interest earned can lead individuals to tilt their investments toward riskier assets that yield capital gains (such as stocks) rather than toward assets that yield interest earnings (such as bonds). Efficiency in investment is maximized when investments are chosen based on their underlying value to the individual, not based on a tax wedge. When individuals choose "too risky" a portfolio because of a tax preference for capital gains, the overall efficiency of investment falls.

23.3

Transfer Taxation

transfer tax A tax levied on the transfer of assets from one individual to another.

gift tax A tax levied on assets that one individual gives to another in the form of a gift.

estate tax A tax levied on the assets of the deceased that are bequeathed to others.

Another important tax on capital in the United States is the **transfer tax** levied on assets passed from one individual to another (most commonly from parents to children). Transfer taxes come in two primary forms. You pay a **gift tax** when you give to any individual a gift worth more than $12,000 in a single year. Any amount above $12,000 must be recorded in your taxes for that year, and those amounts are added up over your lifetime. Then, when you die, remaining assets that are passed on to your heirs are subject to the **estate tax**. The gift and estate taxes are unified under the same tax schedule so that

---

[10] IRS Publication 1304, 2003.

your total estate consists of any assets you leave behind plus the total amount of gifts given over your lifetime (above the $12,000 annual exemption).

For 2006 through 2008, the estate tax exempts the first $2 million of your gifts and estate from taxation and imposes rates ranging from 15–45% on values above that.[11] This exemption level increases each year, and the estate tax is scheduled to disappear in 2010 (although it will then reappear in 2011, as discussed in the Application in Chapter 4, page 111). Importantly, funeral expenses, transfers to spouses, and charitable contributions are all completely deductible from estate taxes. Roughly speaking, the estate tax applies mostly to parents passing large amounts of assets to their children.[12]

Poterba (2001) noted that even though the gift and estate taxes are unified, tax treatment of gifts and estates can differ significantly. One reason is that the tax rates are applied to after-tax amounts of gifts but before-tax amounts of estates. For example, if you had $15,000 to give to your children right now and you face a tax rate of 50%, you could give your children a gift of $10,000, on which you would pay $5,000 of tax. If you left the $15,000 to your children in your estate, however, the entire amount would be taxable so that your children would receive only $7,500. This reasoning suggests that parents would favor gift giving over leaving large estates. Nonetheless, Poterba finds that on average those subject to the estate tax have given gifts over their lifetimes that total only about 5% of the estates they leave behind; wealthy individuals appear to "underuse" the gift tax relative to the estate tax. This may be because they want to keep their assets as a way of ensuring that their children behave properly toward them, lest the children lose their inheritance![13]

The United States is not alone in having transfer taxes, as shown for a sample of nations in Table 23-3. Twenty-six of 30 OECD nations had some form of transfer taxation in 2001. The United States raises a relatively large share of its revenues from transfer taxes: transfer taxes amount to only 0.41%

■ **TABLE 23-3**

Transfer and Wealth Taxes (% of Government Revenue)

	Transfer Taxes	Wealth Taxes	Transfer and Wealth Taxes
Australia	0.00%	0.00%	0.00%
Canada	0.00	0.80	0.80
Finland	0.64	0.15	0.79
France	1.07	0.34	1.41
Germany	0.44	0.03	0.47
Japan	1.14	0.00	1.14
Norway	0.23	1.29	1.52
Spain	0.63	0.44	1.07
Switzerland	0.73	4.60	5.33
United Kingdom	0.62	0.00	0.62
United States	1.01	0.00	1.01
OECD average	0.41	0.48	0.89

Source: Organization for Economic Cooperation and Development (2005a).

The use of transfer taxes and wealth taxes varies widely around the world. On average, the United States has higher transfer taxes than the typical developed nation but lower taxes on wealth.

---

[11] IRS (2005).

[12] If you eventually want to pass large amounts of assets to your grandchildren, first passing them to your children (who in turn pass them on to their children) would result in the application of the estate tax twice. People thus used to give the money directly to their grandchildren so that the estate tax was only applied once. The tax code now includes a generation-skipping transfer tax schedule that is applied in such a situation, effectively closing this loophole.

[13] Nevertheless, Bernheim et al. (2004) and Joulfaian (2005) find evidence that the relative taxation of estates and gifts does significantly affect the timing of transfers.

of revenues raised in the OECD on average, but account for 1.01% of revenues raised in the United States. Thirteen OECD nations, however, also levy a *wealth tax* each year on the value of their citizens' holdings of assets. This tax does not exist in the United States. The average OECD nation raises 0.89% of its revenues from wealth and transfer taxes, somewhat lower than the 1.01% share in the United States.

Why Tax Wealth? Arguments for the Estate Tax

In discussing the estate tax, we must first ask: Why should governments tax the stock of wealth (either annually or at death), rather than tax only the annual flow of income (or consumption, as we discuss in Chapter 25)? There are at least three arguments for taxing wealth. The first is that this is an extremely progressive means of raising revenue. The portion of estates paying the tax has always been fairly limited and, in 2006, it is estimated that only the wealthiest 0.27 percent of all estates (or a total of 6,343 estates) will pay the estate tax. Nonetheless, in 2004, the estate tax raised over $21.5 billion in revenues—enough to finance the discretionary budgets of several cabinet departments. In 2003, among those estates paying the tax, the average effective tax rate was only 19%.[14] Gale and Slemrod (2001a) also note that heirs to estates tend to have income and asset characteristics similar to those of their parents, so the progressive nature of the estate tax does not depend on whether the burden is calculated on the decedent or the recipient.

The second argument is that wealth taxes are necessary to avoid the excessive concentration of wealth and power in society in the hands of a few wealthy dynasties. Many have argued that the existence of a wealth tax is vital in helping to maintain a society's *meritocracy* by ensuring that individuals are rewarded for their talents and not just for the position they were born into. In very strong terms, Frank Keating, president of the American Council of Life Insurers, criticized moves to repeal the tax by stating, "I am institutionally and intestinally against huge blocs of inherited wealth. I don't think we need the Viscount of Enron or the Duke of Microsoft."[15] Piketty and Saez (2006) discussed the evolution of the share of incomes flowing to the very top of the income distribution (e.g., the top 0.1% of incomes) across a broad sample of nations during the twentieth century. They found that in nations with progressive tax systems for both capital income and wealth, there was an enormous reduction in the share of incomes controlled by the very top income earners. This supports the view that wealth and capital taxation deter the long-run concentration of wealth.[16]

---

[14] United for a Fair Economy (2006).

[15] Wall Street Journal (2006).

[16] In recent years, however, there has once again been a sharp rise in the share of incomes going to the highest-income families in some nations (most notably the United States), so that the share of income accruing to the top 0.1% of families is now back to the levels of the early twentieth century. In other nations (such as France and Japan), there has not been a comparable "reconcentration" of wealth.

A third issue that has often been raised by supporters of the estate tax is the claim that allowing children of wealthy families to inherit all their parents' wealth saps them of all motivation to work hard and achieve their own success. As Andrew Carnegie stated in 1891: "The parent who leaves his son enormous wealth generally deadens the talents and energies of his son, and tempts him to lead a less useful and less worthy life than he otherwise would" (Holtz-Eakin et al., 1993). Indeed, Holtz-Eakin et al. found that the larger an individual's inheritance is, the more likely she is to leave the labor force.

Arguments Against the Estate Tax

While the estate tax has many supporters, there are many who think it should be abolished. There are four major arguments made against the estate tax as it is levied in the United States.

A "Death Tax" Is Cruel
The first argument is that it is morally inappropriate to tax individuals upon their death; as Gale and Slemrod (2001b) write, "Compounding the grief of the family of the deceased with a *tax,* of all things, seems a bit heartless, to be sure." Yet, as they point out, death is neither a necessary nor a sufficient condition to trigger transfer taxes in the United States: transfers between living persons can trigger gift taxes, and 98% of those who die pay no estate tax. Moreover, death is a natural time to levy taxes, since it is when we can most straightforwardly compare the lifetime resources of different individuals. As Gale and Slemrod write, "While contemplation of death is not pleasurable, that does not make taxing at death inappropriate. . . . Much of the griping about taxation at death . . . is simply a smokescreen designed to hide opposition to a progressive tax."

The Estate Tax Amounts to Double Taxation
The second argument is that the estate tax represents *double taxation:* you are taxed on income when you earn it, either in the labor market or in taxable interest payments, and then your children are taxed on it again when you die. This outcome is criticized on two grounds. The first is horizontal equity: Why should those paying estate taxes be taxed an extra time on their income? The second is efficiency: the fact that I will be taxed so heavily on my estate may reduce my incentive to save for my children and thus distort my savings decisions. If I am going to lose up to 48% of what I have saved when I die, I may decide to go on a cruise rather than save the money for my children.

There are three problems with this argument, however. First, double taxation is a pervasive feature of the tax system in the United States and around the world. When you use your after-tax income to buy candy at the corner store and pay a sales tax on that purchase, you are being double taxed. Why should one particular form of double taxation be removed or reduced while others are not?

Second, double taxation does not necessarily reduce savings, since there are both income and substitution effects. On the one hand, the rewards for working and saving are reduced through double taxation, so I may earn less (substitution effect). On the other hand, if I value the inheritance I intend to leave for my children, higher taxation could lead me to work or save *more* in order to maintain the after-tax value of that inheritance (income effect).

Finally, the double taxation argument is complicated by the interaction with the step-up in capital gains basis at death. Labor income is indeed taxed twice for those who pay estate tax, once when earned and then again at death. Similarly, interest and other taxable accrued capital income are taxed twice, once when the returns are paid and again at death. Capital gains income, however, may be taxed only once, at death. If individuals leave their capital assets to their children, there is no tax on the accrued capital gains, because the asset's basis is increased (stepped up) when it is transferred. As a result, without an estate tax, income from capital gains passed across generations might escape taxation altogether.

Unfortunately, there is little evidence on the impact of the estate tax on behavior, so we cannot assess whether the double taxation of labor and accrued capital earnings actually affects work or savings decisions.

Administrative Difficulties Another problem with the estate tax is similar to the one raised earlier with taxing capital gains on accrual: to afford the tax, you may be forced to sell the asset. This could be quite a problem with family farms, for example, where the children may want to continue farming when their parents die, but the only way they can afford the estate tax bill is to sell the farm. Although this is a compelling problem in theory, it is not clear that it is a major issue in practice: in 1998, even before exemptions rose under the 2001 tax cut, only 3% of taxable estates were primarily family farms and businesses, and the American Farm Bureau Federation could not provide a single example of a family forced to sell a farm to pay the estate tax.[17] This is perhaps because current law allows some family farms to take up to 14 years to pay their estate taxes.

A potential solution to the problem of forced asset sales would be to exclude most productive assets from estate taxation. One suggestion by the policy analysts at the private Center on Budget and Policy Priorities (and similar to a plan proposed by Senator Daniel Patrick Moynihan in 2000) would be to freeze the estate tax at its planned form in 2009, with a $3.5 million exemption and a top tax rate of 45%. If this were done instead of the planned total repeal in 2010, only the estates of the wealthiest 3 of every 1,000 people who die in 2009 would be taxed, representing only 0.3% of all deaths.[18] Moreover, a recent Congressional Budget Office study has shown that high exemption levels are an effective means of providing estate tax relief to farms and small businesses. The CBO study showed that had the 2009 exemption level been in effect in 2000, fewer than 100 family-owned businesses and only 65 farm estates would have owed any estate tax at all.[19] Also, compared to

---

[17] Friedman and Lee (2003).
[18] Aron-Dine and Friedman (2006).
[19] Friedman and Aron-Dine (2006).

permanent repeal of the estate tax, the revenue implications of this alternative are significant. Permanent repeal would cost the federal government revenues of about $1 trillion from 2012 to 2021, while the alternative would cost $400 billion, only 40% of the cost of repeal.[20].

Compliance and Fairness The final argument made against the estate tax is on grounds of compliance and fairness. There are a number of ways that sophisticated taxpayers can avoid paying the estate tax. One popular method is for parents to set up *trusts* for their children. A trust is a legal arrangement whereby an individual gives a third party (the *trustee*) control of certain assets on the condition that those assets be used to benefit specific people, like his or her children.

Suppose that Kanga made $3 million from her investments and would like to pass that wealth on to her son, Roo. If she gives the wealth to Roo while she's living, she incurs a gift tax, and if she waits until her death, she incurs an estate tax. Kanga is, however, legally permitted to put the $3 million into a trust controlled by Tigger, who is the trustee. As long as Kanga specifies that Tigger must spend the money only on Roo, the funds in this trust are never taxed, but Roo nonetheless receives its full benefits (assuming Tigger is actually trustworthy). Parents can also set up *insurance trusts,* whereby their life insurance policies are placed into trusts so that their children receive the insurance proceeds tax-free.

Another popular (and legal) method of avoiding transfer taxes is to grant one's heirs shares of stock in a new family business. If Bill Gates III had been a parent in 1986 when Microsoft went public, he could have given each of his children 1% of Microsoft's shares without incurring a large gift tax (because the shares weren't very valuable at the company's inception). Had he done so, his children would now be quite wealthy and would have avoided large transfer taxes associated with such wealth (though they would have had to pay a capital gains tax if they sold the stock during their lifetimes). Trusts and stock transfers are thus two ways that individuals well versed in the legal system can legally avoid paying transfer taxes.

Moreover, estate and gift taxes are levied on one type of transfer, cash and property, but not on another type of transfer, services. If I spend $20,000 to pay for a family trip, this is not treated as a gift to my children for the purposes of the gift and estate tax, but if I give that same $20,000 to my children, it is considered a gift and lowers my estate tax exemption.

As a result of these alternatives, some refer to the estate tax as a "voluntary tax": only those too unsophisticated to avoid the tax end up paying it. This is an unfair outcome that violates horizontal equity. Some claim that if a tax cannot be applied fairly, it should not be applied at all. Once again, the costs of such horizontal inequities must be weighed against the benefits of the revenue raised by this tax: Is the unfairness so large that it justifies removing more than $20 billion in revenues a year?

---

[20] Friedman (2006). These estimates imply much larger annual collections from the estate tax in the future because wealth is rising so rapidly for older households in the United States.

A related point is that removing the estate tax may reduce charitable giving in the United States. This is because donations to charity from one's estate are deductible from the estate tax. Almost 10% of charitable giving in the United States comes in the form of donations from estates. If the estate tax were removed, it is possible that this charitable giving could fall because the price of charitable giving has risen: there would no longer be an estate tax against which charitable giving can be deducted. The prediction for charitable giving is unclear, however; removing the estate tax would also make individuals wealthier, and this would have an income effect, leading to increased charitable giving.[21]

23.4

Property Taxation

property tax A tax levied on the value of real estate, including the value of the land and any structures built on the land.

As discussed in Chapter 10, the major source of financing for local governments in the United States is the **property tax,** a tax on the market value of privately owned property which may include land, structures, and machinery as well as other real property such as cars, boats, business inventory, and so on. The types of property subject to taxation vary widely across localities. Land and structures are subject to taxation in all states, but all states exempt government property, and most exempt religious property, charitable properties, cemeteries, and hospitals. In many states, personal property and motor vehicles are also exempt from taxation.[22] Since most property tax revenues are raised from taxing land and homes, we will focus on this aspect of property taxation in the discussion that follows.

Property taxes are levied at a locally determined rate on the *assessed value* of residential and commercial property, which is the value assigned by the jurisdiction, usually the town or city. Localities attempt to match assessed values to market property values in most cases, but this is difficult when a piece of property has not been recently sold. As a result, the effective property tax rate (the ratio of property tax payments to market property values) can deviate significantly from the statutory rate. Effective rates are calculated by multiplying the nominal tax rate by the *assessment ratio,* the percentage of the property's value that is subject to taxation. For example, a nominal tax rate of 2% and an assessment ratio of 50% would yield an effective tax rate of 1%.

The assessment ratio used varies widely across different localities: in 2001, the assessment ratio in Columbia, South Carolina, was only 4%, while in Providence, Rhode Island, it was 100%. Overall, among the largest cities in each state in 2001, the average assessment ratio was 59.0%. There are similarly wide variations in the effective tax rate across jurisdictions in the United States: in 2001, effective rates ranged from a low of 0.37% in Honolulu, Hawaii, to a high of 4.55% in Bridgeport, Connecticut.[23]

---

[21] Bakija, Gale, and Slemrod (2003) estimate that, on net, reducing the estate tax would lower charitable giving.
[22] O'Sullivan, Sexton, and Sheffrin (1995).
[23] Government of the District of Columbia, Office of Tax and Revenue (2002).

While property taxes constitute a fairly limited share of state revenues, they are the single largest source of revenue at the local level and account for more than half of total revenues.[24] In 2005, state and local governments collected $352 billion in property taxes, with approximately 96% of that being accounted for by local government units including counties, cities, and school districts.[25]

There are a number of interesting economic issues raised by property taxation. Some of these issues were covered in Chapter 10, such as the capitalization of property taxes into home prices (with the example of Proposition 13 in California) and the role of property taxes in financing schools. In this chapter, we consider other important issues in property tax policy, such as the incidence of the property tax and different types of property taxation.

Who Bears the Property Tax?

The property tax is a source of much debate at the state and local levels, with a number of states imposing limits on the ability of localities to raise their property taxes. This debate reflects the view that property taxes are costly burdens on average-income home owners. Yet, as we learned in Chapter 19, the incidence of a tax is not determined by who pays the tax bill. So who actually bears the property tax?

The incidence of the property tax has been a source of long-standing debate among public finance economists, as summarized in Zodrow (2001). There are three schools of thought on the incidence of the property tax. The "traditional view" is a partial equilibrium analysis of the property tax. This view highlights that the tax is levied on two factors: land, which is inelastically supplied, and structures (e.g., houses), which are much more elastically supplied. The part of the tax that is levied on land is borne by landowners, as is always the case when a factor is inelastically supplied. But the part of the tax that is levied on structures is more complicated, and the incidence of this structure tax depends on the relative elasticity of supply of structures and of the individuals who want to use those structures. In the long run, if the supply of structures is perfectly elastic, but individual demand for a community is not, this tax will be borne to some extent by residents of the community, renters and owners alike.

The "capital tax" view of property tax incidence (sometimes referred to as the "new view") recognizes the general equilibrium nature of tax incidence. When towns levy property taxes, in the long run they chase capital out of town to other jurisdictions. As capital supply increases in other jurisdictions, for a given level of capital demand, the rate of return to capital falls around the nation (or even around the world). Thus, the average burden of the property tax is borne by capital owners, a fairly well-off group. It remains true under this view, however, that locality-specific deviations from the national

[24] Lorelli (2001).
[25] U.S. Census Bureau (2006d).

average are borne by that locality's land and home owners. Thus, as Zodrow (2001) emphasizes, the "capital tax view" essentially encompasses the traditional view but moves from a partial to a general equilibrium perspective.

Finally, the "benefits tax" view mirrors our discussion of the Tiebout model in Chapter 10. Property taxes are typically used to finance local government spending that is valued by most home owners. As a result, property taxes are to some extent a user fee that supports the Tiebout model: property taxes are the price set by each town to finance the optimal local level of public goods. If, for example, a town is in a perfect Tiebout equilibrium at which all residents of a town value public goods at their tax cost, then there is no burden associated with property taxation; it is simply a price residents pay voluntarily for local public goods.

Thus, the incidence of the property tax depends very much on which is the appropriate model for analyzing the tax. Under the traditional model, the property tax is borne fully by local residents in proportion to their expenditures on housing, and is therefore proportional or somewhat regressive. Under the capital tax view, the common part of the property tax is borne in large part by capital owners, so it is much more progressive. Under the benefits tax view, there is no incidence, since the property tax is simply a price paid for a service received. Existing evidence cannot distinguish among these models, but economic theory suggests that the "capital tax view" has considerable merit, so that the tax may be more progressive than it is typically perceived (Zodrow, 2001).

Types of Property Taxation

Property taxes need not apply equally to all types of property. In particular, two important distinctions can be drawn in levying property taxes.

Residential Homes Versus Businesses The first distinction in designing property taxes is that between taxing residential homes and businesses. Some argue that to encourage economic development, property taxes on businesses should be lower than those imposed on residential homes. It is uncertain, however, whether such tax breaks for businesses deliver enough benefits to local communities to justify the lost tax revenue.

▶ APPLICATION

Property Tax Breaks to Businesses

In recent years, a number of local governments have tried giving property tax breaks (as well as other tax breaks) to local businesses in order to convince them not to move their operations elsewhere. For example, near the end of 2003, Cincinnati gave $52.2 million in tax breaks to Convergys Corporation, a customer service company, to keep the firm from moving its 1,700 jobs across the Ohio River to northern Kentucky, where tax rates were lower. In Missouri, St. Louis County offered Packaging Concepts, Inc., $2.5 million in tax breaks so that the company, intent on leaving its site in the center of St.

Louis, would settle nearby in the southern part of the county. And in February 2004, New York City granted Bank of America $42 million in tax breaks to convince the company to build its 51-story office tower in the center of Manhattan.

Is it worthwhile for governments to offer companies such tax breaks in order to convince them to stay in a particular location? Critics of Bank of America noted that shortly after the tax breaks were announced, the company merged with FleetBoston Financial Corporation, raising the possibility of layoffs. One opponent of the deal was furious that "every year, we're losing tax dollars on this." In 2004, a New York City study found that the city's ten largest banks received $120 million in tax breaks under Mayors Bloomberg and Giuliani while actually cutting 3,000 jobs.

As recently as 2001, urban economist Ed Glaeser concluded that although location-based incentives "seem to be a permanent part of the urban economic landscape, economists do not yet know why these incentives occur and whether they are in fact desirable."[26] A recent study by Greenstone and Moretti (2003), however, suggested that cities successfully attracting large industrial plants are better off. They found that wages grew 1.5% faster in the successful cities than in comparable cities that had lost the competition for these same plants. Greenstone and Moretti also found that property values in the successful cities rose 1.1% faster than they did in the runner-up cities. The authors concluded that successful attraction of industrial plants increases the welfare of local residents and may validate the use of tax breaks to win the competition against other cities. ◄

Regardless of whether tax breaks to attract business are a good idea for any particular location, they are almost certainly a bad deal for the nation as a whole. The nation as a whole would be best served if firms locate where it is most efficient, not where they get the best tax breaks. Moreover, such property tax breaks can lead to a "race to the bottom," whereby the actions of one local government to reduce its property tax (in order to attract businesses) cause other local governments to do the same. This process can lead to a cycle of self-defeating tax cuts that do not have much effect on business location but do substantially lower property tax revenues.

Land Versus Improvements The second distinction that can be drawn in designing property taxes is that between taxing land and taxing the improvements to that land, such as a house, an office building, or a shopping center. This distinction was highlighted by Henry George, a nineteenth-century thinker who believed that the returns earned by labor and capital reflected the productive activity of these factors but that the returns accruing to landowners did not. The landowner is paid solely because he owns the land and not because of any effort put into production. George therefore made a radical proposal: eliminate taxes on labor and capital and replace them with a single tax on the value of land. George did *not* propose to tax improvements on the

---

[26] Glaeser (2001).

land because this approach would undermine his basic premise that ownership, not effort, should be taxed.

George's reasoning is illustrated by Mark Lubold, city councilor of Holyoke, Massachusetts, an old industrial city suffering from a shrinking tax base because of underutilized buildings and vacant lots. Recently, Lubold pointed out that the current property tax system "punishes those who keep up or improve their property with higher taxes while those who let their property go are rewarded with tax decreases." Lubold has been pushing Holyoke to adopt a form of George's ideas by lowering tax rates on buildings but raising them on land. This system, he believes, "would encourage owners of vacant buildings to fix them up, collect rents and conduct business to pay the higher taxes or sell the buildings or land to someone who will." Lubold points to 700 cities around the world that have adopted some form of a land-value tax, including Sydney, Australia, and Cape Town, South Africa. In Harrisburg, Pennsylvania, the number of vacant buildings dropped from 4,000 to 500 after the adoption of a land-value tax.[27]

In another example, Pittsburgh suffered in 1913 from high land prices that discouraged businesses from establishing themselves. To combat this problem, Pittsburgh instituted a system that lowered taxes on buildings and taxed land at six times that rate. Some credit the two-tiered tax system with fueling Pittsburgh's building boom in the 1940s and 1950s. In 2001, however, the land-value system was replaced by one that equalized tax rates on buildings and land. The reason? Assessors had probably been compensating for the high land tax by undervaluing the land itself. When an outside assessor was brought in and declared land values to be double what they had been the year before, taxpayers revolted and politicians scrapped the system.

The fundamental problem with tax systems that try to distinguish the value of land from the value of the assets on that land is that market values cannot be used for taxation: the market values only the total package of land plus assets, not each separately. Administrative mechanisms, such as assessment, must be used to separately value land, and these mechanisms are subject to error and manipulation. This makes the land tax unreliable as a dominant form of revenue raising.[28]

23.5

Conclusion

The impact of the tax code on decisions about how much to save, and in what form to save it, will always be central to debates over tax reform. In this chapter, we have reviewed some of the major aspects of the tax code that affect risk taking and wealth accumulation in the United States. We first highlighted that taxation doesn't necessarily reduce, and under certain assumptions definitely increases, risk taking.

---

[27] Restuccia (2003).
[28] Fitzpatrick (2001).

This theoretical point has important implications for the debate over capital gains taxation. The strongest arguments for the preferential tax treatment of capital gains are that (a) lower capital gains tax rates will "unlock" productive assets, and (b) lower capital gains taxes will encourage entrepreneurship. The existing evidence on the former suggests that such unlocking is not large in the long run. The theoretical discussion suggests that the predictions for entrepreneurship are unclear. Moreover, even if lower capital gains taxation promotes risk taking and entrepreneurship, it does so at the very high cost of providing large subsidies to previous investments.

We also looked at the estate tax, which is a very progressive tax but one that raises difficult issues of horizontal equity and enforcement. Finally, we discussed the uncertain incidence of the property tax and the important issues of taxation of businesses versus residential homes and land versus improvements to that land.

▶ HIGHLIGHTS

- Taxation has an uncertain effect on risk taking. Proportional taxation with a full loss offset would likely increase risk taking, but factors such as limited loss offsets and progressive tax structures can reduce risk taking.

- In addition to wages and interest earned on savings, people earn income in the form of capital gains, which are the returns earned when assets are sold for more than their purchase price. Capital gains are heavily subsidized by realization on accrual and step up in basis at death, and also traditionally have faced a lower marginal tax rate.

- Lowering capital gains tax rates can offset the impact of inflation on asset values, reduce asset "lock-in," and encourage entrepreneurship, but at the cost of giving large tax breaks to past investments. Existing evidence suggests that there is little long-run reduction in the lock-in effect from lower capital gains taxes.

- The estate tax is levied on a small number of the richest estates in the United States and is therefore highly progressive.

- There are several arguments against estate taxation, but each has weaknesses. For example, the estate tax double-taxes labor and interest earnings, but in its favor is the fact that it is the only tax on capital gains for those who pass assets on to their heirs.

- The property tax is the main revenue source for local governments. The economic incidence of the property tax is unclear, but the economic tax incidence is likely to be more progressive than the statutory incidence, since at least part of the tax falls on the owners of land and owners of capital.

- Lowering property taxes on businesses is a popular way for local governments to attract business, but it is inefficient for the nation as a whole.

▶ QUESTIONS AND PROBLEMS

1. The tax system has a 50% tax rate on gains from risky investments, and also allows a deduction at a 50% rate of any losses from risky investments. Which tax policy would increase risk taking more: (a) allowing those deductions on any losses, or (b) limiting the deduction only to losses that offset other gains (no loss offset)?

2. The Job Growth and Tax Relief Reconciliation Act of 2003 (JGTRRA) reduced the rate at which capital gains are taxed, but it includes a "sunset" provision whereby the tax rate will return to its original level in 2009 (unless further action is taken by Congress). How is this sunset provision likely to affect capital gains tax realizations and revenues in 2008 and 2009?

3. President Berry suggests changing the capital gains tax law so that taxes are assessed when the gains are accrued rather than when they are realized. Why would investors tend to oppose this policy change?

4. Prior to 1997, many university professors who moved from expensive places like Boston or San Francisco to low-cost cities like Madison, Wisconsin, or Gainesville, Florida, tended to purchase extremely large houses upon their moves. This tendency was dramatically curtailed after 1997. What feature of the U.S. tax code encouraged this behavior?

5. What is the empirical evidence on whether capital gains tax cuts lead to a permanent increase in capital gains realizations? What does this evidence imply for the prospects of lowering capital gains taxes as a long-term revenue-generation tool?

6. When I spend money on my children's consumption, this transfer is not taxed, but if I make a large direct gift to my children, it is taxed. Why does this represent a horizontal inequity inherent in transfer taxes? Can you think of any policy modifications that could reduce this inequity?

7. Senator Crawford, arguing in favor of capital gains tax cuts, says that reducing capital gains tax rates will stimulate entrepreneurial activity. Senator Long, arguing against these tax cuts, suggests that they will encourage people to engage in riskier behavior and inefficient investment. Evaluate both senators' arguments.

8. When Bill died in 2006, he left his children $200,000 in cash (generated from labor earnings), a $1.1 million home that he had purchased (with labor earnings) for $100,000 in 1980, and $1.2 million in stock that he had purchased (with labor earnings) for $200,000 in 1985. Evaluate the argument that the estate tax represents double taxation of Bill's income.

9. Why does the property tax, as implemented in the United States, provide a disincentive for property owners to improve their property? How would a land tax alter these incentives?

10. The government of Lupostan introduced a policy in which all investments in college education and training are tax-deductible. Describe an empirical test of the effects of this policy on the level of human capital accumulation. What effects would you expect to find from such a policy?

▶ ADVANCED QUESTIONS

11. Estoluania is considering replacing its progressive tax system with a flat tax that would raise equal revenue. How could this change encourage risk-taking behavior? How could it *discourage* risk-taking behavior?

12. A researcher found that when the capital gains tax rate declined, the average bequest size fell as well. How does the tax treatment of capital gains in the United States explain this relationship?

13. Pamplovia raised its estate tax rate from 30% to 50%. However, it "grandfathered" in families whose householders were over 80 years old, allowing these families to be assessed the original 30% estate tax. How could you go about estimating the effects of estate tax rates in Pamplovia on the magnitude of bequests?

14. In some states, a local government that reduces its tax base receives additional aid for local public good provision from the state government. Why

will cities be more likely to offer tax breaks in this circumstance? Why are tax breaks in this case particularly bad for overall welfare?

15. The Economic Growth and Tax Relief Reconciliation Act of 2001 (EGTRRA) lowered the top marginal rate for estate taxation, called for a gradual increase in the estate tax exemption (the amount of an estate that is untaxed) to $3.5 million, and called for a complete elimination of the tax in 2010. However, a sunset provision in the law implies that the estate tax will reappear again in 2011, with an exemption of only $1 million and at a higher marginal rate. How should this sunset provision affect the savings and charitable giving rates of the elderly prior to 2011 and subsequent to 2011?

The **e** icon indicates a question that requires students to apply the empirical economics principles discussed in Chapter 3 and the Empirical Evidence boxes.

Corporate Taxation

24

On June 1, 2004, the Homeland Security Department awarded a $10 billion, decade-long contract to Accenture LLP. The company would help build a "virtual border" around the United States by recording the exit and entry of noncitizens, using digital finger scans and photographs. Eight days later, the House Appropriations Committee voted to block the contract because the company had incorporated in Bermuda to avoid paying U.S. corporate income taxes. Democratic representative Rosa DeLauro, who sponsored the blocking amendment, said, "These companies have an obligation to the United States of America to pay their taxes."[1] An Accenture spokesperson responded that her company had been chosen "based on cost, capability and management criteria. Preventing successful companies from bidding on government contracts just because they are not incorporated in the U.S. rejects the free market principles of the federal procurement system."[2] One week later, the appropriations committee's amendment was voted down in the full House, allowing Accenture to keep the contract.

The strong feelings inspired by the debate over corporate taxation were due in part to the realization that the role of corporate taxation in government revenue has changed dramatically in recent years. Corporations in the United States are taxed on their *net earnings,* the difference between what they earn and what they spend on factors of production. By statute, most corporations face a marginal tax rate of 35%. In practice, numerous features of the corporate tax system (sometimes referred to as loopholes) make effective tax rates much lower than this, and increased use of these loopholes has at least partly led to the significant decline in corporate tax revenues. In 1960, for example, almost one-quarter of federal revenues was raised through the corporate tax, as is shown in the left panel of Figure 24-1 on page 690. This share

---

[1] *Washington Post* (2004), "Washington in Brief," June 17, 2004, p. A4.
[2] Glassman (2004).

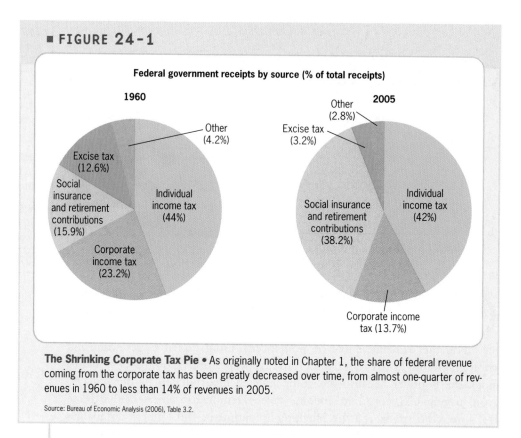

■ FIGURE 24-1

Federal government receipts by source (% of total receipts)

The Shrinking Corporate Tax Pie • As originally noted in Chapter 1, the share of federal revenue coming from the corporate tax has been greatly decreased over time, from almost one-quarter of revenues in 1960 to less than 14% of revenues in 2005.

Source: Bureau of Economic Analysis (2006), Table 3.2.

has changed dramatically over the past several decades, with corporate taxes bringing in less than 14% of federal revenues today, as the right panel shows.

To its detractors, the corporate tax is a major drag on the productivity of the corporate sector, and the reduction in the tax burden on corporations has been a boon to the economy that has led firms to increase their investment in productive assets. To its supporters, the corporate tax is a major safeguard of the overall progressivity of our tax system. By allowing the corporate tax system to erode over time, supporters of corporate taxation argue, we have enriched capitalists at the expense of other taxpayers.

In this chapter, we evaluate these arguments. We begin by discussing the nature of corporations and the arguments for having a corporate tax. We introduce the structure of the corporate tax in the United States and consider the difficulties in defining corporate expenses. We also discuss how to apply the principles of Chapter 19 to assess the ultimate incidence of corporate taxation.

We then focus on two important behavioral effects of the corporate tax. The first is the impact of corporate taxation on a firm's investment decisions. The second is the combined impact of corporate and individual taxation on a firm's decisions about how to finance its business ventures. Finally, we discuss the set of difficult issues raised by taxing corporations that earn their income in many different nations.

24.1
What Are Corporations and Why Do We Tax Them?

In analyzing corporate taxation, it is important to note that not all goods and services are produced by the corporate sector in the United States. There is also a large and robust noncorporate sector consisting of self-employed individuals, partnerships, and other organizational forms that do not seek the protections of incorporation. The noncorporate sector accounts for about one-quarter of sales in the United States.

Within the corporate sector, most of the production is by firms owned by a large number of **shareholders,** individuals who have purchased ownership stakes in a company. The major advantage of incorporation is that it offers the guarantee of *limited liability,* which means that the owners of a firm cannot be held personally responsible for the obligations of the firm. If a corporation fails, the shareholders are not required by law to use their personal assets (such as their homes, jewelry, and so on) to pay the debts of the failed company. The most that shareholders can lose is the amount they have invested in the corporation.

There are two classifications of corporations: S-corporations and C-corporations (the letters refer to the tax schedule used to file tax returns). The major difference between these classifications is the tax system that applies to the firm. Income from an S-corporation is treated as personal income as it is earned and is subject to the individual income tax; income from C-corporations is subject to the corporate income tax as it is earned and may be subject to the individual income tax again as it is distributed to a corporation's shareholders. Our discussion of corporate taxation will focus on C-corporations, which account for most of the production of the corporate sector.

Ownership vs. Control

Most corporations separate *ownership* of the firm from *control* (or management) of the firm. Some corporations are publicly traded on a stock exchange, so any investor can purchase or sell ownership shares in the company. Other corporations are privately held, so only select individuals are able to have an ownership stake.

In either case, shareholders typically do not make the day-to-day decisions on how to run the corporation. Those decisions are made by *managers,* who are hired by the shareholders to run the company. This separation of ownership from control is certainly necessary for large corporations; the thousands of owners of a large company could never get together to make all the decisions needed to run that company on a day-to-day basis. This separation of ownership from control has the disadvantage, however, of giving rise to what economists call an **agency problem:** a misalignment of the interests of the owners and the managers.

Consider, for example, the decision of a corporate manager to buy a jet airliner for his corporate travel. Suppose that the manager knows that it would

shareholders Individuals who have purchased ownership stakes in a company.

agency problem A misalignment of the interests of the owners and the managers of a firm.

be much less expensive for him to take commercial flights for all of his travel than for the company to own its own jet. Thus, it is in the shareholders' interests for the manager to use commercial flights because that would be the best thing for the profitability of the firm. Yet the manager may prefer the jet for comfort and convenience, reasons that have nothing to do with the profitability of the company. Moreover, if the manager has control of the accounting process, he can undoubtedly produce calculations to show the firm's owners that a jet is less costly than commercial flights (by using the most expensive commercial airline prices for comparison rather than the lower prices he would be likely to pay). Thus, the manager may convince the owners to let him buy a jet, even though it is not in their best interests.

This is just a small example of the havoc that the agency problem can cause in corporate settings. Later in this chapter we will discuss the implications of the separation of ownership and control for corporate tax policy.

▶ **APPLICATION**

Executive Compensation and the Agency Problem

A number of corporate executives have made the news in recent years for receiving compensation packages that seem wildly out of proportion to the executives' actual value. How can executives receive such high compensation? There are two possible reasons. First, they may be worth it: after all, these individuals are running some of the most important companies in the world. Nonetheless, this high compensation doesn't seem to be related to superior performance in many cases. For example, in 2004, net income at Eli Lilly fell 29% and its return to shareholders dropped 17%. In that same year, the company's chief executive enjoyed a 41% pay raise that pushed his salary up to $12.5 million. Similarly, in the period from 2001 to 2004, the electronics contract manager Sanmina-SCL lost money in every single year and its shareholders' total return fell by 27% in just 2004—yet in that same year, the pay of its chief executive jumped from $1.2 million to $15 million.[3]

The second possible reason for high executive compensation is that owners of firms have a hard time keeping track of the actual compensation of the firm's managers, and the managers exploit this limitation to compensate themselves well. Owners of corporations try to keep control of executive mismanagement through the use of a **board of directors,** a set of (supposedly independent) individuals who meet periodically to review decisions made by the firm and report back to the broader set of owners on management's performance. Yet these boards of directors are very imperfect control devices. For example, when Richard Grasso retired as head of the New York Stock Exchange and claimed a $187 million severance package, a subsequent report suggested that few directors of the company actually understood Grasso's complicated contract and thus were surprised to find themselves owing him that much money. Other executives may conveniently place their friends

board of directors A set of individuals who meet periodically to review decisions made by a firm's management and report back to the broader set of owners on management's performance.

---
[3] Deutsch (2005).

and allies on the board of directors, reducing the board's ability to effectively monitor those same executives.

At times, executive compensation crosses the line from outrageous to illegal. In March 2006, the *Wall Street Journal* published a report examining the practice of granting *stock options* to top executives in several major companies. Stock options are designed to give managers the incentive to perform well by providing them the right to buy a block of their company's stock at a fixed price, such as the current price (the "strike price"). Thus, if the company's stock price rises, presumably due in some part to good management, the manager can buy his stock at the promised low price, sell at the higher price, and make money; if the stock price falls, the manager simply doesn't "exercise" his option in this way. Thus, companies use stock options a way of motivating managers to improve company performance that has no cost to the company if those managers fail and the company does worse.[4]

Stock options have the disadvantage, however, that the "strike price" can be manipulated to maximize the value of the options. In several cases, the *Journal's* analysis exposed a suspiciously consistent pattern: stock-option grants were often dated *just before* a rise in the company's stock price and often at the bottom of a steep drop, suggesting that the options had been backdated—that is, the grants' dates had been changed to earlier dates on which share prices were low. This backdating is not in the company's interest—the company wants to motivate executives to raise stock prices, not raise executives' rewards because prices were lower at some point in the past. But it is certainly in the interests of executives, whose options are more valuable the lower the strike price.

In one particularly flagrant example, all six of the stock-option grants awarded to Affiliated Computer Services chief executive Jeffrey Rich from 1995 to 2002 were dated directly before a rise in the stock price, yielding a 15% higher return than if they had been granted at each year's average share price. Though Rich and ACS insisted it had been "blind luck," according to the *Journal's* computations, the odds of this happening by chance were around one in a billion.[5]

Spurred by the *Journal's* report, the SEC opened an investigation into the practice of backdating stock options at several U.S. companies and, by May 2006, ten executives or directors at affected companies had been forced to resign.[6] By September 2006, the federal investigation had brought to light possible improper stock-options practices at nearly 100 U.S. companies. In one particularly bizarre example, Cablevision Systems Corp., the country's fifth largest cable operator, was found to have granted and possibly backdated options in the period from 1997 to 2002 for its Vice Chairman, Marc Lustgarten. The twist? Mr. Lustgarten had died in 1999 of pancreatic cancer. Though an investigation is ongoing, many suspect that the posthumously awarded options were meant to enrich Mr. Lustgarten's heirs who were entitled to exercise all stock options

---

[4] For example, suppose that a company's current stock price was $100 per share. Company A grants its CEO 1 million stock options, so that she has the right to buy up to 1 million shares at $100 per share, regardless of the actual stock price. If the stock price falls, she will never exercise (use) these options—they are worthless. But if the stock price rises, say to $150, then she can buy 1 million shares for $100 a share and sell them for $150, making $50 million in profit.

[5] Forelle and Bandler (2006).

[6] *Wall Street Journal* (2006a).

▪ **FIGURE 24-2**

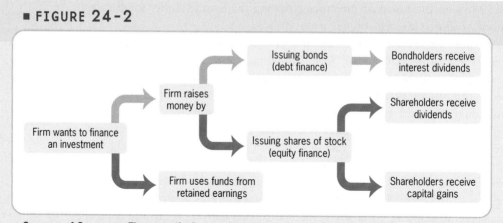

Sources of Corporate Finance • If a firm wants to finance an investment, it can either use its own retained earnings, or raise new funds from the capital market in one of two ways. The first is to issue bonds that pay bondholders periodic interest payments (debt finance). The other is to issue ownership (equity) shares that pay shareholders either through dividends or through capital gains earned on increases in the value of the firm (equity finance).

upon his death. While awarding options has traditionally been justified as a means of giving executives a greater stake in the company's success, the Cablevision example is a striking demonstration of how far the practice has departed from its original purpose. As John Coffee, a professor of law at Columbia University, wryly noted, "Trying to incentivize a corpse suggests they were not complying with the spirit of shareholder-approved stock-option plans."[7]

Agency problems are not unique to the United States. In December 2003, Italian dairy giant Parmalat SpA and its founder, Calisto Tanzi, became engulfed in one of Europe's biggest-ever corporate frauds when the company declared bankruptcy and admitted that a 3.9 billion euro bank account it allegedly held at the Bank of America did not, in fact, exist. Further investigation revealed that Tanzi had led the company in a decade-long fraud involving falsified company accounts and funds siphoned off for personal gain (including at least $1.1 billion doled out to Tanzi family businesses and bank accounts) that left Parmalat with 14 billion euros in debt. To date, trials regarding the scandal are ongoing.[8] ◄

debt finance The raising of funds by borrowing from lenders such as banks, or by selling bonds.

bonds Promises by a corporation to make periodic interest payments, as well as ultimate repayment of principal, to the bondholders (the lenders).

Firm Financing

Firms grow by making investments and reaping the rewards of those investments. To make investments in capital such as new machinery, however, a firm must *finance,* or raise the funds for, the investment. There are three possible channels of corporate financing, as shown in Figure 24-2. The firm can borrow from lenders such as banks; this type of financing is called **debt finance.** This borrowing is often done by selling corporate **bonds,** which are promises

---

[7] Grant, Bandler, & Forelle (2006)
[8] Galloni (2005) and Galloni and Trofimov (2004).

by the corporation to make periodic interest payments (along with an ultimate repayment of principal) to the bondholders (the lenders).

The second source of investment financing is to sell a *share* (a small piece) of ownership in the company for money that can be used to make investments; this type of financing is called **equity finance.** Investors who buy shares in a company can be rewarded in two different ways. One is by receiving a **dividend,** a periodic payment from the company per share owned. The other is by earning a **capital gain** on the shares held as the price rises above the purchase price of the stock.

Finally, firms can finance their investment out of their own **retained earnings**, which are any net profits that are kept by the company rather than paid out to debt or equity holders. Indeed, in recent years there is increasing evidence that a large share, perhaps a majority, of new investment is financed from retained earnings.[9]

Why Do We Have a Corporate Tax?

Why do we have a corporate income tax? After all, as we emphasized in Chapter 19, firms are not entities but combinations of factors. So when we tax "firms," we ultimately tax the factors of production that make up those firms. Wouldn't it be more straightforward to tax the factors (labor and capital) directly, rather than get revenue from them through the convoluted (and uncertain) mechanism of corporate taxation? There are at least two reasons why we might want a separate corporate tax.

Pure Profits Taxation To the extent that corporations have market power, they will earn *pure profits,* returns that exceed payouts to their factors of production (labor and capital). As established by the important analysis of Diamond and Mirlees (1971), a pure profits tax is a much better way to raise revenues than is a tax on factors of production. This is because a pure profits tax does not distort the decision making of a producer, while taxes on labor or capital have distortionary effects of the types discussed in Chapters 21–23 (such as lowering labor supply, savings, or risk taking).

A firm chooses prices and production levels to maximize profits. If the government were to announce tomorrow that it was taking some part of those profits, the optimal choice of price and quantity for the firm would not change; the decision that maximizes pre-tax profits also maximizes after-tax profits: $(1 - \text{tax}) \times \text{profits}$. Pure profits taxes therefore collect revenue without distorting behavior. In addition to being distortion-free, a pure profits tax is very progressive because those receiving the profits from production are likely to be well-off.

While the pure profits tax seems like a good idea, it is not the way the corporate tax works, for two reasons. First, as we see later in the chapter, corporate taxes are not pure profits taxes: firms can minimize their corporate tax burdens by changing their use of inputs. Since corporate taxes cause firms to substitute away from their optimal production pattern, there is a distortion that causes inefficiency.

equity finance The raising of funds by sale of ownership shares in a firm.

dividend The periodic payment that investors receive from the company, per share owned.

capital gain The increase in the price of a share since its purchase.

retained earnings Any net profits that are kept by the company rather than paid out to debt or equity holders.

---

[9] See Rauh (2006) for compelling evidence as well as a review of past literature in this area.

economic profits The difference between a firm's revenues and its economic opportunity costs of production.

accounting profits The difference between a firm's revenues and its reported costs of production.

Second, a pure profits tax should be levied on **economic profits,** the difference between firm revenues and economic costs. It would involve using the type of cost calculations discussed in Chapter 8, appropriately valuing resources at their *opportunity cost* (their use in the next best alternative activity). Yet firms pay taxes on **accounting profits,** the difference between revenues and reported costs. Reported costs can differ from economic costs both because they use prices rather than opportunity costs and because firms can manipulate their accounting practices to vary the amount they report as costs.

Retained Earnings Another rationale for corporate taxation is similar to the arguments we discussed for capital gains: if corporations were not taxed on their earnings, then individuals who owned shares in corporations could simply avoid taxes by having the corporations never pay out their earnings. These earnings would accumulate tax-free inside the corporation, leading to a large tax subsidy to corporate earnings relative to other forms of savings (or other economic activity in general). If corporations paid out those earnings many years later, the present discounted value of the tax burden would be quite low.

24.2

The Structure of the Corporate Tax

In this section, we review the basic structure of the corporate tax. This is a very complicated tax, so we present a simplified version of the structure.

The taxes of any corporation are:

$$\text{Taxes } = ([\text{Revenues} - \text{Expenses}] \times \tau) - \text{Investment tax credit.}$$

We define each element of this expression in turn.

Revenues

These are the revenues the firm earns by selling goods and services to the market.

Expenses

A firm's expenses consist primarily of three components. The first is the *cash-flow costs of doing business.* These costs comprise any expenditures for services or goods over the past year. Examples would include compensation paid to employees, purchases of intermediate inputs to production such as steel or energy, the costs of advertising, rent on buildings, and so on. The second component is *interest payments,* the payments made to those who lend the firm money. Both cash-flow costs and interest payments are deductible from corporate earnings in the period during which they are incurred; the amount spent each year in these categories is subtracted from that year's earnings in computing the firm's tax burden.

depreciation The rate at which capital investments lose their value over time.

The final expense component is **depreciation** on capital investments, the rate at which capital investments lose their value over time. When a company hires a worker for a year at a given salary, it pays the salary for services rendered during the year and can fully deduct those salary payments from taxation.

When the company buys equipment or a new building, however, it is investing in a good that will deliver services for many years. Thus, the tax code does not permit the full costs of the machine to be deducted in the period of purchase. Instead the tax code allows the corporation to deduct from its taxes **depreciation allowances,** which are tax allowances that are designed to approximate the rate at which the capital investment loses its value. Corporations take the depreciation allowances each year for a number of years, thus spreading the cost of the asset over a number of years. The appropriate determination of depreciation allowances is very important for corporate tax policy. How should such longer-lived purchases be treated for tax purposes?

depreciation allowances The amount of money that firms can deduct from their taxes to account for capital investment depreciation.

Economic Depreciation In principle, the tax code should allow firms to deduct **economic depreciation,** the deterioration in the value of the machine each period, as their expense. Consider a firm that is buying a machine this year for $100,000. The machine will wear down gradually over time, so each year the machine will be worth $10,000 less. After ten years, the machine will be worthless, and the firm will have to replace it.

economic depreciation The true deterioration in the value of capital in each period of time.

What is the cost to the firm of using this machine for one year? It is the purchase price ($100,000) minus its value after one year ($90,000). Using the machine for one year essentially costs the firm $10,000, since that is the reduced value of the asset. Since this amount is the firm's cost of using the machine for the year, it is the appropriate expense to deduct from earnings. Just as using a year of labor costs that year's wages, using a year of a machine costs the reduction in the value of the machine over that year.

Depreciation in Practice The problem with implementing economic depreciation in practice is that the true rate of economic depreciation is typically unobserved and varies widely across assets. The economic depreciation of an office building may be quite low because wear and tear on the building is gradual. The economic depreciation of an industrial machine, however, could be much greater because of the wear and tear of the production process.

As a result of these uncertainties, the tax code has adopted a series of **depreciation schedules** for different classes of assets. One approach to depreciation is to take the typical life of an asset—ten years in our example— and divide the amount of depreciation equally into each year of the asset's life. This method is known as *straight-line* depreciation. In our example, this approach would appropriately measure economic depreciation.

depreciation schedules The timetable by which an asset may be depreciated.

In other cases, depreciation may be more rapid. For those cases, the government may offer *accelerated* depreciation schedules. The government could decide to allow firms to depreciate the cost of the machine over a shorter period of time—say, five years in our example instead of ten. Alternatively, within a given time frame the government could allow more front-loaded depreciation, with larger depreciation deductions earlier in the life cycle of the asset. In the extreme case, the government can allow corporations to **expense investments** in physical capital and deduct the entire cost of the asset in the year the investment is made.

expensing investments Deducting the entire cost of the investment from taxes in the year in which the purchase was made.

The key point for modeling the impact of the tax code on investment decisions is that *the value of depreciation deductions rises with the speed with which they are allowed.* This is because the present discounted value (PDV) of any tax break is higher the sooner you get the break.

Imagine that the firm in our example can borrow at a 10% interest rate, so the firm uses 10% as its discount rate for doing PDV calculations. Consider first economic depreciation (which is the same as straight-line depreciation in this case). The PDV of the set of depreciation allowances is:

$$10,000 + \frac{10,000}{1.1} + \frac{10,000}{(1.1)^2} + \ldots + \frac{10,000}{(1.1)^9} = \$61,446$$

Now, imagine instead that the firm is allowed accelerated straight-line depreciation, where it can depreciate $20,000 each year for five years. The PDV of that set of depreciation allowances would be:

$$20,000 + \frac{20,000}{1.1} + \frac{20,000}{(1.1)^2} + \frac{20,000}{(1.1)^3} + \frac{20,000}{(1.1)^4} = \$75,816$$

By speeding up the rate at which the firm can depreciate its machine, the government has allowed the firm to deduct over $14,000 more from its taxable income in present value. At the extreme, with expensing, the PDV of the depreciation deduction is $100,000, since the deduction is all taken in the first period.

▶ APPLICATION

What Is Economic Depreciation? The Case of Personal Computers

Personal computers are an excellent example of the difficulties in defining economic depreciation. Doms et al. (2003) gathered data on the market value of personal computers and modeled it as a function of the age of the PC. They found that the depreciation period for a PC is very rapid, on the order of only five years. Moreover, the depreciation during this period is *exponential,* not linear. They estimate that each period the value of the PC declines by 50% of its value at the start of the period. So after one year, the typical PC is worth only half its purchase value. After two years, it is worth only 25%; after three years, only 12.5%; and it is essentially worthless by the fifth year. This finding suggests that the depreciation schedules for PCs should be not only short but accelerated even within that brief time frame.

The researchers also reached another important conclusion: most of the depreciation of PC value is not due to actual wear and tear on the machine but to the *revaluation of the product* as microprocessors improve. A computer doesn't actually function 50% less well after one year in most cases, but it is worth only half as much because the new models are so much better, at similar prices.

Moreover, even the remaining depreciation caused by factors other than revaluation is also not from physical wear and tear. Instead, it is caused by software advances that are beyond the capability of older machines. This part of the depreciation becomes rapid after just a couple of years of PC life. Thus, economic depreciation is a subtle concept that goes far beyond physical depreciation of the actual machine. Tax policy makers face a daunting task in setting depreciation schedules appropriately across the wide variety of physical assets employed by firms in the United States. ◄

Corporate Tax Rate

Corporations are taxed on their net earnings (earnings minus expenses) according to a roughly progressive tax rate schedule, shown in Figure 24-3. The very smallest firms, with net earnings below $50,000 per year, pay a 15% tax rate. Tax rates then rise with a firm's net earnings, peaking at 39% for firms with net earnings between $100,000 and $335,000, before falling to 35% for firms with earnings of $1.833 million and above. The vast majority of large corporations face the 35% tax rate.[10]

Investment Tax Credit

The final component for computing corporate tax burdens is the **investment tax credit (ITC).** The ITC allows firms to deduct a percentage of their annual qualified investment expenditures from the amount they owe in taxes. The ITC had been a periodic feature of the U.S. corporate tax code but has not been in effect since 1986 (when firms could receive a credit amounting to

investment tax credit (ITC) A credit that allows firms to deduct a percentage of their annual qualified investment expenditures from the taxes they owe.

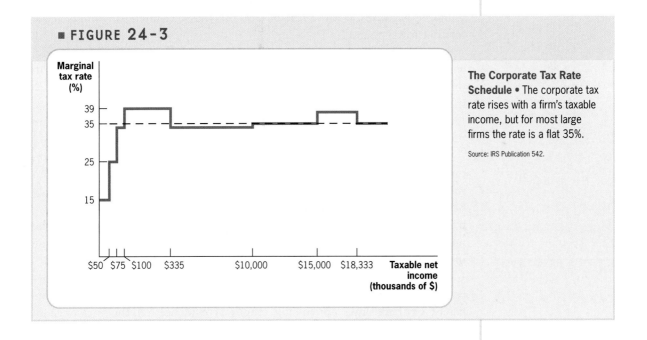

■ FIGURE 24-3

The Corporate Tax Rate Schedule • The corporate tax rate rises with a firm's taxable income, but for most large firms the rate is a flat 35%.

Source: IRS Publication 542.

---

[10] The "bubble" of a higher 39% rate between $100,000 and $335,000 was inserted so that both the average and marginal tax rates on firms above this size would be 35%.

6–10% of their investment expenditures, depending on asset life). While the ITC has not been available for many years, it is a constant source of discussion in corporate tax debates.

24.3

The Incidence of the Corporate Tax

The tools of general equilibrium tax incidence from Chapter 19 can be employed to assess the incidence of the corporate tax. Consider first the effect of the corporate tax on the goods market. A tax on producers will be shifted to consumers if demand for a good is at all inelastic. In turn, elasticity of demand for a good is determined by how easy it is for consumers to reduce their purchases or shift them to goods produced by the noncorporate sector or by foreign producers. Since the corporate sector produces the majority of goods and services in the economy, demand is not likely to be perfectly elastic. Thus, at least some of the corporate tax is reflected in higher prices for consumers. In the long run, as consumers are more able to adjust their purchases, demand will become more elastic and consumers will bear less of the tax.

To the extent that corporations bear some of this tax, we must then assess how the tax is distributed across labor and capital. Since the corporate sector employs such a large share of workers in the United States, it seems likely that the supply of labor to that sector is not perfectly elastic. Therefore, when corporations pay taxes, at least some of the costs may be shifted to workers in the form of lower wages.

In the short run, the capital supply to the corporate sector is fairly inelastic, and capital therefore bears much of the incidence of corporate taxation. In the long run, however, capital is more mobile because investors can turn to the noncorporate sector or to opportunities in other countries' economies. Indeed, capital is more mobile than labor in the long run because workers are unlikely to move abroad in response to lower wages.

Corporate income taxation also has important general equilibrium effects on the noncorporate sector as well, through spillovers. As capital moves from the corporate to the noncorporate sector in the long run, it raises the supply of noncorporate capital, lowering the rate of return in the noncorporate sector until the after-tax return in the corporate sector equals the return in the noncorporate sector. Capital in the noncorporate sector therefore bears some of the incidence of a tax on corporate capital in the form of lower returns.

Thus the burden of the corporate tax is shared by consumers, workers, corporate investors, and noncorporate investors in some proportion. Unfortunately, we have little convincing empirical evidence on the incidence of corporate taxation. The true incidence of the corporate tax remains one of the primary mysteries of public finance. What seems clear, however, is that assuming all the burden of the corporate tax is on investors, as the CBO does (see Chapter 19), is likely to be incorrect.

24.4

The Consequences of the Corporate Tax for Investment

We now turn to discussing the efficiency consequences of the corporate tax. In particular, there is significant concern that the corporate tax may reduce the amount of investment undertaken by firms.

Theoretical Analysis of Corporate Tax and Investment Decisions

To understand the effect of corporate taxation on investment decisions, we begin by modeling the investment decision in a world of no corporate taxes. The investment decision is determined by firms setting the marginal benefits and costs of investment equal on a per-period basis; the firm estimates the return it will get from its investment in each period (the benefit), compares that to the cost of the investment in each period, and invests only if the benefits are larger than the costs.

Suppose that each dollar of investment in a machine produces MP_K cents of additional output in each period (the marginal product of the machine), which is the benefit of investment. In each period, the machine depreciates in value by a linear amount δ per dollar (such as 10¢ for each dollar of machinery investment). This depreciation is not, however, the total cost of the machine to the firm in one period; the firm also has to finance the machine's purchase. As we discussed earlier, there are several ways in which a firm can finance its investments. Suppose this firm finances its investment by selling equity shares in the firm. In return it has to make dividend payments each period of ρ per dollar borrowed. In this case, the total cost of the machine in each period is depreciation + dividend = $\delta + \rho$. If the depreciation rate is 10% and the firm pays out 10% of the value of the investment in dividends (the dividend yield) each period, then the per-period cost of investing \$1 in a machine is $\delta + \rho = \$0.10 + \$0.10 = \$0.20$.

We can analyze the implications of corporate taxation for firm investment decisions graphically. Figure 24-4 (page 702) shows how the marginal cost and marginal benefit curves for investment determine the amount of investment made (K). The marginal benefit curve measures the *actual* return to each dollar of investment in each period, MP_K. Marginal benefit falls as investment increases, due to the assumption of diminishing marginal product; there is a lower return to each additional dollar of investment since there is a lower marginal product of each additional dollar of capital. The marginal cost curve measures the *required* return to each additional dollar of investment each period, or how much the investment must yield in each period in order to cover its costs (of depreciation and financing). The marginal cost is constant at $\delta + \rho = \$0.20$, as shown by the MC_1 curve.

Firms invest until the marginal dollar of investment results in equal costs and benefits, which occurs at point A, with a level of investment K_1. Firms

■ FIGURE 24-4

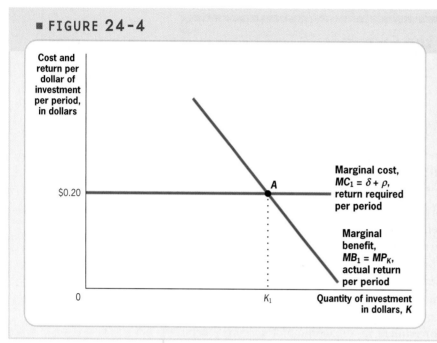

Investment Decisions with No Corporate Tax • With no corporate tax, the firm chooses its investment level by equating the marginal benefit of an additional dollar of investment with its marginal cost. The marginal benefit (MB_1) is equal to the actual return per dollar of investment, the marginal product of capital (MP_K). The marginal cost is equal to the required return per dollar of investment, the sum of depreciation (δ) and financing costs (ρ). This equality initially occurs at point A, with investment level K_1.

invest until the next dollar of investment yields just enough return ($0.20) to cover their costs in each period. If a firm invests less than this amount (to the left of K_1), the marginal return from an additional dollar of investment is above its marginal cost of $0.20, so the firm should invest more; if the firm invests more than this amount (to the right of K_1), the marginal return from that dollar of investment is below its marginal cost of $0.20, so the investment should not be undertaken.

The Effects of a Corporate Tax on Corporate Investment What happens if we introduce taxes into this story? Imagine first that the corporate tax is simply a tax at a rate τ on cash earnings minus labor costs (there are no tax deductions of any type for investment spending). The cash earnings per dollar spent on the machine per period is MP_K, so once this tax is imposed, the earnings per dollar spent on the machine drop to $MP_K \times (1 - \tau)$ (since the new tax must be paid on each dollar of earnings). This reduction in actual return causes the marginal benefit curve to shift down to MB_2, as shown in Figure 24-5: the taxation of corporate earnings has reduced the marginal benefit of investing. The costs per dollar of investment remain at $\delta + \rho$, so the marginal cost curve remains at its initial level. The new optimal investment choice is at point B, and investment falls to K_2.

Firms invest less when the government takes some of their return through corporate taxation. This is because the firm's after-tax actual rate of return on the investment must be large enough to meet the required rate of return, $\delta + \rho$. As a result, the pre-tax rate of return must be higher than it is without taxation, and that only occurs if the firm is investing less. For example, with a tax rate of 50%, the firm must earn $0.40 of return on a dollar of investment to

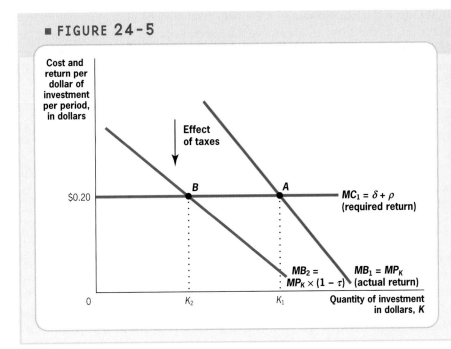

Investment Decision with a Tax on Corporate Income • Taxing corporate profits lowers the benefits of investment to $MP_k \times (1 - \tau)$, so that the marginal benefit curve shifts to MB_2. The firm lowers its investment, moving to point B, and a lower level of investment, K_2.

pay back its $0.20 of cost in depreciation and financing. Thus, the firm must invest less: it should stop investing at the point where the marginal dollar of investment has a $0.40 return rather than continuing to invest until that marginal dollar of investment has a $0.20 return. In this scenario, corporate taxation leads to less investment.

The Effects of Depreciation Allowances and the Investment Tax Credit on Corporate Investment

This description of the effect of taxes on corporate investment does not include the influence of tax deductions for investment, such as depreciation allowances or investment tax credits. These tax deductions act as discounts off the price of investments, lowering the marginal cost by offsetting some of the costs of financing and depreciation.

Recall that depreciation allowances are typically spread out over the purchase year and future years and that to value such streams of benefits we need to consider their present discounted value (PDV). The value of any given depreciation allowance schedule, z, is the PDV of the stream of depreciation allowances associated with a new machine purchase, as a fraction of the purchase price of the machine. If the firm could expense the machine (deduct its full value in the year of purchase), z would be 1.0, since the deduction allowance is 100% of the purchase price. As depreciation allowances are spread out over future years, z falls because the PDV of the depreciation allowances falls as the allowances become more distant.

Depreciation is subtracted from firm earnings in computing the base of corporate taxable income. Each dollar of depreciation allowances therefore saves the firm $\$\tau$ in corporate tax payments, since it lowers the tax base by $1.

If the depreciation allowances for a firm have a PDV of z, they are worth $\$(\tau \times z)$ to the firm. If a firm could expense its investment, for example ($z = 1$), and the firm's corporate tax rate was 35%, the depreciation allowance associated with each \$1 of the machine's purchase price would be worth \$0.35 to the firm in reduced tax payments.

In addition, in the past (but not since 1986) the tax system has allowed corporations to take advantage of an investment tax credit (ITC). The ITC provides the firm with a credit of α cents for each dollar of investment in the year that it makes the investment.

The availability of depreciation allowances and the ITC act as a rebate against the cost of investing. In essence, the cost of each dollar of machine in each period, previously $\delta + \rho$, has fallen to $(\delta + \rho) \times (1 - [\tau \times z] - \alpha)$, because the firm can offset these rebates against its costs of investing.

Figure 24-6 illustrates the effect of depreciation allowances and the ITC on a firm's investment decisions. As in Figure 24-5, the relevant marginal benefit curve for the firm is the after-tax MB_2. The reduction in the required return from depreciation allowances and the ITC lower the MC curve from MC_1 to MC_2, which now has a value of $(\delta + \rho) \times (1 - [\tau \times z] - \alpha)$. To see these changes numerically, return to the example used earlier: with a 10% depreciation rate per period (δ) and a 10% dividend yield (ρ), the pretax marginal cost curve was at \$0.20. Suppose that the depreciation schedule for this investment is such that the PDV of the depreciation allowances is equal to one-half of the purchase price of the machine ($z = 0.5$); that there is a 35% corporate tax rate; and that there is an ITC of 10%. In this case, the cost of each dollar of machine in each period (the return required by the investor on that dollar of investment) has fallen to $0.20 \times (1 - [0.35 \times 0.5] - 0.1) = \$0.145$.

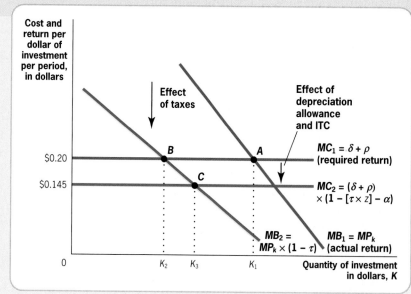

■ FIGURE 24-6

Investment Decisions with Depreciation and the ITC • ITC deduction of depreciation allowances and the existence of an investment tax credit (ITC) lowers the costs of investment from $(\delta + \rho)$ to $(\delta + \rho) \times (1 - [\tau \times z] - \alpha)$, shifting the MC curve down to MC_2. The firm moves to point C, with investment K_3, which is higher than before depreciation and the ITC but lower than in the no-tax world.

The new equilibrium is at point C, with a level of investment of K_3. This is the point at which after-tax marginal costs and after-tax marginal benefits for each dollar of machinery investment in each period are equal (where actual returns (MB_2 curve) equal required returns (MC_2 curve) for the marginal dollar of investment). The level of investment is higher than before depreciation allowances and the ITC (K_2), but remains lower than before taxation (K_1) (although, as we discuss below, it may in some cases be even higher than before taxation). The reduction in marginal benefits from earning after-tax returns exceeds the reduction in marginal costs from having depreciation allowances and the ITC, so investment still falls overall because of corporate taxation.

Effective Corporate Tax Rate Now that we understand how taxes affect a firm's investment decisions, we can summarize mathematically the net impact of the tax system on investment decisions. The effect of taxes is summarized by the **effective corporate tax rate,** the percentage increase in the rate of pre-tax return to capital that is necessitated by taxation. As shown in Figures 24-4 to 24-6, when taxes are imposed, the rate of return earned by the firm on its investments must rise to finance the tax payments. How much it must rise is a function of the tax rate, the treatment of depreciation, and the presence of the ITC. These factors therefore come together to determine the overall effect of taxation on investment decisions.

effective corporate tax rate The percentage increase in the rate of pre-tax return to capital that is necessitated by taxation.

Consider first the simple corporate tax system of Figure 24-5, with a tax at 35% on corporate earnings and no depreciation allowance or ITC. Before taxation, the firm's actual rate of return must be at least the required rate of return of 20%. After this 35% corporate tax, the firm's actual rate of return must be at least $0.2/(1 - 0.35) = 0.307 = 30.7\%$ to meet the required return of 20%. The firm must earn a rate of return that is 35% higher on its investments to pay its taxes and to meet the required return to pay its depreciation and financing obligations. As a result, the effective corporate tax rate is the statutory corporate tax rate, 35%.

More generally, the effective corporate tax rate (ETR) is measured as:

$$\text{ETR} = \frac{F_k \text{ (after tax)} - F_k \text{ (before tax)}}{F_k \text{ (after tax)}}$$

Because of corporate taxes, the marginal product of each dollar of investment F_k must be higher in order to pay its taxes and meet the required rate of return. With no depreciation allowance or ITC, F_k must be 35% higher due to taxation.

Now consider the more realistic corporate tax system in Figure 24-6, with a corporate tax rate of 35%, as well as a depreciation allowance and ITC. In this case, the firm must have a higher rate of return to pay taxes on its earnings, but it can have a lower rate of return since the cost of the machine is subsidized by depreciation and ITC. With depreciation and the ITC, the effective tax rate is:

$$\text{ETR} = \frac{(1 - [\tau \times z] - \alpha)}{(1 - \tau)} - 1$$

For example, if z and α are both zero (the case with no depreciation allowances or ITC), the effective tax rate is τ, the statutory rate. In our example, with $z = 0.5$ and an ITC of 0.1, the effective tax rate is:

$$\text{ETR} = \frac{(0.35 - 0.35 \times 0.5 - 0.1)}{(1 - 0.35 \times 0.5 - 0.1)} = \frac{0.075}{0.725} = 10.3\%$$

Because of the value of the depreciation deductions and the ITC, the effective tax rate is now only 10.3%, despite the 35% statutory rate. That is, the firm must earn a pre-tax rate of return that is only 10.3% higher than the rate it earned before taxation in order to meet its required rate of return of 20%. This is lower than the statutory rate because the ITC and depreciation allowance offset some of the effect of taxation.

Negative Effective Tax Rates

With a large enough z and ITC α, the effective corporate tax rate could be negative. If the firm in our example could expense its machine and deduct the full cost of the machine in the period of purchase, so that $z = 1$, then the effective tax rate would be:

$$\text{ETR} = \frac{(0.35 - 0.35 \times 1 - 0.1)}{(1 - 0.35 \times 1 - 0.1)} = \frac{-0.1}{0.55} = -18.2\%$$

A negative effective tax rate would mean that the MC curve falls so much in Figure 24-6 that point C is to the right of point A, and the firm invests more with taxes (K_3) than it did without them (K_1).[11]

Policy Implications of the Impact of the Corporate Tax on Investment

The mathematics of the previous section show the varied impacts that corporate tax structures can have on firm investment decisions. For any given corporate tax rate, the tax system can be designed to offer very different incentives for investment. A tax system that simply taxed corporate income, with no deductions for depreciation or investment tax credit, would clearly reduce investment levels by lowering the marginal benefit (after-tax return) of each dollar of investment. Allowing depreciation, particularly if it is accelerated, investment tax credits can mitigate or even reverse the negative effect of taxes on investment by lowering the required return to an investment. When a company buys a machine, it receives the embedded tax advantages of having purchased that machine. The faster depreciation is and the larger the investment tax credit is, the larger those tax advantages are.

---

[11] A negative effective corporate tax rate is more likely if the firm has financed its investment with debt rather than equity. Recall that interest payments on a firm's debt are tax-deductible. This deduction lowers even further the cost of financing investment, because financing through debt costs only $\rho \times (1 - \tau)$ rather than the full ρ.

As a result, the effective marginal tax rate for corporations has varied widely during the recent past, from a high of 51% in 1980 to a low of 27% in 2003. Two particularly interesting episodes involve the major tax acts of 1981 and 1986, as reviewed in the Application.

▶**APPLICATION**

The Impact of the 1981 and 1986 Tax Reforms on Investment Incentives

Two of the most important pieces of government legislation of the 1980s were the major tax reform acts of 1981 and 1986. The 1981 tax act introduced a series of new incentives to spur investment by corporate America. Depreciation schedules were made much more rapid and an investment tax credit was introduced. As a result, according to Fullerton (1987), effective tax rates (under certain reasonable assumptions about inflation, financing, and so on) on various capital assets averaged 29%, but the rates on equipment were actually *negative 18%* because of subsidization by the investment tax credit and accelerated depreciation schedules.

Further contributing to the low effective tax rates in the early 1980s were active tax avoidance and/or evasion strategies by corporations. Under the 1981 act, firms could "sell" each other tax breaks, similar to the ways firms can trade pollution permits as we read in chapters 5 and 6. Suppose that one firm had such large investment tax credits and depreciation allowances that it did not have to pay any more tax and still had several million dollars in depreciation allowances left over (beyond what was needed to bring the firm's tax liability to zero). Suppose that another firm had positive taxable earnings. The second firm could actually arrange to buy from the first firm its extra depreciation allowances, and the second firm could then use those depreciation allowances to offset its own earnings!

This point is not just a theoretical curiosity. Occidental Petroleum, with earnings of more than $700 million, managed to have no tax liability in 1981 and sold $30 million of its own tax breaks to a New York insurance company. General Electric managed to buy so many tax credits and depreciation rights that it not only reduced its 1981 tax liability to zero but also received a $100 million refund for past years' payments.[12]

This trading, combined with the accelerated depreciation schedules, led to a study by the research group Citizens for Tax Justice (CTJ).[13] CTJ studied 250 large companies that together earned profits of $56.7 billion from 1981 to 1983. In that period, 128 of the companies paid no federal taxes in at least one of those years. Seventeen companies paid nothing all three years, instead receiving total refunds of $1.2 billion while earning $14.9 billion in profits.

---

[12] Edsall (1982).
[13] McIntyre and Folen (1984).

GE earned $6.5 billion in profits over those three years but claimed $283 million in refunds. CTJ also found that 130 companies had a smaller effective average tax rate on their profits than the average American family: 0.3% compared to 12%.

In response to these types of findings, the Tax Reform Act of 1986 made three significant changes to the corporate tax code. First, it lowered the top tax rate on corporate income from 46% to 34%. Second, it significantly slowed depreciation schedules and ended the ITC (trades of tax breaks across firms had been ended several years earlier). As a result, the average effective tax rate on corporate income rose, from 21% in 1985 to about 28% in 1987.[14] This rise highlights the difficult nature of defining effective tax rates under the corporate tax code; effective rates can rise (as they did here, from 21% to 28%) even as the statutory rate falls (as it did here, from 46% to 34%). Finally, the 1986 act significantly strengthened the corporate version of the Alternative Minimum Tax (AMT) that we discussed for individuals in Chapter 18, providing a means of ensuring some tax payment from companies that were using loopholes to avoid taxation.

Corporate use of legal loopholes in the tax codes seems to have rebounded in the late 1990s, however, and continues to the present day. The 1990s saw a large and growing disparity between *book* income (income reported to owners) and *tax* income (income reported for tax purposes). The ratio between book and tax income was 1.0 in 1992, but by 1998 it had risen to 1.63; corporations were reporting 63% more income to their owners than the amount of income they were reporting for tax purposes, with an aggregate gap of $290 billion. According to Desai (2002), some of this difference is due to different accounting rules between the two sets of reports, but as much as half may be due to corporate tax-sheltering activities. More recently, a 2004 study by the General Accounting Office (GAO) of corporations doing business in the United States found that, from 1996 to 2000, over 61% of U.S.-controlled corporations reported no U.S. tax liability, while 71% of foreign-controlled corporations reported none.[15] ◄

Evidence on Taxes and Investment

There is a large literature investigating the impact of corporate taxes on corporate investment decisions. The conclusion of recent studies is that the investment decision is fairly sensitive to tax incentives, with an elasticity of investment with respect to the effective tax rate on the order of −0.5: as taxes lower the cost of investment by 10%, there is 5% more investment. This sizeable elasticity suggests that corporate tax policy can be a powerful tool in determining investment and that the corporate tax is very far from a pure profits tax.

[14] Maguire (2003).
[15] U.S. General Accounting Office (2004).

24.5

The Consequences of the Corporate Tax for Financing

The corporate tax has efficiency implications beyond the decisions of firms on how much to invest. Another potentially important decision that may be influenced by corporate taxation is how to *finance* that investment. As noted previously, firms have three primary choices for financing investment: they can use retained earnings, they can increase their debt by borrowing, or they can issue equity (ownership shares). Moreover, if a firm chooses the equity route, it has two choices on how to return earnings to investors: it can issue dividends or it can reinvest the funds and try to increase the value of the stock, leading to capital gains. For now, let's leave aside the less interesting case of financing investment through retained earnings, and focus on the impact of taxes on financing investment from new capital.

The Impact of Taxes on Financing

Suppose that a firm needs $10 for an investment that will yield $1 in corporate income each year. The firm wants to finance this investment through debt or equity, and in either case return that $1 to the investor. Figure 24-7 illustrates the impact of taxes on the firm's decision about how to finance that investment (once again ignoring the option, for now, of financing from retained earnings). At the first node, the firm decides to either take on debt or

■ **FIGURE 24-7**

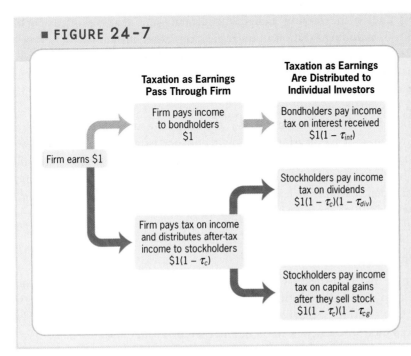

	Taxation as Earnings Pass Through Firm	Taxation as Earnings Are Distributed to Individual Investors

Firm earns $1

Firm pays income to bondholders
$1

Bondholders pay income tax on interest received
$1(1 − τ_{int})

Firm pays tax on income and distributes after-tax income to stockholders
$1(1 − τ_c)

Stockholders pay income tax on dividends
$1(1 − τ_c)(1 − τ_{div})

Stockholders pay income tax on capital gains after they sell stock
$1(1 − τ_c)(1 − τ_{cg})

The Firm's Financing Decision • When the firm wants to finance investment, it can do so either by issuing equity (stocks) or taking on debt (issuing bonds). If the firm takes on debt, then when it earns $1, it pays that $1 to bondholders, but it also subtracts the dollar from its taxable income, so that bondholders get the full $1, on which they pay interest taxes. If the firm issues equity, then when it earns $1, it pays that $1 to equity holders in the form of either dividends or capital gains. In either case, the firm has to pay corporate taxes on the dollar, and individuals then pay either dividend or capital gains taxes when they receive the dollar.

issue equity to finance the $10 investment. If the firm finances with debt (the top branch), it will pay the $1 in interest to bondholders. In this case, the firm will pay no taxes on the $1 in corporate income because interest payments are deductible from firm income for the corporate tax: the $1 in corporate income is offset by $1 in interest payments when computing taxes. The bondholder who has loaned money to the firm therefore receives the full $1, but then has to pay personal taxes on that $1 at the personal income tax rate on interest, τ_{int}, so the bondholder receives $\$1 \times (1 - \tau_{int})$.

Alternatively, the firm can issue equity to finance the investment. In this case, when the firm earns the $1 from the investment, it will not have the interest payment to provide an offsetting deduction for corporate taxation, so it will have to pay corporate taxes on the $1. Thus, only $\$1 \times (1 - \tau_c)$, where τ_c is the corporate tax rate, will get passed to shareholders.

If the firm uses equity finance, it has an additional decision: How should it get the money to the shareholders? With debt, there is no choice—the dollar is simply paid as interest. With equity, the firm has the choice of paying a dividend or retaining the earnings and reinvesting them. If it pays the dollar out as a dividend, then the stockholder has to pay dividend taxes on the dollar. Thus, the stockholder ultimately receives $\$1 \times (1 - \tau_c) \times (1 - \tau_{div})$, where τ_{div} is the personal tax rate on dividend income. This feature is often referred to as the *double taxation of dividends,* with dividends taxed by both the corporate and personal tax systems.

If instead the firm reinvests the $1, the stockholder will possibly reap a capital gain when she sells the stock share. Let's assume that each $1 of reinvestment increases the stock price by $1. In this case, the stockholder receives $\$1 \times (1 - \tau_c) \times (1 - \tau_{cg})$, where τ_{cg} is the *effective* capital gains tax rate. The effective capital gains tax rate is lower than the statutory capital gains tax rate for most investors due to the host of benefits to capital gains that we discussed in Chapter 23, including taxation upon realization rather than accrual and step-up of basis at death. The effective capital gains tax rate has also traditionally been far below the dividend tax rate. As of 2004, the statutory rates on capital gains and dividends are equal, at 15%, but the effective capital gains tax rate remains below the dividend tax rate.

As should be clear from Figure 24-7, the corporate tax structure can play a critical role in a firm's decisions on how to finance its investments. Financing through debt saves corporate taxation of earnings but does not allow individuals to take advantage of low capital gains tax rates. Financing by equity, and paying dividends, seems the least tax efficient route of all. This figure therefore raises two questions about corporate financing.

Why Not All Debt?

A company has two means of financing an investment. If it adds debt, the interest it pays to finance its investment is exempt from corporate taxation. If it adds equity, it pays the corporate tax. So why don't companies simply finance all their investment with debt and thereby avoid corporate taxation?

There are a number of specific answers provided to this question, but they all come down to the key distinction between debt and equity: debt requires fixed payments but equity does not. A firm can choose whether to pay dividends on equity, but it can't choose whether to make its interest payments: it must make them. If the firm doesn't make its interest payments, it defaults on its debts and can be forced into *bankruptcy*. In bankruptcy, all individuals who have invested in a firm can make claims on its remaining assets. Bondholders are the primary claimants; they are first in line to claim whatever assets may remain. Equity holders, in contrast, are only entitled to the resources left over after the bondholders have received their claims.

Imagine that you could choose the grading scheme for this course, and you had two choices. Under one choice you do a problem set each week, and if you ever fail one problem set you fail the course. Under another choice you do a problem set each week, and it is the average grade across all of your problem sets that determines your final grade. Most of us would choose the latter grading scheme because of its greater flexibility.

Likewise, the extra flexibility of equity can raise its value enough to offset its tax disadvantage. Equity finance can provide a "buffer zone" against the risk of bankruptcy; with equity, if times are bad the firm can simply not pay a dividend rather than being forced into bankruptcy. Managers in particular, who often care more about reducing the day-to-day risk of losing their job than about maximizing the return to the distant owners of a company, might prefer equity to debt.

This preference for equity, despite its tax disadvantages, is strengthened by a particular kind of agency problem within the firm: the conflict of interest between debt holders and equity holders. Debt holders are parties who get a fixed return (interest payment) regardless of how well the firm does, so long as the firm doesn't go bankrupt. Equity holders, in contrast, receive a return that is tied to firm performance: the share of earnings that is reinvested in the company grows in value as the company grows in value. In Figure 24-7, we assumed that each dollar reinvested in the firm yielded only a dollar in value. In reality, each dollar of investment earns an uncertain amount. Equity holders suffer when a corporate investment does poorly but benefit when it does well.

For equity holders, however, there is a lower limit to how badly they can lose when the company does poorly: all they can lose is their initial investment if the firm goes bankrupt. On the other hand, there is no upper limit to how well they can do when the company does well. Thus, when equity holders own only a small share of a company, they will want to take excessive risks, because they get a higher return but bear relatively little risk; since they own a small part of the company, they don't have that much money to lose. The possibility of excessive risk taking is a problem because equity holders make the decisions about whom to hire and, potentially, which projects to choose.

Consider a firm that currently has equity of $1 million and debt of $5 million, as shown in the top panel of Table 24-1 (page 712), for a total firm value of $6 million The firm's interest payment on the debt each period is $500,000. The firm currently has earnings of $600,000 per year, so that each

■ **TABLE 24-1**

The Debt vs. Equity Conflict

	Share of financing	Possible gain from investment	Possible loss from investment	Expected return from investment	Should the firm take the risk?
Equity holders	$1 million	$3 million	$2 million	$0.5 million	Yes
Debt holders	$5 million	0	$10 million	−$5 million	No
Equity holders	$5 million	$3 million	$10 million	−$3.5 million	No
Debt holders	$1 million	0	$2 million	−$1 million	No

In the top panel, equity holders control only $1 million of the firm's finances and debt holders control $5 million. The investment under consideration has, from the equity holders' perspective, a potential gain of $3 million and a potential loss of only $2 million, so that the expected return is positive and the investment will be made; but this is a mistake from the debt holders' perspective, since they have no gain and an expected $5 million loss. When equity holders control $5 million of the firm's assets, however, as in the bottom panel, the equity holders will not want to undertake the risky investment.

year it can pay the interest it owes its debt holders and pay the remaining $100,000 of earnings as a dividend to its equity holders.

Suppose that, in addition to this steady flow of earnings, the firm is offered a project that has a 50% chance of yielding $3 million and a 50% chance of losing $6 million. If the investment fails, the firm would go bankrupt, since it would have to sell its $6 million in assets ($5 million of debt and $1 million of equity) to pay the $6 million debt from losing. From an overall firm perspective, this is not a good risk to take. The *expected return* on this investment, the odds of winning times the value if the firm wins, plus the odds of losing times the value if the firm loses, is $(0.5 \times \$3 \text{ million}) + (0.5 \times -\$6 \text{ million}) = -\$1.5$ million, so the firm is better off not taking the investment because it loses money on average.

Now think about the project from the equity holders' perspective. If this investment hits, they get the entire $3 million, since they gain all the benefits from better firm performance. If the investment misses, and the firm goes bankrupt, they lose the $1 million they have invested, plus their dividend payment of $100,000 for each period in the future. At an interest rate of 10%, the present discounted value of this stream of dividend payments is $1 million, so equity holders lose a total of $2 million if the firm goes bankrupt.[16] From the equity holders' perspective, there is a 50% chance they will lose $2 million and a 50% chance they will gain $3 million, for an expected value to the equity holders of $500,000 ($[0.5 \times -\$2 \text{ million}] + [0.5 \times \$3 \text{ million}] = \$500,000$). So they will vote to take on this project.

What about the debt holders? They get nothing if this gamble hits, since the firm already earns enough to pay back its interest payments. But if the

---

[16] Recall from Chapter 4 that the PDV of an infinite stream of future payments is the payment level divided by the interest rate ($100,000/0.1 = \$1,000,000$).

gamble misses and the firm goes bankrupt, they not only lose their $500,000 per year in interest payments, but also their initial $5 million investment. So from their perspective, this is a gamble with a 50% chance of winning zero (if it hits, they still just get their $500,000 interest payment) and a 50% chance of losing $5 million in assets and $5 million PDV of future interest payments. For bondholders, the expected value of this investment is −$5 million.

In this case, there is a clear conflict of interest between equity and debt holders. The equity holders, who own the company and have control over the decision makers if not the decisions, would support taking on this project, while the debt holders would not. This is a problem because the equity share is so small. If the equity share were $5 million and the debt share were $1 million, equity holders wouldn't support this project. This is illustrated in the bottom panel of Table 24-1 (assuming that the firm now pays $500,000 in dividends to equity holders and $100,000 in interest payments to bondholders). In this situation, the equity holders don't want to risk the new investment because they have too much to lose: the expected return on the investment for them is now −$3.5 million. As before, the debt-holders also don't want to make this risky investment, since their expected value remains negative. In this case, the interests of the debt and equity holders are now aligned (they both lose money), and the project is not undertaken.

The key insight here is that *as the fraction of firm financing that is debt rises, the potential for this conflict of interest grows.* This potential grows because as the debt share rises, the debt holders bear a larger and larger share of projects that go bankrupt, while equity holders have a smaller and smaller risk from taking a gamble.

Now, imagine you work for a bank that is looking to loan its money to a small firm. Would you prefer to loan to a firm with 50% equity and 50% debt or one with 10% equity and 90% debt? By the logic of the example we've just explored, you would prefer to loan to the firm with 50% equity: because more of the owners' capital is at risk, they will make more sensible decisions. You worry that if you loan to the firm with only 10% equity it will take crazy risks that have negative expected value for you as the debt holder.

As a result of this agency problem, banks (and other lenders) will charge *higher interest rates on loans to firms as their share of debt financing rises.* These higher interest rates offset the tax advantage of debt, so that firms now face a trade-off: more debt means more tax advantage but potentially higher financing costs because banks fear loans to debt-heavy firms.

The Dividend Paradox

The second major mystery of corporation finance is why firms pay dividends. Having chosen the equity route for financing, if a firm earns $1, it can pay the dollar out as a dividend, triggering dividend income taxes, or it can reinvest the dollar, raising the value of the stock and allowing the recipient to take advantage of preferential capital gains tax rates when she sells her shares. The fact that effective capital gains tax rates are traditionally so much lower than dividend tax rates suggests that firms should reinvest rather than pay dividends, as long as they can find productive reinvestments for the firm. Yet about one-fifth of publicly traded firms pay dividends, though the number has been declining in the last couple of decades. Thus, we have another puzzle—why do firms pay dividends when capital gains are taxed so much less?

Empirical evidence supports two different views about why firms pay dividends, as reviewed by Gordeon and Dietz (2006). The first is an agency theory: investors are willing to live with the tax inefficiency of dividends to get the money out of the hands of managers who suffer from the agency problem. A recent study found that if 25 of the largest long-standing dividend payers in 2002 had never paid them, their cash holdings, currently $160 billion, would be $1.8 trillion! The authors suggest that such large cash stockpiles might be a recipe for disaster because of opportunistic managers, leading to inefficient investment or even outright corruption. Equity owners in that situation may therefore be willing to pay the price of dividend inefficiency to reduce the manager's control over firm assets.[17]

The second is a signaling theory: investors have imperfect information about how well a company is doing, so the managers of the firm pay dividends to signal to investors that the company is doing well. That is, the very fact that managers are willing to "burn money" by paying tax-inefficient dividends must prove that the company has cash to burn! By paying dividends, managers can prove to ill-informed investors that their investment is performing nicely.

How Should Dividends Be Taxed?

An important ongoing debate in tax policy concerns the appropriate tax treatment of dividend income. As we have seen throughout this chapter, the individual tax rate on dividends is typically higher than the effective tax rate on capital gains. According to the logic of Figure 24-7, a high-dividend tax rate can have three effects on firm financing decisions. First, it can reduce the use of dividends to repay equity holders. As reviewed in the Application on page 715, there is clear evidence that the 2003 reduction in dividend taxation led to an increase in dividend payouts.

Second, high-dividend taxes could push firms to choose debt rather than equity financing. Existing evidence suggests that higher-dividend tax rates cause firms to rely more heavily on debt.[18]

Finally, and perhaps most importantly, higher-dividend taxes could reduce investment. For those investors who receive their return in the form of dividends, the effective tax rate on investment will rise as the tax rate on dividends rises. This increase will lead those investors to require a higher pre-tax rate of return on investments, shifting up the marginal cost curve in Figures 24-4 through 24-6, and lowering investment (since, with diminishing marginal product, firms must lower investment to get a higher actual rate of return on the next dollar of investment). This outcome has caused many to argue that the double taxation of dividends lowers the rate of corporate investment in

---

[17] DeAngelo and DeAngelo (2004).
[18] Auerbach (2002).

the United States. Thus, reducing the dividend tax could, in principle, be a strong tool for increasing the nation's level of corporate investment.

This prediction, however, is derived from a model that can't predict why firms would pay dividends in the first place! In fact, both the agency and signaling models predict that higher tax rates on dividends will lead to *more* investment, not less. This is because in both models, dividends are wasteful, and taxing them more highly reduces their use; regardless of whether dividends solve agency problems or act as a signal, as their cost goes up (through higher taxation), they will be used less for that purpose. When firms pay fewer dividends, they have more retained earnings. Recent literature in corporate finance has suggested that the availability of retained earnings is an important, and perhaps the most important, determinant of investment financing.[19] Thus, taxing these inefficient dividend payouts will lead to more investment, not less. Unfortunately, to date there is little convincing evidence on the impact of dividend taxation on investment.

▶ **APPLICATION**

The 2003 Dividend Tax Cut

One of the measures President Bush signed into law on May 28, 2003, under the Jobs and Growth Tax Relief Reconciliation Act, was a reduction in the rate at which dividends are taxed. Previously, dividends were taxed at 38.6%, well above the 20% capital gains rate. The 2003 law, however, reduced both the dividend and capital gains rates to 15%, making dividends significantly more attractive for investors, though the dividend provision expires in 2009, after which dividend tax rates will return to 38.6%.

Proponents of the dividend tax cut believed it would both stimulate the economy and end what they perceived as the unfair practice of taxing corporate income and then taxing it again when that income was paid out in the form of dividends. Bush himself wanted the complete elimination of dividend taxes, arguing that, "ending the double taxation of dividends [along with his other proposed tax cuts] . . . is the best way to make sure this economy grows."[20] In this view, the tax cut would spur companies to offer more dividends and make investing more attractive to investors by placing more money directly in their hands.

Opponents of the dividend tax cut argued, however, that dividends are primarily received by higher income households and that such a tax cut would both worsen the country's fiscal balance and make the tax burden less progressive. Billionaire Warren Buffett noted that under one Senate proposal to eliminate dividend taxes entirely, he could have used his shares of the company Berkshire Hathaway to "receive $310 million in additional income, owe not another dime in federal tax, and see my tax rate plunge to 3%."[21] Although

---

[19] The hypothesis that firm-retained earnings is a central source of investment financing was first tested by Hubbard, Fazzari, and Petersen (1988). Recent strong evidence in support of this view is provided by Lamont (1997), who showed that oil company investments fell when they had less cash on hand due to declining oil prices, and Rauh (2004), who showed that firm investments fell when the government mandated they contribute more to their pension funds.

[20] Powell (2003).

[21] Buffett (2003).

the elimination of dividend taxes did not ultimately pass, the rate reduction did and it was predicted that this reduction would cost the government roughly $80 billion over the next decade.

Several recent papers have studied the impacts of the 2003 tax reduction. There has been a clear rise in dividend payouts, as would be predicted by both the standard model and the two alternative explanations discussed earlier. Chetty and Saez (2006) found that dividend payouts, which had been flat for four years before the policy change, rose by about one-quarter in the wake of this policy change. Moreover, they found that this increase was concentrated in firms whose stockholders benefited most from the lower dividend taxes, as opposed to firms whose primary shareholders are non-taxable institutions (such as pension funds). The key question of whether this tax cut actually raised investment, however, remains unanswered. ◄

Corporate Tax Integration

corporate tax integration
The removal of the corporate tax in order to tax corporate income at the individual (share-holder) level.

While recent legislation has reduced the tax rate on dividends, a larger question remains: Why should the tax system treat corporate income differently depending on how it is returned to shareholders? An alternative approach to corporate tax policy would be **corporate tax integration,** removing the corporate tax and taxing corporate income at the individual level. A typical approach to corporate integration would be to attribute the earnings of the corporation each year to its shareholders, regardless of whether those earnings are paid out as dividends. An individual who owned 5% of a company would be assigned income equal to 5% of the company's earnings at tax time, and the company itself would owe no taxes.

Such an approach would remove any tax favoritism in paying out corporate earnings to shareholders in one manner versus another, since earnings would be taxed at the shareholder level, regardless of how those funds were returned to shareholders. Moreover, this approach would tax corporations just like non-corporate entities, such as partnerships, are taxed. It would remove any bias that the corporate tax may cause in the decision to move between corporate and noncorporate status. Some research suggests that firms choose to move out of the corporate sector as the tax burden on corporations (relative to non-corporate entities) rises.[22] This high elasticity suggests that there may be sub-stantial deadweight loss from firms being in the wrong state of incorporation solely due to tax incentives. Corporate integration would therefore further lower the deadweight loss from corporate taxation.

Such a reform, however, would reduce federal government revenues since all corporate income would be taxed once, not twice, as occurs for equity invest-ment. The tax savings from integration would accrue primarily to the high income investors who hold the most shares in corporations. Thus, as with many reforms to the corporate income tax, the efficiency gains of integration must be offset against the reductions in the vertical equity of the tax system.

---

[22] Goolsbee (2002).

24.6

Treatment of International Corporate Income

Corporations around the world are functioning in an increasingly integrated world product market. As a result, there may be a number of reasons why firms in the United States would want to produce in other nations, such as lower labor costs, lower transportation costs when selling the product in those nations, or a better ability to customize products to local tastes. Firms that operate in multiple countries are called **multinational firms,** and the production arms of the corporation in other nations are called the firm's **subsidiaries.**

Production costs or sales advantages are not the only reason why firms produce goods abroad. The corporate tax structure in the United States and in other nations may also play a role. In this section, we discuss the treatment of international income in the U.S. corporate tax structure.[23]

multinational firms Firms that operate in multiple countries.

subsidiaries The production arms of a corporation that are located in other nations.

How to Tax International Income

There are two basic approaches to taxing corporations that earn income abroad.[24] The first is a **territorial system,** whereby corporations earning income abroad pay tax only to the government of the country in which the income is earned. The second is a **global system,** whereby corporations are taxed by their home countries on their income regardless of where it is earned. About half of OECD nations, including the United States, use the global approach.

U.S. firms therefore pay their U.S. corporate tax obligation wherever their plants or factories are located. Firms can, however, claim any tax payments to foreign governments as a credit against their U.S. taxes. Because of this **foreign tax credit,** firms should, in principle, pay the same tax rate (the U.S. corporate tax rate) regardless of where they locate their subsidiaries. In practice, however, this is not the case, leading to a tax advantage to earning income in other nations. This tax advantage has two causes: the PDV gain of delaying tax payments on income earned in other nations and the ability to shift profits from high- to low-tax nations.

Foreign Dividend Repatriation The first tax advantage of foreign income is that firms are taxed only on their international income when the income is returned, or **repatriated,** from the foreign subsidiary to the U.S. parent company. As a result, U.S. firms will never face U.S. taxes as long as they retain their foreign earnings at their foreign subsidiaries. For a subsidiary in a nation

territorial tax system A tax system in which corporations earning income abroad pay tax only to the government of the country in which the income is earned.

global tax system A tax system in which corporations are taxed by their home countries on their income regardless of where it is earned.

foreign tax credit U.S.-based multinational corporations may claim a credit against their U.S. taxes for any tax payments made to foreign governments when funds are repatriated to the parent.

repatriation The return of income from a foreign country to a corporation's home country.

---

[23] This discussion draws on the review in Gordon and Hines (2002). Another interesting issue discussed in that article, but not reviewed here, is the sensitivity of foreign investment to a nation's tax rates. The available evidence suggests that companies are very sensitive to tax rates in deciding where to locate their investments across countries.

[24] While this discussion is about corporate taxation, many of the concepts introduced here are applicable as well to the tax treatment of individual income earned abroad.

with low corporate tax rates, relative to the United States, this tax structure provides a strong incentive to defer repatriation of earnings. For example, if the foreign nation has a corporate income tax rate of only 10%, while the rate is 35% in the United States, the firm can defer taxation in the amount of 25% of earnings by not repatriating those earnings from the foreign subsidiary back home to the United States. This deferral is a tax advantage because those remaining U.S. taxes (the 25%) are paid in the future when earnings are eventually repatriated, so the present value of tax payments on foreign income is lower than if taxes were paid when the income was earned. If the money is *never* repatriated, the corporation avoids paying any U.S. tax on its foreign earnings altogether.[25] This is very similar to the tax advantage of taxation of capital gains on realization rather than on accrual: the effective rate is lowered because taxes are paid in the future.

► **APPLICATION**

A Tax Holiday for Foreign Profits

The proper taxation of foreign profits was the focus of the debate around the passage of the American Jobs Creation Act of 2004. As indicated by its name, the bill was intended to rejuvenate the economy and create jobs. One of its most important provisions was a one-year reduction of the tax rate on repatriated profits from 35% to 5.25%. The hope was that multinational firms would take advantage of the one-year window by repatriating billions of dollars in profits currently held overseas. By including restrictions on what the repatriated profits could be spent on, lawmakers intended to funnel as much of the incoming money as possible into jobs-producing activities such as research and development. A study partly funded by corporate supporters of the bill concluded that the legislation could add as many as 666,000 new jobs in the two years after its passage.[26] As one of the bill's leading supporters, Senator John Ensign from Nevada said, "There is not a lot of incentive for U.S. companies to bring money back from overseas now because of the high tax penalty. This legislation is exactly the extra boost our economy needs."[27]

Critics of the bill voiced a number of concerns. One of these was the difficulty in controlling how companies would spend the repatriated money. As Christopher Senyek, an accounting analyst at Bear Stearns, explained, "Since cash is fungible, there's really no way to track it."[28] Others were skeptical of the bill's ostensible intention of stimulating the economy. They reasoned that the profits being brought home would simply free up money that would have

---

[25] Desai et al. (2001) compare the behavior of U.S. foreign *subsidiaries,* which do not pay U.S. tax on foreign income until it is repatriated, with that of U.S. foreign *branches,* which do pay tax on income when it is earned, regardless of repatriation. They find that foreign subsidiaries in low-tax locations are significantly less likely to repatriate dividends than are foreign branches in the same country, which is consistent with tax-motivated repatriations.
[26] Groppe (2003).
[27] Andrews (2005).
[28] Aeppel (2005a).

gone into investment and creating jobs anyway. According to Philip L. Swagel, a former chief of staff on President Bush's Council of Economic Advisors, "There will be some stimulative effect because it pumps money into the economy. But you might as well have taken a helicopter over 90210 [Beverly Hills] and pushed the money out the door. That would have stimulated the economy as well." These critics argued that, in the end, the bill would only reward companies who had been most successful in hoarding their profits in overseas tax havens.[29] Related to this final point was a serious concern about the role this bill would play in the larger debate concerning deferral and the U.S. system of international taxation: many worried that allowing this one-time tax holiday would actually further encourage multinationals to keep their profits abroad in the future by raising expectations that Congress might allow other tax holidays further down the road. As George Plesko, an associate professor of accounting at the University of Connecticut in Storrs, put it, "Once you have this precedent, why shouldn't a company expect it to happen again?"[30]

By October 2005, U.S. companies had announced the repatriation of roughly $206 billion—an amount representing nearly $37 billion in lost revenues due to the lower tax rate.[31] However, it was clear that the expected surge in hiring and job creation was not materializing. In one particularly perverse example, Ford Motor Company repatriated $850 million of overseas profits in 2005 under the American Jobs Creation Act, thus saving about $250 million in taxes. Yet in January 2006, the company announced it had cut 10,000 jobs in that same year and was planning to cut 30,000 more.[32] As of this writing, a final evaluation of the bill's effects has not yet been compiled because many companies operate according to the fiscal calendar and thus have been able to extend the deadline for repatriation well into 2006. ◀

Transfer Pricing The second reason why firms with multinational operations may pay less tax is that when a good is produced using inputs from many nations, it is difficult to appropriately attribute the profits earned on that good to any particular nation. In particular, companies will have an incentive to report profits as being earned in nations with low corporate tax rates, and report expenses as being incurred to offset earnings in nations with high corporate tax rates. A company can accomplish this goal by manipulating its **transfer prices,** the amount that any of the company's subsidiaries reimburse any other of the same company's subsidiaries for goods transferred between the two.

Imagine that France levies a 50% tax on corporate profits, compared to the 35% corporate tax rate in the United States. An American computer company has a French subsidiary that manufactures microchips at a cost of $100

transfer prices The amount that one subsidiary of a corporation reimburses another subsidiary of the same corporation for goods transferred between the two.

[29] Weisman (2005).
[30] Aeppel (2005b).
[31] Aeppel (2005a).
[32] Sloan (2006).

each. The American company transfers those microchips to the United States, where it spends another $500 on the rest of the computer, then sells the whole package for $1,000. So the total profit on the transaction is $400. How does the company decide to allocate that $400 in profit between the American parent and the French subsidiary?

The American company could say that the entire $400 profit is due to the microchip, and could transfer $500 to its French subsidiary in exchange for each chip (the cost of $100 plus profits of $400). On paper, the French subsidiary would make a $400 profit (the $500 transfer from the United States minus the $100 cost of producing the chip) and would pay $200 in taxes (0.50 × $400) to the French government. The American company records no profit, since it sells the computer for $1,000 and records costs of $500 to its French subsidiary for the chip and $500 to its U.S. plant for producing the computer.

At the other extreme, the American company could say that none of the $400 profit is due to the microchip and transfer only $100 to its French subsidiary in exchange for each chip. In that case, the French subsidiary makes no profit, while the American company makes $400 in profit on each computer ($1,000 − $500 − $100). The company thus pays only $140 in taxes (0.35 × 400), this time to the U.S. government.

The American company can thus lower its taxes by $60 per computer by transferring only $100 to the French subsidiary. The transfer-pricing problem arising from this practice is that companies will have the incentive to make profits appear as if they were earned in the low-tax country.

The United States and other OECD countries are aware of this problem, and tax authorities in those nations require that in transactions between a firm and its foreign subsidiaries, transfer prices be recorded as if the exchange had occurred at "arm's length," as if two separate, unrelated firms had negotiated the price. In practice, this rule is extremely difficult to enforce and, in many cases, to interpret. There is substantial evidence that corporations manipulate prices and profits across subsidiaries to reduce tax burdens. For example, Collins et al. (1998) found that U.S. multinationals report greater foreign profitability if they face foreign tax rates below those of the United States.

Perhaps the largest recent example of such a scheme involved Glaxo-SmithKline, a drug company based in the United Kingdom that sells the ulcer drug Zantac through subsidiaries in many other nations.[33] Glaxo has a subsidiary in the United States, which is, in this case, the higher-tax country, so it could reduce its taxes by shifting expenses to the United States and profits back to the United Kingdom. According to the U.S. Internal Revenue Service, Glaxo did exactly that by overpaying royalties on Zantac to its British parent company, which did the research and development of the drug. These large royalties led to higher tax payments in Britain and lower tax payments in the United States, since the U.S. subsidiary could deduct the royalties as a cost of doing business. As a result, in January 2004 the IRS demanded payment of

---

[33] Stewart (2004).

$5.2 billion from the company—$2.7 billion in back taxes owed from 1989 to 1996 and $2.5 billion in interest. There will probably be further charges for tax avoidance from 1997 to 2000. To complicate matters, Britain's Inland Revenue (its version of the IRS) has sided with GlaxoSmithKline, saying that the company has paid appropriate taxes on profits in Britain and that further payments would amount to double taxation. It is unclear how the dispute will be resolved.

24.7

Conclusion

Despite the declining importance of the corporate tax as a source of revenue in the United States, it remains an important determinant of the behavior of corporations in the United States. The complicated incentives and disincentives that the corporate tax creates for investment appear to be significant determinants of a firm's investment decisions. And both corporate and personal capital taxation substantially, although not completely, drive a firm's decisions about how to finance its investments.

The United States faces a difficult set of decisions about how to reform its corporate tax system. Despite repeated calls for ending "abusive corporate tax shelters," there has been little movement to end the types of corporate tax loopholes that cause such activity. Given the political economy discussion of Chapter 9, this lack of interest should not be surprising: corporate tax breaks have highly concentrated and powerful supporters, with only the diffuse tax-paying public to oppose them.

▶ HIGHLIGHTS

- Corporations are entities that typically feature separation of ownership from control over daily operations.

- The existence of the corporate tax can be motivated either as a pure profits tax or as the only means of ensuring that corporate earnings do not escape taxation.

- The corporate tax is levied on the difference between earnings and expenses. Defining the depreciation expenses associated with investment is a particularly difficult issue.

- The incidence of the corporate tax is unclear, with the tax falling in unknown proportions on consumers, workers, and owners of corporate capital.

- The corporate tax system has complicated effects on investment incentives. The effective tax rate depends not only on the statutory corporate rate but also on the treatment of depreciation, the investment tax credit, and the nature of investment financing.

- Existing evidence suggests that corporate investment is fairly responsive to effective tax rates on investment earnings.

- Despite a strong tax subsidy to debt, through the ability of firms to deduct interest payments from their corporate taxable income, firms are far from fully debt financed, perhaps due to agency problems. And, despite a strong tax disincentive for firms to pay dividends, they continue to pay them, perhaps as a means of removing money from opportunistic managers.

- The fact that the United States taxes multinational corporations on repatriated reported earnings causes some firms to delay repatriation and to underreport earnings through transfer pricing.

▶ QUESTIONS AND PROBLEMS

1. Gill Bates is the CEO of a large company. His compensation is based on current profitability. He's considering undertaking one of two investments available to the company: (a) one that yields profits of $500 million in each of the next 5 years and none thereafter, and (b) one that yields annual profits of $300 million over 20 years. He selects the first investment. How could this example illustrate the agency problem?

2. You are a manager of a company that just spent $80,000 to purchase a piece of equipment that is expected to function for six years. If you can borrow money at 7%, what is the PDV of the depreciation allowance under the following circumstances?

   a. You can expense the investment.
   b. You depreciate using straight-line depreciation methods.
   c. You depreciate over four years using accelerated straight-line depreciation methods.
   d. You depreciate using an augmented accelerated method in which half of the asset value is depreciated immediately and the other half is straight-line depreciated over the remaining three years.

3. Suppose that new machines cost $504, and the marginal benefit from new machines is $MB = 246 - 6K$, where K is the number of machines purchased. The depreciation rate is 15% and the dividend yield is 10%.

   a. What amount of capital will you purchase? Why?
   b. What amount of capital would you purchase if there were a 25% tax rate on cash earnings minus labor costs?

4. Suppose that dividend yield is 6%, depreciation is 12%, and the corporate tax rate is 35%. What would be the marginal cost of each dollar of machinery investment in the following situations?

   a. Firms are allowed to expense the machine.
   b. There is an investment tax credit of 8%.

5. Why has the effective capital gains tax rate tended to be substantially lower than the dividend tax rate in the United States? Given that this disparity exists, why do so many firms pay dividends?

6. Why are equity holders more likely than debt holders to want firms to engage in risky investments?

7. You conducted a research study and found that corporations that finance their investments with a larger ratio of debt to equity tend to pay higher rates of interest to lenders. Why do you think this practice occurs?

8. The government of Kapitalia changes its tax code to allow for more accelerated depreciation of assets. Would you expect firms to substitute production methods away from capital and toward labor, away from labor and toward capital, or neither? Explain.

9. Consider the psychological effects of dividend signaling. Which would seem a stronger signal of corporate health (or its lack): when a long-standing dividend payer stops paying dividends or when a firm that had not previously paid them begins to do so? Explain.

10. Suppose that all industrialized countries agreed to a compact specifying that the corporate income of multinational firms must be paid to the country where the parent firm is incorporated. What do you expect would happen to the number of multinational firms? Explain your reasoning.

11. Suppose that the corporate income tax rate is 30%, the personal income tax rate on dividend income and the interest tax rate are both 35%, and the capital gains tax rate is 20%. Compare the after-tax returns on each dollar of corporate earnings under three investment financing strategies: (a) the corporation finances by using debt; (b) the corporation finances by issuing equity but does not pay dividends; and (c) the corporation finances by equity and pays all of its income in dividends.

12. Different states have different corporate tax rates. How could you use this to study the elasticity of corporate investment with respect to corporate tax rates? What would be the problems with this approach?

▶ ADVANCED QUESTIONS

13. Megacola faces demand of $Q = 2,200 - 20P$. Its costs are constant at \$5 per unit.

    a. Show that Megacola will not change its behavior if the government introduces a 20% tax on its profits.

    b. Does the existence of firms such as Megacola strengthen or weaken the case for a corporate income tax? Explain.

14. Suppose that the corporate tax rate is 25%, there is an investment tax credit of 10%, the depreciation rate is 5%, and dividend yield is 10%. The official depreciation schedule is such that the PDV of depreciation allowances is 40% of the purchase price of a machine.

    a. Calculate the per-period marginal cost of each dollar that the firm spends on the machine.

    b. If the marginal benefit per period is $MB = 40 - 0.6K$, where K is the number of dollars spent on the machine, what is the optimal amount of machinery purchased?

    c. How would your answer change if the ITC increased to 20%?

15. The legislature in Tuneria has just passed a new law which will provide a large investment tax credit in one year. What pattern of investment would you expect to see over the next two years? What implications would this have for estimates of the elasticity of investment with respect to investment tax credits?

16. Reducing corporate tax rates is often considered as a policy tool to enhance investment. How could the presence of tax loopholes diminish the relationship between corporate tax rates and corporate investment?

The ℯ icon indicates a question that requires students to apply the empirical economics principles discussed in Chapter 3 and the Empirical Evidence boxes.

Fundamental Tax Reform

25

Vying to become the Republican presidential candidate in 1996, demi-billionaire Steve Forbes ran on a platform that emphasized the need for a *flat tax*. Forbes proposed to repeal the current personal and corporate income taxes, as well as the estate tax. A 20% flat tax (scheduled to drop to 17% after two years) would instead be levied on wages, pensions, and self-employment income. All itemized deductions and federal tax credits would be eliminated, but large exemptions would be offered against one's wages ($10,700 per taxpayer, $5,000 per dependent). "Unearned" income, such as interest, capital gains, and dividends, would no longer be taxed, though employer-paid fringe benefits, such as health insurance, would be. During a stump speech in South Carolina, Forbes declared, "The tax code today is nothing more than a cesspool of legalized corruption and special interest legislation. We should replace this monstrosity with a simple flat tax that is a tax cut for all Americans. . . . With a flat tax you'll keep more of what you earn and rip down barriers to job-creating investments so we can create more jobs and better-paying jobs too. This is the way to start to get America moving again."[1]

The appeal of this platform for its many advocates mirrors the dissatisfaction with the fundamental structure of the U.S. income tax. There is no shortage of criticism of the existing income tax: one can find many claims that the tax system is unfair to the poor or to the rich; that it is unfair to single people or to married couples; that it is too easy to evade, or that the government spends too much time harassing honest taxpayers; that it doesn't do enough to promote savings or that it provides too many loopholes for savings; and so on. As a result, fundamental reform of the income tax has become a centerpiece of public debate in recent decades.

In some cases, this debate has led to action. The most notable case was the Tax Reform Act of 1986 (TRA 86). In 1986, the U.S. individual tax code featured 15 tax brackets, ranging from rates of 11% to 50%. In addition, as noted

---

[1] This quote is from a February 29, 1996, speech in Aiken, South Carolina, the transcript of which is at http://www.pbs.org/newshour/bb/election/forbes_3-1.html.

in the previous chapters, there was accelerated depreciation, an investment tax credit, special tax treatment of capital gains, deductions for contributions to IRAs, and a variety of other avenues for avoiding taxes through *tax shelters,* which are activities with no economic value other than as a means for reducing tax payments. TRA 86 radically modified this system. The number of tax brackets was reduced to three, with rates of 15%, 28%, and 33%.[2] Realized capital gains were treated as regular income, IRA deductions were limited (as described in Chapter 22), and tax shelter opportunities were greatly reduced. In short, the tax system was reformed in the direction long advocated by tax analysts: lower rates on a broader base of income.

Many of the features of this reform, however, have been reversed in the subsequent two decades. Sizeable changes to the tax code in 1993, 1997, 2001, and 2003, as well as other minor changes along the way, have reintroduced both more brackets (we now have six tax brackets) and greater opportunity for tax avoidance and evasion. Thus, the time is ripe for once again rethinking the fundamental structure of the individual income tax, and in particular considering a move back to a low-rate, broad-based tax system.

In this chapter, we discuss fundamental tax reform in four steps. First, we discuss the three major arguments for moving to a low-rate, broad-based tax system: tax compliance, tax simplicity, and tax efficiency. Second, we discuss the difficult political and economic barriers to fundamental reform of the tax system. Third, we turn to a specific fundamental reform of the tax system that long has been of interest to public finance economists: moving from an income base to a consumption base for taxation. We discuss the pros and cons of such a switch and look at different alternatives for implementing consumption taxes in practice. Finally, we return to the example that motivated this introduction, the flat tax, and discuss its promises and pitfalls.[3]

"Hi, Mr. Topper. This is the I.R.S. Say, back in April, when you paid your tax, we had no idea of the sort of bills Uncle Sam would be running up, and—well, the long and the short of it is that we have to soak you again."

_25.1

Why Fundamental Tax Reform?

As noted in the introduction, there are three major arguments for fundamental tax reform: to increase tax compliance, to make the tax code simpler, and to improve tax efficiency. In this section, we review each of these goals.

---

[2] There were actually only two marginal rates—15% and 28%. There was a third bracket in practice because people with taxable income of $71,900 to $149,250 had to pay a 5% surcharge on the taxes they owed. For those with taxable incomes over $149,250, the marginal rate dropped back to 28%. This third "bracket" effectively caused some people who were in a middle income bracket to pay higher marginal rates than those in a higher income bracket.

[3] An excellent source for learning about tax reform debates is Slemrod and Bakija (2000).

Improving Tax Compliance

tax compliance Efforts to reduce the evasion of taxes.

tax evasion Illegal nonpayment of taxation.

Tax compliance is the willingness of individuals or corporations to obey the tax laws. To improve tax compliance, the government must reduce the amount of **tax evasion,** which is illegal nonpayment of taxation that takes place under a tax system. It is important to distinguish tax *evasion* from tax *avoidance,* or legal activities undertaken by individuals to shift income from taxable to nontaxable forms. When I buy more health insurance instead of earning wages, or spend my money on a business lunch rather than on a family lunch, I may be engaging in tax *avoidance,* taking action to reduce my tax burden, but fully within the limits of the law. If I simply do not pay the taxes I owe, or if I fail to report income or claim a tax deduction that is not within the limits of the law, then I am *evading taxes.*

▶APPLICATION

Tax Evasion

The distinction between tax *avoidance* and tax *evasion* is a fine one and there is a large community of tax lawyers and judges who struggle daily with this distinction. Nevertheless, clear instances of outright tax evasion do exist.[4] For example:

1. Stanley S. Tollman, a Manhattan hotelier, is now a fugitive from U.S. authorities, hiding in England from tax evasion charges. The 73-year-old Tollman, who once controlled the Days Inn hotel chain and a number of luxury hotels across the world, was indicted in April 2002 for hiding $100 million in profits from the sale of the Days Inn company. The indictment said that taxes were evaded on at least $32 million of income by running the money through secret accounts in the Channel Islands, British tax havens. Tollman's son Brett has since pleaded guilty to federal tax evasion charges, but his father has not returned to the United States.

2. The rich are not the only ones who evade taxes. For years, taxpayers wanting to claim tax exemptions for dependents were required only to fill in the names of their dependents on tax forms, leading to concern that individuals were making up names and claiming exemptions for dependents who did not exist. Indeed, when the 1986 Tax Reform Act required filers to list as well the Social Security numbers of dependents over the age of five, 6 million dependents suddenly disappeared from the tax rolls! Over 11,000 families lost seven or more dependents between 1986 and 1987. Two years later, when the tax law required that the Social Security numbers of child care providers be listed before

"It's funny how two intelligent people can have such opposite interpretations of the tax code!"

---

[4] These examples come from Johnston (2003a), Crenshaw (1991), and Russakoff (1998).

workers could claim their child care tax credits, 2.6 million child care providers disappeared!

3. Tax evasion is particularly common among workers who are paid in cash, which is harder for the IRS to trace. One New York–area house painter knocks hundreds of dollars off his price if his customers pay him in cash because he'll save more than that by not reporting the income on his taxes. The painter claims that "Out of 100 customers a year, at most 1 or 2 want [me] to pay taxes. Out of 1,000 in a dozen or so years, maybe there are 5 or 6." Former IRS commissioner Margaret Richardson tried to find Washington-area window cleaners willing to be paid not in cash but on the books, but eventually gave up, lamenting later, "I had dirty windows for four years." ◄

Theory of Tax Evasion Economists assume that individuals make their decisions to evade taxes in the same rational way that they make other decisions: by trading off the costs and benefits. The benefits of evading taxes are the avoided tax payments. The costs are the risk of getting caught and the penalty to be paid if caught.

This trade-off is illustrated in Figure 25-1, which graphs the marginal benefit and marginal cost per dollar of nonreported income on the vertical axis and the amount of nonreported income (evasion) on the horizontal axis. The marginal benefit per dollar of evasion is the marginal tax rate faced by the evader, since underreporting by \$1 saves tax payments of τ¢. The marginal benefit curve is therefore a horizontal line at τ. In Figure 25-1, the marginal tax rate is

■ **FIGURE 25-1**

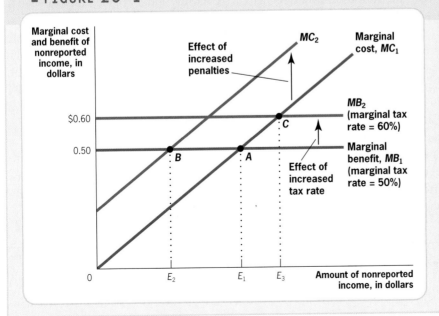

Optimal Tax Evasion • The marginal benefit of evading taxes is the tax payment saved per dollar of evasion, which is the marginal tax rate (initially 50% in this example). The marginal cost of evading is the rising odds of being caught and the larger penalties associated with higher levels of evasion. Optimal evasion occurs when these costs and benefits are equal at E_1. If penalties or odds of getting caught rise, the marginal cost curve shifts in from MC_1 to MC_2, and evasion falls to E_2. If the tax rate goes up, the marginal benefit curve shifts up from MB_1 to MB_2, and evasion rises to E_3.

50%, so the marginal benefit per dollar of evasion, $\tau \cancel{c}$, is a flat curve, MB_1, at $0.50. The marginal cost of evasion is the marginal penalty paid per dollar of evasion times the probability of getting caught. Both the penalty and the probability of getting caught are likely to rise with the amount of evasion, so that the marginal cost of evasion rises with the amount of evasion. The optimal amount of evasion, E_1, is found at point A, the point at which the marginal benefits and costs are equal.

This is an oversimplified model of cheating; some individuals, for example, would never cheat on their taxes regardless of the incentives to do so. The predictions of such a model are nevertheless in accord with common sense. If the penalties for the next dollar of cheating or the probability of getting caught rise, the marginal cost curve shifts up from MC_1 to MC_2 and the optimal amount of evasion is identified by point B. Individuals cheat less, evading an amount E_2. Alternatively, if the marginal tax rate rises to 60% (holding penalties, and thus marginal cost, constant at MC_1), the marginal benefit curve shifts up from MB_1 to MB_2. The optimal amount of evasion at the new marginal tax rate (at point C) rises to E_3, since individuals find it more worthwhile to cheat.[5]

Evidence on Tax Evasion Tax evasion is pervasive in the United States and around the world. In the United States, the most recent estimates place the "tax gap" between taxes owed and taxes paid at $280 billion, or 16.3% of tax revenue in that year (3.2% of GDP).[6] Other developed nations exhibit similar tax gaps; for example, in 1994 New Zealand estimated its own gap at 10.2% of tax revenue and growing. Developing nations fare even worse. The Philippines loses 73% of its individual income tax revenue and 40% of corporate income tax revenue; in Moldova (formerly part of the Soviet Union) the evasion rate jumped from 5% of revenues in 1994 to 35% in 1998 as Moldova began the transition to a free-market economy; and a recent study in Madagascar estimated its tax gap at 60% of total revenues.[7]

Some empirical studies have also found that the predictions of our simple model are borne out. For example, Clotfelter (1983) found that noncompliance is correlated with the marginal tax rate, with an elasticity somewhere between 0.5 and about 3.0; each 1% rise in the marginal tax rate leads to 0.5% to 3% more noncompliance. Perhaps most tellingly, Slemrod, Blumenthal, and Christian (2001) conducted an experiment in which they randomly sent letters to Minnesotans before tax returns were due, some of them threatening an audit (a thorough review of tax records to catch cheating), others appealing to people's consciences to be honest on their returns. The appeals to conscience had no effect, while the audit threats increased reported income for lower- and middle-class families. Interestingly, the audit threat served to *lower* report-

---

[5] Of course, if the government sets penalties as a function of the amount saved on taxes, as opposed to the amount of income evaded, then cheating incentives won't necessarily rise with the tax rate.

[6] U.S. General Accounting Office (2003); $50 billion of these revenues were eventually collected late in subsequent years, so the net tax gap is about $230 billion.

[7] New Zealand example from Giles (1999); Moldova example from Anderson and Carasciuc (1999); Madagascar example from Gray (2001).

ed income for upper-class families: the authors suggest that richer families may have seen the letter as the opening round in a negotiation, leading them to bid low (report low income) at first!

▶ APPLICATION

The 1997 IRS Hearings and Their Fallout for Tax Collection[8]

In September 1997, the Senate Finance Committee held a week of hearings to investigate abuses of taxpayers by the Internal Revenue Service, which collects the nation's taxes. Committee chairman William Roth expected to see "a picture of a troubled agency, one that is losing the confidence of the American people, and one that all too frequently acts as if it were above the law." Indeed, over that week the committee heard all sorts of damning testimony. A New York priest spoke of being hounded by the IRS to pay taxes he didn't owe on a trust set up by his recently deceased mother to help the poor. Investigators found one case of a man who committed suicide after a protracted battle with IRS agents over back taxes. Agents were accused of choosing audit targets based on political or personal considerations.

As a result of these hearings, political pressure for IRS reform grew rapidly. A new IRS commissioner, Charles O. Rossotti, was appointed with the aim of making the agency more taxpayer friendly, and in 1998 President Clinton signed the Taxpayer Bill of Rights, which protected taxpayers and created a congressional watchdog agency, the Treasury Inspector General for Tax Administration, which would function as an independent overseer of the IRS.

Two facts have become clear in the years since the original hearings. First, the testimony that made the IRS seem abusive and out of control actually painted a skewed and perhaps deliberately dishonest picture of the agency's operations. The star witness of the hearings, who had detailed his humiliation at the hands of IRS agents, was most likely involved in serious tax-evasion schemes and ultimately paid $23 million in back taxes. A 2000 General Accounting Office report on the alleged abuses found no corroborating evidence for *any* of the witnesses' testimony of systematic abuse. By that same year, the new watchdog agency set up in 1998 had investigated 830 complaints of harassment by IRS agents and had found many of them to be without merit or even bogus, intended by tax evaders to derail possible audits. Not one reached the legal standard of harassment.

Second, constrained by a lack of financial resources and new obligations under the Taxpayer Bill of Rights, the IRS's enforcement capacities have been severely impaired. From 1997 to 2000, the number of field examiners dropped by two-thirds, the number of collection cases closed fell by one-half, and the number of tax evasion cases pursued (other than for illegal activities such as drugs and terrorism) fell by two-thirds. Whereas in 1977 8% of corporations faced an annual audit, fewer than 1% do now. Between 1995 and 2001,

---

[8] Johnston (2003b).

audit rates of self-employed individuals (a particularly noncompliant group) fell from 4% to 2%. Perhaps most frustrating is the IRS's identification of $30 billion in underpayments, which it would cost only $2 billion to collect if Congress would provide the funding (the IRS knows exactly who owes the money but can't afford to pursue them).

Though the Senate hearings fueled popular resentment of the IRS and the subsequent moves to restrain its powers, the pendulum may be swinging back in the opposite direction. Evidence of corporate tax evasion in particular has Americans calling once again for fairness in the tax system, rather than mere protection. In response, the latest IRS commissioner, Mark Everson, has vowed to make enforcement a priority of his agency. Nonetheless, the damage may already be done. A 2003 survey by the IRS Oversight Board showed that 17% of Americans believe cheating on taxes is acceptable, up from 11% in 1999. ◄

Why Should We Care About Tax Evasion? It is clear that individuals evade taxes, but why should we care? Why not just raise taxes enough to cover the evasion? In principle, the same amount of revenue could be collected in a system with evasion and high rates as in one with no evasion and lower rates.

There are three reasons why we care about tax evasion and should want to reduce it. The first is efficiency. As we have highlighted repeatedly, efficiency is increased by broadening the tax base and lowering the tax rate (unless there is some positive externality to the excluded activity). Tax evasion clearly has no positive externalities, so efficiency will fall if we have to raise the tax rate to cover revenue losses due to cheating. Moreover, since cheating rises as the tax rate rises, raising the tax rate to offset the revenue loss from cheating is partially self-defeating.

The second reason why we care about tax evasion is vertical equity. The wealthy have a much greater scope for tax evasion than do lower-income groups, since much of the income earned by the wealthy is in forms that are not directly reported to the IRS, while most income taxes owed by lower-income groups are directly withheld from their wages. Consequently, cheating as a share of income is likely to be higher among the wealthy, so that a system with cheating will be less vertically equitable than one without. It is difficult to offset this inequity with higher rates on the rich, since this will just increase their cheating.

Finally, tax evasion is one of the clearest violations of horizontal equity that we have discussed in this book. Two individuals in very similar circumstances will be treated differently by the tax code if one is honest and the other is not. This is a clear violation of horizontal equity principles.

Making the Tax Code Simpler

At the end of 2003, the IRS sent taxpaying individuals a 131-page packet with instructions for completing their Form 1040 (the individual income tax form). On page 77 of the instructions, the IRS estimated that it would take between 13 and 14 hours to complete the tax forms, assuming that most income came in the form of wages and that there were no complicated investment activities and no deductions to itemize. Itemizing deductions, according to the IRS, would take another 6 hours; reporting small business activity would take 11 hours; and reporting capital gains would take 8 hours. This is a significant commitment of time and energy for many taxpayers. One study estimated that, in 2000, taxpayers spent 3.2 billion hours and $18.8 billion filling out tax forms, an average of 25.5 hours and $149 per filer.[9] As Slemrod and Bakija (2000) point out, this is the equivalent of "one and a half million hidden, unpaid IRS employees"!

Given these facts, a common rallying cry for tax reform is to increase tax simplicity by eliminating or limiting the complex administrative difficulties associated with paying taxes. Presidential candidate Steve Forbes wanted taxpayers to mail only a postcard to the IRS. General Wesley Clark, attempting to become the Democratic nominee in 2004, trumpeted a plan that would "simplify the tax process, eliminating dozens of pages of forms and boiling hundreds of pages of the tax code down to one easy-to-use form. With this new system, you can figure out whether or not you need to pay taxes just by filling out three lines. The first line is your income. The second line is your marital status. The third line is the number of children you have. . . . [In fact,] under my plan, more than half of America's taxpayers won't need to file any tax forms at all."[10] Table 25-1 compares the current tax system to Steve Forbes's flat-tax proposal, illustrating how much easier tax filing would be in the flat-tax world.

Simplicity of the tax code is clearly an admirable goal in theory. In many cases, tax simplicity is also consistent with other equity and efficiency goals. But in other cases, achieving other worthwhile goals may be incompatible with simplification. In those cases, the government must trade off the benefits of simplification against the costs in impeding other policy goals.

Consider, for example, the inclusion of employer-provided health insurance in the individual tax base. This inclusion might be suggested by a Haig-Simons definition, since these are contributions to an individual's ability to pay taxes. Including employer-provided health insurance would increase tax fairness, as discussed in Chapter 18, as measured by either horizontal or vertical equity. It would most likely increase tax efficiency as well by broadening the base of income subject to taxation and allowing a lower tax rate (unless

■ **TABLE 25-1**

Simplicity Advantages of a Flat Tax

Current tax system	Forbes's flat tax
Gross income (wages, interest, etc.) – Deductions	Wage income – Exemptions
= Adjusted gross income (AGI) – Exemptions – Itemized (or standard) deduction	= Taxable income

= Taxable income
  ⎡ Use income tax schedule
  ⎣ (Figure 18–3)
	⎡ Multiply by 20% ⎤

= Taxes owed – Credits	
= Total tax payment – Withholding	= Total tax payment – Withholding
= Final payment/refund due	= Final payment/refund due

The definition of the tax base is much more complicated under our current income tax system than it would be under a flat tax.

---

[9] Guyton et al. (2003).
[10] From Wesley Clark's campaign Web site, http://www.clark04.com/.

there are strong externality or market failure arguments for subsidizing health insurance in this way).

Yet including employer health insurance spending in the tax base would substantially increase the complexity of the tax code. Employers would have to report to the government and to individuals each year the amount that employers contributed to health insurance on their employees' behalf, which would require extra record keeping and reporting. Individuals would have yet another item to report on their individual income tax. The complications would multiply if, as discussed in Chapter 15, this tax exclusion was not removed but rather capped; then employers and individuals would have to figure out how to pay taxes on just employer spending above that capped level. Thus, achieving tax simplicity may come at the cost of sacrificing other goals of tax reform.

Improving Tax Efficiency

In the optimal income tax model of Chapter 20, the cost of raising tax rates was the potential reduction in labor supply. More generally, what matters for the efficiency cost of taxation is the entire array of behavioral responses to taxation. The motivation for many fundamental reforms, such as the flat tax advocated by Steve Forbes, is to reduce the marginal tax rates that potentially distort decisions on how hard to work, how much to save, or how much risk to take. Moreover, changes in tax rates affect not only decisions on labor supply, savings, and risk taking, but also many other decisions, such as how much child care to use and how much to give to charity.

As we contemplate tax reform, we can summarize this array of behavioral responses to taxation by asking a simple question: How does changing the tax *rate* change tax *revenues*? The overall efficiency of the tax code is a function of the *elasticity of tax revenues with respect to the tax rate*.[11] As this elasticity rises, the deadweight loss from taxation rises, highlighting the equity–efficiency trade-off that underlies the optimal income tax discussion of Chapter 20.

Changing the tax rate changes tax revenues through five channels:

1. **Direct effect:** A higher tax rate raises revenues on a fixed base of taxation.

2. **Indirect effects:**
   a. *Gross income effect:* A higher tax rate may reduce gross income generated by lowering the amount of labor supplied, the savings undertaken, or risk taking. (This was the subject of the research literature discussed in Chapters 21–23.)

direct effect of tax changes A higher tax rate that raises revenues on a fixed base of taxation.

indirect effects of tax changes A higher tax rate that lowers the size of the revenue base on which taxes are levied.

---

[11] As discussed by Saez (2004), this is only strictly true if the substitution into and out of taxed activities is from other untaxed activities, for example, if higher taxes lower revenues because of more leisure instead of more labor, or more compensation through health insurance rather than through wages. But if the substitution is from activities taxed under one system to activities taxed under another, then the analysis is more complicated. For example, several studies have shown that a rise in the individual tax rate relative to the corporate tax rate causes people to shift their business activities from a form taxed by the individual tax system (called S-corporations) to a form taxed by the corporate tax system (called C-corporations).

b. *Reporting effect:* For a given level of gross income, a higher tax rate will cause individuals to reclassify income in ways that are not subject to a tax. Suppose that your employer offers you the choice between a raise of $5,000 and an additional health insurance benefit that will be paid by the employer (and shielded from tax) worth $3,000. If your tax rate is 25%, you will choose the raise and pay $1,250 in tax. If your tax rate is 50%, however, you will choose the new health insurance benefits, so that you pay nothing in tax. Thus, by raising the tax rate, we have lost $1,250 in revenues that we would have raised at a tax rate of 25%.

c. *Income exclusion effect:* For a given reported income, a higher tax rate will cause individuals to take more advantage of the deductions and exclusions from gross income that are used in defining taxable income: people may give more to charity, choose a bigger mortgage, or contribute more to a tax-preferred retirement savings account to avoid taxes as tax rates rise.

d. *Compliance effect:* Finally, higher tax rates may reduce revenues through increased tax evasion.

Thus, the direct effect is offset by the indirect effects in determining the ultimate response of the tax base to a rise in tax rates.

An example of these effects is presented in Figure 25-2. Suppose that Bob earns $45,000 per year in wages and $5,000 per year in cash from mowing his

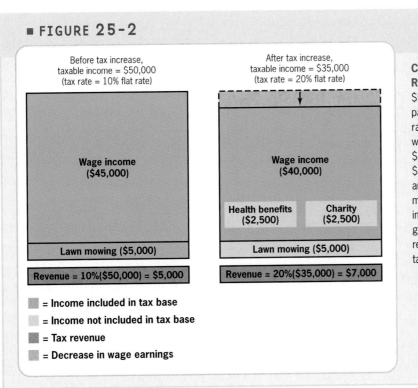

■ FIGURE 25-2

Before tax increase,
taxable income = $50,000
(tax rate = 10% flat rate)

After tax increase,
taxable income = $35,000
(tax rate = 20% flat rate)

Wage income
($45,000)

Wage income
($40,000)

Health benefits
($2,500)

Charity
($2,500)

Lawn mowing ($5,000)

Lawn mowing ($5,000)

Revenue = 10%($50,000) = $5,000

Revenue = 20%($35,000) = $7,000

☐ = Income included in tax base
☐ = Income not included in tax base
☐ = Tax revenue
☐ = Decrease in wage earnings

Changes in the Tax Base as Tax Rates Rise • Bob initially earns $50,000 and has a tax rate of 10%, paying $5,000 in taxes. When the tax rate rises to 20%, Bob reduces his wage earnings to $40,000, gives $2,500 more to charity, substitutes $2,500 in health insurance for wages, and stops reporting $5,000 in lawn-mowing income, so that his taxable income has fallen to $35,000. The government raises only 40% more in revenues ($2,000) despite doubling the tax rate.

neighbors' lawns, yielding a total tax base of $50,000. Initially there is a flat 10% tax on income, so that Bob pays $5,000 a year in taxes. Suppose now that the government tries to double its revenue by raising taxes to 20%. The direct effect of such a tax rate increase would be to raise revenues to $10,000, but Bob offsets this with four indirect responses that erode the tax base: (a) he reduces his work hours so that his wage income drops by $5,000 to $40,000; (b) he negotiates with his employer to shift $2,500 of his salary into health benefits; (c) he contributes $2,500 more to charity; and (d) he stops reporting his $5,000 in lawn-mowing income. These indirect responses lower the tax base from $50,000 to $35,000. The government now takes 20% of only $35,000, or $7,000. The doubling of tax rates has increased revenue by only 40% due to these indirect offsets that have shrunk the tax base.

Evidence on the Revenue Consequences of Higher Tax Rates While there is a long tradition of research on estimating the effect of taxes on the individual components of tax revenue, it wasn't until the late 1980s that economists began to assess the overall impact of taxes on revenues. Since that time, a large number of studies have modeled the impact of changes in individual tax rates on the tax revenues collected from those individuals.

These studies have provided several clear messages about how tax revenues respond to tax rates. First, the indirect effects we listed do offset the direct effect of raising tax rates to a significant degree. While estimates vary, a central estimate is that there is roughly a 4% decline in the base of taxable income for each 10% rise in tax rates. This response implies a significant deadweight loss from income taxation, a fact that motivated the optimal income tax computations discussed in Chapter 20.

Second, most of this response comes from the indirect effects of reporting, income exclusion, and compliance, and not from the indirect effect of gross income earning. Changes in tax rates appear to have relatively modest effects on total gross income; the total amount of income actually generated through work or savings does not respond in a sizeable way to taxation. Rather, most of the estimated effect on taxable income results from the use of tax exclusions, income shifting, and evasion. These findings suggest that it is not only high tax rates but also the lack of a Haig-Simons base (and high compliance) that causes tax inefficiency. If taxes were based on a Haig-Simons base of total income, the tax base would respond much less to changes in tax rates.[12]

Third, most if not all of this response comes from the rich. This should not be surprising, because lower- and middle-class taxpayers have relatively little scope to take advantage of the income reporting, exclusion, and compliance effects. In terms of the income reporting effect, lower- and middle-income families have relatively little control over the form of their compensation, so they can't shift toward tax-favored forms of compensation. In terms of the income exclusion effect, given the income required for expenses of daily liv-

---

[12] Kopczuk (2003) reviews the literature on the responsiveness of the tax base to tax rates and provides evidence that it is indeed the sensitivity of income definitions, and not the actual amount of income generated, that causes tax revenues to be elastic with respect to tax rates.

ing, there is only a limited scope for lower- and middle-income families to shift expenditures toward charity or higher mortgage payments. In terms of the compliance effect, the taxes of middle-income taxpayers are largely collected by withholding the taxes from wage income as it is paid by employers, so that relatively little scope for evasion exists.

Summary: The Benefits of Fundamental Tax Reform

Fundamental tax reform such as a flat tax, or even the system put in place by the Tax Reform Act of 1986, helps address all three of the tax reform goals (increasing tax compliance, simplifying the tax code, and improving tax efficiency). By expanding the tax base and lowering tax rates, fundamental tax reform improves tax compliance and tax efficiency.[13] By ending large numbers of detailed exemptions and deductions from taxation, and taxing different forms of income at the same rate, fundamental tax reform also makes tax filing simpler. So why is it so hard to achieve fundamental tax reform? The next section addresses the political and economic constraints tax reformers encounter.

25.2

The Politics and Economics of Tax Reform

The Tax Reform Act of 1986 moved the United States toward the type of broad-based, low-tax-rate system that has long been advocated by economists. But this "victory" was short-lived. In 1993, the Congress and the Clinton administration increased tax rates on top income earners from 31% to 39.6% and expanded the number of brackets from three to five. In 1997, the Taxpayer Relief Act provided new tax credits for having children, for various educational expenses, and for business research. The capital gains tax rate was also reduced to 20%, though the reduced rate applied only to assets held for at least 18 months (short-term assets would be taxed as earned income), and a $500,000 exclusion of gains on home sales replaced an earlier, less generous provision. Tax reforms in 2001 and 2003 have continued to complicate the tax code, which now has six income tax brackets, varying phaseouts for numerous tax breaks and savings incentives, a refundable child tax credit on top of the usual exemptions, a capital gains law calibrated by seven different tax rates, an alternative minimum tax that applies to growing numbers of taxpayers each year, and tax schedules that change with each year and in some cases expire, only to return the following year.

Why is it so hard to maintain a simple, broad-based tax code? Why do we have so much pressure for particular provisions that deviate from the Haig-Simons standard? There are two explanations, one political and one economic.

---

[13] The increase in tax efficiency is only true if the elasticity of the newly taxed items is not sufficiently higher than the elasticity of items already included in the tax base. The aforementioned research by Kopczuk (2004) suggests that is the case.

Political Pressures for a Complicated Tax Code

As we discussed in Chapter 9, political pressures for policy changes are strongest when the winners from these changes are concentrated, well organized, and have much to gain, and the losers are diffuse and don't lose much per person. Any given deviation from the broad Haig-Simons base may not have dramatic implications for efficiency or equity that are noticeable to the broad set of taxpayers. Yet even a small deviation can deliver large benefits to a concentrated set of taxpayers. The reductions and eventual repeal of the estate tax, for example, will affect only 50,000 households, but it will save those households a total of $30 billion a year.

A particularly strong pressure for tax code complication is the perception of politicians that naïve voters are opposed to new government spending programs but support the same goal when financed by a tax expenditure, despite identical budget implications. President Clinton, for example, came into office in 1992 promising to shift federal spending toward investments such as education and job training, but ended up achieving his goals in this area through "targeted tax cuts" (such as for spending on college education) rather than new spending. As one of his advisers noted, "We discovered very quickly that, even with a Democratically controlled Congress, it was almost impossible to get the spending and investment agenda approved. But the minute we proposed any kind of tax cut, everybody started salivating."[14] Apparently, relabeling a spending program as a tax cut, despite its cost in terms of tax efficiency, has enormous political appeal.

Economic Pressures Against Broadening the Tax Base

While there are clear political pressures in favor of a tax code with many special provisions, economic considerations also can get in the way of removing such provisions and broadening the tax base. As highlighted in these tax chapters, the economy does not take changes to the tax system lying down. Any tax change affects the prices and quantities determined in a variety of goods and factor markets, and these price and quantity changes in turn can lead to equity effects that must be considered as part of tax reform. This is clearly illustrated by the case of **tax shelters,** activities whose sole reason for existence is tax minimization.

tax shelters Activities whose sole reason for existence is tax minimization.

Background: Tax Shelters By the mid-1980s, the tax code had created a number of ways in which savvy investors could legally turn a profit by shielding their money from the IRS. Most of these schemes centered on an asset that for some reason received favorable tax treatment. Investors in real estate could, for example, deduct depreciation expenses rapidly and treat profits as capital gains, 60% of which were tax-exempt. Equipment leasing for moviemaking, scientific research, and other industries qualified for an invest-

---

[14] Chandler (1996).

ment tax credit that could equal up to 10% of the cost of the equipment. Drilling for oil and gas would often yield even better tax treatment because 60% to 80% of the initial investment could be written off as a tax deduction.

Many of these measures had been intended by Congress to encourage investment in real estate and the oil industry, but the distortion of incentives created by these tax shelters caused serious overinvestment in these sectors. The real estate tax breaks could yield $2 of write-offs for every $1 of investment, while equipment-leasing tax breaks yielded $5 for each $1. By the mid-1980s, over $10 billion a year was being invested in such shelters, with over half of that in real estate alone. Despite excess building construction and vacancy rates close to 30%, real estate tax shelters remained profitable for investors. One industry insider estimated that over 75% of investment in independent oil and gas company ventures came through such shelters.[15]

Particularly galling were tax shelters that recorded "paper losses" while actually turning a profit for their investors. For a simple example, imagine that in 1983 Josh had an income of $250,000, placing him well within the 50% tax bracket (which started at $109,400). Let's say Josh decided to invest $100,000 of that income in an oil-drilling venture that yielded no income and was sold for $90,000 one year later. This would seem like a very bad investment, losing $10,000 in one year, but not so in the world of tax shelters, as illustrated in Table 25-2.

The deduction for oil investments allowed Josh to deduct 60% of the initial investment ($60,000) from his 1983 taxes, so that he got a $30,000 tax savings at his 50% marginal tax rate. He could then offset the $10,000 loss against other income one year later, saving him the tax on that other income at a 50% rate, for an additional tax savings of $5,000. Thus, after one year Josh has turned his $100,000 into $90,000 plus $35,000 of tax savings, or $125,000. A 25% annual rate of return on an investment that is losing money—a real example of American ingenuity!

■ TABLE 25-2

Tax Shelters

Action	Result
Invest $100,000 in oil venture Sell oil venture for $90,000 Deduct $60,000 from this year's income Deduct $10,000 loss from next year's income	Lose $10,000 in value Save $30,000 on taxes Save $5,000 on taxes
Net effect	Make $25,000

Even though the investment in a tax shelter loses $10,000 in real value, it generates $35,000 in tax savings, so that on net there is a $25,000 gain from the investment.

Tax shelters became so prevalent that many creative individuals started to pursue truly strange schemes. One oyster farmer, for instance, recruited buyers of young oysters by claiming they could deduct the cost of the oysters up front, pay taxes on the income only two years later when the oysters matured, and treat that income as capital gains. The IRS later ruled that the growth of an oyster did not count as a capital gain![16]

---

[15] Russakoff (1985).
[16] Swardson (1985).

tax capitalization The change in asset prices that occurs due to a change in the tax levied on the stream of returns from that asset.

Transitional Inequities The existence of tax shelters clearly runs in opposition to the three benefits of fundamental tax reform described earlier: tax shelters make tax evasion easier; they make the tax code more complicated; and they make the tax code less efficient. At the same time, taking on tax shelters raises a difficult economic issue because of the type of **tax capitalization** discussed in Chapter 10. Recall that tax capitalization is the change in asset prices that occurs due to a change in the tax levied on the stream of returns from that asset. The fact that tax shelter benefits are capitalized into the value of assets means that ending such shelters can severely punish their owners and cause large horizontal inequities.

Suppose that two apartment buildings are for sale in a city, one in a low-income neighborhood and one in a more affluent neighborhood. The building in the low-income neighborhood is worth only $100,000 because its owners cannot charge enough rent to cover its costs; the building in the more affluent neighborhood is worth $200,000. Suppose also that a special tax provision is introduced that allows individuals who invest in apartment buildings in low-income neighborhoods to take large tax deductions of the type discussed earlier (such as accelerated depreciation or an investment tax credit). Because of these tax benefits, the market value of the building rises to $200,000: the $100,000 of pre-tax value plus a stream of tax benefits valued at $100,000. Felix is a taxpayer who values these tax breaks, so he buys the low-income apartment building for $200,000. At the same time, his friend Rod buys the apartment building in the more affluent neighborhood, which we assume comes with no associated stream of tax benefits, for $200,000.

One year later, the government announces that it is closing this tax shelter for apartment buildings in low-income neighborhoods. The value of Felix's apartment building immediately falls back to $100,000, because there is no longer any associated stream of tax benefits. This is an enormous reduction in Felix's net worth. Moreover, this reduction in net worth does not reduce Felix's tax burden, since the tax code only allows him to deduct up to $3,000 of capital losses from other income each year.

transitional inequities from tax reform Changes in the treatment of similar individuals who have made different decisions in the past and are therefore differentially treated by tax reform.

Felix's sizeable loss is an example of the way that market responses to tax changes can cause **transitional inequities from tax reform**: changes in the treatment of similar individuals who have made different decisions in the past and are therefore differentially treated by tax reform (particularly tax reforms that affect capital asset values). Felix and Rod both invested $200,000 in apartment buildings at the same time, yet due to this tax reform Felix lost $100,000 and Rod lost nothing. This is a large horizontal inequity.

These transitional inequities are an issue in taxation and any other form of government regulation. Suppose that the government announces that a public beach is no longer fit for swimming due to water contamination. This announcement would immediately lower the value of all homes on the beach, whose high prices reflected their previous access to swimming.

Such transitional inequities are a natural feature of any tax reform, which by definition will create winners and losers (unless there is a large overall tax cut that makes everyone better off). This reality led Feldstein (1976) to suggest that tax reforms be infrequent and slowly phased in to minimize the horizontal inequities that arise from frequent and sudden asset price changes.

Concerns about transitional inequity have also led to various forms of compensation through the political process, such as *grandfathering,* whereby those who made decisions under the old tax rules are allowed to continue to benefit from those rules, while the rules are changed for all future decisions (in the previous example, under a grandfathered change Felix would be allowed to keep his tax breaks worth $100,000, but new investors in apartments would not be able to take advantage of those tax breaks). Such compensation is often both inequitable (well-off individuals are usually the ones who benefit from special tax rules) and inefficient (bad features of the tax code are retained to benefit some parties). But compensation may be the necessary grease for the wheel of tax reform. The costs of this compensation must be weighed against the long-run benefits to society of reforming taxes.

▶ APPLICATION

Grandfathering in Virginia

Near the end of 2003, the state of Virginia began the political process of transforming its tax system, in an effort to put its shaky financial house back in order. One particularly costly feature of the system was the automatic $12,000 annual deduction that every Virginian 65 or older received on his or her state income taxes, regardless of wealth or income. Widely derided as a giveaway to seniors, the automatic deduction clearly had the backing of a determined minority of elderly citizens, whom it benefited directly. Thus, when Democratic governor Mark Warner proposed eliminating that deduction, he made sure to include in his plan a clause that allowed seniors currently over 65 to keep the deduction, a true "grandfather" (and grandmother) clause. Even his Republican opponents made sure that their plans included such a clause as well. Virginia's politicians agreed at the time that the so-called senior subtraction was largely untouchable, even though immediate repeal would bring nearly $300 million annually into the state's coffers. As one leader of a retirees' organization ominously stated, "It's on the books, and they'd be in a really bad position if they repealed it."[17] The tax reform eventually passed, with the grandfather clause intact, in April 2004. ◀

The Conundrum

As we have just seen, political and economic pressures are significant barriers to moving to a broad-based system of the type suggested by the Haig-Simons criteria. Political forces are constantly pushing for the use of the tax code to deliver benefits to particular groups, at the cost of potentially inefficient and

---

[17] Melton (2003).

inequitable holes in the tax base. Moreover, once these tax breaks are in place, it is very hard to remove them because they create horizontal inequities for those who made decisions based on the existence of these tax breaks.

Nevertheless, we have seen fundamental tax reform in the not-too-distant past in the Tax Reform Act of 1986. If these barriers can be overcome and more fundamental reform is possible, what directions should it take? In the next sections, we consider the fundamental reform options most discussed by economists.

▶ **APPLICATION**

TRA 86 and Tax Shelters

The treatment of tax shelters in the Tax Reform Act of 1986 presents an interesting case study of the types of compromises required by fundamental tax reform. TRA 86 closed many of the egregious tax shelters that had emerged in the wake of the 1981 tax reform. A straightforward means of doing so would have been to eliminate the tax shelters directly, by stopping the special treatment of oil and gas investments, for example. This reform would have increased equity and efficiency, and would have made the tax code simpler.

Congress, however, found it politically difficult to directly attack these tax shelters, which would have meant angering some of their most important constituents who were taking advantage of these shelters. Instead, Congress addressed the shelter problem indirectly, by dividing income into three categories: ordinary (earned) income, investment income, and passive income. *Passive income* was defined as income in which the individual did not take an active role, such as tax shelters or real estate income. Congress then stipulated that losses from one category of income could not offset income from a second category of income. In this way, individuals could not use tax shelters to completely wipe out their taxable income from other sources. In addition, the Alternative Minimum Tax (AMT) computed income without many of the tax shelter rules available under the ordinary income tax, ensuring that the wealthy paid at least some minimum rate of tax on their income.

These changes were largely effective at ending the most egregious use of tax shelters, but they came at a cost: they made the tax code more complicated. Income now had to be categorized in ways that were not necessary before, and tax burdens now had to be computed twice, once under the ordinary income tax and once under the AMT.

Were these changes in TRA 86 good or not? The answer may be found by comparing the costs of increased complexity with the benefits of a fairer and more efficient tax system that has fewer tax shelter opportunities. One clear lesson is that both goals can be served if politicians take more direct routes to improving the tax code, such as simply removing tax shelters, rather than indirect routes, such as those pursued by TRA 86. ◀

25.3

Consumption Taxation

A radical reform of the current U.S. tax system that is often favored by economists would be to change from taxing income to **taxing consumption,** taxing individuals based not on what they earn but on what they consume. The notion of taxing consumption rather than income can be traced back at least as far as the seventeenth-century philosopher Thomas Hobbes, who wrote in his famous treatise *Leviathan,* "It is fairer to tax people on what they extract from the economy, as roughly measured by their consumption, than to tax them on what they produce for the economy, as roughly measured by their income." In the United States, consumption is taxed to some extent through state and local sales and excise taxes as well as some federal excise taxes, but consumption taxation plays a much larger role in the rest of the world than in the United States: national and subnational governments in the United States receive a lower percentage of tax revenue from consumption taxation than in any other OECD nation, as shown in Figure 25-3.

taxing consumption Taxing individuals based not on what they earn but on what they consume (such as through a sales tax).

Why Might Consumption Make a Better Tax Base?

The sections that follow describe the many forms of consumption taxation. For the purposes of our initial discussion, however, let's assume that we are referring to a retail sales tax of the kind now levied in most U.S. states, but at

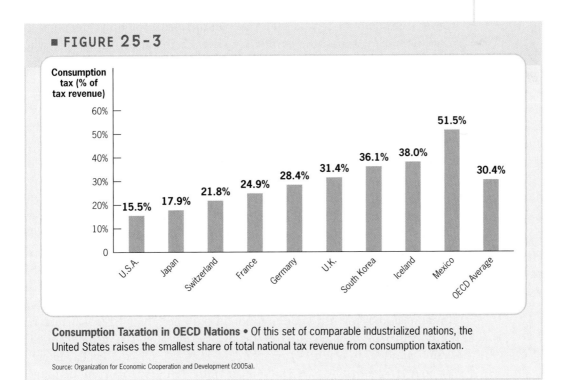

■ FIGURE 25-3

Consumption tax (% of tax revenue)

U.S.A.	15.5%
Japan	17.9%
Switzerland	21.8%
France	24.9%
Germany	28.4%
U.K.	31.4%
South Korea	36.1%
Iceland	38.0%
Mexico	51.5%
OECD Average	30.4%

Consumption Taxation in OECD Nations • Of this set of comparable industrialized nations, the United States raises the smallest share of total national tax revenue from consumption taxation.

Source: Organization for Economic Cooperation and Development (2005a).

a higher level: for example, a federal tax of 35% on all purchases. There are three potential advantages to moving to a consumption tax base.

Improved Efficiency A single-rate sales tax could reduce many of the inefficiencies associated with the current tax system. As highlighted in the first section of this chapter, most of the elasticity of the tax base with respect to tax revenues arises because of "holes" in our tax system, such as the non-taxation of income paid in the form of fringe benefits. Such opportunities for tax avoidance would, in principle, disappear with a national sales tax that included expenditures such as employer-provided health insurance.

A particular source of inefficiency in our current tax system is the lack of a "level playing field" across investment choices. The current tax system penalizes particular forms of savings and favors others. Saving in the form of real estate, for example, is favored through the tax exemption of imputed rents on owner-occupied housing and capital-gains exemption on housing; saving in the form of equity in a corporation is penalized if it is paid out as dividends. These differences in tax burdens can distort savings decisions in the same way that tax wedges always cause individuals to make inefficient decisions. People will save too much in housing and not enough in dividend-paying corporations, relative to the efficiency-maximizing level, because of these tax bonuses and penalties.

A consumption tax would end these types of arbitrary decisions by taxing goods only when consumed. If individuals defer consumption to save, the form of savings does not determine their tax burden because savings would not be taxed no matter what form it takes.

Fairer Treatment of Savers and Less Distortion to Savings Decision A major complaint against the current tax system is that it penalizes those who save relative to those who spend, the implicit motivation for the earlier Hobbes quote. The reduced savings that may result could lead to lower productivity for the U.S. economy, as discussed in Chapter 4. This "pro-consumption" bias would end under a consumption tax system.

Consider two individuals, Homer and Ned, who are identical except for their preferences for saving. Both live for two periods, earning $100 in the first period and nothing in the second period. Homer is impatient: he wants to consume his entire income in the first period and nothing in the second period. Ned is more patient; he wants to consume in both periods. Initially, they are both subject to an income tax, which taxes all labor earnings and interest income at 50%. The interest rate earned on savings is 10%.

Table 25-3 compares the tax burdens on the two men under an income tax regime and a consumption tax regime. Under the income tax regime in the top panel, both individuals have an income tax bill of $50 on their $100 of earnings in period 1. Homer spends his entire after-tax income ($50). Ned, in contrast, chooses to set his consumption in both periods at $25.61, which he accomplishes by saving $24.39 of his first-period after-tax earnings. In the second period, Homer has no income, so he pays no tax. Ned has interest earnings of $2.44, so he pays $1.22 in tax on that interest. In present discounted value (PDV) terms, Homer pays only $50 in taxes across both periods, but Ned pays $51.10. Thus, savers such as Ned are penalized in an income tax regime. This tax treatment of savings is both horizontally inequitable (because Ned is taxed more simply for making a different choice) and inefficient because it may reduce the incentive to save (because savings leads to higher tax payments).

The second panel of Table 25-3 shows the tax outcomes under a consumption tax system, with a tax rate of 100%; for each $1 of consumption you pay $1 in tax. Such a system has no effect on Homer; he continues to consume $50 in the first period, pays his $50 in consumption tax, and then is done. The higher rate of return on savings, however, will lead Ned to save more *in this example.* (Remember from Chapter 23 that whether lower taxation of savings actually leads to more savings is an open question.) He will only consume $25 in the first period, and will pay only $25 in consumption taxation. He will save the remaining $50, earning $5 in interest. His second period consumption will therefore be $27.50, and he will pay $27.50 in consumption taxes. The PDV of his tax payments is now $50, the same as Homer's. The switch to consumption taxation has removed the pro-consumption bias in income taxation and the horizontally inequitable treatment of those who choose to save their income rather than to consume it. Removing this pro-consumption bias may also lead to higher savings levels (if taxation does actually lower savings, which most economists assume is the case) and a more productive economy.

This argument against taxing capital income is even stronger when one moves beyond two periods, as highlighted by the work of Chalmley (1986) and Judd (1985). Consider a consumer who earns $100, and would like to consume $50 today and save the remainder for 10 years at an interest rate of 10%. If there is no capital income taxation, then in 10 years the consumer has $50 \times (1.1)^{10}$ to consume, or $130. If there is a 50% capital income tax, then in 10 years the consumer has only $50 \times (1.05)^{10}$ to consume, or $81. Extending the example to 50 years, in the no-tax world the consumer has *ten times* as much to consume as in the capital income tax world. Thus, Chalmley and Judd pointed out that capital income taxes amount to ever-increasing consumption taxes, causing potentially enormous distortions to consumption and savings decisions.

Simplicity Another advantage of the consumption tax is simplicity. In principle, it is much more straightforward to simply tax individuals on their purchases than on a complicated definition of income. In practice, however, even consumption tax regimes have struggled with different definitional issues such

■ **TABLE 25-3**

Income Versus Consumption Taxation and the Treatment of Savers

	Homer	Ned
Income tax		
Income in period 1	$100	$100
Taxes in period 1	50	50
Consumption in period 1	50	25.61
Savings in period 1	0	24.39
Interest earnings in period 2	0	2.44
Taxes in period 2	0	1.22
Consumption in period 2	0	25.61
PDV of taxes	50	51.10
Consumption tax		
Income in period 1	$100	$100
Taxes in period 1	50	25
Consumption in period 1	50	25
Savings in period 1	0	50
Interest earnings in period 2	0	5
Taxes in period 2	0	27.50
Consumption in period 2	0	27.50
PDV of taxes	50	50

The top panel of the table shows the impact of an income tax on Homer, who consumes all of his income when he earns it, and Ned, who saves some of his income. Ned has a higher present discounted value (PDV) of taxes than Homer under the income tax, since Ned is taxed on both his labor and interest income. When the government moves to a consumption tax in the second panel of the table, both Ned and Homer have the same PDV of taxes.

as the treatment of services and consumer durables (for example, should you be taxed on the entire purchase price of your home or only on the stream of housing services as you consume them over time?).

Why Might Consumption Be a Worse Tax Base?

The efficiency, horizontal equity, and simplicity advantages of consumption taxation are offset by five disadvantages.

Vertical Equity The primary concern with consumption taxation is a reduction of vertical equity. In a simple model (such as that used to analyze Homer's and Ned's situations) individuals consume their entire income at some point during their lives, with no desire to leave inheritances to their children, so income and consumption taxes would have the same burden on rich and poor; they both pay the same share of their lifetime income in taxes.

Clearly, however, this is not the right explanation for consumption behavior in the real world. A central fact about consumption is that the share of income devoted to consumption falls with income: the rich save much more than the poor throughout their lives. Dynan et al. (2004) found that those in the lowest income quintile (the bottom fifth of the income distribution) save 3% of their lifetime income, while those in the highest income quintile save 25% of their lifetime income. The top 1% of the income distribution saves almost half of its lifetime income. As a result, consumption taxes are *regressive:* because the poor consume more of their income, they bear more of the tax burden (relative to their incomes).

If the rich save more over their lives, they must be leaving larger bequests when they die. Thus, it would be simple to resolve the regressivity of consumption taxes by taxing bequests as consumption. If bequests were taxed as consumption, all individuals would end up being taxed on their lifetime resources.

As the debate over the estate tax shows, however, large taxes at death are not politically popular. Taxing bequests as consumption would amount to an enormous extension of the estate tax and would clearly raise opposition, particularly because taxing bequests would likely undo much of the long-run savings incentives arising from taxing consumption (since it would be more costly to save for one's children). As a result, no developed nations that have consumption taxes include bequests in the measure of consumption, and consumption taxes are regressive in practice relative to income taxes.

There are some alternatives for addressing the regressivity of the consumption tax. One would be to move to a progressive *expenditure tax;* as discussed below, such an approach has not been successfully applied in the past. The regressivity of the consumption tax could also potentially be addressed by applying different tax rates to goods based on the income profile of their likely consumers. Staple foods such as bread or milk could be taxed less highly, and luxury goods consumed by the rich could be taxed more highly. The problem with this approach is that it provides the *opposite* policy prescription to that recommended by the Ramsey model of Chapter 20: we would now be exempting the most inelastically demanded goods (staples), and taxing more heavily the most elastically demanded goods (luxuries). Another problem is that this approach adds a new opportunity for vote-maximizing politicians to distort economic choices: politicians from textile states would, for example, lobby hard for clothes to be included in the tax-preferred category. This approach would also present a hornet's nest of difficult decisions about which goods go in which categories: If we have a lower tax rate on bread, which is a necessity good, how do we treat bagels from an expensive delicatessen, which are a luxury good?

Asymmetric Information As discussed in Chapter 17, the government ideally wants to redistribute from high-ability to low-ability individuals, but it has only imperfect measures of ability, such as earnings. By taxing earnings rather than underlying ability, the government induces the moral hazard effect of causing individuals to work less hard. As Saez (2002) observed, however, the highest-ability individuals are also likely to be the ones that save the most. Thus, savings can be used as a *targeting device* for redistributing from high- to low-ability individuals. Saez proves that in such a case the government should tax capital income to some extent to take advantage of this targeting device and efficiently redistribute from high- to low-skill individuals. Thus, introducing these differences across individuals can undo, at least partly, the strong presumption against capital taxation in the dynamic model.[18]

Transition Issues Another major problem with consumption taxes involves transition issues. If we switched today from an income to a consumption tax, people your age (that is, college age) should be roughly indifferent. Your lifetime earnings and consumption are largely ahead of you, so you would pay the same tax either way. Future generations would benefit, since more savings would lead to a larger capital stock, a higher marginal product of labor, and a higher standard of living. The current middle-aged and especially the current elderly would be major losers, however. Those individuals have paid their income taxes, saving some of the after-tax income to finance later consumption. If that consumption is then taxed at a high consumption tax rate, they are taxed twice, once on the income as they earn it and once on the savings as they spend it. This is much worse than the tax treatment of savings under the income tax, since the consumption tax would tax them on their *entire* savings (because it is used to finance consumption), not just the interest earnings.

---

[18] In an important rejoinder to the earlier work of Chalmley and Judd, Golosov et al. (2003) provide a dynamic version of this argument. Once again, we would like to tax highly skilled individuals, but these individuals will earn less if the government is taxing their earnings. But if more highly skilled individuals have higher savings, then by taxing savings we get these highly skilled individuals to work more (so that they have enough money when they retire). Thus, not only can capital income taxation serve to target high ability groups, it can be used to motivate them to work more by reducing their savings.

In a two-period example, suppose individuals work in the first period, earning $200. They consume $100 and save $100 at a 10% interest rate. In the second period, when they are retired, they consume $110. With income taxes at a rate of 50%, they would pay labor taxes on the $200 of labor earnings ($100 of taxes in the first period) and interest taxes on the $10 interest earnings ($5 of taxes in the second period). If a consumption tax were introduced in the second period when they are retired, however, they would still pay the taxes on the $200 of earnings ($100 of taxes in the first period), but would now pay consumption taxes on the entire $110 of consumption they do in the second period ($55 of taxes in the second period). So their total tax payments would rise from $105 to $155 because of the transition to a consumption tax.

It is highly unlikely that politicians would be willing to undertake a policy change that is so detrimental to seniors. As a result, a switch to a consumption tax would likely include some provision to compensate individuals for this double taxation. Such a provision would be costly, however: by some estimates, the *entire efficiency gain* from a consumption tax over the first several generations would be used up if extra taxes had to be raised to make transition payments to existing generations. Moreover, those who are hurt by the transition are the highest-income asset holders in society. So the compensation that undoes these transition costs would actually involve compensating the richest members of society!

Compliance   Suppose that we simply replaced the existing income tax with an expansion of the kinds of sales taxes levied in most states today. According to Gale (1999), this reform would require a sales tax rate on the order of 35%. A major problem with such a large sales tax is compliance. With a high sales tax rate, there would be a strong incentive to conspire with retailers to avoid the tax (for example, by paying a retailer a small side payment to not ring up the sale for tax purposes), or to purchase items through channels that do not bear sales taxes (the "black market"). It is much harder to track consumption expenditures than it is to track income earned, where withholding from paychecks can solve compliance problems for the vast majority of the population.

Cascading   A final problem with a national sales tax is the problem of "cascading" taxation of business inputs. In principle, a sales tax is paid only on retail sales, not on sales of business inputs. In practice, however, many businesses buy their inputs at the retail level. An individual starting a business, for example, might buy a photocopier at an office supply store and have to pay the consumption tax on it. As Slemrod and Bakija (2000, page 213) point out, businesses often pay sales taxes on their inputs and then again when they sell their outputs, so that a cascading problem develops. Goods that require more intermediate steps of production and distribution are taxed more heavily if those steps involve retail purchases (such as someone running a home business that puts together gift baskets of retail goods for hospital patients). This cascade leads both to distortions away from modes of production that involve multiple stages and to a deadweight loss from inefficient production choices; if it would be more efficient to produce using retail purchases, firms might nevertheless choose not to do so because of the tax disadvantage.

In levying their current retail sales taxes, some states in the United States try to avoid this problem by giving businesses a registration number to present when purchasing goods from other firms. This number exempts them from the retail sales tax. This procedure works poorly in practice, however, so that a high percentage of retail sales revenues come from business purchases that should be exempt from retail sales tax.[19]

Designing a Consumption Tax

Different forms of consumption taxation can address the concerns raised with the sales tax approach just discussed.

Value-Added Tax The compliance and cascading problems associated with a large retail sales tax have led most nations with large consumption taxes to adopt instead a **value-added tax (VAT),** also known as a "cascading" consumption tax. The idea of the VAT is to tax goods at each stage of production on the value added to the good at that production stage, rather than only at the point of sale on the final retail value of the good.

value-added tax (VAT) A consumption tax levied on each stage of a good's production on the increase in value of the good at that stage of production.

Table 25-4 presents an example of how a VAT works for a kitchen table that has a retail sales value of $100 and a VAT rate of 20%. If this were a pure sales tax, I would pay $20 tax on the $100 table, which might offer a strong incentive for the retailer and me to conspire to avoid the tax. The VAT proceeds by defining the value added at each stage of production—the difference between the value of what is produced and the price paid for the inputs from other firms—and taxing just the value added.

In this example, the first stage of production is the logger, who cuts down the trees and turns them into lumber that she sells for $25 to a manufacturer. The logger's value added is $25, and so she pays a VAT of $5. The manufacturer then turns the wood into a table and sells it to the retailer for $75. The manufacturer's value added is $50, so he pays a VAT of $10. Finally, the retailer sells the table to me for $100. The value added at the retail stage is $25, so the VAT paid by the retailer is $5.

■ TABLE 25-4

Value-Added Tax in Practice

Agent	Purchase Price	Sale Price	Value Added	Tax Paid (VAT = 20%)
Logger	$0	$25	$25	$5
Manufacturer	25	75	50	10
Retailer	75	100	25	5

Total tax paid: $20

When the logger adds $25 in value to a table through producing the wood, she pays $5.00 in VAT (VAT rate = 20%). The manufacturer then adds $50 in value and pays a VAT of $10.00. Finally, the retailer pays $5.00 in VAT on her $25 in value added.

---

[19] Slemrod and Bakija (2000), p. 10.

In theory, the VAT addresses both the compliance and cascading problems. The total VAT payments are $20, the same as the 20% retail sales tax on the table. But there is an important difference: the tax is now *self-policing,* with each participant in the production chain having a strong incentive to make sure that the other participants report correctly. Any attempt to reduce value added by claiming that a producer either paid more for inputs than he really did or sold the product for less than he really did raises the tax bills of other participants in the production chain. So the participants themselves will ensure that the tax reporting is accurate.

Suppose that the manufacturer tried to cheat by claiming he paid $30 for the wood and sold the table for $60, so that his value added was only $30 (and his tax bill was only $6, rather than the $10 he would pay if he were honest). Then both the logger and the retailer would protest, since this would mean that they would each pay higher value-added taxes. The logger's value added would now appear to be $30 (since she would appear to have a sales price to the manufacturer of $30), and the retailer's value added would now appear to be $40 (since he would appear to have paid only $60 for the table and sold it for $100). This self-policing system ensures that the manufacturer is honest. The only participant who is not policed is the retailer, but now only $5 (one-quarter of the VAT revenues) are paid at the "unpoliced" consumer purchase stage (in contrast to all $20 in the sales tax example).

The VAT also explicitly accounts for the cascading problem by taxing firms only on the value they add, allowing them to deduct from taxation the price they pay for inputs. So firms that use retail inputs are not penalized under a VAT in the way that they might be under a retail sales tax.

While the VAT sounds quite simple in principle, in practice the VAT levied in most developed nations has become the kind of complicated tax system that drives critics of the income tax to distraction. VATs typically have multiple rates and various complicated exemptions, and as a result VAT systems generally cost no less to administer than income tax systems. In Britain, for example, the standard VAT rate is 17.5%, but it is reduced to 5% for home fuel and power. Certain "necessities" have no VAT; these include groceries, children's clothing, books, education, and medical services (with the exception of osteopaths). And, if you expect your business to do less than $80,000 in commerce, you need not even register for VAT with the government. VATs may also have compliance problems that can approach or exceed those involving the income tax in the United States.[20]

Expenditure Tax The common feature of retail sales and value-added taxes is that the taxes are paid at the level of the purchase, with no differentiation according to who is making that purchase. Poor and rich pay the same VAT for the same purchase. It is therefore hard to meet society's demand for progressivity using a sales tax or a VAT. This concern over progressivity has led to

---

[20] Slemrod and Bakija (2000), pp. 215–218.

consideration of an **expenditure tax,** a tax levied on yearly consumption, not yearly income. In essence, an expenditure tax operates in the same way as an income tax, but it replaces the base of taxation with expenditure rather than income.

Such a tax could be designed to be as progressive as the current income tax system while having the benefits of using consumption as a tax base. On the other hand, both the compliance problems and the complex information requirements associated with this sort of tax would be enormous. It would be very difficult to track the expenditures that each family makes during the year, and if families tried to track them the paper trail could get horrible. This is why attempts to implement an expenditure tax in Sri Lanka and India failed completely. In both countries the tax administrations lacked the resources to enforce compliance with the tax, so that taxpayers were able to manipulate their personal figures for spending and saving. Those experiments ended quickly, and even Sweden, which has a very efficient tax administration, eventually concluded that, though an expenditure tax is fairer in principle, it is impossible to enforce.[21]

> **expenditure tax** A consumption tax levied on yearly consumption rather than on specific sales.

Backing Into Consumption Taxation: Cash-Flow Taxation

The previous discussion raised two difficulties: taxing consumption at the point of production leads to progressivity concerns, but taxing expenditure at the individual level has proved administratively infeasible. An alternative approach is to recognize that consumption is equal to income minus savings. Thus, allowing individuals to deduct all savings from their income in computing their tax burden will yield the same outcome as if we had taxed their expenditure. This is the idea behind the **cash-flow tax,** which taxes individuals on the difference between cash income and savings.

> **cash-flow tax** A tax on the difference between cash income and savings.

The advantage of this approach is that it would require the least change to our current system of taxation. The only major difficulty would be in verifying people's claims about how much they saved during the year. This amount could be verified by recognizing for tax purposes only savings done through officially recorded channels, such as bank accounts, stock purchases, and so on.

Indeed, our current tax system has many features of a cash-flow tax. All retirement savings by one's employer and much of the retirement savings on one's own (through IRA and 401(k) accounts) are exempt from taxation. Savings through one's house are also exempt from capital gains taxes up to $500,000. In addition, self-employed individuals can set up Keogh accounts through which they can shield up to 20% of their self-employment income from taxation by saving it for retirement. Retirement savings and housing investments represent the majority of savings for most Americans, so for them this approximates a cash-flow tax.

---

[21] Evidence on India and Sri Lanka from Muten (2001), p. 11; evidence on Sweden from Peter Birch Sorensen's speech, "The Nordic Dual Income Tax—In or Out?" delivered at Working Party 2 on Fiscal Affairs, OECD, June 14, 2001, available at http://www.econ.ku.dk/pbs/diversefiler/oecddual.pdf (p. 6).

A major change needed for moving to a true cash-flow tax, however, would be to allow high-income taxpayers who save in other forms (such as their businesses) to deduct that savings from taxable income. The urge for such a change motivates the desire for the type of large new savings incentives discussed in the introduction of Chapter 22. As described in that chapter, however, these savings incentives would have large revenue costs, and would deliver the majority of their benefits to high-income individuals. Thus, there is significant opposition to moving to a pure cash-flow tax.

25.4

The Flat Tax

Finally, we consider the tax described in the example that opened this chapter, the flat tax, which was first popularized by economists Robert Hall and Alvin Rabushka in 1981.[22] Their plan has several features:

1. Corporations pay a flat-rate VAT on their sales, but *also* get to deduct wage payments to workers from their VAT tax base. There is no corporate income tax.

2. Individuals pay a tax on labor income only, not capital income, at that same flat rate.

3. All tax expenditures would be eliminated (health insurance expenditures would be treated like wage payments, charitable contributions and home mortgage interest would no longer be deductible, and so on) and would be replaced by a single family-level exemption.

The first thing to note about such a plan is that it is closely related to a VAT: the first element is a VAT that exempts wage payments, but the second element involves taxing wage payments at that same VAT rate. Why not just use a VAT? The real insight of this plan was that by taxing the wage income at the individual level, we could introduce progressivity into the tax structure, as the expenditure tax tries to do, but we can do so without actually taxing expenditure. In their plan, Hall and Rabushka proposed a flat tax rate of 19% and an exemption level of $25,000. This allows the plan to exempt the lowest-income earners in society (those with incomes below $25,000) from taxation, allowing for more vertical equity than a VAT or sales tax.

Advantages of a Flat Tax

There are several major advantages of a flat tax. The most important are the efficiency gains from having one flat rate on a broad income definition. This change expands the set of tax sources (such as employer spending on health insurance) and removes many of the avenues that individuals can use to reduce their tax base as tax rates rise (such as raising their home mortgage

---

[22] For a detailed discussion of their proposal, see Hall and Rabushka (1995).

interest payments), allowing the marginal tax rate to stay low and reducing the inefficiency of taxation. Efficiency also rises for the reason highlighted in Chapter 20 and this chapter: the elasticity of taxable revenues is largest for the highest income groups. High-income taxpayers are the ones who will reduce their taxable income the most when tax rates rise. So a rising marginal-rate tax system not only raises deadweight loss by setting a high rate on a narrow base of rich individuals, it also raises deadweight loss by taxing most highly the group with the most elastic supply of taxable income. That is why the optimal income tax computations discussed at the end of Chapter 20 suggest similar, or even lower, marginal rates on the rich than on lower-income groups. Indeed, the type of tax code suggested by those simulations is similar to that suggested by advocates of the flat tax: a large exemption for the poor with a fairly flat marginal rate on everyone else.

Efficiency may rise even further with a flat tax. Savings are excluded from taxation, which may lead to more capital accumulation, although once again we do not know how sensitive savings are to the after-tax interest rate. The flat-tax approach would also remove the corporate income tax, and all of its associated inefficiencies, thus raising corporate investment and making corporate financing more efficient.

Finally, the flat tax would have enormous benefits in terms of simplicity, as illustrated earlier. Compliance would also likely improve because the simpler tax system would make it harder to find ways to evade taxes; for almost all taxpayers, their entire tax bill could be collected through withholding from earnings.

Problems with the Flat Tax

The problems with the flat tax are similar to those raised with consumption taxation. First, while a flat tax can be made fairly progressive for low- and middle-income earners, it will be much less progressive for high-income earners than our current system. Table 25-5 shows the average tax rate on a married couple with two children under our current tax system and under the Hall-Rabushka flat-tax proposal. If this family earns $25,000, it pays no

■ TABLE 25-5

Distributional Implications of the Flat Tax

	Household Income (Married Couple With Two Children)				
	$25,000	$50,000	$100,000	$300,000	$1,000,000
Current tax code (2004)	1.2%	6.9%	13.0%	24.2%	31.7%
Hall-Rabushka flat tax	0%	9.5%	14.3%	17.4%	18.5%

This table shows the average tax rate on families under the current tax code (as of 2004) and the Hall-Rabushka flat tax. For families earning $25,000, the tax burden falls under a flat tax relative to today's tax system. For most other families earning under $100,000, however, tax burdens rise, while for most families with incomes over $100,000, tax burdens fall.

tax under the flat tax; it has an average tax rate of 1.2% under the current income tax. For families earning $50,000 or $100,000, however, the tax burden is higher under the flat tax. The real tax saving accrues to groups with incomes above $100,000. Under the flat-tax proposal just discussed, the average tax rate on a family earning $300,000 is 17.4%, while the average tax rate on a family earning $1 million is not much higher (18.5%). In contrast, under our current income tax system, the average tax rate on those earning $300,000 is 24.2%, and the average tax rate on a family earning $1 million is much larger (31.7%).[23]

This sizeable reduction in vertical equity may be problematic for many voters. A 1996 U.S. Treasury Department study of a flat tax proposed by Representative Dick Armey and Senator Richard Shelby concluded that the total federal tax bill for people with incomes below $200,000 would increase by an average of 11.8%, while the tax bill for those with incomes above $200,000 would fall by 28.3%.[24]

Second, there are difficult transition issues raised by the flat tax. Removing the current set of tax preferences would cause enormous horizontal inequities that would be costly to undo. For example, the removal of the mortgage interest deduction, which is a large subsidy to housing, could lead to a dramatic drop in the value of owning a house, as reflected in house prices. Individuals who suddenly saw a large drop in the value of their most valuable asset would understandably be upset by this change. Similarly, some estimates suggest that there would be enormous disruption to the health insurance market from removing the tax preference to employer-provided health insurance: as many as 20 million persons could lose their health insurance, a group half as large as the existing number of uninsured.[25] These transitional inequities are an inevitable consequence of radical reform, and they should not be the sole reason for opposing reform, but they must be addressed in any politically realistic reform effort.

▶ APPLICATION

The 2005 Panel on Tax Reform

In January, 2005, President Bush appointed the President's Advisory Panel on Federal Tax Reform, charging them to recommend options that would make the tax code "simpler, fairer, and more conducive to economic growth." This panel, consisting of both politicians and tax policy experts, issued a series of recommendations on November 1, 2005, that were generally praised as sensible reforms to our tax code. In particular, the panel proposed several fundamental changes to the structure of the tax code:

---

[23] This assumes that the family takes $12,400 worth of exemptions, as well as the $9,700 standard deduction.
[24] Slemrod and Bakija (2000), p. 10.
[25] Gruber and Lettau (2000).

Move to a broader definition of income and flatter tax rates. As discussed in Chapters 18 and 20, tax efficiency is maximized by a broad income tax base with flat rates. But desires to use the tax code to encourage particular social goals has led to numerous "holes" in the Haig-Simons base. Moreover, those holes, such as the mortgage interest deduction, are often available only to certain taxpayers (those who itemize), and have values that rise with income (since they are deductions rather than credits). The Tax Panel therefore proposed the following changes:

▶ Replace the mortgage interest deduction with a flat 15% credit for all taxpayers for mortgage payments up to the mean home price in the area

▶ Allow a deduction for charitable giving for all taxpayers who give more than 1% of their income (with the goal of subsidizing marginal, rather than inframarginal, gifts to charity)

▶ Limit the exclusion of health insurance premiums from taxation to premiums below the national average level of premiums (for example, employer-provided insurance payments of more than $11,500 for a family would be taxed like wage income)

▶ Remove the deductibility of state and local tax payments

▶ Move from the current system of six brackets to three or four brackets

Simplify and condense complicated aspects of the tax code. Under the current tax code, there are personal exemptions, standard deductions, and child tax credits that all must be computed separately by taxpayers in figuring out their tax burden. The panel proposed replacing these with a single family credit based on family size and marital status. In addition, the current tax code features more than a dozen retirement, education, and health savings plans; the panel proposed to replace these with two accounts, one for retirement savings, and one for preretirement needs such as medical care or education. Finally, the tax panel proposed to abolish the Alternative Minimum Tax, which greatly complicates tax computation for many taxpayers.

Reduce capital taxation. In an effort to promote savings (and thereby growth), the tax panel proposed significantly reducing the double taxation of corporate capital income, either by removing the individual taxation of corporate capital income, or by removing the taxation of corporations.

Despite fears that this report would be highly partisan, these recommendations were generally bipartisan and followed the recommendations that economists of all types have been making for tax reform for years. As evidence of the bipartisan nature of the recommendations, the panel was equally criticized for going too far (by those opposed to reducing capital taxation on equity grounds) and for not going far enough (by those in favor of a pure consumption tax). The one consistent complaint about the analysis was that this plan claimed to be revenue neutral, raising the new revenues necessary to pay for reduced capital taxation and the removal of the AMT. But this revenue neutrality was only true if one assumed that the tax cuts put in place by President Bush in 2001–2003 would be adopted permanently.

If, instead, these tax cuts were allowed to expire, as most are scheduled to do under the current "sunsetting" provisions of the 2001 and 2003 laws, then the current tax system to which this reform is being compared would raise more revenues. The alternative proposed by the panel would then no longer be budget neutral, and the panel would have to suggest higher tax rates to raise the same level of revenues as current law. ◀

25.5
Conclusion

Complaints about the taxation of income in the United States abound. The complications, economic distortions, and redistribution inherent in the U.S. system of income taxation leave many unhappy with the income tax as the nation's primary source of revenue raising. As this chapter has highlighted, however, fundamental reform of the income tax is not easy. Moving to fundamental reform, such as replacing income taxation with consumption taxation or a flat tax, raises difficult issues about the appropriate trade-off between efficiency and equity in our tax code.

▶ **HIGHLIGHTS**

▪ A major problem with the current tax system is compliance, with evasion leading to a large reduction in revenues, tax inefficiency, and horizontal and vertical inequities. Higher tax rates appear to make tax evasion worse.

▪ Tax simplicity is an admirable goal, but it may conflict with other goals, such as tax efficiency.

▪ Higher tax rates appear to lower the tax base, offsetting the revenue gains from higher rates. Most of this reduction in the tax base occurs not through lower gross income, but through lower reported income, more tax avoidance, and more tax evasion, and these effects are largely concentrated at the top of the income distribution.

▪ Reforming taxes can lead to large violations of horizontal equity and can create substantial losers.

▪ A radical revision of our current income tax system favored by many economists is a move to consumption taxation, which would lead to a smaller distortion to savings decisions but would also be less vertically equitable, since the poor consume a higher share of their income.

▪ Consumption taxation can be implemented with a sales tax, a value-added tax (VAT), or a cash-flow tax.

▪ Another fundamental reform favored by many economists is a move to a flat tax, with an exemption and single marginal tax rate. Such a system would improve efficiency, simplicity, and compliance, but would significantly worsen vertical equity and would have very high transitional costs.

▶ QUESTIONS AND PROBLEMS

1. Why would reducing the number of tax brackets reduce the incentives for tax evasion?

2. Describe the advantages of using a value-added tax instead of a sales tax.

3. Compare the two tax systems illustrated in Table 25-5. Describe a taxpayer who would be better off with the existing system than with the flat-tax proposal. Describe a taxpayer who would be better off under the flat-tax system.

4. How would fundamental tax reform likely increase tax efficiency in the United States?

5. Imagine that a $30,000 investment in a good is expected to return you $25,000, and your marginal tax rate is 30%. The government is considering an investment tax credit that reduces the price of the investment. How large would the percentage reduction in the price of the investment have to be for you to make this investment?

6. Tax evasion is particularly common for workers in professions like waiting tables and bartending, where tips make up a substantial fraction of compensation. Use economic theory to explain why this is the case.

7. Describe the equity–efficiency trade-off associated with the Hall-Rabushka flat-tax proposal. How would this trade-off be affected by increasing the exemption level and the flat-tax rate?

8. The government of Tortunia increased its income tax rates by 20% in all tax brackets. The effect of this tax rate increase on total tax revenues works through several pathways. Describe whether you expect the higher tax rate to raise or lower tax revenues through each of the following pathways:

   a. The direct effect of the tax rate increase
   b. The effects of the tax rate increase on personal income
   c. The effects of the tax rate increase on tax evasion or tax avoidance

9. Why would an equitable transition from an income tax to a consumption tax undo some, if not all, of the efficiency gains associated with the introduction of a consumption tax?

▶ ADVANCED QUESTIONS

10. Suppose that the world is populated by people who are identical in every dimension except for their savings behavior. People live for two periods, earning $500 in the first period and nothing in the second period. The income tax on labor earnings and interest income is 40% and the interest rate earned on savings is 8%. There are two types of people. "Hand-to-Mouth" consumers consume everything in the first period, and "Smoothers" split their consumption exactly equally between the two periods.

    a. How much tax would Hand-to-Mouth consumers pay in each of the two periods? How much tax would Smoothers pay in each of the two periods?
    b. Suppose the income tax is replaced by an 80% consumption tax. In this system, for every $1 in consumption, the person is charged $0.80 in tax. How much tax will each type of consumer pay in each period now?

    c. Compare the present value of the taxes paid by the two types of consumers under the two types of tax system. Which tax system is more equitable?

11. What is the difference between tax evasion and tax avoidance? How would you empirically distinguish the two phenomena?

12. Suppose that the tax rate is 30%. Suppose also that the probability of getting caught evading taxes is 10% plus an additional 2.5% for every $1,000 in tax evasion. (Hence, $P = 0.1 + 0.025X$, where X is the number of dollars (in thousands) of evasion.) Individual who are caught evading taxes will be forced to pay the taxes they owe in addition to a $10,000 penalty. How much evasion will a risk-neutral taxpayer engage in? How would your answer change for a risk-averse taxpayer?

13. While proponents of tax simplification argue that a flat tax would be fairer, in other dimensions a flat tax reduces fairness in the tax system. Why is this so?

14. Istalia currently provides a tax credit for families who send their children to college. Faced with dire financial straits, Istalia decides to eliminate this tax credit but to continue to extend it to the families currently taking advantage of it. Given that such a process is inequitable, and that it continues to drain revenues from the government, why is Istalia doing this?

15. Consider two consumption tax systems: (a) one in which all goods are taxed at the same rate, and (b) one in which the "necessities" are not taxed and "luxuries" are taxed at a higher rate. Compare the equity and efficiency of these two systems.

16. When traveling on vacation recently in a country with a large consumption tax, I was presented with a deal: pay cash and get a 10% discount. Given that credit card transactions cost the merchant less than 2%, why did the merchant make me this offer? Would the merchant be more or less likely to make the offer if the country had a value-added tax instead? Explain.

The ℮ icon indicates a question that requires students to apply the empirical economics principles discussed in Chapter 3 and the Empirical Evidence boxes.

absolute deprivation The amount of income the poor have relative to some measure of "minimally acceptable" income.

accounting profits The difference between a firm's revenues and its reported costs of production.

acid rain Rain that is unusually acidic due to contamination by emissions of sulfur dioxide (SO_2) and nitrogen oxide (NO_x).

actuarial adjustments Changes to insurance premiums that insurance companies make in order to compensate for expected expense differences.

actuarially fair premium Insurance premium that is set equal to the insurer's expected payout.

adjusted gross income (AGI) An individual's gross income minus certain deductions, for example, contributions to individual retirement accounts.

adverse selection The fact that insured individuals know more about their risk level than does the insurer might cause those most likely to have the adverse outcome to select insurance, leading insurers to lose money if they offer insurance.

after-tax price The gross price minus the amount of the tax (if producers pay the tax) or plus the amount of the tax (if consumers pay the tax).

agency problem A misalignment of the interests of the owners and the managers of a firm.

Alternative Minimum Tax A tax schedule applied to taxpayers with a high ratio of deductions and exemptions to total income.

altruistic When individuals value the benefits and costs to others in making their consumption choices.

annuity payment A payment that lasts until the recipient's death.

Arrow's Impossibility Theorem There is no social decision (voting) rule that converts individual preferences into a consistent aggregate decision without either (a) restricting preferences or (b) imposing a dictatorship.

attrition Reduction in the size of samples over time, which, if not random, can lead to bias estimates.

automatic stabilization Policies that automatically alter taxes or spending in response to economic fluctuations in order to offset changes in household consumption levels.

average tax rate The percentage of total income that is paid in taxes.

balanced budget incidence Tax incidence analysis that accounts for both the tax and the benefits it brings.

balanced budget requirement (BBR) A law forcing a given government to balance its budget each year (spending = revenue).

basis The purchase price of an asset, for purposes of determining capital gains.

benefit guarantee The cash welfare benefit for individuals with no other income, which may be reduced as income increases.

benefit reduction rate The rate at which welfare benefits are reduced per dollar of other income earned.

benefit taxation Taxation in which individuals are taxed for a public good according to their valuation of the benefit they receive from that good.

bias Any source of difference between treatment and control groups that is correlated with the treatment but is not due to the treatment.

block grant A grant of some fixed amount with no mandate on how it is to be spent.

board of directors A set of individuals who meet periodically to review decisions made by a firm's management and report back to the broader set of owners on management's performance.

bonds Promises by a corporation to make periodic interest payments, as well as ultimate repayment of principal, to the bondholders (the lenders).

broadest definition of tax wedges Any difference between pre- and posttax returns to an activity caused by taxes.

budget constraint A mathematical representation of all the combinations of goods an individual can afford to buy if she spends her entire income.

bureaucracies Organizations of civil servants, such as the U.S. Department of Education or a town's Department of Public Works, that are in charge of carrying out the services of government.

capital accounting A method of measuring the government's fiscal position that accounts for changes in the value of the government's net asset holdings.

capital gain The difference between an asset's purchase price and its sale price. Also, the increase in the price of a share since its purchase.

capital gains Earnings from selling capital assets, such as stocks, paintings, and houses.

capital income taxation The taxes levied on the returns from savings.

cash accounting A method of measuring the government's fiscal position as the difference between current spending and current revenues.

cash–flow accounting Accounting method that calculates costs solely by adding up what the government pays for inputs to a project, and calculates benefits solely by adding up income or government revenues generated by the project.

cash–flow tax A tax on the difference between cash income and savings.

cash welfare Welfare programs that provide cash benefits to recipients.

categorical welfare Welfare programs restricted by some demographic characteristic, such as single motherhood or disability.

causal Two economic variables are causally related if the movement of one causes movement of the other.

charter schools Schools financed with public funds that are not usually under the direct supervision of local school boards or subject to all state regulations for schools.

child care Care provided for children by someone other than the parents of those children.

child support Court-ordered payments from an absent parent to support the upbringing of offspring.

Children's Health Insurance Program (CHIP) Program introduced in 1997 to expand eligibility of children for public health insurance beyond the existing limits of the Medicaid program, generally up to 200% of the poverty line.

Coase Theorem (Part I) When there are well-defined property rights and costless bargaining, then negotiations between the party creating the externality and the party affected by the externality can bring about the socially optimal market quantity.

Coase Theorem (Part II) The efficient solution to an externality does not depend on which party is assigned the property rights, as long as someone is assigned those rights.

commitment devices Devices that help individuals who are aware of their self-control problems fight their bad tendencies.

commodity egalitarianism The principle that society should ensure that individuals meet a set of basic needs, but that beyond that point income distribution is irrelevant.

compensating differentials Additional (or reduced) wage payments to workers to compensate them for the negative (or positive) amenities of a job, such as increased risk of mortality (or a nicer office).

conditional block grant A grant of some fixed amount with a mandate that the money be spent in a particular way.

constrained utility maximization The process of maximizing the well-being (utility) of an individual, subject to her resources (budget constraint).

Consumer Price Index (CPI) An index that captures the change over time in the cost of purchasing a "typical" bundle of goods.

consumer surplus The benefit that consumers derive from consuming a good, above and beyond the price they paid for the good.

consumption smoothing The translation of consumption from periods when consumption is high and thus has low marginal utility to periods when consumption is low and thus has high marginal utility.

consumption tax A tax paid on individual or household consumption of goods (and sometimes services).

contingent valuation Asking individuals to value an option they are not now choosing or do not have the opportunity to choose.

contracting out An approach through which the government retains responsibility for providing a good or service, but hires private sector firms to actually provide the good or service.

control group The set of individuals comparable to the treatment group who are not subject to the intervention being studied.

control variables Variables that are included in cross-sectional regression models to account for differences between treatment and control groups that can lead to bias.

corporate income tax Tax levied on the earnings of corporations.

corporate tax integration The removal of the corporate tax in order to tax corporate income at the individual (shareholder) level.

correlated Two economic variables are correlated if they move together.

corruption The abuse of power by government officials in order to maximize their own personal wealth or that of their associates.

cost-benefit analysis The comparison of costs and benefits of public goods projects to decide if they should be undertaken.

cost-effectiveness analysis For projects that have unmeasurable benefits or are viewed as desirable regardless of the level of benefits, we can compute only their costs and choose the most cost-effective project.

cross-sectional regression analysis Statistical analysis of the relationship between two or more variables exhibited by many individuals at one point in time.

crowd-out As the government provides more of a public good, the private sector will provide less.

current tax incidence The incidence of a tax in relation to an individual's current resources.

cyclically adjusted budget deficit A measure of the government's fiscal position if the economy were operating at full potential GDP.

cycling When majority voting does not deliver a consistent aggregation of individual preferences.

deadweight loss The reduction in social efficiency from denying trades for which benefits exceed costs.

debt The amount a government owes to those who have loaned it money.

debt finance The raising of funds by borrowing from lenders such as banks or by selling bonds.

deficit The amount by which a government's spending exceeds its revenues in a given year.

defined benefit pension plans Pension plans in which workers accrue pension rights during their tenure at the firm, and when they retire the firm pays them a benefit that is a function of that workers' tenure at the firm and of their earnings.

defined contribution pension plans Pension plans in which employers set aside a certain proportion of a worker's earnings (such as 5%) in an investment account, and the worker receives this savings and any accumulated investment earnings when she retires.

demand curve A curve showing the quantity of a good demanded by individuals at each price.

depreciation The rate at which capital investments lose their value over time.

depreciation allowances The amount of money that firms can deduct from their taxes to account for capital investment depreciation.

depreciation schedule The timetable by which an asset may be depreciated.

difference-in-difference estimator The difference between the changes in outcomes for the treatment group that experiences an intervention and the control group that does not.

direct effect of tax changes A higher tax rate that raises revenues on a fixed base of taxation.

direct effects The effects of government interventions that would be predicted if individuals did not change their behavior in response to the interventions.

direct student loans Loans taken directly from the Department of Education.

disability insurance A federal program in which a portion of the Social Security payroll tax is used to pay benefits to workers who have suffered a medical impairment that leaves them unable to work.

discretionary spending Optional spending set by appropriation levels each year, at Congress's discretion.

discretionary stabilization Policy actions taken by the government in response to particular instances of an underperforming or overperforming economy.

dividend The periodic payment that investors receive from the company, per share owned.

dynamic scoring A method used by budget modelers that attempts to model the effect of government policy on both the distribution of total resources and the amount of total resources.

Early Entitlement Age (EEA) The earliest age at which a Social Security recipient can receive reduced benefits.

Earned Income Tax Credit (EITC) A federal income tax policy that subsidizes the wages of low-income earners.

economic depreciation The true deterioration in the value of capital in each period of time.

economic incidence The burden of taxation measured by the change in the resources available to any economic agent as a result of taxation.

economic profits The difference between a firm's revenues and its economic opportunity costs of production.

educational credit market failure The failure of the credit market to make loans that would raise total social surplus by financing productive education.

educational vouchers A fixed amount of money given by the government to families with school-age children, who can spend it at any type of school, public or private.

effective corporate tax rate The percentage increase in the rate of pretax return to capital that is necessitated by taxation.

elasticity of demand The percentage change in the quantity demanded of a good caused by each 1% change in the price of that good.

empirical public finance The use of data and statistical methods to measure the impact of government policy on individuals and markets.

empirical tools The set of tools designed to analyze data and answer questions raised by theoretical analysis.

entitlement spending Mandatory funds for programs for which funding levels are automatically set by the number of eligible recipients, not the discretion of Congress.

equality of opportunity The principle that society should ensure that all individuals have equal opportunities for success, but not focus on the outcomes of choices made.

equity–efficiency trade-off The choice society must make between the total size of the economic pie and its distribution among individuals.

equity finance The raising of funds by sale of ownership shares in a firm.

estate tax A tax levied on the assets of the deceased that are bequeathed to others. Also a form of wealth tax based on the value of the estate left behind when one dies.

ex ante BBR A law forcing either the governor to submit a balanced budget or the legislature to pass a balanced budget, or both, at the start of each fiscal year.

ex post BBR A law forcing a given government to balance its budget by the end of each fiscal year.

excise tax A tax paid on the sales of particular goods, for example, cigarettes or gasoline.

exemption A fixed amount a taxpayer can subtract from AGI for each dependent member of the household, as well as for the taxpayer and the taxpayer's spouse.

expected return The return to a successful investment times the odds of success, plus the return to an unsuccessful investment times the odds of failure.

expected utility model The weighted sum of utilities across states of the world, where the weights are the probabilities of each state occurring.

expenditure tax A consumption tax levied on yearly consumption rather than on specific sales.

expensing investments Deducting the entire cost of the investment from taxes in the year in which the purchase was made.

experience rating Charging a price for insurance that is a function of realized outcomes.

externality Externalities arise whenever the actions of one party make another party worse or better off, yet the first party neither bears the costs nor receives the benefits of doing so.

first-dollar coverage Insurance plans that cover all medical spending, with little or no patient payment.

First Fundamental Theorem of Welfare Economics The competitive equilibrium, where supply equals demand, maximizes social efficiency.

fiscal equalization Policies by which the national government distributes grants to subnational governments in an effort to equalize differences in wealth.

foreign tax credit U.S.-based multinational corporations may claim a credit against their U.S. taxes for any tax payments made to foreign governments.

401(k) accounts Tax-preferred retirement savings vehicles offered by employers, to which employers often match employees' contributions.

four questions of public finance When should the government intervene in the economy? How might the government intervene? What is the effect of those interventions on economic outcomes? Why do governments choose to intervene in the way that they do?

free rider problem When an investment has a personal cost but a common benefit, individuals will underinvest.

Full Benefits Age (FBA) The age at which a Social Security recipient receives full retirement benefits (Primary Insurance Amount).

full shifting When one party in a transaction bears the entire tax burden.

funded Refers to retirement plans in which today's savings are invested in various assets in order to pay future benefits.

general equilibrium tax incidence Analysis that considers the effects on related markets of a tax imposed on one market.

gift tax A tax levied on assets that one individual gives to another in the form of a gift.

global tax system A tax system in which corporations are taxed by their home countries on their income regardless of where it is earned.

government failure The inability or unwillingness of the government to act primarily in the interest of its citizens.

greenhouse effect The process by which gases in the Earth's atmosphere reflect heat from the Sun back to the Earth's surface.

gross income The total of an individual's various sources of income.

gross price The price in the market.

guaranteed student loans Loans taken from private banks for which the banks are guaranteed repayment by the government.

Haig-Simons comprehensive income definition Defines taxable resources as the change in an individual's power to consume during the year.

health maintenance organization (HMO) A health care organization that integrates insurance and delivery of care by, for example, paying its own doctors and hospitals a salary independent of the amount of care they deliver.

health savings account (HSA) A type of insurance arrangement whereby patients face large deductibles, and they put money aside on a tax-free basis to prepay these deductibles.

holdout problem Shared ownership of property rights gives each owner power over all the others.

horizontal equity The principle that similar individuals who make different economic choices should be treated similarly by the tax system.

house price capitalization Incorporation into the price of a house the costs (including local property taxes) and benefits (including local public goods) of living in the house.

human capital A person's stock of skills, which may be increased by further education.

implicit obligation Financial obligations the government has to the future that are not recognized in the annual budgetary process.

impure public goods Goods that satisfy the two public good conditions (non-rival in consumption and non-excludable) to some extent, but not fully.

imputing home earnings Assigning a dollar value to the earnings from work at home.

income effect A rise in the price of a good will typically cause an individual to choose less of all goods because her income can purchase less than before.

indifference curve A graphical representation of all bundles of goods that make an individual equally well off. Because these bundles have equal utility, an individual is indifferent as to which bundle he consumes.

indirect effects The effects of government interventions that arise only because individuals change their behavior in response to the interventions.

indirect effects of tax changes A higher tax rate that lowers the size of the revenue base on which taxes are levied.

individual income tax A tax paid on individual income accrued during the year.

Individual Retirement Account (IRA) A tax-favored retirement savings vehicle primarily for low- and middle-income taxpayers, who make pretax contributions and are then taxed on future withdrawals.

inferior goods Goods for which demand falls as income rises.

information asymmetry The difference in information that is available to sellers and to purchasers in a market.

inframarginal impacts Tax breaks the government gives to those whose behavior is not changed by new tax policy.

in-kind welfare Welfare programs that deliver goods, such as medical care or housing, to recipients.

insurance premiums Money that is paid to an insurer so that an individual will be insured against adverse events.

interest rate The rate of return in the second period on investments made in the first period.

intergenerational equity The treatment of future generations relative to current generations.

intergovernmental grants Payments from one level of government to another.

internality The damage one does to oneself through adverse health (or other) behavior.

internalizing the externality When either private negotiations or government action lead the price to the party to fully reflect the external costs or benefits of that party's actions.

international emissions trading Under the Kyoto treaty, the industrialized signatories are allowed to trade emissions rights among themselves, as long as the total emissions goals are met.

intertemporal budget constraint An equation relating the present discounted value of the government's obligations to the present discounted value of its revenues. Also, the measure of the rate at which individuals can trade off consumption in one period for consumption in another period.

intertemporal choice The choice individuals make about how to allocate their consumption over time.

investment tax credit (ITC) A credit that allows firms to deduct a percentage of their annual qualified investment expenditures from the taxes they owe.

iron triangle There is no way to change either the benefit reduction rate or benefit guarantee to simultaneously encourage work, redistribute more income, and lower costs.

itemized deductions Alternative to the standard deduction, whereby a taxpayer deducts the total amount of money spent on various expenses, such as gifts to charity and interest on home mortgages.

job lock The unwillingness to move to a better job for fear of losing health insurance.

job match quality The marginal product associated with the match of a particular worker with a particular job.

Keogh accounts Retirement savings accounts specifically for the self-employed, under which up to $40,000 per year can be saved on a tax-free basis.

legacy debt The debt incurred by the government because early generations of beneficiaries received much more in benefits than they paid in taxes.

lifetime tax incidence The incidence of a tax in relation to an individual's lifetime resources.

Lindahl pricing An approach to financing public goods in which individuals honestly reveal their willingness to pay and the government charges them that amount to finance the public good.

liquidity constraints Barriers to credit availability that limit the ability of individuals to borrow.

lobbying The expending of resources by certain individuals or groups in an attempt to influence a politician.

lock-in effect In order to minimize the present discounted value of capital gains tax payments, individuals delay selling their capital assets, locking in their assets.

long-term care Health care delivered to the disabled and elderly for their long-term rather than acute needs either in an institutional setting (a nursing home) or in their homes.

lump-sum tax A fixed taxation amount independent of a person's income, consumption of goods and services, or wealth.

magnet schools Special public schools set up to attract talented students or students interested in a particular subject or teaching style.

majority voting The typical mechanism used to aggregate individual votes into a social decision, whereby individual policy options are put to a vote and the option that receives the majority of votes is chosen.

managed care An approach to controlling medical costs using supply-side restrictions such as limited choice of medical provider.

mandate A legal requirement for employers to offer insurance or for individuals to obtain some type of insurance coverage.

marginal cost The incremental cost to a firm of producing one more unit of a good.

marginal deadweight loss The increase in deadweight loss per unit increase in the tax.

marginal impacts Changes in behavior the government hopes to encourage through a given tax incentive.

marginal productivity The impact of a one unit change in any input, holding other inputs constant, on the firm's output.

marginal rate of substitution (MRS) The rate at which a consumer is willing to trade one good for another. The MRS is equal to the slope of the indifference curve, the rate at which the consumer will trade the good on the vertical axis for the good on the horizontal axis.

marginal tax rate The percentage that is paid in taxes of the next dollar earned.

marginal utility The additional increment to utility obtained by consuming an additional unit of a good.

marginal willingness to pay The amount that individuals are willing to pay for the next unit of a good.

market The arena in which demanders and suppliers interact.

market equilibrium The combination of price and quantity that satisfies both demand and supply, determined by the interaction of the supply and demand curves.

market failure A problem that causes the market economy to deliver an outcome that does not maximize efficiency.

marriage tax A rise in the joint tax burden on two individuals from becoming married.

matching grant A grant, the amount of which is tied to the amount of spending by the local community.

means-tested Programs in which eligibility depends on the level of one's current income or assets.

means-tested welfare Welfare programs restricted only by income and asset levels.

median voter The voter whose tastes are in the middle of the set of voters.

Median Voter Theorem Majority voting will yield the outcome preferred by the median voter if preferences are single-peaked.

Medicaid Federal and state program, funded by general tax revenues, that provides health care for poor families, elderly, and disabled.

Medicare Federal program, funded by a payroll tax, that provides health insurance to all elderly over age 65 and disabled persons under age 65.

Medicare Part A Part of the Medicare program that covers inpatient hospital costs and some costs of long-term care; financed from a payroll tax.

Medicare Part B Part of the Medicare program that covers physician expenditures, outpatient hospital expenditures, and other services; financed from enrollee premiums and general revenues.

Medicare Part D Part of the Medicare program that covers prescription drug expenditures.

minimum wage Legally mandated minimum amount that workers must be paid for each hour of work.

models Mathematical or graphical representations of reality.

monopoly markets Markets in which there is only one supplier of a good.

moral hazard Adverse actions taken by individuals or producers in response to insurance against adverse outcomes.

mortgage Agreement to use a certain property, usually a home, as security for a loan.

multinational firms Firms that operate in multiple countries.

national health insurance A system whereby the government provides insurance to all its citizens, as in Canada, without the involvement of a private insurance industry.

natural monopoly A market in which, because of the nature of a good, there is a cost advantage to have only one firm provide the good to all consumers in a market.

negative consumption externality When an individual's consumption reduces the well-being of others who are not compensated by the individual.

negative production externality When a firm's production reduces the well-being of others who are not compensated by the firm.

1970 Clean Air Act Landmark federal legislation that first regulated acid rain–causing emissions by setting maximum standards for atmospheric concentrations of various substances, including SO_2.

no-fault insurance When there is a qualifying injury, the workers' compensation benefits are paid out by the insurer regardless of whether the injury was the worker's or the firm's fault.

nominal interest rate The interest rate earned by a given investment.

nominal prices Prices stated in today's dollars.

non-excludable Individuals cannot deny each other the opportunity to consume a good.

nongroup insurance market The market through which individuals or families buy insurance directly rather than through a group, such as the workplace.

non-rival in consumption One individual's consumption of a good does not affect another's opportunity to consume the good.

normal goods Goods for which demand increases as income rises.

numeraire good A good for which the price is set at $1 in order to model choice between goods, which depends on relative, not absolute, prices.

observational data Data generated by individual behavior observed in the real world, not in the context of deliberately designed experiments.

oligopoly markets Markets in which firms have some market power in setting prices but not as much as a monopolist.

opportunity cost The cost of any purchase is the next best alternative use of that money or the forgone opportunity. Also, the social marginal cost of any resource is the value of that resource in its next best use.

optimal commodity taxation Choosing the tax rates across goods to minimize deadweight loss for a given government revenue requirement.

optimal fiscal federalism The question of which activities should take place at which level of government.

optimal income taxation Choosing the tax rates across income groups to maximize social welfare subject to a government revenue requirement.

ordeal mechanisms Features of welfare programs that make them unattractive, leading to the self-selection of only the most needy recipients.

overtime pay rules Workers in most jobs must legally be paid one and a half times their regular hourly pay if they work more than 40 hours per week.

partial equilibrium tax incidence Analysis that considers the impact of a tax on a market in isolation.

partially experience-rated The tax that finances the UI program rises as firms have more layoffs, but not on a one-for-one basis.

payroll tax A tax levied on income earned on one's job.

pension plan An employer-sponsored plan through which employers and employees save on a (generally) tax-free basis for the employees' retirement.

political economy The theory of how the political process produces decisions that affect individuals and the economy.

pooling equilibrium A market equilibrium in which all types of people buy full insurance even though it is not fairly priced to all individuals.

positive consumption externality When an individual's consumption increases the well-being of others but the individual is not compensated by those others.

positive production externality When a firm's production increases the well-being of others but the firm is not compensated by those others.

poverty line The federal government's standard for measuring absolute deprivation.

precautionary saving model A model of savings that accounts for the fact that individual savings serve at least partly to smooth consumption over future uncertainties.

preexisting distortions Market failures, such as externalities or imperfect competition, that are in place before any government intervention.

preferred provider organization (PPO) A health care organization that lowers care costs by shopping for health care providers on behalf of the insured.

premium support A system of full choice among health care plans for Medicare enrollees, whereby they receive a voucher for a certain amount that they can apply to a range of health insurance options (either paying or receiving the difference between plan premiums and the voucher amount).

present discounted value (PDV) The value of each period's dollar amount in today's terms. A dollar next year is worth $1 + r$ times less than a dollar now because the dollar could earn $r\%$ interest if invested.

primary earners Family members who are the main source of labor income for a household.

private marginal benefit (PMB) The direct benefit to consumers of consuming an additional unit of a good by the consumer.

private marginal cost (PMG) The direct cost to producers of producing an additional unit of a good.

privatization A proposal to reform Social Security by allowing individuals to invest their payroll taxes in various assets through individually controlled accounts.

producer surplus The benefit that producers derive from selling a good, above and beyond the cost of producing that good.

profits The difference between a firm's revenues and costs, maximized when marginal revenues equal marginal costs.

progressive Tax systems in which effective average tax rates rise with income.

property tax A form of wealth tax levied on the value of real estate, including the value of the land and any structures built on the land.

proportional Tax systems in which effective average tax rates do not change with income, so all taxpayers pay the same proportion of their income in taxes.

prospective capital gains tax reduction Capital gains tax cuts that apply only to investments made from this day forward.

Prospective Payment System (PPS) Medicare's system for reimbursing hospitals based on nationally standardized payments for specific diagnoses.

prospective reimbursement The practice of paying providers based on what treating patients should cost, not on what the provider spends.

public choice theory School of thought emphasizing that the government may not act to maximize the well-being of its citizens.

public finance The study of the role of the government in the economy.

public goods Goods for which the investment of any one individual benefits everyone in a larger group.

pure public goods Goods that are perfectly non-rival in consumption and are non-excludable.

quasi-experiments Changes in the economic environment that create nearly identical treatment and control groups for studying the effect of that environmental change, allowing public finance economists to take advantage of randomization created by external forces.

Ramsey Rule To minimize the deadweight loss of a tax system while raising a fixed amount of revenue, taxes should be set across commodities so that the ratio of the marginal deadweight loss to marginal revenue raised is equal across commodities.

randomized trial The ideal type of experiment designed to test causality, whereby a group of individuals is randomly divided into a treatment group, which receives the treatment of interest, and a control group, which does not.

real interest rate The nominal interest rate minus the inflation rate; measures an individual's actual improvement in purchasing power due to savings.

real prices Prices stated in some constant year's dollars.

redistribution The shifting of resources from some groups in society to others.

reduced form estimates Measures of the total impact of an independent variable on a dependent variable, without decomposing the source of that behavior response in terms of underlying utility functions.

referendum A measure placed on the ballot by the government allowing citizens to vote on state laws or constitutional amendments that have already been passed by the state legislature.

refund The difference between the amount withheld from a worker's earnings and the taxes owed if the former is higher.

refundable Describes tax credits that are available to individuals even if they pay few or no taxes.

regression line The line that measures the best linear approximation to the relationship between any two variables.

regressive Tax systems in which effective average tax rates fall with income.

relative income inequality The amount of income the poor have relative to the rich.

rents Payments to resource deliverers that exceed those necessary to employ the resource.

repatriation The return of income from a foreign country to a corporation's home country.

replacement rate The ratio of benefits received to earnings prior to the entitling event.

retained earnings Any net profits that are kept by the company rather than paid out to debt or equity holders.

retirement hazard rate The percentage of workers retiring at a certain age.

retrospective reimbursement Reimbursing physicians for the costs they have already incurred.

returns to education The benefits that accrue to society when students get more schooling or when they get schooling from a higher-quality environment.

revealed preference Letting the actions of individuals reveal their valuation.

risk aversion The extent to which individuals are willing to bear risk.

risk pool The group of individuals who enroll in an insurance plan.

risk premium The amount that risk-averse individuals will pay for insurance above and beyond the actuarially fair price.

Roth IRA A variation on normal IRAs to which taxpayers make after-tax contributions but may then make tax-free withdrawals later in life.

sales taxes Taxes paid by consumers to vendors at the point of sale.

savings The excess of current income over current consumption.

school finance equalization Laws that mandate redistribution of funds across communities in a state to ensure more equal financing of schools.

screening A model that suggests that education provides only a means of separating high- from low-ability individuals and does not actually improve skills.

Second Fundamental Theorem of Welfare Economics Society can attain any efficient outcome by suitably redistributing resources among individuals and then allowing them to freely trade.

secondary earners Workers in the family other than the primary earners.

secondhand smoke Tobacco smoke inhaled by individuals in the vicinity of smokers.

self-control problem An inability to carry out optimal strategies for consumption.

self-insurance The private means of smoothing consumption over adverse events, such as through one's own savings, labor supply of family members, or borrowing from friends.

separating equilibrium A market equilibrium in which different types of people buy different kinds of insurance products designed to reveal their true types.

shareholders Individuals who have purchased ownership stakes in a company.

short-run stabilization issues The role of the government in combating the peaks and troughs of the business cycle.

simulation exercises The numerical simulation of economic agents' behavior based on measured economic parameters in an attempt to determine optimal tax rates or other outcomes of interest.

single-peaked preferences Preferences with only a single local maximum, or peak, so that utility falls as choices move away in any direction from that peak.

SO_2 allowance system The feature of the 1990 amendments to the Clean Air Act that granted plants permits to emit SO_2 in limited quantities and allowed them to trade those permits.

social capital The value of altruistic and communal behavior in society.

social discount rate The appropriate value of r to use in computing *PDV* for social investments.

social insurance programs Government provision of insurance against adverse events to address failures in the private insurance market.

social marginal benefit (SMB) The private marginal benefit to consumers plus any costs associated with the consumption of the good that are imposed on others.

social marginal cost (SMC) The private marginal cost to producers plus any costs associated with the production of the good that are imposed on others.

Social Security A federal program that taxes workers to provide income support to the elderly.

Social Security Wealth The expected present discounted values of a person's future Social Security payments minus the expected present discounted value of a person's payroll tax payments.

social welfare The level of well-being in society.

social welfare function (SWF) A function that combines the utility functions of all individuals into an overall social utility function.

special education Programs to educate disabled children.

standard deduction Fixed amount that a taxpayer can deduct from taxable income.

standardized (structural) budget deficit A long-term measure of the government's fiscal position, with short-term factors removed.

states of the world The set of outcomes that are possible in an uncertain future.

static scoring A method used by budget modelers that assumes that government policy changes only the distribution of total resources, not the amount of total resources.

statutory incidence The burden of a tax borne by the party that sends the check to the government.

structural estimates Estimates of the features that drive individual decisions, such as income and substitution effects or utility parameters.

subsidiaries The production arms of a corporation that are located in other nations.

subsidy Government payment to an individual or firm that lowers the cost of consumption or production, respectively.

substitution effect Holding utility constant, a relative rise in the price of a good will always cause an individual to choose less of that good.

supply curve A curve showing the quantity of a good that firms are willing to supply at each price.

tax-benefit linkages The relationship between the taxes people pay and the government goods and services they get in return.

tax capitalization The change in asset prices that occurs due to a change in the tax levied on the stream of returns from that asset.

tax compliance Efforts to reduce the evasion of taxes.

tax credits Amounts by which taxpayers are allowed to reduce the taxes they owe to the government through spending, for example, on child care.

tax deductions Amounts by which taxpayers are allowed to reduce their taxable income through spending on items such as charitable donations or home mortgage interest.

tax evasion Illegal nonpayment of taxes.

tax expenditures Government revenue losses attributable to tax law provisions that allow special exclusions, exemptions, or deductions from gross income, or that provide a special credit, preferential tax rate, or deferral of liability.

tax incidence Assessing which party (consumers or producers) bears the true burden of a tax.

tax loss offset The extent to which taxpayers can deduct net losses on investments from their taxable income.

tax price For school equalization schemes, the amount of revenue a local district would have to raise in order to gain $1 more of spending.

tax shelters Activities whose sole reason for existence is tax minimization.

tax subsidy to employer-provided health insurance Workers are taxed on their wage compensation but not on compensation in the form of health insurance, leading to a subsidy to health insurance provided through employers.

tax wedge The difference between what consumers pay and what producers receive (net of tax) from a transaction.

taxable income The amount of income left after subtracting exemptions and deductions from adjusted gross income.

taxation on accrual Taxes paid each period on the return earned by an asset in that period.

taxation on realization Taxes paid on an asset's return only when that asset is sold.

taxing consumption Taxing individuals based not on what they earn but on what they consume (such as through a sales tax).

territorial tax system A tax system in which corporations earning income abroad pay tax only to the government of the country in which the income is earned.

theoretical tools The set of tools designed to understand the mechanics behind economic decision making.

time series analysis Analysis of the comovement of two series over time.

total social surplus (social efficiency) The sum of consumer surplus and producer surplus.

transfer prices The amount that one subsidiary of a corporation reimburses another subsidiary of the same corporation for goods transferred between the two.

transfer tax A tax levied on the transfer of assets from one individual to another.

transitional inequities from tax reform Changes in the treatment of similar individuals who have made different decisions in the past and are therefore differentially treated by tax reform.

treatment group The set of individuals who are subject to an intervention being studied.

UI replacement rate The ratio of unemployment insurance benefits to pre-unemployment earnings.

uncompensated care The costs of delivering health care for which providers are not reimbursed.

unemployment insurance A federally mandated, state-run program in which payroll taxes are used to pay benefits to workers laid off by companies.

unfunded Refers to retirement plans in which payments collected from today's workers go directly to today's retirees, instead of being invested in order to pay future benefits.

utility function A mathematical function representing an individual's set of preferences, which translates her well-being from different consumption bundles into units that can be compared in order to determine choice.

value-added tax (VAT) A consumption tax levied on each stage of a good's production on the increase in value of the good at that stage of production.

value of additional government revenues The value of having another dollar in the government's hands relative to its next best use in the private sector.

vertical equity The principle that groups with more resources should pay higher taxes than groups with fewer resources.

voter initiative The placement of legislation on the ballot by citizens.

warm glow model Model of public good provision in which individuals care about both the total amount of the public good and their particular contributions as well.

wealth taxes Taxes paid on the value of the assets, such as real estate or stocks, held by a person or family.

welfare economics The study of the determinants of well-being, or welfare, in society.

withholding The subtraction of estimated taxes owed directly from a worker's earnings.

workers' compensation State-mandated insurance, which firms generally buy from private insurers, that pays for medical costs and lost wages associated with an on-the-job injury.

zoning Restrictions that towns place on the use of real estate.

Acemoglu, Daron. "Why Not a Political Coase Theorem? Social Conflict, Commitment, and Politics." *Journal of Comparative Economics* 31 (December 2003): 620–52.

Acemoglu, Daron, Simon Johnson, and James A. Robinson. "The Colonial Origins of Comparative Development: An Empirical Investigation." *American Economic Review* 91 (December 2001): 1369–1401.

Administration for Children & Families. *Fiscal Year 2004 TANF Financial Data.* 2005.

Administration for Children & Families. *Office of Family Assistance TANF Caseload Data.* Accessed last on June 15, 2006, at http://www.acf.hhs.gov/programs/ofa/caseload/caseloadindex.htm.

Aeppel, Timothy. "Tax Break Brings Billions to U.S., but Impact on Hiring is Unclear." *Wall Street Journal* (October 5, 2005a), p. A1.

Aeppel, Timothy. "Tax Break on Foreign Profits Is Temporary, but Will U.S. Companies Expect an Encore?" *Wall Street Journal* (December 19, 2005b), p. A2.

Ainslie, G., and N. Haslam. "Hyperbolic Discounting." In *Choice Over Time,* edited by G. Loewenstein and J. Elster. New York: Russell Sage Foundation, 1992.

Aizcorbe, Ana M., Arthur B. Kennickell, and Kevin B. Moore. "Recent Changes in U.S. Family Finances: Evidence from the 1998 and 2001 Survey of Consumer Finances." *Federal Reserve Bulletin* 89 (January 2003): 1–32.

Akerlof, George A. "The Market for Lemons: Quality Uncertainty and the Market Mechanism." *Quarterly Journal of Economics* 84 (August 1970): 488–500.

Allen, Mike. "Bush Signs Bill Providing Big Farm Subsidy Increases." *Washington Post* (May 14, 2002), p. A1.

American Cancer Society. *Cancer Facts & Figures 2006.* Atlanta, GA: American Cancer Society, 2006, p. 39.

American Council of Life Insurers. *Life Insurers Fact Book, 2005.* Washington, DC: ACLI, 2005.

American Institute of Certified Public Accountants. *Understanding Social Security Reform: The Issues and Alternatives.* New York: AICPA, March 2005.

Anderson, John E., and Lilia Carasciuc. "Tax Evasion in a Transition Economy: Theory and Empirical Evidence from the Former Soviet Union Republic of Moldova" (September 1999). Accessed at http://ssrn.com/abstract=182812.

Anderson, Lisa R., Jennifer M. Mellor, and Jeffrey Milyo. "Social Capital and Contributions in a Public Goods Experiment." University of Chicago, Harris School Working Paper Series 03.17, 2003.

Anderson, Patricia M., and Phillip B. Levine. "Child Care Costs and Mother's Employment Decisions." In *Finding Jobs: Work and Welfare Reform,* edited by David Card and Rebecca Blank. New York: Russell Sage Foundation, 2000.

Anderson, Patricia M., and Bruce D. Meyer. "The Unemployment Insurance Payroll Tax and Interindustry and Interfirm Subsidies." In *Tax Policy and the Economy,* Vol. 7, edited by J. Poterba. Cambridge, MA: MIT Press, 1993, pp. 111–44.

Anderson, Patricia M., and Bruce D. Meyer. "The Effects of the Unemployment Insurance Payroll Tax on Wages, Employment, Claims and Denials." *Journal of Public Economics* 78 (October 2000): 81–106.

Andreoni, James. "An Experimental Test of the Public-Goods Crowding-Out Hypothesis." *American Economic Review* 83 (December 1993): 1317–27.

Andrews, Edmund L. "U.S. Companies Benefit from One-Time Law on Foreign Profits." *New York Times* (February 1, 2005), p. 1.

Angrist, Joshua, et al. "Vouchers for Private Schooling in Colombia: Evidence from a Randomized Natural Experiment." *American Economic Review* 92 (December 2002): 1535–58.

Aron-Dine, Aviva, and Joel Friedman. "New Estate Tax Anecdotes Dredge Up Old Myth That the Estate Tax Claims Half of an Estate." Washington, DC: Center on Budget and Policy Priorities, June 14, 2006.

Ardagna, Silvia, Francesco Caselli, and Timonhy Lane. "Fiscal Discipline and the Cost of Public Debt Service: Some Estimates from OECD Countries." National Bureau of Economic Research Working Paper 10788, September 2004.

Arrow, Kenneth J. *Social Choice and Individual Values.* New York: Wiley, 1951.

Ashraf, Nava, Dean Karlan, and Wesley Yin. "Tying Odysseus to the Mast: Evidence from a Commitment Savings Product in the Philippines." *Quarterly Journal of Economics* 121 (May 2006): pp. 635–72.

Atkinson, Anthony B., and Joseph E. Stiglitz, "The Structure of Indirect Taxation and Economic Efficiency," *Journal of Public Economics* 1 (1972): 97–119

Attanasio, Orazio P., and Agar Brugiavini. "Social Security and Households' Saving." *Quarterly Journal of Economics* 118 (3, August 2003): 1075–1119.

Attanasio, Orazio P., and Susann Rohwedder. "Pension Wealth and Household Saving: Evidence from Pension Reforms in the United Kingdom." *American Economic Review* 93 (5, December 2003): 1499–1521.

Attanasio, Orazio P., and Guglielmo Weber. "Is Consumption Growth Consistent with Intertemporal Optimization? Evidence from the Consumer Expenditure Survey." *Journal of Political Economy* 103 (December 1995): 1121–57.

Auerbach, Alan J. "Taxation and Corporate Financial Policy." In *Handbook of Public Economics*, Vol. 3, edited by Alan J. Auerbach and Martin Feldstein. Amsterdam: Elsevier, 2002.

Auerbach, Alan J., Jagadeesh Gokhale, and Laurence J. Kotlikoff. "Generational Accounts: A Meaningful Alternative to Deficit Accounting." In *Tax Policy and the Economy*, Vol. 5, edited by David Bradford. Cambridge, MA: MIT Press, 1991.

Auerbach, Alan J., Jagadeesh Gokhale, and Laurence J. Kotlikoff. "Generational Accounting: A Meaningful Way to Evaluate Fiscal Policy." *Journal of Economic Perspectives* 8 (Winter 1994): 73–94.

Baker, Michael, Jonathan Gruber, and Kevin Milligan. "Universal Childcare, Maternal Labor Supply, and Family Well-Being." National Bureau of Economic Research Working Paper 11832, December 2005.

Bakija, Jon M., William G. Gale., and Joel B. Slemrod. "Charitable Bequests and Taxes on Inheritance and Estates: Aggregate Evidence from across States and Time." *American Economic Review* 93 (May 2003): 366–370.

Balz, Dan, and John E. Yang. "Bush Abandons Campaign Pledge, Calls for New Taxes." *Washington Post* (June 27, 1990), p. A1.

Barron, James. "High Cost of Military Parts." *New York Times* (September 1, 1983), p. D1.

Batchelder, Lilly, J. Fred Goldberg, and Peter Orszag. "Efficiency and Tax Incentives: The Case for Refundable Tax Credits." New York Law School mimeo, 2006.

Becker, Gary S., and Kevin M. Murphy. "A Theory of Rational Addiction." *Journal of Political Economy* 96 (August 1988): 675–700.

Berger, Mark C., and Dan A. Black. "Child Care Subsidies, Quality of Care, and the Labor Supply of Low-Income, Single Mothers." *Review of Economics and Statistics* 74 (November 1992): 635–42.

Bergstrom, T. C., J. Roberts, D. L. Rubinfeld, and P. Shapiro. "A Test for Efficiency in the Supply of Public Education." *Journal of Public Economics* 35 (1988): 289–307.

Bernheim, B. Douglas, Robert J. Lemke, and John Karl Scholz. "Do Estate and Gift Taxes Affect the Timing of Private Transfers?" *Journal of Public Economics* 88 (December 2004): 2617–34.

Besley, Timothy, Torsten Persson, and Daniel Sturm. "Political Competition and Economic Performance: Theory and Evidence from the United States." National Bureau of Economic Research Working Paper 11484, July 2005.

Bianchi, Marco, Bjorn Gudmundsson, and Gylfi Zoega. "Iceland's Natural Experiment in Supply-Side Economics." *American Economic Review* 91 (December 2001): 1564–79.

Bifulco, Robert, and Helen F. Ladd. "The Impacts of Charter Schools on Student Achievement: Evidence from North Carolina." University of Connecticut mimeo, June 2004.

Bitler, Marianne, Jonah Gelbach, and Hilary Hoynes. "What Mean Impacts Miss: Distributional Effects of Welfare Reform Experiments." National Bureau of Economic Research Working Paper 10121, November 2003.

Blank, Rebecca. "When Can Public Policy Makers Rely on Private Markets? The Effective Provision of Social Services." *Economic Journal* 110 (March 2000): C34–9.

Blank, Rebecca. "Evaluating Welfare Reform in the United States." *Journal of Economic Literature* 40 (December 2002): 1105–66.

Blank, Rebecca, and David Card. "Recent Trends in Insured and Uninsured Unemployment: Is There an Explanation?" *Quarterly Journal of Economics* 106 (4, 1991).

Blank, Rebecca M., David Card, and Philip K. Robins. "Financial Incentives for Increasing Work and Income among Low-Income Families." In *Finding Jobs: Work and Welfare Reform*, edited by David Card and Rebecca M. Blank. New York: Russell Sage Foundation, 2000, pp. 373–419.

Blau, Francine and Lawrence M. Kahn. "Changes in the Labor Supply Behavior of Married Women: 1980–2000." National Bureau of Economic Research Working Paper 11230, March 2005.

Bohrnstedt, George W., and Brian M. Stecher. "What We Have Learned About Class Size Reduction in California." Sacramento: California Department of Education, September 2002.

Bosworth, Barry, and Gary Burtless. "Supply-Side Consequences of Social Security Reform: Impacts on Saving and Employment." CRR Working Paper 2004-01, January 2004.

Bound, John, Jeffrey Groen, Gabor Kezdi, and Sarah Turner. "Trade in University Training: Cross-State Variation in the Production and Stock of College-Educated Labor." *Journal of Econometrics* 121 (July–August 2004): 143–73.

Bradford, David. "Factor Prices May Be Constant But Factor Returns Are Not." *Economics Letters* 1 (1978): 199–203.

Brennan, Geoffrey, and James M. Buchanan. *The Power to Tax: Analytical Foundations of a Fiscal Constitution.* Cambridge: Cambridge University Press, 1980.

Brown, Warren, and Frank Swoboda. "Government Ends Probe of GM Trucks." *Washington Post* (December 3, 1994), p. A1.

Bruni, Frank. "Bush, in a Broad Attack on Gore, Paints Him as the Candidate of Big Government." *New York Times* (September 17, 2000), sec. 1, p. 22.

Brunner, Eric J. "Free Riders or Easy Riders? An Examination of the Voluntary Provision of Public Radio." *Public Choice* 97 (1998): 587–604.

Brunner, Eric, Jon Sonstelie, and Mark Thayer. "Capitalization and the Voucher: An Analysis of Precinct Returns from California's Proposition 174." *Journal of Urban Economics* 50 (2001): 517–536.

Bryan, Frank M. *Real Democracy: The New England Town Meeting and How It Works.* Chicago: University of Chicago Press, 2003.

Bryant, Nelson. "Trout Feel Sting of Acid Rain." *New York Times* (July 20, 1980), sec. 5, p. 7.

Buchanan, James M., and Gordon Tullock. *The Calculus of Consent: Logical Foundations of Constitutional Democracy.* Ann Arbor: University of Michigan Press, 1962.

Buffett, Warren. "Dividend Voodoo." *Washington Post* (May 20, 2003), p. A19.

Bull, Nicholas, Janet Holtzblatt, James R. Nunns, and Robert Rebelein. "Defining and Measuring Marriage Penalties and Bonuses." U.S. Department of the Treasury, OTA Paper 82-Revised, November 1999.

Bureau of Economic Analysis. *National Income and Product Accounts (NIPA).* Last accessed on July 12, 2006, at http://www.bea.gov/bea/dn/nipaweb/SelectTable.asp?Selected=N.

Bureau of Labor Statistics. "Consumer Price Index." Last accessed on June 21, 2006, at http://www.bls.gov/cpi/home.htm.

Burman, Leonard E. "Roth Conversions as Revenue Raisers: Smoke and Mirrors." *Tax Notes*, May 22, 2006.

Burman, Leonard E., William G. Gale, and Jeffrey Rohaly. "The Expanding Reach of the Individual Alternative Minimum Tax." *Journal of Economic Perspectives* 17 (Spring 2003): 173–86.

Burman, Leonard E., William G. Gale, and Jeff Rohaly. "The Expanding Reach of the Individual Alternative Minimum Tax." Tax Policy Center, May 2005 update.

Burman, Leonard E., and William C. Randolph. "Measuring Permanent Responses to Capital-Gains Tax Changes in Panel Data." *American Economic Review* 84 (September 1994): 794–809.

Burtraw, Dallas, Alan Krupnick, Eric Mansur, David Austin, and Deirdre Farrell. "The Costs and Benefits of Reducing Air Pollutants Related to Acid Rain." Resources for the Future Discussion Paper 97-31-REV (September 1997).

Cancian, Maria, and Deborah Reed. "Changes in Married Couples' Intra-household Distribution of Work and Earnings." Presentation paper for the Population Association of America 2004 Annual Meeting, March 2004.

Card, David, Carlos Dobkin, and Nicole Maestas. "The Impact of Nearly Universal Insurance Coverage on Health Care Utilization and Health: Evidence from Medicare." National Bureau of Economic Research Working Paper 10365, 2004.

Card, David, and A. Abigail Payne. "School Finance Reform, the Distribution of School Spending, and the Distribution of Student Test Scores." *Journal of Public Economics* 83 (January 2002): 49–82.

CBPP, The Concord Coalition, and CED. "Joint Statement in Support of Restoring Pay-As-You-Go Budget Enforcement for Tax Cuts and Entitlements." Washington, DC, April 20, 2004.

Centers for Disease Control and Prevention. "Annual Smoking-Attributable Mortality, Years of Potential Life Lost, and Productivity Losses—United States, 1997–2001. *Morbidity and Morality Weekly Report* 54 (25, July 1, 2005a): 625–628.

Centers for Disease Control and Prevention. *Health, United States, 2005.* Washington, DC: U.S. Government Printing Office, 2005b.

Centers for Disease Control and Prevention. "Infant, Neonatal, and Postnatal Deaths, Percent of Total Deaths, and Mortality Rates for the 15 Leading Causes of Infant Death by Race and Sex: United States, 2003." March 2006a.

Centers for Disease Control and Prevention. "Deaths: Final Data for 2003." *National Vital Statistics Report* 54 (13, April 19, 2006b).

Centers for Medicare and Medicaid Services. "Medicare & You 2006." January 2006a.

Centers for Medicare and Medicaid Services. *The 2006 Annual Report of the Boards of Trustees of the Federal Hospital Insurance and Federal Supplementary Medical Insurance Trust Funds.* Washington, DC, May 1, 2006b.

Centers for Medicare and Medicaid Services. "Health Accounts: National Health Expenditures." Last accessed on June 18, 2006c, at http://www.cms.hhs.gov/NationalHealthExpendData/.

Centers for Medicare and Medicaid Services. "Medicaid Mandatory Eligibility Groups." Last accessed on June 18, 2006d, at http://www.cms.hhs.gov/MedicaidEligibility/.

Chaloupka, F. J., and Kenneth E. Warner. "The Economics of Smoking." In *Handbook of Health Economics*, Vol. 1B, edited by A. J. Culyer and J. P. Newhouse. Amsterdam: Elsevier, 2000, pp. 1539–1628.

Chamley, Christophe. "Optimal Taxation of Capital in General Equilibrium." *Econometrica* 54 (1986): 607–22.

Chandler, Clay. "Are 'Targeted Cuts' on Target?" *Washington Post* (October 20, 1996), p. H1.

Chandler, Clay. "Treasury Official Slams Estate Tax Rollback Effort." *Washington Post* (April 22, 1997), p. C1.

Chandra, Amitabh, Jonathan Gruber, and Robin McKnight. "Medical Price Sensitivity and Optimal Health Insurance for the Elderly." MIT mimeo, 2006.

Chay, Kenneth Y., and Michael Greenstone. "Air Quality, Infant Mortality, and the Clean Air Act of 1970." National Bureau of Economic Research Working Paper 10053, October 2003.

Chay, Kenneth Y., and Michael Greenstone. "Does Air Quality Matter? Evidence from the Housing Market." *Journal of Political Economy* 113 (2, April 2005): 376–424.

Chernew, Michael E., Richard A. Hirth, and David M. Cutler. "Increased Spending on Health Care: How Much Can the United States Afford?" *Health Affairs* 22 (July/August 2003): 15–25.

Chetty, Raj, and Adam Looney. "Consumption Smoothing and the Welfare Consequences of Social Insurance in Developing Economies," National Bureau of Economic Research Working Paper 11709, October 2005.

Chetty, Raj, and Emmanuel Saez. "The Effects of the 2003 Divided Tax Cut on Corporate Behavior: Interpreting the Evidence," *American Economic Review* 96 (May 2006): 124–129.

Chou, Shin-Yi, Jin-Tan Liu, and James K. Hammitt. "National Health Insurance and Precautionary Saving: Evidence from Taiwan." *Journal of Public Economics* 87 (September 2003): 1873–94.

Clotfelter, Charles T. "Tax Evasion and Tax Rates: An Analysis of Individual Returns." *Review of Economics and Statistics* 65 (August 1983): 363–73.

Coase, Ronald H. "The Problem of Social Cost." *Journal of Law and Economics* 3 (1960): 1–44.

Coase, Ronald H. "The Lighthouse in Economics." *Journal of Law and Economics* 17 (October 1974): 357–76.

Coates, Dennis, and Michael Munger. "Legislative Voting and the Economic Theory of Politics." *Southern Economic Journal* 61 (January 1995): 861–72.

Collins, Julie, Deen Kemsley, and Mark Lang. "Cross-Jurisdictional Income Shifting and Earnings Valuation." *Journal of Accounting Research* 36 (Autumn 1998): 209–29.

Congressional Budget Office. "An Analysis of the Administration's Health Proposal." Washington, DC: U.S. Government Printing Office, 1994.

Congressional Budget Office. "For Better or for Worse: Marriage and the Federal Income Tax." Washington, DC: U.S. Government Printing Office, June 1997.

Congressional Budget Office. "Issues in Designing a Prescription Drug Benefit for Medicare." Washington, DC: U.S. Government Printing Office, October 2002.

Congressional Budget Office. "The Economics of Climate Change: A Primer." Washington, DC: U.S. Government Printing Office, 2003a.

Congressional Budget Office. *How CBO Analyzed the Macroeconomic Effects of the President's Budget.* Washington, DC: U.S. Government Printing Office, July 2003b.

Congressional Budget Office. *Historical Effective Tax Rates: 1979 to 2003.* Released December 2005.

Congressional Budget Office. *The Uncertainty of Budget Projections: A Discussion of Data and Methods.* Washington, DC: U.S. Government Printing Office, 2006a.

Congressional Budget Office. *The Budget and Economic Outlook: Fiscal Years 2007 to 2016.* Washington, DC: U.S. Government Printing Office, 2006b.

Congressional Budget Office. *Analytical Perspectives, Budget of the United States, Fiscal Year 2007.* Washington, DC: U.S. Government Printing Office, 2006c.

Crenshaw, Albert B. "An IRS Chiller: Case of the Disappearing Dependents." *Washington Post* (February 14, 1991), p. A21.

Cullen, Julie Berry, and Jonathan Gruber. "Does Unemployment Insurance Crowd Out Spousal Labor Supply?" *Journal of Labor Economics* 18 (July 2000): 546–72.

Cullen, Julie Berry, Brian A. Jacob, and Steven Levitt. "The Effect of School Choice on Student Outcomes: Evidence from Randomized Lotteries." National Bureau of Economic Research Working Paper 10113, November 2003.

Currie, Janet, and Jonathan Gruber. "Saving Babies: The Efficacy and Cost of Recent Changes in the Medicaid Eligibility of Pregnant Women." *Journal of Political Economy* 104 (December 1996a): 1263–96.

Currie, Janet, and Jonathan Gruber. "Health Insurance Eligibility, Utilization of Medical Care, and Child Health." *Quarterly Journal of Economics,* 111 (2, May 1996b): 431–66.

Currie, Janet, and Enrico Moretti. "Mother's Education and the Intergenerational Transmission of Human Capital: Evidence from College Openings." *Quarterly Journal of Economics* 118 (November 2003): 1495–1532.

Cutler, David M. *Your Money or Your Life: Strong Medicine for America's Health Care System.* New York: Oxford University Press, 2004.

Cutler, David M., Mark McClellan, Joseph P. Newhouse, and Dahlia Remler. "Are Medical Prices Declining? Evidence from Heart Attack Treatments." *Quarterly Journal of Economics* 113 (November 1998): 991–1024.

Cutler, David M., and Sarah J. Reber. "Paying for Health Insurance: The Trade-off between Competition and Adverse Selection." *Quarterly Journal of Economics* 113 (May 1998): 433–66.

Davis, Susan A. "We Must Safeguard Employee Pension Programs." *San Diego Union-Tribune* (February 14, 2002), p. B7.

Deacon, Robert T., and Jon Sonstelie. "Rationing by Waiting and the Value of Time: Results from a Natural Experiment." *Journal of Political Economy* 93 (August 1985), pp. 627–47.

DeAngelo, Harry, and Linda DeAngelo. "Dividend Policy, Agency Costs, and Earned Equity." National Bureau of Economic Research Working Paper 10599, July 2004.

Deaton, Angus S. *The Analysis of Household Surveys: A Microeconomic Approach to Development Policy.* Baltimore: Johns Hopkins University Press, 1997.

Deaton, Angus. "Health, Inequality, and Economic Development." *Journal of Economic Literature* 41 (March 2003): 113–58.

Dee, Thomas S. "Are There Civic Returns to Education?" *Journal of Public Economics* 88 (August 2004): 1697–1720.

DellaVigna, Stefano, and Ulrike Malmendier. "Contract Design and Self-Control: Theory and Evidence." *Quarterly Journal of Economics* 119 (May 2004): 353–402.

DeParle, Jason. "Study Finds Many Children Don't Benefit from Credits." *New York Times* (October 2, 2005), sec. 1, p. 20.

Department of Revenue of India—Income Tax Department. "Computation of Income." Last accessed on July 10, 2006, at http://incometaxindia.gov.in/general/computation.asp#c3.

Desai, Mihir A. "The Corporate Profit Base, Tax Sheltering Activity, and the Changing Nature of Employee Compensation." National Bureau of Economic Research Working Paper 8866, April 2002.

Desai, Mihir A., C. Fritz Foley, and James R. Hines Jr. "Repatriation Taxes and Dividend Distortions." National Bureau of Economic Research Working Paper 8507, October 2001.

Deutsch, Claudia H. "My Big Fat C.E.O. Paycheck." *New York Times* (April 3, 2005), sec. 3, p. 1.

Diamond, Peter, and Jonathan Gruber. "Social Security and Retirement in the United States." In *Social Security and Retirement Around the World,* edited by Jonathan Gruber and David A. Wise. Chicago: University of Chicago Press, 1999.

Diamond, Peter, and Jerry Hausman. "Contingent Valuation: Is Some Number Better Than No Number?" *Journal of Economic Perspectives* 8 (Fall 1994): 45–64.

Diamond, Peter A., and James A. Mirrlees. "Optimal Taxation and Public Production: I. Production Efficiency." *American Economic Review* 61 (March 1971): 8–27.

Diamond, Peter A., and Peter R. Orszag. *Saving Social Security: A Balanced Approach.* Washington, DC: Brookings Institution Press, 2004.

Dillon, Sam. "Strongly G.O.P. Utah House Challenges Bush's Signature Education Law." *New York Times* (February 16, 2005a), p. A14.

Dillon, Sam. "Report from States Faults Bush's Education Initiative." *New York Times* (February 24, 2005b), p. A18.

Dillon, Sam. "Education Law Finds Few Fans in Utah." *New York Times* (March 6, 2005c), sec. 1, p. 33.

Dixon, June, and Uffa Fox. *A Personal Biography.* London: Angus and Robertson, 1978.

Djankov, Simeon, Rafael La Porta, Florencio Lopez de Silanes, and Andrei Shleifer. "The Regulation of Entry." *Quarterly Journal of Economics* 117 (February 2002): 1–37.

Domar, Evsey D., and Richard A. Musgrave. "Proportional Income Taxation and Risk-Taking." *Quarterly Journal of Economics* 58 (1944): 388–422.

Dominitz, Jeff, Charles F. Manski, and Jordan Heinz. "'Will Social Security Be There For You?': How Americans Perceive Their Benefits," National Bureau of Economic Research Working Paper 9798, June 2003.

Doms, Mark E., Wendy E. Dunn, and Stephen D. Oliner. "How Fast Do Personal Computers Depreciate? Concepts and New Estimates." Federal Reserve Bank of San Francisco Working Paper, 2003.

Dowding, Keith, Peter John, and Stephen Biggs. "Tiebout: A Survey of the Empirical Literature." *Urban Studies* 31 (May 1994): 767–97.

Dowding, John K., Peter John, and Stephen Biggs. "Residential Mobility in London: A Micro-Level Test of the Behavioural Assumptions of the Tiebout Model." *British Journal of Political Science* 25 (July 1995): 379–97.

Downs, Anthony. *An Economic Theory of Democracy.* New York: HarperCollins, 1957.

Drew, Christopher, and Joseph B. Treaster. "Politics Stalls Plan to Bolster Flood Coverage." *New York Times* (May 15, 2006), p. A1.

Duflo, Esther. "The Medium Run Effects of Educational Expansion: Evidence from a Large School Construction Program in Indonesia." *Journal of Development Economics* 74 (Special Issue, June 2004): 163–97.

Duflo, Esther, William Gale, Jeffrey Liebman, Peter Orszag, and Emmanuel Saez. "Savings Incentives for Low- and Middle-Income Families: Evidence from a Field Experiment with H & R Block." National Bureau of Economic Research Working Paper 11680, October 2005.

Duggan, Mark G. "Hospital Ownership and Public Medical Spending." *Quarterly Journal of Economics* 115 (2000), 1343–1373.

Dynan, Karen E., Jonathan Skinner, and Stephen P. Zeldes. "Do the Rich Save More?" *Journal of Political Economy* 112 (April 2004): 397–444.

Eckholm, Eric. "Government Says Contractor Inflated Its Cost Estimates." *New York Times* (February 10, 2005), p. A19.

Edsall, Thomas B. "Tax Shift Would Hurt GE, Occidental Least." *Washington Post* (August 18, 1982), p. D8.

Edwards, Sebastian, and Alejandra Cox Edwards, "Social Security Privatization Reform and Labor Markets: The Case of Chile," *Economic Development and Cultural Change* 50 (3, April 2002): 465–89.

Egan, Timothy. "Built with Steel, Perhaps, but Greased with Pork." *New York Times* (April 10, 2004), p. A2.

Eichenwald, Kurt. "HCA is Said to Reach a Deal on Settlement of Fraud Case." *New York Times* (December 18, 2002), sec. C, p. 1.

Eissa, Nada, and Hilary Williamson Hoynes. "The Earned Income Tax Credit and the Labor Supply of Married Couples." National Bureau of Economic Research Working Paper 6858, December 1998.

Eissa, Nada, and Jeffery B. Liebman. "Labor Supply Response to the Earned Income Tax Credit." *Quarterly Journal of Economics* 111 (May 1996): 605–37.

Ellerman, A. Denny, Paul L. Joskow, Richard Schmalensee, Juan-Pablo Montero, and Elizabeth M. Bailey. *Markets for Clean Air: The U.S. Acid Rain Program.* New York: Cambridge University Press, 2000.

Ellwood, David T. "The Impact of the Earned Income Tax Credit and Social Policy Reforms on Work, Marriage, and Living Arrangements." *National Tax Journal* 53 (December, 2000): 1063–1106.

Ellwood, David T., and Isabel V. Sawhill. "Fixing the Marriage Penalty in the EITC." *Brookings Economic Papers* (September 20, 2000).

Employee Benefits Research Institute. "Sources of Health Insurance and Characteristics of the Uninsured: Analysis of the March 2005 Current Population Survey." Washington, DC: EBRI Issue Brief 287, 2005.

Energy Information Administration. *International Energy Annual 2003.* Washington DC: U.S. Government Printing Office, 2005.

Engelhardt, Gary V. "Tax Subsidies and Household Saving: Evidence from Canada." *Quarterly Journal of Economics* 111 (November 1996): 1237–68.

Engelhardt, Gary V., and Jonathan Gruber. "Social Security and the Evolution of Elderly Poverty." National Bureau of Economic Research Working Paper 10466, May 2004.

Engen, Eric M., and Jonathan Gruber. "Unemployment Insurance and Precautionary Saving." *Journal of Monetary Economics* 47 (June 2001): 545–79.

Epple, Dennis, and Richard Romano. "Educational Vouchers and Cream Skimming." National Bureau of Economic Research Working Paper 9354, November 2002.

Evans, W. N., M. C. Farelly, and E. Montgomery. "Do Workplace Smoking Bans Reduce Smoking?" *American Economic Review* 89 (1999): 728–747.

Farber, Henry. "What Do We Know About Job Loss in the United States: Evidence from the Displaced Workers Survey 1984–2004," Princeton University Industrial Relations Section Working Paper 498 (January, 2005).

Feldman, Roger, and Bryan E. Dowd. "A New Estimate of the Welfare Loss of Excess Health Insurance." *American Economic Review* 81 (March 1991): 297–301.

Feldstein, Martin S. "The Welfare Loss of Excess Health Insurance." *Journal of Political Economy* 81 (March–April 1973): 251–80.

Feldstein, Martin S. "Social Security, Induced Retirement, and Aggregate Capital Accumulation." *Journal of Political Economy* 82 (5, September/October 1974): 905–26.

Feldstein, Martin S. "On the Theory of Tax Reform." *Journal of Public Economics* 6 (July–August 1976): 77–104.

Feldstein, Martin S., and Daniel Altman. "Unemployment Insurance Savings Accounts." National Bureau of Economic Research Working Paper 6860, December 1998.

FEMA. *National Flood Insurance Program—Program Description.*

Field, Erica. "Educational Debt Burden and Career Choice: Evidence from a Financial Aid Experiment at NYU Law School." National Bureau of Economic Research Working Paper 12282, June 2006.

Figlio, David N. "Political Shirking, Opponent Quality, and Electoral Support." *Public Choice* 103 (June 2000): 271–84.

Figlio, David N., and Lawrence S. Getzler. "Accountability, Ability and Disability: Gaming the System." National Bureau of Economic Research Working Paper 9307, November 2002.

Figlio, David N., and Cecilia Elena Rouse. "Do Accountability and Voucher Threats Improve Low-Performing Schools?" Princeton University mimeo (submitted to *Quarterly Journal of Economics*), June 2004.

Figlio, David N., and Joshua Winicki. "Food for Thought: The Effects of School Accountability Plans on School Nutrition." National Bureau of Economic Research Working Paper 9319, November 2002.

Finkelstein, Amy. "Minimum Standards and Insurance Regulation: Evidence from the Medigap Market." National Bureau of Economic Research Working Paper 8917, May 2002.

Finkelstein, Amy. "Health Policy and Technological Change: Evidence from the Vaccine Industry." National Bureau of Economic Research Working Paper 9460, January 2003.

Finkelstein, Amy, and Robin McKnight. "What Did Medicare Do (and Was It Worth It)?" National Bureau of Economic Research Working Paper 11609, 2005.

Finkelstein, Amy, and James Poterba. "Adverse Selection in Insurance Markets: Policyholder Evidence from the U.K. Annuity Market." *Journal of Political Economy* 112 (1, Part 1, February 2004): 183–208.

Firestone, David. "House Expands Child Credit as Part of a Larger Tax Cut." *New York Times* (June 13, 2003), p. 28.

Fischel, William A. "Did Serrano Cause Proposition 13?" *National Tax Journal* 42 (December 1989): 465–73.

Fisher, Elliot S., David E. Wennberg, Therese A. Stukel, Daniel J. Gottlieb, F. L. Lucas, and Etoile L. Pinder. "The Implications of Regional Variations in Medicare Spending. Part 1: The Content, Quality, and Accessibility of Care." *Annals of Internal Medicine* 138 (4, February 18, 2003a): 273–87.

Fisher, Elliot S., David E. Wennberg, Therese A. Stukel, Daniel J. Gottlieb, F. L. Lucas, and Etoile L. Pinder. "The Implications of Regional Variations in Medicare Spending. Part 2: Health Outcomes and Satisfaction with Care." *Annals of Internal Medicine* 138 (4, February 18, 2003b): 288–98.

Fisher, Franklin M. *The Identification Problem in Econometrics.* Huntington, NY: R. E. Krieger, 1976.

Fitzgerald, J. F., L. F. Fagan, W. M. Tierney, and R. S. Dittus. "Changing Patterns of Hip Fracture Care Before and After Implementation of the Prospective Payment System." *Journal of the American Medical Association* (1987): 218–21.

Fitzpatrick, Dan. "The Tax Grind: New Assessment Structure Packs a Wallop for Some Pittsburgh Businesses." *Pittsburgh Post-Gazette* (April 22, 2001), p. C1.

Fletcher, Deborah. "Intergenerational Conflict and Publicly Provided Goods." PhD Dissertation, University of Florida, May 2003.

Ford, Reuben, David Gyarmati, Kelly Foley, and Doug Tattrie. *Can Work Incentives Pay for Themselves?* Ottawa: Social Research and Demonstration Corporation, 2003.

Forelle, Charles, and James Bandler. "The Perfect Payday—Some CEOs Reap Millions by Landing Stock Options When They Are Most Valuable." *Wall Street Journal* (March 18, 2006), p. A1.

Frankenberg, Erica, and Chungmei Lee. *Race in American Schools: Rapidly Resegregating School Districts.* Cambridge, MA: The Civil Rights Project, Harvard University, 2002.

Friedman, Joel. "The High Cost of Estate Tax Repeal." Washington, DC: Center on Budget and Policy Priorities, June 15, 2006.

Friedman, Joel, and Aviva Aron-Dine. "The State of the Estate Tax as of 2006." Washington, DC: Center on Budget and Policy Priorities, June 2, 2006.

Friedman, Joel, and Robert Greenstein. "Joint Tax Committee Estimate Shows That Tax Gimmick Being Designed to Evade Senate Budget Rules Would Increase Long-Term Deficits." Washington, DC: Center on Budget and Policy Priorities, April 26, 2006.

Friedman, Joel, Richard Kogan, and Robert Greenstein. "New Tax-Cut Law Ultimately Costs as Much as Bush Plan." Washington, DC: Center on Budget and Policy Priorities, June 27, 2001.

Friedman, Joel, and Andrew Lee. "Permanent Repeal of the Estate Tax Would Be Costly, Yet Would Benefit Only a Few, Very Large Estates." Washington, DC: Center on Budget and Policy Priorities, June 17, 2003.

Friedman, Milton. "Prohibition and Drugs." *Newsweek* (May 1, 1972).

Friedman, Milton. "Energy Rhetoric." *Newsweek* (June 13, 1977), p. 82.

Fullerton, Don. "The Indexation of Interest, Depreciation, and Capital Gains and Tax Reform in the United States." *Journal of Public Economics* 32 (February 1987): 25–51.

Furman, Jason. "Tax Reform and Poverty." Center on Budget and Policy Priorities, April 10, 2006.

Gale, William G. "The Required Tax Rate in a National Retail Sales Tax." *National Tax Journal* 52 (September 1999): 443–57.

Gale, William, Jonathan Gruber, and Peter Orszag. "Encouraging Homeownership Through the Tax Code." Brookings Institution mimeo, 2006.

Gale, William G., and Peter R. Orszag. "Economic Effects of Sustained Budget Deficits." *National Tax Journal* 56 (September 2003): 463–85.

Gale, William G., and Peter R. Orszag. "Bush Administration Tax Policy: Distributional Effects." *Tax Notes.* Tax Policy Center, September 27, 2004.

Gale, William G., and John Karl Scholz. "IRAs and Household Saving." *American Economic Review* 84 (1994): 1233–1260.

Gale, William G., and Joel Slemrod. "Rethinking the Estate and Gift Tax: Overview." National Bureau of Economic Research Working Paper 8205, April 2001a.

Gale, William G., and Joel Slemrod. "Rhetoric and Economics in the Estate Tax Debate." *National Tax Journal* 54 (September 2001b): 613–27.

Galloni, Alessandra. "In Parmalat Case, 11 Are Convicted After Plea Deals—Verdict Paves Way for Trial Related to the Fraud That Crippled Dairy Giant." *Wall Street Journal Europe* (June 29, 2005), p. A3.

Galloni, Alessandra, and Yaroslav Trofimov. "Tanzi's Power Games Helped Parmalat Rise, but Didn't Cushion Fall." *Wall Street Journal Europe* (March 8, 2004), p. A1.

Garrett, Bowen, and Sherry Glied. "Does State AFDC Generosity Affect Child SSI Participation?" *Journal of Policy Analysis and Management* 19 (Spring 2000): 275–95.

Geanakoplos, John, Olivia S. Mitchell, and Stephen P. Zeldes. "Social Security Money's Worth." In *Prospects for Social Security Reform,* edited by Olivia S. Mitchell, Robert J. Myers, and Howard Young. Philadelphia: University of Philadelphia Press, 1999.

Gelbach, Jonah B. "Public Schooling for Young Children and Maternal Labor Supply." *American Economic Review* 92 (March 2002): 307–22.

"George Ryan Guilty on All Counts." CBS Broadcasting. CBS2, Chicago (April, 17 2006). Last accessed on June 22, 2006, at http://cbs2chicago.com/politics/local_story_107111835.html.

Giles, David E. A. "Modelling the Hidden Economy and the Tax-Gap in New Zealand." *Empirical Economics* 24 (4, 1999): 621–40.

Gingrich, Newt. "All of Us Together . . . Must Totally Remake the Federal Government." *Washington Post* (April 8, 1995), p. A12.

Glaeser, Edward L. "The Economics of Location-Based Tax Incentives." Discussion Paper 1932. Cambridge, MA: Harvard Institute of Economic Research, 2001.

Glaeser, Edward L. "Should the Government Rebuild New Orleans or Just Give Residents a Check?" *Economists' Voice* 2 (2005).

Glaeser, Edward L. "A Smaller New Orleans." *Boston Globe* (February 1, 2006), p. A13.

Glaeser, Edward L., and Joseph Gyourko. "Zoning's Steep Price." *Regulation* 25 (Fall 2002): 24–30.

Glaeser, Edward L., and Jesse M. Shapiro. "The Benefits of the Home Mortgage Interest Deduction." National Bureau of Economic Research Working Paper 9284, October 2002.

Glassman, Mark. "House Panel Votes to Halt Accenture Pact." *New York Times* (June 10, 2004), p. C3.

Goel, Rajeev K., and Michael A. Nelson. "Corruption and Government Size: A Disaggregated Analysis." *Public Choice* 97 (October 1998): 107–20.

Gokhale, Jagadeesh, and Kent Smetters. *Fiscal and Generational Imbalances: New Budget Measures for New Budget Priorities.* Washington, DC: AEI Press, 2003.

Golosov, Mikhail, Narayana Kocherlakota, and Aleh Tsyvinski. "Optimal Indirect and Capital Taxation." *Review of Economic Studies* 70 (3, 2003): 569–87.

Goolsbee, Austin. "The Impact and Inefficiency of the Corporate Income Tax: Evidence from State Organizational Form Data." National Bureau of Economic Research Working Paper 9141, September 2002.

Gordon, Jane. "New Medicare Rules Causing Many Queries." *New York Times* (November 20, 2005), sec. 14CN, p. 2.

Gordon, Nora. "Do Federal Grants Boost School Spending? Evidence from Title I." *Journal of Public Economics* 88 (August 2004): 1771–1792.

Gordon, Roger, and Martin Dietz. "Dividends and Taxes." National Bureau of Economic Research Working Paper 11292, June 2006.

Gordon, Roger H., and James R. Hines, Jr. "International Taxation." National Bureau of Economic Research Working Paper 8854, April 2002.

Gore, Albert. "Excerpts from Gore's Speech Outlining His Plans for Improving Education." *New York Times* (April 29, 2000), p. A10.

Gottlieb, Martin, Kurt Eichenwald, and Josh Barbanel. "Health Care's Giant: Powerhouse Under Scrutiny." *New York Times* (March 28, 1997), sec. A, p. 1.

Government of the District of Columbia. *Tax Rates and Tax Burdens in the District of Columbia—A Nationwide Comparison.* Office of Tax and Revenue, August 2002.

Gramlich, Edward M., and Daniel L. Rubinfeld. "Micro Estimates of Public Spending Demand Functions and Tests of the Tiebout and Median-Voter Hypotheses." *Journal of Political Economy* 90 (June 1982): 536–60.

Gray, Clive S. "Enhancing Transparency in Tax Administration in Madagascar and Tanzania." Belfer Center for Science and International Affairs, John F. Kennedy School of Government, Harvard University. Africa Economic Policy Discussion Paper 77, August 2001.

Greene, Jay P., Paul E. Peterson, Jiangtao Du, Leesa Boeger, and Curtis L. Frazier. "The Effectiveness of School Choice in Milwaukee: A Secondary Analysis of Data from the Program's Evaluation." University of Houston mimeo, August 1996.

Greenstone, Michael. "The Impacts of Environmental Regulations on Industrial Activity: Evidence from the 1970 and 1977 Clean Air Act Amendments and the Census of Manufacturers." *Journal of Political Economy* 110 (2002): 1175–1219.

Greenstone, Michael, and Enrico Moretti. "Bidding for Industrial Plants: Does Winning a 'Million Dollar Plant' Increase Welfare?" National Bureau of Economic Research Working Paper 9844, July 2003.

Gregg, Judd. "The Safety Valve Has Become a Fire Hose." *Wall Street Journal* (April 18, 2006), p. A18.

Grogger, Jeffrey, and Charles Michalopoulos. "Welfare Dynamics under Time Limits." *Journal of Political Economy* 111 (June 2003): 530–554.

Groppe, Maureen. "Lilly Leading Coalition to Get a Tax Holiday for Foreign Profits." *Garnett News Service* (October 31, 2003).

Grossman, Michael, Robert Kaestner, and Sara Markowitz. "An Investigation of the Effects of Alcohol Policies on Youth STDs." National Bureau of Economic Research Working Paper 10949, December 2004.

Gruber, Jonathan. "The Incidence of Mandated Maternity Benefits." *American Economic Review* 84 (June 1994): 86–102.

Gruber, Jonathan. "The Consumption Smoothing Benefits of Unemployment Insurance." *American Economic Review* 87 (March 1997): 192–205.

Gruber, Jonathan. "Disability Insurance Benefits and Labor Supply." *Journal of Political Economy* 108 (December 2000): 1162–83.

Gruber, Jonathan. "Tobacco at the Crossroads: The Past and Future of Smoking Regulation in the U.S." *Journal of Economic Perspectives* 15 (Spring 2001a): 193–212.

Gruber, Jonathan. "Introduction. In Risky Behavior Among Youths: An Economic Analysis." Chicago: University of Chicago Press, 2001b, pp. 1–28.

Gruber, Jonathan. "The Wealth of the Unemployed." *Industrial and Labor Relations Review* 55 (1, October 2001c): 79–94.

Gruber, Jonathan. "Health Insurance and the Labor Market." In *The Handbook of Health Economics,* edited by Joseph Newhouse and Anthony Culyer. Amsterdam: North Holland, 2001d, pp. 645–706.

Gruber, Jonathan. "Pay or Pray? The Impact of Charitable Subsidies on Religious Attendance." National Bureau of Economic Research Working Paper 10374, March 2004.

Gruber, Jonathan. "A Tax-Based Estimate of the Elasticity of Intertemporal Substitution." National Bureau of Economic Research Working Paper 11945, January 2005.

Gruber, Jonathan. "The Role of Consumer Copayments for Health Care: Lessons from the RAND Health Insurance Experiment and Beyond." MIT mimeo, April 2006.

Gruber, Jonathan, and Botond Koszegi. "Tax Incidence When Individuals Are Time Inconsistent: The Case of Cigarette Excise Taxes," *Journal of Public Economics* 88 (August 2004): 1959–1988.

Gruber, Jonathan, and Alan Krueger. "The Incidence of Mandated Employer-Provided Insurance: Lessons from Workers' Compensation Insurance." In *Tax Policy and the Economy,* Vol. 5, edited by David Bradford. Cambridge, MA: MIT Press, 1991.

Gruber, Jonathan, and Michael Lettau. "How Elastic Is the Firm's Demand for Health Insurance?" *Journal of Public Economics* 88 (July 2004): 1273–93.

Gruber, Jonathan, and Brigitte C. Madrian. "Health Insurance, Labor Supply, and Job Mobility: A Critical Review of the Literature." In *Health Policy and the Uninsured,* edited by Catherine McLaughlin. Washington, DC: Urban Institute Press, 2004, pp. 97–178.

Gruber, Jonathan, and Peter Orszag. "Does the Social Security Earnings Test Affect Labor Supply and Benefits Receipt?" *National Tax Journal* 56 (n4, December 2003): 755–73.

Gruber, Jonathan, and Emmanuel Saez. "The Elasticity of Taxable Income: Evidence and Implications." National Bureau of Economic Research Working Paper 7512, April 2000.

Gruber, Jonathan, and Kosali Simon. "Crowd Out Ten Years Later: Have Recent Public Insurance Expansions Crowded Out Private Health Insurance?" MIT mimeo, 2006.

Gruber, Jonathan, and David A. Wise. "Introduction and Summary." In *Social Security and Retirement around the World,* edited by Jonathan Gruber and David A. Wise. Chicago: University of Chicago Press, 1999.

Gruber, Jonathan, and Aaron Yelowitz. "Public Health Insurance and Private Savings." *Journal of Political Economy* 107 (December 1999): 1249–74.

Grumbach, K., D. Keane, and Andrew Bindman. "Primary Care and Public Emergency Department Overcrowding." *American Journal of Public Health* 83 (March 1993): 372–8.

Gueron, Judith M. "Work and Welfare: Lessons on Employment Programs." *Journal of Economic Perspectives* 4 (Winter 1990): 79–98.

Guyton, John L., John F. O'Hare, Michael P. Stavrianos, and Eric. J. Toder. "Estimating the Compliance Cost of the U.S. Individual Income Tax." Presentation to the National Tax Association Spring Symposium, 2003.

Hall, Robert E. "Intertemporal Substitution in Consumption." *Journal of Political Economy* 96 (April 1988): 339–357.

Hall, Robert E., and Alvin Rabushka. *The Flat Tax.* Stanford, CA: Hoover Institution Press, Stanford University, 1995.

Hanratty, Maria J. "Canadian National Health Insurance and Infant Health." *American Economic Review* 86 (March 1996): 276–84.

Hanushek, Eric A., John F. Kain, and Steven G. Rivkin. "The Impact of Charter Schools on Academic Achievement." Stanford University working paper, December 2002.

Hanushek, Eric A., and Margaret E. Raymond. "The Effect of School Accountability Systems on the Level and Distribution of Student Achievement." *Journal of the European Economic Association* 2 (April–May 2004): 406–15.

Harberger, Arnold C. "Tax Lore for Budding Reformers." In *Reform, Recovery and Growth,* edited by Rudiger Dornbusch and Sebastian Edwards. Chicago: University of Chicago Press, 1995, pp. 291–309.

Hart, Oliver, Andrei Shleifer, and Robert W. Vishny. "The Proper Scope of Government: Theory and Application to Prisons." *Quarterly Journal of Economics* 112 (November 1997): 1127–61.

Hartigan, Patti. "Free Riders Who Don't Share in the Digital Community." *Boston Globe* (August 25, 2000), p. C9.

Hausman, Jerry. "Efficiency Effects on the U.S. Economy from Wireless Taxation." *National Tax Journal* 53 (September 2000): 733–42.

Helsinki Commission. *The Baltic Sea Joint Comprehensive Environmental Action Programme (JCP): Ten Years of Implementation.* Baltic Sea Environment Proceedings 88, 2003.

Herd, Richard, and Chiara Bronchi. "Increasing Efficiency and Reducing Complexity in the Tax System in the United States." OECD Economics Department Working Paper 313, December 2001.

Hersch, Joni. "Smoking Restrictions as a Self-Control Mechanism." *Journal of Risk and Uncertainty* 31 (May 2005): 5–21.

Hesseldahl, Erik. "Public Radio Goes Begging," a March 30, 2001, article located at http://www.forbes.com/2001/03/30/0330pubradio.html.

Hines, James R., and Richard H. Thaler. "The Flypaper Effect." *Journal of Economic Perspectives* 9 (Fall 1995): 217–26.

HM Revenue & Customs. "Notes on Capital Gains Return 2005–06." Last accessed on July 10, 2006, at http://www.hmrc.gov.uk/cgt/index.htm#2.

Holden, Sarah, and Jack VanDerhei. "401(k) Plan Asset Allocation, Account Balances, and Loan Activity in 2002." Employee Benefit Research Institute Issue Brief 261, September 2003.

Holtzblatt, Janet, and Robert Rebelein. "Measuring the Effect of the EITC on Marriage Penalties and Bonuses." *National Tax Journal* 53 (December 2000): 1107–34.

Holtz-Eakin, Douglas, David Joulfian, and Harvey S. Rosen. "The Carnegie Conjecture: Some Empirical Evidence." *Quarterly Journal of Economics* 108 (May 1993): 413–36.

Hotz, V. Joseph, Charles H. Mullin, and John Karl Scholz. "Welfare, Employment and Income: Evidence on the Effects of Benefit Reductions in California." *American Economic Review Papers and Proceedings* (May 2002): 380–4.

Howe, Peter J. "Bush Says Revamp of Saving Plans Aims to Replace IRAs, 401(k)s, Change Tax Rules." *Boston Globe* (February 1, 2003), p. E1.

Hoxby, Caroline M. "Does Competition among Public Schools Benefit Students and Taxpayers?" *American Economic Review* 90 (December 2000): 1209–38.

Hoxby, Caroline M. "All School Finance Equalizations Are Not Created Equal." *Quarterly Journal of Economics* 116 (November 2001): 1189–1231.

Hoxby, Caroline M. "School Choice and School Productivity (or Could School Choice Be a Tide That Lifts All Boats?)." National Bureau of Economic Research Working Paper 8873, April 2002.

Hoxby, Caroline M. "Competition Among Public Schools: A Reply to Rothstein." National Bureau of Economic Research Working Paper 11216, March 2005.

Hoynes, Hilary. "Work, Welfare and Family Structure: What Have We Learned?" In *Fiscal Policy: Lessons from Economic Research,* edited by Alan Auerbach. Cambridge: Cambridge University Press, 1997, pp. 101–46.

Hsieh, Chang-Tai, and Miguel Urquiola. "When Schools Compete, How Do They Compete? An Assessment of Chile's Nationwide School Voucher Program." National Bureau of Economic Research Working Paper 10008, October 2003.

Hubbard, R. Glenn, S. Fazzari, and B. C. Petersen. "Investment, Financing Decisions, and Tax Policy." *American Economic Review* 78 (May 1988): 200–5.

Hubbard, R. Glenn, Jonathan Skinner, and Stephen P. Zeldes. "Precautionary Saving and Social Insurance." *Journal of Political Economy* 103 (April 1995): 360–99.

Hulse, Carl. "Jobless Compensation: Bush Signs Bill to Extend Unemployment Benefits." *New York Times* (January 9, 2003), p. A23.

Hunt, H. Allan. "Benefit Adequacy in State Workers' Compensation Programs." Social Security Bulletin 65 (4, 2004).

Institute of International Education. *Open Doors 2005.* New York: International Institute of Education, 2005.

Insurance Information Institute. *The Fact Book: Property/Casualty Insurance Facts.* New York: The Institute, 2006.

Internal Revenue Service. "Publication 542: Corporations." Washington, DC: U.S. Department of the Treasury, 2003.

Internal Revenue Service. *Statistics of Income 2001, Individual Income Tax Returns,* January 2004. Accessed at http://www.irs.gov/taxstats/article/0,id=96586,00.html.

Internal Revenue Service. *Your Federal Income Tax.* Publication 17 (2005a).

Internal Revenue Service. *Tax Law Changes for Gifts and Estates and Trusts.* November 19, 2005b.

Internal Revenue Service. "Publication 596: Earned Income Credit." Washington, DC: U.S. Department of the Treasury, 2005c.

International Association for the Evaluation of Educational Achievement. *TIMSS 2003 International Mathematics Report.* Boston: International Study Center, Boston College, 2004a.

International Association for the Evaluation of Educational Achievement. *TIMSS 2003 International Science Report.* Boston: International Study Center, Boston College, 2004b.

International Panel on Climate Change. *Climate Change 2001: Impacts, Adaptation, and Vulnerability.* Geneva: United Nations Environment Programme, 2001.

Jacob, Brian A. "Accountability, Incentives and Behavior: The Impact of High-Stakes Testing in the Chicago Public Schools." National Bureau of Economic Research Working Paper 8968, May 2002.

Jacob, Brian A., and Steven D. Levitt. "Catching Cheating Teachers: The Results of an Unusual Experiment in Implementing Theory." National Bureau of Economic Research Working Paper 9414, January 2003.

Jacobsson, Fredrick, Magnus Johannesson, and Lars Borgquist. "Is Altruism Paternalistic?" Linkoping University mimeo, 2005.

Jaeger, David A., and Marianne E. Page. "Degrees Matter: New Evidence on Sheepskin Effects in the Returns to Education." *Review of Economics and Statistics* 78 (November 1996): 733–40.

James, Estelle, James Smalhout, and Dimitri Vittas. "Administrative Costs and the Organization of Individual Account Systems: A Comparative Perspective." In *New Ideas about Old Age Security,* edited by Robert Holzmann and Joseph E. Stiglitz. Washington, DC: World Bank, 2001.

Jenkins, Holman W., Jr. "Business World: Let's Have More Heirs and Heiresses." *Wall Street Journal* (February 21, 2001), p. A27.

Johnson, David S., John M. Rogers, and Lucilla Tan. "A Century of Family Budgets in the United States." *Monthly Labor Review* 124 (May 2001): 28–45.

Johnson, Julia Overturf. "Who's Minding the Kids? Child Care Arrangements: Winter 2002." *Current Population Reports* P70-101. Washington, DC: U.S. Bureau of the Census, October 2005.

Johnston, David Cay. "Tax Fugitive's Son Pleads Guilty to Evasion Charges." *New York Times* (September 6, 2003a), p. C3.

Johnston, David Cay. *Perfectly Legal.* New York: Portfolio, 2003b.

Joint Committee on Taxation. "Estimated Budget Effects of the Conference Agreement on Revenue Provisions of H.R. 2014, the 'Tax Payer Relief Act of 1997.'" Washington, DC: U.S. Government Printing Office, 1997.

Joulfian, David. "Choosing Between Gifts and Bequests: How Taxes Affect the Timing of Wealth Transfers." *Journal of Public Economics* 89 (December 2005): 2069-91.

Joumard, Isabelle, and Per Mathis Kongsrud. "Fiscal Relations across Government Levels." OECD Economic Department Working Paper 375, December 2003.

Journal of Commerce. "Territorial Discrimination Proves Costly for Calif. HMO" (November 18, 1988), p. 9A.

Jowit, Juliette. "Can the Cost of Saving a Life Ever Be Too High?" *Financial Times* (April 3, 2002) p. 16.

Judd, Kenneth L. "Redistributive Taxation in a Perfect Foresight Model." *Journal of Public Economics* 28 (1985): 59-83.

Kaiser Commission on Medicaid and the Uninsured. "The Uninsured: A Primer." Washington, DC: The Kaiser Family Foundation, January 2006.

Kaiser Family Foundation. "Employer Health Benefits—2005 Annual Survey." Menlo Park, CA: The Kaiser Family Foundation, 2005.

Kaiser Family Foundation. *Trends and Indicators in the Changing Health Care Marketplace, 2006 Update.* Accessed at http://www.kff.org/insurance/7031/ti2004-list-set.cfm.

Kaiser Family Foundation. *Seniors' Early Experiences with the Medicare Prescription Drug Benefit.* April 2006a.

Kalt, Joseph P., and Mark A. Zupan. "Capture and Ideology in the Economic Theory of Politics." *American Economic Review* 74 (June 1984): 279–300.

Kearney, Melissa Schettini. "Is There an Effect of Incremental Welfare Benefits on Fertility Behavior? A Look at the Family Cap." *Journal of Human Resources* 39 (Spring 2004): 295–325.

Keeler, Emmett B. "The Value of Remaining Lifetime Is Close to Estimated Values of Life." *Journal of Health Economics* 20 (January 2001): 141–3.

Kemper, Peter, and John Quigley. *The Economies of Refuse Collection.* Cambridge: Ballinger, 1976.

Kindleberger, Richard. "A BID to Restore Downtowns, Tool to Breathe Life into Business Districts Largely Untested in Mass." *Boston Globe* (December 12, 1999), p. G1.

Kingma, Bruce Robert. "An Accurate Measurement of the Crowd-Out Effect, Income Effect, and Price Effect for Charitable Contributions." *Journal of Political Economy* 97 (October 1989): 1197–1207.

Kirwan, Barrett. "The Incidence of U.S. Agricultural Subsidies on Farmland Rental Rates." PhD Dissertation, Massachusetts Institute of Technology, January 2004.

Kling, Jeffrey. "Fundamental Restructuring of Unemployment Insurance: Wage-Loss Insurance and Temporary Earnings Loss Replacement Accounts." Hamilton Project Discussion Paper (September, 2006).

Knight, Brian. "Endogenous Federal Grants and Crowd-Out of State Government Spending: Theory and Evidence from the Federal Highway Aid Program." *American Economic Review* 92 (March 2002): 71–92.

Kocieniewski, David. "Tax Proposal in New Jersey Has Businesses Up in Arms." *New York Times* (April 13, 2002a), p. B1.

Kocieniewski, David. "Governor Says Tax Increase Is Not Cause of Layoffs." *New York Times* (July 11, 2002b), p. B5.

Kolata, Gina. "In Public Health, Definitive Data Can Be Elusive." *New York Times* (April 23, 2002), p. F1.

Kopczuk, Wojciech. "Tax Bases, Tax Rates, and the Elasticity of Reported Income." National Bureau of Economic Research Working Paper 10044 (October, 2003).

Kotlikoff, Laurence J. "Generational Policy" In *The Handbook of Public Economics,* edited by Alan J. Auerbach and Martin Feldstein. New York: North-Holland, 2002.

Krueger, Alan B. "Incentive Effects of Workers' Compensation Insurance." *Journal of Public Economics* 41 (February 1990): 73–99.

Krueger, Alan B. "Workers' Compensation Insurance and the Duration of Workplace Injuries." Mimeo, Princeton University, July 1991.

Krueger, Alan B. "Experimental Estimates of Education Production Functions." *Quarterly Journal of Economics* 114 (May 1999): 497–532.

Krueger, Alan B., and Diane M. Whitmore. "The Effect of Attending a Small Class in the Early Grades on College Test-Taking and Middle School Test Results: Evidence from Project STAR." *Economic Journal* 111 (January 2001): 1–28.

Krugman, Paul. "Outside the Box." *New York Times* (July 11, 2001), p. A17.

Krugman, Paul. "Roads Not Taken." *New York Times* (April 25, 2003), p. A31.

Laibson, David I., Andrea Repetto, and Jeremy Tobacman. "Self-Control and Saving for Retirement." *Brookings Papers on Economic Activity* 1 (1998): 91–172.

Lamont, Owen. "Cash Flow and Investment: Evidence from Internal Capital Markets." *Journal of Finance* 52 (March 1997): 83–109.

Lazear, Edward P. "Educational Production." *Quarterly Journal of Economics* 116 (August 2001): 777–803.

Ledyard, John O. "Public Goods: A Survey of Experimental Research." In *The Handbook of Experimental Economics,* edited by John H. Kagel and Alvin E. Roth. Princeton: Princeton University Press, 1995, pp. 111–94.

Lee, Andrew, and Joel Friedman. "Administration Continues to Rely on Misleading Use of 'Averages' to Describe Tax-Cut Benefits." Washington, DC: Center on Budget and Policy Priorities, May 28, 2003.

Leibson, C. L., J. M. Naessens, M. E. Campion, I. Krishan, and D. J. Ballard. "Trends in Elderly Hospitalization and Readmission Rates for a Geographically Defined Population: Pre- and Post-Prospective Payment." *Journal of the American Geriatrics Society* 39 (1991): 895–904.

Leight, Jessica. "Argentina: Moving On Up?" *Yale Economic Review* (Spring 2006).

Leistikow, Bruce N., Daniel C. Martin, and Christina E. Milano. "Fire Injuries, Disasters, and Costs from Cigarettes and Cigarette Lights: A Global Overview." *Preventive Medicine* 31 (2, August 2000): 91–9.

Leonard, Mary. "Bloc of Senate Democrats Girds for Welfare Fight." *Boston Globe* (May 24, 2002), p. A2.

LeVeaux, Christine, and James C. Garand. "Race-Based Redistricting, Core Constituencies, and Legislative Responsiveness to Constituency Change." *Social Science Quarterly* 84 (March 2003): 32–51.

Levitt, Steven D. "How Do Senators Vote? Disentangling the Role of Voter Preferences, Party Affiliation, and Senate Ideology." *American Economic Review* 86 (June 1996): 425–41.

Lewin Group. *Labor Economic Conditions, Socio-Economic Factors, and the Growth of Applications and Awards for SSDI and SSI Disability Benefits.* Fairfax, VA: Lewin Group, 1995.

Lieber, Ron. "Green Thumb: A New Tax Trick for Your IRA—Rule Change Could Yield a Windfall in 2010—but Will It Last?" *Wall Street Journal*, May 20, 2006.

Liebman, Jeffrey, Maya MacGuiness, and Andrew Samwick. "Nonpartisan Social Security Reform Plan," available as of 2006 at http://www.ksg.harvard.edu/jeffreyliebman/lms_nonpartisan_plan_description.pdf

Lindblom, Mike. "Monorail: It's a Go." *Seattle Times* (November 20, 2002), p. A1.

Lipton, Eric, and Ron Nixon. "Many Contracts for Storm Work Raise Questions." *New York Times* (September 26, 2005), p. A1.

Lochner, Lance, and Enrico Moretti. "The Effect of Education on Crime: Evidence from Prison Inmates, Arrests, and Self-Reports." *American Economic Review* 94 (March 2004): 155–89.

Lorelli, Michael Fitzpatrick. "State and Local Property Taxes." *Special Report.* Washington, DC: The Tax Foundation, August, 2001.

Lundberg, Shelly J., Robert A. Pollak, and Terence J. Wales. "Do Husbands and Wives Pool Their Resources? Evidence from the United Kingdom Child Benefit." *Journal of Human Resources* 32 (Summer 1997): 463–80.

Lurie, N., N. B. Ward, M. F. Shapiro, and R. H. Brook. "Termination from Medi-Cal—Does It Affect Health?" *New England Journal of Medicine* 311 (August 16, 1984): 480–4.

Luttmer, Erso F. P. "Do People Care How Much Their Neighbors Earn? How Relative Earnings Affect Well-Being." National Bureau of Economic Research paper (July 22, 2004). Accessed at http://www.nber.org/~luttmer/relative.pdf.

Lutz, Byron F. "Taxation with Representation: The Incidence of Intergovernmental Grants in a Plebiscite Democracy." Massachusetts Institute of Technology mimeo, October 17, 2004.

Maddison, Angus. *The World Economy: A Millennial Perspective.* Washington, DC: OECD, 2001.

Madrian, Brigitte C. "Employment-Based Health Insurance and Job Mobility: Is There Evidence of Job-Lock?" *Quarterly Journal of Economics* 109 (February 1994): 27–54.

Madrian, Brigitte, and Dennis Shea. "The Power of Suggestion: Inertia in 401(k) Participation and Savings Behavior." *Quarterly Journal of Economics* 116 (November 2001): 1149–87.

Maguire, Steve. "Average Effective Corporate Tax Rates: 1959–2002." Congressional Research Service, September 5, 2003.

Majumdar, Sumit K. "Assessing Comparative Efficiency of the State-Owned Mixed and Private Sectors in Indian Industry." *Public Choice* 96 (July 1998): 1–24.

Mallaby, Sebastian. "Kit's Caboodle." *Washington Post* (June 7, 2004), p. A23.

Mankiw, N. Gregory. *Macroeconomics,* 5th ed. New York: Worth, 2003.

Manning, W. G., E. B. Keeler, J. P. Newhouse, E.M. Sloss, J. Wasserman, and JAMA. "The Taxes of Sin: Do Smokers and Drinkers Pay Their Way?" *Journal of the American Medical Association* 261 (1989): 1604–9.

Manning, W. G., A. Leibowitz, G. A. Goldberg, W. H. Rogers, and J. P. Rogers. "A Controlled Trial of the Effects of a Prepaid Group Practice on Use of Services." *New England Journal of Medicine* 310 (June 7, 1984): 1505–10.

Manning, Willard G., Emmett B. Keeler, Joseph P. Newhouse, Elizabeth M. Sloss, and Jeffrey Wasserman. *The Costs of Poor Health Habits.* Cambridge, MA: Harvard University Press, 1991.

Markowitz, Sara. "Criminal Fights and Alcohol Beverage Control: Evidence from an International Study." National Bureau of Economic Research Working Paper 7481, January 2000a.

Markowitz, Sara. "An Economic Analysis of Alcohol, Drugs and Violent Crime in the National Crime Victimization Survey." National Bureau of Economic Research Working Paper 7692, May 2000b.

Markowitz, Sara, and Michael Grossman. "Alcohol Regulation and Violence Towards Children." National Bureau of Economic Research Working Paper 6359, February 1999.

Markowitz, Sara, Robert Kaestner, and Michael Grossman. "An Investigation of the Effects of Alcohol Consumption and Alcohol Policies on Youth Risky Sexual Behaviors." National Bureau of Economic Research Working Paper 11378, May 2005.

Marquis, G. S., J. P. Habicht, C. F. Lanata, R. E. Black, and K. M. Rasmussen. "Association of Breastfeeding and Stunting in Peruvian Toddlers: An Example of Reverse Causality." *International Journal of Epidemiology* 26 (1997): 349–56.

Marsh, Bill. "Fresh Pork, Coming to a District Near You." *New York Times* (August 7, 2005), sec. 4, p. 3.

Marwell, Gerald, and Ruth E. Ames. "Economists Free Ride, Does Anyone Else? Experiments on the Provision of Public Goods, IV." *Journal of Public Economics* 15 (June 1981): 295–310.

Matsusaka, John G. "Fiscal Effects of the Voter Initiative: Evidence from the Last 30 Years." *Journal of Political Economy* 103 (June 1995): 587–623.

Matsusaka, John. "Direct Democracy Works." *Journal of Economic Perspectives* 19 (Spring 2005): 185–206.

Mauro, Paolo. "Corruption and Growth." *Quarterly Journal of Economics* 110 (August 1995): 681–712.

McCarthy, Eugene J. "Pollution Absolution." *New Republic* 18 (October 29, 1990): 9.

McDonald, Frank. "The BID to Make Times Square Safe." *Irish Times* (August 18, 2001), p. 66.

McDonald, Greg. "Congress Squeezes Maximum Political Mileage from Budget." *Houston Chronicle* (October 21, 1998), p. A8.

McIntyre, Robert S., and Robert Folen. "Corporate Income Taxes in the Reagan Years." Washington, DC: Citizens for Tax Justice, 1984.

McMurrer, Daniel P., and Isabel V. Sawhill. *Economic Mobility in the United States.* Washington, DC: Urban Institute, October 1, 1996.

Medicare Trustees. *2006 Annual Report of the Board of Trustees of the Federal Hospital Insurance and Federal Supplementary Medical Insurance Trust Funds.* Washington, DC: U.S. Government Printing Office, 2006.

Megginson, William L., and Jeffrey M. Netter. "From State to Market: A Survey of Empirical Studies on Privatization." *Journal of Economic Literature* 39 (June 2001): 321–89.

Melton, R. H. "Candidates Guarded on Senior Tax Break." *Washington Post* (September 11, 2003), p. B5.

MetLife Mature Market Institute. "MetLife Market Survey on Nursing Home and Home Care Costs, 2004." Westport, CT, September 2004.

Meyer, Bruce D. "A Quasi-Experimental Approach to the Effects of Unemployment Insurance." National Bureau of Economic Research Working Paper 3159, November 1989.

Meyer, Bruce D. "Unemployment Insurance and Unemployment Spells." *Econometrica* 58 (July 1990): 757–82.

Meyer, Bruce D., and Dan T. Rosenbaum. "Making Single Mothers Work: Recent Tax and Welfare Policy and its Effects." National Bureau of Economic Research Working Paper 7491, January 2000.

Meyer, Bruce D., and James X. Sullivan. "The Effects of Welfare and Tax Reform: The Material Well-Being of Single Mothers in the 1980s and 1990s." *Journal of Public Economics* 88 (July 2004): 1387–1420.

Miller, Gary J., and Terry M. Moe. "Bureaucrats, Legislators, and the Size of Government." *American Political Science Review* 77 (June 1983): 297–322.

Milligan, Kevin, Enrico Moretti, and Philip Oreopoulos. "Does Education Improve Citizenship? Evidence from the United States and the United Kingdom." *Journal of Public Economics* 88 (August 2004): 1667–95.

Mirza, M. M. Q., R. A. Warrick, and N. J. Ericksen. "The Implications of Climate Change on Floods of the Ganges, Brahmaputra and Meghna rivers in Bangladesh." *Climatic Change* 57 (2003): 287–318.

Moffitt, Robert. "Incentive Effects of the U.S. Welfare System: A Review." *Journal of Economic Literature* 30 (March 1992): 1–61.

Moffitt, Robert A. *Means-Tested Transfer Programs in the United States.* Chicago: University of Chicago Press, 2003.

Moretti, Enrico. "Workers' Education, Spillovers, and Productivity: Evidence from Plant-Level Production Functions." *American Economic Review* 94 (June 2004): 656–90.

Morrall, John F., III. "Saving Lives: A Review of the Record." *Journal of Risk and Uncertainty* 27 (December 2003): 221–37.

Mueller, Dennis C. *Public Choice III.* New York: Cambridge University Press, 2003.

Murray, Sheila E., William N. Evans, and Robert M. Schwab. "Education-Finance Reform and the Distribution of Education Resources." *American Economic Review* 88 (September 1998): 789–812.

Muten, Leif. "Taxation of Interest in the European Union." Hamburg Institute of International Economics, HWWA Discussion Paper 124, 2001.

Nataraj, Sita, and John Shoven. "Has the Unified Budget Undermined the Federal Government Trust Funds?" National Bureau of Economic Research Working Paper 10953 (December 2004).

National Academy of Social Insurance. *Workers' Compensation: Benefits, Coverage, and Costs, 2003.* Washington, DC, July 2005.

National Aeronautics and Space Administration Goddard Institute for Space Studies. "Global Annual Mean Surface Air Temperature Change." Accessed at http://data.giss.nasa.gov/gistemp/graphs/Fig.A.pdf.

National Association of Realtors. "Median Sales Price of Existing Single-Family Homes for Metropolitan Areas." July 14, 2006.

National Child Care Information Center. *NCCIC Child Care Database—Early Care and Education Funding.* Last accessed on July 12, 2006, at http://nccic.org/IMS/Search.asp.

National Governors Association. "Food Stamps." FFIS Federal Funds Information for States, 2005.

National Highway Traffic Safety Administration. "Alcohol-Related Fatalities in 2004." Washington, DC: National Center for Statistics and Analysis, 2005.

Newhouse, Joseph P., and Daniel J Byrne. "Did Medicare's Prospective Payment System Cause Length of Stay to Fall?" *Journal of Health Economics* 7 (December 1988): 413–6.

Newhouse, Joseph P., and the Insurance Experiment Group. *Free for All? Lessons from the RAND Health Insurance Experiment.* Cambridge, MA: Harvard University Press, 1993.

New York Times. "S.A.T. Coaching Disparaged" (February 10, 1988), p. B8.

New York Times. "Sham Self-Discipline in the Capitol" (March 17, 2005a), p. 30.

New York Times. "Fixing No Child Left Behind" (April 5, 2005b), p. A22.

New York Times. "The 2000 Campaign: Exchanges Between the Candidates in the Third Presidential Debate" (October 18, 2000), p. A26.

Nichols, Albert L., and Richard J. Zeckhauser. "Targeting Transfers through Restrictions on Recipients." *American Economic Review* 72 (May 1982): 372–7.

Nicita, Alessandro. "Efficiency and Equity of a Marginal Tax Reform: Income, Quality and Price Elasticities for Mexico." World Bank Policy Research Working Paper 3266, April 2004.

Nordhaus, William. "After Kyoto: Alternative Mechanisms to Control Global Warming," *American Economic Review* 96 (May 2006): 31–34.

Nordhaus, William D., and Joseph Boyer. *Warming the World: Economic Models of Global Warming.* Cambridge, MA: MIT Press, 2000.

Nyman, John A. "The Value of Health Insurance: The Access Motive." *Journal of Health Economics* 18 (April 1999): 141–52.

O'Brien, Timothy L. "All's Not Quiet on the Military Supply Front." *New York Times* (January 22, 2006), sec. 3, p. 1.

Oclander, Jorge, and Rosalind Rossi. "Big Kickback Plot Detailed." *Chicago Sun-Times* (December 1, 1995), p. 9.

Office of the Federal Register. *Federal Register,* Vol. 70, No. 155. Washington, DC: U.S. Government Printing Office, August 12, 2005.

Office of the Federal Register. *Federal Register,* Vol. 71. Washington, DC: U.S. Government Printing Office, January 24, 2006.

Office of Management and Budget. *Special Analyses: Budget of the United States Government.* Washington, DC: U.S. Government Printing Office, 1976.

Office of Management and Budget. "Circular No. A-94: Guidelines and Discount Rates for Benefit-Cost Analysis of Federal Programs." Washington, DC: U.S. Government Printing Office, October 29, 1992.

Office of Management and Budget. *Historical Tables: Budget of the United States Government, Fiscal Year 2007.* Washington, DC: U.S. Government Printing Office, 2006a.

Office of Management and Budget. *Analytical Perspectives: Budget of the United States Government, Fiscal Year 2007.* Washington, DC: U.S. Government Printing Office, 2006b.

Okun, Arthur. *Equality and Efficiency: The Big Tradeoff.* Washington, DC: Brookings Institution, 1975.

Olson, Mancur, and Richard Zeckhauser. "An Economic Theory of Alliances." *Review of Economics and Statistics* 48 (August 1966): 266–79.

Oreopoulos, Philip, Marianne E. Page, and Ann Huff Stevens. "Does Human Capital Transfer from Parent to Child? The Intergenerational Effects of Compulsory Schooling." National Bureau of Economic Research Working Paper 10164, December 2003.

Oreskes, Michael. "Support for Bush Declines in Poll." *New York Times* (July 11, 1990), p. A10.

Organisation for Economic Co-operation and Development. *OECD Historical Statistics.* Paris: OECD, 2001.

Organisation for Economic Co-operation and Development. *Agricultural Policies in OECD Countries: A Positive Reform Agenda.* Paris: OECD, 2002a.

Organisation for Economic Co-operation and Development. *Benefits and Wages: OECD Indicators.* Paris: OECD, 2002b.

Organisation for Economic Co-operation and Development. *Revenue Statistics, 1965–2002.* Paris: OECD, 2003.

Organisation for Economic Co-operation and Development. *Revenue Statistics, 1965–2004.* Paris: OECD, 2005a.

Organisation for Economic Co-operation and Development. *Education at a Glance, 2005.* Paris: OECD, September 13, 2005b.

Organisation for Economic Co-operation and Development. *OECD Health Data.* Paris: OECD, October, 2005c.

O'Rourke, Lawrence M. "End to Marriage Tax Penalty?" *Chicago Sun-Times* (March 30, 2001), p. 3.

Orszag, Peter R. "Administrative Costs in Individual Accounts in the United Kingdom." Washington, DC: Center on Budget and Policy Priorities, March 1999.

Orzechowski, William, and R. C. Walker. *The Tax Burden on Tobacco.* Washington, DC: Tobacco Institute, 2003.

O'Sullivan, Arthur, Terri A. Sexton, and Steven M. Sheffrin. *Property Taxes and Tax Revolts.* Cambridge: Cambridge University Press, 1995.

Pargal, Sheoli, Daniel Gilligan, and Mainul Huq. "Private Provision of a Public Good: Social Capital and Solid Waste Management in Dhaka, Bangladesh." World Bank Working Papers—Infrastructure, Telecoms, Power, Water, 2422, August 1, 2000.

Parsons, Donald. O. "Disability Insurance and Male Labor Force Participation: A Response." *Journal of Political Economy* 92 (June 1984): 542–9.

Parsons, Donald O. "Measuring and Deciding Disability." In *Disability and Work: Incentives, Rights and Opportunities,* edited by Caroline L. Weaver. Washington, DC: American Enterprise Institute Press, 1991.

Pasha, Shaheen. "Flood Insurance Rates to Rise." CNN (September 6, 2005).

Pear, Robert. "States Intervene After Drug Plan Hits Early Snags." *New York Times* (January 8, 2006a), sec. 1, p. 1.

Pear, Robert. "In Medicare Debate, Massaging the Facts." *New York Times* (May 23, 2006b), sec. A, p. 21.

Peltzman, Sam. "The Effect of Government Subsidies-in-Kind on Private Expenditures: The Case of Higher Education." *Journal of Political Economy* 81 (January–February 1973): 1–27.

Perciasepe, Robert. Testimony before a subcommittee of the U.S. Senate Committee on Environment and Public Works, October 14, 1999.

Perlstein, Michael. "Ex-cop Gets 21 Months for Fraud." *Times-Picayune* (January 22, 2004), Metro p. 1.

Persson, T., and G. Tabellini. "Constitutional Determinants of Government Spending." Boccom University mimeo, 2000.

Peterson, Steven P., George E. Hoffer, and Edward Millner. "Are Drivers of Airbag Equipped Cars More Aggressive? A Test of the Peltzman Hypotheses." *Journal of Law and Economics* 38 (October 1995): 251–265.

Pigou, A. C. *A Study in Public Finance,* 3rd ed. London: Macmillan, 1947.

Piketty, Thomas, and Emmanuel Saez. "The Evolution of Top Incomes: A Historical and International Perspective." *American Economic Review* 96 (May 2006): 200–205.

Pizer, Steven D., Austin B. Frakt, and Roger Feldman. "Payment Policy and Inefficient Benefits in the Medicare+Choice Program." *International Journal of Health Care Finance and Economics* 3 (2, June 2003): 79–93.

Pollack, Andrew. "Companies Announce Setback in Treatment for Parkinson's." *New York Times* (March 19, 2001), p. C2.

Poterba, James M. "Lifetime Incidence and the Distributional Burden of Excise Taxes." *American Economic Review* 79 (May 1989a): 325–30.

Poterba, James M. "Capital Gains Tax Policy toward Entrepreneurship." *National Tax Journal* 42 (September 1989b): 375–89.

Poterba, James M. "Retail Price Reactions to Changes in State and Local Sales Taxes." *National Tax Journal* 49 (June 1996): 169–79.

Poterba, James M. "Estate and Gift Taxes and Incentives for Inter Vivos Giving in the United States." *Journal of Public Economics* 79 (January 2001): 237–64.

Poterba, James M. "Taxation and Corporate Payout Policy." National Bureau of Economic Research Working Paper 10321, February 2004.

Poterba, James M., Steven F. Venti, and David A. Wise. "Implications of Rising Personal Retirement Saving." In *Frontiers in the Economics of Aging,* edited by David A. Wise. Chicago: University of Chicago Press, 1998a.

Poterba, James M., Steven F. Venti, and David A. Wise. "Personal Retirement Saving Programs and Asset Accumulation: Reconciling the Evidence." In *Frontiers in the Economics of Aging,* edited by David A. Wise. Chicago: University of Chicago Press, 1998b.

Powell, Michael. "Rescue's Just Not Part of the Plan." *Washington Post* (May 4, 2003), p. B1.

Pozen, Robert C. "A 'Progressive' Solution to Social Security." *Wall Street Journal* (March 15, 2005), p. A20.

Quayle, Dan. "After the Riots: Excerpts from Vice President's Speech on Cities and Poverty." *New York Times* (May 20, 1992), p. A20.

Radin, Charles. "Accident Probe Leads to T Overtime Limit." *Boston Globe* (January 8, 1980).

Rauh, Joshua. "Investment and Financing Constraints: Evidence from the Funding of Corporate Pension Plans." *The Journal of Finance* 61 (February, 2006): 33–71.

Rawls, John. *A Theory of Justice.* Cambridge, MA: Belknap Press of Harvard University Press, 1971.

Reid, T. R. "Deduction of the Week." *Washington Post* (November 3, 1981a), p. A21.

Reid, T. R. "Deduction of the Week." *Washington Post* (November 17, 1981b), p. A17.

Restuccia, Paul. "Troubled Cities Eye Land-Value Tax." *Boston Herald* (February 28, 2003), p. 46.

Revkin, Andrew C. "Huge Ice Shelf Is Reported to Break Up in Canada." *New York Times* (September 23, 2003), p. A10.

Rhode, Paul W., and Koleman S. Strumpf. "Assessing the Importance of Tiebout Sorting: Local Heterogeneity from 1850 to 1990." *American Economic Review* 93 (December 2003): 1648–77.

Richardson, Karen. "Warren Buffett Gives $30 Billion to Gates Foundation—Berkshire Hathaway Chairman Donates 85% of His Stock Holdings to Five Charitable Organizations." *Wall Street Journal* (June 26, 2006), p. B1.

Rivlin, Gary. "Patchy Recovery in New Orleans; Some People Return, but Only One in 10 Businesses Has Reopened." *New York Times* (April 5, 2006), p. C1.

Roig-Franzia, Manuel, and Spencer Hsu. "Many Evacuated, but Thousands Still Waiting." *Washington Post* (September 4, 2005), p. A01.

Rosen, Harvey S. "Housing Subsidies: Effects on Housing Decisions, Efficiency, and Equity." In *Handbook of Public Economics,* Vol. 1, edited by Martin Feldstein and Alan Auerbach. Amsterdam: North-Holland, 1985, pp. 375–420.

Rosen, Kenneth T. "The Impact of Proposition 13 on House Prices in Northern California: A Test of the Interjurisdictional Capitalization Hypothesis." *Journal of Political Economy* 90 (February 1982): 191–200.

Rosenbaum, David E. "Lawmakers' Pet Projects (and Not Just for Roads) Find Home in Transportation Bill." *New York Times* (July 30, 2005), p. A11.

Rosin, Hannah. "The Fat Tax." *New Republic* (May 18, 1998), p. 19.

Rothstein, Jesse. "Does Competition among Public Schools Benefit Students and Taxpayers? A Comment on Hoxby (2000)." National Bureau of Economic Research Working Paper 11215, March 2005.

Rothstein, Kevin. "Ex-prison Guard Charged with Workers' Comp Fraud." *Boston Herald* (December 19, 2002), News p. 16.

Rouse, Cecilia. "Private School Vouchers and Student Achievement: An Evaluation of the Milwaukee Parental Choice Program." *Quarterly Journal of Economics* 113 (May 1998): 553–602.

Russakoff, Dale. "Influential Tax-Shelter Industry Concludes Its Busiest Time of Year." *Washington Post* (January 1, 1985), p. A7.

Russakoff, Dale. "Tax Cheats: A Tradition of Omission." *Washington Post* (April 8, 1998), p. A1.

Saez, Emmanuel. "Optimal Income Transfer Programs: Intensive versus Extensive Labor Supply Responses." National Bureau of Economic Research Working Paper 7708, May 2000.

Saez, Emmanuel. "Optimal Progressive Capital Income Taxes in the Infinite Horizon Model," National Bureau of Economic Research Working Paper 9046, July 2002.

Saez, Emmanuel. "Reported Incomes and Marginal Tax Rates, 1960–2000: Evidence and Policy Implications." National Bureau of Economic Research Working Paper 10273, February 2004.

Sangar, David E., and Edmund L. Andrews. "Bush Rules Out a Tax Increase for Gulf Relief." *New York Times* (September 17, 2005), p. A1.

Sawhill, Isabel V., and Wade F. Horn. "How Congress Can Save Marriage." *Knight Ridder* (April 5, 1999).

Schemo, Diana Jean. "20 States Ask for Flexibility in School Law." *New York Times* (February 22, 2006), p. A12.

Schwartz, John. "Levees Rebuilt Just in Time, but Doubts Remain." *New York Times* (May 25, 2006), p. A1.

Sears, David O., and Jack Citrin. *Tax Revolt: Something for Nothing in California.* Cambridge, MA: Harvard University Press, 1982.

Shane, Scott, and Eric Lipton. "Stumbling Storm-Aid Effort Put Tons of Ice on Trips to Nowhere." *New York Times* (October 2, 2005), sec. 1, p. 1.

Sheiner, Louise. "Health Care Costs, Wages and Aging." FEDS Discussion Paper 99-19, January 14, 1999.

Singer, Paul. "Hurricane Season—A Port in a Storm." *National Journal* (May 27, 2006).

Slemrod, Joel, and Jon Bakija. *Taxing Ourselves: A Citizen's Guide to the Great Debate over Tax Reform.* Cambridge, MA: MIT Press, 2000.

Slemrod, Joel, Marsha Blumenthal, and Charles Christian. "Taxpayer Response to an Increased Probability of Audit: Evidence from a Controlled Experiment in Minnesota." *Journal of Public Economics* 79 (March 2001): 455–83.

Sloan, Allan. "Ford Takes a Tax Holiday for 'Jobs Creation.'" *Washington Post* (January 24, 2006), p. D2.

Smith, Robert S. "Mostly on Monday: Is Workers' Compensation Covering Off-the-Job Injuries?" Benefits, Costs, and Cycles in Workers' Compensation Insurance. Norwood: Kluwer, 1989.

Social Security Administration. "Retirement Benefits." SSA Publication No. 05-10035, July 2004.

Social Security Administration. *SSI Annual Statistical Report, 2005.* Released September 2006.

Social Security Administration. *Income of the Population 55 or Older, 2004.* Washington, DC: U.S. Government Printing Office, 2006a.

Social Security Administration. *Annual Statistical Supplement, 2005.* Washington, DC: U.S. Government Printing Office, 2006b.

Social Security Advisory Board. *Social Security: Why Action Should Be Taken Soon.* Washington, DC: U.S. Government Printing Office, 2001.

Social Security Trustees. *The 2006 Annual Report of the Board of Trustees of the Federal Old-Age and Survivors Insurance and Federal Disability Insurance Trust Funds.* Washington, DC: U.S. Government Printing Office, 2006.

Stamler, Bernard. "The Gray Area for Nonprofits, Where Legal Is Questionable." *New York Times* (November 17, 2003), p. F2.

State of Vermont. "Rate Schedule." Department of Labor, 2005.

Steinberg, Richard. "Does Government Spending Crowd Out Donations? Interpreting the Evidence." *Annals of Public and Cooperative Economics* 62 (October–December 1991): 591–617.

Steiner, Janet, and Robert E. Schiller. *The Condition of Public Education.* Springfield, IL: Illinois State Board of Education, 2003.

Steuerle, C. Eugene, and Jon M. Bakija. *Retooling Social Security for the 21st Century.* Washington, DC: Urban Institute Press, 1994.

Stewart, Heather. "Glaxo Hit by $5bn US Tax Demand." *The Guardian* (January 8, 2004), p. 19.

Stolberg, Sheryl Gay, and Edmund L. Andrews. "New Criticism Falls on 'Supplemental' Bills." *New York Times* (April 23, 2006), sec. A, p. 16.

Stone, Andrea. "AARP Endorsement Boosts GOP's Prescription-Drug Plan." *USA Today* (November 18, 2003), p. 11A.

Stratmann, Thomas. "Logrolling in the U.S. Congress." *Economic Inquiry* 33 (July 1995): 441–56.

Stratmann, Thomas. "Congressional Voting over Legislative Careers: Shifting Positions and Changing Constraints." *American Political Science Review* 94 (September 2000): 665–76.

Straub, John D. "Fundraising and Crowd-Out of Charitable Contributions: New Evidence from Contributions to Public Radio." Texas A&M Department of Economics Working Paper, 2003.

Summers, Lawrence H. "Capital Taxation and Accumulation in a Life Cycle Growth Model." *American Economic Review* 71 (September 1981): 533–44.

Summers, Lawrence H. "Some Simple Economics of Mandated Benefits." *American Economic Review* 79 (May 1989): 177–83.

Swardson, Anne. "Oysters Promoted as Tasty Tax Shelter." *Washington Post* (September 9, 1985), p. 1.

Swardson, Anne. "Court Backs IRS on Rabbi's Tax Deduction." *Washington Post* (March 28, 1986), p. A13.

Taxpayers for Common Sense. *Database of Earmarks in Conference Agreement to the Transportation Bill.* August 12, 2005. Available at http://www.taxpayer.net/Transportation/safetealu/states.htm.

Teske, Paul, Mark Schneider, Michael Mintrom, and Samuel Best. "Establishing the Micro Foundations of a Macro Theory: Information, Movers, and the Competitive Local Market for Public Goods." *American Political Science Review* 87 (September 1993): 702–13.

Thaler, Richard H., and Shlomo Benartzi. "Save More Tomorrow: Using Behavioral Economics to Increase Employee Saving." *Journal of Political Economy* 112 (Part 2 Supplement, February 2004): 164–87.

Thompson, Bob. "Sharing the Wealth?" *Washington Post* (April 13, 2003), p. W8.

Tiebout, Charles. "A Pure Theory of Local Expenditures." *Journal of Political Economy* 64 (October 1956): 416–24.

Times (London). "Thieves Put Spoke in Freewheeling Dream." April 20, 1994.

Topel, Robert H. "On Layoffs and Unemployment Insurance." *American Economic Review* 73 (September 1983): 541–559.

Tyler, John H., Richard J. Murnane, and John B. Willett. "Estimating the Labor Market Signaling Value of the GED." *Quarterly Journal of Economics* 115 (May 2000): 431–68.

United for a Fair Economy. *America's Wealth Gap and the Case for Preserving the Estate Tax.* Boston: United for a Fair Economy, April 2006.

United Nations Development Programme. *Human Development Report 2005.* New York: United Nations Development Programme, 2005.

United Nations Environment Programme. "Backgrounder: Basic Facts and Data on the Science and Politics of Ozone Protection." August, 2003. Accessed at http://www.unep.org/ozone/pdf/Press-Backgrounder.pdf.

United Nations Environment Programme. "Summary of Issues for Discussion by the Open-ended Working Group of the Parties to the Montreal Protocol." July 6, 2006. Accessed at http://www.unep.ch/ozone/Meeting_Documents/oewg/26oewg/OEWG-26-2E.pdf.

U.S. Bureau of the Census. *Statistical Abstract of the United States: 1962,* 82nd ed. Washington, DC: U.S. Government Printing Office, 1962.

U.S. Bureau of the Census. *Statistical Abstract of the United States: 2003,* 123rd ed. Washington, DC: U.S. Government Printing Office, 2003.

U.S. Bureau of the Census. *Families and Living Arrangements—2003 March CPS* (September 15, 2004). Accessed at http://www.census.gov/population/www/socdemo/hh-fam.html.

U.S. Bureau of the Census. *Income, Poverty, and Health Insurance Coverage in the United States: 2004.* Washington, DC: U.S. Government Printing Office, 2005a.

U.S. Bureau of the Census. *Historical Poverty Tables* (May 13, 2005b). Accessed at http://www.census.gov/hhes/www/income/histinc/histpovtb.html.

U.S. Bureau of the Census. *Historical Income Tables* (December 20, 2005c). Accessed at http://www.census.gov/hhes/www/income/histinc/histinctb.html.

U.S. Bureau of the Census. *Statistical Abstract of the United States: 2006,* 125th ed. Washington, DC: U.S. Government Printing Office, 2006a.

U.S. Bureau of the Census. *State and Local Government Finances: 2002–03* (May 31, 2006b). Accessed at http://www.census.gov/govs/www/estimate03.html.

U.S. Bureau of the Census. *Population Estimates.* Last accessed on June 17, 2006c, at http://www.census.gov/popest/estimates.php.

U.S. Bureau of the Census. *Quarterly Summary of State and Local Government Tax Revenue.* Last accessed on July 12, 2006d, at http://www.census.gov/govs/www/qtax.html.

U.S. Bureau of Labor. *Women in the Labor Force: A Databook.* U.S. Bureau of Labor Statistics, May 2005.

U.S. Department of Agriculture—Food and Nutrition Service. "Nutrition Program Facts—National School Lunch Program." September 2005a.

U.S. Department of Agriculture—Food and Nutrition Service. "Nutrition Program Facts—The School Breakfast Program." September 2005b.

U.S. Department of Agriculture—Food and Nutrition Service. "WIC Program National Level Annual Summary." Last accessed on June 15, 2006, at http://www.fns.usda.gov/pd/wisummary.htm.

U.S. Department of Education. *Twenty-fifth Annual Report to Congress on the Implementation of the Individuals with Disabilities Education Act.* Washington, DC, 2003.

U.S. Department of Education. *Digest of Educations Statistics, 2005.* Washington, DC, 2006a.

U.S. Department of Education. *2004–2005 Title IV/Federal Pell Grant End of Year Report.* Washington, DC, 2006b.

U.S. Department of Education. *The Student Guide 2006–2007.* Washington, DC, 2006c.

U.S. Department of Health and Human Services. *Temporary Assistance for Needy Families Program: Fifth Annual Report to Congress.* Washington, DC: U.S. Government Printing Office, 2003a.

U.S. Department of Health and Human Services. *Temporary Assistance for Needy Families Program: Sixth Annual Report to Congress.* Washington, DC: U.S. Government Printing Office, 2004.

U.S. Department of Health and Human Services. *Indicators of Welfare Dependence: Annual Report to Congress.* Washington, DC: U.S. Government Printing Office, 2005.

U.S. Department of Health and Human Services—Health Resources and Services Administration. "New Jersey Medicaid & S-CHIP Eligibility." Last accessed on June 18, 2006, at http://www.hrsa.gov/reimbursement/states/New-Jersey-Eligibility.htm.

U.S. Department of Housing and Urban Development. "FY 2006 Income Limits."

U.S. Department of Housing and Urban Development. *Fiscal Year 2007 Budget Summary.* Washington, DC, February 2006.

U.S. Department of Justice. "Alcohol and Crime: An Analysis of National Data on the Prevalence of Alcohol Involvement in Crime." NCJ-168632 (April 1998).

U.S. Department of Labor. *Unemployment Insurance Chart Book.* Washington DC: October, 2004.

U.S. Department of Labor. *State Workers' Compensation Laws* (July 1, 2005a). Accessed at http://www.dol.gov/esa/regs/statutes/owcp/stwclaw/stwclaw.htm.

U.S. Department of Labor. *Historical Labor Participation Rates* (December 7, 2005b). Accessed at http://www.bls.gov/emp/emplab04.htm.

U.S. Department of Labor. *Unemployment Insurance Data Summary* (March 2006a). Last accessed on June 28, 2006, at http://workforcesecurity.doleta.gov/unemploy/content/data.asp.

U.S. Department of Labor. *Comparison of State Unemployment Insurance Laws 2005* (April 2006b). Accessed at http://www.ows.doleta.gov/unemploy/uilawcompar/2005/comparison2005.asp.

U.S. Department of Labor. "OSHA Facts Sheet—December 2004." Last accessed on June 16, 2006c, at http://www.osha.gov/as/opa/oshafacts.html.

U.S. Department of Transportation. *2004 Status of the Nation's Highways, Bridges, and Transit: Conditions and Performance.* Washington, DC: U.S. Government Printing Office, 2004.

U.S. Department of Transportation—Federal Highway Administration. *Financing Federal-Aid Highways: The Highway Trust Fund.* Last accessed on June 27, 2006, at http://www.fhwa.dot.gov/reports/fifahiwy/fifahi05.htm.

U.S. Department of the Treasury. "President's Budget Proposes Bold Tax-Free Savings and Retirement Security Opportunities for All Americans." Press Statement KD-3816 (January 31, 2003a).

U.S. Department of the Treasury. "Long-Term Capital Gains and Taxes Paid on Long-Term Capital Gains, 1977–2001." Office of Tax Policy, September 2003b.

U.S. Department of the Treasury. "Capital Gains and Taxes Paid on Capital Gains for Returns with Positive Net Capital Gains, 1954–2003." Office of Tax Policy, January 2006.

U.S. Environmental Protection Agency. *Light-Duty Automotive Technology and Fuel Economy Trends: 1975–2005.* Washington, DC: U.S. Government Printing Office, 2005.

U.S. General Accounting Office. *Financial Audit: IRS's Fiscal Years 2003 and 2002 Financial Statements,* GAO-04-126. Washington, DC, 2003.

U.S. General Accounting Office. *Tax Administration: Comparison of the Reported Tax Liabilities of Foreign- and U.S.-Controlled Corporations, 1996–2000,* GAO-04-358. Washington DC, 2004.

U.S. House of Representatives Committee on Ways and Means. *2004 Green Book.* Washington, DC, 2004.

U.S. Joint Committee on Taxation. "Overview of Present Law and Economic Analysis Relating to Marginal Tax Rates and the President's Individual Income Tax Rate Proposals." JCX-6-01. Washington, DC (March 6, 2001).

U.S. Joint Committee on Taxation. *Estimates of Federal Tax Expenditures for Fiscal Years 2006-2010.* Washington, DC: U.S. Government Printing Office, 2006.

U.S. Office of Personnel Management. *Federal Civilian Workforce Statistics: The Fact Book, 2005 Edition.* Washington, DC: U.S. Government Printing Office, 2006.

Viscusi, W. Kip. "The Value of Risks to Life and Health." *Journal of Economic Literature* 31 (December 1993): 1912–46.

Viscusi, W. Kip. "Cigarette Taxation and the Social Consequences of Smoking." In *Tax Policy and the Economy,* edited by James Poterba. National Bureau of Economic Research, Vol. 9 (1995), pp. 51–101.

Viscusi, W. Kip, and Joseph E. Aldy. "The Value of a Statistical Life: A Critical Review of Market Estimates throughout the World." *Journal of Risk and Uncertainty* 27 (August 2003): 5–76.

Wald, Matthew L. "Battle Swirls on Security at A-Plants." *New York Times* (August 6, 2004a), p. A15.

Wald, Matthew L. "Security Drill at Weapons Plant Raises Safety Questions." *New York Times* (December 21, 2004b), p. A22.

Wallis, John Joseph, and Wallace E. Oates. "The Impact of the New Deal on American Federalism." In *The Defining Moment: The Great Depression and the American Economy in the Twentieth Century,* edited by Michael D. Bordo, Claudia Goldin, and Eugene N. White. Chicago: University of Chicago Press, 1998.

Wall Street Journal. "Hot Topic: Probing Stock-Options Backdating" (May 27, 2006a), p. A5.

Wall Street Journal. "Taxes Everlasting" (June 8, 2006b), p. A18.

Washington, Ebonya. "Female Socialization: How Daughters Influence Their Legislator Fathers' Votes on Women's Issues." MIT Research in Progress, July 2004.

Washington Post. "San Jose's Choice: Tax Retrenchment Hurts Needy Most" (September 18, 1983), p. A1.

Washington Post. "Stealth Tax Reform" (February 4, 2003), p. A24.

Washington Post. "Washington in Brief" (June 17, 2004), p. A4.

Weisman, Jonathan. "Break on Foreign-Profit Tax Means Billions to U.S. Firms." *Washington Post* (August 19, 2005), p. D1.

Winslow, C. M., D. H. Solomon, M. R. Chassin, J. Kosecoff, N. J. Merrick, and R. H. Brook. "The Appropriateness of Carotid Endarterectomy." *New England Journal of Medicine* 318 (March 24, 1988): 721–7.

Witte, John F. "Achievement Effects of the Milwaukee Voucher Program." University of Wisconsin at Madison mimeo, January 1997.

Wood, David L., and Philip A. Brunell. "Measles Control in the United States: Problems of the Past and Challenges for the Future." *Clinical Microbiology Reviews* 8 (April 1995): 260–67.

Woodbury, Stephen A., and Robert G. Spiegelman. "Bonuses to Workers and Employers to Reduce Unemployment: Randomized Trials in Illinois." *American Economic Review* 77 (September 1987): 513–30.

Woodward, Bob. "Origin of the Tax Pledge." *Washington Post* (October 4, 1992), p. A1.

Woolhandler, S., T. Campbell, and D. U. Himmelstein. "Costs of Health Care Administration in the United States and Canada." *New England Journal of Medicine* 349 (August 21, 2003): 768–75.

World Bank. *World Development Indicators.* Washington, DC: Development Data Group, The World Bank, 2006.

World Health Organization. "Why Is Tobacco a Health Priority?" Last accessed on June 2, 2006, at http://www.who.int/tobacco/health_priority/en/index.html.

Writing Group for the Women's Health Initiative Investigators. "Risks and Benefits of Estrogen Plus Progestin in Healthy Postmenopausal Women." *Journal of the American Medical Association,* 288 (2002): 321–333.

Zodrow, George. "The Property Tax as a Capital Tax: A Room with Three Views." *National Tax Journal* 54 (March 2001): 139–56.